FRANZ SCHUBERT – THE COMPLETE SONGS

FRANZ SCHUBERT
THE COMPLETE SONGS
VOLUME THREE
SCHWANENGESANG–Z
CATALOGUES AND ADDENDA

GRAHAM JOHNSON

translations of the song texts by Richard Wigmore

WITHDRAWN

YALE UNIVERSITY PRESS
NEW HAVEN AND LONDON

The publisher acknowledges the generous sponsorship of the Guildhall School & Music Drama, London, without which the publication of this work would not have been possible.

Deepest gratitude also to the Marilyn Horne Foundation, a US nonprofit organization devoted exclusively to the art of song, for its support and encouragement of this publication.

Copyright © 2014 Yale University

All rights reserved. This book may not be reproduced in whole or in part, in any form (beyond that copying permitted by Sections 107 and 108 of the U.S. Copyright Law and except by reviewers for the public press) without written permission from the publishers.

For information about this and other Yale University Press publications, please contact:

U.S. office: sales.press@yale.edu   www.yalebooks.com
Europe Office: sales@yaleup.co.uk   www.yalebooks.co.uk

Set in 10/12 pt Minion by Toppan Best-set Premedia Limited
Printed in Great Britain by TJ International Ltd, Padstow, Cornwall

Library of Congress Control Number: 2013931540

ISBN   978-0-300-11267-2

A catalogue record for this book is available from the British Library.

Published with assistance from the Annie Burr Lewis Fund

[II/484] For kind permission to reproduce an extract from Detlev Glanert's *Einsamkeit* © Copyright 2009 by Boosey & Hawkes Music Publishers Ltd the author and publishers gratefully acknowledge Boosey & Hawkes Music Publishers.
[III/83] For kind permission to reprint lines from Jeremy Reed's translation of Georg Phillipp Friedrich von Hardenberg's *Nachthymne* from *Novalis: Hymns to the Night* (1989) the author and publishers gratefully acknowledge the Enitharmon Press, London.

FRANZ SCHUBERT: The Complete Songs represents Graham Johnson's considerable reworking and expansion of the programme notes for the first issue of the Hyperion Schubert series where each disc appeared under a singer's name. By the time of the second issue of the series the decision was taken by Hyperion not to reissue the notes in booklet form because the present publication by Yale University Press was already mooted and in preparation.

10 9 8 7 6 5 4 3 2 1

S

SCHWANENGESANG
(Senn) Op. 23 no. 3, **D744** [H490]
A♭ major   Autumn? 1822

Swansong

'Wie klag' ich's aus
'Das Sterbegefühl,
'Das auflösend
'Durch die Glieder rinnt?'

'Wie sing' ich's aus
'Das Werdegefühl,
'Das erlösend
'Dich, o Geist, anweht?'

Er klagt', er sang,[1]
Vernichtungsbang,
Verklärungsfroh,
Bis das Leben floh.

Das bedeutet des Schwanen Gesang![2]

'How shall I lament
The presentiment of death,
The dissolution that flows
Through my limbs?'

'How shall I express in song
The feeling of new life
That redeems you
With its breath, o spirit?'

It lamented, it sang,
Fearful of extinction,
Joyously awaiting transfiguration,
Until life fled.

That is the meaning of the swan's song!

JOHANN CHRYSOSTOMUS SENN (1795–1857)

This is the second of Schubert's two Senn solo settings (1822). See the poet's biography for a chronological list of all the Senn settings.

This text is to be found in the printed edition of Senn's *Gedichte* under the title *Schwanenlied*, but this book was published only in 1838, long after Schubert's death. There is good reason to believe that the poems were brought to Schubert in manuscript by a mutual friend, perhaps Franz von Bruchmann, who visited Senn in the autumn of 1822. Two years earlier the fiery young poet had been exiled in his native Tyrol for alleged political offences – in reality little

---

[1] Senn writes (*Gedichte*, 1838) '*Es* klagt, *es* sang'.
[2] Senn writes (*Gedichte*, 1838) 'Das *ist* des Schwanen Gesang!'

more than being cheeky to the police when his lodgings were searched and impressing them with his cleverness in interviews. In the minds of the authorities, an opinionated and adroit young man with liberal views was a very real danger. Schubert had been a school-fellow of Senn and sympathized with his anti-authoritarian views. The settings were published in August 1823 as part of Op. 23, a set that also included a bitter song of disillusionment with love (Platen's *Die Liebe hat gelogen* D751) and *Schatzgräbers Begehr* D761 by Schober where the treasure-hunter digs his own grave and longs to lie in it. (It seems that the censor's office over-looked the fact that the third of these poets had been officially exiled. Even so, Walther Dürr designates these songs *Lieder für den verbannten Freund* – songs for an exiled friend.)

There is nothing to prove that Schubert set the Senn poems immediately he received them. We have no firm dates for any of the Op. 23 lieder and it may well be that some of these dark songs, and *Schwanengesang* in particular, were composed in the spring of 1823. They would thus be contemporary with Schubert's health crisis and the poem entitled 'Mein Gebet' ('My Prayer'). The longing for destruction in order to find transfiguration in Senn's lyric finds an exact echo with the last of Schubert's own lines of verse at that time (*see* SCHUBERT, THE COMPOSER AS POET). The composer had become, in his own way, as much an establishment exile as poor Senn. Not only are the poet's words (a 'presentiment of death' and the 'dissolution that flows through my limbs') uncomfortably near Schubert's own circumstances, but the music itself has an immediacy that suggests a heightened subjective response. The song shares the *alla breve* dactylic pace of *Der Tod und das Mädchen* D531 (the death motif rhythm is invoked), but these two gigantic miniatures stand at opposite poles. In the Claudius setting the mastery of Death is delineated in the inhuman ease and gliding simplicity of his harmony; the Senn setting bristles with the tortured chromaticism of vulnerability and all-too-human emotion.

The key signature of A flat major disguises the fact that the song begins in A flat minor and is poised throughout between the 'hard' and 'soft' versions of this tonality – thus the tonic minor moves to the dominant in b. 1, and a wistful answering phrase, an octave lower, repeats this progression with the tonic major falling to the dominant. John Reed observes that the song inhabits the same tonal country as the Impromptus D935 and D899/4 of the Moments Musicaux – A flat major and minor, C flat major/minor and D flat major/minor. There is a positively Wagnerian moment on the word 'auflösend': an unusually dense bank of accidentals flattens and dissolves the harmony, black notes on the keyboard changing all to white. Perhaps this chord was considered too difficult to decipher by the publisher Leidesdorf, hence the natural signs (instead of double flats) in the song's first edition that were perpetuated in the Peters Edition. Actually, this pile-up of natural signs makes for a better musical pun because the German for the naturalization of flats is 'auflösen'.

The atmosphere of world-weary resignation in this song in preparation for death (also a kind of resolution of a suspension or discord) is both oppressive and inspiring; a stoic courage and a pride, inherent in the underlying dactylic rhythm, shines through the music. The two bars on an E flat pedal (bb. 9 and 10, the beginning of Senn's second verse) have a nobility about them; the swan himself is the narrator (or the swan-musician) and according to that creature's status its utterance is sacred and royal. The spread chords at bb. 12–13 seem to be played by a minstrel accompanying himself on a harp. Since the Mayrhofer setting *Nachtstück* D672, where the old minstrel strides into the forest to surrender his life to nature, Schubert probably associated the renunciation of life with the elegiac possibilities of this ancient instrument.

The song has an ABA structure with the A part modified on repetition. 'Er klagt', er sang' (b. 13) follows the notes of the first verse for only a bar; at 'Vernichtungsbang' and 'Verklärungs-froh' (bb. 15–16) the vocal line becomes more impassioned and higher in tessitura – where the first verse discussed the possibility of a swansong, this is the real thing. This music is less rage against the dying of the light and more a steely determination that the singing will be ever more striking as the light fails. A two-bar interlude (bb. 18–19) brings the section to a close and initiates what might seem at first to be another strophe (a repeat of the very first bar of the song). In fact Senn provides a dangling line in his poem that is meant to be a summing-up and coda. Schubert makes the long mournful setting of 'Das' (b. 20) a wonderful upbeat to the poet's final line which here suggests a solemn confirmation of death, as if in a coroner's report. The two bars of postlude are placed in the depths of the piano in a way that prophesies the ending of *Ihr Bild* (in *Schwanengesang* D957/9).

The printing of the poem makes clear that the first eight lines (in inverted commas) are spoken by the dying swan, the remainder of the poem by an observer or narrator. In August 1823, just after the publication of the Op. 23 lieder, Schubert wrote to Schober, 'I rather doubt whether I shall ever be well again'. Whether *Schwanengesang* was written just before or during Schubert's crisis, it has the air of a wounded bird's promise to sing ceaselessly and 'Verklärungs-froh' for the time that is left to him. The wildly beautiful song of Oscar Wilde's nightingale, with its heart pressed against the rose thorn of life, seems an appropriate image for Schubert's creativity in these troubled years of his life. It is perhaps irreverent with a song of this seriousness to remind the listener of Samuel Coleridge's contemporary lines: 'Swans sing before they die – 'twere no bad thing / Should certain persons die before they sing'.

Autograph:	Staatsbibliothek Preussischer Kulturbesitz, Berlin
First edition:	Published as Op. 23 no. 3 by Sauer & Leidesdorf in August 1823 (P46)
Publication reviews:	*Allgemeine musikalische Zeitung* (Leipzig) No. 26 (24 June 1824) cols 425–8 [Waidelich/Hilmar Dokumente I No. 282; Deutsch Doc. Biog. No. 479]
Subsequent editions:	Peters: Vol. 4/21; AGA XX 407: Vol. 7/16; NSA IV: Vol. 2/8; Bärenreiter: Vol. 1/138
Bibliography:	Reed 1985, p. 497 Youens 2008, pp. 30–33
Discography and timing:	Fischer-Dieskau II 5[7] 2'22 Hyperion I 11[2] Hyperion II 25[16] 2'28 Brigitte Fassbaender

← *Gott in Natur* D757 *Wer sich der Einsamkeit ergibt* D₂478/1 →

SCHWANENGESANG Swansong
(Rellstab, Heine and Seidl)
August and October 1828
D957 & D965A

The opening of *Liebesbotschaft* from the first edition of *Schwanengesang* (1829).

In Greek mythology the legend of the swansong goes back to Phaethon, son of Helios, who perished attempting to drive his father's chariot across the heavens. As Cycnus, son of Sthenelus, mourned the death of Phaethon in song, Apollo changed him into a swan and placed him among the stars.

Schubert was well aware of the significance of the term swansong – the proverbial final performance of the swan who knows he is about to die and gathers all his strength for one last utterance. As early as 1815 the composer set *Schwangesang* D318 to a poem by Kosegarten on this theme, and in 1822 or 1823 he composed *Schwanengesang* D744 to a poem by his exiled friend Johann Senn. At that stage he could never have dreamed that two important sets of songs by very different poets would be published together under that title in the year after his death.

The genesis of this work has a great deal to do with a famous composer's death, but Beethoven's rather than Schubert's. The commentary on *Auf dem Strom* D943, discusses the psychological depth of Schubert's link with Beethoven (who had died in 1827) in the last year of his own life. It is curious, but understandable, that he seems to have been more engaged with thoughts of Beethoven and his music *after* that composer's death than before it: the remark ascribed to Schubert – 'Who can do anything after Beethoven?' – dates from much earlier, and in 1828 he was setting about answering his own question. He needed to exorcise the ghost of his great contemporary, the better to move on and occupy his natural place as Vienna's leading composer, and homage seemed the best way to pay his dues, even if that homage was accomplished with, as Walther Dürr says, 'typically Schubertian reserve'.

In the spring of 1825 the poet and music critic Ludwig Rellstab (qv) had visited Vienna and left handwritten copies of some of his poems in Beethoven's possession in the hope that the master would set them – which he never did of course. After Beethoven's death his amanuensis, Anton Schindler, claimed to have handed the poems over to Schubert for composition. However, in his memoirs (*Aus meinem Leben*, 1861), Ludwig Rellstab puts a different slant on the story: he received the poems back from Schindler full of pencil markings in Beethoven's hand 'showing those that pleased him the most, and those that he handed on to Schubert for composition'. In this version of events Beethoven personally singled Schubert out for the great task, whereas Schindler, in his story, casts himself as the intermediary and inspired matchmaker between composer and text. He also claimed credit for introducing a batch of Schubert's published songs to Beethoven during the great man's final illness. It is not inconceivable that Rellstab received the copies of his poems back from Schindler only when Schubert had finished with them, but in the absence of the pages in question we cannot know whether the pencil markings mentioned by Rellstab are indeed Beethoven's (or Schubert's), nor whether the selection corresponds to the songs set by the younger composer. In any case, Schindler is such an unreliable source that it remains an open question whether he furnished Schubert with copies of the poems at all, or only wished he had done so many years later (he died in 1864). In favour of Schindler's version of events is the improbability that Schubert at this stage of his career would have decided to set the lyrics of a distant Berliner like Rellstab, neither a friend nor a great poet, without a strong external reason for doing so (*see* RELLSTAB).

Schindler fails to tell us how many poems were passed to Schubert, and why the composer chose to set the ones he did. The suitability of *Auf dem Strom* for a concert given on the first anniversary of Beethoven's death is discussed in the article for that song. But when he came to plan another group of songs on these Rellstab poems, what thoughts guided the composer's choice? He had already written two highly integrated cycles (*Die schöne Müllerin* D795 and *Winterreise* D911) and Deutsch suggested that he probably wanted to avoid composing another work with a connecting narrative because of a hitherto supportive critic's unfavourable response to *Winterreise* ('true song should unfold itself in single flowers'). Whatever Franz Stoepel of Munich wrote, it would in any case have been impossible to cap *Winterreise* before that work had even been published.

In 1816 Beethoven had published his *An die ferne Geliebte* cycle Op. 98, the mastery and success of which must have cut Schubert to the quick: throughout 1815 and for most of 1816 he must have thought himself unassailable in the uniquely beautiful fortress of song he had built for himself, brick by brick, in those amazingly productive years. Here at least Beethoven (who ruled all other realms of music) held no sway. And suddenly – out of the blue as it were – Beethoven produced a stunning new work of such innovative splendour that it must have haunted Schubert for the remainder of his career. In 1818 he had composed something of a riposte to *An die ferne Geliebte*, the song-cantata *Einsamkeit* D620 to the words of Mayrhofer. Like the Beethoven cycle this consisted of six linked sections, a garland of songs by a single poet on a single theme. What Schubert had not yet done, however, was to marry the best of both worlds: to write a cycle of separate free-standing songs united not by a storyline (as in the two Müller cycles), but by a theme flexible enough to give unity in diversity. Such a cycle could surely employ the theme of the distant beloved in various guises as a way of both paying tribute to Beethoven and putting this old rivalry (an entirely private matter for Schubert) to rest.

Is it only by chance that over every song in *Schwanengesang* hovers the presence of the distant beloved – not one, but an entire gallery of them? In *Liebesbotschaft* and *In der Ferne* the lover sends messages to her by water and on the breeze; in *Kriegers Ahnung* the soldier bids his distant spouse or lover farewell (he is about to die in battle), and in *Ständchen* the serenader is separated from the object of his affection and never permitted to scale the balcony; *Frühlingssehnsucht* links longing for the advent of spring with a hopeless desire for the presence of the loved one; *Aufenthalt* is awash with tears born of loveless sorrow, and *Abschied*, however seemingly merry, is a song of parting which bids love farewell before a journey (even the darkest symphonic work must have its scherzo). The Rellstab setting *Herbst* D945 (not included in the cycle), with its memories of faded love, also fits into this theme. The other possible Rellstab scherzo, the fragment *Lebensmut* D937 (and categorically not part of *Schwanengesang*) is the only song that could not, in any conceivable way, be made to fit into such an anthology. Was it excluded from the cycle and never finished for this reason?

Whether by chance or planning, this 'ferne Geliebte' theme continues into the Heine cycle: *Der Atlas* is Heine's alter ego who has gambled on love and lost; *Ihr Bild*, *Die Stadt* and *Der Doppelgänger* similarly describe the loss of love and the terrible distance between estranged lovers – in the last case a visit to her former house occasions a premonition of death. *Am Meer* concerns memories of a terrible parting (after a terrible coming together), and even *Das Fischermädchen* is arguably about love on the rebound, a search for a fleeting substitute for a love that has been lost back home. This 'theme' may even be extended into the song that was placed at the end of the cycle by the publisher Haslinger: the owner of the carrier pigeon in *Die Taubenpost* sends love out in terms of longing, but receives nothing back. Throughout this sequence 'she' is absent, unable to respond even if able to listen, as in *Ständchen*; she is separated by distance, the impenetrable wall of a house, convention, even death perhaps, but she is not *there*. Only in two songs, *Abschied* and *Das Fischermädchen*, can we sense any possibility of a colloquy and even then we sense that flirtation is a means of escaping the pain of a greater love nearer to home. If there were a single title that covered the theme of these songs it might be *An die fernen Geliebten*. If it were true that Schubert was still in love with Karoline Esterházy and felt – correctly – that he could never aspire to her hand, the shared experience of unattainable love would have been another link with his great predecessor via the title of a song cycle.

We shall never be certain about Schubert's intention regarding the publication of these songs. It is true that he offered the six Heine settings in their own right to the German publisher Probst in October 1828 (songs that were 'extraordinarily well-received here' as he assured Probst), and from this one might infer he intended to publish the Rellstab and Heine cycles separately. At this time he seems to have been desperately keen to widen his list of publishers to escape a stultifying Viennese exclusivity. He was possibly willing to compromise over an initial idea for a large and inclusive cycle in order to sell a shorter work in Germany with texts by one of the most modish poets of the time (Probst showed no interest in the offer). We would be more certain of Schubert's intentions if he had offered the Rellstab cycle separately to Probst as well. It is also possible that the publisher Haslinger visited the composer in the last weeks of his life (while Schubert was correcting the proofs of *Winterreise* for Haslinger's firm) and that they spoke about the Rellstab and Heine settings and how they might be published. This would certainly not have been as *Franz Schuberts Schwanen-Gesang* (their eventual designation in print), but as a cycle perhaps dedicated to the composer's friends (an idea that goes back to an – unauthenticated – quote from Josef von Spaun). As with *Auf dem Strom*, any link with Beethoven would have remained a private matter of respectful homage between Schubert and the shade of the composer who both inspired and intimidated him more than any other. But it could not have been lost on Schubert that in dealing with Tobias Haslinger, also his publisher for *Winterreise*, he was moving ever closer to the man who had been at the nerve centre of Beethoven's creative orbit: Haslinger had published that composer's Opp. 90–101, 112–18, 136–8 and several others.

Poets:	Ludwig Rellstab (1799–1860) songs I–VII; Heinrich Heine (1797–1856) songs VIII–XIII; Johann Gabriel Seidl (1804–1875) song XIV
Autographs:	Pierpont Morgan Library, New York (fair copy of all fourteen songs); Song XIV also at Wienbibliothek im Rathaus, Vienna (rough sketch on two staves)
First edition:	Published in two volumes by Tobias Haslinger, Vienna in May 1829
Publication reviews:	*Allgemeine musikalische Zeitung* (Leipzig), No. 40 (7 October 1829), col. 653ff. [Waidelich/Hilmar Dokumente I No. 747]
Subsequent editions:	Peters: Vol. 1/122–69; AGA XX 554–67: Vol. 9/134–85; NSA IV: Vol. 14/96–168; Bärenreiter: Vol. 4/120–76
Arrangements:	*6 Heine Lieder* arr. Friedrich Goldmann (1941–2009) for baritone solo and orchestra (1997)
Bibliography:	Chusid 2000 Chusid 2000[2] Hilmar-Voit 1991, p. 48 (Rellstab songs) & 50 (Heine Songs) Kohlhäufl 1999, pp. 159–60 (Seidl) Newbould 1997, pp. 310–15

SEVEN SONGS TO POEMS BY LUDWIG RELLSTAB

I LIEBESBOTSCHAFT   Love's message
D957/1 [H670]
G major

(75 bars)

Rauschendes Bächlein,
So silbern und hell,
Eilst zur Geliebten
So munter und schnell?
Ach, trautes Bächlein,
Mein Bote sei Du;
Bringe die Grüsse
Des Fernen ihr zu.

All' ihre Blumen
Im Garten gepflegt,
Die sie so lieblich
Am Busen trägt,
Und ihre Rosen
In purpurner Glut,
Bächlein, erquicke
Mit kühlender Flut.

Wenn sie am Ufer,
In Träume versenkt,
Meiner gedenkend,
Das Köpfchen hängt;
Tröste die Süsse
Mit freundlichem Blick,
Denn der Geliebte
Kehrt bald zurück.

Neigt sich die Sonne
Mit rötlichem Schein,
Wiege das Liebchen
In Schlummer ein.
Rausche sie murmelnd
In süsse Ruh,
Flüstre ihr Träume
Der Liebe zu.

Murmuring brook,
So silver and bright,
Do you hasten, so lively and swift,
To my beloved?
Ah, sweet brook,
Be my messenger.
Bring her greetings
From her distant lover.

All the flowers,
Tended in her garden,
Which she wears so charmingly
On her breast,
And her roses
With their crimson glow:
Refresh them, brooklet,
With your cooling waters.

When on your banks
Lost in dreams,
Thinking of me,
She hangs her head;
Comfort my sweetheart
With a kindly glance,
For her beloved
Will soon return.

When the sun
Sinks in a red flush,
Lull my sweetheart
To sleep.
With your soft murmurings
Bring her sweet repose,
And whisper
Dreams of love.

LUDWIG RELLSTAB (1799–1860); poem written before 1825

This is the fourth of Schubert's ten Rellstab solo settings (1827–8). See the poet's biography for a chronological list of all the Rellstab settings.

This music reflects perfection in its watery surface – a classical perfection in a pastoral frame, appropriate for Beethoven and the possible provenance of the Rellstab poems directly from that master's desk. The intense subjective whimsy of *Die schöne Müllerin* D795 and the tragic melancholy of *Winterreise* are more important milestones in the history of the Romantic style, but no matter – it was very much Schubert's own decision to differentiate the manner of these Rellstab songs from those of their predecessors. Einstein remarks that *Liebesbotschaft* was written as a result of 'a new emphasis which transforms the song into a recital piece'. By this does he mean that a song with neither narrative context, nor characters with names or roles, becomes something nearer to chamber music? Although *Liebesbotschaft* is in the same key of G major as *Wohin?* D795/2, the Rellstab stream, also pressed into service as love's messenger, is several degrees cooler than Müller's, and inhabited neither by water nixies nor the spirit of German folksong. If anything the mood here is nearer the G major coda of *Eifersucht und Stolz* D795/15 from the same cycle, where the miller boy imagines himself playing pretty songs to children on a reed pipe, a fabricated pastoral idyll unrelated to his real story. But at least we have followed that story with growing empathy. As much as we adore the music of *Liebesbotschaft*, the narrator and his gardening paramour are stock characters, a slightly updated Damon and Chloë. Once the song is over they cease to live in our imagination or concern.

In exchange for this lack of interest in the song's background, at least as far as the poetry is concerned, we find a foreground of melting beauty and elegance. Schubert is able to take any character, however wooden, and breathe life into it; thus the narrator emerges, if not as a *Sturm und Drang* lover, as someone courtly and affectionate, a lieder-singing Don Ottavio. Rellstab has given Schubert all the help he initially needs by providing a stream – the last in which our composer was to dip his toe – which is murmuring, silver and bright. With this as his inspiration Schubert works his miracle, beginning with the movement of the glinting water in the piano. It is difficult to believe that the whole song did not derive from this flawless five-bar introduction, but the sketch (printed in NSA Volume 14b p. 286), one of the few we possess for a major Schubert song, tells us otherwise. The composer is often parsimonious with his music paper, but here, for once, he is extravagant. The song is planned on three staves and Schubert concerns himself only with the vocal line, leaving large white gaps for the piano part – on a map, after all, these empty spaces would signify water! Of the accompaniment only a desultory six bars are sketched, scattered in groups of two throughout the piece (at bb. 30–1 for instance), and even these are as bare as a skeleton, as if an aide-memoire for something he already has in his head.

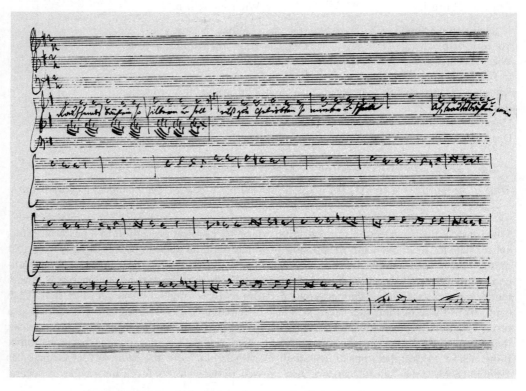

Sketch for *Liebesbotschaft*, the first of two sparsely filled sides of manuscript paper.

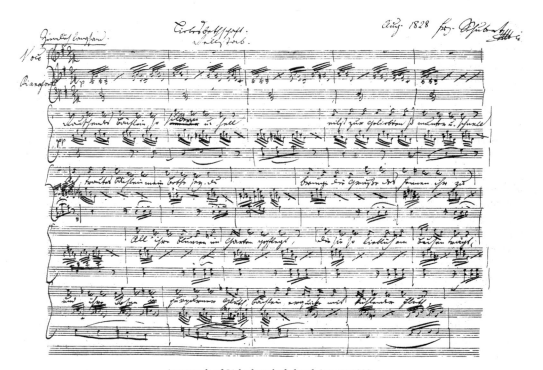

Autograph of *Liebesbotschaft* dated August 1828.

The voice part on the other hand is already perfectly formed, scarcely different from the final version – a melody that seems to have been conceived on the spot and without revision. The composer bothers to write the word underlay for only two and a half lines of poetry, but it is clear that he is working with the poet's poem by his side. If we were only allowed to glimpse the scene at Schubert's desk it would tell us much: if he were consulting a handwritten piece of paper it would confirm that he used copies of the poem prepared by Rellstab for Beethoven in 1825; if it were a book we would know the composer used the published edition of Rellstab's poems from 1827, proving false Schindler's claims to have given him the poems.

The priorities of this sketch are clear. Here is proof that Schubert regarded song-writing as tune first and foremost; the melody had to be established before anything else. In this sketch, however, he leaves an entire three-line stave blank before beginning the vocal line – a sign that he planned a substantial introduction. What he eventually wrote to fill in this space is unique in his songs. The first seeming anomaly is the use of the words 'Ziemlich langsam' (rather slow) for music that bristles with demisemiquaver figurations – a black thicket which usually signifies virtuosic speed, particularly in Romantic music. This marking led the soprano Elena Gerhardt (1883–1961) to ask Gerald Moore to play the introduction at a snail's pace, but anyone aware of eighteenth- and nineteenth-century practices would know that in this $\frac{2}{4}$ the crotchet is meant to be taken as the 'rather slow' beat (no matter how many smaller notes are made to fit into the larger unit), and that the marking does not refer to how the music should *sound*, so much as how it should be *measured*. This is one of many instances where Schubert, himself born in the eighteenth century, reveals himself as Salieri's pupil. We have only to turn to the songs of Beethoven to find demisemiquavers, and the seemingly contradictory marking 'Andante vivace' in the Metastasio setting *Lebensgenuss* (Op. 82 no. 5); the famous *Wonne der Wehmut* (Goethe,

Op. 83 no. 1) is also in $\frac{2}{4}$ and marked 'Andante espressivo'. Generations of singers have slowed this piece down into four ponderous beats in a bar, making the accompanying demisemiquavers sound lugubrious. They are meant to flow without sounding hasty or snatched, and so it is with the opening of *Liebesbotschaft*.

This musicological point is worth making because it is one of the things that establishes the song's classical poise within its adventurousness – a typically Schubertian compromise between old and new, humility and initiative, giving way and forging ahead, conservation and renewal, and between the musical worlds of one composer born in 1770 and another born in 1797. Schubert honoured the past with almost every note he wrote and here was no exception, particularly as he set out to write a work that was associated in his mind with Beethoven. On the other hand the innovation, quiet and muted though it may be, is staggering. Thousands of composers have given the piano an aquatic role, but even in competition with himself, Schubert here achieves a high-water mark. Over a riverbed of left-hand fifths, as constant as a steady current, the stream flows imperturbably, its movement visible (and audible) in figurations rippling up the stave and down again. In more than one song from this period (e.g. *Frühlingssehnsucht* – the third in the Rellstab set) the composer has been fascinated by subtle harmonic changes hidden within chord patterns in the accompaniment. So it is here, with the pianist's fingers limning in touches of unexpected harmony which fill out the texture and make it sparkle (including that famous and unexpectedly concealed G sharp at the end of b. 3 that has tripped up so many pianists!)

As soon as the voice enters with its matchless but simple melody, the piano adopts the role of the solicitous *cavaliere servente*. The poet's concern for the well-being of his beloved is mirrored in the piano's cradling of the voice. It supports the singer in undulations that produce euphonious sixths in combination with the vocal line, and echoes each of the singer's opening phrases with music that suggests the sighing of distant horn-calls, reinforcing the underlying pastoral convention. This conversational pattern of two bars of singing followed by one of pianistic commentary continues throughout the poem's first strophe. Right from the beginning the music is suffused with a tinge of melancholy – a state of mind largely disguised by the energy of the rippling and the enthusiasm of the singer. Nevertheless the words 'so silbern und hell' shift briefly into A minor (b. 7), and 'Ach, trautes Bächlein, / Mein Bote sei Du' are cast in E minor (b. 12), the relative minor of the tonic key. This adds an element of rueful longing, resignation as much as ardour, which contributes to the sense of deep feelings held in check. After all, Don Ottavio with his patrician reserve never lays a finger on Donna Anna.

For the second strophe, from b. 18, the music moves sideways into the subdominant, C major. This shift makes something magical and other-worldly of the lover's garden and her flowers that spring into life thanks to mezzo staccato quavers in the pianist's left hand. (The very word 'gepflegt' suggests work in the garden, as if the gentle digging of the piano's left-hand semiquavers might be done with a miniature hoe.) The narrator cannot see this pastoral retreat from his vantage point upstream, leaving him (and us) free to make something Elysian of it in our minds. Mention of roses prompts Schubert, who has written his fair share of flower songs, to perfumed eloquence: the last two lines of the strophe are set twice, and each time the word 'Rosen' produces a leap of a fifth for the voice, the second a third higher than the first (bb. 22 and 26). It is as if the singer has suddenly become intoxicated with the fragrances of a summer evening. The passionate setting of 'purpurner Glut' (b. 27) produces a wonderful sighing fall on 'Glut', but even this glowing image is described with a shift into a wilting D minor. We realize that the singer is separated from the fulfilment of his dream; he is not in the garden, but only able to dream about surrendering to the aroma of the flowers worn on the beloved's breast.

The third strophe is introduced by an interlude where two bars alternate between G[7] and C major (bb. 30 and 31) with a tiny left-hand motif of gentle yearning semiquavers (this was included, albeit notated in the treble clef, in the song's sketch discussed above). As soon as the singer enters the music sinks into A minor – E minor – G minor for 'Wenn sie am Ufer, / In Träume versenkt' (bb. 32–5), an exquisitely doleful progression, each chord change sinking deeper into slumber. The speed of the vocal line has exactly halved (crotchets and quavers rather than quavers and semiquavers), a wonderful use of musical augmentation to depict sleep and dreams. Meanwhile the stream murmurs on in the original pulse. The third and fourth lines of this verse ('Meiner gedenkend, / Das Köpfchen hängt', from b. 36) are set to music a third lower in pitch than the first and second – one of the composer's loveliest sequences, and absolutely descriptive of the words.

When quick note values return to the vocal line ('Tröste die Süsse / Mit freundlichem Blick') semiquavers nudge up the stave as if on a quest – searching and scanning for the sight of a familiar face. The repetition of these words sounds a note of desperation, always hidden by the classical poise that makes some people, including Capell, think of this song as 'amiable' and 'placid'. The stream is at its most ruffled here with frequent changes of harmony, a turbulence suggesting that the reuniting of these lovers will be no simple matter. The phrase 'Kehrt bald zurück' ('Will soon return', bb. 44–5) plays a special role here (the same word 'zurück' pulled the vocal line away from modulation in the first strophe of *Auf dem Strom* D943): it is sung to a cadence that moves into B major but it prompts one of the composer's most magical returns to the home key, a musical pun on the meaning of 'zurück' which inspires tears rather than laughter. The little group of semiquavers in octaves in the left hand that paves the way back to G major (b. 50, the only such tremor from the riverbed in the entire song) sets up to perfection this heartbreakingly beautiful cadence.

The last verse is virtually a repeat of the first – the song's form is ABCA – and it is a triumph of strophic management. All the inflections of the new words are just as appropriately set, as if the music had been minted freshly for them. For example, 'Rauschen', used here as a soporific, and is entirely different from the beguiling verb describing the stream in *Wohin* D795/2. The withdrawal into E minor for 'Flüstre ihr Träume / Der Liebe zu' at bb. 61–2 suggests the intimacy of lovers' secrets, and the leap of a tenth on 'Träume' ('Grüsse' in the equivalent passage in the first verse) is a magical thing, a gift to a singer in command of his *mezza voce*. The coda passage is a repeat of the poem's final line, and for this the music moves into C major. Although this is not really a surprise (the music for the second strophe also began in this way) the subdominant is an intimate locale (from b. 64) for the words 'Flüstre ihr Träume', suggesting the exchange of almost sacred confidences. The final descending melisma on dotted rhythms for 'Liebe' (b. 67) is as affecting as a deeply sincere bow of homage.

The postlude is an elaboration of the prelude, bringing the music full circle – an absolutely perfect circle drawn freehand by a great master. If the song seems, at one level, framed by an old-fashioned pastoral convention, something contrived in comparison to the spontaneity of almost any song in *Winterreise*, we have to remember that some of the greatest works of art have been accomplished within the conventions of artificiality. Yes, we may notice the difference, but we still love this music very much, and would not be without it for the world.

First edition:	Published by Tobias Haslinger, Vienna in May 1829, Volume 1, no. 1 (P204)
Subsequent editions:	Peters: Vol. 1/122; AGA XX 554: Vol. 9/134; NSA IV: Vol. 14a/96, Sketch 14b/286; Bärenreiter: Vol. 4/120
Further settings and arrangements:	Ludwig Berger (1777–1839) *Liebesbotschaft* Op. 17 no. 1 (date unknown)
	Carl Friedrich Girschner (1794–1860) *Liebesbotschaft* Op. 25 no. 4 (1839)
	Arr. Franz Liszt (1811–1886) for solo piano, no. 10 of

Schwanengesang (1838–9) [*see* TRANSCRIPTIONS]
Karl Wilhelm Taubert (1811–1891) *Liebesbotschaft* Op. 17 no. 10
(1880)
Arr. Leopold Godowsky (1870–1938) for solo piano, *Love's
message* (1927, 2nd revised edition 1937) [*see* TRANSCRIPTIONS]

Discography and timing: Fischer-Dieskau III 3[1]   2'48
                       Hyperion I 37[6]
                       Hyperion II 37[1]   2'55   John Mark Ainsley

← *Glaube, Hoffnung und Liebe* D955   *Kriegers Ahnung* D957/2 →

II KRIEGERS AHNUNG   Warrior's premonition
D957/2 [H671]
C minor

(122 bars)

In tiefer Ruh liegt um mich her	In deep repose my comrades in arms
Der Waffenbrüder Kreis;	Lie in a circle around me;
Mir ist das Herz so bang und schwer,	My heart is so anxious and heavy,
Von Sehnsucht mir so heiss.	So ardent with longing.
Wie hab' ich oft so süss geträumt[1]	How often I have dreamt sweetly
An ihrem Busen warm!	Upon her warm breast!
Wie freundlich schien des Herdes Glut,	How cheerful the fireside glow seemed
Lag sie in meinem Arm!	When she lay in my arms.
Hier, wo der Flammen düstrer Schein[2]	Here, where the sombre glimmer of the flames,
Ach! nur auf Waffen spielt,	Alas, plays only on weapons,
Hier fühlt die Brust sich ganz allein,	Here the heart feels utterly alone;
Der Wehmut Träne quillt.	A tear of sadness wells up.
Herz! Dass der Trost Dich nicht verlässt!	Heart, may comfort not forsake you;
Es ruft noch manche Schlacht –	Many a battle still calls.
Bald ruh ich wohl und schlafe fest,	Soon I shall surely rest and sleep deeply.
Herzliebste – Gute Nacht!	Beloved, goodnight!

LUDWIG RELLSTAB (1799–1860); poem written before 1825

*This is the fifth of Schubert's ten Rellstab solo settings (1827–8). See the poet's biography for a
chronological list of all the Rellstab settings.*

---

[1] Rellstab writes 'Wie hab' ich oft so süss *geruht*' (to rhyme with the 'Glut' in the strophe's third line).
[2] Rellstab writes 'Hier wo der *Flamme* düstrer Schein'.

Schubert, the composer of the famous Marches Militaires D733, grew up against a background of war; his home city was the host of the Congress whose task it was to redraw the map of Europe in the wake of Napoleon's defeat. Austria was caught up in these conflicts during his childhood, and the composer's first song masterpiece, *Gretchen am Spinnrade* D118, dates from the very week in which the first anniversary of the emperor's victory over the French forces was marked by Vienna's biggest triumphal celebration. One of his most admired poets, Theodor Körner, had died in this war of liberation, and for a number of years in the composer's adolescence the streets of Vienna must have been full of walking wounded. In the Schubert song canon there is fighting aplenty from a number of historical epochs and locales: noble Ossianic warriors fighting the Romans; bloodthirsty ballads and songs of noble knights and ladies; battle and drinking songs, often for male chorus, including one inspired by Wallenstein and the Thirty Years War, *Der Wallensteiner Lanzknecht beim Trunk* D931; and of course songs like Körner's *Gebet während der Schlacht* D171 where the battle poem dates from the composer's own lifetime. In a letter written from Schubert's long holiday in Upper Austria in 1825, where he visited the site of the bloody massacre of the Bavarians by the Tyroleans in 1809, he expresses a profound distaste for the horrors of war, particularly conflicts associated with religion. Nevertheless, his interest in soldiery (he himself was too short, and short-sighted, for military service) seems to have focused on medieval chivalry and Christian versus Muslim conflict as exemplified by the Crusades: the opera *Fierabras* D796 is the biggest work on this theme, but such songs as *Romanze des Richard Löwen-herz* D907 from Scott's *Ivanhoe*, *Der Kreuzzug* D932, and the unfinished opera *Der Graf von Gleichen* D918 show a continuing fascination with this period in history.

The soldier in *Kriegers Ahnung* is without background – he might be a Greek or Roman. The two other songs by Schubert that describe soldiers facing certain death are *Amphiaraos* D166 (Körner) and *Hektors Abschied* D312 (Schiller); perhaps Rellstab's line about soldiers sleeping in a circle is a clue in this regard. This 'Krieger' might be a Crusader, or he might be fighting in a contemporary setting, although there is a gravity about him that suggests the nobility of a knight of yore. The homesickness of every serving solider, alongside memories of happier times, are combined with foreboding that he will soon have to pay the ultimate price as a warrior and patriot. The song is a prophecy of Mahler's obsession with soldiers' songs and with the cruel fate of lovers described in that composer's *Wo die schönen Trompeten blasen* (1898), and *Revelge* (1899). *Der Tamboursg'sell* is also filled with compassion for the deserter, a small man caught up in the war machine and destroyed by it.

Curiously enough, the very opening strikes a Mahlerian note – C minor chords in ⅜ that suggest the shudder of muffled drums or even the clanking of armour. C minor is also a dramatic key for Beethoven – we have mentioned the *Marcia funebre* from the 'Eroica' Symphony Op. 55 in connection with *Auf dem Strom* D943, but here one is reminded of the opening of the 'Pathé-tique' Sonata Op. 13, as well as the frisson of the opening of Schubert's own Piano Sonata in C minor D958. The song is divided into sections marked by the different verses, and the structure is unlike any of the other Rellstab settings. This is not only Schubert's last war song; it represents his last essay in sectional song composition where changes of key, metre and tempo are used in preference to a single seamless structure. To an extent this is 'old-fashioned' Schubert, a type of song that, in formal terms at least, he would have been more likely to have written ten or twelve years earlier. The celebrated *Der Wanderer* D489 of 1816 comes to mind and, as in that master-piece, Schubert takes his time to establish a mood of heavy foreboding before the entry of the voice.

How heavy the mood should be here is another matter. A great deal of the efficacy of the piece depends on the marking 'Nicht zu langsam'. Some commentators have talked about a death march at the beginning (a curious description of music in ⅜) and this, allied with the opening words ('In tiefer Ruh') has encouraged in some performers an impossibly slow tempo coupled with a Wagnerian interpretation, as if such a song could only be sung by a hoary Gurnemanz. If the composer intended this song to be performed by the singer who has just delighted us with *Liebesbotschaft* – a young man in love, and not necessarily a bearded old warrior – a lighter approach is justified. (This point is especially relevant when one considers the relatively rare occurrence of a performance of this set of songs by a tenor; of all the songs in *Schwanengesang* this is the only one that baritones are able to sing without transposition, and hearing them able to revel in the tessitura has accustomed us to darker, and thus older-seeming, colours.) The tempo should be a slow one-in-the-bar which enables a good singer to encompass the opening phrase in one breath; it also gives a twitch of angst to the dotted-rhythm opening which should not be merely grandly somnolent. There is an aspect of the *scena* here, as is usually the case when Schubert divides a song into sections, and with this come certain theatrical flourishes: the portentous 'dirty work afoot' harmonies of 'Mir ist das Herz so bang und schwer' (bb. 15–17) are taken from an earlier Schubert, and the turn that decorates 'Sehnsucht mir so heiss' (set almost as a free cadenza, bb. 20–21) might have been written for Vogl, enabling him to re-live, with his customary pathos, a great moment in the opera house. This first section ends with a four-bar interlude (bb. 25–8) where the rhythmic motif of the introduction places us firmly in the dominant.

We might now expect a second verse in C minor, but instead of a V–I progression we slip a semitone upwards into A flat major. This is marked by a new tempo indication ('Etwas schneller'). As he calls here for only a moderate change of speed Schubert surely did not wish the first section to be too slow. (In many a performance this section – crotchet for crotchet – is taken at about three times the speed of the opening.) The composer avoids a new key signature, perhaps in an attempt to preserve a sense of unity. The music blossoms into gentle triplets, tendrils of caress and intimacy which, together with the change of key, suggest past happiness. As in *Winterreise* D911, the harshness of the present in the minor key is mitigated by the beauty of major-key memories. The entwining of voice and piano in euphonious sixths at 'An ihrem Busen warm!' (bb. 33–5) and 'Lag sie in meinem Arm!' (bb. 37–9) looks back to *Liebesbotschaft*: the lovers' dreamy reactions to thoughts of their paramours are remarkably similar, as are the descending harmonic sequences on the repeats of these phrases. This has led us into D flat major via a passage in the key of G flat (in this context a shift that suggests uxorious intimacy) from b. 39; a short interlude of rocking arpeggios in D flat major in the middle of the piano gives way to triplets on low D flats (at the end of b. 42) which pulsate ominously in the bass. To change the scene back to the unpleasant reality of the military camp with cinematic speed these D flats are suddenly re-spelled as acerbic C sharps (b. 43). This is the pivot that moves the music for the third verse into F sharp minor.

The dark mood of *Aufenthalt* D957/5, a song about lonely isolation, appears here as a pre-echo. The pulsating triplets also have much in common with the panic-stricken fourth verse of *Auf dem Strom* that describes a one-way journey to the unknown regions of death, and also with *Fahrt zum Hades* D526. The horror of the soldier's situation is aptly illustrated at 'Hier fühlt die Brust sich ganz allein' (b. 50) by a sudden harmonic shift from the first inversion of F sharp minor (with A as the bass note) into the root position of A minor. This bleak harmony prevails for three bars of merciless triplets before falling to the even more dismal reaches of F minor in first inversion. From this bedrock of depression the music surges upwards, both in terms of harmony and vocal tessitura, to depict the soldier's tears rising to the surface, as if from the deepest of hidden wells. The sob of the first 'Der Wehmut Tränen quillt' (bb. 54–7) is somewhat stifled, but the high F of 'Wehmut' on the repeat of these words gives full voice to his emotions.

How easily might Schubert have set the concluding verse – certainly not even Rellstab at his most inspired – in a sentimental and lachrymose manner. But the composer realizes that something exceptional is called for to enliven the song. Firstly, the music must expand to encompass all that happens rather too quickly in these short concluding lines (the battles still to be fought, the premonition of death that lies at the heart of the piece, the soldier's farewell). The space and power needed to express all this is achieved by various verbal repetitions as well as another change of tempo ('Geschwind, unruhig' from b. 61) and key signature. This resolves three flats into naturals – thus C major – but we hear this tonality only briefly at the song's most intimate passage, the words 'Bald ruh ich wohl'. Otherwise the section is a sea of churning accompanying sextuplets pivoting around G, the dominant of C major, as well as A minor and its dominant. Both valour and panic are suggested by this music, a considerable expressive achievement. Mention of many a battle ('manche Schlacht') produces a four-bar interlude of the greatest energy (bb. 69–72), and we find ourselves in the thick of the fighting with swords whirring all around us. (Here the pianist's fingers are reminded of the accompaniment of *Am Feierabend* D795/5 from *Die schöne Müllerin* that represents crushing of another sort – instead of metal clanking on metal, the grinding of mill-wheels, stone against stone.) The harmonies, like the protagonist, seem trapped in a situation where there is no resolution.

And then the power of imagination instantly switches the scene from battlefield to bedroom. This is the sort of magical moment of instantaneous release, unique to song (or film), of which neither opera nor theatre is capable. The vocal line, suddenly hushed, emerges like a burst of starlight at the top of the stave. Supported by the purity of C major (albeit not in its root position, which would have turned fantasy into something more palpable) the soldier rests his head on the breast of the beloved; the setting of 'Bald ruh ich wohl' and 'und schlafe fest' achieve temporary if chilling repose in the middle of the maelstrom. Gentle triplets replace the scurrying sextuplets of the battle music and ties across the bar lines suspend the passage of time (have the words 'ruh' and 'schlafe' ever been more lingeringly and audaciously set than at bb. 73–4 and 77–8?) That the soldier knows his fate all too well is emphasized by 'Herzliebste – Gute Nacht!' The pathos here is that of the prisoner dreaming in the condemned cell, and Schubert has found such a perfect means of describing peace in the eye of the storm that he repeats the entire passage with some small adjustments. Actually this is no idle whim – the scale of the song and the grandeur of the events and the emotions surrounding them require this expansive prolongation. (Schubert being Schubert, the repetition is not exact; at this stage of his life he is never lazy enough to 'cut and paste' an earlier piece of music, but will always recompose it to fit its new circumstances.) We have another opportunity to experience the *mezza voce* magic of 'Bald ruh ich wohl' and the heady dreams of 'und schlafe fest'. As before, 'Herzliebste – Gute Nacht' follows these words, this time harmonized in A flat major (bb. 107–10). This is to prepare us for a return to the music of the opening. We remember that C minor to A flat major had been the pathway (between Verses 1 and 2) into the soldier's dream-world; now A flat major to C minor in the reverse direction points the way, irreversibly, back to reality.

If performers get their tempo relationships right, the dotted crotchet of the 'Geschwind' will more or less equal the crotchet of the returning Tempo I. The word 'Herzliebste' is set across this change of metre, but there should be no radical change of pulse. In this way Schubert ensures a smooth transition between two sections which should melt into each other without a percep- tible break. As both premonitions of violence and dreams of peace fade into the background, we find ourselves once again in the military camp with drums shuddering as an ominous portent of the morrow. These words of farewell hang in the air – a hopeless and final message to a distant beloved.

How successful is this song? Fine as it is, it misses inclusion in the list of Schubert's indis- pensable masterpieces. It is touched with greatness in many ways, and abounds with details that could only have come from the pen of the mature Schubert. But Capell puts his finger on the problem when he writes that 'Schubert's treatment is felt to be, if not perfunctory, at least exterior'. For at least part of this the poet is to blame: a convincing depiction of 'a soldier and afeared' is beyond Rellstab's powers, for he is no Shakespeare. There is something formal about the poem, something slightly contrived and theatrical, and this stands between us and complete belief in this character. We need more time, and more music, to become acquainted with the torment of such a protagonist. As it is, his music moves us greatly, but he himself moves in and out of our ken too quickly to register as anything more substantial than a transitory phantom.

First edition:	Published by Tobias Haslinger, Vienna in May 1829, Volume 1, no. 2 (P205)
Subsequent editions:	Peters: I/126; AGA XX 555: Vol. 9/139; NSA IV: Vol. 14a/103; Bärenreiter: Vol. 4/125
Further settings and arrangements:	Ludwig Berger (1777–1839) *Des Kriegers Ahnung* Op. 17 no. 3 Arr. Franz Liszt (1811–1886) for solo piano, no. 14 of *Schwanengesang* (1838–9) [*see* TRANSCRIPTIONS]
Discography and timing:	Fischer-Dieskau III 3[2] 4'34
	Hyperion I 37[7]
	Hyperion II 37[2] 5'16 John Mark Ainsley

← *Liebesbotschaft* D957/1   *Frühlingssehnsucht* D957/3 →

III FRÜHLINGSSEHNSUCHT   Spring longing
D957/3 [H672]
B♭ major

(103 bars)

Säuselnde Lüfte   Whispering breezes,
Wehend so mild,   Blowing so gently,
Blumiger Düfte   Exuding the fragrance
Atmend erfüllt!   Of flowers,
Wie haucht Ihr mich wonnig begrüssend an! How blissful to me is your welcoming breath!
Wie habt Ihr dem pochenden Herzen getan?   What have you done to my beating heart?
Es möchte Euch folgen auf luftiger Bahn,   It yearns to follow you on your airy path.
Wohin?   Where to?

   Bächlein, so munter   Silver brooklets,
Rauschend zumal,   Also babbling so merrily,
Wollen hinunter[1]   Seek the valley
Silbern ins Tal.   Below.
Die schwebende Welle, dort eilt sie dahin! The surging current rushes down there
Tief spiegeln sich Fluren und Himmel darin. The fields and the sky are deeply mirrored there.
Was ziehst Du mich, sehnend verlangender   Why yearning, craving senses, do you draw me
   Sinn,
Hinab?   Downwards?

---

[1] Rellstab writes '*Wallen* hinunter' – brooklets that 'seethe' or 'charm' did not, it seems, fit Schubert's musical conception.

Grüssender Sonne	Sparkling gold
Spielendes Gold,	Of the welcoming sun,
Hoffende Wonne	You bring the fair joy
Bringest du hold.	Of hope.
Wie labt mich Dein selig begrüssendes Bild!	How your happy, welcoming countenance
	refreshes me!
Es lächelt am tiefblauen Himmel so mild	It smiles so benignly in the deep blue sky
Und hat mir das Auge mit Tränen gefüllt!	And yet has filled my eyes with tears.
Warum?	Why?
Grünend umkränzet	The woods and hills
Wälder und Höh'!	Are wreathed in green.
Schimmernd erglänzet	Snowy blossom
Blütenschnee!	Shimmers and gleams.
So dränget sich Alles zum bräutlichen Licht;	All things strain towards the bridal light;
Es schwellen die Keime, die Knospe bricht;	Seeds swell, buds burst;
Sie haben gefunden, was ihnen gebricht:	They have found what they lacked:
Und Du?	And you?
Rastloses Sehnen!	Restless longing,
Wünschendes Herz,	Yearning heart,
Immer nur Tränen,	Are there always only tears,
Klage und Schmerz?	Complaints and pain?
Auch ich bin mir schwellender Triebe bewusst!	I too am aware of swelling impulses!
Wer stillet mir endlich die drängende Lust?	Who at last will still my urgent desire?
Nur D u befreist den Lenz in der Brust,[2]	Only *you* can free spring in my heart,
Nur Du!	Only you!

LUDWIG RELLSTAB (1799–1860); poem written before 1825

This is the sixth of Schubert's ten Rellstab solo settings (1827–8). See the poet's biography for a chronological list of all the Rellstab settings.

The sketch for *Liebesbotschaft* had been a 'hole in one' from the point of view of the vocal line at least: what we see as Schubert's first thoughts have become the song more or less as we know and love it. The sketch for *Frühlingssehnsucht*, however (which Richard Capell confuses with the one for *Liebesbotschaft*), is of completely unfamiliar music: a wafting melody in D major with a time signature of ⅜ – very much in the mood and metre of the Leitner setting *Wolke und Quelle* D896B from 1827. After five bars there is a change into common time with a gently chugging melody for 'Wie haucht Ihr mich wonnig begrüssend an!' Schubert breaks off this sketch just before the greatest problem in the song – how to set the rhetorical 'Wohin?'. It is just as well that he abandoned these first ideas: one has already sensed that the awkward gear change between ⅜ and ¼ is unworkable. This leisurely music was discarded in favour of the celebrated ²⁄₄ moto perpetuo in B flat major. Whether the composition of another contemporary spring song (*Bei dir allein!* D866/2) played a part in its re-casting is a moot point.

In *Liebesbotschaft* water is the medium through which the lover sends messages to the distant inamorata. Although water features in the second verse of *Frühlingssehnsucht*, the poem begins

---

[2] Rellstab writes 'Nur D u *befreiet* den Lenz in der Brust'.

with whispering breezes. Once he had decided to compose essentially a strophic song, Schubert had to find an accompaniment that would do for these, as well as for babbling brooks (Verse 2), glinting sunlight (Verse 3), bursting buds (Verse 4) and restless longing (Verse 5). From that point of view these all-purpose triplets work triumphantly well. The common denominator is energy combined with delicacy: at the correct tempo the piano writing makes a whirlwind effect that does not preclude a swiftly woven filigree of harmonic detail, and the vocal line is cast in Schubert's favourite dactylic rhythm. The interaction of this duple metre with the unceasing triplets of the accompaniment further energizes the song's texture. The composer favours dactyls to depict the workings of nature – indeed anything, including the advent of death (*Der Tod und das Mädchen* D531), which is beyond man's control. A dactylic song like *Die Sterne* D939 is a humming dynamo of electric energy; the march of spring in *Trockne Blumen* D795/18 an implacable cortège. Similarly, in *Frühlingssehnsucht* there is no stopping the stirrings of nature. This makes the freeze-frame effect on the various questioning words that end each strophe especially arresting.

The twelve-bar *Vorspiel* is a masterful depiction of mounting excitement and rising sap. For two bars we hear only pulsating triplets in B flat major; in the third bar the bare B flats in the bass stave are adorned, like sprouting buds on a trellis, with a rising line in an inner voice – the tenor line of the accompaniment; this sets up a euphonious colloquy with the alto line in the right hand which, in turn, nudges the soprano line up the stave as the chords become louder and fuller. For a moment, before the decrescendo that prepares us for the entrance of the voice, we experience in these triplets the exultant frisson of vernal triumph. (The only other spring-song introduction that can offer a comparable build-up is *L'Hiver a cessé* from Fauré's *La Bonne Chanson* Op. 61 no. 9.) Once the singer enters, the vocal line is supported in the bass line with chords that move in sequences of thirds, fifths and sixths – horn-calls which underline the outdoor nature of the song, and are typical of the pastoral frame which characterizes *Liebesbotschaft*. The conversational nature of these horn-calls when heard as interludes (for example the two-bar phrase after 'Blumiger Düfte / atmend erfüllt!' bb. 21–2) also harks back to bb. 8 and 11 of that song and reminds us that Schubert may have originally intended *Frühlingssehnsucht* to be the second in the Rellstab cycle. (The sequence of the sketches implies this at any rate.)

As the strophe progresses the music achieves a passionate sweep that is very different, for instance, from the gentle swaying of the Pollak setting *Frühlingslied* D919 from 1827. In some ways this is a *Rastlose Liebe* D138 sound-alike. The prevailing B flat major moves towards a cadence in A flat major (b. 41) – a moment's respite for the singer at 'Herzen getan?' as a fermata brings the accompaniment to a brief pause. Then as the music slips back into B flat major for 'Es möchte euch folgen', the vocal line is supported with a new rhythmic vigour, a dotted quaver + semiquaver figure that sounds a seasonal fanfare beneath the singer's passionate outpourings. At a repeat of these words the music moves into D minor (b. 46), adding grim determination to the idea of a journey that may be hazardous. It is here that the grand surprise comes, the song's masterstroke. The problem of how to set that awkward 'Wohin?' is solved by bringing the tumultuous onslaught of the song to a sudden halt. (This pause for thought is much more successful than the passage of similar introspection in the Goethe song *Willkommen und Abschied* D767.) The singer's Ds (on 'luftiger Bahn') creep up a semitone to E flat on 'Wohin?' (bb. 49–50), supported by a shift into the dark and distant key of A flat minor. The repeat of this enquiry resolves on to E flat major, decorated with a pleading, and dismally bereft, F flat appoggiatura (b. 52). A four-bar interlude of two groups of tied half-minims echoes the singer's dismay (his sense of isolation is illustrated, even visually, by those white and empty bars). Thus we are led back to B flat major and the equally sudden resumption of the moto perpetuo.

Thereafter, or at least for the next three verses, the song is strophic; all the new words fit the music to perfection. The water imagery of the second strophe is appropriately mirrored by an accompaniment that bubbles and gurgles as easily as it whispers and blows. The elongated word at the end of the strophe is this time the rather more sinister 'Hinab?'; the first upward inflection seems initially to be a question and then, on the downward repeat, comes an answer illustrating the direction of the word's meaning (i.e. 'Downwards? Downwards!'). As Schubert composed this passage was he reminded of *Der Müller und der Bach* D795/19 and the suicidal miller boy of *Die schöne Müllerin*? The connection between water imagery and the brook that lures young men to their graves suggests that Rellstab, derivative poet as he was, knew his friend Wilhelm Müller's *Die schöne Müllerin* poems long before they were printed in 1821. At the end of the third verse 'Warum?' also seems ideally set; this is the culmination of a strophe where the light-fingered accompaniment has admirably reflected the glinting sun. Such brightness serves only to emphasize an inner darkness – there is the ache of tears in this music, and it becomes clear that the one thing missing in the protagonist's life is the presence of the distant beloved. In the fourth verse the dotted rhythms are particularly suited to celebrate the successful quest of the swelling buds which have found the bridal light. We sense a wedding ceremony in the air for everyone except the singer whose forlorn repeats of 'Und Du?' are addressed to himself. This change of thought gives rise to a final verse where the poet allows his observations of nature to give way to more subjective musings.

Self-pity dictates that the fifth verse should begin as a *minore* variant of the other four (from b. 103). Schubert first darkens the colour of this section by flattening the harmonies; he then screws the tension tighter by repeating the same words in a major key in a much higher tessitura – high G flats and Fs (bb. 115–16). This repetition of 'Rastloses Sehnen! / Wünschendes Herz' is veritably heroic, worthy of an operatic tenor. The passage of twenty 'rogue' bars that classifies this song as a *modified* strophic setting has been short but telling. We are soon back on familiar ground at b. 122 with 'Auch ich bin mir schwellender Triebe bewusst!' This is a return of the 'triumph' music with its dotted rhythms that we have encountered at the end of all the preceding verses. The final 'Du!' is addressed to the distant beloved, and there is something hopeless in this; we shall never know whether she heeds these pleas, but her compliance cannot be taken for granted. This ambivalence – the pleasure in thinking of her, the pain in her absence – is reflected in how this final '<u>Du</u>' is harmonized: a bar of E flat major (b. 140) is followed by one in E flat minor (b. 141). 'Nur Du!' again, and this time a sung F clouded by the uncertainty of F7 harmony for two bars. This last, highly unconventional as a clinching gesture, leaves the whole question of her reciprocation hanging in the air. Although the piano closes the song in a flourish of broken chords in B flat major there is no forte of triumph: the hushed final cadence with a suggestion of E flat minor (b. 147) is an ominous touch – a cold shiver of rejection passing over the surface of the music. Hindsight makes us realize that we have detected the seed of doubt everywhere in this music, and that its passion and enthusiasm have been a vain attempt to divert our attention from the central emptiness in the narrator's life.

First edition:	Published by Tobias Haslinger, Vienna in May 1829, Volume 1, no. 3 (P206)
Subsequent editions:	Peters: I/131; AGA XX 556: Vol. 9/144; NSA IV: Vol. 14a/111, Sketch 14b/289; Bärenreiter: Vol. 4/131
Arrangements:	Arr. Franz Liszt (1811–1886) for solo piano, no. 9 of *Schwanengesang* (1838–9) [*see* TRANSCRIPTIONS]
Discography and timing:	Fischer-Dieskau III 3³ 3'17
	Hyperion I 37⁸
	Hyperion II 37³ 3'53 John Mark Ainsley

← *Kriegers Ahnung* D957/2   *Ständchen* D957/4 →

IV STÄNDCHEN   Serenade
D957/4 [H673]
D minor

(50 bars)

Leise flehen meine Lieder	Softly my songs plead
Durch die Nacht zu Dir;	Through the night to you;
In den stillen Hain hernieder,	Down into the silent grove,
Liebchen, komm' zu mir!	Beloved, come to me!

Flüsternd schlanke Wipfel rauschen   Slender treetops whisper and rustle
In des Mondes Licht;   In the moonlight;
Des Verräters feindlich Lauschen   My darling, do not fear
Fürchte, Holde, nicht.   That the hostile betrayer will overhear us.

Hörst die Nachtigallen schlagen?   Do you hear the nightingales call?
Ach! sie flehen Dich,   Ah, they are imploring you;
Mit der Töne süssen Klagen   With their sweet, plaintive songs
Flehen sie für mich.   They are imploring for me.

Sie verstehn des Busens Sehnen,   They understand the heart's yearning,
Kennen Liebesschmerz,   They know the pain of love;
Rühren mit den Silbertönen   With their silvery notes
Jedes weiche Herz.   They touch every tender heart.

Lass auch D i r die Brust bewegen,   Let *your* heart, too, be moved,
Liebchen, höre mich!   Beloved, hear me!
Bebend harr' ich Dir entgegen!   Trembling, I await you!
Komm', beglücke mich!   Come, make me happy!

LUDWIG RELLSTAB (1799–1860); poem written before 1825

This is the seventh of Schubert's ten Rellstab solo settings (1827–8). See the poet's biography for a chronological list of all the Rellstab settings.

This is probably the most famous serenade in the world, but the cost of such fame to the music has been high. It has become so hackneyed, and such a symbol of Schubert in his *Lilac Time* incarnation, that one must always make a conscious effort to hear it with fresh ears. The piece has been subject to a staggering number of instrumental arrangements and one cannot help but think of Richard Tauber dressed up as Schubert and singing it to Hannerl, Haiderl or Hederl in the *Dreimäderlhaus* as he blinks amiably 'durch die Brille'. (This is no disrespect to a great singer, incidentally. The entrepreneurs of the time simply capitalized on the fortuitous similarity of his build and appearance to those of the composer and, as they say, who can buck the market?) The music, usually in wordless adaptations, is still employed as one of the theme songs of *Alt Wien* and the queasy Viennese *Sehnsucht* that is piped into shopping malls.

The main effect of this popular accessibility has been to make us hear in this serenade something free and easy where it is assumed that the urgent requests of the lover have a naturally happy ending. It is so much a set piece, and the melody is so enchanting, that we can forget all too easily that it is written in the minor key, and that it is full of that silver-toned melancholy (not sob-tinged sentimentality) that is rather more profound than thousands of glib, heart-on-sleeve interpretations would signify. Its vaunted similarity to Don Giovanni's 'Deh, vieni alla finestra' is confined to the tonality of D – Schubert's song *An die Laute* D905 owes more to this Mozartian inspiration. Another Mozartian influence might be the slow movement of the Piano Concerto in A major K488 where, if the wistful opening melody in ⅜ triplets is only distantly related to Schubert's serenade, the mood of the whole seems a fitting inspiration to a younger composer planning to write a piece in the minor key where passion and discretion, hope and disappointment, are all entwined. The point is that the serenader of the Rellstab *Ständchen* is no heartless seducer, assured and convinced of success; the music is shot through with uncertainty and vulnerability, and it is this which makes it a quintessentially Schubertian creation.

We hear the serenader's lute or guitar first – gently rocking staccato chords (they are actually marked 'staccatissimo' as if to suggest a plectrum rather than the brush of a finger) underpinned by bass minims. In a ⅜ bar this allocates an important rest to the left hand on the third beat of bar, an addition of light and air to a texture that can be swamped by over-use of the pedal and glutinous instrumental adaptations. These quietly resonating lower notes are the foundation of the work's poise and energy; in the manner of a ground bass they establish a spacious momentum, a hypnotic sway that is as responsible for the song's popularity as its melody. After a four-bar introduction we hear the famous tune which, like other heart-stopping moments in the Rellstab songs, is made up of a falling sequence: thus the weaving melodic phrase for 'Leise flehen' is repeated a tone lower (except for the top D) for 'meine Lieder'. This is followed by the clinching two-bar cadence (V–I) of 'Durch die Nacht zu Dir' (bb. 7–8), which is duly echoed by the piano. As in *Liebesbotschaft* and *Frühlingssehnsucht* the accompaniment has a conversational role, mulling over what has gone before in affectionate reiteration. The next two lines of poetry continue the long arch of the melody and include a superb opportunity for the tenor to display his *mezza voce* and feeling for words on the lightly touched high F of 'stillen Hain' (b. 11). The descending phrase 'Liebchen, komm' zu mir!' (bb. 13–14) is in the relative major (how touching this is – we can almost *feel* the singer's tenderness) and is once again echoed with an interlude. The guitar motif of the accompaniment moves into the left hand during these interpolations, and there is no reason to assume that this is suddenly legato – the plucked staccati are surely intended to be heard as such throughout. Pianists with foot welded to the pedal, beware!

Schubert uses two of Rellstab's strophes for each of his musical ones. Thus 'Flüsternd schlanke Wipfel rauschen' (from b. 17) is the beginning of the first verse's middle section beginning in the dominant of the home key. The return to D minor via A⁷ at 'Wipfel rauschen' allows for a touch of drama (even more appropriate for the matching passage of the next phrase – 'Des Verräters feindlich Lauschen') but once again it is the juxtaposition of major and minor that works its magic spell. What could be more poetic than the moon? The switch to B flat major (VI) in b. 19 for 'In des Mondes Licht' bathes the music in the softest light. The entwining of voice and accompaniment in dreamy thirds at the repeat of these words makes something almost palpably liquid of this imagery. The volatile temperament of the singer (for there is something Italian about the very concept of a serenade) allows a forte outburst on the repeat of 'Fürchte, Holde, nicht' (bb. 27–8). It seems the singer is prepared to die for his beloved and take on any number of treacherous interlopers.

The eight-bar interlude that now follows is one of the great Schubertian miracles. Derived in the most subtle manner from the singer's unfolding melody, it is the musical essence of the preceding serenade compressed into instrumental, rather than vocal, terms. The apotheosis of the echo, it is typical of the Rellstab songs. The echo also contains an echo of itself: the *minore* statement of the first four bars (bb. 28–32) melts into a major-key reiteration of the same material (bb. 32–6), the effect of which is indescribably wistful. This is one of those songs where we can almost feel how tenderly Schubert, if he had been given the chance, might have made love. And how seldom such chances seem to have come his way, if ever, is also writ large in this music.

Thus the sound of the nightingale, which is the subject of the third and fourth verses of the poem (the song's second musical strophe), is the 'schmelzend Ach' of which Hölty wrote in *An die Nachtigall* D196, the 'voix de notre désespoir' that Verlaine immortalized in *En sourdine* set by Fauré, Hahn and Debussy. This is the last of the many appearances of this bird in Schubert's songs, and perhaps the most beautiful. So enthused is the listener with the music that he scarcely notices the presence of this little songster who defines the mood of the whole of this *Ständchen*. The point is that the nightingale's song represents the sorrow of unhappy love rather than its fulfilment, what Coleridge calls 'Philomela's pity-pleading strains'. The interlude after 'Ach! sie flehen Dich' seems especially appropriate (bb. 9–10 in the repeat), the dying fall of the piano's echoing phrase doing service for an imitation of birdsong at eventide. In musical terms this is all a strophic repeat of the song's first page, but the new words bring new delight: the jump of a sixth up to the word 'Töne' set to a dotted crotchet (b. 11) seems a built-in illustration of tonal beauties per se, whether from the throat of man or bird; the clinging harmonies in thirds at the repeat of 'Kennen Liebesschmerz' denote the twinned complicity of souls who suffer pain in parallel; and the change into D major at 'Silbertönen' (b. 24) is a moment of real magic. The equivalent passage in the first verse (Rellstab's second, at 'feindlich Lauschen') is not special in the same way; surely this is an instance when the composer planned ahead and engineered a colour change with the words of the second strophe in mind. This is the sweetest piece of silver ever to have crossed a larynx, and it deserves a *palme d'or*.

The music is suddenly disrupted with an abrupt change of mood, as if the singer's patience is at an end. He changes tactics by trying something more forceful than seductive charm. In performance these pleas, which have in them something of a command, almost always result in a faster tempo for the following eight bars, a change that is not actually marked by the composer, but which is so time-honoured as to have become almost de rigueur. From the point of view of the performer's *amour-propre* this music is a masterstroke. Anna Milder once wrote to Schubert of his songs that 'all this endless beauty cannot be sung to the public' (letter of 8 March 1825), meaning there had to be an element of showmanship to keep the man in the street interested. The closing bars of this song (particularly the forte passage of 'Bebend harr' ich Dir entgegen!', bb. 33–4) give the singer a chance to show his mettle as a tenor worthy of the name. There is an element of macho theatricality here which is lacking in very many of the greatest Schubert lieder, and this ardent peroration may indeed be a contributing factor to the song's enduring popularity. Briefly the music enters into the more thrusting regions of a sharp key: launched by the turbulence of the diminished harmonies under 'Liebchen, höre mich!' (bb. 31–2) the music clambers on to the impassioned heights of a cadence leading to B minor. For a moment the singer is on a high, trembling with passionate expectation. The two-bar interlude after 'Dir entgegen' (bb. 35–6, the same rising phrase harmonized first in E minor then in B minor) is, for once, also forte. And then a descent into reality. The juxtaposition in b. 37 of G major for the first 'Komm', beglücke mich!' makes for music that is crestfallen and rueful. At b. 39 the singer rallies for another 'Komm', beglücke mich!', once again forte, where the euphonious thirds between voice and piano seem to be a metaphor for imagined sexual unity. But at the third appearance of these words (without the 'komm'), Schubert himself comes into view, revealed as

Illustration (1933) by Anton Pieck for *Ständchen*

the little man who has loved and lost: the melancholy descent of the final 'Beglücke mich!' is spread over three bars (bb. 41–4), the second and third syllables of this hopeless request each taking an entire bar.

This texture, suddenly bare, allows the strumming guitar staccati to re-establish themselves in our consciousness. We are back where we started, with the beloved as unattainable as ever. It has been a serenade in vain, a 'vergebliches Ständchen', like some of the greatest in the lieder repertoire. A shortened version of the interlude between musical Verses 1 and 2 brings the song to a close; there is no play between minor and major here, only the instrumental reduction of the serenade supported by guitar chords gently oscillating in the tonic, subdominant and dominant of D major. But it would be a complacent listener who imagined that this quiet withdrawal in the major key betokened happiness or calm. The thought of love's fulfilment is blissful, but the chances of dreams turning into reality are slim. If we have the ears to listen, Schubert can use such sweet harmonies to sadder effect than anyone else.

First edition:	Published by Tobias Haslinger, Vienna in May 1829, Volume 1, no. 4 (P207)
Subsequent editions:	Peters: I/135; AGA XX 557: Vol. 9/148; NSA IV: Vol. 14a/118, Ornamented version ('Veränderung') 14b/290; Bärenreiter: Vol. 4/136
Further settings and arrangements:	Franz Lachner (1803–1890) *Ständchen* Op. 49 no. 6 (1836) Arr. Franz Liszt (1811–1886) for solo piano, no. 7 of *Schwanengesang* (1838–9) [*see* TRANSCRIPTIONS] Judith Weir (b. 1954) *Ständchen* (1997) Arr. Tilman Hoppstock (b. 1961) for guitar accompaniment, in *Franz Schubert: 110 Lieder* (2009)
Discography and timing:	Fischer-Dieskau III 3⁴ 3'53
	Hyperion I 37⁹
	Hyperion II 37⁴ 4'03 John Mark Ainsley

← *Frühlingssehnsucht* D957/3   *Aufenthalt* D957/5 →

V AUFENTHALT   Stopping place
D957/5 [H674]
E minor

Rau-schen-der Strom,   brau-sen-der Wald,

(141 bars)

Rauschender Strom,	**S**urging river,
Brausender Wald,	Roaring forest,
Starrender Fels	Immovable rock,
Mein Aufenthalt.	My resting place.

Wie sich die Welle	As wave
An Welle reiht,	Follows wave,
Fliessen die Tränen	So my tears flow,
Mir ewig erneut.	Ever renewed.
Hoch in den Kronen	As the high treetops
Wogend sich's regt,	Stir and heave,
So unaufhörlich	So my heart
Mein Herze schlägt.	Beats incessantly.
Und wie des Felsen	Like the rock's
Uraltes Erz,	Age-old ore
Ewig derselbe	My sorrow remains
Bleibet mein Schmerz.	Forever the same.
Rauschender Strom,	Surging river,
Brausender Wald,	Roaring forest,
Starrender Fels	Immovable rock,
Mein Aufenthalt.	My resting place.

LUDWIG RELLSTAB (1799–1860); poem written before 1825

This is the eighth of Schubert's ten Rellstab solo settings (1827–8). See the poet's biography for a chronological list of all the Rellstab settings.

This E minor song is one of the great favourites of the set, particularly for amateur baritones who enjoy a dramatic outing. The song has *attitude*, and addresses the world with a portentously glowering gaze. It also has the advantage of very short phrases, and countless singers with little breath control have been able to roar its opening pages with some emotional credibility, if little beauty of tone. Its suitability for any voice in the original key is questionable: too low to lie well for most tenors, it embraces high Gs that baritones tend to avoid in lieder performance, particularly when soft as in this song's middle section. Accordingly the lower voices transpose the song into D minor which adds an even darker colour to its inherently doom-laden scenario. Someone who has heard this song often in performance (where it can sound like an aria from *Don Carlos*) would be surprised to see how much of it is marked 'piano'. The song rises in its later stages to anguished utterance, but a lot of it is meant to be *innig*. A tenor voice essaying the original key is unable to dig deep into the music in the manner of the lower voices.

This is a much faster song than *Der Wanderer* D489 but the woeful introspection of both works gives them something in common. The dotted rhythm of the opening vocal phrase of *Aufenthalt*, as well as the downward leaps in the vocal line, are prophesied in *Laura am Klavier* D388 at the lines 'Rauschende, schäumende Giessbäche wälzen' (bb. 73–5). *Aufenthalt* also reminds us of other songs from 1828. The opening words, 'Rauschender Strom', hint that we may find here some of the musical characteristics of *Auf dem Strom* D943, and so we do. Of course the surging river is only one of the aspects of nature described in *Aufenthalt*, which is not usually classified as one of Schubert's water lieder. But the flowing movement of water has inspired the work's *Bewegung*, and the two songs share a similar tempo and a similar grandeur; the fourth verse of *Auf dem Strom* (which mentions tears, as does the second of this song) throbs with a similarly insistent triplet accompaniment and sense of high drama.

The other song brought to mind by *Aufenthalt* is *Herbst* D945. The shared E minor tonality is an obvious link, and the simple but eloquent left hand that engages in a colloquy with the voice, sometimes with melody, sometimes through rhythmic imitation, is a feature common to both songs. In *Herbst* the piano's right hand rustles in semiquaver sextuplets, and these perform the same harmonic function as the relentless triplets in *Aufenthalt*. Indeed, the colours of the songs are so alike, both reflecting introspection and deep pessimism, that it is impossible to imagine a properly varied *Schwanengesang* (surely one of the glories of the cycle) which includes both songs. Perhaps Schubert regarded *Herbst* as a study for *Aufenthalt*, which is why the former song disappeared from view for so many years.

We have already spoken of the short bursts of melody separated by rests that are a characteristic of this song. They are a result, of course, of the poem's tendency to describe different pictures in short dactylic bursts in successive lines ('Rauschender Strom / Brausender Wald'). The poem is usually printed incorrectly in order to save space in recital programmes, but in this case it is clear that the versification, the look of the poem on the page, has a great deal to do with the song's musical shape. From the beginning there is a deliberately engineered conflict between the duplets of the vocal line and the triplets of the accompaniment. The songs of Brahms also rely for much of their expressive strength on this dichotomy and that composer's first published song, *Liebestreu* Op. 3 no. 1, clearly owes something to *Aufenthalt*. In both lieder the struggle not to be swept away by the water imagery, or by the sadness of events, is mirrored by the battle between the two note values. The fixated narrator sits tight – in the Brahms stubbornly unmoved from love's devotion, in the Schubert wedded to unchanging sorrow. As Richard Capell puts it, 'It is necessary to preserve the squareness of the $\frac{2}{4}$ subjects against the unceasing triplets – to maintain one's foothold, so to say, against the beating wind and rain.' In the prelude the left hand pushes against those right-hand triplets in a fight to be heard, resolutely refusing to be drawn into their rhythm. The voice has dotted rhythms that should sound resolute – an instance when quaver + semiquaver dotted rhythm does not quite equate to the first and last note of a triplet as was often (but clearly not always) the practice in Schubert's time.

The opening vocal melody is delivered in a succession of short bursts separated by rests but it somehow adds up to a marvellous continuous melody with a wide range and an impressive rhetorical sweep. This poem is extremely pithy, so Schubert freely repeats words and whole phrases in each verse. Without this the song would be over in a flash, and extremely lightweight. The singer's dotted rhythm is echoed by the piano's left hand which propels the voice forward to its next utterance. A significant stretch of the music is grounded on an E pedal (within only six bars, bb. 14–19, this encompasses chords of E minor, E major, E^7 and second inversions of both A major and minor). All these changes of harmony give the music turbulence, but the use of a pedal point makes it appear simultaneously anchored, an exact analogy for the protagonist's state of mind – stubbornly inconsolable in the midst of the storm. This is also the source of the stentorian grandeur of the song. The danger here is a pomposity which is unusual for this composer. From this point of view the windswept *Herbst* seems more typically Schubertian.

The second verse is set to new music that is a superb realization of stormy waters; the vocal line even looks tidal on the page: 'Wie sich die Welle' starts on a low B, jumps a sixth to the G above, recedes to the same B before leaping a seventh like a wave breaking on the shore of the stave. This vocal waxing and waning continues with the musical description of the poet's tears. The words 'Fliessen die Tränen / Mir ewig erneut' are heard three times, the second of which (bb. 35–9) is a raw outburst that still sounds surprising today, a wail-like cry from the heart with the word 'Tränen' elongated to three minims, accompanied by three bars of unremitting A^7 chords hammered out mercilessly (bb. 37–9). This is a harmony that we had not expected to hear so suddenly juxtaposed to the G major of the preceding 'Fliessen'. Then in b. 40 the bass note of A rises to A sharp, the leading note of B minor, triggering a shift into that key. The eight-bar interlude (bb. 48–55) is an upper pedal on B with the piano harmonies rising chromatically beneath it. In this rather original way the composer steers us into the third strophe and a new key, G major, so that this B becomes the third of the scale.

For the third strophe, new music again. A heartfelt tune, in G major, of the greatest simplicity and nobility, marked piano moreover – hardly an oasis of emotional calm, but music of dignity and introspection. The doubling of the entire vocal line by the piano's left hand from b. 56 (so that the melody is also the bass line, something that is especially meaningful and relatively rare in Schubert) is extremely affecting. The narrator's beating heart is heard in the piano's incessant right-hand triplets and the rather etiolated texture brought about by this doubling allows us to glimpse his loneliness and sensitivity. Without this window into his soul we might have thought him merely a misanthropic brute. The decorative cadence at the end of the verse at the third and final 'Herze schlägt' (bb. 74–6) is the only moment in the entire song where the singer allows himself to be wooed into the triplet rhythm of his accompanist.

The shape of the song now reveals itself as a palindrome. So far we have had three verses and the form has been ABC. The remaining two strophes use music that is already familiar, thus the whole is ABCBA. The fourth verse uses a repeat of the 'wave' music; this is effective enough despite the fact that the new imagery of the rock's age-old ore is less suited to a passage that was so obviously crafted to depict the tidal flux of 'Welle an Welle'. Finally, the clinching recapitulation of the first verse is not the composer's own repeat: it is Rellstab himself who brings the poem full circle, thus creating Schubert's musical shape for him. But there is one more surprise, and a disturbing one: for the setting of the second of the phrases with the words 'Starrender Fels', we hear a sudden juxtaposition of E minor (home key) harmony (b. 123) with no fewer than four fortissimo bars of C minor triplets (bb. 124–7) under 'Fels'. Even the most sophisticated of ears could hardly have expected this brutal switch. The musicologist Richard Kramer sees it as 'a harmony without antecedent, with no apparent justification'. In seeking such a justification he sees a reference to the C minor opening of *Kriegers Ahnung*. Others like Edward Cone see this use of the flattened submediant as typical of other moments in the Rellstab songs. From the expressive point of view an enormous emphasis, almost a talismanic power, has been given to the word 'Fels': this rock is more than a sheer cliff-face; surely it is symbolic of a stone blocking the way, the cause of the impasse of the emotions, the boulder the singer has to shoulder, Atlas-like. And perhaps his 'Aufenthalt' is the end of the road, the place where he discovers that any way further forward is blocked to him. (The English title is often rendered as 'resting place', too peaceful and comfortable a connotation.) Little wonder that the protagonist allows himself a moment of rage and despair with music that is high, loud and jarring. The final repeat of 'Brausender Wald, mein Aufenthalt' from b. 130 is far less dramatic ('Starrender Fels' is omitted, presumably because it would have been impossible to cap the previous outburst) but it allows the voice to rise and fall in a mournful melisma, something of which the ascetic vocal line has so far been rigorously free. This in turn is imitated by the piano's left hand – and then of course we realize that this is the same music as for the introduction. Not for the first time in a Rellstab song, we feel that we have come full circle.

This is the only *Schwanengesang* song that has neither a female ingredient nor mention of love. But the very absence of such an element is symptomatic of the mental block with which the singer is confronted. The theory about a cycle of 'distant beloved' poems might have been stronger if this character had addressed his plaint to the woman of his dreams. Instead we find someone tormented and out of step with society and then, as now, we suspect that this tension might be explained by failure in love or romance. Perhaps it suited Schubert to include at least one song where the reason for the character's emotional disorientation remains an open question. The failure of love, after all, takes many forms, as does the persona of the distant beloved.

First edition:	Published by Tobias Haslinger, Vienna in May 1829, Volume 1, no. 5 (P208)
First known performance:	30 January 1829, Musikverein, Vienna. The concert was organized by Anna Fröhlich to celebrate Schubert's music and raise money to construct a monument in his memory, and was repeated on 5 March 1829 in the same venue. Soloist: Johann Michael Vogl (see Waidelich/Hilmar Dokumente I No. 687 and Deutsch No. xxvi for full concert programme)
Performance reviews:	*Der Sammler* (Vienna) No. 23 (21 February 1829), p. 92 [Waidelich/Hilmar Dokumente I No. 698] *Monatsbericht der Gesellschaft der Musikfreunde des Oesterreichischen Kaiserstaates* (Vienna, March 1829), pp. 41–6 [Waidelich/Hilmar Dokumente I No. 703]
Subsequent editions:	Peters: I/138; AGA XX 558: Vol. 9/151; NSA IV: Vol. 14a/121; Bärenreiter: Vol. 4/139
Further settings and arrangements:	Heinrich August Marschner (1795–1861) *Aufenthalt* Op. 76 no. 4 (1834) Arr. Franz Liszt (1811–1886) for solo piano, no. 3 of *Schwanengesang* (1838–9) [*see* TRANSCRIPTIONS]
Discography and timing:	Fischer-Dieskau III 3[5] 3'23 Hyperion I 37[10] Hyperion II 37[5] 3'35 John Mark Ainsley

← *Ständchen* D957/4   *In der Ferne* D957/6 →

VI IN DER FERNE   Far away
D957/6 [H675]
B minor – B major

Wehe dem Fliehenden	Woe to him who flees,
Welt hinaus ziehenden!—	Who journeys forth into the world,
Fremde durchmessenden,	Who travels through strange lands,
Heimat vergessenden,	Forgetting his native land,
Mutterhaus hassenden,	Spurning his mother's home,
Freunde verlassenden	Forsaking his friends:
Folget kein Segen, ach!	Alas, no blessing follows him
Auf ihren Wegen nach!	On his way!

Herze, das sehnende,	The yearning heart,
Auge, das tränende,	The tearful eye,
Sehnsucht, nie endende,	Endless longing
Heimwärts sich wendende!	Turning homewards!
Busen, der wallende,	The surging breast,
Klage, verhallende,	The dying lament,
Abendstern, blinkender,	The evening star, twinkling
Hoffnungslos sinkender!	And sinking without hope!
Lüfte, ihr säuselnden,	Whispering breezes,
Wellen sanft kräuselnden,	Gently ruffled waves,
Sonnenstrahl, eilender,	Darting sunbeams,
Nirgend verweilender:	Lingering nowhere:
Die mir mit Schmerze, ach!	Send her, who broke
Dies treue Herze brach—	My faithful heart with pain,
Grüsst von dem Fliehenden	Greetings from him who is fleeing
Welt hinaus ziehenden!	And journeying forth into the world!

LUDWIG RELLSTAB (1799–1860); poem written before 1825

This is the ninth of Schubert's ten Rellstab solo settings (1827–8). See the poet's biography for a chronological list of all the Rellstab settings.

Here we have a more anguished message to the 'ferne Geliebte' than Beethoven would have thought appropriate to send in a song. Times had changed. Between that composer's cycle (1816) and the *Schwanengesang* lies Schubert's darker romanticism. The Berliner Rellstab, though himself hardly the most original of poets, would have been aware of the latest literary developments. Among these would have been *Winterreise* by his old friend Wilhelm Müller which was available in book form in 1824, a year before Rellstab gave his poems to Beethoven. Müller's winter traveller goes out into the hostile world, embarking on his journey as a result of a failed relationship. In the last four lines of *In der Ferne* the narrator, similarly driven to a life of distant travel, sends a bitterly gallant message to the girl who has broken his heart. These words might easily have come from the character who bids his faithless lover goodnight at the beginning of *Winterreise*.

Would that the poet had been satisfied, however, with a metre and form of expression as direct as Müller's! Instead we have one of the strangest and most 'worked' of all the poems that Schubert set, an exercise in clever literary artifice, and a veritable feast of adjectival present participles and internal rhymes. (Capell, with a disdain for Victorian curlicues, refers to a 'Swinburnian revel of triple rhymes'.) The effect is both extravagant and contracted – a flowery telegraphese where every thought is curtailed as a result of the verb form that dangles disconsolately at the end of each line. If the poet is too shell-shocked to put together a sequence of coherent thoughts, he still has the self-possession to play verbal games reminiscent of Rückert on a bad day. He also distances himself from the circumstances described; only the 'mir' in the final strophe gives the game away and informs us that this is his own plight. Rellstab was clearly proud of his virtuosity in rhyming, although the final result, especially when read out loud, walks a thin line between romantic obsession and unintentional comedy (one's soulful attention begins to falter somewhere around 'blinkender' and 'sinkender'). One doubts very much whether Schubert would have chosen to set this poetry if it had come his way without the Beethoven connection. And only a brave composer at the height of his powers would be prepared to take on such a disjointed series of images in end-stopped lines that do nothing to help the music hang together.

Fortunately Schubert *was* at the height of his powers, and if it is true that he was looking to make an *An die ferne Geliebte* for modern times, the poem was ideal for his purposes. Like *Aufenthalt* it achieves a type of majesty unique to certain Rellstab songs (one also thinks of *Kriegers Ahnung*), a grandeur both imposing and moving, yet at the same time somewhat stiff – no, that is an exaggeration: 'at one remove' would be a better description. This has nothing to do with Schubert's use of harmony as such: he explores new harmonic regions in a manner of which Beethoven would not have dreamed (certainly in his lieder) and this aspect of the songs is new and startling. But it is as if Schubert is so intent on creating masterful musical constructions, music to impress the shade of Beethoven, perhaps, that he is less concerned to fashion his creatures out of flesh and blood. His usual flair for dramatic truth is quite different from the quasi-operatic stance of some of these characters. Although in many ways they are larger than life, there is also something theoretical about them, as if they were archetypes rather than real people. (Is *Fidelio*, for all its greatness, not an opera of archetypes? Indeed, is this not at the core of its greatness?) This 'statuary' style, passionate and imposing yet remote at the same time, is not absolutely new for Schubert; we noticed it much earlier in his output, particularly in some of the grander Schiller settings that have also called on a Beethovenian mood and musical vocabulary. For the more epic Rellstab poems one feels that the musical solutions are the result of a controlled experiment, and certainly not a sign of Schubert losing his inimitable touch. We only have to remember that Beethoven's finest songs (and these are many and beautiful) are very different from Schubert's at his most typical. The Rellstab poems were originally Beethoven's texts and, in setting these, Schubert seems to have thought himself into a Beethovenian state of mind.

The dramatic opening of this song is a good illustration of this. The listener's attention is summoned, in a thoroughly symphonic manner, by an opening on the fifth degree of the scale. Measured unison F sharps are filled out by creeping left-hand semiquavers, ushering in what at first sounds like a plagal cadence in the key of F sharp but is soon revealed as the dominant of the home key, B minor. Brandishing the dominant at the listener as an opening gesture is rare in lieder (only *Letzte Hoffnung* D911/16 from *Winterreise* comes to mind in the songs of the mature Schubert) but it is typical of the arresting opening of Beethoven overtures such as *Leonore 3* Op. 62, *Coriolan* or *Egmont* Op. 84 no. 1 (we know that the last two of these were familiar to Schubert). But of course Schubert remains Schubert, as is the case for any composer who attempts a stylization. The choice of key is a sign of this. He has selected a tonality which was his eventual choice for *Einsamkeit* D911/12, and a first choice for *Der Leiermann* D911/24, both from *Winterreise* – a key which, according to John Reed, denotes for this composer 'physical and mental suffering, loneliness, alienation and derangement'. The sombre, brooding mood of an earlier Schubertian outcast in B minor – *Der Unglückliche* D713 – also comes to mind.

After two bars (the tempo marking is 'Ziemlich langsam') this strident introductory F sharp is capped by an even more gloomy G natural (b. 3) which is also filled out after a bar, this time by diminished-seventh harmony. A return to a repeat of the opening bars grounded in F sharp sets the scene in a way that is both dramatic and formal. The time signature is ¾ and anyone who has attempted to sing this song knows that the 'Ziemlich langsam' must refer to a slowish one-in-the-bar tempo, rather than three painfully dragging crotchets. This is confirmed by the fact that most of the four-bar phrases must be accomplished within a single breath. The vocal line (grounded in or around repeated F sharps in depressive fashion, cf. the opening of *Der Doppelgänger*) is minimalist – or, rather, it seems to be almost spoken. We have to wait to hear the melody as a totality: it emerges over a long span rather than proudly announcing itself in these opening bars. The alternation of tonic and dominant harmonies is a strong feature here, as are the striding octave basses that emphasize the music's down-in-the-mouth character. There is a fermata (Schubert's translation of the poet's solitary use of a hyphen) after the first two lines of the poem (b. 12); in this way the protagonist seems to enter the stage after the overture, announce himself, and then get on with the rest of the song.

All this might be called old-fashioned were it not for a general mood of suicidal gloom that is hardly classical. The song seems to cultivate a deliberate monotony, particularly in terms of rhythm. Of course here the composer is the poet's prisoner, for there is nothing to be done with this metre but to set line after line of music in the same pulse – three crotchet beats followed by dotted crotchet + quaver and another crotchet. Harmony must provide the variety, and the setting of 'Mutterhaus hassenden' (bb. 17–18) is a case in point. The change here from B minor to B flat major(!) would have done Berlioz credit. This wrench contains such venom that we would not be surprised if, in setting it, the composer had called on unhappy memories of his own 'Mutterhaus' or, more particularly, 'Vaterhaus'.

This extraordinary dislocation has a deeper musical purpose, and this is a planned slide into anarchy of sorts. It is the beginning of a long chromatic descent in the bass between B natural and F sharp in the course of six bars. At 'Wegen nach!' (b. 23) the left hand reaches the first inversion of D major, opening the doorway into a return to its relative minor, the home key of B. Such a long arch, a tortured progress that moves in steps, albeit with strange harmonic surprises, again brings Berlioz to mind (one of whose strongest inspirations was also one of Schubert's – the monumental operatic architecture of Gluck). The extraordinary vocal plunge of a fifth on the second 'Wegen nach!' (after holding an F sharp on the first syllable for seven-and-a-half beats) seems better suited to the second verse's 'sinkender'. This is surely another illustration of how Schubert has learned to plan ahead in the writing of strophic songs.

And this song *is* strophic, at first completely, and then much modified. The second verse, introduced by an interlude that is a repeat of the *Vorspiel*, is an exact musical repeat of the first. The dislocated harmony which was so powerful for 'Mutterhaus hassenden' is less effective for 'Busen, der wallende' (bb. 46–7), but this is a trade-off for the remarkably apt setting of 'sink-ender' already mentioned. Once again we hear the ominous seven-bar interlude (from b. 59), and by now we must admit to the power of music that seems to grow in stature with each succeeding anguished phrase. This is Schubert the sophisticated symphonic structuralist at work.

The change to the key signature of B major for the first of two complete (and different) settings of the poet's last verse comes just in time to cast a ray of redeeming sunlight on this dark tableau. Mention of breezes prompts a lambent murmur of right-hand semiquavers against left-hand triplets (from b. 66). The effect of this accompaniment, in the tessitura and tonality of the piano writing of *Nacht und Träume* D827, is curiously Brahmsian. The meshing of different note values, while descriptive of both wind and wave, is hardly typical of Schubert's piano writing with voice and a new, almost impressionist, note is struck. The vocal line, and even the harmonic movement that supports it, is made up of new material, but it is all cleverly derived from what has gone before. It is evident that a creative hand is seeking to give unity, both to the song and to the Rellstab settings as a whole: the euphonious interaction of descending sixths heard between voice and piano at 'Sonnenstrahl, eilender' (from b. 70) is a feature found in a number of the other Rellstab songs, as is the echoing commentary of the piano after 'Die mir mit Schmerze, ach!' (b. 76), and again after 'Dies treue Herze brach' (b. 79). (This conversational aspect of the piano writing will achieve even greater importance in the song's concluding verse.)

Of course this ray of happier B major cannot last long; it cedes to B minor for mention of pain and a broken heart, and the strophe seems destined to end in the minor. It is a poignant surprise then that the word 'ziehenden' (bb. 85–7) changes from minor back to major in the course of its setting. It is as if the vocal line has been stroked with a consolatory caress. The frequent switches between minor and major here are like the sun appearing, disappearing and then reappearing from behind a cloud.

The presence of natural beauty is the source of this consolation, of course, and now Schubert repeats the words for Rellstab's third verse to make his fourth. The tenor voice comes into its own at last (and the baritone is challenged to an exacting use of *mezza voce*). After a single bar of gentle oscillations in B major (b. 88), we hear the same words ('Lüfte, ihr säuselnden'), this time raised to a higher tessitura and a higher power. The effect of this change of register is magical, and the single bar of piano interlude (b. 94) provides an echo that is other-worldly, largely due to the unusual spacing of the chords in both hands – an almost dissonant rumble in the bass and an eloquent dying fall much higher in the treble. On 'Nirgend verweilen<u>der</u>' there is a sudden change of harmonic direction: the F sharp bass that had seemed to promise a comfortable modulation back to B major creeps up a semitone to F double-sharp (b. 100) and we find ourselves poised first on the edge of G sharp minor and then engulfed by it. This has the effect of a promise broken, a betrayal expressed in musical terms, and it announces a coda of tensely varied harmonic exploration. Through one door lies happiness, through another an end to all hope. Once again it is the word 'ziehenden', with all its implied movement and capacity for change, that is a pivotal point. Its first appearance in this strophe (bb. 109–11) is harmonized by a 6–4 in B major followed by F sharp[7]. Instead of leading to B major (or minor) this rises to the unlikely but upbeat regions of G major. Oh blessed hope! Through this canal the vocal line breaks out triumphantly at b. 112 into the open seas of C major (the flattened supertonic) with an ecstatically rising scale on 'Welt hinaus'. But one should expect no permanent happiness from Neapolitan chicanery something as ominously named as the flattened supertonic: the second 'ziehenden' that has appeared in b. 113 slips back into the home key and the extended cadence that carries it there is mercilessly and grimly elongated. The piano, once it has reached the

Autograph of *In der Ferne* (conclusion) and *Abschied* (beginning).

concluding B minor, simply stays there; its triplets, as if attempting to swamp the voice, are hammered out fortissimo and roll on to a single concluding chord once the vocal line has ceased. This is perhaps the most brutal of all Schubert's postludes, the rejection of the final appeal, the end of the road or, as John Reed says, 'a final slamming of the door against the fugitive'.

First edition:	Published by Tobias Haslinger, Vienna in May 1829, Volume 1, no. 6 (P209)
Subsequent editions:	Peters: I/142; AGA XX 559: Vol. 9/156; NSA IV: Vol. 14a/126; Bärenreiter: Vol. 4/144
Arrangements:	Arr. Franz Liszt (1811–1886) for solo piano, no. 6 of *Schwanengesang* (1838–9) [*see* TRANSCRIPTIONS]
Discography and timing:	Fischer-Dieskau III 3[6] 5'32
	Hyperion I 37[11] 6'04 John Mark Ainsley
	Hyperion II 37[6]

← *Aufenthalt* D957/5   *Abschied* D957/7 →

VII ABSCHIED   Farewell
D957/7 [H676]
E♭ major

(167 bars)

Ade, Du muntre, Du fröhliche Stadt, Ade!	Farewell, lively, cheerful town, farewell!
Schon scharret mein Rösslein mit lustigem Fuss;	Already my horse is happily pawing the ground.
Jetzt nimm noch den letzten, den scheidenden Gruss;[1]	Take now my final good wishes on parting.
Du hast mich wohl niemals noch traurig gesehn,[2]	I know you have never seen me sad;
So kann es auch jetzt nicht beim Abschied geschehn.	Nor will you now as I depart.
Ade, Du muntre u.s.w. . . .	Farewell! etc. . . .
Ade, Ihr Bäume, Ihr Gärten so grün, Ade!	Farewell, trees and gardens so green, farewell!
Nun reit' ich am silbernen Strome entlang,	Now I ride along the silver stream;
Weit schallend ertönet mein Abschiedsgesang;	My song of farewell echoes far and wide.
Nie habt Ihr ein trauriges Lied gehört,[3]	You have never heard a sad song;
So wird Euch auch keines beim Scheiden beschert.	Nor shall you do so at parting.
Ade, Ihr Bäume u.s.w. . . .	Farewell! etc. . . .

[1] Rellstab writes 'Jetzt nimm *meinen* Letzten, den scheidenden Gruss'.
[2] Rellstab writes 'Du hast mich wohl *nimmermehr* traurig gesehen'.
[3] Rellstab writes 'Nie habt Ihr ein *klagendes* Lied gehört'.

Ade, Ihr freundlichen Mägdlein dort, Ade![4]
Was schaut Ihr aus blumenumduftetem Haus
Mit schelmischen, lockenden Blicken heraus?
Wie sonst, so grüss' ich und schaue mich um,
Doch nimmer wend' ich mein Rösslein um.[5]
  Ade, Ihr freundlichen u.s.w. . . .

Ade, liebe Sonne, so gehst Du zur Ruh', Ade!
Nun schimmert der blinkenden Sterne Gold.
Wie bin ich Euch Sternlein am Himmel
  so hold;
Durchziehn wir die Welt auch weit und breit,
Ihr gebt überall uns das treue Geleit.
  Ade, liebe Sonne u.s.w. . . .

Ade, Du schimmerndes Fensterlein
  hell, Ade!
Du glänzest so traulich mit dämmerndem
  Schein
Und ladest so freundlich ins Hüttchen uns ein.
Vorüber, ach, ritt ich so manches Mal
Und wär' es denn heute zum letzten Mal?
  Ade, Du schimmerndes u.s.w. . . .

Ade, Ihr Sterne, verhüllet Euch grau! Ade!

Des Fensterlein trübes, verschimmerndes
  Licht[6]
Ersetzt Ihr unzähligen Sterne mir nicht;
Darf ich h i e r nicht weilen, muss h i e r
  vorbei,
Was hilft es, folgt Ihr mir noch so treu![7]

Ade, Ihr Sterne, verhüllet Euch grau! Ade!

Farewell, charming maidens, farewell!
Why do you look out with roguish, enticing eyes
From houses fragrant with flowers?
I greet you as before, and look back;
But never will I turn my horse back.
  Farewell! etc. . . .

Farewell, dear sun, as you go to rest, farewell!
Now the stars twinkle with shimmering gold.
How fond I am of you, little stars in the sky;

Though we travel the whole world, far and wide,
Everywhere you faithfully escort us.
  Farewell! etc. . . .

Farewell, little window gleaming brightly,
  farewell!
You shine so cosily with your soft light,

And invite us so kindly into the cottage.
Ah, I have ridden past you so often,
And yet today might be the last time.
  Farewell! etc. . . .

Farewell, stars, veil yourselves in grey!
  Farewell!
You numberless stars cannot replace for us

The little window's dim, fading light;
If I cannot linger *here*, if I must ride on,

How can you help me, though you follow me so
  faithfully?
Farewell, stars, veil yourselves in grey! Farewell!

LUDWIG RELLSTAB (1799–1860); poem written before 1825

This is the last of Schubert's ten Rellstab solo settings (1827–8). See the poet's biography for a chronological list of all the Rellstab settings.

This is the last of Schubert's *Abschied* lieder and, on a superficial level at least, the merriest. One has to work rather hard at bidding farewell in such an upbeat manner. Saying goodbye, as Schubert's winter traveller knew only too well, is usually not a happy business: the composer's own poem for Franz von Schober's temporary departure from Vienna (*Abschied* – 'Lebe wohl! Du lieber Freund!', D578, 1817) prompts a song that is simple and poignant – it is even cast in

---

[4] Schubert changes Rellstab's 'Mägdelein' to 'Mägdlein'.
[5] Rellstab writes 'Doch *nimmermehr* wend' ich mein *Rösselein* um'.
[6] Rellstab writes 'Des *Fensterleins* trübes verschimmerndes Licht'.
[7] Rellstab writes 'Was hilft es *mir*, folgt Ihr mir noch so treu!'

the desolate key of B minor; *Abschied. Nach einer Wallfahrtsarie* D475 (Mayrhofer, 1816), with its haunting horn-calls, has a soulful spaciousness which reflects the pilgrims' journey over distant mountains; the recitation *Leb' wohl du schöne Erde (Abschied von der Erde)* D829 (Pratobevera, 1826) is Schubert's only essay in piano-accompanied melodrama – a touching valediction spoken on the threshold of death. The contrast between these profound songs and this seemingly uncomplicated *Abschied* is great. There are of course other happy songs of farewell in the lieder repertoire – Schumann's *Der Knabe mit dem Wunderhorn* Op. 30 no. 1 (Geibel) comes to mind, as well as his *Wanderlied* Op. 35 no. 3 where the poet Kerner proposes 'a last glass of sparkling wine'. And of course there is Mahler's rollicking *Scheiden und Meiden* from *Des Knaben Wunderhorn* where the words insist that parting is a sad thing but the music is both hearty and heartless, a contradiction that lends a dark and sinister aspect typical of that composer's view of folksong.

   Mahler's setting is at full gallop; one can hear warhorses thundering through the town. This *Abschied* is not nearly so frantically energetic, but it does feature a horse-ride, the last of a number of Schubert songs to do so. The famous *Erlkönig* D328 was the first, followed by *Willkommen und Abschied* D767 and *Auf der Bruck* D853. In each case the poet announces an equestrian element at the beginning of the poem – 'Wer reitet so spät . . . ?' (Goethe), '. . . geschwind zu Pferde' (also Goethe), '. . . mein gutes Roß' (Schulze) – and the composer follows suit with figurations in the accompaniment to depict the ride. The 'gutes Roß' of *Auf der Bruck* is a sturdier steed than the 'Rösslein' of this *Abschied*, a trusty little horse that paws the ground at the beginning of the poem. But his canter pervades the music, or rather the *idea* of it. As many commentators have pointed out, it is useless to base a song's tempo on a calculation of actual physical movement (a walk by a millstream will be of no help in gauging the correct speed of *Das Wandern* D795/1 from *Die schöne Müllerin* for example). Many an interpretation of this *Abschied* has been ruined by too fast a tempo and gabbled words in well-meaning imitation of a steeplechase; singer and pianist alike can all too easily be riding for a fall. The song needs to be elegant and perky, gallant and contained within a 'mässig' or moderato tempo from the very beginning. Even at a reasonable tempo its unremitting moto perpetuo takes its toll on various technical aspects of singing – breathing and diction chief among them. I have known one singer tie himself so tightly in knots in this song that he lost his voice. If the vocalist tends to hurrying, accompanists must jockey for a more reasonable speed in rehearsal. It is pointless to lock songs into a stable tempo only after the hoarse have bolted.

   So closely has Schubert's music been forged to this poem (like hoof and horseshoe) that few people take the trouble to read the Rellstab as poetry. Separated from Schubert's music, there is a note of melancholy in the words, a determination not to be sad at this final parting but an indication that all is not well in the narrator's life. Indeed, we might even find echoes here of *Winterreise* D911 – the winter traveller is also capable of adopting a cheery stance, half in irony and half in an attempt to make the best of a tragic situation. The last verse is particularly revealing in this respect: in addressing the stars who are commanded to 'veil themselves in grey' the poet wonders what use they can be to him 'If I cannot linger here, if I must ride on'. Even the beauty of the numberless stars cannot rival the chink of light in the little window of the beloved's house. Like *Gute Nacht* D911/1 from *Winterreise*, this is a nocturnal song of farewell, where the compulsion inherent in the emphasized words of 'Darf ich h i e r nicht weilen, muss h i e r vorbei' implies a strong reason for departure. And with that there is the possibility of a sad, even tragic, background to the story. If we read between the lines we find a scenario that includes a 'ferne Geliebte', or at least an estranged one.

   Not for the first time in these Rellstab songs we notice that Schubert is less interested in delving deep into the background and psychology of his characters than in creating a musical shape worthy of important songs which, in turn, are meant to be worthy of Beethoven's memory. He almost certainly felt that in some of these texts there was a limit to the emotional nuances that could be reflected in music. It is true that he marks the last strophe of *Abschied* with a new and beautiful harmonic shift (discussed below), and there are plenty of felicitous details that show he knows exactly what is going on in the singer's mind, but his interest in this poem is formal in every sense. This succession of words trips off the tongue – or should do so with any luck. (How one pities the singer who has to memorize this song, a nightmare ride through confusing musical crossroads and across a minefield of text.) But this patter is well suited to the moto perpetuo the composer has planned for his sheerly *musical* purpose. Schubert wishes to write nothing less (though perhaps a little more) than a light-hearted finale to his 'symphonic' song cycle – and what better epilogue could there be than music that jogs and trots into the distance as the horseman makes his *adieux*.

The key is E flat major, also the key of Beethoven's Piano Sonata 'Les Adieux', Op. 81a, where the sound of the departing stagecoach's post horn appears in the opening chords (above them Beethoven writes the word 'Lebewohl'). Even in *Winterreise* the mood is momentarily lifted by the post horn sounding in merry fashion, and we should not be too surprised that the composer has chosen to mitigate the mood of *In der Ferne* with something lighter; between these two songs there is the same sequence of keys (B minor to E flat major) as there is between *Einsamkeit* and *Die Post* in *Winterreise* D911/12 and 13.

And so we begin our journey with a marking of 'Mässig geschwind' and an eight-bar prelude where the quavers are marked 'staccatissimo', the better to glint and glance, jump and prance. Sometimes in single notes and sometimes in chords, the right hand ranges across the stave in a manner that challenges most pianists' sense of keyboard geography to the full. The left hand adds a piquant lift to the chugging motor rhythm – mostly separate quavers marking each beat in different registers, and then suddenly, often on the fourth beat of the bar, a cheeky duplet, like a bump in the otherwise even terrain negotiated with an added fillip of equine energy. We can almost feel the saddle lifting under us; unlike the four-square gallop of *Auf der Bruck*, the sway of the ride, the side-to-side movement of horse and rider, and the relaxed pleasure this denotes, are built into the music.

The voice enters on 'Ade', the first of this word's countless appearances, set in almost every possible part of the vocal register. The German 'Ade' of folk music is traditionally set to a rising fourth, and thus Schubert gamely begins; but as the song progresses we will hear thirds on this word (mostly minor, both ascending and descending), a sixth (the opening of the second and fourth verses), as well as seconds. The horse's impatience is perfectly described: the vocal line rises and falls three times, like a hoof lifting a few inches before scraping the ground. The movement of harmony throughout shows Schubert at his most dazzling; we can scarcely keep up with the changes and how meticulously apposite they are for the words. Any number of deft passing excursions are made from the tonic, touching on subdominant and dominant, but bigger shifts are kept for more expressive purposes. Thus the appearance of the relative minor at 'So kann es auch jetzt nicht beim Abschied geschehn' (bb. 21–3) is like the obscuring of sunlight by a passing cloud. This seems appropriate for a moment when the singing of a sad song is mooted, even if it is immediately dismissed as impossible. The final line of the strophe is a repeat of the first, as suggested by the poet who prints the verse's final line as 'Ade, Du muntre u.s.w.' (a shortening of 'und so weiter' ('etc.')). Schubert sets this *envoi* in F minor (bb. 24–6), a use of the supertonic that wonderfully conveys a sense of distance. We can almost hear the narrator disappear as he rides away. The quick return to E flat major for the last 'Ade!' (Schubert's own addition) has the almost comic dislocation of a Doppler effect.

The second verse is different. After an interlude modelled on the song's beginning, a nervous twitch in quavers in the left hand, like a tiny nudge of the bridle, steers the music into A flat major (from b. 36). This is a happy turning off the main highway: the Elysian fields of the subdominant are suited to a description of green gardens and silver streams. Various delicious harmonic excursions and diversions return the music to A flat major at the end of the verse. We note the falling interval of this final 'Ade' and wonder why this is pitched in reverse, as it were. (The answer is in Verse 4, a strophic repeat of this one, which bids farewell to the setting sun, something impossible to paint with an ascending interval!)

Verse 3 is a repeat of the music for Verse 1; here the charming maidens of the town, flagrant flirts all (if we are to believe 'Mit schelmischen, lockenden Blicken') are mentioned, surely significantly, in the plural. These 'freundlichen Mägdlein' are not, however, the cause of the singer's departure. We gather in the course of the song that there is one in particular who is responsible for that, and she is not among these flibbertigibbets. The little excursion into the relative minor at the end of this verse throws a beam of light on the singer's decision to depart – this is one of the moments when, reading between the lines, we gather that there might once have been a good reason for him to stay.

Verse 4 is a repeat of the music for Verse 2, and once again the subdominant is explored with appropriate effect. The glint and twinkle of sun and stars is masterfully reflected in the darting *Bewegung* of the accompaniment, a classic example of Schubert's ability to accommodate multitudes of contradictory ideas within one all-purpose piano motif. Here we forget the narrator's pony for a moment, and see instead the horse-drawn chariot of Apollo as it traverses the sky. But the rhetorical question 'Und wär' es denn heute zum letzten Mal?' in the next verse, tinged in C minor, is another half-teasing, half-serious, intimation that this departure is not without its pain and difficulties.

So far the form has been ABABA, but the last strophe is different. Another letter is called for, a C for Coda, even though the section finishes with a return to the constituents of A. No matter how much Schubert wants to write a symphonic finale, a lifelong sensitivity to words means he can't help but create magic for a verse that suddenly marks out the narrator as a poet and fellow sufferer, and not just 'one of the lads'. E flat major turns into E flat minor (from b. 130) and then the relative major of that key, C flat major. This move (it sounds as if it were B major of course) after so much E flat major is indescribably poetic, as if we have been spirited to another planet. Here are encapsulated all the 'might-have-beens' of the song: the narrator addresses the stars, and in so doing he allows himself briefly to dream of another, kinder destiny. 'Darf ich h i e r' (bb. 144–5) brings him down to earth with a new-found determination to leave after all, the temptation to linger peremptorily vanquished. The E flat[7] of this chord is not quite 'home', but it moves him out of the dream-world back to A flat minor (b. 146), and thence to E flat minor (b. 149). It is at the second 'h i er' (and with a triumphantly defiant two-beat flash of E flat major in b. 150) that he embraces the stark reality of the tonic. Then quickly follows the advent of C minor to colour 'muss h i e r vorbei'. The words 'Was hilft es, folgt Ihr mir noch so treu!' are revealing: the singer has tried to be so carefree throughout, but his last words as he disappears finally into the distance inform us that something has happened that not even the help of the heavens can redress.

As has been pointed out, it is not as if Schubert completely ignores these nuances; indeed, he follows the poem's various contours meticulously. But he is not to be deflected from constructing a shape that will give pleasure to the public. We all thank him for this, and admit to listening to this song with tapping foot and smiling eye without giving a second thought to whatever problems the protagonist carries away with him. At the end of the Rellstab cycle we find perhaps the best illustration of the limitations of Schubert's engagement with this poet: in terms of his involvement with Rellstab's characters he seems to say 'so far and no further'. Thus his relationship to the words is 'at one remove', despite lavishing on them his greatest art.

Another cantering song in E flat major, also set in a beautiful small town, owes much to this *Abschied*: Hugo Wolf's Mörike setting *Auf einer Wanderung* where the similarly staccato accompaniment combines an equestrian rhythm with the hop-skip-and-jump of the narrator's delighted heart.

First edition:	Published by Tobias Haslinger, Vienna in May 1829, Volume 2, no. 1 (P210)
Subsequent editions:	Peters: I/146; AGA XX 560: Vol. 9/160; NSA IV: Vol. 14a/133; Bärenreiter: Vol. 4/149
Further settings and arrangements:	Arr. Franz Liszt (1811–1886) for solo piano, no. 5 of *Schwanengesang* (1838–9) [*see* TRANSCRIPTIONS] Karl Wilhelm Taubert (1811–1891) *Abschied* Op. 186 no. 6 (1875)
Discography and timing:	Fischer-Dieskau III 3[7] 4'23 Hyperion I 37[12] Hyperion II 37[7] 4'48 John Mark Ainsley

←— *In der Ferne* D957/6   *Der Atlas* D957/8 —→

Whether by accident or design, the *Schwanengesang* is a Janus-like work that looks backwards as well as forwards. The seven settings of the poems of Ludwig Rellstab honour the poet's connection with Beethoven, and establish Schubert's right to be the great man's successor. Just as Beethoven had proved himself the greatest composer in Vienna by making thirty-three sublime piano variations of Diabelli's 'Schusterfleck' (Op. 120), a cobbler's patch of a theme, we sense that these Rellstab poems would have been set in masterly fashion, whatever their intrinsic merits, sheerly as a question of Schubertian *amour-propre*. The composer has given his all to a poet who, in other circumstances, might not have detained him long. Such is the musical mastery displayed here that the listener knows that he is hearing great music whether or not he understands the words (millions have listened to *Ständchen* as a purely instrumental piece of music). This is not to say that the words are unimportant in these works, or to deny that they have given rise to inspired musical analogies, but the listener's enjoyment in the irresistible flow of vocal chamber music is paramount. This is the work of a genius in his thirties, at the height of his youthful powers, and of whom much more is expected. The Rellstab songs are, if you like, the lieder equivalent of Beethoven's 'Razumovsky' Quartets Op. 59 – forgetting for the moment that those were products of Beethoven's middle period, and that Schubert was already in his final year. The Rellstab songs, surely, represent the genius of a vital young man, not someone nearing his death – someone who should, by rights, have been in the midst of his own 'middle period', even if other works of 1827 and 1828 suggest a 'late period'.

We know, however, that the last music that Schubert heard before he died in his brother's house was a performance of a much later work by Beethoven: he had begged for a string quartet by that composer far removed from the 'Razumovsky' style – the great C sharp minor, Op. 131. Poor, ill Schubert became so excited by this music – indeed, he was one of the very few people in Vienna who would have been able to fathom its greatness – that the players feared he would have a seizure. Beethoven was counted an avant-garde composer as much as a guardian of the sacred flame of Haydn and Mozart, and the fearlessness and sublimity of these last quartets must have played their part in encouraging Schubert into similar bravery in his song explorations – certainly in terms of an avant-garde element within a cycle written in Beethoven's honour. That composer's example showed that it was not for a great creator to sit on his laurels: he had to lead the public, by the ear if necessary, into the future. In the following six Heine settings Schubert does just this. These songs are so far removed from Rellstab's that we might as well compare landscape with moonscape. That poet's words had been expanded into music. But in the unfamiliar light and shadow of this vast, lunar terrain the strangely powerful words by a new icon of romanticism are telescoped into some of the most powerfully concise and economical songs ever written. Thus the Rellstab *Abschied* could be seen, in the context of this cycle, as a farewell to the past, and the rumblings of *Der Atlas* as heralding the music of the future, both representing different sides of the same creative coin.

And Heine was very much the poet of the future. He had everything to appeal to the Schubertians. By the agenda of the reading circle at the beginning of 1828 we know how much they were enthused by his work; Franz von Schober conducted these readings, and how this poet *manqué*, with his lumbering and pretentious *Paligenesien* sonnets, must have envied Heine – so well-travelled, so amusing, such a martyr to the pains of love (and respected, not derided for it), so *talented*. Heine must have seemed the man of the moment and, in many ways, he was. Here was humour and irony, the deepest feeling as well as the lightest touch, a mastery of prose as much as of poetry, a modern voice that boded ill for the forces of political repression and cultural philistinism. And there was a pithy mode of expression in his poetry which had a Goethe-like directness and suitability for musical setting. Heine's was a name unknown to Beethoven, and it was up to Schubert to introduce them to each other.

SIX SONGS TO POEMS BY HEINRICH HEINE

VIII Der ATLAS[1]   Atlas
D957/8 [H677]
G minor

(56 bars)

Ich unglücksel'ger Atlas! eine Welt,	I, unhappy Atlas, must bear a world,
Die ganze Welt der Schmerzen muss ich tragen.	The whole world of sorrows.
Ich trage Unerträgliches, und brechen	I bear the unbearable, and my heart
Will mir das Herz im Leibe.	Would break within my body.
Du stolzes Herz! du hast es ja gewollt,	Proud heart, you wished it so!
Du wolltest glücklich sein, unendlich glücklich	You wished to be happy, endlessly happy,
Oder unendlich elend, stolzes Herz,	Or endlessly wretched, proud heart!
Und jetzo bist du elend.	And now you are wretched!

HEINRICH HEINE (1797–1856); poem written in 1823/4

This is the first of Schubert's six Heine solo settings (1828). See the poet's biography for a chronological list all of the Heine settings.

---

[1] The punctuation and versifictation of the six Heine songs have been taken from Schubert's most probable source: *Reisebilder*, Erster Theil, 1826.

In these few lines (none of the poems has a heading, and Schubert provides his own) are united the worlds of classicism and romanticism. The story of Atlas is one that might have been explored by Mayrhofer in his Hellenic mode; he would have retold his version of the legend – as in *Memnon* D541 or *Atys* D585. But Heine is more modern in his far sharper use of metaphor, more interested in his own mythologized present than in the mythological past. He is less concerned with the fate of the Titan Atlas (condemned by Zeus to hold up the sky as a punishment for a revolt against Olympus) than with his own troubles. So it always is with the greatest 'ich'-centred poet of them all. He shoulders so much grief that, with typically unashamed exaggeration, he claims to know what it is to shoulder the weight of the whole world. Schubert shows that he understands this distinction between *a* world ('eine Welt') of sorrow and *the* world as a globe-like entity: the song's title is not *Atlas* but <u>*Der Atlas*</u>. This Atlas is a human being who has suffered much. Who can this unhappy giant be?

That he is an important and commanding figure is evident from the opening bars. This is a drum roll for a great man as much as for the severity of the Titan's plight and an acknowledgement of the composer's reading of the classics. That this dramatic opening also represents a symphonic overture and curtain-raiser to the group (*pace* countless arguments for its reordering within the set of six) is also likely. The key is G minor, a tonality which, according to John Reed, Schubert associates with valiant struggles and losing battles. The right hand is awash with tremolo figurations – by no means the first time they have been heard in Schubert's songs, but the first where they have been given such prominent status. The left hand is heavy with a motif in mighty octaves. This begins with two crotchet Gs, then a quick jump of a third to a B flat (a semiquaver right at the end of b. 1) and a plunge to the F sharp below (the first beat of b. 2). This plangent accented passing note resolves back on G after a beat. The right hand shadows

Autograph of *Der Atlas*.

the harmonic changes implied by the left. This circular motif, which we will find elsewhere in the Heine songs, is small but very powerful. The descent of a diminished fourth is repeated, as if to add insult to injury. A semiquaver upbeat and two further resounding low Gs complete the four-bar prelude. The effect is both monumental and unsteady, as if Atlas has to shuffle from one position to another in order to keep a grip. For the duration of those accented F sharps we sense the world teetering precariously, spinning for a moment on an uncertain footing before settling back on its G minor axis.

This important left-hand figure sounds strangely familiar, and it derives, as we might have suspected, from a late work by Beethoven. We have mentioned the inspiration of the C sharp minor String Quartet Op. 131, but here Schubert is drawn to the late Piano Sonata in C minor Op. 111. The *Maestoso* opening of that work has the piano crashing down to a low F sharp in the bass in impetuous dotted rhythm. Even more important is the theme of the *Allegro con brio ed appassionato*, revealed in the bass clef in bb. 20 to 22. In these notes – the rise of a minor third, the fall of a diminished fourth, a return to the tonic – lies the kernel of the melody for *Der Atlas*.

The vocal line ('Ich unglücksel'ger Atlas', from b. 4) mirrors the melody of the left-hand introduction. Indeed, the pianist now doubles the vocal line, as if one were manacled to the other, underlining the unremitting nature of the Titan's baleful task. Heine's poem, too pithy for Schubert's imposing purposes, is expanded by repetition from the very beginning, an insistence that emphasizes the idea of 'stuck here and going nowhere'. The phrase 'Die ganze Welt der Schmerzen muss ich tragen' is repeated at b. 10 as a contraction ('Die ganze Welt muss ich tragen') which depicts the hero for a moment in his mythological role rather than as a metaphor for Heine himself. But the repetition has another function: the hero is like someone with a life sentence obsessively persuading himself to get used to the idea. The vocal tessitura is weighted towards the bottom of the stave, appropriate to someone so bowed down with problems, but both settings of 'Die ganze Welt' heave the vocal line up to an E flat at the top of the stave; the interval of a minor sixth from 'die' to 'ganze' charts the upward sweep of a wider view, and the burden of a global responsibility.

Atlas was the first weightlifter. History does not relate whether this was a sport with which Schubert was acquainted in Vienna – as a spectator of course! But what now follows is a graphic depiction in music of someone lifting weights first to waist level and then, with superhuman effort, high into the air for a few moments before dropping them to the ground. Perhaps Schubert imagined the moment when Atlas first manoeuvred the globe on to his shoulders. Thus 'Unerträgliches' shifts between G for the voice (b. 16) and then a G sharp supported by diminished seventh harmony (b. 17) as the challenge is taken and the burden lifted halfway. A quaver's gasp and an extraordinary burst of energy follows as voice and piano swiftly launch the phrase 'und brechen / Will mir das Herz' up the stave (bb. 17–21). The augmented second at 'Herz im' is the ultimate muscular wrench that culminates in the defiant high F sharp of 'Leibe' (b. 19). Here something heavy seems held aloft at huge cost (no singer finds this passage easy) until the final 'be' of 'Leibe' falls an exhausted fifth with the suddenness of a weightlifter who has reached the limit of his strength. Leo Black notes the voice doubling piano in this passage and states that 'subjection to an ineluctable law could scarcely be more pressingly depicted. . . After all that effort, all that pride, Atlas has proved incapable of bearing the world's woes.' In any case, the effect is terrific: words and music describe great physical and emotional stress. The change of direction in the harmony (flats in G minor are replaced by a slew of sharps in the vocal line which steer the music to F sharp major, and thence to B minor) is a superb example of how tension and effort can be added to music (or taken away) by the smallest nudge of the harmonic tiller.

The song's middle section is Heine's second verse. The rattling right-hand demisemiquaver oscillations cease in favour of triplets shared between the hands. An unexpected sharpening of a semitone lifts the music into B major (from b. 22); there is something grimly heroic about this, defiant at the same time as infinitely world-weary. The accented left-hand quavers trace a motif which is a major-key variant of the opening music in the bass clef. In rhythms as tightly bound as the wrists of a condemned prisoner the singer addresses himself off the cuff – 'It's all your own fault', he tells his heart. 'You gambled and lost. You wanted everything or nothing, and now you have nothing!' The wail of diminished harmony for 'un<u>endlich</u> glücklich' (bb. 28–30) is balanced by an even more desperate, but quieter, 'unendlich elend' (bb. 33–5).

Heine's well-known tendency is to end poems with a throwaway line or unexpected rapier thrust. Here the final *coup de grâce* is the 'Und jetzo bist du elend', as if to say 'You lived life at the extremes, you gambled, and look – it's your own fault, so live with it!' In a reading of the poem (and forgetting the music for a moment) the final 'elend' is a fragment of Jewish humour at its darkest, a type of self-directed *Schadenfreude*. This effect is made stronger here by the fact that this lyric is unrhymed. Every other poem in the Heine cycle has an ABCB structure but here it is without rhyme and ends in mid-air; Atlas' perpetual plight seems dismissed with a shrug. In Schubert's song, however, the repeat of 'unendlich elend' and a new shift of harmony mean that the ironic 'stolzes Herz' at the end of the strophe's third line actually sounds like a call to action and the beginning of a brave new thought. Heine had meant to imply, surely, that his once proud heart had been humbled, leaving us to pity him. But Schubert's dotted rhythms at 'stolzes Herz' underline continuing pride. And 'Und jetzo bist du elend' is the most dramatic phrase in the piece with a high G for '<u>jetzo</u>' and a very strong V–I cadence on 'elend.' Hardly a throwaway line – and more of a sledgehammer blow than a rapier thrust.

Contrary to the pithy spirit of the poem, Schubert repeats the first verse in a musical contraction of the opening strophe. The voice is enmeshed with the bass octaves with even more constricting effect. We have heard all this material before apart from the truly grandiose (one might be tempted to say Wagnerian) climactic phrase that includes a high A flat ('Die ganze Welt der <u>Schmerzen</u> muss ich tragen', bb. 48–52). The raw power of this passage strikes a new note in Schubert's music as the character seems to emerge with a blood-curdling cry of pain from the frame that has hitherto contained him. The hammered insistence on the flattened supertonic – also in the piano – is so much larger than life that it would be tempting to lecture the composer on Heine's use of exaggeration for ironic effect. But by now the mythological character, and the shade of Beethoven that has hovered over the piece throughout, have taken over. The thundering postlude would not be out of place in Wolf's *Prometheus* (who was Atlas' brother-Titan).

We have got to know Heine better through Robert Schumann and other later composers. We are familiar with his pathos and his self-conscious pose, his ability to conjure vast imagery (look at the last of the *Dichterliebe* Op. 48 songs with its giants and saints, cathedrals and coffins) as a frame for his obsessive examination of every small detail of his emotive life, itself based as much on fiction as fact. If Schubert is not quite on Heine's wavelength here it is because he has taken the poem at face value, possibly attracted to it in the first place as a means of paying tribute to Beethoven. He comes from a generation where words mean more or less what they say. In any case, no composer has ever truly mastered the glint of Heine's malicious irony (something which is almost impossible adequately to convey in music), not even Robert Schumann. Nevertheless, *Der Atlas* is a miracle on its own terms. It is only sad that we will never find out what Schubert might have made of Heine on closer and more protracted acquaintance. In the meantime we are left pondering one of Susan Youens's many powerful aperçus on the nature of the attraction between Schubert and the Heine poems he chose to set:

For Schubert, who made some sort of erotic bid for happiness and lost hugely, whose burden of terminal illness could no more be relinquished than could Atlas's burdens of globe and sky, who knew he was a Titan of music, this poem might well have had personal meaning.

First edition:	Published by Tobias Haslinger, Vienna in May 1829, Volume 2, no. 2 (P211)
Subsequent editions:	Peters: I/151; AGA XX 561: Vol. 9/167; NSA IV: Vol. 14a/142; Bärenreiter: Vol. 4/157
Bibliography:	Youens 2007, pp. 11–22
Further settings and arrangements:	7 further settings and 13 arrangements in Metzner 1992, including
	Vesque von Püttlingen (1803–1883) *Ich unglücksel'ger Atlas* from *Die Heimkehr*, no. 24 (1851)
	Arr. Franz Liszt (1811–1886) for solo piano, no. 11 of *Schwanengesang* (1838–9) [*see* TRANSCRIPTIONS]
	Reinhold Moritzovich Glière (1875–1956) *Jo Atlas, zlopoluchnyi* Op. 58 no. 7 (1912)
Discography and timing:	Fischer-Dieskau III 3⁸ 2'15
	Hyperion I 37¹⁴
	Hyperion II 37⁸ 2'13 Anthony Rolfe Johnson

← *Abschied* D957/7   *Ihr Bild* D957/9 →

IX IHR BILD   Her portrait
D957/9 [H678]
B♭ minor

Ich stand in dunkeln Träu - men und stärrt' ihr Bild - nis an,

(36 bars)

Ich stand in dunkeln Träumen, Und starrt' ihr Bildnis an,[1] Und das geliebte Antlitz Heimlich zu leben begann.	I stood in dark dreams, Gazing at her picture, And that beloved face Began mysteriously to come alive.
Um ihre Lippen zog sich Ein Lächeln wunderbar, Und wie von Wehmutstränen Erglänzte ihr Augenpaar.	Around her lips played A wondrous smile, And her eyes glistened, As though with melancholy tears.
Auch meine Tränen flossen Mir von den Wangen herab – Und ach, ich kann es nicht glauben, Dass ich Dich verloren hab'!	My tears, too, flowed Down my cheeks. And oh – I cannot believe That I have lost you!

[1] Heine writes 'Und *starrte* ihr Bildnis an'.

HEINRICH HEINE (1797–1856); poem written in 1823/4

This is the second of Schubert's six Heine solo settings (1828). See the poet's biography for a chronological list all of the Heine settings.

Many of Schubert's songs have been ignored by the critics and musicologists, but a great deal has been written about these relatively bare thirty-six bars. They have made a deep impression on everyone because this song seems to represent the very bleakness of Schubert's approaching end. Here is a new stylistic departure that marks the beginning of a journey, all the more poignant because we know that it cannot be continued. After the start of the group with *Der Atlas*, an anguished fanfare in music, we realize that Schubert's new partnership with Heine ranks with his collaboration with Goethe and Müller: this is a poet powerful enough to make a difference to how the music *sounds*.

The key is B flat minor, but never was there a more 'difficult' key signature heading a more transparent piece of music. (The E flat minor of Schumann's *Ich hab' im Traum geweinet* Op. 48 no. 3 – a Heine setting from *Dichterliebe* – comes to mind as a parallel.) The piano begins with a dotted minim B flat (an octave shared between the hands) followed by a rest; and then exactly the same again – the same note and the same rest. These two bars were the subject of an enthusiastic passage in *Der Tonwille* (1921) by Heinrich Schenker, perhaps the most famous name in musical analysis. He proposed that these two B flats were what we would now call a tonal analogue for the act of looking at something. To give the tonic note once in a bare unison is one thing; to repeat it is to imply a second, more searching stare.

It is rare for the formidable and rigorous Schenker to be lost for diagrams, putting his usual analytical apparatus to one side in favour of commenting on the relationship of words to music in this way. But, as he himself says, there is no other way to explain how Schubert 'shows himself the true magician who binds a secret thread around the exterior situation (here, the staring at a picture), around the soul of the unhappy love, and around us'. What is an unusual way of looking at things for Schenker, however, is common enough for vocal performers. One has to sing and play (as much as stare at) the song picture to realize that there is a vast vocabulary of Schubertian word-to-music responses where a verbal idea gives rise to a chord, a phrase, a figuration, a modulation, a turn of phrase, a tonality and so on. New 'expressions' in this 'language' were continually minted by the composer, becoming part of an established vocabulary of tonal analogues to which he continually returned, refining and elaborating the grammar of his own secret song-writing language. Harmonic analysis (in the conventional sense) of songs by the great lieder composers can begin only after a discussion of the text and the musical responses brought to birth by those words. In this field, harmony and form are servants of the word, not of a purely musical idea. For unless words were put to music that had already been composed, this would be to put the cart before the horse.

So yes, of course, the reiteration of these two 'gathering' minims may well imply a stare, or deepening concentration, Schubert's response to the stillness of the past tense of the verb 'stand' and the colour of the adjective 'dunkeln'. But we note too that the doubling of voice and piano in much of this song has its own meaning – it is, in John Reed's words, 'an image of loneliness and deprivation'. Schubertians have come to this conclusion by comparing many passages in the canon where the same musical device mirrors similarly bleak emotion. The shape of the vocal line for 'Ich stand in dunkeln Träumen', with its rise of a minor third followed by a dip to the leading note and back to the tonic, seems to have been derived from the motif that pervades *Der Atlas*, and is announced in thundering left-hand octaves in the opening of that song. As with some of the 'fingerprints' that unite the Rellstab songs, this interest in cyclical musical procedures linking one song with another is an idea, like so many others in 1828, that Schubert might later have developed to an astonishing degree. The shudder of double-dotted rhythm (rare in Schubert's songs) at 'starrt' ihr Bildnis an' adds an edge of suspense, even horror, to a scenario which has a supernatural element, even if only in the narrator's mind. The piano interlude in left-hand octaves at the bottom of the keyboard (bb. 6–8) echoes the double-dotted fragment of vocal melody that we have just heard. The effect is not dissimilar to the ominous trills that punctuate the opening melodic statements of the B flat major Piano Sonata D960.

At 'das geliebte Antlitz' (bb. 9–10) the music softens into the major key, a shift familiar from the *Winterreise* D911 songs where minor tonality represents unpleasant reality, major a retreat into happy memories of the past. The marshalling of all his concentration (depicted by the continual unisons and doublings) enables the poet to cross the threshold separating the viewer of the picture from its subject. Whether he imagines his lover comes to life, or she actually does so, lies within the realm of poetic licence or perhaps religious belief like icons in the Catholic Church that supposedly weep or bleed. Either way, the bare textures of the music gradually fill out with new growth; after 'Heimlich zu leben begann' (bb. 11–12) the piano interlude begins with a bare left-hand B flat; the addition of an adjacent semitone creates a minor second (A–B flat), which is followed by a major second (A flat–B flat); then the right hand joins in, resulting in a chord in three parts. Suddenly we have a bar of four-part harmony, music so domestic and sweet as to be playable on the parlour harmonium. This is to see an outline fleshed out before our eyes, a tree of life sprouting shoots as bare twigs become covered in green foliage.

The poem's second verse describes the animation of the beloved's features. The modulation from B flat major to G flat major is simply achieved, but it is wonderfully effective, and we feel drawn into an intimate and mysterious relationship with the smiling woman. The poet's engagement with her is equally strange, and our ignorance of the background between them enhances the enigma. This is eloquent rather than genial music, with an undertow of the deepest pathos. The economy of the writing for voice and piano is almost unprecedented in Schubert – at times the vocal line seems scarcely harmonized. But this is a calculated modesty: the singer is made to sound awestruck, humble and grateful for this stolen moment and, yes, utterly repentant (for what misdemeanour or failing we shall never know, but that is typical of Heine). After 'Lächeln wunderbar' there is a tiny motif in falling thirds for the pianist (b. 18), a brief musical twitch for a Mona Lisa smile. These twitches, interpolations and interruptions would make a chapter of their own in Schubert's music. Here one is reminded of the middle section of the slow movement of the G major String Quartet D887, from b. 52, with those extraordinary tiny shudders for the first violin and viola in unison.

The *minore* colouring for 'Wehmutstränen' (bb. 19–20) is equally masterful, and the helplessness of the narrator could not be more apparent in the minimalist accompanying texture. The 'Augenpaar' are decorated with a glinting mordent in the vocal line (b. 21), followed by another falling staccato figuration at b. 22 (tears glistening or tears dropping?) – exactly the same notes in thirds and in G flat major as at b. 18. Both of these interjections, in one sense hopelessly easy to play, represent a real challenge to the pianist and seem somehow inadequate to the situation, indicative perhaps of the protagonist's helplessness. There is no possible opportunity to make anything expressive of these tiny touches – the barest of the *Winterreise* songs seems florid in comparison.

The pianist has a similar problem in introducing the poem's last verse. This is perhaps Schubert's most inscrutable interlude, containing a detail which one longs to have heard Schubert play himself. Instead of a recapitulation of the two bare B flat unisons of the opening we have fuller chords – both on B flat as before, but filled out with portentous minor-key harmonies. We fancy we hear a ghost of the smile in the semiquaver D flats at bb. 22 and 23 played by the right-hand little finger as a fleeting anacrusis to each chord. How to make something, without undue exaggeration, of these chords with their curious upbeats has perplexed every pianist who has played this music.

The music for the poem's third verse is an exact repeat of the first, and it is an important part of the conception that the song should be a simple ABA structure. The prosody of 'Mir von den Wangen herab' (bb. 26–7) is not ideal (the unimportant 'von' is awkwardly emphasized by a long note value) but such a detail seems not to matter in the ongoing tread of the music and the inevitability of its shape. This return to the music of the opening tells us that the moment of closeness and intimacy with 'her portrait', more a Proustian trick of memory than magic or witchcraft, perhaps, is over. We now return to the initial mood of distance and exclusion. The black despair of 'Und ach, ich kann es nicht glauben / Dass ich dich verloren hab'!' is expressed in the major key, and it sounds more toweringly woeful than it would have in the minor.

The postlude is the same music as for the blossoming tree of life at bb. 12–14, but it is inflected into B flat minor, and marked forte with stentorian significance. Such a tragic song has to end in the minor, but it was brilliantly perceptive of Schubert to allow the singer to finish in the major; this bitter-sweetness exactly captures the poet's masochism, and his almost triumphant relish in the inevitability of his own misfortune. From every viewpoint this song is a masterpiece, but perhaps most of all for its ability to enter into Heine's strangely self-torturing emotional world. Perhaps Franz von Schober deserves some of the credit for this – after all it was probably his reading of the poem in the *Lesegesellschaft* that acquainted Schubert with it in the first place.

First edition:	Published by Tobias Haslinger, Vienna in May 1829, Volume 2, no. 3 (P212)
Subsequent editions:	Peters: I/154; AGA XX 562: Vol. 9/170; NSA IV: Vol. 14a/146; Bärenreiter: Vol. 4/160
Bibliography:	Youens 2007, pp. 22–45
Further settings and arrangements:	89 further settings and 32 arrangements in Metzner 1992, including
	Vesque von Püttlingen (1803–1883) *Ihr Bild* from *Die Heimkehr*, no. 23 (1851)
	Franz Lachner (1803–1890) *Ihr Bildnis* Op. 33 no. 14 (1832)
	Arr. Franz Liszt (1811–1886) for solo piano, no. 8 of *Schwanengesang* (1838–9) [*see* TRANSCRIPTIONS]
	Karl Wilhelm Taubert (1811–1891) *Ihr Bild* Op. 17 no. 9 (1880)
	Clara Schumann (1819–1896) *Ich stand in dunkeln Träumen* (first version *Ihr Bildnis*, 1840), Op. 13 no. 1 (1844)
	Edvard Grieg (1843–1907) *Ich stand in dunkeln Träumen* Op. 2 no. 3 (1861)
	Hugo Wolf (1860–1901) *Ich stand in dunkeln Träumen* from *Liederstrauss* (1878)
	Arr. Anton Webern (1883–1945) for voice and orchestra (1903) [*see* ORCHESTRATIONS]
	Arr. Tilman Hoppstock (b. 1961) for guitar accompaniment, in *Franz Schubert: 110 Lieder* (2009)
Discography and timing:	Fischer-Dieskau III 3[9] 2'53
	Hyperion I 37[15]
	Hyperion II 37[9] 2'53 Anthony Rolfe Johnson

← *Der Atlas* D957/8   *Das Fischermädchen* D957/10 →

X Das FISCHERMÄDCHEN
D957/10 [H679]
A♭ major

The fisher maiden

Du schönes Fischermädchen,
Treibe den Kahn ans Land;
Komm zu mir und setze dich nieder,
Wir kosen Hand in Hand.

Leg' an mein Herz dein Köpfchen,
Und fürchte dich nicht zu sehr;
Vertrau'st du dich doch sorglos
Täglich dem wilden Meer.

Mein Herz gleicht ganz dem Meere,
Hat Sturm und Ebb' und Flut,
Und manche schöne Perle
In seiner Tiefe ruht.

Lovely fisher maiden,
Bring your boat to the shore;
Come and sit beside me,
And hand in hand we shall talk of love.

Lay your little head on my heart
And do not be too afraid;
For each day you trust yourself
Without a care to the turbulent sea.

My heart is just like the sea.
It has its storms, its ebbs and its flows;
And many a lovely pearl
Rests in its depths.

HEINRICH HEINE (1797–1856); poem written in 1823/4

This is the third of Schubert's six Heine solo settings (1828). See the poet's biography for a chronological list all of the Heine settings.

This enchanting serenade is the apotheosis of the barcarolle – at least until Gabriel Fauré, after Chopin's single contribution to the genre, adopted that form for thirteen magnificent piano works some fifty years later. Other Schubert love songs in 𝄴 (*Alinde* D904, *Abendlied für die Entfernte* D856), beautiful as they are, somehow miss the boat in comparison to these undulations that are not so much waterborne as water-aware. The pianist's right hand floats and weaves, the chords changing shape like so much flotsam and jetsam on the song's surface, the modulations a metaphor for the new patterns brought about by each incursion of the rolling tide. One of these brings into view the boat of the fisher girl returning to dry land. There is nothing violent here (although the words refer to storms at sea in the last verse), just the gentle bobbing of waves, and all the time in the world to spin a yarn. We are in full view of the beach, for the song takes place at the water's edge – the site of Schumann's Heine setting *Abends am Strand* Op. 45 no. 3 when young men tell second-hand tall stories about exotic, faraway lands. These may lead (they hope) to first-hand experience in quite a different terrain: these travellers' tales are meant, after all, to impress the girls, the daughters of working fishermen who help with the boats and the daily catch.

And this poem is also about fishing for a catch. Heine is a city boy on holiday, out for a good time with a local girl. To seduce her he will use whatever sweet talk is necessary, inventing suitably simplistic metaphors to make her feel at home, for these are words designed to traverse barriers of class and education. In Dickens's *David Copperfield* the good-looking Steerforth would have used similar poetic conceits to woo poor, susceptible Little Em'ly on the beach at Great Yarmouth as he plotted to seduce her and then, inevitably, abandon her. Thus here we have a love song that is not a love song, words not meaning what they say, and once again Schubert fails to appreciate Heine's irony, taking the words of a manipulative rogue as if they were sincerely meant. But Heine can be as po-faced as you please, while laughing at himself, his readers and his own chutzpah: how could *any* composer put all those layers into music? Not even the acutely literary Schubert was prepared for the new cynicism that had entered the soul of romanticism, and there were many (Karl Kraus in his *Heine und die Folgen*, 1910, for example) who never forgave this poet for what they took to be the poisoning of the German literary well. (*Vergiftet sind meine Lieder* – 'Poisoned are my songs' – is after all the title of one of Liszt's Heine settings.)

Fischer-Dieskau talks of the song's 'delicate sultrinesss' and its 'touch of impertinence'. He marries the music and poem in a compromise that is typical of today's performers of this song, making Schubert a touch less sincere, and Heine a touch more, until they meet somewhere in the middle. Some singers even contrive to perform this affectionate song heartlessly, with a rapacious gleam in the eye and an underlying sneer – a type of *Don Giovanni* serenade. This attempt to rewrite Schubert is the oldest trap in the world for a lieder singer who believes he has a clearer insight into the words than the composer himself. If you do not agree with an interpretation of the words, the only solution is to make another setting of them yourself; attitude, diction, acting cannot alter the heart of a song such as this. (Such impositions should arguably also be denied to directors working in the opera world, although it is true that way-out productions which distort the composer's original intentions occasionally yield interesting results.)

Schubert's *Das Fischermädchen*, if not Heine's, is a genuinely charming serenade, suffused with a gentle longing, and it must be sung as if the singer really cares about the outcome; if he manages to plight his troth the result could be the life of a happily married couple in a cottage by the sea. But, until then, the singer has no luck with the fisher girl: far from being an easy catch, she is as unattainable as any of the women Schubert is said to have longed for. For all the physical proximity suggested by the words, the fisher girl is, in effect, as distant as any 'distant beloved', for Schubert's music makes her so. She is certainly as distant as the lover serenaded in the corresponding song in the Rellstab cycle, *Ständchen*. We detect in both pieces that note of lifelong, rueful melancholy that suffuses anything by Schubert with a sexual undertone. For whatever reason, the hunt is not his métier; he would sooner skirt the challenge than challenge a rival for the skirt. Like the miller boy, he finds hunters unsympathetic. The compensations are many, however: fulfilment is not on the agenda, but longing, and its myriad nuances, become an art form in their own right.

The song is in A flat major, a key according to John Reed which denotes secure and reciprocated love in Schubert's songs. If that is so, this quality of affection is something sought in this music rather than attained. There is a veil of pleading and sadness over the music, a mood extraordinary for a work nominally in the major key. 'Nominally' because phrases like 'Komm zu mir und setze dich nieder' (Verse 1, bb. 13–15) and 'Und manche schöne Perle' (Verse 3, bb. 59–61) are harmonized by supertonic harmony – in this case chords of B flat minor. The song inhabits 'flat'-sounding (and thus soulful rather than merry) keys, and the magical modulation of the second verse into C flat major (from b. 29) accentuates this fact. Even the barcarolle *Bewegung* ('Etwas geschwind') implies control and consideration rather than passionate powers of persuasion. The rise to the high G flat at 'kosen Hand in Hand' (Verse 1, b. 21) may well suggest the swinging back and forth of entwined arms; in the other two strophes it is less ebullient. But there is no lack of gallantry (not for the first time the character of Don Ottavio comes to mind): after this upward scoop the elegant descent back to the home key (sometimes ornamented with a mordent, as in the NSA, b. 22) is typical of an Italianate *serenata* at its most winning.

We have already spoken of the shift into C flat major for the second verse. The piano interlude that ushers this in (bb. 23–9) is quite simply one of the loveliest that Schubert was ever to write. Playing this one can imagine the composer's expression as he scans the face of a lover, the better to read and understand what he sees there before embarking on the song's next verse. As different thoughts flash across Schubert's face, one mood yielding to another, there are moments of hesitation and lingering, excuses for the tiny moments of rubato with which his inspired changes of harmonic direction are lovingly tagged by his interpreters. If the look of a lover, full of gentle concern for the beloved's welfare, can be translated into music, here it is. The long favoured use of the flattened mediant (C flat major in the key of A flat) makes this strophe appear an oasis of intimacy; the words are set to music of such matchless generosity that we forget that the poet, in saying them, has no objection to the girl risking her life daily at sea, as long as she returns from the storms to bring him pleasure.

The final verse is almost an exact repeat of the first. The robust words 'Sturm und Ebb' und Flut' are well suited to the straightforward A flat arpeggio with which they mount the stave (bb. 51–3). Here even the lyricism of Schubert's music cannot disguise the self-regarding narcissism of the text. '*Mein* Herz', says the poet, and that is all that interests him. A man as self-centred as Heine might have written interesting music if he had been capable, but it would never have been *this* music. Apart from this mismatch, the song is a great one, and occupies an important place in the set – a ray of sunlight glinting on the sea after two songs of exceptional intensity, and before yet another dark and strange *fantasia*. The postlude is a reappearance of the prelude with an added couple of bars to bring the song to a gently wafting conclusion.

First edition:	Published by Tobias Haslinger, Vienna in May 1829, Volume 2, no. 4 (P213)
Subsequent editions:	Peters: I/156; AGA XX 563: Vol. 9/172; NSA IV: Vol. 14a/148; Bärenreiter: Vol. 4/162
Bibliography:	Youens 2007, pp. 45–53
Further settings and arrangements:	26 further settings and 37 arrangements in Metzner 1992, including
	Giacomo Meyerbeer (1791–1864) *Komm!* (1837)
	Franz Grillparzer (1791–1872) *Das Fischermädchen* (date unknown)
	Carl Loewe (1796–1869) *Du schönes Fischermädchen* Op. 9 no. 5 (1832)
	Vesque von Püttlingen (1803–1883) *Du schönes Fischermädchen* from *Die Heimkehr*, no. 8 (1851)
	Arr. Franz Liszt (1811–1886) for solo piano, no. 2 of *Schwanengesang* (1838–9) [*see* TRANSCRIPTIONS]
	Franz Lachner (1803–1890) *Das Fischermädchen* Op. 33 no. 10 (1832)
	Alexander Borodin (1834–1887) *Krasavitsa-ribachka* (trans. Kropotkin), also with cello (*c.* 1854)
	Samuel Coleridge-Taylor (1875–1912) *My pretty fishermaiden* (published 1918)

Reinhold Moritzovich Glière (1875–1956) *Du schönes Fischermädchen* Op. 58 no. 6 (1912)
Arr. Tilman Hoppstock (b. 1961) for guitar accompaniment, in *Franz Schubert: 110 Lieder* (2009)

Discography and timing: Fischer-Dieskau III 3[10]   2'03
Pears-Britten 2[1]
Hyperion I 37[16]
Hyperion II 37[10]   2'27   Anthony Rolfe Johnson

← *Ihr Bild* D957/9   *Die Stadt* D957/11 →

XI Die STADT   The town
D957/11 [H680]
C minor

Am fernen Horizonte	On the distant horizon
Erscheint, wie ein Nebelbild,	Appears, like a misty vision,
Die Stadt mit ihren Türmen	The town with its turrets,
In Abenddämmrung gehüllt.	Shrouded in dusk.

Ein feuchter Windzug kräuselt	A damp wind ruffles
Die graue Wasserbahn;	The grey stretch of water.
Mit traurigem Takte rudert	With mournful strokes
Der Schiffer in meinem Kahn.	The boatman rows my boat.

Die Sonne hebt sich noch einmal	Radiant, the sun rises once more
Leuchtend vom Boden empor,	From the earth,
Und zeigt mir jene Stelle,	And shows me that place
Wo ich das Liebste verlor.	Where I lost my beloved.

HEINRICH HEINE (1797–1856); poem written in 1823/4

This is the fourth of Schubert's six Heine solo settings (1828). See the poet's biography for a chronological list all of the Heine settings.

This is one of the strangest songs that Schubert ever composed. Only *Der Leiermann* D911/24 at the end of *Winterreise* can compare with it as music which suppresses harmonic and rhythmic variety to depict the one-track obsessions of someone *in extremis*. The music is so minimalist here that it might almost be an aria from an imaginary John Adams opera entitled *Heine in Hamburg*. The music, much of it deliberately indeterminate and grey, is based on repetitions of

Illustration (1935) by Anton Pieck for *Die Stadt*.

cells. Despite its simplicity, the creation of this music must also have repeatedly exercised the grey cells of the composer: for many commentators this is the masterpiece of the set – here is music even more bare and concentrated than that for *Ihr Bild*. The word 'impressionism' comes to mind because there seems only to be an impression or sketch of a 'real' song (the play between reality and unreality is a feature of the text); the harmonies of *Die Stadt* appear to be a mere sketch of what is implied on the printed page. The misty visions described in the poem seem worthy of Whistler or Turner, and are depicted with similarly airy brushstrokes. The scurrying diminished-seventh arpeggio that recurs unaltered no fewer than *seventeen* times during the course of the song might have been part of a Debussy Prelude or *Estampe* were it not for its refusal to modulate or ingratiate in any way. Images of wind, water and suddenly emerging sunlight suggest Monet, perhaps.

Mention of such composers and painters of later generations makes one wonder whether, as Susan Youens has suggested, there is a possibility that 'Heine's lost beloved . . . [is] nothing less than the entire Romantic poetic project or poetry itself', and whether Schubert's response was deliberately to evoke a worn-out, or 'verschöpft', harmonic system, a musical dead end. On the other hand, beneath the blurred and atmospheric contours of *Die Stadt* is a core of sharp seriousness that is very much part of German values in the earlier part of the nineteenth century. The town with its turrets on the horizon is painted by, if anyone, Caspar David Friedrich, and the song, for all its avant-garde vagaries, takes its place as one of the proud icons of German romanticism.

The town of Hamburg, the scene of Heine's humiliation in love, is the villain of the piece, as well as its title. The nameless town in *Rückblick* D911/8 from *Winterreise* is unpleasant enough, but only because of its heartbreaking personal associations. In this song, *Die Stadt* is the site of Heine's unhappiness which has come about in the context of the host city's cold impersonality. Indeed one is made to feel that the town is something callous and uncaring in itself. This is a glimpse of the society of the future and a world Schubert was never to know, with its steam trains, factories and gas lighting. In *Die Stadt* he imagined a city that loomed in the distance, large and forbidding, repository of a thousand secrets and heartbreaks, nearer Blake's nightmare descriptions of London in the 1820s than Vienna in the same period. In 1828 Schubert's home city was still an eighteenth-century town in many ways – there was no pollution, no steam power, gas or electricity. It was a town of political repression, but the Industrial Revolution had, as yet, largely passed it by. We sense that Schubert sees Hamburg not as he sees his beloved Vienna: here is a *modern* city, the kind he would not have liked to live in. The mood is tense, neurotic, dangerous, unhealthy. Those fixated arpeggios sound a note of claustrophobia, their diminished harmony a type of pollution.

Heine's words are set without repetitions – here there are no rhetorical verbal repeats as there had been in *Der Atlas* – and the simplicity of the music, combined with the stark strength of its peroration, convey the poet's loss with the almost offhand concision of Heine at his most bleak. There is much talk of a 'new Schubert' with this song. To tell the truth, a new 'new Schubert' seems to be born with each Heine setting, so strange and compulsive are they, and so different from each other, and from the songs that have gone before. That the poet has caused his own personality to be deeply reflected in the music (an influence on composers that only the greatest poets can wield) is without question.

The time signature is ⅜, the tempo marking 'Mässig geschwind'. Soft rolling Cs, demisemiquavers in split octaves, oscillate in the left hand for the first beat. The second and third beats are solitary quavers on low Cs. This procedure is repeated exactly for the second bar, recalling the stasis in the introduction to *Ihr Bild*. Bars 3, 4 and 5 feature the same music, each bar a repeat of its predecessor. The same Cs oscillate beneath a right-hand arpeggio that swirls up and down the octave based on the diminished chord on A natural. There are eight notes in the bass and nine in the treble, so these figurations, as they mesh together, never sound tritely tidy, and they are not meant to. We are reminded that the narrator is sitting in a boat which is being rowed by an oarsman, the Hamburg equivalent of Charon, underworld ferryman: the second and third beats of each bar are given over to a rowing motif made up of the same diminished harmony. This is an accented figure of two descending quavers, the first of which is a chord, the second a solitary A – these drooping, sigh-like movements are heard in bb. 3–5, first in the treble stave, and then an octave lower in the bass. The plashing chords seem to represent the oar plying the water, but nothing happens to take the stationary vessel from one point to another. It is caught immobile in time and space, the water as viscous as the Styx. We are reminded that Schubert's great *Gruppe aus dem Tartarus* D583 also features shivering piano figurations in an ominous C minor.

For the sight of the imposing town, misty music is replaced by a definite melodic outline. The double-dotted crotchet-note figurations that appeared in *Ihr Bild* (at 'starrt' ihr Bildnis an') were unusual for Schubert, but here they are again for 'Am fernen Horizonte'. The act of staring, or in this case scanning the horizon, a feature of both songs. The distance between the vocal line and the bass-clef harmonies (at 'Erscheint, wie ein Nebelbild', bb. 8–10), as well as the pervasive dotted rhythms, is strongly reminiscent of the first page of *Die Nebensonnen* D911/23 from *Winterreise* where the winter traveller looks into the distance as he counts three suns in the sky. The idea of effortful concentration on a distant focal point is common to all three songs. Harmonies shift grandly, but simply, between C minor and its dominant and subdominant. The old-fashioned Handelian rhythms, prompted by mention of the city with its imposing towers and palaces, are descriptive of civic pomp and circumstance. This is the almost operatic backdrop to the failure of the poet's affair.

The second verse begins with mention of the 'feuchter Windzug'. This is of course represented by the arpeggio motif that has appeared in bars 3 and 4 of the *Vorspiel*. But nothing, surely, could prepare us for the use of this bar no fewer than eleven times as an accompaniment for a vocal line, also fashioned from diminished harmony, which swirls down the stave in woebegone sequences a third apart from each other (bb. 17–19, bb. 19–21, bb. 21–3, bb. 23–5). This withdrawn music has the effect of a slowly spiralling leaf caught in the autumn wind. With the words 'in meinem Kahn' the voice reaches C at the bottom of the treble stave (bb. 24–5). The lowest point in the song thus represents the height of its introspection.

The arrival of the sun occasions another *forte pomposo* passage with a solemn oratorio-like tread. The music is similar to that for the first strophe, but in a higher and grander tessitura. The flattened supertonic, such a feature of these songs, is magnificently jarring for 'Und zeigt mir jene Stelle' (bb. 32–3). The impression is of someone unhinged with grief, and the high G for 'Liebste verlor' is one of the great and chilling pay-off moments of *Schwanengesang* in terms of sheer vocal power. Capell correctly analyses why this is a particularly effective setting as far as Heine is concerned: 'The cry of the poet's loss on the 6–4 minor chord is uttered wildly; but lost is lost, and there is no more to be said.' Here then is a workable musical equivalent of Heine's 'sting in the tail'. One can imagine, if the poem were to be read, the words 'Where I lost my beloved' being said more quietly as a clinching throwaway. But one of the strangest features of this song is the composer's decision to make things in the distance appear in sharp (and loud) musical focus, and things in near vision – the boat, the rowing, the water – hazy and indistinct. This bizarre reversal of perspectives shows us that the past (the distant city, and memories of his lost love) is the only place where the narrator has been truly alive.

The song ends with the same five bars with which it began. There is an important new point – the very last note of all. This is a single minim C with a fermata on the last beat. Schubert thus avoids his obligation, as a good and well brought-up pupil of Salieri's composition class, to resolve the discord of the last diminished seventh. The music moves directly from the diminished chord to that solitary low C. Are we supposed to imagine a C major or minor chord there? Maybe we hear only an impression of one. Is this as flagrant a breach of the rules as one suspects? We must wait until the next song to find out.

First edition:	Published by Tobias Haslinger, Vienna in May 1829, Volume 2, no. 5 (P214)
Subsequent editions:	Peters: I/159; AGA XX 564: Vol. 9/175; NSA IV: Vol. 14a/152; Bärenreiter: Vol. 4/165
Bibliography:	Youens 2007, pp. 53–63
Further settings and arrangements:	26 further settings and 12 arrangements in Metzner 1992, including
	Vesque von Püttlingen (1803–1883) *Die Stadt* from *Die Heimkehr*, no. 6 (1851)
	Franz Lachner (1803–1890) *Am fernen Horizonte*
	Felix Mendelssohn (1809–1847) *Wasserfahrt* for TTBB, Op. 50 no. 4 (1838)
	Arr. Franz Liszt (1811–1886) for solo piano, no. 1 of *Schwanengesang* (1838–9) [*see* TRANSCRIPTIONS]
	Robert Franz (1815–1892) *Am fernen Horizonte* Op. 37 no. 3 (1866)
	Arr. Tilman Hoppstock (b. 1961) for guitar accompaniment, in *Franz Schubert: 110 Lieder* (2009)
Discography and timing:	Fischer-Dieskau III 3[11] 2'55
	Hyperion I 37[17]
	Hyperion II 37[11] 2'51 Anthony Rolfe Johnson

← *Das Fischermädchen* D957/10   *Am Meer* D957/12 →

XII AM MEER   By the sea
D957/12 [H681]
C major

(45 bars)

Das Meer erglänzte weit hinaus,	The sea glittered far and wide
Im letzten Abendscheine;	In the sun's dying rays;
Wir sassen am einsamen Fischerhaus,	We sat by the fisherman's lonely house;
Wir sassen stumm und alleine.	We sat silent and alone.
Der Nebel stieg, das Wasser schwoll,	The mist rose, the waters swelled,
Die Möwe flog hin und wieder;	A seagull flew to and fro.
Aus deinen Augen, liebevoll,	From your loving eyes
Fielen die Tränen nieder.	The tears fell.

Ich sah sie fallen auf deine Hand,	I saw them fall on your hand.
Und bin aufs Knie gesunken;	I sank upon my knee;
Ich hab' von deiner weissen Hand	From your white hand
Die Tränen fortgetrunken.	I drank away the tears.

Seit jener Stunde verzehrt sich mein Leib,	Since that hour my body is consumed
Die Seele stirbt vor Sehnen;—	And my soul dies of longing.
Mich hat das unglücksel'ge Weib	That wretched woman
Vergiftet mit ihren Tränen.	Has poisoned me with her tears.

HEINRICH HEINE (1797–1856); poem written in 1823/4

This is the fifth of Schubert's six Heine solo settings (1828). See the poet's biography for a chronological list all of the Heine settings.

According to the rules of classical harmony, the single low C minim after a diminished-seventh harmony at the end of *Die Stadt* has left that song's closing harmony unresolved. What follows is the strongest possible argument that Schubert's order for the songs in this Heine group was his own, and not in the least fortuitous. *Am Meer* opens with the chord of the German sixth in C major (C + A flat + C + D sharp + F sharp + C) which immediately resolves on to the tonic. If this is played immediately after *Die Stadt*, the final chord of that song is resolved by the first of this one as we move from C minor to C major. The manuscript reveals that Schubert had originally 'spelled' this opening chord as: C + A flat + <u>E flat</u> + C + F sharp + C. This adds weight to the theory that he regarded the two songs as harmonically related, and that he wished them to be linked in performance. It shows that the composer, by his inmost nature, was no confrontational revolutionary. He is cheeky enough to make us think he is an anarchist, but then he slyly backtracks, acknowledging convention in a way that surprises (and delights) us.

The opening also reminds us of another work in C major, the contemporary String Quintet D956, where the music fills out into a similar chord after the opening unison Cs. The alternation of these two pivoting tonalities is familiar as a symphonic motif, and Schubert did not invent it. But in both works it signals a certain majesty and C major grandeur. *Am Meer* is short in length (only two pages in the Peters Edition and in the AGA) but massive in effect – the broad,

Autograph of *Die Stadt* (conclusion) and *Am Meer* (beginning).

open vistas and endless shoreline of Heine's beloved North Sea are built into the music. Schubert's personal experience of water was confined to streams and lakes but, as in *Meeres Stille* D216, he was somehow able to conjure vast stretches of sea, sand and sky in music in this great 'empty' key (both settings of the Adriatic *Gondelfahrer* D808 and 809 are also in C major). If he had heard more of Heine's *Reisebilder* read aloud by Schober he would have known how the poet felt about this part of North Germany near Cuxhaven ('I love the sea like my soul', and 'The sea is my soul', Heine wrote to his publisher Campe). One fancies that the ache of that love is built into this music, the backdrop as important as the sad relationship described in the foreground.

Heine's four strophes are treated as two identical musical verses, each of which is divided into two parts, the first reflective, the second more active. Unless these Heine songs date from much earlier in 1828, this is Schubert's last strophic song, the final example of a form that had prompted him to so much expressive music. Often this was a means of exercising a discipline over his own prolix tendencies; to use a comparison from instrumental music, the strophic song encouraged the composer to favour the sonata or rondo form over the freedom of the fantasia. It was usually easy enough for Schubert to write new music for a new verse of poetry, but the strophic form had taught him to hone and polish what he had already written, and the intellectual challenge of creating diversity in unity was also a stimulus. But we may ask ourselves why the song is cast in this form at all.

The poem, a strange and difficult one with a 'sting in the tail' – that sudden change of mood the Germans call 'Stimmungsbreching' – is partly an evocation of atmosphere and partly a narrative. The poem takes place by the seashore and the woman is a 'Fischermädchen', a holiday romance rather than someone permanently involved in the poet's life. At first, the description of the lovers ('silent and alone') is static; then it is counterpointed by a great deal of movement (rising mists, swelling waves, flying seagulls, falling tears). In the third verse the lovers are less fixed to the spot; the poet falls to his knees and the strange tear-drinking episode takes place. The consequences of this are couched in the most ambiguous terms in the final stanza: is the poet a victim of some supernatural power, the woman a Lorelei? Is his 'poisoning' merely a metaphor for being addicted to the beloved and unable to live without her, or does it hint at venereal illness? (A phrase like 'verzehrt sich mein Leib' might have reminded Schubert of his own fateful encounter.) Or is Heine simply playing with the reader by balancing the overwhelming sentiment of the first three strophes with a sudden pistol shot of a line, a slap in the face for the woman who is dismissed as an 'unglücksel'ge Weib' – perhaps in a wave of post-coital misogyny. In terms of the poetry at least, this description of the physical consequences of the poet's impetuous tear-drinking, an exchange of body fluids, is a descent into bathos. We are left with the feeling that Heine himself might have delivered this final line with a bitter smile of self-deprecation.

The other thing we notice about the poem (though perhaps not at first, so vivid are the descriptions) is that the whole story is recounted in the past tense, something on which Schubert chooses to concentrate. It is true that at the end Heine tells us that his body continues to be consumed, and that he is dying of longing, but there is no telling how long ago the scene had been enacted. Schubert's timeless music swathes the poem not only in sea mists, but also in the mists of time. The only difference between these lines and a strange fairy tale is the word 'wir' (we) that casts the singer in a first-person narrative role. But it is the fairy-tale aspect that appeals to Schubert, and it solves the problem of how to deal with the awkward final strophe: any irony or 'contemporary' viewpoint is ironed out in favour of a heartfelt ending. This narrator is caught in the web of a story like the Flying Dutchman (another Heine creation as it happens); it is as if he recounts the strange sequence of events time and time again – perhaps, like the Ancient Mariner – to whoever will listen to another performance of the song. And in so doing, his music becomes a magical incantation rather than a realistic description of obsession and betrayal. It is the grandeur of the song's resignation, somehow loftily removed from the immediacies of human strife, that encourages this interpretation.

As if to frame this set piece, the opening chords sound like an overture (they are repeated at the end of the song, as if slowly bringing the curtain down on the story). The entry of the voice follows a fermata, but the vocal line begins without fuss or prevarication. This is Schubert in his *Das Wirtshaus* D911/21 or *Die Nebensonnen* D911/23 mode where the doubling of voice by piano, as well as a rhythm that would not be out of place in a hymnal, adds to the poetic power of the whole. The tessitura, as Capell points out, is demandingly high – not of the kind seriously to challenge the high tenor Ludwig Tietze (cf. the Rellstab *Lebensmut* D937 among other songs) but requiring a firm, sustained line and marvellous breath control. This eloquent placing of the voice, perhaps a third higher than the average lied tessitura, gives the song a certain operatic dimension in terms of added tension and 'stretch'. This contributes to the formality of the music's effect, rather than making it more immediate. The lied, after all, is usually pitched nearer to the tessitura of human speech.

C major is a key in which one may luxuriate in consonance, and the vocal line (as often in *Schwanengesang*) is enriched by sounding in thirds and sixths with the accompaniment. (This is another song that could easily have had a horn obbligato like *Auf dem Strom*.) Euphony of this kind can sound commonplace and sentimental, but it can also strike a lofty note; Mahler exploited it to marvellous effect in songs of the utmost pathos. (A great composer like Poulenc could also make music of the café unbearably poignant.) Heine's pathos is surely part of the expressive legacy of the Jewish tradition he shared with Mahler. In July 1828, probably at about the time he was writing this song, Schubert set Psalm 92 (D953) for his friend the rabbi and cantor, Salomon Sulzer. To do so he must have listened to Jewish liturgical music and learned something about Hebrew. This is worth mentioning here because if the plaintive sound of cantorial music is to be found anywhere in Schubert's lieder, it is in the elegiac desperation of *Am Meer*, the very tessitura of the voice appropriate for a call to prayer. (Even the decorations at the ends of the words Abend<u>scheine</u> (b. 6) and ge<u>sunken</u> (b. 27) have the inbuilt flourishes of that tradition.) If prayer played a part in the song's genesis (and this would involve Schubert's having chosen to show in musical terms that he understood something of the poet's Jewish background) it would go some way towards explaining the ritualistic nature of the music.

The poem's second verse is set differently (the song's structure is ABAB). The music changes from C major to C minor, and the accompaniment becomes ruffled in oscillating demisemiquavers as the sea is whipped into foam by the wind (bb. 12–18). The poetic image is one of mist ('Der Nebel stieg') and these obfuscating ripples of sound suit this perfectly. (It is questionable whether or not these tremolandi are measured. Schubert is here poised between the classical and Romantic traditions; the other song with a similarly windswept middle section is the Collin setting *Wehmut* D772 where it is clear that measured sextuplets are required.) The descent of the solitary seagull ('Die Möwe flog hin und wieder', bb. 16–18) is a marvellous picture: the vast expanses of grey sky which it mournfully traverses are almost visible in the downward sweep of the vocal line. Maritime observation now ceases in favour of the beloved whose weeping is described in a passage of the highest Romantic melancholy, a heaviness of emotion we associate with a later part of the century than Schubert's. Indeed, Mahler could easily have incorporated the music for 'Fielen die Tränen nieder' (bb. 21–2) into his own songs. This musical phrase is made up of two identical falling figures, each with an added accent in the vocal line, a marking uncharacteristic of Schubert. The fervid tone of pleading as the phrases are repeated in almost gestural terms would not seem inappropriate to accompany the tearing of clothing in grief-stricken ritual.

'Nieder' finishes in the dominant. It is a simple matter to return to the tonic after a single bar's interlude. (This is an echo of the preceding cadence with its touch of C minor harmony.) The extraordinary events of the poet's third verse are described in music that has previously painted the couple sitting silent and alone in the sunset. Such is the momentum of the song's construction in sheerly musical terms, however, that the music seems inevitable, and unarguably appropriate for the words. The idea of a prayer, the feeling that there *is* something religious about this music, returns powerfully when the poet kneels before his lover as if she were a holy icon. Fervent worship has never been more intensely described in song, the vast simplicity of the emotion underpinned by grave and beautiful switches between tonic and dominant. The drinking of tears from someone's hand is a disturbing concept – a subverted holy communion of wafer and wine where everlasting life is replaced with everlasting death – but in this sublime musical context it is an occurrence we accept without question.

The second musical strophe now continues into the poet's fourth verse. Once again tremolandi begin to shiver (from b. 33), this time describing the workings of a dreadful inner sickness. The idea of the body being consumed ('verzehrt sich mein Leib') is brilliantly caught in the busy piano writing, the whirring demisemiquavers like an onslaught of overactive cells destroying the body from within. By now the momentum of expressive emotion that has built up is such that Schubert seems not to care that the strophic structure has resulted in the faulty accentuation of 'Mich hat das unglücksel'ge Weib' (a dotted crotchet on the unimportant 'hat', b. 40). The parallel sixths of 'unglücksel'ge Weib' are again Mahlerian, this time uncannily prophetic of the mood of *Oft denk' ich, sie sind nur ausgegangen!* from *Kindertotenlieder*. The final 'Vergiftet mit ihren Tränen' is set to the same doleful music, suggestive of ritual, as before.

The embellishment (b. 43) of the final 'Tränen' (unlike the first verse) adds a new expressive detail. (We are reminded that Brahms, at the end of his *Sapphische Ode* Op. 94 no. 4, sets the closing 'Tränen' with exactly the same turn, as if in loving homage to Schubert.) But the old-fashioned nature of the ornament (again arguably cantorial) distances us from the immediacy of the emotion in an extraordinary way. This is part of the song's strange magic, for *Am Meer* is monumental rather than touching in the usual Schubertian sense. The two bars of postlude (German sixths resolving into C major) add to the sense of mystery. These chords offer little sense of release. On the contrary, in ending as it began, the song leaves us hanging in the air. The narrator's fate is suspended into eternity and he will be doomed to repeat his ritual of misfortune like a ghost that can never be laid to rest. This circular aspect of the poems seems to be a sub-theme of the Heine cycle as a whole: *Der Atlas* is doomed to hold the world on his shoulders for eternity; one senses that the coming-to-life of *Ihr Bild* will be re-enacted time and time again; the courtship of *Das Fischermädchen* will never come to a satisfactory conclusion; and the distant horizon of *Die Stadt* will be scanned ceaselessly, and in vain. As for *Der Doppelgänger*, the singer will forever stand wringing his hands in that haunted street. Or will he? If *Am Meer* resolves *Die Stadt* in harmonic terms, it solves nothing of its textual mystery. We will find quietus only in the closing bars of the final song.

Max Kalbeck (qv Vol. II/895) mentions a lost orchestration of this song by Johannes Brahms ('Stockhausen once had it').

First edition:	Published by Tobias Haslinger, Vienna in May 1829, Volume 2, no. 6 (P215)
Subsequent editions:	Peters: I/162; AGA XX 565: Vol. 9/178; NSA IV: Vol. 14a/156; Bärenreiter: Vol. 4/168
Bibliography:	Youens 2007, pp. 63–74
Further settings and arrangements:	101 further settings and 129 arrangements in Metzner 1992, including

Vesque von Püttlingen (1803–1883) *Die vergifteten Tränen* from
Die Heimkehr, no. 14 (1851)
Fanny Mendelssohn (1805–1847) *Am Meer* (1838)
Arr. Franz Liszt (1811–1886) for solo piano, no. 4 of
Schwanengesang (1838–9) [*see* TRANSCRIPTIONS]
Zdeněk Fibich (1850–1900) *Am Meer* (1866)
Arr. Tilman Hoppstock (b. 1961) for guitar accompaniment, in
Franz Schubert: 110 Lieder (2009)

Discography and timing: Fischer-Dieskau III 3[12]   4'35
Hyperion I 37[18]
Hyperion II 37[12]   3'56   Anthony Rolfe Johnson

←— *Die Stadt* D957/11   *Der Doppelgänger* D957/13 —→

XIII Der DOPPELGÄNGER   The wraith
D957/13 [H682]
B minor

Still ist die Nacht, es ruhen die Gassen,
In diesem Hause wohnte mein Schatz;
Sie hat schon längst die Stadt verlassen,
Doch steht noch das Haus auf demselben Platz.

Da steht auch ein Mensch und starrt in
   die Höhe,
Und ringt die Hände, vor Schmerzensgewalt;
Mir graust es, wenn ich sein Antlitz sehe, –
Der Mond zeigt mir meine eigne Gestalt.

Du Doppelgänger! du bleicher Geselle![1]
Was äffst du nach mein Liebesleid,
Das mich gequält auf dieser Stelle,
So manche Nacht, in alter Zeit?

The night is still, the streets are at rest;
In this house lived my sweetheart.
She has long since left the town,
But the house still stands on the selfsame spot.

A man stands there too, staring up,
And wringing his hands in anguish;
I shudder when I see his face –
The moon shows me my own form!

You wraith, pallid companion,
Why do you ape the pain of my love
Which tormented me on this very spot,
So many a night, in days long past?

---

[1] Heine in both *Reisebilder* (1826) and *Buch der Lieder* (1827) writes 'Du *Doppelt*gänger! du bleicher Geselle!' This was also the form of the word used by Jean Paul in *Siebenkäs*. Schubert chose to use a more modern variation.

HEINRICH HEINE (1797–1856); poem written in 1823/4

This is the last of Schubert's six Heine solo settings (1828). See the poet's biography for a chronological list all of the Heine settings.

The German word 'Doppeltgänger' was an invention of the writer Jean Paul Richter; it appears in his *Siebenkäs* (1796) where the eponymous hero of the novel has a deathly double named Leibgeber. Heine no doubt discovered the word in that novel but there is no shortage of historical sightings of the phenomenon which an article in *Nature* (September 2006) tentatively ascribes to a temporary malfunction of the left temporoparietal junction of the brain, and not necessarily the result of schizophrenia or paranoia. In *Dichtung und Wahrheit* Goethe describes riding to see Friederike Brion (*see Willkommen und Abschied* D767) and seeing his own figure coming towards him on horseback wearing the very clothes that he was to wear for his final visit to Friederike some years later. This was a harmless vision but a doppelgänger is usually thought to prophesy the death of the person whose ghostly double appears. John Donne was said to have seen his wife thus before she died in childbirth; Wilhelm Müller describes in his *Tagebuch* (14 November 1815) how he was startled to see a woman in the street who was the double of a female relative; Abraham Lincoln saw himself in a vision which he interpreted as meaning that he would not survive his second term as president, and Shelley claimed to have seen his own double shortly before his death by drowning. In the first act of that poet's *Prometheus Unbound* (1818) he describes someone who 'Met his own image walking in the garden . . . / For know there are two worlds of life and death: / One that which thou beholdest; but the other / Is underneath the grave, where do inhabit / The shadows of all forms that think and live, / Till death unite them and they part no more.' This passage would have been well known to the Pre-Raphaelite poet–painter Dante Gabriel Rossetti whose canvas entitled *How they met themselves* depicts lovers, arm in arm, encountering their own ghostly doubles.

Schubert's setting of Heine's poem is one of the most famous songs of all time. Like many of the greatest creations in art, it astounds by its simplicity as much as its complexity. The composer's long apprenticeship had been unlike that of lesser mortals certainly – so many masterpieces were created along the way that to speak of his indenture seems nonsense. But even the greatest composers set themselves aims, and the determination to improve is not confined to those with lesser gifts. Schubert's complex posthumous relationship with Beethoven, which had been so much a feature of 1828, was born of a combination of just such humility, as well as healthy ambition. From the beginning he had pursued the ideals of clarity and concision married to the greatest expressiveness. In this structural context he treated his fathomless gift for melody, *pur sang*, almost as an irrelevance. Of course that talent is inextricably bound up with his genius, but it is possible to see in the apparent tunelessness of *Der Doppelgänger* the culmination of a lifetime's hard work. Close listening (and remember we have the advantage of sophisticated twenty-first-century ears) reveals what Schubert was aiming at: melody not for its own sake, but subject to the words, and truthful to their contours; spoken song and sung speech so convincing and powerful that we cease to notice which is which.

Die schöne Müllerin D795 and *Winterreise* D911 had already proved his mastery of this terrain. He had conquered much new territory; each peak scaled had seemed the highest yet, an exploratory *ne plus ultra*. But until the very last month of his life there was always another door opening out on to a new vista. In some ways the songs of *Schwanengesang*, for all their brooding intensity, are the result of a more relaxed mastery where innovative daring is handled with a lighter, more varied touch than encountered in *Winterreise*. Schubert seems not to shoulder the world like *Der Atlas*, but to have it in the palm of his hand. Doubtless Beethoven's death, leaving the field clear for a successor, had much to do with his new confidence. Acutely

Illustration (1935) for *Der Doppelgänger* by Anton Pieck.

aware of his mortality since the onset of his illness, it is a moot point whether this awareness was further heightened in those fabulously creative months of 1828. One can understand why this has become a biographical commonplace, for it might help to explain the composer's prescience at this stage of his life: in 1828 he is a step ahead of everyone (including us, the listeners). The scope of his vision seems uncanny, even uncomfortable. Nowhere is this more apparent than in *Der Doppelgänger*; on the threshold of his own death, he seems to anticipate the thought and aims of his great successors. If a time machine had transported him to the desks of Wagner and Wolf, one senses he would have found their marriage of word and tone comprehensible, and related to his own.

And yet *Der Doppelgänger*, as if this spectre were desirous of including the whole of music in his all-encompassing arms, owes almost as much to the past as to the future. It does, after all, end with the words 'in alter Zeit' ('in days long past'). Schubert had written songs in the old style before (*Vom Mitleiden Mariä* D632, *Pax vobiscum* D551 among others) but the cantus firmus of this song, a four-bar passacaglia that is at the heart of the music's sinister progress, is almost unprecedented in his output. How much Schubert knew about early music is difficult to ascertain, but it is known that he had access to Raphael Kiesewetter's remarkable library of vocal scores from earlier centuries. Perhaps he had been influenced by the loan of Handel's complete works, a *Gesamtausgabe* that had once belonged to Beethoven. Christopher Gibbs has pointed out the possible inspiration of the C sharp minor fugue from Book 1 of Bach's *Das wohltemperierte Klavier* BWV 849. Whatever the inspiration, whether Handel via Beethoven, or the prospect of studying fugue with Simon Sechter, *Der Doppelgänger* is unique in being one of Schubert's most avant-garde works at the same time as one in which the techniques of the past are given a new prominence.

As we have said, the cantus firmus of this song – with a hint of *Dies irae* according to Capell (1928), more like *Miserere nobis* says Black (2003) – is almost unprecedented, but not quite. The same theme in dotted minims, this time in C minor (C – B natural – E flat – D), is announced as a fugal subject at the beginning of the 'Agnus Dei' of Schubert's E flat major Mass (D950, June 1828). That work was written for the church in the Alsergrund where Beethoven's body had been taken on the day of his funeral in March 1827 (it seems that in 1828 most Schubertian paths lead to Beethoven, including that composer's use of fugue in many of his late works). In Schubert's Mass the fugal exposition of this theme is dark, even menacing, the soul-searching of the syphilitic only too aware of the meaning of 'peccata mundi'. After yielding to a smoothly consolatory movement in E flat major ('Dona nobis pacem') the 'Doppelgänger' theme is recapitulated in an E flat minor contrapuntal passage of towering majesty. A final 'Dona nobis pacem', a short movement of eerie beauty, brings the Mass to a close, and the composer allows himself (bb. 221–2) to set the word 'pacem' to a haunting derivative (G – A flat – C – B natural) of the chromatic motif. Schubert had sometimes quoted his songs in instrumental works. If, as seems likely, the Heine songs date to after June 1828, the process is here reversed. But what is the significance of the quotation?

The tormented narrator of the song is in search of a solution to his heartbreak; he sees his ghostly double – a sure sign, according to German folklore, of his own impending death. This will at least bring peace and release from pain. In Schubert's mind the 'Doppelgänger' motif is resolved by the idea of 'Dona nobis pacem', just as it had been in his Mass: 'Give us – and all those that suffer and are in pain – peace'. If the first song in the Heine group, *Der Atlas*, personifies the Beethovenian struggle, it might not be too fanciful to see in the last song the ghost of a requiem for that composer's troubled soul, and for the entire cast of troubled characters in the Heine lieder. The sublime eloquence of the postlude, eight chords in eight bars as significant as any Schubert wrote, betokens a journey so profound as to make this a possibility. This could well signify a wordless 'Dona nobis pacem' which would explain why the matchlessly moving major-key ending of *Der Doppelgänger* seems to be the only true moment of resolution and release in the entire group of six songs. Without this explanation the apparently unmotivated (so to speak) *tierce de Picardie* with which the work ends seems perplexing.

The key is Schubert's woebegone tonality of B minor. That famous four-dotted-minim figure begins its weary, but strictly measured, trudge through the music: I – V (in first inversion) – I (in first inversion without the tonic, so the chord could also masquerade as D major with a missing A natural) and V (second inversion). And then the same pattern again. Over this the voice enters (b. 5) in a taut obbligato, a monotone ('Still ist die Nacht'), leading to a tiny descending phrase on a tonic chord arpeggio for 'es ruhen die Gassen'. Suspense and fear are evident in the strictly controlled dotted rhythms. The third appearance of the four-bar passacaglia (as well as the fifth) is altered to include the chord of D major on b. 11 (under 'wohnte mein Schatz'). Over this the vocal line quickens with creepy melisma, as if the singer were breaking out in a cold sweat. An interlude in the piano (b. 13) echoes the shudder implicit in the voice as, at the last moment, an F sharp^7 chord is embellished with a tiny tremor.

And so it goes on, the third and fourth lines of the strophe a musical repeat of the first and second with the subtle addition of even more ghoulish ornament. The sight of the spot where his lover's home stands is enough to give the singer a nasty turn (at the words 'auf demselben Platz', b. 21). Because of the independent menace of the bass passacaglia, voice and piano seem to have led separate lives from the beginning of the song. But they are entwined at the same time, as if part of a masterly contrapuntal weave. Martin Chusid in his enlightening *Companion to Schwanengesang: History, Analysis, Performance* (2000) avers that the skeletal dotted minims of the piano part might be taken to embody the spectre. If this is the case, the ghostly double has hovered unseen (but not unheard) from the beginning and will only be confronted by the singer at the song's climax.

This meeting takes place at the end of the second verse where the culminative tension generated by passacaglia technique (how well Purcell understood this!) comes into its own. At b. 25 the singer first notices what he takes to be a man ('Da steht auch ein Mensch') and finds the stranger's overwrought actions immediately disturbing. Despite the narrator's alarm, the imperturbable ground bass tells us that the ghost has not been recognized. The singer becomes more frightened, a heightening of tension generated by a substantial rise in vocal tessitura in bb. 29–30 at 'Und ringt die Hände', but still voice and piano go their separate ways and recognition is delayed. The agonized setting across the barline of 'Schmerzensgewalt' (bb. 31–3) is pure genius; a change of harmony halfway through the word 'Schmerz' (part of the merciless passacaglia but altered – D major to F sharp^7 with a horribly flattened bass on C natural) is like a vicious punch in the stomach. The second half of the verse at last signifies the moment of recognition. 'Meine eigne Gestalt' engenders a veritable shriek of horror (bb. 39–42), the pianist hammering out a chord where a tiny alteration of a semitone connects and locks with the singer's raw high G at the top of the stave. This is like the *Titanic* connecting with the iceberg of her destiny, something Thomas Hardy described at the end of a poem with the title 'Convergence of the Twain':

> IX
> Alien they seemed to be:
> No mortal eye could see
> The intimate wedding of their later history,
>
> X
> Or sign that they were bent
> By paths coincident
> On being anon twin halves of one august event,

XI
Till the Spinner of the Years
Said 'Now!' And each one hears,
And consummation comes, and jars two hemispheres.

This face to face confrontation, the 'jarring of two hemispheres' in *Der Doppelgänger*, where voice and piano come together at last, is one of the most frightening moments in music. When this 'august event' is compared with the unfolding facts of Schubert's destiny and imminent death it becomes even more chilling. It is as if in wanting so much to honour the dead Beethoven, in wanting so much to occupy his place, in *wanting so much to be like him*, Schubert suddenly catches sight of how their destinies are indeed the same – but not in the way he had hoped. What lay in store was not the honoured position of Vienna's greatest composer in the years to come, but a one-way ticket to the Währinger cemetery where their graves would lie side by side.

This is fanciful hindsight of course, but a song like this encourages such thoughts. The final stanza is no less astonishing. It is new in several ways: at last the accompaniment is allowed to break out of the repetitive pattern. As the spectre is addressed directly ('Du Doppelgänger, du bleicher Geselle!') the underlying harmonies rise in dotted minims, a semitone at a time. This progress in bb. 43–7 from B minor up to D sharp minor leads to the beginning of the furious question: 'Was äffst du nach mein Liebesleid?' The brutal use of the coarse 'äfft' (der Affe is an ape) is like a verbal slap across the face – it suggests something repulsive and subhuman in the ghostly apparition's movements. Schubert's direction that this music should be sung and played in the context of an extended accelerando is extremely rare in his songs (*Gretchen am Spinnrade* D118 is another famous example, thus it occurs in the first great dramatic song and the last). There are cadences at 'Liebesleid' and 'Stelle' on the dominant of D sharp (thus A sharp major) which sounds like B flat major in the context of B minor (cf. the use of this contrast in *In der Ferne*). The return to B minor at b. 52 for the high and held F sharp on 'So manche Nacht' encapsulates the wail of someone caught up in a curse condemning them to suffer eternal damnation. And as if to remind us in closing that the song owes its existence to early music, the cadence at 'in alter Zeit' is extended into a decorated melismatic flourish (bb. 53–6) that is gravely formal and infinitely woeful. Brahms quotes this baleful cadence at the end of his song from 1867, *Herbstgefühl* Op. 48 no. 7 (on the words 'stirbt sie auch'). Some forty years after the song's composition, *Der Doppelgänger* had already achieved an almost talismanic significance for Schubert's admirers. It occupies a special place in his output that in itself has no double – a terrifying glimpse into the future outside the realms of beauty, charm or melodic memorability.

The postlude has already been discussed, but the C major chord at b. 59 is one of those Schubertian harmonies that we might imagine has the power to stop planets in their courses. The flattened supertonic is frequently to be found in Schubert's songs, but it is in the sound-world of Heine's lyrics that it seems unbelievably poignant and significant.

First edition:	Published by Tobias Haslinger, Vienna in May 1829, Volume 2, no. 7 (P216)
Subsequent editions:	Peters: I/164; AGA XX 566: Vol. 9/180; NSA IV: Vol. 14a/159; Bärenreiter: Vol. 4/170
Bibliography:	Youens 2007, pp. 74–84
Further settings and arrangements:	11 further settings and 18 arrangements in Metzner 1992, including
	Adolf Fredrik Lindblad (1801–1878) *Ny godtköpsupplaga* from *Sånger och visor* (pub. 1878–90)
	Vesque von Püttlingen (1803–1883) *Der Doppelgänger* from *Die Heimkehr*, no. 20 (1851)

Arr. Franz Liszt (1811–1886) for solo piano, no. 12 of
Schwanengesang (1838–9) [*see* TRANSCRIPTIONS]
Philipp Graf zu Eulenberg (1857–1921) *Still ist die Nacht, es ruhen die Gassen* (*c.* 1895)
Arr. Tilman Hoppstock (b. 1961) for guitar accompaniment, in
Franz Schubert: 110 Lieder (2009)

Discography and timing: Fischer-Dieskau III 3¹³   4'25
Hyperion I 37¹⁹
Hyperion II 37¹³   3'41   Anthony Rolfe Johnson

← *Am Meer* D957/12   *Der Hirt auf dem Felsen* D965 →

SONG TO A POEM BY JOHANN GABRIEL SEIDL

XIV Die TAUBENPOST   The pigeon-post
D965A [H684]
G major

(105 bars)

Ich hab' eine Brieftaub' in meinem Sold,	I have a carrier-pigeon in my pay,
Die ist gar ergeben und treu,	Devoted and true;
Sie nimmt mir nie das Ziel zu kurz,	She never stops short of her goal
Und fliegt auch nie vorbei.	And never flies too far.
Ich sende sie vieltausendmal	Each day I send her out
Auf Kundschaft täglich hinaus,	A thousand times on reconnaissance,
Vorbei an manchem lieben Ort,	Past many a beloved spot,
Bis zu der Liebsten Haus.	To my sweetheart's house.
Dort schaut sie zum Fenster heimlich hinein,	There she peeps furtively in at the window,
Belauscht ihren Blick und Schritt,	Observing her every look and step,
Gibt meine Grüsse scherzend ab	Conveys my greeting breezily,
Und nimmt die ihren mit.	And brings hers back to me.
Kein Briefchen brauch' ich zu schreiben mehr,	I no longer need to write a note,
Die Träne selbst geb' ich ihr:	I can give her my very tears;
O sie verträgt sie sicher nicht,	She will certainly not deliver them wrongly,
Gar eifrig dient sie mir.	So eagerly does she serve me.
Bei Tag, bei Nacht, im Wachen, im Traum,[1]	Day or night, awake or dreaming,
Ihr gilt das alles gleich:	It is all the same to her;
Wenn sie nur wandern, wandern kann,	As long as she can roam
Dann ist sie überreich!	She is richly contented.

[1] Seidl (*Natur and Herz*, 1853) writes 'Bei Tag, bei Nacht, im Wachen *und* Traum'.

Sie wird nicht müd, sie wird nicht matt,	She never grows tired or faint,
Der Weg ist stets ihr neu;	The route is always fresh to her;
Sie braucht nicht Lockung, braucht nicht Lohn,	She needs no enticement or reward,
D i e Taub' ist so mir treu!	So true is *this* pigeon to me.

D'rum heg' ich sie auch so treu an der Brust,	I cherish her as truly in my heart,
Versichert des schönsten Gewinns;	Certain of the fairest prize;
Sie heisst – die Sehnsucht! Kennt ihr sie? –	Her name is – Longing! Do you know her?
Die Botin treuen Sinns.	The messenger of constancy.

JOHANN GABRIEL SEIDL (1804–1875)

This is the last of of Schubert's twelve Seidl solo settings (1826–8). See the poet's biography for a chronological list of all the Seidl settings.

Schubert's last song reminds us that the composer was himself a pianist who loved to accompany singers. The lilt (one may almost say 'swing') of the piano writing is exhilarating despite the fact that the music neither stirs nor excites. It does, however, move in every sense. The marking is 'Ziemlich langsam', but like *Liebesbotschaft*, in the same key and with the same marking, the music is written two-in-the-bar (in this case *alla breve*). From this pull in opposite directions comes the humane compromise of which this composer is master: a saunter of well-being and optimism moderated by a shadow of doubt – something gentle and wistful. And it is this *Bewegung*, so often found in the songs of the composer's maturity, that is at the heart of many a Schubertian miracle.

This is a major-key song that should be happy – at least on paper. But like that similar masterpiece, *Frühlingsglaube* D686, the singer's radiant optimism only serves to remind the listener of the sadness that lies behind the bravery. In that song of spring the determination to believe that change is just around the corner is admirable, but the music tells us that this optimism is misplaced. The combination of self-delusion and gentle rapture engenders our compassion. Similarly, the lover too shy to woo with word and gesture, who sends forth his affection day after day in the form of mute and fluttering longing, is someone whose constancy we can admire, but only with tender concern for his real happiness. Like the nightingale in Wilde's fairy tale, there are those who press their hearts to the rose-thorn and sing with exultant happiness, and Schubert is one of them. Neither *Frühlingsglaube* nor *Die Taubenpost* makes any attempt to burden the listener with behind-the-scenes pain; on the contrary, we might imagine that here is unalloyed joy until we read – or listen – between the lines. And then we are almost embarrassed to feel pity, so dignified seem the bright-eyed singers of both songs. We know something they perhaps do not: that spring will never arrive and that one day soon the pigeon will fade away on its homeward journey. *How* we become aware of this is Schubertian mystery, somehow audible in the music. Thus Schubert engages our pity without asking for it; and the radiance of the music draws us even closer to the hidden suffering.

Most composers are masters of manipulation, of moving the listener with myriad tricks of harmony and dramatic context. Schubert composed his fair share of music with a canny eye on audience response, and knew how to use musical techniques to conjure any effect (and reaction) he chose. But on many occasions, and often in reaction to a poem that chimes with his own feelings, he withdraws into a world of his own where the listener, no longer a 'client' to be delighted and persuaded, becomes an observer on the periphery. It is at these times that Schubert writes songs without giving a thought to the effect they will make on the public. In the earlier years this sometimes led to lieder or ballads, over-long and little suited to the recital platform, which only Schubertians can love (and love them we do). But at other times, and especially as he got older, the composer seems to have been able, from time to time, to confide something to manuscript paper that is so artlessly *true*, so unaffectedly vulnerable, that we, like the carrier pigeon, find ourselves peeping through the window of a beloved soul.

The great cycles are not of this ilk – they are too important to have been written while lost in dreamy confessional mode. (Although Schubert was far ahead of his listeners' tastes in *Winterreise* D911, he was still able to envisage the winter traveller recounting his pain to the world.) Smaller songs, like diary entries rather than novels, are another matter, and *Die Tauben-post*, probably written in the wake of the great Heine songs, continues the *An die ferne Geliebte* mood of the other *Schwanengesang* songs with an important difference. The characters in that collection (whether warrior or weightlifter, serenader or haunted lover) are little to do with Schubert himself; they invoke the shade of Beethoven, the muse of Heine, and so on. But *Die Taubenpost* is one of those transparent songs that speak in the composer's own voice. The effect of this in a performance of the cycle as a whole is suddenly to reintroduce Schubert himself; he comes before the curtain to speak the *envoi* which brings the work to a close. It is even possible that he told the publisher Haslinger that he wanted a fourteen-song cycle ('to be dedicated to his friends', as Spaun says) rather than an unlucky thirteen. It also fitted in exactly with the linking 'theme' of a homage to the 'ferne Geliebte'. But it is much more likely that it was Haslinger himself who added the song to the set at the time of publication in May 1829. It had already made an impression at a Schubertiad in January of that year when Vogl sang a number of songs in memory of the deceased composer.

What had made Schubert read these words, and lose himself in them, is perhaps not difficult to imagine. It is said that he remained, until the end, hopelessly in love with Countess Karoline Esterházy to whom, he claimed, all of his works were dedicated without his needing to say so. Apart from these, what could he send her? Letters with ardent declarations of love? Certainly not, for this was almost certainly a one-sided passion where all the constraints of difference in social station forbade even a formal expression of romantic admiration. In any case the composer seems to have been in love with what Karoline represented – musicality, sensitivity, an irre-proachable womanliness to complement his longed-for, masculine (Beethovenian) indepen-dence – as much as for the person she actually was.

No, all Schubert could really send Karoline were his thoughts, and his longing. And like the owner of the carrier pigeon in *Die Taubenpost*, he seems contented to do so without thought of reciprocation. This pigeon, the poet tells us, no longer needs to carry letters to assure the beloved of his devotion. All is now wordless, including, alas, the imagined replies brought back by the bird to its endlessly patient master. This has become a metaphor in some people's minds, mine certainly, for the very nature of Schubert's art which is about endless giving, and ceaseless generosity, all without thought of reward. As Hans Gál (in *Franz Schubert and the Essence of Melody*) puts it:

Fate, which thrust this precious vessel of grace defenceless into the world, gave him the capacity to rejoice, and this it was that made him rich. From his wealth he drew the love that lives within his melodies, the love he never received and always so lavishly poured forth.

Die Taubenpost happens to be Schubert's last song, but this is not what makes it so moving. We would have been moved at any time by a song that drew attention, unintentionally and in enchanting metaphor, to the gap between what Schubert gave and the little he received back. It is true that such an evaluation turned out to be a timely, and fitting (and wonderfully elegant) farewell. But Schubert's willingness to keep sending the pigeon on its ultimately thankless missions is a sign that he himself wrote this song in no valedictory sense. We catch him not at a tragic moment, surely, but at a crossroads of what may nearly pass for contentment. Things were going well, give or take, as always, a few setbacks. He had laid claim with a succession of important works to Beethoven's mantle, and a metaphorical cloakroom attendant at the Musik-verein was surely on the point of handing it over to his safekeeping. He was composing 'like a god' (to use his own words after a good patch in 1818) and, *if only he could get over this patch of illness* and return to Schober's house, he would be able to begin reaping the rewards of all the hard work of 1828.

Thus *Die Taubenpost* is really a song by someone who accepts the status quo with a rueful smile. To be in love with love, to have a guiding star, however distant, is better than being gloomy and cynical. And so there is a lift to the music from the very first bars. The four-bar introduction is a masterly essay in how an unremarkable sequence of chords, switching between tonic and dominant, can be turned into magic. The sparing use of root-position chords is part of the secret, as is a wonderful use of syncopation: each bar kicks off with a jaunty note in the bass and on the beat; the right hand follows a quaver later, off the beat, the music lightened by the bounce of chords not merely marked staccato, but staccatissimo. (The reason why the song is syncopated at all becomes clearer later.) The left hand, almost in the manner of honky-tonk jazz pianism of a later century, leaps or strides many a cheeky tenth. The pianist is usually afraid of those sudden forays into the bass register, but if he remains relaxed the gambol pays off. In the right hand there is no sign of conventional melody, but the vamping chords constitute as memorable a pattern of notes as could be desired. Once again, here is the Schubertian sleight of hand where melody is accompaniment, and accompaniment melody.

The undated sketch of this song, printed in NSA Volume 14b p. 195, has a bare vocal line and various accompanying figures added in aide-memoire fashion; it reveals that the composer

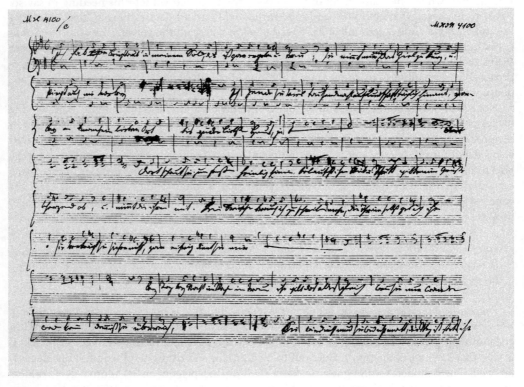

Autograph sketch of *Die Taubenpost* showing Schubert's method of planning a song on two staves, vocal line and bass line.

had initially had the voice (at 'Ich hab'') begin on the tonic, two Gs. These were later changed to Bs, and what a masterstroke this was. The first sounds grounded and ordinary, the second already on the wing. The vocal line is set partially in dactylic rhythm, a logical outcome of the linking of this pulse with the workings of nature – the attraction and desire felt by the narrator, routine and instinct on the pigeon's part. Underneath the first sentence the piano has a syncopated phrase, derived from the introduction but with an important embellishment (offbeat crotchet + quaver + a lilting three-note motif: dotted quaver + semiquaver + quaver). This is an important part of the accompaniment for verses 1, 4 and 5, when the pigeon is at home and not on one of its journeys. In this figure Schubert, like some nineteenth-century Messiaen, has transcribed the song of the wood pigeon whose offbeat 'signature tune' in the wild is also syncopated, and ends with a similar little roulade. (I am grateful to my colleague Simon Keenlyside, an expert ornithologist who, when I first suspected this link, sang me various pigeon calls over the phone from Salzburg.) Thus it appears to be birdsong that has inspired the entire *Bewegung* of *Die Taubenpost*; even the clearly marked alternation of legato chords with staccato in the introduction makes better sense when heard as a sound bite of outdoor life. This is, after all, the composer who built the sounds of the cricket into his music (*Der Einsame* D800), as well as that of the quail (*Der Wachtelschlag* D742) and various larks, cuckoos and nightingales.

This has not begun as a song rich in modulation, but this is perhaps because the carrier pigeon is safely grounded at home and cooing away for most of the first verse. At 'Und fliegt auch nie vorbei' ('And never flies too far') there is a shift (bb. 12–13) to B major (cf. the shift from G to B major in *Der Musensohn* D764) for the first of numerous enchanting interludes. Schubert uses two of Seidl's verses to make one musical verse. Thus 'Ich sende sie vieltausendmal'

(bb. 15–16) begins the second half of the ongoing, seamless melody which has taken possession of the song almost without our noticing. The inevitability of the rise and fall of this unfolding tune is sheer Schubertian delight. The first 'Bis zu der Liebsten Haus' (bb. 22–3) shifts into the relative minor of the home key but then, led by a downward flight of winged semiquavers in the piano (another enchanting accompanying motif that recurs four times in the course of the song), the repeat of these words leads back to the tonic.

A five-bar interlude (bb. 25–9), based partially on familiar motifs in the accompaniment and partly on the melodic line, leads to the song's second verse (Seidl's third and fourth). How marvellously the pedal on D for eight bars (bb. 30–37) conveys the pigeon transfixed at the lover's window, curious as a peeping tomtit! The pianist's finger keeps returning to D in the left hand, as if retaining a precarious grip on the windowsill. The sudden shift from D major into B flat major at 'Kein Briefchen brauch' ich zu schreiben mehr' (b. 38) sounds both grateful and loving. The following four

Die Taubenpost.

Illustration from the almanac *Aurora* (1844).

lines of poetry remain in this key, and the dotted rhythm cooing motif – used in this song to signal the bird's safe return to home base – is heard again. But the music itself only returns to the tonic after another five-bar interlude, perhaps the most wonderful of the piano links in the piece. The way the modulation from B flat major to G major is engineered in this *Zwischenspiel* (bb. 47–51) is breathtaking in its elegance (it almost seems obvious, but only Schubert could have accomplished it, and only after hard work – this much the sketch reveals). The song is a study not so much in harmonic adventurousness as in the subtle permutations of harmony that stem from various inversions of the tonic, subdominant and dominant chords.

The strophic element of the song now comes into its own. Seidl's Verses 5 and 6 are set to more or less the same music as his Verses 1 and 2, everything fitting to perfection in terms of accentuation and meaning. But this structure in pairs leaves one verse over in a poem of seven stanzas, and this Schubert sets as his coda. In the home straits of his song-writing career, and in the process of saying farewell without knowing it, he writes a final page of such ravishing beauty that it is difficult to think how any conscious valediction could have been more eloquent. It is the yearning of this page, and its sadness with a gentle smile, that has led so many people to imagine that Schubert knew the time had come to say goodbye. At first we expect a repeat of the music for the poet's Verses 3 and 4, but we soon realize that Schubert the magician is at work in a peroration worthy of Prospero. Once again the sketch shows how he refined his original thoughts to achieve optimum effect. Harmonic change now engineers a more urgent note. 'D'rum heg' ich sie auch so treu an der Brust' (from b. 71) leads to a modulation into the intimate regions of the subdominant (C major) at 'Versichert des schönsten Gewinns' (bb. 73–6). From here to A major for 'Sie heisst – die Sehnsucht!' is a short journey but an unexpected one with a built-in hesitation, the apotheosis of the Schubertian hiatus, that points towards a new turning and a shaft of light at the end of the tunnel. The appoggiatura lean on 'die <u>Sehnsucht</u>' in this context (and when we hear it later on a different accented passing note) is quite simply the most touching setting of this key word in the entire song repertoire. 'Kennt ihr sie?' (we hear this twice) might have come from the lips of Goethe's Mignon in her 'Kennst du das Land?' lyric, so searching and vulnerable is the gaze behind the repeated question. The music seems to scan the face of the person addressed ('Do you know it . . . *do* you? . . . please tell me!'). 'Die Botin treuen Sinns' is full of the greatest tenderness, as well as pride. This bird, this emotion, is the narrator's very life and love.

And then, from b. 86, the same words over again, but this time 'schönsten Gewinns' leads us into E flat (by b. 90) rather than C major. As if hovering in mid-flight, the piano remains suspended in this tonality for two bars. This time 'Sie heisst . . . die Sehnsucht' (the gap between the phrases both signifies and *causes* a lump in the throat) returns the music to the tonic key – an inadequate description of a musical miracle that is simultaneously unexpected and inevitable. In this passage we hear Schubert's own longing soft and clear; what it has cost him to do without reciprocal love for so many years; how a young man, tormented and irretrievably wounded by sexual temptation, has lost neither his capacity for tenderness, nor the romantic idealism that has remained, despite everything, a source of hope and joy. The remaining music, including the beautiful postlude, is fashioned from what has gone before. This blend of happiness and wistfulness sets the seal, gently and without ceremony, on a composer's entire song-writing career, indeed his entire creative life. That Haslinger felt that *Die Taubenpost* deserved to be rescued from its orphan status, and to become part of Schubert's last published song cycle, was more than a money-making ploy. It shows a glimmer of understanding of the inner, private Schubert that was rare in the hard world of music publishing (compare Diabelli's insensitivities, as well as Probst's). The termination of a collaboration between composer and publisher that was clearly growing in understanding was one of the many losses that the catastrophe of Schubert's death in November 1828 brought in its train.

The lyric appeared for the first time in print in Seidl's *Natur und Herz* (1853), an anthology of poems, most of which had already been published in almanacs and periodicals. The next poem in this collection is entitled *Vöglein – mein Bote* where the theme of a little bird as love's messenger is continued to enchanting and breathless effect. This is not specifically a carrier pigeon but a few pages later there is another poem, *Die Brieftaube*, which once again describes the affectionate relationship between just such a bird and its grateful owner (we begin to wonder if the poet may have had some personal experience of sending love letters in this way). The narrator pounces on the message delivered from his beloved; the pigeon resting on his breast has been entrusted with thousands of greetings and kisses, and in the branches of that tree there may one day be another little pigeon to assuage the bird's own longing. This would be a just reward. He who has served love truly is surely worthy of receiving true love back.

At the core of the almost unbearable poignancy of *Die Taubenpost*, Schubert's not Seidl's, is the message that the truly deserving do not always get what is due to them – not in this life, anyway. This dutiful carrier pigeon, having given unflinching service, is unlikely to find the reward of happiness that the poet predicts in *Die Brieftaube*. Like Schubert it will bravely continue doing the task for which it exists, but that enduring cheerfulness in the major key is as haunting as anything in minor mode and can unexpectedly break the heart.

First edition:	Published by Tobias Haslinger, Vienna in May 1829, Volume 2, no. 8 (P217)
First known performance:	30 January 1829, Musikverein, Vienna. The concert was organized by Anna Fröhlich in order to celebrate Schubert's music and raise money to construct a monument in his memory, and was repeated on 5 March 1829 in the same venue. Soloist: Johann Michael Vogl (See Waidelich/Hilmar Dokumente I No. 687 and Deutsch No. xxvi for full concert programme)
Performance reviews:	*Der Sammler* (Vienna) No. 23 (21 February 1829), p. 92 [Waidelich/Hilmar Dokumente I No. 698] *Monatsbericht der Gesellschaft der Musikfreunde des Oesterreichischen Kaiserstaates* (Vienna, March 1829), pp. 41–6 [Waidelich/Hilmar Dokumente I No. 703]
Subsequent editions:	Peters: I/166; AGA XX 567: Vol. 9/182; NSA IV: Vol. 14a/162, Sketch 14b/295; Bärenreiter: Vol. 4/172
Bibliography:	Hilmar-Voit 1991, p. 52 Youens 2002, pp. 404–14
Arrangements:	Arr. Franz Liszt (1811–1886) for solo piano, no. 13 of *Schwanengesang* (1838–9) [*see* TRANSCRIPTIONS]
Discography and timing:	Fischer-Dieskau III 3[14] 3'35 Hyperion I 37[20] Hyperion II 37[15] 3'34 Anthony Rolfe Johnson

← *Der Hirt auf dem Felsen* D965

THE PUBLICATION OF *SCHWANENGESANG*

On 17 December 1828, less than a month after Schubert's death, Tobias Haslinger made a down payment to Ferdinand Schubert for the fourteen songs that comprise *Schwanengesang*. He was the first to purchase music from the composer's *Nachlass*, even though he was soon to be overtaken by Diabelli in this regard. In January 1829 Haslinger announced that he intended to offer the music on subscription; subscribers would receive an ornamental flyleaf on which would be written their individual names, thus personalizing their copy of the cycle and at the same time assembling a roll call of the composer's mourners and admirers. Haslinger enrolled 158 subscribers who ordered 180 copies. In May 1829 the work was advertised. Each of the two volumes had thick light-blue paper covers to which were stuck square white labels (in the manner of the two *Winterreise* volumes with their oblong labels on green paper covers, *see* below), leaving the figures 1 and 2 – signifiying volumes one and two of the set – to be inked in by hand. The title was *Schwanen-Gesang* on the outer labels and *Schwanengesang* on the main

The cover of the first edition of *Schwangesang* (1829). Light blue paper with glued-on printed vignette in white card with hand-numbering.

Prænumerations Exemplar (subscribers' sheet) for copies of the first edition of *Schwanengesang* that had been paid for in advance. The name of the subscriber was filled in on this page.

title page, where the words 'Letztes Werk' (Last Work) appeared instead of an opus number. Unlike *Winterreise*, each song was assigned a separate title page (for example, XIV| Die Taubenpost| von| Franz Schubert). Subscribers found in their copies (the recto of the front flyleaf of the first volume) an extra page with a vignette of weeping willow, swan and setting sun, all under a rainbow-shaped heading 'Prænumerations Exemplar'. These copies, exceedingly rare, are much prized by present-day collectors.

THE PERFORMING ORDER OF *SCHWANENGESANG*

As with Hugo Wolf's *Italienisches Liederbuch*, there have been myriad suggestions for a new performing order for this cycle, and almost every singer and pianist team has found their own solution. I have come to believe that Wolf's own order works better than any other, and the same applies to the published order of the Schubert cycle, but one perhaps needs many years of experimenting with alternatives before reaching this conclusion. Of course the Rellstab and Heine parts of the work often appear separately in recitals, the latter far more frequently than the former. The work as a whole is insufficiently long to make for an entire evening's programme so these fourteen songs (almost always reordered and separated into their constituent poets) are sometimes complemented by further Seidl settings (to go with *Die Taubenpost*) or by some of the other songs that were composed in Schubert's final year. The Rellstab *Herbst* D945 is a natural favourite for this, as is the *Lebensmut* fragment D937. Occasionally, if the singer is a tenor, it is possible to present Rellstab's *Auf dem Strom* D943 with horn on the same programme. A reordering of the Heine set is much more of a contentious issue than for the Rellstab. Sometimes a performing order after the sequence in Heine's *Reisebilder* is proposed, thus (numbering Heine's poems in Roman numerals) VIII D957/10, XIV D957/12, XVI D957/11, XX D957/13, XXIII D957/9 XXIV D957/8. This is only slightly different from the performing order recommended by Elmar Budde (where 12 and 11 change places). In this case the juxtaposed songs delineate a rising and falling shape of tonalities from A flat major up to C major via C minor, and then a downward trajectory of three minor keys (provided the songs are sung either in their original tonalities or are consistently transposed). Both these orders retain the water-theme link between songs X–XII in the published cycle.

SCHWANGESANG
(KOSEGARTEN) **D318** [H197]
F minor   19 October 1815

Swansong

Endlich stehn die Pforten offen,	At last the gates are open;
Endlich winkt das kühle Grab,	At last the cool grave beckons,
Und nach langem Fürchten, Hoffen,	And after long fears and hopes

Neig' ich mich die Nacht hinab.	I drift down towards night.
Durchgewacht sind nun die Tage	An end now to the awareness
Meines Lebens. Süsse Ruh	Constant throughout the days of my life;
Drückt nach ausgeweinter Klage	After weeping in lamentation, now sweet peace
Mir die müden Wimpern zu.	Closes my weary eyelids.
[...5...]	[...5...]
Ewig wird die Nacht nicht dauern,	The night will not last forever,
Ewig dieser Schlummer nicht.	Nor will this sleep.
Hinter jenen Gräberschauern	Beyond the terror of the grave
Dämmert unauslöschlich Licht.	An eternal light dawns.
Aber bis das Licht mir funkle,	But until that light shines for me,
Bis ein schönrer Tag mir lacht,	Until a fairer day smiles upon me,
Sink' ich ruhig in die dunkle,	I will sink peacefully
Stille, kühle Schlummernacht.	Into the cool, silent night of sleep.

LUDWIG KOSEGARTEN (1758–1818); poem written in December 1775

This is the nineteenth of Schubert's twenty-one Kosegarten solo settings (1815–17). See the poet's biography for a chronological list of all the Kosegarten settings, as well as a discussion of Morten Solvik's Kosegarten Liederkreis and this song's place within it.

This is one of several Schubertian graveside elegies, this time spoken in the first person as the poet prepares to meet his end. Although Kosegarten's poem does not directly relate to war, the composer's mind was running on the theme of patriotism and noble death at the time. It is easy to see how he would have perceived an analogy between the soul preparing to make its last journey and the soldier preparing for his inevitable end as in *Gebet während der Schlacht* D171 and *Amphiaraos* D166, both composed earlier in 1815. (*Kriegers Ahnung* D957/2 from *Schwanengesang* from 1828 is the last and greatest of such songs.)

Another song on this theme of departure into immortality is *Hektors Abschied* D312, a mythological hero's swansong and farewell to his wife, also composed on 19 October 1815. There were no fewer than eight songs written on that day: the others are *Die Sterne* D313, the magisterially beautiful *Nachtgesang* D314, the two *An Rosa* songs D315 and D316, *Idens Schwanenlied* D317 and *Luisens Antwort* D319. Apart from the Schiller setting about Hector and Andromache, all the poems were by Kosegarten, for this was the height of the composer's intense four-month 'fling' with that poet. In terms of its key and mood (not to mention its title) this *Schwangesang* is most closely related to *Idens Schwanenlied*. The music has a grave quality of simplicity suggesting the wisdom of a Sarastro and the acceptance of the inevitable by a brave philosopher with a belief in the afterlife. The word-painting of 'das kühle Grab' in b. 4 is apposite (a beguiling melisma decorated with an acciaccatura that softens the threat of the grave) as are the graceful dip in the vocal line (as in *Ossians Lied nach dem Falle Nathos* D278) to illustrate 'Neig' ich mich die Nacht hinab' (bb. 6–8) and the touching high note for 'Süsse Ruh' in b. 11. At the passage beginning with the word 'Ruh' (b. 12) we notice the dactylic rhythm (a minim followed by two crotchets) of Death's tread, the rhythm that would permeate *Der Tod und das Mädchen* D531 sixteen months later. The calm of this is interrupted by the sudden despairing upward leap of 'Klage' in b. 14, as if at the last minute the singer is experiencing a stab of fear despite his faith in the afterlife. The piano's postlude (bb. 17–21) re-establishes a mood of sepulchral peace, once again prophesying the later famous song. In these early years Schubert's composing unconscious was in the process of forming a vast vocabulary (sometimes borrowed from other sources, particularly Mozart) of tonal analogues and motifs, a library of words-to-music correspondences. A study of seemingly unimportant songs like *Schwangesang* in relation to the later masterpieces bears this out again and again.

Kosegarten's poem has seven substantial strophes. These are printed in the AGA but not laid under the music as they are in the generous printing of the NSA. Translated above are strophes 1 and 7, as recorded in the Hyperion Edition.

Autograph:	Wienbibliothek im Rathaus, Vienna (first draft)
	Irvine Gilmore Music Library, Yale University, New Haven (fair copy)
First edition:	Published as part of the AGA in 1895 (P604)
Subsequent editions:	Not in Peters; AGA XX 165: Vol. 3/150; NSA IV: Vol. 9/164
Discography and timing:	Fischer-Dieskau I 5^{38} 2'47
	Hyperion I 20^5
	Hyperion II 11^9 2'48 Michael George

← *Idens Schwanenlied* D317   *Luisens Antwort* D319 →

SCHWEIZERLIED
(GOETHE) **D559** [H368]   Swiss song
F major   May 1817

(12 bars)

Uf'm Bergli	I sat
Bin i gsässe,[1]	On the mountainside
Ha de Vögle	Watching
Zu geschaut;	the birds;
Hänt gesunge,	They sang,
Hänt gesprunge,	They hopped,
Hänt's Nästli	They built
Gebaut	Their nests.
In ä Garte	I stood
Bin i gstande,[2]	In a garden,

---

[1] Goethe writes (*Gedichte*, 1815) 'Bin i *gesässe*'.
[2] Goethe writes (*Gedichte*, 1815) 'Bin i *gestande*'.

Ha de Imbli	Watching
Zu geschaut;	The bees;
Hänt gebrummet,	They hummed,
Hänt gesummet,	They buzzed,
Hänt Zelli	They built
Gebaut.	Their cells.
Uf d'Wiese	I walked
Bin i gange,	In the meadow,
Lugt' i Summer –	Looking at
Vögle a;	The butterflies;
Hänt gesoge,	They sucked,
Hänt gefloge,	They flew,
Gar zue schön hänt's	And they did it
Getan.	Very prettily.
Und da kummt nu	Then Hansel
Der Hansel,	Comes along
Und da zeig i	And I show him
Em froh,	Gaily
Wie sie's machen,	How they do it;
Und mer lachen,	And we laugh,
Und machen's	And do
Au so.	As they do.

JOHANN WOLFGANG VON GOETHE (1749–1832); poem written in early 1811

This is the fifty-second of Schubert's seventy-five Goethe solo settings (1814–26). See the poet's biography for a chronological list of all the Goethe settings.

This song is a real little charmer, although during the Hyperion recording sessions the Swiss soprano Edith Mathis witheringly remarked that Goethe's attempts at Swiss German, the so-called *Schwytzerdütsch*, were not nearly as accurate as they might have been; it seems a German enters this territory at his peril. Any visitor to Switzerland knows how different the German language is in that country and also how speakers of *Hochdeutsch* tend to patronize and dismiss the Swiss dialect.

Fox Strangways, the well-known British translator of the Schubert songs into English, chose to put this song into Devonian dialect. Shakespearian echoes of comic characters with Mummerset accents come to mind, and this hearty bonhomie is appropriate for the way that the composer has set the poem. Schubert's Viennese *Ländler* and waltzes are generally more gracious and less rustic than this, but music from the sophisticated big city is bound to differ from that of the 'provinces'. In *Schweizerlied* we hear suggestions of cowbells and clog dancing, yodels and thigh-slapping on the strong second beat of the bar – in other words all the clichés of this type of character piece. The composer seems to have had as much fun setting it as the poet had writing it. Schubert being Schubert, the tune is marvellously infectious and although it may have been Goethe's intention to have fun at the expense of the Swiss, the end result is merely an affectionate salute to neighbours across the mountains. As with his Italian evocations, the composer seems to be no less in love with a musical style because it makes him smile. Despite the simplicity of the piano writing, it is amazing that in the spacing of the chords and in the intervals of the vocal line, Schubert creates a vivid thumbnail sketch, executed in a flash by the hand of a master. Unlike Goethe, the composer never had the opportunity to visit Switzerland, and the song pre-dates by eight years his own mountain holiday in Upper Austria where he might have heard folk music similar to this. The poem was inspired by a Swiss folksong *Uff em Bergli bin i gsesse* (in 1806 in *Des Knaben Wunderhorn* there had been a similar poem printed, beginning *Auf'm Bergle bin ich gesessen*) although Goethe also seems to veer into the Swabian. From the beginning Schubert's melody seems to owe something to the same folksong. Walburga Litschauer, the great expert on Schubert's dance music, tells us the accented second beat of the bar in this song is typical of the Viennese *Ländler* around 1820.

The song shares a four-sided manuscript with two other songs – *Liebhaber in allen Gestalten* D558 and *Der Goldschmiedsgesell* D560. They are not individually dated beyond simply the month of May, but there is no reason to suppose that all three were not composed on the same day in 1817 in a single rush of creativity – and what an enchanting May day it must have been, to judge by the music.

Autograph:	Conservatoire collection, Bibliothèque Nationale, Paris
First edition:	Published as Vol. 7 no. 16 in Friedlaender's edition by Peters, Leipzig in 1885 (P487)
Subsequent editions:	Peters: Vol. 7/36; AGA XX 121: Vol. 3/48; NSA IV: Vol. 11/139
Bibliography:	Capell 1928, p. 104
	Liedlexikon 2012, p. 461
	Einstein 1951, p. 111
Discography and timing:	Fischer-Dieskau —
	Hyperion I 21[14]
	Hyperion II 19[2] 1'20 Edith Mathis

⟵ *Liebhaber in allen Gestalten* D558   *Der Goldschmiedsgesell* D560 ⟶

SCHWERTLIED
(Körner) **D170** [H78]   Song of the sword
C major   12 March 1815

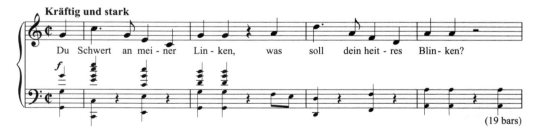

(19 bars)

Du Schwert an meiner Linken,	Sword at my left side,
Was soll dein heit'res Blinken?	Why do you shine so brightly?
Schaust mich so freundlich an,	Your friendly gaze
Hab' meine Freude dran.	Brings me joy.
Hurrah!	Hurrah!

'Mich trägt ein wackrer Reiter,
Drum blink' ich auch so heiter,
  Bin freien Mannes Wehr,
  Das freut dem Schwerte sehr.'
    Hurrah!

Ja, gutes Schwert, frei bin ich,
Und liebe dich, herzinnig,
  Als wärst du mir getraut,
  Als eine liebe Braut.
    Hurrah!

[. . . 2 . . .]

'O seliges Umfangen!
Ich harre mit Verlangen,
  Du Bräut'gam hole mich,
  Mein Kränzchen bleibt für dich.'
    Hurrah!

[. . . 4 . . .]

So komm den aus der Scheide,
Du Reiters Augenweide,
  Heraus, mein Schwert, heraus,
  Führ' dich in's Vaterhaus.
    Hurrah!

'Ach herrlich ist's im Freien,
In rüst'gen Hochzeitsreihen.
  Wie glänzt im Sonnenstrahl
  So bräutlich hell der Stahl!'
    Hurrah!

[. . . 2 . . .]

Drum drückt den liebeheissen
Bräutlichen Mund von Eisen
  An eure Lippen fest.
  Fluch! wer die Braut verlässt.
    Hurrah!

Nun lasst das Liebchen singen,
Dass helle Funken springen!
  Der Hochzeitsmorgen graut –
  Hurrah, du Eisenbraut!
    Hurrah!

'I am worn by a valiant knight,
That is why I shine so brightly.
  I defend a free man,
  Which is a sword's great joy.'
    Hurrah!

Yes, good sword, I am free,
And I love you with all my heart,
  As if you were betrothed to me
  As my beloved bride.
    Hurrah!

[. . . 2 . . .]

'O blissful embrace!
I wait longingly.
  O bridegroom, come take me,
  My wreath remains for you alone.'
    Hurrah!

[. . . 4 . . .]

Come out, then, from your sheath,
A treat for a knight's eyes!
  Out, my sword, out.
  I lead you into the parental home.
    Hurrah!

'How glorious it is in the open air,
In the spirited wedding dance.
  How brightly the bridal steel
  Gleams in the sun's rays.'
    Hurrah!

[. . . 2 . . .]

Then press the passionate
Bridal mouth of iron
  Tightly to your lips.
  Cursed be the man who abandons his bride.
    Hurrah!

Now let my beloved sing
So that bright sparks fly!
  The wedding morning dawns;
  Hurrah, you bride of iron!
    Hurrah!

Wenige Stunden vor dem Tode des
Verfaſſers gedichtet.

u Schwert an meiner Linken,

Was ſoll dein heit'res Blinken?

Schauſt mich ſo freundlich an,

Hab' meine Freude dran.

Hurrah!*

Illustration for *Schwertlied* from the Prachtausgabe of Körner's works (1882).

THEODOR KÖRNER (1791–1813); poem written 24–6 August 1813

Schwertlied is almost always performed as a choral piece; but the work's designation is 'for single voice or chorus'. Accordingly, the work is listed here as the fifth of Schubert's sixteen solo Körner settings (1815–18) rather than as an ensemble. See the poet's biography for a chronological list of all the Körner settings.

This poem stands at the end of the collection of *Leyer und Schwert*. An annotation tells us that it was written a few hours before the death of the poet, a fact that did not deter the composer from making a hearty song out of the text, originally sixteen verses long. There is as usual, however, a chilling mirthlessness about this typically Teutonic marriage between death and celebration, as if the steel that is about to enter the unfortunate singer's body has already entered his soul. For English-speaking listeners the accentuation of the word 'Hurrah' with an accent on the first syllable sounds unusual. Schubert stipulates that the rattling of swords should accompany the jubilation at this final chorus ('Bei dem Hurrah wird mit den Schwerten geklirrt'). For the Hyperion recording, despite the warlike lineage of the label's name in terms of Greek mythology, the clanking of a hundred swords was left to the listener's imagination. It is interesting to imagine how the requisite sounds might have been conjured by the composer and his friends when, and if, this piece was sung ('Any old iron?') at a musical party. Are we to assume that, just as many an average American today keeps a gun in the house, most Viennese householders could put their hands on a sword with relative ease?

Illustration for Korner's *Schwertlied* by Rudolf Eichstaedt.

In itself the song is a stirring enough solo for a young tenor promoted from the choral ranks. The tempestuous piano writing displays a Beethovenian manner, and the abrupt chords of the postlude suggest swords hacking through the air as they counter the parry and thrust of an imaginary enemy. The category of this piece is hard to decide: is it a solo work or a choral one? The AGA decided for the former (thus publishing in Series XX), the NSA the latter (Series III). The AGA prints all sixteen strophes of Körner's poem, with only the first two laid under music. The Hyperion recording offered the first two verses and the last. Three strophes are certainly sufficient in terms of musical performance, but they cannot convey the extraordinary lovers' dialogue in Körner's poem between the soldier and his sword – the deadly weapon is cast as a bride who has been languishing, unused, before being rescued by marriage. This adds a bizarre but powerful erotic impulse to the idea of dying for the Fatherland. The strophes printed here – 1, 2, 3, 6, 11, 12, 15, 16 – better convey the spirit of the poem than was practical in the recording studio.

Autograph:	Houghton Library, Harvard University, Cambridge, MA
First edition:	Published in August Reismann's *Franz Schubert. Sein Leben und seine Werke* in 1873 (P466)
Subsequent editions:	Not in Peters; AGA XX 54: Vol. 2/78; NSA III: Vol. 3
Discography and timing:	Hyperion I 20[20] 1'27 John Mark Ainsley & The London
	Hyperion II 5[18] Schubert Chorale (dir. Stephen Layton)

← *Trinklied vor der Schlacht* D169   *Gebet während der Schlacht* D171 →

SCHWESTERGRUSS

Sister's greeting

(BRUCHMANN) **D762** [H498]
F♯ minor   November 1822

(79 bars)

(1) Im Mondenschein   In the moonlight
      Wall' ich auf und ab,   I wander up and down
      Seh' Totenbein'   Seeing dead bones
      Und stilles Grab.   And a silent grave.

(2) Im Geisterhauch   In the ghostly breeze
      Vorüber bebt's,   Something floats past,
      Wie Flamm' und Rauch   Flickering
      Vorüber schwebt's;   Like flame and smoke.

(3)   Aus Nebeltrug
      Steigt eine Gestalt,
      Ohn' Sünd' und Lug
      Vorüber wallt,

From the deluding mists
A figure rises,
Without sin or falsehood,
And drifts past.

(4)   Das Aug' so blau,
      Der Blick so gross
      Wie in Himmelsau,
      Wie in Gottes Schoss;

Such blue eyes,
Such a noble gaze,
As in the fields of heaven,
As in the lap of God.

(5)   Ein weiss Gewand
      Bedeckt das Bild,
      In zarter Hand
      Eine Lilie quillt.

A white garment
Covers the apparition.
From its delicate hand
Springs a lily.

(6)   Im Geisterhauch
      Sie zu mir spricht:
      'Ich wand're schon
      Im reinen Licht,

In a ghostly whisper
She speaks to me:
'Already I walk
In the pure light.

(7)   Seh Mond und Sonn'
      Zu meinem Fuss
      Und leb' in Wonn',
      In Engelkuss;

'I see the moon and the sun
At my feet,
And live in bliss,
Kissed by angels.

(8)   Und all' die Lust,
      Die ich empfind',
      Nicht deine Brust
      Kennt, Menschenkind!

'Your heart, child of man,
Cannot know
How great is the joy
I feel.

(9)   Wenn du nicht lässt
      Den Erdengott,
      Bevor dich fasst
      Der grause Tod.'

'Unless you relinquish
The earth's false gods
Before fearful death
Seizes you.'

(10) So tönt die Luft,
      So saust der Wind,
      Zu den Sternen ruft
      Das Himmelskind,

Thus the air echoes;
Thus the wind whistles;
The child of heaven
Calls to the stars.

(11) Und eh' sie flieht,
      Die weiss' Gestalt,
      In frischer Blüt'
      Sie sich entfalt':

And before she flees
Her white form
Is enfolded
In fresh flowers.

(12) In reiner Flamm'
      Schwebt sie empor,
      Ohne Schmerz und Harm,
      Zu der Engel Chor.

She floats up
In pure flame,
Without pain or grief,
To the choir of angels.

(13)   Die Nacht verhüllt   Night veils
        Den heil'gen Ort,   The holy place;
        Von Gott erfüllt   Filled with God,
        Sing' ich das Wort.   I sing the Word.

FRANZ VON BRUCHMANN (1798–1867); poem written after July 1820

This is the fourth of Schubert's five Bruchmann solo settings (1822–3). See the poet's biography for a chronological list of all the Bruchmann settings.

On 22 October 1822 the painter Moritz von Schwind wrote to Franz von Schober telling him about a Schubertiad that was due to be held on 10 November by one of the Bruchmann daughters, Justina, in honour of her mother. Mention was made of Frau von Bruchmann's lingering grief at the loss of her other daughter, Sybilla, who had died on 18 July 1820. Franz von Bruchmann, their brother, had written a poem in which he recounts his spiritual contact with his sister's ghost. It is likely that the singer Vogl sang Schubert's setting of this poem at the November Schubertiad.

The poet's mother, the older Justina von Bruchmann (1774–1840), must have been pleased by the occasion (and by the distinguished Vogl's performing *Schwestergruss*). Schubert's Op. 20 songs, published in April 1823, were dedicated to Frau von Bruchmann, who was likely to have paid the composer a sum of money as was customary for a compliment of this kind. The inclusion in that opus of *Sei mir gegrüsst* D741, where loved ones are parted by the chasm between life and death, was no doubt meant as another bow to the memory of the 'entriss'ne' Sybilla, torn away from her family. All in all, *Schwestergruss* would have pleased (and perhaps also mystified) the bereaved relatives. The dead girl's memory was honoured but her living brother, whose spiritual struggle had somewhat hijacked the occasion, even more so.

Bruchmann took as his model one of the greatest pieces of Romantic literature, the *Hymnen an die Nacht* of Novalis (qv), a sequence of prose and poetry that commemorates the poet's rapt spiritual attachment to his fiancée Sophie von Kühn who died tragically young. In the third of these, Novalis stands alone on a barren hill, 'driven by desperation to review the insignificance of my life':

> . . . *the place around me levitated; and over this region my released and reborn spirit hovered. The hill became a cloud of dust – and through the cloud I saw my love's transfigured features. In those eyes rested infinity – I took those hands, and my tears became a glittering galaxy. The future opened, and aeons disappeared into the distance, like a travelling storm. With her I contemplated the prospect of a new life. It was the first and only dream, and from then on I've felt immutable trust in the night heaven, and its bride, the light.*[1]

Schubert's extraordinary setting of Novalis's *Nachthymne* D687 nearly three years earlier (part of the fourth *Hymnen an die Nacht*), as well as the four *Hymne* from the *Geistliche Lieder* D659–662, are shining evidence of the composer's admiration for and knowledge of Novalis. Bruchmann's language and imagery would have been more familiar to Schubert than to Richard Capell who calls the poem 'intolerably vulgar'. But it might well have struck members of the Schubert circle as self-regarding and frankly ridiculous that Franz von Bruchmann, minor poet, had cast himself in a Novalis-like role on the death of his sister. In any case, Novalis's poem has nothing to do with the guilt-ridden Catholicism with which Bruchmann was soon to identify.

---

[1] Translation by Jeremy Reed from Novalis, *Hymns to the Night* (London, 1989), p. 21.

However, there were all sorts of reasons for making the occasion work: Schober was secretly involved with Bruchmann's other sister and was possibly the moving spirit behind the whole idea of a Schubertiad to honour the memory of Sybilla. Schober and Justina were clearly hoping that brother Franz (who was an old friend, after all) would support their romance once he found out about it, and so it was important to keep him onside. The extent of Schubert's complicity in all this is impossible to identify, but Schober and Schubert were at their closest at this time, only a month or so before the composer discovered his illness.

In the opening two bars the softly chiming unison C sharps (long–short–short, tapped out twice like a message from the dead at a seance) tell us something extraordinary is about to happen. Although dactylic rhythm is not a feature that pervades this song like some others, its presence here announces that something of import is afoot, and we might have guessed that the text is about death and a maiden. And, as so often when this composer begins with measured octaves, his music immediately suggests suspense and commands us to sit up and take notice. The bareness of texture is a deliberate ploy so that the song can gradually open up and expand in complexity and intensity. This gives the music the effect of approaching from a distance, becoming more detailed as it gets nearer, appropriate for a poem where the spirit of the poet's sister seems slowly to materialize before she speaks and then fades and vanishes. In this way the ghost of Sybilla von Bruchmann is conjured out of thin air.

After those opening two bars we hear that the tonality is F sharp minor, rather an unusual key for Schubert. A melody doubled in the alto and bass voices slips under the shelter of those tolling C sharp dactyls (one of Schubert's inspired upper pedal points). The melancholy lilt seems strangely familiar, and Beethoven comes to mind: in the Allegretto of the Seventh Symphony Op. 92 (b. 27) the viola, in similar fashion, insinuates a counter-melody under the second violins' upper pedal in dactylic rhythm. And then, returning to *Schwestergruss*, we hear that this inner melody in bb. 3–4, a mournful tune with rising sequences, is a minor-key variant of the 'Eroica' theme. This tune appears not only in the last movement of the symphony but also, before that, in Beethoven's ballet *Die Geschöpfe des Prometheus* Op. 43, and a set of variations for piano (Op. 35).

We shall never know whether there was a conscious decision to bow to Beethoven in this song, or whether the similarities are merely coincidental. After five and a half bars of introduction, and with the moonlit entry of the voice, we first hear the quaver triplets that pervade the song – mostly in the right hand, sometimes in the left, occasionally in the inner voices of a texture which, from time to time, approximates to that of a string quartet. Schubert has it in mind to compose a continuous song – not strophic in any sense but bound together by motifs. Once we have embarked on this journey, the musical momentum keeps going in an amazing manner, always propelled forward, albeit gently, by those ceaseless triplets. Richard Capell and Fischer-Dieskau here observe a similarity to the triplets of *Erlkönig* D328; it is true that both songs have a supernatural theme, but there is nothing in the gliding mood of *Schwestergruss* to remind us of a horse's thundering hooves.

Verse 1: The restless movement implied by 'Wall' ich auf und ab' (I wander up and down) is caught wonderfully by the *Bewegung* that manages to be both still – as if awestruck by the moonlit graveyard – and turbulent. Here Schubert's empathy unveils the self-tormenting Bruchmann in search of a faith, and we hear his inner turmoil as he seeks an answer to life's (and death's) mysteries. After the vocal announcement of the 'Eroica' theme, Schubert employs every aspect of harmonic technique available to him: at b. 6 the crunch between the glacial stillness of 'Totenbein' / Und stilles Grab' (repeated Ds in the voice part) and the chromatic descent in the right-hand accompaniment is a perfect analogue for an inner shudder. We know we are in for one of the 'heavenly length' songs when the composer sets the words twice; the long melody alternates between stasis (as a pedal note) or shadowing the exceptionally inventive and eloquent bass line in thirds and sixths. This strophe ends in F sharp major, a cadence on 'stilles Grab' in b. 16 that introduces a four-bar interlude (bb. 17–20). Here the right hand sings in beatific melody, first with a major inflection (again that 'Eroica' theme), then with a minor-key colour, while the triplet motif is assigned to the viola tessitura – this is one of the song's several string quartet-like passages.

Verses 2–6: Once he has set the mood in expansive manner, Schubert uses words at a much faster rate: the poet's verses run together as if in continuous narrative. With the change into D major, Sybilla von Bruchmann's ghost floats into the music. To prepare for this supernatural moment the piano writing abandons the treble clef entirely at b. 21 and sinks to the bottom of the instrument. This distance between the tessitura of voice and piano enhances the mystery of this spellbound nocturne, as in *Nacht und Träume* D827. Caught in the magic web of music that develops organically one phrase from the next, we scarcely notice that there is no tune to speak of: rather the melody is derived and evolved from various cells, chief of which is the 'Eroica' theme, exploited for its rhythm as much as for its melody. Schubert incorporates the first half of Bruchmann's sixth strophe into this section, reserving the change of key signature (b. 41) for the first words of the singing wraith.

Verses 6–9: This is the last of Schubert's depictions of ghostly voices from the dead. The two versions of Schiller's *Thekla (eine Geisterstimme)* D73 and D595 come to mind, as do the exquisite passages for the disembodied Vinvela in *Cronnan* D282. Something unusual has to happen here, and for only the second time in his lieder (the other occasion is for another night piece, *Die Mondnacht* D238) the composer goes into a key signature of six sharps. We have touched on F sharp major already, but now we find ourselves officially 'on the other side', glimpsing heaven through the portals of an exotic tonality bristling with accidentals, each sharp sign a heavenly portcullis that separates the purified dead from the sinning living. Here there is a bass pedal for six bars (perpetually gently pulsating quavers in bb. 41–6) on a left-hand C sharp. The right hand contents itself with spread chords as the voice of the angel is accompanied by a harp. Schubert does not allow her to sing with the freedom of a living person: the dynamic is *ppp* and the repetitive melody, anchored around a pivotal A sharp, has a very small range, as if her appearance takes place within the breadth of a single beam of light (cf. the second *Thekla* setting, D595). The whole of this passage is deliberately unsophisticated, as if heaven equates with child-like innocence and utterance. There is a tiny but significant shift in harmony at b. 51 for the finger-pointing 'du' ('Wenn du nicht lässt / Den Erdengott'); mention of this 'god of this earth' is an all-embracing euphemism for whatever aspect of the poet's own life was making him increasingly guilty. The threatened retribution – 'Der grause Tod' – calls for the only diminished harmonies in the piece (b. 54).

Verses 10–12: From b. 55 the main 'Eroica' motif deep in the piano's left hand provides the melody for an ominous two-bar interlude. Now that the spirit has delivered her message, the singer is released from fear and awe and able to express the ecstasy of revelation; from b. 56 the vocal line moves into a higher tessitura and stays there. This page provides real technical challenges to the singer with its constant excursions to F sharps at the top of the stave. At 'So tönt die Luft, / So saust der Wind' (bb. 56–8) an accompaniment descending in semitones against a held vocal line magically evokes the moan and sweep of the wind (the C sharp/D clash that we heard earlier). Otherwise the harmonic direction of this music is ever upward; sometimes the accompanying triplets remind us of the introduction to *Nähe des Geliebten* D162 where the movement of triplets opens one harmonic vista after another. Sybilla is first encircled with flowers and then floats aloft: it takes a genius to deal convincingly with a divine ascension in musical terms – it is hard enough in a genuinely religious work – but Schubert *is* a genius and he manages it. He demands a great deal of his singer who must be suffused with joy at this point – a tall order when the phrase 'Zu der Engel Chor', with its long melisma on 'Engel', is among the hardest he ever wrote (bb. 66–8). Although it only rises to an F sharp, the placement of the preceding phrase makes this line, from the singer's viewpoint, seem to ascend into the stratosphere.

Verse 13: The song's coda is solemn, lyrical and transfigured – everything that such a piece needs to make it believable (or nearly believable). For the first time canonic imitation is used between voice and piano, as if the singer is responding to the divine message – having heard it he will make it part of his life. The postlude goes on singing the tune of the vocal line as if to illustrate the zeal of the poet who now claims to be 'filled with God' and who resolves to 'sing the Word'. As the song comes to its end, even staunch unbelievers feel raised to a higher power.

The emergence of biographical detail in songs and their performance was not as unusual in the Schubert circle as we might suppose: the composer was able to set Mayrhofer's *Geheimnis* D491 (which praises his musical genius) without embarrassment; Schober's *Pilgerweise* D789 seems to have taken as its theme the tragedy of Schubert's sickness and struggle to survive. The composer evidently regarded this element of self-dramatization as part and parcel of being a member of a group of artists who brought their own works to their gatherings, works inspired by the events that affected them all and which were the subject of discussion and sometimes gossip.

But even taking all this into account, this impossibly mawkish poem has in it the seeds that would cause an irreparable estrangement between Bruchmann and the rest of the Schubertians, including the composer. When the poet discovered in 1824 that Justina was secretly engaged to Franz von Schober, he broke the relationship up, much to the dismay of Schwind and Schubert who sided with Schober in the most dramatic rift the circle was ever to experience. Bruchmann was always searching for the 'meaning of life'; he had even travelled to Erlangen in Bavaria (such journeys were forbidden to students by Austrian law) to hear the lectures of Schelling. There he met up with the great poet August von Platen (qv) who had perhaps previously met him in Vienna (Kupelwieser's drawings of Bruchmann show a good-looking, even rather pretty, young man, and Platen might well have been smitten). We thus owe two Platen settings to Schubert's friendship with Bruchmann, as well as the four important songs (apart from *Schwestergruss*) from this period of 1822–3: *Der zürnende Barde* D785, *An die Leier* D737, *Im Haine* D738 and *Am See* D746. Bruchmann may also have played a large part in introducing Schubert to the poetry of Friedrich Schlegel. But religious conversion and renunciation of earthly sin were in the air, and Bruchmann's relationship with his closest friend, the exiled Johann Senn, was also severed in the interest of holiness. It is possible that Bruchmann's tussle with the enigmatic 'Erdengott' mentioned in the song was in reality a struggle to control, and then eradicate, his own homosexual feelings. All this intensity and self-examination were probably anathema to Schubert; proselytizing is boring, particularly moralizing based on guilt, and Bruchmann had the makings of a gigantic bore. But it is possible that the composer's own despair at discovering his illness put him temporarily in the mood for a lyric offering some kind of salvation even at the expense of divine retribution.

Once Bruchmann renounced his former life and returned to Catholicism he had nothing more to do with the Schubertians. He was married for a short time, but his wife died. He then became a Redemptorist priest in 1833, going on to a life in the church where he held several important positions in the hierarchy. A late photograph of him shows a sumptuously dressed and rather sour-looking prelate.

Autograph:	Wienbibliothek im Rathaus, Vienna
First edition:	Published as Book 23 no. 1 of the *Nachlass* by Diabelli, Vienna in July 1833 (P303)
Subsequent editions:	Peters: Vol. 7/38; AGA XX 413: Vol. 7/38; NSA IV: Vol. 13/51
Bibliography:	Capell 1928, pp. 174–5
	Einstein 1951, p. 253
	Fischer-Dieskau 1977, pp. 185–6
	Kohlhäufl 1999, p. 275
Discography and timing:	Fischer-Dieskau —

Hyperion I 35[2]
Hyperion II 26[3]   6'47   Geraldine McGreevy

← *Schatzgräbers Begehr* D761   *Schicksalslenker, blicke nieder* D763 →

SIR WALTER SCOTT (1771–1832)

THE GERMAN TRANSLATIONS

S1 *Der Pirat* aus dem Englischen des Walter Scott, übersetzt von S. H. Spiker, Zweiter Band, Berlin bei Duncker und Humblot, 1822

S2 *Das Fräulein vom See* Ein Gedicht in sechs Gesängen von Walter Scott. Aus dem Englischen und mit einer historichen Einleitung und Anmerkungen von D. Adam Storck, Professor in Bremen, Essen bei C. D. Badeker, 1819

[According to Ernst Hilmar (*Franz Schubert in his time* p. 101) Karoline Pichler (qv) had also made a translation of *The Lady of the Lake*.]

S3 *Das Fräulein vom See*. Ein Gedicht in sechs Gesängen von Walter Scott. Aus dem Englischen, und mit einer historichen Einleitung und Anmerkungen von D. Adam Storck, weiland Professor in Bremen. Zweite, vom Uebersetzer selbst noch verbesserte Auflage. Essen, bei C. D. Badeker, 1823

Certain readings in the 1823 edition in *Ellens erster Gesang* make it more likely that Schubert had this second (1823) edition, or the later reprint by the Viennese firm Mausberger, to hand. Both editions included Storck's detailed sixty-page introduction to the background of the story in Scottish history.

S4 *Ivanhoe*. Nach dem Englischen von Walter Scott. Neue verbesserte Auflage, Erster Theil. Wien Gedruckt bey Anton Strauss 1825

There is no translator mentioned in this Viennese edition, although the translation is identical with the one issued in Germany in Leipzig (1820) by Karl Ludwig Methusalem Müller (1771–1837) (qv): *Ivanhoe. Nach dem Englischen des Walter Scott von K. L. Meth. Müller, Zweyter Teil*, Leipzig: J. C. Hinrichs'sche Buchhandlung, 1820. It seems likely that the more recent Viennese edition was Schubert's source, and not the older German volume.

THE ENGLISH SOURCES

S5 *Tales of My Landlord.* Third Series collected and Arranged by Jedediah Cleishbotham, Schoolmaster and Parish-Clerk of Gandercleugh. In Four Volumes. Volumes III and IV. *A Legend of Montrose.* Edinburgh, Printed for Archiibald Constable and Co. Edinburgh. Longman, Hurst, Rees, Orme and Brown, Paternoster Row; and Hurst, Robinson, and Co., 90 Cheapside London. 1819

S6 *The Pirate* By the author of 'Waverley' and 'Kenilworth' &c. In three Volumes. Volume II. Edinburgh, Printed for Archibald Constable and Co. Ltd and Hurst, Robinson and Co., London, 1822

S7 *The Lady of the Lake* a Poem By Walter Scott, Esq. Printed for John Ballantyne And Co. Edinburgh and Longman, Hurst, Rees, and Orme, and William Miller, London by James Ballantyne & Co., Edinburgh, 1810

S8 *Ivanhoe, A Romance* By the Author of Waverley &c. In Three Volumes. Volume II. Edinburgh, Printed for Archibald Constable and Co.; and John Ballantyne, Edinburgh; and Hurts, Robinson, and Co. London, 1821

TALES OF MY LANDLORD,

Third Series,

COLLECTED AND ARRANGED

BY

JEDEDIAH CLEISHBOTHAM,

SCHOOLMASTER AND PARISH-CLERK OF GANDERCLEUGH.

Hear, Land o' Cakes and brither Scots,
Frae Maidenkirk to Jonny Groats',
If there's a hole in a' your coats,
    I rede ye tent it,
A chiel's amang you takin' notes,
    An' faith he'll prent it.
                                BURNS.

IN FOUR VOLUMES.

VOL. III.

EDINBURGH :

PRINTED FOR ARCHIBALD CONSTABLE AND CO. EDINBURGH ;

LONGMAN, HURST, REES, ORME, AND BROWN, PATERNOSTER-ROW ;
AND HURST, ROBINSON, AND CO. 90, CHEAPSIDE, LONDON.

1819.

First edition of *A Legend of Montrose* (Edinburgh, 1819).

THE SONGS

1825?	*Lied der Anne Lyle* D830 [S5: Chapter XIII pp. 277–8] O. E. Deutsch averred that Sophie May was the translator by her of this poem. And yet, quite another translation by her of Anne Lyle's lyric is to be found in *Allan Mac-Aulay, der Seher des Hochlandes. Eine Legende aus den Kriegen des Montrose von Walter Scott. Aus dem Englischen übersetzt von Sophie May.* Wien Mausberger's Druck und Verlag, 1826. For an argument that raises the possibility of Craigher von Jachelutta as translator of the song, *see* commentary on *Lied der Anne Lyle.*
1825	*Gesang der Norna* D831 [S1: pp. 150–51] [S6: Chapter Five, p. 126] *Bootgesang* D835 Op. 52 no. 3 Quartet (TTBB) with piano [S2: from 'Zweiter Gesang: Die Insel' pp. 67–9] [S3: pp. 63–5] [S7: Canto Second 'The Island' XIX pp. 69–70] *Coronach* D836 Choral Song (SSA) with piano [S2: from Dritter Gesang 'Das Aufgebot' pp. 116–17 with subtitle 'Todtengesang'] [S3: pp. 109–10] [S7: Canto Third 'The Gathering' XVI pp. 117–18]
April–July 1825	*Ellens Gesang I* D837 [S2: from 'Erster Gesang, Die Jagd'] [S3: pp. 33–4] [S7: Canto First, 'The Chase' XXXI pp. 38–9]

Ellens Gesang II D838 [S2: from
'Erster Gesang, Die Jagd' pp. 37–8]
[S3: p. 35] [S7: Canto First 'The
Chase' XXXII pp. 39–40]

Lied des gefangenen Jägers D843 [S2:
from Sechster Gesang, 'Die
Wachtstube' pp. 285–6] [S3:
pp. 263–4] [S7: Canto Sixth, 'The
Guard-Room' XXIV pp. 38–9]

April 1825   Ellens Gesang III D839 [S2: from
Dritter Gesang, 'Das Aufgebot'
pp. 135–6, with title 'Hymne an
die Jungfrau'] [S3: pp. 127–8] [S7:
Canto Third 'The Gathering' XXIX
pp. 136–7]

Normans Gesang D846 [S1: from
Dritter Gesang 'Das Aufgebot'
pp. 126–7] [S2: pp. 118–19] [S7:
Canto Third 'The Gathering' XXIII
pp. 127–8]

March 1826   Romanze des Richard Löwenherz D907
[S4: pp. 242–4] [S8: Chapter III pp.
43–5 under the title of The Crusader's
Return]

THE

PIRATE.

BY THE AUTHOR OF "WAVERLEY,
KENILWORTH," &c.

Nothing in him ——
But doth suffer a sea-change.
            Tempest.

IN THREE VOLUMES.

VOL. I.

EDINBURGH:
PRINTED FOR ARCHIBALD CONSTABLE AND CO.;
AND HURST, ROBINSON, AND CO.,
LONDON.

1822.

First edition of *The Pirate* (Edinburgh, 1822).
This edition was issued before Scott's
authorship had been acknowledged in Britain.

Walter Scott was born in Edinburgh on 15
August 1771. Like a number of his contemporaries in Germany who had elected to become
poets, Scott had initially been steered towards
becoming a lawyer and was called to the bar
in 1792. He was fascinated by the very things
that were yet to interest the publishers in
literary London – old Scottish tales and ballads
from the Border country. He was an implacable
enemy of France but was fascinated by the
courtly literature of that country when it was
connected with Scotland, although at this early
stage of his career he was unenthusiastic about
the Highlands and Highlanders. He was proud
to be of fair-haired Saxon stock, the race driven
northwards by the Norman enemy; the troublesome Celts, the Jacobite rebels of 1745, were
unreliable traitors. Scott was in favour of the
Union and was in some ways a patriotic
Hanoverian. Some of his earliest literary
work was translating from German, including
the poetry of Bürger and Goethe (*Götz von*

Berlichingen). He married a woman of French
descent, Margaret Charpentier, in 1797, and
was awarded a baronetcy in 1822. His first great
epic poem was *The Lay of the Last Minstrel*,
published in 1805; *Marmion* followed in 1808.

During the Napoleonic Wars the celebrated
gallantry of the Highland Regiments in the
Peninsular Wars brought about a radical
change of mind in Scott concerning his
northern countrymen. The author soon
became an ardent advocate of a Scotland
united by the complementary talents of Saxons
and Celts, a country that would be stronger
and more influential as a result (nothing would
have upset him more, however, than the efforts
of Scottish politicians to achieve independence
from England). In order to bring accuracy and
detail to his writings Scott set about turning
himself into the foremost scholar of Highland
lore and history. *The Lady of the Lake* (significantly set at a time in history before religion
was a divisive issue) was a peace offering, and

Walter Scott, frontispiece to *Urania* (1827).

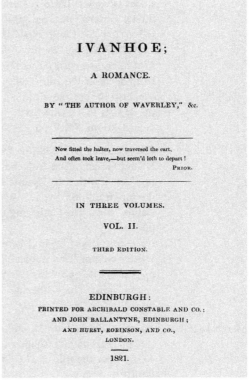

An early edition of *Ivanhoe* (Edinburgh, 1821). This edition was issued before Scott's authorship had been acknowledged.

paean of praise, to his previously undervalued Celtic compatriots. The storyline takes place during a war between the King of Scotland and his Highland subjects that leads to a just and honourable peace. Between 1805 and 1810 publications of poetic epics created something of a sensation, but it was the novels rather than the long narrative poems that were soon to bring about an extraordinary Scott-mania in battle-weary Europe.

Nevertheless, Scott readily acknowledged that Lord Byron, with *Childe Harold* in 1812, had beaten him as a poet. He refused the offer of the poet-laureateship in 1813, and became a novelist. He was unwilling, however, to risk his great reputation as a serious poet when embarking on a career as a mere storyteller in prose. He thus issued his novels anonymously, and the author of these works was known as 'The Great Unknown'. There was increasing speculation about their authorship, which was

only officially acknowledged in 1827 by Scott himself as far as the British market was concerned. In the German translations of the novels (such as *Der Pirat* and *Ivanhoe* read by Schubert), however, there was no diffidence about identifying the author. Indeed there was a Viennese edition of many of Scott's novels by 1825.

Waverley was the first of these 'anonymous' novels, published in 1814, and it gave its name to the series of Scott novels as a whole. It is now agreed that his masterpieces in this series were *The Antiquary* and *Old Mortality* (both 1816) and *The Heart of Midlothian* (1818). In 1819 he published the second series of *Tales of My Landlord*; one of these was *A Legend of Montrose* (from which Schubert selected a text), and another was *The Bride of Lammermoor* from which Donizetti fashioned his most famous opera, *Lucia di Lammermoor*. (For

Tales of My Landlord Scott's pseudonym was Jedediah Cleishbotham, but only, it seems, for the British reading public.) Also published in 1819 was *Ivanhoe*, the novel set in the time of the Crusades perhaps Scott's most enduring achievement. In 1822 he published *Peveril of the Peak* where the deaf–mute Fenella is directly inspired by Mignon from *Wilhelm Meister*. Scott is likely to have read Goethe's novel in the original some time between 1795 and 1810, and it also seems to have influenced *The Lady of the Lake*: Ellen Douglas and her father (who accompanies her singing on the harp) were perhaps modelled on the duetting characters of Mignon and the Harper. Like Mignon there is something other-worldly about Ellen, and both father-harpists were disgraced exiles.

To list the titles of the novels 'by the author of Waverley' would take up an entire page. By 1826 Scott had made a great deal of money but then disaster struck. In that year the author, who was a partner in the publishing firm of Ballantyne, became caught up in the bankruptcy of the sister firm of Constable & Co.

and found himself personally liable for a debt of £114,000. This is an enormous sum even today, and in Scott's time the equivalent of many millions of pounds. In an incredibly stoic manner Scott determined to pay off the debt by the power of his pen; he managed to do so by unstinting hard work and the writing of many books, but the effort and stress involved undoubtedly shortened his life. In 1811 he had purchased Abbotsford on the Tweed where he built himself a beautiful mansion – a baronial castle in fact. His tireless determination to avoid the consequences of bankruptcy was a matter of honour, but it was also motivated by the desire to keep Abbotsford within his ownership, and in this he narrowly succeeded. Scott died in this great house that had cost him so dear on 21 September 1832.

Scott was immeasurably helped by the enthusiasm for the works of Ossian (*see* MACPHERSON) that had in a sense put Scotland on the literary map for Continental readers. The exploits of the ancient warriors of Fingal had enchanted an entire generation of German, French and Italian readers, and so Scott

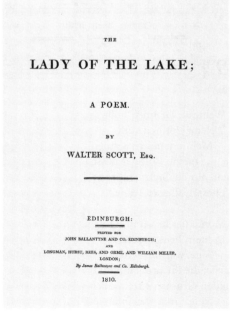

First edition of *The Lady of the Lake* (Edinburgh, 1810) with its author as a frontispiece.

provided a sequel – excitingly written poetry and prose concerning Fingal's descendants who had a similar spirit and dash in war and conflict. Scott's flair for storytelling was backed by a formidable apparatus of learning and scholarly information. The poetry of James Macpherson ('Ossian') came Schubert's way in 1815 and, less than a decade later, in August 1823, a letter to Franz von Schober from the composer, by now struggling with the symptoms of his illness, tells of how he is reading Walter Scott. By this time many of the poems and novels were available to German-speakers in quite a wide choice of translations. Readers were enthralled by the new concept of the historical novel, with highly worked-out plots and a wealth of authentic detail. Schubert, concerned daily with poetry in the setting of his songs, clearly liked to relax by reading novels. We know, for example, that he was enthused by the American novelist James Fenimore Cooper – in translation of course – on his deathbed. The influence of the singer Johann Michael Vogl on Schubert's reading habits in this period is not to be underestimated. Vogl, a student of the English language, was apparently able to read Scott in the original. What really piqued Schubert's interest in *The Lady of the Lake*, however, may have been the success enjoyed in Vienna by his rival Rossini in an opera on the same story, *La Donna del lago*, which starred Henriette Sontag, a singer much admired by Schubert. This was the first of Scott's works to be turned into an opera. Composers such as Bellini, Bizet, Boieldieu, Donizetti, Flotow, Marschner, Nicolai and Sullivan were to write operas, choral works and incidental music based on Scott.

Das SEHNEN   Longing
(KOSEGARTEN) **D231** [H122]
A minor   8 July 1815

(13 bars)

Wehmut, die mich hüllt,
Welche Gottheit stillt
   Mein unendlich Sehnen!
Die ihr meine Wimper nässt,
Namenlosen Gram entpresst,
   Fliesset, fliesset Tränen!

Mond, der lieb und traut
In mein Fenster schaut,
   Sage, was mir fehle!
Sterne, die ihr droben blinkt,
Holden Gruss mir freundlich winkt,
   Nennt mir, was mich quäle!

[...]

O Melancholy that envelops me,
What god can still
   My boundless longing?
You that moisten my eyelashes,
And draw from me nameless grief.
   Flow, you tears, flow!

O Moon, gazing fondly and tenderly
Through my window,
   Say, what is the matter with me?
Stars, shining up above,
Sending me your sweet, kindly greeting,
   Tell me what torments me!

[...]

In die Ferne strebt, Wie auf Flügeln schwebt Mein erhöhtes Wesen. Fremder Zug, geheime Kraft, Namenlose Leidenschaft, Lass, ach lass genesen!	As if on hovering wings, My uplifted being Is drawn into the distance. Strange stirrings, secret power, Nameless passion, O let me be well again!
Ängstender beklemmt Mich die Wehmut, hemmt Atem mir und Rede Einsam schmachten, o der Pein! O des Grams, allein zu sein In des Lebens Öde!	Melancholy oppresses me Still more fearfully, stifling My breath and my speech, O the pain of languishing in solitude! O the grief of being alone In life's wilderness!
[. . . 2 . . .]	[. . . 2 . . .]

LUDWIG KOSEGARTEN (1758–1818)

This is the sixth of Schubert's twenty-one Kosegarten solo settings (1815–17). See the poet's biography for a chronological list of all the Kosegarten settings, as well as a discussion of Morten Solvik's Kosegarten Liederkreis and this song's place within it.

Like Verlaine's *Il pleure dans mon cœur* (set by both Debussy and Fauré), this little poem of 'spleen' describes what would now be termed depression; the title of 'longing' implies an ardent desire for release from such a condition. This heartfelt wish to lift the mists of melancholy is touchingly described by the poet (surely one of Kosegarten's most self-revealing poems), and Schubert follows suit with a little plaint in his very special key of A minor (suitably anchored, as if trapped, in the home tonality for the opening two bars of the song). This tonality inevitably brings Goethe's Mignon to mind.

The melodic line for the 'Namenlosen Gram' at bb. 4–8, descending and then ascending again in the same region of the stave, is repetitive with great effect. It is as if the singer is caught and weighed down by emotions and is seeking a way out of a maze. The 'Etwas geschwind' marking is ideal: there must be a touch of angst in the tempo, but also an apathy which has no use for purposeful speed. Schubert often reveals to much acclaim his understanding of the feminine psyche (as in *Gretchen am Spinnrade* D118), but here is a song that is completely unknown (ignored by Fischer-Dieskau in his survey, for example), not by any means solely a woman's song, that describes a tormented condition that clearly claimed countless sufferers in earlier centuries, as well as our own. The lack of any consolatory change into A major in this song is an eloquent indication of Schubert's customary empathy.

Kosegarten's poem is headed *Sehnsucht* in later editions of the poems. All of its seven strophes fit the music with perfect ease, although a performance with all of these would scarcely be justified. Elly Ameling selected strophes 1, 2, and 4 for the Hyperion Edition; these are surely adequate if the music is given room to breathe, and if the marking of 'Etwas geschwind' is interpreted moderately. Strophe 5, perhaps the most desperate in the poem, has been added above.

Autographs:	Private possession, Canada (first draft) Wienbibliothek im Rathaus, Vienna (fair copy)
First edition:	Published as Op. post. 172 no. 4 by C. A. Spina, Vienna in 1865 (P404)

Subsequent editions: Peters: Vol. 6/101; AGA XX 94: Vol. 2/177; NSA IV: Vol. 8/122
Discography and timing: Fischer-Dieskau —
                         Hyperion I 7[13]
                         Hyperion II 8[5]   1'18   Elly Ameling

← *Die Täuschung* D230   *Hymne an den Unendlichen* D232 →

SEHNSUCHT (I)   Longing
(SCHILLER) **D52** [H23]
D minor – F major   15–17 April 1813

(148 bars)

Ach, aus dieses Tales Gründen,
  Die der kalte Nebel drückt,
Könnt ich doch den Ausgang finden,
  Ach wie fühlt' ich mich beglückt!
Dort erblick' ich schön Hügel,
  Ewig jung und ewig grün!
Hätt' ich Schwingen hätt ich Flügel,
  Nach den Hügeln zög' ich hin.

Harmonien hör' ich klingen,
  Töne süsser Himmelsruh,
Und die leichten Winde bringen
  Mir der Düfte Balsam zu,
Gold'ne Früchte seh' ich glühen
  Winkend zwischen dunkelm Laub,
Und die Blumen, die dort blühen,
  Werden keines Winters Raub.

Ach wie schön muss sich's ergehen
  Dort im ew'gen Sonnenschein,
Und die Luft auf jenen Höhen
  O wie labend muss sie sein!
Doch mir wehrt des Stromes Toben,
  Der ergrimmt dazwischen braust,
Seine Wellen sind gehoben,
  Dass die Seele mir ergraust.

Ah, if only I could find a way out
  From the depths of this valley.
Oppressed by cold mists,
  How happy I would feel!
Yonder I see lovely hills,
  Ever young and ever green!
If I had pinions, if I had wings
  I would fly to those hills.

I hear harmonious sounds,
  Notes of sweet, celestial peace,
And the gentle breezes bring me
  The scent of balsam.
I see golden fruits glowing,
  Beckoning amid dark leaves,
And the flowers which bloom there
  Will never be winter's prey.

Ah, how beautiful it must feel to wander
  There in the eternal sunshine;
And the air on those hills,
  How refreshing it must feel.
But I am barred by the raging torrent
  Which foams angrily between us,
Its waves tower up,
  Striking fear into my soul.

Einen Nachen seh ich schwanken,	I see a boat pitching,
Aber ach! der Fährmann fehlt.	But alas! There is no boatman.
Frisch hinein und ohne Wanken,	Jump in without hesitation!
Seine Segel sind beseelt.	The sails are billowing.
Du musst glauben, du musst wagen,	You must trust, and you must dare,
Denn die Götter leihn kein Pfand,	For the gods grant no pledge;
Nur ein Wunder kann dich tragen	Only a miracle can convey you
In das schöne Wunderland.	To the miraculous land of beauty.

FRIEDRICH VON SCHILLER (1759–1805); poem written in 1802

This is the fourth of Schubert's forty-four Schiller solo settings (1811–24). See the poet's biography for a chronological list of all the Schiller settings.

Between the two versions of this song (the second setting is D636) there is a gap of eight years. With the exception of different versions of some of the Mignon lyrics (the first from 1815, the sixth from 1826) these two settings of *Sehnsucht* are separated by a greater gulf of time, experience and style than any other pair of Schubert songs sharing a text.

The poem was first published in the almanac *Taschenbuch für Damen 1803*. If any lyric by Schiller were to be nominated as typical of the work that appealed to the composer, it would be this. It contains a happy mixture of the romantic description of nature, gentle yet resonant on the ear, and the rugged determination of *Sturm und Drang* – a marriage of the feminine and masculine that befits Schiller's status as an important playwright, as renowned for his creation of Amalia, Thekla and Maria Stuart as of Franz and Karl Moor, Wallenstein and Don Carlos.

Verses 1–2: The key is D minor and, without any piano introduction, we plunge into the poem. There is something to be said for this shock tactic when the first word is a dramatic 'Ach'. The sixteen-year-old composer is not yet a master of melody or rhythm: the descending vocal arpeggio of the opening (bb. 2–4) is rather uninventive, and the word-setting of 'Die der kalte Nebel drückt' (a succession of alternating minims and crotchets) does not do full justice to the scansion. After the interpolation of five bars of rather lame recitative, 'Hätt' ich Schwingen, hätt' ich Flügel' is based on another arpeggio (A major, bb. 25–8) with deft piano embellishments on the same chord. One cannot avoid the impression that the singer is as much in search of a tune as an exit from the claustrophobic valley. By casting the song in the bass clef, Schubert has definitely envisioned his singer in heroic mould. With the second verse the words 'Harmonien hör' ich klingen' are all set within the chord of A major, as if to illustrate that the matching notes within a tonic chord are what harmony is all about. An air of importance is enhanced by a confidently rolling accompaniment for 'Töne süsser Himmelsruh' (in the left hand from b. 37), the words set to a phrase of appropriate heavenly length. The vocal line of 'Gold'ne Früchte' (bb. 53–6) is suggestive, even in its appearance on the page, of fruit hanging heavy on the bough; there is an appropriately glowing diminished seventh harmony for 'glühen' bb. 59–60, and euphony of sixths and tenths for the idyllic repetition of 'Werden keines Winters Raub' (bb. 70–73).

Verse 3: The first four lines are recitative – not perhaps Schubert's most inventive use of the genre. In D636 these lines are incorporated into the seraphic B flat section, all the better to lead to the contrasting water music (churning semiquavers) which the imagery at the second half of the verse requires. In D52, however, the setting of 'Doch mir wehrt des Stromes Toben' (from b. 82, marked Andante) shows that Schubert is not yet a master of the aquatic genre. There is drama aplenty in these thunderous chords and noble vocal line, but no fluidity. It is as if the waves of the Red Sea have been parted by Moses and are standing stiffly to attention.

Verse 4: With a change at b. 89 to four flats and a marking of 'Allegro agitato ma non troppo', the young Schubert suddenly strikes form. The accompaniment of the 'Allegro agitato' (quavers in the left hand alternating with pairs of semiquavers in the right) is extraordinarily illustrative of a small boat pitching and tossing in stormy waters. The harmony is so anchored (in F minor) that we know the boat is moored in the harbour and awaiting its crew. This is more subtly indicated in D636, with less movement in the bass line, but one scarcely notices this detail in the sweep of the whole. In D52 we note how the little semiquaver motif in the right hand becomes more anguished (larger intervals, higher leaps) when it is discovered that 'der Fährmann fehlt' (bb. 94–9). The vocal line stretches into longer note values to indicate emptiness, a lack of a boatman and the momentary dejection of not knowing what to do. It is here that the older, more mature Schubert joins hands with his younger self. So satisfied was he with the last section of his youthful composition that he incorporated the music beginning 'Frisch hinein und ohne Wanken' ('Più allegro', b. 103) almost note for note into the later setting, D636. The key is different, pianistic details have been changed and the note values halved, but in essence the music is the same until the end of the song. According to the musicologist Bertha Schnapper in her *Die Gesänge des jungen Schubert*, the young composer was using a traditional march tune in this section, but even if this is so it is a borrowing that has stood the test of time. The music is both bracing and, in its optimism and strength, typical of the call to spiritual arms that lies at the heart of many of Schubert's Schiller songs. (*See also* the Senn setting *Selige Welt* D743.)

Autograph:	Staatsbibliothek Preussischer Kulturbesitz, Berlin (first draft)
First edition:	Published as No. 1 of *Sechs bisher ungedrückte Lieder* by Wilhelm Müller, Berlin in 1868 (P413)
Subsequent editions:	Not in Peters; AGA XX 9: Vol. 1/62; NSA IV: Vol. 2b/241; Bärenreiter: Vol. 2/200
Bibliography:	Capell 1928, p. 81
	Fischer-Dieskau 1977, p. 141
	Schnapper 1937, pp. 119–20
Discography and timing:	Fischer-Dieskau I 1[6] 4'11
	Hyperion I 16[14]
	Hyperion II 2[19] 4'26 Thomas Allen

← *Die Schatten* D50   *Verklärung* D59 →

SEHNSUCHT (II)   Longing
(SCHILLER) OP. 39, **D636** [H461]

The song exists in three versions, the third of which is discussed below:
(1) Beginning? of 1821; (2) Date unknown; (3) Appeared in 1826

(1)	'Ziemlich geschwind'	B minor	¢	[111 bars]
(2)	'Nicht zu schnell'	B minor	¢	[119 bars]

(3)   B minor

(119 bars)

See previous entry for poem and translation

FRIEDRICH VON SCHILLER (1759–1805); poem written in 1802

This is the forty-first of Schubert's forty-four Schiller solo settings (1811–24). See the poet's biography for a chronological list of all the Schiller settings.

This is Schubert's second setting, composed some eight years after the first, although we are not entirely certain about the date (the Schubert scholar Paul Mies dated it as early as 1817). However, we do know that the song was ready to be performed on 8 February 1821 at a concert for the Musikverein, sung by Josef Götz (qv SINGERS). As if it were music composed for a special occasion this mini-cantata has the stylized trappings and grandeur of a set piece within an imaginary opera. It may also seem somewhat formulaic and old-fashioned, but it was an augury of the work's future popularity with singers that the composer prepared another fair copy for the bass, Adalbert Rotter – almost certainly at Rotter's request. The version for Götz was written in the treble clef (first version, NSA Vol. 2b p. 251) and that for Rotter (second version, NSA Vol 2b p. 258) in the bass clef. When Schubert came to publish the song in February 1826 (third version, Vol 2a p. 165) he chose the treble clef – perhaps not at the publisher's insistence, as Mandyczewski suggests, but because he had not ruled out a performance of the work by a female singer. Indeed, the song was performed in public by Josefine Fröhlich in January 1825 at the Musikverein, and by Louise Weiss at the same venue two years later. In the following century it was a favourite song of Dame Janet Baker who used to transpose it up into C minor.

Verse 1: This setting is a quintessential example of Schubert's musical response to a fine Schiller text. This is also to say that there is some invocation of the spirit of Beethoven – direct, manly and no-nonsense, and lyrical in a distinctively sinewy way. Six bars of introduction for the piano alone set the scene perfectly: a two-bar motif aspiring upwards and falling back in bb. 1–2, then repeating the pattern in a higher sequence. After this there are an extra two bars that redirect the ear, via the dominant, to the home key of B minor for the singer's first impassioned 'Ach'. The accompaniment, like some impatient steed, paws the ground in quavers that alternate between the hands, supporting a vocal line that is determined and moderately impassioned in the mid-stave. The rise in semitones for 'Könnt ich doch den Ausgang finden' (bb. 12–13) betokens the poet trying to find an exit while shaking free from his shackles. The first four lines of the opening strophe unfold between bb. 7 and 18 when the music modulates into G major with a change of key signature – this is the 'Ausgang' for which the singer longs, even if it is only imaginary. Here the vocal line is introduced by a two-bar motif that is built around the notes of a simple G major arpeggio in a musical phrase that Beethoven might have used. In comparison with Schubert's usual inventiveness, this courtly pattern of notes borders on banality, but it is somehow saved by the freshness and intensity of its context. The vocal line is naive, and deliberately so – the beauty of the hills, ever youthful and green, is described as if to wide-eyed children. At b. 25 the line 'Hätt' ich Schwingen' generates a certain amount of tension that is underpinned by two bars of A^7 harmony, as if the voice were attempting lift-off, and not quite succeeding in getting the foothold in D major that would enable this.

Verse 2: At b. 22 there is a change to the two flats of B flat major, and the sudden switch from G major (in a more ethereal pianistic texture, higher in the stave) is perfect for an aural change of scenery. The music of the spheres ('Harmonien hör' ich klingen') resounds prettily – if rather conventionally – in this passage. There is scarcely anything here in terms of musical vocabulary that might not have been composed by Haydn twenty years earlier – although the cheeky little 'wind motif' in the piano from b. 36 announces the future world of Schubert's *West-östlicher Divan* settings, and the song *Geheimes* D719. A melismatic mention of 'Balsam' (b. 42) shifts the music into F major – the dominant of this subsection in B flat major. After this, a rather *pomposo* mention of 'Gold'ne Früchte' in an effulgently voiced A flat major (b. 44) opens a passage that leads the ear through winding pathways to the flowering orchard where winter is unknown. By b. 52 this has reached E flat major via G minor. After this, a tacked-on bar with an F^7 chord (b. 57) enables a return to the little silvery dotted rhythm figure in B flat major – a fanfare of a gentle kind – that we first encountered at the beginning of Strophe 2 (b. 33).

Verse 3: The first half of Strophe 3 is given over to music we have already heard, thus bb. 58–68 are an exact musical repeat of bb. 33–43, and the architectural shape of the whole is rendered stronger by this interweaving of material. In a brilliant piece of musical planning, Schubert engineers things so that the 'Geheimes' motif (*see* above) for the 'gentle breezes' mentioned in b. 40 does equal service for the 'air on those hills' in b. 64. In both cases the piano figuration suggests the gentle scuffing of tiny gusts of wind trying time and again to lift leaves up into the air, and only partly succeeding. These breezes are clearly meant to be bearers of fragrances rather than harbingers of storms. At b. 69 F major darkens into F minor and at b. 70, amidst D^7 oscillations, we suddenly find ourselves in the wild and watery world of *Der Taucher* D77, perhaps Schubert's most famous extended Schiller ballad. During three bars (bb. 70–72) of stormy interlude, the pianist's left hand is pressed into service to simulate a succession of breakers with different bass notes that launch themselves at the rocky wall of semiquavers in the upper stave. From b. 73 the key of G minor is established for five bars – the left hand in staccato quavers chiming in striding tenths with the busy semiquavers of the right. After this, the bottom drops out of the riverbed: G in the bass descends to G flat (b. 78) and thence to F (b. 79), F flat (b. 80), E flat (b. 81), D flat (b. 82), C flat (b. 83). The result is a kind of musical Hokusai wave where the unmanned boat is storm-tossed on a watery cauldron of shifting harmonies. The C flat, the third degree of the scale of A flat minor, changes enharmonically to B natural, and suddenly we discover we have reached B major – conveniently the dominant of the key of E major that is announced by the new key signature in four sharps.

Verse 4: The final strophe is marked 'Schnell' and Schubert, most unusually, returns to the melody that he had used for these words in D52. There is no precedent for this selective repetition in other songs where the different settings are years apart. In the earlier work the marking is simply 'Più allegro', the key is F major, not E major, and the music is notated in double the note values that we encounter here. In other respects the music is very much the same. Whether or not this march derives from a popular march, as has been suggested (*see* commentary for D52 above), it clearly still fitted the bill for Schiller's words as far as the older Schubert was concerned. In the later song the coda is more extensively – and effectively – worked out, particularly in terms of the pianistic flourishes of the short and energetic postlude. After declaiming to the skies his or her lesson in idealistic optimism ('You must trust, and you must dare'), the singer sweeps off the stage in a blaze of glory. There has been impressive entrance music at the beginning of the song, and this little cantata is capped by an equally exciting coda; it only lacks the conventional slower movement that is common in works of this kind. The abiding impression is of music expertly crafted and excitingly made, hammered and chiselled out of the marble of Schiller's edifying genius. But while the stormy gusts described by the poet are powerful enough, they are dutifully, rather than lovingly, enacted in musical terms by the composer and in the song as a whole, governed by the classical age at the expense of the Romantic, we miss the breath of ordinary humanity and ineffable truth with which Schubert is capable of animating his greatest vocal works. It is, of course, a marvellous song and it might seem unfair to split hairs like this. It might also be unfair, if true, to remark that in admiring Schiller's influence on this music we are aware of the lack of an equivalent warmth and individuality that animates the Goethe settings.

Autograph:	British Library, London (fragment; first version)
	Library of Congress, Washington (fair copy for A. Rotter; second version)
Publication:	First published as part of the NSA in 1975 (P763; first version)
	First published as part of the AGA in 1895 (P683; second version)
	First published as Op. 39 by A. Pennauer, Vienna in February 1826 (P86; third version)
First known performance:	8 February 1821, *Abend-Unterhaltung* of the Gesellschaft der Musikfreunde at the Musikverein, Vienna. Soloist: Josef Götz (see Waidelich/Hilmar Dokumente I No. 70 for full concert programme)
Publication reviews:	*Allgemeine musikalische Zeitung* (Leipzig), No. 29 (19 July 1826), col. 480 [Waidelich/Hilmar Dokumente I No. 397; Deutsch Doc. Biog. No. 680]
	Musikalische Eilpost (Weimar), Vol. 1 No. 17 (1826), p. 133 [Waidelich/Hilmar Dokumente I No. 434; Deutsch Doc. Biog. No. 699]
Subsequent editions:	Peters: Vol. 2/86; AGA XX 357a & b: Vol. 6/29; NSA IV: Vol. 2a/165; Bärenreiter: Vol. 2/53
Bibliography:	Capell 1928, p. 157
	Einstein 1951, p. 190
	Fischer-Dieskau 1977, p. 141
Further settings:	Ferdinand Ries (1784–1838) *Sehnsucht* Op. 35 no. 4 (1811)
	Benedict Randhartinger (1802–1893) *Sehnsucht* [date unknown]
Discography and timing:	Fischer-Dieskau II 2^{17} 4'20
	Hyperion I 1^{19}
	Hyperion II 24^3 4'29 Janet Baker

← *Im Walde* D708   *Die gefangenen Sänger* D712 →

SEHNSUCHT (Was zieht mir das Herz so?) Longing
(GOETHE) **D123** [H54]
G major   3 December 1814

Colorado College Library
Colorado Springs, Colorado

(69 bars)

Was zieht mir das Herz so?	What is it that tugs at my heart so?
Was zieht mich hinaus?	What lures me outside,
Und windet und schraubt mich	Twisting and wrenching me
Aus Zimmer und Haus?	Out of my room and my home?
Wie dort sich die Wolken	Look how the clouds over there
Am Felsen verziehn,[1]	Are being distorted by the rocks.
Da möcht ich hinüber,	I would like to cross over there,
Da möcht ich wohl hin!	I would like to go there!
Nun wiegt sich der Raben	Now the ravens hover
Geselliger Flug;	In gregarious flight;
Ich mische mich drunter	I join them
Und folge dem Zug.	And follow their course.
Und Berg und Gemäuer	We fly above mountains
Umfittigen wir,	And ruins;
Sie weilet da drunten,	She dwells below;
Ich spähe nach ihr.	I look out for her.
Da kommt sie und wandelt;	There she comes, strolling along;
Ich eile sobald,	I immediately hasten,
Ein singender Vogel,	Like a singing bird,
Im buschigten Wald.[2]	To the bushy wood.
Sie weilet und horchet	She lingers and listens,
Und lächelt mit sich:	Smiling to herself:
'Er singet so lieblich	'He sings so charmingly,
Und singt es an mich.'	And sings to me!'
Die scheidende Sonne	The departing sun
Vergüldet die Höh'n,[3]	Gilds the hills;
Die sinnende Schöne	The musing beauty
Sie lässt es geschehen.[4]	Does not heed it.
Sie wandelt am Bache	She strolls by the brook,
Die Wiesen entlang,	Through the meadows;
Und finster und finstrer	Darker and darker
Umschlingt sich der Gang.	Grows the winding path.
Auf einmal erschein' ich,	Suddenly I appear,
Ein blinkender Stern.	A shining star.

[1] Goethe writes (*Gedichte*, Wien, 1810) '*Um* Felsen verziehn'.
[2] Goethe writes (*Gedichte*, Wien, 1810) '*Zum* buschigten Wald'.
[3] Goethe writes (*Gedichte*, Wien, 1810) '*Verguldet* die Höh'n (without umlaut).
[4] Goethe writes (*Gedichte*, Wien, 1810) 'Sie lässt es *geschehn*'.

'Was glänzet da droben?	'What is that sparkling up there,
So nah und so fern?'	So near and yet so far?'
Und hast du mit Staunen	And when, with astonishment,
Das Leuchten erblickt;	You catch sight of its light,
Ich lieg dir zu Füssen,	I shall lie at your feet.
Da bin ich beglückt!	There I shall be contented!

JOHANN WOLFGANG VON GOETHE (1749–1832); poem written before 18 December 1802

This is the fifth of Schubert's seventy-five Goethe solo settings (1814–26). See the poet's biography for a chronological list of all the Goethe settings.

A lesser composer, following *Gretchen am Spinnrade* D118, would have attempted other songs in that vein, as if he were mining a seam of gold. But with Schubert's response to texts, there is never a formula; even the name Goethe was no 'Open, Sesame' to a stockpile of flawless jewels. Schubert had found the means to weave Gretchen, her predicament and her spinning wheel into a seamless unity but with other poems he was sometimes less lucky. His failures are ever honourable (to call them failures at all is only to judge them by the standards of his acknowledged masterpieces) and it is always interesting to see what he was aiming at as, in Capell's words, 'he hesitated, he experimented, he fumbled'.

Goethe himself (and the whole North German school of song composers) was critical of those musicians who allowed their musical fancies to detract from the attention due to the poems. This setting is a demonstration of what Goethe feared most about music's power to submerge his lyrics.

Schubert made a recitative out of Matthisson's *Trost. An Elisa* D97 and few today would bemoan the fact that stilted classical metre has been swept aside in favour of 'staging' the poem effectively. But when the lively, breathless, culminative impact of Goethe's anapaestic rhythm for *Sehnsucht* is vitiated by Schubert's stop-go alternation between recitative, aria and piano interlude, including twelve quick excursions to other keys, there is valid cause for complaint. Beethoven came closer in his setting of 1810 (Op. 83 no. 2), and Schubert seems to have gone to great lengths to try something different. It may be that he simply found the internal rhythm of the poem too relentless for comfortable musical expression and was doing his best to take some of the wind out of its sails; it has a passionate bluster that fits a Beethovenian mindset more than a Schubertian one.

It cannot be denied that some of Schubert's episodes within the setting are charmingly done: the swift flight of the ravens in Verse 2 (the sudden 'Ziemlich geschwind' in b. 10) and the music for the flowing brook in Verse 4 (from b. 44) give some intimation of how the song may have been set as an enchanting moto perpetuo. The interlude for the singing bird (Verse 3, 'Lieblich' from b. 26) is in some ways admirable (the poem after all mentions lingering and listening, and we are made to do both), but its music-box effect adds an arch touch of eighteenth-century *bergerette* to what is in fact a tempestuously Romantic poem. (We think of the minstrel's equally classical aria comparing himself to the singing bird in *Der Sänger* D149, composed a few months later.) The interlude for the setting sun – 'Ziemlich langsam' from b. 36 (an image better and more economically handled in *Adelaide* D95) – kills stone-dead any culminative rhythmic impetus the piece may have had; yet when taking this passage on its own merits, the poet's shining star reverberates in empty space with the simplest and most telling of musical means. Also excellent is the depiction of astonishment in the last verse: the 'Langsam' in ⅜ from b. 58 ('Und hast du mit Staunen') is in fact a fragment of a slow waltz, and a clever means of returning to the rumbustious tempo that closes the piece as the poet throws himself at his beloved's feet (a precipitous downward scale in the postlude in bb. 66–7). Goethe's poem, with its onrushing metrical sweep, is weighed down with rather too much fussy musical detail. Nevertheless, the composer was pleased enough with the song to consider letting Goethe see it. It was included in the second album assembled for the poet (which was never sent to Weimar).

Autograph:	Wienbibliothek im Rathaus, Vienna (first draft and fair copy)
First edition:	Published as Book 37 no. 2 of the *Nachlass* by Diabelli, Vienna in June 1842 (P347)
Subsequent editions:	Peters: Vol. 6/10; AGA XX 35: Vol. 1/206; NSA IV: Vol. 7/60; Bärenreiter: Vol. 6/6
Bibliography:	Capell 1928, pp. 43 & 69
	Fischer-Dieskau 1977, p. 37
Further settings:	Ludwig van Beethoven (1770–1827) *Sehnsucht* Op. 83 no. 2 (1810)
Discography and timing:	Fischer-Dieskau I 2[16] 3'00
	Hyperion I 12[18]
	Hyperion II 4[10] 3'17 Adrian Thompson

← *Ammenlied* D122   *Am See* D124 →

SEHNSUCHT   Longing
(Mignon) (I)
in 2 versions ('Nur wer die Sehnsucht kennt')
(GOETHE) **D310** [H190 & H190A]

(1)   A♭ major   18 October 1815

(35 bars)

(2)   F major   18 October 1815

(39 bars)

Nur wer die Sehnsucht kennt	Only he who knows longing
Weiss, was ich leide!	Knows what I suffer.
Allein und abgetrennt	Alone, cut off
Von aller Freude,	From all joy,
Seh' ich an's Firmament	I gaze at the firmament
Nach jener Seite.	In that direction
Ach! der mich liebt und kennt	Ah, he who loves and knows me
Ist in der Weite.	Is far away.
Es schwindelt mir, es brennt	I feel giddy,
Mein Eingeweide.	My vitals are aflame.
Nur wer die Sehnsucht kennt	Only he who knows longing
Weiss, was ich leide!	Knows what I suffer.

JOHANN WOLFGANG VON GOETHE (1749–1832); poem written in June 1785

These are the thirtieth and thirty-first of Schubert's seventy-five Goethe solo settings (1814–26).
See the poet's biography for a chronological list of all the Goethe settings.

This poem has always been irresistible to composers. From the poet's own circle Reichardt and Zelter set it; Beethoven attempted it no fewer than four times in 1807–8, and both Kreutzer and Loewe found music for it (the latter as early as 1816–18, more or less contemporary with Schubert's earlier excursions into *Wilhelm Meister*). In later years it was tackled by Schumann, Tchaikovsky and Wolf, whose setting shows Mignon at perhaps her most unhinged. Goethe describes his text as a duet, the words softly shared by Mignon and the Harper. Schubert followed this direction in one setting (D877/1), as did both Reichardt and Zelter.

There is no text on which Schubert worked harder to find a definitive musical solution. Innumerable composers have grappled with this elusive poem. Schubert's struggles are heroic and deeply involved, as if he identified strongly with Mignon's plight: her sufferings, like his, were private ones, a burden of woe unshared. His definitive A minor setting in 1826 (D877/4) was in a way the simplest, refined down to the absolute essentials. After the setting composed in one day discussed here (almost two settings, so widely do the two versions diverge in places) the composer tried twice again in 1816, and then spent a decade thinking how best to catch the spirit of the girl's grief in music before composing D877/4, as well as the magnificent duet for soprano and tenor, D877/1 (*see* GESANGE AUS WILHELM MEISTER).

FIRST VERSION (A flat major):

The young composer seems over-conscious of the celebrity of the lyric and ties himself up in knots setting it to music. There is no introduction and the rather static melody in A flat with which the song begins is recapitulated in b. 20. Even by Schubert's standards six changes of key signature, often mid-bar, within thirty-six bars (A flat to E and back, and then to B minor via a kaleidoscopic series of enharmonic modulations) is excessive. This is an early example of the composer's predilection in the key of A flat for settling on the flattened third degree of the scale, i.e. C flat major here disguised as B major – no doubt his instinctive musical reaction to Mignon's restlessness and unhappiness. The lines 'Es schwindelt mir, es brennt / Mein Eingeweide' at the heart of the poem present a problem. The words are over too quickly for Schubert to make much of them. It is probable that a deeper rereading of the poem alerted him to their importance, and this seems to have been the main reason that he returned to the text on the same day. The six-bar piano postlude is eloquent and heartfelt, if a little bit over-classical for the mood of the lyric as a whole.

SECOND VERSION (F major):

In this song Schubert places the voice in a less hysterical and more reflective tessitura. Much of the first section is merely a transposition of the first version, but he does away with any change of key signature in the interests of unity of thought. Tremolandi, starting in A flat minor (from b. 16) are used to heighten the emotional temperature of the difficult words beginning 'Es schwindelt mir': the singer is pushed down into chest voice and repeats the words 'es brennt / Mein Eingeweide' (bb. 18–19, then 19–20) which gives more time for the passage to make an effect, although it is still not really satisfactory. The recapitulation of the main melody is set up by a piano interlude where bare oscillating demisemiquavers change into triplets; underneath these a line of chromatically ascending left-hand quavers ushers in the voice, now accompanied in triplets, in the home key of F major. This gives the vocal line an ornate Italianate sweep that suggests cantilena (Mignon is, after all, Italian). This is really an ornamented variant, rather than a repeat, of the opening material; in fact the emotional embroidery of Mignon's line now bears little resemblance to the beginning of the song.

A rather wild excursion into A flat minor returns via F minor to F major in time for the postlude. This passage is energized, and given pathos, by throbbing triplets, although the music seems rather anodyne in comparison to the wild flights of vocal fancy in the immediately preceding bars. The effect is one of 'work in progress' with this lyric, as indeed was the case. Nevertheless, the composer liked this second attempt well enough to include it in the second album of songs assembled for Goethe which, in the end, was never sent to Weimar.

For a complete list of songs relating to *Wilhelm Meister*, see MIGNON LIEDER and HARFNER-LIEDER. *See also* WILHELM MEISTERS LEHRJAHRE.

Autographs:	In private possession (first version)
	Österreichische Nationalbibliothek, Vienna (second version)
Publication:	First published as part of the AGA in 1895 (P596; first version)
	First published as part of the AGA in 1895 (P597; second version)
Subsequent editions:	Not in Peters; AGA XX 158a & b: Vol. 3/126 & 128; NSA IV: Vol. 3b/218 & 220; Bärenreiter: Vol. 2/220 & 222
Discography and timing:	Fischer-Dieskau —
	Hyperion I 7^{23} & 7^{24} 2'23
	Hyperion II 11^1 & 11^2 2'29 Elly Ameling

←— *Das gestörte Glück* D309   *Hektors Abschied* D312 —→

SEHNSUCHT (Mignon) (II)   Longing
('Nur wer die Sehnsucht kennt')
(GOETHE) **D359** [H211]
D minor   1816

(45 bars)

See previous entry for poem and translation

Johann Wolfgang von Goethe (1749–1832); poem written in June 1785

This is the thirty-seventh of Schubert's seventy-five Goethe solo settings (1814–26). See the poet's biography for a chronological list of all the Goethe settings.

Schubert set this poem no fewer than six times. The first setting, D310, exists in two versions (A flat major and F major) and dates from 18 October 1815. For this second setting in D minor the composer has not yet settled on the final tonality for Mignon, A minor. This was already a feature of his Harper songs of 1816 (and the relationship of Mignon and the Harper as father and daughter makes it appropriate that they should share the DNA of tonality) but by now we can recognize other features of his final thoughts as if they are gradually materializing before our ears. The time signature of 𝄴 makes its first appearance; flowing triplets support most of the vocal line; the immobile staccato chords that support the line 'Ach! der mich liebt und kennt' (from b. 16) are similar to those in the final setting, D877/4; the section beginning 'Es schwindelt mir' (b. 24) is supported by excited demisemiquavers, and the phrase 'es brennt / Mein Einge- weide' is repeated. We can certainly see the outline of the song we know so well taking shape strongly in the composer's mind (*see* Gesänge Aus Wilhelm Meister). Indeed, at the reprise of 'Nur wer die Sehnsucht kennt', Schubert, in b. 31, hits on the exact rhythm (with a two-semiquaver shudder on 'Sehn<u>su</u>cht') which he was definitively to use ten years later.

Despite the impression of a work in transition, this setting is effective and moving in its own right. The tessitura is much higher than D877/4 so the effect is more operatic, less introverted. In her two 1816 manifestations (*see also* D481) Mignon takes centre stage in a way that is perhaps contrary to her waif-like character. A beautiful touch, unique to this setting, is the sequential repeat of the words beginning 'Ach! der mich liebt und kennt', the first phrase bb. 17–20 in C major, the second, bb. 21–4, most affectingly in B major. These words are not repeated in any of the other solo songs, only the duet setting. This semitone slip downwards is a mournful dislocation that implies distance, admirably serving the sense of the words 'in der Weite.'

For a complete list of songs relating to *Wilhelm Meister*, see Mignon Lieder and Harfner-lieder. *See also* Wilhelm Meisters Lehrjahre.

Autograph:	Missing or lost
First edition:	Published as No. 13 of *Neueste Folge nachgelassener Lieder und Gesänge* by J. P. Gotthard, Vienna in 1872 (P439)
Subsequent editions:	Not in Peters; AGA XX 260: Vol. 4/200; NSA IV: Vol. 3b/222; Bärenreiter: Vol. 2/224
Discography and timing:	Fischer-Dieskau —
	Hyperion I 24[16]
	Hyperion II 12[6] 2'18 Christine Schäfer

← *Die Nacht* D358   *Hoffnung* D295 →

~∾~∾~∾~∾~∾~

SEHNSUCHT (Mignon) (III)   Longing
('Nur wer die Sehnsucht kennt')
(Goethe) **D481** [H298]
A minor   September 1816

Nur   wer die   Sehn - sucht kennt,   weiss,___ was ich__ lei - de,

(45 bars)

See Sehnsucht (I) D310 *for poem and translation*

JOHANN WOLFGANG VON GOETHE (1749–1832); poem written in June 1785

This is the forty-second of Schubert's seventy-five Goethe solo settings (1814–26). See the poet's biography for a chronological list of all the Goethe settings.

This must surely have been designed as a companion piece for the Harper's song D478/2 (the 'Etwas geschwind' version of *Wer nie sein Brot mit Tränen ass*). It shares both the key (A minor) and time signature (²⁄₄) with that song, as well as the relentless semiquavers in the accompaniment that provide both songs with impetus and energy. Perhaps Schubert had it in mind in 1816 to integrate Mignon's songs into a *Wilhelm Meister* cycle and – as was to be the case with the *Gesänge des Harfners* published as Op. 12 in 1822 – the tonality of A minor was to be the unifying key. What the song lacks is a long, spun vocal line that is memorable enough to engage our emotions. There is a great deal of harmonic activity and ingenuity, and Mignon's emotions brush the borders of many keys (the accompaniment bristles with sharps and flats); but all this frenetic activity merely dissipates the intensity of the lyric which has at its heart a core of simplicity and world-weary resignation. The recapitulation of the tune for the last two lines of the lyric (which we hear three times in both D359 and D481) is accompanied by sextuplets. Schubert could not resist his favourite A minor/A major axis and much of this section (from b. 24) is ambivalently poised between the two. Towards the end there is an unequivocal modulation into A major for the piano's postlude (from b. 38) which undulates and sighs in ravishing manner, as if Mignon accepts her fate with a gentle smile shining through tears. This piano writing is surely the most beautiful and original feature of the setting.

    This third setting of Mignon's lyric seems further from the final setting (D877/4, *see* GESANGE AUS WILHELM MEISTER) than the second D359 (also dated 1816, although we do not know in which month) – this despite the fact that D359 is in D minor rather than A minor. It is easy to see why Mandyczewski in the AGA ordered them differently from Deutsch, even if mistakenly. *See* SEHNSUCHT (Mignon) (I) (II) and (IV).

Autograph: Conservatoire collection, Bibliothèque Nationale, Paris
First edition: Published as part of the AGA in 1895 (P656)
Subsequent editions: Not in Peters; AGA XX 259: Vol. 4/198; NSA IV: Vol. 3b/224;
                          Bärenreiter: Vol. 2/226
Discography and timing: Fischer-Dieskau   —
                          Hyperion I 24[19]
                          Hyperion II 15[25]   2'00   Christine Schäfer

←— *Mignon (So lasst mich scheinen)* D469   *Liedesend* D473 —→

SEHNSUCHT (Mignon) (IV)
('Nur wer die Sehnsucht kennt')
(GOETHE) **D656** [H424+]
B minor – E major   April 1819

Longing   Quintet, TTBBB
(Unaccompanied)

(63 bars)

See Sehnsucht (I) D310 *for poem and translation*

JOHANN WOLFGANG VON GOETHE (1749–1832); poem written in June 1785

Schubert's unaccompanied male choruses do not normally lie within the scope of this book, but an exception has been made in this case because it was the only one of six settings of this poem that Schubert placed outside the ambit of the piano-accompanied repertoire. For the same reason this vocal quintet for two tenors and three basses was recorded for the Hyperion Edition.

The assignation of Mignon's fragile and feminine text to five hearty male voices may seem bizarre, but this chorus is a work of the composer's maturity and he understood that the lyric had a universal significance outside its dramatic context in Goethe's *Wilhelm Meister*. Thinking about the lines where Mignon gazes into the firmament, the composer places her outside her normal milieu of the drawing room in this setting. An unaccompanied chorus resonates more freely and wildly than a vocal line grounded by the piano (a delicate instrument – even more so in Schubert's time – which has to be kept indoors for the sake of its health). A chorus can be sung in the mountains, or under the stars; the message of Mignon's longing and loneliness can be sung to the moon or flung into the firmament – 'in die Weite' (to modify Goethe slightly with a change of case from dative to accusative) even though there is no response beyond the dying echo.

It is clear that Schubert has thought a great deal about this sumptuous setting. It is his only male chorus in five parts: the key is E major and the first tenor line is quite demandingly high while the second bass line goes down to low Es. There is a certain contrapuntal inter-reaction between the tenors and basses, particularly at 'Ach! der mich liebt und kennt' (from b. 12) where different parts of the chorus illustrate the idea of two people separated by a chasm (in this case different clefs) attempting to communicate. The setting of 'Weite' (marked fortissimo with a diminuendo to piano, bb. 19–21) is taxing but highly effective. At 'Es schwindelt mir' (from the upbeat to b. 22) there is a daring canonic effect of great modernity, the entire twelve-bar passage marked pianissimo. At b. 32 Schubert recapitulates the first eight lines of the poem, once again emphasizing the broad idea of gazing into the firmament. He then repeats 'Nur wer die Sehnsucht kennt / Weiss, was ich leide!' no fewer than four times, each set differently with a new emotional inflection, rising to a high and anguished crescendo for the third time, and then dying with great pianissimo pathos at the final bars. This is a beautifully crafted piece of work with the kind of spatial grandeur denied to a single voice with piano; but one is nevertheless reminded that this composer needed the possibilities of the lone individual voice pitting itself against the piano to work his most profound vocal magic.

For a complete list of songs relating to *Wilhelm Meister, see* Mignon Lieder and Harfner-
lieder. *See also* Wilhelm Meisters Lehrjahre.

Autograph:	Missing or lost
First edition:	Published as Heft (Vol.) 33 of *Chöre von Franz Schubert mit und ohne Begleitung* by Friedrich Schreiber (Spina's successor), Vienna in 1867
First known performance:	5 January 1838, Vienna, under the direction of Johann Herbeck
Subsequent editions:	AGA XVI 35: p. 185; NSA III: Vol. 4
Bibliography:	Capell 1928, pp. 219–20
	Einstein 1951, pp. 306–7
Discography and timing:	Hyperion I 24[20] 3'11 The London Schubert Chorale
	Hyperion II 21[20] (dir. Stephen Layton)

← *Der Jüngling am Bache* D638   *Geistliches Lied ('Marie')* D658 →

SEHNSUCHT   Longing

(Mayrhofer) Op. 8 no. 2, **D516** [H341]
C major – G major   Spring 1817?

(42 bars)

Der Lerche wolkennahe Lieder	The larks' songs up near the clouds
Erschmettern zu des Winters Flucht,	Ring out as winter flees;
Die Erde hüllt in Samt die Glieder,	The earth wraps her limbs in velvet,
Und Blüten bilden rote Frucht.	And red fruit forms from the blossoms.
Nur du, o sturmbewegte Seele,	You alone, storm-tossed soul,
Nur du bist blütenlos, in dich gekehrt,	Do not flower; turned in on yourself,
Und wirst in goldner Frühlingshelle	You are consumed by deep longing
Von tiefer Sehnsucht aufgezehrt.	Amid spring's golden radiance.
Nie wird, was du verlangst, entkeimen	What you crave will never burgeon
Dem Boden, Idealen fremd;	From this earth, alien to ideals,
Der trotzig deinen schönsten Träumen	Which defiantly opposes its raw strength
Die rohe Kraft entgegenstemmt.[1]	To your fairest dreams.
Du ringst dich matt mit seiner Härte,	You grow weary struggling with its harshness,
Vom Wunsche heftiger entbrannt:	Ever more inflamed by the desire
Mit Kranichen ein strebender Gefährte,[2]	To journey to a kinder land,
Zu wandern in ein milder Land.	As aspiring companion to the cranes.

[1] Mayrhofer writes (*Gedichte*, 1824) 'Die *rauhe* Kraft entgegenstemmt'. For an explanation of the background to these alternative Mayrhofer readings see Editorial Note at the beginning of Johann Mayrhofer.
[2] In a misprint of the AGA, the positive meaning of 'strebender' (aspiring) is rendered negative by 'sterbender' (dying).

JOHANN MAYRHOFER (1787–1836)

This is the fifteenth of Schubert's forty-seven Mayrhofer solo settings (1814–24). See the poet's biography for a chronological list of all the Mayrhofer settings.

This song of spring – one of the finest of the Mayrhofer settings, and yet one of the least performed – seems much influenced by the Italian style, at least in the beginning. It is as if the composer can imagine the birds longing for warmer climes 'wo die Zitronen blühn' (in Mignon's words) and disporting themselves in the musical style of the land to which they aspire. The left-hand accompaniment reminds us of another song of longing to escape to pastures new, *Drang in die Ferne* D770; similar long leaps between the bass notes on the beat and the accompanying pianistic vamp suggest the dance of life and the relentless drive of natural forces beyond one's control. The right-hand melody plunges and dips as if in flight, and the vocal line follows suit with a similar display of aerobatic exuberance. Trills in the piano part add to an impression of a pleasantly showy song, yet not a particularly Schubertian one, despite the grace of the melody built around chords of the tonic and dominant seventh. This is perhaps what Einstein means when he writes that the song begins in an 'almost pedantic and superficial style'. However, the modulation into A flat on the mention of the word 'Samt' (velvet) in b. 10 is a nice touch, as is the way in which the vocal line flowers in melismatic tendrils before our ears on 'Blüten bilden rote Frucht' (bb. 12–13).

The fifth to eighth lines of the poem are another matter (in fact each quatrain in this song, a poem of two verses treated as four musical verses, has a different atmosphere appropriate to the words). Without warning A flat major yields to E major on 'Nur *du*, o sturmbewegte Seele' (b. 14) and there is a stentorian, even haranguing tone that seems to look the listener straight in the eye, as if the accusation of barrenness were being made in a court of law. Such disparities among the moods of the four sections probably explain why most commentators find a certain lack of conviction in this setting, although Einstein, who was an expert on the Italian madrigal, considers the contrast between the unselfconscious awakening of nature in the first verse and the private tragedy of the individual of the second to be 'in the manner of Petrarch'. He is reminded of Monteverdi's setting of that poet in the five-part madrigal *Zefiro torna* that 'paints the same contrast'. John Reed points out that the declamatory nature of the Schober setting *Todesmusik* D758 here comes to mind, and it is true that Robert Holl, that most informed of Schubert singers, likes to include both these rare songs in the same recital. In complete contrast to the comfortable setting of 'Blüten bilden rote Frucht' a few moments earlier, where singer and pianist are happily entwined, the voice on 'Nur du bist blütenlos' sits perilous and lonely, high on the stave (bb. 15–17), while the piano growls in sulky triplets far away in a deeper register.

The third quatrain (with a change to two sharps at b. 24) is in the manner of *Der Unglückliche* D713 (cf. the passage in that song beginning 'Versenke dich in deines Kummers Tiefen'), a work in which a wall of persistently repeated triplets make their point with finger-jabbing urgency, as if they represent an edict of fate that the accused finds impossible to reverse. Another song in which this same triplet motif can be heard is the celebrated *Der Wanderer* D489 that was composed six months earlier at the most. This is all music of outcasts. The 'rohe Kraft' (raw strength) of the philistine (bb. 30–33) prompts sforzato chords – one of the very rare occasions, it seems, when Schubert actually wants a harsh or ugly sound from the piano. The poet is trapped in a living hell (in this verse the atmosphere is claustrophobic as if the voice is unable to find a way out of the chromatic maze) and one is reminded of similar bursts of rough sound in *Gruppe aus dem Tartarus* D583, also from 1817.

For the final four lines of the poem an exit is found, as unexpected as it is unannounced. After flying frantically in every direction searching for a way out of a building, it is as if the bird suddenly finds a chink through which it can escape into the aether. This is the effect of a sudden change to G major at the double bar line on b. 34; on one side of this lies prison, on the other freedom. What is extraordinary is the way in which Schubert somehow makes it clear in the dreamlike tone of the music (via a hugely extended dominant pedal, bb. 33–9) that it is only in the imagination that the singer's tortured soul is allowed to escape to be with the cranes. In this music, blissfully happy, but also removed from reality, the vocal line suddenly finds itself in smooth flight, unexpectedly reunited with its piano mate which joins it in ecstatic convoy, shadowing it in lovingly consonant thirds and sixths. The three bars of postlude are as pithy a picture as we could possibly have of the crane taking wing (less agile than the lark ascending – the composer here finds ideal music for birds of a different size). It is an apotheosis worthy of Ganymede, as well as Schubert's slightly later response to the idea of that boy's journey heavenward. Political alienation alone seldom produces words of such heartache and it is hard not to feel that the poet is making a veiled statement about the loneliness and lack of flowering in his own sexuality. The question remains open as to whether Schubert himself is merely empathetic to the poet's viewpoint, that of a close friend, or whether the imagery tells something of his own story.

There is a fascinating sixteen-bar sketch for Mayrhofer's *Sehnsucht* printed in the NSA (Volume 1b, p. 290) which shows the composer's way of working on a song of this kind, making it clear that the vocal line was composed before any of the accompaniment's details. Two bars of right-hand introduction (later discarded) use a figuration that is similar to *Der Schäfer und der Reiter* D517, an exactly contemporary song. The accompaniment as Schubert eventually created it is the result of later thought and was obviously written out once the vocal line had been completed.

Autograph:	Wienbibliothek im Rathaus, Vienna (fair copy)
First edition:	Published as Op. 8 no. 2 by Cappi & Diabelli, Vienna in May 1822 (P22)
Dedicatee:	Johann Karl Grafen Esterházy von Galántha
Subsequent editions:	Peters: Vol. 2/22; AGA XX 386: Vol. 6/130; NSA IV: Vol. 1a/73; Bärenreiter: Vol. 1/60
Bibliography:	Einstein 1951, pp. 193–4
	Fischer-Dieskau 1977, p. 204
	Youens 1996, pp. 194–8
Discography and timing:	Fischer-Dieskau II 4[6] 3'11
	Hyperion I 21[2]
	Hyperion II 17[19] 2'57 Edith Mathis

← *Augenlied* D297   *Schlaflied* D527 →

SEHNSUCHT (Die Scheibe friert)   Longing
(SEIDL) OP. 105 NO. 4, **D879** [H597]
D minor   March 1826

Nicht zu geschwind

Die Schei-be friert, der Wind ist rauh, der nächt'-ge Him-mel rein und blau:

(89 bars)

Die Scheibe friert, der Wind ist rauh,
Der nächt'ge Himmel rein und blau:
Ich sitz' in meinem Kämmerlein
Und schau' ins reine Blau hinein!

Mir fehlt etwas, das fühl' ich gut,
Mir fehlt mein Lieb, das treue Blut:
Und will ich in die Sterne sehn,
Muss stets das Aug' mir übergehn!

Mein Lieb, wo weilst du nur so fern,
Mein schöner Stern, mein Augenstern?
Du weisst, dich lieb' und brauch' ich ja, –
Die Träne tritt mir wieder nah.

Da quält' ich mich so manchen Tag,
Weil mir kein Lied gelingen mag, –
Weil's nimmer sich erzwingen lässt
Und frei hinsäuselt, wie der West!

Wie mild mich's wieder grad' durchglüht! –
Sieh' nur das ist ja schon ein Lied!
Wenn mich mein Los vom Liebchen warf,
Dann fühl' ich, dass ich singen darf.

The window pane freezes, the wind is harsh,
The night sky clear and blue.
I sit in my little room
Gazing out into the clear blueness.

Something is missing, I feel only too well;
My love is missing, my true love.
And when I look at the stars
My eyes constantly fill with tears.

My love, where are you, so far away,
My fair star, my darling?
You know that I love you and need you;
Again tears well up within me.

For many a day I have suffered
Because no song of mine has turned out well,
Because none can be forced anymore
To murmur freely, like the west wind.

How gentle the glow that again warms me!
Behold – a song!
Though my fate has cast me far from my beloved,
Yet I feel that I can still sing.

JOHANN GABRIEL SEIDL (1804–1875)

This is the seventh of Schubert's twelve Seidl solo settings (1826–8). See the poet's biography for a chronological list of all the Seidl settings.

On first hearing, this song seems to be related to *Erstarrung* D911/4 from *Winterreise*; one could perhaps almost hear in it a sketch for that later work. John Reed calls it the first of Schubert's *Winterreise* songs. He also finds the song ominous and sombre, hearing in its opening bars a quotation of the composer's 'death motif' in D minor. I think it is rather too easy to exaggerate the work's link with the last great cycle (if there is one) and thereby see in it something dark and disturbing. Like *Der Wanderer an den Mond* D870 by the same poet, *Sehnsucht* begins in the minor key true enough, but the major-key passages (and the song ends in the major) suggest a problem solved, or at least eased, a chink of light in the darkness, a healing of the soul. In this case, by the end of the song, a writer's block has also been released.

Only a non-pianist would equate the triplet accompaniment of this song with that of *Erstarrung*. The effect is similar, but the technical challenge very different. The first note of each triplet ingeniously changes to chime with the vocal line and alter the harmony, but the second and third notes of the *Sehnsucht* triplet comprise a rising octave rather than the falling one more usually demanded (in *Erstarrung*, for example) and which most experienced pianists can play as naturally and automatically as an Alberti bass. Schubert obviously prides himself on giving each of his songs a unique accompaniment; in *Sehnsucht* this reversal of the expected (a brain-teaser to be compared to patting one's head and rubbing one's stomach simultaneously) is a trick he plays but once on his song accompanists, and once is enough. It gives *Sehnsucht* a slightly yet crucially different feel from the many other songs accompanied by triplets. In fact it is a good thing if the new pattern somewhat slows down the pianist's fingers. The 'Ziemlich schnell' of *Erstarrung* is quite different from the 'Nicht zu geschwind' of this *Sehnsucht*, a song that can be ruined by too fast a performing tempo. Its chief glory is the strength of the roving bass line, an icy staccato at the outset to offset the legato effect of the wind depicted by the right hand. It seems obvious that Schubert sketched this skeletal bass, together with the vocal line, before coming up with accompanying details.

The change at Verse 2 ('Mir fehlt mein Lieb' bb. 22–3) into the submediant at the mention of the poet's distant love is similar to the change into F major (also the submediant of that song) at 'Wo find ich eine Blüte' in *Erstarrung* D911/4. It is memory of another song in *Winterreise* that is prompted by Verse 3, however: the beautiful melting into D major from D minor (at b. 35) recalls that most magical of moments in *Gute Nacht* D911/1 where the same two keys change places in the singer's mind. It seems that Schubert was especially touched by the tenderness of the phrase 'Mein schöner Stern, mein Augenstern?', bb. 36–8, a poetic image that had also earlier inspired Friedrich Rückert – and subsequently Schumann with his *Mein schöner Stern* Op. 101 no. 4 in 1849. Simple as it may sound, the little piano interlude that follows (just before 'Du weisst, dich lieb', at bb. 38–40) is a masterpiece of subtlety and pianistic trickiness, as are similar inner-voiced passages for the piano after the singer pauses briefly for breath. We return to the minor for the tears (b. 45) that take us into Verse 4, and then, although this is in no way a strict strophic song (details are changed all the time in order to set the words with greater naturalness) we modulate once more to the major at the end of b. 65.

A second glance shows us that we have reached D major this time via F major (rather than directly from D minor), making the caressing tone of the end even more special. Suddenly we realize that the song is not only about love but about the nature of creativity and the freezing of the creative impulses that stands in the way of poets and composers who, engulfed by 'Sehnsucht', fruitlessly attempt to rediscover their Muse. Indeed, it seems that the winter storm is not entirely an ill wind – the pain of separation has enabled a song to come into being. 'I feel that I can still sing', says the poet, whatever the dreadful odds. These words placed into Schubert's own mouth via this lied are poignantly apt in regard to the lonely personal circumstances in which he composed a great deal of his work. As Walt Whitman wrote in 1860, and published in *Calamus*:

> But now I think there is no unreturn'd love, the pay is certain one way or another,
> (I loved a certain person ardently and my love was not return'd;
> Yet out of that I have written these songs.)

Autographs:	Library of Congress, Washington (first 71 bars); Wienbibliothek im Rathaus, Vienna (remainder of song)
First edition:	Published as Op. 105 no. 4 by Josef Czerny, Vienna in November 1828 (P177)
Publication reviews:	*Allgemeiner Musikalischer Anzeiger* (Vienna), No. 5 (31 January 1829), p. 19f. [Waidelich/Hilmar Dokumente I No. 688]
Subsequent editions:	Peters: Vol. 4/100; AGA XX 493: Vol. 8/179; NSA IV: Vol. 5a/96; Bärenreiter: Vol. 4/16
Bibliography:	Capell 1928, p. 221
	Fischer-Dieskau 1977, p. 238
Discography and timing:	Fischer-Dieskau II 8[2] 3'14
	Hyperion I 15[15]
	Hyperion II 32[3] 2'28 Margaret Price

← *Am Fenster* D878   *Fischerweise* D881 →

SEHNSUCHT DER LIEBE

Love's yearning

(KÖRNER) **D180** [H85]
E minor   8 April 1815

Ruhig. Langsam

Wie die Nacht mit heil'-gem Be-ben auf der still-en Er-de liegt!

(79 bars)

Wie die Nacht mit heil'gem Beben	Lo, how with solemn trembling
Auf der stillen Erde liegt!	Night lies over the silent world.
Wie sie sanft der Seele Streben,	How gently it lulls the soul, its strivings,
Üpp'ge Kraft und volles Leben	Its abundant strength and rich life,
In den süssen Schlummer wiegt!	To sweet slumber!
Aber mit ewig neuen Schmerzen	But with ever-new pain
Regt sich die Sehnsucht in meiner Brust.	Yearning stirs within my breast.
Schlummern auch alle Gefühle im Herzen,	Though all feeling slumbers in my heart,
Schweigt in der Seele Qual und Lust –	Though anguish and pleasure are silent in my soul,
Sehnsucht der Liebe schlummert nie,	Love's yearning never slumbers;
Sehnsucht der Liebe wacht spät und früh.	Love's yearning lies awake early and late.
[. . . 2 . . .]	[. . . 2 . . .]
Tief, im süssen, heil'gen Schweigen,	In sweet, holy silence
Ruht die Welt und atmet kaum,	The world rests deeply, scarcely breathing;
Und die schönsten Bilder steigen	The loveliest images rise
Aus des Lebens buntem Reigen,	From the brightly coloured dance of life,
Und lebendig wird der Traum.	And dreams come alive.
Aber auch in des Traumes Gestalten	But even amid the images of dreams
Winkt mir die Sehnsucht, die schmerzliche, zu,	Painful yearning beckons to me,
Und ohn' Erbarmen, mit tiefen Gewalten,	And without pity, with violent force,
Stört sie das Herz aus der wonnigen Ruh':	It wrenches the heart from blissful rest.
Sehnsucht der Liebe schlummert nie,	Love's yearning never slumbers;
Sehnsucht der Liebe wacht spät und früh.	Love's yearning lies awake early and late.
So entschwebt der Kreis der Horen	Thus the circle of the hours floats by
Bis der Tag im Osten graut.	Until day dawns in the east.
Da erhebt sich, neu geboren,	Then, new-born, the bride of heaven
Aus des Morgens Rosentoren,	Arises radiant and glowing
Glühend hell die Himmels-Braut.	From the rosy portals of morning.

Aber die Sehnsucht nach dir im Herzen[1]	But the longing for you within my heart
Ist mit dem Morgen nur stärker erwacht;	Is only awakened more strongly with the morning;
Ewig verjüngen sich meine Schmerzen,	My sorrows are forever rejuvenated.
Quälen den Tag und quälen die Nacht:	They torment me night and day.
Sehnsucht der Liebe schlummert nie,	Love's longing never slumbers;
Sehnsucht der Liebe wacht spät und früh.	Love's longing lies awake early and late.

THEODOR KÖRNER (1791–1813)

This is the tenth of Schubert's sixteen Körner solo settings (1815–18). See the poet's biography for a chronological list of all the Körner settings.

Music of night and mystery is ushered in with a slow march that, in the piano writing at least (bb. 1–2), momentarily resembles the quasi-passacaglia figure of *Der Doppelgänger* D957/13 in a benign incarnation. The vocal line in this passage also traces this melodic trajectory. The first twelve bars of the song are a hymn to night of the greatest depth and seriousness. From b. 6 the accompaniment throbs in gently supportive quavers while the vocal melody is courtly and restrained. We imagine that we have the measure of the piece – one of those rather old-fashioned Schubert songs cast in classical mould – but this impression has been created the more to surprise us. The change at the upbeat to b. 13 is spectacular. The marking is suddenly 'Schnell' with a new time signature of ⅜. This scheme reflects the metrical plan of the poem where the first, third, fifth and seventh verses are made up of slow trochees, and the even-numbered verses contain quicker dactyls (Schubert's ability to plan out a song according to the metre of the poem already shows an astonishing sophistication).

To introduce this new section, a three-bar piano interlude descends in a diminished seventh arpeggio on G sharp. The last thing we expect, and at this speed, is a sudden F natural high in the vocal line (on the word 'Aber') on the first inversion of an F major chord, with vibrant semiquavers rattling the pianist's wrists. With almost unseemly haste we now move through A[7] to B flat major – the shift between these two chords rendering a marvellous twinge at '[. . .] neuen Schmerzen'. This is dramatic enough, but something much more audacious is on the way: at b. 22 a seemingly alien D sharp on the word 'Regt' is an immediate follow-on from an interlude bar of B flat major. The bass line of the accompaniment remains fixed on B flat; the right hand, drawn into the singer's orbit, oscillates on F sharp and D sharp. The ear hears this as an appoggiatura on a first inversion of F sharp major where the left hand B flat has suddenly changed to an A sharp. For two bars this split orthography remains – sharps in the right hand (and vocal line), flats in the left. What is most unexpected, however, is the rise in the left hand (after two bars) of a semitone to *B natural*, so that the key phrase in the song, 'Sehnsucht der Liebe' comes out of its flattened shell and explodes like a shooting star at the height of the stave.

The change of harmony has freed the vocal line, turning it into something unpredictable. How ardent this seems, and how unhinged! The falling sequences of bb. 30–45 are rather more conventional, albeit anguished. But the two-bar interlude of throbbing E major triplets at bb. 46–7 announces a strange new twist. As if from nowhere the voice pings out another totally unexpected note (this time a high G natural) on the word '<u>Sehn</u>(sucht)' in b. 48, and hangs on up there for three entire bars while the piano slips from that E major chord to G[7] in third inversion (on a D), then a tone lower to C major and then C minor. What a roller-coaster ride this is! The final 'Sehnsucht der Liebe' (including another high G for the singer, this time in b. 58) is harmonized in C major, slipping down into C minor and thence back to G major through an

---

[1] Körner writes 'Aber die Sehnsucht *in meinem* Herzen'.

extended 6-4. The panting postlude (bb. 64–9), all passion spent, reverts to a piano dynamic and alternates octaves with sixths, the whole song ending on rueful plagal alternations as if the longing caused by love is something holy as well as painful. The other Körner settings are well known for their passionate utterance, but the musical dislocations of this song, with its bold modulations, are well and truly a musical match for the disorientated and restless longing of the poem. This is a song that deserves to be much better known.

Körner's poem has four strophes, each with an antistrophe, thus eight verses of poetry in all. Printed here are 1, 2, 5, 6, 7 and 8 as recorded for the Hyperion Edition.

Autograph: Aoyama Junior College, Osaka (fragment)
First edition: Published as part of the AGA in 1895 (P558)
Subsequent editions: Not in Peters; AGA XX 60: Vol. 2/92; NSA IV: Vol. 8/32;
                              Bärenreiter: Vol. 6/126
Bibliography: Youens 1996, pp. 132–6
Discography and timing: Fischer-Dieskau I 3[12]   3'17   (first four strophes only)
                              Hyperion I 4[7]
                              Hyperion II 6[4]   4'56   Philip Langridge

← *Liebesrausch* D179   *Die erste Liebe* D182 →

SEI MIR GEGRÜSST   I greet you
(Rückert) Op. 20 no. 1, **D741** [H495]
B♭ major End of 1821–Autumn 1822

O du Entriss'ne mir und meinem Kusse!
  Sei mir gegrüsst!
  Sei mir geküsst!
Erreichbar nur meinem Sehnsuchtsgrusse!
  Sei mir gegrüsst!
  Sei mir geküsst!

Du von der Hand der Liebe diesem Herzen
  Gegeb'ne! du
  Von dieser Brust
Genomm'ne mir! mit diesem Tränengusse
  Sei mir gegrüsst!
  Sei mir geküsst!

You who were torn from me and my kisses,
  I greet you!
  I kiss you!
You, whom only my yearning greeting can reach,
  I greet you!
  I kiss you!

You who were bestowed on this heart
  By the hand of love,
  You who were taken
From my breast! With this flood of tears
  I greet you!
  I kiss you!

Zum Trotz der Ferne, die sich, feindlich trennend,	Defying the distance that, hostile and divisive,
Hat zwischen mich	Has come
Und dich gestellt;	Between you and me;
Dem Neid der Schicksalsmächte zum Verdrusse	Frustrating the envious powers of fate,
Sei mir gegrüsst!	I greet you!
Sei mir geküsst!	I kiss you!
Wie du mir je im schönsten Lenz der Liebe	As in love's fairest spring
Mit Gruss und Kuss	You once came to me
Entgegen kamst,	With greetings and kisses,
Mit meiner Seele glühendstem Ergusse,	So with all the fervour of my soul
Sei mir gegrüsst!	I greet you!
Sei mir geküsst!	I kiss you!
Ein Hauch der Liebe tilget Räum' und Zeiten,	One breath of love dissolves time and space,
Ich bin bei dir	And I am with you,
Du bist bei mir,	You are with me;
Ich halte dich in dieses Arms Umschlusse,	I hold you closely in my arms' embrace,
Sei mir gegrüsst!	I greet you!
Sei mir geküsst!	I kiss you!

FRIEDRICH RÜCKERT (1788–1866); poem written in 1819

This is the first of Schubert's six Rückert solo settings (1822–3). See the poet's biography for a chronological list of all the Rückert settings.

Rückert's poems may have come up at one of Schober's readings for the Schubert circle; or perhaps it was Schubert's friend Franz von Bruchmann (qv; the song is dedicated to Bruchmann's mother) who drew the composer's attention to a new volume of poems by that poet entitled *Östliche Rosen* which had been published in Germany at the beginning of 1822. It had appeared hot on the heels of the Persian-inspired *Ghasalen* (1821) by Bruchmann's friend Platen, and both collections bowed low in the direction of Goethe's *West-östlicher Divan* of 1819. Schubert selected this untitled poem written in Persian ghazal form and, not surprisingly, he chose the first line of the refrain as the song's title. The chief characteristic of this type of verse is the constant repetition of a key phrase.

That this song is problematic for performers may come as something of a surprise to those who like their Schubert effulgently romantic. Gerald Moore confessed to me that, of all the well-known Schubert songs, this was the one he liked the least. The line between a fine performance and one which tips the scale into sentimentality is a fine one, and the music can all too easily appear cloyingly self-indulgent, a failing that rarely muddies the clear waters of Schubertian creativity. It is interesting to read in Cosima Wagner's *Tagebuch* (for 15 January 1875) that Wagner had found certain Schubert songs that were performed for him 'beautiful beyond proportion', especially *Sei mir gegrüsst* which he considered Schubert's most beautiful song. 'It moved us to tears', adds Cosima. It is even possible that Rückert's last verse lingered in the master's mind and inspired a line in the libretto of *Parsifal* (*see* below).

The augmented second which we hear in the very first bar of the melody later became a Romantic cliché in self-consciously soulful music; as Capell says, 'such chromaticisms were overworked by the generation that followed Schubert to the point of wearying the world' – although this was hardly Schubert's fault. Added to this, the tempo 'Langsam' (exacerbated by most performers' tendency to exaggerate this composer's slow tempo markings) and the seemingly unending repetitiveness of those key words can all too easily sound laborious. We wearily come to the conclusion, as the singer once again climbs the stave for the greeting ('gegrüsst', as at bb. 12–13), and descends it for the kissing ('geküsst', as at bb. 14–15), that this lover is a bore – he protests his adoration too much, and after a while we cease to believe him. Many a valiant singer, trapped within a draggingly slow tempo, has attempted to traverse this song's heavenly length, his fixed smile of adoration slipping by the second, as he negotiates the not inconsiderable technical difficulties of the music.

Capell, in a remarkably eloquent note, makes a case for the song: 'There is a moment in youth when the fire of profane desire burns so clear as to be spiritual, and the carnal thing is sacred. In this glow the superb song was conceived. There are serenades playful, frivolous, persuasive, cynical. This one is noble.' The song is undoubtedly noble, but it is hardly a serenade. Admittedly there is a certain similarity to the celebrated Rellstab *Ständchen* D957/4 (both songs are in ⅜ and have mezzo staccato quavers in the accompaniment), and perhaps this is why generations of performers have come to see the work as a radiant love song. But even a superficial reading of the poem shows starkly unhappy images: the feminine verbal noun 'Entriss'ne' (the one torn away); the 'Tränengusse' (flood of tears); the 'hostile and divisive' distance that separates the lovers; the 'envious powers of fate', and so on. In most 'serenade' performances these words come across as self-indulgent hyperbole. But it is clear that a catastrophe has given rise to this lyric – this is no commonplace lover standing with his lute beneath a balcony. Conventionally, the singer has to be smilingly aglow with love as he sings, and it is this that is in conflict with the distinct thread of bitterness, loneliness and abandonment that runs through the words. Perhaps, considering the poem's oriental background, two doomed young lovers have been separated by the jealous edict ('the envious powers of fate') of a cruel sultan? What is not clear is whether the 'time and space' that separate the two can ever be traversed by human beings.

If we accept the possibility that this poem, from the poet who wrote the *Kindertotenlieder*, is an elegy after the death of a loved one, many of the conflicting images become clearer. (The dedication of the song to Bruchmann's mother makes sense in this regard: she had lost her daughter Sybilla in 1820, the same girl who later prompted the composition of the ghostly *Schwestergruss* D762.) It is also significant that the vignette that decorates the poem in *Östliche Rosen* (where each of the many designs seems to have been chosen to go with the words) looks very like a funeral wreath.

Vignette for this poem from Rückert's *Östliche Rosen* (1822).

Only the poet's 'yearning greeting' can reach his beloved who was snatched from his breast, suggesting a final parting: the person to whom the song is addressed is already on the other side of the Great Divide. The phrase 'tilget Räum' und Zeiten' evokes the same idea. And this image, in turn, brings Eurydice to mind: the whole of this poem might be Orpheus' serenade to his lost wife, a lieder version of Gluck's 'Che farò senza Euridice' and, like that masterpiece, also in a major key which is infinitely capable of sadness and pathos. If 'Sei mir gegrüsst! / Sei mir geküsst!' is heard as a litany of bereavement, the obsessiveness of the many repeats seems less banal. The bar of echo for 'Sei mir geküsst!' comes across as someone lovingly dwelling on a wistful memory: he will never kiss her again. There are real moments of anger and passion (the setting of 'mit diesem Tränengusse' (bb. 36–8) is almost a sob of emotion) and it is this energy that keeps the piece moving, the desire to reach out and touch someone in another world bringing an urgency. Such a change of emphasis makes an enormous difference to the performer: charming the audience should not be the first priority. It goes without saying that this interpretation goes utterly against the 'schmalzy' (and superficial) way with this song that has become the established Viennese convention.

Schubert wrote another ghazal in this period, the Platen setting *Du liebst mich nicht* D756. In that song the repetitions of the title phrase suggest someone unhinged by the break-up of a relationship, and the harmonic excursions illustrate the torment caused by deep and complex feelings. There is something of the same feeling in *Sei mir gegrüsst* – it is full of harmonic twists, excursions and surprises which are, again, more explicable in the broader context of bereavement. The form is rather sophisticated, a combination of strophic and *durchkomponiert* techniques, with a strong feeling of a rondo with variations. The poem's five verses are translated, in musical terms, into an alternating ABABA, where A is the familiar melody and B is a second idea, an intense and *innig* melody grounded on a dominant pedal – at least for a while. Of course the two appearances of the B section (bb. 30–44 and bb. 61–77) follow different harmonic pathways as Schubert gives way to the inspiration of the moment, and the second appearance of A (from b. 45) is essentially in the minor key.

The most moving moment of the song occurs in the last verse, a much modified version of A, with the words 'Ein Hauch der Liebe tilget Räum' und Zeiten' (from b. 78). This mention of 'time and space' is perhaps prophetic of Wagner's words ('Zum Raum wird hier die Zeit') that introduce the transformation music of *Parsifal*. A moving sequential setting of 'Ich bin bei dir / Du bist bei mir' (bb. 82–5) lifts the piece, given a fine performance, on to a more exalted plane. This is the moment of healing and resolution, the passage like balm poured upon the aching wound of the singer's grief. The wild fortissimo outburst of 'Ich halte dich in dieses Arms Umschlusse' (bb. 86–9) that immediately follows seems to challenge the Fates themselves in a final gesture of defiance. In this singer's mind the grave has been overcome. This recalls the passion of Novalis for his beloved Sophie who died in her teens. Rückert certainly knew the Novalis poems, and the almost mystical reuniting of lovers separated by death is often to be found in the literature of the time. If *Sei mir gegrüsst* is taken seriously on this level it can be seen as approaching the metaphysical grandeur of such songs as Schlegel's *Fülle der Liebe* D854.

Many Schubert lieder were performed with guitar accompaniment but this is the only song in the canon that is linked with a contemporary performance with harp accompaniment. The memoirs of the singer and stage producer Ludwig Josef Cramolini (quoted in NSA Vol. 1/xix) recount how he was approached by the harpist Capus von Pichelstein and asked to perform the song as a serenade at a social gathering. According to Cramolini, Schubert himself coached the pair in the singer's home and after the performance congratulated Cramolini with the kind of words that one is accustomed to read rather too frequently in singers' autobiographies: 'No-one can sing this song as well as you, you brought tears to all our eyes'. The whole of this story seems so unlikely that it may very well be true; the fact that Cramolini mentions that the song came from Rückert's *Östliche Rosen* strikes an authentic note.

Autograph:	Missing or lost
First edition:	Published as Op. 20 no. 1 by Sauer & Leidesdorf, Vienna in April 1823 (P36)
Dedicatee:	Justina von Bruchmann
First known performance:	27 December 1828, at a memorial for Schubert in Linz, organized by Abbé Luigi Tomazolli. Soloist: 'Frau v. R.' (See Waidelich/Hilmar Dokumente I No. 719)

Subsequent editions: Peters: Vol. 1/190; AGA XX 400: Vol. 6/214; NSA IV: Vol. 1/137;
                       Bärenreiter: Vol. 1/108
Bibliography: Capell 1928, pp. 170–71
                       Fischer-Dieskau 1977, pp. 251–2
                       Voss 1999, pp. 122–30
Arrangements: Arr. Franz Liszt (1811–1886) for solo piano, no. 1 of *Lieder von
                       Schubert* (1837–8) [*see* TRANSCRIPTIONS]
                       Arr. Tilman Hoppstock (b. 1961) for guitar accompaniment, in
                       Franz Schubert: 110 Lieder (2009)
Discography and timing: Fischer-Dieskau II 4[16]   3'52
                       Hyperion I 28[8]
                       Hyperion II 25[21]   4'39   Maarten Koningsberger

←— *An die Türen will ich schleichen* D$_2$478/3   *Todesmusik* D758 —→

JOHANN GABRIEL SEIDL (1804–1875)

THE POETIC SOURCES
S1 [Outer cover] *Dichtungen* von Joh. Gabr. Seidl, Erster Theil. [Title page] *Balladen, Romanzen,
Sagen und Lieder* von Johann Gabriel Seidl, Wien, Druck und Verlag von J. P. Sollinger, 1826

This first volume was advertised in the *Wiener Zeitschrift* on 30 August 1825 with a binding in
coloured paper in the manner of a volume from a 'Damenbibliothek'.

S2 [Outer cover] *Dichtungen* von Joh. Gabr. Seidl, Zweiter Theil. [Title page] *Lieder der Nacht,
Elegien aus Alfons von Lamartine, Die Deutung* von Johann Gabriel Seidl, Wien, Druck und
Verlag von J. P. Sollinger, 1826

This little volume, like S1, was advertised in the *Wiener Zeitschrift* in October 1825. The propor-
tions of the book, with a cover on which a rectangular bordered pattern is printed, matches the
appearance of the book of poems held in Schubert's right hand, the composer's arm draped over
the back of a chair, in the famous Rieder portrait of late 1825.

S3 *Lieder der Nacht* von Johann Gabriel Seidl. Zweite, verbesserte und vermehrte Auflage. Wien
1851. Druck und Verlag von J. B. Sollinger's Witwe, Tuchlauben No. 439

S4 *Natur und Herz – (Lyrische Nachlese)* von Johann Gabriel Seidl, Stuttgart, Hallberger, 1853

S5 *Joh. Gabr. Seidls gesammelte Schriften*. Herausgegeben von Hans Max. Band I–VI Wien,
Wilhelm Braumüller, 1877–1881

THE SONGS
1826   *Widerspruch* D865 (Quartet for TTBB and piano and solo song) [S1: pp. 191–2,
            no. 3 of *Jägerlieder*] [S5: Volume I pp. 179–80]
            Wiegenlied D867 [S1: pp. 143–4] [S5: Volume I pp. 162–3]
            Das Zügenglöcklein D871 [S2: pp. 26–7] [S5: Volume I pp. 33–4]

Der Wanderer an den Mond D870 [S2: pp. 24–5] [S3: pp. 23–5 – with line altered from S1: 'Aus Ostens Wieg' in Westens Grab'] [S5: Volume I p. 31 with the same alteration]

March 1826 *Im Freien* D880 [S2: pp. 45–6] [S3: pp. 48–9] [not reprinted in S5]
Am Fenster D878 [S2: pp. 5–6] [S5: Volume I p. 25]
Sehnsucht D879 [S2: p. 31] [S3: pp. 108–9] [not reprinted in S5]

September 1826 *Nachthelle* D892 (Song for tenor solo, TTBB chorus and piano) [S2: p. 35] [S3: p. 42] [S5: Volume I pp. 38–9]
Grab und Mond D893 (Quartet TTBB) [S2: p. 41] [S3: pp. 30–31] [S5: Volume I p. 41]

1828? *Die Unterscheidung* D866/1 *Vier Refrain-Lieder* No. 1 [This poem appeared in an almanac entitled *Das Veilchen* (1835) with the title *Gretchens Abscheu vor der Liebe*. Otherwise the poems of the *Refrain-Lieder* were handed over to Schubert in handwritten form and were not printed separately from their music in the poet's lifetime]
Bei dir allein! D866/2, *Vier Refrain-Lieder* No. 2
Die Männer sind mechant! D866/3, *Vier Refrain-Lieder* No. 3
Irdisches Glück D866/4, *Vier Refrain-Lieder* No. 4

October 1828 *Die Taubenpost* D965A [S4: p. 209] [S5: Volume IV pp. 338–9]

Mention should also be made of another Seidl setting for unaccompanied voices that lies outside the scope of this book: *Nachtgesang in Walde* D913 (Quartet TTBB) and horn, April 1827

Johann Gabriel Seidl was born on 21 June 1804 in Vienna. His father, after whom he was named, was a lawyer, his mother was Anna Seidl (née Lettner). He went to good schools – the Normalhauptschule bei St Anna and the Akademische Gymnasium where both Bruchmann and Schober had earlier been students. Seidl was seven years younger than Schubert and, as such, the contemporary of Moritz von Schwind, Franz Lachner, Eduard von Bauernfeld and Vesque von Püttlingen. These younger men were destined to belong to the second generation of Schubertians, coming into the composer's ken in the 1820s and revitalizing the sociable activities of the circle once many members of the original cadre had left Vienna or married (or both). Only one of those mentioned above, Bauernfeld, provided the composer with a text to set to music, whereas there are fifteen Schubert settings of poems by Seidl, who was nowhere near as close a friend to the composer as Schwind and Lachner, for example. Simply living in Vienna and being a successful young artist was no automatic guarantee of intimacy with Schubert.

As a schoolboy Seidl was exceptionally precocious and prolific. He had been a published poet in almanacs under various pseudonyms (such as 'Siegl' or 'Meta Communis') from the age of sixteen. This literary facility saved him and his mother from penury when the poet's father suddenly died in 1823, leaving the family penniless. Seidl gave up his place at university (where he had been studying philosophy and law) and became a peripatetic teacher, giving lessons in private houses. His career intersects with Schubert's between 1824 and 1828, a stressful time for both men for entirely different reasons. This is the least documented period in Seidl's reasonably long life and none of his biographers, nor Schubert's, have anything to say regarding a friendship between the two. As we shall see, the composer whom Seidl really admired was Weber, a proven genius of the opera stage and thus of far greater interest to a young and ambitious writer.

The poet's first appearance in the Schubert documents is a letter to the composer written on 1 July 1824. This concerns a play by Seidl called *Der kurze Mantel* (The Short Cloak) which Schubert had apparently agreed to consider as an opera libretto. Seidl's letter attempts to galvanize the composer into action ('for heaven's sake, hurry up') and is full of theatre gossip and information about casting, money and operatic politics. On this evidence one senses that the twenty-year-old Seidl, spurred on by need and ambition sharpened by misfortune, had become a skilled 'operator', but not so skilled as to avoid annoying those on whom he exerted pressure. There is a scarcely concealed desperation in 'do not let yourself regret your promise' when Schubert's clearly casual agreement could hardly have been construed as a promise. In such a way, young writers pushed their way through Viennese social and literary barriers before achieving acceptance and success in the capital city.

In fact, Seidl knew Vienna and its environs so well that he published a guide to the beauties of the towns and villages surrounding the city as an alphabetical gazetteer (*Wiens Umgebungen*, 1826). In later years he was also to publish a famous guide to the Tyrol (*Wanderungen durch Tyrol und Steyermark*, Leipzig, Wigand, 1840), a collection that includes poems and folksongs and hovers between topography and belles-lettres. In this respect Seidl took his cue from Aloys Schreiber (qv), another Schubert poet renowned as a writer of guide books.

Schubert seems to have kept Seidl at something of a distance; in the surviving letters the two use the polite 'Sie' form with each other. On the other hand, Seidl seems quickly to have become accepted on more familiar terms by Carl Maria von Weber, who was something of a Schubertian bugbear. Herein lies a possible reason for Seidl's failure to win Schubert over to his side to any intimate degree. In 1823 the composer's face-to-face lack of enthusiasm for Weber's new opera *Euryanthe* had so displeased the master from Dresden who, rather to his discredit, was not impressed by Schubert's honesty, that any hopes that Schubert might have had for a performance of his opera *Alfonso und Estrella* D732 in that city were immediately dashed. In Seidl's *Dichtungen*

(Volume 1 pp. 160–62), only a few pages away from the text for *Wiegenlied* D867, there is a resoundingly ebullient hymn, a *Festgesang*, in honour of the composer of *Euryanthe*. Indeed Seidl heaps extravagant praise on the very opera that Schubert had frankly pronounced less good than *Der Freischütz*. Seidl was clearly aware that the libretto for *Euryanthe* by Helmina von Chézy could be improved upon and his poem was no doubt sent to Weber in the hope of a future collaboration.

Another possible reason for the distance between Schubert and Seidl may have been a matter of political sympathies. At twenty-two the poet was, according to Susan Youens, 'already an old fogey in the making and slightly illiberal in temperament'. The composer was clearly not charmed by Seidl personally as he was by Schwind and Bauernfeld who were, by contrast, liberals and beloved friends, and the astute Seidl was far removed from the reckless fire and idealism of the exiled Johann Senn. By this time Schubert had had enough of opera libretti (in due course he would work on his last such venture with Bauernfeld) and so he did not compose music for *Der kurze Mantel*. (In the end Seidl had to persuade no fewer than three other composers to take on an act each.) As for the poetry, Schubert seems to have read what Seidl sent him, sometimes enjoying it, sometimes not.

The ability of this young man to absorb other poets' styles was dazzling. While still in his teens he had translated most beautifully from Lamartine and Sheridan, Thomas Moore and Southey, not to mention all the Greek and Latin authors he could lay his hands on. In terms of oriental pastiche he could almost out-Rückert Rückert, and his command of the ballad style of Schiller was impressive. That Goethe was his main influence is hardly surprising and in a poem like *Im Freien* this is very evident. His interest in folksong (he was a master of dialects and transcribing them in his own special fashion) gave him considerable individuality in the Viennese literary scene of the time; later on this corner of a market that was largely of his own creation would furnish him with some of his best-remembered successes (for example *Flinserln*, 1828).

Young Seidl was well aware that musical settings of his poems would bring his name before the public, and he is likely to have bombarded composers systematically with literary material in the hope of rousing their interest. One cannot blame him for such industry in the light of his straitened circumstances. In this respect Seidl seems to have been exceedingly 'modern' in the conduct of his career – the use of a mailing list, the systematic cultivation of a well-nurtured social network and so on. The temperamental differences between him and Schubert in this regard were, once again, considerable.

The twenty-two-year-old Seidl lent Schubert a copy of his newly published *Dichtungen* (1826) in three volumes. The first volume of the collection was well reviewed in the *Wiener Zeitschrift* on 29 October 1825, very early for

Seidl's *Lieder der Nacht*, the second volume of the poet's *Dichtungen* (1826).

an 1826 publication as was the custom of the time. Perhaps to his own surprise, Schubert discovered two poems for musical setting in this first volume, and seven in the second – thus nine poems for solo songs were excavated from two of these slim Seidl volumes (the third consisted of short stories). Schubert's days of setting Goethe were over and he seems to have found pleasure in the poetry of someone who unashamedly took Goethe as his model, but with a discernible Austrian accent. In a single bound Seidl, a young fellow Austrian (and a professional in a way that dilettantes like Bruchmann and Schober were not) had entered the lists of Schubert's collaborator-poets, achieving immortality at one remove.

In the English version of Deutsch's Documentary Biography (1946) there is no further epistolary contact between Schubert and Seidl after the *kurze Mantel* reminder. But a letter that only came to light in 1956 is published in the German version of the documents (1964). This dates from 4 August 1828, three and a half months before the composer's death. The missive begins 'Dear Herr Gabriel. Enclosed with this letter I am sending you back your poems. I could not discover in them any poetic qualities whatsoever, or anything suitable for music.' This has sometimes been taken as a slap in the face for the overambitious Seidl, but the poet had not published anything of real significance since the *Dichtungen* of 1826 so it is hard to imagine what new book was part of the parcel of papers returned to him (*if* the book was new, that is, or even a book). And it is difficult to see why Schubert would have caused gratuitous offence to someone to whom he recently owed no fewer than eleven of his compositions. Furthermore the note is signed 'Ihr Verehrer, Frz. Schubert' – your admirer. It is perfectly possible that composer and poet are sharing a joke: in saying that there was *nothing* of interest in the poetry, Schubert is being amusingly ironic about how *much* he had found to set to music in the little volumes that were lent to him nearly two years earlier and were presumably being returned to the poet only now. In any event, Seidl and Schubert had still not exchanged the familiar 'Du' form whereby acquaintance turns to friendship. From this letter we also discover that the return of the books had a quid pro quo: Seidl had in his possession the manuscripts for the songs *Widerspruch* D865 and *Wiegenlied* D867 (he was an able tenor himself and had perhaps wished to perform these songs) and Schubert wanted them back so that they could be published.

That is one theory at least. It is also possible that Schubert, in August 1828, was genuinely dissatisfied with whatever poems in manuscript (not a printed book) he had received from Seidl for a completely new project that was clearly getting on his nerves. This involved setting poems by Seidl that had not yet reached print (and were not destined to do so in his lifetime). The publisher Thaddäus Weigl had hoped to persuade Schubert to compose some down-to-earth songs that would be well received in the popular market, and it is not hard to imagine the savvy Seidl setting up the deal and pulling the strings, bringing together publisher and composer in a way that ensured he could write the texts. The composing of these completely untypical songs (*Vier Refrain-Lieder* D866/1–4) would probably have made Schubert very grumpy – enough to reject the 'popular' poems on offer by Seidl (thus the contentious letter) who might well have had to burn the midnight oil to provide others that might have appealed to the composer more. Seidl was so prolific and so clever at versification that he could have sent dozens of unpublished poems to Schubert over a period of weeks in the hope that some of them might appeal to him. *Die Unterscheidung* and *Die Männer sind mechant!* were exactly the type of risqué texts that Weigl had in mind for this project; but it is clear that *Bei dir allein!* and *Irdisches Glück* were chosen from a portfolio of work that rather broadened the parameters originally laid down by the publisher in search of downmarket profit. It is surely likely that one of the poems sent to Schubert at this time, perhaps in the hope that he would see something amusing and popular in it (Viennese working men had their own carrier pigeons), was *Die Taubenpost*, and that the composer

quietly set this lyric aside for a greater musical destiny altogether.

When Schubert died, Seidl was the first to leap to his desk to write a graveside panegyric, quicker than either Schlechta or Schober, both authors of similar poems. One can perhaps imagine Schober's disdain for the sharply clever but slightly down-at-heel Seidl, and this may be another reason Schubert kept him somewhat at arm's length. Seidl's *Meinem Freunde Franz Schubert*, written the day before the composer's funeral, was published in the *Wiener Zeitschrift* on 6 December 1828; at twelve rather fulsome and lengthy strophes (with reference to 'Mein Schubert') one could be forgiven for thinking that Schubert and Seidl had been the closest friends in all the world. The poem is full of the narrative 'ich' that places Seidl at the forefront of events. It is hard to defend Seidl here from charges of opportunism, but his unusual use of the word 'Doppelgänger' in Verse 6, as a means to describe the poet's mirroring role in a composer's life, gives one pause for thought. The song of that name was only to be published in 1829. We assume that Seidl was in touch with Schubert in August 1828 over the *Vier Refrain-Lieder*, but if he knew about the Heine settings composed more or less at the same time this indicates a different level of friendship. It remains possible that Seidl had gradually become closer to Schubert out of the sight of the documents or any corroborating evidence.

With all this literary activity one might imagine Seidl to be already famous and well-to-do by 1828, but his contributions to various almanacs, however ubiquitous, were poorly paid. He was as yet little known by the public at large, although he had been avidly sowing the seeds of his future reputation. The fact is that he was in desperate need of a steady job, and life in Vienna had provided no security at all. The death of Schubert (and also the hope of further collaborations with him) seems to have marked a turning point for the poet. He appears to have been grateful to have been appointed to a rather humble teaching position in Cilli in Styria (now Celje in Slovenia). He married his beloved Therese in 1829 and made the move soon afterwards, staying there until 1840 and becoming close friends with that fine poet Karl von Leitner (qv), resident in Graz. In fact Seidl became an honorary Styrian, travelling the length and breadth of that province and exploring every corner. His travels took him as far south as Venice and the discovery of Roman remains in Cilli initiated his fascination with archaeology (this would stand him in good stead for his later appointment in Vienna as a museum curator). From a personal, rather than professional, point of view this was an idyllic phase in his life; his children, a son and daughter, were born in Cilli. He continued to edit the almanac *Aurora* and its yearly appearance would have been a reminder to the Viennese public of his existence.

Seidl might easily have lived out the rest of his life in relative obscurity in Styria, so the success of a new collection of poems, *Bifolien*,

Johann Gabriel Seidl from *Album österreichischer Dichter* (1850).

in 1836 must have come as a welcome surprise. His reputation also received a substantial and unexpected lift in Germany with a highly favourable entry in *Die Poesie und die Poeten in Österreich*, a survey of Austrian literature made in the same year by the acerbic critic Julius Seidlitz (the pseudonym of Isaac Jeitteles, 1794–1857, exiled from Austria and writing from Leipzig). Seidlitz admitted, in his comically grudging manner, that he had nothing but praise for the poet's work. Seidl's output seems often to have given rise to such modified rapture, although modified by what exactly is hard to define – perhaps simply a lack of true originality. In 1840 false news of Seidl's death somehow arrived in Vienna from Styria, resulting in a series of newspaper obituaries that included glowing retrospective accounts of his talents and achievements going back to the 1820s. On such accidents depend many of life's turning points. Important members of the Viennese establishment took note of a name they had somehow forgotten, and Seidl's hour had come. Once the mistake was revealed he returned to Vienna in triumph in August 1840. For the next thirty years he rose through the ranks of civil-service distinction and academic honour with unerring brilliance. His literary output continued to be large and various, and he also became a book censor in the office in which Mayrhofer had worked until 1836. In 1854 he provided a revised text for Haydn's 'Gott erhalte Franz den Kaiser' and this led to the kind of fame where his name was taught in schools. In 1856 he was appointed custodian of the 'Schatzkammer', the imperial collection of coins and other small treasures, a task to which he was more than equal in terms of scholarship. He was created a Hofrat in 1874 and died the following year, on 18 July. Born in 1804 and dying in 1875, he was an exact contemporary of the very much greater Swabian poet Eduard Mörike. In 1892 he was interred with honour in the new Zentralfriedhof in Vienna and in 1904 there were even celebrations in the city for his centenary.

Seidl is no longer remembered as the Austrian national treasure he once undoubtedly was. In matters of linguistics and translation he was not the genius that Rückert was, nor a technical magician in the class of Platen, nor an innovator like Heine, and his novels and works for the theatre lack psychological depth. But Seidl *was* talented and supremely hard-working. Moreover, he was clearly a man who attracted the personal admiration, even devotion, of such figures as Karl von Leitner (qv) and the great Viennese writer Adalbert Stifter. In the years after Schubert's death there are many witnesses to his modesty, probity and generosity. Seidl's literary achievements are all perfectly honourable, and sometimes far more than that; fighting against difficult conditions in his early life, he worked with admirable vigour and discipline to establish himself as a poet. Both his career and his considerable talent are utterly representative of the zeitgeist in which he worked. This both limited him and gave him the opportunity to flourish in the comfortably urbane milieu of which he was a tactical master. It is impossible to imagine Seidl as anything other than Viennese, with all the pros and cons of that designation.

It was Seidl's good luck to have been set to music by Schubert in 1826 and 1828 when the result was one masterpiece after another. He might have been surprised that he is now chiefly remembered because of his slightly uneasy connection (or so it seems) with a composer who had never enjoyed an operatic success. That Schubert set more of Seidl's poems than, say, Schlechta's, is proof that being the composer's close friend was not a guarantee of more musical settings, particularly in the last five years of his life. Even if Schubert preferred other company to Seidl's, he was astute enough to value the verse. An accident of history meant that Seidl's son Karl (1830–1861) married Karoline Schubert, the composer's niece. If Schubert had lived and attended this wedding it might have been an opportunity for these two old collaborators, now part of the same family, to exchange the 'Du' at last.

Bibliography: Fuchs, 1904
Seidlitz [Jeitteles] 1837, Vol. 2, pp. 67–72
Youens 2002, pp. 363–414

SELAM CYCLE

(*See also* AN DIE GELIEBTE D303, LABETRANK DER LIEBE D302, DIE MACHT DER LIEBE D308, MEIN GRUSS AN DEN MAI D305, SKOLIE D306, DIE STERNENWELTEN D307, WIEGENLIED D304)

The anthology *Selam, Ein Almanach für Freunde des Mannigfaltigen auf das Jahr 1814* was edited by the poet Ignaz Castelli (qv) and published by Anton Strauss in Vienna. This small volume was the source of eleven Schubert settings by seven different poets. In addition to the seven songs listed above, it included *Die Sterne* (Fellinger) D176, *Vergebliche Liebe* D177, *Die erste Liebe* D182 (all songs from April 1815), as well as *Das gestörte Glück* D309 which was composed alongside the other seven songs of 15 October 1815.

In an article of 1989 'Lieder aus dem "Selam". Ein Schubertsches Liederheft' and in his introduction to Volume 9 of the NSA (p. XVI), Walter Dürr advances the idea that seven of the eight songs composed by Schubert on 15 October 1815 (D302–D308) might be thought of as a small cycle, and that they may well have been imagined by Schubert as such. In this progression of songs (*Labetrank der Liebe* (Stoll) D302, *An die Geliebte* (Stoll) D303, *Wiegenlied* (Körner) D304, *Mein Gruss an den Mai* (Kumpf) D305, *Skolie* (Deinhard-Deinhardstein) D306, *Die*

Sternenwelten (Fellinger) D307 and *Die Macht der Liebe* (Kalchberg) D308, Dürr traces the idea of love as a gift from heaven (D302–3), experienced in various ways in earthly life (D304–6) and finally connected to heavenly powers (D307–8). The Körner setting *Das gestörte Glück* D309, composed on the same day, was excluded from this collection seemingly because its playful tone did not match the seriousness of the other songs.

Dürr supports his theory that these songs might belong together as a set, a bouquet rather than a cycle, by noting that they were carefully written out as fair copies in a single book (once in the Wertisch collection and now in the Österreichische Nationalbibliothek) and that, contrary to his normal practice when writing many songs in one manuscript, Schubert dated each song separately, as if making a special point of the day's significance. On the other hand this fact could also underline the independence of each song, none of which was numbered (as was the case in Schubert's later cycles). John Reed pointed out that 15 October was the name-day of Therese Grob and it is quite possible that this was the inspiration behind the songs. It is clear, however, that neither the book of songs nor an additional fair copy of *Labetrank der Liebe* came into the possession of Therese or her family. If Schubert had indeed thought of making a cycle of this kind as early as October 1815, well before Beethoven published *An die ferne Geliebte* Op. 98 in 1816, one can imagine his disappointment at having been pipped at the post by the older composer's unexpected coup when he himself had already had a similar idea.

SELIGE WELT   Blessed world
(Senn) Op. 23 no. 2, **D743** [H491]
A♭ major   Autumn? 1822

(21 bars)

Ich treibe auf des Lebens Meer,	I drift upon life's sea;
Ich sitze gemut in meinem Kahn,	I sit comfortably in my boat,
Nicht Ziel, noch Steuer, hin und her,	Without destination, without tiller, moving to and fro,
Wie die Strömung reisst, wie die Winde gahn.	As the current takes me, as the winds blow.
Eine selige Insel sucht der Wahn,	Folly seeks a blessed isle,
Doch eine ist es nicht.	But no such isle exists.
Du lande gläubig überall an,	Be trusting, land wherever
Wo sich Wasser an Erde bricht.	Water breaks against the shore.

JOHANN CHRYSOSTOMUS SENN (1795–1857)

This is the first of Schubert's two Senn solo settings (1822). See the poet's biography for a chronological list of the Senn settings.

This song is a miniature that brandishes a mighty fist. It is over in the twinkling of an eye (a mere twenty-one bars) but it is no less a portrait of the poet Senn, friend of the composer's youth, than the Platen songs are true to the character of that poet. This is the prototype of songs from *Winterreise* like *Mut!* D911/22 or *Der stürmische Morgen* D911/18, other short, sharp shocks in Schubert's output. The music is compact and muscular, like Senn himself; it states its case with an economy of language and directness (also typical of the poet). It then vanishes as suddenly from the scene as Senn himself – exiled from Vienna as a result of the paranoia of the police state. It is possible that the poem was brought back to Vienna from the Tyrol by Senn's closest friend, Franz von Bruchmann. It is not to be found in the volume of *Gedichte* published in Innsbruck in 1838, probably for political reasons; had the book appeared ten years later, a different political climate might have enabled its inclusion.

The frequent doubling of vocal line and accompaniment (a characteristic of *Mut!*) is indicative of strength of purpose. The key is A flat major and it is interesting to note that the only other Senn setting, *Schwanengesang* D744, is in the same tonality. The opening of the song (bb. 1–2) shares with the Mayrhofer setting *Der Schiffer* D536 a finger-flexing ability to create a melodic individuality out of what are essentially decorated arpeggio figurations. The choice of key implies that, in Schubert's mind at least, something about Senn's utterance had the force and eloquence of nature. In common with other A flat songs on sensual subjects such as *Ganymed* D544 and *Versunken* D715, there is a middle section in C flat major. Schubert usually reserves this for moments of surrender; here it is the luxury and folly of dreaming of Cythera, the non-existent blessed isle of Aphrodite, which transports us into the distant and unrealistic tonalities of illusion. Newbould points out the futility of this: 'three times a key-implication is brusquely cancelled – C flat major, G major and E minor are all denied, and C minor supervenes. Thus hopes of finding an island paradise – each one glimpsed in the mind's eye as a beckoning remote key – are dashed.' This miniature 'Invitation au voyage' passage is seldom sung lyrically – or piano – enough by baritones, many of whom feel they must snarl their way through the piece. The chords in palpitating semiquavers (bb. 10–16) should create an effect of a shimmering chimera. The relative plain sailing between b. 10 and halfway through b. 14 is suddenly sabotaged as if by unexpected storms and treacherous currents (bb. 14–16, with sforzato markings). It is as if a commanding hand at the tiller has been needed to prevent a terrible accident. Resounding unison octaves on E flat in both hands in b. 17 signal the return of sense and pragmatism, and the sturdy tune of the opening replaces what has been an interlude of fantasy and lyricism. The whole song is about coping with real life, as opposed to the life you might wish to have in fantasy; bravely accepting one's fate and seeing where you end up – a mixture of aggressive bravery and passive stoicism. It is no surprise that the song shares a manuscript with *Heliopolis II* D754, music of similar bite and heroism.

Autograph:	Staatsbibliothek Preussischer Kulturbesitz (headed *Selige Welt. Von Senn*, undated)
First edition:	Published as Op. 23 no. 2 by Sauer & Leidesdorf, Vienna in August 1823 (P45)
Publication reviews:	*Allgemeine Musikalische Zeitung* (Leipzig), No. 26 (24 June 1824), col. 425–8 [Waidelich/Hilmar Dokumente I No. 282; Deutsch Doc. Biog. No. 479]
Subsequent editions:	Peters: Vol. 4/19; AGA XX 406: Vol. 7/14; NSA IV: Vol. 2/6; Bärenreiter: Vol. 1/137
Bibliography:	Fischer-Dieskau 1977, p. 157
	Kohlhäufl 1999, pp. 124–6
	Newbould 1997, p. 157

Discography and timing: Fischer-Dieskau II 5[6]   1'09

                     Hyperion I 28[15] & 2[6]   1'04   Maarten Koningsberger

                                           1'02   Stephen Varcoe

                     Hyperion II 25[17]   1'04   Maarten Koningsberger

← *Schwanengesang* D744   *Wer sich der Einsamkeit ergibt* D₂478/1 →

SELIGKEIT   Bliss
(HÖLTY) **D433** [H260]
E major   May 1816

(40 bars)

Freuden sonder Zahl	Joys beyond number
Blühn im Himmelssaal	Bloom in the vaults of heaven
Engeln und Verklärten,	For angels and the transfigured,
Wie die Väter lehrten.	As our fathers taught.
Oh, da möcht' ich sein	Ah, there I should like to be,
Und mich ewig freun![1]	Forever rejoicing!
Jedem lächelt traut	Upon each a heavenly bride
Eine Himmelsbraut;	Smiles tenderly;
Harf' und Psalter klinget,	Harp and psalter sound;
Und man tanzt und singet.	There is dancing and singing.
Oh, da möcht' ich sein	Oh, there I should like to be
Und mich ewig freun!	Forever rejoicing!
Lieber bleib' ich hier,	I would sooner stay here
Lächelt Laura mir	If Laura smiles on me
Einen Blick, der saget,	With a look that says
Dass ich ausgeklaget.	I have ceased grieving.
Selig dann mit Ihr	Blissfully then with her
Bleib' ich ewig hier!	I will remain forever here!

LUDWIG HÖLTY (1748–1776); poem written 12 February 1773. Adapted for publication in
1804 by JOHANN HEINRICH VOSS (1751–1826)

*This is the twentieth of Schubert's twenty-three Hölty solo settings (1813–16). See the poet's
biography for a chronological list of all the Hölty settings.*

[1] Hölty/Voss writes (*Gedichte*, 1804) 'Und mich freun, mich freun'.

This is an ironic description of a Christian, angelic heaven. It is in the same key, E major, as the long Schiller setting *Elysium* D584, a tonality Schubert favours to depict transfiguration, both serious and tongue-in-cheek. The introductory music is so well known that most singers do not even bother to announce the encore's title; twelve bars of delicious meandering semiquavers in the piano, underpinned by a left-hand waltz rhythm (there is a marvellously unexpected shift to G sharp major in b. 6) set the foot tapping and lighten the heart. Tiny inflections of waltz-rubato are allowed in a piece such as this, designed to tease, but only the truly skilled know how to provide charm-inflection without inflation. Of course this is a very different joy from the pagan celebrations, the everlasting wedding feast promised in the *Elysium*, and this music takes itself rather less seriously than Schiller the classicist's poems about the ancient world. If this text, written for the twenty-fifth meeting of the Göttingen Hainbund and read aloud to Hölty's brother poets, owes anything to another poet it is Petrarch and his *Canzoniere* where the transfigured Laura remains unreachable. Hölty makes the point that he can be with *his* Laura because love has turned earth into heaven.

The bliss described by Hölty has something whimsical and coy about it, but it also has the earthiness of a Ländler: its tempo is slower than a waltz (as if the text is being coaxed out of the singer) but it has more glide than a country dance. Although the long accented passing notes resolving downwards, a dotted crotchet falling to a crotchet in bb. 15–16, 19–20, 23–4 and 27–8 are almost outrageously manipulative, the artlessness of this music is full of the high art that defies definition.

The song was unknown until 1895 but since then has become one of the most famous of all Schubert 'lollipops'. Elisabeth Schumann, who made it her own between the wars, was able to carry off the song as a masterpiece of soubrette charm. It was a favourite encore of Rita Streich who, in singing 'Bleib ich ewig hier' (accompanied by a curtsey to match the downward sweep of the final vocal roulade), assured her audiences of her undying willingness to stay on stage just as long as they continued to applaud – the 'hier' suddenly referring to that heaven on earth, the concert platform. This coy approach can give the proscenium arch an unintended meaning. Hölty's words can also lend themselves to a more passionately masculine advocacy and Fischer-Dieskau and Schreier made the alluring Laura the focus of their interpretations. What is delightful about the poem is that it does not permit heads (or souls) to remain permanently in the clouds, and we are returned to the safety of terra firma. Laura's beauties are after all palpable, even if on seeing her we imagine we have died and gone to heaven. The wry philosophy has its explosive implications for the dangers of modern life. Even if the singer has been promised an array of virgins in the afterlife he would be well advised to calm down and keep hold of a living person he can be sure of.

Autograph:	Österreichische Nationalbibliothek, Vienna
First edition:	Published as part of the AGA in 1895 (P641)
Subsequent editions:	Peters: Vol. 7/11; AGA XX 225: Vol. 4/108; NSA IV: Vol. 10/162
Arrangements:	Arr. Tilman Hoppstock (b. 1961) for guitar accompaniment, in *Franz Schubert: 110 Lieder* (2009)
Discography and timing:	Fischer-Dieskau I 7[15] 1'50
	Hyperion I 11[19]
	Hyperion II 14[12] 2'03 Brigitte Fassbaender

← *Der Leidende (Klage)* D432ʙ   *Erntelied* D434 →

SELMA UND SELMAR
(KLOPSTOCK) **D286** [H172]

Selma and Selmar   Duet

The song exists in two versions, the second of which is discussed below:
(1) Date unknown; (2) 14 September 1815

(1)   'Etwas langsam, innig'   F major   ¾   [20 bars]

(2)   F major

Wei-ne du nicht, o, die ich in-nig lie-be,

(20 bars)

Selmar:
  Weine du nicht, o, die ich innig liebe,
Dass ein trauriger Tag von dir mich scheidet!
Wenn nun wieder Hesperus dir dort lächelt,
Komm' ich Glücklicher, wieder!

Selma:
  Aber in dunkler Nacht ersteigst du Felsen,
Schwebst in täuschender dunkler Nacht auf
  Wassern!
Teilt' ich nur mit dir die Gefahr zu sterben;

Würd', ich Glückliche, weinen?

Selmar:
  Do not weep, my most truly beloved,
Because a sad day separates me from you.
When Hesperus, there, once more smiles on you
I shall return a happy man.

Selma:
  But in the dark night you climb the rocks;
In night's deceptive darkness you range over the
  waters!
If I could now share with you the danger of
  death,
Would I then, a happy woman, weep?

FRIEDRICH GOTTLOB KLOPSTOCK (1724–1803); poem written in summer? 1766

*Selma und Selmar is a musical dialogue between two characters who never sing simultaneously
(a performance for a single singer taking both male and female roles would thus be a possibility).
This duet is accordingly listed here as the third of Schubert's thirteen Klopstock solo settings
(1815–16). See the poet's biography for a chronological list of all the Klopstock settings.*

This is one of the many duets in the Schubert repertoire where two singers (in this case first
male, then female) never conjoin. In this strophic song the first verse is sung by Selmar, the
second by Selma. In terms of inner radiance and beauty of melody the piece outdoes another
Klopstock setting, the more complex and elaborately theatrical *Hermann und Thusnelda* D322,
composed just over a month later. Whether or not Klopstock himself was influenced by Ossian
in the writing of the poem, it is likely that Schubert, in the midst of his high Ossianic phase,
was attracted to it by its indeterminate historical background, and to this extent he must have
classed it as having something to do with Ossian. Even *Hermann und Thusnelda* is Ossianic to
the extent that the race of early German heroes must have seemed connected to the noble race
of warriors whose existence was promulgated by the Celtic bard. In any case, Selma is a word
used by Ossian, albeit as the name for Fingal's castle or capital city, deriving from the Gaelic
'Sealla-math', meaning 'beautiful view or prospect'. Selma (as in the soprano Selma Kurz) became
popular as a girl's name in Germany.

The piece has the mood of a stately minuet. The poem, in which a male lover reassures his troubled paramour, is strongly reminiscent of Klopstock's *Furcht der Geliebten* D285 where it is Cidli who is enjoined not to weep. The melody is touching, rather in the baroque manner of *Bist du bei mir*, attributed to Bach. The music is written in Schubert's antique style, his means of acknowledging that the poem he is setting is not a 'modern' one. Selmar sings his strophe first, and Selma's music is an exact repeat. This is different from Christian Neefe's setting of 1776 where the first verse is in the major and the second in the minor.

John Reed finds it puzzling that the second version of the song should be marked 'Etwas geschwind' ('rather fast'). In Schubert's first version (identical to the second apart from the brief two-bar introduction) the tempo marking is 'Etwas langsam, innig'. Reed finds this preferable for a 'solemn hymn-like setting'. Performers of Schubert songs learn, however, that the composer's tempo markings are never to do with a song's *mood* but rather, in the old-fashioned Italian manner taught by Salieri, with *pulse*. Thus a song may seem fast but have a slow background pulse and marking, as in the rippling and playful *Liebesbotschaft* D957/1 from *Schwanengesang*, 'Ziemlich langsam'. In that case the basic unit of the crotchet *is* slow within $\frac{2}{4}$, despite the demisemiquavers that fill out the beats to depict the glittering water. *Selma und Selmar* is an example of the converse: the crotchets glide by rather quickly when measured by the metronome – try beating them in three and the tempo will indeed be 'Etwas geschwind'. Because there are no semiquavers, however, the *effect* is of a slow song. The original marking of 'Etwas langsam' probably encouraged the song's earliest performers (if there were any, who knows?) to essay too slow a tempo where the four-bar phrases were unsingable in a single breath. The composer's second thoughts can be understood when seen in this light.

It is worth noting, however, that in Volume 9 of the NSA Walther Dürr makes a case for a reordering of the versions, and believes that the one marked 'Etwas geschwind', long accepted as the second, is in fact the first. While acknowledging that songs with piano introductions are usually second versions, he argues that Schubert usually dates the first versions of his songs rather than later ones. In this case it would mean that the version marked 'Etwas geschwind' came first. The question remains open.

Autograph:	Staatsbibliothek Preussischer Kulturbesitz, Berlin (second version as above, first version as in NSA)
	The first version (as listed above, the second as in NSA) is derived from a copy of the music in Albert Stadler's album
Publication:	First published as part of the AGA in 1895 (P582; first version)
	First published as Book 28 no. 2 of the *Nachlass* by Diabelli, Vienna in April 1837 (P316; second version)
Subsequent editions:	Peters: Vol. 5/158; AGA XX 140a & b: Vol. 3/74; NSA IV: Vol. 9/60 & 61
Bibliography:	Clerk 1870, Vol. 1, p. 76
Arrangements:	Arr. Tilman Hoppstock (b. 1961) for guitar accompaniment, in *Franz Schubert: 110 Lieder* (2009)
Discography and timing:	Deutsche Grammophon
	Schubert Duette 1'30 Janet Baker & Dietrich Fischer-Dieskau
	Hyperion I 22[24] 1'41 Lorna Anderson & Jamie MacDougall
	Hyperion II 10[7]

←— *Furcht der Geliebten ('An Cidli')* D285   *Vaterlandslied* D287 —→

JOHANN CHRYSOSTOMUS SENN (1795–1857)

THE POETIC SOURCES
The two Senn poems set by Schubert were almost certainly brought back in manuscript to Vienna from the Tyrol by Franz von Bruchmann and handed over to the composer.

LATER POETIC EDITION
S1 *Gedichte von Johann Senn*. Innsbruck in der Wagner'schen Buchhandlung, 1838

THE SONGS
Autumn? 1822   *Selige Welt* D743
                Schwanengesang D744 [S1: p. 15 with title of 'Schwanenlied' and footnote, 'In Musik gesetzt von Fr. Schubert']

Johann Senn was born in Pfunds in the Tyrol on 1 April 1795 (there is some disagreement on this date, and it is often given as 1792, but Goedeke and other sources are categoric). Two years older than Schubert, he was a proud and patriotic Tyrolean. His father, Franz Michael Senn (1762–1813), was in the judiciary and was a political activist for the independence of the Tyrol in the uprisings against the French and Bavarians in 1809. His family moved to Vienna in 1810 and the boy was sent to the Stadtkonvikt where Schubert was also a pupil. He is thus numbered among the composer's earliest and most lively friends. Senn was loved for his freedom of thought, his fearless intellectual vivacity and his affectionate nature.

Senn's father was murdered in 1813, but this family tragedy was only the beginning of the boy's troubles. Metternich's police, fearful of student-fermented rebellion in Vienna, were suspicious of all young people who gathered regularly at inns. The murder of the playwright Kotzebue in March 1819 was the excuse to set about the enactment of repressive legislation – the Karlsbad Decrees – by which liberty of speech and of the press were abolished throughout German-speaking lands. A letter of July 1819 from the British diplomat Sir Robert Gordon to the British premier Lord Castelreagh clearly delineates the paranoia of the Austrian government, all the more eloquent because Gordon was generally in sympathy with Metternich's conservative agenda: 'Nothing can surpass Prince Metternich's activity in collecting facts and informa-

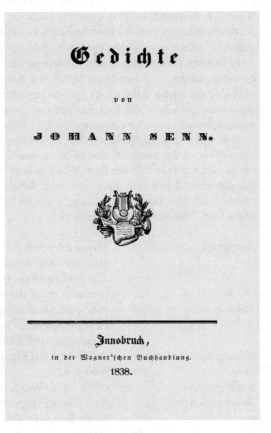

Senn's *Gedichte* (Innsbruck, 1838).

tion upon the inward feelings of the people; with a habit of making these researches he has acquired a taste for them . . . The secrecy with which the task is indulged leads him to attach too great importance to his discoveries. Phantoms are conjured up and magnified in the

Johann Senn, pencil drawing, 1820, by Leopold Kupelwieser.

was about to return to Salzburg. By the time the police arrived there were only five people left at Senn's apartment, including the poet himself, and all were arrested. One of these, as luck would have it, was 'the school assistant Schubert from the Rossau'. The police commissioner Leopold Ferstl (later ennobled with the title of Ferstl von Försenau) complained of Senn's 'defiant and offensive behaviour' during questioning, and another three – the law student Streinsberg, a young man named Zechenter from Cilli in Slovenia, and 'the son of the merchant Bruchmann' were all in the mood to confront their accusers, no doubt emboldened by a night of drinking and greatly irritated by the injustice of heavy-handed police interference. The memorandum of the police chief refers to their 'outrageous and criminal behaviour'.

Schubert was of little interest to the authorities and it is likely that he kept his head down during the incident, but he must have remembered this terrifying brush with the police for the rest of his life, for Metternich's agents had a reputation for extreme brutality. These four all received official warnings and their parents were notified (one can imagine the scenes of paternal rage in the Schubert household) but Senn fared much worse. Apart from the 'evidence' of the diary, it did not help at all that a police examiner, almost admiringly, labelled him a genius – the very worst kind of young opponent for the security of the state. It seems he was condemned not because he had broken the law but because there was perceived to be a danger of him doing so in the future. Once he was in the hands of the authorities, events snowballed and the poet's own pugnacious personality clearly did him no favours. Senn was kept imprisoned for fourteen months in Vienna and was then exiled back to his native Tyrol. While the poet was fiercely patriotic to his home region, to the point of being a separatist, Vienna was the only significant cultural centre of the nation, and a young artist cut off from his friends and important artistic influences lived in a wilderness – scenically beautiful, certainly, but unconducive to intellectual development. This single setback so early in

dark, which probably if exposed to light would sink into insignificance; and his informers naturally exaggerate their reports, aware that their profit is to be commensurate with the display of their phantasmagoria.' No neater summation could be found of the witch-hunt that led up to Senn's arrest. Certain students who met together were identified by the authorities as potentially dangerous and there may have been an informer within the Schubert circle. There was a raid on premises at which Senn was not present, but police confiscated a friend's diary in which had been written, 'Senn is the only man I regard as capable of being able to die for an idea.' This simple sentence made him a prime target for the attentions of the authorities, and according to Bruchmann's later communication with him ('you were torn from our midst early in the morning, never to return') there was a dawn raid on the poet's home on 20 January 1820 following a student party ('a wildly spent night' in Bruchmann's words) in honour of one Alois Fischer who his career literally ruined his life. A decade later the Viennese count Anastasius Grün would anonymously write (and publish in Germany) his *Spaziergänge eines Wiener Poeten* which was openly critical of the Metternich regime. Metternich's police traced the book back to Grün and, no doubt because he was an aristocrat, allowed him to compromise and recant. Senn, who would have been an important part of the movement culminating in the revolution of 1848, was accorded no such deference.

He made ends meet in Innsbrück by writing but he was forbidden to teach privately, being considered a potentially bad influence on the young. The local police went out of their way to harass Senn and make his life as unpleasant as possible. Bruchmann, devoted to the poet, kept in touch with him and lent him money, regarding Senn as something of a Christ-like figure who had been sacrificed to pay for the sins of the entire Schubert circle. But the friendship between these two men, utterly different in temperament, dissolved as Bruchmann's political and religious beliefs became more right wing and hard line. Before this happened, however, Bruchmann visited Senn in September 1822 and brought back at least two of the poet's manuscripts, passing them on to Schubert for musical setting. It is interesting that it was probably also Bruchmann who was the middleman in the arranging for two of Platen's poems to be set after encountering the poet in Erlangen; Bruchmann emerges in this version of the story as something of a secret agent engaged in subterfuge with political (Senn) and sexual (Platen) outcasts – in later life these were roles with which he would have been horrified to have been identified.

It seems that the Vienna circle of friends kept in close clandestine touch with Senn for some years after his exile, and that his thoughts and opinions continued to exert an influence on them. In the autumn of 1823 Schubert's Op. 23 was published – the poet's two songs (*Selige Welt* and *Schwanengesang*) were the central panel of a collection of four with Platen's *Die Liebe hat gelogen* D751 and Schober's *Schatzgräbers Begehr* D761 on either side. The poet's name is printed on both songs, but Schubert was unable to dedicate the entire set to Senn as he had planned. This might have been due to an immediate embargo from the censor's office, but the wheels of bureaucracy usually revolve in more obtuse ways – perhaps it was impossible to obtain written permission from the dedicatee, necessary for all song publications in Austria, because the exiled person in question was prohibited from engaging in correspondence with government departments.

For the poet himself, the long-term consequences of that exile from Vienna were continuing financial hardship and artistic frustration. Senn later served as a common soldier, and for a while even joined that secret revolutionary army, the Carbonari, in Italy, progressing through the ranks. Having no means of making money from his writings, he became increasingly bitter in his dealings with people and eventually turned to drink. We do not know a great deal about Schubert's feelings for Senn, but he must have regarded his old friend with the kind of admiration reserved for those who share one's own beliefs and suffer monstrous ill-treatment on that account – 'there, but for the grace of God, go I'. The poet's reputation no doubt took on something of a mythical status with this group of angry young men, ashamed that they, unlike Senn, had been cowed into submission by the state. If this strong-willed and admirably straightforward poet had remained in Vienna, the whole balance of the composer's circle might have been different; it is even possible that Franz von Schober would not have achieved quite the same influence over Schubert if Senn had been there to offer a counterbalance. The poet's autobiographical sketch written in 1849 mentions Schubert with nostalgia (according to Schober, Senn dreamed of Schubert in 1830), and he also wrote a sonnet (*see* below) when news reached him of Schubert's death. It is one of the few contemporary pieces written about Schubert that demonstrates an awareness that the composer's work had been achieved at an enormous personal cost. Senn died in Innsbruck on 30 September 1857.

An S. den Tondichter.

Apollo's Wort war einst vor dir erklungen:
'Ich will zum heil'gen Sänger ein dich weihen,
'Wenn du entsagst dem blüh'nden Lebensreihen,
'Nur staunend singst, von ew'ger Gottlust
  trunken.'

Er sprach's. Du warst in Andacht hingesunken,

Sein Wollen konnt' nur Müssen dir verleihen;
Im Leben solltest du zum Kind gedeihen,

Doch im Gesang hast Orpheus du erschwungen.

Gelöst dein irdisch Sein in Harmonien,

Entschwebest du auf der Begeist'rung Flügel
Zu des Olympos schneebedeckten Höhen.

Und wenn du schwebst voll trunkner Fantasien,
Entsinket dir des eignen Lebens Zügel,
Und süsse Töne müssen dich verwehen!

To S the Tone Poet

Apollo's word once resounded before you:
'I shall consecrate you as a sacred singer.
If you renounce life's spirited dance
And astonish with your singing, drunk with
  eternal divine joy.'

Thus he spoke. You sank to your knees in
  reverence;
His will could only be your command.
In life you would flourish in childlike
  innocence,
But in song you flew as high as Orpheus.

Your earthly existence is dissolved in
  harmonies,
You float on the wings of rapture
To the snow-clad heights of Olympus.

And when you soar, intoxicated with fantasies,
The yoke of your own life slip away,
And sweet music must carry you aloft!

Bibliography: Dürhammer 1999, pp. 98, 199 & 309

SERAFINA AN IHR KLAVIER *see* AN MEIN KLAVIER D342

SERBATE, O DEI CUSTODI   Guard, o ye gods
(METASTASIO) **D35/3** [H14]
C major   (Compostion exercise) 10 December 1812

(93 bars)

Serbate, o Dei custodi
Della Romana sorte
In Tito il Giusto, il forte,
L'onor di nostra età.
Voi gl'immortali allori

Guard, o ye gods,
Custodians of Rome's destiny.
Titus, the just and the strong,
Is the honour of our age.
Guard for Rome's sake the immortal laurels

Su la Cesarea chioma	On the brow of Caesar;
Voi custodite a Roma	Preserve for Rome's sake,
La sua felicità.	His happiness.
Fu vostro un sì gran dono,	Yours was such a great gift;
Sia lungo il dono vostro.	May it last long.
L'invidii al mondo nostro	May times to come
Il mondo che verrà.	Envy our age because of him.

PIETRO METASTASIO (1698–1782); poem written in 1734

This is the third of Schubert's fourteen Metastasio solo settings (1812–27). See the poet's biography for a chronological list of all the Metastasio settings.

In D35 there are three settings of this text from Metastasio's *La clemenza di Tito* – the first two are choral, firstly for four solo voices, and then for chorus (as the poet had intended in his libretto). But Schubert was then assigned the much more sophisticated task of creating a noble aria for tenor in opera seria style. This shows another side of Salieri's teaching regime for the young Schubert, an extension of the gentle cosseting that had so far required him to construct only melodious little pieces. Many of the arias and ensembles he had written for *Quell' innocente figlio* D17 and *Entra l'uomo allor che nasce* D33 (qqv) could be performed by good amateur singers. But here we have something much longer and more heroic, and definitely the province of the operatic professional.

At first Schubert was not asked to write accompaniments for any of the exercises undertaken for Salieri; here, however, the piano's introduction and postlude are both the composer's own, as well as the vocal and bass lines. The musicologist Alfred Orel (1889–1967) made the realization recorded for the Hyperion Edition. Orel's commentary on this work, and in particular on Salieri's many suggestions and improvements, shows that Schubert's schoolfriend Anton Holzapfel was wide of the mark in depicting the Italian as a lazy and uninterested teacher. On the contrary, he went into great detail in his 'marking', and Schubert would have picked up much that was useful during these sessions of change and revision. Salieri helped Schubert achieve what the teenager had not managed before – a large and heroic through-composed aria, difficult to sing certainly, but not stupidly impossible (like passages in some of the earlier ballads). It is well conceived for the larger tenor voice, and capable of generating considerable musical excitement. If the melodic invention is nowhere near what we have come to expect of Schubert, it should be remembered that he was writing an exercise in C major celebratory pomp with little room for subtle touches of human feeling.

The choice of text in favour of a heroic emperor may well have been influenced by the political events of the time. Napoleon's catastrophic lack of success in Russia had refocused the hopes of Austrians on the Emperor Franz I who was now preparing for the so-called 'Befreiungskrieg' – the war of liberation against French domination. Naturally, it would be interesting to know if Schubert knew the Mozart opera at this stage (he certainly never saw a production of it), but one thing is certain: he set the aria from Metastasio's original, not from Mozart's libretto which uses a shortened version of this choral text, adapted by Caterino Mazzolà for the Mozart opera's first performance in Prague in 1791. It is more likely that Salieri knew the text because his own teacher Gluck had set it as early as 1752.

| Autograph: | Destroyed in 1945 |
| First edition: | Realized from the bass line by Alfred Orel and first published in his *Der junge Schubert* in 1940 and subsequently as part of the NSA in 1986 (P797) |

Subsequent editions: Not in Peters; Not in AGA; NSA VIII: Vol. 2/232 (Orel's
                            completion)
Discography and timing: Fischer-Dieskau   —
                            Hyperion I 33^{10}
                            Hyperion II 2^{10} 3'24   Adrian Thompson

← *Entra l'uomo allor che nasce (Aria di Abramo) D33/2*   *Die Advokaten D37* →

SEUFZER   Sighs
(HÖLTY) **D198** [H100]
G minor   22 May 1815

(65 bars)

Die Nachtigall	The nightingale
Singt überall	Sings everywhere
Auf grünen Reisen.	On green boughs
Die besten Weisen,	Her loveliest songs
Dass ringsum Wald	That all around woods
Und Ufer schallt.	And river banks resound.
Manch junges Paar	Many young couples
Geht dort, wo klar	Stroll where
Das Bächlein rauschet,	The limpid brook murmurs.
Und steht und lauschet	They stop and listen
Mit frohem Sinn	Joyfully
Der Sängerin.	To the songstress.
Ich höre bang'	But gloomily
Im düstern Gang	On the dark path
Der Nachtigallen	I hear the nightingales'
Gesange schallen;	Echoing song.
Denn ach! allein	For alas, I wander
Irr' ich im Hain.	Alone in the grove.

LUDWIG HÖLTY (1748–1776); poem written 18 February 1773. Adapted for publication in
1804 by JOHANN HEINRICH VOSS (1751–1826)

*This is the sixth of Schubert's twenty-three Hölty solo settings (1813–16). See the poet's biography
for a chronological list of all the Hölty settings.*

Seufzer was written on the same day as *An die Nachtigall* D196 and *An die Apfelbäume, wo ich Julien erblickte* D197. The construction of the poems could not be more different: the long unrhymed classical lines of *An die Apfelbäume* are here replaced by rhymed folk-like ones, and it is fascinating to see that Schubert's musical creativity could not help but be influenced by the look of the words on the printed page. The poem itself was so much changed by Hölty's well-meaning, but sometimes misguided, editor Voss, that its metre and the opening four lines are all that remains of the original poem (which was entitled *Die Nachtigall*). Schubert was not to know about this act of creative editing, but it is the metre that has influenced him the most. An example of this is the lines 'Und steht und lauschet [bb. 28–31] . . . mit frohem Sinn [bb. 32–5] . . . Sängerin [bb. 36–9]' which are part of a single sentence as far as their meaning is concerned, but which Schubert separates by quaver rests. This is in deference both to Hölty's line-breaks and to the dramatic truth, in musical terms, of needing time (at least a couple of quavers' worth) for the young couple to be pleasurably astonished by the song of the nightingale.

The melody enhances the feminine rhyme by sequence or echo at the twinned lines ending 'Reisen' (b. 7) and 'Weisen' (b. 11), 'rauschet' (b. 27) and 'lauschet' (b. 31), and 'Nachtigallen' (bb. 45–8) and 'schallen' (b. 51). The stretched-out time signature of 𝄵 of *An die Apfelbäume, wo ich Julien erblickte* is here replaced by the much shorter-breathed 𝄴. It seems that lofty contemplations on love like *An die Apfelbäume* merit compound time signatures, but the simplicities of nature, like folksong, are best contained by bar lengths simple and unpretentious. Perhaps Schubert heard the real-life nightingale's song in this rhythm; the Claudius setting *An die Nachtigall* D497 is also in 𝄴, and the Hölty setting of the same name has the pastoral 'swing' of 𝄵. There is a ripple of water about this music, and it is interesting to see that Schubert looked beyond the first verse for a background that would determine the song's *Bewegung*, and found the presence of water in the second strophe ('wo klar / Das Bächlein rauschet' bb. 23–7). Accordingly the stream in gently undulating semiquavers runs unobtrusively throughout the song. This is a perfect miniature, a neglected little jewel, where poetic and musical matter are perfectly matched.

Autograph:	Conservatoire collection, Bibliothèque Nationale, Paris
First edition:	First published as part of the AGA in 1895 (P563)
Subsequent editions:	Not in Peters; AGA XX 74: Vol. 2/120; NSA IV: Vol. 8/54
Discography and timing:	Fischer-Dieskau I 3²³ 1'05
	Hyperion I 10⁷
	Hyperion II 6²⁰ 1'26 Martyn Hill

← *An die Apfelbäume, wo ich Julien erblickte* D197   *Auf den Tod einer Nachtigall* D201 →

WILLIAM SHAKESPEARE (1564–1616)

THE TRANSLATIONS
S1 *William Shakspeare's* [sic] *Saemtliche Dramatische Werke*, übersetzt im Metrum des Originals. XXXVI Bändchen. Wien. Druck und Verlag von J. P. Sollinger, 1825. *Antonius und Cleopatra* von Ferd. V. Mayerhofer Titel und Vignetten lithographirt bei Joseph Trentsensky in Wien

The spelling of 'Shakspeare' for this edition was also common in nineteenth-century England. As late as 1864 there were Staffordshire statuettes of the Bard inscribed with this spelling.

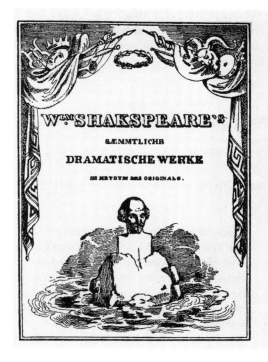

Designs by Moritz von Schwind for the front and back covers of the Viennese Shakespeare Edition – thirty-seven small booklets bound in brown card, each with a different vignette (of English design) on the internal title pages.

S2 *William Shakspeare's* [sic] *Saemtliche Dramatische Werke*, übersetzt im Metrum des Originals. XXVI Bändchen. Wien. Druck und Verlag von J. P. Sollinger, 1825. *Cymbelin* von A. W. Schlegel. Titel und Vignetten lithographirt bei Joseph Trentsensky in Wien

S3 *William Shakspeare's* [sic] *Saemtliche Dramatische Werke*, übersetzt im Metrum des Originals. II Bändchen. Wien. Druck und Verlag von J. P. Sollinger, 1825. *Die beiden Edelleute von Verona* von Bauernfeld. Titel und Vignetten lithographirt bei Joseph Trentsensky in Wien

S4 *William Shakspeare's* [sic] *sämmtliche dramatische Werke* Übersetzt im Metrum des Originals in einem Bande nebst Supplement, enthaltend Shakspeare's Leben, nebst Anmerkungen und kritischen Erläuterungen zu seinen Werken Wien, Zu haben bei Rudolph Sammer, Buchhändler, 1826

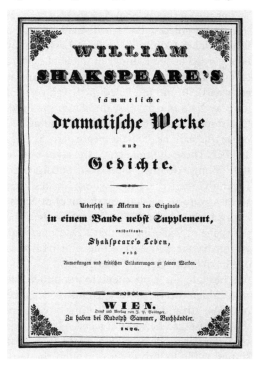

Title page of the single-volume Viennese edition of Shakespeare (1826).

This is a handsome one-volume edition of the Wiener Shakespeare Ausgabe in Gr 8vo format, very much bigger than the small paperbacks of the individual plays, without vignettes, and issued by a different publisher in a completely reset text. It is not impossible that the Schober family acquired this volume and that it was Schubert's source.

THE SONGS

July 1826   *Trinklied* ('Bacchus, feister Fürst des Weins') D888 [S1: Act II Scene 7 p. 47 sung by
             Enobarbus] [S4: p. 864]
             Ständchen ('Horch! horch! die Lerch'') D889 [S2: Act II Scene 3 p. 33, sung by a
             musician urged on by Cloten] [S4: p. 606]
             Gesang (An Silvia) D891 [S3: Act IV Scene 2 p. 55, sung by chorus] [S4: p. 32]

Shakespeare was baptized in Stratford-on-Avon on 26 April 1564 and died on 23 April (?) 1616. It seems unnecessary here to provide English-speaking readers with an outline of Shakespeare's life story. Suffice it to say that of the plays from which Schubert took lyrics, *The Two Gentlemen of Verona* was unknown before 1623; *Cymbeline* was first published in 1623 but was performed in 1611; *Antony and Cleopatra* was registered in 1608, but the Folio text was first published in 1623.

For the Germans, Shakespeare was perhaps the single greatest literary discovery from a foreign land. Gotthold Ephraim Lessing may be regarded as the founder of the Shakespeare cult in Germany: he praises Shakespeare as early as 1750, and modelled the blank verse of his play *Nathan der Weise* on that of the Bard. Christoph Martin Wieland had published prose translations of Shakespeare plays as early as 1762. These did not escape the attentions of the young Goethe who also encountered Johann Gottfried Herder (whose Shakespeare studies were of crucial importance) at Strasbourg University in 1770. Goethe wrote: 'The first page of Shakespeare that I read made me aware that he and I were one . . . I had been one born blind who first sees the light . . . I did not hesitate for a moment to renounce the rule-ridden theatre of the ancients . . . I leaped into free air and for the first time was aware that I possessed hands and feet . . . In the face of Shakespeare I acknowledge that I am a poor sinner, while he prophesies through the pure force of nature.' Goethe was inspired in

numerous works by the Bard's example, above all in *Faust*: the 'Erdgeist' comes from Caesar's ghost; Faust's brawling is suggested by the carousings of Prince Hal; Juliet's Nurse has inspired Martha, the widow-companion of Gretchen, whose lovelorn distress, in turn, is modelled on Ophelia; Faust's duel with Valentin comes from Romeo's with Tybalt; and so on. A major part of *Wilhelm Meisters Lehrjahre* is concerned with the mounting of a production of *Hamlet*. As far as contemporary German taste is concerned, the selection of this work for such detailed attention signals the victory of Shakespearean drama over the neoclassicism of French theatre. Goethe's great colleague and friend Friedrich Schiller was also mightily taken with Shakespeare. At the beginning of his career the character of Franz Moor in *Die Räuber* resembles Richard III and, at the end of it, Wilhelm Tell seems influenced by the Bard's Julius Caesar.

The next translator of importance was August von Schlegel who by 1810 had published no fewer than seventeen of Shakespeare's plays. This monumental work was completed in 1825–33 by Graf Wolf Heinrich Baudissin and his wife Dorothea under the supervision of Ludwig Tieck, Dorothea's father. Thus a further nineteen plays were added to an edition that became standard for over a century. It is at this point in the story that Schubert appears – all too briefly. It is easy to take instantly to a poet who has been translated into a modern language and it was thus that Shakespeare appeared peculiarly contem-

Shakespeare welcomes Schiller into heaven, frontispiece of the almanac *Minerva* (1820).

We do not know exactly when Schubert was first aware of a poet whose name graces many early nineteenth-century German publications. For example, the almanac *Urania* from 1823 (wherein Schubert first discovered the *Winterreise* poems) contains six handsome plates of scenes from *King Lear*, *Othello* and *Macbeth* with passages translated from the English by J. H. Voss (qv). Ilija Dürhammer notes that the Shakespeare *Sonnets* were read aloud in the reading circle hosted by Schober and the mysterious dedicatee of these love poems was no doubt discussed. By the time Schubert came to set some of the Shakespearean lyrics, there had appeared a special pocket-sized Viennese edition of the Bard's works (1825–6), each play issued separately with a title page and vignette. These small drawings were not by Moritz von Schwind, as is sometimes claimed, but by John Thurston (1774–1822) whose illustrations (six for each play), published in London in 1825, were turned into engravings that could be 'adapted to all editions'. Schwind did, however, provide the front and back designs for the light-brown paper covers of this Viennese Shakespeare edition, incorporating Thurston's sketch of Shakespeare's head, and placing it on a stone plinth. Only eleven of the plays in this edition (the same Viennese firm of Trentsensky issued the plays of Caldéron in thirty-six equally small booklets) were newly translated; for other plays (*Cymbeline* among them) the publisher relied on extant translations by August von Schlegel and others. Of the three songs Schubert set to music, two of the translators were known to him personally (Bauernfeld and Mayerhofer von Grünbühel) which certainly contributed to his interest in these particular versions of the lyrics. The singer Johann Michael Vogl could read English in the original and was undoubtedly a Shakespeare enthusiast – another reason for Schubert to have composed these songs.

porary to German-speakers, something denied English audiences of the nineteenth century who had to deal with a vocabulary, idiom and style that was no longer in everyday use. One can only surmise what further lyrics by Shakespeare Schubert might have set had he lived longer. In the sweep and variety of his lieder, Schubert displays a breadth of imagination and human sympathy that is also found in the Shakespeare plays; in this respect the adjectives Shakespearean and Schubertian, usually used to very different purpose, might be almost interchangeable.

SHILRIK UND VINVELA   Shilric and Vinvela   Duet
(OSSIAN–MACPHERSON/HAROLD) **D293** [H178]

The song exists in two versions, the second of which is discussed below:
(1) 20 September 1815; (2) Date unknown

(1)   'Nicht zu geschwind'   B♭ major – A major   **C**   [195 bars]

(2)   B♭ major – A major

(196 bars)

The English translation given here is Ossian's original, despite tiny variations.

Vinvela:

Mein Geliebter ist ein Sohn des Hügels; er verfolgt die fliehenden Hirsche; die Doggen schnauben um ihn; die Senn seines Bogens schwirrt in dem Wind. Ruhst du bei der Quelle des Felsen oder beim Rauschen des Bergstroms? Der Schilf neigt sich im Wind, der Nebel fliegt über die Heide; ich will ihm ungesehn nahn; ich will ihn betrachten vom Felsen herab. Ich sah dich zuerst liebreich bei der veralteten Eiche von Branno; schlank kehrtest du vom Jagen zurück, unter allen deinen Freunden der schönste.

Vinvela:

My love is a son of the hill. He pursues the fleeing deer. His dogs are panting around him; his bow-string sounds in the wind. Dost thou rest by the fountain of the rock, or by the noise of the mountain stream? The rushes are nodding to the wind, the mist flies over the heath. I will approach my love unseen; I will behold him from the rock. Lovely I saw thee first by the aged oak of Branno; thou wert returning tall from the chase; the fairest among thy friends.

Shilrik:

Was ist's für eine Stimme, die ich höre? Sie gleicht dem Hauche des Sommers! Ich sitz nicht beim neigenden Schilfe; ich hör nicht die Quelle des Felsen. Ferne, ferne o Vinvela, geh ich zu den Kriegen von Fingal: meine Doggen begleiten mich nicht; ich trete nicht mehr auf den Hügel. Ich seh dich nicht mehr von der Höhe, zierlich schreitend am Strome der Fläche; schimmernd, wie der Bogen des Himmels; wie der Mond auf der westlichen Welle.

Shilric:

What voice is that I hear? that voice like the summer wind! I sit not by the nodding rushes; I hear not the sound of the rock. Afar Vinvela, afar, I go to the war of Fingal. My dogs attend me no more. No more I tread the hill. No more from on high I see thee, fair moving by the stream of the plain; bright as the bow of heaven; as the moon on the western wave.

Vinvela:

So bist du gegangen, o Shilrik! Ich bin allein
auf dem Hügel! man sieht die Hirsche am
Rande des Gipfels, sie grasen furchtlos
hinweg; sie fürchten die Winde nicht mehr;
nicht mehr den brausenden Baum. Der Jäger
ist weit in der Ferne; er ist im Felde der
Gräber. Ihr Fremden! ihr Söhne der Wellen!
O schont meines liebreichen Shilrik!

Shilrik:

Wenn ich im Felde muss fallen, heb hoch,
O Vinvela, mein Grab. Graue Steine und ein
Hügel von Erde; sollen mich, bei der
Nachwelt bezeichnen. Wenn der Jäger beim
Haufen wird sitzen, wenn er zu Mittag seine
Speise geneusst, wird er sagen: 'Ein Krieger
ruht hier,' und mein Ruhm soll leben in
seinem Lob. Erinn're dich meiner, o Vinvela,
wenn ich auf Erden erlieg!

Vinvela:

Ja! ich werd' mich deiner erinnern; ach! mein
Shilrik wird fallen! Mein Geliebter! Was soll
ich tun, wenn du auf ewig vergingest? Ich
werd' diese Hügel am Mittag durchstreichen:
die schweigende Heide durchziehn. Dort
werd' ich den Platz deiner Ruh, wenn du von
der Jagd zurückkehrtest beschaun. Ach! mein
Shilrik wird fallen; aber ich werd' meines
Shilriks gedenken.

Vinvela:

Then thou art gone, O Shilric! I am alone on the
hill! The deer are seen on the brow; void of fear
they graze along. No more they dread the wind,
no more the rustling tree. The hunter is far
removed; he is in the field of graves. Strangers!
Sons of the waves! Spare my lovely Shilric!

Shilric:

If fall I must in the field, raise high my grave,
Vinvela. Grey stones and heaped-up earth shall
mark me to future times. When the hunter shall
sit by the mound, and produce his food at noon,
'Some warrior rests here,' he will say; and my
fame shall live in his praise. Remember me,
Vinvela, when low on earth I lie!

Vinvela:

Yes! I will remember thee, alas! my Shilric will
fall! What shall I do, my love! when thou art for
ever gone? Through these hills I will go at noon:
I will go through the silent heath. There I will
see the place of thy rest, returning from the
chase. Alas! my Shilric will fall; but I will
remember Shilric.

JAMES MACPHERSON ('OSSIAN') (1736–1796), translated by EDMUND, BARON VON HAROLD
(1737–1800)

Shilrik und Vinvela *is a musical dialogue between two characters who never sing simultaneously
(a performance for a single singer taking both male and female roles would thus be a possibility).*
*This work is accordingly listed here as the fifth of Schubert's ten Ossian–Macpherson solo
settings (1815–17). See the poet's biography (under Macpherson) for a chronological list of all the
Ossian settings.*

The first German translations (from the English of James Macpherson) of this supposedly Gaelic
verse were published in 1764. So powerful was their influence that Goethe asked his readers to
believe that the hero's suicide in his *Die Leiden des jungen Werthers* was precipitated, in part, by
his reading of Ossian with Charlotte. The role of the ancient bard, still apparent in poems by
Schubert's contemporaries nearly fifty years later, was inspired by the appearance of these epic
poems. The minstrel was seen as a worldwide figure going back to the beginning of time; he
was a priest-like idealist whose disinterested love of art and truth reminded men that they had
lost touch with the higher spiritual (though not specifically Christian) values of yore.

What was it in the works of Macpherson–Ossian that appealed to so many writers, musicians and painters, and to Schubert in particular? His first Macpherson setting, *Kolmas Klage* D217, dates from 1815, as does his first foray into the Greek myths, Körner's *Amphiaraos* D166. Perhaps wind-swept, misty Scotland was a northern counterpart, in Schubert's mind, to the southern lands of ancient civilizations; if Greece was the cradle of rational thought and intellectual exploration, Ossian's warriors signposted a romantic age full of feeling, the more authentic for being untutored and instinctive. The last books Schubert ever read were by James Fenimore Cooper whose Red Indians embody the attraction of the 'noble savage'. If ancient Greece meant clarity, warmth and light, Fingal's Scotland was shrouded by the mists of time, cold and more closely related to the sagas of the north in which all German-speakers feel the background of their race. The warriors of Greece were capable of great heroism, but Ossian's heroes were idealistically upright, trusty and true, with all the good, and none of the bad, of primitive peoples. The Rev. Archibald Clerk, defending Macpherson's integrity as late as 1870, writes of Ossian's female characters: 'in purity, dignity and tenderness [they are] immeasurably superior to the coarse, scolding, fighting goddesses of Homer'. Clark also informs us that the name Shilric, or Silric, derives from the Gaelic 'Sìol Rìgh' which means 'one of a royal race'. Vinvela (or Binvela, also Binvel) is from the Gaelic 'Binnbheul', meaning 'melodious mouth'.

In *Carric-Thura*, a subsection of Macpherson's *Fingal* (1762, p. 194) we encounter the following footnote: 'One should think that the parts of Shilric and Vinvela were represented by Cronnan and Minona, whose very names denote that they were singers, who performed in public. Cronnan signifies *a mournful sound*, Minona, or Min-'óon, *soft air*. All the dramatic poems of Ossian appear to have been performed before Fingal upon solemn occasions.'

Verse 1 (Vinvela): The introduction bears a disconcerting similarity to 'God Save the King', probably coincidental, unless Schubert had heard the tune hammered out at the first performance of Beethoven's 'Battle' Symphony Op. 91 in December 1813, or perhaps all around Vienna in celebration of the Allied victory at Waterloo a few months before he wrote this ballad. Shilric and Vinvela were, after all, British citizens in the broadest sense. All the musical illustrations precede what they describe, in the manner of Haydn's *Die Schöpfung*: in the piano interlude at bb. 7–10 the flight of the deer (two of them, male and female, in canonic imitation); in bb. 12–16 the panting dogs (the modulation between two bouts of panting suggests great doggy eagerness to please); and at bb. 17–18 the fluttering of reverberating bow strings. In b. 20 there is a change to 'Langsam' that sets up a $\frac{3}{4}$ signature. At b. 21 the aria beginning 'Ruhst du bei der Quelle des Felsen', a duet between the vocal line and a cello in the pianist's left hand, is a ravishing example of Schubert's water and nature music. There is a change of direction when Vinvela goes to look for Shilric, deciding that she would get a better vantage point if she were to 'behold him from the rock'. At b. 36 there is a four-bar interlude (marked 'Geschwind') before 'Ich sah dich zuerst liebreich' where the climbing modulations echo the astonishing piano music in Haydn's *Arianna a Naxos*, whose heroine climbs to a high vantage point from where she sees the departure of the treacherous Theseus' ship. This is followed by a recitative (bb. 40–50) that ends with a melting setting of 'der schönste' (and a sudden 'Langsam'); Schubert seems stricken by Shilric's beauty through Vinvela's eyes.

Verse 2 (Shilric): We are not certain, as is often the way with this poetry, if we are dealing with Shilric in person, or whether it is his spirit who speaks in the manner of Mahler's *Wo die schönen Trompeten blasen*, a genre of *Des Knaben Wunderhorn* poem much influenced by Ossian. At b. 51 the marking is 'Mässig geschwind', with a change to a single sharp in the key signature. Here a wonderful little figure – a crotchet followed by a dotted minim in rising sequences – is a perfect tonal analogue for the pricking up of Shilric's ears before the lines 'Was ist's für eine Stimme . . . ?' (b. 55). There follows an eloquent flowing plaint, accompanied by double thirds marked 'Etwas langsam' ('Ich sitz nicht beim neigenden Schilfe' from b. 61), of the type heard in the mourning music for the warrior killed at the end of the Kenner *Ballade* D134. The dogs pant dutifully in the piano writing as soon as they are mentioned (from b. 71). With the phrase 'schimmernd, wie der Bogen des Himmels, wie der Mond auf der westlichen Seite', the cupola of heavenly skies and the moon on the waters inspire a magical ten bars of infinite tenderness and rapture (bb. 79–88).

Verse 3 (Vinvela): This is a set-piece aria (with a change of marking to 'Langsam' and a change of key to G minor) that lacks some of the spontaneity of the recitatives. It has an old-fashioned eighteenth-century air, Gluckian and rather grandiose, as if Schubert is attempting to depict the stoicism of former times. 'Felde der Gräber' (b. 103) plunges the voice to an all-time low with the worms. But the following 'Ihr Fremden! ihr Söhne der Wellen!' (bb. 104–8) is somehow much more personal – a twice-repeated phrase of Mozartian beauty and poise.

Verse 4 (Shilric): This is steadfast music with another change of key, this time to F minor. The marking, 'Mit Würde', describes exactly the sense of patriotic duty. Shilric must master his fears with a heavy heart but a determined will – the latter admirably depicted by the purposeful bass in left-hand strides. The sixths between voice and accompaniment of 'Graue Steine' (bb. 123–4) are stonily uncompromising. From b. 131 the casual everyday quality of the recitative 'Wenn der Jäger beim Haufen wird sitzen' is lifted into the realms of immortal fame and memory (Shilric's own imagined place in the history of his people) by a shift from F minor into a hushed G flat (the marvellous phrase 'Ein Krieger ruht hier', marked 'Langsam' at bb. 133–4). Shilric's last arioso to his beloved, 'Erinn're dich meiner, o Vinvela' (from b. 136) achieves a genuinely lofty tone; it begins in E flat minor and by b. 148 has returned the music to an F minor chord on a semibreve with fermata.

Verse 5 (Vinvela): Without any ado, Vinvela starts her final aria in A major with the marking 'Ziemlich geschwind'. This gives a sudden lift to the proceedings that some have found inappropriate for one who imagines herself to be a war widow ('Not altogether sorry to be rid of him', writes John Reed, tongue-in-cheek). This music begins with the same heady defiance, both of death and its supposed ability to kill love, that we find in the Schiller setting *Hektors Abschied* D312 written less than a month later. But it conveys a more subtle mixture of emotions than most battle paeans. 'Ich werd' diese Hügel am Mittag durchstreichen' (from b. 163) says Vinvela: this announcement of her intention to wander the hills at noon sets up the scenario for the song's narrative sequel, *Cronnan* D282, which, although composed a fortnight earlier, actually takes up the narrative thread after a gap of only twenty lines. In *Cronnan* we discover that Shilric (impersonated by the singer named Cronnan) has survived the battle, and that Vinvela (impersonated by the singer Minona) has expired with grief, believing him to be dead. This close connection between the two songs was ignored in the publication order of the Ossian settings in the *Nachlass*, and has been ignored ever since.

The piece does not end in a blaze of glory; we are left, rather, with the emptiness of Vinvela's supposed bereavement. The postlude in simple minims (bb. 192–6) consigns Shilric softly to immortality in her breast; it is the Celtic counterpart to the heavenly means by which Ganymede will be lifted to immortality, two years later, on a cloud of rising minims in the final bars of his song D544. In a passage like this we see that the mythologies of Ossian and those of the ancient Greeks are taken equally seriously in Schubert's mind. Ganymede's apotheosis rises heavenward, whereas Shilric's metaphorical burial deep in Vinevela's mind moves inexorably downwards.

Although this song has been recorded as a duet in modern times there is nothing in the autograph that directs that it is to be performed as such. Male singers of former times were certainly more comfortable in assuming female characters in the process of narrative storytelling and Johann Michael Vogl gloried in singing Ellen Douglas's *Ave Maria* (*Ellens Gesang III*) D839.

Autographs:	Gesellschaft der Musikfreunde, Vienna (first 7 pages; first version); Wienbibliothek im Rathaus, Vienna (remainder of song; first version) Missing or lost (second version)
Publication:	Published as part of the NSA in 2011 (first version) Published as Book 4 no. 1 of the *Nachlass* by Diabelli, Vienna in July 1830 (P244; second version)
Publication reviews:	Rellstab 'Ueberblick der Erzeugnisse', *Iris im Gebiete der Tonkunst* (Berlin) No. 39 (12 November 1830) [Waidelich/Hilmar Dokumente II No. 784b]
Subsequent editions:	Peters: Vol. 4/192; AGA XX 146: Vol. 3/100; NSA IV: Vol. 9/90 & 100
Bibliography:	Clerk 1870, Vol. 1, pp. 179 & 180
Discography and timing:	Hyperion I 13[7]
	Hyperion II 10[13] 9'47 Marie McLaughlin & Thomas Hampson

← *Dem Unendlichen* (first version) D291   *Dem Unendlichen* (second version) D291 →

SIE IN JEDEM LIEDE   She in every song
(LEITNER) **D896A** [H650]
(Fragment) B♭ major   Autumn 1827 or later

Nehm ich die Har- fe,   fol-gend dem Dran-ge   sü-sser Ge-füh- le,   denk ich auch dein.

(115 bars)

Nehm' ich die Harfe,	When I take up my harp,
Folgend dem Drange	Prompted
Süsser Gefühle,	By sweet feelings,
Denk' ich auch dein.	I think of you too,
Mädchen! und glaub', es	Maiden; and believe me,
Können ja lange.	There cannot long
Ohne die Harfe	Be minstrels
Sänger nicht sein.	Without harps.
Wähn' ich im Liede	When in my songs
Siedler und Klause,	I imagine I see
Burg und Turniere	Once more before me
Wieder zu schau'n;	Crofters' and monks' cells,
Prangst mit Barette und	Castles and tournaments,
Starrender Krause	You are there on the balcony
Du am Balkone	Among the ladies,
Zwischen den Frau'n.	Resplendent in your cap and starched ruff.

Preis' ich der Alpen
Friedliche Lüfte,
Hoch ob des Thales
Wildem Gebraus;
Füllst du als Sennin
Trillernd die Klüfte,
Lachst aus dem kleinen
Hölzernen Haus.

When I praise the peaceful
Alpine breezes,
High above the valley's
Wild commotion,
You as dairymaid fill the ravines
With your trilling,
You laugh from within
The little wooden house.

Sing' ich von schönen
Wasser-Jungfrauen,
Einsam im Mondschein
Schwimmend im See;
Schwebst du bei ihnen
Unten im Blauen,
Streckst mir entgegen
Arme von Schnee.

When I sing
Of the fair water-nymphs
Swimming alone
In the moonlit sea,
You glide along with them
In the blue waters,
Holding out
Your snow-white arms to me.

Überall nahe
Weilest, du Liebe,
Mir in der Dichtung
Rosigem Land';
Ach, nur im Leben,[1]
Strenge und trübe,
Trennt uns des Schicksals
Feindliche Hand.

Everywhere you are close to me,
My love,
In the rosy land
Of poetry.
Ah, only in life,
Harsh and gloomy,
Does the hostile hand of fate
Sunder us.

KARL GOTTFRIED VON LEITNER (1800–1890)

This is the third of Schubert's eleven Leitner solo settings (1822–3 and 1827–8). See the poet's biography for a chronological list of all the Leitner settings.

This fragment song is blessed with something lacking in the other two Leitner fragments (D896 and D896b): in bb. 15–20, again in bb. 35–41 and yet again in bb. 56–60, the composer has sketched variants on the same enchanting little melody in the piano stave as an interlude for the song (and thus, as in Van Hoorickx's version, also a possible piano introduction). In a matter of a few seconds an idea can come to Schubert that would have occurred to no one else at any time in musical history; even this lilting little ascent, hardly more than a dactylic dallying around the bare bones of a B flat major arpeggio, is touched by the unique and radiant felicity of his genius. The first half of the vocal line is also dactylic; it descends the stave in gentle sequences as a counterpart to the piano's melody.

Of the sketches ascribed to Leitner texts, the editors of the NSA were in 1988 least convinced by Van Hoorickx's suggestion that this is the correct poem for the music. Walther Dürr argues with some justification that the threefold repetition of each last line of the poem's strophes is hardly typical. On the other hand, in the first verse the crestfallen melodic descent on the two repetitions of 'Ohne die Harfe / Sänger nicht sein' and the final 'ohne Harfe' strikes a

[1] Leitner writes (*Gedichte* 1857) 'Nur *in des Lebens / Wirrem Getriebe*'.

convincingly rueful note, and one can justify the repetition and ornamentation of 'Du am Balkone' in the second verse as an illustration of courtly love. Further details seem to fit this text well: if there has to be a sudden high A flat in the second verse, where better than at b. 23 for the heroic exertion of 'Turniere' (tournaments)? The modulation into G major (at b. 42) lends a breath of fresh air to the alpine breezes of Verse 3; the mention of water nymphs and the moonlit sea of the fourth verse coincides with the song's exploration of its most distant and mysterious flat-key tonalities; the tenorial extravagances of the peroration seem an appropriately dramatic reaction to the 'hostile hand of fate'. In fact so many details happily fit the music that it is unlikely to be merely coincidental, and the *Liedlexikon* (Dürr et al. 2012) prints the Leitner text without further comment. One notices that the poem is a type of compendium of some of Schubert's favourite imagery: time-travelling in the second verse with its monks, knights and ladies; echoing music for mountain and valley in the third, the dairymaid a sort of Shepherdess on the Rock; and enchanted water-nixies in the fourth that look back to *Die schöne Müllerin* D795.

This song has all the ingredients of another *Das Lied im Grünen* D917 where meandering countryside pathways are replaced by Disneyland crossroads leading off to various lands of fairy tale, each with its own theme. Of course in this version of the song there are awkward corners that do not entirely convince: some of these difficulties lie with the speed of the composer's mind and the absence of his later revising hand – but only some of them. No one else can be Schubert, and to guess correctly what miracles of harmonic invention the composer had in mind as he made this sketch is impossible. Goodness knows what fabulous song he himself might have made of this had he chosen to spend a few more hours with it!

The hugely demanding vocal tessitura suggests the tenor Ludwig Tietze. It is perhaps significant that neither Tietze's name, nor an unusually high tessitura, is associated with the early gestation of *Winterreise* D911 that was contemporary with these Leitner songs. Although Schubert composed that cycle in tenor keys, Tietze seems to have been nowhere on hand when the composer sang the music through to his friends during the autumn of 1827. This, taken together with the abandonment of these three high-lying Leitner songs, suggests the possibility of a temporary estrangement between singer and composer at the time. Perhaps the tenor felt he was being taken for granted. By the beginning of 1828 he was once again involved with the performance of Schubert's music, including the first song from *Winterreise*, but if Tietze's evaluation of Schubert after his death as a not particularly great composer is anything to go by, a simmering resentment remained.

Autograph:	Wienbibliothek im Rathaus, Vienna (fragment)
First edition:	Published as part of the NSA in 1988. Performing version by Reinhard Van Hoorickx (P804)
Subsequent editions:	Not in Peters; Not in AGA; NSA IV: Vol. 14b/273; Not in Bärenreiter
Discography and timing:	Fischer-Dieskau —
	Hyperion I 36[10]
	Hyperion II 35[3] 4'31 Michael Schade

← *Fröhliches Scheiden* D896   *Das Weinen* D926 →

SIEBEN GESÄNGE AUS WALTER SCOTT'S FRÄULEIN VOM SEE

(Seven Songs from Walter Scott's The Lady of the Lake)
SIR WALTER SCOTT (1771–1832); poem written in 1810, and translated by Philipp Adam
Storck (1780–1822) in 1819 OP. 52 **D837**, **D838**, **D835**, **D836**, **D846**, **D839**, **D843**
1825 (*see* individual songs for more specific dating)

The seven numbers from Scott's *The Lady of the Lake* were among the triumphs of the extended
summer holiday of 1825, although Schubert had almost certainly begun composing them before
mid-May when he set off on his long journey, the first ever lieder tour, with singer Johann
Michael Vogl, his companion and performing colleague. Vogl, who was conversant with the
English language, probably encouraged the composer to write them. The enthusiasm of the
actress and singer Sophie Müller for Walter Scott may also have played a part: this set of songs
might have been designed to appeal to her. The composer and Vogl had made various visits to
Müller's home in Vienna during this year, usually taking a mixture of old and new songs for
performance. If Schubert envisaged Sophie singing Ellen's songs, it is reasonable to suppose that
the two solo pieces for male voice were meant for the distinguished baritone. The other important factor in Schubert's decision to tackle this subject was undoubtedly the huge success of
Rossini's opera after the Scott epic poem, *La donna del lago*, composed in 1819 and given its
first performance in Vienna by Barbaia's Italian company in May 1823. Luigi Lablache, later to
be one of Schubert's favourite singers, took the role of Ellen's father 'Douglas d'Angus' and the
role of 'Elena' was taken with enormous aplomb by the young Henriette Sontag at the beginning
of her career. This was the singer on whom Schubert had his eye for the important co-title role
of his opera *Alfonso und Estrella* – although these hopes came to nothing.

From the point of view of the German-speaking world it appears that the Rossini opera
heightened the public's interest in reading
translations of Scott's epic poem. The second
edition (1827) of Willibald Alexis's translation contains the frontispiece printed here of
Sontag in the title role of *La donna del lago*.
This book was issued in Zwickau by Robert
Schumann's family publishing business, so it
is a measure of how quickly Sontag had
become famous. It is a translation, incidentally, that Schubert might easily have chosen
to set to music instead of Adam Storck's, had
he known it in time. Schubert's young friend
Moritz von Schwind was commissioned by
the publishers Sauer & Leidesdorf to provide
a vignette for the vocal score of the Rossini
work published in 1824 by the company (*see*
below, p. 152). For this engraving Schwind
took the Traunsee just south of Gmunden,
Upper Austria, as his model for Lake Katrine
in the Scottish Highlands, and it is possible
that Schubert did the same in terms of imaginative response to a locale. The composition
of the Scott songs is connected with Schubert's
visits with Vogl in 1825 to Schloss Ebenzw-
eyer on the shore of the Traunsee, the home
of Florian Maximillian Clodi (1740–1828)

Henriette Sontag as Elena in Rossini's *La donna del lago*,
frontispiece to the translation of *The Lady of the Lake* by
Willibald Alexis (Leipzig, 1827).

and his daughter Therese Clodi (*c.* 1801–1847). She was known to the Schubert circle as 'Das Fräulein vom See', not only because she lived on the shore of a beautiful lake, but because she looked after her very elderly father there – as did Ellen Douglas in Scott's poem.

It is likely that Schubert was able to study the Rossini work even if he was too unwell or too absorbed in composing *Fierabras* D796 to catch one of several performances during this and the following season. The result seems to have been a determination to do something different from Rossini, a kind of lieder riposte to that composer's efforts on behalf of the Scottish poet, and a refusal to let him off Scott-free for playing fast and loose with an important piece of literature. Schubert's work goes back to the actual words of the poet (albeit in German translation) and is the biggest assemblage of songs he planned in a single opus, apart from the two Müller cycles. That he was aiming to make a substantial impression with the work is obvious; that he was attempting to trace the outline of a dramatic story through a sequence of songs, and in a way that was consciously different from the opera, also seems likely. Perhaps the composer had originally intended to set more of the lyrics embedded in Scott's epic poem (thus constituting a greater overview of the story), or perhaps these were the only poems in the work that appealed to him (to set the twenty-seven strophes of *The Ballad of Alice Brand* from Canto IV would have been a mighty and disproportionate task). Nevertheless, this group of seven songs and ensembles seems to have been a gauntlet thrown down on behalf of the emerging world of lieder performance (a Cinderella of an art form) in competitive defiance of its operatic elder and domineering (if not exactly ugly!) sister. Schubert's Op. 52 has something of an operatic cast, and separate choruses for male and female voices (there are five solo songs for three different characters – Ellen, Norman and Malcolm – with the addition of two choral songs). No other lied opus combines choral music with solos in quite this way, and it is possible that Schubert hoped for a complete performance at a Musikverein concert where part songs were performed as frequently as solos.

Schubert probably had high hopes of these songs being well received in Britain, the land which had been so beneficial to Haydn and Beethoven and, accordingly, a version with Scott's original words was engraved in smaller notes and published as an *ossia* (with the exception of *Normans Gesang* which proved impossible to adapt). *Lied des gefangenen Jägers* required so much alteration (Scott's iambic tetrameters were a bad fit for the anapaests of the music) that it was printed separately. Perhaps the poet Craigher von Jachelutta, or even the Anglophile Vogl, supervised these versions, but it seems that their English was not quite good enough to give Schubert accurate help in the correct accentuation of the language. This 'translation' back to the original failed to yield the expected success or profit in the land of its intended market.

Walther Dürr (Dürr/Feil 1991, p. 122) sees parallels between the political situation in Scotland in the time of James V (the conflict of religion and nationalism) and the underlying conflict between the middle and ruling classes in Europe following the defeat of Napoleon. Scott could scarcely have intended this similarity to be drawn in a work written in 1810, long before the defeat of Napoleon, but it is certainly possible that Scott's European readers were in a mood to be reminded that such internecine political conflicts were as old as the Scottish hills.

Autograph:	Missing or lost
First edition:	Published as Op. 52 by Artaria, Vienna in April 1826
Dedicatee:	Sophie Gräfin von Weissenwolf
First known performance:	It is possible that these songs received their first performance at an *Abend-Unterhaltung* in Gmunden in June 1825, performed by Johann Michael Vogl and Nanette Wolf. See Waidelich/Hilmar Dokumente II No. 333b
Publication reviews:	*Allgemeiner musikalischer Anzeiger* (Frankfurt), No. 2 (8 July 1826), p. 10f. [Waidelich/Hilmar Dokumente I No. 395]

I ELLENS GESANG I
(Raste Krieger, Krieg ist aus)
OP. 52 NO. 1, **D837** [H564]
Db major   April–July 1825

Ellen's Song I

(176 bars)

A literal translation of Storck's translation is given here.
Scott's original poem is printed below in italics.

Raste Krieger! Krieg ist aus,	Rest, warrior! Your war is over,
Schlaf den Schlaf, nichts wird dich wecken,	Sleep the sleep, nothing shall wake you;
Träume nicht von wildem Strauss	Do not dream of the fierce battle
Nicht von Tag und Nacht voll Schrecken.	Of days and nights filled with terrors.
In der Insel Zauberhallen	In the island's enchanted halls
Wird ein weicher Schlafgesang	A soft lullaby
Um das müde Haupt dir wallen	Shall caress your weary head
Zu der Zauberharfe Klang.	To the strains of a magic harp.
Feen mit unsichtbaren Händen	Fairies with unseen hands
Werden auf dein Lager hin	Shall strew upon your bed
Holde Schlummerblumen senden,	Sweet flowers of sleep
Die im Zauberlande blühn.	That bloom in the enchanted land.
Raste Krieger, Krieg ist aus,	Rest, warrior! Your war is over.
Schlaf den Schlaf, nichts wird dich wecken.	Sleep the sleep, nothing shall wake you;
Träume nicht von wildem Strauss,	Do not dream of the fierce battle
Nicht von Tag und Nacht voll Schrecken.	Of days and nights filled with terrors.
Nicht der Trommel wildes Rasen,	Neither the wild crash of drums,
Nicht des Kriegs gebietend Wort,	Nor the summons to battle,
Nicht der Todeshörner Blasen	Nor the blaring of death's horns
Scheuchen deinen Schlummer fort.	Shall frighten away your sleep.
Nicht das Stampfen wilder Pferde,	Neither the stomping of frenzied horses,
Nicht der Schreckensruf der Wacht,	Nor the sentry's fearful cry,
Nicht das Bild von Tagsbeschwerde	Nor a vision of the day's cares
Stören deine stille Nacht.	Shall disturb your tranquil night.
Doch der Lerche Morgensänge	Yet the lark's morning song
Wecken sanft dein schlummernd Ohr,	Shall gently awaken your slumbering ear,
Und des Sumpfgefieders Klänge	And the sounds of marsh birds
Steigend aus Geschilf und Rohr.	Soaring from reeds and rushes.

Raste Krieger! Krieg ist aus,
Schlaf den Schlaf, nichts wird dich wecken
Träume nicht von wildem Strauss,
Nicht von Tag und Nacht voll Schrecken.

Rest, warrior! Your war is over,
Sleep the sleep, nothing shall wake you.
Do not dream of the fierce battle,
Of days and nights filled with terrors.

Song

Soldier rest! thy warfare o'er,
Sleep the sleep that knows not breaking;
Dream of battled fields no more,
Days of danger, nights of waking.

No rude sound shall reach thine ear,
Armour's clang, or war-steed champing,
Trump nor pibroch summon here
Mustering clan, or squadron tramping.

In our isle's enchanted hall,
Hands unseen thy couch are strewing,
Fairy strains of music fall,
Every sense in slumber dewing,

Yet the lark's shrill fife may come
At the day-break from the fallow,
And the bittern sound his drum.
Booming from the sedgy shallow.

Soldier rest! thy warfare o'er,
Dream of fighting fields no more:
Sleep the sleep that knows not breaking,
Morn of toil, nor night of waking.

Ruder sounds shall none be near
Guards nor warders challenge here,
Here's no war-steeds neigh and champing,
Shouting clans, or squadrons stamping.

This is the third of Schubert's eight Scott solo settings (1825–6). See the poet's biography for a chronological list of all the Scott settings.

The historical background to Scott's *The Lady of the Lake* is a complicated one, but it can be summarized and simplified to some extent. King James V (1512–1542) was heir to a kingdom torn apart by factions, pro English and pro French. The Earl of Angus, Archibald Douglas (the eponymous hero of Loewe's well-known ballad – 1857 – to a poem of Theodor Fontane) had

Vignette by Moritz von Schwind for the Viennese vocal score of Rossini's *La donna del lago* (1824).

been banished to England. The king then outlawed the entire Douglas clan, including the Earl of Bothwell who had been his mentor (or perhaps *this* is Archibald Douglas? The sources, including Scott, are confused and contradictory as is often the case with history that is a palimpsest of legend and balladry). Here Scott allows himself some fictional licence. The elderly Douglas who features in this poem represents the entire outlawed Douglas clan. He has refused to leave his beloved homeland and, together with his wife and daughter (the beautiful Ellen Douglas), he is given refuge and a hiding place by Roderick Dhu, chief of the Clan-Alpine, who is enamoured of Ellen and defies the king in open rebellion. This story thus takes place sometime after 1530 when Scotland was a Roman Catholic monarchy under the rule of James V who attempted to stem the tide of the Reformation. He died in 1542, defeated by Henry VIII's troops at the battle of Solway Moss. On the battlefield news was brought to him of the birth of his daughter, the future (and ill-fated) Mary Queen of Scots.

Scott tells us that it was the custom of both James IV and James V to walk through their kingdoms in disguise, the better to understand their subjects. At the opening of *The Lady of the Lake*, the king, James V, disguised as James Fitz-James, 'the Knight of Snowdon', is hunting in the vicinity of Loch Katrine (the name derives, Scott suggests, from the 'caterans' or robbers who infested the area in earlier times). The king has discovered the beauties of this area by accident after losing his steed and becoming separated from his hunting companions. Climbing up a precipice, he catches sight for the first time of the bay with its islands which, in the failing light, seem like an enchanted part of another world. (Scott's descriptions of this area brought hundreds of visitors to the Trossachs within weeks of the poem's publication.) As 'Fitz-James' prepares to sleep in the open, a small skiff crosses the lake, rowed by a beautiful dark-haired young woman dressed in the plaid of a chieftain's daughter – 'And ne'er did Grecian chisel trace / A Nymph, a Naiad or a Grace / Of finer form, or lovelier face'.

Ellen on Lake Katrine at the beginning of *The Lady of the Lake*. Illustration by Howard Chandler Christy, 1910.

This is Ellen Douglas who has briefly emerged from hiding; she has heard the sound of a hunting horn and taken it to be a signal from her lover, Malcolm Graeme, whom she expects to meet on the shore. Instead Fitz-James, the king in disguise, introduces himself without revealing his true identity. In the solemn tradition of guest-friendship of those parts, Ellen invites him home, and they row the boat back to a small rocky island in the middle of the loch. There, hidden away, is a 'rustic bower', a makeshift house of wood and matting, half castle, half hermitage. Fitz-James recognizes an old sword as belonging to the banished earl, but says nothing. Ellen's mother, Dame Margaret, is deeply courteous, but all enquiries about the head of the house are lightly turned away. Ellen playfully claims that she and her mother cast spells on wandering knights; as if to prove her point she begins to sing:

She sung, and still a harp unseen
Fill'd up the symphony between.

An exceptionally full, sixty-five-page background article to the history of Scotland was published by Adam Storck as an introduction to his German translation (1819, second edition 1823) of the Scott poem, and we should assume that Schubert read it. He was also clearly aware of the context of this set of poems in the story as a whole. Performers who treat this song as a dirge, or battle requiem for a dead soldier, have not been equally well informed. There is no threat of death in this poem: Ellen sings to Fitz-James in order to draw attention away from the awkward subject of her father's whereabouts. In welcoming her mysterious visitor she attempts to enchant him, more or less tongue-in-cheek, with beguiling music worthy of a Scottish Lorelei. But she is not a malevolent spirit and she lacks the Lorelei's guile. She is in fact far more closely related to the character of Goethe's Mignon.

Schubert knew that in these mysterious circumstances, and in this strange hideaway, Ellen's music would have to make time stand still. The marking is 'Mässig' so the crotchet beat is not slow, and the music not portentous. Nevertheless, the first section of the piece (in fact the first appearance of a recurring rondo) is massively dignified and encompasses a world of feeling, or other-worldly feeling, in a span of thirty bars: arches of sound on slowly moving harmonic foundations progress in stately fashion from one chord to the next with a preponderance of tonic, dominant and subdominant harmony. All is grand simplicity. Mention of a great warrior has prompted Schubert to return to an idea from his musical past: the opening ritornello in D flat (the characterful accompaniment, but not the vocal line) is taken, sometimes note for note, from Thusnelda's hymn (marked 'Mit heiligem Jubel') for the victorious return of her husband, the Teutonic warrior Arminius (*Hermann und Thusnelda*, Klopstock, D322, October 1815, bb. 84–111). A decade later, Schubert allows this old military music to float in a new guise of spell-induced fancy.

At b. 31 (Verse 2 of the poem) there is a new marking of 'Langsam', but the time signature is 'alla breve'. (The effect is to engineer a quaver = quaver tempo between the two sections, and a completely smooth musical transition.) The key signature changes to three sharps, but the initial description of the island's magic halls plays on the fact that D flat major and C sharp major are enharmonically identical. The accompaniment here is simplicity itself – gently oscillating quavers that support a vocal line of spun gold. The harmonic movement is once again spacious, the majority of bars containing a single chord blissfully elongated beneath the voice by the accompanying quavers. The movement of harmony, however, is gravely moving. At bb. 44–8 there is a piano interlude of great eloquence, as if the composer has imagined a horn solo for the pianist's left hand. The poem's third verse is more or less an exact repeat of the second (bb. 48–65), even more magical in being heard a second time, including that soulful horn interlude in A major, the third of the scale (C sharp) being the pivot point for a return to D flat major. Leo Black hears this 'horn' solo as something potentially played on the cello, and points out that this kind of interlude, with an eloquent singing melody placed in the middle of the musical texture, reappears in a famous piece of solo piano music – in the 'second subject' of the Impromptu in A flat major D935/2 (1827).

Verse 4 is a second appearance of the 'Raste Krieger' music; the key signature changes back to five flats and we revert to triple time. Musicans hearing this song for the first time would have now realized that it is written in a spacious rondo form. At b. 92 there is a change back to three sharps, but instead of 'Langsam' the music for Verse 5 is marked 'Geschwind'. At just the right moment, hypnotic calm is broken by the martial sounds of battle; the poet lists what will *not* disturb the warrior but the composer, as if to lay potential dangers at rest like a Celtic shaman, invokes the potential disturbances in musical illustration, the better to negate them. The change of pace is effected by an accompaniment that suggests stamping steeds – a repetitive right-hand figuration of a speedy dactyl, a quaver plus two semiquavers. This dominates the *Bewegung* from bb. 92–9; in this latter bar the tempo marking changes to 'Langsamer' and the pianist must make a smooth transition to accompanying quavers (and a remarkable modulation into C major). In this way we are spirited from the imaginary battlefield directly into the ministrations of Ellen herself, and the peace of sleep and rest. A rumble of danger in the far distance is to be heard in the piano's left hand timpani (bb. 102–3 and 103–4).

Verse 6 is a musical repeat of Verse 5. Thus at b. 110 there is a return to a 'Geschwind' tempo that is, once again, moderated by the 'Langsamer' direction. This time the gallop evaporates and sinks (at b. 118) into the calm of B flat major (rather than C major) at the words 'deine stille Nacht'. The effect of this brilliantly planned tonal architecture is that the warrior is invited to fall into an ever deeper sleep. At the end of this section the harmony changes from B flat major to B flat minor before 'Doch der Lerche Morgensänge' and we are drawn down into an even more distant part of the subterranean caverns of dreams. In a masterstroke of tempo engineering the music for Verse 7 (from b. 127) is slower still, a second 'Langsamer' piled on the first. Mention of the lark and bittern (famous for its booming calls across the marshes) produces music completely inappropriate for the ornithologist, but of a rare and fragile beauty for the Schubertian. Ellen speaks here with a rare compassion, as if she were indeed soothing the brow of a wounded warrior, slowly bringing him back to life with the most tender nursing. At bb. 139–43 the A major horn interlude makes its final appearance. By the simple expedient of raising the piano's bass line by an octave, Schubert gives the accompaniment a magically etiolated sound for the third and final appearance of the rondo refrain (bb. 134–66). This piano writing sounds like Tennyson's 'horns of Elfland faintly blowing'. There is a remarkably hypnotic coda; as the accompaniment slowly sinks back to the lower regions of the keyboard, a final repetition of the poem's opening line is set on a murmured phrase that is all but a monotone. There is scarcely a bar of this long song that does not contribute to its other-worldly effect.

It is possible to graft this vocal line on to Scott's original text, but Storck's translation is eight lines longer. It was Storck, incidentally, who turned the song into a rondo in his relatively free translation (by repeating the first verse as the last) and Schubert followed suit. That the eleven-year-old Felix Mendelssohn came across Storck's translation of Scott hot off the press some five years before Schubert is an indication that Scott's huge popularity throughout Europe was at its peak somewhat before the songs were composed. Mendelssohn's setting (1820) is extremely simple in comparison (G major, $\frac{2}{4}$ as opposed to Schubert's triple measure), but it has a charm of its own.

First edition:	Published as Op. 52 no. 1 by Artaria, Vienna in April 1826 (P87)
Subsequent editions:	Peters: Vol. 3/16; AGA XX 471: Vol. 8/70; NSA IV: Vol. 3a/7; Bärenreiter: Vol. 2/74
Bibliography:	Black 1997, p. 8
	Capell 1928, p. 209
	Einstein 1951, p. 301
Further settings and arrangements:	Felix Mendelssohn (1809–1847) *Raste Kreiger! Krieg ist aus* (1820)
	Arr. Colin Matthews (b. 1946) for voice and chamber ensemble, *Ellens drei Gesänge* (1984)
Discography and timing:	Fischer-Dieskau —
	Hyperion I 13[12]
	Hyperion II 30[1] 8'34 Marie McLaughlin

← *Totengräbers Heimwehe* D842   *Ellens Gesang II* D838 →

II ELLENS GESANG II
(Jäger, ruhe von der Jagd)
Op. 52 no. 2, **D838** [H565]
Eb major   April–July 1825

Ellen's Song II

(80 bars)

A literal translation of Storck's translation is given here.
Scott's original poem is printed below in italics.

Jäger, ruhe von der Jagd!
Weicher Schlummer soll dich decken,
    Träume nicht, wenn Sonn' erwacht,
Dass Jagdhörner dich erwecken.

Schlaf! der Hirsch ruht in der Höhle,
Bei dir sind die Hunde wach,
    Schlaf, nicht quäl' es deine Seele,
Dass dein edles Ross erlag.

Jäger, ruhe von der Jagd!
Weicher Schlummer soll dich decken;
    Wenn der junge Tag erwacht,
Wird kein Jägerhorn dich wecken.

Huntsman, rest from the chase!
Gentle slumber shall cover you;
    Do not dream that when the sun rises
Hunting horns shall wake you:

Sleep! The stag rests in his den,
Your hounds lie awake beside you;
    Sleep! Let it not torment your soul
That your noble steed has perished.

Huntsman, rest from the chase!
Gentle slumber shall cover you;
    When the new day dawns
No hunting horn shall wake you.

> *Song*
> *'Huntsman, rest! thy chase is done,*
> *   While our slumbrous spells assail ye,*
> *Dream not, with the rising sun,*
> *   Bugles here shall sound reveillé.*
> *Sleep! the deer is in his den;*
> *   Sleep! Thy hounds are by thee lying;*
> *Sleep! nor dream in yonder glen,*
> *   How thy gallant steed lay dying.*
> *Huntsman, rest! thy chase is done,*
> *Think not of the rising sun,*
> *For at dawning to assail ye*
> *Here no bugles sound reveillé.*

This is the fourth of Schubert's eight Scott solo settings (1825–6). See the poet's biography for a
chronological list of all the Scott settings.

In the first canto of Scott's *The Lady of the Lake*, Ellen's second song is a continuation of the first; the heading is 'Song continued', and the two pieces are separated by only a few lines of narration to give Ellen pause for breath. Directly after it is sung, the bed of Fitz-James (in reality the King of Scotland in disguise) is prepared and decked with mountain heather. His dreams are disturbed by the beauty of Ellen, and memories of the loyalty of her father. Schubert's marking of 'Etwas geschwind' has encouraged many a performer, perhaps a bit embarrassed at the length of Ellen's first song, to turn *Jäger, ruhe von der Jagd!* into a scherzo by way of contrast, and jaunty, even ebullient, performances have unfortunately become the norm. Interpretative help is at hand in the form of a letter written by Anton Ottenwalt to Josef von Spaun from Linz in July 1825. Ottenwalt's articulate and perspicacious impressions of the Scott songs were formed by hearing the composer himself play the accompaniments:

> *Jägers Ruhe. Another slumber song, . . . in the accompaniment, the tune of horns, I should say, like the echoes of a hunting song in a beautiful dream . . . The most generally appealing by the loveliness of its melody and the rocking horn music . . . My dear fellow, how we wished each time that you could hear it! If only we could send those tunes into your dreams, as we ourselves hear them around us deep into the night.*

The emotions aroused in Ottenwalt by a song he links with gentle dreams (as indeed the words suggest) are far from the Highland fling mood of many a performance. It is a dance of delight, perhaps, but one that is conjured by Ellen's 'slumbrous spells'. The dotted rhythms that pervade the accompaniment have to trip gently, rather than jump and jolt. At b. 18, and again at b. 40, the horn motif combines with that of a galloping steed (as explored from b. 92 in the first of Ellen's songs); this too must remain within the realms of dreams, avoiding what seems like an invitation to a bracing canter across the keyboard. The key is E flat, with the horn calls that are always evoked by that tonality (cf. Beethoven's Sonata Op. 81a, 'Les Adieux'). Sleep is a land through the looking glass, where the conscious and unconscious diverge. The first horn call, which rises upwards (b. 1), is answered by one that falls (b. 2). As the vocal line climbs in the refrain, the piano beneath it moves in mirroring contrary motion (b. 8).

The song has a simple ABA form with a middle verse that magically modulates into C minor (b. 34). This is prepared by a wonderful transition (bb. 32–3) where a B flat^7 chord melts into a first inversion of G major on a B natural, and thence into the new key with C as the bass. For this moment of unexpected musical suspense the pianist's rhythm must be immaculate; these rising semitones are an analogue for a door slowly opening into a new chamber of the unconscious. The setting of the following passage (beginning 'Schlaf! der Hirsch ruht in der Höhle, from b. 34) seems whispered in secretive mood, the breath held for fear of disturbing the dreaming hunter. As in Ellen's first song, the composer cannot resist illustrating what is not supposed to disturb the dreamer (urgent horn calls with a suggestion of stamping steeds). In performance these should be nothing more than distant shadows of a drama. Nightmares are heard to recede during the word 'Schlaf' set to a dotted minim (b. 44) as peace is restored, a long diminuendo over two bars. Once again the shifting of the bass line in a rise of a semitone (in this case from C flat to C natural) plays an important part in suggesting different layers of consciousness. The arrival of 'Seele' in the home key (albeit in a dreamy second inversion) at b. 46 seems a return to security. The song's gentle dance rhythm and the repetition of question and answer phrases suggest folk music dreamed up on the magic carpet of Schubert's travelling imagination, each song provided with a different itinerary. The music's gentle lilt has an essentially Scottish feel; the same may be said of another Scott setting in three flats, *Lied der Anne Lyle* D830.

First edition:	Published as Op. 52 no. 2 by Artaria, Vienna in April 1826 (P88)
Subsequent editions:	Peters: Vol. 3/22; AGA XX 472: Vol. 8/78; NSA IV: Vol. 3a/40; Bärenreiter: Vol. 2/83
Arrangements:	Arr. Johannes Brahms (1833–1897) for voice and wind instruments (1862); also arr. for voice and female choir and wind instruments (1873?) [*see* ORCHESTRATIONS]
	Arr. Colin Matthews (b. 1946) for voice and chamber ensemble, *Ellens drei Gesänge* (1984)
Discography and timing:	Fischer-Dieskau —

Hyperion I 13¹³

Hyperion II 30²   3'32   Marie McLaughlin

← *Ellens Gesang I* D837   *Bootgesang* D835 →

III BOOTGESANG   Boat song   Quartet, TTBB

OP. 52 NO. 3, **D835** [H566]

C minor   1825

A literal translation of Storck's translation is given here.
Scott's original poem is printed below in italics.

Triumph, er naht, Heil, Heil dem Helden,
  Stets grünende Fichte, gesegnet seist du!
Lang, lang blüh in seinem hellschimmernden
  Banner,
    O Baum, du Schutz und Schmuck unsers
    Stamms!
      Tränk ihn, Himmel, mit deinem Tau,
      Spend ihm, Erde, neuen Saft,
    Dass freudig er knosp' und weit sich
    verbreite,
      Und jedes Hochlands Tal
      Schalle jauchzend zurück:
'Es lebe Sir Roderick, Clan Alpines Held!'

[. . . 3 . . .]

Rejoice, he approches! Hail to the hero!
  Evergreen spruce, you are blessed!
Long, long may you bloom on his bright-shining
  banner,
    O tree, protector and jewel of our clan!

    Water it, heaven, with your dew;
    Give it fresh sap, earth,
  That it may bud joyfully and spread its
  branches wide,
And let every Highland valley
  Echo resoundingly:
'Long live Sir Roderick, Clan-Alpine's hero!'

[. . . 3 . . .]

Boat Song
Hail to the chief who in triumph advances,
Honoured and blessed be the ever-green pine!
Long may the tree in his banner that glances,
Flourish, the shelter and grace of our line!
Heaven send it happy dew,
Earth lend it sap anew,
Gayly to bourgeon, and broadly to grow,
While every highland glen,
Sends our shout back agen,
'Roderigh Vich Alpine dhu, ho! ieroe!'

This poem occurs in Canto II of *The Lady of the Lake*. A loyal song is raised to the chieftain of the clan, Roderick Dhu (i.e. Black Roderick or Roderick the dark-skinned) as he returns home by boat on Lake Katrine. Roderick is the older of the suitors of Ellen Douglas, the beautiful heroine of this long narrative poem. Ellen is also the central figure in the group of solo songs for soprano that Schubert wrote on these Scott texts.

Scott introduces the *Boat Song* with these lines:

The war-pipes ceased; but lake and hill
Were busy with their echoes still,
And when they slept, a vocal strain
Bade their hoarse chorus wake again,
While loud an hundred clans-men raise
Their voices in their chieftain's praise.
Each boat-man, bending to his oar,
With measured sweep the burthen bore,
In such wild cadence, as the breeze
Makes through December's leafless trees:
The chorus first could Allan know,
'Roderigh Vich Alpine, ho! iro!'.
And near, and nearer as they rowed,
Distinct the martial ditty flowed.

The music manages to capture a robust Scottish flavour. Beethoven was still making versions of folksongs with piano trio accompaniment for George Thompson of Edinburgh in 1825; perhaps Schubert knew some of that master's earlier arrangements. But there is little in those works that hints at the rugged Scottish landscape evoked in this craggy music. The gruff tonality proclaims that these clansmen are not to be trifled with, and the doubled octave unisons of the accompaniment give the music a stern sense of resolve. There is also doughty use of the strident dotted rhythms associated by Schubert with warfare. This is very much a march rather than the rowing music (two dips of the oar for each line of poetry) ingeniously envisaged by Scott, for this smoother metre is lost in Storck's translation. The truculent mood of the minor-key opening thaws to a note of radiant admiration in a blaze of C major. No Scottish rugby supporters have ever greeted their heroes with more enthusiasm.

Scott's poem contains four verses: only the first is printed here. The opening phrase of the song's bilingual first edition suffices to illustrate Schubert's problems with English accentuation: the essential word 'Hail' is thrown away on a semiquaver while 'to' is set to a dotted quaver.

This poem was at one time extremely famous. The first line of the original may strike some as familiar – particularly Americans. It is of course the title of the 'theme tune' of the president of the United States, the musical motto ('Hail to the Chief') that accompanies his public appearances. The song is thought to be by an English composer, James Sanderson; it was published in America in 1812 (thus pre-dating Schubert's setting by thirteen years) although no English printed copy of the music is extant. It is not known exactly when it became the presidential theme-tune but it was first heard at an inauguration in 1845.

First edition: Published as Op. 52 no. 3 by Artaria, Vienna in April 1826 (P89)
Subsequent editions: AGA XVI 10: p. 89; NSA IV: Vol. 3a/26
Further setting: James Sanderson (1769–1841) *Hail to the Chief* (c. 1812)
Discography and timing: Hyperion I 35^{15} The London Schubert Chorale (dir.
                          Hyperion II 30^3 1'28   Stephen Layton)

← *Ellens Gesang II* D838   *Coronach* D836 →

IV CORONACH (Totengesang der   Coronach: Threnody of   Trio, SSA
Frauen und Mädchen)   women and maidens   (Chorlied)
OP. 52 NO. 4, **D836** [H567]
F minor   1825

A literal translation of Storck's translation is given here.
Scott's original poem is printed below in italics.

Er ist uns geschieden vom Berg und   He is gone from our mountains and forests
    vom Walde
Wie versiegte Quelle, als Not uns bedrängte.   Like a dried up spring, in our direst need.
Die Quelle wird fliessen, genährt von   The spring will flow again, nourished by the rain.
    dem Regen,
Uns scheint nie mehr Freude, dem Duncan   But joy will shine no more for us, and no
    kein Morgen.   morning will dawn for Duncan.
Die Hand des Schnitters nimmt reife Ähren,   The hand of the reaper takes ripe ears of corn,
Unser Trauergesang klagt blühende Jugend.   Our lament mourns the bloom of youth.
Der Herbstwind treibt Blätter, die gelben,   The autumn wind scatters leaves, yellow and
    die welken,   withered;
Es blüht' unsre Blume, als Mehltau sie welkte. Your flower was in full bloom when mildew
                                                 tainted it.

    Ihr flüchtigen Füsse, du Rat in Bedrängnis,   Swift feet, counsel in distress,
Du Arm im Streite, wie tief ist dein   Strong arm in battle – how deep is your slumber.
    Schlummer.

Wie Tau auf den Bergen, wie Schaum auf
   dem Bache,
Wie Blas' auf der Welle bist ewig geschieden.

Like dew on the mountains, like foam on the
   stream,
Like surf on the waves, you have gone forever.

He is gone on the mountain
   He is lost to the forest.
Like a summer-dried fountain,
   When our need was the sorest.
The font, re-appearing,
   From the rain-drops shall borrow
But to us comes no cheering,
   To Duncan no morrow!

The hand of the reaper
   Takes the ears that are hoary,
But the voice of the weeper
   Wails manhood in glory;
The autumn winds rushing
   Waft the leaves that are searest,
But our flower was in flushing,
   When blighting was nearest.

Fleet foot on the correi,[1]
   Sage counsel in cumber,
Red hand in the foray,
   How sound is thy slumber!
Like the dew on the mountain,
   Like the foam on the river,
Like the bubble on the fountain,
   Thou art gone, and for ever!

At the beginning of Canto III of Scott's *The Lady of the Lake*, Roderick Dhu sends out the summons for a vast gathering of his clan. In swiftly paced verse that generates real excitement, Scott describes the clansmen, far and wide, each abandoning his work to answer the call to arms. As a sideshow to this summons, the narrative focuses for some stanzas on a family bereavement: the arrival of the messenger coincides with the funeral of Duncan, one of Roderick's bravest soldiers. He is mourned by his family and followers, and the 'stripling son' of the once intrepid warrior goes to war in his father's stead. This is one of numerous sub-plots with which the author enriches his vast poem; another side-story in this section of the poem ('The Gathering') concerns Norman and his bride-to-be, Mary, the background to *Normans Gesang* D846. Scott introduces the *Coronach* (in his own gloss 'a wild expression of lamentation poured forth by the mourners over the body of a departed friend') with these lines:

Within the hall, where torches ray
Supply the excluded beams of day,
Lies Duncan on his lowly bier,
And o'er him streams his widow's tear.

[1] Or *corri*: the hollow side of the hill, where game usually lies. (Scott's own footnote.)

> *His stripling son stands mournful by,*
> *His youngest weeps, but knows not why;*
> *The village maids, and matrons round*
> *The dismal coronach resound.*

Schubert's music for this lament of 'village maids and matrons' is a three-part female chorus (something unique in his output) of the deepest seriousness, the rumbling left-hand basses signifying the muffled drum of funeral music. Clashes of A flat against G (b. 3) and D flat against C (b. 4) emphasize the mourners' anguish. Schubert has here made a remarkable, and purely instinctive, attempt to capture the sound of Celtic keening. But unlike *Bootgesang* there is no raw edge to the music; instead there is a hushed dignity leading to forte passages that are heartfelt rather than a 'wild expression of lamentation'. An interest in the music and words of peasant peoples would develop throughout Europe into a real study of folksong, but only some time after the composer's death. Nevertheless, Schubert is trying his best to respond to age-old traditions beyond his ken. He was already a practised armchair-traveller to the Scottish north; his settings of the so-called Scottish minstrel Ossian were among the most inspired songs of his youth, and here he draws on that experience. As in *Bootgesang*, the music is simple and stoic as befits the people who sing it, but it has its own magic. Even straightforward changes between minor and major (here from F minor to the relative major of A flat, thence to F major) are affecting beyond the economy of their means.

First edition:	Published as Op. 52 no. 4 by Artaria, Vienna in April 1826 (P90)
Subsequent editions:	AGA XVIII 1: p. 1; NSA IV: Vol. 3a/34
Arrangements:	Arr. Hans Zender (b. 1936) 'Coronach, der Gondelfahrer, Nachthelle, Schubert-Chöre, 23. Psalm für Chor und Orchester' (1986)

Discography and timing: Hyperion I 35[16]   5'03   Patricia Rozario, Lorna Anderson & Hyperion II 30[4]   Catherine Wyn-Rogers

← *Bootgesang* D835   *Normans Gesang* D846 →

V NORMANS GESANG   Norman's song
Op. 52 no. 5, **D846** [H568]
C minor   April 1825

A literal translation of Storck's translation is given here.
Scott's original poem is printed below in italics.

Die Nacht bricht bald herein, dann leg' ich mich zur Ruh,	Soon night will fall. Then I shall lie down to rest;
Die Heide ist mein Lager, das Farnkraut deckt mich zu,	The heath shall be my bed, the bracken shall cover me.

Mich lullt der Wache Tritt wohl in den
    Schlaf hinein.
Ach, muss so weit von dir, Maria, Holde, sein.

Und wird es morgen Abend, und kommt
    die trübe Zeit,
Dann ist vielleicht mein Lager der blutig
    rote Plaid,
Mein Abendlied verstummet, du schleichst
    dann trüb und bang,
Maria, mich wecken kann nicht dein
    Totensang.[1]

So musst ich von dir scheiden, du holde, süsse
    Braut?
Wie magst du nach mir rufen, wie magst du
    weinen laut,
Ach, denken darf ich nicht an deinen herben
    Schmerz,
Ach, denken darf ich nicht an dein getreues
    Herz.

Nein, zärtlich treues Sehnen darf hegen
    Norman nicht,
Wenn in den Feind Clan-Alpine wie Sturm
    und Hagel bricht,
Wie ein gespannter Bogen sein mutig Herz
    dann sei,
Sein Fuss, Maria, wie der Pfeil so rasch und
    frei!

Wohl wird die Stunde kommen, wo nicht die
    Sonne scheint,
Du wankst zu deinem Norman, dein holdes
    Auge weint:
Doch fall ich in der Schlacht, hüllt
    Todesschauer mich,
O glaub, mein letzter Seufzer, Maria, ist für
    dich.

Doch kehr ich siegreich wieder aus kühner
    Männerschlacht,
Dann grüssen wir so freudig das Nahn der
    stillen Nacht,

The sentry's tread shall lull me to sleep.

Alas, I must be so far from you, Mary.

Come tomorrow evening, come the bleak hour,

My bed may be the blood-red plaid;

My vesper song will cease, and you, Mary,

Will creep about, gloomy and troubled; your
    threnody will not waken me.

Thus I had to leave you, fair, sweet bride.

Though you may call out for me, though you
    may weep aloud,
I cannot, alas, think of your bitter suffering,

I cannot, alas, think of your faithful heart.

No, Norman cannot feel tender, devoted longing,

When Clan-Alpine bursts like hail and tempest
    on the foe;
His bold heart must be then like a drawn bow,

His foot, Mary, as swift and free as an arrow.

A time will come when the sun does not shine,

You will stumble towards your Norman, your fair
    eyes will weep;
But if I fall in battle, if grim death shrouds me,

Believe this, Mary: my last sigh shall be for you.

But if I return victorious from the brave battle,

How joyfully we shall greet the approach of the
    silent night.

---

[1] Storck's original translation reads 'Maria, *ach* mich wecken'.

Das Lager ist bereitet, uns winkt die süsse
  Ruh
Der Hänfling singt Brautlieder, Maria, hold
  uns zu.

The bed is prepared, sweet repose beckons to us;

Soon, Mary, the linnet will sing us wedding
  songs.

Song
The heath this night must be my bed,
The bracken curtain for my head,
My lullaby the warder's tread,
    Far, far from love and thee, Mary;
To-morrow eve, more stilly laid,
My couch may be my bloody plaid,
My vesper song, thy wail, sweet maid!
    It will not waken me, Mary!
I may not, dare not, fancy now
The grief that clouds thy lovely brow;
I dare not think upon thy vow,
    And all it promised me, Mary.
No fond regret must Norman know;
When bursts Clan-Alpine on the foe,
His heart must be like bended bow,
    His foot like arrow free, Mary.
A time will come with feeling fraught,
For, if I fall in battle fought,
Thy hapless lover's dying thought
    Shall be a thought on thee, Mary.
And if returned from conquered foes,
How blithely will the evening close,
How sweet the linnet sing repose,
    To my young bride and me, Mary!

This is the fifth of Schubert's eight Scott solo settings (1825–6). See the poet's biography for a chronological list of all the Scott settings.

The tale of the gallant Norman, 'heir of Armandave', is one of the various fragmentary sub-plots that embroider the main narrative of Walter Scott's *The Lady of the Lake*. The author no doubt included it to press home the point that loyalty to clan and chief were paramount in sixteenth-century Highland life. Like Annot Lyle, in the Schubert song named after her from Scott's *The Legend of Montrose* (D830), Norman faces a conflict between love and duty, a variant of the incompatibility of sex and religion. The overall theme of this epic poem, apart from the central love story of Ellen Douglas and Malcolm Graeme, is the battle between crown and clan at a time when Scotland was rent by internecine strife. The reconciliation brought about by the wisdom of a merciful king is Scott's broad historical lesson. Norman owes his allegiance to Roderick Dhu, chief of the Clan-Alpine and sworn enemy of James V of Scotland. No sooner has he come out of the church with his bride Maria, than Angus the heir of Duncraggen appears with a fiery cross (having swum a turbulent stream to reach the chapel – all excellently recounted) to summon Norman to arms. Certainly the least attractive legacy of *The Lady of the Lake* was the adoption of the burning cross of this poem by the American Ku Klux Klan.

The text gave Schubert the chance to compose one of the two famous horse-riding songs of 1825 (the other is Schulze's *Auf der Bruck* D853), and one of the most effective of a favourite genre that includes *Willkommen und Abschied* D767 and *Erlkönig* D328. Like those songs, *Normans Gesang* is a moto perpetuo, full of grim resolve. Its accompaniment is more authentically equestrian than the others, and we feel the rider bounce in the saddle as the horse gallops over uneven ground. The composer made it the finale of a group of Scott songs which he performed with Vogl in Linz in late July 1825. Anton Ottenwalt wrote to Josef von Spaun about this informal concert in a letter of 27 July; his remarks on *Normans Gesang* are worth quoting in full:

> *The warrior with his sacrificial torch, the summons to arms, sings as he fares across the country. Hurrying without respite he thinks of his errand, of the bride he has left at the altar, of the morrow's combat, of victory, of reunion . . . Schubert himself regards this as the best of the Scott songs. Vogl himself interprets it heavily (a syllable, often a word, to each note) but splendidly.*

Modern listeners would perhaps place Ellen's songs on a higher plane than Norman's horse-ride, but Schubert must have been proud of the symphonic scheme – artfully modified repetition, and the avoidance of monotony by changes of key at just the right moments – which holds a long song together. The Scott settings are all characterized by an inspired use of ostinati that unify long stretches of rhapsodic melodic invention; the first verse of *Normans Gesang* stays in the home key of C minor until an excursion into the G major dominant and a totally new second tune at b. 20. This pattern is repeated for Verses 3 and 4, and seems set to govern Verses 5 and 6 also, until the dream of victory and reunion prompts an unexpected and touching modulation to C major for the last strophe (b. 81 with upbeat). When we hear this music we are somehow made to feel that we may be listening to Norman's swansong. Schubert has exactly understood

Vignette for *Normans Gesang* on the title page of Carl Czerny's solo piano arrangement (1838).

the young knight's character – he is the salt of the earth, simple without being stupid, romantic without being sentimental. He invokes his bride's name, Mary, at the end of the verses like a sacred litany; as he does so the vocal line blooms into high-lying melisma (the only such lyrical moments in this taxing piece, while elsewhere, as Vogl discovered to his cost, the singer's challenge is to sing a word on every note at a rather fast tempo). The final 'Maria' is embellished with a turn as if in knightly homage (b. 100). It seems careless of Scott not to let his readers know whether Mary ever sees her groom again; all we know is that the Battle of Beal' an Duine in which Norman fights was an extremely bloody one.

First edition: Published as Op. 52 no. 5 by Artaria, Vienna in April 1826 (P91)
First known performance: 8 March 1827, *Abend-Unterhaltung* of the Gesellschaft der
                                Musikfreunde, Vienna. Soloist: Ludwig Tietze, accompanied by

Franz Schubert (see Waidelich/Hilmar Dokumente I No. 459 for full concert programme)

Contemporary reviews: *Berliner allgemeine musikalische Zeitung*, No. 23 (6 June 1827), p. 182 [Waidelich/Hilmar Dokumente I No. 506; Deutsch Doc. Biog. No. 849]

Subsequent editions: Peters: Vol. 2/99; AGA XX 473: Vol. 8/82; NSA IV: Vol. 3a/42; Bärenreiter: Vol. 2/86

Bibliography: Capell 1928, p. 211
                        Fischer-Dieskau 1977, p. 221

Discography and timing: Fischer-Dieskau II 7[4]   3'11
                        Hyperion I 13[11]
                        Hyperion II 30[5]   3'34   Thomas Hampson

← *Coronach* D836   *Ellens Gesang III* D839 →

VI ELLENS GESANG III (Ave Maria)   Ellen's Song III
Op. 52 no. 6, **D839** [H569]
B♭ major   April 1825

A literal translation of Storck's translation is given here.
Scott's original poem is printed below in italics.

Ave Maria! Jungfrau mild,
Erhöre einer Jungfrau Flehen,
Aus diesem Felsen starr und wild
Soll mein Gebet zu dir hinwehen.
Wir schlafen sicher bis zum Morgen,
Ob Menschen noch so grausam sind.
O Jungfrau, sieh der Jungfrau Sorgen,
O Mutter, hör ein bittend Kind!
                    Ave Maria!

Ave Maria! Unbefleckt!
Wenn wir auf diesen Fels hinsinken
Zum Schlaf, und uns dein Schutz bedeckt
Wird weich der harte Fels uns dünken.
Du lächelst, Rosendüfte wehen
In dieser dumpfen Felsenkluft,

Ave Maria! Maiden mild!
Listen to a maiden's entreaty
From this wild unyielding rock
My prayer shall be wafted to you.
We shall sleep safely until morning,
However cruel men may be.
O Maiden, behold a maiden's cares,
O Mother, hear a suppliant child!
                    Ave Maria!

Ave Maria! Undefiled!
When we sink down upon this rock
To sleep, and your protection hovers over us,
The hard rock shall seem soft to us.
You smile, and the fragrance of roses
Wafts through this musty cavern.

O Mutter, höre Kindes Flehen,
O Jungfrau, eine Jungfrau ruft!
                    Ave Maria!

  Ave Maria! Reine Magd!
Der Erde und der Luft Dämonen,
Von deines Auges Huld verjagt,
Sie können hier nicht bei uns wohnen.
Wir woll'n uns still dem Schicksal beugen,
Da uns dein heil'ger Trost anweht;
Der Jungfrau wolle hold dich neigen,
Dem Kind, das für den Vater fleht.
                    Ave Maria!

O Mother, hear a suppliant child,
O Maiden, a maiden cries to you!
                    Ave Maria!

  Ave Maria! Purest Maiden!
Demons of the earth and air,
Banished by the grace of your gaze,
Cannot dwell with us here.
Let us silently bow to our fate,
Since your holy comfort touches us;
Incline in grace to a maiden,
To a child that prays for its father.
                    Ave Maria!

Hymn to the Vivgin
Ave Maria! maiden mild!
Listen to a maiden's prayer;
Thou canst hear though from the wild;
Thou canst save amid despair.
Safe may we sleep beneath thy care,
Though banish'd, outcast, and reviled –
Maiden! hear a maiden's prayer;
Mother, hear a suppliant child!
                    Ave Maria!

Ave Maria! undefiled!
The flinty couch we now must share,
Shall seem with down of eider piled,
If thy protection hover there.
The murky cavern's heavy air
Shall breathe of balm if thou hast smiled;
Then, maiden! hear a maiden's prayer,
Mother, list a suppliant child!
                    Ave Maria!

Ave Maria! stainless styled!
Foul demons of the earth and air,
From this their wonted haunt exiled,
Shall flee before thy presence fair.
We bow us to our lot of care,
Beneath thy guidance reconciled;
Hear for a maid a maiden's prayer,
And for a father hear a child!
                    Ave Maria!

This is the sixth of Schubert's eight Scott solo settings (1825–6). See the poet's biography for a chronological list of all the Scott settings.

The song was an immediate favourite in the Schubert circle. It was composed in Upper Austria when the composer was on holiday with the singer Vogl, an excursion that incorporated the first-ever lied recital tour. In a letter to his father of 25 July 1825, Schubert writes, 'They wondered greatly at my piety which I expressed in a hymn to the Holy Virgin and which, it appears, grips every soul and turns it to devotion. I think this is due to the fact that I have never forced devotion in myself and never compose hymns or prayers of that kind unless it overcomes me unawares; but then it is usually the right and true devotion.' Six weeks later Schubert mentions the song again, this time to his brother Ferdinand. In an age less touchy about sexing songs, he and Vogl have been performing it everywhere: 'The manner in which Vogl sings and I accompany, as though we were one at such a moment, is something quite new and unheard-of for these people.'

Such is the worldwide popularity of this song, and so often has it been performed with Latin text in church, that most people never connect it with Ellen Douglas and the plight of her father. In the third canto of Scott's epic poem this prayer follows hard on the heels of Norman's summons to arms (*see Normans Gesang*). When the conflict between the king (whom Ellen still does not realize is none other than Fitz-James) and Roderick Dhu comes to a head, the heroine joins her father in hiding in his rocky eyrie, fit more for wolf or wildcat than for human habitation. Roderick Dhu, whose love of Ellen is unrequited, lingers in the vicinity and overhears her 'melting voice' which, harp-accompanied, seems to be that of an angel. An illustration in the *Rheinisches Taschenbuch für 1824* depicts Ellen singing to her bearded father's accompaniment – he is the Allan-Bane mentioned in the lines that lead into the song – while the head of Roderick, concealed in the shrubbery, is to be seen as he overhears the song. If Scott had read Goethe's *Wilhelm Meister* some time after 1795 it is quite possible that the angelic Ellen and her harp-playing father were modelled on that seminal father-and-daughter duo of the lieder repertoire, Mignon and the Harper.

Ellen singing 'Ave Maria', accompanied on the harp by her father. Secretly listening is Roderick Dhu. From *Rheinisches Taschenbuch*, 1824.

Scott, ever conscious of Scotland's splintered factions, reminds his nineteenth-century English readers that Ellen is a Highlander and a devout Catholic like all other Scots at that time. The whole story takes place when the ongoing strife between the clans was between Lowland Saxon and Highland Celt just before the forces of the Reformation changed Scotland for ever. It was the daughter of King James V, Mary Stuart, Queen of Scots (a heroine for Germans because of Schiller's play of 1800) who was later to lose the battle for state Catholicism.

There is no doubt that Schubert, not conventionally religious, has been inspired to write a piece that reflects Ellen's character and purity as much as that of the Virgin to whom she prays; her supplication to the Heavenly Mother is mirrored by her selfless devotion to her beleaguered father on earth. Perhaps a devotion celebrating human goodness and love, as much as divine love, is what Schubert meant by 'a right and true devotion' when writing to his father. The song, hypnotically strophic, has the same ineffable span as the opening pages of Ellen's first song. The prayer is occasioned by the deepest sorrow and anxiety on the part of Ellen, yet the music glows with confidence as if the character were taking refuge in a liturgical prayer. (This has none of the drama that can be found in *Die junge Nonne* D828, but in a much earlier song, *Die Nonne* D208, the prophetic piano interlude at bb. 34–40 is a seraphic succession of triplets based on a tonic pedal to depict the same immovable devotion felt by Ellen.) The vocal line reflects maidenly sorrow and religious faith, but in the flowering of melismas (for example, 'Jungfrau' in b. 4) we hear also the ecstasy of a young woman with her whole future before her, a woman in love. This music does not deny that religious ecstasy and erotic impulse can be closely related. Despite her fears, Ellen (or Schubert) believes that life is, after all, beautiful. This would exactly suit the mood of a summer during which the composer must have felt he was at last waking up from a nightmare of sickness and a dismal medical prognosis.

In the ineffable unfolding of this music, modulations never seem engineered: everything feels inevitable and in its right place. The song can be easily ruined by gratuitous rubato in the pianist's pervasive sextuplet figurations. Capell suggests that this accompaniment was inspired by the *Bewegung* of one of Bach's cantatas; whether or not this is true, the music requires the unselfconscious flow of the pre-Romantic age. This style has sometimes been referred to as Bach's unstoppable 'sewing machine', but *Ave Maria* is powered rather by Gretchen's spinning wheel raised to a higher and calmer power. This floating accompaniment is not a mirror of Ellen's unhappiness; its movement seems governed by a cosmic energy more universal than the interpretative fancy of any particular performer. Each verse is really one long paragraph, flowing ineluctably to the final cadence of repeated litany – as if nothing can interrupt the line of communication between the supplicant and the Virgin Mary herself. Singer and pianist are at one and in the grip of something extraordinary when performing this song, and audiences sensed this when they heard Vogl with Schubert at the piano at various informal concerts in Upper Austria in the summer of 1825. The first public performance was given by the soprano Theresia Josephi at an evening concert of the Gesellschaft der Musikfreunde in Vienna. The date was 31 January 1828, Schubert's thirty-first birthday, and his last.

It was not long before Schubert's setting was taken to be a religious song per se, its composer forgotten by those who have associated the melody with a timeless hymn to a Latin text with organ accompaniment. Is it the purest luck that the Latin prayer fits the English and German words, or must we simply thank Scott for casting his original in a way that more or less encompasses the length and breadth of its liturgical inspiration? Schubert's music has been heard in countless instrumental versions and the depths of kitsch to which some of these arrangements descend are breathtaking. Robert Holl has in his possession a beautifully written-out orchestral score in the hand of Schubert's elder brother Ferdinand, who was a sometime composer. Here Scott is dispensed with in favour of Latin, but other details (a four-part chorus at the end adds a series of 'Amens') demonstrate that the temptation to wring every aspect of religious sentimentality out of this music was indulged early on. Almost comical is Ferdinand's addition of timpani – a thud on the first beat of each bar of the introduction, and a drum roll on the refrain with a crescendo leading to the emphasized vowel 'Ave Maria'. The animated movie *Fantasia* (1940) concludes with a vast singing processional of wraith-like pilgrims moving first through misty mountainous landscapes and then vast Piranesi-like cathedral structures. But it is hard to censure Walt Disney for this treatment of the song (with a newly grafted English text) when something equally cloying was produced by a member of the composer's own family a century earlier. As early as 1820 (five years before Schubert set this lyric) the eleven-year-old Felix Mendelssohn set the same translation to music (D minor, $\frac{6}{8}$) in a musical style that was derived from his teacher Carl Friedrich Zelter and his love of Bach. The word 'mild' (within the phrase 'Ave Maria! Jungfrau mild') occasions from the young composer six bars of melismas in the Bachian oratorio style. Felix's sister Fanny composed a setting of the same text, perhaps more distinguished, with generous piano arpeggios in imitation of the accompanying harp, the instrument played, according to Scott, by Ellen's aged father while the concealed Roderick Dhu looked on longingly, transported by Ellen's beauty.

First edition:	Published as Op. 52 no. 6 by Artaria, Vienna in April 1826 (P92)
First known performance:	31 January 1828, *Abend-Unterhaltung* of the Gesellschaft der Musikfreunde, Vienna. Soloist: Theresia Josephi (see Waidelich/ Hilmar Dokumente I No. 580 for full concert programme)
Subsequent editions:	Peters: Vol. 1/206; AGA XX 474: Vol. 8/90; NSA IV: Vol. 3a/50; Bärenreiter: Vol. 2/91
Bibliography:	Black 2003, p. 116 (for the Piano Sonata in C major D840 written directly after this song) Capell 1928, pp. 210–11 Einstein 1951, p. 302 Fischer-Dieskau 1977, p. 212
Further settings and arrangements:	Fanny Mendelssohn (1805–1847) *Ave Maria* (1832) Felix Mendelssohn (1809–1847) *Ave Maria* (c. 1820) Arr. Franz Liszt (1811–1886) for solo piano, no. 12 of *Lieder von Schubert* (1837–8) [*see* Transcriptions] Arr. Colin Matthews (b. 1946) for voice and chamber ensemble, *Ellens drei Gesänge* (1984)
Discography and timing:	Fischer-Dieskau — Hyperion I 13[14] Hyperion II 30[6] 6'09 Marie McLaughlin

← *Normans Gesang* D846   *Lied des gefangenen Jägers* D843 →

VII LIED DES GEFANGENEN JÄGERS
Op. 52 no. 7, **D843** [H570]
D minor   April–July 1825

Song of the imprisoned huntsman

(32 bars)

A literal translation of Storck's translation is given here.
Scott's original poem is printed below in italics.

Mein Ross so müd' in dem Stalle sich steht,
Mein Falk ist der Kapp und der Stange so leid,
Mein müssiges Windspiel sein Futter
verschmäht,
Und mich kränkt des Turmes Einsamkeit.
Ach wär' ich nur, wo ich zuvor bin gewesen,
Die Hirschjagd wäre so recht mein Wesen,
Den Bluthund los, gespannt den Bogen:
Ja, solchem Leben bin ich gewogen.

My horse is so weary of his stall;
My hawk is so tired of perch and hood;
My idle greyhound spurns his food,

And I am sick of this tower's solitude.
I wish I were as I have been before;
Hunting the hart is truly in my nature,
With bloodhound free and bow drawn:
Yes, I favour such a life.

Ich hasse der Turmuhr schläfrigen Klang,
Ich mag nicht seh'n, wie die Zeit verstreicht,
Wenn Zoll um Zoll die Mauer entlang
Der Sonnenstrahl so langsam schleicht.
Sonst pflegte die Lerche den Morgen
zu bringen
Die dunkle Dohle zur Ruh' mich zu singen,
In dieses Schlosses Königshallen,
Da kann kein Ort mir je gefallen.[1]

I hate the drowsy chime of the steeple clock,
I care not to see how time passes
As, inch by inch along the wall,
The sunbeams crawl so slowly.
Once the lark would herald the morning,

And the dark rook sings me to rest.
In the kingly halls of this castle
I can find nowhere that pleases me.

Früh, wenn der Lerche Lied erschallt,
Sonn ich mich nicht in Ellens Blick,
Nicht folg ich dem flüchtigen Hirsch durch
den Wald,
Und kehre, wenn Abend taut, zurück.
Nicht schallt mir ihr frohes Willkommen
entgegen,
Nicht kann ich das Wild ihr zu Füssen mehr
legen,
Nicht mehr wird der Abend uns selig
entschweben,
Dahin ist Lieben und Leben.

At early morning, when the lark's song echoes,
I do not sun myself in Ellen's eyes;
Nor do I pursue the fleet deer through the forest

And return home with the evening dew.
No joyful welcome rings in my ears,

I cannot lay my catch at her feet;

No more will evening float past in bliss.

Love and life are lost.

My hawk is tired of perch and hood,
My idle greyhound loathes his food,
My horse is weary of his stall,
And I am sick of captive thrall
I wish I were, as I have been,
Hunting the hart in forest green,
With bended bow and bloodhound free,
For that's the life is meet for me.

I hate to learn the ebb of time
From yon dull steeple's drowsy chime,

[1] Storck's original translation of this line reads '*Ist kein Ort, der mir kann gefallen*'.

> *Or mark it as the sunbeams crawl,*
> *Inch after inch, along the wall.*
> *The lark was wont my matins ring,*
> *The sable rook my vespers sing;*
> *These towers, although a king's they be,*
> *Have not a hall of joy for me.*
>
> *No more at dawning morn I rise,*
> *And sun myself in Ellen's eyes,*
> *Drive the fleet deer the forest through,*
> *And homeward wend with evening dew;*
> *A blithesome welcome blithely meet,*
> *And lay my trophies at her feet,*
> *While fled the eve on wing of glee, –*
> *That life is lost to love and me!*

This is the seventh of Schubert's eight Scott solo settings (1825–6). See the poet's biography for a chronological list of all the Scott settings.

This ballad appears in the sixth and last canto of *The Lady of the Lake*, almost at the end of Scott's long epic. Ellen Douglas, on a mission to Stirling Castle, finds herself in a 'latticed bower' beneath one of the castle turrets:

> But sudden, see, she lifts her head!
> The window seeks with cautious tread!
> What distant music has the power
> To win her in this woeful hour!
> 'Twas from the turret that o'er hung
> Her latticed bower, the strain was sung.

As this song wafts down from the tower she recognizes the voice of her beloved Malcolm Graeme (or Malcolm Groem as the Rossini opera has it, a trouser role for mezzo soprano, and in the 1980s one of Marilyn Horne's great assumptions). This incident, reminiscent of the story of Blondel and the imprisoned Richard the Lionheart, soon leads to a happy ending. Ellen's protector, James Fitz-James (who is also the mysterious guest to whom the first two of *Ellens Gesänge* had been addressed in the poem's opening canto) is at last revealed as none other than the King of Scotland himself. He duly pardons both Ellen's father, Lord James of Douglas, and Graeme. With regal generosity he gives Ellen's hand in marriage to his former enemy.

> His chain of gold the King unstrung,
> The links o'er Malcolm's neck he flung,
> Then gently drew the glittering band,
> And laid the clasp on Ellen's hand.

Richard Capell's commentary criticizes what he takes to be the song's weaknesses and, in doing so, points out its strengths. He begins by acknowledging that 'the chivalric rhythm and the bold tune start well' but he finds the song 'cloying'. He continues: 'The song is, for one thing, contained within an octave. The pianoforte never rises above a D on the treble stave, and all modulation is denied.' In using the words 'contained' and 'denied' Capell effectively sums up Malcolm Graeme's plight as a prisoner and Schubert's response to it. He might have realized that the boundaries within which this song moves were not imposed by the limits of the composer's abilities, but by the King of Scotland's prison cell.

The introduction is stirring and regal – six bars recall the sound of the distant hunting-horns that so tantalize the singer. The pervasive polonaise rhythm is effective for the same reason that it is so moving in the music of Chopin: it is a dance of contained, steel-sprung energy with overtones of pride and

Vignette for *Lied des gefangenen Jägers* on the title page of Carl Czerny's solo piano arrangement (1838).

defiance, also associated with the struggle for liberation of a nation in servitude. It is also likely that Rossini played a part in the rhythm selected for this song: the sprung dactyls of Malcolm's *La mia spada* from the finale of Act I of *La donna del lago* evoke his pride and independence. The same aria in E flat major also probably influenced the rhythmic shape of *Ellens Gesang II* D838. In the summer of 1825 Anton Ottenwalt in Linz heard Schubert play *Lied des gefangenen jägers*; in a letter to Josef von Spaun (27 July 1825) he recalls the accompaniment: 'How shall I describe those angrily throbbing, briefly cut-off chords? I am almost ashamed at having taken it into my head to write about it.' The unbiddable Malcolm Graeme embodies the stubborness of the Scottish clans, jealous of their independence and notoriously unwilling to acknowledge fealty to a central authority. Adam Storck's translation of *The Lady of the Lake* opens with a sixty-five-page essay designed to furnish the German-speaking reader with the historical background necessary to understand Scott's poem. If Schubert read this (and there is no reason to suppose he did not) he would have known of Malcolm Graeme's proud lineage, his youthful resentment against the royal family and his frustration at not being able to do anything about it.

As in the opening of *Totengräbers Heimwehe* D842, also governed by a tightly structured motivic accompaniment, the shape of the vocal line emerges apparently by chance: in neither song is the protagonist in a mood to embark on a melody, his discomfort of paramount importance, yet the sum total of his seemingly spontaneous phrases, as if muttered in anger rather than sung, amounts to something memorable – not a conventional tune, perhaps, but a compelling melodic pattern. The accompanying piano motifs dictate a voice part moulded to their harmonic movement – banks of repeated notes climbing in steps up the stave, but soon reaching their ceiling. Schubert knows that anything above the baritone's vocal *passaggio* will sound, if well sung, heroic and unconstrained; accordingly, the prisoner's voice never goes higher than a D. The descending phrase on 'Und mich kränkt des Turmes Einsamkeit' (bb. 12–14) is a text-book example of Schubert's use of a vocal line doubled by piano octaves to denote loneliness or abandonment. The answering phrase in the piano interlude, also in double octaves (bb. 14–16), mounts the stave as a mirror image, a powerful analogue for someone pacing up and down the length of a tiny cell.

Schubert must have been aware that the first four lines of each strophe refer to the prisoner's present circumstances, and the next four to past happiness. He responds by changing to the major key (in the manner of certain songs in *Winterreise* D911) as Malcolm's mind is flooded with the comfort of sweeter memories before returning to hateful reality. After four lines of bemoaning his fate, tiny verbal signposts (the conditional 'wär', the nostalgic 'zuvor' and 'sonst', the regretful threefold 'nicht' and 'dahin') lead us back into memories of happier times. This is genuinely affecting and, as little as we know of Malcolm's character, the composer manages to depict him as someone who will prove to be a tender and loving consort for Ellen. (His macho devotion to blood sports, less fashionable in our own time, was required of an aristocratic gentleman warrior in Ellen's epoch, as well as Schubert's.)

As in all Schubert's best strophic songs, the later verses fit the music surprisingly well. There are tiny adjustments, and 'Ich hasse der Turmuhr schläfrigen Klang' at bb. 31–3 is fitted out with extra semiquavers that suggest a vehemence absent from the equivalent passage in the first verse. The crawling sunbeams symbolizing the slow passing of time at bb. 37–9 are also well suited to dragging unison octaves, and the arrival of dawn is aptly reflected by the gentle glow of the major key at 'Sonst pflegte die Lerche den Morgen zu bringen' (from b. 41); here the semiquaver pulsations in the accompaniment are heard to twitter like birds, a reminder that Schubert's greatest accompaniments can be multi purpose. In the third verse the darting melisma in semiquavers on 'Hirsch durch den Wald' at b. 62 is as nervous as a hounded stag, and the descending scale passage at 'ihr zu Füssen mehr legen' (b. 70) is perfect for gallantly laying something precious at the beloved's feet. The bitterness of 'Dahin ist Lieben und Leben' from b. 72, and the postlude, now a pale piano echo of the more defiant introduction, bring this superb piece of song-theatre to a close. If the public experiences a sense of constraint in this music, as Capell did, the composer has entirely succeeded in his aims.

First edition:	Published as Op. 52 no. 7 by Artaria, Vienna in April 1826 (P93)
First known performance:	8 February 1827, *Abend-Unterhaltung* of the Gesellschaft der Musikfreunde, Vienna. Soloist: Johann Karl Schoberlechner (see Waidelich/Hilmar Dokumente I No. 450 for full concert programme)
Contemporary reviews:	*Allgemeine Musikalische Zeitung* (Leipzig) No. 14 (4 April 1827) col. 234f. [Waidelich/Hilmar Dokumente I No. 469; Deutsch Doc. Biog. No. 805]
	The Harmonicon (London), July 1827 [Waidelich/Hilmar Dokumente I No. 510; Deutsch Doc. Biog. No. 797]
Subsequent editions:	Peters: Vol. 2/106; AGA XX 475: Vol. 8/92; NSA IV: Vol. 3/54; Bärenreiter: Vol. 2/94
Bibliography:	Capell 1928, p. 212
	Einstein 1951, pp. 301–2
	Fischer-Dieskau 1977, pp. 212–13
	Rode-Breynann 1999, pp. 31–45
Discography and timing:	Fischer-Dieskau II 7[5] 2'55
	Hyperion I 35[17]
	Hyperion II 30[7] 3'26 Thomas Hampson

← *Ellens Gesang III* D839   *Das Heimweh* D851 →

Der SIEG
(MAYRHOFER) **D805** [H547]
F major   March 1824

(55 bars)

O unbewölktes Leben!	O unclouded life,
So rein und tief und klar.	So pure, so deep and clear!
Uralte Träume schweben	Age-old dreams float
Auf Blumen wunderbar.	Miraculously over the flowers.
Der Geist zerbrach die Schranken,	The spirit broke the fetters
Des Körpers träges Blei;	Of the body's inert leaden mass;
Er waltet gross und frei.	It roams great and free.
Es laben die Gedanken	The mind is refreshed
An Edens Früchten sich;	By the fruits of Paradise;
Der alte Fluch entwich.	The ancient curse is no more.
Was ich auch je gelitten,	Whatever I may have suffered,
Die Palme ist erstritten,	The palm is now won
Gestillet mein Verlangen.	And my longing stilled.
Die Musen selber sangen	The Muses themselves sang
Die Sphinx in Todesschlaf,[1]	The sphinx to the sleep of death,
Und meine Hand, – sie traf.	And my hand struck the blow.
O unbewölktes Leben!	O unclouded life,
So rein und tief und klar.	So pure, so deep and clear!
Uralte Träume schweben	Age-old dreams float
Auf Blumen wunderbar.	Miraculously over the flowers.

JOHANN MAYRHOFER (1787–1836)

This is the forty-fourth of Schubert's forty-seven Mayrhofer solo settings (1814–24). See the poet's biography for a chronological list of all the Mayrhofer settings.

In March 1824 Schubert, recuperating from the primary and secondary stages of his venereal illness, was still suffering from bouts of deep depression as is shown by a heart-rending letter he wrote at the end of this month to his friend, the painter Kupelwieser, in Rome ('I feel myself to be the most unhappy and wretched creature in the world . . . whom love and friendship have nothing to offer but pain'). In the meantime life went on, and so did the composition of songs – above all the great Mayrhofer settings that were conceived after the appearance of the

---

[1] Mayrhofer writes (*Gedichte*, 1824) 'Die *Schlang*' in Todesschlaf'. It is likely that the sphinx as set by Schubert was included in an earlier version of the poem and stems from the poet himself and that for this song Schubert was working from a handwritten copy. For an explanation of the background to these alternative Mayrhofer readings see Editorial Note at the beginning of Johann MAYRHOFER.

poet's *Gedichte* in print. We first hear of *Der Sieg* in a letter written by Moritz von Schwind to Franz von Schober on 6 March 1824. This document comes from a time when Schubert's friends clearly felt, with some relief, that he was on the mend at last. Schubert was benefiting from a diet which, if it did little to cure his malady, at least reduced his weight and consumption of alcohol.

> *Schubert is really doing well. He says that a few days into the new treatment he felt things were taking a turn for the better and everything had changed. He still lives on panada [bread boiled to a pulp in water and flavoured] one day and a schnitzel the next and drinks copious amounts of tea. He also frequently goes bathing and on top of it all keeps inhumanly busy. On Saturday a new quartet is to be performed at Schuppanzigh's who is absolutely delighted and is said to have been working especially hard learning his part. For a long time now he has been working on an octet, with the utmost resolution. If you drop by during the day, he says, 'Hello, how are you? – Good!' and then goes on writing, at which point you leave again. Two of Müller's poems he has set most beautifully, and three of Mayrhofer's, whose poems have already been published, Gondelfahrt [sic], Abendstern and Sieg. The last I didn't, in fact, know all that well and had always recalled it as a richly blossoming song with something of a romance about it ['ein reiches blühendes fast märchenhaftes Lied'],* but now it is serious, weightily Egyptian, but nevertheless so warm, round, grand and genuine.*

There are a number of interesting points raised by this letter, one of the few on-the-spot reports of Schubert's way of working: concentrated and oblivious to social distractions when he wished to be. Exactly which numbers from Müller's *Die schöne Müllerin* D795 particularly appealed to Schwind we shall never know; it seems that these songs from 1823 had been relatively slow to filter through to members of the circle. The puzzled reference to *Der Sieg* may concern two different performances of the same new song, each emphasizing different aspects of it, as can often happen. Deutsch suggests that Schwind, in describing *Der Sieg* as 'Egyptian', is comparing the noble tone and tempo of the work with a much earlier Mayrhofer setting, *Memnon* D541, about the ancient legend ascribed to the statue of the great pharaoh on Luxor's west bank. But he is just as likely to be referring to the song's similarity (with the same low F in b. 38) to Sarastro's *O Isis und Osiris* from Mozart's *Die Zauberflöte*. It is also likely that Schwind, not unnaturally, associated the word 'Sphinx' with Egypt. (Schubert's manuscript shows that he wrote this word rather than Mayrhofer's 'Schlang'' and it is printed thus in both the AGA and NSA.) However, according to Robert Holl, the use of 'Sphinx' here not only stems from that creature's famous riddles and its association with the Oedipus legend; it could well go back to Schubert's reading (perhaps with Mayrhofer in the earlier years of their friendship, *see Liane* D298) of Jean Paul's great novel *Titan* where it is designated as an old curse and frustration (something like Winston Churchill's famous 'black dog') that eats away at the heart of the hero Albano. It seems that Mayrhofer changed the poem for the printed version in 1824 (which only appeared in October of that year). The poet, perhaps in touch directly with Diabelli in 1833 before the song appeared in print, asked for this change to be incorporated in the song's first edition. The image of the snake, after all, and not the Sphinx, is associated with the old curse of Eden.

Der Sieg is one of the most neglected of the Mayrhofer songs, and also one of the most revealing. Schwind's description of it as 'so warm, round, grand and genuine' is exactly right in musical terms, but he appears to have paid little attention to the gruesome aspect of the words in the middle section. (It is amazing what some listeners will overlook in the presence of a good tune.) Written in the bass clef, like quite a number of the lieder of this period, it might well have

---

* It is possible that Schwind, in using the word 'Lied' in this passage, is referring to Mayrhofer's poem before Schubert set it to music.

been conceived for Vogl, although at this period Schubert was in touch with his sometime Hungarian employer Count Esterházy who was also a bass. It has the mood of a solemn chorale (the 'St Anthony' theme used by Brahms comes to mind) and mention of a saint is appropriate, for this is Mayrhofer's vision of an afterlife, free from the shackles of earthly existence. His victory is that he has chosen when and how to make his exit – in fact he has had the courage to commit suicide. Here is an indication that this drastic step had been on the poet's mind long before he killed himself in 1836. Unlike the nightmare vision of his own *Fahrt zum Hades* D526, he finds himself in heaven rather than hell. Mention of Eden, and Schubert's response to it (the organ-accompanied tone of the song's opening and close) implies that the poet has the Christian heaven in mind, notwithstanding a suicide's ineligibility to enter therein. The F major tonality prophesies the graveside chorale of *Das Wirtshaus* D911/21 from *Winterreise*. The transfiguration of the poet is musically arranged in such a way as to make of this singing angel a patriarchal figure of enormous understanding and benignity, not unlike the eastern magus who sings the Rückert setting *Greisengesang* D778.

The first verse is a noble melody in F major. 'Age-old dreams' sink to the bottom of the stave in bb. 9–10, as if going back to their roots, and flowers bloom higher on the stave with the gracious ornamentation of the word 'wunderbar' (bb. 11–12). After this hymn-like strophe, the middle section is a flashback to the events that led to this heavenly state. There is a change to ⅜ and the marking is 'Etwas bewegter'. This passage, less melodic than the opening, begins in C major and is leaden with portentous dotted rhythms appropriate to the image of 'Des Körpers träges Blei' (bb. 16–18). This is the music of moral struggle, oratorio-like arioso, to be found in such songs as the Schiller setting *Der Kampf* D594. What the poet meant by 'Der alte Fluch' (the ancient curse) we shall never be sure, but if meant in a Christian context, its conjunction with images of Eden and the snake might refer to original sin and God's curse on the serpent in Genesis 3:14.

But Mayrhofer's Eden also owes something to Greek mythology: the line could have been spoken by a benighted Orestes, one of the poet's favourite characters. In the context of suicide, it seems to refer to everything that made the poet's life a misery on earth, and one cannot help but think that this includes his suppressed sexuality. The sense of sustained heroism on the dotted minim in b. 32 on 'Gestillet mein Verlangen', sung fortissimo, is truly majestic. The verse about the 'Musen' and the 'Schlang' (or Sphinx, *see* above) implies that Mayrhofer's art made it possible for him to appease and control the serpent of sin. The low tessitura of this phrase is eerily effective. The sudden self-inflicted blow of 'Und meine Hand, – sie traf' (bb. 39–40) is a truly dramatic moment, the vocal line climbing the stave as though rising to the ultimate challenge. Once the suicidal blow has been dealt, the music is suspended in mid-air as four dotted minim chords in the accompaniment go through various transformations from sharps to flats and then naturals, as if the poet's blow melts into the magician's magic touch: D flat^7 slips into the second inversion of F sharp major; this in turn changes to A^7 in first inversion on C sharp and then, with a miraculous slip of a semitone to C natural in the bass, the C^7 chord that prepares a return to the F major of the opening. The poet's action ('Und meine Hand – sie traf') has solved the mystery of the ancients: everything has been clarified and revealed to him and we can trace the journey of the transfigured soul as it prepares itself for another existence.

The last verse is an exact repetition of the first. As with *Pilgerweise* D789 this recapitulation is in the original poem and not simply the composer's own idea, and it sets the seal on a song of deceptive simplicity. It is possible that Schubert treated this theme of transition into a new life as a type of 'Heiliger Dankgesang' – a hymn of thanks, as in Beethoven's String Quartet Op. 132, for what he took to be his recovery from serious illness (see the first two sentences quoted in the Schwind letter above). Life in at least the beginning of March 1824 must have felt 'unclouded' in comparison to the nightmare of 1823, and the self-destruction of the middle verse might be taken to refer to the destruction of a disease raging within. If this was so it was an optimism that was not to last the month. At the end of March Schubert penned his famous letter to his friend Kupelwieser where he compared himself to the inconsolable character of Gretchen in Goethe's *Faust*, his life shattered and in ruins.

Autograph:	Gesellschaft der Musikfreunde, Vienna
First edition:	Published as Book 22 no. 1 of the *Nachlass* by Diabelli, Vienna in June 1833 (P299)
Subsequent editions:	Peters: Vol. 5/122; AGA XX 458: Vol. 8/16; NSA IV: Vol. 13/136
Bibliography:	Capell 1928, p. 204
	Fischer-Dieskau 1977, p. 193
	Youens 1996, pp. 214–18
Arrangements:	Arr. Tilman Hoppstock (b. 1961) for guitar accompaniment, in *Franz Schubert: 110 Lieder* (2009)
Discography and timing:	Fischer-Dieskau II 6[13] 2'53
	Hyperion I 35[11]
	Hyperion II 29[2] 2'37 Neil Davies

← *Abendstern* D806   *Auflösung* D807 →

⁓⁓⁓⁓⁓⁓⁓⁓⁓⁓

JOHANN PETRUS SILBERT (1772–1844)

THE POETIC SOURCES
S1 *Die heilige Lyra* von Johann Petrus Silbert. Wien 1819, Gedruckt bey Anton Strauss, Zu haben beym Verfasser (Grünangergasse Nro. 893) und in Commission bey Jacob Mayer und Comp.

THE SONGS
February 1819   *Abendbilder* D650 [S1: pp. 180–81]
              Himmelsfunken D651 [S1: pp. 214–15]

Johann Silbert was born in Kolmar in Alsace on 29 March 1772. In his teens he moved to Mainz, going to school and university there, then went to live in Austria in 1817. He spent some years as a secondary-school teacher in the Transylvanian towns of Klausenberg (Cluj) and Kronstadt (Brasov) before moving to Vienna where he was Professor of French at the Polytechnisches Institut. He was an avid theologian and a friend and devout follower of the celebrated Redemptorist pastor Clemens Maria Hofbauer (1751–1820) who was canonized as a saint in 1909 and later became patron saint of Vienna. At the time that Silbert wrote the collection entitled *Die heilige Lyra* (from which Schubert chose his two settings) Hofbauer was coming to the end of his life, having established his own monastery. Hofbauer was known to be a supporter of the ideals of the Enlightenment and had experienced problems with the police on this account. This alone would have made his work (and that of his disciples, including Silbert) required reading for someone like Franz von Bruchmann who later became a Redemptorist priest himself. It is likely that the *Bildung* circle, of which Schubert was a part, discussed recently published books, and that Silbert's collection (essentially modest in comparison to the ground-breaking writings of Novalis) came to the composer's notice in this way. Silbert died on 26 December 1844 in Vienna.

Die heilige Lyra by Johannes P. Silbert (Vienna, second edition, 1820).

J. P. Silbert, engraving by Gustav Leybold after a drawing by Leopold Kupelwieser.

SING-ÜBUNGEN
D619 [H400]
C major   July 1818

Singing exercises (wordless)   Duet

With all the exercises that Schubert wrote for Salieri as a young student (pedagogical works that he produced right up to 1816, and possibly beyond), it is a novelty to come across the composer as a teacher in his own right. Schubert found himself in Zseliz, Hungary, in the summer of 1818, working as music instructor to the two young countesses Esterházy – Marie (1802–1837) and Karoline (1805–1851).

It is well known that Count Esterházy (1777–1834) was extremely interested in music, and that he and his wife, Countess Rosine, were reasonably gifted singers. Quite naturally they also wanted their daughters to sing competently, and the encouragement of their talents in this direction had, in all probability, been Schubert's responsibility from the spring of 1818 when he is likely to have visited the girls in their *Stadtpalais* in Vienna (earning a precious two Gulden an hour for his work). One may conjecture that Schubert had asked his colleague, Johann Michael Vogl, himself a famous singing teacher, for some pointers in this regard, but one must not forget that the boys of the Hofkapelle, students at the Imperial Konvikt where Schubert received his education, had also had singing tuition, and that the composer counted himself a singer of sorts. This did not stop him from setting impossible vocal tasks in some of the early ballads, but by the middle of 1818 (and in stark contrast to works written before 1814) he was well tuned in to matters of vocal range and comfort.

Nevertheless, in writing these singing exercises (in fact one continuous piece of music) Schubert set his two charges a very difficult task. They must have struggled with this piece – unless the standard of singing among teenage girls was thoroughly professional (it would have had to be much higher than might be found today among a similar age group). It is true that singers of the epoch began their stage careers much earlier than is the present custom, but we do not hear of the Esterházy girls pursuing virtuoso careers (not that women of their station would have been allowed to do so), nor do we have any documentary evidence that the *Sing-Übungen* became a 'party piece', which would surely have happened if the work had been a real success with its dedicatees.

From the casting of the vocal quartet *Gebet* D815, which dates from Schubert's second visit to Zseliz in 1824, we know that Marie Esterházy sang soprano, and that her sister Karoline, like her mother, was an alto. And yet, at first glance, this piece is definitely written for two sopranos of equal range. A closer look brings an interesting perspective: the second part visits the same high Gs heard from the first singer, but less often, and when they occur it is never quite in the same exposed way. Both parts visit the middle and the top of the stave (the piece is a thorough work out for both singers), but it seems that Schubert's intention is to encourage young Karoline to work on her top by making her follow, and imitate, her elder sister who had more of a natural ability in that register. The exquisite tact inherent in a piece written for sisters (who no doubt were subject to all the usual sibling rivalries) is that Schubert in no way makes the younger singer feel any less challenged. As a result, however, the long flowing four-bar phrases (one relentlessly succeeding the other, requiring great breath control), as well as the coloratura passages, with all they require of the diaphragm, would have been too much, certainly for the younger countess. But the fact that the composer already defended and encouraged thirteen-year-old Karoline, with whom his name was later to be linked in romantic terms, seems undeniable.

The piece is written on three staves: two vocal staves with figured bass. Here we have a clear illustration of Schubert's wonderful ability to write an interesting bass line, something on which all his songs depend. (We would notice this more often if our minds and ears were not usually diverted by the felicities of the right-hand piano part, usually the last to be composed. In this case, of course, the music for the right hand can be simple or fancy as the pianist realizing the figured bass chooses.) The interchange of bass-line triplets with the twists and turns of the girls' vocal lines is masterful, the one bouncing off the other like a demanding three-sided ball game. It is as if the composer, who would have improvised the accompaniment from the bass line, were dancing with the young countesses, teasing them and leading them on; his enjoyment at this prospect, tinged with the erotic musical symbolism of these entwined lines, is obvious. This is perhaps what accounts for the piece's length and complexity.

The plural title, 'Singing Exercises', is puzzling. But this is surely linked with the question of how one may perform this wordless piece. Sometimes such exercises are sung merely to 'la', but here we are not given any clue. If there is more than one exercise contained in this piece, it must be to do with the mastering and matching of vowel sounds in the various registers that is one of a singer's first tasks. Accordingly the two sopranos might have varied the vowels throughout the piece, changing from 'ah' to 'ee' and 'oo', and so on.

Incidentally, the idea of a music master to two high-born sisters, each trying to outdo the other – and trying to hide the fact in a barrage of arch dissembling – is brilliantly caught by E. T. A. Hoffmann in one of his Kreisler stories. (In this case the siblings are unmusical to a comical degree.) This emphasizes the fact (also celebrated by Molière in *Le bourgeois gentil-homme*) that it was far from unusual for genuinely talented musicians to be enlisted to flatter the amateur aspirations of the idle rich. Schubert was lucky that his own experiences in this role seem to have been more positive than usual.

Autograph:	Houghton Library, Harvard University, Cambridge, MA
First edition:	Published as part of the AGA in 1892 (P526)
Subsequent editions:	AGA XIX 36: p. 95; NSA VIII: Vol. 2/40
Discography and timing:	Fischer-Dieskau —

Deutsche Grammophon *Schubert Duette*	3'56	Janet Baker & Dietrich Fischer-Dieskau
Hyperion I 34[10] Hyperion II 20[9]	3'52	Patricia Rozario & Lorna Anderson

← *Grablied für die Mutter* D616   *Einsamkeit* D620 →

SINGERS

DURING THE COMPOSER'S OWN LIFETIME
The first singing voice that Franz Schubert would have heard was that of his mother, **Elisabeth Katharina Schubert**, née Vietz (1756–1812). Born and brought up in Silesia, she would have known folk melodies from the Sudetenland that were far from the staple fare of the Viennese.

Who knows what music was sung to amuse, pacify and enchant her infant son? In a fascinating passage in *Franz Schubert: Music and Belief* (2003, pp. 45–6), Leo Black points out that the Himmelpfortgrund lay between two streams, and that there was a wash house very near to where Schubert was born. While these *Waschweiber* went about their work the child was likely to have heard the singing voices of 'cheerful, vocalizing Viennese femininity . . . the mixed breath of melody and the common folk'.

As a boy Schubert was a singer himself: he won a scholarship to the Imperial Konvikt as a member of what is now known as the Vienna Boys' Choir, and was required to take part in the sung masses at the Hofkapelle, among other vocal duties. In return he was educated at a school far finer than the one run by his father. Additionally, the young composer was considered exceptional enough to warrant private tuition with the Imperial Kapellmeister, Antonio Salieri. A surviving piece of manuscript paper in Salieri's hand, clearly written out for Schubert's benefit, shows the vocal ranges of the four different types of singers: soprano, alto, tenor and bass (*see* Vol. II/622). Perhaps the Italian master had been alarmed by some of the unreasonable demands, in terms of tessitura, that the young Schubert had already made of his singers – as yet an imaginary cohort of artists. It was Schubert himself who sang his early songs to his schoolfriends, no doubt accompanying himself at the piano. The composer's voice broke a few months after his fifteenth birthday; an inscription on the alto part of a Mass in C major by Peter Winter (1754–1825) reads, 'Schubert, Franz, crowed for the last time, 26th July, 1812.' We know of occasions throughout Schubert's life when he sang his own songs for friends (for example, the first informal performance of *Winterreise* D911 in 1827 that bewildered members of his circle who were expecting less downhearted music). The composer seems to have been a strangely versatile singer. Josef Hüttenbrenner remarked that he had 'an unusually high voice' and Thekla von Gumpert in her memoirs claimed that her husband, Franz von Schober, had described the singing voice of the young Schubert, heard in the Hofburg *c.* 1812, as more powerful than that of the other boy singers. Anselm Hüttenbrenner remembered how useful Schubert was when they sight-read old scores together at Salieri's: he could sing baritone or tenor and, if necessary, alto and soprano as well (he had an astonishing ability to sing falsetto). For the birthday of Johann Michael Vogl (*see* below) in 1819 in Steyr he sang the modest baritone part in a cantata (D666) especially written for the event.

From perhaps as early as 1810 Schubert began to visit the opera, thanks to the generosity of wealthier older friends, Josef von Spaun in particular. By 1812 he had seen two operas by Joseph Weigl (*Das Waisenhaus* and *Die Schweizerfamilie*), Boieldieu (*Jean de Paris*), Cherubini (*Médée*), Spontini (*La vestale*) and Mozart's *Die Zauberflöte*, not to mention Isouard's *Aschenbrödel*, a version of the Cinderella story. The high point of this youthful opera-going was Gluck's *Iphigenie in Tauris* (in German) in January 1813, shortly before his sixteenth birthday. The roles of Orestes and Iphigenia on that occasion were taken by a pair of singers who were to play a crucial part in Schubert's life, particularly the baritone who sang Orestes. This was Johann Michael Vogl, while Anna Milder-Hauptmann was his Iphigenia. It was said that Schubert in the company of the famous poet Theodor Körner, overhearing negative criticism of the two singers in a café after the performance, angrily jumped up and spoke in their defence. He had become a fan of Vogl in particular, and was to meet him four years later in circumstances that he would never have dreamed possible.

It could not have been long after this incident that Schubert first encountered the girl, and singer, with whom he was said to have been very much in love in his teenage years. **Therese Grob** (1798–1875) was a soprano in the choir of the Lichtenthal church, Schubert's local place of worship (a short walking distance from his home in the Säulengasse) where he had received music lessons as a boy from the organist Michael Holzer. Schubert's Mass in F major D105 was performed in this church with Therese as soprano soloist, as well as the *Salve Regina* in F D223.

It may be that a work like *Gretchen am Spinn-rade* D118 was composed with Therese in mind, but the Therese Grob Album (a collection of sixteen songs purportedly put together for her in November 1816, *see* AUTOGRAPHS, ALBUMS AND COLLECTIONS) contains no music as dramatic or demanding as this seminal Goethe setting. Another Schubert friend who was something of a singer was the poet **Franz von Schlechta** (qv). He sang in the lost cantata *Prometheus* D451 in 1816, and then wrote a poem about it afterwards, the publication of which was the first time that Schubert's name had appeared in print.

It was all very well for Schubert to depend on his singing friends for performances, but his music called for the advocacy of an experienced professional. Undoubtedly the most important collaborator of the composer's life was the baritone **Johann Michael Vogl** (1768–1840) who might be dubbed the first-ever full-time lieder singer – at least in the later years of his career. Born in Steyr, he sang

Therese Grob in later life, unsigned oil painting.

in the church choir as a boy soprano and studied at the gymnasium in Kremsmünster. He went to Vienna in order to read law but soon turned his attention to singing professionally. From 1794 he was a member of the Kärntnertortheater where he excelled in a number of important operatic assumptions that required vocal skill and personal *gravitas*; the only role that reputedly defeated him was that of Pizarro in Beethoven's *Fidelio*. His imposing personality enabled him to win the support of influential friends, including members of the aristocracy. Vogl had a commanding presence and a way with words – a performing charisma that suggested that this idol of the composer's early years (Schubert had seen him first in Weigl's *Das Waisenhaus*, and then as Orestes in Gluck's *Iphigenie*) might be a suitable champion for the growing number of Schubert songs, many of them as yet unperformed. A plot was hatched between Franz von Schober (qv) and Josef von Spaun (qv) to bring the singer and the twenty-year-old composer together, aided by Schober's brother-in-law, the Italian tenor **Giuseppe Siboni** (1780–1839) who was a colleague of Vogl's at the Kärntnertortheater. Vogl, not quite fifty, was coming to the end of his stage career; as it turned out his retirement would be hastened by the ascendancy of the Italian opera in Vienna, a vogue that would render him (and many other German singers) more or less out of work.

In the autumn of 1817 the important meeting between composer and singer at last took place. Vogl had not been easily persuaded that he should waste his time auditioning a young hopeful. Tall and very pompous, he was almost unbelievably patronizing in his attitude to Schubert. There was a pile of (no doubt carefully pre-arranged) song manuscripts on the piano, and he began to read through these in a mood of amused condescension. The first piece he was said to have read was the Mayrhofer setting *Augenlied* D297, granting it faint praise – 'nicht übel' ('not bad at all'). Vogl went on to read Goethe's *Ganymed* D544 and the magnificent Mayrhofer setting *Memnon* D541.

Mayrhofer was also clearly involved in the campaign to win Vogl to Schubert's cause; he provided the composer with a number of classically inspired texts that would appeal to the singer's learned temperament and remind the public of a celebrated operatic Orestes. (Some years later the dedication of the Op. 6 songs to Vogl, including two fine Mayrhofer settings, set the seal on this three-way collaboration.) The singer understood Greek and Latin (Marcus Aurelius was a favourite author); he was known as 'Greek Bird' or *Rara avis* to his colleagues – a pun on the fact that the German for bird is 'Vogel'. He also read English, prided himself on his knowledge of philosophy and was even a moderately fluent composer.

Vogl's initial reaction to what must have been an astonishing afternoon of sight-reading was somewhat equivocal. But he was clearly fascinated that someone of such undistinguished appearance, and so shy a disposition, should have produced music of this kind. His immediate advice to Schubert was not to be so retiring and to be more of an actor or performer ('Komödiant') – a direction, in today's terms, to 'play the game' with greater confidence. Throughout his life (the remaining twenty or so years of which were increasingly dominated by Schubert's music), Vogl found it difficult to reconcile the musical glories that came his way, one great song after another, with the physical reality of a little man who failed to fit the singer's conception of how a genius should look and behave (Vogl was ever the thespian in search of a larger than life production). He put forward the theory that Schubert composed in a somnambulant state, and that he was merely a conduit, scarcely aware of the import of the music that passed through him. Vogl knew his Plato and this idea is clearly derived from the Greek philosopher's description in the *Ion* of the god taking possession of the artist who is so powerfully inspired that he is unaware of what he is doing, or how. Vogl was not the only one to try to explain the Schubert phenomenon in this way, but his attitude reveals his most irritating side – grandeur and snobbery combined with a tendency, typical of certain distinguished performers, to see life as an autobiographical play in which other people had merely supporting roles. Dickens would have made much of such a character; Vogl may indeed remind us of Vincent Crummles, a ham actor, centre of his own universe, comical to others if not to himself, but kind enough to befriend Nicholas Nickelby when that young man was down on his luck. Nicholas of course became very fond of and grateful to Mr Crummles, and Schubert's loyalty to Vogl was similarly steadfast.

Vogl was basically good-hearted, and this significantly redeems him. After his initial hauteur had warmed into musical enthusiasm, he was unfailingly kind to the composer – although a cynic might detect in this a measure of self-interest. He clearly realized that Schubert was his guide down a new pathway that had miraculously opened up for him, effectively a new career. The composer was welcomed into Vogl's home, introduced to his influential friends and no doubt lectured on all manner of things by his new mentor. If Schubert found this tiresome at times, he also learned a great deal from Vogl, if not about music itself, then about the 'business' of music, as well as literature and aesthetics. Above all, he valued the way the older man interpreted his songs, even tacitly allowing the singer to ornament his work in the quixotic and self-indulgent manner of the

Vogl accompanied by Schubert, detail from
Schubertabend bei Josef Ritter von Spaun, a sepia drawing,
1868, by Moritz von Schwind.

eighteenth-century *divo*. This was a compulsion that partly derived from Vogl's own unfulfilled ambitions as a composer, a habit that Schubert put up with rather than encouraged. Before Vogl was more or less forced to retire from the Kärntnertortheater, Schubert wrote him an opera, or rather a *Singspiel* – *Die Zwillingsbrüder* D647, premiered in June 1820 – where the singer took both leading roles as the eponymous twin brothers. The composition of such a vehicle, received with some success, shows that Schubert already had the full measure of the man in terms of both his abilities and the vanity that often goes hand in hand with a successful career on the stage.

The female lead in *Die Zwillingsbrüder* was taken by **Betty Vio** (1808–1872) a famous young singer of the time who perhaps also performed Schubert's lieder. The great operatic soprano **Nanette Schechner** (1806–1860), a singer from Munich who conquered Vienna and who was admired by Schubert for her vocal resemblance to Anna Milder-Hauptmann (*see* below), never seems to have shown an interest in the composer's songs. Franz von Schober joined in what he called the 'hymn of praise' for Schechner and she was mooted for a role in Schubert's opera *Der Graf von Gleichen* D918 (with a libretto by Bauernfeld); she had left Vienna, however, by the time Schubert began the composition – which he never completed. Hüttenbrenner remembered an evening dining in Schechner's company when Schubert was a fellow guest. Her presence in the Schubert story is a reminder that in terms of 'casting', the composer, having successfully recruited Vogl, often allowed his songs to look after themselves; if his interest in Schechner was typical, he paid closer attention to selecting and recruiting singers for his operas.

Another important singer was **Karoline Unger** (1803–1877) whom Schubert was said to have briefly coached for the role of Dorabella (in *Mädchentreu*, the German language version of *Così fan tutte*, where the character was renamed Isabella) at the Kärntnertortheater during his brief

Vogl and Schubert 'going out to battle and victory'. Drawing by Franz von Schober.

spell there as repetiteur in April 1821. Karoline was the daughter of Karl Unger (qv), one of the composer's poets, and she was a student of Vogl's from 1825, having first studied with Mozart's sister-in-law, Aloysia Lange. After her marriage she became a composer herself, using her married name Sabatier. Unger was one of the important early interpreters of Schubert's lieder, although she seems to have been active in this field only after the composer's death. She was briefly engaged to the poet Nikolaus Lenau, who described Karoline's performances of *Gretchen am Spinnrade* and *Der Wanderer* D489 as 'a vocal storm of passion'. The French tenor Adolph Nourrit (*see* below), whom she met in Venice in 1838, noted with approval that she 'had been brought up to revere Schubert'.

Johann Michael Vogl retired officially from the Kärntnertortheater at the beginning of December 1821, making his last operatic appearance in June 1822. He was still ambitious and energetic and his second career came to him like manna from heaven. On three occasions (the summers of 1819, 1823 and the gloriously extended summer holiday of 1825) Vogl took Schubert with him on holidays to Upper Austria as his companion and accompanist. As a performer of Schubert's songs the singer was welcomed into homes and monasteries where he was treated as a returning hero and favourite son. In September 1825 Schubert wrote to his brother Ferdinand, 'the manner in which Vogl sings, and I accompany him, and the way in which we seem at such a moment to be *one*, is something quite new and unfamiliar'. In one sentence the composer thus describes, if not the birth of the lied, then the birth of lied performance as we know it.

On the first of these journeys (1819) Schubert made the acquaintance of the Koller family in Steyr; the daughter of the house **Josefine** (or **Josefa**) **Koller** (1801–1874) was a pianist and amateur singer. The composer later provided a song, *Namenstagslied* D695, for the name-day of Josefine's father, Josef von Koller (1780–1864). These first-ever lieder tours, where singer and pianist travelled and worked in tandem, brought genuine joy, relaxation and fulfilment to Schubert's life. In the wake of the composer's terrible illness Vogl seems to have behaved with humanity and an admirable practicality in aiding his recuperation.

Back in Vienna, Vogl was a frequent performer at parties and Schubertiads and the composer was often his accompanist. There were performances at the homes of Karl von Enderes, Franz von Bruchmann, Josef von Spaun, Josef Witteczek and

Karoline Unger, engraving after Josef Kriehuber.

others. The *Vier Canzonen* D688 of 1820 – four Italian ariettas – were eminently suitable for a promising singer, if not yet a prima donna. The manuscript was presented to **Franziska Roner von Ehrenwerth** (1795–1890) who was to become the wife of Josef von Spaun in 1828. It is entirely likely that the music was specially crafted to the budding vocal abilities of a woman who was the beloved of one of Schubert's dearest friends. At a gathering at the home of Karl Pinterics in 1822 Schubert was persuaded to accompany a singer in the service of Prince von Schwarzenberg, **Franz Stohl** (1799–1882). Stohl remembered how Schubert's accompanying of *Der Zwerg* D771 had 'inflamed' and inspired him, as well as the 'unassuming, taciturn and almost bashful'

Schubert ('no flatterer'), saying, 'There is one more person who understands me' – although such memories are not always to be trusted.

Schubert and Vogl were particularly fond of a young Mannheim-born actress named **Sophie Müller** (1803–1830) who seems also to have been an amateur singer of rare distinction. She had arrived in the imperial city in 1822 to take up a contract at the Burgtheater. On several occasions in 1825 Vogl and Schubert visited her, playing new songs to her, and she sang them with equal enthusiasm. The biography of the beautiful Sophie by the poet Johann Mailáth (qv) contains entries from her diary for 1825 that detail these visits:

25 February 1825: Vogl and Schubert ate with us for the first time today; afterwards Vogl sang several of Schiller's poems set by Schubert.

1 March 1825: Vogl and Schubert came in the afternoon and brought new songs from Der Pirat, *also* Die Rose. *Vogl sang from memory* Gruppe aus dem Tartarus; *wonderful.* [There is only one song from Scott's *Der Pirat* – Gesang der Norna D831.]

2 March 1825: After lunch Schubert came; I sang with him until nearly six o'clock, then drove to the theatre.

3 March 1825: After lunch Schubert came and brought a new song, Die junge Nonne. *Later Vogl came and I sang it to him; it is splendidly composed. Old Lange* [Josef Lange who had painted Mozart's last portrait] *joined us too. We had music until towards 7 o'clock when the gentlemen left.*

7 March 1825: Vogl came to lunch, and with Schubert at 5 o'clock; they brought several new songs, among which Fragment aus dem Aeschylus, Ihr Grab, Die Forelle *and* Der Einsame *are excellent. They left at 7.30.*

30 March 1825: Schubert and Vogl came for the last time today. Vogl leaves for his country seat at Steyr.

20 April 1825: Schubert came today; I tried several new songs: Der Einsame, Die böse Farbe, Drang in die Ferne. [Vogl left for Steyr shortly after 30 March, so Schubert visited Sophie alone with a number of songs under his arm. He was soon to join Vogl in Upper Austria for the greatest holiday of his life.]

Sophie Müller, drawing by Josef Kriehuber.

Elsewhere in her diary (January 1826) Sophie Müller mentions the famous Teltscher lithograph of the composer and also hearing the Schulze songs. She writes of hearing the second half of Schubert's *The Lady of the Lake* settings of Walter Scott. In June 1826 she wryly notes Vogl's intention to marry Kunigunde Rosa. In October 1826 she pays Schubert two florins, almost certainly for a piece of printed music. Schubert also went to see her perform at the Burgtheater and she was on the subscribers' list for *Schwanengesang* D957 and 965A. Her early

Katharina Fröhlich (Grillparzer's fiancée) and Josefine Fröhlich, pastel drawings by Heinrich.

death was considered a catastrophe for the artistic life of Vienna.

Also important in the Schubert circle (from 1820 onwards) were the Fröhlich sisters, Anna, Barbara, Katharina and Josefine. Of these Katharina was famously the long-standing fiancée of the poet Grillparzer, though she never married him. **Anna Fröhlich** (1793–1880) was both singer and pianist (she studied the piano with Hummel and singing with Siboni); from 1819 to 1854 she taught singing and piano at the Vienna Conservatoire and was accomplished enough to accompany *Erlkönig*. **Josefine Fröhlich** (1803–1878) was also a singing pupil of Siboni and had a significant career at the Royal Opera in Copenhagen. She took part as the alto soloist in the first performance of the choral *Ständchen* D920, composed by Schubert at the behest of the formidable Anna.

Like Sophie Müller, but of an older generation, **Antonie Adamberger** (1790–1867) was a singing actress. Unlike Müller she was a

Antonie Adamberger, engraved from a miniature painting by Monforno.

native of Vienna. Long before Schubert met her she had taken the role of Klärchen in Goethe's *Egmont*, a play with incidental music by Beethoven (Op. 84), singing the songs *Die Trommel gerühret* and *Freudvoll und leidvoll* (the latter text also set by Schubert as *Die Liebe* D210) in that production. She had been betrothed to the poet Theodor Körner before he was killed in battle in 1813. Antonie and her husband, Josef Cales von Arneth, attended the famous Schubertiad at the home of Josef von Spaun on 15 December 1826, and Antonie sang Schubert songs at her own party for Spaun and his friends given on 20 April 1827. She also performed Schubert's songs at St Florian in 1826. Some three years earlier Vogl, accompanied by Schubert, had given a concert at the same monastery. Antonie had retired from the stage as soon as she got married in 1817.

The much more famous **Anna Milder** (1785–1838) had been Beethoven's first Leonore in 1805. She had chosen to continue her life as a professional diva after she married Peter Hauptmann in 1810 (the marriage did not last). Unlike the younger soprano, Wilhelmine Schröder-Devrient (*see* below), Anna Milder-Hauptmann was not much of an actress. She played a bigger, though rather less sympathetic, role in Schubert's life than Sophie Müller, or even the Fröhlichs. In a letter to his friends from Zseliz (8 September 1818) Schubert confirms that for him Milder is an 'irreplaceable' singer. He adds, 'She sings best and trills worst of all.' She was a 'big beast' in the singer's jungle, an early protégée of the *Zauberflöte* librettist Emanuel Schikaneder. She was a pupil of Vogl and a famous singer in Berlin where she was a friend of Zelter, Goethe's intimate correspondent. Schubert had been a fan of Milder's singing since his boyhood, and it is to her credit that when she returned to Vienna on tour in 1824 she sought him out, having become aware of his prowess as a song composer. She first attempted to reach him through Johann Schickh, the proprietor and editor of the *Wiener Zeitschrift*, but failed (the composer was away in Zseliz). She wanted him to make a setting for her of a poem by Karl von Leitner (qv), the Styrian poet, but this project came to nothing. Schubert was interested in winning her support for his opera *Alfonso und Estrella* D732, but this was hindered by the fact that the lead role in that work did not suit Milder's kind of voice. She warned Schubert in a letter that the 'endless beauties' of his songs were not really suitable for a public that demanded more in the way of vocal excitement. (This was when she was in possession of both *Suleika* songs, D717 and D720, as well as *Geheimes* D719.) It is clear that it was she, not only her public, that craved this excitement, and that her enthusiasm for Schubert's music was guided by a very singery, and ever-practical, self-interest. The second *Suleika* song D717 and *Der Hirt auf dem Felsen* D965 appear to have been composed for Milder's voice, both works having show-off components. The latter score reached her only after Schubert's death and was given its first performance in Riga in 1830. The diva had shown little interest in *Alfonso und Estrella* D732, but the choice of storyline for Schubert's last, and incomplete, opera, *Der Graf von Gleichen*, seems to have been a reaction to a letter from her of 8 March 1825 where she suggests that he treat an 'oriental subject'.

In terms of collaborating with famous opera singers Schubert had an easier, or at least more congenial, time with the Neapolitan-born **Luigi Lablache** (1794–1858), the most famous bass of his generation. After working with both Donizetti and Bellini he had come to the Kärntnertortheater in 1823 to take up a position as the lead bass in Domenico Barabaia's new Italian company. Lablache heard the vocal quartet *Der Gondelfahrer* D809 at the home of Frau von Lászny (*see* DEDICATEES) and was so delighted

Luigi Lablache by Josef Kriehuber, 1827.

with it that he insisted on taking part in a repeat performance where he sang the second bass part. Lablache signed a piece of paper (Vienna, 30 April 1827) that stated he was agreeable to Schubert's dedication to him of the three Italian songs of Op. 83 – *L'incanto degli occhi* D902/1, *Il traditor deluso* (D902/2) and *Il modo di prender moglie* D902/3. These are perhaps the greatest of all Schubert's Italian stylizations, music that veritably exudes the affection and admiration the composer felt for their dedicatee (*see* DREI GESÄNGE FÜR BASS-STIMME MIT KLAVIER).

The other professional operatic bass who had some connection with Schubert was the wealthy, Viennese-born **Josef Preisinger** (1792–1865) who specialized in the Italian repertoire (he played Basilio in Rossini's *Il barbiere di Siviglia*, among other roles) and was also an amateur composer. He worked variously in Graz, Pressburg (Bratislava), Prague and other cities in Germany and France. At the *Abend-Unterhaltungen* of the Gesellschaft der Musikfreunde, Preisinger gave the first performances of two important Schubert songs: *Gruppe aus dem Tartarus* D583 (8 March 1821, repeated at another evening concert on 19 December 1822) and *Der Zwerg* (13 November 1823). He also took part in ensemble performances of the horn-accompanied *Nachtgesang im Walde* D913, and of the orchestrally accompanied *Gesang der Geister über den Wassern* D714 given at the home of Ignaz von Sonnleithner in March 1821.

In those days the difference between professional and amateur singers was far less marked than in our own time. Few people would have doubted Lablache's skills, but other home-grown artists were more controversial. This brings the discussion back to the art of Johann Michael Vogl. As a famous opera singer of the past, he was worshipped by some, but the younger Schubertians, such as Moritz von Schwind, came to think of him as 'an elderly fop', a bit of a phoney and a figure of fun. As a younger man Vogl had been gifted with a naturally beautiful voice and a fine presence, but as a singer *pur sang* he lacked knowledge of formal singing technique or *bel canto* ('nicht die entfernteste Idee' – 'not the remotest idea' – according to Leopold von Sonnleithner). As time went on, he sang as well as he could, and in entirely his own manner. On occasion Vogl was technically challenged by Schubert's musical demands; he asked, for example, that the composer insert an extra bar of interlude in *Erlkönig* so that he could recover his breath (later singers have had cause for gratitude). Beautiful and affecting enunciation was clearly a speciality; as he got older he was able to rely less and less on his vocal prowess, and songs sometimes seemed more recited than vocalized. This gave his performances an 'arty' slant that was criticized in certain quarters for its pretentiousness and lack of voice. But there were many who believed this kind of wholehearted, even over-the-top, engagement with the poem was essential to the art of the lied. That Schubert himself valued Vogl highly is without question. Until meeting Vogl he had sung his own songs to his friends: it was a role he was prepared to hand over to the older man. The scholar Till Gerrit Waidelich notes that the opening of Act 2 of the opera *Alfonso und Estrella* (the short recitative into the aria of the Wolkenmädchen) gave Schubert, and his librettist Franz von Schober, a chance to pay tribute to the special powers of Vogl and his role in giving voice to the composer's songs with soulful intensity (and this despite the fact that Vogl was opposed to the writing of this opera in the first place):

Alfonso:	*Alfonso:*
O sing' mir Vater, noch einmal	O sing to me again, father,
Das schöne Lied vom Wolkenmädchen!	The fair song of the cloud-maiden!
Troila:	*Troila:*
Schon sollst du es selber singen.	But you should sing it yourself.

Alfonso:
Wohl weiss ich es, doch fehlt mir noch die Kraft

Und deine seelenvolle Weise.

Troila:
So horch denn!

Alfonso:
Indeed I know the song, but I lack both the
   strength
And your soulful way of singing.

Troila:
Listen then!

To Schubert's amusement the old bachelor Vogl had married, in his late fifties, and had had a daughter. As late as 1834 he sang *Erlkönig* in public and Bauernfeld remembered that he had sung *Winterreise* at the home of Karl von Enderes in about 1839. Vogl died in Vienna on 20 November 1840, almost twelve years to the day after Schubert's death.

It is interesting that each succeeding generation of the musical public, when listening to song and appraising its practitioners, has tended either inordinately to admire or detest the more rarefied artists of Vogl's kind. A century and a half later the public that continued to value, for example, the art of Schwarzkopf and Fischer-Dieskau at the end of their respective careers, was happy to trade vocal youthfulness for the sort of vivid textual (and musical) insight that had been considered a mark of Vogl's authenticity.

On the other hand, those who simply wanted good 'honest' singing, the sound of a fine, fresh voice creating sumptuous legato lines of melody, favoured less affected singers for Schubert's songs, and not necessarily full-time professionals. The first usually to be named in this category was the tenor **Ludwig Tietze** – often spelled Titze – (1797–1850) who was Schubert's exact contemporary. Sonnleithner was scathing about the Bohemian-born tenor's lack of general culture, vocal finesse and dramatic instincts, but he admitted that Tietze was a naturally gifted singer. This was good enough for Schubert, who accompanied the tenor on a number of occasions. Tietze gave the first public performances at the Gesellschaft der Musikfreunde of *Rastlose Liebe* D138 (29 January 1824), *Der Einsame* D800 (23 November

Ludwig Tietze, a lithograph by Gabriel Decker.

1826), *Normans Gesang* D846 (8 March 1827), *Im Freien* D880 (6 May 1827) and *Gute Nacht* from *Winterreise* D911/1 (10 January 1828). At the Landhaus he performed for the first time *Romanze des Richard Löwenherz* D907 (2 February 1828). He was entrusted with the fiendishly high tenor solo in *Nachthelle* D892 (25 January 1827) and the premiere of *Auf dem Strom* D943 in the public concert of Schubert's works given on 26 March 1828. In the absence of a suitable soprano he even gave the first performance of *Mirjams Siegesgesang* D942 at Schubert's memorial concert on 30 January 1829.

According to (the sometimes unreliable) Josef Hüttenbrenner, Tietze was 'Schubert's greatest enemy'; the tenor apparently deemed Schubert as unworthy of a requiem mass to be celebrated in his memory, considering him merely a 'song poet' rather than a 'great composer'. Although Tietze is the dedicatee of the *Offertorium* D136, published in June 1825 (the singer would no doubt have regarded a bigger work of this kind more his due), not one of the great lieder he performed so regularly is dedicated to him. It seems clear that this possessor of an extremely useful voice was every inch a 'tenor', and that Schubert considered him a colleague rather than a close friend. Nevertheless, Tietze continued to give first public performances after Schubert's death: *Der blinde Knabe* D833 (8 January 1829), *Drang in die Ferne* D770 (19 February 1829) and *An mein Herz* D860 (7 February 1833). He was accompanied in *Erlkönig* and *Liebesbotschaft* D957/1 by Franz Liszt (29 April 1838). The review for Liszt was splendid, of course, but Tietze is congratulated merely for 'holding his own' against such a performance.

Mention must also be made of the singers who specialized in Schubert's music for male quartet. Works like *Die Nachtigall* D724, *Das Dörfchen* D598 and *Geist der Liebe* D747 were almost as popular as *Erlkönig*, and each of the singers who sang in the regular quartet ensemble also sang solo lieder from time to time. Two were already in their forties, and two were more or less contemporaries of Schubert's. Like the composer's parents they had all been born in the Bohemian or Moravian regions of the empire, and had come to Vienna to make their fortunes with varying success.

Josef Barth (1781–1865) had been an official of the Schwarzenberg household, and became a tenor in the court chapel. When *Das Dörfchen* was published, Schubert dedicated it to him; the quartet clearly owed its enthusiastic reception in part to the skills of this first tenor. The second tenor was **Johann Karl Umlauff** (1796–1861), a singing student of Vogl. He was apparently offered an engagement at the Kärntnertortheater in 1821 but turned it down in favour of pursuing a career as a lawyer, eventually achieving financial success and ennoblement. (He claimed to have argued with Schubert over the prosody of *Der Wanderer* D489, and seems to have been surprised when the composer was unwilling to submit to suggestions for improvements.) He spent his later years in Romania, singing Schubert songs translated into French and the local language. The second bass was **Wenzel Nejebse** (1796–1865), an amateur singer

The singers Josef Barth (*left*) and Josef Götz (*right*). Pastel drawings by Princess Pauline von Schwarzenberg.

but a dedicated one, who took part in a number of Schubert first performances. In his professional life he worked first in the censor's office and then the treasury. Nejebse was one of the subscribers to the first edition of *Schwanengesang*, and was a founder member of the Wiener Männergesang-Verein.

The first bass, also something of a composer, was perhaps the most fascinating of the four. Like his younger colleague Umlauff, **Josef Götz** (1787–1822) studied law, and like Barth was a member of the Schwarzenberg household. (The drawings opposite of the two singers are by the Princess Pauline.) He decided to embark on an operatic career and became a well-liked Doctor Bartolo in Rossini's *Il Barbiere di Siviglia*. Sadly, his career as a professional singer was very short-lived. Due to a deterioration in health, he had to give up singing some six months after the Kärntnertortheater performance of *Das Dörfchen*, and he died in early 1822 of venereal disease. This was a sad end for a handsome man of thirty-five, and it must have been distressing for Schubert who knew Götz quite well: the bass had given the first performance of *Sehnsucht* (Schiller) D636, in February 1821, and had taken part in other pieces such as the lost cantata *Prometheus* and, of course, *Die Nachtigall*. When Schubert discovered that he himself had syphilis at the end of 1822 or early in 1823, Götz's demise must have been fresh in his mind, and a grisly reminder of what he himself might expect to suffer.

The vocal teams who sang the quartets changed personnel according to availability. On occasion, another bass replaced Nejebse, someone who was to become almost as famous as Schubert in his own right – **Johann Nepomuk Nestroy** (1801–1862). Nestroy had been a fellow pupil at the Imperial Konvikt, though younger than Schubert. After a failed attempt to follow law, he made his way as a singer with considerable success, and performed in a number of the composer's male-voice quartets as first bass. He also took part in performances of *Fidelio* and Meyerbeer's *Il Crociato in Egitto* when Schubert was an unimpressed member of the audience. But singing was only one of Nestroy's skills. Schubert was never to know him at the height of his success as a comic actor, playwright and wit; he became renowned for his sarcastic wordplay and farces based on the old Viennese traditions of *Volkskomödie*. Nestroy, eventually acknowledged as the greatest satirist of the age, penned pieces making fun of such writers as Grillparzer and Hebbel. He frequently sang in Schubert's four-part ensembles and when he moved to

Johann Nestroy, photograph from the 1840s.

Amsterdam, already on his way to theatrical renown, he took part there in further performances of this music that he clearly loved. A humorous reference to *Der Wanderer* D489 occurs in his magic play *Die Familien Zwirn, Knieriem und Leim* (1834).

Another replacement singer in quartet concerts, this time a high tenor, was **Anton Haizinger** (1796–1869), much admired for his technique and his ability to sing coloratura. As far as his connection with Schubert was concerned, he took part in various quartets and in Leopold von Sonnleithner's concerts. He was, however, considerably more successful than most of the singers in these ensembles. Haizinger was internationally famous as a Rossini tenor and as a singer of

Mozart, Weber and Beethoven (the tenor part in the Ninth Symphony); his career took him as far afield as London and St Petersburg. Haizinger's son, **Anton Haizinger the Younger**, was a soldier by profession (a Feld-Marschall-Leutnant) but also a famed salon singer at the time of Brahms (he was a baritone). He sang Schubert and Loewe almost exclusively and was considered utterly different from his rather more suave contemporary, Julius Stockhausen (*see* below). He seems to have been a 'one-off' in terms of tone, gestures, dramatic delivery and so on. Hanslick thought his singing 'manly and expressive', citing Haizinger's gripping performances of songs like *Der Zwerg, Die Allmacht* D852 and *Kriegers Ahnung* D957/2. For the composer Karl Goldmark in his youth, Haizinger was the last representative of a dying school of singing – 'this is how the Schubert interpreter Vogl must have sung'. Haizinger died in 1891.

Anton Haizinger the Younger.

After this brief departure from the singer-scene contemporary with Schubert himself, we return to a singer only a year older than the composer, and one of his most important colleagues from as early as 1818. He is mentioned separately here, largely because he kept himself apart from the hurly-burly of Viennese musical life. He belonged to a different social milieu from that of any of the other fine Schubert singers, and although he was graciously kind with Schubert and clearly loved his music, there seems never to have been a question of a close friendship, or of his taking part in public concerts. This was the tenorial baritone (or baritonal tenor), **Carl Freihherr von Schönstein** (1796–1876). Schubert first met this cultivated young artist in the summer of 1818 in Zseliz, the summer residence of the Esterházy family in Hungary. The twenty-one-year-old composer was engaged as music tutor at the time to the two daughters of Count Esterházy (the whole family were amateur singers in their own right; *see* commentaries on *Sing-Übungen* D619 and *Gebet* D815, the latter composed in 1824, during Schubert's second Zseliz visit).

Carl von Schönstein, lithograph by Kriehuber, 1841.

The aristocratic Schönstein had been mainly interested in singing Italian music (he had been well taught, and was a sensitive and imaginative musician), but after his meeting with Schubert he gradually became an enthusiastic advocate for the new lieder style; according to Spaun he modelled his interpretations of Schubert's songs on Vogl's. His birth and rank enabled him to perform at the social gatherings of the highest citizens in the land, and he also made appearances, sometimes at Vogl's side, at the grander Schubertiads – those for example that were given by well-born hosts like Josef von Spaun. Schönstein was the dedicatee of *Die schöne Müllerin* D795, and Schubert seems to have had the singer's voice in mind while composing the cycle. Schönstein later averred that after their meeting, Schubert more or less wrote all his songs in a tessitura to suit him – although this remark may have in it a trace of aristocratic presumption. It is true that a tenor-baritone of this *Fach* can normally encompass the songs in their original tonality; certain songs had to be transposed for Vogl after all, and the high-key edition of Schubert's lieder usually avoid the heights and depths of the stave, keeping to a medium tessitura that would have suited Schönstein's voice. (Schubert had to transpose *Rastlose Liebe* down a tone for Schönstein, however.) In 1838, a decade after Schubert's death, Franz Liszt was much taken by Schönstein's singing and praised his ability to give himself entirely to the music while forgetting what impression his singing may be making on the listener. More than one commentator has mentioned Schönstein's ability to bring tears to the listener's eyes with his voice and artistry. Apart from *Die schöne Müllerin* he sang such songs as *Der zürnenden Diana* D707, *Das Lied im Grünen* D917, *Der Winterabend* D938 and *An die Musik* D547.

There were many other contemporary singers in Vienna whose names appear in the Schubert documents – certainly too many for them all to be mentioned in an article of limited size. Some of these, such as **Franz Siebert**, **Franz Rosner** and **Josef Gottdank**, were associated with the few public performances of Schubert's operas, and sometimes part songs, rather than his solo lieder. The tenor **Franz Jäger** (1796–1852) first sang the higher-key version of *Schäfers Klagelied* D121 at a concert at the 'Zum römischen Kaiser' on 28 February 1819, the first public performance of any of Schubert's songs. **Ferdinand Walcher** (1799–1873) was introduced to the Schubert circle by those assiduous diarists of the later Schubert circle, the Hartmann brothers. Walcher scribbled a single sentence about Schubert's lack of belief in God that has often been quoted, and he performed *Drang in die Ferne* and *Auf dem Wasser zu singen* D774.

The older tenor **August, Ritter von Gymnich** (1786–1821) was a friend of Sonnleithner and was recruited to the Schubertian cause by the younger man; he was subsequently close to the Fröhlichs. Gymnich sang Schubert's music several times in public, but seems to have restricted his repertoire to *Erlkönig*, and *Der Wanderer* D489. The bass-baritone **Johann Karl Schoberlechner** (1800–1879) (pictured overleaf) was fond of performing opera solos and ensembles at concerts, but he was also a relatively late addition to the Schubertian lieder-singing ranks. He was on hand to give public performances of such songs as *Der Zwerg* (21 December 1826 and again on 11 December 1827), *An Schwager Kronos* D369 (first performance 11 January 1827), *Lied des gefangenen Jägers* D843 (first performance 8 February of the same year), *Der Kampf* D594 (first performance 6 December 1827) and two songs from *Winterreise* – *Der Lindenbaum* D911/5 and *Im Dorfe* D911/17 (first performances 22 January 1829). He took part in the Schubert memorial concerts in January and March 1829.

One of the most gratifying fan letters that Schubert ever received ('To Franz Schubert, famous composer in Vienna') came from Breslau on 4 June 1828. It was written by the highly gifted **Johann Theodor Mosewius** (1788–1858), a theatre and music director, actor, composer, singer and singing teacher whom Schubert seems to have known through Schober who had lived in Breslau for a period. Mosewius expressed his special admiration for the two Müller cycles (at a time when *Die schöne Müllerin* was still little known and the published first part of *Winterreise* was only six months old). On the same day Mosewius wrote to Schober speaking of Schubert's 'unsurpassed' talent and explaining that he had assigned Schubert songs to his students. According to Schilling's encyclopaedia, Mosewius was an educated singer of solid ability; he frequently

Johann Karl Schoberlechner, lithograph by Josef Teltscher, 1827.

performed Schubert's songs at a time when their value (as he put it when writing to the composer) continued to be 'more and more appreciated in our formerly one-dimensional North'.

Mention should also be made of the singer **Carl Adam Bader** (1789–1870) who, in November 1827, sang *Erlkönig* in the Singakademie in Berlin, even further north, accompanied by Felix Mendelssohn – a collision of two musical worlds, the conflicting lied traditions of Austria and North Germany. The eighteen-year-old composer, pupil of Zelter and fan of Reichardt, was able to play Schubert's accompaniment marvellously but seems to have been immune to the song's qualities. The Hohenems-born cantor, the tenor **Salomon Sulzer** (1804–1890) is discussed in the commentary for *Der 92. Psalm* D953. The Swedish tenor **Isaac Albert Berg** (1803–1886) was responsible for the performance of the Swedish folksong that Schubert subsequently used as a theme for the slow movement of his E flat major Piano Trio D929.

So that the impression is not one of end-to-end impressive vocal achievements, the tenor **Ferdinand Schimon** (1797–1852) should be mentioned. A portraitist of no little ability (he made a fine likeness of Beethoven), he was supposedly encouraged by Schubert to take up singing professionally, and the composer wrote for him the role of Palmerin in the opera *Die Zauberharfe* D644. On the night of the premiere (19 August 1820) he apparently made a mess of his aria which was cut from subsequent performances. He went on to sing *comprimario* (character) roles at the Munich opera, but like so many who dream of becoming singers, he ended up finding success in a different field – in this case by returning to his earlier life as a painter.

There are some singers, no less well known at the time, whose dates have come down to us incomplete (or not at all). The soprano **Sophie Linhart** was a pupil of Anselm Hüttenbrenner and sang *Gretchen am Spinnrade* at Ignaz Sonnleithner's on 2 March 1821 (on 20 February 1823 she sang the same song at the Musikverein). On 26 March 1821 Leopold von Sonnleithner wrote a testy letter to Schubert's factotum of the time, Josef Hüttenbrenner, asking him to ensure that Schubert turned up to rehearse with Sophie. The song to be accompanied was *Der Jüngling auf dem Hügel* D702 with a text by Josef's brother Heinrich. Linhart later sang under her married name of Schuller. The bass **Adalbert Rotter** (b. 1800) must have done something to please Schubert as he received a fair copy of the autograph of the Schiller setting *Sehnsucht* D636 from the composer himself on 24 April 1824. To this autograph, in the manner of a younger student noting the performance of an older master, Rotter added the information that Vogl had sung the song on 24 October of the same year. The tenor **Franz Ruess** sang *Erlkönig* and *Die abgeblühte Linde* D514 in concerts in 1821 and 1823. Other Schubert singers were **Jakob Rauscher** (b. 1803) of Graz, a well-known Jaquino in *Fidelio*, a certain **Herr Ruprecht** (*c.* 1822) whom we know to have been a court singer, and an ageing but, according to the press, capable tenor, **Herr Fausky**, also of Graz. Names such as these flit in and out of the documents as a reminder of what an incredibly lively musical life was enjoyed by the Viennese in Schubert's lifetime.

Despite all the singers mentioned above, Vogl, Tietze and Schönstein seem to have been by far the most important from Schubert's point of view, with the possible addition of Schoberlechner. At Schubert's only public concert of his works on 26 March 1828, Vogl gave first performances of *Der Kreuzzug* D932, *Die Allmacht* D852, *Die Sterne* D939 and *Fragment aus dem Aeschylus* D450. The two baritones (Vogl and Schoberlechner) and tenor (Tietze) performed alongside each other at the Schubert memorial concert held on 30 January 1829. On that occasion Vogl gave the first performances of two Schubert songs from *Schwanengesang* (*Aufenthalt* and *Die Taubenpost* D957/5 and D965A) and Schoberlechner performed *Die Allmacht* D852.

BETWEEN SCHUBERT'S DEATH AND THE GRAMOPHONE

Like Anna Milder-Hauptmann, **Wilhelmine Schröder-Devrient** (1804–1860) was a famous Leonore in *Fidelio*. Schubert saw her in this role in 1822, and attempted to meet her via the good offices of Vogl; he almost certainly had her in mind for his opera *Alfonso und Estrella*. We are not sure if such a meeting ever took place, but one biographer has her singing Schubert songs in Vienna as early as June 1821. To Schröder-Devrient belongs the glory of having convinced the elderly Goethe of the importance of Franz Schubert's music; this was in April 1830 in Weimar, and the song was of course *Erlkönig*. The poet had heard it once before, in 1826, but it was the power of Devrient's performance that revealed to him the song's achievement as an artistic whole. At last Franz Schubert, whose attempts at communication he had ignored since 1816, was for him, as the Germans say, 'ein Begriff', a name to reckon with. The same song was performed by Devrient in London in 1831, and by 1835 she had become a renowned singer and champion of Schubert's lieder. In Leipzig her standing as a Schubert singer was rivalled only by **Elisa Meerti** (1817–1878), praised by the *Neue Zeitschrift für Musik*. As well as her public performances of the songs, Devrient also sang them in salons and private homes, such as that of the Carus family, friends of the young Robert Schumann, and she was the 'singing idol' of the young Clara. In a diary entry for March

Wilhelmine Schröder-Devrient, lithograph by Eduard Cramolini, 1835.

Josef Staudigl Sr, pencil drawing by Schlieferdecker.

1841, Schumann wrote that it was her performance of the Schubert songs that had pleased him best of all, and that her singing voice was able to move her listeners to tears. She had the knack of making the composer, and his music, seem as important as her celebrated self; in November 1842 the effect of one of her performances is noted in the diary of Heinrich Brockhaus: 'Ein grosses Genie, dieser Schubert'. She was considered a mistress of the art of declamatory song with perfect intonation and faultless diction, even when singing high notes.

In terms of male singers to follow in the immediate footsteps of Vogl, the most important was the Viennese bass **Josef Staudigl** (1807–1861). He had started out studying theology and went so far as to become a novice, but he turned his attention to singing with quickly successful results. He sang the songs of Schubert (including *Gruppe aus dem Tartarus* D583 and *Grenzen der Menschheit* D716) with enormous confidence and took this repertoire to England where it met with great success. He was hailed by the press as the 'Great Master of the German Lied' (the London *Times* referred to him as 'unapproachable as a bass singer, with a voice sonorous and of amazing scope') and he was clearly a highly exciting performer. The old Schubertians, like Leopold von Sonnleithner and Josef von Spaun, were rather less impressed: Sonnleithner felt that Staudigl's performances were too dramatic and arbitrary, somehow cheapening the music. He much preferred the singing of **Henriette von Spaun**, Josef von Spaun's niece, which he described as 'simple and natural'. Spaun himself wrote that Staudigl was not even to be compared with Vogl, despite all the public applause, averring that Vogl's classical education enabled him to render the Schubert songs with greater spiritual depth than Staudigl. The singer, who was also a talented painter, ended his life unhappily in a mental asylum near Vienna. His son Josef Staudigl the younger (1850–1916) was also a singer of Schubert's songs but he never enjoyed the same reputation as his father.

The accolade of being the first important Schubert singer outside German-speaking countries, and without any connection to Vienna, belongs to the French tenor **Adolphe Nourrit** (1802–1839). He first heard the songs of Schubert in 1833 as arranged and played by Franz Liszt,

and the experience seems to have furnished him with a burning mission in life. His early performances included *Ellens Gesang III* (*Ave Maria*) D839 at the salon of the *romance* composer
Louise Puget in 1834, *Die junge Nonne* D828 at the Paris Conservatoire and *Erlkönig* at the
Opéra Comique, in Berlioz's orchestration, the last two both in 1835. He busied himself with
commissioning better French translations for the song texts, and by 1839 he was saluted by
Berlioz in the *Journal des Débats* for his exemplary work in introducing Schubert to French
audiences. This Schubert movement had an incalculable effect on the development of the French
mélodie and the vocal works with piano of such composers as Gounod, and later Bizet. Contemporary reviews saluted his performances as something quite extraordinary, especially when he
was accompanied by Liszt. Nourrit lost his voice as a result of forcing it to sing high notes off
the chest, like his stronger-voiced colleague, Gilbert Duprez. Depressed by his inability to pursue
his career, he committed suicide. Chopin accompanied *Die Gestirne* D444 – a favourite song of
Nourrit – at the singer's funeral.

Nourrit's pupil, the tenor **Pierre François de Wartel** (1806–1882), was counted among the
finest Schubert interpreters of his time. Between 1831 and 1846 he had an engagement at the
Paris Opéra, but this did not prevent him from travelling abroad with his wife as accompanist
(Atala Thérèse Wartel, 1814–1865), giving song recitals as far afield as Warsaw, Prague and St
Petersburg. He was undaunted by the prospect of singing Schubert in French to German-
speaking audiences, and performed in Dresden, Berlin and Vienna itself in 1842 where the press
marvelled that a Frenchman was able to champion this music so persuasively. Wartel included
cycles like *Winterreise* and *Schwanengesang* in his repertoire, admirably continuing the pioneering
work of Nourrit. A few years after Wartel's appearance in Vienna, the Austrian public heard for
the first time (1846) the singing of the Swedish nightingale **Jenny Lind** (1820–1887). In the
1853–4 season she sang *Frühlingsglaube* D686, and the great critic Hanslick, lost for words for
once, described her art as 'softly elegiac'. She was one of the first singers, accompanied by her
husband, the composer Otto Goldschmidt, to perform *Die schöne Müllerin* as a complete cycle.
Jenny Lind was a favourite of Robert and Clara Schumann; their highly enthusiastic verdicts on
her singing remain the best testament to her powers as a lieder artist. The Schumanns were
initially equally enthusiastic about the singing of Pauline Garcia, sister of Maria Malibran; she
was the dedicatee of Schumann's Op. 24 Heine cycle, and was to become known under her

The lied in France: Adolphe Nourrit (after a drawing of A. Collin, 1824) and Pierre François de Wartel, lithograph by
Josef Kriehuber, 1843.

married name of **Pauline Viardot** (1821–1901). In publishing a *recueil* of forty Schubert songs in later years (with French translations by her friend Louis Pomey), Viardot was also to influence Schubert's reception in France. It is notable, however, that in a diary entry for September 1840, in the second week of her marriage, Clara Schumann professed herself dissatisfied with the young Garcia's performance of *Gretchen am Spinnrade*, and that by 1843 Robert Schumann, though admiring her lively musicianship, thought her inclination to the Italian style ill suited the German repertoire. This is one of the earliest testimonies to the fact that not all great and famous singers are automatically good lieder singers.

With **Julius Stockhausen** (1826–1906) we cross over into the epoch of another avid Schubertian, Johannes Brahms, whose cycle *Die schöne Magelone* Op. 33 was composed for this gifted baritone. Stockhausen was born in Paris and his godfather, the Parisian violist, organist and composer Chrétien Urhan (1790–1845) was responsible for introducing the young singer to the glories of Schubert's lieder. (It was also Urhan who first alerted Franz Liszt to Schubert's songs.) Stockhausen may have taken *Winterreise* to London as early as 1851 and performed *Die schöne Müllerin* complete in Vienna in 1856. This latter work became his calling card in countless performances – Hamburg, accompanied by Brahms (1861), Cologne with an audience of 2,000 (1864), St Petersburg accompanied by Anton Rubinstein (1866). In each case an actress read the Müller texts, including the poem's prologue and epilogue, that were not set by Schubert. In the fickle Vienna of the 1860s, a new edition was issued by the publisher Spina that replaced the name of Schubert's original dedicatee (Carl von Schönstein) with Stockhausen's, so closely identified with this work had the baritone become. Baron Schönstein, the aggrieved elderly tenor,

The doubly dedicated Spina edition of *Die schöne Müllerin*

Julius Stockhausen, lithograph by Hans Canon, 1854.

objected mightily – and with reason. Spina
made a tactful compromise with the name of
Schönstein retained as dedicatee in italics, but
with 'as sung by Julius Stockhausen' in bold
type.

Brahms made instrumental accompaniments for Stockhausen of the songs *Memnon*
D541, *Geheimes* D719, *An Schwager Kronos*
D369 and *Greisengesang* D778. Stockhausen
was counted the Schubert singer par excellence
of his time (although the elderly Spaun, stubbornly true to the old ideals, still found him
wanting in dramatic energy in comparison
with Vogl). His performances of Schubert in
the Crystal Palace series in London (alongside
such singers as **Amalie Joachim**, **Sophie Löwe**
and **George Henschel**) were noted by Sir
George Grove. His pupils at the Frankfurt
Conservatoire (where Clara Schumann also
taught) included the singers **Raimund von Zur
Mühlen** (1854–1931) who was eventually
responsible for establishing a lieder-singing
and -teaching tradition in England, and the
Dutch-born baritone **Johannes Messchaert**
(1857–1922), who numbered among the
greatest of the performers of the two great
Müller cycles, and whose distant successor
Fischer-Dieskau considered himself to be.
Another famous pupil of Stockhausen was
Helen Magnus (1840–1914), born in
Hamburg but engaged at the Hofoper in
Vienna from 1876. She was a famous Brahms
interpreter but the composer Karl Goldmark
recalls hearing her sing *Alinde*. Beside him sat
Schubert's friend Eduard von Bauernfeld who
had not heard the song since Schubert's own
time and was very moved by Magnus's perfor-
mance. Under her married name of von
Hornbostel, Helen Magnus founded a choir
that was eventually conducted by Eusebius
Mandyczewski [*see* SCHOLARS]. She also
funded a foundation to support gifted female
lieder singers.

In Vienna a school of singing began to
grow where the study of Schubert lieder was
held to be of great importance. One of the
greatest of all Viennese singing teachers was
the composer and scholar **Josef Gänsbacher**
(1829–1911) whose father, Johann, had been

Johannes Messchaert.

Ludwig Wüllner.

a well-known Tyrolean composer. Gänsbacher was one of the editors of the Breitkopf & Härtel Schubert *Gesamtausgabe*. Of his many pupils mention should be made of the Viennese soprano **Marie Wilt** (1831–1891) who was a protégée of the Schubertian Johann Herbeck [*see* SCHOLARS] and who was counted among the greatest vocal talents of her time. Wilt's starry career and eventual suicide seem typical of the artistic maelstrom that was *fin de siècle* Vienna. It was at about this time that the mystique of the 'Viennese' Schubert took hold – the composer whose music could only be truly understood by studying and working in the town of his birth.

Nevertheless, Schubert interpreters abounded outside Vienna. The baritone **Walter Gura** (1842–1906) made a name for himself in Munich and Breslau. A younger contemporary of Stockhausen's, and who denied being influenced by him, was the bass **Ludwig Wüllner** (1858–1938) (pictured above, p. 201). Born in Münster, he was the son of a famous Wagner conductor. He was among the first singers to perform the Schubert ballad repertoire (the earlier, longer songs) and to organize 'Historical Schubert Evenings' in Munich. He apparently sang in an improvisatory style, having never heard, or cared to hear, Stockhausen and the Viennese tradition that he had inherited. The singer had considerable success, with numerous Schubert performances in England and the USA. Such blithe isolationism would never again be possible after the invention of the gramophone record.

SCHUBERT IN THE 'GOLDEN AGE' OF RECORDING

From the beginning of the twentieth century all the great singers' voices, and many of their forays into Schubert interpretation, were preserved on disc. Apart from the rare early cylinders, these recordings were made on shellac in various sizes (mainly 10 and 12 inch) and to be played at various speeds – although this variety of choice stabilized to a standard 78 r.p.m.

The enormous and comprehensive study of Schubert songs recorded on shellac assembled by Karsten Lehl (2002) reveals the extent of the veritable explosion of Schubert performance after the turn of the century. From this time on it becomes increasingly difficult to identify the most important performers in the onslaught of singers' names, all jostling for equal attention on myriad ancient record labels. In the second half of the century, the greatest singers were hand-picked by powerful recording companies, and the recording of lieder became a highly selective process reserved for the vocal and musical elect. But before that it had been a kind of free-for-all – a condition that seems to have come full-circle in the twenty-first century with the gradual collapse of the commercial disc, and the proliferation of different technological options for the storage and transfer of musical data.

To dip into Lehl's monumental catalogue is instructive, if somewhat alarming. There were early recordings, for example, of *Gretchen am Spinnrade* by **Carlotta Roeder** (1901?), **Maria Gay**, 1879–1941 (1903) and **Johanna Gadski**, 1872–1932 (1908); of *Schäfers Klagelied* by **Peter Michailowitsch** (1902); of *Rastlose Liebe* by **Edyth Walker**, 1870–1950 (1902); of *Der Fischer* D225 and *Heidenröslein* D257 with an anonymous singer (1897–1902, for Pathé records); of *Heidenröslein* and *Ellens Gesang III* (*Ave Maria*) D839 by **Edith Clegg** (1898); of *Erlkönig* D328 by at least eighteen singers before the First World War including **David Bispham**, 1857–1921, **Lilli Lehmann**, 1848–1929, **Lillian Nordica**, 1857–1914, **Robert Radford**, 1874–1933, **Ernestine Schumann-Heink**, 1861–1936 and **Sir George Henschel**, 1850–1934; in the same period, of *Am Tage aller Seelen* (*Litanei*) D343 by at least ten singers; of *Der Wanderer* D489 by over twenty-five singers, also before the First World War; of *Der Tod und das Mädchen* D531 by fifteen singers; of *An die Musik* D547 by eleven singers; of *Die Forelle* D550 by four singers; of *Du bist die Ruh* D776 by thirteen singers including **Julia Culp**, **Lilli Lehmann**, **Giovanni Zenatello** and **Karl Erb**. The redoubtable length and breadth of Lehl's catalogue (which extends to the beginning of the LP era) means that what is mentioned above is highly selective and almost arbitrary (no recordings after 1913 are included, and no song after D776) but it gives some idea of the revolution in the dissemination of Schubert's music brought about by the gramophone.

Gustav Walter (1834–1910) was among the earliest singers, though by no means *the* earliest, as is sometimes claimed, to record a Schubert song. He was, however, the oldest singer whose voice is preserved singing one of these lieder. In 1905, at the age of seventy-one, he made three discs for G & T in Vienna that included a performance of *Am Meer* D957/12. A friend of Brahms, the Bohemian-born baritone started out as a worker in a sugar factory but became an opera singer in Brno, and from there obtained a contract at the Wiener Hofoper where he worked between 1867 and 1887. He was mainly a Mozart singer, although he also sang the role of Udolin in the 1867 performance of *Die Verschworenen* D787, and the eponymous hero in a production of *Alfonso und Estrella*. It is sometimes claimed that Walter had studied with Vogl – as indeed he had, but it was with Franz Vogl of Prague. Johann Michael Vogl of Vienna had died in 1840 and could not have taught Walter unless the latter had taken singing lessons at the age of six. On his retirement from the opera house in 1887, at the age of fifty-three, Walter began a new career as a lieder singer, sometimes accompanied by Brahms. In the period 1873–5 he performed *Die schöne Müllerin* over thirty times, placing himself next to the slightly older Stockhausen as the most important Schubert singer of his generation. His performance of *Winterreise* went back to the order of the poems as published by the poet Müller; Walter's justification was that this reordering was in the honoured tradition of Vogl's literary awareness and learning – and which Vogl we might ask? Certainly it was the older Vogl who left behind copies of Schubert's songs embellished with mostly superfluous ornamentation. In both cases Schubert's original should have been left to stand exactly as it was composed.

On the recording Walter's voice is bright and lyrical for his age, and the performance avoids the prevailing interpretative pathos that is typical of the period. The same cannot be said of the 1902 recordings of songs from *Die schöne Müllerin* and *Winterreise* by the Viennese-trained tenor **Franz Naval** (1865–1939) for the Talking Machine Company. Naval was a pupil of the famous Viennese singing teacher Josef Gänsbacher (*see* above) and his romanticized rubato, his constant changes of tempi and his portamenti may owe more to his own taste than to that of his teacher. Nevertheless, it seems that within less than sixty years of Schubert's death the performing style of his songs had utterly changed and taken on the contemporary characteristics of *fin de siècle* sentimentality (*see* RUBATO).

The baritone **Julius von Raatz-Brockmann** (1870–1944) was a protégé of Cosima Wagner. His voice is preserved on records made for the firm of Anker & Odeon. In 1913 he recorded twelve songs from *Winterreise*, the first attempt to place even a part of this song cycle on disc.

Like Gustav Walter, **Karl Erb** (1877–1958), the first Palestrina in Pfitzner's opera, was still fresh of voice and heart after his seventieth year. My mentor and teacher, Gerald Moore (*see* PIANISTS), used to recount the sheer

The tenor Karl Erb.

Elena Gerhardt in 1939. The photograph by Dorothy Wilding is dedicated to Gerald Moore.

pleasure of making music with this singer when he was already past the age of sixty. He had recorded *Nähe des Geliebten* D162, *Ganymed* and *Auf der Riesenkoppe* D611 for Odeon as early as 1912. Fischer-Dieskau has written that many listeners realized the beauty of the lied for the first time thanks to Erb. His unusual and reedy voice, hardly beautiful in its own right, yet beautiful because of what he did with it, was ideal for lieder. The famous recording of *Des Fischers Liebesglück* D933 is one of the finest indications of Erb's sense of imagination, and his command of a daring rubato that manages to remain eminently Schubertian.

Elena Gerhardt (1883–1961), born in Leipzig and initially the protégée of the conductor Arthur Nikisch, was one of the greatest and most influential of lieder singers, although it is generally accepted that her recordings do not do her justice. Those who actually heard her (the critic Desmond Shawe-Taylor cited her *Winterreise* as the best he had ever heard) or played for her (Gerald Moore was a smitten admirer of her art) testify to Gerhardt's unique communicative power. I trained at the Royal Academy of Music in the early 1970s and regard myself as a Gerhardt grand-pupil, alongside Dame Felicity Lott. (Gerhardt taught the RAM's leading singing teacher, the mezzo soprano lieder singer Flora Nielsen, herself a recording artist.) Gerhardt was the first to devote a complete recital to a particular composer, such as Schubert or Wolf, and she was also the first woman singer to give a full performance of *Winterreise* D911. Her first Schubert recordings date from 1911 and her accompanists included Nikisch himself, Ivor Newton, Conrad Valentijn Bos (with whom she recorded eight songs from *Winterreise* in 1928 and many Wolf songs in 1931) and finally, and most happily, Gerald Moore. She left Germany and lived in England during the Second World War; her husband, erstwhile head of Leipzig radio, was an outspoken opponent of the Nazis and was lucky enough to escape their retribution. (Neither the singer nor her husband was Jewish.) Gerhardt herself had an enormous sense of humour and an earthy love of life, and she was much loved by her many pupils and accompanists.

By the 1930s, the millstream of fine singers working on Schubert's songs had turned into an overflowing Rhine or Danube. As far as the listener is concerned, historical research was replaced by a subjective reaction that was available to anyone who encountered a recorded performance. In the past, only those who had heard a singer in the opera house or concert hall had the right to pass comment on their art. There is indeed a difference between hearing a singer 'live' and knowing one only through recordings (the case of Elena Gerhardt comes to mind), but it is a subtlety increasingly blurred by technological advances. In this period Schubert songs were served up to the public in any number of inauthentic arrangements, and the standard of performance was wildly uneven. There was never a shortage of opera singers who attempted Schubertian performance with differing success. The more interesting of these include such names as **Leo Slezak**, **John McCormack**, **Herbert Janssen**, **Kirsten Flagstad** – great singers all, who were able to bring something to repertoire carefully selected to suit them. Nevertheless, it is still possible to identify with gratitude the names of those who kept the Schubert tradition alive as handed down by the great lieder singers of the past. It goes without saying that all the singers listed below gave song recitals around the world; but in terms of evaluating their achievements, their recorded legacy now takes precedence, not always helpfully, over the memories of those who experienced their work at first hand. Such a list in a short article of this kind has to be highly selective, often unfairly so.

Elisabeth Schumann (1888–1952) was one of the most beloved of Schubert singers, the lightness of her voice and her sunny, light-of-heart temperament ideal for the songs that were not too dramatic or heavy. She retired in 1951, singing songs from *Die schöne Müllerin* in her last working season, but her recorded legacy numbers nearly fifty Schubert songs – not many by the standards of the LP or CD eras perhaps, but hugely impressive at the time of 78s.

Lotte Lehmann (1888–1976), besides possessing one of the most beautiful voices in recorded history, was an all-encompassing powerhouse of energy and activity; she was a great opera singer who brought to the lied (and Schubert) a commitment equal to her work on stage – a style brimming over with energy that was not, in this repertoire at least, always unreservedly admired. After her emigration to the United States she became an inspiring teacher. Her larger-than-life passion for creativity extended to painting, embroidery, stained glass and book illustration – often with lieder-related subjects. Her large recorded legacy includes twenty-two Schubert songs.

Heinrich Schlusnus (1888–1952) was a much-recorded baritone, and one of the most successful of all time. His considerable vocal gifts were the source of enormous joy to his many listeners, although a certain naivety of interpretation and heaviness of rhythm, while prized by admirers as a kind of deliberate interpretative simplicity, have been criticized. Schlusnus recorded nearly as many Schubert songs as Elisabeth Schumann, but few if any of these have been considered definitive performances of the works concerned.

Elisabeth Schumann, portrait by Lotte Meitner-Graf.

Lotte Lehmann.

Richard Tauber (1891–1948) was a phenomenally gifted tenor but earned the distrust of some serious Schubertians for the part he played in cheapening the image of Schubert with his

Richard Tauber as Schubert in the British film *Blossom Time* (1934).

The tenor Julius Patzak.

appearances as the composer in the musical *Das Dreimäderlhaus*, followed by the English version *Lilac Time* and various cinematic spin-offs. With his short build, monocle and tendency to corpulence, Tauber was a natural for the role; his failure to resist the commercial pressures that enabled him to earn a lot of money playing a cheery and bespectacled Schubert can be explained by the sad decline in his health that took from him the ability to appear in heavier operatic roles – Mozart's Don Ottavio had been a speciality. He was a kind and charming man and a great musician (someone no less distinguished than Elisabeth Schwarzkopf used to rave about the privilege of having worked with him), and many of his earlier Schubert recordings with piano belie any misguided attempt to pigeonhole him as a mere populist.

Heinrich Rehkemper (1894–1949) was a fine baritone of the old school, a mainstay of the Munich Opera and a favourite recital partner of Richard Strauss. His recorded legacy includes twenty-seven Schubert songs. More inspired perhaps was the singing of **Julius Patzak** (1898–1974), individual of voice, a Viennese version of Peter Pears – though with a grander vocal endowment – and a personal charisma that quickly made avid fans of his listeners. He was accompanied in some important recordings (including *Die schöne Müllerin*) by Michael Raucheisen (*see* PIANISTS) and he recorded a *Winterreise* at the age of seventy with Jörg Demus. Another gifted Viennese tenor – less individual and compelling than Patzak, but charming of voice – was **Anton Dermota** (1910–1989); he was also an assiduous collector of manuscripts, including Schubertiana.

To the baritone **Gerhard Hüsch** (1901–1984) belonged the privilege of being the official star voice and lieder singer of German HMV during the 1930s. His recordings of the great Schubert song cycles were exported around the world at the height of the 78 era, winning Schubert countless new fans in Europe, America and the Far East. The composer's enthusiastically loyal following found among the wartime generation of the British listening public had been nurtured by Hüsch's widely available recordings. Handsome of appearance and beguiling of voice and diction, Hüsch, like Schlusnus, was much admired. A more cultivated lieder singer than Schlusnus, and musically better organized, he shared with him a manliness of approach that disdained weakness or neurosis, a stance

The baritone Gerhard Hüsch.

The bass Hans Hotter.

so pointedly aristocratic as to at times preclude flexibility and spontaneity. For flashes of imaginative vulnerability and the depiction of instability at the heart of the great cycles, the listener would have to go back to singers who had represented a different Germany, like Karl Erb, or wait for the era of post-war singers like Fischer-Dieskau, Souzay or Pears. In the early 1950s Hüsch had a second career as a recording artist for the Victor Label in Japan where he was especially popular; he was also a renowned teacher, and the accompanist Geoffrey Parsons (*see* PIANISTS), among many others in the post-war years, counted Hüsch his mentor and master.

A more enduring career, one that successfully negotiated the political changes of a new Germany, was that of **Hans Hotter** (1909–2003), whose monumental success was the result of an unlikely marriage between singing opera of the grandest kind (he was the greatest Wotan of his time) and the interpretation of the most sensitive and intimate of songs, including those of Schubert. Hotter's mastery of his own instrument and his extraordinary vocal range enabled him to excel in *Winterreise* as well as other Schubert songs. His ability to soften and colour the voice was combined with an enviable intimacy of diction. All these attributes were passed on to Hotter's most distinguished lieder-singing pupil, the Dutch bass-baritone **Robert Holl** (b. 1947), a Schubert master for modern times in terms of the depth of his knowledge and scholarship, and one who can move between the role of Gurnemanz and singing Schubert with a navigational ease born of years of experience.

The bass-baritone Robert Holl, photographed by Stephan Helmreich.

SCHUBERT IN THE AGE OF THE LP

With the advent of the long-playing record everything changed in terms of the Schubert repertoire. Whereas singers had previously prepared two songs per recording session, one for each
side of a 78, they were now required to find, learn and perform a sufficient number to fill two
sides of a long-playing record. (The demand for new material would grow even more with the
eventual advent of the CD.) The advantages of this, in terms of broadening people's awareness
of the Schubert repertoire, were many, but it also meant that there were now almost too many
recorded offerings for the public to focus on, as they might have on a single side of a 78, played
again and again. The listener now became aware that the best lieder singers were increasingly
groomed and engaged exclusively by the top record labels: the lead players in this field were the
English EMI, Decca (also an English label), Deutsche Grammophon Gesellschaft (DGG) and
the Dutch firm Philips. For many decades the lieder fan who purchased records made by these
companies would be assured of hearing mostly fine performances, almost always the best available. (This was to change in the 1980s with the advent of smaller firms with equally high technical standards.) An unfortunate by-product of this slimming-down of the number of artists
recorded was that there were many fine ones left out in the cold. If they were shut out of the
exclusive club of the big record labels they could only reach audiences in live concerts. But this
is where radio began to play a role as patron, particularly the Third Programme in London,
and the best of the German and Dutch radio stations. Highly informed radio producers, like
that fine Schubertian Leo Black in London, were able to support and encourage the work of
emerging artists or older singers who had been ignored by the recording establishment. That
aspect of Schubertian performance encouraged and fostered by the radio stations deserves a
chapter to itself. One remembers, for example, that fine soprano **Ilse Wolf** (1921–1999) whose
reputation was made by the BBC.

It is at this point that a new and indispensable name comes into the history of lieder performance: **Dietrich Fischer-Dieskau** (1925–2012) began with 78s but his career dominated the entire
LP era. Here was a singer for the new post-war age – someone with a personality strong enough
to explore new paths while preserving a seamless link with the best of the German musical past.
The Second World War was a recent and terrible memory; with the English accompanist Gerald
Moore by his side, Fischer-Dieskau represented a new artistic consensus whereby the German
lied was given back to the world, as if released at last from a twelve-year prison sentence and
free to travel as an international ambassador of peace and enlightenment. (In fact the performance of Schubert's songs in German had been a constant feature of musical life in wartime
Britain and America, a very different state of affairs from the 'patriotic' hatred of anything to
do with the German language during the First World War.) An early 78 recording of *Nacht und
Träume* D827, where Fischer-Dieskau sings in a pianissimo *mezza voce*, announces a distinct
change of regime. At the time, forthright older singers like Hüsch dismissed this new approach
as 'whispering' and under-sung, but the public, listening to the gramophone in the intimacy of
their own homes, yearned for transcendental scene-painting of this kind, where the voice was
servant of the emotions, not to mention of the composer's often ignored pianissimo markings.
Fischer-Dieskau knew how to use the microphone to beguiling effect in his soft singing, and
his listening public enjoyed an intimate relationship with his voice.

But rapt and contemplative *Innigkeit* was only one of his many moods and colours. With an
array of pianists, and a seemingly endless ability to invent song programmes, Fischer-Dieskau
vigorously set about his life's work of chronicling the lied in recordings – indeed, he was to
become the art form's *encyclopédiste*. Every singer or pianist who has planned a lieder programme
since his time has been in his debt for the availability of a recording of almost any song in the
repertoire. There will be those who argue that they don't enjoy reading encyclopaedias cover to
cover, or that in his thirst to survey the length and breadth of the bigger picture, this singer

Dietrich Fischer-Dieskau rehearsing with Gerald Moore, *c.* 1971.

skimmed over the depths of the shyer treasures that lie concealed on the way, songs that are more deserving of patient and prolonged attention. One might compare Fischer-Dieskau's industry with the restlessness of the singer Vogl in September 1825, a powerhouse of energy and determination: 'There was no inducing Vogl to view Salzburg with its salt mines', wrote the rueful Schubert, somewhat dismayed by his singer's willpower, 'His great soul . . . urged him on to Gastein, like a wanderer in a dark night who yearns for a ray of light'. Vogl was merely searching for the holy grail of a cure for his gout, but some of Fidi's activity seemed similarly driven as he strove to make a survey of every aspect of the song catalogue. Or thus it must have seemed to his astonished accompanists, like Gerald Moore, who had hitherto only known singers with a repertoire of a hundred rather than a few thousand songs.

The impression left by a Fischer-Dieskau recital was hardly different from that of listening to his recordings: one could only salute his beguilingly mellifluous voice, his wonderful diction, enviable technical control, a refined sense of style and a creative use of rhythm – in short, a level of mastery that one encounters seldom in any performing discipline. On the other hand, there will always be musicians of a different temperament who prefer to travel more slowly, sitting by the roadside carefully examining every petal of the wayside flowers (although it might be argued that they are only able to do so because a pathway through the field has already been beaten by a more intrepid explorer). These song-botanists who move at a less ambitious pace strive for interpretations that are less adroitly surveyed and triumphantly encompassed, music-making of less width, perhaps, but – it must be admitted – sometimes greater depth.

Schubert once asked despairingly, 'Who can do anything after Beethoven?' Younger baritones, indeed all lieder singers, often felt the same about Fischer-Dieskau who stood before them like an immovable colossus. When André Gide was asked to name the greatest French poet, his reply was 'Victor Hugo, hélas'. For anyone tempted to add that 'alas' to a similar admission of Fischer-Dieskau's supremacy, it is notable that Gide's original answer concerned a creative giant rather than a mere performer – and it is within this heroic league, outside the realm of other lieder singers of his generation, that Fischer-Dieskau's achievement must be assessed. Whatever cavils have emerged against him, there can be no doubt that his lifelong service to Schubert – and a host of other composers – marks him out as the most important lied exponent of the twentieth century, and perhaps of all time. With Gerald Moore he recorded over 500 Schubert songs for DGG between 1969 and 1971, and he made multifarious recordings of Schubert lieder with many other pianists, both before and since. A list of these is in itself an indication of the length and breadth of the singer's Schubertian career: Daniel Barenboim, Alfred Brendel, Benjamin Britten, Jörg Demus, Karl Engel, Christoph Eschenbach, Hartmut Höll, Joachim Kaiser, Hertha Klust, Murray Perahia, Maurizio Pollini, Hermann Reutter, Sviatoslav Richter, Wolfgang Sawallisch, András Schiff, Norman Shetler, Günther Weissenborn. In the case of *Winterreise* alone, Fischer-Dieskau made six LP versions between 1951 and 1985, and since then nine further versions for CD. Added to this is his writing – the singer published many books on song-related topics including *Auf den Spuren der Schubert-Lieder* (1971). He also pursued something of a career as a conductor, and counted painting among his hobbies.

Fischer-Dieskau's slightly younger contemporary **Hermann Prey** (1929–1998) was arguably endowed with a finer baritone voice, per se, and some listeners preferred his straightforward simplicity of approach – that of the typical *Wanderbursch*, the young man, as in *Die schöne Müllerin*, who sets out on the road of life and sings off-the-cuff about his experiences. In this way Prey's musical viewpoints had more in common with an earlier generation of German baritones, like Schlusnus, and occasional uncertainties of intonation also harked back to former times. Nevertheless, Prey was a devoted and tenacious Schubertian, initiating any number of performing projects (particularly a pet idea of presenting all of the composer's works chronologically, a concept that foundered more than once, and in more than one festival, when confronted with the realities of box office). He frequently gave recitals where Schubert was the only composer on the programme, and held many a master class in lied interpretation. His recorded output of Schubert songs concentrated on the three great cycles.

The tenor **Fritz Wunderlich** (1930–1966) is still talked about as one of the great might-have-beens of lieder interpretation. Like Grillparzer writing of Schubert after his early death, one may say that 'the art of music here entombed a rich possession, but even fairer hopes'. The singing of Wunderlich on record is wonderfully natural and unaffected; it is from the heart, not spoiled by false pathos and has, in short, an intrinsic elegance and style that suits Schubert perfectly. And all this takes for granted the beauty of his instrument. How much more he would have achieved if he had had the chance to collaborate with, say, Gerald Moore, is incalculable; a few more years of work would have enabled him to grow into interpretations of greater insight and depth. What remains of his recorded legacy, however, some sixteen assorted Schubert songs and *Die schöne Müllerin*, is precious to the Schubertian.

The soprano who was perhaps Fischer-Dieskau's most talented female contemporary as a lieder singer – and certainly the most glamorous and famous – was **Elisabeth Schwarzkopf** (1915–2006). She was a pupil in Berlin of Maria Ivogün and her husband, the accompanist and sovereign programme planner, Michael Raucheisen (*see* PIANISTS). From the beginning of Schwarzkopf's career Schubert was an important part of her recitals, although her Schubertian legacy in terms of recordings pales before Fischer-Dieskau's, like that of any other singer of the period. She left only about two dozen Schubert songs on disc accompanied by Edwin Fischer, Gerald Moore and Geoffrey Parsons. There are many fine performances on these records, all coached, bar by bar, by her husband, the recording producer Walter Legge, but Schwarzkopf was not the purely instinctive Schubert singer that, for example, Elisabeth Schumann had been. The unrehearsed performance with Geoffrey Parsons of *Erlkönig* D328, recorded on a whim at the end of a session, is perhaps the most chillingly memorable. With her extraordinary passion for the blending of word and tone, Schwarzkopf was above all the Wolf singer par excellence; some listeners found her Schubert over-inflected – too calculated and lacking in spontaneity – for there was never an artist who, goaded by her husband, more relished dissecting her music-making in merciless self-castigation (with the pianist's failings analysed in like manner). It might be argued that Schubert benefits from a more forgiving approach. I am reminded of the story told me by the great Spanish singer **Victoria de Los Angeles** who described taking a Schubert song to study with Elena Gerhardt: 'It is not at all how *I* do it,' said Gerhardt, 'but what you do is enchanting . . . don't change a note.' This remark, so different from Clara Schumann's disapproving verdict on the style of Pauline Viardot's singing, gives pause for thought: one feels that Schubert himself might have made room at the table for the idiosyncratic interpretation of his songs by those who came from other traditions than his own, provided they were sung with a full heart. Such was the charm and sincerity of de Los Angeles that he might even have overlooked what was unidiomatic in her lieder singing.

In the late 1940s, and early '50s, there were German-speaking sopranos, younger than Schwarzkopf, who were gifted Schubertians – for example, the charm and fluid grace of the singing, at its best, of **Irmgard Seefried** (1919–1988) is not to be forgotten. The mezzo soprano **Christa Ludwig** (b. 1928), perhaps the greatest vocal talent of her generation, was another discovery of the great entrepreneur and talent scout Walter Legge. Apart from the glamour of her celebrated opera career, she was a Schubert singer of considerable experience, recording some thirty songs with Irwin Gage, and about a dozen others with Geoffrey Parsons. She also recorded *Winterreise* more than once.

When Fischer-Dieskau embarked on his survey of the Schubert songs for DGG he invited **Janet Baker** (b. 1933) to record the women's songs with him, as part of the complete set. This she eagerly agreed to but, to her fury, she was prevented from doing so by her contractual obligations to EMI. As a result the women's songs never appeared on the DGG project. Attempting partly to redress the balance, EMI released *A Schubert Evening with Janet Baker* (1971) accompanied by Gerald Moore, a selection of some of the songs that would have been included on the much larger Fischer-Dieskau collaboration, and in 1987 the same singer was on the first of thirty-seven CDs recorded for the Hyperion Schubert Edition. In 1978 the soprano **Gundula Janowitz** (b. 1938) embarked on a DGG project with Irwin Gage to record all of the 'missing' Schubert songs for women. This was never completed, but the fifty-two items presented in 'Volume 1' represent a considerable achievement. A further fifteen Schubert songs were recorded by Janowitz with the accompanist Charles Spencer.

A separate note must be made of the singers who worked chiefly in the German Democratic Republic and who for a long time did not have access to the career opportunities offered by the West. The world-renowned tenor **Peter Schreier** (b. 1935) from Dresden was an exception, as was **Olaf Bär** (b. 1957) from the younger generation – the latter baritone won the Walter Grüner lieder competition in London that put him on the international map and resulted in a contract with EMI. Less lucky were fine artists like the baritone **Siegfried Lorenz** (b. 1945) whose considerable Schubertian achievements remained largely under-appreciated outside his home country.

This brief survey of Schubertian singers ends with the advent of the CD, but not before a paragraph concerning fine Schubert singers of the LP era who were not of German or Austrian birth. It was inevitable that because Fischer-Dieskau was a baritone, other baritones would be compared with him – almost always unfavourably. Thanks to a contract with Philips, the French high baritone **Gérard Souzay** (1918–2004) was able to record Schubert songs at a distance from Fischer-Dieskau, and in very much his own manner, having less to fear from the comparison than one might imagine. He was a singer of refinement and charm whose way with Schubert, and extensive experience with a wide tranche of the repertoire, offered complementary, rather than competitive, interpretations. His Schubertian performances with Dalton Baldwin, without pretending to be towering or definitive statements, enticed the ear and touched the heart in a way that might have even given his great German contemporary occasional pause for thought. Souzay's career is a reminder of the special niche that Schubert has always enjoyed in the musical history of France. Other French-speaking singers from France had recorded Schubert songs of course (among them **Georges Thill** and **Charles Panzéra**) but it was Souzay who seemed to be the worthy successor to the tradition of those first great French Schubert singers of the nineteenth century, Nourrit and Wartel.

Chief among the non-German tenors, partly because of a lifelong partnership with perhaps the greatest of all accompanists, was Sir **Peter Pears** (1910–1986). There had been a succession of Schubert singers in England going back to the tenor Sir **Charles Santley** (1834–1922), a singer valued in this composer by Sir George Grove, and the dapper baritone **Harry Plunket-Greene** (1865–1936) who was the first Englishman to perform *Winterreise* complete in public (Robert Louis Stevenson heard him do so and wrote *The Vagabond* from *Songs of Travel* as a result). Pears, less conventional by far (he came from a generation that challenged Victorian values) was nevertheless profoundly English (what used to be termed a 'gentleman') as well as something of a Renaissance man in terms of his general culture. His singing in both German and his own language was the crowning glory of an English tenorial tradition, utterly different from its German equivalent, that went back to Santley's time and had included such great artists as John Coates and Gervase Elwes. With Benjamin Britten, Pears made a single 78 of two Schubert songs for HMV in 1950, and thereafter they recorded their Schubert repertoire for Decca – a short 45r.p.m. recital, an LP of *Die schöne Müllerin*, a boxed set with *Winterreise* together with Schumann's *Dichterliebe* Op. 48, and a miscellaneous recital of more rare songs that was made shortly before Britten's final illness when he lost the ability to play the piano. Pears and Britten were undaunted by strictly German-speaking performing traditions and they reserved their awe and affection for the music, rather than for other interpretations of it. Their English confidence and common sense, combined with high art, often made for something daring and unique. Pears as a singer of Schubert could be matchlessly eloquent with Britten in the two Müller cycles, and in *Die schöne Müllerin* later in life with Murray Perahia. It was thanks to a performance of *Winterreise* at the Maltings, Snape in 1972 (Britten's last) that I experienced a truly Damascene conversion to Schubert and decided that my life should by devoted to song.

Other English tenors who have made a sensitive contribution to the Schubertian recorded legacy include in particular **Ian Partridge** (b. 1938), partnered by his sister Jennifer. **Richard Lewis** (1914–1990) performed a remarkable *Auf den Strom* with Dennis Brain. Among British baritones who have sung Schubert with notable success are **John Shirley-Quirk** (b. 1931) and **Benjamin Luxon** (b. 1937). The Danish tenor **Axel Schiøtz** (1906–1975) was famous for a brightly sung and sunnily sincere *Die schöne Müllerin*. Two tenors from Switzerland with very different backgrounds recorded sensitive Schubert recitals in different generations – **Hugues Cuénod** (1902–2010) and **Ernst Haefliger** (1919–2007). The American tenor **Robert White** (b. 1936) recorded a fine album of Schubert lieder in 1989, and one must salute the Schubertian achievements of the American soprano **Jessye Norman** (b. 1945). I remember an all-Schubert recital by her at the Queen Elizabeth Hall on 1 January 1978, accompanied by Dalton Baldwin, as a particularly splendid achievement. Occasions such as these, while less permanent than recordings, are still capable of surpassing the pleasures of the gramophone.

SCHUBERT IN THE CD ERA
Other books have surveyed the rich Schubertian discography of recent years, and their authors have been able to do so with greater impartiality than I can muster. In any case, it seemed that no sooner had the age of the CD arrived than technology became ever more sophisticated; there should now perhaps be a large article on Schubert downloads and performances on YouTube. At the end of this volume there is a note concerning the making of the Hyperion Edition; I have permitted myself to list there the sixty or so artists who took part in the Schubert recording project (1987–2001) but it is hardly fitting for an accompanist to comment on the performances of colleagues and friends. There were a number of singers who were unable to take part in the series when invited, and a few whose exclusion was regrettable (even Schubert wrote a finite number of songs). It goes without saying that the contributions to the Hyperion Series of the late **Arleen Auger** (1939–1993), **Elizabeth Connell** (1946–2011), **Anthony Rolfe Johnson** (1940–2010), **Philip Langridge** (1939–2010), **Lucia Popp** (1939–1993) and **Dame Margaret Price** (1941–2011) will be long remembered. The work of such remarkable senior artists and distinguished Schubertians as **Elly Ameling** (b. 1934), **Dame Janet Baker** (b. 1933), **Brigitte Fassbaender** (b. 1939), **Edith Mathis** (b. 1938), **Ann Murray** (b. 1949), **Peter Schreier** (b. 1935) and **Sarah Walker** (b. 1943) continues to astonish. They may have now retired from the recital platform, but their recorded presence is a daily fact of life. All these artists, and the many who continue to sing, some of them still at the height of their careers, are worthy of extended praise and evaluation – but perhaps not within the context of this book (there is a complete list of all artists on pp. 874–5 of this volume). Today there is of course an exciting new generation of wonderfully gifted Schubert singers – so many, in fact, that to attempt to list them would be invidious. They will certainly make their own important contributions to the ongoing Schubertian cause. One thing we can be certain of is that this is a composer who will never be short of interpreters.

SKOLIE

Skolion (drinking song)

(Deinhard-Deinhardstein) **D306** [H186]
B♭ major   15 October 1815

(18 bars)

Lasst im Morgenstrahl des Mai'n	Let us in the light of the May morning
Uns der Blume Leben freun,	Enjoy life's flower
Eh' ihr Duft entweichet!	Before its fragrance fades!
Haucht er in den Busen Qual,	If it should breathe sorrows into our hearts
Glüht ein Dämon im Pokal,	A spirit glows within the cup
Der sie leicht verscheuchet.	That will effortlessly banish them.
Schnell wie uns die Freude küsst,	No sooner does joy kiss us
Winkt der Tod, und sie zerfliesst;	Than death beckons; and it flees.
Dürfen wir ihn scheuen?	Should we fear death?
Von den Mädchenlippen winkt	From maidens' lips the breath of life
Lebensatem, wer ihn trinkt,	Entices us; he who drinks it
Lächelt seinem Dräuen.	Can smile at death's threats.

JOHANN LUDWIG VON DEINHARD-DEINHARDSTEIN (1794–1859)

This is Schubert's only setting of a Deinhard-Deinhardstein text. See the poet's biography. See also the article for Selam.

A 'skolion' (originally a Greek word) is a drinking song where the cup is passed around from drinker to drinker. This is pleasant cheery music in B flat major with a hearty vocal line, a masculine, German version of Herrick's 'Gather ye rosebuds while ye may' with alcohol to oil the wheels of its *carpe diem* philosophy. John Reed has noticed that Schubert songs written in this key have a certain rhythmic energy and impetus. *Skolie* is a little ditty which achieves its bracing energy through left-hand semiquavers that bustle and weave in impressive fashion. The piano writing in bb. 4–6 even suggests a touch of inebriation. The whole of this miniature recalls the Beethoven of *Die Wut über den verlornen Groschen* Op. 129 ('Rage over a lost penny'), a piano piece that displays a similar combination of what Reed calls the 'vernacular style' in its melody, and a sophisticated pianistic ingenuity in its depiction of the commotion of the crowd. This piece may be more often heard if it were to be performed as part of Walther Dürr's proposed *Selam* cycle (qv) – seven songs composed on 15 October 1815, of which this is the fifth.

Autograph:	Österreichische Nationalbibliothek, Vienna (first draft)
First edition:	Published as part of the AGA in 1895 (P593)
Subsequent editions:	Not in Peters; AGA XX 154: Vol. 3/120; NSA IV: Vol. 9/142

Discography and timing: Fischer-Dieskau I 5³⁰ 1'03
                         Hyperion I 22¹⁷
                         Hyperion II 10²²   0'58   Jamie MacDougall

←— *Mein Gruss an den Mai* D305   *Die Sternenwelten* D307 —→

SKOLIE   Skolion (drinking song)
(MATTHISSON) **D507** [H323]
G major   December 1816

(20 bars)

Mädchen entsiegelten,	The girls have unsealed
Brüder, die Flaschen;	The bottles, brothers;
Auf! die geflügelten	Come, let us snatch
Freuden zu haschen,	Winged joys
Locken und Becher von Rosen umglüht.	Curls, and cups rimmed with glowing roses.
Auf! eh' die moosigen	Come, before the mossy
Hügel uns winken,	Mound calls us,
Wonne von rosigen	Let us drink bliss
Lippen zu trinken;	From rosy lips,
Huldigung Allem, was jugendlich blüht!	And do homage to all in the bloom of youth.

FRIEDRICH VON MATTHISSON (1761–1831); poem written in 1791

This is the twenty-sixth of Schubert's twenty-nine Matthisson solo settings (1812–17). See the poet's biography for a chronological list of all the Matthisson settings.

This merry little ditty, written no doubt for an end-of-year party, has a distinguished parentage. Einstein remarked that it was 'almost identical' to Zumsteeg's 1796 setting (republished in the fifth book of the *Kleine Balladen und Lieder* in 1803). The key is the same, certainly, and the time signature of ⅜, but Schubert's setting is, if anything, simpler than Zumsteeg's, who for one of his musical strophes uses two of Matthisson's verses. Schubert also refrains from interludes and his setting is tighter and leaner. In his second bar Zumsteeg changes harmony, but Schubert stays resolutely in the tonic key of G major. The effect of this is to make a homage of a different kind: in Schubert's hands the song bears a strong resemblance to Figaro's 'Se vuol ballare' from *Le Nozze di Figaro*. The words 'Brüder, die Flaschen' in b. 4 have the same rhythmic bite as 'Signor Contino'. There is an appropriately eighteenth-century feel to this music, particularly in the postlude. 'Skolion' is a Greek word for a drinking song in which the cup is passed round, and the communal aspect of the setting means that there is a strong possibility that it was written for Ignaz Assmayr, a fellow Salieri pupil alongside Schubert, in whose possession the autograph remained. Anselm Hüttenbrenner remembers that a group of young composers, including Assmayr, used to meet on Thursday evenings to go through male voice quartets that had been composed by one or other of their number. Naturally, a song like this could equally be performed in unison chorus. This is Schubert's second *Skolie*; the other, with a text by Deinhard-Deinhardstein, D306, is from October 1815.

Autograph:	New York Public Library
First edition:	Published as part of the AGA in 1895 (P664)
Subsequent editions:	Not in Peters; AGA XX 283: Vol. 4/249; NSA IV: Vol. 11/52
Discography and timing:	Fischer-Dieskau I 9^2 0'53
	Hyperion I 23^{29}
	Hyperion II 17^1 0'53 Christoph Prégardien

← *Mailied* D503   *Lebenslied* D508 →

SO LASST MICH SCHEINEN *see* MIGNON (SO LASST MICH SCHEINEN, BIS ICH WERDE) D469 and D727 and *GESÄNGE AUS WILHELM MEISTER* D877/3

Die SOMMERNACHT   The summer night
(KLOPSTOCK) **D289** [H175]

The song exists in two versions, the second of which is discussed below:
(1) 14 September 1815; (2) Date unknown, probably 1816

(1) 'Nicht zu langsam'   C major   **C**   [26 bars]

(2) C major

Wenn der Schimmer von dem Monde nun herab	When the moon's soft light
In die Wälder sich ergiesst, und Gerüche	Shines into the woods,
Mit den Düften von der Linde	And the scent of the lime tree
In den Kühlungen wehn;	Is wafted in the cool breezes:
So umschatten mich Gedanken an das Grab	Then my mind is overshadowed by thoughts
Meiner Geliebten, und ich seh' im Walde[1]	Of my beloved's grave; in the forest

[1] Schubert disturbs Klopstock's metre with his alterations in this line; the original reads, '*Der* Geliebten, und ich *sah in dem* Walde'.

Nur es dämmern, und es weht mir	I see only the growing dusk; and the blossom's fragrance
Von der Blüte nicht her.	Does not reach me.
Ich genoss einst, o ihr Toten, es mit euch!	Spirits of the dead, with you I once cherished it!
Wie umwehten uns der Duft und die Kühlung,	How the fragrance and the cool breezes caressed us,
Wie verschönt warst du von dem Monde,	How you, beautiful nature,
Du, o schöne Natur!	Were transfigured by the moonlight!

FRIEDRICH GOTTLOB KLOPSTOCK (1724–1803); poem written in July 1766

This is the sixth of Schubert's thirteen Klopstock solo settings (1815–16) See the poet's biography for a chronological list of all the Klopstock settings.

The poet's thoughts of his beloved's grave spread like a shroud over his mind, numbing his eyesight and sense of smell. The fragrance of the lime tree fails to reach him, the moonlight is powerless to illuminate the darkness: all he can see is the dark of the forest. How different was everything when she was still alive! In those days the poet and his consort bathed in the scents of the outdoors and admired nature's beauties by moonlight.

This is a sublime example of *recitativo in tempo*, and a song which has been consistently undervalued, not even rating a mention in Capell's book. Perhaps this is because the music, as magical as it is, does not last long enough to do justice to the depth of the poem. Schubert might well have known Gluck's setting which ends adventurously in the dominant. The opening thirds and sixths of this setting, the concord of moonlight euphony, are also shot through with the chromatics of human emotion and bereavement. This passage is reminiscent of the recitative that begins the Ossian setting *Die Nacht* D534 from two years later. There are many beautiful touches; thus in the piano music of b. 6 the moonlight pours (as it were, drop by drop) into the wood in mezzo-staccato falling semiquavers after the word 'ergiesst', and the fragrance from the flowers is wafted into the music via diminished chord harmonies, a crotchet falling to a quaver under the word 'dämmern' in b. 14. This is prophetic of *Dass sie hier gewesen* D775, Schubert's greatest song about lingering fragrance, and another masterful mix of perfumed recitative and lyrical line. The point of the poem is that the bereaved narrator does not smell the fragrances of nature, so preoccupied with his grief is he; but Schubert cannot resist illustrating what passes the poet by.

The little arioso from 'Wie umwehten uns der Duft' that finishes the piece (bb. 21–6) is quite simply Schubert of the highest quality; gratitude for nature prompts the singer to launch, at last, into a legato outpouring of classically poised melody. The effect is like a soothing balm ('der Duft und die Kühlung') healing the wounds of loss. Bereavement has the power to teach us how to value the beauties of the here and now with a heightened humility and intensity. The poet had lost his wife in childbirth but in this grammatical context the word 'Geliebten' is not necessarily feminine and singular, and it might also be that Klopstock's beloved (plural) friends were those who had died in defence of the fatherland. The singular 'Grab' can have a plural intention in both German and English (as in the phrase 'Sie liegen alle im Grab' – they are all in the grave). There is a mixture of moonlit introspection and patriotism, for which this poet was renowned, in the companion piece to this poem (also set by Gluck), *Die frühen Gräber* D290.

The tiny differences between the first and second versions of the song are instructive: for the second version, a bar shorter than the first, Schubert had cut and refined his original thoughts. The sequential repeat of 'Ich genoss es einst mit euch' (bb. 20–21) is deemed unnecesary – too sentimental perhaps – and left-hand octaves in the final bars are slimmed down to single notes, creating a sparer texture that seems more fitting to Klopstock's poem. This is one of those early Schubert songs where it is possible to ornament passages marked 'Recit' with appoggiature: at the beginning of bb. 5, 8, 11, 13 – all of these suggested in *ossia* staves in NSA.

Autograph:	Staatsbibliothek Preussischer Kulturbesitz, Berlin (first version)
Publication:	First published as part of the AGA in 1895 (P586; first version)
	First published as part of the AGA in 1895 (P587; second version)
Subsequent editions:	Not in Peters; AGA XX 143a & b: Vol. 3/80 & 82; NSA IV: Vol. 9/67 & 69
Bibliography:	Einstein 1951, p. 111
Discography and timing:	Fischer-Dieskau I 5[22] 2'43
	Hyperion I 8[4]
	Hyperion II 10[10] 3'07 Sarah Walker

←— *An Sie D288*   *Die frühen Gräber D290* —→

SON FRA L'ONDE   I am among the waves
(Metastasio) **D78** [H28]
C minor   18 September 1813

(61 bars)

Son fra l'onde in mezzo al mare,	I am among the waves in the midst of the sea,
E al furor di doppio vento	A prey to the fury of fierce winds;
Or resisto, or mi sgomento	Now I am resolute, now I tremble,
Fra la speme, e fra l'orror.	Vacillating between hope and terror.
Per la fè, per la tua vita	Now I fear for your faith, for your life,
Or pavento, or sono ardita,	Now I am emboldened;
E ritrovo egual martire	And yet I find equal suffering
Nell' ardire e nel timor.	In boldness and in fear.

PIETRO METASTASIO (1698–1782); poem written in 1721

This is the sixth of Schubert's fourteen Metastasio solo settings (1812–27). See the poet's biography for a chronological list of all the Metastasio settings.

This is one of the most accomplished of the Metastasio settings, the most sophisticated of all from 1813, and a rival to *Vedi quanto adoro* settings of 1816 D510. It is sung by Venere (Venus) in Metastasio's *Gli orti Esperidi*, and if Salieri selected this text for his pupil he could not have made a better choice. He must have been astonished by the flair and imagination with which

Schubert responded to the plight of the goddess who claims to be tossed by the waves, trembling between hope and terror. Was it just coincidence that only the day before composing this aria (the manuscripts are clearly dated) Schubert began work on his most ambitious ballad, Schiller's *Der Taucher* D77? This long and elaborate work is about the young knight who recklessly dives off a cliff into the most dangerous depths of the sea in order to rescue the king's goblet. From the point of view of pianistic illustration this is also a work devoted to water in its most dramatic moods. *Son fra l'onde* appears to be a study for *Der Taucher*, and in it can be detected a level of confidence that was no doubt inspired by the young composer's engagement with his exciting new project. Compare, for example, the accompanying figurations at 'Per la fè, per la tua vita / Or pavento, or sono ardita' (bb. 22–31) with the stormy water music (also in C minor) for the sixth strophe of *Der Taucher* (from b. 215 of that work, 'Und es wallet und siedet und brauset und zischt'). And in other aspects of *Son fra l'onde*, the composer seems to have the wind behind him. The vocal line is notable for its muscular strength and the eloquence of its long-spanned phrases. The length of each is beautifully judged for the singer's breath, and the tessitura is ideal for a more dramatic voice. There is no sign here of the unreasonable vocal demands that marred the earlier ballads. For this, we have Salieri, that old operatic pro, to thank.

We have no way of knowing whether Schubert took his German songs to Salieri. Legend has it that *Hagars Klage* first aroused the old boy's interest in Schubert, but it has also been assumed that the ballads after this were composed behind his back. If this is so, it is an extraordinary coincidence that the two texts match up in such a way, and in such close chronological proximity. One can well imagine the following scenario: Schubert takes Salieri his first sketches of *Der Taucher*; the Italian is interested and impressed, but he insists that he does not know enough about German to help with pieces of this kind and is only prepared to mark the exercises with Italian words. However, he suddenly remembers that Metastasio wrote a text about the stormy sea, and sets it forthwith as Schubert's next exercise.

Another possible explanation is that Schubert had been lent a number of books containing Metastasio texts, and that he was permitted to make his own text selections for his exercises. This was almost certainly the case with the large number of Schiller exercises for vocal trio written in 1813, and it may have extended, after a while, to the Italian texts. Having embarked on *Der Taucher*, and being forced to break off from it in order to prepare a new exercise for Salieri, it would have been quite understandable if Schubert had been drawn to this turbulent and watery poem.

It is the last of the extant composition exercises from 1813. There are no more surviving manuscripts until we rediscover the connection with Salieri through documents from 1816. Unless Salieri decided that Schubert had 'graduated' in this area of study at the age of sixteen, it is possible that in 1814–15, two years incredibly rich in lieder and ballad settings, Salieri set Schubert further Italian exercises that are now lost to us.

Autograph:	Wienbibliothek im Rathaus, Vienna
First edition:	Published as part of the AGA in 1895 (P704)
Subsequent editions:	Not in Peters; AGA XX 572: Vol. 10/36; NSA IV: Vol. 6/150; Bärenreiter: Vol. 5/98 (high voice edition only)
Discography and timing:	Fischer-Dieskau —
	Hyperion I 33[16]
	Hyperion II 2[25] 1'53 Ann Murray

← *Pensa, che questo istante* D76   *Verschwunden sind die Schmerzen* D88 →

SONETT I
(PETRARCH/A. VON SCHLEGEL) **D628** [H407]
B♭ major   November 1818

Sonnet I

(80 bars)

A literal translation of Schlegel's translation is given here.
Petrarch's original poem is printed below in italics.

Apollo, lebet noch dein hold Verlangen,
   Das an thessal'scher Flut die blonden Haare

In dir entflammt, und ists im Lauf der Jahre

Nicht unter in Vergessenheit gegangen:

Vor Frost und Nebeln, welche feindlich hangen,
   Solang' sich uns dein Antlitz birgt, das klare,

Jetzt dies geehrte heil'ge Laub bewahre,
Wo du zuerst und ich dann ward gefangen.

Und durch die Kraft von dem verliebten Hoffen,

Das in der Jugend nicht dich liess vergehen,
Lass, von dem Druck befreit, die Luft erwarmen.
So werden wir, vom Staunen froh getroffen,
   Im Grünen uns're Herrin sitzen seh'n,

Und sich beschatten mir den eignen Armen.

Apollo, if the sweet desire
   With which her blonde hair inflamed you by the waters.

Of Thessaly still lives; and if, in the course of the years,

It has not sunk into oblivion:

Then preserve from the hostile frost and mist,
   Which appear when your bright face is concealed,

This revered and hallowed tree,
Where first you, then I, were taken captive.

And, by the power of those impassioned hopes

Which in your youth saved you from death,
Let the air grow warm, freed from an icy grasp.
Thus, in joyful astonishment,
   We shall behold our mistress seated on the grass,

Shading herself with her own arms.

SONETTO XXXIV

Apollo, s'ancor vive il bel desio
Che t'infiammava a le tessaliche onde,
E se non hai l'amate chiome bionde,
   Volgendo gli anni, già poste in oblio;

Dal pigro gielo e dal tempo aspro e rio,
Che dura quanto 'l tuo viso s'asconde,
Difendi or l'onorata e sacra fronde,
   Ove tu prima, e poi fu' invescato io;

E per vertù de l'amorosa speme
Che ti sostenne ne la vita acerba,
  Di queste impression' l'aere disgrombra:

Sì vedrem poi per meraviglia inseme
Seder la Donna nostra sopra l'erba
  E far de le sue braccia a se stessa ombra.

FRANCESCO PETRARCA (1304–1374), translated by AUGUST VON SCHLEGEL (1767–1845)

This is the first of Schubert's three solo settings of Petrarch (1818), and the fourth of his ten August von Schlegel solo settings (1816–26). See the biographies of both Petrarch and August von Schlegel for a chronological list of settings in each case.

August von Schlegel was mainly known as a translator through his astonishingly prolific work on Shakespeare, but with a book entitled *Blumensträusse Italiänischer, Spanischer, und Portugiesischer Poesie* (1804) he extended his exploration of foreign languages to include this celebrated region of Italian literature. He skilfully preserves the formal rhyme scheme of the Petrarchan sonnet, a lyrical poem of fourteen lines. The first eight lines ('octave' or 'octet') are rhymed ABBAABBA; the rhyme scheme of the closing six lines ('sestet') varies – it may be CDECDE, CDCCDC or CDEDCE. For five centuries major poets have been sonneteers; the form originated in thirteenth-century Sicily and was influenced by the love poetry of the Provençal troubadours. From there it spread to Tuscany and found its highest expression in the work of Petrarch who wrote no fewer than 317 sonnets, addressed to his idealized beloved, Laura. As Einstein points out, Schubert was the first composer in the German musical tradition to tackle this type of poem – 'a notoriously difficult exercise', as Reed rightly says. Petrarch's sonnets had been set by countless Italian composers of the sixteenth century, but always in parts where the eight-line octet and six-line sestet were treated as separate entities. Schubert's North German forerunners Reichardt and Zelter had never attempted such a setting, and the only other significant nineteenth-century songs with these texts are those by Franz Liszt in the original Italian, pieces that stand completely outside the lieder tradition despite their undeniable beauty. In this, as in so many respects, Schubert was a pioneer; his astonishing range of interests and sympathies, as demonstrated by his forays into this literature alone, should silence those who accuse him of being unaware of the difference between a great poem and a bad one. Schubert might have been guilty of indulgence for the poetic outpourings of his circle, but generosity to amateur efforts is not synonymous with a lack of literary discernment, and neither is a young man's desire to take on great literature, however intractable it may be to musical setting.

There is no doubt that Schubert had heard of Petrarch before he came across this poem, and he almost certainly knew the famous and touching story of the poet's unswerving devotion to a young girl he had glimpsed in an Avignon church and worshipped from afar for the rest of his life. Although the magical name Laura is not actually mentioned in these sonnets, Schlegel adds a note that this 'geehrte heil'ge Laub' is the laurel tree ('lauro') which Petrarch often used as a metaphor for Laura, and that the poem is in fact a prayer to Apollo to restore her to health after an illness. In any case Schubert knew that this love at a distance had inspired later literature; he himself had already set poems by both Matthisson and Schiller (e.g. *Die Betende* D102 and *Die Entzückung an Laura* D577) where the name Laura is apostrophized in more modern dress, and where the tone of devotion from afar derives from Petrarch. In setting these texts Schubert was being very 'modern', as Einstein points out; the rediscovery of the Middle Ages was one of the achievements of romanticism, and it is perhaps paradoxical that the young composer was moved to greater experimental daring with old texts such as these than he would have been with contemporary poets – always excepting his friend Mayrhofer, of course, who was also a translator of Petrarch's sonnets.

Schubert's work on the big ballads of his teenage years, as well as on Mayrhofer texts like *Liedesend* D473, *Iphigenia* D573 and *Fragment aus dem Aeschylus* D450, stands him in good stead when he tackles these poems – he was used to making a free sequence of musical movements to encompass the changing moods and metres of a text. We begin here with a recitative where the piano plays little part. In this opening address to Apollo, Schubert seems to have been aiming at the Attic simplicity of an unaccompanied vocal line, although he could not resist a tiny sighing motif on the piano after 'Verlangen' (b. 3). There is an expressive descent down the stave at 'in Vergessenheit gegangen' (b. 9) that chimes well with the English translation, 'sunk into oblivion'. At b. 10 with 'Frost und Nebeln' the marking

Apollo depicted in *Der Mythos alter Dichter* (1815).

changes to 'Geschwind' in ¾ time, and there is a dotted-rhythm shudder in the accompaniment reminiscent of Purcell's famous Cold Scene in *King Arthur*. The spacious ('Langsamer') setting of 'Wo du zuerst [pause for an interlude of four sighing quavers] und ich dann [pause for another interlude] ward gefangen' is superbly expressive of love at first sight, the afflicted lover literally rendered immobile by beauty. The change in the weather at 'die Luft erwarmen' (bb. 41–3) is mirrored by a stately motif in the piano, warmed into life by delicious little trills in bb. 44 and 46.

Another short patch of recitative ('So werden wir, vom Staunen froh getroffen') depicts the astonishment of both Petrarch and Apollo, and leads us into the most extended lyrical outpouring of the work. The piece has been nominally in the key of B flat throughout, but not until the final two lines of aria can we now hear this, so capricious and varied have been the harmonic changes. The page of music beginning 'Im Grünen uns're Herrin sitzen seh'n' (from b. 50, marked 'Mässig') is Schubert at his most gentle and affectionate; we are freed from the rigours of duple time, just as Laura is delivered from her sickness, and the music wafts in graceful ¾. The idea of the laurel tree providing its own shade inspires a more or less flat roof of minims and crotchets in the stave at the first 'Und sich beschatten' (the vocal line appears thus on the printed page, bb. 58–61), and fronds of leafy melisma (bb. 65 and 71) on the repeat of those words. The gently rocking quavers of the postlude extend the feeling that love is something holy and mysterious; perhaps it is the suspensions that make this music curiously prophetic of the piano writing in *Du bist die Ruh* D776. In both that song and this sonnet, the poets are struck by a similar sense of wonder and worship.

Autograph:	Wienbibliothek im Rathaus, Vienna (fair copy)
First edition:	Published as part of the AGA in 1895 (P680)
Subsequent editions:	Not in Peters; AGA XX 345: Vol. 5/225; NSA IV: Vol. 12/52
Bibliography:	Capell 1928, pp. 145–6
	Einstein 1951, pp. 185–6
	Fischer-Dieskau 1977, pp. 114–15
Discography and timing:	Fischer-Dieskau II 2[8] 2'54
	Hyperion I 27[5]
	Hyperion II 21[1] 3'01 Matthias Goerne

← *Lob der Tränen* D711   *Sonett II* D629 →

SONETT II   Sonnet II
(PETRARCH/A. VON SCHLEGEL) **D629** [H408]
G minor   November 1818

A literal translation of Schlegel's translation is given here.
Petrarch's original poem is printed below in italics.

Allein, nachdenklich, wie gelähmt vom Krampfe,	Alone, pensive, as if lamed by cramp,
Durchmess' ich öde Felder, schleichend träge,	I trudge wearily across the desolate fields,
Und wend' umher den Blick, zu fliehn die Stege,	And cast my gaze around, that I may avoid those paths
Wo eine Menschenspur den Sand nur stampfe.	Where human footprints are impressed in the sand.
Nicht andre Schutzwehr find' ich mir im Kampfe	In my battle I find no other defence
Vor dem Erspäh'n des Volks in alle Wege,	Against people who observe me wherever I go;
Weil man im Tun, wo keine Freude rege,	For in my actions, devoid of joy,
Von aussen lieset, wie ich innen dampfe.	They see from without how I burn inwardly.

So dass ich glaube jetzt, Berg und Gefilde,

   Und Fluss und Waldung weiss, aus welchen Stoffen

   Mein Leben sei, das sich verhehlt jedweden.

Doch find' ich nicht so rauhe Weg' und wilde,

   Dass nicht der Liebesgott mich stets getroffen.

   Und führt mit mir, und ich mit ihm dann Reden.

So that I now believe that mountains and pastures,

   Rivers and forests, know what stuff

   My life is made of, though it is concealed from others.

But I do not find a path so rough and wild

   That the god of love does not constantly find me

   And converse with me, and I with him.

SONETTO XXXV

Solo e pensoso i più deserti campi
Vo mesurando a passi tardi e lenti;
E gli occhi porto per fuggire intenti
   Ove vestigio uman l'arena stampi.

Altro schermo non trovo che mi scampi
Dal manifesto accorger de le genti;
Perché negli atti d'alegrezza spenti
   Di fuor si legge com'io dentro avvampi:

Sì ch'io mi credo omai che monti e piagge
E fiumi e selve sappian di che tempre
   Sia la mia vita, ch'è celata altrui.

Ma pur sì aspre vie né sì selvagge
Cercar non so, ch'Amor non venga sempre
   Ragionando con meco, ed io co lui.

FRANCESCO PETRARCA (1304–1374), translated by AUGUST VON SCHLEGEL (1767–1845)

This is the second of Schubert's three solo settings of Petrarch (1818), and the fifth of his ten August von Schlegel solo settings (1816–26). See the biographies of both Petrarch and August von Schlegel for a chronological list of settings in each case.

The opening figuration in the accompaniment feels familiar to the pianist – something about the way the inner voices in the right hand are doubled by the left, and appear to pivot around a central obsessive harmonic point, while longer notes are held at the extremities of each hand. A search in the deeply embedded finger-memory of the Schubertian (players know that there is such a thing) unearths a passage from the Schiller setting *Gruppe aus dem Tartarus* D583, Dante-inspired rather than Petrarch. At the words 'Folgen tränend seinem Trauerlauf' (bb. 40–46, a text which is also about the idea of making a journey under emotional stress) we find music with the same characteristics. More than ever we are aware of Schubert's highly sophisticated motivic language, an unconscious process whereby similar poetic images produce the same musical response – in general terms, if not always in detail. There are times when different composers share this language as if it has been passed down from one generation to another like a spoken dialect (this phenomenon is discussed in detail in Deryck Cooke's *The Language of Music*, a work that needs a sequel devoted to vocal music and the great lieder composers). An example of this is at 'schleichend träge' (b. 7), where we have quavers, syncopated so as to be a semiquaver apart; thus Schubert depicts Petrarch's weary limbs in exactly the way that Schumann was to paint Heine's (cf. *Schöne Wiege meiner Leiden* Op. 24 no. 5 at the passage 'Und die Glieder matt und träge / Schlepp' ich'). This is so important an image to Schubert that the word 'Schleichend' appears in the tempo marking. That this 'schleichend' is Schlegel's invention and does not appear in the original Petrarch, and that Schubert ascribes the sonnet to Schlegel, rather than its Italian author, on the autograph, shows that the composer seems not to have had access to the original text.

At 'Nicht andre Schutzwehr' (b. 13) a few bars of more or less unaccompanied recitative are introduced that quickly change (at 'wo keine Freude rege') to a more measured section (marked 'Unruhig'), with impatiently alternating quavers under the pianist's hands. The interlude after 'dampfe', the first phrase more rhetorical (bb. 21–2), the answering echo suppressed and more menacing (bb. 22–3), is worthy of *Der greise Kopf* D911/14 from *Winterreise*. At 'So dass ich glaube jetzt', Schubert experiments with a curious accompanimental figure from b. 24 – a triplet shared between the hands (first and third notes in the left hand, second in the right), a distribution to be found nowhere else in the songs; the effect is curiously like a limp, and we remember the 'gelähmt vom Krampfe' of the first line (an image incidentally furnished by Schlegel, for it is not to be found in the original Petrarch). For this section we have modulated to the key of G flat major, a shift remote from the tonic of G minor and thus suggestive of a cloud cuckoo land of fantasy and escape where the poet is able to converse with mountains, rivers and forests. We emerge from this and return to G minor for the last section (marked 'Etwas Langsamer').

As in *Sonett I* D628, Schubert has reserved his greatest inspiration for the last two lines, an envoi of infinite tenderness. We move into § and, in similar fashion to the first piece, the change of time signature (in this case from simple to compound time) adds a lilt that suggests, in splendidly ambiguous Schubertian manner, the blessings of love as well as the pains. 'Dass nicht der Liebesgott mich stets getroffen' is accompanied by a beautiful falling counter-melody in the piano's left hand; this sounds like a cello solo high on the fingerboard, and the effect of the whole is floating and ethereal. We see the god of love hovering around the poet's head, conversing with Petrarch in mid-flight. The solitary man is encouraged back into conversation with the ornamented setting of 'Reden': semiquavers signify words tumbling from a mouth too long condemned to silence. The vocal line ends in B flat major, but a tiny postlude changes everything as the music is inflected back into G minor. This is very much in the manner of the song *Erster Verlust* D226 where, after the singer brings the song to a close (or so he thinks) in A flat major, the pianist in a single bar of accompaniment gently but firmly seals the singer's fate in F minor.

It is curious that no one seems to have noticed that this song in its subject matter, and in its grandeur, is a miniature *Winterreise* D911 nine years in advance. Read as a poem, Petrarch's sonnet (among his most celebrated works) is extremely appropriate to the character of Schubert *in extremis*, and to his lonely path as a creator and human being. There is enough testimony to Schubert's sensuality for us to know that the urgings of the god of love were ever-present, and one may be sure that there was much about his private life that was concealed from others. It is significant that this poem was also translated by Schubert's great friend Mayrhofer (published in the almanac *Fortuna* in 1828), although with considerably less skill than Schlegel, and probably using the older poet's translation as a model. It is easy to see why Mayrhofer was interested in this sonnet, for one can read into it not only the plight of a man hopelessly in love but also that of one who is condemned to find love only on the wild paths, and who is forced by public scrutiny into concealing his very nature. Petrarch's image of burning inwardly, and concealing all, also brings Mayrhofer's *Memnon* D541 to mind.

Autograph: Wienbibliothek im Rathaus, Vienna (fair copy)
First edition: Published as part of the AGA in 1895 (P681)
Subsequent editions: Not in Peters; AGA XX 346: Vol. 5/228; NSA IV: Vol. 12/49
Discography and timing: Fischer-Dieskau II 2[9]   2'52
                              Hyperion I 27[6]
                              Hyperion II 21[2]   2'50   Matthias Goerne

← *Sonett I* D628   *Sonett III* D630 →

SONETT III   Sonnet III
(PETRARCH/GRIES) **D630** [H409]
C major   December 1818

Sehr langsam

Nun - mehr, da Him- mel, Er - de schweigt und Win - de,

(83 bars)

A literal translation of Gries's translation is given here. Petrarch's original poem is printed below in italics.

Nunmehr da Himmel, Erde schweigt und Winde,
  Gefieder, Wild, des Schlummers Bande tragen,
  Die Nacht im Kreise führt den Sternenwagen,
  Und still das Meer sich senkt in seine Gründe:

Nun wach' ich, nun sinn' ich, glüh' und wein und finde[1]
  Nur sie, die mich verfolgt mit süssen Plagen.
  Krieg ist mein Zustand, Zorn und Missbehagen;
  Nur, denk' ich s i e, winkt Friede mir gelinde.

Now that heaven and earth are silent, and winds,
  Birds and beasts are fettered by sleep,
  Night drives the starry chariot in its orbit,
  And the sea sinks calmly into its depths.

Now I wake, think, burn and weep, and find
  Only her, who pursues me with sweet torment.
  War is my state, anger and unease;
  But when I think of *her*, peace beckons gently to me.

[1] The original Gries translation is 'Nun wach ich, *sinne, glühe, wein'*, und finde'.

So strömt, was mich ernährt, das Süss' und
   Herbe,
   Aus eines einz'gen Quells lebend'gem
      Strahle,
   Dieselbe Hand gibt Heilung mir und
      Wunden.
Und dass mein Leiden nie ein Ziel
   erreiche,[2]
   Sterb' und ersteh' ich täglich tausend Male;

So weit entfernt noch bin ich zu gesunden.

So all that nourishes me, both sweet and bitter,

   Flows from the living radiance of a single
      source,
   And the same hand both heals and wounds
      me.
And since my suffering never reaches its end

   I die and rise again a thousand times each
      day,
So far am I still from being cured.

SONETTO CLXIV

Or che' l ciel e la terra e' l vento tace,
E le fere e gli augelli il sonno affrena,
Notte il carro stellato in giro mena,
   E nel suo letto il mar senz' onda giace;

Vegghio, penso, ardo, piango; e chi mi sface
Sempre m'è innanzi per mia dolce pena:
Guerra è 'l mio stato, d'ira e di duol piena;
   E sol di lei pensando ho qualche pace.

Così sol d'una chiara fonte viva
Move 'l dolce e l'amaro ond' io mi pasco;
   Una man sola mi risana e punge.

E perchè 'l mio martir non giunga a riva,
Mille volte il dì moro e mille nasco;
   Tanto da la salute mia son lunge.

FRANCESCO PETRARCA (1304–1374), translated by JOHANN DIEDERICH GRIES (1775–1842)

This is the third of Schubert's three solo settings of Petrarch (1818), and his only setting of a Gries text. See the biographies of both Petrarch and Gries for a chronological list of settings in each case.

In the 1817 Mayrhofer setting *Erlafsee* D586, an expressive falling sixth in the piano introduction, and again in the opening of the vocal line, is emblematic of the beauty and silence of a lake 'Am stillen Erlafsee'. In *Sonett III* the same interval is used to even greater effect; this time there is a sequence of descending sixths in piano and voice because the canvas is larger, yet the images are similar: silence, watery depths, the sinking sun and the emotional ambivalence of 'so wohl, so weh''. This phrase in *Erlafsee* is matched by the Petrarch/Gries 'dolce e l'amaro / Süss' und Herbe' ('both sweet and bitter' in bb. 32–4). Another 1818 song (composed two months earlier) comes to mind, this time in C minor rather than C major – *Blondel zu Marien* D626. Also in ⅛ and marked 'Sehr langsam', it has similarly ornate vocal writing with Italianate

---

[2] The Gries translation reads 'Und dass mein Leiden nie ein Ziel *erwerbe*' ('earn' or 'win'), a rhyme scheme here ignored by Schubert.

melismas, and an accompaniment that suggests an operatic aria. It is obvious that Petrarch's nationality is not lost on the composer even if he wrongly believed he was setting Dante (see below). The music in general is reminiscent of other grand Schubert nocturnes: the introduction to *Der Unglückliche* D713 (Pichler) is foreshadowed in the triplet-quaver repeated chords that dominate the accompaniment in this sonnet's first page, heralds of night's mystery in both pieces; the impressive slide downwards in b. 10 of the voice on 'senkt in seine Gründe', a scale that the piano continues to even murkier depths, is worthy of *Freiwilliges Versinken* D700 (Mayrhofer). One is tempted to compare this Petrarch setting with no fewer than four other Schubert songs in the space of a few lines, and measure its achievements first and foremost in comparison to other fine works. But *Sonett III* is vintage Schubert of the period in its own right, and worthy of much more serious consideration than it has previously been accorded.

After a splendid page evoking the beauties of night, the words 'Nun wach' ich, nun sinn' ich' are ushered in by a tiny bridge passage, an arpeggio plus a chromatic scale in the piano (second half of b. 11), which seems to raise the curtain on a picture of Petrarch himself. We hear him gently emerging from his slumbers, the sweetness of the half-waking state evoked by the same leaning chromatics that imply obsession. The dotted crotchets on 'Nun', an unimportant word that Schubert repeats and which would not usually be accorded such a protracted setting, underlines not only the sense of 'only now' but also illustrates the stretching of tired limbs. Not until Wolf's *Schon streckt' ich aus im Bett die müden Glieder* from the *Italienisches Liederbuch* (1896) would a composer again strike this mood of glowing devotion combined with sleepiness. The vocal line goes on to climb high in the stave in b. 16 and modulates to A flat in a manner suggesting that it has a wilful direction of its own which surprises the singer, the perfect analogue for 'sweet torment' out of control. 'Krieg ist mein Zustand, Zorn und Missbehagen' (bb. 18–21) produces appropriately agitated music initially in A flat minor, quasi-recitative with staccato bass notes and rumbling piano figurations, which brings us back via C sharp major to the home key of C major in first inversion.

This sets up another interlude in which the singer can enter the A flat major world where he dreams of Laura. The bridge to this arioso is the phrase 'Nur, denk' ich s i e' which is repeated in a rising sequence punctuated by soft mezzo staccato triplets (bb. 23–4). These bars of recitative, moving from F minor to B flat minor and thence into A flat major, contain all the wonder and sweetness of Petrarch's love for Laura; they seem saturated with the exotic fragrance of the beloved, and it is no wonder that they bring to mind the perfume of *Dass sie hier gewesen* D775. The arioso itself (beginning 'winkt Friede mir gelinde') is of great tenderness, as if Schubert has really thought himself into the poet's predicament. Something about the demanding tessitura of 'winkt Friede mir' suggests happiness out of reach: the peace that beckons is only a chimera.

The Italian sonnet is traditionally composed of the opposition of two moods. The first eight lines (octet) state a problem, ask a question or express an emotional tension. The last six lines (sestet) resolve the problem, answer the question or relieve the tension. For this sonnet's clinching sestet Schubert has planned a masterly return to the dropping sixth motif of the opening, beginning with an elongated setting of the word 'So' (b. 30). Thus there is a sense of summing up, of drawing the strands of the poet's argument together with an even greater sense of architectural design than in the other two sonnet settings. This is no real repetition of the opening music, however, for the motif is used as an upbeat to a different melody, now in § (marked 'Etwas bewegt') where the accompaniment flows in watery semiquavers that reflect the poet's idea that all emotions, sad and happy, flow from a single source. We have arrived at last at the main aria of the piece, for in these Petrarch settings Schubert reserves the most lyrical music for the final section. As we have already seen, the flattened inflection of 'Süss' und Herbe' is reminiscent of the 'so wohl, so weh" at the end of *Erlafsee*. The extraordinary tonal ambiguity and wandering between keys at 'Dieselbe Hand gibt Heilung mir und Wunden' (bb. 38–43) suggests the helplessness of someone in the grip of a fever, so disorientated and lovelorn that he has no idea where to put himself. A similarly wayward piano interlude brings us to the chord of G major (b. 49) and the middle section of the aria. The singer has a D (on 'und') and for a moment we expect a passage in G major, but the piano diverts this note into forming a part of its B flat major chord at b. 50. We are launched into an Italianate middle section with a touch of the sob of operatic desperation implied by the singer's ardently repeated notes see-sawing around that pulsating D. The suspended animation of this line, where the singer is caught within the upper third of the stave, turning hither and thither in a fruitless attempt to find an escape, illustrates the poet's metaphor about being trapped between living and dying, an exalted state such as we find in the Novalis *Nachthymne* D687 setting. The denuded setting of 'So weit entfernt noch' (from b. 57), with its implication of A minor in 𝄽 rhythm, is strongly prophetic of 'Ach! der mich liebt und kennt / Ist in der Weite' from *Lied der Mignon* of 1826 (D877/4).

With the words 'zu gesunden' Petrarch's sonnet ends, but Schubert decides on a repeat in the interests of musical symmetry. We thus return to the beginning of the sestet and from b. 62 hear the aria once again ('So strömt, was mich ernährt') but musically modified: 'gibt Heilung mir und Wunden' here stays in C major (bb. 74–6) rather than modulating into G. This enables the construction of a closing section of gentle dreaminess, the plagal oscillation between F major and C major emphasizing the holy nature of the poet's love for Laura. It is perhaps only on this final page that we feel let down: this ending, beautiful though it is, does not seem worthy of a work of this size, and one so full of musical riches (although it might be argued that to conclude with a whimper is true to the helplessness described by the poem). *Sonett III* just misses being a Schubertian masterpiece – the twenty-one-year-old composer has attempted something extremely ambitious, and by and large has succeeded.

Sonett III was translated by J. D. Gries. It appears in the *Blumensträusse Italianischer, Spanischer, und Portugiesischer Poesie*, the same anthology of translations from the Romance languages where Schubert found his two other Petrarch poems and for which Schlegel was both contributor and editor. In a moment of abstraction Schubert wrote Dante's name at the head of this manuscript. Capell points out that there is a line in the *Inferno* ('Mentre che 'l vento, come fa, si tace') which bears a passing resemblance to the opening line of this sonnet. This was perhaps why Mandyczewski in the *Gesamtausgabe* also ascribes the poem to Dante – a rare mistake from such a scrupulous editor. Schubert's experiments with the sonnet form when working on these Petrarch settings stood him in good stead when he set a sonnet by Goethe later in 1819 – *Die Liebende schreibt* D673.

Autograph:	Wienbibliothek im Rathaus, Vienna (first draft)
First edition:	Published as part of the AGA in 1895 (P682)
Subsequent editions:	Not in Peters; AGA XX 347: Vol. 5/231; NSA IV: Vol. 12/56
Further setting:	Claudio Monteverdi (1567–1643) *Or che 'l cielo e la terra e 'l vento tace*, madrigal for 6 voices from *Madrigali guerrieri e amoroso, Libro ottavo* (1638). First popularized by Nadia Boulanger's recording (1937)
Discography and timing:	Fischer-Dieskau II 2[10] 5'33
	Hyperion I 27[7]
	Hyperion II 21[3] 6'32 Matthias Goerne

← *Sonett II* D629   *Blanka* D631 →

Die SONNE STEIGT *see* KLAGE (DIE SONNE STEIGT) D415

JOSEF VON SPAUN (1788–1865)

THE POETIC SOURCE
This poem certainly was handed over to Schubert in autograph. It was never printed.

THE SONG
March 1817   *Der Jüngling und der Tod* D545

Josef von Spaun would have been rather embarrassed to have been counted among Schubert's poets as a result of what he would have regarded as his meagre poetic efforts. He is of their number simply because Schubert was so fond of him that he set his words to music as an affectionate act of gratitude for years of friendship and support.

Spaun was born into a well-to-do and semi-noble Linz family on 11 November 1788. In her youth his mother had been a semi-professional singer which probably accounts for the tender attention he always paid to music. He was a good nine years older than Schubert and the two met because Spaun, while pursuing his legal studies in Vienna from 1805, boarded at the Stadtkonvikt. In return for his lodgings he was responsible for running the school orchestra as well as playing in the second violins. He seems to have occupied the position somewhere between unofficial school prefect and junior teacher. Schubert arrived at the Konvikt in September 1808 aged eleven and Spaun, who was nineteen, met him there in November at the school's evening musical gatherings. From the very beginning the older boy took an interest in the youngster's talent (it was at this stage that Schubert shyly played him a minuet of his own composition). The young composer came to regard Spaun as his closest ally at the Konvikt. This was the first stage of a friendship that seems to have been uniquely marked by instalments. Spaun left Vienna for Linz in 1809 to take up the first of many posts in his fifty-two-year civil service career.

Spaun returned to Vienna in 1811 and remained there for a decade. This was a crucial period for Schubert of course, and Spaun found that his young protégé had come along in leaps and bounds. The composer was now devouring book after book of the ballads and songs (*Kleine Balladen und Lieder*) of Zumsteeg, both imitating and improving on them. Spaun ensured that Schubert had enough music paper on which to write his increasingly adventurous compositions. It was Spaun who took Schubert to the opera (an outing that was otherwise unaffordable for the teenager) and the pair saw works by Joseph Weigl (*Die Schweizerfamilie* and *Das Waisenhaus*) and Gluck's *Iphigenie in Tauris* (the opera's title in German). Here the young Schubert had the unforgettable experience of hearing Anna Milder-Hauptmann and Johann Michael Vogl as Iphigenia and Orestes. On the same evening he met the poet Theodor Körner through Spaun's good offices. Schubert's achievements of 1814 to 1816 must have left Spaun breathless, and one knows that the music itself was his greatest reward. He now had every proud reason to introduce his young friend to the cream of his acquaintance – the poet Matthäus von Collin who was Spaun's cousin, and the poet Johann Mayrhofer who was Spaun's oldest friend from his early Linz days (the meeting with Schubert took place at the end of 1814). Many other people of importance to Schubert, including the artists Leopold Kupelwieser and Moritz von Schwind, and the poet and gifted dilettante Franz von Schober, came into his ken because of Spaun. Winning the great singer Vogl to Schubert's cause in 1817 seems to have been a carefully orchestrated Spaun–Schober collaboration. It was through Spaun that Schubert composed his cantata *Prometheus* D451 (sadly lost to us) in honour of Spaun's former teacher Heinrich Josef Watteroth.

In 1816 Spaun was behind a significant effort to contact Goethe on Schubert's behalf. It was Spaun who wrote the covering letter to the great poet with the parcel that included a book of song masterpieces (they were returned forthwith). Spaun had informed Goethe of a project whereby Schubert would publish separate books of songs devoted to different poets with Goethe himself at the apex. Goethe's failure to answer Spaun's letter may have had something to do with the fact that the lion of Weimar knew that Spaun's uncle, Franz Seraphicus, who lived in Munich, was a virulent opponent of his work. This is only one theory: Goethe may simply have been busy, or disinclined to engage with musicians after a bad experience with an arrogant Carl Eberwein who had written *Faust* music in June 1816; or the poet might have been preoccupied with the very recent death of his wife Christiane. The parcel seems to have been sent at the worst possible time. In 1817 Schubert set one of Spaun's own poems, something that came about because of Spaun's enthusiasm for the Claudius setting *Der Tod und das Mädchen* D531.

In 1821 Spaun returned to his home town of Linz where he was appointed to a position in the customs office. His initial failure to keep in touch with his friends in Vienna resulted in the comic aria *Herrn Josef von Spaun, Assessor in Linz* D749 for which von Collin wrote the text. There is a grain of truth in the comic exaggeration of forsaken comradeship in this parody of Italian opera, for Spaun's absence from Vienna must have been keenly felt by his devoted circle: this was the very period (1821–6) when Schubert would have badly needed advice and comfort in times of illness and tribulation. Spaun briefly returned to Vienna in the winter of 1824–5 but he had been away from the city when Schubert became, according to some observers, more licentious in his behaviour, contracting syphilis as a result. In the meantime the songs of Opus 13 (*Der Alpenjäger* D524, *Der Schäfer und der Reiter* D517 and *Lob der Tränen* D711) were dedicated to Spaun who enthusiastically ensured that there was a fan base for Schubert in Linz. His younger brother Anton von Spaun (1790–1849), friend and collaborator of Mayrhofer, was far more of a writer and literary intellectual and it is astonishing that Schubert never set Anton's poetry which was highly valued and circulated within

the Schubert circle. All of Spaun's family (his brothers Anton, Franz and Max, and his sister Marie – later married to Anton Ottenwalt) were joyfully recruited to the Schubertian cause. Anton Stadler, sometime poet, was also a part of this circle. The composer was made an honorary member of the Linz Gesellschaft der Musikfreunde. In 1825 Spaun was posted to Lemberg (Lvov) where he made another circle of friends who were later furnished with Schubert's music.

Spaun at last returned to Vienna at the beginning of July 1826. He became director of the state lottery in 1841 and, although he did not approve of gambling, he was as ever a scrupulous servant of the state. In the last two years of Schubert's life the friendship became even stronger. Spaun hosted some magnificent Schubertiads (the famous Moritz von Schwind painting of a Schubertiad records an occasion in 1826 where Spaun was the host) and Schubert dedicated to his friend the Piano

Josef von Spaun, oil Painting by Leopold Kupelwieser

Sonata in G major D894. The last great Schubertiad of all took place in January 1828 in honour of Spaun's fiancée, Franziska Roner von Ehrenwerth for whom Schubert had written the *Vier Canzonen* D688 eight years earlier. The couple married in April 1828 and had five children, the last of whom died in 1920. Unlike Schober, Spaun visited Schubert on his deathbed, seemingly unaware that his friend was in mortal danger. 'There is really nothing the matter with me', Schubert had said to him, 'only I am so exhausted I feel as if I were going to fall through the bed.' There was a Schubertiad in the composer's memory at Spaun's house on 23 December 1828, the day of the memorial service.

It is generally agreed that the composer never had a better friend than the generous and stable Spaun. Above all he was a man of tremendous kindness. If he lacked the fantasy and daredevil freedom of some of Schubert's other friends, notably Schober, his written memories of the composer have proved the most reliable, and his judicious ability to see the events and personae of the epoch in perspective show him to have been a man of tolerance, insight and loyalty. There has perhaps been no better

brief summation of Schubert's song-writing achievements than these words of Spaun: 'In this category he stands unexcelled, even unapproached . . . Every one of his songs is in reality a poem on the poems he set to music. Who among those who had the good fortune to hear some of his greatest songs does not remember how this music made a long familiar poem new for him, how it was suddenly revealed to him and penetrated to his very depth?' Some of Spaun's qualities of judgement were fostered by the self-discipline that stems from a life in public service; he seems not to have particularly enjoyed his various jobs, but he discharged them all with admirably unpompous rectitude. If there is someone among Schubert's many contemporary friends and acquaintances who should have been the recipient of an imaginary Schubert Prize, Spaun's candicacy as the senior Schubertian, the first and perhaps the best, towers above everyone else. His personal verdict on the composer ('. . . an affectionate son and brother, and a loyal friend. He was a kind, magnanimous, good man') might equally be posterity's verdict on Josef von Spaun. He died in his beloved Linz on 25 November 1865 (*see* also FRIENDS AND FAMILY).

Bibliography: Liedlexikon 2012, p. 862

FRIEDRICH SPEE VON LANGENFELD (1591–1635)

THE SOURCE
S1 *Poetisches Taschenbuch für das Jahr 1806 von Friedrich Schlegel* (1805)

THE SONG
December 1818   *Vom Mitleiden Mariä* D632 [S1: pp. 200–1]

This religious poet, born near Düsseldorf of a noble family, became a Jesuit in 1610. During his lifetime the re-establishment of Roman Catholicism in his home region of north-west Germany was a process fraught with difficulty, and he survived an assassination attempt in 1629. As a result of his experiences officiating at

the burning of witches he became convinced of the injustice against many innocent women and wrote an anonymous attack (*Cautio criminalis*, 1631) on the judicial system. He died of plague while tending the sick in Trier. His writing, in which the beauties of Nature play a large part, is more in the Franciscan than Jesuit tradition.

Friedrich von Spee.

In his *Poetisches Taschenbuch* of 1806, Friedrich von Schlegel, who would soon become an enthusiastic Catholic convert, was enraptured with Spee's poetry and published a selection of twenty-three poems under the heading *Trutznachtigall. Eine Auswahl geistlicher Volkslieder nach Friedrich Spee und einigen andern.* Despite mentioning a 'few other' writers, these introductory words give the false impression that the poems in this *Taschenbuch* (now a great bibliophilic rarity, but clearly in Schubert's possession for at least a short time) are all from Spee's seminal collection *Trutznachtigall, oder Geistliches-Poetisch Lustwäldlein*, a posthumous collection of lyrics published in 1649.

In fact, *Vom Mitleiden Mariä* is one of seven of the lyrics that do not appear in

Trutznachtigall. Schlegel covered himself by mentioning a few other authors in his foreword, and also by confessing that he has made changes here and there in the original material, some of it earlier than Spee, some more recent. Nevertheless, Hans Eichner, the editor of the *Dichtungen* volume of the *Kritische Friedrich-Schlegel-Ausgabe*, has pointed out that the poem is Schlegel's reworking of verses 2, 3 and 4 of *Von unser lieben Frawen [Frauen] mit Leiden*, a hymn that is generally ascribed to Spee, whether or not Schlegel knew this. Schlegel is likely to have found the text either in the *Geistliches Psalterlein der Societät Jesu* (Köln, 1647) or in a book of Catholic church songs and hymns. These strophes run as follows, and may be compared to Schlegel's text for *Vom Mitleiden Mariä* as an indication of the kind of modernizing changes to which the later poet subjected the older master's original words (the spelling of the original has been conserved in this case):

Als bey dem Creutz Maria stund,
Weh vber weh jhr Hertz empfundt,
Vnd schmertzen über schmertzen,
Das gantze Leyden Christi stundt,
Gedruckt in jhrem Hertzen.

Sie schawt jhrn Sohn an bleich vnd Todt,
Und überall von Wunden roht,
Am Creutz vnschuldig hangen,
Gedenck wie dieser Schmertzliche Todt,
Ihr sey zu Hertzen gangen.

In Christi Haupt durch Bein und Hirn,
Durch Augen, Ohren Schlaff und Stirn,
Viel scharpffe dornen stochen:
Dem Sohn die Dornen Haupt vnd Stirn,
Das Hertz der Mutter brochen.

The complete hymn text of eight strophes can be found in NSA Volume XII pp. 240–1.

SAMUEL HEINRICH SPIKER (1786–1858)

THE TRANSLATION
S1 *Der Pirat* aus dem Englischen des Walter Scott, übersetzt von S. H. Spiker, Zweiter Band, Berlin bei Duncker und Humblot, 1822

THE ENGLISH SOURCE
S2 *The Pirate* By the author of Waverley and Kenilworth &c. In three Volumes. Volume II. Edinburgh Printed for Archibald Constable and Co. Ltd and Hurst, Robinson and Co., London, 1822

THE SONG
1825   *Gesang der Norna* D831 Op. 85 no. 2 [S1: pp. 150–51] [S2: Chapter five, p. 126]

Samuel Spiker was born in Berlin on 24 December 1786. He was librarian at the Royal Prussian Library, a position that made him extremely grand. His nickname was Lord Spiker – something that came about because he had toured the British Isles in 1816 (writing a two-volume work about his tour, *Reise durch England, Wales und Schottland*, published in Leipzig in 1818). He had also translated Shakespeare. In his capacity as the Prussian

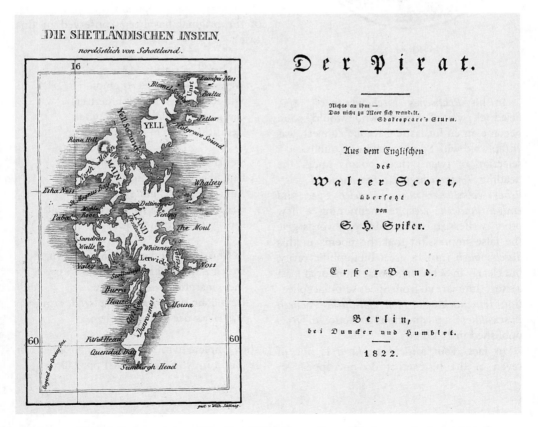

Title page of S. H. Spiker's translation of *The Pirate* (1822). *Nornas Gesang* is in the second volume of this three-volume translation.

king's personal envoy, Spiker was dispatched to Vienna in 1826 to receive the copy of Beethoven's Ninth Symphony, a work dedicated to his employer, King Friedrich Wilhelm III of Prussia. His Viennese visit was a little too early to have come across the Scott song to his translation composed by Schubert in 1825, but only published in March 1828. Spiker edited his own newspaper in Berlin. He died there on 24 May 1858.

Die SPINNERIN
(GOETHE) **D247** [H139]
B minor   August 1815

The spinner

(247 bars)

Als ich still und ruhig spann,
Ohne nur zu stocken,
Trat ein schöner junger Mann
Nahe mir zum Rocken.

As I spun, silently and calmly,
Without stopping,
A fair young man
Approached me at my distaff.

Lobte, was zu loben war:
Sollte das was schaden?
Mein dem Flachse gleiches Haar,
Und den gleichen Faden.

He duly complimented me
What harm could that do?
On my flaxen hair
And on the flaxen thread.

Ruhig war er nicht dabei,
Liess es nicht beim Alten;
Und der Faden riss entzwei,
Den ich lang' erhalten.

But he was not content with that,
And would not let things be.
And the thread which I had long kept intact
Snapped in two.

Und des Flachses Stein-Gewicht
Gab noch viele Zahlen;
Aber, ach! ich konnte nicht
Mehr mit ihnen prahlen.

And the flax-stone's weight
Produced many more threads;
But, alas, I could no longer
Boast about them.

Als ich sie zum Weber trug,
Fühlt' ich was sich regen,
Und mein armes Herze schlug
Mit geschwindern Schlägen.

When I took them to the weaver
I felt something stir,
And my poor heart beat
More quickly.

Nun, beim heissen Sonnenstich,
Bring' ich's auf die Bleiche,
Und mit Mühe bück' ich mich
Nach dem nächsten Teiche.

Now, in the scorching sun,
I take my work out to be bleached,
And with great effort
I bend over the nearest pool.

Die Spinnerin.

Als ich still und ruhig spann,
Ohne nur zu stocken,
Trat ein schöner junger Mann
Nahe mir zum Rocken.

Lobte, was zu loben war,
Sollte das was schaden?
Mein dem Flachse gleiches Haar,
Und den gleichen Faden.

Ruhig war er nicht dabei,
Ließ es nicht beim Alten;
Und der Faden riß entzwei,
Den ich lang' erhalten.

Und des Flachses Steingewicht
Gab noch viele Zahlen;
Aber, ach! ich konnte nicht
Mehr mit ihnen prahlen.

Als ich sie zum Weber trug,
Fühlt' ich was sich regen,
Und mein armes Herze schlug
Mit geschwindern Schlägen.

Nun beim heißen Sonnenstich,
Bring' ich's auf die Bleiche,
Und mit Mühe bück' ich mich
Nach dem nächsten Teiche.

Was ich in dem Kämmerlein
Still und fein gesponnen,
Kommt—wie kann es anders seyn?
Endlich an die Sonnen.

Die Spinnerin by Eugen Neureuther (1829–30).

Was ich in dem Kämmerlein	What I had spun so quietly and finely
Still und fein gesponnen,	In my little room
Kommt – wie kann es anders sein? –	Will at length – how can it be otherwise? –
Endlich an die Sonnen.	Come out into the light of day.

JOHANN WOLFGANG VON GOETHE (1749–1832); poem written no later than 1795

This is the twentieth of Schubert's seventy-five Goethe solo settings (1814–6). See the poet's biography for a chronological list of all the Goethe settings.

This poem (heartily disliked by Goethe's contemporary Herder, probably on account of its openly sexual story) is ideal material for a strophic song; indeed any attempt to find a through-composed solution would result in something narratively unmanageable, more like an opera. The words are supremely understated, as is the drama and sense of tragedy, and something nearer folksong than lied seems entirely fitting. The girl too, simple without being stupid, would be likely to sing something repetitive like this, while burying herself in her work. Schubert has found his principal ideas here from the idea of spinning: the semiquavers are truly spun, like flaxen thread, delicately woven, passing through the stave's warp and weft. The original key is impossible for anyone but the highest and chirpiest of sopranos, and even then the tessitura is uncomfortable for the phonation of comprehensible words. This is perhaps why so few singers take up this masterpiece – for a masterpiece it is. On top of this it also presents the usual daunting challenges of colouring and memorizing strophic songs. Despite the simplicity of the music, the story is a tragic one of seduction, exploitation and disgrace (for this is undoubtedly what the girl faces when her secret is discovered). But the narrative is recounted without senti-mentality or self-pity, and is all the more moving for that. John Reed calls this 'a triumphant vindication of Goethe's views on the supremacy of the strophic song'. It was the fourth item in an album of Goethe settings that Josef von Spaun sent to the great poet in 1816 but, like the rest, it went unnoticed and unacknowledged. It was also one of only two songs sent to Goethe that were passed over for publication in the composer's lifetime – in this case, perhaps, on account of the poem's subject matter. It is one of Schubert's most effective strophic settings in that the drudgery of repetition, the feeling that one of life's sad old stories is happening yet again, is built into the repetitive nature of the music.

Autograph:	Staatsbibliothek Preussischer Kulturbesitz, Berlin (fair copy for Goethe)
First edition:	Published as Op. post. 118 no. 6 by Josef Czerny, Vienna in June 1829 (P227)
Publication reviews:	*Berliner allgemeine musikalische Zeitung*, No. 44 (31 October 1829) p. 347 [Waidelich/Hilmar Dokumente I No. 750]
Subsequent editions:	Peters: Vol. 4/151; AGA XX 119: Vol. 3/44; NSA IV: Vol. 8/174
Bibliography:	Einstein 1951, p. 111
	Fischer-Dieskau 1977, p. 53
Discography and timing:	Fischer-Dieskau —
	Hyperion I 7[14] 2'43 Elly Ameling
	Hyperion II 8[25]

← *Claudine von Villa Bella* II   *Der Gott und die Bajadere* D254 →
  Liebe schwärmt auf allen Wegen D239/6

SPRACHE DER LIEBE[1]
(A. von Schlegel) **D410** [H245]
E major   April 1816

The language of love

(33 bars)

Lass dich mit gelinden Schlägen	Let me touch you with gentle strokes,
Rühren, meine zarte Laute!	My tender lute!
Da die Nacht hernieder taute,	Now that the dewy night has fallen
Müssen wir Gelispel pflegen.	We must talk in whispers.
Wie sich deine Töne regen,	As your notes vibrate,
Wie sie atmen, klagen, stöhnen,	As they breathe, lament, moan,
Wallt das Herz zu meiner Schönen,	So my heart flows to my beloved,
Bringt ihr aus der Seele Tiefen	Bringing here from the depths of my soul
Alle Schmerzen, welche schliefen;	All the sorrows that were slumbering.
Liebe denkt in süssen Tönen.	Love thinks in sweet music.
[... 3 ...]	[... 3 ...]

AUGUST WILHELM VON SCHLEGEL (1767–1845); poem written in 1802

*This is the third of Schubert's ten August von Schlegel solo settings (1816–25.) See the poet's
biography for a chronological list of all the August von Schlegel settings.*

The language of love turns out to be music, of course, and this is perhaps the least known of
the songs that Schubert wrote about his own art. Works like *An die Musik* D547, *Trost im Liede*
D546 and *An mein Klavier* D342 are serene contemplations on music's powers to heal and
enchant. In *Sprache der Liebe*, on the other hand, melody excites and goads the lover into action,
and by the end of the song we feel that music is an aphrodisiac for the consummation of
passionate feelings. The poem's first line inspires a lute-like introduction, the music of tuning
up – a tiny phrase repeated, and then expanded to a slightly higher point in the stave (b. 3),
followed by the typical spread chord that denotes an instrument ready for use. Mandyczewski
printed this passage in small notes, believing it not to be authentic, but authentic it is, and it
suits the song perfectly – which is more than can be said for other spurious introductions added
in posthumous editions.

The time signature is §, suggestive of dance, and Schubert often employs this Ländler rhythm
for songs with a cheeky glint in the eye (cf. *Seligkeit* D433 where analogies with heaven are used
for flirtatious purposes). *Sprache der Liebe* begins in traditional serenade vein, but it is soon
apparent that the composer has other things in mind for the song apart from a pretty tune with

---

[1] Schlegel's title is *Die Sprache der Liebe*. After a four-line quotation of Ludwig Tieck, four strophes are printed under
the heading 'Erste Weise' (first Air). The poem as printed above is the first strophe of 'Zweite Weise' (second Air).

simple quaver accompaniment. In b. 7, the bar before 'Da die Nacht hernieder taute', the pianist has a tiny interlude, hands together in conspiratorial octaves. After this, night falls in the vocal line as the melody sinks deeper into the stave; mention of whispering ('Müssen wir Gelispel pflegen') prompts rustling semiquavers in the accompaniment. The music has briefly modulated into the dominant (B major) at 'zarte Laute' and now it moves in typically Schubertian fashion to G major (b. 12).

The next section gives rise to a squeeze-box progression of chromatics where the flattened minor-key inflections on the verbs 'atmen' (b. 15) and 'stöhnen' (b. 16) paint the sighs of the woebegone lover. Love has become indistinguishable from music in his mind, and the initial discretion of the serenader is forgotten. The ear is teased by the breathless depiction of the poet's heart flowing to the beloved with the help of music. We are made to wait for the return to the home key, and the final cadence of consummation is artfully prolonged. In this way the listener is tantalized along with the impatient lover. In the accompaniment, the change from quavers to semiquavers (first in the inner voices from b. 20, and then gradually in the piano's right hand) is cleverly planned to make the final eight bars especially passionate.

At the end the piece vibrates with strummed chords in both hands, as if a forest fire has broken out in the thicket of semiquavers, the blaze of harmonies emblematic of the telepathic powers of music. The vocal line is made up of short phrases ('Alle Schmerzen', 'welche schliefen' and so on) depicting breathlessness and excitement. The words 'Liebe denkt in süssen Tönen' state the crucial point of the poem, that feelings are more powerful than words, and that music is nearer to a state of feeling than any mere verbal expression. This phrase, which is set three times using sequence and rhythmic elaboration to increase intensity, was a quotation from Ludwig Tieck, printed by Schlegel as a motto above his poem. At the final 'süssen Tönen' the vocal line blossoms into an effusion of semiquavers (at b. 31) and an ornamental triplet, before nosediving into the lap of the stave with an elongated and syncopated setting of 'Tönen' (bb. 32–3). The effect is of the final gasp of a satisfied lover, home at last, passion finally spent. Underneath the singer the accompaniment continues to race in pounding heartbeats of amorous exertion. It is only on the last syllable of the last word that we really feel we have reached the tonic with a final delighted shudder.

There are repeat marks in this music, implying that Schubert had all four of Schlegel's strophes in mind for this setting. The problem is that it is difficult to make the words fit the music. The editors of the NSA have printed a version of the notes ('a suggestion of the editors') where the three following verses of Schlegel's poem have been adapted to fit the music (NSA Vol. 10 p. 362, example 9).

Autograph:	Wienbibliothek im Rathaus, Vienna (fair copy)
First edition:	Published as Op. post. 115 no. 3 by M. J. Leidesdorf, Vienna in June 1829 (P220)
Subsequent editions:	Peters: Vol. 4/142; AGA XX 207: Vol. 4/78; NSA IV: Vol. 10/136
Bibliography:	Capell 1928, pp. 125–6
Discography and timing:	Fischer-Dieskau I 6[28] 1'31
	Pears–Britten 2[2] 1'53
	Hyperion I 27[3] 1'25 Matthias Goerne
	Hyperion II 13[21]

← *Die verfehlte Stunde* D409   *Der Herbstabend* D405 →

ALBERT STADLER (1794–1888)

THE POETIC SOURCES
All the Stadler poems that Schubert set to music were given to Schubert in manuscript.

THE SONGS
2 July 1815	*Lieb Minna* D222
For 10 August 1819	*Cantate zum Geburtstag des Sängers Johann Michael Vogl* D666
For 19 March 1820	*Namenstagslied* D695

Albert Stadler was born in Steyr, Upper Austria on 4 April 1794. He attended Kremsmünster School between 1806 and 1812, and in 1812 he moved to Vienna to study at the university. Like Spaun, he boarded at the Stadtkonvikt without actually being a pupil there, and came into contact with Schubert whose talent he appreciated from early on (Stadler himself was a very able composer). So perspicacious was his estimate of Schubert that he collected copies of the songs composed between 1813 and 1817 which proved invaluable when the collected edition was being prepared some seventy years later (*see* AUTOGRAPHS, ALBUMS AND COLLECTIONS). In 1817 Stadler left Vienna with the score of *Der Strom* D565 in hand, marked 'a memento of friendship', and began work as a civil servant in Steyr. From there he moved to Linz in 1821 and thence to Salzburg in 1845.

Stadler was clearly close to Schubert during that *annus mirabilis* of 1815. He provided the composer with a libretto for the *Singspiel Fernando* D220, and also for the song *Lieb Minna* D222. He seems to have possessed a handwritten volume of verses suitable for musical setting (perhaps including his own) and it is possible that Schubert found the poems there for certain Salis-Seewis texts such as *Der Jüngling an der Quelle* D300 and *Pflügerlied* D392. This 'Liederbuch' is mentioned on Stadler's copy of the latter song as the source of further verses not written under the music. The intensity of the amateur poet's connection with the composer was not maintained after 1817, although they were always pleased to see each other in Steyr and Linz. Schubert and Stadler were reunited in the summer of 1819 when the composer went on holiday for the first time to Upper Austria in the company of the singer Vogl. At this time Schubert was a guest at the home of Stadler's uncle, Albert Schellmann. During this visit the composer set Stadler's poem in honour of Vogl's birthday. This was a miniature cantata, a vocal trio with piano D666. For the celebratory performance on 10 August, Stadler accompanied while Schubert sang the tenor line, Josefine Koller the soprano and Bernhard Benedict the bass. Once Schubert had returned to Vienna, Stadler asked him to compose a song for Josefine to sing to her father, Josef von Koller on his name-day. Schubert provided the *Namenstagslied* D695 for the domestic performance on 19 March 1820.

While at Linz, Stadler was extremely active in the affairs of the Gesellschaft der Musik-

Albert Stadler in later life.

freunde (of which Schubert was to become an honorary member). He was in contact with the Spaun and Ottenwalt families who had strong Schubert connections and in June 1823, when Schubert came to Linz for a recuperative holiday at the height of his health crisis, Stadler introduced him to the Hartmann family who were to become among the composer's deepest and – like Stadler himself – most perceptive admirers. (From late 1826, the Vienna diaries of the two Hartmann sons, Fritz and Franz, were to be an invaluable source of Schubertian documentary material.) Stadler and the composer met up for the last time in the summer of 1825 when Schubert and Vogl, during the course of their extensive summer holiday, made Linz their base. At the beginning of October a visit was made to the Weissenwolf family at Schloss Steyregg, not far from Linz (on this occasion the composer shared a room with Stadler). This introduction, like several of the meetings in Schubert's life when Stadler was the middle man, was a fruitful one. The Weissenwolfs (Count Johann and Countess Sophie) opened their doors to Schubert and Vogl on various occasions over the summer. This connection with the nobility was bound to have pleased the composer's family back in Vienna: 'The countess is a great admirer of my humble self, has all my songs, and sings some of them quite prettily . . . The Walter Scott songs made such an impression on her that she even made it clear that it would by no means displease her if I were to dedicate them to her', Schubert wrote to his father and step-mother. That this dedication for the *Sieben Gesänge aus Walter Scott's Fräulein vom See* Op. 52 (D835–9, 843, 846) came about as planned (no doubt accompanied, as was customary, by a gift from the dedicatee) would certainly have been a source of pleasure to Stadler. This was to be his last service to Schubert during the composer's lifetime, but he continued to promote the music of his friend throughout the many years remaining to him. Some of Stadler's own songs were printed (settings of Körner, Heine and Leitner). He died in Vienna on 5 December 1888.

Die STADT *see SCHWANENGESANG* D957/11

STÄNDCHEN ('Horch! horch! die Lerch')   Serenade 'Hark, hark, the lark'
(**SHAKESPEARE**) **D889** [H604]
C major   July 1826

(46 bars)

Horch! horch! die Lerch' im Ätherblau;	Hark, hark! the lark at heaven's gate sings,
Und Phöbus, neu erweckt,	And Phoebus 'gins arise,
Tränkt seine Rosse mit dem Tau,	His steeds to water at those springs
Der Blumenkelche deckt;	On chalic'd flowers that lies;
Der Ringelblume Knospe schleusst	And winking Mary-buds begin
Die goldnen Äuglein auf;	To ope their golden eyes;

Mit allem, was da reizend ist,	With everything that pretty is,
Du süsse Maid, steh auf!	My lady sweet, arise;
Steh auf; steh auf!	Arise, arise!

WILLIAM SHAKESPEARE (1564–1616), translated by AUGUST WILHELM VON SCHLEGEL (1767–1845); published in Vol. 26 of the Viennese edition of Shakespeare's plays in 1825

This is the second of Schubert's three Shakespeare solo settings (1826) and the last of his ten August von Schlegel solo settings (1816–25). See the biographies of both Shakespeare and August von Schlegel for a chronological list of settings in each case.

The lyric comes from *Cymbeline* Act II Scene 3. Against his wishes, Cymbeline's daughter, the beautiful Imogen, has married Posthumus Leonatus, a poor but worthy gentleman who has been banished to Italy. The queen, Cymbeline's second wife, has ambitions for her lumpish son Cloten, and wishes him to marry Imogen and assume the throne. The plot concerns the attempts by various characters to despoil the love between Posthumus and Imogen. An Italian, Iachimo/Giacomo (or Jachimo in the German version), in the manner of a Don Alfonso, has wagered that no woman can be faithful. Posthumus, in the manner of a Ferrando or a Gugliemo (the parallels are with Mozart's *Così fan tutte* of course) accepts the challenge. On arriving in Britain, Iachimo soon realizes that the only way to win his wager is to hide in Imogen's bedchamber and take note of convincing details whereby he can persuade the husband that he has slept with the wife: he steals her bracelet and takes note of a mole on her left breast. Later in the same scene, while Imogen is asleep, Cloten enters with musicians in a clumsy attempt to woo her.

> CLOTEN: *I would this music would come. I am advised to give her music o' the morning; they say it will penetrate. Come on, tune. If you penetrate her with your fingering, so; we'll try with tongue too. If none will do, let her remain; but I'll never give o'er. First, a very excellent, good-conceited thing; after, a wonderful sweet air with admirable rich words to it; and then let her consider.*

> MUSICIAN: *Hark, hark! the lark at heaven's gate sings . . .*

Thus double entendre of the bawdiest kind introduces a song that was very dear to the Victorians (it might have been something composed by Arthur Sullivan for this was the type of Schubert he adored and emulated) and which played its part in early Schubert reception in a more prudish England than Shakespeare's. Like *Gesang (An Silvia)* D891, this is a creation from the holiday in Währing in the summer of 1826. Perhaps Schubert had received copies of the recently issued Viennese Shakespeare edition directly from Bauernfeld or perhaps the well-to-do Schober had these small volumes in the house. This was a period that found Schubert composing not very prolifically, but like a god. How effortless it all sounds, this tender serenade with the chirruping of the lark evoked by a delicate semiquaver motif that also brings to mind tiny elfin trumpets announcing the dawning of a new day. These piano figurations are as delicate as dew drops on an exquisite summer morning, and they have already been prophesied in *Die Rose* D745 (at the phrase 'Es kam die Morgenröte', also descriptive of dawn and opening flower buds), a Friedrich von Schlegel setting from 1822. The cheekily genial music of *An Silvia* has given way to something much more ethereal. The song as the composer intended it (without the two extra verses written by Friedrich Reil for the second Diabelli edition of 1835) is over in a trice, as transitory as the best British weather.

Cloten's serenade from *Cymbeline* from *The Library Shakespeare* illustrated by Gilbert, Cruikshank and Dudley.
Cloten's musicians serenade Imogen.

The song is in C major, but we hear the tonic chord in root position only rarely. So much is written over a dominant pedal that the listener feels suspended in that dream-world – half-sleeping, half-waking – in which Imogen finds herself. At the repeat of 'Der Blumenkelche deckt' (bb. 17–18) there is a real modulation to the dominant, but this yields immediately to an E flat pedal which leads us to the key of A flat major, a harmonic excursion favoured in many of Schubert's C major songs (cf. *Gondelfahrer* D808). At 'Der Ringelblume Knospe schleusst' we are drawn tonally into the secret world of flowers, the composer revelling in the pathetic fallacy with the same sense of wonder that is heard in some of Schumann's flower songs, above all *Am leuchtenden Sommermorgen* from *Dichterliebe* Op. 48 No. 12. As the serenade progresses it gathers momentum and enthusiasm with the heat of the rising sun, coinciding with the return of the tonic key (albeit in first inversion) for the forte 'steh auf' of bb. 29–30. Delicate pleas give way to an outburst of energy where the invitation to arise becomes a command. Capell is amusing here: 'Imogen would have been altogether too startled at being bidden arise by the interval of a seventh [at 'Steh auf' bb. 30–31 and 34–5] and could only have taken the aubade for a brawl.' This may be true in an inept performance but with a fine singer, and with each successive 'auf' underpinned by a different bass harmony (always avoiding being earthed on the tonic), the vocal line soars like a lark in the clear air. The return of the prelude as a postlude restores the decorum and the sense of musicians gently tapping on the window to rouse the stay-abed. Like the serenade to Silvia, this is a masterpiece of economy and delight.

The autographs of this song, *Gesang (An Silvia)* and *Hippolits Lied* D890 were written in an unusually small musical notebook with the stave lines hand-drawn in pencil. A story about Schubert writing a song on the back of a menu in the Währing beer garden, having suddenly found a text that pleased him, and composing it among the tumult of a busy Sunday lunch, is to be read in Kreissle's biography. The source of the story, Josef Doppler, who worked for the publisher Spina, probably added a few details, and changed a few as well, in order to make his anecdote more startling, Schubert's small notebook that he took on his walks evolving into a menu card. Sadly, such embellishment of personal reminiscences communicated years after the event became a commonplace.

Autograph:	Wienbibliothek im Rathaus, Vienna (first draft)
First edition:	Published as Book 7 no. 4 of the *Nachlass* by Diabelli, Vienna in October 1830 (P253)
Subsequent editions:	Peters: Vol. 1/234; AGA XX 503: Vol. 8/228; NSA IV: Vol. 14/18
Bibliography:	Capell 1928, pp. 224–5
	Fischer-Dieskau 1977, p. 233
Arrangements:	Arr. Franz Liszt (1811–1886) for solo piano, no. 9 of *Lieder von Schubert* (1837–8) [*see* TRANSCRIPTIONS]
	Arr. Arnold Schoenberg (1874–1951) for voice, clarinet, bassoon, mandolin, guitar and string quartet (1921) [*see* ORCHESTRATIONS]
Discography and timing:	Fischer-Dieskau II 8[12] 1'38
	Hyperion I 26[13]
	Hyperion II 32[10] 1'33 Christine Schäfer

← *Trinklied D888*   *Gesang (An Silvia) D891* →

STÄNDCHEN (Zögernd leise)   Serenade   Alto solo & male/female
(GRILLPARZER) **D920** [H629]   chorus

The song exists in two versions, both of which are discussed below:
(1) July 1827; (2) July 1827

(1)   F major [For A solo and TTBB]

(2)   F major [For A solo and SSAA]

Zögernd, leise[1]	Softly, hesitantly,
In des Dunkels nächt'ger Hülle[2]	Cloaked in night's darkness,
Sind wir hier;	We have come here,
Und den Finger sanft gekrümmt,	And with fingers gently curled,
Leise, leise,	Softly, softly
Pochen wir	We knock
An des Liebchens Kammertür.	On the beloved's bedroom door.
Doch nun steigend,	But now, our emotion rising,
Schwellend, schwellend,[3]	Swelling,
Hebend mit vereinter Stimme, laut,[4]	Surging, with united voice
Rufen aus wir hochvertraut:	We call out loud, in warm friendship:
Schlaf' du nicht,	'Do not sleep
Wenn der Neigung Stimme spricht!	when the voice of affection speaks!'
Sucht' ein Weiser nah' und ferne	Once a wise man with his lantern
Menschen einst mit der Laterne;	Sought people near and far;
Wie viel selt'ner dann als Gold,	How much rarer, then, than gold
Menschen uns geneigt und hold?	Are people who are fondly disposed towards us?
D'rum, wenn Freundschaft, Liebe spricht	And so, when friendship and love speak,
Freundin, Liebchen, schlaf' du nicht! –	Do not sleep, friend, beloved!
Aber was in allen Reichen	But what in all the world's realms
Wär' dem Schlummer zu vergleichen?	Can be compared to sleep?
[(. . . 2 lines . . .)][5]	[(. . . 2 lines . . .)]
D'rum statt Worten und statt Gaben,	And so, instead of words and gifts,
Sollst du nun auch Ruhe haben;	You shall now have rest.
Noch ein Grüsschen, noch ein Wort,	Just one more greeting, one more word;
Es verstummt die frohe Weise,	And our happy song ceases.
Leise, leise,	Softly, softly
Schleichen wir uns wieder fort.[6]	We steal away again.

FRANZ GRILLPARZER (1791–1872); poem written in July 1827

The circumstances surrounding the birth of this delicious *pièce d'occasion* tell us a good deal about Schubert's personality, and about how his friends tended to regard him as an effortlessly flowing, and inexhaustible, fount of entertainment and amusement. One must remember that the song was 'commissioned' at the time the composer was working on his last opera, *Der Graf von Gleichen* D918, and he probably had to interrupt work on that big piece (which he never finished) to write it. This was, after all, the year of very great music, of *Winterreise* D911 for example, a task that took a great amount of effort and spiritual introspection. *Ständchen* was

---

[1] Grillparzer writes (*Gedichte*, 1872) 'Zögend *stille*'.
[2] In the second version 'In des Dunkels nächt' ger *Stille*'. In neither version is Grillparzer's original half-rhyme 'Hülle'–'Stille' observed.
[3] Grillparzer writes (*Gedichte*, 1872) '*Hebend*, schwellend'.
[4] Schubert adds 'Hebend' to Grillparzer's line (the word has been displaced from the previous line) and he changes the punctuation. Grillparzer's original reads 'Mit vereinter Stimme, laut'.
[5] The lines are 'Was du hast und weisst und bist / Zahlt nicht, was der Schlaf vergisst' ('what you have and know and are / count for nothing they are forgotten in sleep'.
[6] Schubert adds a 'ja' to the final line with the repetition of the words 'schleichen wir' ('schleichen wir, *ja* schleichen wir uns wieder fort'), although this is only in the first version.

conceived as a surprise tribute for the twenty-fourth birthday of Louise Gosmar (1803–1858). An entry in the diary of Franz von Hartmann for February 1827 implies that Fräulein Gosmar was knowledgeable about Schubert's music and liked it. She was born of a prosperous Jewish family, and was later to marry Leopold von Sonnleithner, an admirer of Schubert's who played a key role in brokering the deal that first brought the composer's songs to the printed page in 1821. This birthday was hardly an event in the composer's intimate circle, but Gosmar and her prospective husband were rich and important enough for her singing teacher, Anna Fröhlich, to go to quite a bit of trouble on her behalf. This included enlisting Schubert to write music to the poem that Grillparzer (who was part of the Sonnleithner family) had already provided. Let the redoubtable Anna, on this evidence the Lilian Baylis of Biedermeier Vienna, continue the story in her own words:

> I said to him 'Look Schubert, you must set this to music for me' . . . He looked at the sheet of paper for a while and finally said 'There, it is finished now, I've got it already.' And only three days later he really did bring it to me, finished, set for mezzo soprano (that is my sister Pepi [Josefine Fröhlich]) and four men's voices. At this I said to him 'No, Schubert, I can't use it like this, it's meant to be a tribute from Fräulein Gosmar's women friends only. You must write me the chorus for women's voices.' I remember quite clearly saying this to him; he was sitting over there in the right-hand window recess of the ante-room. – And soon afterwards he brought it to me, set for Pepi's voice and women's chorus . . .

On 11 August 1827 three carriages transported the chorus of ladies from Vienna to Döbling, and a piano was secretly moved into the front garden to surprise the celebrant. The Fröhlich sisters were disappointed that Schubert did not turn up to this first performance. He would also have escaped the second had they not sent someone to track him down to his favourite coffee house and haul him to the concert. In Schubertian annals this behaviour is always put down to forgetfulness; time and time again, and always taken at his word, the composer used this excuse to protect himself from company and events that were unnecessary to him and his work. It is perhaps the one negative trait of the Viennese character, unjustly renowned for dissembling perhaps, but with a reputation for guile nevertheless, that we find in Schubert. On this occasion he is hardly to be blamed.

We must, however, be grateful to the importunate Fröhlich sisters. Both versions of the song are beautiful; if the setting for men's chorus is to be preferred, it is because Schubert first envisioned the piece with these forces. The idea of a group of women prowling around at night to sing to the 'Freundin' would have seemed faintly ridiculous to a composer steeped in the gallant tradition of the nocturnal serenade in staccato semiquavers. A tentative tiptoe dalliance, with the lightest of knocks on the door, is superbly conveyed by the gentle but pointed moto perpetuo accompaniment. The words 'steigend [b. 15], schwellend [b. 16], hebend [b. 17]' are made for music and modulation, and Schubert exploits this to the full. The masterful quasi-fugal passage between bb. 28 and 31 and then bb. 36 and 39 (somehow perfect for the solemn searchings of a short-sighted wise man with swinging lantern – as if an academic schooled in the rigours of old-fashioned music) is a bow to the Men in Armour in *Die Zauberflöte*, and an indication that Schubert was finding counterpoint more and more interesting (he soon arranged to take lessons in it from the acknowledged Viennese expert, Simon Sechter). In fact Grillparzer is here referring to the story of Diogenes, who went around with his lantern lighted in daylight hours, explaining that he was seeking 'einen Menschen' – a human worthy of being called so. Grillparzer playfully ignores the cynic's taunts and turns the lofty singular concept of 'Man' into the plural – 'people' – people moreover who are loving ('geneigt und hold').

Friendship and love ('Freundschaft, Liebe' in bb. 44–5) cut a swathe through the pedantry, and the purest melody returns. An extraordinary touch of humour is the composer's built-in smile acknowledging the length of the piece. Just when the serenaded sweetheart is promised rest, and we think the proceedings are to be wound up, we are warned in bb. 64–6 of one more greeting, one more word ('Noch ein Grüsschen, noch ein Wort') and the music sets off again. The exit is charmingly managed in quasi-operatic style; indeed this work has something in common with the haunting nocturnal chorus, 'Still noch decket uns die Nacht' that opens *Alfonso und Estrella* D732.

The revision of this work – changing male chorus into female – entailed more hard work than anyone realized. The piano part, it is true, stays the same (there are some articulation differences between the versions) but the composer ensures that the part-writing for the second version (SSAA) takes careful account of the balance of sonorities within the new forces. It seems possible that he had also been taken to task for overtaxing the soloist (perhaps further observations from the exigent Anna Fröhlich?) because the second version is less demanding in terms of tessitura; there is also slightly more recovery time between the solo passages. In b. 23 the dotted-rhythm setting of 'Schlaf du nicht' is a new detail prefacing a fortissimo high D flat in b. 24 (not a more dramatic F, as in the first version). Unlike the first version the singer takes a rest in bb. 30–31 and again in bb. 38–9. In bb. 40–41 the repeat of the phrase 'Wie viel seltner dann als Gold / Menschen uns geneigt und hold' is now sung as a solo without choral competition (bb. 32–3). In b. 44 Schubert makes an adjustment whereby a tricky to execute piece of word-setting is simplified. In the first version a clash between the final syllables of the words 'spricht' (chorus) and 'Freund*schaft*' (soloist) was avoided by double dotting the solo singer's minim on 'Freund' so that -schaft is set to a quaver sung after the choral 'spricht'. For the second version Schubert abandons this refinement (or perhaps he thought it fussy) and allows the two words to sound together. In b. 52 the vocal line on 'Liebchen, schlaf du nicht' is recast in a graceful and curvaceous rising and falling phrase. In b. 71 the rhythm and word-setting are simplified, replacing a more difficult chromatic ascent in the first version; the composer no longer needs to add a rhetorical 'ja' to Grillparzer's text. Decisions such as these are unlikely to have taken Schubert a great deal of time but they show what a thorough craftsman he was. What they cannot indicate is whether the composer preferred the second version (required of him) over the one he first wrote. This seems unlikely.

Here and there Schubert changes Grillparzer's words (it is of course possible that the poet changed them himself between the composition of the music and the very late publication of his *Gedichte* in 1872). These changes are detailed in the footnotes to the poem.

Autographs:	Wienbibliothek im Rathaus, Vienna (first version)
	Music Academy Library [Mushino Ongaku Diagaku], Tokyo (second version)
Publication:	First published as part of the AGA in 1891 (P510; first version)
	First published as Op. post. 135 by Diabelli, Vienna in *c.* 1840 (P330; second version)
First known performance:	Version with female voices performed 24 January 1828, *Abend-Unterhaltung* of the Gesellschaft der Musikfreunde, Vienna. Soloist: Josefine Fröhlich (see Waidelich/Hilmar Dokumente I No. 570 for full concert programme). Fröhlich had previously performed this song privately in Döbling on 11 August 1827 (see Deutsch Doc. Biog. No. 921)

Contemporary reviews:	*Allgemeine Musikalische Zeitung* (Leipzig) No. 13 (26 March 1828), col. 206 [Waidelich/Hilmar Dokumente I No. 605; Deutsch Doc. Biog. No. 1017]
Subsequent editions:	AGA XIX 14: p. 108 (first version), XVIII 4, p. 20 (second version); NSA III: Vol. 3
Arrangements:	Arr. Felix Mottl (1856–1911) for voices and orchestra, *Ständchen* (1891) [see ORCHESTRATIONS]
Discography and timing:	Hyperion I 8[16] 6'02 Sarah Walker with male Hyperion II 33[17] chorus

← *Das Lied im Grünen* D917   *L'incanto degli occhi* D902/1 →

STÄNDCHEN (Rellstab) *see SCHWANENGESANG* D957/4

Die STERBENDE
(MATTHISSON) **D186** [H88]
A♭ major   May 1815

The dying girl

(25 bars)

Heil! dies ist die letzte Zähre,
  Die der Müden Aug' entfällt!
Schon entschattet sich die Sphäre
  Ihrer heimatlichen Welt.
Leicht, wie Frühlingsnebel schwinden,
  Ist des Lebens Traum entflohn,
Paradiesesblumen winden
  Seraphim zum Kranze schon!

[...]

Horch! im heilgen Hain der Palmen,
  Wo der Strom des Lebens fliesst,
Tönt es in der Engel Psalmen:
  Schwesterseele, sei gegrüsst!
Die empor mit Adlerschnelle
  Zu des Lichtes Urquell stieg;
Tod! wo ist dein Stachel? Hölle!
  Stolze Hölle! wo dein Sieg?

Hail! This is the last tear
  To fall from the weary girl's eyes.
Already the sphere of her familiar world
  Is shadowed.
The dream of life has fled
  As lightly as spring mists vanish;
Already seraphim are weaving flowers of paradise
  Into a wreath.

[...]

Hark! In the holy land of palms
  Where the stream of life flows,
The angels' psalms resound:
  'Greetings, sisterly soul!
You have risen up, swift as an eagle,
  To the source of light.
Death, where is your sting? Hell,
  Proud hell, where is your victory?'

FRIEDRICH VON MATTHISSON (1761–1831); poem written in 1780

This is the seventeenth of Schubert's twenty-nine Matthisson solo settings (1812–17). See the poet's biography for a chronological list of all the Matthisson settings.

On paper there is nothing to this song at all although the opening word 'Heil' is a startling beginning. Apart from a pleasant modulation to Schubert's beloved subdominant in b. 9 it seems an anaemic, rather colourless chorale. Then one realizes that these apparently dull qualities can be turned to the performers' advantage (provided the singer is skilful enough): a dying girl is hardly likely to be other than pale and withdrawn, and her vision of the next life is appropriately outlined by music of piety and simplicity. The insubstantial nature of life, like spring mists, is painted in a vocal line that is without a bass at 'Leicht, wie Frühlingsnebel' (b. 10–11) and then supported by tolling bells in E flat octaves (in the left hand at bb. 11–12; cf. the passing bells, also on E♭, in *Das Zügenglöcklein* D871). The piano part under the line 'Ist des Lebens Traum entflohn' is broken by airy rests, as if already afloat, separate from the world, and at peace. With the dying fall of the postlude to the last verse ('Stolze Hölle! wo dein Sieg', a passage imitated by Matthisson from Herder via Alexander Pope) we can almost hear the girl's spirit leaving her body. The poem is about Elisa, who is also addressed in *Trost. An Elisa* D97. Matthisson's friend Rosenfeld had died young and his fiancée, Elisa had, in turn, died of a broken heart. There is certainly no raging against the dying light here, only the most maidenly of expirations. How deliberately different this is from that other moment of death, valiant rather than resigned, in *Verklärung* D59, the younger Schubert's 1813 setting of Herder's translation of Pope's lines, concluding with a much more pugnacious 'O Death! where is thy sting?'

Matthisson's poem has three strophes, of which 1 and 3 are printed above. In the Hyperion Edition Elly Ameling sings 'Wo *ist* dein Sieg' at the end of the song (as printed in the AGA, but incorrect in terms of Matthisson's metre). This third strophe does not appear in Schubert's autograph (only the first has an underlay) so the additional word is one of the few literary errors on Mandyczewski's part. In fact it is possible to sing the metrically correct 'Wo dein Sieg' by allocating to 'Wo' two sung notes – and this is exactly how it has appeared, belatedly, in the NSA in 2009.

The first eleven bars are vigorously struck through on the autograph, probably by the composer himself. Eusebius Mandyczewski (AGA *Revisionsbericht*, Series XX p. 17) believed that Schubert, frustrated by some aspect of the music's unsuitability for a later strophe, intended to cancel the entire setting. There is a possibility, of course, that he found the end result sentimental, even tasteless. Matthisson's use of his friend's dying fiancée as a theme may seem exploitative to present-day readers. It is a rare editor, however, who is prepared to throw away a Schubert song, however problematic.

Autograph:	In private possession, Vienna
First edition:	Published as part of the AGA in 1895 (P559)
Subsequent editions:	Not in Peters; AGA XX 65: Vol. 2/100; NSA IV: Vol. 8/40
Bibliography:	Hoorickx 1976, p. 156
Discography and timing:	Fischer-Dieskau —

Hyperion I 7[6]
Hyperion II 6[7]   2'43   Elly Ameling

← *Trinklied* D183   *Stimme der Liebe* D187 →

Die STERNE

(FELLINGER) **D176** [H82]

A♭ major   6 April 1815

The stars

Lieblich, ziemlich langsam

Was fun - kelt ihr so mild mich an? ihr Ster - ne, hold __ und hehr! __

(19 bars)

Was funkelt ihr so mild mich an?
Ihr Sterne, hold und hehr!
Was treibet euch auf dunkler Bahn
Im ätherblauen Meer?
Wie Gottes Augen schaut ihr dort,
Aus Ost und West, aus Süd und Nord,
So freundlich auf mich her.

Und überall umblinkt ihr mich
Mit sanftem Dämmerlicht,
Die Sonne hebt im Morgen sich,
Doch ihr verlasst mich nicht,
Wenn kaum der Abend wieder graut,
So blickt ihr mir, so fromm und traut,
Schon wieder ins Gesicht.

Willkommen denn, willkommen mir!
Ihr Freunde, still und bleich!
Wie lichte Geister wandelt ihr
Durch euer weites Reich,
Und ach! vielleicht begrüsset mich
Ein edler, der zu früh verblich,
Ein treuer Freund aus euch!

Vielleicht wird einst mein Aufenthalt
Im hellen Sirius,
Wenn diese kleine Wurmgestalt
Die Hülle wechseln muss;
Vielleicht erhebt der Funke Geist
Wenn diese schwache Form zerreisst,
Sich auf zum Uranus!

O lächelt nur! o winket nur,
Mir still zu euch hinan!
Mich führet Mutter Allnatur

Why do you sparkle so gently at me,
You stars, so noble and so fair;
What drives you on your dark course
Through the blue ocean of the ether?
Like the eyes of God,
From east and west, north and south,
You gaze kindly down on me.

Everywhere you bathe me
In soft, dusky light.
The sun rises in the morning,
But you never forsake me.
Evening hardly darkens
Before you shine, so pure and tender,
Once more upon my face.

Welcome then, welcome
Friends, pale and silent!
Like shining spirits you wander
Through your vast realm.
And ah, perhaps a noble, faithful friend,
Who perished too soon,
May greet me from among you!

Perhaps one day my abode
Will be upon bright Sirius,
When this small wormlike frame
Must change its skin;
Perhaps, when this feeble form is torn apart,
The spirit will rise like a spark
Up to Uranus.

O smile! O beckon me silently
Towards you!
Mother Nature guides me

Nach ihrem grossen Plan;	According to her great plan;
Mich kümmert nicht der Welten Fall,	The end of the world does not trouble me,
Wenn ich nur dort die Lieben all'	If only I can find all my loved ones
Vereinet finden kann.	United there.

JOHANN GEORG FELLINGER (1781–1816); poem written in 1812

This is the first of Schubert's three Fellinger solo settings (1815). See the poet's biography for a chronological list of all the Fellinger settings.

This enchanting and graceful little strophic song, a lilting *berceuse*, is a worthy companion to Schubert's other starry songs and it veritably glints with evening light (the marking is 'Lieblich', cf. the much later *Der liebliche Stern* D861). The mood of piety and gratitude precisely reflects Fellinger's verses, and is cheery without losing the sense of awe that characterizes Schubert's nature songs with a religious overtone. The accompaniment with its semi-staccato open fifths in the bass, quietly insistent (Schubert seems to understand that there are pulsations in the emanation of light); these support a right hand that delightedly dances in the heavens. The gazing eyes of God ('Wie Gottes Augen schaut ihr dort') twinkle high in the stratosphere of the keyboard (bb. 9–12), leaping octaves in an enchantingly cheeky dotted rhythm. The four-bar postlude is one of artful simplicity – one might imagine it easy to imitate Schubert in this mode until someone tries to do so, inevitably unsuccessfully. The final two bars of the piano part are an ascending arpeggio directing our gaze ever upwards and encompassing two octaves.

Fellinger's poem has five strophes of which 1, 2, and 5 were recorded for the Hyperion Edition.

Autograph:	In private possession, Princeton, NJ
First edition:	Published as No. 30 of *Neueste Folge nachgelassener Lieder und Gesänge* by J. P. Gotthard, Vienna in 1872 (P456)
Subsequent editions:	Not in Peters; AGA XX 57: Vol. 2/86; NSA IV: Vol. 8/25; Bärenreiter: Vol. 6/120
Discography and timing:	Fischer-Dieskau I 3[9] 2'32
	Hyperion I 19[10] 2'50 Felicity Lott
	Hyperion II 6[1]

← *Das war ich (I)* D174   *Vergebliche Liebe* D177 →

Die STERNE   The stars

(KOSEGARTEN) **D313** [H192]
B♭ major   19 October 1815

(20 bars)

Wie wohl ist mir im Dunkeln!	How happy I am in the darkness!
Wie weht die laue Nacht!	How warm the night breeze!
Die Sterne Gottes funkeln	God's stars glitter
In feierlicher Pracht.	In their solemn splendour.
Komm', Ida, komm' ins Freie,	Come, Ida, into the open air
Und lass in jene Bläue	And let us gaze up in wonder
Und lass zu jenen Höhn	At the blue sky
Uns staunend aufwärts sehn.	And at those peaks.
[. . .]	[. . .]
O Sterne Gottes, Zeugen	God's stars, witnesses
Und Boten bessrer Welt,	And harbingers of a better world,
Ihr heisst den Aufruhr schweigen,	You silence the tumult
Der unsern Busen schwellt.	Which fills our breast.
Ich seh' hinauf, ihr Hehren,	I gaze up, lofty stars,
Zu euren lichten Sphären,	To your shining spheres,
Und Ahndung bessrer Lust[1]	And a presentiment of higher bliss
Stillt die empörte Brust.	Calms my incensed heart.
[. . . 4 . . .]	[. . . 4 . . .]
O Sterne Gottes, Boten	God's stars, messengers
Und Bürger bessrer Welt,	And citizens of a better world,
Die ihr die Nacht der Toten	Who brighten the night of the dead
Zu milder Dämm'rung hellt!	To a soft half-light.
Umschimmert sanft die Stätte,	Cast your gentle radiance around me
Wo ich aus stillem Bette	When I awaken from my silent bed
Und süssem Schlaf' erwach	And sweet slumber
Zu Edens schönerm Tag!	To a fairer day in Eden.

LUDWIG KOSEGARTEN (1758–1818)

This is the fourteenth of Schubert's twenty-one Kosegarten solo settings (1815–17). See the poet's biography for a chronological list of all the Kosegarten settings, as well as a discussion of Morten Solvik's Kosegarten Liederkreis and this song's place within it.

This song has remained thoroughly, and inexplicably, unappreciated by commentators. It captures, using the simplest musical means, the feelings of exaltation and rapture that run through almost all of the Schubert songs on this theme. The opening words, 'Wie wohl ist mir im Dunkeln!', suggest the intimacy of the narrator at peace with the world, hugging to himself the feelings that no one can take from him – a communing with nature that provides some of mankind's most transcendental experiences, as well as some of Schubert's greatest works. That it should have been written on the same piece of music paper as the light-hearted and somewhat risqué Körner setting, *Das gestörte Glück* D309, is a small indication of the composer's Protean nature.

[1]Kosegarten writes '*Ahnung*' rather than '*Ahndung*'.

The song is made up of a hymn tune but it flies free of the modest church-like resonances of works of this type with the attenuated starry tessitura of its vocal line. In this respect it is reminiscent of the 1819 Mayrhofer masterpiece *Die Sternennächte* D670 where the voice also seems suspended in outer space. To achieve this feeling of other-worldliness the opening bars are made to seem almost ungrounded, without a strong bass line; it is only on the words 'feierli-cher Pracht' (bb. 6–8) that substantial forte chords add majesty to what has been hitherto an ethereal picture. The invitation from b. 8 to Ida ('Komm', Ida, komm' ins Freie') begins on the supertonic of the home key of B flat but by b. 12 we have reached the distant key of A flat. Experts have commented on this being an unusual feature but without discussing what led to it. It is Schubert's desire, surely, to evoke the colour blue – radiant and in the far distance – that has prompted this change, and it suggests mystery and wonder 'in jene Bläue' as well as a warmth of colour quite different from that of the silvery stars. The phrase 'zu jenen Höhn' at the end of the first strophe (bb. 13–14) aspires to the heights and the top of the vocal compass. The final vocal cadence seems rather more special in the *ossia* (printed in the NSA) with its downward jump of a fifth. The postlude (bb. 16–20) is very simple, yet miraculous. No one could say why a succession of chords that at first sight seem to have come from a hymnal has such a profound effect. It is enough to acknowledge that Schubert is master of using the most economical means to achieve the deepest things. These four bars preceded by an upbeat (marked forte) are worthy not only of the majesty of the heavens but of the humility of the star-struck amateur astronomer.

There are eight strophes in Kosegarten's poem of which 1, 3 and 8 (as recorded for the Hyperion Edition) are printed and translated above.

Autograph:	Houghton Library, Harvard University, Cambridge, MA (fair copy)
	In private possession (first draft)
First edition:	Published as part of the AGA in 1895 (P599)
Subsequent editions:	Not in Peters; AGA XX 160: Vol. 3/142; NSA IV: Vol. 9/148
Discography and timing:	Fischer-Dieskau I 5³⁴ 2'06 (first two strophes only)

Discography and timing: Fischer-Dieskau I 5^{34} 2'06   (first two strophes only)
Hyperion I 22^{19}
Hyperion II 11^{4} 3'21   Jamie MacDougall

← *Hektors Abschied* D312   *Nachtgesang* D314 →

Die STERNE   The stars
(F. VON SCHLEGEL) **D684** [H440]
E♭ major   1819? Or 1820

Du staunest, o Mensch, was heilig wir strahlen?	You marvel, O man, at our sacred radiance?
O folgtest du nur den himmlischen Mächten,[1]	If only you followed the heavenly powers
Vernähmest du besser, was freundlich wir blinken,	You would understand better how benignly we twinkle,
Wie wären verschwunden die irdischen Qualen!	How earthly suffering would vanish!
Dann flösse die Liebe aus ewigen Schalen,	Then love would flow from eternal vessels,
Es atmeten alle in reinen Azuren,	All would breathe the pure azure,
Das lichtblaue Meer umschwebte die Fluren,	The light-blue sea would lap about the meadows,
Und funkelten Sterne auf den heimischen Talen.[2]	And stars would sparkle in our native valleys.
Aus göttlicher Quelle sind alle genommen,	All spring from a divine source;
Ist jegliches Wesen nicht eines im Chore?	Is not all creation united in the choir?
Nun sind ja geöffnet die himmlischen Tore,	Now the heavenly gates are open,
Was soll denn das bange Verzagen noch frommen?	Of what avail is timorous despair?
O wäret ihr schon zur Tiefe geklommen,	If you had already climbed to the depths
So sähet das Haupt ihr von Sternen umflogen	You would see the stars circling around your head,
Und spielend um's Herz die kindlichen Wogen,	And the childlike waves, unruffled by life's storms,
Zu denen die Stürme des Lebens nicht kommen.	Playing about your heart.

FRIEDRICH VON SCHLEGEL (1772–1829); poem written in 1800/1801

This is the the the sixth of Schubert's sixteen Friedrich von Schlegel solo settings (1818–25). See the poet's biography for a chronological list of all the Friedrich von Schlegel settings. See also the article about the cycle of which this song is part – Abendröte.

This is one of the most powerful of the Schlegel settings. Capell groups it together with the song *Abendröte* D690 under the adjective 'visionary', and it is true that both works share that quality, aided by the depth of their respective poems. Whether or not Schubert intended both strophes of *Die Sterne* to be sung is not altogether clear. The Peters Edition follows the posthumous first edition and prints only one strophe of Schlegel's poem. However, there is no doubt that the song makes better sense with the complete text. The second verse reinforces the Schlegelian philosophy to which we have been introduced at the beginning of the poet's cycle – the concept of all creation united in the choir of life.

As in much of Schubert's music of this period (1818–20), this song has a strong Italian influence; it is linked in this way to *Der Fluss* D693. On the printed page it has the look of an operatic cantilena to the point that interesting verbal prosody seems to have been sacrificed for the smoothness of the vocal line, and where the composer has been content to allow most of the accompaniment to consist of rather bland triplets. This, however, is to reckon without divine inspiration, for this simplicity is highly sophisticated and intentional. The stars are not light-

---

[1]Schlegel writes 'O folgest du nur den himmlischen *Winken*' (to rhyme with 'blinken' in the following line).
[2]Schlegel writes 'Und funkelten *Stern*' auf den heimischen Talen'.

weight human beings whose rhythms move hither and thither; their radiance is for all time and undisturbed by temporal considerations. Thus they sing 'unruffled by life's storms' and, in the right performers' larynx and hands, this song radiates peace and a celestial aura that is both touching and impersonal in the sense that it is above all human strife.

The key is E flat major, and it is interesting that Schubert was later to choose this tonality again for his other great song about the stars, *Die Sterne* D939 of Leitner. The opening bar is a simple triplet arpeggio in the home key of E flat, followed by a spread-chord dotted minim on the same notes, three beats in all (in 𝄴 time). This is followed by a bar where the same music is crucially modified by sharpening the B flat to a B natural, thus making an augmented triad on the dominant that Richard Kramer has noted is something of a code in the Schlegel settings. (This thumbprint is also found in *Der Fluss*, *Die Gebüsche* D646 and *Sonett III* D629.) We stay on that augmented chord for a pregnant two beats, the effect of which is to suggest the gradual opening up of a natural mystery, as if we were being allowed to pass through the portals of the heavens. This impression of being led somewhere, of being taken by the hand into a sacred shrine, continues with the remainder of the introduction as it moves from the subdominant (b. 3) back to the tonic.

The stars then begin their address. The dotted-rhythm triplets we hear in the accompaniment in these opening bars derive from Schubert's response to the verb 'staunen', and express mankind's astonished reaction to the radiance of the stars; the piano thus asks voiceless questions on behalf of perplexed humanity, as the stars gently reprove us, light of heart and with hearts of light. With the fifth line and from the upbeat to b. 13 ('Dann flösse die Liebe aus ewigen Schalen') we come to the core of the song – something of a starry manifesto. For this music, which is in the subdominant key of A flat major, the deepest peace reigns: all bumpy rhythms are ironed out in the accompaniment (nothing but triplets underpin this aria) and the voice part broadens to a point where only a vocal star can manage the long-breathed phrases. It is here that Schubert defies the normal rules of prosody by giving a dotted crotchet (six in all) to each of the syllables 'flös - se die Lie - be aus'. How superb this is to convey the generous outpouring of love to starving mankind; the sound is spread as smoothly across the stave as butter on heavenly bread. It is unreasonable, of course, that after these two bars the singer should be required to extend this line and rise, without further breath, to the top of the phrase, hold an appropriately long note for 'e – wigen' (eternal, b. 15) and then descend to 'Schalen' without gasping or fainting. With scarcely pause for breath, and as if to illustrate the difference between inhalation and exhalation, the same musical phrase is inverted, another six dotted crotchets (descending three at a time) for 'at - me - ten al - le in' plus another crowning phrase on 'rei - nen Azuren'. And so the song continues on its way, each phrase the most stringent test of singing technique, and each sublimely beautiful when sung well. The pianist, with not much to do, can only listen in astonishment, as described by the poem, along with the rest of mankind.

This is one of those songs where virtuosic demands constitute something of a spiritual challenge, the surmounting of which is part of the music's power. The singer with the breath control needed to execute these phrases seems synonymous with someone who has 'seen the light'. With these musical difficulties it is little wonder that the piece did not find a publisher in Schubert's lifetime. By the time of its composition Schubert was a master of the strophic song (his apprenticeship in this area had been completed in 1815/16 when he acquired his ability to find music that equally suited all the strophes of a poem). In the second verse we notice details that seem specially arranged for the new words: 'Nun sind ja geöffnet die himmlischen Tore' is supported by a piano line that blossoms outwards, opening up like a gate as it gently climbs the stave (bb. 8–10); the airy setting of 'von Sternen umflogen' (bb. 19–20) is particulary appropriate for the image of stars circling around the singer's head, high in the tessitura, each note a jewel in the constellation's diadem.

The lack of a postlude in a song of this significance makes the ending feel rather peremptory. Although there is nothing to authorize it, the pianist is tempted to return to the beginning and play the introduction again. (Diabelli's solution, when publishing the song in the *Nachlass*, was to elongate the cadence.) Perhaps Schubert was right to end the music in mid-heaven, as if leaving the stars to their eternal work while mankind is unable to maintain indefinite contact with their wavelength. A postlude with its almost inevitable rallentando might imply that these wise immortals are somehow or other under our control.

Autograph:	Missing or lost
First edition:	Published as Book 48 no. 1 of the *Nachlass* by Diabelli, Vienna in Spring 1850 (P380)
Subsequent editions:	Peters: Vol. 6/58; AGA XX 378: Vol. 6/102; NSA IV: Vol. 12/131
Bibliography:	Capell 1928, p. 166
	Kramer 1994, pp. 211–12
Discography and timing:	Fischer-Dieskau II 3[20] 3'51
	Hyperion I 27[17]
	Hyperion II 22[15] 5'08 Matthias Goerne

← *Über allen Zauber Liebe* D682   *Morgenlied* D685 →

Die STERNE   The stars
(LEITNER) OP. 96 NO. 1, **D939** [H658]
E♭ major   January 1828

(188 bars)

(1) Wie blitzen   How brightly
Die Sterne   The stars
So hell durch die Nacht!   Glitter through the night!
Bin oft schon   I have often
Darüber   Been aroused by them
Vom Schlummer erwacht.   From slumber.

(2) Doch schelt' ich   But I do not chide
Die lichten   The shining beings
Gebilde drum nicht,   For that,
Sie üben   For they
Im Stillen   Quietly perform
Manch' heilsame Pflicht.   Many a healing task.

(3)	Sie wallen	They wander
	Hoch oben	High above
	In Engelgestalt,	In the form of angels;
	Sie leuchten	They light
	Dem Pilger	The pilgrim's way
	Durch Heiden und Wald.	Through heath and wood.

(4)	Sie schweben	They hover
	Als Boten	Like harbingers
	Der Liebe umher,	Of love,
	Und tragen	And often
	Oft Küsse	Bear kisses
	Weit über das Meer.	Far across the sea.

(5)	Sie blicken[1]	They gaze
	Dem Dulder	Tenderly
	Recht mild in's Gesicht,	Into the sufferer's face,
	Und säumen	And fringe
	Die Tränen	His tears
	Mit silbernem Licht.	With silver light;

(6)	Und weisen	And comfortingly,
	Von Gräbern	Gently,
	Gar tröstlich und hold	Direct us away from the grave,
	Uns hinter	Beyond
	Das Blaue	The azure
	Mit Fingern von Gold.	With fingers of gold.

(7)	So sei denn	I bless you,
	Gesegnet,	Radiant throng!
	Du strahlige Schar!	Long may you shine
	Und leuchte	Upon me
	Mir lange	With your clear,
	Noch freundlich und klar.	Pleasing light!

(8)	Und wenn ich	And if one day
	Einst liebe,	I fall in love,
	Seid hold dem Verein,	Then smile upon the bond,
	Und Euer	And let
	Geflimmer	Your twinkling
	Lasst Segen uns sein.	Be a blessing upon us.

For the Reclam Edition of Leitner's *Gedichte* (*c.* 1890) the versification of this poem is changed to something rather more conventional in appearance: lines 1 and 2 are run together to make a single line, also lines 4 and 5. This makes for a succession of four-line strophes infintely less evocative than the original.

---

[1] Leitner writes 'Sie *flimmern*'.

KARL GOTTFRIED VON LEITNER (1800–1890); poem written in 1819

This is the last of Schubert's eleven Leitner solo settings (1822–3 and 1827–8). See the poet's biography for a chronological list of all the Leitner settings.

One of the best-loved of all the composer's nature depictions, this song effortlessly combines the cosy and the universal. This is definitely a view of the heavens from Styria where the poet appropriates the stars as his own and imagines them as good and worthy citizens of the heavens – twinkling philanthropists performing many a charitable task in that cheery context where one member of the community sees it as his duty to look after another. These stars shine down on a world that is 'artless and sincere' (Schubert's words to Marie Pachler when describing how he found Graz different from Vienna). In this part of Austria the pilgrim still walks earnestly through the wood; it is still accepted that God is in his heaven which is situated, like the stars themselves, in the azure above; and falling in love is still something that happens once in a lifetime, where a lasting bond is sealed with a celestial blessing.

The earlier commentators have been less than kind about Leitner. Capell refers to his sentiments as 'feeble-minded' and Einstein as 'pedantic and sentimental'. But Schubert is quite obviously charmed by this view of life from the safety of uncynical Styria, and responds to it with a full heart – if occasionally with a smile. The poetry fits happily with the composer's own experience of Graz as a place apart; his fortnight there in 1827 was somehow caught in a time warp that made the harmless anachronisms of Leitner's verse perfectly valid. Besides, Schubert is often in two minds about many things: during the autumn of 1827 he penned *Im Dorfe* D911/17 from *Winterreise* where a traveller standing outside in the cold pours scorn on bourgeois values and those who dream safely in cushioned beds; from the same period comes Leitner's *Der Winterabend* D938, a touching hymn to moonlight and past love sung from inside a warm, comfortable house by an honest citizen from a Biedermeier world who would have regarded that frozen misanthrope as a disconcerting visitor from another world.

One could not be a song composer in search of different texts without a certain element of Keats's 'negative capability' – an openness to make of oneself a blank sheet of paper waiting for the imprint of inspiration and experience from another source. Thus it is no surprise that the same composer could set to music the dark and comfortless pronouncements of the choral setting by Seidl, *Grab und Mond* D893, and *Die Sterne* where the narrator seems not to have a moment of doubt about his faith in a divinely ordered world. Schubert acts as a roving reporter in sound, scurrying around to gather up different sides of the same story: in the Schlegel setting *Die Sterne* D684 the words are directed to mankind by the stars themselves, and in the Leitner song the compliment is returned as an earthbound human being pays tribute to these heavenly bodies. The paradox is that in the prayer-like music for Schlegel's singing stars the awe of mankind is reflected, and in the Leitner setting, where the words are put in the mouth of a mere mortal, we hear the energy and movement of the stars themselves.

The key is E flat major and the time signature $\frac{2}{4}$ with a marking of 'Etwas geschwind'. The moderating 'etwas' is of the essence for finding the correct tempo: this song has given its performers more trouble than most in this respect – too fast and the music rushes and gabbles (the piece is often performed as if it were written with half the number of bar lines in an *alla breve* $\frac{2}{2}$); too slow and the sparkle of the heavenly bodies becomes sluggish. The short length of the bars is related to the versification of the text that is seldom printed correctly. Here is a clear case of the power of the appearance of the words on the printed page to influence the music. Apart from writing in dactylic metre, Leitner uses very short lines where pairs of words often stand alone, isolated like tiny stars, each contributing a single moment of sparkle to the night sky. Although Schubert runs the first three lines of the poem together to make a single musical phrase, the $\frac{2}{4}$ time signature, and the resulting proliferation of bar lines, provide strong beats (for example on 'blitzen' and 'Sterne' in the first verse) which preserve something of the poet's telegraphese. The placing of the piano's interludes also creates short, separate vocal phrases that shine separately, each in its own little galaxy.

As Capell observes, *Die Sterne* is 'a light and airy relation' of the Allegretto of Beethoven's Seventh Symphony Op. 92, that movement in measured dactyls (crotchet + two quavers or long–short–short) which was to be assimilated and recycled in so many ways by a Schubert enamoured of the musical energy generated by these pulsations within a moto perpetuo. In his own vocabulary of tonal analogues, a word-to-music language already fluent in his adolescence, and increasingly sophisticated over the years, the forward propulsion of dactylic metre measures the continuous spin of nature at work, the hidden, throbbing dynamo that powers those aspects of human existence over which we are powerless. Death strides or glides purposefully in this rhythm (*Der Tod und das Mädchen* D531, the Senn *Schwanengesang* D744 and another Leitner setting, *Vor meiner Wiege* D927). The sad and incontrovertible fact of love's betrayal, deadly in its own way, *Die Liebe hat gelogen* D751, has a similar *Bewegung*. The seasons too can be heard to march in this rhythm (as in the triumphant return of Maytime at the end of *Trockne Blumen* D795/18 from *Die schöne Müllerin*), and the world turns in dactyls as it gathers all, great and small, into its lap (*Lied 'Die Mutter Erde'* D788).

Die Sterne is similarly cosmic, the movement of the stars being sometimes immutable, sometimes variable, but always beyond human control. It is the sublime, hidden motor of the universe, ticking away and secretly performing this 'heilsame Pflicht', a steady musical hum, linking the centuries together, hums ancient and modern as it were. Death is mentioned but in a comforting way – that final journey remains a distant prospect in the song's astrological chart. After all, the poet has not yet found a partner for life's dance. In the meantime, the passing of time, the unrelenting tick-tock that makes something finite even of light years (or Leitner years perhaps) continues apace. Mention should be made here of the fifth of the *Moments musicaux* D780 – the 'Allegro vivace' in F minor, a piano piece contemporary with *Die Sterne*, which employs an insistent dactylic rhythm without any literary justification – although one might imagine that this determined, even furious, music concerns a fateful fiat of one kind of another.

The first thing we hear in this song is a musical translation of flickering sparks of distantly generated energy. The stars radiate electricity but the music seems to bristle with a measurable current, as if transmitting a message in Morse code from extraterrestrial beings. The sense of immense distance between the source of the message and its recipients is emphasized by the chain of modulations through which the sixteen-bar introduction passes. Here the repeated E flat major chords (with G at the top) seem at first to be a purely rhythmic gesture, but it soon becomes clear that these insistent notes (we hear ten of them) are part of a gradually changing tune: lift-off in slow motion. These dancing Gs are in the treble supplanted in b. 5 by seven B flats followed by four B naturals (from b. 7) which lead via a circular detour to ten repeated Cs (from b. 9). Onward and ever upward! These notes pulsate away (always in dactylic rhythm) while the harmony underneath changes from C^7 to F^7. As the right-hand melody progresses even further up the stave (D – E flat – F in b. 12) the harmonies move to B flat^7 and thence back to E flat, the completion of the full harmonic circle effected by a diabolically delicate little turn under the pianist's dancing fingers. (This decoration in the manner of something from a Haydn piano sonata is famously tricky, as is a similar mordent in the accompaniment for *Lachen und Weinen* D777.)

The journey implied by the introduction is both tiny and immense. Everything lies so closely under the pianist's hands that the vast expanses of space can be negotiated from the centre of the keyboard. But each link in this chain seems to represent a passage through a new galaxy where melody and harmony conjoin to give the impression of new vistas opening up in the music. That something should sound simultaneously so lofty and so friendly is a Schubertian miracle. The vocal line from b. 17 for 'Wie blitzen / Die Sterne / So hell durch die Nacht' sails easily up the stave, its shape a contraction of the more gradual ascent of the introduction. As the voice remains poised in space for 'Nacht' (bb. 21–2) the piano in b. 22 echoes the tail end of the vocal phrase in the alto line of its four-part texture. (These answering phrases are one of the song's many touches of genius – they imply a moment's lag as beams from distant planets take their time to reach us.) The poem's fourth, fifth and sixth lines ('Bin oft schon / Darüber / Vom Schlummer erwacht') make up the answering phrase to the first; this is a completion of a musical sentence, but the interjection of the little interlude sets it apart so that it sounds like a reply echoing across mountains and valleys or even galaxies.

The beginning of the second verse moves suddenly into C major (from b. 31), one of those astral turnings that are part of this song's magic. The composer then repeats the last three lines for a further little exploratory foray (bb. 42–6) which returns to E flat on 'heilsame Pflicht'. This music for the second half of Verse 2 turns out to be one of the two 'refrains' that bind the song together (the first is in fact the music for the entire first verse). Between every two of Leitner's strophes Schubert repeats the *Vorspiel* as an interlude.

The repetitive elements in this song make it seem as fixed in eternity as the stars themselves. Verses 1, 3, 5 and 7 share the same music, as do the second halves of verses 2, 4 and 6. Within this ordered universe the deviations and astral bends are all the more noticeable. Of the song's most magical moments one should single out the daring and ravishing excursion into the outer space of C flat major (from b. 76), before a safe return to the home ship docked in E flat (Verse 4), and the way the music for Verse 6 inclines earthwards in a moment of compassion (the change to G major from b. 121 is like a healing balm in sound). The words 'Und weisen / Von Gräbern / Gar tröstlich und hold' are set in such a way – a tiny flaw this – as to suggest that it is the graves, rather than the stars, that are 'tröstlich und hold' (a great artist like Robert Holl knows how to avoid this by changing colour between the lines while making an infinitesimal gap between them). This is followed by a return to impersonal cheeriness where heaven is signalled 'Mit Fingern von Gold' in merry, unconcerned music in E flat major. These contrasting sections affirm that the stars are both watching over us, and impervious to our fate. That Schubert is able simultaneously to convey both tenderness and indifference is the measure of a masterpiece, out of this world in every way.

Autograph:	State Archive Třbron, Jindřichův Hradec, Czech Republic
First edition:	Published as Op. 96 no. 1 by Schober's Lithographisches Institut, Vienna in Summer 1828 (P165)
Dedicatee:	Maria Karoline Fürstin von Kinsky
First known performance:	26 March 1828 at the Musikverein, Vienna as part of the Schubert 'Privatkonzert'. Soloist: Johann Michael Vogl (see Waidelich/Hilmar Dokumente I No. 603 for full concert programme)
Contemporary reviews:	*Allgemeine Musikalische Zeitung* (Leipzig), No. 19 (7 May 1828), col. 307f. [Waidelich/Hilmar Dokumente I No. 613; Deutsch Doc. Biog. No. 1067]
	Abend-Zeitung (Dresden), No. 141 (12 June 1828), p. 564 [Waidelich/Hilmar Dokumente I No. 620]
	Allgemeine Musikalische Zeitung (Berlin), No. 27 (2 July 1828), p. 215 [Waidelich/Hilmar Dokumente I No. 624; Deutsch Doc. Biog. No. 1069]

Subsequent editions:	Peters: Vol. 3/182; AGA XX 552: Vol. 9/125; NSA IV: Vol. 5/54; Bärenreiter: Vol. 3/186
Bibliography:	Capell 1928, p. 246
	Einstein 1951, p. 352
	Fischer-Dieskau 1977, p. 273
	Newbould 1997, p. 309
	Youens 2002, pp. 265–73

Discography and timing: Fischer-Dieskau II 9[13]   3'11

Hyperion I 6[13] & 36[13]   3'30   Anthony Rolfe Johnson
                             3'19   Juliane Banse

Hyperion II 35[11]   3'19   Juliane Banse

← *Der Winterabend* D938   *Der Tanz* D826 →

Die STERNENNÄCHTE   The starry nights
(MAYRHOFER) **D670** [H433]

The song exists in two versions, the first of which is discussed below:
(1) October 1819; (2) Date unknown

(1)   D♭ major

(56 bars)

(2)   'Sanft'   B♭ major   § [56 bars]

In monderhellten Nächten[1]	On moonlit nights
Mit dem Geschick zu rechten,	My heart has learnt
Hat diese Brust verlernt.	Not to quarrel with fate.
Der Himmel, reich besternt,	The heavens, rich with stars,
Umwoget mich mit Frieden;	Leave me in peace
Da denk ich: Auch hienieden	And I think: even here on earth
Gedeihet manche Blume;	Many a flower blooms;
Und frischer schaut der stumme,	And my silent, troubled gaze
Sonst trübe Blick hinauf	Brightens as it contemplates
Zu ew'ger Sterne Lauf.	The stars' eternal course.

[1]Mayrhofer writes (*Gedichte*, 1824) 'In *Mond erhellten* Nächten'. For an explanation of the background to these alternative Mayrhofer readings see Editorial Note at the beginning of Johann MAYRHOFER.

Auf ihnen bluten Herzen,[2]	On them, too, hearts bleed;
Auf ihnen quälen Schmerzen,	On them pain torments;
Sie aber strahlen heiter,	But they shine serenely on.
So schliess' ich selig weiter:	And so I happily conclude:
Auch unsre kleine Erde,	Even our little earth,
Voll Misston und Gefährde,	Full of discord and danger,
Sich als ein heiter Licht	Is a bright light
In's Diadem verflicht;	Woven into this diadem;
So werden Sterne	Stars are made thus
Durch die Ferne!	By distance!

JOHANN MAYRHOFER (1787–1836)

This is the thirty-fourth of Schubert's forty-seven Mayrhofer solo settings (1814–24). See the poet's biography for a chronological list of all the Mayrhofer settings.

The argument of the poem is simple enough: our problems recede when we see them at a distance and within a larger perspective. Mayrhofer, in his curious way, predicts space travel and the bird's-eye view of the astronauts when he imagines how beautiful and twinkingly friendly our own planet must seem from a faraway star. There is also in the poet's tone a note of earnest humility (Einstein calls it 'spiritual fervour') and a stumbling after the larger truths of life which the composer has caught perfectly. In this song we can hear Mayrhofer's introspective pessimism, certainly, but we can also hear what a dear fellow he was (obviously dear to Schubert too) and how he struggled to make the most of the cards that had been dealt him (we gain something of the same insight during a fine performance of *Nachtviolen* D752). The song is half hymn of gratitude and half plaint, and in this twilight world of merged feelings poet and composer are particularly well matched.

In musical terms everything is unearthly perfection in this song, from the disposition of the chords (another example of a great deal of music in the aerial treble clef) to the placing of the exquisite single trill in the piano part before the entry of the voice. Once the vocal line has begun it seems suspended on a thread of silver, a balancing act on a moonbeam. For the second verse (the composer creates an ABA form from the poet's two verses) the music comes down to earth as it reflects the poet's mortal concerns. The passage beginning 'Auf ihnen bluten Herzen' (from b. 31) is heart-rendingly chromatic, the better to contrast with the happy diatonic melody ('Sie aber strahlen heiter') describing the ever hopeful stars who do not allow accidental meteors to enter their orbit. The reprise is set up with astonishing simplicity and once more it is as if we tread on moonbeams. The closing lines 'So werden Sterne / Durch die Ferne' is a superb piece of poetic shorthand in a language often given to prolixity. Its understatement, and the humble acceptance of the miracles of nature that it implies, make for a moving coda. Even the final bar of piano writing sounds unbearably eloquent and full of meaning.

This is one of the great Mayrhofer songs, although it is curiously neglected in performance – perhaps because of the difficulty of its tessitura. In the key of D flat this jewel of a setting is bathed in a translucent light – it is as if we are hearing, in that gentle § pulse, the music of the spheres. The NSA prints a second version (Volume 12 p. 216) which is different in sundry details. This version is in B flat (it was published and first appears thus also in the Peters Edition) and the marking is 'Sanft'. As Walther Dürr points out, such a marking was unlikely to have

---

[2]Schubert sets the first two lines of this strophe in the reverse order from that in Mayrhofer's *Gedichte* 1824; the strophe begins 'Auf ihnen quälen Schmerzen / Auf ihnen bluten Herzen'.

emanated from a publisher, so it seems that Schubert had some hand in overseeing the copy. The upward scale on 'strahlen' in b. 38 was adopted as an ossia in the D flat major version in the AGA (and thus recorded in the Hyperion Edition). The question arises whether this was a decoration of the singer Vogl. The change from major to minor on the word 'trübe' in b. 27 is also unlikely to have been editorial. The second key of B flat major certainly makes the song accessible to more singers, but the colour of the composer's first thoughts in D flat major are unquestionably more magical. Although the song first appeared in D flat major in the AGA this was a cobbled-together edition incorporating details of the B flat version. The song in its authentic and original D flat tonality appeared thus for the first time only in the NSA in 1996.

Autographs:	Staatsbibliothek Preussischer Kulturbesitz, Berlin (first part; first version) Conservatoire collection, Bibliothèque Nationale, Paris (second part; first version)
Publication:	First published as part of the NSA in 1996 (P809; first version) First published as Op. post. 165 no. 2 by C. A. Spina in 1862 (P397; second version). Details of this version were incorporated into the AGA version in D flat major
Subsequent editions:	Peters: Vol. 6/88; AGA XX 366: Vol. 6/58; NSA IV: Vol. 12/111 & 216
Bibliography:	Capell 1928, p. 161 Einstein 1951, pp. 191–2 Youens 1996, pp. 205–9
Discography and timing:	Fischer-Dieskau II 3[9] 2'46 Hyperion I 19[11] Hyperion II 22[8] 2'57 Felicity Lott

← *Beim Winde D669*   *Trost D671* →

Die STERNENWELTEN   The starry worlds
(JARNIK/FELLINGER) **D307** [H187]
F major   15 October 1815

(25 bars)

Oben drehen sich die grossen	High above, the great
Unbekannten Welten dort,	Unknown worlds revolve;
Und dem Sonnenlicht umflossen	Bathed in the sun's light
Kreisen sie die Bahnen fort –!	They circle in their course.
Traulich reihet sich der Sterne	Around them, in harmonious array,
Zahlenloses Heer ringsum,	Spreads the numberless host of stars;

Sieht sich lächelnd durch die Ferne,	Smiling they gaze at each other from afar
Und verbreitet Gottes Ruhm.	And proclaim widely the glory of God.

Eine lichte Strasse gleitet	A path of light glides up
Durch das weite Blau herauf,	Through the vast blue firmament,
Und die Macht der Gottheit leitet	And the power of God gently guides
Schwebend hier den Sternenlauf;	The course of the stars;
Alles hat sich zugeründet,	Everything has attained perfection,
Alles wogt in Glanz und Brand,	Everything swirls in light and fire,
Und dies grosse All verkündet	And this great universe proclaims
Eine hohe Bildnerhand.	The hand of the sublime Architect.

[. . .]	[. . .]

JOHANN GEORG FELLINGER (1781–1816), translated from the poem of URBAN JARNIK
(1774–1844); poem written in 1812–13

This is the last of Schubert's three Fellinger solo settings (1815) and his only setting of a text after Urban Jarnik. See Fellinger's biography for a chronological list of all the Fellinger settings, and Jarnik's biography for further information about the poet. See also the article for Selam.

15 October 1815 was one of the most prolific dates in the entire history of the lied. With a small book of poems in his pocket, Schubert was mobile – as long as he had music paper to hand, he could have composed these eight songs anywhere. It might seem to have been a day of reckless literary promiscuity, but perhaps the composer was building more than castles in the air. Eight songs composed, and most by different poets: two by Stoll, and then on to Körner, Kumpf, Deinhard-Deinhardstein, Fellinger (this song), followed by a return visit to Körner. This is a young man who is suddenly intoxicated with his song-writing powers and anxious to try every-thing within reach: there are love songs, a lullaby, two hymns to May (understandable in the chill of October) and a risqué ditty (*Das gestörte Glück* D309) about endless vain attempts to bag sexual prey. It is the raciness of Körner that seems the odd man out in this almost idealisti-cally romantic scenario. All the texts were taken from a single source: the Viennese almanac *Selam* for 1814 issued by Ignaz Castelli. It is Walther Dürr's belief (see NSA Vol. 9 p. xvi) that Schubert had it in mind to write a set of songs, a *Selam* cycle (qv), of seven settings. Within that putative collection, *Die Sternenwelten* was the sixth, the weightiest song, the apex of the construc-tion that led to an epilogue.

On the printed page the song looks extremely simple, but that is characteristic of many a mighty hymn. The vocal range is lower than would suit a normal soprano, but there are unex-pected high notes to put off ambitious contralti. This is perhaps an argument that might be raised against Dürr's cycle theory – that on one day Schubert was not only changing poets, philosophies and outlooks with the insouciance of a great all-encompassing actor, but he was also changing casts with the canniness of an actor-manager. To find a singer capable of all the songs, though not impossible, would not be easy. Long before his collaboration with great artists like Vogl and Milder, he could only dream of the sumptuous range of voices at a composer's disposal: in the fantasy world where a composer writes his music, the greatest performances are to be had. At the beginning of his song writing career in 1811 Schubert had little idea of vocal tessitura, but once his friend Spaun began taking him to the opera he developed a feeling for vocal *Fach* unrivalled by any of the other great lieder composers.

The text of *Die Sternenwelten* shows that in this period praise of God was utterly compatible with all sorts of scientific, even space-exploring, curiosity. But mention of the 'sublime Architect' produces music in the old oratorio style: dotted rhythms, baroque-like ornamentations and a remarkable little accompanying figure that doubles the voice at the very beginning of the song and appears in the left hand more than once in *pomposo* imitation. The bar of interlude reinforcing the cadence halfway through the song (at b. 9) is also indicative of the grandeur of church music. The smiling left-hand imitation after 'Sieht sich lächelnd' (between bb. 17 and 18), as well as the canonically conceived postlude, are astonishingly carefully crafted for a day filled with so much musical activity. The song is a strange mixture of joy and melancholy – tender and subdued but with an imposing grandeur that belies its spareness of texture. The prosody of the first verse is convincing, whereas the words of the second verse can be made to fit the music only by tinkering with the allocation of syllables to the musical line (at 'dies grosse All verkündet', for example).

There is a third verse in Fellinger's poem. The original Slovenian text with the title 'Svésdishzhe' (beginning 'Turkej gori se nesnáni / Vélki svéti súzhejo') is printed in Schochow 1974, Volume 1 pp. 88–9; its author is Urban Jarnik (1784–1844) (qv).

Autograph:	Österreichische Nationalbibliothek, Vienna (first draft)
First edition:	Published as part of the AGA in 1895 (P594)
Subsequent editions:	Not in Peters; AGA XX 155: Vol. 3/121; NSA IV: Vol. 9/143
Discography and timing:	Fischer-Dieskau I 5³¹ 1'23 (first strophe only)

Discography and timing: Fischer-Dieskau I 5^{31} 1'23 (first strophe only)
Hyperion I 5^{12}
Hyperion II 10^{23} 3'17 Elizabeth Connell

← *Skolie* D306   *Die Macht der Liebe* D308 →

STIMME DER LIEBE (I)   The voice of love
(MATTHISSON) **D187** [H89]
F major   May 1815

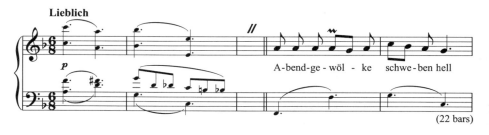

Abendgewölke schweben hell
Am bepurpurten Himmel;
Hesperus schaut, mit Liebesblick
Durch den blühenden Lindenhain,
Und sein prophetisches Trauerlied
Zirpt im Kraute das Heimchen!

Evening clouds float brightly
Through the crimson sky.
Hesperus looks lovingly
Through the flowering lime grove,
And in the grass the cricket
Chirps his prophetic threnody!

Freuden der Liebe harren dein!	The joys of love await you!
Flüstern leise die Winde;	The winds whisper softly;
Freuden der Liebe harren dein!	The joys of love await you!
Tönt die Kehle der Nachtigall;	Thus sings the nightingale.
Hoch von dem Sternengewölb' herab	From the high starry vaults
Hallt mir Stimme der Liebe.	The voice of love echoes down to me.
Aus der Platanen Labyrinth	From the labyrinth of plane trees
Wandelt Laura, die Holde!	Comes fair Laura!
Blumen entspriessen dem Zephyrtritt,	Flowers bloom at her airy footsteps,
Und wie Sphärengesangeston	And like the music of the spheres
Bebt von den Rosen der Lippe mir	Towards me from her rose lips
Süsse Stimme der Liebe!	Floats the sweet voice of love.

FRIEDRICH VON MATTHISSON (1761–1831); poem written in 1777

This is the eighteenth of Schubert's twenty-nine Matthisson solo settings (1812–17). See the poet's biography for a chronological list of all the Matthisson settings.

As always, when Schubert is in this serenely fluent mood we are tempted to think of Mozart, and one need go no further than the letter duet of the Countess and Susanna from *Le Nozze di Figaro* K492 to find the influence here. There are one or two felicitous touches apart from the ease and inevitability of the melody: the unusually chromatic introduction (falling scales such as are to be found in b. 2 and then in bb. 3–4 are not often encountered in Schubert's songs in such an undisguised state) is entirely suitable to depict the floating of the evening clouds. The upward inflection in the vocal line at bb. 8 and 16 is enchanting and a real test for a singer to execute elegantly. The chirp of cricket song is painted not only by drier (and carefully phrased) arpeggios in the accompaniment, but also by the voice: the second time the words 'Zirpt im Kraute das Heimchen' appear there is a chromatic inflection at b. 17, and when they are heard yet again, there is a fanciful plunge from an F to a surprising B natural (bb. 19–20). In the third strophe the word 'süsse' is set to the same falling interval – and this seems either suggestively naughty or ominous. We are reminded that the chirping of crickets can be interpreted as a presentiment of death, and that this tritone emphasizes the ominous nature of the cricket's 'prophetic threnody'. A footnote in the NSA points out that the introduction of the song is probably not meant to be repeated between the strophes.

Autograph:	Wienbibliothek im Rathaus, Vienna (first draft)
First edition:	Published as part of the AGA in 1894 (P560)
Subsequent editions:	Not in Peters; AGA XX 63: Vol. 2/98; NSA IV: Vol. 10/148
Bibliography:	Hoorickx 1976, p. 156
Discography and timing:	Fischer-Dieskau I 3[15] 1'44
	Hyperion I 7[3]
	Hyperion II 6[8] 2'11 Elly Ameling

← *Die Sterbende* D186   *Naturgenuss* D188 →

STIMME DER LIEBE (II)
(MATTHISSON) **D418** [H254]
G major   29 April 1816

The voice of love

(14 bars)

See previous entry for poem and translation

FRIEDRICH VON MATTHISSON (1761–1831); poem written in 1777

This is the twenty-fourth of Schubert's twenty-nine Matthisson solo settings (1812–17). See the poet's biography for a chronological list of all the Matthisson settings.

The first version of this song from 1815 is a melodic delight with its gentle Mozartian elegance, but here we have much more overt urgency. Capell calls this song 'placid', which may apply to the first version but surely not to this reworking of the text. It resembles, on the printed page, the reflective litany of Goethe's *Nähe des Geliebten* D162, and the great inner passion stoking that song, strophe by strophe, to ever more rapturous emotion, also pulsates through *Stimme der Liebe*: we hear the ebullience of nature on the move. The accompaniment is superbly suited to many an idea in the poem. Firstly, its rolling progress (impossible for the singer if it is too slow) conveys the ecstasy of the whole, and it is appropriate also for the song of crickets, throbbing with the vibrancy of a summer night, more recklessly than in the homely chirruping of *Der Einsame* D800. In the second verse the idea of whispering and rustling can also be caught by the piano (with a change of dynamic of course), and the idea of the airy footsteps of the 'Zephyrtritt' goes equally well with the piano's pacings. John Reed correctly points out that such an accompaniment became a cliché in nineteenth-century song, but here it is used with convincing freshness. On top of these ardent pulsations there is an open-hearted vocal line is enriched with a wonderful sequence that begins (bb. 5–6) with Hesperus' lordly overview (D minor to A minor), answered by a move through the blossoming linden grove (C minor to G major, bb. 7–8), and we have a page of absolutely inimitable Schubert.

Autograph: Pierpont Morgan Library, New York (incomplete first draft)
First edition: Published as part of the AGA in 1895 (P634)
Subsequent editions: Not in Peters; AGA XX 214: Vol. 4/90; NSA IV: Vol. 10/149
Discography and timing: Fischer-Dieskau   —
                              Hyperion I 8[3]
                              Hyperion II 14[5]   2'01   Sarah Walker

← *Klage (Die Sonne steigt)* D415   *Julius an Theone* D419 →

STIMME DER LIEBE
(STOLBERG) **D412** [H248]

The voice of love

The song exists in two versions, the second of which is discussed below:
(1) April 1816; (2) April 1816

(1)   No tempo indication   E major   ¢   [30 bars]

(2)   D major

(32 bars)

Meine Selinde! denn mit Engelsstimme	My Selinde! For love sings to me
Singt die Liebe mir zu: sie wird die Deine!	With an angel's voice: She will be yours
Sie wird die Meine! Himmel und Erde schwinden![1]	She will be mine! Heaven and earth vanish!
Meine Selinde!	My Selinde!
Tränen der Sehnsucht, die auf blassen Wangen	Tears of longing which quivered
Bebten, fallen herab als Freudentränen!	On pale cheeks fall as tears of joy!
Denn mir tönt die himmlische Stimme: deine	For the heavenly voice sings to me:
Wird sie! die Deine!	She will be yours, yours!

FRIEDRICH LEOPOLD, GRAF ZU STOLBERG-STOLBERG (1750–1819); poem written in 1775

This is the fifth of Schubert's nine Stolberg solo settings (1815–23). See the poet's biography for a chronological list of all the Stolberg settings.

This is certainly one of the most highly praised songs of 1816. All the commentators make a point of singling it out for special analysis and commendation. It is easy to see why: within these two pages and thirty-two bars we encompass a roller coaster of emotion and passionate involvement. This begins rather anonymously (bare pianissimo triplet chords in thirds in the right hand with the shy entry of a rising motif in the left hand in b. 2) and finishes in an even more withdrawn manner – three short chords marked ppp. Between these hushed extremities a veritable volcano of emotion erupts before our ears.

Triplet accompaniments that drive the music ineluctably forward were much favoured by Schubert in the 1815–17 period – not only in the celebrated *Erlkönig* D328 but also for *Nähe des Geliebten* D162, *Der Herbstabend* D405, the famous *Der Wanderer* D489, *Die Einsiedelei* D393, *An den Tod* D518, *Fahrt zum Hades* D526 and so on. The key word that inspired Schubert here was 'Engelsstimme' – the angel's voice announced in b. 4 that says 'She will be yours!' These throbbing triplets that dominate the first section of the song resume towards the end on mention of 'die himmlische Stimme' bb. 24–5. The composer quite obviously does not see this angel as a breezy little putto in a baroque fantasy, but rather as a heaven-sent messenger with a trumpet,

---

[1] Stolberg writes 'Wird die Meine!' Schubert repeats the pronoun 'sie' already used in the poem's second line.

and this gives the song its visionary, not to say ecstatically religious, air. It seems to belong to the same family as *Die Gestirne* D444 (June 1816) where field and forest sing the Lord's praise, and the celebrated *Die Allmacht* D852 of 1825 where earth and heaven proclaim Jehovah's might. The shifts of key are enough to make us giddy and the final return to the home key of D major right at the end is effected by a passage with a heroic sung high A (b. 27). This is a man who feels life and love to the very limit, and the vocal challenges of a song hardly ever heard in recital programmes reflect this. The whole thing only lasts a minute and a half, but we are drawn into a world of romantic obsession. There is a symphonic feel to this music as though the piano left-hand figure that proposes a rhythm for 'Meine Selinde' (and which returns when these words are repeated in bb. 14–15) should be played by the cellos, the triplets generating a huge motor-rhythm energy as if played by a full wind section. The only criticism of this remarkable song would be one of proportion in relation to style and content; the imposing stature of the work feels crowded by the relatively slender slot of time and space it occupies.

It is also interesting that as probably the most ardent love song of 1816 it is not included in the collection put together for Therese Grob in November of that year. John Reed suggests that this could well be a sign that the relationship had cooled by then and that Schubert thought it no longer appropriate to copy out such a song for her. Perhaps her parents would have been shocked by anything as bold as this; after all it was precisely because the young composer did *not* have the right to say 'You are mine!' that the relationship (if any) is said to have foundered. And it is also true that any young lover is unlikely to place into his beloved's hands a song in praise of another woman, even if this 'Selinde' is part of Stolberg's history rather than Schubert's.

Autograph:	In private possession
Publication:	First published as part of the NSA in 2002 (P835; first version)
	First published as Book 29 no. 1 of the *Nachlass* by Diabelli,
	Vienna in June 1838 (P320; second version)
Subsequent editions:	Peters: Vol. 3/200; AGA XX 210: Vol. 4/82; NSA IV: Vol. 10/140 &
	142
Bibliography:	Capell 1928, p. 119
	Einstein 1951, p. 134
	Fischer-Dieskau 1977, p. 68
Discography and timing:	Fischer-Dieskau I 7[1] 1'51
	Hyperion I 23[8]
	Hyperion II 13[24] 1'25 Christoph Prégardien

← *Daphne am Bach* D411   *Romanze* D144 →

FRIEDRICH LEOPOLD, GRAF ZU STOLBERG-STOLBERG (1750–1819)

THE POETIC SOURCES
The literary source of the Stolberg songs from 1815 and January 1816 remains a mystery. For the April 1816 songs Schubert could have used S1. It is clear that he probably used either S2 or S3 below for the 1823 songs.

THE POEMS IN EARLIER AND LATER EDITIONS
S1 *Gedichte der Brüder Christian und Friedrich Leopold Grafen zu Stolberg.* Herausgegeben von Heinrich Christian Boie, mit Kupfern. Leipzig in der Weygandschen Buchhandlung, 1779.

S2 *Gedichte der Brüder Christian und Friedrich Leopold Grafen zu Stolberg*, Erstes Bändchen, Drittes Bändchen, Wien 1818 im Verlage bey Leopold Grund

This edition is too late to have been the source of the Stolberg settings (except of course *Auf dem Wasser zu singen*) but it is possible that there was an earlier Viennese edition.

S3 *Gedichte der Brüder Christian und Friedrich Leopold Grafen zu Stolberg*, Erster Theil und Zweyter Theil, Wien, 1821 Im Verlage J. B. Wallishausser. Hamburg bei Perthes und Besser

S4 *Vier Tragodien des Aeschylos* übersetzt von Friedrich Leopold Graf zu Stolberg. Hamburg bei Friedrich Perthes, 1802

THE SONGS

24 August 1815   *Morgenlied* D266 [S2: Drittes Bändchen pp. 125–7] [S3: Zweiter Theil pp. 113–15]

28 August 1815   *Abendlied* D276 [S2: Drittes Bändchen pp. 109–12] [S3: Zweiter Theil pp. 123–5]

15 January 1816   *An die Natur* D372 [S2: Drittes Bändchen pp. 2–3] [S3: Erster Theil p. 113] This poem was probably known to Schubert when a student as it was included (pp. 71–2) in *Sammlung Deutscher Beyspiele für Bildung des Styls*, a textbook from his schooldays, a source of other early settings.

Gedichte by the brothers Christian und Friedrich Leopold Stolberg, Viennese edition (1818).

April 1816	*Daphne am Bach* D411 [S1: pp. 97–8] [S2: Erstes Bändchen pp. 64–5] [S3: Erster Theil pp. 83–4]
	Stimme der Liebe D412 [S1: p. 90] [S2: Erstes Bändchen, p. 59] [S3: Erster Theil p. 77]
	Romanze D144 [S2: Erstes Bändchen, pp. 42–4] [S3: Erster Theil pp. 56–9] [This song is a fragment of 7 bars completed by Reinhard Van Hoorickx]
	Lied in der Abwesenheit D416 [S1: p. 146] [S2: Erstes Bändchen p. 93] [S3: Erster Theil p. 126]
June 1816	*Fragment aus dem Aeschylus* D450 (Mayrhofer). The translation made from Aeschylus by Mayrhofer was strongly influenced by Stolberg's translation [S4: pp. 268–9]
April 1823	*Lied ('Die Mutter Erde')* D788 [S2: Drittes Bändchen p. 229 under the title 'Lied'] [S3: Erster Teil p. 265 under the title 'Lied']
1823	*Auf dem Wasser zu singen* D774 Op. 72 [S2: Drittes Bändchen pp. 360–61 with title *Lied auf dem Wasser zu singen* 'Für meine Agnes'] [S3: pp. 319–20 with title *Lied auf dem Wasser zu singen* 'Für meine Agnes']

Friedrich Leopold Graf zu Stolberg, painting by J. B. Lampi.

Friedrich Leopold, Graf zu Stolberg-Stolberg was born in Denmark on 7 November 1750. He worked on various literary ventures with his brother Christian (1748–1821); they were thus forerunners of such celebrated fraternal collaborations as the Schlegels, Grimms and Goncourts. Both Stolberg brothers, as admirers of Klopstock, were members of the Göttingen Hainbund. They travelled to Switzerland in 1775 with Goethe who, although exactly the same age, found them disturbingly unruly. Friedrich Leopold's translation of Homer's *Iliad* made him famous in Germany, and although the brothers published their poems together in 1779, Christian began to be counted the less significantly talented of the two. In 1781 Leopold married Agnes von Witzleben (1761–1788), the Muse of his poetry who died in her twenties. It was on their honeymoon that he wrote *Auf dem Wasser zu singen* and dedicated it to her ('für meine Agnes'). This Stolberg had a strong Danish connection in his career and he worked for a time as a diplomat, and as far afield as Russia. In 1800 he converted to Catholicism with his second wife, Sophie, and his children, and settled in Münster. He had begun as an indefatigable hater of political tyranny but the events of the French Revolu-

tion changed his attitudes somewhat. He remained an enthusiastic translator of Homer, Aeschylus, and even Ossian (1806) but he now chastised Schiller, and even Goethe, for the type of 'pagan' poetry that emanated from Weimar (and which Schubert delighted to set). In retrospect he would no doubt have regretted translating some of the dialogues of Plato in 1795, but these *Auserlesene Gespräche des Platon* (published in Vienna in 1803) were admired in the Schubert circle. The volume began with *Phaedrus* (Phaedros), a discourse on love known almost by heart by those attracted to the same sex and quoted by Aschenbach in Thomas Mann's *Death in Venice* (although not there in Stolberg's translation). Stolberg's change of religious viewpoint, accompanied by a shift from liberal to reactionary views, brings to mind the volte-face of Friedrich von Schlegel (more or less at the same time) with its similar effect of mystifying and alienating former friends and allies. Stolberg had an extended feud with his former ally Johann Heinrich Voss (qv) that was a cause célèbre throughout literary Germany. In 1816 Stolberg moved to Sondermühlen bei Osnabrück where he died on 5 December 1819.

JOSEPH LUDWIG STOLL (1777–1815)

THE POETIC SOURCE
S1 *Selam. Ein Almanach für Freunde des Mannigfaltigen auf das Jahr 1814.* Von I. F. Castelli. Wien Gedruckt und in Verlage bey Anton Strauss

THE SONGS
15 October 1815   *Labetrank der Liebe* D302 [S1: p. 204]
                   An die Geliebte D303 [S1: p. 205]

Joseph Ludwig Stoll (sometimes wrongly named as Johann Stoll) was born in Vienna on 31 March 1777. His father, the distinguished physician Maximilian Stoll, died when his son was nine years old. Stoll terminated his studies and went on a grand tour of Europe that used up his large inheritance. For the theatre in

Weimar he wrote various light-hearted plays in the French style and came to the notice of Goethe who recommended him for a position at Vienna's Burgtheater in 1807. In Vienna he met up with Seckendorff and the friends edited the journal *Prometheus*. On account of the war with the French this lasted for only six issues. He wangled a pension from the occupying Napoleon as the son of the distinguished doctor. This caused resentment in the Burgtheater, and among Austrian patriots, and Stoll was dismissed from his post. Encouraged by the publication of the first volume of his *Poetische Schriften* in Heidelberg in 1811, and as his pension was no longer remitted in Vienna, Stoll raised money with the help of Beethoven for a move to Paris. The declining fortunes of France under Napoleon forced him to return to Vienna where he died in poverty on 22 June 1815 (according to Oskar Wolff, 22 January). The compassionate and moving poem from Ludwig Uhland's *Gedichte* (1815) entitled *Auf einen verhungerten Dichter* ('On a starved poet') refers to Stoll and his unfortunate career. Grillparzer had regarded him simply as a wastrel. A few of his works stayed in the repertoire. In February 1824 Stoll's *Scherz und Ernst* was one of the plays in which Franz von Schober appeared as an actor while pursuing his dreams of a stage career in Breslau. Schubert set two Stoll poems from *Selam* 1814, but there are no grounds for believing that the text of *Lambertine* D301, composed a few days earlier, is by Stoll. It has, however, long been attributed to him.

PHILIPP ADAM STORCK (1778–1822)

THE TRANSLATION

S1 *Das Fräulein vom See* Ein Gedicht in sechs Gesängen von Walter Scott. Aus dem Englischen und mit einer historischen Einleitung und Anmerkungen von D [Doktor]. Adam Storck. Weiland Professor in Bremen. Zweite vom Uebersetzer selbst noch verbesserte Auflage. Essen bei G. D. Bädeker, 1823

The first edition of this translation issued by the same publisher in 1819, printed more spaciously in slightly larger format and on better paper, was almost certainly not the one Schubert used. This is indicated by certain revisions made by Storck in the translation of *Ellens dritte Gesang* (*Ave Maria*) as set by Schubert.

THE ENGLISH SOURCE

S2 *The Lady of the Lake* Poem By Walter Scott, Esq. Printed for John Ballantyne And Co. Edinburgh and Longman, Hurst, Rees, and Orme, and William Miller, London by James Ballantyne & Co., Edinburgh, 1810.

THE SONGS

See Scott for the list of seven settings from *The Lady of the Lake* translated by Storck.

Philipp Adam Storck, son of a Protestant minister, was born in Traben, in the Mosel region, on 19 October 1778. He studied philology at Giessen and Jena and taught at the commercial college (Handelsschule) in Hagen; in 1810 he became director of the same institution and in 1817 moved on to teach history, modern languages (including English) and commerce at the Handelsschule in Bremen. He quickly became an expert on the history of the Bremen region, a fact that is reflected in his publications including the posthumously published *Ansichten der freien Hansestadt Bremen und ihrer Umgebungen* (1827). Storck translated two other works by Scott, *The Lay of the Last Minstrel* (translated as *Der letzte Minstrel*, 1820) and *Rokeby* (translated as *Burg Rokeby*, 1822). Storck died at a relatively young age, like his father before him, on 19 April 1822, and work on the *Rokeby* translation was completed by an anonymous collaborator. His immortality, such as it is, has been assured only by his connection with Schubert's Scott songs. It might not have been so, for there was another, rather more inspired, translation of the Scott poem – entitled *Die Jungfrau vom See* – on sale from 1822, published by Gebrüder Schumann in Zwickau. This book might easily have fallen instead into the composer's hands.

It was among the very first works of Willibald Alexis, the pen name of Georg Wilhelm Häring (1798–1871), a poet later set by Brahms, whose first two historical novels were falsely ascribed to Scott himself ('nach dem Englischen des Walter Scott'). That a talented writer was prepared to pass off his own work as Scott's is an indication of the public craze in German-speaking lands for this author.

Der STROM   The river

(ANONYMOUS) **D565** [H375]
D minor   June? or Autumn 1817

Mein Leben wälzt sich murrend fort,	My life rolls grumbling onward,
Es steigt und fällt in krausen Wogen,	Rising and falling in undulating waves,
Hier bäumt es sich, jagt nieder dort	Here rearing up, there darting down,
In wilden Zügen, hohen Bogen.	In wild jerks and high arches.
Das stille Tal, das grüne Feld	Through the silent valley, the green fields,
Durchrauscht es nun mit leisem Beben,	It rushes, gently pulsating
Sich Ruh ersehnend, ruhige Welt,	Longing for peace
Ergötzt es sich am ruhigen Leben.	And delight in this tranquil life.
Doch nimmer findend, was es sucht,	But never finding what it seeks,
Und immer sehnend tost es weiter,	And ever yearning, my life rages on;
Unmutig rollt's auf steter Flucht,	Without pleasure ever fleeing
Wird nimmer froh, wird nimmer heiter.	Never to be content, never happy.

ANONYMOUS/UNKNOWN

This is the fifteenth of Schubert's nineteen solo settings of an anonymous poet. See Anonymous/ Unknown for a chronological list of all the songs for which the poets are unknown.

Like the contemporary Mayrhofer setting *Fahrt zum Hades* D526, this is a relentless D minor journey to the abyss, but the river of life is more turbulent than the viscous depths of the Styx. For sheer harmonic audacity there is no water music like this in all Schubert: it unleashes itself with the power of a tightly coiled spring, the piano part clattering in turbulent semiquavers where, in certain sections, the harmony changes on every crotchet and shifts in almost every bar. A glance at the poem is sufficient to see why the composer's predisposition towards modulation is here given unbridled licence. The words 'krausen Wogen' (bb. 13–15) were obviously Schubert's starting point: the curling waves lash against the climbing and plunging vocal line with unruly abandon. There is a moment of comparative respite at the beginning of the second verse as repeated As in the vocal line (from bb. 24–8) burrow their way through a valley ('Das stille Tal, das grüne Feld') flanked by a bank of semiquavers. The third verse with its dizzy modulations recalls a similar passage in the Schiller setting *Der Pilgrim* D794 – the fruitless search for the answer to life is common to both songs. If we were to hear the piano introduction with an innocent ear, Schubert would not be the first composer to come to mind; this stormy movement suggests rather the style of a later Romantic master like Schumann, or even Brahms. It is interesting that Brahms owned a manuscript of this song and put it forward for publication in 1876. In terms of its modernity it could easily have been written in that year.

The authorship of this poem is a puzzle. Schubert either wrote the song as a token of friendship for Albert Stadler (a friend from his schooldays who moved to Steyr in 1817) or he gave Stadler the manuscript as a farewell gift. Stadler (a composer who occasionally turned his hand to poetry) has been considered a possible author, as has another poet from the circle, Anton Ottenwalt. Recent research on Ottenwalt's poetry has revealed an overall literary style that does not chime with *Der Strom*; Stadler, however, in the absence of a better candidate, remains the most probable author of the poem. Ernst Hilmar thinks that Schubert himself could be the author of this text that has the quality of a diary entry. This brings to mind the great Schulze settings of 1825–6.

In 1876 when the song was first published by Wilhelm Fritsch of Leipzig, Johannes Brahms (who owned the autograph) appended the following musicological note:

> *The present song from Schubert's manuscript in the possession of Johannes Brahms, carries in addition the title 'As remembrance for Herr Stadler'. Another song on the same pages (Das Grab of Salis for male chorus) is marked 'June 1817'. The style of the manuscript and a place in the text ('ruhige Welt' etc.) suggest that words and music were written down as a result of one spontaneous impulse.*

This typically Brahmsian oblique reference to bb. 35–6 concerns the place on the autograph where Schubert had to indent the continuation of the song by some inches – a third of the page in fact – as a result of a massive ink-blot. Brahms took this accident to be a sign of the excitement of the white heat of compositional inspiration.

Autograph:	Wienbibliothek im Rathaus, Vienna (first draft)
First edition:	Published in *Blätter für Hausmusik* by E. W. Fritsch, Leipzig in 1876 and subsequently as Vol. 7 no. 29 in Friedlaender's edition by Peters, Leipzig in 1887 (P493)
Subsequent editions:	Peters: Vol. 7/65; AGA XX 234: Vol. 5/123; NSA IV: Vol. 11/154
Bibliography:	Capell 1928, pp. 143–4
Discography and timing:	Fischer-Dieskau II 1[9] 1'36
	Hyperion I 2[9]
	Hyperion II 19[9] 1'31 Stephen Varcoe

← *Gretchen im Zwinger* (*Gretchens Bitte*) D564   *Der Jüngling an der Quelle* D300 →

STROPHE AUS 'DIE GÖTTER GRIECHENLANDS'
(SCHILLER) **D677** [H438]

Strophe from 'The gods of Greece'

The song exists in two versions, the second of which is discussed below:
(1) November 1819; (2) November 1819

(1)   No tempo indication   A minor   ¾   [53 bars]

(2)   A minor

(52 bars)

[(. . . 11 . . .)]

[(. . . 11 . . .)]

Schöne Welt, wo bist du? Kehre wieder
Holdes Blütenalter der Natur!
Ach, nur in dem Feenland der Lieder
Lebt noch deine fabelhafte Spur.
Ausgestorben trauert das Gefilde,
Keine Gottheit zeigt sich meinem Blick,
Ach, von jenem lebenwarmen Bilde
Blieb der Schatten nur zurück.

Fair world, where are you? Return again,
Sweet springtime of nature!
Alas, only in the magic land of song
Does your fabled memory live on.
The desolate fields mourn,
No god reveals himself to me;
Of that warm, living image
Only a shadow has remained.

[(. . . 4 . . .)]

[(. . . 4 . . .)]

FRIEDRICH VON SCHILLER (1759–1805); poem written February/March 1788

This is the fortieth of Schubert's forty-four Schiller solo settings (1811–24). See the poet's biography for a chronological list of all the Schiller settings.

In 1770 Herder, one of the youthful Goethe's professors in Strasbourg, had warned his brilliant pupil that he would have to learn Greek in order to understand the eternal verities. Although Goethe never mastered the language, he wrote a number of poems exploring classical myths. Schubert set only the twelfth of sixteen strophes of *Die Götter Griechenlands* (1788) by Goethe's younger contemporary Schiller who averred that something had died in the soul of man if the old Grecian gods were indeed dead. In our own time, Isaiah Berlin, citing not only Schiller, but also Hölderlin, Hegel, Friedrich Schlegel and even Marx, summed up what he calls 'the great myth of the Greeks' as viewed from the standpoint of the Romantic age: 'Once upon a time we were integral, we were Greeks . . . We were children playing in the sunlight, we did not distinguish between necessity and freedom, between passion and reason, and this was a happy and innocent time. But this time is past, innocence is gone, life no longer offers us these things; what we are now offered as a description of the universe is nothing but a grim causal treadmill.'

Schubert and his circle, citizens of a police state in everything but name, might have viewed themselves as working that treadmill. The composer was sharing accommodation with Mayrhofer when this song was written, and perhaps it was that poet who had brought this particular strophe to Schubert's attention. If any of Schiller's words might have been written with an aching heart by the Viennese poet himself, it is these. The remainder of Schiller's *Die Götter Griechenlands* mentions mythical characters such as Helios, Orestes, Philoctetes and Castor and Pollux, all of whom had inspired Mayrhofer poems of their own. The subject is classical but, in presenting us with a fragment – a single strophe set to music that sounds mysteriously incomplete, an amalgam of poetry and music that raises more questions than it answers – Schubert creates a quintessentially Romantic work of art, according to the precepts of many scholars from Friedrich Schlegel to Charles Rosen in *The Romantic Generation* (1996). It is thus a song as much about the musical future as the historical past: its opening seems to come from nowhere; its ending fades into uncertainty. These are auguries of *Im wunderschönen Monat Mai* Op. 48 no. 1 from Schumann's *Dichterliebe* (1840) which takes place within the confines of a timeless month, equally open-ended and unrecoverable.

The music conveys a feeling of loss, and of being lost on a journey through time. In *Erstarrung* D911/4 from *Winterreise* the traveller searches in vain in the snow-covered grass for her footsteps and mementos of past love. Here it is as if we are ruefully contemplating a fragment of ancient pottery, all that remains of a vanished civilization. With only one of sixteen strophes to hand, our chances of finding the missing pieces are remote. The rapturous consolation that John Keats described in his *Ode on a Grecian Urn*, more or less contemporary with Schubert's song, is denied us. The artefact hymned by Keats (writing in England, a country admired for its political freedom) is preserved in all its glory, but Schiller's concern, more dangerous for the repressive governments of Europe, is broken ideas rather than an intact work of art in a museum.

The remote, other-worldly quality of the song is achieved by the lack of an anchored bass in the *minore* sections where everything is built on the 6-4 chord; what is missing is the root position. The change to A major, and the arrival of an underlying tonic (halfway through b. 4), suddenly brings the dream into focus. This visionary major-key tonality is only mock reality, as in *Die Nebensonnen* D911/23 from *Winterreise* where illusory suns shine in the same key. Mention of 'the magic land of song' transports us into the submediant, F sharp major (bb. 14–15); the effect is one of hallucinatory happiness that fades with a crestfallen and forlorn F sharp minor at the repeat of the words. Flat reality is all that is left after the transitory bubble of hope has been pricked.

For the second four lines we find ourselves back in A minor and the deserted fields of present-day Greece. The section beginning at b. 24 ('Ausgestorben trauert das Gefilde') has the feeling and rhythm of the Greek open-circle dance known as the *syrtos*. Here, as the shade of Schubert meets the contemporary Greek composer Theodorakis, the piano writing intertwines with the singer's melody, itself ornamented with weaving melismas that are far removed from the austere musical style of the opening. There is a brief instrumental interlude as if a reedy oboe were accompanied by plucked strings in the piano's staccato left hand. Schubert could easily have heard Greek folk music in one of the Viennese tavernas run by refugees and émigrés from the Peloponnese. Here he seems to be depicting the tragic contrast between the glories of ancient Greece and its modern downtrodden status as a colony of the Ottoman Empire. The struggle for Greek independence was to break out two years later, in 1821, but it was already a hotly discussed policital theme; Mayrhofer and Schubert would probably have shared the belief of such writers as Wilhelm Müller (cf. the middle section of *Pause* D795/12) and Lord Byron that

Greece was entitled to its independence from Austria's old enemy, Turkey. This song has always been discussed for its philosophical and aesthetic significance, but seldom in the light of the ongoing political struggle where a small country was dominated by the machinations of empire. Artists in Vienna, repressed by their own government, might well have felt 'We are all Greeks now.' Schubert's encounter with Metternich's secret police in March 1820 (with serious consequences for the poet Johann Senn) was only a few months away.

The piano's wan imitation of the vocal line after 'Blieb der Schatten nur zurück' (bb. 34–5) is the perfect musical metaphor for a shadow cast at the distance of a bar, of an era out of step with the ideals of a golden age. This is a transitional passage that leads us back into the past and a recapitulation of the opening words. In musical terms it is a virtual repetition of the opening – four bars in the minor key and seven, with upbeat, in a transfigured A major. There is a *minore* coda consisting of five beats with upbeat – another 'Schöne Welt', and this time 'wo bist du?' repeated, as words and music die on the singer's breath. There are two versions of the song. In the first there is a slightly altered interlude in bb. 22–3, but the biggest difference lies in the very last bar where Schubert leaves the A minor chord at the end unresolved in its second inversion – a measure of his compositional daring in 1819. In the second version a final A in both hands is added to resolve the chord and bring the song to a close.

In the early months of 1824, five years after the composition of the song, Schubert was exceptionally depressed and touchy. In a rare outbreak of temper and violence, he confided in a notebook that he envied Nero's ability to do away with his enemies to a musical accompaniment (this was the last of his various written allusions to classical history). It was during this time that he wrote his *Octet* D803 and his A minor String Quartet D804, both of which quote the dotted-rhythm motif of the opening of *Strophe aus 'Die Götter Griechenlands'*. In the *Octet* this appears in the beginning of the last movement, *Andante molto*, a baleful F minor outburst, almost a wail, preceded by a shivering cello tremolo. The third movement of the string quartet, the Allegretto *Menuetto*, begins with an unequivocal quotation, a fragment of melody that proves far more pervasive. This is the wavering motif in dotted rhythm (E–D–E), announced by the cello at the bottom of the bass stave and taken up by other strings – the same notes that have opened the song, only this time three octaves lower. The cello writing is gently urgent and somewhat ominous: danger is afoot in this dance movement, and a brooding resentment can be detected in that bass-clef drone that prevents the music from finding a resolution in the tonic. This is music that warns as much as it laments, the dark underside of idealized nostalgia. At almost exactly the same time Schubert wrote a desperate letter to his friend Leopold Kupelwieser in Rome, the sad theme of which was 'Beautiful and happy days of yore, where are you now?' In July he wrote to his brother Ferdinand, his prose seeming just as susceptible as his music to changes between minor and major: 'It is no longer that happy time during which each object seems to us to be surrounded by the shining aura of youth, but a period of fateful recognition of miserable reality, which I endeavour to beautify as much as possible by my imagination.' In quoting the opening of the 1819 song in chamber music works from 1824, Schubert was referring to a time before his illness, to days which, despite their drawbacks, were comparatively carefree and optimistic. The high-flown aesthetic and political issues heatedly debated by the Mayrhofer circle were now recognized as a luxury. Nostalgia for his own healthy past was as much an impossible dream for the composer as any philosophical *Sehnsucht* for ancient times.

Autograph:	Wienbibliothek im Rathaus (headed *Strophe von Schiller*)
Publication:	First published as part of the AGA in 1895 (P686; first version)
	First published as Book 42 no. 1 of the *Nachlass* by Diabelli, Vienna in 1848 (P359; second version)

Subsequent editions:	Peters: Vol. 6/30; AGA XX 371a & b: Vol. 6/76 & 78; NSA IV: Vol. 12/126 & 128
Bibliography:	Berlin 1999, p. 87
	Capell 1928, p. 158
	Einstein 1951, p. 190
	Newbould 1997, p. 161
Arrangements:	Arr. Tilman Hoppstock (b. 1961) for guitar accompaniment, in *Franz Schubert: 110 Lieder* (2009)
Discography and timing:	Fischer-Dieskau II 3[13] 3'46
	Hyperion I 14[1]
	Hyperion II 22[13] 3'51 Thomas Hampson

←— *Nachtstück* D672   *Über allen Zauber Liebe* D682 —→

STROPHIC SONGS

A strophic song (as opposed to a through-composed song) is one in which all verses of the poem are sung to the same music. Hymns and chorales are strophic and so are the vast majority of folksongs and folk ballads. The concept of a strophic composition goes back to the odes of classical antiquity. Strophic lieder are very much a feature of eighteenth-century German art song and Schubert, a transitional figure between the classical and Romantic periods, wrote songs like these as a result of the example of his musical forebears. The strophic song presents not only a formidable challenge to the composer (who has to find a musical setting that is equally apt for each verse of the poem) but also for the singer. The task of memorizing the song, and making it interesting, is much more difficult because the same music is attached to different words – or, rather, the words of the different verses do not have music that is unique to them. How much the singer is required to paint and point the differences in the text via music that is essentially unchanging, at least on paper, is at the heart of the modern performer's dilemma.

As a very young composer Schubert resisted the form in favour of larger, rambling musical structures. Overflowing with youthful musical ideas he was not initially drawn to composing strophic songs – he preferred long, through-composed ballads where he could follow the vagaries of the poem at will. In these early compositional adventures he was inspired by the example of Johann Rudolf Zumsteeg of Stuttgart (1760–1802) whose extended ballads were copied, and soon excelled, by the younger composer. Schubert was aware, however, that song (as opposed to ballad) composition, as it was understood in North Germany and by the Berlin school of lieder, was essentially a strophic art where the discipline and resourcefulness of the composer were almost submissively put at the disposal of the poet so as not to overshadow the words with superfluous musical detail. This type of modest composition had its roots in classically inspired order and discipline but it was deemed more musically accessible to ordinary people than through-composed art songs, also more closely connected to folksong. Goethe admired lieder of this kind – settings of his own words by his friends Johann Friedrich Reichardt, Carl Friedrich Zelter and others. Schubert came to value the taut eloquence of the best of these strophic songs, very different from the extended ballads of the prolix Zumsteeg (who, to be fair, was also capable of writing strophic lieder, just as Reichardt and Zelter also composed numerous ballads).

Schubert wrote his first strophic songs in 1814. In his later teens (1815–16), he increasingly became a master of the medium and became skilful with the form like no other composer before or since. With consummate skill he went on to write strophic songs within his two great

Müller song cycles (1823 and 1827), and he composed strophic songs to the end of his career. The ingenious way that he was able to compress his endlessly imaginative responses to words within the strict confines of the strophic form resulted in numerous masterpieces all the more moving for their formal concision and relative economy of means. The greatest Schubert strophic songs have an inevitability and timelessness where the form enhances, rather than limits, the composer's options. The listener is scarcely aware of counting the verses, so enchantingly cogent is the progress of one to the next, so delightful is it to hear the same music again, coloured and inflected with new words. Modern performers nevertheless sometimes elect to omit some of the strophes, particularly in songs where there is no narrative necessity for encompassing all of them.

Schubert composed about 230 purely strophic songs (depending on whether one counts the fragments); a great many more contain strophic elements and are modified in various ways in terms of vocal and pianistic detail. Schubert began his strophic experiments in the autumn of 1814 with the poet Matthisson: *Erinnerung* D98 has a recitative at its heart but its first three verses, and the last two, are strophic. The first version of the same poet's *Lied aus der Ferne* D107 has a strophic section in the second and third verses (the second version of this song from 1816 is entirely strophic). The first song that stands on its own as entirely strophic is the mesmeric Goethe setting *Nachtgesang* D119, composed on 30 November 1814. The same poet's *Trost in Tränen* D120, also strophic, followed suit on the same day. Many strophic settings of the poets Theodor Körner and Ludwig Kosegarten were composed in 1815, as well as famous texts of Goethe (*Nähe des Geliebten* D162, *Der Fischer* D225, *Die Spinnerin* D247, *Der Gott und die Bajadere* D254, *Der Rattenfänger* D255, *Der Schatzgräber* D256, *Heidenröslein* D257). Other significant poets set in strophic compositions were Gabriele von Baumberg, Friedrich Schiller (*Des Mädchens Klage* D191), Matthias Claudius (*An die Nachtigall* D196) and Klopstock.

1816 saw more Goethe lieder: *Der König in Thule* D367, *Jägers Abendlied* D368 – the first purporting to be a ballad from antiquity, and thus inevitably strophic, the second the plaint of a simple working man, and thus related to folksong. These strophic songs nestle among the Goethe masterpieces of 1816 written in through-composed forms. In Schiller's *Ritter Toggenburg* D397 the composer creates an extended strophic song in binary form at the end of the ballad to depict the vigil of the knight as he waits for a sign from his beloved. He sits outside the convent 'for many long years'; in this case the strophic form is an ideal means to depict the unchanging devotion of Toggenburg, faithful unto death, over such a long period. (Schubert has been criticized for being unimaginative in how he chose to conclude this work, but the opposite is true.) Apart from Goethe's close friend Schiller, there was now a whole range of poets whom Schubert judged as suitable for strophic setting in terms of their own eighteenth-century backgrounds: Schubart, Jacobi, Hölty, Salis-Seewis, Uz, Claudius. The setting of August von Schlegel's passionate and eventful *Die verfehlte Stunde* D409 as a strophic song is an extraordinary, if rather unlikely, achievement. From the autumn of 1816 comes a sequence of strophic settings to Mayrhofer texts: *Rückweg* D476, *Alte Liebe rostet nie* D477, *Der Hirt* D490, *Zum Punsche* D492.

The composition of strophic Goethe settings continued in 1817: *Liebhaber in allen Gestalten* D558, *Schweizerlied* D559, *Der Goldschmiedsgesell* D560. Schubert chose to set his own poem of farewell, addressed to his friend Franz von Schober, as a strophic song – *Abschied* D578. The poets Claudius, Salis-Seewis, Matthisson and Schiller (*Thekla* D595) continue to feature, as well as strophic settings by poets within his own circle – Mayrhofer, Schober and Ottenwalt. This may be considered the end of Schubert's apprenticeship in this difficult medium. The number of strophic settings now drops off; mastery has been achieved and no more practice is necessary. Schubert was now able to write a strophic song at any appropriate time, one of his many formal options.

The mature masterpieces in Schubert's song output that are strophic date from 1817 onwards – *An die Musik* D547, Schreiber's *Das Marienbild* D623, Schlegel's *Vom Mitleiden Mariä* D632, Silbert's *Himmelsfunken* D651, Uhland's *Frühlingsglaube* D686 (1820), settings from Friedrich von Schlegel's *Abendröte* (*Die Sterne* D684, *Der Fluss* D693), Stolberg's *Auf dem Wasser zu singen* D774 (1823) and selected songs from the two Müller song cycles. In *Die schöne Müllerin* (D795, 1823) ten of the twenty songs, half the cycle in fact, are entirely strophic (nos 1, 7, 8, 9, 10, 13, 14, 16, 17, 20) and these songs may be considered the apotheosis of strophic song as an art form. In *Winterreise* D911 (1827), on the other hand, there are only three more or less straightforward strophic songs, *Wasserflut, Rast* and *Frühlingstraum* (nos 6, 10 and 11), although the opening *Gute Nacht* begins as such with four minor-key verses before embarking on a fifth in the major. The cycle as a whole is a masterful demonstration of what can be achieved by modifying and varying the rules of strophic composition.

In the years between the two cycles (1825–6) the great strophic songs are fewer but all significant: Schiller's *Dithyrambe* D801, Scott's *Ellens dritter Gesang III (Ave Maria)* D839 and the same poet's *Lied des gefangenen Jägers* D843. Three songs from Ernst Schulze's *Poetisches Tagebuch* (*Um Mitternacht* D862, *Im Jänner 1817* D876, *Lebensmut* D883) are entirely strophic, although all the Schulze settings are subtle variations on the strophic theme, the famous *Im Frühling* D882 actually a set of variations. In the later years it might seem that the strophic song is on the wane as far as Schubert is concerned, but he never dropped it entirely. A jewel of a serenade, *Gesang (An Silvia)* D891 (1826), is strophic. There are at least five strophic songs worth mentioning from 1827: *An die Laute* D905, *Der Wallensteiner Lanzknecht beim Trunk* D911, and the curiously effective *Eine altschottische Ballade* D923, the Schober setting *Jägers Liebeslied* D909, and the wonderful Leitner setting, *Des Fischers Liebesglück* D933 – a musical triumph despite, or perhaps on account of, the restrictions of its form.

In the last summer of his life Schubert composed the *Vier Refrain-Lieder* D866, light-hearted songs meant for the popular market, three of which are strophic. It is perhaps one of these that is Schubert's last strophic song – but that honour might also belong to the Leitner setting *Das Weinen* D926, or the Rellstab setting *Herbst* D945 which, despite its proximity to the modernity of the ground-breaking Heine settings, is an entirely old-fashioned strophic song with repeat marks (though hardly old-fashioned in other ways). Here, as on countless other occasions, the composer has taken extraordinary care to find music that will be relevant for the poem's different verses.

The art of performing strophic songs is sadly more or less lost to us. The classicist Mary Beard was asked (*The Guardian*, 16 March 2013), 'If you could bring something extinct back to life, what would you choose?' Her reply was, 'A live Latin-speaker.' My reply would be, 'A live – and distinguished – singer of strophic songs in Vienna, circa 1820.' Of course, it would be tempting to ask to hear the charismatic baritone Johann Michael Vogl, a retired opera singer born in 1768 (*see* FRIENDS AND FAMILY and SINGERS). Vogl was somewhat overbearing (his documented foppery and exaggerations were detested by some, admired by others), an amateur composer determined to put his personal mark on any music he performed. The consensus seems to be that, in the manner of any younger accompanist working with an older celebrity, Schubert held his tongue while judging Vogl's advocacy of his songs to be important enough to allow the singer his head in matters of interpretation – the composer clearly valued the singer's intelligence, his profound and imaginative engagement with the text and his undoubted artistry.

Nevertheless, given only one go with a time machine, I would prefer to hear the songs of, say, *Die schöne Müllerin* D795 sung by a less theatrical personality (the tenor Carl von Schönstein, for example, born in 1797), and accompanied by Schubert himself. This performance would almost certainly be more indicative of the composer's own tastes. The amount of interpretative licence taken by both singer and pianist would be of crucial interest. In the opening

Das Wandern how much variation would we hear in the piano part regarding the difference between water, mill-wheels and millstones? Would Schönstein vary the tempo and dynamics of the strophic repeats in the songs in the interest of the narrative? Would the last song, *Des Baches Wiegenlied*, be a quiet moto perpetuo or would the tempo be varied according to the events described in the poem? How free could the singer and pianist be, either individually or together? How much would be spontaneous, invented on the spot, in terms of word-painting, how much worked out in advance and during rehearsal?

It is here that a distinction must be made between ornamentation and the differentiation of verses in the singing of strophic songs. Vogl ornamented both strophic and non-strophic songs in *Die schöne Müllerin* (the corrupt 1830 Diabelli edition survives to give us a watered-down version of how he did so), but there was almost certainly a rather more modern tradition (with younger singers like Schönstein) whereby performing variations were made between strophes without indulging in ornaments or decorations, employing instead more subtle shifts of time, emphasis, dynamics and vocal colour. The insertion of pauses between phrases is a kind of grey area between the two different approaches. In Vogl's copy of the strophic song *Der Fischer* D225, for example, apart from a few added ornaments for the later verses, the first verse is sprinkled with supplementary *fermate* and there are three in the final ten bars alone. We can only imagine what was conveyed in dramatic terms during these, what sort of expressions were on the singer's face (Vogl regarded himself as a great actor, and so did many others) and how far the story was made theatrical at the expense of the music. From the point of view of musical architecture alone it would seem that the whole point of a strophic song was to create a concise musical unity; it would surely be pointless to destroy this in performance. Apart from the eloquent, even impassioned, testimony of people like Sonnleithner (*see* RUBATO) we cannot know the boundaries of what was permitted in the interest of strophic variation in Schubert's own mind. We have a clearer idea of performing practice fifty years earlier, but times were changing and in the figure of Beethoven the modern composer exerted a different kind of control over his material and how it was performed. We only discuss the ornamenting of Schubert's songs because of Vogl's surviving manuscripts (*see* ORNAMENTATION), but as far as I am aware no one talks about ornamenting Beethoven's *An die ferne Geliebte* Op. 98 beyond the many decorative touches that are already to be found in that score. According to Sonnleithner, Schubert himself did not permit gratuitous and unmarked tempo changes in his own music.

From what we can gather from Schubert's contemporaries about the directness, simplicity and sheer beauty of his playing and his sense of rhythm, as well as his disinclination to exaggeration, the performance of his songs was definitely not an interpretative free-for-all. But without having been there to hear a contemporary performance or, more importantly, having grown up in a musical world where the eighteenth century was a fairly recent memory, we have no way of knowing, much less understanding, the prevailing Viennese standards of song performance in Schubert's own time. Is it possible that there was no standard at all, that each artist was very different, that in these years when the lied was emerging as a modern art form there was a kind of anarchy prevailing in its performance? It would take a brave, even foolhardy, modern performer to plunge into a recreation of a past that is scarcely knowable. In my view the surviving material indications of how Schubert's music was changed and ornamented in performance fails to approach, much less improve, the original unadorned score in terms of beauty, interest or impact – but of course this is very much the reaction of a musician born in the twentieth century.

Der STÜRMISCHE MORGEN *see* WINTERREISE D911/18

SULEIKA I (Suleikas erster Gesang)   Zuleika I
(WILLEMER/GOETHE) OP. 14 NO. 1, **D720** [H468]

The song exists in two versions, the second of which is discussed below:
(1) March 1821; (2) appeared December 1822

(1)   'Etwas lebhaft'   B minor $\frac{3}{4}$ [142 bars]

(2)   B minor – B major

Was bedeutet die Bewegung?	What does this stirring portend?
Bringt der Ost mir frohe Kunde?	Is the east wind bringing me joyful tidings?
Seiner Schwingen frische Regung	The refreshing motion of its wings
Kühlt des Herzens tiefe Wunde.	Cools the heart's deep wound.
Kosend spielt er mit dem Staube,	It plays caressingly with the dust,
Jagt ihn auf in leichten Wölkchen,	Throwing it up in light clouds,
Treibt zur sichern Rebenlaube	And drives the happy swarm of insects
Der Insekten frohes Völkchen.	To the safety of the vine leaves.
Lindert sanft der Sonne Glühen,	It gently tempers the burning heat of the sun,
Kühlt auch mir die heissen Wangen,	And cools my hot cheeks;
Küsst die Reben noch im Fliehen,	Even as it flies it kisses the vines
Die auf Feld und Hügel prangen.	That adorn the fields and hillsides.
Und mir bringt sein leises Flüstern[1]	And its soft whispering brings me
Von dem Freunde tausend Grüsse;	A thousand greetings from my beloved;
Eh' noch diese Hügel düstern,	Before these hills grow dark
Grüssen mich wohl tausend Küsse.	I shall be greeted by a thousand kisses.
Und so kannst du weiter ziehen!	Now you may pass on,
Diene Freunden und Betrübten.	And serve the happy and the sad;
Dort wo hohe Mauern glühen,	There, where high walls glow,
Dort find' ich bald den Vielgeliebten.	I shall soon find my dearly beloved.
Ach, die wahre Herzenskunde,	Ah, the true message of the heart,
Liebeshauch, erfrischtes Leben	The breath of love, renewed life
Wird mir nur aus seinem Munde,	Will come to me only from his lips,
Kann mir nur sein Atem geben.	Can be given to me only by his breath.

---

[1] For the original text (the fourth and fifth verses of the poem) see Marianne von WILLEMER.

MARIANNE VON WILLEMER (1784–1860), attributed to and adapted by JOHANN WOLFGANG
VON GOETHE (1749–1832); original poem written 23 September 1815

*This is the sixtieth of Schubert's seventy-five Goethe solo settings (1814–26) or, in this case,
poems attributed to Goethe. Without the composer realizing it, this was also the first of his two
settings (1821–4?) of poems by the as-yet-unacknowledged Marianne von Willemer. See the
biographies of both Goethe and Willemer for a chronological list of settings in each case.*

When the forces of nature join forces with the
erotic energies of an eastern temptress, the
results are bound to be spectacular. This song,
and its companion setting D717, are among
the best-known of Schubert's lieder, and are as
difficult to perform as they are adequately to
describe. From the very beginning we realize
we are in for something extraordinary: the
piano, in its guise as the East Wind, rustles
sinuously across both staves as it ascends from
the depths of the keyboard, spending its
energy in two dotted minim chords (bb. 4–5)
that are rolled under the pianist's fingers – a
force of nature suddenly contained as if at the
heroine's command. (Ambiguity and disguise
figure strongly in these Zuleika songs where
the protagonists wear oriental garb and everything is a symbol for something else.) These
wonderful five bars are redolent of the East
Wind certainly (and one remembers that
Goethe lives in the east – of Germany – in
Weimar, and his beloved Marianne von
Willemer (qv) near Frankfurt to the west) but
the curling left-hand figurations rising from
the depths of the instrument might also be
heard as a wind-swept metaphor for the stirrings of sexual desire. Something very similar
to this introductory passage is found in the

Goethe's autograph of *Was beduetet die Bewegung?*,
adapting the original poem of Marianne von Willemer.

Andantino section of the fragmentary *Fantasie in C* D905 (probably composed between 1821
and 1823). Here the same key and time signatures preside over a wonderfully sensual passage
of uninterrupted left-hand semiquavers, deliciously murmuring in the lower and middle regions
of the bass clef. There are eight bars of this music, the first of which is an entirely chromatic
scale, followed by other fanciful chromatically inflected meanderings.

The song's key (B minor, symbolic in Schubert of love and longing) and its characteristically
punctuated left-hand rhythm are those of the 'Unfinished' Symphony D759. In her opening
lines, Zuleika asks two questions in the home tonality – 'Was bedeutet die Bewegung?' and
'Bringt der Ost mir frohe Kunde?' – the second inflected upwards at the end to suggest that she
expects an answer. The balancing phrase from b. 13 brings a reply in the relative major. The
repeat of the last two lines of this strophe (from b. 18) is a marvel of tenderness; the triplets in
the vocal line (first heard here at '<u>frische</u> Regung') are a sultry feature of the song, suggesting
arabesques or moorish melismas that subtly evoke the quasi-oriental provenance of the poem.

Accents on the first beat of every bar (bb. 6–71 and 82–108), long ignored or misread as decrescendo markings, contribute enormously to the exotic eastern flavour, a bodily inflection as if the sinuous Zuleika were dancing before our eyes. For the second verse, her gaze shifts to the world about her – Goethe the scientist and botanist has been her teacher after all – and, momentarily distracted from the intensity of her longing, she smiles in the major key at the workings of nature. From b. 27 the domain of the insects is placed under a musical microscope, and each of the accompaniment's black semiquavers on the page represents a bustling ant. Aurally, this impression is aided by the word-setting and a quick succession of busy consonants; in the piano we hear something like the repetitive hum of a thousand tiny exotic creatures as they disport themselves in the dust surrounding the vine leaves. This is followed by a welcome musical repetition of the first verse (from b. 42); the wind cools the heat of Zuleika's cheeks as it kisses the vines. In Verse 4 the real romantic message of the East Wind reveals itself to the singer whose newly minted vocal line astride an already familiar accompaniment (the same as Verse 2, so b. 27 and b. 62) stretches out to receive it like a body yielding to a caress. At 'Von dem Freunde tausend Grüsse' (bb. 66–9) and 'Grüssen mich wohl tausend Küsse' (bb. 76–9) the voice is teased into gently repetitive undulations of foreplay as it cleaves to the piano line in hunting-horn thirds and sixths.

Of course all this is a prelude to the song's climax of Verse 5 – waves of mounting passion where the first two lines of the strophe are repeated in two magnificent sequences, one a semitone higher than the other (bb. 84–7 and bb. 88–91). A plateau is reached at b. 92 on 'Dort . . . dort [the word-repeat is Schubert's] wo hohen Mauern glühen'. The voice's E rises to F in b. 94, then F sharp in b. 96; the piano's left hand also rises in semitones to meet the vocal invitation/ challenge with all the exciting consequences of a whirlwind chromatic journey through the senses. After a massively exciting upbeat on b. 96 ('Dort find' ich . . .') the two halves conjoin in *two* shuddering climaxes on 'bald den Vielgeliebten' (bb. 97–9). The first of these, on the word 'bald' (b. 97), seems to be the high point until we realize that it is on an inconclusive second inversion of F sharp major; a moment later, in a second spurt of energy at b. 99, we reach the root position of the temporary tonic, itself the dominant of the home key. Schubert had written nothing as openly impassioned as this for a woman's voice since the climax of *Gretchen am Spinnrade* D118. That work had been shot through with the bitter-sweet anguish of sexual awakening; here there is only the delighted expectation of practised reciprocation. True enough, it is the rapture of *fantasy* of union, but who was better placed than Schubert to fantasize alongside the poets about the kind of reciprocated love which, as far as we know, he was never to enjoy in reality? The ten bars of piano interlude (bb. 99–108) that lead into the final verse allow racing pulses and heartbeats to descend into a warm glow of quietus and detumescence. This passage where the pianist must take over from the passion of the voice, and not allow the feeling accumulated by the singer to fade away in mechanical note-spinning, is one of the most challenging for accompanists.

In the final section (from b. 109 and marked 'Etwas langsamer') it is as if the voice rests satiated on the piano's shoulder and the throbbing heartbeat of a gentle F sharp pedal; this is Schubert's 'extase langoureuse' and 'fatigue amoureuse' long before Debussy, in the first of his *Ariettes oubliées*, attempted to capture Verlaine's post-coital mood (warmth, security, fear that this bliss might not continue for ever). Above all this music is about *feeling*, for sensation alone is never enough for any true lover or Schubertian. In Brahms's opinion this was one piece where music truly added something and deepened Goethe's words (he meant Willemer's), all the other poems being so complete in themselves. In this intimate sarabande, triplets and a single ornamental turn (b. 119) grace the vocal line the better to let it flow and unfold in its intensely private inner contentment. We hear the same twelve bars of music twice, the only important difference being in the tessitura of the right-hand accompaniment which is an octave higher as the soul and spirit gradually surface from the depths. Diminished sevenths on 'Wird mir nur aus seinem Munde' (bb. 127–8) and 'Kann mir nur sein Atem geben' (bb. 129–32) perfume this music with the presence of Hatem (thus the pun on 'Atem', breath) who is the longed-for lover. Zuleika's words are repeated one last time as the vocal line winds the piece down to its conclusion and melts into the sleep and dreams of fulfilment. The F sharp pedal is now to be heard in both bass and treble and continues until b. 138, six bars from the end, where the home key of B major arrives at last on the final 'erfrischtes <u>Leben</u>'. John Reed, quoting Blake, sees in this music 'the lineaments of gratified desire', and he is surely right. Schubert's imagination has allowed the two lovers to conjoin where the disparity in their ages, as well as geographical distance, has defeated them in real life.

On 26 April 1825 Marianne wrote to Goethe (whom she had now not met up with in person for a decade), reporting that in attempting to buy a Beethoven song from a local music shop, she had been sent 'a really lovely song on the East Wind and *Geheimes* from the Divan'. This was obviously Schubert's Op. 14 published in 1822. She did not mention the identity of the composer, so once again Schubert's name was destined to fail to make an impression on Goethe. Brahms agreed with Marianne's verdict, as have thousands of others since, considering it the 'loveliest song ever written'. His own song *Von ewiger Liebe* Op. 43 no. 1 (also in B minor/major) owes much to this *Suleika* in terms of its breadth and structure.

The NSA prints an earlier version of *Suleika I*. This was clearly the composer's first draft that he revised when preparing the song for publication at the end of 1822. This is a classic example of how Schubert's revising eye was able to 'tweak' already marvellous music and prepare it for its voyage into the outside world: newly added articulation marks, dynamics and occasional changes in the accompaniment all add to the music's stature. One of the most noticeable differences is his addition of dotted rhythm to the piano writing in the last section (from b. 108). The synchronization of the piano with the voice in dotted rhythm lifts and transforms the power of the vocal line in a way that is scarcely credible. One has only to play Schubert's first thoughts in this passage to see how leaden they are in comparison to the final version; it is often in these tiny last-minute changes that Schubert has some of his best ideas. If he had lived to see all his songs through the press in this manner we would no doubt have been astounded at what he could achieve in terms of sprucing up old manuscripts, in some cases the work of minutes rather than hours.

Towards the end of 1822 the gifted young artist Moritz von Schwind (*see* FRIENDS AND FAMILY) designed a vignette for the first edition of this song based on a portrait of his beloved Anna (or Netti) Hönig. In the end the publishers Cappi & Diabelli did not use his illustration and the design was lost.

Autograph:	Österreichische Nationalbibliothek, Vienna (first draft, headed *Suleika. Göthe*)
Publication:	First published as part of the NSA in 1970 (P745; first version)
	First published as Op. 14 no. 1 by Cappi & Diabelli, Vienna in December 1822 (P34; second version)
Dedicatee:	Franz von Schober
Subsequent editions:	Peters: Vol. 2/38; AGA XX 396: Vol. 6/194; NSA IV: Vol. 1a/108 & Vol. 1b/239; Bärenreiter: Vol. 1/86
Bibliography:	Capell 1928, p. 156
	Einstein 1951, p. 219
	Fischer-Dieskau 1977, pp. 144–6
	Gülke 1991, pp. 124–9
	Newbould 1997, pp. 157–8

Further settings: Felix Mendelssohn (1809–1847) *Suleika* Op. 57 no. 3 (1839?)
Discography and timing: Fischer-Dieskau   —
                           Hyperion I 19[17]
                           Hyperion II 24[10]   5'31   Felicity Lott

←— *Geheimes* D719   *Suleika II* D717 →

SULEIKA II (Suleikas zweiter Gesang)   Zuleika II (Zuleika's second song)
(WILLEMER/GOETHE) OP. 31, **D717** [H469]
B♭ major   March 1821? or December 1824?

(186 bars)

Ach, um deine feuchten Schwingen,	Ah, West Wind, how I envy you
West, wie sehr ich dich beneide:	Your moist wings;
Denn du kannst ihm Kunde bringen	For you can bring him word
Was ich in der Trennung leide!	Of what I suffer separated from him.
Die Bewegung deiner Flügel	The motion of your wings
Weckt im Busen stilles Sehnen;	Awakens a silent longing within my breast.
Blumen, Auen, Wald und Hügel	Flowers, meadows, woods and hills
Stehn bei deinem Hauch in Tränen.	Grow tearful at your breath.
Doch dein mildes sanftes Wehen	But your mild, gentle breeze
Kühlt die wunden Augenlider;	Cools my sore eyelids;
Ach, für Leid müsst' ich vergehen,	Ah, I should die of grief
Hofft' ich nicht zu sehn ihn wieder.	If I had no hope of seeing him again.
Eile denn zu meinem Lieben,	Hasten then to my beloved
Spreche sanft zu seinem Herzen;	Speak softly to his heart —
Doch vermeid' ihn zu betrüben	But be careful not to distress him,
Und verbirg ihm meine Schmerzen.	And conceal my suffering from him.
Sag ihm, aber sag's bescheiden:	Tell him, but tell him humbly,
Seine Liebe sei mein Leben,	That his love is my life,
Freudiges Gefühl von beiden	And that his presence will bring me
Wird mir seine Nähe geben.	A joyous sense of both.

MARIANNE VON WILLEMER (1784–1860), attributed to and adapted by JOHANN WOLFGANG
VON GOETHE (1749–1832); original poem written in September 1815

*This is the sixty-first of Schubert's seventy-five Goethe solo settings (1814–26) or, in this case,
poems attributed to Goethe. Without the composer realizing it, this was also the second of his
two settings (1821–4?) of poems by the as-yet-unacknowledged Marianne von Willemer. See the
biographies of both Goethe and Willemer for a chronological list of settings in each case.*

On 24 December 1824 Schubert received a letter from Anna Milder, celebrated opera singer
and musical heroine of his youth. She had tried, and failed, to meet him in Vienna through the
good offices of Johann Schickh, editor of the *Wiener Zeitschrift für Kunst und Mode* which had
published a number of Schubert songs as fold-out supplements. One of the most recent of these
was *Drang in die Ferne* D770 with a poem by Leitner. Schickh seems to have been a Leitner
enthusiast: did he encourage Milder to ask Schubert to set another Leitner poem, *Der Jüngling
und der Nachtschmetterling*, which she enclosed in her letter?

The composer was in a difficult position. There was nothing he liked less than being pres-
sured to set a poem chosen by someone else, and it was only on rare occasions that he succumbed.
In this respect he was almost always impervious to celebrity and worldly power; only friendship
was able to exert any sense of obligation. He was, however, capable of occasional perspicacity
when it came to furthering his career, particularly in his fruitless quest to be a successful opera
composer. It is obvious that in Leitner's poem, 'The Youth and the Moth'[1], Milder saw the chance
of a display piece requiring her to flit up and down across the stave in capricious and virtuoso
fashion. 'I take the liberty', she coyly wrote in her letter, 'of making the single suggestion that
the composition should be addressed to a wide public.' Schubert had revered Milder's artistry
in her younger days, and she might have been be a powerful ally in Berlin where he hoped to
see his opera *Alfonso und Estrella* D732 staged. It was clear that he would have to write a piece
for her, but he drew the line at 'The Moth'.

He was almost certainly unaware that Milder was on cordial terms with Marianne von
Willemer who was known to be the inspiration of Goethe's Zuleika. (The revelation that Marianne was actually the author of these lines came only decades later.) There is every reason to
suppose, as Milder is the song's dedicatee, that Schubert believed that *Suleika II* would suit her
down to the ground and that the piece would be a 'sweetener' for the main project on his mind
– the staging of his opera with her help and influence. Whether Schubert wrote the piece
expressly for Milder (as she claimed), or whether he had composed it some four years earlier,
together with his other music with texts from Goethe's *West-östlicher Divan* (qv), remains a
matter of musicological debate. A Berlin review from June 1825, in which it is stated that the
song was written especially for Mme Milder and that Schubert had dedicated the 'Manuskript'
to her, is perhaps nothing more than supposition. The following commentary comes up with
various reasons for favouring both schools of thought.

The receipt of the two scores, a song and an opera, one slight and the other bulky, was
acknowledged by the singer on 8 March 1825. From this letter we learn that she already
possessed a printed copy of *Suleika I* D720, and that she was 'moved to tears' by *Suleika II* (here
perhaps confusing one song with the other). Nevertheless, she says, 'All this endless beauty
cannot be sung to the public, since the crowd only wants treats for the ear.' (The expressive
German neologism 'Ohrenschmaus' might be translated as 'ear-candy' in modern times.) Clearly,
she still hankered after 'The Moth', and suggested a Goethe poem for setting, also ignored by
Schubert. Her lightning verdict on the unsuitability for Berlin of *Alfonso und Estrella* was bitterly

---

[1] In Leitner's *Gedichte* (1825) this poem, *Der Jüngling und der Nachtschmetterling* is only three pages away from the text
of Schubert's immortal *Die Sterne* D969, and next to *Der Wallensteiner Lanzknecht beim Trunk* D931.

disappointing for the composer. In an authentic example of the centuries-old language of diva-speak she writes, 'If I should have the pleasure of being able to appear in one of your operas, it would doubtless have to be suited to my individuality and contain, for example, a part for a queen, a mother or a peasant woman.' To be fair to Milder, the insensitivity of this letter was balanced by one of 28 June 1825 (which arrived when Schubert was away on holiday with Vogl) in which she recounts in rapturous mood how she had sung *Suleika II* and *Erlkönig* D328 in a concert in Berlin on 9 June with marked success.

It is generally conceded that this song is less touching as a piece of music than *Suleika I*, marvellously inventive and unusual though it certainly is. For a start, there is less vulnerability to it. In the first Zuleika song, the protagonist waits for news and hangs breathlessly on Hatem's wind-borne message; in the second, however, despite the bereft tone of some of the words, the music implies that Zuleika is mistress of the situation – it is she who is using the West Wind as her messenger and her almost imperious wish (who could disobey a diva capable of a high B flat?) is its command. The miracle of *Suleika I* is that it manages to be both epic and intensely personal – we are drawn to the heart of her longing in a way that would be inconceivable in an aria. On the other hand, *Suleika II* seems almost certainly deliberately shaped as a virtuoso display piece for both voice and piano (and it is this that makes many people believe that the piece was indeed written expressly for Milder). When Schubert is in the mood to show that he can write public as opposed to private songs, an operatic dimension creeps in at the expense perhaps of the still small voice, not dependent on show or scale, that lies at the heart of his greatest lieder. On the other hand, this song is no empty vehicle for high notes and digital dexterity – it is filled with the most sumptuous and subtle detail. When the two *Suleikas* are performed as a pair the second provides an effective foil to the profundities of the first.

A number of the reviews of the time emphasize the oriental character of the piece and the piano writing is certainly unique in all Schubert. The broken octaves that sidle around the keyboard do splendid service in simulating the wind, and there is a voluptuous feminine sway, redolent of the harem, in this music. In the right hand tiny bells attached to headdresses and ankle bracelets seem to be tinkling in the breeze. Janissary music (emulating the Turkish sultan's body-guards with their bells, cymbals and drums) was still very much the rage in Vienna, and a number of Viennese piano makers made instruments that incorporated janissary effects. Such effects seem to be built already into Schubert's music without the need for further mechanical colourings.

The shape of the opening vocal line ('Ach, um deine feuchten Schwingen') recalls 'Ach, die wahre Herzenskunde' in *Suleika I* (in speeded-up metamorphosis), although the mood and the key are quite different. The chromatically rising phrase on 'Was ich in der Trennung leide' (bb. 21–3) is also reminiscent of passages in *Suleika I*. These similarities are used as ammunition by those who believe both songs date from 1821, but Schubert would have been perfectly capable of returning to his *Suleika* frame of mind after a three-year gap. In any case, if both *Suleika* songs had been written in March 1821 (as the Deutsch catalogue and the NSA suggest) why had they not been published as a pair at the end of 1822?

The last two lines of the strophe are repeated; there is a great deal more repetition of lines and whole verses in this piece than in *Suleika I*, adding to the quasi operatic character of the piece. The accompaniment of the second verse shrinks in scope as does the range of the vocal line – as if Zuleika were drawing the West Wind nearer to her in order to address it in confidence. The spar-kling beauties of 'Blumen, Auen, Wald und Hügel' (from b. 49) are all innocence in F major (stac-cato quavers in the left hand like drops of dew) but on the repeat of the words a shift into D flat major (from b. 60) colours the scenery into an exotic landscape worthy of the roses of Ispahan.

The repeat of 'Stehn bei deinem Hauch in Tränen' (D flat major at bb. 70–71, D flat minor at bb. 72–3), has the words 'Hauch' and 'Tränen' ('breath' and 'tears') eloquently prolonged. There follows (bb. 76–83) a piano interlude with a melting return to the music of Verse 1. This sophisticated variation of strophic song technique is the same as that used in *Suleika I*. The music for this verse is the same as Verse 1 until the heart-stopping interrupted cadence on 'sehn ihn <u>wieder</u>' (this last word in b. 100) that seems to sum up all the ache of Zuleika's hopes; the song hurtles passionately forward through a number of keys as the last two lines of the verse are repeated in rapturous vocal embroidery, then repeated yet again. The piano interlude at the end of this section with its juxtaposed G major (bb. 120–21) and G minor figurations (bb. 122–3) sounds particularly eastern in inspiration. This element of pastiche and a certain staginess prevents the music from moving us as much as does the equivalent piano interlude in *Suleika I*.

The closing movement of this miniature cantata ('Etwas geschwinder' from b. 129), comprising the last two verses of the poem, is as much a virtuosic scherzo as the closing of *Suleika I* is a beguiling nocturne. The shape and rhythm of the vocal line at 'Eile denn zu meinem Lieben' seems to derive from the first Zuleika's 'Und so kannst du weiter ziehen!' (bb. 84–5 in that song). The pianist's life now becomes really difficult: instead of a tricky leap once in a bar the left hand here has to plunge to the bottom of the keyboard at every beat; on top of this, the right hand has a dancing, clipped, three-note figure that entails rapid repetition of the first two of three semiquavers – a succession of quick alternations between the second finger and thumb of the right hand followed by the little finger stretching up the octave. It is a task that Gerald Moore in a letter to me likened to walking a tightrope. This movement no doubt influenced Johannes Brahms in the closing 'Vivace, ma non troppo' section of *Wie soll ich die Freude, die Wonne denn tragen?*, the sixth song in his Tieck cycle, *Die schöne Magelone*, Op. 33. In Brahms's *cabaletta*, similar verbal imagery about hurrying forward (windborne messages in *Suleika*, rowing through the water in the Brahms) inspires a pattern of repeated semiquavers influenced by those to be found in its Schubertian model. Perhaps it was the large canvas of Schubert songs in contrasting tempi (like the two *Suleika* lieder) that encouraged Brahms to attempt the portmanteau settings of the Magelone legend.

One might imagine here that Schubert is wearing his composer of dance music hat (the influence of Milder's 'wide public' again?); the brisk tempo and left-hand leaps make this a ⅜ relative of the *Galopp*. Alternation of B flat major and minor is again reminiscent of the same device in the peroration of *Suleika I*. The words for the last verse, 'Sag ihm, aber sag's bescheiden', initially herald another drawing-in of the reins: a shift into G minor at b. 160, wonderfully betokening modesty and discretion, gives the pianist a moment of respite from left-hand athletics – but only for four bars; 'Freudiges Gefühl von beiden' signals a note of triumph and panting (of pianist and repeated words) which leads ineluctably to a crowning high B flat for the soprano in b. 168 – Milder's pay-off. To end here would have been too obvious and an artistic defeat for Schubert. The coda (from b. 171, marked 'Mit halber Stimme' – with half voice) is a repeat of the first two lines of the last verse ('Sag ihm, aber sag's bescheiden') and it restores a mood of dreamy delicacy to a work which has negotiated the minefield known to every composer who has undertaken a commission to someone else's specifications. (Well, that is *if* the piece really had been composed specially for Milder.) The negotiation of the 'ritard.' marked in b. 172 is a problem: does it refer only to the humility of the phrase 'Sag ihm . . . aber bescheiden' or does it govern the remaining fourteen bars as they slowly wind down? Most performers opt for the general anaesthetic, but I have come to favour the local applied to the 'bescheiden' phrase, the wind momentarily tempered rather than becalmed.

Would the work have been even greater had Schubert not attempted to satisfy Milder (again, *if* he had attempted to do so)? Was she even aware of the concessions he had made to her sense of self-importance? At least we have something a great deal more satisfying than a fluttering vocalise in imitation of a moth. Schubert might have had this song 'on the stocks' that he realized would suit her. However, *Suleika II* is patently such a diva's piece that, whatever the evidence to support its composition in 1821, one suspects this was not the case. For a discussion of Schubert's further entanglements with Anna Milder the reader is referred to the commentary on *Der Hirt auf dem Felsen* D965.

Autograph:	Missing or lost
First edition:	Published as Op. 31 by A. Pennauer, Vienna in August 1825 (P85)
Dedicatee:	Anna Milder
First known performance:	9 June 1825, Jagorscher Saal, Berlin. Soloist: Anna Milder, accompanied by her sister, Jeanette Bürde (see Waidelich/Hilmar Dokumente II No. 337a)
Contemporary reviews:	*Königlich privilegirte Berlinische Zeitung* No. 133 (11 June 1825) [Waidelich/Hilmar Dokumente I No. 338]
	Berlinische Nachrichten No. 133 (11 June 1825) [Waidelich/ Hilmar Dokumente I No. 339; Deutsch Doc. Biog. No. 559]
	Königlich privilegirte Berlinische Zeitung No. 135 (14 June 1825) [Waidelich/Hilmar Dokumente I No. 340]
	Allgemeine Musikalische Zeitung (Leipzig), No. 31 (3 August 1825), col. 526f. [Waidelich/Hilmar Dokumente I No. 344]
	The Harmonicon (London), No. 35 (November 1825), p. 211 [Waidelich/Hilmar Dokumente I No. 352]
Subsequent editions:	Peters: Vol. 2/68; AGA XX 397: Vol. 6/201; NSA IV: Vol. 2a/97; Bärenreiter: Vol. 2/4
Bibliography:	Fischer-Dieskau 1977, pp. 145–6
Further settings:	Carl Friedrich Zelter (1758–1832) *Suleika* (1820)
	Benedict Randhartinger (1802–1893) *Suleika* [date unknown]
	Fanny Mendelssohn (1805–1847) *Suleika* (1836)
	Felix Mendelssohn (1809–1847) *Suleika* Op. 34 no. 4 (1836)
Discography and timing:	Fischer-Dieskau —
	Hyperion I 19^{18}
	Hyperion II 24^{11} 4'25 Felicity Lott

← *Suleika I* D720   *Im Gegenwärtigen Vergangenes* D710 →

LUDWIG VON SZÉCHÉNYI (1781–1855)

THE POETIC SOURCES
The poems came to Schubert in handwritten form, almost certainly through friends who were intermediaries between the aristocratic poet and the composer.

THE SONGS
1817? 1821?   *Die abgeblühte Linde* D514 Op. 7 no. 1
               Der Flug der Zeit D515 Op. 7 no. 2

Ludwig, Graf von Széchényi von Sárvári-Felsö-Vidék was born in Horpács, Hungary, on 6 November 1781. He was an amateur poet and musician, and high steward to the Arch-duchess Sophie. His brother Stephan was a prominent Hungarian statesman who founded the Hungarian National Museum and Library. After Széchényi came to live in Vienna he became an influential member of the Gesellschaft der Musikfreunde. He was also something of a composer. Schubert set only two of his poems, neither of which was published as a text.

Viennese musical politics being what they were, it is possible that at the end of 1821 the publication of the Op. 7 songs (*Der Tod und das Mädchen* D531 and the two Széchényi settings, the whole opus dedicated to the poet) successfully cleared the way for Schubert's election to full membership of the Gesellschaft in March 1822. The composer might well have been urged by friends to compose – and quickly publish – these songs so that he could obtain the considerable advantages that full membership of the Gesellschaft der Musikfreunde would bring him. This course of action could have been recommended by the song composer Benedict Randhartinger, a school contemporary of Schubert's, who was Széchényi's private secretary at the time.

On the other hand, it is possible that Schubert had encountered Széchényi through another Hungarian count, Karl Esterházy, and as early as 1817. If so, the Széchényi songs

Ludwig Széchenyi, 1848.

might date from that year as contemporary works of *Der Tod und das Mädchen*. Even if this were the case, the selection of these slight works over others more worthy of early publication might still have been made for political reasons – musical politics, that is. There is no surviving record of any personal contact between poet and composer. Széchényi died on 7 February 1855.

SZENE AUS 'FAUST'
(GOETHE) **D126** [H56]

Scene from *Faust*   Solo & chorus

The song exists in two versions, the second of which is discussed below:
(1) December 1814; (2) 12 December 1814

(1) 'Sehr langsam'   C major – B♭ minor   **C**   [98 bars]

(2)   C major – B♭ minor

Dom. Amt, Orgel und Gesang. Gretchen unter vielem Volke. Böser Geist.

(100 bars)

Böser Geist:

Wie anders, Gretchen, war dir's,
Als du noch voll Unschuld
Hier zum Altar trat'st,
Aus dem vergriffenen Büchelchen
Gebete lalltest,
Halb Kinderspiele,
Halb Gott im Herzen!
Gretchen! Wo steht dein Kopf?
In deinem Herzen, welche Missetat?
Bet'st du für deiner Mutter Seele,
Die durch dich zur langen,
Langen Pein hinüberschlief?
Auf deiner Schwelle wessen Blut?
Und unter deinem Herzen
Regt sich's nicht quillend schon,
Und ängstigt dich und sich
Mit ahnungsvoller Gegenwart?

Gretchen:

Weh! Weh!
Wär' ich der Gedanken los,
Die mir herüber und hinüber gehen
Wider mich!

Chor:

Dies irae, dies illa,
Solvet saeclum in favilla.

Böser Geist:

Grimm fasst dich!
Die Posaune tönt!
Die Gräber beben!
Und dein Herz, aus Aschenruh
Zu Flammenqualen wieder aufgeschaffen,
Bebt auf!

Gretchen:

Wär' ich hier weg!
Mir ist als ob die Orgel mir
Den Atem versetzte,
Gesang mein Herz
Im Tiefsten löste.

Chor:

Judex ergo cum sedebit,
Quidquid latet adparebit,
Nil inultum remanebit.

Evil Spirit:

How differently you felt, Gretchen,
When, still full of innocence,
You came to the altar here,
Mumbling prayers
From your worn little book,
Half playing children's games,
Half with God in your heart.
Gretchen! What are you thinking of?
What sin lies within your heart?
Do you pray for the soul of your mother,
Who because of you
Overslept into a long, long agony?
And whose blood lies on your threshold?
And beneath your heart
Does not something already stir and swell,
Tormenting itself and you
With its foreboding presence?

Gretchen:

Alas! Alas!
If only I could be free of the thoughts
Which run to and fro in my mind,
Against my will.

Chorus:

Day of wrath! O day of mourning!
See fulfilled the prophets' warning.

Evil Spirit:

Anguish grips you!
The trumpet sounds,
The graves tremble!
And your heart, stirred up again
From ashen peace to blazing torment,
Trembles likewise!

Gretchen:

If only I could escape from here!
I feel as if the organ
Were taking my breath away,
And the singing dissolving my heart
In its depths.

Chorus:

When the Judge his seat attaineth,
And each hidden deed arraigneth,
Nothing unavenged remaineth.

Gretchen:	*Gretchen:*
Mir wird so eng!	I am so afraid!
Die Mauern-Pfeiler befangen mich!	The pillars of the walls are constricting me!
Das Gewölbe drängt mich! – Luft!	The vault presses down on me! – Air!
Böser Geist:	*Evil Spirit:*
Verbirg dich! Sünd' und Schande	Hide yourself! Shame and sin
Bleibt nicht verborgen.	Will not remain hidden.
Luft? Licht? Wehe dir!	Air? Light? Woe upon you!
Chor:	*Chorus:*
Quid sum miser tunc dicturus?	What shall I, frail one, be pleading?
Quem patronum rogaturus?	Who for me be interceding,
Cum vix justus sit securus.	When the just are mercy needing?
Böser Geist:	*Evil Spirit:*
Ihr Antlitz wenden	The blessed turn their faces
Verklärte von dir ab.	From you.
Die Hände dir zu reichen,	The pure shudder
Schauert's den Reinen.	To reach out their hands to you.
Weh!	Woe!
Chor:	*Chorus:*
Quid sum miser tunc dicturus?	What shall I, frail one, be pleading?
Quem patronem rogaturus?	Who for me be interceding?

JOHANN WOLFGANG VON GOETHE (1749–1832); poem written before 1775

This is the sixth of Schubert's seventy-five Goethe solo settings (1814–26). Szene aus 'Faust' is strictly speaking an ensemble piece, but as a piano-accompanied piece with significant solo passages it is listed here as one of the lieder. See the poet's biography for a complete list of all the Goethe settings.

Faust (qv), the drama in two parts that occupied Goethe for most of his life, is central to his achievement as a poet. In Part One, which Schubert encountered in 1814 (Part Two was to be published only after his death), readers are entranced by a compendium of philosophy and verse styles, noble and popular as the scenes shift from one locale to the other with bewildering speed and diversity. Fortunately a lieder composer can make light of the logistics of theatrical staging, and six weeks after composing *Gretchen am Spinnrade* D118 Schubert seized on this scene.

Above the music the composer writes the words that are simply Goethe's stage-directions transferred to manuscript paper: 'Dom. Amt, Orgel und Gesang. Gretchen unter vielem Volke. Böser Geist' ('Within a cathedral, organ and song. Gretchen among many people. The Evil Spirit'). Missing here are the words that place the Evil Spirit behind the tormented girl: 'Böser Geist *hinter* Gretchen'. Perhaps Schubert omitted these because he could not envisage one singer standing behind the other during a performance with piano. He had already composed the Matthisson *Romanze* D114 but *Szene aus 'Faust'* was a stepping stone to the extravagances of his Zumsteeg-inspired ballad style – opera-in-the-home where he conjured many of the effects of a larger staging with the limited cast of singer and pianist. The first version of this work, somewhat nearer to an orchestrally accompanied conception, is discussed at the end of this article.

Gretchen has entered the cathedral following the death of her brother Valentin who has been killed in a duel with Faust. Valentin's dying words to Gretchen (who had hoped to receive his forgiveness) reproached her for a relationship with Faust that had brought dishonour to the family. She has sought quiet refuge in the cathedral but, by chance, she has entered it during the celebration of a Requiem mass and finds that the words of the 'Dies Irae' (carefully selected for this purpose by Goethe) apply directly to her. The first thing that strikes the listener of today is that Schubert's treatment of the text denotes an operatic style that has not yet been invented, a flexible and flowing mixture of arioso and recitative with a premonition of Wagner's harmonic audacity and expressive power. It is as if Mephistopheles himself has emboldened the composer to look into the future.

The two-bar introduction consists of a pair of ascending three-note phrases that sidle up to the heroine with malicious intent. Gretchen never directly answers the 'Böser Geist' or acknowledges his presence – whether he is invisible to her is uncertain. Does she hear his devilish voice whispering in her ear, or do his

Detail from *Marguerite à l'église* (Gretchen in the church), illustration by Eugène Delacroix for Gérard de Nerval's translation of *Faust* (1828).

taunts masquerade as the workings of her own conscience? At first he speaks in seductive tones of honeyed sympathy, like a torturer persuading his victim to relax, all the better to surprise her later with the sudden onslaught of pain. The second syllable of the words 'Altar' (b. 4) and the phrase '*Gott im* Herzen' (b. 8) drop a fourth as if the sneering 'Böser Geist' were placing them in inverted commas to mock their import. Other words risible to the Devil, like 'heart' (b. 13) and 'soul' (b. 17), are similarly negatively inflected with drooping intervals. After bb. 10–11, sinister bars of chromatically rising harmonies before 'Gretchen! Wo steht dein Kopf', the 'Böser Geist' accuses Gretchen of murder: so that she could keep an assignation with Faust the hapless girl had administered a sleeping draught to her mother, not realizing that it would be fatal. The rest of the world may have regarded the circumstances of her mother's death merely as mysterious, but the 'Böser Geist' – and thus Gretchen's own conscience – knows better.

Mention of her mother's death leads to thoughts of her own impending maternal role, something that is horrendously unwelcome and will lead to her murdering her child. It is perhaps here that the spirit plants in her the seed of this terrible idea. The already-threatened baby stirs within her, and Schubert miraculously invents a figure, a slow writhing trill in tenths (bb. 24 and 26) to depict this. The young composer's knowledge of childbirth is to be expected (he came from a large family with a history of infant mortality) but this passage is chillingly, almost indecently, graphic; it is hardly surprising that this work was never sent to Goethe or proposed for publication in Schubert's lifetime.

In all three of her frenzied interruptions of Mephistopheles's taunts, Gretchen, at the end of her tether, sings in a high tessitura – a shrill contrast to the baritone's almost casual ease of utterance. In bb. 29–30 the words 'Weh! Weh! / Wär' ich' (D flat, D natural, E flat) are accompanied by three ascending diminished sevenths leading to a chord of E flat on 'los' (halfway through b. 30). In mirroring Gretchen's plight even as they support her vocal ascent, the fingers of the pianist's right hand, with every successive quaver chord, make an effort to break free from the constricted space assigned to them on the stave. They try shifting notes in the middle of the chord, moving the thumb and little finger into different harmonic permutations, until they break out into the temporary clearing of a G major chord in b. 32. This moment of respite is quickly countermanded by the C minor chorus of 'Dies irae', sung only too aptly ('Langsam' from b. 33) by members of the congregation. Condemned on all sides, Gretchen is caught between the Devil and the Holy See. The implacable strength of the chorale rhythm contrasts with the wayward indiscipline of her anguished thoughts.

From b. 45 the Evil Spirit throws off all pretence at gentleness ('Grimm fast dich! / Die Posaune tönt!). The horrors of judgement at the resurrection, last trump and all, are gloatingly described, and lead to further self-laceration on Gretchen's part as she negotiates the chromatic high wire. The judgemental chorus is heard again at b. 55 ('Wie oben'), and for the third time Schubert finds constricted music of fear and claustrophobia for his poor heroine ('Mir wird so eng!' at b. 69). In calling for air and fighting for breath, the voice claws its way out of a mass of suffocating chromatic debris, but only temporarily. The word 'Luft!' (b. 72) on an unresolved seventh chord is the last we hear of Gretchen, for it is here that she faints. In the last line of the scene in Goethe, Gretchen calls for smelling salts ('Nachbarin! Euer Fläschchen!'), but Schubert wisely avoids setting these words to music. It is only in the hushed commentary of the last choral refrain (for the first time marked piano at b. 94) that the composer allows a touch of compassion for his stricken heroine. And here he leaves her until early 1816, and the song *Der König in Thule* D367 which harks back to an earlier scene in the play. After this Schubert set *Gretchen im Zwinger* D564 in May 1817. The scene in the cathedral with the 'Böser Geist' is the last time we encounter Gretchen in Goethe's play until we find her in chains in prison, and condemned to death for infanticide. Lorraine Byrne writes that Gretchen's suffering in the *Dom* scene 'serves as a sharp rebuke to the sentimentalized Roman Catholicism portrayed by many contemporary male writers'.

Schubert's first version of this setting dates from a few days earlier in December 1814. It is a fascinating sliver from the Schubertian workbench. This version is printed in the NSA (Volume 7 p. 196) on three staves – and thus appears in the normal song format. In the autograph Schubert goes onto three staves for bb. 16–23, but the printing in the AGA (Volume 1 p. 215) is reproduced on two staves throughout and gives a clearer idea of what Schubert's original looked like, a way of working whereby songs were often conceived in a kind of preliminary shorthand. (Other surviving examples of such sketches include *Liebesbotschaft* D957/1 and *Die Taubenpost* D956A from *Schwanengesang*.) There are a few additional quasi-orchestral indications ('Orgelton', 'Tromboni') that mirror the poet's ideas found in the text, and also serve to inspire the pianist to search for colour. In the two-stave printing (thus in AGA and not NSA) the outbursts from the Requiem Mass suggest a choir singing in four parts instead of a single vocal line accompanied by four-part piano writing. Not unexpectedly the second version improves and refines the vocal line and accompaniment, and firmly returns the work to the milieu of solo song by bringing the vocal ranges of the two characters closer together. Of course this richly dramatic work can still be performed as a duet with chorus (as recorded for the Hyperion Edition) but the final version is modified in such a way as to enable a single voice to sing both roles as well as the unison chorus.

In modern times both Christine Schäfer and Christopher Maltman have performed the work as a solo; her flexible soprano is ideal for the purpose, and his high baritone easily encompasses the notes for the heroine. On the modern concert platform Gretchen's rising panic, when expressed with a touch of baritone falsetto, might all too easily suggest camp parody to the listener searching for laughs (it depends, surely on how well it is done). In Schubert's own time a singer of Vogl's larger-than-life theatricality would have impersonated Gretchen without hesitation.

See also FAUST.

Autographs:	Conservatoire collection, Bibliothèque Nationale, Paris (first version); Musée royal de Mariemont, Belgium (second version); Staatsbibliothek Preussischer Kulturbesitz, Berlin (marked 'Sketch for a further setting')
Publication:	First published in August Reismann's *Franz Schubert. Sein Leben und seine Werke* in 1873 (P467; first version) First published as Book 20 no. 2 of the *Nachlass* by Diabelli, Vienna in December 1832 (P295; second version)
Subsequent editions:	Peters: Vol. 5/108; AGA XX 37a & b: Vol. 1/215; NSA IV: Vol. 7/71 & 196; Bärenreiter: Vol. 6/15 & 132
Bibliography:	Byrne 2003, p. 329 Fischer-Dieskau 1977, p. 37 Hirsch 1993, pp. 28–37 Winter 1978, p. 500
Further Settings:	Robert Schumann (1810–1856) *Scene im Dom*, No. 3 of *Scenen aus Goethes Faust* WoO3 (1844–53) Charles Gounod (1818–1893) *Faust*, Act IV Scene 3 'Souviens-toi du passé?' (1859, rev. 1860, 1861, 1869)

Discography and timing:

Deutsche Grammophon *Schubert Duette*	6'31	Janet Baker, Dietrich Fischer-Dieskau & members of the RIAS Chamber Choir
Hyperion I 13[5] Hyperion II 4[12]	7'26	Thomas Hampson, Marie McLaughlin & members of The New Company

← *Am See* D124   *Ballade* D134 →

T

TÄGLICH ZU SINGEN
(Claudius) **D533** [H348]
F major   February 1817

To be sung daily

Ich dan - ke Gott, und freu - e mich wie's Kind zur Weih-nachts - ga - be,

(13 bars)

Ich danke Gott, und freue mich
    Wie's Kind zur Weihnachtsgabe,
Dass ich hier bin! Und dass ich dich,[1]
    Schön menschlich Antlitz! habe;

Dass ich die Sonne, Berg und Meer,
    Und Laub und Gras kann sehen,
Und abends unterm Sternenheer
    Und lieben Monde gehen;

[. . .]

Ich danke Gott mit Saitenspiel,
    Dass ich kein König worden;
Ich wär' geschmeichelt worden viel,
    Und wär' vielleicht verdorben.

[. . . 4 . . .]

Gott gebe mir nur jeden Tag,
    So viel ich darf zum Leben.
Er gibt's dem Sperling auf dem Dach;
    Wie sollt' er's mir nicht geben!

I thank God, and rejoice
    Like a child at Christmas.
That I am here! And that I possess
    The fair countenance of mankind

That I can see sun, mountains and the sea,
    Leaves and grass,
And can walk in the evening
    Beneath the host of stars and the beloved moon.

[. . .]

To the sound of strings I thank God
    That I am not a king;
I would have been greatly flattered
    And would perhaps have been corrupted.

[. . . 4 . . .]

May God give me each day,
    Just so much as I need for my life.
He gives this to the sparrow on the roof;
    Why should he not give it to me!

Matthias Claudius (1740–1815); poem published in 1778

This is the last of Schubert's thirteen Claudius solo settings (1816–17). See the poet's biography for a chronological list of all the Claudius settings.

It is a measure of Schubert's astonishing versatility that this little song was composed between *Der Tod und das Mädchen* D531 and the epic Ossian setting *Die Nacht* D534; *Ganymed* D544 lay a short while in the future. Only in his imagination could the composer roam Scottish

[1] Claudius has 'Dass ich *bin, bin!*'

moors and Elysian fields, but *Täglich zu singen* inhabits milieux with which he was more familiar – the church and the schoolroom. Schubert had at last broken free from the drudgery of teaching but the very title of *Täglich zu singen* suggests the litany of the classroom: the old-fashioned harmony with a hint of contrapuntal didacticism underlines old-fashioned values, and although one is sure that Schubert was no stringent disciplinarian, the little interlude-postlude (bb. 10–13) wags fingers of emphatic authority. The origin of the words is biblical of course, and the lyric refers to the psalms of David (the beginning of Verse 4) and the New Testament in Verse 9. According to Fischer-Dieskau, Claudius had in mind Gellert's *Morgen-gesang* 'Mein erst Gefühl sei Preis und Dank' when penning these words – albeit for singing in a Lutheran rather than a Catholic church. In its own sturdy way the poet's gratitude to the heavenly father for the beauties of life is the equal of Goethe's pantheism via Ganymede, if rather more soberly expressed. The Reichardt setting, the fifth of *Oden und Lieder von Klop-stock, Stolberg, Claudius und Hölty* (Berlin, 1779), is also in F major, but in compound time. In the absence of a marking for the Schubert song, Reichardt's paradoxical 'Ruhig und heiter' will do reasonably well, with more of an emphasis on the 'heiter'.

The poem has nine strophes. The NSA prints four verses laid under the music (apparently those chosen by the composer), all printed and translated above. These are 1, 2, 4 and 9 of the poet's original. The Hyperion recording contents itself with 1, 2 and 9.

Autograph:	University Library of Lund, Sweden (first draft)
First edition:	Published as a solo piano arrangement entitled 'Ich danke Gott' by Kratochwill, Vienna in 1876; and with vocal line as part of the AGA in 1895 (P472)
Subsequent editions:	Not in Peters; AGA XX 304: Vol. 5/38; NSA IV: Vol. 11/89
Further settings & arrangements:	Johann Abraham Peter Schulz (1747–1800) *Täglich zu singen* (1782–90)
	Johann Friedrich Reichardt (1752–1814) *Täglich zu singen* (1778–9)
	Arr. Tilman Hoppstock (b. 1961) for guitar accompaniment, in *Franz Schubert: 110 Lieder* (2009)
Discography and timing:	Fischer-Dieskau I 9²¹ 1'13 (first two strophes only)
	Hyperion I 5⁸
	Hyperion II 17²⁶ 1'28 Elizabeth Connell

← *Der Tod und das Mädchen* D531   *Die Nacht* D534 →

Die TÄUSCHUNG   Illusion
(KOSEGARTEN) **D230** [H121]
E major   7 July 1815

Im Er-len-busch, im Tan-nen-hain, im Sonn- und Mond- und Ster-nen-schein

(14 bars)

Im Erlenbusch, im Tannenhain,
Im Sonn- und Mond- und Sternenschein
Umlächelt mich ein Bildnis.
Vor seinem Lächeln klärt sich schnell
Die Dämmerung in Himmelhell,
In Paradies die Wildnis.

In the alder grove, in the pine wood,
By the light of sun, moon and stars,
An image smiles upon me.
At that smile
Dusk quickly changes to celestial brightness,
And the wilderness turns to paradise.

Es säuselt in der Abendluft,
Es dämmert in dem Morgenduft,
Es tanzet auf der Aue.
Es flötet in der Wachtelschlag,
Und spiegelt sich im klaren Bach,
Und badet sich im Taue.

It whispers in the evening air;
It drowses in the morning fragrance;
It dances in the meadow;
It sings in the song of the quail;
It is reflected in the clear brook,
And bathes in the dew.

[...]

[...]

Ich öffn' ihm sehnend meinen Arm,
Und streb' es traut und liebewarm
An meine Brust zu drücken.
Ich hasch' und hasche leere Luft,
Und nichtig, wie ein Nebelduft
Entwallt es meinen Blicken.

I open my arms to it longingly,
And strive to press it
Tenderly, ardently, to my breast.
I snatch at it, and snatch empty air,
And it drifts from my sight,
As insubstantial as mist.

Wer bist du, holdes Luftgebild,
Das engelhold und engelmild
Mit Schmerz und Lust mich tränket?
Bist du ein Bote bessrer Welt,
Der mich aus deinem öden Feld
In seine Heimat winket?

Who are you, sweet ethereal creature
Who with angelic grace and tenderness,
Floods me with pain and joy?
Are you a messenger from a better world,
Calling me from this desolate land
To your own country?

O fleuch voran! Ich folge dir.
Bei dir ist Seligkeit, nicht hier;
Sprich, wo ich dich erfasse,
Und ewig aller Pein entrückt,
Umstrickend dich, von dir umstrickt,
Dich nimmer, nimmer lasse.

O flee hence! I shall follow you!
Bliss is with you, not here!
Tell me where I may hold you,
And never, ever leave you,
Eternally freed from all pain,
Embracing and embraced by you!

LUDWIG KOSEGARTEN (1758–1818); poem written in 1787

This is the fifth of Schubert's twenty-one Kosegarten solo settings (1815–17). See the poet's biography for a chronological list of all the Kosegarten settings, as well as a discussion of Morten Solvik's Kosegarten Liederkreis and this song's place within it.

An enchanting song this, one of those little Schubertian jewels that are always a happy surprise to encounter in those pages of the *Gesamtausgabe* ignored by all but the avid enthusiast. Schubert found Kosegarten one of his most potent sources of inspiration in 1815; between June and October of that year he composed no fewer than twenty settings. While all are strophic and none are of ground-breaking originality, these songs have a gentle sweetness and inner radiance that achieves a modest and endearing perfection. For songs with this unpretentious feel it seems that E major was the composer's favourite key. According to John Reed it is the Schubertian tonality of innocence and joy, and it is used for six of the Kosegarten settings from this year. The same key dominates a group of the 1816 strophic settings such as Hölty's *Seligkeit* D433 and *Erntelied* D434 which border on folksong. In mood and key *Die Täuschung* is similar to *Die Erscheinung* D229, another Kosegarten setting written on the same day, but in its gentle and confidential tone it also prefigures two Hölty settings from May 1816, *Die frühe Liebe* D430 and *Blumenlied* D431.

Among the felicities of *Die Täuschung* is the gently rocking accompaniment for the left hand in quavers; the right hand enters at the end of the first bar and forms a delicate descant throughout, flute music that dances gravely over the slightly old-fashioned Alberti bass. The first thing we hear in the accompaniment's treble is a sighing motif of five notes, signifying perhaps the gentle sound of the pastoral pipe, or a mysterious smiling presence hovering high over the picture. The second half of the strophe (from 'Vor seinem Lächeln klärt sich schnell') provides transformation music (from b. 6) that reaches its apogee on a high A on the first syllable of 'Paradies' (b. 11). The clarity and tessitura of this radiant passage suggests purity, but its chromaticism betokens deception; it is accompanied by the piano with a delightful right-hand motif of descending thirds phrased into gentle sighs and tremulous trills. The reverse of the song's coin of simplicity is a gently exquisite sensuality; perhaps that is also a part of the 'deception' at its heart. There is no sign here of the unhinged parody of Viennese *Gemütlichkeit* that characterizes the waltz song which, but for the lack of a definite article, is this song's namesake – *Täuschung* from *Winterreise* D911/19.

Kosegarten's poem has six strophes. Two of these are laid under music in the AGA and the rest printed at the bottom of the page. In the NSA all are printed beneath the stave which is a great deal easier for the singer. Translated here are 1, 2, 4, 5 and 6. For the Hyperion Edition 1, 2 and 6 were performed.

Autograph:	Wienbibliothek im Rathaus, Vienna (fair copy)
First edition:	Published as a supplement to *Zellners Blätter für Musik, Theater und Kunst* in 1855; subsequently issued as Op. post. 165 no. 4 by C. A. Spina, Vienna in 1862 (P399)
Subsequent editions:	Peters: Vol. 6/93; AGA XX 93: Vol. 2/176; NSA IV: Vol. 8/120
Discography and timing:	Fischer-Dieskau I 4[11] 1'39
	Hyperion I 20[12]
	Hyperion II 8[4] 1'41 Patricia Rozario

⟵ *Die Erscheinung (Erinnerung)* D229   *Das Sehnen* D231 ⟶

TÄUSCHUNG *see* WINTERREISE D911/19

Des TAGES WEIHE *see* SCHICKSALSLENKER, BLICKE NIEDER D763

Der TANZ

The dance   Quartet, SATB

(SCHNITZER VON MEERAU?) **D826** [H659]
C major   Early 1828?

(26 bars)

Es redet und träumet die Jugend so viel	Youth talks and dreams so much
Von Tanzen, Galoppen, Gelagen,	Of dancing, capering and carousing;
Auf einmal erreicht sie ein trügliches Ziel,	Then all of a sudden it reaches its illusory goal,
Da hört man sie seufzen und klagen.	And we hear it sighing and complaining.
Bald schmerzet der Hals,	Now the pain is in the throat,
Und bald schmerzet die Brust,	Now it's in the chest;
Verschwunden ist alle die himmlische Lust.	Vanished are all heavenly joys.
'Nur einmal noch kehr' mir Gesundheit zurück!'	'Give me back my health just this once!'
So flehet vom Himmel der hoffende Blick.	The imploring gaze beseeches heaven!
Jüngst wähnt' auch ein Fräulein mit trüben Gefühl,	Recently a young lady, profoundly despondent,
Schon hätte ihr Stündlein geschlagen,	Thought that her last hour had come.
Doch stand noch das Rädchen der Parze nicht still,	But the wheel of the fates had not yet stopped,
Nun schöner die Freuden ihr tagen.	And now joys dawn all the fairer.
Drum Freunde, erhebet den frohen Gesang,	So, friends, raise your voices in joyful song,
Es lebe die teure Irene noch lang!	May dear Irene live many a long year!
Sie denke zwar oft as das falsche Geschick,	However often she recalls the caprice of fate,
Doch trübe sich nimmer ihr heiterer Blick.	May her merry look never grow dark.

KOLUMBAN SCHNITZER VON MEERAU (dates not known)

This is one of the rare songs that lead us directly into the dance world of Schubert's contemporaries (his dance music remains his least-known and most underestimated body of work). It is a merry romp in a bouncing §, bristling with energy and good spirits. The fanfare-like introduction in a bright C major forgoes any unnecessary subtlety; the best thing about this chorus is its rousing and infectious tune. The vocal lines are unusually straightforward; there is no attempt at contrapuntal interplay between the parts, and the soprano line is doubled throughout in the pianist's right hand, with the addition of cheeky mordents and semiquaver elaborations. A delightful touch is the complete lack of postlude; the music comes to an end with a sudden and bracing flourish of three unison Cs in the piano – two semiquavers and a quaver.

Closely related to *Der Tanz* is *Al par del ruscelleto* D936, a short Italian cantata with chorus and piano-duet accompaniment, also in C major. This was composed at the end of 1827 to celebrate the recovery of Irene Kiesewetter (1811–1872) from serious illness. Her father Raphael Georg Kiesewetter von Wiesenbrunn (1773–1850) was an important official in Viennese life, and a friend of Leopold von Sonnleithner who played a key role in arranging to have Schubert's songs printed for the first time. While recent scholarship posits that *Der Tanz* was composed more or less at the same time, or slightly after Irene's recovery, thus in early 1828, it was the opinion of Kreissle von Hellborn and Otto Erich Deutsch that this vocal quartet was written in

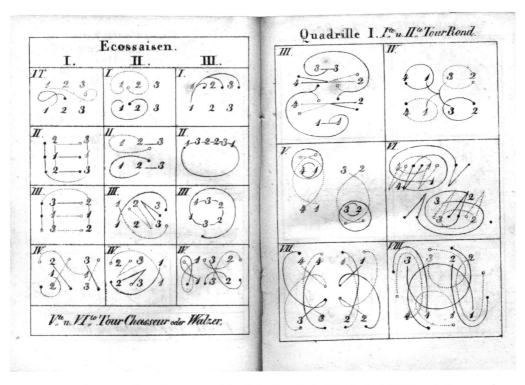

Dance figures ('Tanztouren') for Ecossaises and Quadrilles from *Becker's Taschenbuch* (1818); such choreographic diagrams were a frequent feature of almanacs of the time.

1825 as a light-hearted warning to Irene concerning her unquenchable passion for dancing. A piece like this would also have been welcomed by the Schubertians at the end of this year of lively parties. Against this theory is the fact that Irene was only fourteen in 1825 and that the second verse of the piece (printed for the first time in the NSA in 1996, too late to be recorded for the Hyperion Edition) refers directly to Irene and, by implication, to her health. She survived this crisis to become an accomplished accompanist of Schubert's songs. The poem's authorship remains far from certain – the name Schnitzer is mentioned on a copy of the music, and the only person of that name in the fringe of the Schubert circle is one Kolumban Schnitzer von Meerau, although almost nothing is known about him. The opening lines of the poem are a parody of the well-known Schiller poem *Hoffnung*, set twice by Schubert (D251 and D637).

Autograph:	Wienbibliothek im Rathaus, Vienna
First edition:	Published as part of the AGA in 1892 (P517)
Subsequent editions:	AGA XVII 14: p. 228; NSA III: Vol. 2a/191
Discography and timing:	

Deutsche Grammophon *Schubert-Quartette*	0'52	Elly Ameling, Janet Baker, Peter Schreier & Dietrich Fischer-Dieskau
Hyperion I 35[18] Hyperion II 35[12]	1'43	Patricia Rozario, Catherine Denley, Ian Bostridge & Michael George

←— *Die Sterne* D939   *Auf dem Strom* D943 —→

Die TAUBENPOST *see SCHWANENGESANG* D965A

Der TAUCHER   The diver
(SCHILLER) **D77**[1] [H29]

The song exists in two versions, the second of which is discussed below:
(1) 5 April 1814 (D77); (2) completed beginning of 1815 (D111)

(1) 'Allegro'   C major – D minor   **C**   [575 bars]

(2) C major – D minor

(605 bars)

The text printed below follows that of the second version

(1)	Wer wagt es, Rittersmann oder Knapp, Zu tauchen in diesen Schlund? Einen goldnen Becher werf ich hinab. Verschlungen schon hat ihn der 　　schwarze Mund. Wer mir den Becher kann wieder zeigen, Er mag ihn behalten, er ist sein eigen.	'Who will dare, knight or squire, To dive into this abyss? I hurl this golden goblet down, The black mouth has already devoured it. He who can show me the goblet again, May keep it, it is his.'
(2)	Der König spricht es und wirft von 　　der Höh Der Klippe, die schroff und steil Hinaushängt in die unendliche See, Den Becher in der Charybde Geheul. 'Wer ist der Beherzte, ich frage wieder, Zu tauchen in diese Tiefe nieder?'	Thus the king speaks, and from the top Of the cliff which juts abruptly and steeply Into the endless sea, he hurls the goblet into the howling Charybdis. 'Who is there brave enough, I ask once more, To dive down into the depths?'
(3)	Und die Ritter, die Knappen um ihm her, Vernehmen's und schweigen still, Sehen hinab in das wilde Meer, Und keiner den Becher gewinnen will. Und der König zum dritten Mal wieder 　　fraget: Ist keiner, der sich hinunter waget?	And the knights and squires around him Listen, and keep silent, Looking down into the turbulent sea, And none desires to win the goblet. And the king asks a third time: 'Is there no one who will dare the depths?'
(4)	Doch alles noch stumm bleibt wie zuvor, Und ein Edelknecht, sanft und keck, Tritt aus der Knappen zagendem Chor. Und den Gürtel wirft er, den Mantel weg, Und alle die Männer umher und Frauen Auf den herrlichen Jüngling verwundert 　　schaun.	But all remain silent as before, Then a young squire, gentle and bold, Steps from the hesitant throng, Throws off his belt and cloak. And all the men and women around him Gaze in astonishment at the fine youth.

[1] In the first edition of the Deutsch catalogue the second version of *Der Taucher* is given the separate number D111.

(5) Und wie er tritt an des Felsen Hang,
   Und blickt in den Schlund hinab,
   Die Wasser, die sie hinunter schlang,
   Die Charybde jetzt brüllend wiedergab,
   Und wie mit des fernen Donners Getose
   Entstürzen sie schäumend dem finstern
      Schosse.

And as he steps to the cliff's edge,
And looks down into the abyss,
The waters which Charybdis devoured
She now regurgitates, roaring
And, as if with the rumbling of distant thunder,
They rush foaming from the black womb.

(6) Und es wallet und siedet und brauset
      und zischt,
   Wie wenn Wasser mit Feuer sich mengt,
   Bis zum Himmel spritzet der dampfende
      Gischt,
   Und Flut auf Flut sich ohn' Ende drängt,
   Und will sich nimmer erschöpfen und
      leeren,
   Als wollte das Meer noch ein Meer
      gebären.

The waters seethe and boil, rage and hiss
As if they were mixed with fire,
The steaming spray gushes up to the heavens,
And flood piles upon flood ceaselessly,
Never exhausting itself, never emptying,
As if the sea would beget yet another sea.

(7) Doch endlich, da legt sich die wilde
      Gewalt,
   Und schwarz aus dem weissen Schaum
   Klafft hinunter ein gähnender Spalt,
   Grundlos als ging's in den Höllenraum,
   Und reissend sieht man die brandenden
      Wogen
   Hinab in den strudelnden Trichter
      gezogen.

But at length the turbulent force abates,
And black from the white foam
A yawning rift gapes deep down,
Bottomless, as if it led to hell's domain;
And you see the tumultuous foaming waves,
Sucked down into the seething crater.

(8) Jetzt schnell, eh' die Brandung
      wiederkehrt,[2]
   Der Jüngling sich Gott befiehlt,
   Und – ein Schrei des Entsetzens wird
      rings gehört,
   Und schon hat ihn der Wirbel
      hinweggespült,
   Und geheimnisvoll über dem kühnen
      Schwimmer
   Schliesst sich der Rachen, er zeigt sich
      nimmer.

Now swiftly, before the surge returns,
The youth commends himself to God,
And – a cry of horror is heard all around –
The whirlpool has already borne him away,
And over the bold swimmer, mysteriously,
The gaping abyss closes; he will never be seen
   again.

(9) Und stille wird's über dem
      Wasserschlund,
   In der Tiefe nur brauset es hohl,
   Und bebend hört man von Mund
      zu Mund:
   Hochherziger Jüngling, fahre wohl!

Calm descends over the watery abyss.
Only in the depths is there a hollow roar,
And the words falter from mouth to mouth:
'Valiant youth, farewell!'

[2] Schiller writes 'widerkehret'.

Und hohler und hohler hört man's heulen,
Und es harrt noch mit bangem, mit
   schrecklichem Weilen.

The roar grows ever more hollow,
And they wait, anxious and fearful.

(10)   Und wärfst du die Krone selber hinein
Und sprächst: wer mir bringet die Kron,
Er soll sie tragen und König sein,
Mich gelüstete nicht nach dem teuren
   Lohn.
Was die heulende Tiefe da unten verhehle,
Das erzählt keine lebende glückliche Seele.

Even if you threw in the crown itself
and said, 'Whoever brings me this crown,
Shall wear it and be king,' –
I would not covet the precious reward.

What the howling depths may conceal,
No living soul will ever tell.

(11)   Wohl manches Fahrzeug, vom Strudel
   gefasst,
Schoss gäh in die Tiefe hinab,
Doch zerschmettert nur rangen, sich
   Kiel und Mast
Hervor aus dem alles verschlingenden
   Grab—
Und heller und heller, wie Sturmes Sausen
Hört man's näher und immer näher
   brausen.

Many a vessel, caught by the whirlpool,

Has plunged sheer into the depths,
Yet only wrecked keels and masts

Have struggled out of the all-consuming grave.

Like the rushing of a storm,
The roaring grows ever closer and more vivid.

(12)   Und es wallet und siedet und brauset
   und zischt,
Wie wenn Wasser mit Feuer sich mengt,
Bis zum Himmel spritzet der dampfende
   Gischt,
Und Well' auf Well' sich ohn' Ende drängt,
Und wie mit des fernen Donners Getose
Entstürzt es brüllend dem finstren
   Schosse.

The waters seethe and boil, rage and hiss,

As if they were mixed with fire,
The steaming spray gushes up to the heavens

And flood piles on flood, ceaselessly,
And, as if with the rumbling of distant thunder,
The waters rush foaming from the black womb.

(13)   Und sieh! aus dem finster flutenden
   Schoss
Da hebet sich's schwanenweiss,
Und ein Arm und ein glänzender Nacken
   wird bloss,
Und es rudert mit Kraft und mit
   emsigem Fleiss,
Und er ist's, und hoch in seiner Linken
Schwingt er den Becher mit freudigem
   Winken.

But look! from the dark watery womb

A form rises, as white as a swan,
An arm and a glistening neck are revealed,

Rowing powerfully, and with energetic zeal,

It is he! and high in his left hand
He joyfully waves the goblet.

(14)   Und atmete lang und atmete tief,
Und begrüsste das himmlische Licht.
Mit Frohlocken es einer dem andern rief,
Er lebt! Er ist da! Es behielt ihn nicht.

He breathes long, he breathes deeply,
And greets the heavenly light.
Rejoicing they call to each other:
'He's alive! He's here! The abyss did not keep
   him!

Aus dem Grab, aus der strudelnden
  Wasserhöhle
Hat der Brave gerettet die lebende Seele.

From the grave, the swirling watery cavern,
The brave man has saved his living soul.'

(15) Und er kommt, es umringt ihn die
  jubelnde Schar,
Zu des Königs Füssen er sinkt,
Den Becher reicht er ihm knieend dar,
Und der König der lieblichen Tochter
  winkt,
Die füllt ihn mit funkelndem Wein bis
  zum Rande,
Und der Jüngling sich also zum König
  wandte:

He approaches, the joyous throng surround
  him;
And he falls down at the king's feet,
Kneeling, he hands him the goblet,
And the king signals to his charming daughter

Who fills it to the brim with sparkling wine;

Then the youth turns to the king:

(16) Lange lebe der König! Es freue sich,[3]
Wer da atmet im rosigten Licht!
Aber da unten aber ist's fürchterlich,[4]
Und der Mensch versuche die Götter
  nicht,
Und begehre nimmer und nimmer zu
  schauen,
Was sie gnädig bedecken mit Nacht
  und Grauen.

'Long live the king! Rejoice,
Whoever breathes this rosy light!
But down below it is terrible,
And man should never tempt the gods

Nor should ever desire to see

What they graciously conceal in night and
  horror.

(17) Es riss mich hinunter blitzesschnell.
Da stürzt' mir aus felsigem Schacht,
Entgegen ein reissender Quell:[5]
Mich packte des Doppelstrom's
  wütende Macht,
Und wie einen Kreisel mit
  schwindelndem Drehen
Trieb mich's um, ich konnte nicht
  widerstehn.

'It tore me down as fast as lightning –
Then, from a rocky shaft
A torrential flood poured towards me:
I was seized by the double current's raging
  force,
And, like the giddy whirling of a top,

It hurled me round; I could not resist.

(18) Da zeigte mir Gott, zu dem ich rief,
In der höchsten schrecklichen Not,
Emporragend ein Felsenriff,[6]
Das erfasst' ich behend und entrann
  dem Tod,
Und da hing auch der Becher an
  spitzen Korallen,
Sonst wär' er ins Bodenlose gefallen.

'Then God, to whom I cried,
Showed me, at the height of my dire distress,
A rocky reef, rising from the depths,
I swiftly gripped it and escaped death –

And there, too, the goblet hung on coral lips,

Or else it would have fallen into the bottomless
  ocean.

---

[3] Schiller writes '*Lang* lebe der König'.
[4] Schiler writes '*Da unten aber* ist's fürchterlich'.
[5] Schiller writes '*Wildflutend* entgegen ein reissender Quell'.
[6] Schiller writes '*Aus der Tiefe ragend* ein Felsenriff'.

(19)	Denn unter mir lag's noch, Bergetief,
	In purpurner Finsternis da,
	Und ob's hier dem Ohre gleich ewig
	schlief,
	Das Auge mit Schaudern hinunter sah,
	Wie's von Salamandern und Molchen
	und Drachen
	Sich regte in dem furchtbaren
	Höllenrachen.[7]

'For below me still it lay, fathomlessly deep,
There in purple darkness,
And even if, for the ear, there was eternal calm
here,
The eye looked down with dread,
At the salamanders and dragons

Inhabiting the terrifying caverns of hell.

(20) Schwarz wimmelten da, im grausen
Gemisch,
Zu scheusslichen Klumpen geballt,
Der stachlichte Roche, der Klippenfisch,
Des Hammers greuliche Ungestalt,
Und dräuend wies mir die grimmigen
Zähne
Der entsetzliche Hai, des Meeres Hyäne.

'Black, in a ghastly melée,

Massed in horrifying clumps,
Teemed the stinging roach, the fish of the cliff,
The hammerhead, hideously misshapen,
And, threatening me with his wrathful teeth,

The gruesome shark, the hyena of the sea.

(21) Und da hing ich und war mir's mit
Grausen bewusst,[8]
Von der menschlichen Hilfe so weit,
Unter Larven die einzige fühlende Brust,
Allein in der grässlichen Einsamkeit,
Tief unter dem Schall der menschlichen
Rede
Bei den Ungeheuern der traurigen Öde.

'And there I hung, terrifyingly conscious

How far I was from human help;
Among larvae the only living heart,
Alone in terrible solitude,
Deep beneath the sound of human speech

With the monsters of that dismal wilderness.

(22) Und schaudernd dacht' ich's, da kroch's
heran,
Regte hundert Gelenke zugleich,
Will schnappen nach mir; in des
Schreckens Wahn
Lass' ich los der Koralle umklammerten
Zweig,
Gleich fasst mich der Strudel mit
rasendem Toben,
Doch es war mir zum Heil, er riss mich
nach oben.

'And, with a shudder, I thought it was creeping
along,
Moving hundreds of limbs at once,
It wanted to grab me – in a terrifying frenzy

I let go of the coral's clinging branch:

At once the whirlpool seized me with raging
force,
But it was my salvation, pulling me upwards.'

(23) Der König darob sich verwundert schier,
Und spricht: Der Becher ist dein,
Und diesen Ring noch bestimm' ich dir,
Geschmückt mit dem köstlichsten
Edelgestein,
Versuchst du's noch einmal und bringst
mir Kunde,

At this the king is greatly amazed,
And says, 'The goblet is yours,
And this ring, too, I will give you,
Adorned with the most precious stones,

If you try once more, and bring me news

---

[7] Schiller writes 'Sich *regt*'; Schubert adds another awkward syllable to the metrical line.
[8] Schiller writes 'und *war's mir*'.

Was du sahst auf des Meers tief unterstem Grunde.	Of what you have seen on the deepest sea's deepest bed.'
(24) Das hörte die Tochter mit weichem Gefühl,	His daughter hears this with tenderness,
Und mit schmeichelndem Munde sie fleht;	And implores with coaxing words:
'Lass, Vater, genug sein das grausame Spiel,	'Father, let the cruel game cease!
Er hat euch bestanden, was keiner besteht,	He has endured for you what no other could endure,
Und könnt ihr des Herzens Gelüsten nicht zähmen!	And if you cannot tame the desire of your heart,
So mögen die Ritter den Knappen beschämen.'	Then let the knights shame the squire.'
(25) Drauf der König greift nach dem Becher schnell,	Thereupon the king quickly seizes the goblet,
In den Strudel ihn schleudert hinein;	And hurls it into the whirlpool:
Und schaffst du den Becher mir wieder zur Stell,	'If you return the goblet to this spot,
So sollst du der trefflichste Ritter mir sein,	You shall be my noblest knight.
Und sollst sie als Ehgemahl heut' noch umarmen,	And you shall embrace as a bride this very day
Die jetzt für dich bittet mit zartem Erbarmen.	The one who now pleads for you with tender pity.'
(26) Da ergreift's ihm die Seele mit Himmelsgewalt,	Now his soul is seized with heavenly power,
Und es blitzt aus den Augen ihm kühn,	And his eyes flash boldly,
Und es siehet erröten die schöne Gestalt,	And he sees the fair creature blush,
Und sieht sie erbleichen und sinken hin,	Then grow pale and swoon –
Da treibt's ihn, den köstlichen Preis zu erwerben,	This impels him to gain the precious prize
Und stürzt hinunter auf Leben und Sterben.	And he plunges down, to life or death.
(27) Wohl hört man die Brandung, wohl kehrt sie zurück,	The foaming waves are heard, they return,
Sie verkündigt der donnernde Schall,	Heralded by the thunderous roar –
Da bückt sich's hinunter mit liebendem Blick,	She leans over with loving gaze:
Es kommen, es kommen die Wasser all,	The waves keep on returning,
Sie rauschen herauf, sie rauschen nieder,	Surging, they rise and fall;
Doch den Jüngling bringt keines wieder.[9]	Yet not one will will bring back the youth.

---

[9] The word 'Doch' in this line is Schubert's own addition.

FRIEDRICH VON SCHILLER (1759–1805); poem completed 14 June 1797

This is the sixth of Schubert's forty-four Schiller solo settings (1811–24). See the poet's biography for a chronological list of all the Schiller settings.

Schubert's experiments with opera in the home are still much misunderstood and undervalued. The miracle of compression and distillation in his songs of two or three pages was made possible by his apprenticeship in the 'song theatre' – which is to say the enormous ballads of the earlier years of his career. Here we see Schubert in his workshop, sleeves rolled up, stage-managing every aspect of scene-change and lighting. Like the Shakespeare of the early histories, he is learning how to combine the art of storytelling with the creation of believable characters. But perhaps a more modern analogy suits Schubert's talents better: in composing operas of the imagination he was actually a pioneer of film techniques. Cutting and splicing, crowd scenes, special effects, long shots and close-ups, miraculously instantaneous scene changes – all are to be found in the ballads of his teenage years. A certain lack of dramatic drive and pacing has undermined the success of his operas in the theatre: largely thanks to flat-footed librettists, he gets stuck in scenes from which, in a ballad, he could extricate himself in a trice. So much of his music deals with emotion in close-up, and tiny yet telling nuances, that it is little wonder that he found the conventions of opera clumsy and inhibiting. His unique gift would have responded better to the cracking pace of film scripts than to wooden libretti requiring trundling shifts of scenery behind an opera-house curtain. Apart from its unhappy ending, *Der Taucher* would be the perfect subject for an Indiana Jones movie. It has everything: a villainous tyrant, a pretty and compassionate princess, whirlpools and sea monsters, and a young hero who, having proved either invincible or plain lucky, perishes in the tragic finale. With today's world-wide demand for escapist films, it is easy to understand why Schubert's century, innocent of cinema, responded with enthusiasm first to poetry and then to compositions like this.

Schubert worked hard over two years at writing and rewriting *Der Taucher*. The first version (D77) was begun on 17 September 1813 and completed on 5 April 1814. The second version was finished in August 1814. Early in 1815 the composer made a copy with further changes in two crucial passages. These revisions have survived in a copy of a copy belonging to Johann Leopold Ebner. For the definitive version published in Volume 6 of the NSA the editors used the Ebner copy, adding missing details that were transferred from the second version and further details (dynamics and so on) from the first. Diabelli's posthumous first edition in the *Nachlass* (qv) took as its basis Schubert's first version (D77) and grafted on the big piano interlude from the second (the 'Prestissimo' passage beginning at b. 503). This compromise was reprinted in the Peters Edition and was recorded by Fischer-Dieskau and Moore. Schubert's second and third thoughts – as published in the NSA as D111'[10] – are superior in many details, above all in the use of silence at dramatic points, and in employing contrasting dynamics. Old-fashioned mannerisms are discarded and passages are compressed into recitative that in the first version hang fire as long-winded arioso. Moreover, Italian markings are replaced by German.

Schiller's twenty-seven-verse epic, perhaps inspired by an early version of the Beowulf saga, was written in the year of the composer's birth and it is possible that Schubert was familiar with it long before he set it to music.

Verse 1: In pompous dotted rhythm the king strides centre stage, peremptory and capricious in imperious recitative. Schiller shows how absolute monarchs are able to play with the lives of

---

[10] NSA Vol. 6 was published in 1969. Since then the second Deutsch catalogue (1978) directed that both versions of the song are D77.

their subjects at whim. From the rumbling octaves in the bass from b. 5 we hear the turbulent waters of the black-mouthed abyss. As the king announces his intention of throwing a precious goblet over the edge, the piano writing plunges downwards (bb. 9–10) in a C major arpeggio. At b. 12 a D minor staccato arpeggio springs upwards, the opposite direction illustrating the monarch's idea of a game of catch with a human retriever.

Verses 2–4: At b. 17, with a marking of 'tempo moderato', direct speech yields to the voice of the narrator. In the accompaniment's swirling semiquavers we hear the king's milling entourage and their astonishment as he hurls the cup into the sea (an E major arpeggio at bb. 22–3). The words 'in der Charybde Geheul' are mirrored by a piano interlude that emphasizes the super-natural horror of the challenge. (The locale is taken directly from the twelfth canto of Homer's *Odyssey* and Michael Kube in *Liedlexikon*, 2012, p. 38 believes that Schiller had seen an illustra-tion of this passage in Athanasius Kircher's *Mundus subterraneus*.) The king's words are met by a bar of cowed silence at b. 41 (an inspired amendment of Schubert's earlier, notier, ideas). This is followed by the cravenly tentative music describing the frightened entourage; the left-hand appoggiaturas somehow suggest their shifty embarrassment. The king asks, for a third time, who will dare to undertake this task and is again met by silence, illustrated by the musical timidity of the interlude between bb. 65 and 68. With a change of key signature into A flat major at b. 69 the hero emerges, 'ein Edelknecht', supported by clean, naive semibreve chords. In a matter-of-fact way he removes his belt and cloak, to the astonishment of the assembled throng. The chromatically rising interlude at bb. 83–6 suggests disbelief as well as excitement – some courtiers are horrified, but others prepare to enjoy a Coliseum-like spectacle at the tyrant's behest.

Verses 5–7: At b. 87 there is a double bar line and a change of key signature to G minor for twenty-five bars that provide an extended upbeat to the long C minor passage that will follow. Here Schubert is thinking tactically in long harmonic paragraphs. The brave youth now has a few moments in which to survey the terrain and realize the extent of his terrible task. When the change to C minor comes, at b. 112 ('con espressione'), the horror of the challenge is grimly outlined by the sort of music that served the cause of melodrama (including silent film accom-paniment) for more than a century afterwards. The seething C minor whirlpool at Verse 6 ('Und es wallet und siedet und brauset und zischt') is a major structural force in the song. As the waters momentarily subside the music thins out for the interlude between bb. 131 and 137 and the yawning rift engendered by the whirlpool is revealed in a sequence of cavernous wide-open semibreve chords (for 'ein gähnender Spalt' at b. 147 until b. 152) in C flat major. Marie-Agnes Dittrich has pointed out the similarity of the falling passage (bb. 145–8) to the music for the falling leaf (including exact tonalities) in *Letzte Hoffnung* D911/16 from *Winterreise* (at bb. 25–7).

Verses 8–12: From b. 163 ('Jetzt schnell, eh' die Brandung widerkehrt') recitative hurries the story along. As the youth takes the plunge an unexpected fortissimo diminished chord in the treble register (b. 166) screams on behalf of the frightened female spectators. This is followed by suspense: the flats of C minor melt into naturals and from b. 173 a passage marked 'Adagio' reflects the horror of the aristocratic audience as a shivering demisemiquaver motif alternates between the hands in a succession of keys. The chorus rates the hero's chances at nought. (In the first version Schubert had made this scene lyrical with arioso to little dramatic effect.) The poem reflects, as if preparing an obituary for the foolhardy youth, on the dangers of the whirl-pool, with the observers averring that if the crown itself were on offer in those dangerous depths, nothing would induce them to take the risk. Because Schiller writes this in the first person on behalf of the agonized entourage, it is the narrator who seems to be allowing himself a moment

Der Taucher from *Handzeichnungen um Dichtungen der deutschen Classiker* by Eugen Neureuther (1832).

of reflection. From b. 202 the waters begin to surge up again in a gradual chromatic spiral; an interlude (bb. 209–14) leads to a return (with a change of key signature back to C minor) to the music for Verse 6 (b. 215). While the young man, now beneath the surface, experiences at first hand horrors that he had previously only surveyed from the edge of the cliff, the king and his entourage, including the narrator, can only see (and hear) what has already been described – masterful grounds for recapitulation.

Verses 13–14: Once again the waters subside, drained away before their furious return – such is the tidal cycle of the whirlpool. The thinning musical texture – the change from the depiction of horror to the illustration of a miracle – precedes the appearance of a white hand and arm and then, bit by bit, the rest of the diver. It is tempting to think that Schumann might have known Schubert's supremely dramatic response to this image: the writing on the wall by a disembodied hand at Belshazzar's Feast (in the Heine setting *Belsatzar* Op. 57) is depicted in similarly ascending chromaticism, and in a section also beginning 'Und sieh!', as at bb. 238–9. At bb. 254–5 there is music of triumph ('Und er ist's') for the returning hero. For the young man this is a holy moment. The harmonies breathe deep and long together with him in gratitude for life; the tempo marking is 'Più andante' from b. 263, and E flat major has replaced C minor. This passage was triumphantly forte in the first version, but in the second its hushed radiance provides a moment of respite in the ballad's hurly-burly. At b. 269 there is a change of key signature to four sharps, new harmonic terrain that prompts an aria of gratitude and general rejoicing (beginning 'Mit Frohlocken es einer dem andern rief', marked 'Con moto' at b. 276) in a mood of sunny geniality.

Verses 15–20: The youth kneels at the feet of his sovereign. For the first time we glimpse the beautiful princess who is commanded to fill the rescued goblet with wine. Unlike the first version where the exhausted boy manages an unlikely formal aria, free recitative here propels the story forward. The young man salutes the king in a passage of arisoso (bb. 306–10) before describing the horrors he has survived. As his storytelling warms up, so does the music (the marking at b. 331 is 'Più mosso'). The narrative of what the intrepid diver has seen in the netherworld is at the heart of the work. As he describes the goblet teetering on the coral reef, it hangs precariously on the vocal line; in this marvellous passage (bb. 356–65) the suspense is almost palpable – as if too much movement from the performers will dislodge the goblet and send it spiralling into the depths. The ominous music of the threatening monsters of the deep slithers in oily passage-work; no mercurial semiquavers here, only massive caterpillar shapes in ascending and descending quavers visible even on the stave, two bars long (as at bb. 381–2, and every two bars until b. 390). This music of sinuous menace culminates in a vision of the hammerhead shark whose presence is painted by the punitive pun of hammer blows in the accompaniment's left hand, three successive sforzati in b. 409 by way of passing illustration.

Verses 21–2: The youth hangs on for dear life, the tremolando at b. 415 pregnant with fear. His solitude is depicted with hushed music reverberating in the watery void. Time stands still in a blur of semiquavers (marked 'Adagio con moto', with a return to the key signature of C minor) anchored by the tolling notes of the bass (bb. 421–4). It is the calm before the storm of the final narrative. This is a gabbled descriptive recitative (from b. 426), the most agitated vocal line in the piece, and something of a catharsis. It is as if the youth, now approaching the finishing line, realizes that the horrors of the deep are even more frightening in the telling than in the experiencing of them. In the young hero's description of his deliverance back to safety, borne to the surface by the vortical flow of a swirling wave (bb. 433–6), Schubert's use of swift recitative mirrors Schiller's terse narrative style. The decisive cadence establishing E flat on 'oben' (bb. 435–6) is the young man's way of saying, 'Well, there you have it!' The court

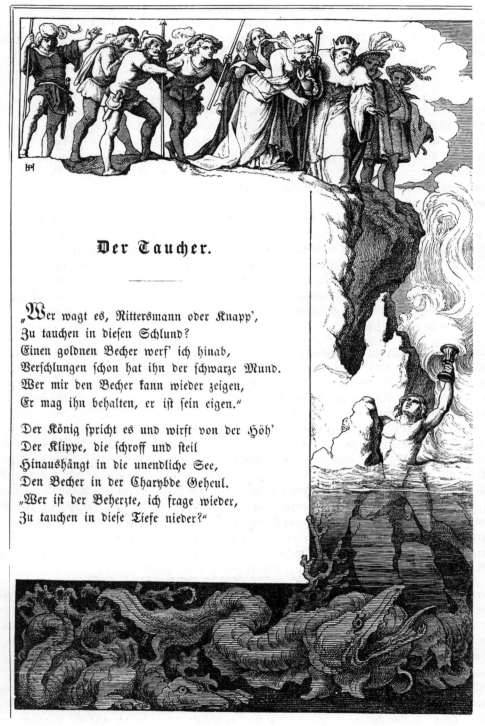

Der Taucher.

„Wer wagt es, Rittersmann oder Knapp',
Zu tauchen in diesen Schlund?
Einen goldnen Becher werf' ich hinab,
Verschlungen schon hat ihn der schwarze Mund.
Wer mir den Becher kann wieder zeigen,
Er mag ihn behalten, er ist sein eigen."

Der König spricht es und wirft von der Höh'
Der Klippe, die schroff und steil
Hinaushängt in die unendliche See,
Den Becher in der Charybde Geheul.
„Wer ist der Beherzte, ich frage wieder,
Zu tauchen in diese Tiefe nieder?"

Illustration for *Der Taucher* (the return of the Diver in Verse 13) by Heinrich Plüddemann from *Deutsches Balladenbuch* (1861).

hears the end of the tale in stunned silence (seven crotchets' rest in bb. 436–7) before the music resumes with tentative quavers and dominant–tonic cadences ('What happens now?' 'What will the king's reaction be?'). This generates far more tension than the equivalent passage in the first version.

Verses 23–5: The youth's descriptions have been fatally fascinating and the king, as if he were a scientifically curious Renaissance monarch, wants more first-hand information about the depths. In the recitative between bb. 443 and 451 the game is changed to 'double or nothing' and the youth is challenged to dive once again into the abyss. In a marvellously feminine aria in a new key signature of D flat major, marked 'Andante con moto' and inflected with gentle chromaticisms (beginning at b. 452), the princess tugs at the sleeve of her father with music of telling sweetness, begging for mercy on the youth's behalf. Schubert and Puccini stand almost a century apart, but if Schubert had been writing an opera rather than a ballad he might have composed a Biedermeier equivalent of Puccini's 'O mio babbino caro' (*Gianni Schicchi*) where feminine entreaties are similarly employed in an attempt to shift paternal hard-heartedness. This music leads us into G major which engineers a return to C major at b. 472 ('Allegro moderato') and a recapitulation of the music for Verse 2. The king speaks to the youth from the beginning of b. 479 (marked 'Recit.'), offering him a knighthood and his daughter's hand in marriage if he jumps once again into the whirlpool. The last line of this passage gave Schubert great trouble. In the earlier version he makes the king, reflecting the plea for mercy from his daughter, sing the words 'mit zartem Erbarmen' (bb. 486–7) tenderly, with a graceful apoggiatura. Here a brutal modulation gives them a contemptuous irony. (This detail is elucidated by Walther Dürr in the introduction to Volume 6 of the NSA.) Thanks to Schubert's revising hand, we can see that paternal jealousy has played a concealed part in his cruelty.

Verses 26–7: The young man is clearly and suddenly in love, as can be heard in the obsessive, almost panting music for bb. 492–7. That these feelings may be reciprocated is intimated by the princess's swoon at b. 497. Inflamed by her beauty the youth throws himself again into the abyss (bb. 500–503) – significantly without the well-timed preparation that had characterized his first assay. The massive piano interlude ('Prestissimo' at b. 503) of forty tempestuous bars in D minor recalls another Schiller setting, *Gruppe aus dem Tartarus* D583, in its diabolical energy. This miniature piano concerto is the major structural difference between the two versions, and it is no surprise that Diabelli appropriated it for his composite publication of 1831 – it is highly effective without being impossible to play. At b. 530 the semiquavers desist in favour of palpitating quavers in one hand, semibreves in the other. This portentous combination, phrases falling and rising as if caught within the compass of the same diminished seventh, is eerily reminiscent of the accompaniment to the final words of the Commendatore in Mozart's *Don Giovanni* – 'Ah! tempo più non v'è'. (This closing scene of the opera was to influence Schubert to the end of his career, *see Der stürmische Morgen* D911/18.)

As if this masculine music depicting the horrors facing the diver is not exceptional enough, Schubert now writes a feminine counterpart – an exceptionally beautiful thirteen-bar wordless vignette of the princess's grief. Here Schubert adds to Schiller's scenario; we know already that she has a heart far bigger than her father's, but it is the composer who informs us that she is as passionately involved with the young man as he with her. This marvellous interlude begins in b. 543 (with upbeat) and is marked 'Compatiente' and, in another version, 'Bedauernd'. Einstein had in mind this tearfully chromatic passage when he described the harmonic resources of *Der Taucher* as being far in advance of Schubert's time: 'there is nothing like them until we reach the Wagner of *Tristan* and *The Ring*'. This is not quite true: for two bars the diminished chords here are exactly those that open the accompaniment of *Dass sie hier gewesen* D775. At b. 556 (Tempo I) the seething whirlpool music of verses 6 and 12 now reappears transposed into D minor, and there would be some excuse for regarding this as the first Schubertian use of that tonality for a dangerous journey that will end in death. When the voice reappears at b. 564 it is after no fewer than sixty-one bars of piano interlude, which must stand as a record in any kind of Schubert setting. The inevitable outcome is described, accompanied by stormy music which gradually softens to become the background to a requiem postlude. Again, immeasurably superior to the first version, this elegy has a tune floating, oboe-like, above the semiquavers (from b. 592), which are themselves anchored on a tonic pedal for fourteen bars. This hushed music is like a wreath floating on a watery grave.

Autographs:	In private possession (first version)
	Missing or lost (second version)
Publication:	First published as Book 12 of the *Nachlass* by Diabelli, Vienna in June 1831 (P275; first version)
	First published as part of the AGA in 1894 (P534; second version)
Subsequent editions:	Peters: Vol. 5/49; AGA XX 12a & b: Vol. 1/73 & 102; NSA IV: Vol. 6/78 & 114; Bärenreiter: Vol. 5/66 (high voice), 64 (medium/low voice)
Bibliography:	Capell 1928, p. 81
	Dittrich 2007, pp. 179–81
	Dürr, Introduction to NSA IV Volume 6 pp. XVI–XVIII
	Hirsch 1993, pp. 72–81
	Schnapper 1937, pp. 60–62
Discography and timing:	Fischer-Dieskau I 1[9] 23'54
	Hyperion I 2[13]
	Hyperion II 3[1] 24'50 Stephen Varcoe

←— *Verschwunden sind die Schmerzen* D88   *Don Gayseros I* D93/1 —→

TEMPO AND EXPRESSION MARKINGS

The list of German words below is a mixture of nouns (with capital letters), adjectives, adverbs, a few prepositions, and conjunctions. In German, adjectives are also used as uninflected adverbs. In musical markings there are also a number of present and past participles used as adjectives and adverbs. The same ambiguity between adjectives and adverbs exists in the use of tempo markings in English. The (imaginary) musical marking 'Sad and gentle, flowing' uses two adjectives and a present participle to tell the performer that the music must sound sadly gentle (or gently sad) whilst still flowing; it therefore must be played (and this could also be the composer's direction to the performers) 'Sadly, gently and in a flowing manner' – a phrase that in itself could also appear at the top of a piece of music.

For the purposes of this article it is assumed that the reader possesses a working knowledge of musical terms in Italian and that these need no further explication here.

ängstlich	fearful, nervously
Affekt	passion, emotion
allmählich	gradually
Andacht, andächtig	(religious) devotion, devoutly
Anmut(h)	charm, grace
Ausdruck	expression
bedauernd	pitying, sorrowing

behaglich	comfortable, agreeably
beinahe	almost, as in 'Beinahe die vorige Bewegung' (in almost the same tempo as previously)
bewegt	moved (both in terms of motion and emotion, the former in the case of tempo markings)
Bewegung	movement, gait, motion, as in 'In sanfter Bewegung' (gently moving forward), 'Mit steigender Bewegung' (with mounting urgency), 'Mässig in gehender Bewegung' (at a moderate walking pace)
bis	up to, until, as in 'bis Ende' (to the end)
declamiert	declaimed
doch	yet, nevertheless
drängend	pressing or driving forward
düster	gloomily
Eile, eilig	haste, hurried
Empfindung	feeling, sensation, emotion
erhaben	elevated, lofty, sublimely
Erinnerung	memory
ernst	seriously
erzählend	narrating (as in a story)
etwas	somewhat, rather
feierlich	solemn, ceremonial, festive
Feuer, feuerlich or feurig	fire, fiery, with ardour
freudig	glad, joyfully
frei	free
frisch	brisk, fresh, lively
froh	joyfully
fromm	pious, devoutly
Gefühl	feeling, as in 'Mit Gefühl' (with feeling)
gehend	going or walking at a steady pace (andante)
gemässigt	measured, moderate (like 'mässig')
geschwind, geschwinder	swiftly, quickly, more quickly
Grauen	horror, as in 'Mit Grauen' (with horror, dread)
heilig	sacred, holy
heiter	serene, clear and bright, also cheerful, jolly, joyful, even 'comic'
herzlich	tenderly, lovingly, sincerely
höchstem	high
innig	warm, tender, fervently
Innigkeit	fervour or 'inwardness', tenderness
Jubel	jubilation
klagend	lamenting, plaintively
Kraft, kräftig	strength, powerful, as in 'Mit aller Kraft' (at full strength)
kraftvoll	vigorously
langsam, langsamer	slowly, slower
Laune	mood or temper, as in 'Guter Laune' (in a good mood)
lebhaft	lively
Leidenschaft	passion as in 'Mit Leidenschaft' (passionately)
leise	light, gently
Liebes-Affekt	loving emotion

lieblich	delightful, charmingly
lustig	jolly, jovially
mässig, mässiger	moderate, at a more moderate pace
Majestät, majestätisch	majesty, majestically
mit	with
munter	cheerful, sprightly, wide awake
nachgehend	following
nicht zu	not too
romanzenartig	in the manner of a narrative ballad
Rührung	emotion, the stirring of emotion
ruhig	peaceful, restful
sanft/sanfter	softly, more gently
schauerlich	awful, gruesome, causing a shudder
scherzhaft	playfully
schleichend	lingering, slinking
schmerzlich, schmerzlicher	painful, more painfully
schnell, schneller	fast, faster
schreitend	striding
schwärmerisch	fanciful, enthusiastic, ecstatic
Sehnsucht	longing for something (often unattainable) as in 'Langsam mit schwärmerischer Sehnsucht' (slow and with ecstatic longing)
sehr	very
stark	strongly
steigen	to rise
Stimme	voice, as in 'mit leiser Stimme' (in a gentle voice)
stürmisch	stormy, stormily
tändelnd	playfully
Takt	bar, measure, beat as in 'In Takte' (in strict time)
trauernd	grieving, mourning
traurig	sad, sadly
unruhig	restlessly
Unruhig, klagend. Im Zeitmasse wachsend bis zur Haltung	Restless, plaintive. Growing (accelerating) in tempo until the fermata [D196]
unschuldig	innocently
vergnügt	delighted, content
vertrauensvoll	trustingly, confidently
vom Zeichen	from the sign ('dal segno)
von ferne	from afar
wachsend	growing
wehmütig	sadly
Wehmut	melancholy, sadness
werden	to become, as in 'geschwinder werden' (getting faster)
wie oben	as above
wild	fierce, wildly
Würde	dignity, as in 'Mit stiller Würde' (with quiet dignity)
zart	tender, tenderly
Zeitmass	tempo, thus 'Im Zeitmasse' (in tempo), 'im ersten Zeitmasse' (tempo primo), 'Zeitmass des Marsches' (in march time)

ziemlich	rather, somewhat (the word can also imply 'very' in present-day colloquial German – the English equivalent would be 'pretty fast', a cause of confusion to some performers)[1]
zögernd	hesitatingly, lingeringly
zu	too (as well as to)
zurückhaltend	holding back, making a rallentando

For the experienced Schubertian there is no doubt that the composer's tempo markings (sometimes also incorporating an indication of the musical mood) play a vital role in determining both speed and character of each of the songs. Over the years the performer develops a feeling for these markings and what they actually mean in practical terms. Schubert, as in so much else of his output, employed a language that he made his own and customized using the templates of Salieri, Mozart and Beethoven among others. This way of communicating his musical wishes to posterity makes perfect sense (or at least much better sense than many other composers) once the 'code' has been examined, if not entirely cracked. The use of these tempo markings for music of similar speeds is surprisingly consistent (if not unfailingly so), and it is often useful to compare one 'Etwas langsam' or 'Mässig' with another, providing the time signature is the same, especially when practical experience has confirmed the effectiveness of at least one of the tempi. An understanding of the use of *alla breve* markings (when four beats are counted in a pulse of two) is an essential adjunct to determining the correct tempo of any piece.

Unlike those of the later Romantic composers, the tempo markings provided by Schubert were not necessarily associated with the overall effect on the ear made by the music – these markings were often less concerned with how the music *sounded* (fast or slow) than with a sequence of more hard-headed mathematical calculations. The marking – slow or fast – refers to *the tempo of the beat*, whether a crotchet, minim or, occasionally, quaver. For example, if a crotchet beat is filled up with rippling demisemiquavers (as is the case of the song *Liebesbotschaft* D957/1 with its marking 'Ziemlich langsam') the song may *sound* fast to the innocent ear, but in terms of its underlying crotchet pulse it can only be considered 'Rather slow'. It is thus labelled because Schubert had been taught to think in terms whereby a bird's-eye view is taken of tempo. In fact, it is extremely helpful to performers to begin to feel *Liebesbotschaft* in a slow two-in-a-bar where the demisemiquavers are treated as passing ornamentation, rather than as something thematically important – which they are not. In order to find the secrets of interpreting Schubert's tempo markings it is important that performers learn that they must not respond automatically to slow or fast markings with slow or fast music-making – that is before checking the pulse in which the marking has been conceived and measured by the composer.

Another important lesson taught by these markings is one of overall *moderation*; this, in so far as it refers to extremes of tempo, is something of a Viennese characteristic, and the same can be said of performing Brahms. The performer eventually learns that most 'fast' Schubert songs are slower than one thinks, and most 'slow' songs faster. Singing is to do with words and breath: too fast a tempo and words are unintelligible and gabbled; too slow and the flow of the music is impeded, and melody and meaning fail to coalesce. In Schubert's tempo markings the language of moderation is to be found almost everywhere. The word 'etwas' (rather or 'a little') stands at the head of no fewer than seventy-one songs, as if the composer were placing a moderating sign by way of warning above his instructions to the performers. On thirty-six other occasions he uses the words 'Nichts zu . . .' (Not too . . .). While the Italian 'Moderato' occurs

[1] In nineteenth-century German usage, 'Es ziemt sich nicht' means 'it is not proper' or 'seemly'. Thus 'ziemlich schnell' could also mean 'appropriately' or 'suitably fast' – in other words, fast enough to suit the poem. With this reading, the word still calls for moderation.

six times, the German word for the same thing – 'Mässig' – occurs in 139 instances: ninety-three times on its own and forty-six times in combination with other directions. Another moderating word is 'Ziemlich' (as in 'Ziemlich geschwind' – 'pretty fast', or 'on the fast side'). We find this word used in thirty-three instances in the song markings as applied to both fast and slow tempi.

TEMPO MARKINGS INCORPORATING MOOD
The following markings are one-offs except where otherwise indicated:

Allegro furioso
Behaglich
Düster, mässig langsam
Erhaben; Ernst; Etwas geschwind, freudig; Etwas geschwind mit Anmuth; Etwas geschwind mit Feuer; Etwas geschwind und sehr unruhig; Etwas geschwind, zart; Etwas langsam, unschuldig
Feierlich; Feurig (7); Freudig; Froh, doch mit Majestät
Geschwind, kraftvoll; Geschwind und feurig; Guter Laune
Heiter (2)
Klagend (6)
Langsam feierlich (6); Langsam lieblich (2); Langsam mit Andacht; Langsam mit heiliger Sehnsucht; Langsam mit schwärmerischer Sehnsucht; Langsam schleichend; Langsam traurig; Langsam (von ferne); Langsam wehmütig; Langsam zart (3); Lebhaft, herzlich; Lieblich (6); Lieblich klagend; Lustig (3)
Mässig, ernst; Mässig, erzählend, trauernd; Mässig, fröhlich; Mässig, heiter (3), Mässig, herzlich; Mässig in schmerzlicher Erinnerung; Mässig mit Innigkeit; Mässig mit Kraft; Mässig lieblich (4); Mässig, lustig; Mässig ruhig; Mässig, unruhig; Mässig, zart; Majestätisch, nicht zu langsam; Mit Andacht; Mit Empfindung; Mit heiliger Rührung (2); Mit Liebes-Affekt; Mit Majestät, sehr langsam; Mit Wehmut, langsam
Nicht zu geschwind, doch feurig (2); Nicht zu geschwind, doch kräftig; Nicht zu geschwind, lieblich; Nicht zu langsam, klagend
Ruhig (8); Ruhig und fromm; Ruhig, zart
Sanft (3); Scherzhaft; Sehr langsam, ängstlich; Sehr langsam, mit Kraft; Sehr langsam, schmerzlich; Sehr langsam, schwärmerisch; Sehr langsam, wehmütig
Tändelnd, sehr leise; Trauernd; Traurig (3)
Unruhig, klagend (2); Unschuldig
Vergnügt; Vertrauensvoll
Wehmütig
Zart; Zart langsam; Zart, lieblich; Ziemlich langsam, feierlich

AN APPROXIMATE HIERARCHY OF TEMPO MARKINGS
The statistics in this article regarding the frequency of tempo markings pertain only to those indicated at the beginnings of songs. The changes of tempi frequently to be found in longer songs are not accounted for.

In the broadest possible terms the tempo range of Schubert songs is expressed in the following range of markings, here arranged in ascending order from very slow to fast (there are forty-three 'Sehr langsam' markings, but no song is marked 'Sehr schnell' – indeed the marking 'Schnell' is used remarkably seldom). It must be noted that there is no real difference between some of the markings that are listed here next to each other – for example, 'Etwas geschwind' and 'Ziemlich geschwind'. The brackets after the markings refer to the number of Schubert songs thus marked.

Sehr langsam (43); Adagio (4)
Langsam (110)
Etwas langsam (22)
Nicht zu langsam (18); Andante (23)
Mässig (139); Moderato (9)
Allegretto (11); Nicht zu geschwind (15); Etwas geschwind (50)
Ziemlich geschwind (13)
Geschwind (16); Allegro (14); Nicht zu schnell (3)
Schnell (5)

There are no fewer than fifty-six songs without a tempo indication, and ninety-five with Italian markings. These are mainly conventional compounds of terms incorporating various shades and modifications of Adagio (8), Allegretto (11), Allegro (24), Andante (39), Larghetto (2), Moderato (6) and Maestoso (2). There is one example each of Ad libitum, Cantabile maestoso, Largo, Marcia, Risoluto, Sostenuto. On one occasion Schubert uses the French term 'Un peu animé'.

Sometimes the composer will create a one-off tempo marking that is specially tailored to the piece in hand: Frisch, doch nicht zu schnell; Gehend; In mässiger Bewegung; In sanfter Bewegung; Mässig in gehender Bewegung; Mit drängender Eile. Markings like 'Ruhig' (and 'Unruhig') as well as 'Scherzhaft' are indicative of both mood and tempo.

METRONOME MARKINGS

There are no metronome markings to be found on Schubert song autographs, but the composer allocated them to twenty-one of his printed songs – the first seven opus numbers issued in 1821 and the song *Drang in die Ferne* Op. 71, D770. It is at least a possibility (though rather unlikely) that the publisher was responsible for some of these, or perhaps those in the Schubertian circle (like Leopold von Sonnleithner, or the composer's sometime factotum Josef Hüttenbrenner) who might have regarded the relatively new phenomenon of the metronome mark as a sine qua non of serious musical publication. As soon as Schubert became independent of the consortium who had arranged publication of songs on his behalf, he seems to have abandoned metronome marks – in his lieder at least. On the other hand, the opera *Alfonso und Estrella* D732 was given extensive metronome markings for practical reasons (the need for the work to be rehearsed in an opera house far away from Vienna and without the composer's presence), and the *Deutsche Messe* D872 was ascribed markings while the composer played it through at the piano. If there were any doubts about the authenticity of the songs' metronome markings it might be in relation to the three songs of Opus 7. Here the markings seem unusually quick and more quirky than in the other song-sets. This particularly pertains to the rushed rum-ti-tum tempo suggested for *Der Flug der Zeit* Op. 7 no. 2, D515 (the music scarcely has time to breathe), and the controversial and seldom obeyed marking, relatively fast, for *Der Tod und das Mädchen* Op. 7 no. 3, D531.

Even if Schubert eventually decided that metronome marks were more trouble than they were worth (and this seems to have been the case), the twenty surviving instances give a unique insight into the range of tempi that the composer associated with various frequently returning tempo indications.

The very slow songs ('Sehr Langsam')

Sehr langsam, Common time *alla breve* (𝄵), ♩ = 63 (*Der Wanderer* Op. 4 no. 1, D489)
Sehr langsam, leise, $\frac{3}{4}$, ♪ = 63 (*Jägers Abendlied* Op. 3 no. 4, D368)
Clive Brown in his essay *Schubert's Tempo Conventions* is at pains to point out that one cannot always take for granted the ratio of 2:1 for *alla breve* vs common time markings:

The treatment of ₵ alla breve *was a particular cause of confusion with many late 18th-century and 19th-century composers. Some used* ₵ alla breve *to indicate a slightly faster tempo than* **C**, *some used it to mean literally twice as fast as* **C**, *while others seem to have regarded* ₵ alla breve *and* **C** *as having a 2:1 ratio at slow tempo, but converging progressively as the tempo increased . . . Schubert broadly shared Beethoven's view that at slow to moderate speeds there was a 2:1 relationship . . .*

In the case of the two songs named above, the calibration of most metronomes did not permit the marking of a minim = 31.5 (in the first) or a crotchet = 31.5 (in the second). In *Der Wanderer* the indicated tempo is rather faster than the deadly slow speed sometimes attempted in this song. The triplets move forward at 63 to the crotchet, although the *alla breve* marking (where the minim is the preferred beat) is an indication that the composer would indeed have preferred to mark the song as minim = 31.5; certainly the performer should think of it in two beats to the bar rather than four. In fact performing experience shows that the ideal tempo of a famous 'Sehr langsam' song without a metronome marking – *Das Wirtshaus* from *Winterreise* D911/21 – is more or less at the speed of a crotchet = 31.5, or a quaver = 63. This suggests that 'Sehr langsam' was often associated with exactly this tempo throughout Schubert's career, and that tempi a great deal slower than this lie substantially outside his creative range (at least as far as songs are concerned) – largely because of the problem of reconciling melodic continuity with the finite nature of breath and human lung capacity.

Sehr langsam, ängstlich, Common time *alla breve,* ♩ = 72 (*Meeres Stille* Op. 3 no. 2, D216)
As the song is written almost entirely in semibreves it may seem curious to give the metronome marking in crotchets. If it is counted in the minims indicated by the *alla breve* time signature, the marking would be 36 to the crotchet. This is somewhat faster than the two songs above, also marked Sehr langsam. Perhaps the added element of fear (indicated by the word 'ängstlich') adds a certain frisson of speed to the song. The sea and wind are static, but the fear of being becalmed may have played a part in the slightly fleeter choice of tempo.

Sehr langsam, schwärmerisch, Common time *alla breve,* ♩ = 50 (*Memnon* Op. 6 no. 1, D541)
This is another instance of a song in an *alla breve* time signature that is given a metronome marking to the crotchet rather than to the minim. Once again the marking (minim = 25) would be impossible to find on a metronome, where the minimum calibration is 40. The static nature of the great and immovable statue of Memnon makes this one of the slowest of the songs to which a metronome marking was assigned – the triplets in this song are the same speed as the quavers grouped in triplets in *Nähe des Geliebten* D162.

Sehr langsam, wehmütig, Common time, ♩ = 54 (*Erster Verlust* Op. 5 no. 4, D226)
This is a song where the first three bars, after the opening 'Ach', have to be sung in one breath – and this fact, above all, dictates the tempo. Although the composer has marked it in four-in-a-bar (common time) to preserve it from too airy and light-hearted a pulse, it is surely an *alla breve* piece in every other way. Thus the real metronome marking intended is minim = 27. This is a slower minim pulse (weighed down by the marking 'wehmütig' in terms of mood) than the first two songs in the 'Sehr langsam' category but not as slow as the minim in *Memnon*.

From the above examples it is clear that this sampling of 'very slow' songs from Schubert's output reveals a range from 25 to 36 – mostly calculated here (for the sake of comparison) to the prevailing pulse of the minim, but in the case of *Jägers Abendlied*, to the crotchet.

The slow songs ('Langsam')

Langsam, mit Ausdruck, Common time, ♩ = 50 (*Wandrers Nachtlied*, Op. 4 no. 3, D224)
Langsam, feierlich mit Anmut, ¹²⁄₈, ♩. = 50 (*Nähe des Geliebten* Op. 5 no. 2, D162)
Langsam, ³⁄₄, ♩ = 50 (*Am Grabe Anselmos* Op. 6 no. 3, D504)
Langsam, Common time, ♩ = 54 (*Antigone und Oedip* Op. 6 no. 2, D542)

The four songs marked 'Langsam' all have pulses measured in crotchets (in one instance a dotted crotchet). From this it is clear that the range of 'Langsam' is crotchet = between 50 and 54. On paper this means that the crotchet pulse is the same here as it is for such 'Sehr langsam' songs as *Memnon* and *Erster Verlust*. The secret of the difference is in the performer's way of thinking of the song (and even phrasing it): in both *Memnon* and *Erster Verlust* the effect is *alla breve* and the governing pulse is a very slow minim rather than a merely slow crotchet.

The songs in moderate tempo

Mässig, ⁶⁄₈, ♪ = 120 (*Schäfers Klagelied*, Op. 3 no. 1, D121)

Schubert must have thought hard about this unusual metromome marking which is in effect dotted crotchet = 40. It is an example of how hard it is to use the metronome system to convey a required musical effect. Even at the seemingly speedy marking of quaver = 120 the musical effect is still of a moderato song. On the one hand the composer probably wanted to avoid too much of a lilt to this *sicilienne*, thus the indication of pulse that concentrates on the quaver. On the other hand, a marking of 40 might have suggested too slow a song (an impression counter-manded also by the direction 'Mässig') and a lugubrious atmosphere. The gentle melancholy of this song lies between the two extremes.

Mässig, Common time *alla breve*, ♩ = 54 (*Der Tod und das Mädchen* Op. 7 no. 3, D531)

This must be the most widely disregarded metronome marking of all time and its authenticity may be open to question (*see* above). It is rare to hear a singer and pianist (the latter responsible for the all-important prelude and postlude) who are willing to forego the portentous musical apparatus of death (and a slow, foreboding tempo) in favour of what the composer seems to require on the printed page: something menacing but inexorable, not exactly swift, but not slow either. Schubert could have clearly marked this music crotchet = 108 but he chose not to because he did not want to encourage a hectic mood – death must glide rather than stride, and all must be measured. The correct tempo for the flustered 'Etwas geschwinder' passage (beginning at b. 8) is a strong argument for the validity of the main tempo: if performers take a much slower view of the 'death' theme, the middle section (the maiden's entreaty) needs to be very much faster – double the tempo, or more – to be effective. But Schubert has only marked 'etwas (somewhat) geschwinder'. Such detective work is sometimes needed to uncover or confirm the composer's intentions. None of this applies, however, if this marking was a straightforward mistake.

Mässig, ²⁄₄, ♩ = 60 (*Der Fischer* Op. 5 no. 3, D225)
This seems to be the classic moderato tempo for a Schubert song.

Ziemlich langsam, Common time *alla breve*, ♩ = 63 (*Morgenlied* Op. 4 no. 2, D685)

This is an example of a song with a slowish marking ('Ziemlich langsam') that makes a lively effect in performance. The metronome per crotchet would have been 126, but Schubert no doubt considered that this would encourage performers to make something too hectic of the music. There are only two other songs with a 'Ziemlich langsam' marking, one of them the famous *Liebesbotschaft* D957/1 from *Schwanengesang*, a song written in 1828 in ²⁄₄ time, rather than the ³⁄₄ of *Morgenlied* composed in 1820. In fact crotchet = 63 would be an ideal tempo for

Liebesbotschaft, showing that there is a consistency of marking between two songs written eight years apart.

Etwas langsam, $\frac{2}{4}$, $\quad$ = 66 (*Der König in Thule* Op. 5 no. 5, D367)
This is as good an example as any of an 'Etwas langsam' song, actually more 'moderato' than langsam, that has an inexorable flow despite the marking. There is something about the breadth of the vocal line and the poise of the music that renders it stately despite the relatively fast pulse.

Lieblich, $\frac{2}{4}$, $\quad$ = 66 (*Heidenröslein* Op. 3 no. 3, D257)
This is the only song with a metronome indication that is accompanied by a mood, rather than a tempo, direction. It has the same pulse as *Der König in Thule* but to have marked it 'Etwas langsam' would have given the wrong impression regarding the sprightly nature of the youth and his audacious relationship with the rose. There are relatively few quavers in *Der König in Thule* of course (none in the accompaniment) whereas *Heidenröslein* is made up of quavers and semiquavers. This gives the impression that the latter song is much faster than the former, although they share the same 'Mässig' pulse.

Mässig, Common time, $\quad$ = 92 (*Die abgeblühte Linde* Op. 7 no. 1, D514)
This song demonstrates the difficulties of metronome markings and, as mentioned above, there is a possibility that the marking is not authentic. The piece is divided into two sections and it is not altogether clear whether the marking refers only to the opening recitative or to the following cantilena as well. It is actually this music (following b. 18) that constitutes the heart of the piece. The composer changes the time signature from common time to *alla breve*, so we assume that this section is to be sung at a seemingly slow minim = 46. In fact with the number of quavers that enliven this little aria the musical effect is moderato because it is neither fast nor slow. This is an example of a relatively fast marking applied to a song of moderate movement.

From these songs it is clear that the marking 'Mässig' encompasses metronome marks somewhere between 60 and 92, with the possibility that the $\quad$ = 92 of *Die abgeblühte Linde* is inauthentic or a mistake. This may seem a rather broad spectrum, but the majority of songs in this tempo category would have metronome markings between 60 and 72 to the crotchet. *Wohin?* from *Die schöne Müllerin*, for example, perhaps the most famous of all Schubert's 'Mässig' songs, falls into precisely this range of tempo possibility.

The reasonably fast and fast songs
Nicht zu geschwind, $\frac{6}{8}$, $\quad$. = 72 (*Gretchen am Spinnrade*, Op. 2, D118)
Gretchen's spinning wheel whirs perfectly effectively at this tempo reflecting Gretchen's seated position and her confused state of mind, and Schubert is right to add his warning that fast should not be *too* fast. The semiquavers that fill the beats provide evidence of her excitement and anguish. This is an example of a song that might sound 'fast' to the listener, but that is underpinned with a pulse of only moderately fast dotted crotchets. This holding-back of the tempo (and of the performers' temptations to make something almost uncontrollably tempestuous of the song) lies at the centre of authentic Schubertian interpretation.

Etwas geschwind $\frac{6}{8}$, $\quad$. = 76 (*Drang in die Ferne* Op. 71, D770)

Etwas geschwind, $\frac{6}{8}$, $\quad$. = 112 (*Der Flug der Zeit* Op. 7 no. 2, D515)
There are sadly no songs with the marking 'Geschwind' to which Schubert gave metronome markings. Here the marking of 112 to the dotted crotchet seems very fast for only 'Etwas

geschwind'. Indeed, it is difficult to believe in this rollicking tempo that engenders a certain inelegance in the piano style and in the vocal declamation of the piece. (*See* above for mention of the possible inauthenticity of the Op. 7 markings.) If we consider *Das Fischermädchen* D957/10, another 'Etwas geschwind' song in $\frac{6}{8}$, we can see how musically disastrous it would be to perform this charming barcarolle at dotted crotchet = 112. The tempo envisaged by the composer is surely crotchet = *c*. 76–84 for both songs.

For the fast songs in the range incorporating the word 'geschwind' (Nicht zu geschwind, Etwas geschwind, Ziemlich geschwind, Geschwind) the metronome marks lie between about 92 and 120. This may seem a broad width of possibilities but it encompasses a range of styles.

The very fast songs
Schnell, Common time, ♩ = 152 (*Erlkönig*, Op. 1, D328)
Schnell, $\frac{2}{4}$, ♩ = 152 (*Rastlose Liebe* Op. 5 no. 1, D138)
There can be no doubt about the relationship between the markings of 'Schnell' and the shared crotchet pulse of these two songs. Another song marked Schnell is *Der Strom* D565; it would be reasonable to suppose that this work could be performed at a speed in the range of crotchet = 140–52.

THE WHIRLWIND SCHUBERT – A MODERN TENDENCY

The Schubert songs can work at any number of speeds as pieces of instrumental music; in the case of the faster songs gifted pianists are often tempted to perform them as bracing scherzi or virtuoso études (songs such as *An Schwager Kronos* D369, *Auf der Bruck* D853, *Auflösung* D807 – to limit myself merely to letter A). But there is always a more moderate tempo that makes sense when the poem (its meaning and clarity) are taken into account, as well as the ability of the singer to put the words across. The inexperienced accompanist who rejoices in playing Schubert simply for the music and less for the words is bound to misjudge many of these tempi. It is also possible that an inexperienced Schubert singer would demand faster tempi in order to make life easier as far as breathing or phrasing are concerned; some of the most diffi- cult Schubert songs are rendered far easier in technical terms for the singer when performed ridiculously fast. When German is not the accompanist's language, and when it does not offend him (or her) to hear the singer verge on incomprehensibility, the temptation to rush is exacer- bated. I was a juror at a lieder competition, in 2012, where the tendency of the competitors was overwhelmingly to hurry the Schubert songs; this was discussed at length with my fellow- jurors Gundula Janowitz, Kurt Widmer, Birgid Steinberger and Robert Holl – all highly expe- rienced Schubertians. Perhaps the strain and adrenaline of competition circumstances are unfavourable to the centred and more contemplative nature of many of the Schubert lieder. My colleagues and I agreed that within this single week of the competition many of the Schubert songs were performed at what I termed 'broadband' speeds, significantly too fast and, although there was a general tendency among younger performers to opt for fast (and loud) perform- ances with most music, the problem seemed worse with Schubert than with other composers. In the following list of songs the first metronome mark is the one which I would recommend (approximately) for performance (in full consideration of their texts and their musical chal- lenges), the second (the tempo in square brackets) the one actually adopted by the competitors (I do not list performers of songs at tempi different to those I favour, but which nevertheless worked):

Abschied (Rellstab) D957/7 'Mässig geschwind', crotchet beat: *c*. 140 [200+]
Alinde (Rochlitz) D904 'Mässig', dotted-crotchet beat: *c*. 58 [66]

Am See (Bruchmann) D746 'Mässig', dotted-crotchet beat: *c*. 46 [52]
An Schwager Kronos (Goethe) D369 'Nicht zu schnell', dotted-crotchet beat: 92 [106]
Auf dem See (Goethe) D543 'Mässig', dotted-crotchet beat: 56 [66]
Auf der Bruck (Schulze) D853 'Geschwind', crotchet beat: 92 [106]
Auflösung (Mayrhofer) D807 'Nicht zu geschwind', crotchet beat: 126 [144]
Bei dir allein! (Seidl) D866/2 'Nicht zu geschwind, doch feurig', crotchet beat: 138 [160]
Delphine (Schutz) D857/1 'Mässige Bewegung', crotchet beat: *c*. 84 [100]
Der Einsame (Lappe) D800 'Mässig, ruhig', crotchet beat: 76 [88]
Ellens Gesang I (Scott tr. Storck) D837 'Mässig', crotchet beat: 76 [86]
Fischerweise (Schlechta) D881 'Etwas geschwind', minim beat: 84 [104]
Geheimnis (Mayrhofer) D491 'Mässig geschwind', crotchet beat: 106 [136]
Gretchen am Spinnrade (Goethe) D118 'Nicht zu geschwind', crotchet beat: Schubert's published
    marking 72 [84]
Gretchen am Zwinger (Goethe) D564 'Sehr langsam', crotchet beat: 40 [48]
Im Walde (Schlegel) D708 'Geschwind', crotchet beat: 128 [144]
Liebesbotschaft (Rellstab) D957/1 'Ziemlich langsam', crotchet beat: 58 [66]
Die Männer sind mechant (Seidl) D866/3 'Etwas langsam', dotted crotchet beat: 54 [66]
Normans Gesang (Scott tr. Storck) D846 'Geschwind', crotchet beat: *c*. 120 [134]
Sehnsucht (Schiller) D636 'Ziemlich geschwind', crotchet beat: 112 [132]
Suleika I (Willemer/Goethe) D720 'Etwas lebhaft', crotchet beat: 104 [116]
Suleika II (Willemer/Goethe) D717 'Mässige Bewegung', crotchet beat: 86 [104]
Totengräbers Heimwehe (Craigher) D842 'Unruhige Bewegung, doch nicht schnell', crotchet
    beat: *c*. 76 [88]
Willkommen und Abschied (Goethe) D767 'Geschwind', crotchet beat: 120 [152].

In the competitors' performance the metronome speed of *Erlkönig* D328 (marked 'Schnell') was adopted for *Willkommen und Abschied*, marked 'Geschwind' (there is no extant Schubert metronome marking for 'Geschwind'). The first and last songs in this list were whirlwind performances by the same aspiring pianist, the singer sailing through the songs with no care for the words or their meanings, and as if borne on a magic carpet rather than a horse. We are perhaps losing, with each succeeding generation, a feel for the genuine mode of nine-teenth-century transport. In stark contrast, only four Schubert songs were performed too slowly: *An den Mond* (Hölty) D193, 'Langsam, wehmuthig', dotted-crotchet beat: 46 [40]; *Du bist die Ruh* (Rückert) D776 'Langsam', quaver beat: 58 [50]; *Du liebst mich nicht* (Platen) D756 'Mässig', crotchet beat: 63 [50]; *Heimliches Lieben* (Klenke) D922, 'Mässig', crotchet beat: 76 [66]. The tendency for pianists to drag this music stems from an uncertain feeling for Schu-bertian style and a veering towards sentimentality at the expense of line and musical coherence. The very fact that Schubert affixed no metronome marks to the majority of his songs indicates that he acknowledged the danger of pedantry in these matters. The only 'right' and 'wrong' tempi are those that sound convincing or unconvincing, taking quite a number of factors into account. Even if artists' decision-making comes down to a matter of taste (inargauble this, although tastes change and develop over the years), text-related musical atmosphere and the comprehensibility of text are also inarguable factors. The important thing for performers (and for pianists in particular) is that their choice of tempo should represent forethought and control, and not just the first adrenalin-influenced speed that comes to hand, or under the fingers. Armed with knowledge of Schubertian performing-practice and style, artists are in a stronger position to come to a decision that will suit both them and the composer.

Bibliography: Brown 1998, pp. 1–15

THEKLA (EINE GEISTERSTIMME) I   Thekla (a phantom voice)
(SCHILLER) **D73** [H25]
G major   22–3 August 1813

Wo ich sei, und wo mich hingewendet,
Als mein flücht'ger Schatten dir entschwebt?
Hab' ich nicht beschlossen und geendet,
Hab' ich nicht geliebet und gelebt?

Willst du nach den Nachtigallen fragen,
Die mit seelenvoller Melodie
Dich entzückten in des Lenzes Tagen,
Nur so lang' sie liebten, waren sie.

Ob ich den Verlorenen gefunden?
Glaube mir, ich bin mit ihm vereint,
Wo sich nicht mehr trennt, was sich verbunden,

Dort wo keine Träne wird geweint.

Dorten wirst auch du uns wieder finden,
Wenn dein Lieben unserm Lieben gleicht,
Dort ist auch der Vater frei von Sünden,
Den der blut'ge Mord nicht mehr erreicht.

Und er fühlt, dass ihn kein Wahn betrogen,
Als er aufwärts zu den Sternen sah,
Denn wie jeder wägt, wird ihm gewogen,
Wer es glaubt, dem ist das Heil'ge nah.

Wort gehalten wird in jenen Räumen

Jedem schönen gläubigen Gefühl,
Wage du, zu irren und zu träumen,
Hoher Sinn liegt oft in kind'schem Spiel.[1]

You ask me where I am, where I turned to
When my fleeting shadow vanished,
Have I not finished, reached my end?
Have I not loved and lived?

Would you ask after the nightingales
Who, with soulful melodies,
Delighted you in the days of spring?
They lived only as long as they loved.

Did I find my lost beloved?
Believe me, I am united with him
In the place where those who have formed a
    bond are never separated,
Where no tears are shed.

There you too will find us again.
When your love is as our love;
There too is our father, free from sin,
Whom bloody murder can no longer strike.

And he senses that he was not deluded
When he gazed up at the stars,
For as a man judges, so he shall be judged;
Whoever believes this is close to holiness.

High above, in those vaults, every fine,
    faithful promise
will be kept;
Dare to err, and to dream;
Often a higher meaning lies behind childlike
    play.

---

[1] In the second setting D595, this line ends '*im kind'schen* Spiel'.

FRIEDRICH VON SCHILLER (1759–1805); poem written in 1802

This is the fifth of Schubert's forty-four Schiller solo settings (1811–24). See the poet's biography for a chronological list of all the Schiller settings.

In answer to public entreaties, Schiller wrote this poem as a kind of sequel to his trilogy of plays *Wallenstein*. In the plays Thekla, daughter of their hero, the famous Bohemian general Albrecht von Wallenstein, is in love with (Schiller's fictional) Max Piccolomini. The pair are Romeo-and-Juliet-like figures – in love but from houses that will become sworn enemies. The drama ends with Wallenstein assassinated (by an Irish or Scottish mercenary in February 1634) and Max dying a hero's death. Now, in the poem Thekla, as a voice from another world, ties up the loose ends of the story – in the third strophe referring to her lost Max, and in the fourth to her murdered father whose downfall was partly caused by his belief in astrology (hence the reference to the stars in the fifth). Schubert set the poem twice – the second time was in 1817 (D595).

In the later version the melody is in hypnotic ⅜ time, alternating between major and minor; the vocal line imprisoned within the compass of a fourth. A seance-like intensity is built into that hushed music whereas in D73 the exact pacing and shaping of Thekla's answers are left more to the imagination of the singer working within the framework of recitative.

Schubert seems to have taken as a key to this setting Schiller's second-last line 'Wage du, zu irren und zu träumen'. The composer does indeed dare to wander, and the performers must dare to dream. The music paints a wraith slipping in and out of focus: she speaks as if from limbo in hushed recitatives, and reassures us about her new home in more anchored arioso. Schubert marks the difference between the two styles of vocal delivery (essentially a question followed by an answer) with mercurial changes between the markings 'Recit' (as in the opening) and 'In tempo moderato' (at b. 5 and then simply 'Tempo' after that).

The epic nature of Thekla's tragedy seems implicit in the music that somehow conveys lofti-ness; yet the commentators, who are unlikely to have heard this song performed, have hardly found it worthy of notice. It is true that playing through this music at the piano gives no sense of the power it can attain when the notes are filled out with vocal colour in a singer's response to the words. This is one of Schubert's enigmatic creations where only the sound of the voice can bring to life passages that are static at the keyboard. Singers at play can sometimes reveal secrets locked away from even assiduous scholars – a point that is at the heart of Thekla's message, via Schiller, to the public.

Schubert has rightly received homage from all quarters for having composed *Gretchen am Spinnrade* D118 at the age of seventeen. 'What an understanding of female psychology!' say all the commentators. *Thekla* is a far less dramatic creation than *Gretchen* but that this music was written by a sixteen-year-old boy seems almost equally praiseworthy. The composer has completely grasped the highly strung nature of this wounded and fragile heroine and the way that her feelings, other-worldly as they are, veer between a kind of spiritual trepidation in the recitatives, and confidence in the arioso passages.

Autograph:	Stiftelsen Musikkulturens Främjande, Stockholm (fair copy)
First edition:	Published as No. 2 of *Sechs bisher ungedrückte Lieder* by Wilhelm Müller, Berlin in 1868 (P414)
Subsequent editions:	Not in Peters; AGA XX 11: Vol. 1/152; NSA IV: Vol. 2b/230; Bärenreiter: Vol. 3/218

Discography and timing: Fischer-Dieskau   —
                          Hyperion I 1²
                          Hyperion II 2²²   3'53   Janet Baker

← *Ein jugendlicher Maienschwung* D61   *Trinklied* D75 →

THEKLA (EINE GEISTERSTIMME) II   Thekla (a phantom voice)
(SCHILLER) OP. 88 NO. 2 **D595** [H393]

The song exists in two versions, the second of which is discussed below:
(1) November 1817; (2) appeared December 1827

(1)   'Langsam (von ferne)'   C♯ minor   ¾   [18 bars]

(2)   C minor

See previous entry for poem and translation

FRIEDRICH VON SCHILLER (1759–1805); poem written in 1802

*This is the thirty-sixth of Schubert's forty-four Schiller solo settings (1811–24). See the poet's
biography for a chronological list of all the Schiller settings.*

Schubert's first attempt at this poem where Wallenstein's daughter answers questions about her
eternal dwelling (D73, *see* commentary above) is a marvel of imaginative freedom, an inspired
recitative, astonishing for a sixteen-year-old boy. (For Thekla's story in greater detail *see* the
commentary to *Des Mädchens Klage* D191.) He returned to the text four years later with very
different ideas. In both versions we sense an attempt to depict the timelessness appropriate to
the utterance of a disembodied spirit. In 1813 he had achieved this by making the voice part
'timeless', in that a recitative is liberated from the pedantry of the bar line. In the second version
it is the use of a ground bass and unashamed repetition (as in *Der Doppelgänger* D957/13, another
song about a ghostly presence) which evokes the spirit's litany. Schubert's harmonic sequence
bears an uncanny resemblance to the ground known as 'La Folia'. In France this is known as
'Folie d'Espagne' and in England 'Farinelli's ground'. Schubert might well have heard this hypnotic
harmonic sequence from his erstwhile teacher Salieri. The 'Folia' ground usually underpins a
type of sarabande in ¾ time and, in common with each of Thekla's sung phrases, is eight bars
long. It may well be that in using a ground of seventeenth-century type, Schubert is attempting
to place the music of Thekla in the authentic seventeenth-century context of Wallenstein and

the Piccolomini of Schiller's plays. This would make it one of the composer's few uses of historical pastiche – *Vedi quanto t'adoro (Didone abbandonata)* D510 is another.

The use of so ancient a musical device is in any case appropriate to depict Thekla's heavenly abode – as old as time itself. The vocal line veers between the minor and the major but is limited to a range of two overlapping fourths: B–E and B flat–E flat. The effect of these high-lying, repetitious phrases (tiring for any singer) is somewhat bizarre and unearthly, which was Schubert's intention. We feel we are in the hushed atmosphere of a seance. At a concert given in the Rittersaal at the Hohenems Festival, Arleen Auger performed this song from an offstage balcony, giving the type of ethereal yet dramatic effect that would have gone down well at one of the composer's Schubertiads. Leo Black writes about the reappearance of this Thekla theme in the 'Miserere Nobis' section of the Mass in E flat D950, positing fascinating reasons for the quotation (including Schubert's friendship with Therese Grob). It seems perfectly possible that Schubert regarded this music, the ghostly outpourings of a lost soul, as suitable for a Miserere.

Thekla in *Die Piccolomini,* Act III Scene 9, as depicted in *Taschenbuch auf das Jahr 1804,* edited by Wieland und Goethe.

An earlier version of this song, printed in the NSA (Volume 4b p. 235), has the marking 'Langsam (von ferne)'. The key is C sharp minor/major and the music is even more constrained and repetitious in that the subtle harmonic musical variety provided by bb. 25–40 of the second version is not present in the composer's first thoughts. On the other hand this setting only uses the poem's first two strophes, and with music as mantra-like as this, two strophes are undoubtedly sufficient. There are also links, perhaps merely fortuitous, between the melody of the vocal line at bb. 18–21 and the Ottenwalt setting *Der Knabe in der Wiege* D579 (also in C major) at bb. 25–8.

Autograph:	Conservatoire collection, Bibliothèque Nationale, Paris (first version)
Publication:	First published as part of the AGA in 1895 (P679; first version) First published as Op. 88 no. 2 by Thaddäus Weigl, Vienna in December 1827 (P138; second version)
Subsequent editions:	Peters: Vol. 2/168; AGA XX 334a & b: Vol. 5/177; NSA IV: Vol. 4a/102 (second version), Vol. 4b/235 (first version); Bärenreiter: Vol. 3/70
Bibliography:	Black 2003, pp. 166–7 Capell 1928, p. 131 Fischer-Dieskau 1977, pp. 100–101 Newbould 1997, pp. 158–9

Discography and timing: Fischer-Dieskau   —
                            Hyperion I 9[11]   5'35   Arleen Auger
                            Hyperion I 11[9]   4'07   Brigitte Fassbaender
                            Hyperion II 20[2]   5'35   Arleen Auger

← Der Kampf D594   Das Dörfchen D598 →

JOHANN LUDWIG TIECK (1773–1853)

THE POETIC SOURCE

Musen-Almanach für das Jahr 1802. Herausgegeben von A. W. Schlegel und L. Tieck. Tübingen, in der Cotta'schen Buchhandlung, 1802

THE SONG

Early 1819   *Abend* D645 [p. 113]

Ludwig Tieck was born on 31 May 1773 in Berlin. He studied philosophy and theology in Halle, Göttingen and Erlangen (numbering Wackenroder and Nicolai among his teachers) before moving to Jena where he encountered Herder, Friedrich Schlegel and Novalis, as well as Fichte and Schelling. He also knew Schiller and Goethe. He quickly became renowned for his skills as a novelist, fabulist and writer of comedies, sometimes using the allegorical name of 'Peter Leberecht'. He visited Vienna in 1808 and was one of the few great German writers of the period to travel to England (in 1817) where he studied Shakespeare; both he and his daughter Dorothea were deeply involved in the preparation (with August von Schlegel and Wolf Graf Baudissin) of German translations of the complete works of Shakespeare, although it was Dorothea who did the larger proportion of the work.

From about 1820 he was counted as the most important German poet after Goethe (Kohlhäufl, *Liedlexikon* 2012, p. 863). Tieck's most important official position was as Dramaturg at the Dresden Hoftheater where he became, according to Oskar Wolff, 'the pride of the city'. In this position he showed an interest in mounting a production of Schubert's opera *Alfonso und Estrella* D732, but this came to nothing. That Tieck was aware of Schubert is attested by an article he wrote for the *Dresdner*

Ludwig Tieck, after a drawing by Griesmann, from *Musenalmanach für das Jahr 1831* edited by Amadeus Wendt.

Theaterzeitung in February 1828 where the composer's name is bracketed with that of Conradin Kreutzer as an important Viennese composer. The small number of Tieck songs in the lieder repertoire demonstrate that Schubert was not the only composer who found his writing almost too rich and dense in word-music to encourage musical setting. The best-known Tieck settings, the fifteen songs of Brahms's mighty cycle *Die schöne Magelone* Op. 33, occur within a much longer prose narrative (part of a collection entitled *Phantasus*), where the poems are fashioned in deliberately simple ballad style to suggest medieval minstrelsy. Tieck was considered unequalled in his ability to evoke the strength and simplicity of this period in modern literary terms, and he was equally famous for taking any and every aspect of foreign writing and turning it into something new in German literature. These 'Peter Leberecht' poems selected by Brahms lend themselves more easily to musical setting than the Tieck lyrics that Schubert encountered (without notable success) in 1819. Despite the poets of the so-called 'Junges Deutschland' making fun of him for being old-fashioned, Tieck was named in Oskar Wolff's encyclopaedia of German literature (1846) as easily the country's greatest living poet. He died in Berlin on 28 April 1853.

Bibliography: Wolff 1846, vol. 7, p. 316

CHRISTOPH AUGUST TIEDGE (1752–1841)

THE POETIC SOURCE
Taschenbuch zum geselligen Vergnügen herausgegeben von W. G. Becker für 1795. Mit Churfürstl. Sächsischem Privilegio. Leipzig bei Voss und Compagnie.

The same almanac is also the source of the Cowley/Ratschky setting *Der Weiberfreund* D271 composed on the same day. The poem for *An die Sonne* is published with the inscription 'Die Komposition ist von Herrn Kapellmeister Seydelmann'. This clearly refers to a musical insert to the almanac by Franz Seydelmann of Dresden (1748–1806).

THE SONG
25 August 1815   *An die Sonne* D272 [pp. 223–4]

Christoph August Tiedge was born on 14 December 1752 in Gardelegen bei Magdeburg. He studied law in Halle and lived in Quedlinburg. After the death of his wife in 1797 he was the private tutor and secretary to the wealthy Countess Elisa von Recke whom he accompanied to Italy, and with whom he later lived in Dresden. Tiedge had an unusually long life but his reputation was made in his earlier years as poet of the religious and philosophical epic *Urania: Über Gott, Unsterblichkeit und Freiheit* (1801), a work influenced by Immanuel Kant.

C. A. Tiedge, engraving after a painting by Friedrich Weitsch.

Beethoven wrote two of his most interesting songs to a text from that celebrated work – different versions of *An die Hoffnung* (Op. 32, 1805 and Op. 94, 1815). There are no fewer than eight volumes of Tiedge's collected works, although his writing, judged by posterity to be banal and cliché-ridden, has largely fallen into neglect since the first half of the nineteenth century. The poet died in Dresden on 8 March 1841.

TIEFES LEID *see* IM JÄNNER 1817 D876

TISCHLERLIED[1]

(Anonymous) **D274** [H161]
C major   25 August 1815

Carpenter's song

(18 bars)

Mein Handwerk geht durch alle Welt	My craftsmanship travels the world over
Und bringt mir manchen Taler Geld,	And brings me many a thaler,
Dess bin ich hoch vergnügt.	Which makes me very happy.
Den Tischler braucht ein jeder Stand.	Men of all ranks need a joiner.
Schon wird das Kind durch meine Hand	Even the baby is rocked to gentle sleep
In sanften Schlaf gewiegt.	In my own handiwork.
Das Bette zu der Hochzeitnacht	The bed for the wedding night
Wird auch durch meinen Fleiss gemacht	Is also built and finely painted
Und künstlich angemalt.	By my hard work.
Ein Geizhals sei auch noch so karg,	However mean the miser may be
Er braucht am Ende einen Sarg,	He still needs a coffin in the end,
Und der wird gut bezahlt.	And for it I am well paid.
Drum hab' ich immer frohen Mut	So I am always cheerful,
Und mache meine Arbeit gut,	And do my work well
Es sei Tisch oder Schrank.	Whether I am making a table or a cupboard.
Und wer bei mir brav viel bestellt	And to all those who place good orders with me
Und zahlt mir immer bares Geld,	And always pay in cash
Dem sag' ich grossen Dank.	I am deeply grateful.

[1] There is a variant version of this song published as a possible second version in the NSA, Vol. 9. The marking is 'Mässig', there is a two-bar introduction, and in the last six bars there are marked differences. As this version only ever appeared in 1850 when the song was first published, its authenticity is questionable. *See* NSA Vol. 9 p. xix.

ANONYMOUS/UNKNOWN

This is the fifth of Schubert's nineteen solo settings of an anonymous poet.
See Anonymous/Unknown for a chronological list of all the songs for which the poets
are unknown.

This song is a product of that extraordinarily fecund day, 25 August 1815. It is also one of the most ingenious of Schubert's pieces depicting working-class folk. The carpenter tells us that his work is at the bottom of everything; it supports us in our cradles and encloses us in our coffins. His craft is all simplicity and lack of pretension, and what could be more fundamental to the work of the musician than the bass line in that simplest of keys, C major? Accordingly, Schubert sets this anonymous text in such a way that the singer *is* the bottom line; the voice furnishes the foundation of the whole song in the same way that a carpenter provides a solid floor for his customers. Of course this bass line is also the tune, and rather a good one at that. For much of the song the pianist only uses the right hand; this simple one-handed staccato accompaniment in combination with the voice in somewhat lugubrious mood provides an apt sound-picture of knocking-on-wood as the carpenter hammers home his simple philosophy. There is nothing very lyrical here apart from a rocking motion, bb. 11–12, at the end of the first verse, mirrored in the postlude, to signify the gentle movement of the wooden cradle. All in all, this workman takes after his material: he is wooden. But Schubert cleverly paints a musical portrait of a man who is good at his work and proud of his skill, a man who underpins our society. If nineteenth-century tradesmen operated cheque accounts the preference shown for cash payment in the last verse would have made of the protagonist a forerunner of the tax-dodging tradesmen of our own times. In this instance, however, he simply wishes to avoid waiting endlessly for the rich to settle their bills. Schubert, no doubt, also preferred cash in hand. Like Shakespeare he is on the side of the simple man.

Autograph:	Wienbibliothek im Rathaus (first version)
First edition:	Published as Book 48 no. 7 of the *Nachlass* by Diabelli, Vienna in 1850 (P386)
Subsequent editions:	Peters: Vol. 6/67; AGA XX 131: Vol. 3/60; NSA IV: Vol. 9/20 (first version) & 21 (second version)
Bibliography:	Black 2001, p. 89, an example of 'bass doubling voice'
Arrangements:	Arr. Tilman Hoppstock (b. 1961) for guitar accompaniment, in *Franz Schubert: 110 Lieder* (2009)
Discography and timing:	Fischer-Dieskau I 5[14] 1'34
	Hyperion I 20[28]
	Hyperion II 9[22] 1'58 Michael George

← *Lilla an die Morgenröte* D273   *Totenkranz für ein Kind* D275 →

TISCHLIED   Drinking song

(GOETHE) **D234** [H126]
C major   15 July 1815

Mich ergreift, ich weiss nicht wie,	I am overcome, I know not how,
Himmlisches Behagen.	With a sense of heavenly well-being.
Will mich's etwa gar hinauf	Shall I perhaps be borne aloft
Zu den Sternen tragen?	To the stars?
Doch ich bleibe lieber hier,	But, to be honest,
Kann ich redlich sagen,	I would rather stay here
Beim Gesang und Glase Wein	Beating on the table,
Auf den Tisch zu schlagen.	With a song and a glass of wine.

Wundert euch, ihr Freunde, nicht,	Do not wonder, friends,
Wie ich mich gebärde,	At my behaviour;
Wirklich es ist allerliebst	It is truly delightful
Auf der lieben Erde;	On this dear earth.
Darum schwör' ich feierlich	So I swear solemnly,
Und ohn' alle Fährde,	And without risking my soul,
Dass ich mich nicht freventlich	That I shall not wantonly
Wegbegeben werde.	Take my leave.

Da wir aber allzumal	But since we are all
So beisammen weilen,	Gathered together,
Dächt' ich, klänge der Pokal	I would have thought that the cup should resound
Zu des Dichters Zeilen.	To the poet's lines.
Gute Freunde ziehen fort,	Good friends are going away,
Wohl ein hundert Meilen,	A hundred miles or so,
Darum soll man hier am Ort	So we must hasten to clink glasses
Anzustossen eilen.	While we are here.

[. . . 5 . . .]   [. . . 5 . . .]

JOHANN WOLFGANG VON GOETHE (1749–1832); poem written by 22 February 1802

*This is the nineteenth of Schubert's seventy-five Goethe solo settings (1814–26). See the poet's
biography for a chronological list of all the Goethe settings.*

A jolly little song this, in the best German tradition of mixing homespun philosophy with the beer flagon and punchbowl – although the poem was in fact written for a state occasion in Weimar in 1802. It is a companion piece for the various lyrics of the hale-and-hearty kind published in the almanacs by other poets. These include Schiller's various *Punschlieder*, two of which Schubert also set in the summer of 1815 – one solo, one choral piece (D253 and D277). Schiller's example in this respect might have inspired Goethe to such effusion, although the older man, more accustomed to female companionship than male camaraderie at this stage of his life (could one really imagine the older Goethe beating on a table?), was somewhat less at home with this genre. In any case the verses were penned tongue-in-cheek as a character piece rather than a heartfelt credo. The words fit the tune (included in an anthology of 1782 by the composer J. A. P. Schulz) of the medieval drinking song *Mihi est propostium in taberna mori* ascribed to Walter Map or Mapes. The poet Bürger later parodied this and here Goethe takes his turn too. The words were sufficiently well known to be quoted and altered by Marianne von Willemer in 1823, written under a print of Frankfurt sent to Goethe, and the poet did her the honour of writing a quatrain that derived in turn from that parody. Schubert thought enough of the song to include it in the second lieder album, prepared for Goethe in 1816 but not sent to the poet after the first was returned. The tune is pleasant enough, and the swashbuckling postlude, with its ascent to the top of the stave followed by a downward rush, is one of the composer's best inspirations in this hearty vein.

For the Hyperion Edition the first two verses of the poem were recorded. There are eight printed in the old *Gesamtausgabe* of which strophes 1, 2 and 3 are printed above with translation.

Autograph:	Wienbibliothek im Rathaus, Vienna
First edition:	Published as Op. post. 118 no. 3 by Josef Czerny, Vienna in June 1829 (P224)
Subsequent editions:	Not in Peters; AGA XX 97: Vol. 2/182; NSA IV: Vol. 9
Bibliography:	Byrne 2003, pp. 189–92
	Sternfeld 1979, pp. 13–15, 112
Further settings & arrangements:	Johann Friedrich Reichardt (1752–1814) *Tischlied* (1809)
	Carl Friedrich Zelter (1758–1832) *Tischlied* (1807)
	Traugott Maximilian Eberwein (1775–1831) *Tischlied* (1810)
	Ferdinand Ries (1784–1838) *Tischlied* Op. 32 no. 6 (1811)
	Arr. Tilman Hoppstock (b. 1961) for guitar accompaniment, in *Franz Schubert: 110 Lieder* (2009)
Discography and timing:	Fischer-Dieskau I 4[14] 2'07 (four strophes only)
	Hyperion I 24[7]
	Hyperion II 8[9] 1'29 Simon Keenlyside

← *Der Abend* D221   *Das Abendrot* D236 →

Der TOD OSCARS

The death of Oscar

('Ossian'–Macpherson/Harold) **D375** [H223]

C minor   February 1816

(289 bars)

1. Warum öffnest du wieder, Erzeugter von Alpin, die Quelle meiner Wehmut, da du mich fragst, wie Oscar erlag? Meine Augen sind von Tränen erblindet. Aber Erinnerung strahlt aus meinem Herzen. Wie kann ich den traurigen Tod des Führers der Krieger erzählen!

Why openest thou afresh the spring of my grief, O son of Alpin, inquiring how Oscar fell? My eyes are blind with tears, but memory beams on my heart. How can I relate the mournful death of the head of the people!

2. Führer der Helden, o Oscar, mein Sohn, soll ich dich nicht mehr erblicken! er fiel wie der Mond in einem Sturm, wie die Sonne in der Mitte ihres Laufs, wenn Wolken vom Schoose der Wogen sich heben; wenn das Dunkel des Sturms Ardanniders Felsen einhüllt. Wie eine alte Eiche von Morven, vermodre ich einsam auf meiner Stelle. Der Windstoss hat mir die Äste entrissen; mich schrecken die Flügel des Nordes. Führer der Helden, o Oscar, mein Sohn, soll ich dich nicht mehr erblicken!

Chief of the warriors, Oscar, my son, shall I see thee no more! He fell as the moon in a storm; as the sun from the midst of his course, when clouds rise from the waste of the waves, when the blackness of the storm enwraps the rocks of Ardannider. Like an ancient oak on Morven, I moulder alone in my place. The blast hath lopped my branches away; and I tremble at the wings of the north. Chief of the warriors, Oscar, my son! shall I see thee no more!

Der Held, o Alpins Erzeugter, fiel nicht friedlich, wie Gras auf dem Feld, der Mächtigen Blut befärbte sein Schwert, er riss sich, mit Tod, durch die Reihen ihres Stolzes, aber Oscar, Erzeugter von Caruth, du bist unrühmlich gefallen! deine Rechte erschlug keinen Feind. Deinen Speer befleckte das Blut deines Freunds.

But, son of Alpin, the hero fell not harmless as the grass of the field; the blood of the mighty was on his sword, and he travelled with death through the ranks of their pride. But Oscar, thou son of Caruth, thou hast fallen low! No enemy fell by thy hand. Thy spear was stained with the blood of thy friend.

3. Eins war Dermid und Oscar: sie mähten die Schlachten zusammen. Ihre Freundschaft war stark, wie ihr Eisen, und im Felde wandelte der Tod zwischen ihnen. Sie fuhren gegen den Feind, wie zwei Felsen die von Ardvens Stirne sich stürzen. Ihr Schwert war vom Blute der Tapfern befärbt: Krieger erbebten bei ihrem Namen. Wer glich Oscarn, als Dermid? und wer Dermid als Oscar!

Dermid and Oscar were one: They reaped the battle together. Their friendship was strong as their steel; and death walked between them to the field. They came on the foe like two rocks falling from the brows of Ardven. Their swords were stained with the blood of the valiant: warriors fainted at their names. Who was equal to Oscar but Dermid? and who to Dermid but Oscar!

Sie erlegten den mächtigen Dargo im Feld,
Dargo, der nie aus dem Kampfe entfloh. Seine
Tochter war schön, wie der Morgen, sanft wie
der Strahl des Abends.

4. Ihre Augen glichen zwei Sternen im Regen:
ihr Atem dem Hauche des Frühlings. Ihr
Busen, wie neugefall'ner Schnee, der auf der
wiegenden Heide sich wälzt. Sie ward von den
Helden gesehn, und geliebt, ihre Seelen wurden
ans Mädchen geheftet. Jeder liebte sie, gleich
seinem Ruhm, sie wollte jeder besitzen, oder
sterben. Aber ihr Herz wählte Oscarn; Caruths
Erzeugter war der Jüngling ihrer Liebe. Sie
vergass das Blut ihres Vaters. Und liebte die
Rechte, die ihn erschlug.

5. 'Caruths Sohn,' sprach Dermid, 'ich liebe, o
Oscar! ich liebe dies Mädchen. Aber ihre Seele
hängt an dir; und nichts kann Dermiden
heilen. Hier durchdring diesen Busen, o Oscar;
hilf deinem Freund mit deinem Schwert.' 'Nie
soll mein Schwert, Diarans Sohn! nie soll es mit
Dermids Blute befleckt sein.' 'Wer ist dann
würdig mich zu erlegen, o Oscar, Caruths
Sohn! lass nicht mein Leben unrühmlich
vergehen, lass niemand, als Oscar, mich töten.
Schick mich mit Ehre zum Grab, und Ruhm
begleite meinen Tod.'

6. 'Dermid brauch deine Klinge; Diarans
Erzeugter schwing deinen Stahl. O fiel ich mit
dir! dass mein Tod von Dermids Rechte
herrühre!' Sie fochten beim Bache des Bergs,
bei Brannos Strom. Blut färbte die fliessenden
Fluten, und ronn um die bemoosten Steine.
Dermid der Stattliche fiel, er fiel, und lächelte
im Tod!

7. 'Und fällst du, Erzeuger Diarans, fällst du
durch die Rechte von Oscar! Dermid, der nie
im Kriege gewichen, seh ich dich also erliegen?'
– Er ging, und kehrte zum Mädchen seiner
Liebe. Er kehrte, aber sie vernahm seinen
Jammer.
    Warum dies Dunkel, Sohn von Caruth! was
überschattet deine mächtige Seele?
    Einst war ich, o Mädchen, im Bogen
berühmt, aber meinen Ruhm hab ich itzo

They killed mighty Dargo in the field: Dargo
who never fled in war. His daughter was fair as
the morn; mild as the beam of night.

Her eyes, like two stars in a shower: her breath,
the gale of spring: her breasts as the new-fallen
snow floating on the moving heath. The
warriors saw her, and loved; their souls were
fixed on the maid. Each loved her as his fame;
each must possess her or die. But her soul was
fixed on Oscar; the son of Caruth was the
youth of her love. She forgot the blood of her
father; and loved the hand that slew him.

'Son of Caruth,' said Dermid, 'I love; O Oscar, I
love this maid. But her soul cleaveth unto thee;
and nothing can heal Dermid. Here, pierce this
bosom, Oscar; relieve me, my friend, with thy
sword.' 'My sword, son of Diaran, shall never be
stained with the blood of Dermid.' 'Who then is
worthy to slay me, O Oscar, son of Caruth? Let
not my life pass away unknown. Let none but
Oscar slay me. Send me with honour to the
grave, and let my death be renowned.'

'Dermid, make use of thy sword; son of Diaran,
wield thy steel. Would that I fell with thee! that
my death came from the hand of Dermid!'
They fought by the brook of the mountain, by
the streams of Branno. Blood tinged the
running water, and curled round the mossy
stones. The stately Dermid fell; he fell, and
smiled in death.

'And fallest thou, son of Diaran, fallest thou by
Oscar's hand! Dermid who never yielded in
war, thus do I see thee fall!' – He went, and
returned to the maid of his love; he returned,
but she perceived his grief.

    Why that gloom, son of Caruth? What
shades thy mighty soul?
    Though once renowned for the bow, O maid,
I have lost my fame. Fixed on the tree by the

verloren. Am Baum, beim Bache des Hügels, hängt der Schild des mutigen Gormurs, Gormurs, den ich im Kampfe erschlug. Ich habe den Tag vergebens verzehrt, und konnte ihn nicht mit meinem Pfeil durchdringen.

Lass mich, Erzeugter von Caruth, die Kunst der Tochter von Dargo versuchen. Meine Rechte lernte den Bogen zu spannen, in meiner Kunst frohlockte mein Vater.

Sie ging, er stand hinter dem Schild. Es zischte ihr Pfeil, er durchdrang seine Brust.

8. Heil der schneeweissen Rechten; auch Heil diesem eibenen Bogen; wer, als Dargos Tochter war wert, Caruths Erzeugten zu töten? Leg mich ins Grab, meine Schönste; leg mich an Dermids Seite. Oscar, versetzte das Mädchen, meine Seel' ist die Seele des mächtigen Dargo. Ich kann dem Tode mit Freude begegnen. Ich kann meine Traurigkeit enden. Sie durchstiess ihren weissen Busen mit Stahl. Sie fiel, bebte, und starb!

Ihre Gräber liegen beim Bache des Hügels; ihr Grabmal bedeckt der ungleiche Schatten einer Birke. Oft grasen die astigen Söhne des Bergs an ihren grünenden Gräbern. Wenn der Mittag seine glühenden Flammen ausstreut, und Schweigen alle die Hügel beherrscht.

brook of the hill is the shield of the valiant Gormur, whom I slew in battle. I have wasted the day in vain, nor could my arrow pierce it.

Let me try, son of Caruth, the skill of Dargo's daughter. My hands were taught the bow: my father delighted in my skill.

She went. He stood behind the shield. Her arrow flew, and pierced his breast.

Blessed be that hand of snow, and blessed that bow of yew! Who but the daughter of Dargo was worthy to slay the son of Caruth? Lay me in the earth, my fair one; lay me by the side of Dermid. Oscar! the maid replied, I have the soul of the mighty Dargo. Well pleased I can meet death. My sorrow I can end. – She pierced her white bosom with the steel. She fell; she trembled, and died.

By the brook of the hill their graves are laid; a birch's unequal shade covers their tomb. Often on their green earthen tombs the branchy sons of the mountain feed, when midday is all in flames, and silence over all the hills.

JAMES MACPHERSON ('OSSIAN') (1736–1796), translated by EDMUND, BARON VON HAROLD (1737–1800) in 1782

This is the eighth of Schubert's ten Ossian–Macpherson solo settings (1815–17). See the poet's biography (under Macpherson) for a chronological list of all the Ossian settings.

Shortly after Schubert's death Anton Diabelli (a composer, but first and foremost a publisher and businessman) bought a large number of Schubert's manuscripts from the composer's brother Ferdinand. Diabelli proceeded to publish these in more than fifty slim volumes over some twenty years (1830–50) before turning over the remaining items to another publisher. But it was the Ossian songs that took pride of place. They inaugurated Diabelli's Nachlass (qv) series (the first five volumes are given over to them), no doubt because they were thought to be good Schubert as well as saleable. In 1830 the public's appetite for the Ossianic style was not what it had been forty years earlier, but Ossian was still more famous in Germany than most other British poets apart from Shakespeare, and the young Schubert's prose poems set as a mixture of dramatic recitative and arioso were daring and innovative. Wagner was a highly impressionable student in Leipzig at the time and it is possible that he knew the Schubert ballads better than we imagine: their publication coincided with the period when he was in the process of forming his own style. The Nachlass, and these settings in particular, received much publicity and critical attention throughout Germany, and there are moments when the

Wagnerian music drama, and even aspects of its harmonic vocabulary, seems foretold by the free-roaming fantasy of the young Viennese master. Alfred Einstein also comments on this in his biography of Schubert.

There is something outmoded, even faintly ridiculous, about this 'Celtic twilight' world of moors, mists and heroes. One thinks of *Wuthering Heights*, or *Rebecca* perhaps, as filmed in black and white in the 1940s. In these movies one accepts the larger-than-life performances (some of which border on caricature) because of the bleak and stormy locales, the sheer romantic sweep of events and the skill of the direction. Similarly, however 'fake' one may judge Ossian to be, the poetry clearly serves its purpose in enabling Schubert to have a grand time as dramaturg and general regisseur. The composer recycled the bleak and atmospheric moods of the Ossian settings into many a song, and without this apprenticeship he would have been less able to capture the atmosphere of wintry discontent in *Winterreise* D911.

Der Tod Oscars is perhaps the least likely of the Ossian settings to win an Oscar, lacking as it does the spellbound atmosphere of *Die Nacht* D534, the melodic sweep of *Kolmas Klage* D217, the ghostly evocations of *Lodas Gespenst* D150 and the sheer symphonic sweep and formal unity of *Cronnan* D282. But what it does have is the best story. Instead of a generalized mood picture, blurred around the edges, we have an easy-to-follow passionate tale about two men who loved the same girl, but who loved honour and each other more. The story has resonances of David and Jonathan, Virgil's Nisus and Euryalus who perished in battle together, and the Sacred Band of Thebes. As such it belongs to the same world as Mayrhofer's songs of Greek antiquity (*Uraniens Flucht* D554 comes to mind) although Schiller's *Die Bürgschaft* D246 elevates friendship to this quasi-sacred level too. Schubert had also long been aware of the friendship between Orestes and Pylades as nobly depicted in Gluck's *Iphigenie auf Tauris* (1779).

In *Der Tod Oscars* Dermid and Oscar are both fiercely attracted to the daughter of Dargo and fight to the death over her. The tragedy here is that, in killing Dermid, Oscar proves the point that 'each man kills the thing he loves' (to quote another Oscar). Schubert's music depicts the pair's manly prowess with great ease, but the vulnerability and tenderness of Oscar, a man guilt-ridden and bereft without his friend, are also painted unselfconsciously and naturally.

The publisher Diabelli, no doubt disapproving of Harold's translation of Macpherson into rather unsatisfactory German, hired Schubert's old friend Leopold von Sonnleithner to revise the texts that Schubert set, a vandalism that Sonnleithner lived to regret. This is the stuff of scholastic nightmare. Where an original manuscript survives it is relatively easy to reinstate the original words; in the case of *Der Tod Oscars* (the autograph is lost) we cannot be sure who is responsible – Sonnleithner or perhaps Schubert himself – for the deviations from the original translation. In Volume 10 of the NSA, words printed in italics supplement the Nachlass text; these are to be taken as *probably* the text that Schubert originally set.

For the purposes of this commentary the poem as printed above has been divided into sections that correspond to the musical sections of Schubert's setting. The 'poem' was originally printed in continuous prose.

Verse 1: The ballad opens with an impassioned little introduction in the piano – two sequential phrases and a third bar that falls to a diminished chord. The work opens rhetorically in midstream; before the song starts we have to imagine a question put to Oscar's father about his son's death. This initiates a burst of emotion suggesting welling tears and a painful surge of memory. The marking at the beginning of the song is 'Mässig, in schmerzlicher Erinnerung' (*Moderato, in painful recollection*). The phrase 'Meine Augen sind von Tränen erblindet' (My eyes are blind with tears) is set to a descending chromatic phrase that changes direction on 'erblindet' (b. 9) as if to suggest a tear-stained face turning upwards and warming to the narrative task (it is astonishing how Schubert's music can powerfully suggest body language). This opening section, an extended recitative in the grand manner, ends (bb. 11–13) on a question: 'Wie kann ich . . . erzählen!' ('How shall I find a way to tell this tale?'). Having asked himself this, the old bard seems to come to a decision with the semibreve chord of b. 14, as if to say 'Ah, now I have it – thus!'

Verse 2: This hefty E flat major chord on a semibreve announces the real beginning of the narrative in which the old seer partially addresses his interlocutor (the son of Alpin) and partially speaks directly to Oscar himself as might a fond parent imagining their child were still alive. A march-like motif ('Mässig bewegt') begins at 'Führer der Helden' and for the first two bars the voice is doubled by the piano in a sort of vocative unison. Each phrase begins forte with great resolve for two bars (as at bb. 15–16 and 19–20) and is balanced by another two bars (bb. 17–18 and 21–2) that taper into a wistful piano, as if the narrator lacks the heart to continue in martial mode. This arioso section, like a battle hymn from times long past, is broken up by snatches of recitative that take Alpin's son into the narrator's confidence as if at last the *real* story of what happened is being told. It is like evenings in Vienna (Walter Legge told me he had experienced such when he was a young man) where the visitor is told by one of the city's old survivors that, contrary to whatever they may have thought or read, *here* is the truth – hidden secrets, perhaps, about Schubert, Mahler, Wolf, Berg et al., handed down by word of mouth, but never printed in books.

Verse 3: At 'Eins war Dermid und Oscar' there is a change of key signature (for the first time) from E flat to F. For Schubert this signifies a time change in the narrative. The mourning is over and we now begin to come to grips with the story itself by going right back to the beginning and discovering the strength of friendship between the two warriors. This music manages to be both straightforward and tender. The setting of 'Wer glich Oscarn, als Dermid?' followed by 'und wer Dermid als Oscar!' (bb. 83–6) is strangely moving. The phrases are absolutely sequential and symmetrical; they belong to each other (thus suggesting that the two warriors are also indivisible) and they balance each other. In the same way the two names scan (a heavy syllable followed by a light). Schubert follows 'und wer Dermid als Oscar' with two pairs of chords in the piano that silently recite the two names, the first pair in b. 87 (dominant to tonic in the key of F) answered and complemented by the second in b. 88 (the same harmonies resolving an octave lower), a perfect tonal analogue for two hearts joined as one. A simple recitative (from b. 89) introduces the enemy Dargo who is quickly dispatched. Just as quickly his daughter is introduced. (bb. 93–5). The arioso from b. 96 – marked 'Sanft' (softly) in response to the sentence in the bar before describing the girl as 'sanft wie der Strahl des Abends' – is in a gently luminous B flat.

Verse 4: This music praises the girl's eyes that are like stars. The tune and the dotted rhythm of the accompaniment are strongly prophetic of the Mayrhofer song Nachtviolen D752 which also describes eyes using metaphors taken from nature. At 'Ihr Busen, wie neugefall'ner Schnee' the music drifts gently downwards to match the snowflake imagery, and at 'der auf der wiegenden Heide sich wälzt' the accompaniment cradles the vocal line with affectionate solicitude. The two heroes fall in love with her suddenly and unexpectedly: the harmonic foundations of the two chords under 'Sie ward von den Helden gesehn, und geliebt' (bb. 109–11) lie only a semitone apart but are enough to signal the irrevocable change in their lives. This shift into G flat major continues for 'Jeder liebte sie, gleich seinem Ruhm' ('Each loved her as his fame'). These words are, significantly, set twice, the second tune (bb. 115–16) a sequence of the first, as if even in this the two men are twinned and it has always been inevitable that they should pursue the same girl. The girl's own reactions ('Aber ihr Herz wählte Oscarn' – 'but her heart chose Oscar' in Macpherson's original) are tenderly shown by a sensual shift from C flat major (B) to E major and an arioso marked 'Mässig' (from b. 120); for a moment we glimpse her discomfort in being more attracted to one of the men than the other. A veil is drawn over the fact that she seems strongly drawn to the very man who has just killed her father.

Verse 5: The next aria (still in E major, from b. 130), '"Caruths Sohn," sprach Dermid', is marked 'Etwas geschwind'. The subject matter is the deadly rivalry for a woman's hand but Schubert's chromatic shifts (the music is almost like a three-part invention *à la* Bach) perfectly captures the anguish and guilt felt by both men and also their tenderness for each other. Their conversation is neither loud nor angry – even this catastrophe does not essentially ruin their friendship. In an extended exchange between the two characters in direct speech, Dermid wishes to be killed, but only by Oscar who naturally declines.

Verse 6: Oscar is eventually persuaded to fight. At b. 159 E major yields to E flat major and three loud martial chords that will form the musical basis, on various pitches, of the cut and thrust of their fight. 'Dermid, brauch deine Klinge' ('Make use of thy sword') says Oscar. 'Would that I fell with thee! that my death came from the hand of Dermid.' The piano's battle music, rather Beethovenian in manner (dotted rhythms alternating with the three-chord motif), is among the best of its genre in Schubert's ballads. When blood begins to run, and after the words 'und ronn um die bemoosten Steine', it is clear from a diminished chord in the piano music exactly when Dermid's body sinks to the ground (bb. 186–7). The cadence at bb. 189–90 for 'fiel, und lächelte im Tod' (fell, and smiled in death), suddenly marked 'Langsam', is exquisite. This passage brings to mind A. E. Housman's lines about the soldier and foeman:

> That took the sabre straight and took it striking
> And laughed and kissed his hand to me and died.

Verse 7: The fight is followed by a recitative from b. 192 ('Und fällst du, Erzeugter Diarans'). A criticism of the remainder of this piece may be that the death of Dermid seems to knock the stuffing out of the music as well as out of Oscar. A mournful interlude after 'seh ich dich also erliegen?' (bb. 195–6) has the quality of music for a Passion or Stabat Mater with a slightly old-fashioned chromatic character. (Schubert was to write *Stabat mater* D383 to a Klopstock text in the same month.) At b. 208 there is an unintentionally insensitive question from the maiden at the centre of this story: 'Why that gloom, son of Caruth?' A strangely jaunty ⅜ aria in A flat major follows ('Einst war ich, o Mädchen, im Bogen berühmt' – 'Once renowned for the bow, o maid, I have lost my fame'). It is the music of dissembling and forced jollity. At 'Am Baum, beim Bache des Hügels, hängt der Schild' ('fixed on the tree by the brook of the hill is the shield'), dotted rhythms re-establish the martial character of the music at the same time as suggesting a shield suspended in mid-air and slightly shuddering in the wind. The somewhat Amazonian daughter of Drago (as we learn in bb. 238–40) is accomplished at archery so Oscar cleverly tricks her into trying out the bow so that she should kill him. The whole of this section sounds like a casual game, as indeed it must seem to be to the duped girl. After 'in meiner Kunst frohlockte mein Vater' a rather remarkable seven-bar piano interlude (bb. 245–52) turns and tightens the screw of harmonic tension in such a way as to suggest the winding-up of a crossbow (the very existence of this weapon in ancient times is a typically Ossianic anachronism). It is all over in a flash and the arrow pierces Oscar's breast ('Langsam' for bb. 254–5).

Verses 8–9: Here the most disjointed and surprising harmonic juxtaposition takes place. After being hit in four flats, Oscar delivers his swansong ('Heil, der schneeweissen Rechten') in four sharps (E major), as if suddenly transfigured by his *Liebestod*. His last request is to be buried next to Dermid (bb. 263–4). The girl is made of stern stuff and in an aria marked 'Etwas geschwind' (from b. 268) she determines to kill herself too, perhaps in desperation that her beauty was not consolation enough for the death of Oscar's friend. At this point the accumulation of deaths is proving somewhat comic. Nevertheless, 'Sie fiel, bebte, und starb' is set to another noble cadence (bb. 273–4) that leads the music back to an E flat major key signature. The postlude (from b. 275 and 'Ihre Gräber liegen beim Bache des Hügels') is in the composer's best Ossianic style with a gravity worthy of an aged narrator. From b. 282 the demisemiquaver oscillations that accompany 'Wenn der Mittag seine glühenden Flammen ausstreut' (when midday is all in flames) flicker in masterful illustration, reminiscent of *Cronnan* D282 where the same figuration describes the movement of leaves and waves.

Autograph:	Missing or lost
First edition:	Published as Book 5 of the *Nachlass* by Diabelli, Vienna in July 1830 (P247)
Publication review:	L. Rellstab 'Ueberblick der Erzeugnisse', *Iris im Gebiete der Tonkunst* (Berlin) No. 39 (12 November 1830) [Waidelich/Hilmar Dokumente II No. 784b]
Subsequent editions:	Peters: Vol. 4/204; AGA XX 187: Vol. 4/7; NSA IV: Vol. 10/25
Discography and timing:	Fischer-Dieskau —
	Hyperion I 23[1]
	Hyperion II 12[18] 16'37 Christoph Prégardien

← *An Schwager Kronos* D369   *Lorma* D376 →

Der TOD UND DAS MÄDCHEN   Death and the maiden
(CLAUDIUS) OP. 7 NO. 3, **D531** [H347]
D minor   February 1817

(43 bars)

Das Mädchen:
Vorüber, ach, vorüber!
Geh, wilder Knochenmann!
Ich bin noch jung, geh, Lieber!
Und rühre mich nicht an.

Der Tod:
Gib deine Hand, du schön und zart Gebild!
Bin Freund und komme nicht zu strafen.
Sei gutes Muts! Ich bin nicht wild,
Sollst sanft in meinen Armen schlafen!

The Maiden:
Pass by, ah, pass by!
Away, cruel Death!
I am still young; leave me, dear God[1]
And do not touch me.

Death:
Give me your hand, you lovely, tender creature.
I am your friend, and come not to chastise.
Be of good courage. I am not cruel;
You shall sleep softly in my arms.

---

[1] See commentary for a discussion of the poet's use of 'geh, Lieber'.

Claudius's autograph of *Der Tod und das Mädchen* (1775).

MATTHIAS CLAUDIUS (1740–1815); poem published in 1775

This is the eleventh of Schubert's thirteen Claudius solo settings (1816–17). See the poet's biography for a chronological list of all the Claudius settings.

The ritornello of this justly famous song is built on a repetitive and obsessive rhythm – a note followed by two of half its length. The equivalent in poetry is the dactyl, a metrical foot within which a stressed syllable is followed by two unaccented ones. Schubert used dactylic rhythm throughout his song-writing career, most often to depict the motor energy of the inscrutable forces of nature. Here Death, in his role of Grim Reaper, presses the rhythm into his relentlessly disinterested service. It is noticeable that the metronome mark for the first edition is considerably faster (and less sentimental) than the tempi that result from most performers' initial, over-romanticized, inclinations. It is, however, not impossible that this marking is not the composer's own, or that it is inaccurate (*see* TEMPO AND EXPRESSION MARKINGS).

It is interesting to note that death in German – der Tod – is a masculine noun (unlike 'la mort' in French for example) and this contrast between male executioner and female victim lends the scenario a certain eroticism. The girl, clearly fatally ill, remains attractively vulnerable on her deathbed (something that in itself is shocking) and Schubert's music for such a damsel in distress would pull at the heartstrings of any *cavaliere servente*. Death is duly implacable in the performance of his timeless and perpetual duty, but he is not impervious to the girl's beauty (he addresses her as 'du schön und zart Gebild'). It is notable that in Schubert's Josef von Spaun setting, *Der Jüngling und der Tod* D545, Death only arrives after an agonized request from the young man who longs for release. Spaun's inference is that if this youth had been a beautiful young woman, no such special pleading to be gathered up would have been necessary.

Grotesque sexual interplay between skeletons and maidens is to be seen in much medieval and Renaissance art – in the memento mori and vanitas canvases of, for example, the early sixteenth-century German, Hans Baldung Grien, paintings Schubert could easily have seen in the Viennese museums. Claudius had also probably seen some of the pervasive erotic

Der Tod nach einer Frau greifend (Death taking hold of a woman) by Daniel Hopfer the Elder (1470–1536), a picture that was in Goethe's personal collection.

iconography on this subject (the Daniel Hopfer gouache illustrated here, for example, was in Goethe's private collection). In Schubert's *Der Tod und das Mädchen* a shadow of sexual frisson is only fleetingly evident in touches of harmonic sensuality in Death's riposte to the girl's pleas.

In this proffered contract between Death and the surrendering maiden there are no threats of hellfire; the Protestant Claudius has imagined a fast-track approach to eternal rest without the intervention of priests, last rites and Purgatory. Lessing and Herder had come to the conclusion that the idea of Death as a punishment was a superstitious aspect of Christianity that contrasted enormously with the personification of Death by the Greeks as a beautiful youth. Surely the Christianity of reason should depict death as gentle and consoling? The girl in this song gives up the ghost suddenly and unshriven. Practising Catholics, however, may have considered this worse than an agonizing Death, and it is perhaps ironic that the song's autograph was destroyed by a priest, albeit one with generous if philistine intentions (*see* below).

Claudius placed a picture of Death as a skeleton ('Freund Hain') as the frontispiece of his works. 'So he appears in our church', wrote the poet, 'as much as I've always pictured him from childhood on . . . This way, I believe, he is quite beautiful, and if only one gazes at him long enough, he'll finally look entirely friendly.' One is reminded that in his poem the maiden, terrified by the 'wilder Knochenmann' in the first part of her outburst, addresses Death as 'dear one' ('Lieber') in the very next line. (That is if one takes the word 'Lieber' literally, rather than as a contraction of 'du lieber Gott' – a translator's conundrum.) Is she commanding or begging Death to leave her alone 'for God's sake', or attempting to flirt with him in the hope of receiving his mercy? In any case she is both repulsed and fascinated by him.

The key is D minor, the tonality of death since Mozart wrote the Commendatore's music in *Don Giovanni*, an opera (like almost all of Mozart's stage works) by which Schubert was mightily influenced. Christoph Wolff has written of Schubert's use of 'the oracle topos of eighteenth-century opera seria' in conceiving the voice of Death, and this goes back to such operas as Gluck's *Alceste* where the pronouncements of the oracle are given in 'liturgical recitation-tone' (cf. the closing bars of *Der Wanderer* D489 and the end of *Antigone und Oedip* D542).

In *Der Tod und das Mädchen*, music to underpin such a pronouncement had to be found and Schubert chooses to begin his song with an introduction that will later serve to accompany the voice. In the opening bars the pianist's hands, bunched closely together in the region of the bass clef, hardly move: the left pivots impassively between tonic and dominant; in the right the harmonies change imperceptibly under the fingers, always coming back to the same D minor chord, wherever they stray. Whichever way you look at it, Death has his victim in his grasp; try as she might to find an exit, there is no escape. For this passage, both claustrophobic and agoraphobic, a constricted prison cell and a bleak moonscape, the pianist is appointed death's plenipotentiary. This is one of the most tactile of all songs to play: the accompanist has to weigh each change within the chords as carefully as if judging a life held precariously in the balance. Similarly, Death the puppeteer manipulates human destinies with the tiniest of hand shifts.

After eight bars of piano introduction (enough of Death's tune – precisely half in fact – to be a calling card) there is a sudden change of tempo ('Etwas geschwinder' from the upbeat to b. 9) for the vocal entry. This section has operatic overtones in that it is inspired by accompanied recitative. The maiden, in short breathy gasps, and with the racing pulse of fear and delirium, begs for mercy, but the repeat of the words 'Und rühre mich nicht an' (bb. 16–19) shows that the game is up. In a protracted descent of a minor sixth over four bars in the vocal line (bb. 16–19) she loses the battle, fading away before our very ears. During an ominous interlude of two bars (bb. 20–21), Death advances by a number of paces, as if to the edge of the girl's bedside, and proceeds to take charge of the situation as only he can. The double bar line here is the gate between life and death – no fearsome portcullis, but a small, secret door. It takes only a minim's rest, moderated by a fermata, to slip the latch.

The same singer is now tasked to enunciate Death's words in the tempo in which the song has begun. It is surely a mistake to turn this piece into a duet: the song is too small to remain a unity with two singers, and so the variation of colour must come from within the structure, and from a single performer. A female singer, at home in the depiction of the maiden, will have to achieve a very special gravitas in this new role. This casting occasionally succeeds, as with

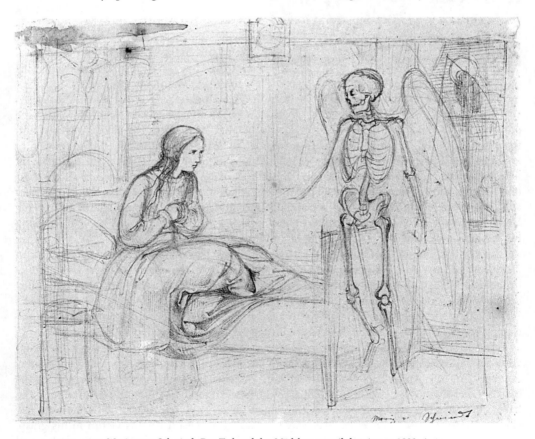

Moritz von Schwind, *Der Tod und das Mädchen*, pencil drawing, *c.* 1823–4.

the somewhat unsettling interpretation of the American contralto Marian Anderson, with her booming, yet unearthly, low D at the end. But it is more usual for a baritone or bass to portray, with varying degress of success, the fear-induced femininity necessary in the first part of the song before embarking more comfortably on the music that lies naturally for the lower male voices.

The returning tempo of Death is, of course, infinitely more measured than the music for the terrified girl ('Das erste Zeitmass' from b. 22). It is as if the spectre has successfully invaded the maiden's body, and her voice, and requisitioned both for his ends. We hear the whole of Death's tune this time (bb. 22–37), and in suitably oracular style. With the maiden's body in his arms, he is now allowed to enter into consolatory harmonic realms that are as simple as they are astonishing: for the crucial words 'nicht zu strafen' an extraordinary cadence into F major at bb. 27–9; a plagal shift to B flat ('Sei gutes Muts!', b. 30), almost holy in its gentle concern; and then a slow and uneluctable progress back to the D major of the final vocal cadence. The arrival in the tonic major at b. 37 appears to signify a merciful release. It says something for the power of Schubert's conception that the low D of 'schlafen', when this is within the singer's ability (the ossia of the higher D is considered an honourable enough alternative) suggests ineffable and eternal peace rather than the abyss of the grave. This depends of course on the singer observing the pianissimo marking of the entire section, without the stentorian grandstanding that is the default setting of a certain kind of operatic bass. The seven-bar postlude (including one bar of overlap with the vocal part) is a major-key variant of the introduction. Although the actual notes present no difficulty, the challenge lies in the balancing of the chords, the control of dynamics and the retention of the other-worldly mood hopefully established by the singer.

The autograph of the first version of this song (there is no surviving autograph for the published version) had originally been the property of Ferdinand Schubert who passed it on to his half-brother, Andreas, who had become a priest. On leaving his position as a teacher at the Schottengymnasium in Vienna, Andreas (whose religious name was Pater Hermann Schubert) thought it a good idea to cut up the first page of *Der Tod und das Mädchen* into eight pieces (the other pages have not survived at all) and distribute them as souvenirs. It is possible that these pieces were later further subdivided by their subsequent owners. Andreas Schubert kept one piece of this autograph; it was inherited by his niece whose family sold it at auction in 1922 to the Musikverein. This segment included the first two and a half bars of the prelude and the tempo marking 'Mässig'. (On the back of this was the third strophe of *Das Lied vom Reifen* D532 (qv), another Claudius setting.) Five further pieces of the autograph found their way into the possession of the Musikverein over the years, including the fragment containing Schubert's signature and the date of the song. A seventh fragment appeared briefly for auction in Vienna in 1961 and was sold to someone in the United States, but not before being photographed to make a facsimile. The eighth fragment, which contains the piano part of bb. 10–11, has never been found. The autograph in possession of the Gesellschaft der Musikfreunde (pictured in NSA Vol. 1a p. XXXI) is thus a reconstruction of the first page of the work whereby six of the fragments are re-assembled to make up a single page.

Seven years after writing this song Schubert was to compose his String Quartet in D minor (D810), in which he used the song's ritornello as the basis for the second movement variations, and where Death's theme in various subtle rhythmic metamorphoses is the seed and starting point for the other movements.

| Autographs: | Gesellschaft der Musikfreunde, Vienna (six of eight fragments); one fragment in private possession; one missing or lost |
| First edition: | Published as Op. 7 no. 3 by Cappi & Diabelli, Vienna in November 1821 (P20) |

Dedicatee:	Ludwig Széchényi von Sarvári-Felsö-Vidék
Contemporary reviews:	*Allgemeine musikalische Zeitung* (Vienna) No. 6 (19 January 1822), col. 43ff. [Waidelich/Hilmar Dokumente I No. 142; Deutsch Doc. Biog. No. 270]
	F. von Hentl 'Blick auf Schubert's Lieder', *Wiener Zeitschrift für Kunst, Literatur, Theater und Mode* No. 36 (23 March 1822), p. 289f. [Waidelich/Hilmar Dokumente I No. 146; Deutsch Doc. Biog. No. 278]
Subsequent editions:	Peters: Vol. 1/221; AGA XX 302: Vol. 5/35; NSA IV: Vol. 1a/66; Bärenreiter: Vol. 1/54
Bibliography:	Capell 1928, pp. 134–5
	Fischer-Dieskau 1977, pp. 85–6
	Newbould 1997, p. 160
	Wolff 1982, pp. 143–71
Further settings & arrangements:	Siegfried Matthus (b. 1934) *Das Mädchen und der Tod* for string quartet (1996–7)
	Algirdas Martinaitis (b. 1950) *Der Tod und das Mädchen* for string quartet (1997)
	Arr. Tilman Hoppstock (b. 1961) for guitar accompaniment, in *Franz Schubert: 110 Lieder* (2009)
Discography and timing:	Fischer-Dieskau I 9¹⁹ 2'30
	Hyperion I 11¹
	Hyperion II 17²⁵ 2'34 Brigitte Fassbaender

←— *Das Lied vom Reifen* D532   *Täglich zu singen* D533 —→

TODESMUSIK   Death music
(SCHOBER) OP. 108 NO. 2, **D758** [H496]

The song exists in two versions, the second of which is discussed below:
(1) September 1822; (2) beginning of 1828?

(1)   'Langsam, feierlich'   G♭ major   ₵   [103 bars]

(2)   G major

(26 bars)

In des Todes Feierstunde,	In the solemn hour of death,
Wenn ich einst von hinnen scheide,[1]	When one day I depart hence

[1] Either Schubert himself inserted this line and the next into Schober's poem, or Schober removed them from an earlier version when he came to prepare his *Gedichte* (1842) for publication.

Und den Kampf, den letzten leide,	And suffer my last battle,
Senke, heilige Kamöne,	Then, sacred muse, let your tranquil songs
Noch einmal die stillen Lieder,	And pure tones
Noch einmal die reinen Töne[2]	Descend one more time
Auf die tiefe Abschiedswunde	To heal the deep wound of parting
Meines Busens heilend nieder.	Within my heart.
Hebe aus dem ird'schen Ringen	Raise my pure, anguished soul
Die bedrängte reine Seele,	From this earthly struggle;
Trage sie auf deinen Schwingen:	Bear it on your wings
Dass sie sich dem Licht vermähle.—	To be united with the light.—
O da werden mich die Klänge	Then harmonies will enfold me
Süss und wonnevoll umwehen,[3]	In sweet bliss,
Und die Ketten, die ich sprenge,	And the chains which I shall break
Werden still und leicht vergehen.	Will vanish, silently, lightly.
Alles Grosse werd' ich sehen,	I shall behold all the greatness
Das im Leben mich beglückte,	That gave me joy in life;
Alles Schöne, das mir blühte,	All the beauty that flowered for me
Wird verherrlicht vor mir stehen.	Will be glorified before me.
Jeden Stern, der mir erglühte,	Those tones will bring back to me
Der mit freundlichem Gefunkel	Every star that shone for me,
Durch das grauenvolle Dunkel[4]	That with its friendly light
Meines kurzen Weges blickte,	Looked down upon my brief journey
Jede Blume, die ihn schmückte,	Through the fearful darkness,
Werden mir die Töne bringen.	And every flower that adorned my path.
Und die schrecklichen Minuten,	And those terrifying minutes
Wo ich schmerzlich könnte bluten,	When I might have bled in agony
Werden mich mit Lust umklingen,	Will envelop me with joyous sounds.
Und Verklärung werd' ich sehen,	I shall behold
Ausgegossen über allen Dingen.	All things transfigured.
So in Wonne werd' ich untergehen,	Thus I shall perish in bliss,
Süss verschlungen von der Freude Fluten.	Sweetly engulfed by waves of joy.

FRANZ VON SCHOBER (1796–1882)

This is the eighth of Schubert's fourteen Schober solo settings (1815–27). See the poet's biography for a chronological list of all the Schober settings.

Franz von Schober was not the most celebrated of the Schubert poets (although he was one of the composer's greatest friends), but there are several Schober settings that are beloved songs, including *An die Musik* D547 and *Am Bach im Frühlinge* D361. On the other hand, *Todesmusik* has stubbornly remained among the unknown Schubert lieder, although it is certainly more interesting as a piece of music than its neglect suggests. Schober aims for a mystical tone that imitates Novalis (cf. *Nachthymne* D687), even though the depiction of music as comforter in the final hours was no doubt conceived as a compliment to Schubert, born of a genuine enthusiasm for the beauty of his music. (The poem was almost certainly written specifically to suit

[2] Schober (1842) writes 'Noch einmal die *süssen* Töne'.
[3] Schober (1842) writes '*Traut* und wonnevoll umwehen'.
[4] Schober (1842) writes 'Durch das *hoffnungslose* Dunkel'.

musical setting.) Schober still had some sixty years to live when he wrote it, and nothing that we know of his life inclines us to be convinced by the self-dramatizing second and third lines, for example, where he suffers his 'last battle', as if on a great personal crusade. (This section was removed when Schober came to prepare the poem for publication in 1842.) The 'pure, anguished soul' is also a preposterously sentimental idea, particularly in relation to this man as we have come to know him. In short, the whole poem is made faintly ridiculous by the self-importance of its amateur writer.

Nevertheless, Schubert took the words at face value and, as always with the poetry of his friends, transcended its limitations. He was almost certainly attracted by the possibilities the words gave him to take us into the starlit world of the music of the spheres, and in this he does not disappoint. In July 1822 the composer had had a strange and fantastic dream, Novalis-like, that he wrote down. Part of the dream is as follows:

> And one day I had news of a gentle maiden who had just died. And a circle formed around her grave in which many youths and old men walked as though in everlasting bliss. They spoke softly so as not to awaken the maiden. . . . But I went to the gravestone with slow steps and lowered gaze, filled with devotion and firm belief, and before I was aware of it, I found myself in the circle, which uttered a wondrously lovely sound; and I felt as though eternal bliss were gathered together in a single moment.

It is surely not impossible that the poem for *Todesmusik* was the result of discussions between the composer and his poet-confidant regarding the meaning and significance of this extraordinary dream.

The song is in a number of sections, in the manner of an operatic aria; indeed, for the most part the vocal writing calls on Italian *bel canto* style, and challenges the singer to show great breath control and technical flexibility. This, as much as anything else, has counted against the song's popularity. The original printed key is G major, although the first version (printed in Volume 5b of the NSA, p. 241) is in G flat major, and this was almost certainly changed simply to facilitate the access of the song to pianists who might have been put off by six flats (a similar change from G flat to G major was effected for the famous *Impromptu* D899/3). The introduction suggests four-part wind music, the prologue to a solemn chorale. (Comparisons with *Das Wirtshaus* D911/21 from *Winterreise* come to mind – a much greater song, but one where we are also made aware of the Austrian tradition of wind and brass music played at outdoor funerals.) As in *Das Wirtshaus*, a conventional and unexceptional opening phrase (the first three notes) is ennobled by a slightly altered repetition, where the seemingly banal addition of a seventh chord evokes the shadow of pathos and doubt. The melody itself might almost have been made for community singing: a beautiful, hymn-like tune, it also resembles (intentionally) the solemn choruses about love and death that German students and secret societies were given to singing when in their cups. In b. 7, in the third beat of the accompaniment (under the word 'von'), the NSA reading (from the first version) of an E flat at the top of the left-hand chord, rather than an E natural, is to be preferred. At 'einmal die stillen Lieder' (bb. 13–14) the vocal line becomes more adventurously soloistic and breaks into running quavers, revealing the essentially nimble nature of the song. (Despite the 'Langsam, feierlich' marking, the song is *alla breve*; a sanctimonious, sluggish tempo defeats the listener's patience.) Schober, showing off his learning, invokes the obscure Kamöne: this is usually encountered in the plural, Kamönen (*Camenae* in Latin, and related to *carmen*, the word for song). These were water goddesses linked to the Muses, known for the sweetness of their music.

Mention of the 'pure, anguished soul' follows a change into three flats, including one of Schubert's many ominous left-hand trills that betoken a shiver at the contemplation of the infinite (b. 21). But we soon pull ourselves together, switch into E flat major and launch into a good example of the composer's heroic style. This is epic music in the manner of *An die Leier* D737, *Mut!* D911/22 from *Winterreise*, and martial passages in various pieces of chamber music and piano duets; but it is short-lived. At 'O da werden mich die Klänge / Süss und wonnevoll umwehen' we find the sort of music-related imagery that Schober wrote especially for Schubert. This is accompanied by a change to F sharp major and the first of the flowing triplets in the accompaniment (from b. 31) that will more or less dominate the song from now on. The vocal line is a fascinating cantilena which moves so fluently that we can only classify it as something between recitative and aria; indeed, this is an example of Schubert's ability to rework what is essentially the material of connecting recitative in any guise he chooses. There is some contrast between major and minor key at 'die Ketten, die ich sprenge' (bb. 34–6), with added sforzati, to match the uncomfortable intrusion of clanging chains. The vocal writing on 'still und leicht vergehen', each word embroidered by melisma, borders on Italianate coloratura.

At 'Alles Grosse werd' ich sehen', a double bar and change of key signature to F sharp minor signals a return to the heroic music that made a brief appearance earlier. This strutting may seem a little lame for the import of the words until one realizes that this *pomposo* passage is meant to depict the emptiness of worldly fame – all form and no substance. Even earthly beauty ('Alles Schöne, das mir blühte') is given short shrift as we move towards our heavenly goal.

We cross the threshold into real Schubertian magic with a move into B flat major on 'verherrlicht vor mir <u>stehen</u>' (bb. 49–51); it is to this moment that the music has been leading and, at the narrator's death, the song comes to life. Softly pulsating triplets denote all-pervasive starlight and we are reminded of Beethoven's 1820 song *Abendlied unterm gestirnten Himmel* WoO 150, which Schubert knew. Relatively rare in this composer, the voice becomes like a chamber-music instrument charged with the decorated repetition of the music of the opening chorale: the singer must execute this ornate line (with arpeggios up and down the stave at the repeat of 'Jede Blume, die ihn schmückte . . . Jeden Stern, der mir erglühte', bb. 59–63) with all the dexterity and elegance of phrasing that one might expect from an able string player. The pianist's left hand has pointed quavers, standing in for a pizzicato cello. The melody that has opened the song does indeed now seem raised to a higher power. Our primary impression is the similarity of this music to the first movement of the B flat major Piano Trio D898; the composer seeks to confer on this song the grandeur of an instrumental peroration. It is as if he feels that, when confronted with the music of the spheres, we no longer need words – instead we are subsumed by the purest of music. As if to underline this state of ecstasy where one line melts into another, Schubert freely repeats 'Jeden Stern, der mir erglühte' out of sequence (bb. 66–8), and adds it to the list which culminates in 'Werden mir die Töne bringen' (bb. 71–4). All of this is confusing for those attempting to follow the poem, but we are no longer in control of sentences; it is as if we are tripping on flower-power and floating through the heavens on speed.

At 'Und die schrecklichen Minuten' there are six bars of suitably dramatic triplets, and again moments of Schubert's chamber music come to mind. We return to the home key via B minor – the second inversion of that key (b. 79) melts into the first inversion of D^7 (b. 80), arriving back at G major at 'Werden mich mit Lust umklingen'. A stentorian four-bar interlude – left-hand trombones – marks the passage into another world (bb. 86–9), before the final verse, 'So in Wonne werd' ich untergehen', which is a remarkable page of music: ethereal, sweet, profound and somehow floating calmly to nescience. Or perhaps to heaven, for the poem is cleverly written so as not to exclude a reading of it as an advertisement for a Christian afterlife. Poet and composer surely intended something more pagan, however. The wide-spaced intervals of the repeat of 'Wonne werd' ich untergehen' (bb. 94–5) recall the closing page of *Memnon* D541. Another song that comes to mind is *Des Sängers Habe* D832 where triplets prophetic of the same B flat major Piano Trio weave their magic in similar way.

Todesmusik is not a great song, perhaps, but it contains great things. It is remarkable for turning a musical cliché on its head: the florid vocal line, a style more often found in Italian opera arias for empty display purposes, is here used to denote delirium and dreamlike unconsciousness. Although mention of ether is a medical anachronism as far as Schubert is concerned, the taking of opium was not unknown in Vienna and Schober would have been the kind of person to try it out. In any event this song is about surrendering to the all-enveloping drug of music in order to ensure a peaceful death for the votary of the Muse.

Autograph:	Schubert-Bund, Vienna (first draft in G flat major)
Publication:	First published as part of the NSA in 1985 (P793; first version)
	First published as Op. 93 no. 2 by M. J. Leidesdorf, Vienna in
	January 1829; later corrected to Op. 108. The song had been
	advertised at Easter 1828 as part of Op. 93, but was not issued
	until after Schubert's death (P194; second version). The title of the
	song is incorrectly given as *Todeskuss*.
Subsequent editions:	Peters: Vol. 4/112; AGA XX 411: Vol. 7/30; NSA IV: Vol. 5a/126 &
	Vol. 5b/241; Bärenreiter: Vol. 4/38
Bibliography:	Capell 1928, p. 174
	Porter 1961, p. 112
Discography and timing:	Fischer-Dieskau II 5¹⁰ 5'53
	Hyperion I 28¹⁴
	Hyperion II 26¹ 5'19 Maarten Koningberger

←— *Sei mir gegrüsst* D741   *Schatzgräbers Begehr* D761 —→

TODTENMARSCH *see* GRABLIED AUF EINEN SOLDATEN D454

TODTENOPFER *see* ERINNERUNG D101

TONALITY AND TRANSPOSITION

Any consideration of tonality in Schubert's songs is bedevilled by the fact that more often than not audiences hear them in transposed keys. This is a fact of life when dealing with singers: without transpositions, the baritone Dietrich Fischer-Dieskau would never have been able to encompass the Schubert recordings of the 1970s (more complete than any survey that had hitherto been attempted), a set of discs that did so much to promote knowledge of the composer's songs in modern times. I possess the set of volumes (the AGA of Mandyczewski) used for these recordings by the famous pianist Gerald Moore who worked with Fischer-Dieskau. There are markings throughout as to which keys the great accompanist had to use for each recording. Moore was of a generation so used to transposition that he could read songs in other keys from the printed page, sometimes transposing as much as a major third down at sight. Not everyone is able to do this, and from the last quarter of the nineteenth century the Leipzig firm of Peters sold volumes of songs printed in alternative keys – middle, low and very low for the first volume of their widely used edition, and middle and low for volumes 2 and 3. Useful as these volumes were, many Schubert lieder were still available in only one key – the original (although a slim volume of transposed songs selected from Peters volumes 4 to 7 was published at a later date). The decision by Bärenreiter to publish all of Schubert's lieder in three keys – high, medium and low – (regardless of the song's original key) represents a new departure.

Purists may insist on original keys for this or any other composer's songs, but this is to live in an ivory tower far from the real singing world. Schubert himself inhabited a world of singers and prided himself on his abilities as an accompanist. He would have been the first to acknowledge that lower-voiced singers needed to transpose, preferring to have a great singer like Vogl (or Fischer-Dieskau) sing his songs in a lower key than not sing them at all. Schubert was capable of making transpositions of his own music, and of compromising on keys when it came to a song's publication. This is just as well because a great deal of compromising went on after his death when Diabelli and others prepared a large number of songs for posthumous publication. This is not to say that *Du liebst mich nicht* D756 is not more effective in its unusual and strangely tortured original key of G sharp minor than the easier to read A minor of its 1826 publication; and it goes without saying that *Die Sternennächte* D670 sounds infinitely better in its starry original key of D flat major rather than the less challenging, and relatively earthbound, key of B flat as when it appeared in its first edition, and subsequently in the Peters Edition.

Clearly when it is possible to hear a Schubert song in its original key (and this usually means a performer with a high, rather than a low, voice) we should take it as a bonus that is always fascinating and rewarding; but it would be an exaggeration to claim that a Schubert song can lose its validity simply by being transposed in performance. Of course the question of how far it is transposed is vital because shifting a song down by a third or, heaven forbid, a fourth, can radically change everything about it, including its viability on the keyboard. The difference between a song in its original and its transposed versions is usually a tone lower in the case of a well-produced baritone voice (this pertains to the great cycles), and occasionally a tone and a half (a minor third). In the fourth, and lowest, version of the Volume 1 songs in the Peters Edition (the printed hierarchy is high voice, middle voice, bass voice and lower bass) the pianistic opening of *Das Wandern* (from *Die schöne Müllerin*) is actually placed higher in the keyboard than it is in the original key. The tonal shift is a fourth down from the B flat major of the original to F major below: the only trouble is that there *is* no 'below' because the piano runs out of bass notes – therefore the only option is to relocate the whole accompaniment a fifth *higher* than the original key.

As a teacher and colleague I have sometimes accused bass-baritones or mezzos of extricating themselves from difficulty by treating a transposition as a get-out clause, an option that is not available to tenors or sopranos who must traditionally sing songs in the original high key. If a song like *Rastlose Liebe* D138 is difficult for the higher voices in E major (with its high As) it is only fair that it should be correspondingly challenging when sung by lower voices. And yet the Peters middle-voice option for this song is C major (rather than D major, as in Schubert's own written-out transposition). The key of C major for *Rastlose Liebe* necessitates high Fs for baritones rather than the high Gs (in D major) that would be the equivalent of the tenor's challenges. A number of medium- or lower-voiced singers have an easier time than they should in this repertoire, and seldom are audiences or judges actually aware of the specifics of transposition. Many a baritone has been tempted into using the bass volume, not because he is a genuine bass but because he can get away with cruising through a Schubert song in a tonality that involves less exposure of his technical shortcomings. The trouble is that the chosen key often sounds dull and fails to capture much of the excitement and colour of the composer's original intention. The further one transposes away from the original, the more this is likely to happen.

Lower-voiced singers who have good technique can sometimes feel themselves imprisoned by the choice of keys that have been available in the Peters Edition for more than a century. The whole of this edition was conceived first and foremost for music-loving amateurs in the days when everyone – uncles, aunts, parents and grandparents – wanted to have a go at singing the Schubert songs. Max Friedlaender understood his market *c.* 1890 but in some cases the tonalities chosen are simply not challenging enough for the professional. Once a song's original key has been abandoned because it is too high, there is no musicological merit in clinging to a lower (or higher) key simply because it happens to be one of the available printed options. In this situation the ability of the accompanist to transpose and offer alternatives to the printed keys is paramount, requiring a quick ear and a developed understanding of the vocal potential of individual singers.

SCHUBERT'S TONAL VOCABULARY

The fact is that Schubert always chose his keys for a reason: they seemed to him to be fitting tonalities for the emotions aroused by the text and for the song he had it in mind to write. This also means that he had a clear idea of the tonal characteristics of each key. This was a partly subjective reaction, and partly inherited from the great composers who had preceded him and who had selected certain keys for music that became forever identified in his mind's eye (or ear) with those tonalities. Thus we find G minor not only a natural choice for Schubert's *Menuetto* from his 5th Symphony D485 (music indebted tonally, and also melodically, to Mozart's *Menuetto* in *his* G minor symphony K550), but also for songs inspired by Pamina's aria 'Ach, ich fühl's' from *Die Zauberflöte* K620. D minor, on the other hand, is a *Don Giovanni* K527 key and clearly identfied by Schubert with the appearance of the statue of the Commendatore, and also with *Requiem* K626. While these tonal flavourings go back to Mozart, there were many others that looked to Beethoven, Gluck and lesser composers, and some of Schubert's tonal reactions were entirely his own. Christian Friedrich Schubart's pronouncements on tonality indicate that Schubert had been brought up within a musical culture that took the idea of tonal colouring seriously, and that there was a widespread acceptance that some keys were more suitable than others for the expression of certain emotions and for the creation of specific moods and atmospheres. As Schubart says, 'Every key is either coloured or not coloured. One draws innocence and simplicity with uncoloured keys. Soft, melancholy feelings with flat keys, wild and strong passions with sharp keys' (*Ideen zu einer Ästhetik der Tonkunst* 1806, reprinted Leipzig, 1924, p. 261). It is interesting to see when and how Schubart's conception of tonality matches Schubert's (in some cases in almost uncanny fashion) and when it is utterly different. The separate, alphabetical articles on each of the various tonalities, both major and minor, in Schilling's *Encylopädie der gesammten musikalischen Wissenschaften oder Universal-Lexicon der Tonkunst* of 1840 (references below) purport to be far more scientific than Schubart's, but Dr Schilling unashamedly incorporates Schubart's ideas freely into his articles, along with some of his own. It is also clear that the tuning of pianos using equal temperament was not nearly as widespread in the early nineteenth century as one might imagine, and that there was a perceived difference between two keys such as F sharp major and G flat major. Occasionally the tonality of a piece seems to have been determined by other reasons, such as keyboard geography. Any pianist will testify to the fact that *Die Forelle* D550 is very much harder to play in any key other than the original D flat major, and that the propinquity of G flat and G natural on the keyboard, and the ease with which the sextuplet figuration of the song's accompaniment lies under the hand in D flat major (and not other keys) suggests the composer had discovered a pleasing pattern in that key that might suggest a fish splashing under and over the waterline.

One of the purposes of this book is to suggest what may have been going through Schubert's mind when he composed his songs. Tonality, therefore, has to be considered as one of the choices that was open to him when he picked up his pen. The compilation of a list such as is printed below is highly personal, and depends on a subjective reaction to the songs and their core expressive purpose. It could be argued that pitch has changed since Schubert's time and that in the modern era keys sound quite differently. There are those who dismiss key-colour speculations by today's artists as nonsense precisely because the Hertz numbers for a particular key fail to tally between the different centuries. That great Schubertian Hans Gál, in reviewing *Der Charakter der Tonarten* ('The Characteristic of Keys') by Paul Mies, in 1950, offers an explanation that goes some way to explain the conundrum:

> Strike a common chord in C major and one in F sharp major (on the piano), and you will do it with a noticeable difference of touch. The elevated position of the black keys results in one's rarely using the same bluntness and vigour as one applies to the white keys. You will notice that a passage in C major will stimulate a brilliant, 'objective' non-legato of elastically jumping fingers, whereas the same passage, played, say, in B major or in D flat will rather invite an expressive legato, thanks to the combination of white and black keys and the much easier action of the thumb. In the string ensemble a similarly 'objective', insensitive element inheres in the use of the open strings, c, d, e, g, a, which coincide with five of the even white keys of the piano. The peculiar way in which white keys, or open strings, are combined in different tonalities, offers an explanation for a development of certain characters of expression connected with them – independent of the actual pitch.
>
> The most decisive fact, however, in the development of such characters ... is the unconscious heritage . . . the tradition of style . . . the influence of one composer on another. If a nineteenth-century composer sets out to write an heroic symphony, would he not be tempted to do so in E flat as Richard Strauss actually did in his Heldenleben? Would this, then, justify the assumption that the heroic character is immanent in this key? Obviously not; it would merely mean that the composer was, consciously or unconsciously, influenced by the archetype of a heroic piece of music, Beethoven's Eroica.

In this article I attempt to guess what Schubert might have heard in the various tonalities, even if today's C major is actually yesterday's B major, or thereabouts. Modern composers may hear different things in these keys entirely, but some of them will have been influenced by the uses to which earlier composers put them. Probably for this reason there is more agreement across the centuries concerning the mood and atmosphere of tonalities than science may lead us to expect. The difference in absolute terms between our D major, for instance, and Mozart's may well be less important than its place within the hierarchy of keys, both flat and sharp, which is an unchanging relationship.

The songs given here form only a selective list. Fuller listings of songs sorted into their tonalities can be found in John Reed's *Schubert Song Companion* (1985, from p. 484). In the tally of settings printed below, a number of episodic songs without any sense of tonal unity have been omitted from the reckoning.

C MAJOR: *Dawn and eternity* [43 solo songs]
Schubart is close to Schubert in this case: 'C major is completely pure. Its characteristics are innocence, simplicity, naivety and the speech of children'; Reed: 'normality and sanity'. One also thinks of the closing lines of Browning's *Abt Vogler* (1864): 'For my resting place is found, / The C major of this life: so, now I will try to sleep'.

The leaves drained of colour and the white hair of *Die abgeblühte Linde* D514
The playful innocence of *Der Knabe in der Wiege* D579
The fathomless reaches of timeless eternity ('Ewigkeit') as threatened in the second part of
    Gruppe aus dem Tartarus D583

The simple, receptive piety of *Das Marienbild* D623

The innocent devotion of *Nachtviolen* D752

The boundless future opportunities for the young lover, the *tabula rasa* of *Halt!* D795/3

The artlessness bordering on gaucherie in the pure morning light of *Morgengruss* D795/8

The unfathomable grandeur, like a blinding flash of white light, of *Die Allmacht* D852

The purity of the morning aubade of Shakespeare's *Ständchen* D889

The wide open spaces and untrammelled horizons of *Am Meer* D957/12, *Meeres Stille* D216, and of the beach opening of *Der entsühnte Orest* D699

C MINOR: *Phantoms and fantasies* [26 solo songs]

Only some aspects of Schubart's classification are close to Schubert: 'Declaration of love and at the same time the plaint of unhappy love. The languishing, longing, and sighs of the love-drunk soul lies in this key'; Reed: 'the sinister aspect of nature'; Schilling compares the tonality to the fate of Shakespeare's sleeping Desdemona waking up to confront her destiny.

The ghosts and supernatural skulduggery in *Der Geistertanz* D15 and D116

The tragedy of the bereaved *Cronnan* D282; the appearance of the ghost of Vinvela in this song, and of the ghost *Thekla* D595

The incomprehensible betrayal of *Die Liebe hat gelogen* D751

The predatory nature of both man and nature as feverishly imagined in *Der Jäger* D795/14 and *Die Krähe* D911/15

The benumbed panic of *Erstarrung* D911/4 and the prematurely aged grief of *Der greise Kopf* D911/14 – both brought about by a failed love affair

The fears and premonitions of *Kriegers Ahnung* D957/2

The bleak and inhospitable mirage of a distant, heartless city in *Die Stadt* D957/11

D FLAT MAJOR: *Music of the spheres* [6 solo songs]

Schubart talks of this being a very special, even 'cock-eyed' tonality, capable of all sorts of unusual expressive characteristics, and some of the shades between sadness and wonder: 'It cannot laugh, but it can smile; it cannot weep but it can grimace.' Schubert uses the key for music that can only be termed 'other-worldly'. Reed: 'contemplative and expressive'; Schilling says this tonality suggests 'the sounds of spirits, ethereal speech emanating from a veiled source'. The writer of this passage, Schilling himself, might almost have had *Memnon* in mind, although it seems unlikely.

A magical music fit for the blue flower of Novalis in *Am Bach im Frühlinge* D361

The hovering of the beloved's sweet image as the hunter gazes into the moon in *Jägers Abendlied* D368

The spirit of the slain Greek hero, now contained within a statue in Egypt, is daily given voice in *Memnon* D541 thanks to the warmth of the sun's rays at dawn

Music for the starry heavens in *Die Sternennächte* D670

In *Ellens Gesang I* D837 the dutiful daughter aims to spirit suspicion away regarding her father by entrancing her guest with music magical enough to make time stand still

C SHARP MAJOR: There are no Schubert songs in this key

C SHARP MINOR: *Mind journeys* [4 solo songs]

Schubart writes of 'the plaints of repentance, intimate communication with God, with friends and with the playmates of life . . . the sighs of dissatisfied friendship and love'; Schilling describes *in extenso* how Schubert's song *Der Wanderer* typifies the characteristics of this tonality.

The imaginary journey through life initiated by *Genügsamkeit* D143

The most famous traveller's journey in *Der Wanderer* D489, a metaphor for displacement and alienation

The youth longs to take his leave of life and depart on his final journey in *Der Jüngling und der Tod* D545

The rise of Mahomet in *Mahomets Gesang* D549 described metaphorically as a stream turning gradually into a mighty river as it gathers its tributaries

D MAJOR: *Philosophers and fishermen* [25 solo songs]

Schubart is not in accord with Schubert in this case: 'The key of triumphs and hallelujas, battle-cries celebrating victory . . . the key for symphonies and marches commissioned for celebratory occasions'; Reed 1985, p. 486: 'unblemished masterpieces of pure song'; Schilling links the tonality, as often in Schubert, with masculine pursuits: 'Ruhe und Frieden des Herzens . . . die männlich erhabene Grazie' ('Repose and the heart's peace . . . manly, noble grace'). Leo Black points out that this sentence encapsulates the qualities of Schubert's D major Piano Sonata D850.

The energetic enthusiasm of those in love with their work in *Fischerlied* D351 and *Fischerweise* D881

The visionary and heightened philosophical reflections of *An die Musik* D547, *Der Sänger* D149, of Schlegel's *Der Wanderer* D649 and the Novalis *Nachthymne* D687

The courage, determination and idealism (with a touch of fanaticism) of *Der Pilgrim* D794

The bright-eyed (and sadly misplaced) confidence of *Mein!* D795/11

The entranced parental love of *Der Vater mit dem Kind* D906

The monastic reflections of *Der Kreuzzug* D932

D MINOR: *Fear and longing* [29 solo songs]

Some aspects of Schubart are close to Schubert in this case: 'melancholy femininity [cf. Schubert's choice of D minor for *Gretchen am Spinnrade*], brooding spleen and gloom'; Reed: 'courage and resolution'; Schilling links the tonality with Mozart's *Don Giovanni* and the same composer's furious aria for the Queen of the Night ('Der Hölle Rache') in *Die Zauberflöte* D620.

The yearning of *Gretchen am Spinnrade* D118

The resignation of *Der König in Thule* D367

The grim determination of *An Schwager Kronos* D369 and of *Gute Nacht* D911/1

The terrifying inevitability of both *Der Tod und das Mädchen* D531 and *Fahrt zum Hades* D526

The turbulence of *Der Strom* D565, the wild drama of *Über Wildemann* D884

The premonitions of mortality of *Wehmut* D772

The pent-up frustration of *Lied des gefangenen Jägers* D843 and of Seidl's *Sehnsucht* D879

The swirling, threatening grandeur of winter in *Der stürmische Morgen* D911/18

E FLAT MAJOR: *Awe and devotion (military, emotional, religious)* [33 solo songs]

Schubart writes of 'the tonality of love, of reverence, of devoted colloquy with God, because its three flats are expressive of the Holy Trinity'; Schilling associates this tonality with the awestruck lyricism of Tamino's 'Dies Bildnis ist bezaubernd schön' in Mozart's *Die Zauberflöte* as well as being the 'Feldton' – the tonality of horns and brass instruments, and thus of military or battle music. The presence of the trinity of three flats as pointed out by Schubart makes this an ideal key for music of a religious nature, and also for Masonic music (cf. the use of this tonality in Mozart's *Die Zauberflöte*).

Excited admiration for the heroic Arminius on the part of his bloodthirsty wife in *Hermann und Thusnelda* D322

Religious devotion in *Am Tage aller Seelen (Litanei)* D343 and in *Glaube, Hoffnung und Liebe* D955

The contemplation of sunset in *An die untergehende Sonne* D457

A hymn to the salutary powers of nature in *Auf dem See* D543

A reminder of the smallness of mankind in comparison to the might of nature in *Auf der Donau* D553

The stars speak to mankind in *Die Sterne* D684, and are contemplated from afar in *Die Sterne* D939

Devotion to the spouse and a declaration of love in *Du bist die Ruh* D776

E FLAT MINOR: *Public lamentation* [4 solo songs]

Schubert: 'If ghosts were able to speak, they would do so in this tonality'; Schilling 1840 (under dis or D sharp minor) associates this tonality with 'Bangigkeit . . . Seelendrang . . . Verzweiflung, die schwärzeste Schwermut' ('anxiety . . . the soul's longing . . . despair and the blackest melancholy') and so on.

The use of the mourning key of E flat minor for ironic and comic purposes in *Klage um Ali Bey* D496A

The stylized – and somewhat formally expressed – grief for the poet's dead son in *Am Grabe Anselmos* D504

A song with a famous theatrical and operatic background (cf. the Grétry opera *Richard Cœur de Lion*) in *Blondel zu Marien* D626

The provision of a song (*Bertas Lied in der Nacht* D653) for Grillparzer's play about an ancestral ghost, *Die Ahnfrau*

E MAJOR: *Al fresco celebrations* [36 solo songs]

Schubart is quite close to Schubert: 'Open rejoicing, smiling joy, and nevertheless, not quite complete enjoyment lie in E major'; Reed: 'innocence and joy'; Schilling links the tonality with Mozart's *Die Zauberflöte* and the aria of Sarastro 'In diesen heil'gen Hallen' as well as 'Sacred love, openness . . . pure happiness and joy, rejoicing and dance'.

The stormy excitement of love reflected by nature in *Rastlose Liebe* D138

The Schillerian rejoicing of *An die Freude* D189 and *Elysium* D584

The state of heavenly bliss in *Seligkeit* D433

The harvest celebrations of *Erntelied* D434

The energy of the rustling forest in *Im Walde (Waldesnacht)* D708

The infinite consolation of nature (and the triumph of the brook in luring the miller boy to its depths) in *Des Baches Wiegenlied* D795/20

The sweet and sacred memories of *Der Lindenbaum* D911/5

E MINOR: *Cold comfort in nature's company* [15 solo songs]

Schubart's description is not close to Schubert (*see* note on Schilling below); Reed: 'sadness, depression and nostalgia'; Schilling simply quotes Schubart: 'Naive, feminine, innocent declarations of love. Sighs accompanied by few tears.'

The outdoor life on the hillside during a funeral in *Der Jüngling auf dem Hügel* D702

The birth and death of flowers in *Der Blumen Schmerz* D731, the resurrection of dead flowers in *Trockne Blumen* D795/18

The whistling wind and cold rain of *Im Jänner 1817* D876
The splitting of hard rock and the spilling of hidden springs in *Heiss mich nicht reden* D877/2
The stream of tears in *Wasserflut* D911/6
The tempestuous, wind-swept voyage of *Schiffers Scheidelied* D910
The frozen stream that mirrors the frozen torrent of feelings in *Auf dem Flusse* D911/7
The depiction of the chill winds and leafless trees of autumn in *Herbst* D945

F MAJOR: *Pastoral scenes* [48 solo songs]

Schubart: 'Readiness to please and peacefulness'; Reed: 'evening, autumn, the stars, hope, consolation; also with sleep'; Schilling mentions 'Ein Mädchen oder Weibchen' from *Die Zauberflöte* as well as Beethoven's Pastoral Symphony Op. 68 and the closing pages of *Fidelio*.

The nostalgic idyll, under the linden tree, of *Abends unter der Linde* D235 and D237
The idealized, almost picture-book countryside depicted in *Der Alpenjäger* D524 and of *Erlafsee* D586
The immense peace and relaxation of *Schlaflied* D527
The wings of harmony as consolation and protection in *Trost im Liede* D546
The idyllic natural scene after a storm in *Nach einem Gewitter* D561
The longed-for unclouded life and recovery through nature of *Der Sieg* D805
The gentle farewells of *Leb wohl, du schöne Erde* D829
The world-weary longing for rest and safety in *Das Wirtshaus* D911/21

F MINOR: *The dark before the light* [18 solo songs]

Schubart's description encompasses some of Schubert's use of the tonality: 'Deep depression, the wailing of corpses . . . and longing for the grave' (cf. *Totengräbers Heimwehe*); Reed: 'regret, bitterness or nostalgia'; Schilling mentions Florestan's aria in prison (*Fidelio*). In a passage that might have been written with the bell effect of *Die junge Nonne* in mind, Schilling also speaks of 'F minor with its pure dominant of C major, that conveys more clearly than any other tonality a presentiment of the indescribable release to be experienced on the other side of the grave'.

The moon conceals her light from the stricken lover in *An den Mond* D193
The beauties of the past lamented and re-experienced in *Erster Verlust* D226
A lover promises to join his dead beloved beyond the grave in *Der Herbstabend* D405
In the midst of a raging storm the young nun searches for inner peace in *Die junge Nonne* D828
The soothsayer at last permitted to give voice to her ancient woes in *Gesang der Norna* D831
The gravedigger seeks redemption in *Totengräbers Heimwehe* D842
The traveller's red-hot tears melt ice and snow in *Gefrorne Tränen* D957/3

G FLAT MAJOR: *Idealized love* [6 solo songs]

Schubart's definition talks of the overcoming of insuperable difficulties, climbing mountains and breathing freely after having done so. In this respect *Iphigenia* is a larger than life character who has suffered much. Reed: 'a profound sense of peace and harmony'; no separate article in Schilling where G flat major is considered together with F sharp major. The song *Lied des Orpheus* D474 begins in G flat major (the key signature lasts only twenty-one bars). In this passage Orpheus sings of his lyre that has been 'crowned by the gods' and capable of magical things.

A hymn of praise and devotion to the beloved in *Nähe des Geliebten* D162
A paean to the 'star of love, image of splendour' in *Der Morgenstern* D172

A prayer for the balm of heavenly peace in *Wandrers Nachtlied* D224
Man is inspired to hope for better things in *Hoffnung* D251
The sixteen-year-old girl who inspired *Phidile* D500 (Therese Grob perhaps) is clearly put on a
    pedestal by the composer
Memories of the beloved fields of Hellas and its flowers, and a prayer to Diana in *Iphigenia* D573
The mellifluous triumph over death in *Todesmusik* (first version) D758

F SHARP MAJOR: *The far side of the moon* [1 solo song]
Schilling emphasizes that this key is brighter and sharper than its enharmonic equivalent of G
flat major.

Moonbeams, spots of light cascading from the gently stirring leaves in *Die Mondnacht* D238
Schubert employs this highly unusual key signature on two other occasions within longer songs:
    in *Schwestergruss* D762 it serves to illustrate the spirit's description of how she walks in the
    pure light, moon and sun at her feet; in *Totengräber-Weise* D869 it accompanies the grave-
    digger's description of love's tears transformed into the colour of heavenly blue.

F SHARP MINOR: *Intimations of mortality* [5 solo songs]
Schubart says of this key that it is 'a dark tonality, resentment and discontent is its
language', while Schubert's use of it has an exalted spiritual dimension; Reed: 'a Romantic key';
Schilling mentions a widespread use of the tonality, singling out Beethoven's *Fidelio* and Spohr's
Faust.

The ailing poet's eyes are drawn heavenwards by the nightingale's song in *An die Nachtigall*
    D196
Elegy for the death of a nightingale in *Auf den Tod einer Nachtigall* D201
Franz von Bruchmann is confronted by the spirit of his dead sister in *Schwestergruss* D762
In *Pilgerweise* D789 the pilgrim speaks of his painful journey as the threads of his happiness
    break one by one.
A gravedigger describes to his charges what challenges await them 'on the other side' in *Toten-
    gräber-Weise* D869

G MAJOR: *Loving contentment* [53 solo songs]
Schubart's description of the key is remarkably similar to Schubert's use of it: 'Everything
country-like, idyllic, pastoral hymns, every peaceful and gratifying passion, every gentle expression of gratitude for true friendship and love'; Reed: 'affectionate lyricism'; Schilling points out
the open-hearted simplicity of G major as one of Papageno's keys (together with F major) and
that it is the tonality of 'ruhige und befriedigte Leidenschaft und treue Liebe' ('tranquil and
contented passion, and true love').

The gentle and hidden language of nature in *Die Gebüsche* D646
The genial sharing of music and happiness in *Der Musensohn* D764 (notwithstanding the *Sehn-
    sucht* of the song's final strophe)
On the brink of falling in love in *Danksagung an den Bach* D795/4
The serenity and happiness of life at home beside the fire in *Der Einsame* D800
The bliss of lovers' reunion in *Wiedersehn* D855
Springtime memories of love in *Im Frühling* D882 and *Über allen Zauber Liebe* D682
The most gentle and playfully insinuating of love songs, *Liebesbotschaft* D957/1
The imperturbable loyalty of the carrier pigeon in *Die Taubenpost* D965A

G MINOR: *Fighting fate's decree* [30 solo songs]

Schubart speaks of 'Displeasure, discomfort . . . ill-feeling, rancour, dislike': 'fortitude'; Schilling cites the G minor arias in the first and second acts of Mozart's *Così fan tutte*. Also very influential for Schubert was this tonality in Pamina's great aria in *Die Zauberflöte* (cf. melodic shape of *Misero pargoletto* D45.)

The epic struggle of *Amphiaraos* D166 to escape the death predicted for him by the gods

The father's fruitless struggle to save his son in *Erlkönig* D328, the mother's lament in *Misero pargoletto* D42 and another mother's frenzied attempts to find her lost daughter in *Lied* (Mutter geht durch ihre Kammern) D373

The wounded pride of the miller boy in *Eifersucht und Stolz* D795/15 and his broken, suicidal lament in *Der Müller und der Bach* D795/19

The traveller's doughty attempt to find consolation in addressing the moon in *Der Wanderer an den Mond* D870

The signpost to death that drives the winter traveller into the wilderness in *Der Wegweiser* D911/20

The anguished poet with the weight of the world on his shoulders in *Der Atlas* D957/8

A FLAT MAJOR: *Love: secret and reciprocated* [37 solo songs]

Schubart's concept of this key is almost comically different from Schubert's: 'the tonality of Death and the Grave, putrescence, the last judgement, eternity lies in its periphery'; Reed: 'faith in the power of nature to revive and renew'; Schilling also describes this tonality quite differently from the way Schubert uses it – although he mentions Agathe's 'Und ob die Wolke sie verhülle' (*Der Freischütz*) and the prison scene in *Fidelio* (when the key of F minor alternates with that of A flat major at the beginning of the second Act to depict 'the longing of the prisoners for eternal rest').

The open-hearted paean of praise to *Adelaide* D95

The lover binds a ring of roses around his sleeping lover in *Das Rosenband* D280

A beautiful boy is enveloped in the arms of the god-like nature in *Ganymed* D544

In *Versunken* D715 a man plays with the abundant tresses of his beloved. In *Geheimes* D719, a man rejoices in a secret relationship with a beautiful girl

The loving relationship between man and his Maker in *Im Abendrot* D799

The lover on horseback counts the days he is away from his lover in *Auf der Bruck* D853

The city dweller serenades the fisher girl in *Das Fischermädchen* D957/10

A FLAT MINOR: *Altered states*

No Schubert songs are officially in A flat minor but the composer wrote two songs – *Auf dem Wasser zu singen* D774 and *Schwanengesang* D744 – with significant passages in the key that act as a foil to the main tonality of A flat major. Both songs are of a metaphysical nature and refer to the recycling of the human soul: in the first, the inconstancy of time (a vocal E flat harmonized in A flat minor) is defeated by an escape on glorious wings (the same E flat harmonized in A flat major); in the second, the swan sings its final song (A flat minor) while awaiting deliverance and rejoicing in its transfiguration (A flat major).

G SHARP MINOR: *Double-sharp desperation* [2 solo songs]

Schubart talks of the key being 'sullen' and 'a heart pressed to the point of suffocation'. The latter well describes the Platen setting *Du liebst mich nicht*. Schilling notes that very few composers make use of the tonality, and little wonder. It is a 'Jammerklage, die im Doppelkreuze hinaufseufzt' – its double sharps are a sign of the battle that is at work in its harmonies, every-thing in its tonal colour is wearisome and achieves expressivity only with difficulty.

The suppressed grief of *An Mignon* (first version) D161 – transposed to G minor for publication as Op. 19 no. 2

The unhinged anguish of *Du liebst mich nicht* (first version) D756 – transposed to A minor for publication Op. 59 no. 1

A MAJOR: *Geniality and gratitude* [47 solo songs]

Schubart describes 'declarations of innocent love, contentment with one's lot in life; the hope of lovers at their parting of seeing each other again; youthful merriment and trust in God'; Reed: 'perfection of form . . . complete equality of voice and keyboard'; Schilling points out that this tonality is suitable for innocent merriment and for pure, reciprocated love (Mozart's use of this key for Don Giovanni's 'Là ci darem la mano' is counted cleverly ironic, as if Zerlina is meant to be fooled by this display of musical sincerity).

A gentle paean of praise to the piano in *An mein Klavier* D342

An outpouring of philosophical gratitude in *An den Mond in einer Herbstnacht* D614

An enraptured description of the lover's eyes compared to flowers in *Des Müllers Blumen* D795/9

A description of a genial gathering on Olympus in *Dithyrambe* D801

The erotic outpourings of a virgin on the brink of sensual experience in *Delphine* D857

A song of praise to the beautiful beloved in *Gesang (An Silvia)* D891

Awaking to memories of a glorious dream about the beloved in *Frühlingstraum* D911/11

A paean to the beauties of the countryside in *Das Lied im Grünen* D917

A MINOR: *Schöne Welt, wo bist du? Irretrievable loss* [30 solo songs]

Schubart's definition in no way encompasses the importance of this tonality for Schubert: 'Demure femininity and softness of character'; Reed: 'disenchantment, alienation and derange-ment'; Schilling says that this tonality is said to have a moderating influence whereby playfulness melds with seriousness and joy mingles with sadness. This aspect of the change between the keys of A major and A minor (and vice versa) is often to be found in the Schubert songs.

The journey into the realm of peace in *Lied (ins stille Land)* D403

The demented wanderings of the harper at the end of *Wilhelm Meisters Lehrjahre* in *An die Türen* D478/3 (all three of the Harper's songs D478 are in A minor)

The emotional plight and suicide of the castrated *Atys* D585 whose 'femininity' (*see* Schubart, above) is a source of guilt and anguish

The lament for the past glories of ancient Greece in *Strophe aus 'Die Götter Griechenlands'* D677

A jealous dwarf kills his royal lover aboard a boat at twilight in *Der Zwerg* D771

The desolation and loneliness of a solitary star in *Abendstern* D806

The yearning for the love of someone 'in der Weite' in *Lied der Mignon* D877/4

The agony of a young man after the suicide of his only beloved in *Hippolits Lied* D890

The distraught reaction of the winter traveller as he reacts to being spurned by his beloved in favour of a rich husband in *Die Wetterfahne* D911/2

The strangely compelling music of the hurdy-gurdy player who stands barefoot on the ice in *Der Leiermann* D911/24. Here there is a loss of sensation in the player's frozen fingers as well as a loss of melody and of harmony

B FLAT MAJOR: *Hope: confidence in the future, come what may . . .* [48 solo songs]

Schubart's definition of this key is simple, but it entirely chimes with Schubert's use of it, whilst hardly encompassing the depths and subtleties of the tonality for the composer: 'Light-hearted love, a good conscience, hope, a glimpse into a better world'; Reed: 'a sort of rhythmic virtuosity'; Schilling notes that this tonality is suited to 'würdiger Ernst', although quite different from the greater, more sublime seriousness of E flat major.

Faith in spring and change in *Frühlingsglaube* (first version) D686 (in Schubert's original key).

A message of love is sent, assured of a loving response, in *Suleika II* D717

The young miller happily sets off on a journey in *Das Wandern* D795/1 and hopefully looks forward to a relationship with the miller girl in *Mit dem grünen Lautenbande* D795/13

The poor blind boy pronounces that 'Whilst thus I sing, I am a king' in *Der blinde Knabe* D833

Ellen Douglas prays to the virgin in *Ellens III Gesang (Ave Maria)* D839 and seems calmly certain of divine protection

Happy memories of marriage help the widower come to terms with his bereavement in *Der Winterabend* D938, as he enjoys his contemplative solitude

The mountain shepherd is confident he will see his girlfriend in the coming spring in *Der Hirt auf dem Felsen* D965

B FLAT MINOR: *Private lamentation, profane and sacred* [8 solo songs]
Schubart describes B flat minor quite differently from Schubert's use of the tonality: it 'mocks God and the whole world and it suggests preparations for suicide'.

The anguished Gretchen begs the Mater dolorosa for forgiveness and guidance in *Gretchen im Zwinger* D564

In a series of three songs with religious texts (*Geistliches Lied* D660, *Geistliches Lied* D661 and *Der 13. Psalm* D663) the singer ('I have sorrow in my heart daily') longs for a closer relationship with God

The anguish of *Im Walde* D834 – the narrator has lost his beloved and believes himself to be a wanderer who will never find rest again

The singer confronts the loss of a loved one whose picture seems to come to life in a miraculous way. He addresses her directly in *Ihr Bild* D957/9

B MAJOR: *Eros and transfiguration (on a watery background)* [8 solo songs]
Schubart writes of the 'scorn, temperament, jealousy' inherent in this tonality. Of the Schubert songs the only one that might fit this classification is *Die böse Farbe* from *Die schöne Müllerin*; Reed: 'B minor and B major stand at the ambivalent centre of Schubert's emotional world.' Schilling refers to this 'strongly coloured tonality that encourages wild passions – a tonality the colour of fire or burning yellow'. Schubert seems to use the key of B major with much more sensual care.

In *Alte Liebe rostet nie* D477 the poet Mayrhofer journeys throughout the world in search of love and finds nothing to rival a mother's love

In *Am Strome* D539 and *Der Fluss* D693 the course of two rivers is a metaphor for the singer's life – he longs for kinder shores in the first; in the second, the pure silver stream will bring him renewal

In *Der Neugierige* D795/6 the miller boy begs the gently flowing brook to tell him if his life will be changed for ever because the miller girl loves him

The same brook thunders with anger at the girl's inconstancy in *Die böse Farbe* D795/17

The miraculous dreams, possibly erotic, that lift people's lives out of the ordinary in *Nacht und Träume* D827

Mignon, dressed as an angel, sings her song of transfiguration: *Lied der Mignon* ('So lasst mich scheinen' D877/3

B MINOR: *Suffering, mental and physical (with a major-key antidote)* [21 solo songs]

According to Schubart this is the key of 'patience, of quietly awaiting the finger of fate and submission to God's will'. This is very far from how Schubert sees this key on the whole. One of the most depressed songs from *Winterreise, Einsamkeit* D911/2, fits into this category but it was initially composed in D minor. Schilling underlines the importance and power of this tonality, as well as its difficulties for instrumentalists.

In *Die Spinnerin* D247 a young girl at the spinning wheel recounts the circumstances of her seduction and her still-concealed pregnancy

The physical pain endured by the wounded eponymous *Philoktet* D540

The doomed unhappiness of *Der Unglückliche* D713

Suleika is separated by distance from her lover, Hatem (*Suleika I* D720) – she receives a wind-borne message and is reunited with him in spirit (in a rapturous B major coda)

The downside of ageing in *Greisengesang* D778 (with a more optimistic viewpoint expressed in B major)

The dragging steps, alone and friendless, of *Einsamkeit* D911/12

In *Vor meiner Wiege* D927 an old cradle prompts thoughts of the poet's mother – he recalls the joy he felt as she suckled him (B major), and agonizes over her future death

The presentiment of death on encountering oneself in double-vision in *Der Doppelgänger* D957/13

Bibliography: Gál 1950
                 Reed 1985, pp. 484–94
                 Schilling 1840 (separate alphabetical articles on tonalities)
                 Schubart 1806

TOTENGESANG DER FRAUEN UND MÄDCHEN *see SIEBEN GESÄNGE AUS WALTER SCOTT'S FRÄULEIN VOM SEE* D863 (CORONACH)

TOTENGRÄBERLIED   Gravedigger's song
(HÖLTY) **D44** [H20]
G major   19 January 1813

(90 bars)

Grabe, Spaten, grabe!	Dig, spade, dig!
Alles, was ich habe,	All that I have
Dank' ich Spaten, dir!	I owe to you, spade!
Reich' und arme Leute	Both rich and poor
Werden meine Beute,	Become my booty,
Kommen einst zu mir.	Come to me in the end.
Weiland gross und edel,	Great and noble,
Nickte dieser Schädel	This skull once
Keinem Grusse Dank.	Acknowledged no greeting.
Dieses Beingerippe	This skeleton
Ohne Wang' und Lippe	Without cheeks or lips
Hatte Gold und Rang.	Possessed gold and high rank.
Jener Kopf mit Haaren	Only a few years ago
War vor wenig Jahren	That head with hair
Schön, wie Engel sind.	Was as lovely as those of angels.
Tausend junge Fentchen	A thousand young fops
Leckten ihm das Händchen,	Would kiss her little hands
Gafften sich halb blind.	And grow half blind staring at her.
Grabe, Spaten, grabe!	Dig, spade, dig.
Alles, was ich habe,	For all that I have
Dank' ich Spaten, dir!	I thank you, spade!
Reich' und arme Leute	Both rich and poor
Werden meine Beute,	Become my booty,
Kommen einst zu mir!	Come to me in the end.

LUDWIG HÖLTY (1748–1776); poem written in 1775

This is the first of Schubert's twenty-three Hölty solo settings (1813–16). See the poet's biography for a chronological list of all the Hölty settings.

One cannot say that this is the first song with which a great German poet joins Schubert's work list. That would be to ignore the Schiller settings *Leichenfantasie* D7 and *Der Jüngling am Bache* D30. But after the likes of Baumberg, Schücking, Pfeffel and Rochlitz it was high time that another mainstream literary figure joined the Schubertian throng. The first of these had been Friedrich von Matthisson, but the two 'gothic horror' fragments of 1812 (*Der Geistertanz* D15 and D15A) were not typical of the composer's later relationship with that poet. It seems that a school textbook, an anthology of poetry printed in Vienna and entitled *Sammlung Deutscher Beyspiele zur Bildung des Styls*, brought *Totengräberlied* to Schubert's attention, alongside Schiller's *Dithyrambe* D47 and Matthisson's *Die Schatten* D50. In Ludwig Hölty, Schubert had a long-distance partnership (in terms of both time and place) initiated by *Totengräberlied*, and he was to return to the great eighteenth-century poet some twenty-two times. Among these settings of charm and freshness (for there is a certain Arcadian flavour to Hölty in which Schubert delights) are a handful of masterpieces.

If this is not one of them, it marks the beginning of the composer's fascination with what might be termed songs of the working people. These musical vignettes take us beyond Vienna's drawing rooms and palaces into the Shakespearean world of homespun philosophers, naive and

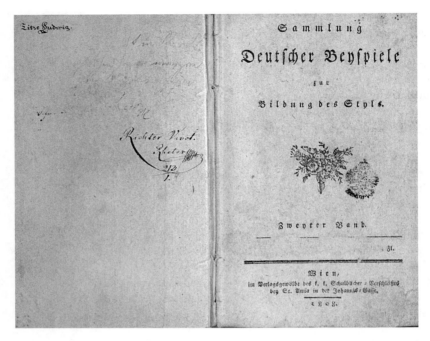

Sammlung Deutscher Beyspiele zur Bildung des Styls, a school textbook published in Vienna in 1808. In the top left-hand corner of the facing page is the neat signature 'Titze Ludwig'. This copy seems to have been used by Schubert's tenor, Ludwig Titze (or Tietze) during his school career.

poor by the standards of their masters but wiser by far in their down-to-earth appreciation of life's truths. The following list of Schubert's 'occupational' songs includes neither the drinking songs nor the war songs, which are also full of philosophical viewpoints, nor the various songs that reflect on life without letting us know the trade or occupation of the singer.

Schäfers Klagelied (Goethe) D121 (1814) shepherd
Ammenlied (Lubi) D122 (1814) nursemaid
Jägers Abendlied (Goethe) D215 (1815) hunter
Wer kauft Liebesgötter (Goethe) D261 (1815) street-hawker
Tischlerlied (unknown) D274 (1815) carpenter
Fischerlied (Salis-Seewis) D351 (1816) fisherman
Jägers Abendlied (Goethe) D368 (1816) hunter
Pflügerlied (Salis-Seewis) D392 (1816) ploughman
Der Hirt (Mayrhofer) D490 (1816) shepherd
Der Alpenjäger (Mayrhofer) D524 (1817) alpine hunter
Wie Ulfru fischt (Mayrhofer) D525 (1817) fisherman
Der Schiffer (Mayrhofer) D536 (1817?) boatman
Der Goldschmiedsgesell (Goethe) D560 (1817) goldsmith
Fischerlied (Salis-Seewis) D562 (1817) fisherman
Der Schiffer (Schlegel) D694 (1820) boatman
Totengräbers Heimwehe (Craigher) D842 (1825) gravedigger
Totengräber-Weise (Schlechta) D869 (1826) gravedigger
Fischerweise (Schlechta) D881 (1826) fisherman
Jägers Liebeslied (Schober) D909 (1827) hunter

This list of songs mirrors contemporary literary preoccupations with the extraordinary qualities of ordinary people, a lesson that Goethe, among many others, learned from Shakespeare. From the musical point of view we know that the young Schubert was a fan of such Viennese popular opera composers as Joseph Weigl (1766–1846), but this was still considered high-class music. Apart from the example of *Singspiele*, Schubert no doubt picked up countless popular ditties sung on Viennese street corners by folk singers, the so-called *Bänkelsänger*. These works depicting (as described by a contemporary witness) 'the illustrated presentation of all the ages of man, the wicked world, the man who is beaten by his wife, and vice versa, a microscopic enlargement of the flea, and such' were printed as broadsides and hawked on the streets. Till Gerrit Waidelich (*Schubert Liedlexikon*, p. 213) informs us that Goethe's friend, the composer Maximilian Eberwein (1775–1831, *see* COMPOSERS) made entire song cycles of poems by Ernst Friedrich Conradi relating to people of various stations and temperaments; it is clear that workers were a treasure trove for middle-class poets and musicians in the late Enlightenment years, and Schubert had inherited something of a tradition.

It is clear from all this that in composing this song of the merry gravedigger – a living oxymoron perhaps, but no fool – the influence of such people as Salieri and Zumsteeg were far from the young composer's mind. The soulful first setting in E minor of this text for unaccompanied male voice trio (D38, AGA XIX p. 76) has something of the Metastasio exercises about it, but in this solo setting we find Schubert on a day off. The opening refrain ('Grabe, Spaten, grabe!') is addressed to the spade, tool of the protagonist's trade. It was the composer's idea to separate the first line from the rest of the poem with an exclamation mark, thus setting up the opening six-note flourish, wide-ranging and marked 'ad libitum' (bb. 1–2). Appropriately, the tessitura digs deep into the bass clef. This is in fact a witty touch because it leads us to expect a different type of song, and it is rather surprising that this moment of E minor gloom is peremptorily banished and followed by a ditty marked 'Allegro con moto'.

Gravediggers' songs are usually plaintive or intense but gnashing of teeth and wailing are banished here. The first verse finishes in G major with chirrupy flourishes in the piano part (bb. 14–19), for all the world as if this occupation were no more sinister than that of Papageno the birdcatcher. The second verse begins in C major at b. 20 and shifts into A minor (from b. 27) after three lines. He knows where the bodies are buried, as they say, and this change of key perfectly maps the geography of the graveyard as the gravedigger moves around his patch showing us his buried treasure. The interlude after this strophe includes three loud octave Cs, deep in the bass (bb. 36–7), as if a spade were suddenly striking bone. With the third verse we encounter erstwhile feminine charms, and this initiates an ingratiating accompaniment in the oh-so-refined semiquavers of bb. 34–7. Irony there is here, certainly, but in the relish of the setting, perhaps a hint of misogyny – Eve, afterall, being the fount of all mankind's woes. This verse ends with the words 'Gafften sich halb blind' (bb. 60–61). In the following interlude, it is fascinating for the Schubertian to identify a pre-echo of the accompaniment of a masterpiece from 1825, *Der blinde Knabe* D833. Here we find similarly phrased exploratory semiquavers in the right hand, and the same staccato quavers in the left, as if a blind man's stick (or spade) were testing for the next step (bb. 62–5). The final strophe is an exact repetition of the first, including the E minor 'ad libitum' invocation, with the addition of a few extra bars at the end by way of coda. In these G major *gruppetti*, preceded by grace notes, we hear another 1825 song prophesied – *Der Einsame* D800. This motif, rather like a quiet chuckle, reflects the contentment of someone extremely happy with his lot.

Autograph:	University Library of Lund, Sweden
First edition:	Published as part of the AGA in 1894 (P532)
Subsequent editions:	Not in Peters; AGA XX 7: Vol. 1/54; NSA IV: Vol. 7/18; Bärenreiter: Vol. 5/56 (high voice), 52 (medium/low voice)

Bibliography: Capell 1928, pp. 80–1
Discography and timing: Fischer-Dieskau I 1⁴   2'15
                            Hyperion I 33¹²
                            Hyperion II 2¹⁶   2'25   Stephen Varcoe

← *Misero pargoletto* D42   *Dithyrambe* D47 →

TOTENGRÄBERS HEIMWEHE[1]   Gravedigger's homesickness
(CRAIGHER) **D842** [H563]
F minor – F major   April 1825

(86 bars)

O Menschheit — o Leben! —	O mankind, O life!
Was soll's? — o was soll's?!	To what purpose? To what purpose?
Grabe aus — scharre zu!	Dig out, fill in!
Tag und Nacht keine Ruh'! —	No rest, day and night!
Das Treiben, das Drängen —[2]	This urgency, this haste,
Wohin? o wohin?! — —	Where does it lead? Where?
'Ins Grab — tief hinab!' —	'Into the grave, deep down!'
O Schicksal — o traurige Pflicht —	O fate, O sad duty,
Ich trag's länger nicht! — —	I can bear it no longer!
Wann wirst du mir schlagen,	When will you strike for me,
O Stunde der Ruh?! —	Hour of peace?!
O Tod! komm und drücke	O death, come and close
Die Augen mir zu! — —	My eyes!
Im Leben, da ist's ach! so schwül! —[3]	Life, alas, is so sultry, so oppressive!
Im Grabe — so friedlich, so kühl!	The grave is so peaceful, so cool!
Doch ach, wer legt mich hinein? —	But, ah, who will lay me there?
Ich stehe allein! — so ganz allein!! —[4]	I stand alone, quite alone!
Von allen verlassen	By all forsaken,
Dem Tod nur verwandt,	Kin to death alone,
Verweil' ich am Rande —	I tarry on the brink,

[1] Craigher's title in *Poetische Betrachtungen in freyen Stunden von Nicolaus* (1828) is *Gräbers Heimwehe*.
[2] Craigher has 'Das *Drängen*, das *Treiben*'.
[3] Craigher has no 'ach' in this line; clearly Schubert's own addition.
[4] Craigher has '*steh*' rather than 'stehe' as set by Schubert.

Das Kreuz in der Hand,
Und starre mit sehnendem Blick,
Hinab, ins tiefe Grab! —

O Heimat des Friedens,
Der Seligen Land!
An dich knüpft die Seele
Ein magisches Band. —
Du winkst mir von ferne,
Du ewiges Licht: —
Es schwinden die Sterne —
Das Auge schon bricht! — —
Ich sinke — ich sinke! — Ihr Lieben —
    Ich komme! — — —[5]

Cross in hand,
Staring longingly down
Into the deep grave!

O homeland of peace,
Land of the blessed!
A magic bond
Binds my soul to you.
You beckon to me from afar,
Eternal light;
The stars vanish,
My eyes already grow dim.
I am sinking, I am sinking! Loved ones —
    I come! — — —

JOHANN NICOLAUS CRAIGHER DE JACHELUTTA (1797–1855); poem written in 1822

This is the last of Schubert's three Craigher solo settings (1825). See the poet's biography for a chronological list of all the Craigher settings.

This is one of the mightiest of the Schubert songs, and the final pages achieve a musical depth and transfiguration that are impossible to describe. How much Craigher de Jachelutta had to do with the song's success is another matter. 'Graveyard Poetry' is an expression used by German scholars for a genre of poem beloved by the 'Göttingen Hainbund poets' (such as Hölty) and inspired by the *Night Thoughts* of the eighteenth-century writer Edward Young. Of course the gravedigger is a Shakespearean subject, but not even an accredited Hamlet could recite this poem without provoking mirth. A serious rendition of such a scene might just have been possible in the reading circles of Schubert's day, but this text, with all its rhetorical hyphens suggesting over-the-top performance, is adequate neither as stageable drama nor as poetry. Even the author seems to have been uncertain of its reception, publishing his work under the pseudonym of 'Nicolaus' in 1828. By the time this collection of poems appeared in print, Craigher's hopes for a long-standing professional association with Schubert had long since evaporated. It had been mooted that they should establish a regular working connection, particularly in terms of translations of lieder for the foreign market, but the composer seems to have lost interest in the idea after setting only three Craigher texts. Perhaps Schubert extricated himself from the arrangement in order to avoid having to set more.

    In Schubert's hands, however, a poem that would have proved an insuperable handicap to any other composer makes perfect sense. Such is the effect of this music that we are grateful to Craigher for writing lyrics, however divorced from reality, that occasioned these flights of musical fancy. As a translator and poet he had a neat line in the bathetic: the Cibber-inspired blind boy (*Der blinde Knabe* D833), and his own inventions of the young nun (*Die junge Nonne* D828) and gravedigger are all cardboard stereotypes that shamelessly seek to manipulate the emotions. But in each of these three songs Craigher provides stagey yet strong characters. And fortunately he wrote them at a time when Schubert was in full Shakespearean flight.

    These tear-jerkers were a real departure from the *innig* world of *Die schöne Müllerin* D795, the cycle which, to Schubert's bitter disappointment, had scarcely been noticed when it was published. The sentimentality of the Craigher settings seems calculated to appeal to a wider

---

[5] Schubert repeats the poem's last line to read 'Ich komme *ich komm!*'

market; this was also surely the reason why a collaboration with a hack like Craigher made sense. The ambition to unite great art with an unashamedly populist streak surfaces from time to time in Schubert's career, and the results are disappointing from the point of view of commercial reward. If 1825 was the year of the large canvas – the 'Great' Symphony D944, the long holiday in Upper Austria, the wide vistas of the *Fräulein vom See* cycle Op. 52 – it was also the year of big songs, not necessarily in terms of length but certainly in terms of emotional weight. And we cannot complain that the Craigher songs are less than masterpieces: we all allow ourselves a tear for the blind boy; we follow the young nun in each phase of her struggle and are uplifted by her 'Alleluias' whatever our religion (or lack of it); and we take the gravedigger very seriously. And this despite the fact that at one moment he is a sour-tempered old codger working himself into a mud-stained frenzy, and at the next a visionary whose ascension to heaven might have been envied by Ganymede or the Virgin Mary. Here is a perfect illustration to Oscar Wilde's observation: 'We are all in the gutter, but some of us are looking at the stars.'

These 1825 songs represent a crucial bridge between Schubert's two great cycles – *Die schöne Müllerin* of 1823 and *Winterreise* D911 of 1827. The winter traveller, with the enormous depth and pity of his plight, needed a prototype. In *Totengräbers Heimwehe* we encounter a monumental, even lofty, dimension to the protagonist's angst which is not to be found in the earlier Müller cycle: here the anger and disdain of *Gute Nacht* D911/1 and *Die Wetterfahne* D911/2, the drained death wish of *Der greise Kopf* D911/14 and the visionary longing of *Das Wirtshaus* D911/21 (all from *Winterreise*) are prefigured.

The key is F minor, the marking 'Unruhige Bewegung, doch nicht schnell' ('Restless movement, though not fast'). The first feature we detect in the heavily chordal accompaniment is a fragment of left-hand melody, a four-note cell of quavers, an ascent of the stave from tonic to the minor third above, and then a drop back to the tonic. This circular figuration in octaves, repeated on various pitches and in various keys, dominates the accompaniment of much of the song's first section. The music seethes with physical activity; the accents on the first and third beats of the bar denote the connecting crunch between one surface and another, in this case spade with gravel. The harmonic movement is restless but all within a tightly circumscribed area: this hard work is taking place at a fixed point, although the contrasting images of 'dig out' and 'fill in' are also depicted in the two contrasting groups of four quavers, one higher in pitch than the other within each bar. The vocal line comes in short gasps, as if out of breath, and its truculent tone is hardly a surprise: Schubert's gruff introduction has prepared us for a misanthrope.

From 'O Menschheit' until 'Grabe aus — scharre zu!' the pulsations of the singer's line slowly ascend the stave one note at a time. While scarcely original or melodically interesting, it is indicative of a mounting sense of emotion. Within these four bars we realize we are in the presence of a towering figure – if not in actual stature, then in terms of willpower. This page does not have a tune to speak of but is an example of Schubert's arioso at its greatest – word-setting so compelling that we simply fail to notice the absence of real melody. Schubertian recitative has become so melodic, and Schubertian melody so attuned to the rise and fall of textual nuance, that the boundaries are blurred in the interests of a type of symphonic unity – a Wagnerian achievement *avant la lettre*. The second two lines of the first strophe (from 'Das Treiben, das Drängen') are set to almost the same music – the gravedigger's job is necessarily repetitive – although the words 'tief hinab!' occasion a descent to the bottom of the stave at b. 14. 'Tag and Nacht keine Ruh'!' he complains. Does he work both day and night, or are his nights sleepless or ruined by nightmare? It is as if the whole of society is dying around him (a flu epidemic, or even the plague) and his unseen masters are driving him ever onwards. His job could be taken as a metaphor for the stress of any Sisyphean task – indeed for the pressures and exigencies of life itself.

The music of the second strophe lifts us from the soil and gruesome tasks at hand into the mind and heart of the gravedigger. Here is a surprise for the student baritone who has read through this music for the first time and found the first page eminently singable. The shift of tessitura and the introduction of weaving semiquavers placed awkwardly high in the vocal line immediately weed out the men from the boys: this passage requires a flexible control of *mezza voce* and coloratura in the *passaggio*. Instead of outbursts of huffing and puffing, there is a plaintive legato counter-melody to those pervasive accompanying quavers, now marked piano, and more pleading than thrusting. Everything is higher-pitched, including the piano writing, and the effect is infinitely more vulnerable, tearful even. This is underlined by the ever-restless bass line that rises a semitone every few bars and tightens the screws of tension until the climactic point of 'O Tod! komm und drücke / Die Augen mir zu!' (bb. 19–22). There then follows a *Zwischenspiel* (bb. 24–6) looking back to the introduction and continuing the symphonic momentum that binds the work together.

This moment of reflection has undermined the gravedigger's lust for work. At the start of the third strophe the familiar F minor motor-rhythm of the accompaniment begins in the bass, but it sticks in its tracks, as if freeze-framed on a juddering video. A musical shudder – a motif of three bass notes, something refusing to develop into its former completeness – provides a convulsive memory of that back-breaking toil. Similarly fixed on F minor the vocal setting of 'Im Leben, da ist's ach! so schwül' is all on a single note (C) with the word 'schwül' set to a wailing sharpened sixth (D natural, in b. 29). The effect of this unresolved phrase is eerie and other-worldly, a musical moonscape. The left-hand silences, sudden rests in the bass clef, yawn like the open grave – dug but not yet filled in. What follows, the phrase 'Im Grabe so friedlich, so kühl', superbly counterbalances this address to a dark void. (The imagery of schwül/kühl for life/death is also to be found in the Stolberg setting *Lied (Des Lebens Tag ist schwer)* D788, and of course in the Heine poem *Der Tod, das ist die kühle Nacht* Op. 96 no. 1 set by Brahms.) Here is the first note of comfort and sweetness heard in the whole song. And how powerful it is that for the first time the left hand abandons its restless quavers in favour of cool and restful minims. But the repose is brief, dreamed-of rather than attained. This phrase has brought the music into E flat major at b. 31 and we are set for another rising sequence (beginning 'Doch ach, wer legt mich hinein?') where the bass is continually punctuated by that three-note motif. The gravedigger fears that he, who has buried so many, will have no one to see him into his final resting place. The vocal line between bb. 32 and 36 rises in anguished semitones from B natural to D while the harmony shifts in stages from E flat major, settling on G major, the dominant of C minor, where it stays for five bars (bb. 36–40). All pretence at melody has been abandoned in these obsessive, chant-like phrases. After the second 'wer legt mich hinein?' a roof of repeated Gs in the piano covers ominous stirrings in the bass, the ghost of that twitching three-note motif.

When this composer prepares as long an upbeat phrase as this, a questioning dominant if ever there was one, we know that he has something special up his sleeve. There is a change of tempo ('Langsamer' – slower) and a new key signature – C minor, a tonality associated in Schubert with tragedy and sinister events. The words 'Von allen verlassen / Dem Tod nur verwandt' initiate an extraordinarily sombre passage where the voice, falling in a long melodic sigh over four bars, is doubled in both hands by the piano. All is lassitude and infinite weariness. This mournful tune also features mordents, adding a shudder to the piano writing. We hear something very like this ominous phrase quoted in a work that is almost contemporary – the first movement of the Piano Sonata in A minor, D845. And we cannot fail to be reminded also of *Der greise Kopf* D911/14, that great and hugely pessimistic song, also in C minor, at the heart of *Winterreise*. There the phrase 'Wie weit noch bis zur Bahre!' ('How far it is still to the grave') is similarly accompanied in double octaves, overlaid with shakes of fear. The connection between the plights of gravedigger and winter traveller is clear – both long for release into another, better, world. No such luck for

Müller's hero; his creator was the better poet. The gravedigger's wish, however, is about to be granted. Having fiercely wielded a mean shovel a few minutes earlier, he is suddenly weak enough to give up the ghost. As in *Die junge Nonne*, an entire lifetime is lived in the progress of a single song. The second phrase in this section (beginning 'Und starre mit sehnendem Blick') seems to be a repeat of the first, but Schubert allows the vocal line to drop unexpectedly to a low A natural in b. 48, and it is this note that proves to be the portal to heaven.

It is as if the composer has turned a key that opens a door into another realm. Everything so far has been deeply felt, but nothing has prepared us for the musical glory that follows. The voice's bare A on 'Grab', poised over the edge of the grave/stave, is echoed deeply in the piano bass by an octave on the same note; this is followed by a gentle and sumptuous A major chord. The new marking is 'Noch langsamer'. From this foundation a new melody spirals, simple but unaccountably affecting, beginning its eloquent ascent in the inner voice of the accompaniment, like a stately cello line. This is a new, slower, symphonic *Bewegung*, replacing the one that has gone before. Above it, as if in the first and second violins, dactylic rhythm echoes the Allegretto movement of Beethoven's Seventh Symphony Op. 92, a favourite Schubertian source of inspiration. This interlude ends in F major in b. 53, but at the entry of the voice ('O Heimat des Friedens, / Der Seligen Land!') there is a return to A major and the beginning of what is effectively a vocal rerun of the wonderful phrase we have just heard in the piano. The vocal line climbs a ninth in the course of three bars, making the setting of 'An dich knüpft die Seele / Ein magisches Band. —' one of the most technically testing phrases for a baritone in the lieder repertoire. The sense of longing and aspiration which floods this hushed music, if properly sung, is awe-inspiring. The change to D major for 'Du winkst mir von Ferne' (bb. 59–60), and the circular progression that returns to F major for the repeat of 'ewiges Licht' is even more magical. This slow dance, the nature of which is emphasized by the mezzo-staccato articulation of the accompanying figuration, a metaphor for the blinking of starlight, is a pavane of transformation, truly music of the spheres.

These stars now disappear in their courses as the world fades from the dying man's sight. As diminished chords throb in the piano's right hand, the words 'Es schwinden . . . die Sterne' are set to two dipping diminished fifths, phrases that are separated by a void where the pianist's left hand provides an answering rising diminished fifth (bb. 63–4). This colloquy of phrases is prophesied, at pitch (F and B natural) in *Einsamkeit* D620 (bb. 84–6) on the words 'ist der Ruhe . . . zartes Glück'. Repose and happiness are dreams equally unattainable for Mayrhofer's seminary novice and Craigher's gravedigger yearning for a heavenly destination. As he raises his gaze, as if stretching upwards, the stars bend sympathetically down towards him. The enormity of these celestial galaxies of 1825 can be clearly discerned through music. At b. 66 a modulation takes the phrase 'Das Auge schon bricht!' into B minor. Another diminished seventh is broached from this distant key, and the colloquy of diminished intervals is repeated a tone lower than before. This eerie conversation between earth and the distant stars suspends the music in outer space. Then the words 'Ich sinke' (bb. 70–71) are harmonized to another diminished seventh, a tone lower still, as the piano's left hand echoes their two-stage descent with ever-lower bass notes throbbing in quavers. This is part of the hidden counterpoint in the music, inner parts that move with a sense of unearthly lightness, each voice like a planet spinning within its own orbit. The repetition of those words allows the vocal line to reach its lowest point at b. 72 before it changes direction and moves upwards.

On 'Ihr Lieben — / Ich komme!' (the first of six repetitions of these words) the gravedigger, already in a transfigured state, has glimpsed the faces of loved ones 'on the other side'. His soul rises from his now redundant body to greet them. The ascent up this arpeggio is both harmonically (F major and C^7) and melodically simple, but in this context its effect is radiant and grandiose. No one is laughing at the old gravedigger's ridiculous poem now. There is another appearance of the repeated falling intervals set to 'Ich sinke', but this is a case of *reculer pour mieux sauter*: in bb. 77–8 the singer is once again required to touch on high Fs at the top of the stave, a vocal feat whose perilous difficulty plays its part in the suspense, and in the depiction of a goal rapturously attained. As in the Mayrhofer setting *Nachtstück* D672, the old man on his death becomes subsumed into the body of the music. Craigher's poem breaks off deliberately, the implication being that we have lost the gravedigger's sentence in mid-flight. With the repeated calls of 'Ich komme, ich komm'!' the vocal line trails away accordingly in the middle of the texture. Above and below the piano writing throbs with the rhythm to which the stars might dance in their eternal round. Rarely in his songs does Schubert use the extremes of the keyboard in this unearthly way. The wide gap between the lowest bass note and the highest chord seems symbolic of the distance between the mire of the graveyard and the starlit galaxies that have to be traversed by that troubled soul. As a pious afterthought Craigher had placed (Verse 3) a crucifix in the old man's hand as a vade mecum for the journey, but this is not what permits his ascent. Schubert's immortal music has enabled even pigs to fly, and the old ham has been blessed with an escape that is as lucky as it is sublime.

Autograph:	Wienbibliothek im Rathaus, Vienna (first draft)
First edition:	Published as Book 24 no. 2 of the *Nachlass* by Diabelli, Vienna in September 1833 (P306). The title above is that quoted in the first edition, the poem, the Deutsch catalogue and the NSA. Only the Peters Edition gives 'Heimweh' which accounts for the everyday omission of the last syllable
Subsequent editions:	Peters: Vol. 5/143; AGA XX 467: Vol. 8/50; NSA IV: Vol. 13/157
Bibliography:	Capell 1928, pp. 206–7
	Fischer-Dieskau 1977, pp. 228–9
Discography and timing:	Fischer-Dieskau II 7[1] 6'04
	Hyperion I 35[14]
	Hyperion II 29[18] 6'58 Christopher Maltman

← *Der blinde Knabe* D833   *Ellens Gesang I* D837 →

TOTENGRÄBER-WEISE   Gravedigger's song
(SCHLECHTA) **D869** [H592]
F♯ minor – F♯ major   1826

(119 bars)

Nicht so düster und so bleich,	Not so sad and pale,
Schläfer in der Truhe,	Sleeper in your chest;
Wohnest nun im stillen Reich[1]	You now dwell in the silent kingdom
Gottgeweihter Ruhe![2]	Of God-dedicated rest.

[1] The original Schlechta is restored here as in the NSA. The Nachlass and Peters Edition print '*Unter Schollen leicht und weicht*' ('Beneath the soft, light earth').
[2] In Nachlass and Peters Edition: '*Leg' ich dich zur* Ruhe'.

Wird der Leib des Wurmes Raub	Though the body is a prey to worms
Und ein Spiel den Winden,	And a plaything of the winds,
Muss das Herz selbst noch als Staub	The heart, even as dust,
Leben und empfinden.	Will live on and feel.
Jetzt beginnet dein Gericht;[3]	Now your judgement begins,
Gleichend deinem Leben	Resembling your life,
Werden, dunkel oder licht,	Dark or bright,
Träume dich umschweben.	Dreams will hover about you.
Jeder Laut, der dich verklagt	Every sound that accuses you
Als den Quell der Schmerzen,	Of being a source of pain
Wird ein scharfer Dolch und nagt	Will become a sharp dagger,
Sich zu deinem Herzen.	Piercing you to the heart.
Doch der Liebe Tränentau,	But the dewy tears of love
Der dein Grab besprühet,	That are sprinkled on your grave
Färbt sich an des Himmels Blau,	Will be coloured by the blue of heaven,
Knospet auf und blühet.	And bud and flower.
Im Gesange lebt der Held,	The hero lives in song,
Und zu seinem Ruhme	And to honour him
Brennet hoch im Sternenfeld[4]	A flower of fire
Eine Feuerblume.	Gleams high above in the field of stars.
Schlafe, bis der Engel ruft,	Sleep until the angel calls,
Bis Posaunen klingen,	Until the trumpets sound,
Und die Leiber sich der Gruft	And the bodies rise from the grave
Jugendlich entschwingen!	Rejuvenated!

FRANZ XAVER VON SCHLECHTA (1796–1875)

This is the fifth of Schubert's six Schlechta solo settings (1815–26). See the poet's biography for a chronological list of all the Schlechta settings.

This song, like all the other settings of this poet, is a victim of Schlechta's continual textual revisions. Schubert set the poem from his printed *Gedichte* (1824), but the poet (one has the impression of someone always fiddling in the background with last-minute changes to a not very distinguished text) undoubtedly introduced various textual 'improvements' that were taken up by the AGA; it was this version that was recorded for the Hyperion Edition. The NSA restores Schlechta's original text as printed here; footnotes detail the text as sung by generations of lieder singers, but not the one that Schubert himself knew.

The commentators are agreed that this work is somewhat problematic. 'The song is singularly lacking in charm', writes Capell, 'while at the same time being so stamped with Schubert's ingeniousness and originality'. Einstein writes of it as 'a compendium of Schubert's favourite modulations'.

---

[3] See above: '*Denn der Herr sitzt zu* Gericht'.
[4] See above: '*Schimmert*' ['gleams'] hoch *in* Sternenfeld.

Leo Black, on the other hand, disagrees. He sees no modulation in this song, but regards it as one of Schubert's finest essays in touching rapidly on the most outlying tonal areas within his unquestioned tonic (Black 1997, p. 13):

> A key in classical music is like a house with many rooms, originally inhabited by someone who lived for the most part in one particular room or suite. Comes a new tenant, who goes far more often into some of those the old one had scarcely entered, and occasionally into parts of the house never previously opened up. He also finds or builds passageways to get him from one room to another faster than any previous owner would have thought possible. To pause for a moment in the doorway of a remote room before moving back toward a main one is not to modulate, it is simply to explore: a matter of harmonic colour where a true modulation is a matter of structure. Haydn was a supreme master at opening doors, showing what could lie beyond them and then closing them again, so too Mozart . . . What Schubert had was both the inclination and the ability to pay flying visits to his remoter rooms, which he could reach with surprising speed.

Having achieved such success with another song about a gravedigger (*Totengräbers Heimwehe* D842 of April 1825) it seems extraordinary that Schubert should go over (or under) the same ground, and write a song on a similar subject. A closer reading shows the two texts to be very different: in *Totengräbers Heimwehe* the gravedigger longs for release from his task and achieves this, in exalted musical fashion, in the song's final pages. In *Totengräber-Weise* we have a man who is grimly happy in his work and who stays with it to the bitter end, dispensing philosophical thoughts the while in the manner of a Shakespeare rustic. He is articulate beyond his station and our expectations and, thanks to Schubert rather than to the more devout Schlechta, there are flashes of grim humour. Indeed, notwithstanding the decidedly unfunny imagery of the poem, this viewpoint of the song as black comedy can even encompass mention of a resurrection that is wilfully sarcastic, with the gravedigger a kind of rough Shakespearian character mocking the hopes of the dead for an afterlife as he unceremoniously buries them. This too is the mood of the very early Hölty setting, *Totengräberlied* D44.

In *Totengräbers Heimwehe* we had encountered a complex character, a misfit in his unhappy profession; in this 'sequel' there is nothing about this different gravedigger's personality – only his thoughts about death and the afterlife. This is perhaps what makes *Totengräber-Weise* a curiously impersonal song (unless it is expanded by adventurous interpretative ingenuity as described above, although this could hardly have been the intention of Schlechta who was insufficiently sophisticated, and far too Catholic, to write with such deliberately perverse intent). On the face of it the gravedigger is a professional who remorselessly digs as he sings, and whose thoughts about heaven, based on a simple but unshakeable faith, do not permit him to stop his work for an instant. There is thus something hard and intractable about the shape of the music, with its four-square and relentless rhythmical patterns. If Capell complains about a lack of charm, it has to be said that the gravedigger's occupation is hardly a charming one. Here Schubert attempts to write a truthful rather than a beguiling song.

We hear the sound of spade against earth throughout. The right-hand harmonies are scrunched together as two surfaces, notes in a chord jostling for primacy, are made to strike each other. Accents marked on the first and third beats of the bar emphasize the unremitting rhythm of a hard, thankless occupation. The shift in tessitura between two-bar blocks of the accompaniment (bb. 1–2 as contrasted with bb. 3–5, or bb. 33–4 with bb. 35–7) betokens the movement of earth shovelled from above into the abyss as it gradually obscures the coffin. The vocal line underlines this: in the octave leap at the beginning (bb. 7–8) we hear the contrast of the dark of 'düster' and pale of 'bleich', and see the gravedigger's heaving gesture as another spadeful of earth hits its mark. The distance between heaven and earth is also signified by this difference between treble and bass clef, as well as by the thrice-occurring switch of key signature between F sharp minor and F sharp major.

A lesser composer would have made this piece completely strophic, but this is a good example of the modified strophic song in Schubert's mature style, where there is nothing automatic about his response to the words. As on other occasions, the composer seems to have started off with a strict strophic song in mind, but the temptation to mirror various details as the text unfolds has proved irresistible. Having taken two of Schlechta's verses to make one musical verse of his own, Schubert is content, at the beginning of the third verse (from b. 40), to re-use the magisterial music of 'Nicht so düster und so bleich' for 'Denn der Herr sitzt zu Gericht' or, in Schlechta's revision, 'Jetzt beginnet dein Gericht'. The fourth verse (from b. 50) begins with the same music as the second, but the image of a sharp dagger ('scharfer Dolch') piercing the heart unleashes a slew of chromatics: the rise in semitones on the lines 'und nagt / Sich zu deinem Herzen' (bb. 55–8) depicts the tortures of hell as the victim whines in pain. Here, with the striding full-handed chords in the accompaniment, we are put in mind of the implacable march of Schiller's setting *Der Pilgrim* D794.

The poem has three more verses to go and Schubert maps out his plan. The final two verses will have the same musical shape as the first two, but a seven-verse poem defies the easy symmetry of groupings by two. This spare middle verse ('Doch der Liebe Tränentau' from b. 64) occasions another shift into F sharp major that is utterly in tune with its theme of tears of love and flowers. The interlude after this strophe ascends into the most ethereal regions of the keyboard in bb. 80–82, as if to paint the azure regions of the 'Himmels Blau'. The sixth verse has poetic resonances that are reminiscent of *Des Sängers Habe* D832. (Of course the two songs are by the same poet who may well have discussed mortality with Schubert and offered up these verses specially tailored so to be meaningful to his friend; we can only imagine Schubert's daily inner struggle with thoughts of the grave at this stage of his life.) With the shift of the accompaniment into the bass at 'Bis Posaunen klingen' (bb. 95–7) we have a marvel-lous change of sonority suggestive of trombones which recalls not only the last trump but also the graveside music for brass ensemble so common at Austrian burials and celebrations of All Souls' Day. (Beethoven wrote *Equali* for four trombones for such occasions.) And so the song continues without pause for breath, the occasional shaft of light high in the treble clef miti-gating the grim thoughts of dust and worm. The accompaniment to the last words ('Jugendlich entschwingen') jumps as high as the compass of Schubert's piano allowed (bb. 107–9), a moment of blissful and other-worldly contrast to what has gone before. The postlude is an elongated version of the prelude; in its progression by stages from the top of the keyboard to the bottom it encapsulates the struggle inherent in the song between life and death, heaven and hell, the open grave and the finished burial mound. As the song ends deep in the bass clef, it is thoughts of 'ashes to ashes and dust to dust' that set their seal on the music, triumphing over brighter hopes.

Autograph:	Library of Congress, Washington (fair copy)
First edition:	Published as Book 15 no. 3 of the *Nachlass* by Diabelli, Vienna in January 1832 (P282)
Subsequent editions:	Peters: Vol. 3/155; AGA XX 496: Vol. 8/198; NSA IV: Vol. 14a/2
Bibliography:	Black 1997, p. 13
	Capell 1928, pp. 214–15
	Einstein 1951, pp. 303–4
	Fischer-Dieskau 1977, p. 239
	Porter 1961, pp. 105–6
	Youens 2002, pp. 352–63

Discography and timing: Fischer-Dieskau II 8[5]   4'55
                          Hyperion I 26[10]
                          Hyperion II 31[15]   5'03   Richard Jackson

← *Wiegenlied* D867   *Das Zügenglöcklein* D871 →

Das TOTENHEMDCHEN *see* DUBIOUS, MISATTRIBUTED AND LOST SONGS

TOTENKRANZ FÜR EIN KIND   Wreath for a dead child
(MATTHISSON) **D275** [H162]
G minor   25 August 1815

(14 bars)

Sanft wehn, im Hauch der Abendluft,	In the evening breeze the spring grass
Die Frühlingshalm' auf deiner Gruft,	Waves gently upon your grave
Wo Sehnsuchtstränen fallen.	Where tears of longing fall.
Nie soll, bis uns der Tod befreit,	Never, until death frees us,
Die Wolke der Vergessenheit	Shall the mists of oblivion
Dein holdes Bild umwallen!	Shroud your sweet image.
Wohl dir, obgleich entknospet kaum,	Happy you, though your blossom was barely unfolded,
Von Erdenlust und Sinnentraum,	You left behind earthly pleasure and sensual dreams,
Von Schmerz und Wahn geschieden!	Sorrow and illusion.
Du schläfst in Ruh'; wir wanken irr'	You sleep in peace; we stumble,
Und unstätbang' im Weltgewirr',	Confused and troubled, through the turmoil of this world,
Und haben selten Frieden.	And seldom know peace.

FRIEDRICH VON MATTHISSON (1761–1831); poem written in 1792/3

This is the twentieth of Schubert's twenty-nine Matthisson solo settings (1812–17). See the poet's
biography for a chronological list of all the Matthisson settings.

In the annals of Schubertian productivity 25 August 1815 was a marvellous day. No fewer than nine songs by various poets were composed. The male quartet *Trinklied* D267 is first on Deutsch's list, followed by another work for the same forces but of an utterly different character, the miners' chorus *Bergknappenlied* D268. Next was *Das Leben* D269, another part-song, this time for trio, followed by Gabriele von Baumberg's *An die Sonne* D270, a poem from Abraham Cowley's *The Mistress* (*Der Weiberfreund* in Ratschky's translation) D271, Tiedge's *An die Sonne*

D272, *Lilla an die Morgenröte* D273 and *Tischlerlied* D274. *Totenkranz für ein Kind* is last in this list of astonishingly variable poetic provenances and stylistic moods.

It was apparently a tradition in medieval Germany to adorn a dead child with a wreath. Matthisson meant his words to be a verbal equivalent of this old-fashioned homage. Child mortality was a constant part of life in households of the early nineteenth century, and Schubert was no stranger to graveside contemplation himself at the burials of several brothers and sisters. As late as 1817 the composer lost a half-brother named Theodor who was only seven months old. The key of *Totenkranz für ein Kind* is G minor, and John Reed revealingly writes that this tonality 'often expresses the fortitude of those whose lot is a battle against fate or the supernatural'. It is in this key that the young Schubert bemoans Metastasio's *Misero pargoletto* D42. The father who rides through the night in an attempt to save his son (*Erlkönig* D328) has something in common with the parents who have lost their child in *Lied* (Mutter geht durch ihre Kammern) D373 from de la Motte Fouqué's *Undine* (both songs are in G minor) as well as the bereft mourners in this little song. As befits its subject matter the music is modest yet deeply felt. Most of the vocal line is doubled by the piano which contributes to a mood of nursery simplicity. There is a gentle tenderness here well suited to paint the haunting 'holdes Bild' of the child. The only trace of semiquaver decoration in a vocal line of crotchets and quavers occurs on a tiny *gruppetto* on the word 'fallen' (b. 6), a turn of phrase that in its gentle flourish was to become something of a Schubertian hallmark. The composer's markings of 'Etwas geschwind' and *alla breve* avoid any sense of lugubrious tragedy. Schubert was to write his best-known elegy for a dead child, *Am Grabe Anselmos* D504, in November 1816. His patient and forbearing relationship with Faust, little son of the Pachler family in Graz in 1827, shows us what an affectionate father the composer might have been.

Autograph:	Wienbibliothek im Rathaus (first version)
First edition:	Published as part of the AGA in 1895 (P577)
Subsequent editions:	Not in Peters; AGA XX 132: Vol. 3/61; NSA IV: Vol. 9/22
Further settings:	Felix Mendelssohn (1809–1847) *Sanft weh'n im Hauch der Abendluft* (1822)
Discography and timing:	Fischer-Dieskau I 5[15] 1'34
	Hyperion I 20[6]
	Hyperion II 9[23] 1'40 Patricia Rozario

← *Tischlerlied* D274   *Abendlied* D276 →

TRÄNENREGEN *see Die SCHÖNE MÜLLERIN* D795/10

TRANSCRIPTIONS AND ARRANGEMENTS FOR PIANO, INSTRUMENTS AND VOICES: A SELECTIVE SURVEY

Almost as soon as Schubert's songs were first heard in Vienna there was the desire to transcribe them – many music lovers wanted the pleasure of listening to this music or playing it on their own instruments. In due course, the commercial advantages of a piece of music appearing in various saleable guises became clear to the publishers. Sometimes singer and pianist were replaced by violinist and pianist, cellist and pianist, flautist and pianist; sometimes it was the pianist who was replaced by a guitarist or organist. Often it was a solo pianist who played the song with the vocal line incorporated under the fingers – almost always in a simple manner –

and sometimes the song was arranged for piano duet. On occasion the text of the song was provided in an underlay, but this was by no means always the case. There was an essential domestic modesty in such transformations that limited them to the intimacies of the drawing room, but transcriptions also had their place in the concert hall: the songs were sometimes arranged for chorus, with and without piano accompaniment, and on occasion they were orchestrated (*see* ORCHESTRATIONS). The apogee of the Schubert song transcription, however, was the magical and impressive transformations effected by certain virtuoso pianists who were also composers. By the twentieth century, when Leopold Godowksy and Serge Rachmaninoff made their transcriptions, Schubert's songs were known everywhere, and these great pianists were providing variations on music that was already iconic. They were also unashamedly following in the footsteps of the pioneering and pivotal figure in this field, Franz Liszt, whose transcriptions brought Schubert's music to the attention of an otherwise indifferent wider public (something still necessary in the 1840s when Schubert was not yet universally acknowledged as one of the great composers). Mere proselytizing, however worthy and necessary, was clearly insufficient for a man of Liszt's irrepressible genius, and from the beginning he reserved the right to stamp these transcriptions with his own personality and to make of them something interesting and challenging in their own right. He seems scarcely to have noticed that his arrangements were more or less unplayable by most lesser mortals. It could well be argued that members of the public took more notice of Schubert's melodies when they were presented to them in a manner that commanded awed attention on account of a spellbinding performance at the keyboard.

Franz Liszt, a photograph taken by Hermann Biow in Hamburg in 1843.

It was not of course Liszt who invented the age-old musical concept of making variations on a theme whereby a tune (often a modest one, such as the one by Diabelli that served Beethoven for his mighty set of Thirty-three Variations, or 'Veränderungen' Op. 120 – Transformations) was enriched by being clothed in the ever-more fantastic garb woven by a great composer's imagination. Perhaps the first transcription of a Schubert song was made in March 1827 when Johann Nepomuk Hummel, moved to tears by the performance of the baritone Vogl accompanied by Schubert himself, improvised masterfully on *Der blinde Knabe* D833. In order to pay his tribute Hummel made, in effect, a transcription of the song on the spot, and the gesture was the highest compliment one composer could pay another. Liszt was no doubt also moved to tears by many a Schubert song, and his tribute to them, and to the posthumous Schubert, was made in the same spirit of wonder and enthusiasm.

Transcriptions have to be divided into two main categories – straightforward, simple renditions of a song for different solo instruments, with and without accompaniment, and the conjuring with variations and virtuosity that seems to have been initiated by Liszt and much imitated since (not that Liszt was incapable of his own version of unruffled simplicity when he considered it appropriate). In terms of numbers, it is the practical transcription – sometimes even deliberately simplified – that wins hands down. Well into the middle of the twentieth century *The World's Encyclopaedia of Recorded Music* (1966) shows us that there was a market for recordings of a handful of Schubert song titles in any number of literal arrangements: recordings of *Ave Maria* (*Ellens Gesang III* D839) were available in five orchestral versions, a version for violin and orchestra (Nathan Milstein), two versions for violin and piano (Yehudi Menuhin and Jascha Heifitz), one for viola and organ (William Primrose), three for cello and piano, four for organ solo and one for guitar. Such arrangements were obviously considered money-spinners and of interest even to serious artists. Similar statistics exist for the *Ständchen* D957/4 from *Schwanengesang* D957/4 and for the famous *Wiegenlied* D498. Schubert often attracted the attention of close harmony ensembles such as the famous German group from the 1930s, The Comedian Harmonists (who recorded, among other things, *Heidenröslein* D257), and the Viennese–American cabaret singer Greta Keller (1903–1977) was probably not the only singer to make swing adaptions of Schubert songs (*Ständchen*, *Am Meer* D957/12, *Der Neugierige* D795/6, *Die Krähe* D911/15 and a hilariously zany *Der Leiermann* D911/24), dating from 1939–40. In about 1958, my first encounter with a Schubert song was *An die Musik* D547 in a solo piano arrangement by Gerald Moore – theme music for the only classical requests programme, *Let's Be Serious*, on Rhodesian radio.

Schubert was aware of the power of his own vocal melodies and of their suitability for variation. Four of his songs famously reappear in his chamber music: the fourth movement of the Piano Quintet ('The Trout', D667) consists of variations on *Die Forelle* D550, the song *Strophe aus 'Die Götter Griechenlands'* D677 pervades the third movement of the String Quartet in A minor D804 and makes an appearance in the Octet D803, *Der Tod und das Mädchen* D531 appears in the second movement of the 'Death and the Maiden' String Quartet in D minor D810, and variations on *Sei mir gegrüsst* D741 form the second movement of the *Fantasie in C* for Violin and Piano D934. While more sophisticated music lovers must have been delighted to hear their favourite songs given a new and different lease of life, ordinary members of the public also benefited from straightforward transcriptions whereby they could enjoy the original songs at home with whatever resources were available. In Schubert's lifetime quite a number of lieder appeared with guitar accompaniment and a few (such as *Lob der Tränen* D711 and *Die Post* D911/13) in arrangements for solo guitar by one Johann Caspar Mertz. The composer's older brother Ferdinand arranged some sixty works including orchestrations of certain songs (*see* ORCHESTRATIONS), some of these with Schubert's knowledge, some without.

The catalogue of Schubert's works by Gustav Nottebohm (1874) gives us an enormously useful glimpse into the world of transcriptions and arrangements for the fifty or so years after the composer's death. The senior figure on these pages is the composer–businessman **Anton Diabelli** (1781–1858) who owned the publishing rights to so much of Schubert's music. The transcriptions published by his firm were more likely to have been done by underlings than by his own hand – whole series of works including the piano transcriptions both for two hands and four hands (*Wiener Lieblingstücke*, *Lieder im leichten Styl*), the songs arranged for violin and piano in *Concordance für Violine concertant* in multiple volumes, and the series known as *Productionen*, again in many volumes, which featured flute and piano transcriptions. Diabelli's constant presence in these Nottebohm listings was necessary to keep up with the competition; such was the power of Schubert's melodies to enchant the public that lesser mortals with an eye to commercial success wasted little time in exploiting the great composer's productions (and the absence of copyright laws) in making arrangements designed to appeal to amateur musicians of every persuasion.

Carl Czerny (1791–1857) was a famous Viennese pianist, composer and pedagogue. His studies for the development of virtuosity have remained famous and his musical worth has been re-evaluated in recent years. His choice of Schubert song for piano transcription shows a discerning knowledge of the repertoire: in the main Czerny seems to have deliberately avoided the songs that Liszt transcribed. The works he chose for arrangement are all masterpieces, but by no means the best-known or the most instantly popular: *An Schwager Kronos* D369, *Der blinde Knabe* D833, *Drang in die Ferne* D770, *Erster Verlust* D226, *Fischerweise* D881, *Gruppe aus dem Tartarus* D583, *Heimliches Lieben* D922, *Jägers Abendlied* D368, *Lied des gefangenen Jägers* D843, *Das Lied im Grünen* D917, *Normans Gesang* D846, *Schlummerlied* (Schlaflied) D527, *Vor meiner Wiege*. Czerny also added a piano part to a posthumous publication of a Schubert chorus – qv *Trinklied* D356. Czerny's arrangements appeared as early as 1829 and were published by Diabelli and by Charles Richault in Paris.

Leopold Jansa (1795–1875) was a Viennese violinist who spent some years in London in exile on account of his sympathy for Hungarian independence. He arranged *Winterreise* complete for violin and piano, as well as for cello and piano.

Friedrich August Kummer (1797–1879) was a distinguished Dresden musician who made transcriptions of Schubert songs for cello and piano.

The Russian violinist **Aleksey Lvov** (1798–1870) made a version for violin and piano of *Auf dem Wasser zu singen* D774. **Carl Georg Lickl** (1801–1877) was a Viennese composer (mainly of church music) and a virtuoso performer on the physharmonika (reed organ). His Schubert transcriptions are for this instrument and piano, or for two pianos. Like Czerny, his choice of titles shows a measure of discernment and a knowledge of Schubert's wider output. It is curious to see Lickl taking an interest in a song like *Fülle der Liebe* D854 (seldom performed today) while ignoring an evergreen favourite like *Im Frühling* D882 for which Nottebohm lists no transcriptions.

Robert Wittmann (b. 1804) was born in Dresden where he was a member of the Kreuzschule as a boy. He was a fine pianist but was better known as a cellist. He was a student of Friedrich Kummer (*see* above). He moved to Leipzig as a teacher and it was there, probably some time in the 1860s, and perhaps because of his connection with Kummer, that he was commissioned by Edition Peters to make solo piano versions of the two Müller cycles, as well as eighty songs in the firm's well-known first volume of Schubert lieder. These unfussy but effective arrangements were published in four books but were also offered bound together in the same format and sequence offered by Peters in their song volume, the three cycles followed by twenty-two 'ausgewählte Lieder'.

R. Wittmann's solo piano transcriptions of Schubert's songs, published by Peters in Leipzig.

Ernst David Wagner (1806–1883) was an expert in musical pedagogy; he was one of the first to arrange Schubert songs in transcriptions 'in leichtem Styl' for young musicians.

Georg Wilhlem Teschner (1809–1883), pupil of Zelter, Klein and Berger in Berlin, was an expert in choral music of every kind. He arranged thirty-six lieder for mixed choir (SATB).

As has already been mentioned, the name of **Franz Liszt** (1811–1886) stands at the epicentre of the history of Schubert transcriptions. In Nottebohm's Schubert catalogue, his name and his arrangements (there listed generally as 'Übertragungen') take their place in modest alphabetical order among other composers, most of the latter now consigned to oblivion. Liszt's fifty-five song transcriptions stand out from all the others, not merely because of his pianistic powers, but because he was fascinated by this music irrespective of its commercial possibilities. His irrepressible ebullience and fecundity of musical production incorporated an unusual mixture – the vanity (or, at the least, the *amour-propre*) of the virtuoso, and the passionate enthusiasm of the humble music-lover who was capable of recognizing, and serving, genius greater than his own. His career was financially successful enough for him to indulge his passion for Schubert, in many respects entirely altruistically. He was in the position to pay tribute to the composer's genius at the same time as incorporating the compositional fruits of his own pianistic ascendancy. This enabled him simultaneously to amaze his listeners with his piano playing while educating them in the matter of Schubert's greatness. It would be no exaggeration to claim that thousands of listeners sought out the printed music of a Schubert song only after having heard Liszt lavish upon it his special attention in the concert hall. Liszt, the great popularizer of the time, played a crucial part in establishing Schubert as a great composer, worthy, for example, of a having his statue in the Stadtpark in Vienna: this was erected in 1872 with scarcely a word of argument, a consensus that could never have been reached in the late 1830s. Liszt's public commitment to Schubert was initiated in a series of eight charity concerts in Vienna on behalf of the Hungarian flood victims of 1838. He had begun work on these song transcriptions (his own term, whereby a more or less faithful arrangement was differentiated from the more elaborate 'paraphrase') in 1837 at the urging of Chrétien Urhan (1790–1845, a violist and composer of German descent resident in Paris, who was influenced by Schubert and counted among his friends Berlioz and Meyerbeer). Of course Liszt was only one of a number of artists who burnished Schubert's posthumous reputation, but he was by far the most celebrated. The period between Schubert's death and that iconic statue in the Stadtpark found Liszt at the height of his performing powers – the years of his so-called 'transcendental execution'. The puristic musicology and scholarship that pronounced Liszt's transcriptions in questionable taste became more influential after his death, and continued into what the pianist and scholar Leslie Howard has witheringly called the 'museum-culture-minded twentieth century'; a situation that has now changed, and very much for the better.

The full scope of Liszt's services to the cause lies beyond the scope of this article, but the conductor of the C major Symphony D944 – uncut – and the opera *Alfonso und Estrella* D732, the editor of the piano music, the arranger of dances and pianos duets, the prospective biographer, is nothing less than a Schubertian hero. Because this book is only about Schubert, this is not the place to discuss Liszt's other song transcriptions, nor his multifarious efforts on behalf of deservingly notable talents such as Robert Franz, nor his large-scale service to diverse contemporaries Weber, Berlioz and Verdi, not to mention Wagner. Suffice it to say that the energy of the man simply beggars belief. But it has always been his lot that the whiff of his wizardry has suggested a not entirely honest legerdemain, and engendered in many a listener a kind of bemused distrust. Such is the inevitable fate of charismatic, larger than life figures.

Liszt's transcriptions of Schubert songs belong to three main types: firstly, relatively simple renditions of accompaniment and vocal line – some of the greatest songs are given this treatment; secondly, a theme and variations whereby a simpler first strophe is succeeded by pianistic elaboration; thirdly, and this is by far the most controversial (and the most interesting) aspect of his arrangements, a much freer and more fantastical approach whereby he attempts to re-create in solo pianistic terms the emotional effects of a great singer's interpretation of a song, even if it means departing considerably from the literal musical text. There are few people who would now deny that pieces of this kind are often considerable works of art in their own right.

THE LISZT SCHUBERT SONG TRANSCRIPTIONS (in alphabetical order)

Die Allmacht D852: for tenor, male chorus and orchestra (*see* ORCHESTRATIONS), Liszt also issued it for tenor, male chorus and piano.

Am Tage aller Seelen (Litanei) D343: a single piano version, 1840. As with all the transcriptions in this group of *Geistliche Lieder*, an underlay of the German text is given at the beginning of the transcription before it becomes musically elaborate.

Liszt's transcription of *Auf dem Wasser zu singen* (1838).

Auf dem Wasser zu singen D774: two publications for solo piano of a single version, 1837. The vocal line is brought out between the thumbs of both hands, sometimes chiming in thirds and tenths in different registers, and retaining much of the original glistening of water-inspired undulation. After the fifth page begins a gradual accelerando that culminates in the *molto agitato* of the closing pages and the *molto strepito* plunging octaves which lead to the final statement of the ecstatic *Nachspiel*.

Du bist die Ruh D776: two solo piano versions, 1837, both of which remain still and gently decorated. Only the two vocal climaxes, where the singer climbs to the high A flat, are given the 'piano concerto' treatment of roving fortissimo chords splashing up and down the keyboard – a less hackneyed device in Liszt's earlier career than it seems now. Not even this exaggeration is to be found, however, in the third version (1879) where the pianistic exuberance at the climaxes is greatly reduced so as not to disturb the overall mood of peace created in the song.

Ellens Gesang III ('Ave Maria') (*see Sieben Gesänge aus Walter Scott's Fräulein vom See*, no. 5) D839: two solo piano versions, *c.* 1837, in the exalted manner ('religioso') that is a barnstorming cliché now, but which no doubt sounded novel and uplifting at the time. Walt Disney exploited the same highly sentimental aspect of this song in the arrangement for the film *Fantasia* (1940). In the second version in particular the purity and simplicity of Ellen Douglas, the Highland heroine as created by Walter Scott who prays for her father's safety, are sacrificed to the grandeur of Mariolatry as if viewed from within the Sistine Chapel. The music written out on three staves (the melody framed from above and below by chords in sextuplets) might have been written for

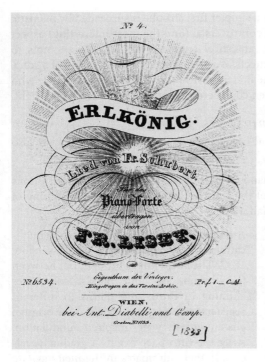

Liszt's transcription of *Der Erlkönig* (1838).

Liszt's transcription of *Frühlingsglaube* (1838).

massed male voice choir. Only at the extended end of the first version, with its ruminative and strangely touching meanderings marked 'piano', are we reminded of the private nature of prayer. That this passage, the farthest from Schubert's original, should best express the spirit of the song, is one of the paradoxes of the transcriber's art.

Erlkönig D328: three solo piano versions, 1837–8. Liszt adds further challenges for the pianist, quite apart from having to incorporate the vocal line throughout. This is a magnificent transcription (marked 'Dramatico' at the beginning) where the gargantuan effort of the pianist equates to that of the father who rides through the night with his sick child. Simply to have heard Liszt play this at a concert would have been enough to convince a listener of Schubert's greatness – and to give Liszt his credit, that is exactly what his arrangement was designed to do. In the closing two pages (marked 'il più presto possible' and 'sempre tumultuoso') even Liszt alternates quavers with triplets to make the passage more playable.

Die Forelle D550: four solo piano versions, 1844. At first one imagines that this is Liszt in *Liebestraum* mood, but the famous tune soon emerges and is treated to various variations with interpolated moments of cadenza filigree. It is clear that Liszt's intention is to conjure unashamedly with a melody that has already become iconic.

Frühlingsglaube D686: three solo piano versions, undated. There are a few moments of virtuoso note-spinning in an interpolated shadow of a cadenza at the end of the arrangement, but *Frühlingsglaube* is allowed to make its own musical point without too much interference. The third version of 1879 is perhaps the most *innig* and Schubertian.

Die Gestirne D444: three solo piano versions, 1840. This song, related in poetic content to *Die Allmacht*, is accorded a quasi orchestral treatment with all the attendant grandeur of throbbing chord and cascading arpeggio – to the extent that the shape of the original melody is all but obscured by ecstatic pianism.

This relatively obscure song was performed at Chopin's funeral in 1849, and it is possible that the great composer may have come to know this music solely through Liszt's positively incandescent arrangement. It was after all at Nohant, home of George Sand, that Liszt first worked at these transcriptions while the Countess Marie d'Agoult rendered the German poems into French to enable him to understand them.

Gondelfahrer D809: one solo piano version of the Schubert quartet, not the solo song, 1883. This lovely and serene product of Liszt's old age is his farewell to the art of Schubert song transcription. It is faithful to the limpid insouciance of the original male-voice quartet where one voice dovetails with another like ripple melting into wave on the Venetian lagoon. The shimmer of moonlight is wonderfully suggested by decorative touches high in the keyboard, and Liszt's signature is placed hauntingly on the arrangement at the very end when we return unexpectedly to the bell-tower chiming midnight (without achieving the twelve strokes, however, that Schubert also denies us in the quartet setting).

Gretchen am Spinnrade D118: two solo piano versions, 1837–8. This is more or less a faithful rendition of the original although the semiquaver sextuplet accompaniment and the vocal line are combined in such a way that the melody, picked out by the right hand, sounds a semiquaver after the bar line. In the two last pages a faithfully transcribed song turns into something more symphonic in terms of sound and scale. The later version of the transcription has a short introduction abstracted from the middle of the work.

Himmelsfunken D651: one version, 1840. The theme of the first verse gives way to two variations – the first of these (on three staves) with a staccato accompaniment, no doubt to reflect the sparkle of heavenly lights ('Funken'), the second with a more lusciously chromatic background.

Die junge Nonne D828: a single solo piano version, 1837–8. Liszt, in homage to Schubert, laboured to preserve the sense and shape of the original. The change of melody right at the end (for the final 'Alleluia') is perhaps an unnecessary touch, but elsewhere the transcriber has admirably disciplined himself to provide for the listener something similar to hearing a fine singer perform this work.

Lob der Tränen D711: a single solo piano version, 1837. The first verse is simply transcribed with the melody in the tenor region of the keyboard; in the second this is transferred to the soprano register with some embellishments. Liszt relies on the shapeliness of the once-famous melody (the song is more or less neglected by present-day recitalists) to make its impression.

Des Mädchens Klage D191: a single solo piano version, 1844. A strophic song converted to a massive theme and variations. It strays far from the classical rigours of the Schiller setting that was this music's inspiration. Liszt was not the only great composer to find something overwhelmingly dramatic in this song – Modest Musorgsky was reputed to have accompanied it in a hair-raisingly exciting manner.

Meeres Stille D216: three solo piano versions, c. 1837. This is perhaps an over-grandiose arrangement of a simple song. Nevertheless Liszt (who took an unusual amount of trouble to get this transcription right as he perceived it) successfully conveys the angst of the becalmed sailor and the potentially tragic consequences of the lack of wind at sea. The grand sweep of the arpeggios conveys the breadth of the horizon and the depth of the ocean, but actually no more effectively than in Schubert's original accompaniment. The growling bass chromaticisms in the first version, more sea monster than becalmed sea, were later prudently excised.

Rastlose Liebe D138: a single solo piano version, 1837–8. A transcription full of technical challenges (very tricky leaps from one part of the keyboard to another), as swift and intense as the original. The opening six bars are exactly the same as the introduction to the song, and were clearly considered difficult enough to leave exactly as they were; the same applies to the postlude. Singers and accompanists would do well to note Liszt's direction for the middle section of the song (beginning 'Alle das Neigen / Von Herzen zu Herzen') which is good advice: 'amoroso non troppo agitato'.

Hymne – Geisterchor aus Rosamunde D797/4

A single piano version, 1840, from *Vier geistliche Lieder*, this is one of the most curious choices for a transcription that Liszt ever made, and certainly his most obscure. The music is almost unknown, and has remained so, but it was belatedly published as part of Op. 26 in 1828, one of four numbers that were issued with piano accompaniment, including the famous *Romanze* and the almost equally forgotten choruses for shepherds and hunters in that opus. Liszt was wrong to suppose, in dubbing this a hymn, that these spirits were of a Christian nature: in the play they sing from the depths, not the heights, and they are more magical than religious.

Die Rose D745: three solo piano versions, 1838. The first verse is faithfully and simply transcribed, but in each version the second verse ushers in some of Liszt's most original writing with throbbing and deliberately disjointed syncopations and strange, piquant harmonies. It is curious that this rather simple and relatively little-known song should have given rise to some of Liszt's most daring transcriptions. The individual embroidery and breadth of thread varies from version to version, but all three are deliciously adventurous in their own ways, even if the extrovert pianism of some of the first version permits us to forget for a moment the fragility of the flower.

Apart from the handful of composers who made complete versions, most arrangers, including Liszt, were selective about which songs from **Die Schöne Müllerin** D795 they chose to transcribe. *Pause* was by far the least popular song, followed by *Des Baches Wiegenlied* and *Eifersucht und Stolz*, and Liszt was very unusual in choosing *Der Jäger*. On the other hand the first two songs in the cycle (*Das Wandern* and *Wohin?*) were exceedingly popular, as were *Der Neugierige* (although this song did not tempt Liszt), *Trockne Blumen* and *Der Müller und der Bach*.

Liszt's treatment of Schubert's three song cycles was to make of them pianistic sequences in their own right, although *Schwanengesang* was the only work of this kind to receive from him a full transcription. The composer chose six out of the twenty songs of *Die schöne Müllerin* (*Das Wandern, Der Müller und der Bach, Der Jäger, Die böse Farbe, Wohin?, Ungeduld* – in that order) and made from them an integrated work that is entirely unconcerned with the narrative sequence of the cycle. It is one of Liszt's characteristics that he takes Schubert's original tonalities very seriously (if he changed them this was normally associated with how one song could felicitously 'segue' into another when two numbers were run together) and he rearranges the songs into a garland where the strength and inevitability of the key scheme is of primary importance.

Das Wandern D795/1: two solo piano versions, 1846, 1879. This arrangement is in Schubert's original key of B flat. Despite all the pianistic activity it has charm and a certain serenity. Liszt's arrangement is two verses shorter than the original song. The second version of 1879 suggests that the young miller's propensity to perambulate has become the fond memory of a somewhat older man, a nostalgia for the high jinks of his younger days.

Wohin? D795/2: two solo piano versions, 1846. This prettily decorated arrangement strangely follows *Die böse Farbe* in Liszt's work – as if we were going backwards in Schubert's cycle in narrative terms. The transcription is in G major, Schubert's original key, and the melody is cleverly divided between the inner fingers of the two hands.

Ungeduld D795/7: three solo piano versions, 1844, 1879. Normally Liszt's second thoughts are simpler than his earlier inspirations but here the opposite is the case. There is a most exceptional and surprising coda to the second version ('extremely blue' in Leslie Howard's words), probably Liszt's sly comment on the fact that, for all the boy's ardent enthusiasm, his passion for the miller girl is doomed.

Der Jäger D795/14: This swift and formidable study in octaves and deft trills, in the original key of C minor, is placed on either side of the more substantial *Die böse Farbe* in Liszt's suite of Müllerin songs, thus framing that pivotal song (*see* below). There are two versions of this piece, both from 1846.

Die böse Farbe D795/17: two solo piano versions, 1846. At first we hear the tune of the song (in C major/minor rather than its original B major tonality) trumpeted out without the sextuplet accompaniment of the original, but these pulsations appear with a virtuosic and treacherous ebullience later in the arrangement. The return of *Der Jäger* is appropriate enough at the end – it is after all the hunter who has been the underlying cause of the miller boy's anguish.

Trockne Blumen D795/18: a single solo piano version, 1844, in C minor rather than the E minor of Schubert's original. The frozen and emotionally numb effect of the melody and its deliberately stark accompaniment is vitiated by Liszt's decorations in the second strophe. The high and tinny tessitura of the music when it proliferates in semiquavers – it becomes far too dance-like here – seems unworthy of the miller boy's grief and the strange majesty of the poetic conception. When Liszt so often veers towards the lugubrious, it is strange that his version of a dark and heartbreaking song here seems rather lightweight.

Der Müller und der Bach D795/19: two solo piano versions, 1846, 1879. This theme with gentle variations (in Schubert's original key of G minor) is held to be one of the finest of all Liszt's Schubert transcriptions, above all in the restraint and simplicity of the second version.

Liszt transcribed all fourteen songs of **Schwanengesang** D957 and his arrangements were eagerly issued by Tobias Haslinger of Vienna who had been the publisher of the original work. Throughout the cycle Liszt offers *ossia* staves for most of the music thus making allowances for pianists less accomplished than himself. This means that two versions of varying difficulty are published one on top of the other, rather confusingly for the eye. The less difficult version could not, however, be described as easy.

Unlike the Müller cycles, there is no narrative thread in these songs that might be

Liszt in 1856.

broken by Liszt's interventions and he seems unconcerned about attempting to separate the Rellstab settings from the Heine – two entirely different worlds of literary endeavour. Nevertheless, Liszt was always aware of the main thrust of a song's meaning, and it is probably no coincidence that he sets both these poets in his own lieder – Rellstab three times and Heine repeatedly. Liszt's *Schwanengesang – Vierzehn Lieder von Franz Schubert* adopts the following order: *Die Stadt, Das Fischermädchen, Aufenthalt, Am Meer, Abschied, In der Ferne, Ständchen, Ihr Bild, Frühlingssehnsucht, Liebesbotschaft, Der Atlas, Der Doppelgänger, Die Taubenpost, Kriegers Ahnung.* Except in the case of the four versions of *Ständchen*, these songs were all issued in two essentially similar solo versions in 1838/9.

Liebesbotschaft D957/1 [tenth in Liszt's sequence]: Liszt plays at shifting the vocal line from tenor to soprano in the course of an arrangement that is fairly faithful to Schubert, even if somewhat lugubrious and less translucent than its peerless original.

Kriegers Ahnung D957/2 [last in Liszt's sequence]: This is a symphonic poem of a transcription. It seems a curious piece to have chosen as the grand closing number for these *Vierzehn Lieder*, but Liszt has clearly been touched by the subject – a soldier's presentiments of doom and his 'Sehnsucht' for his loved one. The fleeting cadenza passages sound like frissons of fear or phantom shadows – pianistic embroidery on the darkness of the Schubert original. The passages where the soldier imagines himself back in his wife's arms are of a most lucid simplicity, a huge contrast to the warlike effects elsewhere in the transcription. It is clear that the composer wished to leave this mood of desperation hanging in the air as the prevailing flavour of the entire cycle – or at least in his version of it.

Frühlingssehnsucht D957/3 [ninth in Liszt's sequence]: This follows on without break from the transcription of *Ihr Bild* which fails to receive its final chord as the two songs are enjambed. This is a ferocious pianistic study in daunting challenges for the left hand as it leaps above and below the right in feats of nigh-impossible hand-crossing.

Ständchen D957/4 [seventh in Liszt's sequence]: four solo-piano versions, *c.* 1837 and 1838–9. Liszt is at first content to leave the beauty of Schubert's melody to speak for itself. In the second verse the tune is voiced down the octave and the canonic writing that ornaments the song's third and fourth verses is a gentle and teasing (if inauthentic) delight.

Aufenthalt D957/5 [third in Liszt's sequence]: The listener feels the shape and grandeur of the original song, if somewhat magnified. Indeed, Liszt's manner is ideal for this stormy essay in romantic word-painting.

In der Ferne D957/6 [sixth in Liszt's sequence]: The complexity of this arrangement necessitates a slower overall tempo than that required by a singer. The tune is so extended, and so portentous in manner, that Schubert's overall shape and the sheer urgency of his emotional agenda are hard to discern. One might call to mind a vast imaginary figure of Schubert, the artist as hero as depicted by Liszt, grimly traversing the bleak and limitless horizon.

Abschied D957/7 [fifth in Liszt's sequence]: This is fairly straightforward, in the original tonality of E flat major, but the textures are heavier and richer than Schubert's. There seems to be a surfeit of detail and too rich an overlay of chordal extravagance to capture the light-hearted trot of the singer's pony. Liszt cannot resist the temptation of thundering triplets, carried away by the foot-tapping moto perpetuo.

Der Atlas D957/8 [eleventh in Liszt's sequence]: The imagery and scale of the song's suffering fits the Lisztian manner like a glove. The pianist, Atlas-like, must shoulder the music's virtuosic challenges as part and parcel of the transcription's power.

Ihr Bild D957/9 [eighth in Liszt's sequence]: A very straightforward transcription, sounding at one point something like a Bach chorale. Such reticence is followed by the highly ornate arrangement of *Frühlingssehnsucht*. Liszt thus juxtaposes songs in B flat minor and B flat major, no doubt led to do so by their original tonalities. But from a textual and stylistic viewpoint the two songs have little in common.

Das Fischermädchen D957/10 [second in Liszt's sequence]: Liszt relies on the melody (written on a third stave in the bass clef, as if for a baritone) to makes its effect, although he cannot resist adding an extra final verse with a filigree of embellishments. These flowery blandishments tend to depict the singing protagonist as a devious and sweet-talking seducer, but whether or not this is a deliberate effect (Liszt was himself a famous seducer of women) is uncertain.

Die Stadt D957/11 [first in Liszt's sequence]: Liszt chose this mysterious and imposing song to open his book of *Schwanengesang* transcriptions. It is an arrangement in the grand manner which inclines to melodrama. He was one of the very few pianists of the time who was interested in this song as material for transcription. It was clearly far too avant-garde for most tastes.

Am Meer D957/12 [fourth in Liszt's sequence]: Liszt relies on the nobility of Schubert's original to make its point, considering further embroidery unnecessary to underline the pathos. His tremolos coincide with Schubert's own, and the broad open reaches of C major correspond exactly to the composer's original.

Der Doppelgänger D957/13 [twelfth in Liszt's sequence]: This is a relatively simple transcription and Liszt clearly knew that he had to do very little to capitalize on the drama and anguish built into the bare bones of the song. What he perhaps failed to realize was how much the dramatic quality of this music depends on the sheerly physical qualities that separate the sound of the human voice from that of the piano. The climax of the song, lacking the tension of the voice at full stretch, is disappointingly bland, with the piano unable to sustain the aural drama of long notes as a singer can, particularly at the top of the stave. It was perhaps in recognition of this that in 1860 Liszt orchestrated the song's accompaniment in an unusual manner as No. 5 of his *Sechs Lieder von Schubert* (*see* ORCHESTRATIONS).

Die Taubenpost D865A [thirteenth in Liszt's sequence]: Liszt clearly regards this beautiful melody with real affection. As sometimes happens in these pieces, the clever pianistic art of placing the vocal line between the hands, in the middle of the texture, slows the tempo and thickens the aerial texture of a Schubert song. The effect is to make the arrangement like a reminiscence of *Die Taubenpost*, or a meditation on it, rather than its immediate artless self.

Sei mir gegrüsst D741: single solo piano version, 1837–8. Schubert's own harmonic shifts in this song are exceptional enough for Liszt to feel no need to add modernistic touches. There are discreet passages, as if gently harp-accompanied, as well as barnstorming handfuls of chords where the melody is doubled in octaves between the hands.

Ständchen ('*Horch! Horch! die Lerch*') D889: two solo piano versions, 1837–8 and 1879. In B flat major instead of Schubert's original C major, this is one of Liszt's most charming and witty transcriptions. There is only one genuine strophe of Shakespeare in the Schubert setting, but Liszt allows himself a variation of great ingenuity and pianistic invention. In the first version the mood becomes perhaps a little loud and rambunctious for the sentiments of an aubade (marked fortissimo, *con fuoco* and, later, *marcatissimo*); accordingly, the 1879 version is more fragile and contained – altogether a delight.

Der Wanderer D489: two solo piano versions, 1837–8, 1879. This is a key work for Liszt both personally and musically. It begins simply (although chords throb in both hands, not only the right) but grows in complexity as the music moves forward, beginning with ominous chromatic interpolations in the left hand (interpreting no doubt 'es braust das Meer'). The middle section of the song is once again simple, with the wanderer's plaint accompanied as if by chords swept by the fingers across the strings of a minstrel's harp. Trills begin to rumble in the background and seraphic chordal writing introduces the section 'Wo bist du, mein geliebtes Land'. But this decoration (and the coruscating cadenza in right-hand octaves before the last appearance of 'Ich wandle still') does nothing to obscure the shape of a *durchkomponiert* song and the music ends faithfully where it should. It is as if Liszt reveres the music too much to add to it or change its form.

The number of composers choosing to transcribe a Schubert song is some indication of its contemporary popularity. Of **Winterreise** D911, *Gute Nacht* was a clear favourite as were *Der Lindenbaum*, *Die Post* and *Das Wirtshaus*. Completely ignored (except by those few composers who made transcriptions of the entire cycle) were *Die Wetterfahne*, *Auf dem Flusse* (surprisingly), *Rückblick* (rather less surprisingly), *Rast*, *Der greise Kopf*, *Die Krähe* (again, surprisingly) and *Letzte Hoffnung*. Only Liszt and Stephen Heller seem to have been interested in *Im Dorfe*. As he had with *Die schöne Müllerin*, Liszt took a selective view of *Winterreise*, choosing twelve songs from the twenty-four – four from the first book composed by Schubert in February 1827 (1, 4, 5 and 6) and eight from the second (13, 17, 18, 19, 21, 22, 23, 24) composed in November of the same year. Schubert's original structure is disregarded and a new sequence established (*Gute Nacht, Die Nebensonnen, Mut, Die Post, Erstarrung, Wasserflut, Der Lindenbaum, Der Leiermann, Täuschung, Das Wirtshaus, Der stürmsiche Morgen, Im Dorfe*). This reveals a strong ground plan in terms of interconnecting tonalities. Liszt's *Winterreise* thus begins with the same song as Schubert's, but ends with *Im Dorfe* (with a reprise of *Der stürmische Morgen* as a postlude), having used the famous last song, *Der Leiermann*, as a bridge passage into *Täuschung*. These twelve transcriptions were issued by the Viennese firm of Tobias Haslinger who had published the original *Winterreise* cycle in 1828. Except where otherwise noted, single versions of these transcriptions date from 1839.

Gute Nacht D911/1 [first in Liszt's sequence]: A very serious and unadorned opening (ingeniously notated on three staves) yields to a second verse that is hauntingly varied and embellished. By the third verse the semiquavers are cascading in every direction, and the gait of the trudging traveller is lost. The nobility of the change into the major key towards the end is vitiated by superfluous decoration.

Erstarrung D911/4 [fifth in Liszt's sequence]: The incorporation of the vocal melody into the piano part is both original and eccentric, displacing it from the beat in a manner that seems to drag it behind the bar line and emphasize it in a pathetic way. The notation on three staves is also unusual with exceptionally long stems for the melody notes concealed in the accompanying triplets. This is one of the most original arrangements of the set.

Der Lindenbaum D911/5 [seventh in Liszt's sequence]: two essentially similar solo piano versions, 1839. The florid piano writing of the original introduction is rendered more ornate still by a left-hand trill; a palimpsest of effects follows – chromatic scales that wrap themselves around the melody like gentle tendrils, then a more heavy-duty armoury of palpitating chords for the storm that is central to the song. A continuing right-hand trill high (B–C sharp) in the treble dominates the final verse like the ethereal closing pages of the 'Arietta' in Beethoven's Piano Sonata Op. 111.

Wasserflut D911/6 [sixth in Liszt's sequence]: Perhaps the most literal of these transcriptions, a sign that Liszt had great confidence in this music to make its point without further elaboration.

Die Post D911/13 [fourth in Liszt's sequence]: This is essentially a straightforward transcription with one or two extra musical interpolations, tiny palpitations of 'mein Herz' which mirror the narrator's inner doubts like self-questioning sighs.

Im Dorfe D911/17 [last in Liszt's sequence]: Liszt clearly regarded this great song as one of the most interesting of the cycle. It brings his suite of *Winterreise* transcriptions to an end (apart from the virtuosic recapitulation of *Der stürmische Morgen*) and begins with great simplicity and minimum added pianistic detail. This mood of restraint, apart from one or two decorative touches, is maintained throughout.

Der stürmische Morgen D911/18 [eleventh in Liszt's sequence]: two essentially similar solo piano versions, 1839. In Liszt's *Winterreise* set this song appears both before and after *Im Dorfe*. The descending arpeggios in diminished seventh harmony, familiar in the original accompaniment, are here extended down the keyboard to almost comic effect, as if the player were in danger of falling off. At the very end, after we have heard *Im Dorfe*, these rattling arpeggios are cranked up in ever-rising tonal shifts to bring Liszt's twelve-song version of the cycle to a finish in a real wintry flurry.

Täuschung D911/19 [ninth in Liszt's sequence]: This song in a rather simple, only moderately ornamented version follows directly from *Der Leiermann*. Liszt obviously relished the suggestion of an upper pedal in the piano writing of the right hand (echoes of his *Das Sterbeglöcklein; see Das Zügenglöcklein*) as well as a chance to juxtapose songs in A minor and A major.

Das Wirtshaus D911/21 [tenth in Liszt's sequence]: two essentially similar solo piano versions, 1839. The beauty and pathos of the chorale-like melody clearly bewitched Liszt. He allows the powerful melodic line to speak for itself at first, but then cannot resist embellishment and even significant alterations of harmony. These are sometimes so daringly 'blue' that here and there they resemble the jazz chords of quite another era. The final passage of the first version is bathed in tremolos and trills and achieves a particularly Lisztian pianistic transcendence – clearly his tribute to the uplifting effect that Schubert's music had on him.

Mut D911/22 [third in Liszt's sequence]: two essentially similar solo piano versions, 1839. Just when the listener, or challenged player, imagines this to be a straightforward transcription, there is an outbreak of devilish decorative detail that embellishes the courage and determination of the original.

Die Nebensonnen D911/23 [second in Liszt's sequence]: three solo piano versions, 1839. The transcription of the melody is essentially simple at first, but at the change into the minor key and with a section marked 'Recit: patetico', it changes into greater rhetorical majesty. This almost triumphant and ornate outpouring seems far from the haunted whisperings of a broken man in a song mostly marked pianissimo, but then Liszt thinks in larger theatrical terms, and Müller's scenario as a progressive narrative decline is not his concern. Although he is by no means unaware of the poems' meanings, Liszt's response is first and foremost to the melodic and harmonic riches of Schubert's songs, each one taken on its own musical terms. Here he transposes Schubert's A major original, unusually, into B flat major.

Der Leiermann D911/24 [eighth in Liszt's sequence]: This song is reduced to its bare bones – it had not yet acquired the huge expressionistic and psychological significance ascribed to it by later generations of listeners. Here it serves as a shortened introduction to *Täuschung*.

Das Zügenglöcklein D871: a single solo piano version, 1844. This is perhaps the most intricate and freest of all the Liszt Schubert song transcriptions. The title *Zügenglöcklein* was an Austrianism for *Das Sterbeglöcklein*, the passing bell which is Liszt's title. The tune of the song is not particularly famous, and it is not one of Schubert's most memorable melodies, yet it has definite and recognizable harmonic contours and fascinating use of an upper pedal note. This frees Liszt to build a substantial set of variations around the idea of these thoughts of death at eventide where every trick of the trade in terms of his pianistic eloquence is employed to make a work of considerable refinement and invention.

The famous pianist **Sigismund Thalberg** (1812–1874) made arrangements of *Die Post* D911/13 and *Täuschung* D911/19 from *Winterreise*.

The Hungarian-born, Paris-based, **Stephen Heller** (1813–1888) was admired by Schumann and was a friend of Chopin and Liszt. Heller transcribed thirty Schubert songs for solo piano in his Op. 30 alone (when other opus numbers are added the tally is nearer to fifty), choosing many of the same titles selected by Liszt. Heller's transcriptions date from 1844 to 1847 which suggests that he followed closely in the master's footsteps. He was not immune to the salon fashions of the time: his transcription of *Die Forelle* (Op. 33) is a *Caprice brillant*, of *Die Post* (Op. 35) an *Improvisata* and of *Lob der Tränen* (Op. 36) a *Morceau de salon*. It is interesting that he adopted Liszt's practice of incorporating several Schubert songs within a larger structure: the *Fantasiestück* Op. 54 has the subtitle of *Grande Fantaisie auf Lieder von Schubert*. It was thanks to Heller that Bizet and Massenet came to know the Schubert songs.

Louis Winkler (b. 1813) was organist in Braunschweig. For piano duet he arranged *An Emma* D113 (not encountered elsewhere), *Auf dem Wasser zu singen* D774, *Erlkönig* D328, *Die Forelle* D550, *Frühlingsglaube* D686, *Gretchen am Spinnrade* D118 and *Der Wanderer* D489. The Berlin composer **Theodor Oesten** (1813–1879) received a reproving entry in Mendel-Reissmann's *Musikalisches Lexikon* for betraying his own talent by becoming too commercial in his aims – he made many hundreds of transcriptions. His Schubert-inspired arrangements are of all the usual titles, although he is one of the very few to have tackled *Der Tod und das Mädchen* D531 and *Der König in Thule* D367. He was the only composer who made a transcription of *Ellens Gesang I* D837 and the Kosegarten setting *Erinnerung* D229. **Heinrich Cramer** (b. 1816) – no relation of the infinitely more famous Johann Baptist Cramer – was a similar hack and regarded by his contemporaries as such. He made solo piano arrangements of *Abschied* D957/7 (Rellstab), *Auf dem Wasser zu singen*, *Drang in die Ferne* D770, *Des Mädchens Klage* D191.

Alexandre Batta (1816–1902) was a Belgian cellist who arranged several Schubert songs for cello and piano. **Fritz Spindler** (1817–1905) was a respected Saxon composer who made numerous Schubert transcriptions. The titles that show some individual initiative on Spindler's part in straying from the well-trodden Lisztian path are *Der Alpenjäger* D524, *An die Musik*, *Auf dem See* D543, *Der König in Thule* D367, *Lachen und Weinen*

Cover of Stephen Heller's transcription of *Die Forelle*.

D777, *Normans Gesang* D846, *Die Sterne* D939, *Wandrers Nachtlied I* D224 and *Wandrers Nach-tlied II* D768.

Franz Abt (1818–1885), choirmaster at Zurich and later conductor in Braunschweig, was a noted expert in choral music. His arrangements of Schubert songs are mostly for SATB and piano. **Friedrich Ferdinand Brissler** (1818–1893) was considered an expert in the composition and arrangement of piano music for four hands. He made a duet version of *Erlkönig*.

The French composer **Charles Gounod** (1818–1893) made an arrangement for violin, cello, physharmonika and piano of *Die junge Nonne*.

Louis Köhler (1820–1886), born in Braunschweig, was another arranger of piano duets. He was a pupil of Sechter and the pianist Bocklet in Vienna (both colleagues of Schubert, of course) and became professor in Königsberg. His duet arrangements include *Erlkönig* D328, *Die Forelle* D550, *Die junge Nonne* D828, *Nacht und Träume* D827 and *Der Wanderer*. He transcribed *Ellens dritter Gesang* D839 for piano and cello (or violin) and harmonium.

The violinist **Michael (Miska) Hauser** (1822–1887) was born in Pressburg and died in Vienna. He toured South America, California and Australia and wrote a book about his world-wide journeys. Hauser arranged a large number of Schubert songs for violin and piano – all the usual ones, as well as others seldom found on the transcriber's table. The latter included *Der Leiermann* at a time when this strange masterpiece was ignored by most arrangers. Hauser is by far the most prolific of the violinist arrangers of Schubert songs, though Nottebohm informs us that one **B. Hunyadi** arranged *Erlkönig* for unaccompanied violin.

Carl Reinecke (1824–1910), famous conductor, composer and teacher who finished his career and life in Leipzig, arranged the whole of *Die schöne Müllerin* D795 for solo piano, and orchestrated *Der Hirt auf dem Felsen* D965.

The Belgian cellist **Guillaume Paque** (1825–1876) who lived and worked in both Madrid and London transcribed three uncommon Schubert songs for cello and piano: *Am See* D746 (Bruchmann), *Erlafsee* D586 and *Der Blumenbrief* D672. **Joseph Stransky** (d. 1872) also contributed cello arrangements including two Seidl settings, *Wiegenlied* D867 and *Sehnsucht* D879, that were not arranged elsewhere, as well as Mayrhofer's *Nachtstück* D672.

Alexander Wilhelm Gottschlag (1827–1908), friend and colleague of Liszt in Weimar, transcribed *Das Marienbild* D623 and *Vom Mitleiden Mariä* D632 for organ.

The violinist **Friedrich Hermann** (1828–1907) was born in Frankfurt and lived in Leipzig. He was commissioned by Peters to make a complete edition of *Die schöne Müllerin* for the following forces: violin and piano, solo piano, flute and piano and cello and piano. *Schwanengesang* was issued complete for both violin and cello with piano.

Johann Herbeck (1831–1877), the most famous Schubertian in this article after Liszt, arranged *Jagdlied* D521 from *Die Nacht* for four male voices, and for mixed choir the songs *Vom Mitleiden Mariä*, *Am Tage aller Seelen (Litanei)* and *Himmelsfunken* D651. A fuller account of Herbeck is given under SCHOLARS.

Karl Bial (1833–1892) was conductor at the Kroll in Berlin. He made a number of arrangements for harmonium including *Das Wirtshaus* from *Winterreise* D911/2. The composers **L. Montlevrin** and **P. Renk** made several transcriptions for zither.

Géza Zichy (1849–1924) was a Hungarian count, friend of Liszt and probably the first person in history to create a career as a pianist for left-hand repertoire (Zichy had lost his hand in a hunting accident as a young man). Zichy's transcription of *Erlkönig* for the left hand alone was famous for its difficulty and ingenuity.

In the last thirty years of the nineteenth century it became increasingly unfashionable, and also perhaps unnecessary, to transcribe the lieder of Schubert. Instead composers attempted to add instrumental colour and their own individuality to Schubert's original thoughts. This is a trend that began with Berlioz and continued with Brahms, and it carries on very much to the present day (see ORCHESTRATIONS).

There remain for consideration, however, two pianists, both princes of the keyboard, who contributed to the field of Schubert song transcription for solo piano – the first much more substantially than the second.

Leopold Godowsky

Leopold Godowsky (1870–1938) was, like Liszt, among the greatest pianists of his time. The American critic Harold Schonberg described Godowsky as having 'the most perfect pianistic mechanism of the period and very likely of all time'. He was 'the master of us all' according to no less a pianist than Josef Hofmann, who was the dedicatee of Godowsky's twelve transcriptions of Schubert songs which were first published in 1927, and reissued in a revised edition in 1937. The entire vocal line in the original key was printed separately for each song, with the text printed in both German and English. Godowsky was born into a poor Polish family but enjoyed one of the most international careers in an epoch when artists moved between countries and various homes with even greater freedom than they do in the modern age. He was a protégé of Saint-Saëns as a young man in Paris (where he encountered Gounod, Fauré and Massenet among many others) and went on to live, and marry, in the United States. In 1900 he returned to Europe where he gave one of the most sensational piano recitals in the concert history of Berlin and overnight became one of the highest-priced instrumentalists in the world. His encores included his hair-raising difficult arrangements of Chopin's Études where two of that composer's studies, one in each hand, were famously combined. Godowsky made his base in Berlin, and later Vienna, before moving back to America in 1914. He was famously gregarious and hospitable and numbered countless great artists of the time as his friends, including other pianists. Among his guests and admirers were to be found luminaries such as Busoni, Scriabin, Mahler, Prokofiev, Lehár, Stravinsky, Gershwin and Rachmaninoff.

In the foreword to his *Schubert Songs, freely transcribed for the piano*, Godowsky writes:

My aim in transcribing these twelve songs of Schubert was not merely to transplant them from the voice to the piano: it was to create piano compositions out of the vocal material, to comment upon and interpret the songs as a composer would treat a theme when writing free variations. I tried in vain to find a suitable term to describe correctly the character of my work. I have had to revert to the vague and colourless designation of 'free transcription'. To those who are open-minded, sympathetic and understanding, these Schubert versions will proclaim my love and veneration for the composer and his immortal songs . . . A masterpiece is indestructible. It remains untarnished whether transcribed, arranged or paraphrased, and its intrinsic value, having the necessary vitality to sustain its interest, cannot be impaired . . .

Novels are dramatized and dramas are novelized. Why should musicians be denied the privileges of comment, criticism, dissertation, discussion, and display of imaginative faculties when transcribing, arranging, or paraphrasing a standard work! Why should the literary man alone enjoy all the prerogatives! Shakespeare built his plays upon borrowed themes, and Molière said: 'Je prends mon bien où je le trouve'.

THE GODOWSKY SCHUBERT TRANSCRIPTIONS

An Mignon D161: Godowsky makes much of Schubert's rather inconsequential two-bar introduction and repeats this between each of his five strophes – the same number as in the Schubert song. Inspired by the sad and languishing mood of the words of the final verse, he does something that Schubert, restricted by his strophic accompaniment, is unable to do: he simplifies the music to plaintive triplets played pianissimo. The effect of this, disappointing as a finale for the average barnstorming pianist, must have been magical in Godowsky's own performance. The key is F minor.

Am Tage aller Seelen (Litanei) D343: This is an almost comic mismatch between the tranquillity of the original and the transcendental virtuosity of the arrangement. Godowsky himself might have been able to play all these notes while retaining the pianissimo of the markings, but in most hands this hectic grandiloquence, despite being pianistically ingenious, seems very distant from the Schubert. The transcription is in F major, a tone up from the original.

Die Forelle D550: In the key of B flat major ('Allegretto vivace') rather than the D flat of the original, this song is ideal for Godowsky's treatment with a whimsical four-bar introduction and a shape that faithfully reflects that of the original. The drama of the trout's demise occasions greater pyrotechnics. The four-bar postlude, an ascending arabesque in whirlwind triplets, is entirely Godowsky's and typical of his pianistic legerdemain in preludes and postludes of this kind.

Heidenröslein D257: This is a charming transcription, faithful to the original, where the insouciance of the added chromatic harmony, although clearly anachronistic as far as Schubert is concerned, adds something to the portrait of the happy-go-lucky young man and his imprudent courtship of the rose. In its gently sly imperturbability the music is reminiscent of the *Wohin?* transcription of Rachmaninoff (*see* below).

Die junge Nonne D828: In this palimpsest of pianistically demanding detail, the noble spirit, as well as the melody, of the Schubert is lost although the original F minor tonality is retained. Godowsky is at his best, it seems, when transcribing strophic songs with memorable melodies and less complex original accompaniments. To capture both elements at the same time results in overkill.

Das Wandern D795/1 from *Die Schöne Müllerin*: As in Schubert's original there are five verses, each increasingly pianistically demanding. In the fourth strophe the melody is placed in the left hand, and the final verse is wreathed in semiquaver triplets as if prophesying the miller's meeting with the brook in the next song, *Wohin?* This arrangement is in G major, a sixth higher than the original.

Wohin? D795/2: Marked 'Allegretto mormorando', with a chromatic two-bar introduction, this transcription, despite its pianistic complexity, is faithful to the mood and spirit of the song, and also its correct tempo. It is impossible to play this music in the clipped and hurried tempo sometimes incorrectly adopted for the original by singers and pianists. It is clear that Godowsky knew these songs not from the score alone, but from attending recitals given by fine singers.

Ungeduld D795/7: The perpetual internal chromatic movement of the triplets, the layers of imitative counterpoint as the verses progress, the increasingly outrageous demands made on the pianist's dexterity, make this a veritable showpiece to bring the composer's collection of transcriptions to a joyful close. We note here in particular how Godowsky writes for a completely independent left hand which is expected to be as ambidextrously able as the right. For the final strophe right-hand semiquavers are combined with left-hand triplets as the music whirrs to its dizzying conclusion.

Morgengruss D795/8: Godowsky's transcription is in G flat major, far from the song's original C major. It is three, rather than four, strophes long – for the last of these, the poet's fourth verse, he is clearly inspired by the words 'Die Lerche wirbelt in der Luft' where the lark ascends and twitters in the higher reaches of the keyboard. The mounting intensity of the writing is an accurate reflection of the miller boy's emotions and the proliferation of his romantic fantasies concerning the maid of the mill. In a performance of the song cycle this hopeless adoration of the girl, to the point of unhealthy obsession, would be up to the singer to convey. Here the complexity of the piano writing admirably conveys the anomaly of someone singing a simple melody overlaid with a tormented emotional agenda, although Godowsky's own recording of this work is remarkably peaceful and seraphic – a beautiful singing tone, and the lightest of touches for the accompanying filigree.

Liebesbotschaft D957/1 from *Schwanengesang*: Godowsky changes the demisemiquavers of the original into semiquavers, but otherwise this is a relatively straightforward (though by no means easy to play) transcription. The vocal line is placed in the tenor register of the keyboard and shared between the hands.

Wiegenlied D498: This beguiling tune, also quoted by Richard Strauss in the opera *Ariadne auf Naxos*, occasions a quiet and gentle transcription (in E flat rather than A flat) overlaid with non-Schubertian chromaticisms and canonic affects, with the melody appearing in the left hand and between the hands.

Gute Nacht D911/1 from *Winterreise*: Godowsky's love of imitative counterpoint and richness of texture is reflected here, but this arrangement, rather unlike Liszt's, remains faithful to the serious mood and length of the original although it is transposed up a tone into E minor. At the beginning of Verse 4, Godowsky reserves the celebrated change into the major key for the vocal line ('*ppp* dolcissimimo') on the fourth beat of the bar rather than the accompaniment on the first beat, a deviation that shows Schubert to have been more inspired. There is little to compare with the heartbreaking poignancy of that preparatory nimbus of D major that in the original underlies and supports the entry of the voice three quavers later.

Serge Rachmaninoff (1873–1943) made wonderful recordings of two of the Liszt song transcriptions – *Das Wandern* and *Ständchen*. In 1925 he composed his only transcription of a Schubert song, **Wohin?** D795/2 It is in the original key of G major and maintains the imperturbable rhythm (with the exception of a tiny cadenza on the third page) of Schubert's sextuplets in semiquavers. The charm of the arrangement is less dependent on velocity of finger than on Rachmaninoff's rueful harmonic twists. These add an anachronistically 'blue' or jazzy note to the shy vocal melody which is transcribed more or less at pitch as it appears on the printed score, thus sounding an octave higher than the tenor or baritone voice. The composer's own recorded performance of this piece, apparently a trifle but in reality extremely tricky to play, is marvellously nonchalant, seeming to cost him no effort at all. The postlude evaporates into thin air, and with it pretty much the whole tradition of song transcription by the great composer–pianists – although the British pianist Stephen Hough has revived it in recent years.

It is perhaps appropriate that a postlude to this article should be provided by two famous accompanists. The first of these, **Michael Raucheisen** (1889–1984), was the leading German *Lied-*

begleiter between the wars (*see* PIANISTS). In 1927 he made three charming arrangements for the husband and wife team, the soprano Maria Ivogün and the tenor Karl Erb. *Frühlingsgesang* D740, *Der Gondelfahrer* D809 (the same work transcribed by Liszt at the end of his career) and *Die Nachtigall* were all male-voice quartets which Raucheisen arranged as duets for two high voices and piano. Raucheisen's English counterpart was **Gerald Moore** (1899–1987) who enjoyed the pre-eminent place among accompanists in the post-war years. Universal Edition published six Schubert songs edited by Moore in which suggestions for rubato and other interpretative details were incorporated in the scores. In the early 1960s Oxford University Press published a number of songs in solo piano arrangements by Moore, including Schubert's *An die Musik* D547. It was this arrangement that he chose to play at the Royal Festival Hall, the last music to be heard in his famous farewell recital of February 1967.

TRANSPOSITION *see* TONALITY AND TRANSPOSITION

TRAUER DER LIEBE   Love's sorrows
(JACOBI) **D465** [H291]

The song exists in two versions, both of which are discussed below:
(1) August 1816; (2) November 1816?

(1)   A♭ major

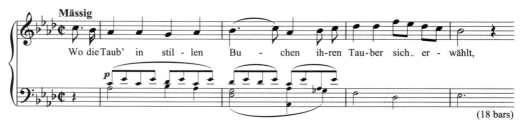

(18 bars)

(2)   'Mässig'   A♭ major   ₵   [20 bars]

Wo die Taub' in stillen Buchen	When the dove, in silent beeches,
Ihren Tauber sich erwählt,	Chooses her mate,
Wo sich Nachtigallen suchen,	Where nightingales seek one another
Und die Rebe sich vermählt;	And vines intertwine;
Wo die Bäche sich vereinen,	Where streams meet
Ging ich oft mit leichtem Scherz,	I often walked, in gentle melancholy,
Ging ich oft mit bangem Weinen,	Or with anxious tears
Suchte mir ein liebend Herz.	In search of a loving heart.
O, da gab die finstre Laube	There the dark foliage
Leisen Trost im Abendschein;	Gave gentle comfort in the glow of evening;
O, da kam ein süsser Glaube	With the light of morning
Mit dem Morgenglanz im Hain;	A sweet belief came to me in the grove;
Da vernahm ich's in den Winden,	I heard it in the winds,

Ihr Geflüster lehrte mich:	Their whispering told me
Dass ich suchen sollt und finden,	That I should search
Finden, holde Liebe, dich!	And find you, fairest love.
Aber ach! wo blieb auf Erden,	But alas, where on earth
Holde Liebe, deine Spur?	Did any trace of you remain?
Lieben, um geliebt zu werden,	To love, in order to be loved in turn,
Ist das Los der Engel nur.	Is the fate of angels alone.
Statt der Wonne fand ich Schmerzen,	Instead of happiness I found only sorrow.
Hing an dem, was mich verliess;	And clung to that which deserted me;
Frieden gibt den treuen Herzen	Peace is given to faithful hearts
Nur ein künftig Paradies.	Only in a future paradise.

JOHANN GEORG JACOBI (1740–1814); poem written between 1775 and 1782

This is the fifth of Schubert's seven Jacobi solo settings (1816). See the poet's biography for a chronological list of all the Jacobi settings.

John Reed calls the style of the music demotic, and if this song reminds us of *Die Zauberflöte* it is because the spirit of Mozart hovers gently over Schubert when he decides to ravish us with the simplest of vocal lines, inimitable and unanswerable. The minor key makes no appearance in this piece, which is surprising for such a melancholy poem, but of course Schubert always avoided the obvious means of expressing unhappiness through music. There is pathos here (note the exceptional harmonization of the word 'Weinen' in b. 14) but nothing exceeds the pastoral frame laid down by the conventions of the poetry. There are two versions printed in the NSA; the first, dated August 1816, is the version long accepted as definitive. The second 'Fassung' with a probable date of November 1816 was written out for the Therese Grob song album. This has tiny differences in the markings, an important chordal difference at 'Weinen' (b. 14 where the B flat bass note is missing from what had been a chord of a fifth), and a four-bar (instead of a two-bar) postlude. This is also unexpectedly Mozartian: the dotted rhythms and the shape of the melody irresistibly recall the march music that Figaro sings to Cherubino – 'Non più andrai' from *Le nozze di Figaro*.

It is unlikely that the Jacobi songs of August 1816 were conceived as a set, but four of them make a remarkable little sequence that works well in performance, particularly in terms of tonalities. In this progression the love song *An Chloen* D462 in A flat major is followed by the joyous *Hochzeit-Lied* D463 in E flat major; then the slow *In der Mitternacht* D464 (also in E flat major, yet conveniently beginning in C minor) makes a fine contrast of mood before a return to A flat major for *Trauer der Liebe*. It is impossible to argue that this was ever Schubert's intention, but such a juxtaposition might plausibly bring a group of neglected Schubert songs to the recital platform in a workable grouping.

Autographs:	Conservatoire collection, Bibliothèque Nationale, Paris (first version)
	In private possession in Switzerland (second version; Therese Grob songbook)
Publication:	First published as a solo piano arrangement by Kratochwill, Vienna in 1876; and with vocal line as Vol. 7 no. 11 in Friedlaender's edition by Peters, Leipzig in 1885 (P475; first version)
	First published as part of the NSA in 2002 (P840; second version)

Subsequent editions:	Peters: Vol. 7/26; AGA XX 247: Vol. 4/152; NSA IV: Vol. 10/206 & 208
Discography and timing:	Fischer-Dieskau I 7³³ 1'55
	Hyperion I 8¹²
	Hyperion II 15¹⁸ 1'54 Sarah Walker

← *In der Mitternacht* D464   *Die Perle* D466 →

TRAUER UMFLIESST MEIN LEBEN *see* KLAGE D371

Der TRAUM   The dream
(Hölty) **D213** [H107]
A major   17 June 1815

(17 bars)

Mir träumt', ich war ein Vögelein,	I dreamt I was a little bird,
Und flog auf ihren Schoss;¹	And flew on to her lap,
Und zupft' ihr, um nicht lass zu sein,	And, so as not to be idle,
Die Busenschleifen los;	Loosened the bows around her breast.
Und flog, mit gaukelhaftem Flug,	Then I flitted playfully
Dann auf die weisse Hand,	On to her white hand
Dann wieder auf das Busentuch,	Then back on to her bodice,
Und pickt' am roten Band.	And pecked at its red ribbon.
Dann schwebt' ich auf ihr blondes Haar,	Then I glided on to her fair hair
Und zwitscherte vor Lust,	And twittered with pleasure
Und ruhte, wann ich müde war,	And when I grew weary
An ihrer weissen Brust.	I rested on her white breast.
Kein Veilchenbett' im Paradies	There is no violet bed in paradise
Geht diesem Lager vor.	Which can surpass that resting place.
Wie schlief sich's da so süss, so süss	How sweetly I would sleep
An ihres Busens Flor!	On her beauteous breast.
Sie spielte, wie ich tiefer sank,	As I sank deeper she fondled me
Mit leisem Fingerschlag,	With a gentle touch of her fingers
Der mir durch Leib und Leben drang,	That ran through my body and soul,

¹ Punctuation is according to the Viennese edition of Hölty's poems (Kaulfuss und Armbruster, 1815).

Mich frohen Schlummrer wach.	Awakening me from my happy slumber.
Sah mich so wunderfreundlich an,	She gazed at me with such wondrous kindness,
Und bot den Mund mir dar,	And offered me her lips
Dass ich es nicht beschreiben kann,	That I cannot describe
Wie froh, wie froh ich war.	How happy I was.
Da trippelt' ich auf einem Bein,	Then I hopped about on one leg
Und hatte so mein Spiel	As a game
Und spielt' ihr mit dem Flügelein	And with my little wings
Die rote Wange kühl.	Playfully cooled her red cheeks.
Doch ach! Kein Erdenglück besteht,	But, alas, no earthly happiness endures,
Tag sei es oder Nacht!	Whether it be day or night!
Schnell war mein süsser Traum verweht,	Swiftly my dream vanished,
Und ich war aufgewacht.	And I awoke.

LUDWIG HÖLTY (1748–1776); poem written in 1775

This is the tenth of Schubert's twenty-three Hölty solo settings (1813–16). See the poet's biography for a chronological list of all the Hölty settings.

Some of Schubert's most irresistible outdoor music is in A major, including such different works as the famous *Das Lied im Grünen* D917 and Hölty's love song among the apple trees, *An die Apfelbäume, wo ich Julien erblickte* D197. It is no surprise that the composer also associates the flight of birds, the epitome of outdoor freedom, with this key, notably the 1820 Schlegel setting *Die Vögel* D691, and the same poet's *Der Knabe* D692, in which a boy dreams about how wonderful it would be to be free as a bird. This song is a rather more frank, even lascivious, version of a young man's fantasies about 'birds', but the key is still A major. It is strange that the ornithological music it most resembles is not by Schubert at all, but by Brahms: in the sixth of the *Liebeslieder* waltzes Op. 52 'Ein kleiner, hübscher Vogel', an A major song in a cheeky, loping gait, the singer also fantasizes about being a bird. But then Brahms knew his Schubert, and drew from him: *Der Traum* appeared in Vienna in 1865 (three years before the composition of the Brahms waltzes) as Schubert's posthumous Op. 172, an opus number put together by the publisher Spina, and also including *Die Vögel*.

On the printed page in the AGA the song appears to be from a much earlier age. There is no separate vocal line: the voice doubles the piano in the manner of Haydn's German songs, or many of the works of Reichardt and Zelter. In the absence of an autograph we have to rely on Albert Stadler's copy of the song, and it is Stadler who notated the song in this way. Whether Schubert himself intended to do so is a moot point; perhaps the short-score version copied by Stadler was only the composer's interim sketch as opposed to the finished article. The NSA presents the song in the normal manner on three staves. It is likely that the ornamentation in the vocal line is not also meant for the piano – to perform such decoration with accurate ensemble is well-nigh impossible.

The sheer Viennese charm of the music stems from Mozart and that most famous of bird-catchers, Papageno. There could be no stronger evidence of Schubert's astonishing unpredict-ability in the matter of length and content of his songs than this little gem of an erotic dream's place directly after the gigantic *Adelwold und Emma* D211 in the Deutsch catalogue. Perhaps after living with Emma's much vaunted purity for nine days, the young composer needed to get to grips with a 'bird' untrammelled by a gilded cage.

Autograph: Missing or lost
First edition: Published as Op. post. 172 no. 1 by C. A. Spina in 1865 (P401)
Subsequent editions: Peters: Vol. 6/96; AGA XX 80: Vol. 2/158; NSA IV: Vol. 8/100
Discography and timing: Fischer-Dieskau I 4^2 1'24   (first two strophes only)
                              Hyperion I 10^{14}
                              Hyperion II 7^6 2'19   Martyn Hill

← *Die Nonne* D211   *Die Laube* D214 →

TRINKLIED (Freunde, sammelt euch im Kreise)   Drinking song   Quartet, TTBB
(SCHÄFFER?) **D75** [H26]
C major   29 August 1813

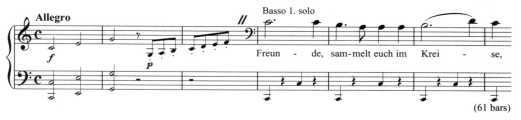

(61 bars)

Freunde, sammelt euch im Kreise,   Friends, gather in a circle.
Freut euch nach der Väter Weise,   Rejoice in the manner of our fathers;
Stimmt in lautem Jubel ein.   Join in loud jubilation.

Freundschaft reicht den Wonnebecher   Friendship offers the cup of joy
Zum Genuss dem frohen Zecher,   For the happy toper's pleasure;
Perlend blinkt der gold'ne Wein.   The golden, sparkling wine beckons.

Schliesst in dieser Feierstunde   In this hour of celebration
Hand in Hand zum trauten Bunde,   Join your hands in convivial union;
Freunde, stimmet fröhlich ein,   Friends, lend your joyful voices;
Lasst uns alle Brüder sein!   Let us all be brothers.

Freunde, seht die Gläser blinken,   Friends, behold the gleaming glasses.
Knaben mögen Wasser trinken,   Let boys drink water;
Männer trinken edlen Wein.   Men drink noble wine.

Wie der gold'ne Saft der Reben   May our life always be
Sei auch immer unser Leben,   Strong and robust, gentle and pure
Stark und kräftig, mild und rein.   To honour our bond of friendship.

Unsern Freundesbund zu ehren   Let us empty our glasses!
Lasset uns die Gläser leeren!   May our life and our wine
Stark und kräftig, mild und rein   Always be strong and robust,
Sei das Leben, sei der Wein!   Gentle and pure.

FRIEDRICH SCHÄFFER? (1772–1800)

This jolly little piece is the first of a number of drinking songs in the Schubert catalogue that demonstrate a continuing enthusiasm for this bibulous pastime. The unaccompanied songs in this list marked with an asterisk fall outside the scope of these commentaries:

Trinklied (Castelli) for tenor, male voice chorus and piano, D148 (1815)
Trinklied (Zettler) for single voices, chorus and piano, D183 (1815)
*Trinklied im Winter (Hölty) for trio of unaccompanied male voices, D242 (1815)
Trinklied (unknown) quartet for male voices and piano, D267 (1815)
Trinklied (unknown) fragment for voice and male chorus, D356 (1816)
*Trinklied (Herr Bacchus ist ein braver Mann) Male trio D426 (1816, disappeared since 1858)
*Trinklied im Mai (Hölty) for trio of unaccompanied male voices, D427 (1816)
Trinklied (Shakespeare) for solo voice and piano, D888 (1826)
*Trinklied aus dem 16. Jahrhundert (Gräffer) for quartet of unaccompanied male voices, D847 (1825)

In addition to these *Trinklieder* there are two songs in praise of punch entitled *Punschlied*, and the glories of the grape are extolled in a number of other songs, for example the two settings of Schiller's *Dithyrambe* D47 and D801. The first of these, D47, begins in a similar way to this song with its loud fanfare of tonic, mediant and dominant – perhaps a drinking motif. Although there is every sign that this prototype *Trinklied* is a *pièce d'occasion* (specially written for a gathering, probably of his school chums during their holiday break), Schubertian individuality is not inaudible. True, there is a bow to traditional formulae in the opening contrasts of forte chords and scurrying piano quavers (like the opening of a Beethoven piano sonata), but there is a compact elegance about the music (and a practised way of writing for the bass voice and chorus) demonstrating that the vine is not the only thing capable of bearing fruit. If he was temporarily on holiday from Salieri's influence (and the high-flown texts of Metastasio he was required to set as composition exercises), these Italian masters had definitely helped the young Schubert to attain a new level of proficiency.

   This was the sort of thing that the composer was capable of putting together in an hour on the day of the party, but in the absence of a photocopier he would also have had to write out the parts. He was soon to become even busier. The season of 1813–14 was about to begin, and with it a new and exciting period of his musical life. This clinking of glasses heralds the close of adolescence and the beginning of Schubert's emotional and musical independence. But even at this early stage of his life, sadness is inextricably mixed with jollity. Only three days earlier (and the news had probably not yet reached Vienna), one of his heroes, the poet Theodor Körner, had been killed in battle.

Autograph: In private possession
First edition: Published as Book 45 no. 2 of the *Nachlass* by Diabelli, Vienna in
                               January 1850 (P371)
Subsequent editions: AGA XVI 16: p. 128; NSA III: Vol. 3
Discography and timing: Hyperion I 33[17]   Michael George with John Mark Ainsley,
                               Hyperion II 2[23]   2'59   Jamie MacDougall & Simon Keenlyside

← *Thekla (eine Geisterstimme)* D73   *Pensa, che questo istante* D76 →

TRINKLIED

(Castelli) **D148** [H63]

C major   February 1815

Drinking song   Tenor & TTB chorus

(28 bars)

Eine Stimme:	One voice:
Brüder! unser Erdenwallen	Brothers, our earthly wandering
Ist ein ew'ges S t e i g e n , F a l l e n ,	Is eternal *climbing and falling*,
Bald hinauf, und bald hinab;	Now up, now down.
In dem drängenden Gewühle	Amid life's teeming throng
Giebt's der Gruben gar so viele,	There are so many hollows,
Und die letzte ist das Grab.	And the last one is the grave.

C h o r :	Chorus:
Darum, Brüder! schenket ein,	So, brothers, fill your glasses.
Muss es schon gesunken sein,	If we're to go under soon,
Sinken wir berauscht vom Wein.	Let's go under intoxicated by wine.

[. . . 7 . . .]   [. . . 7 . . .]

Ignaz Franz Castelli (1781–1862)

This ensemble was composed shortly after Schubert's eighteenth birthday. The regular appearance of convivial drinking songs in 1815 suggests that the composer was writing these choruses for his schoolfriends who, like many young men on the threshold of adult life, were not strangers to experimental over-indulgence when it came to alcohol. The term 'Schubertiad' refers strictly speaking to the musical gatherings of 1821 and later, but there is little doubt that these celebrated parties were the climactic point of a long-established tradition of music-making, dancing and alcohol that had begun in Schubert's teens.

Schubert's source for this work was the almanac *Selam* for 1815. This volume provided him with more than the text: as a supplement to the pocket-sized publication was a printed setting of the words by Antonio Saleiri for solo tenor, unison male choir and piano. Salieri, as was his wont, wrote the vocal line in the old-fashioned soprano clef, but the publishers of *Selam* printed it in the G clef which would make for merry cacophony if uncorrected. Nevertheless, Schubert was clearly inspired enough by this example to choose the same key of C major for his setting and to emulate certain aspects of Salieri's layout, if not his casting (Schubert adds a second tenor and bass as soloists). The opening is a miniature fanfare of horn-like successions of thirds and sixths appropriate to C major, beloved of classical composers for works of ceremony and pomp. In a good many songs of this type, the pleasures of drinking are justified by a lugubrious *carpe diem* philosophy. This jolly little ditty is simple and hearty enough to have been sung by singers well on their way to inebriation, but like most of Schubert's occasional music it still shows the hand of a young master in its response to words.

There is a Beethovenian strength both in the vigorous interplay between vocal line and bass and in the swirling, busy semiquavers of the piano's right hand which spring to life in response to the words 'In dem drängenden Gewühle' – 'Amid life's teeming throng' (bb. 8–10). The verbal noun 'Steigen' (climb) in b. 5 is set to an ascending fourth, and 'Fallen' in b. 6 to a falling third, a response to the emphasis that double-spacing gives to these words in the printed text. A similarly appropriate 'up' illustrates 'Bald hinauf' (bb. 6–7) followed by a 'down' for 'und bald hinab' (bb. 7–8). The modulation at the end of the solo section into A minor (at 'Und die letzte ist das Grab', bb. 13–14) is rather witty – an unwelcome shock at the end of life's tunnel with the pianist's left hand digging deeper than usual into the bottom reaches of the bass clef. The grave is after all the largest pitfall we will encounter. The chorus begins at b. 15 earnestly in A minor for 'Darum, Brüder! schenket ein', returning to the major for the happier image of 'Sinken wir berauscht vom Wein'. A pedal point on C adds to the tenacious, Beethovenian aspect of the piece at the repetition of 'Darum, Brüder!' (b. 20), and the final 'Sinken wir berauscht vom Wein' is followed by a two-bar postlude, descending thirds that scuttle crablike down the keyboard. The effect of this is humorous, as if a succession of drinkers were sinking like ninepins into unconsciousness, each with a happy grin on his face. Schubert himself would scarcely have been able to play this lively and detailed accompaniment if he had been drunk at the time.

The original poem contains eight strophes, each with a chorus; only one of these is printed in the AGA but whether or not this represents the wishes of Schubert and his friends when in their cups is debatable.

Autograph:	Missing or lost
First edition:	Published as Op. 130 no. 2 by Josef Czerny, Vienna in November 1830; subsequently corrected to Op. post. 131 no. 2 (P256)
Subsequent editions:	Peters: Vol. 4/159; AGA XIX 8: p. 59; NSA III: Vol. 3
Bibliography:	Litschauer 2001

| Discography and timing: | Deutsche Grammophon *Schubert-Terzette* | 1'12 | Peter Schreier, Horst Laubenthal & Dietrich Fischer-Dieskau |
| | Hyperion I 22[1] Hyperion II 5[2] | 1'09 | Jamie MacDougall with John Mark Ainsley, Simon Keenlyside & Michael George |

←— *Der Liedler* D209   *Auf einen Kirchhof* D151 —→

~~~~~~~~~~~~~~~~

TRINKLIED   Drinking song
(ZETTLER) **D183** [H87]
G major   12 April 1815

Ihr Freun - de und_ du_ gold' - ner_ Wein, ver - sü - sset_ mir das Le - ben;

(17 bars)

Ihr Freunde und du, gold'ner Wein!	You, friends, and you, golden wine,
Versüsset mir das Leben:	Make my life sweeter.
Ohn' euch, Beglücker, wäre fein!—[1]	Without you, bestowers of joy, it would be a fine thing!
Ich stets in Angst und Beben.	I would live in fear and trembling.
'Ohne Freunde, ohne Wein,	'Without friends, without wine,
Möcht' ich nicht im Leben sein.'	I should not wish to live!'
Wer Tausende in Kisten schliesst,	The man who locks thousands in his chest,
Nach Mehrerem nur trachtet,	Who endeavours only to increase them,
Der Freunde Not und sich vergisst—	Forgetting himself and the plight of his friends,
Sei reich! von uns verachtet	Let him be rich, despised by us!
'Ohne Freunde, ohne Wein,	'Without friends, without wine,
Mag ein Andrer reicher sein!'	Let another man be rich!'
Ohn' allen Freund, was ist der Held?	What is the hero without a friend?
Was sind des Reichs Magnaten?	What are the great men of the realm?
Was ist ein Herr der ganzen Welt?—	What is the master of the whole world?
Sind alle schlecht berathen!	They are all poorly counselled!
'Ohne Freunde, ohne Wein,	'Without friends, without wine,
Mag ich selbst nicht Kaiser sein!'	I should not even wish to be Emperor!'
Und muss einst an der Zukunft Port	And if one day in the future
Dem Leib die Seel' entschweben:	My soul must leave my body,
So wink' mir aus der Sel'gen Hort	Then let a friend and the juice of the vine
Ein Freund und Saft der Reben:	Greet me in the refuge of the blessed.
'Sonst mag ohne Freund und Wein	'Otherwise, without a friend and without wine
Ich auch nicht in Himmel sein.'	I should not even wish to be in heaven!'

ALOIS ZETTLER (1778–1828)

This is Schubert's only setting of Alois Zettler. See the poet's biography.

This piece (composed on the same day as the astonishingly more complex *Die erste Liebe* D182) is designated as a 'song with chorus' by Witteczek, the famous contemporary collector of Schubert autographs. Because its vocal line remains firmly in the middle of the stave (and is thus suitable for tenors, baritones and basses in a common-denominator tessitura) the performance recorded by Hyperion allowed each of four solo male singers to take a turn as soloist. This chimes well with Witteczek's description of the work as a 'Rundgesang', or roundelay. As is usual in German drinking songs, the Grim Reaper makes an appearance in the last strophe. Zettler finally concludes that he prefers to stay on earth rather than go to heaven, a sentiment also voiced by the poet Hölty in the much more famous *Seligkeit* D433.

The tune is attractive and instantly memorable – just the thing for a gathering of men with more serious matters on their minds (imbibing chief among them) than the mastering of musical complexities. The accompaniment of the verses consists of robust chords to support the refrains and quavers that flow as freely as the refreshment on tap. The number of notes in the accompaniment presupposes a pianist who is prepared to drink much less than his confrères. One

---

[1] In the 1836 printed edition of this poem (edited by Kuffner) this and the following line read: '*Von euch getrennt und krank zu sein! — / Dies Denken macht mich beben*'.

might argue that Schubert the pianist was, on these occasions, the 'designated driver' – forced to sit and watch the pleasures of others and always on hand to transport them to another realm. Such it seems was the composer's selflessness on these occasions as the provider of music for social gatherings.

Autograph:	Missing or lost
First edition:	Published as Vol. 7 no. 30 in Friedlaender's edition by Peters, Leipzig in 1887 (P494)
Subsequent editions:	Peters: Vol. 7/69; AGA XX 62: Vol. 2/97; NSA IV: Vol. 8
Discography and timing:	Fischer-Dieskau I 3[14] 1'27 (strophes 1, 3 and 4 only)
	Hyperion I 20[31] 2'06 John Mark Ainsley, Jamie MacDougall, Simon Keenlyside &
	Hyperion II 6[6] Michael George

⟵ *Die erste Liebe* D182   *Die Sterbende* D186 ⟶

TRINKLIED
(ANONYMOUS) D267 [H154]
B♭ major   25 August 1815

Drinking song   Quartet, TTBB

(16 bars)

Auf! Jeder sei nun froh und sorgenfrei!	Come! Let every man be glad and carefree!
Ist noch Jemand, der mit Gram	And if there's anyone who came to us
Schwer im Herzen zu uns kam:	With grief weighing on his heart,
Auf! auf! er sei	Come, let him now be
Nun froh und sorgenfrei!	Glad and carefree!

ANONYMOUS/UNKNOWN

The marking for this bracing little song is 'Feurig' ('fiery'), and yet the dynamic for the introduction to this chorus for four men's voices is pianissimo. Schubert obviously relished the contrast between these four bars from the piano and the sudden fortissimo surprise when the voices enter the fray at b. 5. The accompaniment's left hand has restlessly moving staccato quavers, sometimes in single notes and sometimes doubled in octaves, suggesting an orchestral accompaniment with *détaché* bowing from the lower strings. The repeat mark is the only encouragement necessary to sing these cheerful anonymous words again. The text promises happiness and comfort to anyone coming to this gathering who is burdened with care.

How well, and for how long, have these words kept their promise! For those of any political awareness, life under Metternich was uncomfortable in spiritual terms, and for the early Schubertians even simple music of this kind must have seemed a refuge of sanity and goodness.

Despite being without freedom of speech and thought, and the benefit of the gas lamp, much less electric light, the musical citizens of Vienna seem not to have gone without when it came to enlightenment and radiance. These lucky beneficiaries of a miraculous combination of creativity and sociability simply walked through a door and encountered first performances of countless pieces of life-enhancing music, created in many cases specifically for their enjoyment.

Autograph:	Wienbibliothek im Rathaus, Vienna
First edition:	Published as No. 2 of *Neueste Folge nachgelassener, mehrstimmiger Gesänge mit und ohne Begleitung von Franz Schubert* by J. P. Gotthard, Vienna in 1872 (P511)
Subsequent editions:	AGA XVI 17: p. 131; NSA III: Vol. 3
Discography and timing:	Hyperion I 20³² 1'13 John Mark Ainsley, Jamie MacDougall, Hyperion II 9¹⁵ Simon Keenlyside & Michael George

← *Morgenlied D266*   *Bergknappenlied D268* →

TRINKLIED   Drinking song   Tenor solo & choir, TTBB
(Anonymous) **D356** [not in Hyperion]
D major   Fragment, 1816

(59 bars)

Funkelnd im Becher	Sparkling in the goblet,
So helle so hold,	So bright and fair,
Blinket hochschäumend,	The gold of the delicious sweet grapes
Blinkt perlend das Gold	Glistens,
Der süssen, der köstlichen Reben.	Bubbling and foaming.
Es glänzet auch uns wohl	As bright as the grape's
So freundlich, so hold,	Refreshing gold
Hell wie der Reben	Gleams for us, too,
Erquickendes Gold	Delightful and fair,
Das wogende herrliche Leben.	The glorious surge of life.
Drum, freudiger Zecher,	So, happy topers,
Erhebet die Becher,	Raise your goblets,
Es funkelt der Wein	The wine sparkles,
Wohl so freundlich, so hold,	Delightful and fair,
Es funkelt das wogende	The surge of life
Leben wie Gold!	Sparkles like gold.
Trinket! Trinket!	Drink! Drink!

Anonymous/Unknown

This fragment ranks as one of Schubert's least-known pieces for the reason that it has not been published since it appeared in 1844 in a supplement of a Viennese music journal with a piano part added by Carl Czerny. (This new accompaniment by Czerny was written on to Schubert's surviving manuscript.) The nature of the solo writing at the beginning shows that there was certainly an original piano accompaniment that has since disappeared. Czerny's version has a number of chromatic inflections that sound somewhat anachronistic. There is likely to have been at least one further pair of solo verses and another chorus.

The music was not included in the AGA, and at the time of writing it has not yet been issued by the NSA. It also seems to have escaped the attention of Reinhard Van Hoorickx, and was not recorded for the Hyperion Edition. The hearty music is in simple drinking-song style; the high-lying solo tenor encompasses a few decorations, such as the demisemiquaver melisma on the word 'hell'. The first two verses of the poem (as printed above) are sung as a solo where the vocal line ends in the dominant; the four-part male chorus replies with a stirring passage in $\frac{2}{4}$ where the concluding 'Trinket!' (repeated) occasions a pair of V-I cadences supported by Czerny's tremolando accompaniment.

Autograph:	Wienbibliothek im Rathaus, Vienna (first draft without piano accompaniment)
First edition:	Published by Pietro Mechetti as a supplement to the *Allgemeine Wiener Musikzeitung*, vol. IV no. 66 on 1 June 1844
Subsequent editions:	Not in AGA; NSA III: Vol. 3
Discography and timing:	Hyperion —

TRINKLIED (Bacchus, feister Fürst   Drinking song
des Weins) (Shakespeare) **D888** [H603]
C major   July 1826

(29 bars)

A literal translation of the German translation is given here. Shakespeare's original
text is printed below in italics.

Bacchus, feister Fürst des Weins,	Bacchus, plump prince of wine,
Komm mit Augen hellen Scheins.	Come with brightly shining eyes.
Uns're Sorg' ersäuf' dein Fass,	Let your vat drown our cares,
Und dein Laub uns krönen lass.	And your leaves crown us.
Füll' uns, bis die Welt sich dreht!	Fill us till the world spins round!
Füll' uns, bis die Welt sich dreht!	Fill us till the world spins round!

Song
Come, thou monarch of the vine,
Plumpy Bacchus with pink eyne!
In thy fats our cares be drown'd,
With thy grapes our hairs be crown'd:
Cup us, till the world go round,
Cup us, till the world go round!

WILLIAM SHAKESPEARE (1564–1616), trans. FERDINAND MAYERHOFER VON GRÜNBÜHEL (1798–1869) and EDUARD VON BAUERNFELD (1802–1890)

This is the first of Schubert's three Shakespeare solo settings (1826) and the first of three Bauernfeld solo settings (1826–7). See both poets' biographies.

This lyric comes from *Antony and Cleopatra* Act II Scene 7. Antony accompanies Octavius, Caesar and Lepidus to Misenum, Sicily, where they meet Pompey who invites them for a night of feasting aboard his galley. Menas, Pompey's lieutenant, whispers to his master that by killing all his guests Pompey could become ruler of the world. Pompey rejects this idea but wishes that Menas had acted on his own initiative. In the middle of these events the poem, 'Come, thou monarch of the vine' (sung by a boy) is introduced thus:

> ENOBARBUS (to Antony)
> Ha, my brave Emperor,
> Shall we dance now the Egyptian bacchanals,
> And celebrate our drink?

> POMPEY
> Let's ha't, good soldier.

Illustration from *The Library Shakespeare* for 'Bacchus, god of mirth and wine' from *Antony and Cleopatra*.

ANTONY
Come, let's all take hands,
Till that conquering wine hath steep'd our sense
In soft and delicate Lethe.

ENOBARBUS
All take hands.
Make battery to our ears with the loud music:
The while I'll place you; then the boy shall sing,
The holding every man shall beat as loud
As his strong sides can volley.
(Music plays. Enobarbus places them hand in hand)

Although Capell hears Handel in this song, and Fischer-Dieskau Mozart's Osmin, the music is in Schubert's familiar C major drinking-song vein, with the added suggestion of drunkenness. It is not the boy who sings in Schubert's mind, but a group of rabble-rousing, carousing soldiers. Having read the play carefully, he places them aboard a ship which, although not at sea, is still subject to the movement of the tidal waters. The doubling of the voice part on the piano seems partly for security, as if the revellers must summon all their willpower to steady themselves after too much wine. There is nothing so serious as the deep and earnest concentration of the truly drunk. The setting of 'bis die Welt sich dreht' is a hocketing succession of quavers, a semitone apart and progressively higher in the voice, as if suggestive of boozy hiccups, blurred vision and spinning horizons. The mordent on 'feister' adds to the sense of inebriated jollity, and the vocal line is lubricated by quavers that suggest slurred speech. After the supreme effort to articulate the minims at 'Füll' uns' for the third time, the rest of the phrase ('bis die Welt sich dreht') slides in an out-of-control gush towards the tonic (it would be anachronistic to speak also of the gin). The postlude and introduction are identical: the opening *pomposo* fanfares are appropriate to music on a princely barge, but they give way in the closing bars ('Time, gentlemen, please!') to fourteen of the most disorientated and comic quavers the composer ever wrote (bb. 27–9). It is as if the right hand were lashing out in vain to clutch at a steadying handrail, accompanied by crotchets in the left hand which attempt to regain a foothold on a deck heaving with chromatic swells. After a repetition of this verse (the composer indicates repeat marks despite the fact that there is only one strophe) we are left to assume that it is not only the deck that heaves. Schubert writes as a man who knows scenes such as these at first hand.

Autograph:	Wienbibliothek im Rathaus, Vienna (first draft)
First edition:	Published as Book 48 no. 4 of the *Nachlass* by Diabelli, Vienna in 1850 (P383)
Subsequent editions:	Peters: Vol. 6/63; AGA XX 502: Vol. 8/227; NSA IV: Vol. 14a/16
Bibliography:	Capell 1928, p. 224
	Fischer-Dieskau 1977, p. 233
Discography and timing:	Fischer-Dieskau II 8[11] 0'49
	Hyperion I 26[14]
	Hyperion II 32[9] 1'24 Richard Jackson

← *Dithyrambe* D801   *Ständchen* D889 →

TRINKLIED VOR DER SCHLACHT
(KÖRNER) **D169** [H77]
A minor   12 March 1815

Drinking song
before battle

2 unison
choirs

(15 bars)

Schlacht, du brichst an!	The battle commences!
Grüsst sie in freudigem Kreise,	Greet it in joyful company,
Laut nach Germanischer Weise.	Heartily, in true German style.
Brüder, heran!	Come, brothers!
Noch perlt der Wein;	The wine still sparkles;
Eh' die Posaunen erdröhnen,	Before the trumpets resound
Lasst uns das Leben versöhnen,	Let us appease life.
Brüder, schenkt ein!	Brothers, fill your glasses!
[. . . 3 . . .]	[. . . 3 . . .]
Schlacht ruft: Hinaus!	The battle calls! Away!
Horch, die Trompeten werben.	Hark, the trumpet enlists us.
Vorwärts, auf Leben und Sterben!	Forward march for life or death!
Brüder, trinkt aus!	Brothers, drink up!

THEODOR KÖRNER (1791–1813); poem written in 1813

Illustration for *Trinklied vor dem Schlacht* by R. Eichstädt
in a late nineteenth-century edition of Körner's *Leyer und
Schwert*.

The unique thing about this piece in
Schubert's output is its casting for two unison
choirs, and the use of a type of antiphonal
arrangement that would sound well from
different corners of St Mark's in Venice, *à la*
Monteverdi. It seems that two German
squadrons placed at different parts of the
battlefield are mustering their courage for
the onslaught, a reminder of those incidents
during the First World War when soldiers
in the trenches from opposing sides sang
together. Körner's *Leyer und Schwert* – to
judge by the numbers of sumptuously gilded
editions to be found in all the second-hand
bookshops of Germany – enjoyed its greatest
posthumous vogue in the years between
Bismarck's establishment of the Reich and
the beginning of that same war.

English-speaking people sometimes
find it difficult to tune into the inevitable

Nach der Weise: Feinde ringsum.

Schlacht, du brichst an!
Grüßt sie in freudigem Kreise
Laut nach germanischer Weise.
Brüder, heran!

Noch perlt der Wein;
Eh' die Posaunen erdröhnen,
Laßt uns das Leben versöhnen.
Brüder, schenkt ein!

Gott Vater hört,   Vaterlands Hort,
Was an des Grabes Thoren   Woll'n wir's aus glühenden Ketten
Vaterlands Söhne geschworen.   Todt oder siegend erretten. —
Brüder, ihr schwört!   Handschlag und Wort!

Illustration for Körner's *Trinklied vor der Schlacht* (1882).

connection between heavy drinking and the pondering of mortality that lies at the heart of this kind of Teutonic conviviality. It seems altogether natural in a German drinking song to see the affirmation of brotherhood and the sharing of wine as a prelude to 'crossing the bar'. At least there is nothing lachrymose or sentimental about this setting with its energy derived from the rolling left-hand basses that simulate the rumbling of drums. It has something of the same grim triumphant mood as *Die Trommel gerühret*, Klärchen's song from Beethoven's music for Goethe's *Egmont* Op. 84. The music is marked 'Schnell und feurig' and the speed and fiery nature of this little chorus betokens great bravado until the end of the strophe and the final high A in b. 13. There is a hint of panic and terror in this note because of its tessitura; after all, it is just as unlikely that a regiment will be full of heroes as it is that the average men's chorus will be overflowing with heroic tenors. No doubt Schubert designed this ending to propel the singers headlong into battle, but musicians are not often the best warriors.

The poem, the second-last in Körner's *Leyer und Schwert*, was written to fit an extant tune with words by Karl Gottlob Cramer (1758–1817). This *Kriegslied* beginning 'Feinde rings um!' was later set by the Bohemian composer Franz Gläser who was Schubert's contemporary in Vienna; Körner must have known and sung a much earlier setting of Cramer's words.

Körner's poem has six strophes. 1, 2, and 6 are given here as recorded in the Hyperion Edition.

Autograph:	Houghton Library, Harvard University, Cambridge, MA
First edition:	Published as part of the AGA in 1895 (P557)
Subsequent editions:	AGA XX 53: Vol. 2/76; NSA III: Vol. 3
Discography and timing:	Hyperion I 20[19] 1'05 The London Schubert Chorale (dir.
	Hyperion II 5[17] Stephen Layton)

← *Jesus Christus unser Heiland* D168A   *Schwertlied* D170 →

TROCKNE BLUMEN *see Die SCHÖNE MÜLLERIN* D795/18

TROST
Consolation

(ANONYMOUS) **D523** [H336]
E major   January 1817

(15 bars)

Nimmer lange weil' ich hier,
Komme bald hinauf zu dir;
Tief und still fühl' ich's in mir:
Nimmer lange weil' ich hier.

I shall not tarry here much longer,
Soon I shall come to you above;
Deeply, silently I feel within me:
I shall not tarry here much longer.

Komme bald hinauf zu dir,
Schmerzen, Qualen, für und für
Wüten in dem Busen mir;
Komme bald hinauf zu dir.

Soon I shall come to you above;
Sorrow and torment forever
Rage in my breast;
Soon I shall come to you above.

Tief und still fühl' ich's in mir:
Eines heissen Dranges Gier
Zehrt die Flamm' im Innern hier,
Tief und still fühl' ich's in mir.

Deeply, silently I feel within me:
The flame of ardent desire
Consumes my innermost being.
Deeply, silently I feel it within me.

Nimmer lange weil' ich hier . . .

I shall not tarry here much longer . . .

ANONYMOUS/UNKNOWN

This is the thirteenth of Schubert's nineteen settings of an anonymous poet. See Anonymous/ Unknown for a chronological list of all the songs for which the poets are unknown.

This haunting little song with an ingenious anonymous poem written as a variant of the *triolet* form, is completely overlooked by commentators and programme makers. It is a superb example of Schubert's ability to write something memorable and touching without seeming to try. There is an enormous sense of anguished longing and aspiring for release in this music, but how the composer achieves it is almost beyond analysis. He lavished so much care over strophic songs in his formative years that such mastery of distillation and concision was clearly hard-won rather than something taken for granted. The progress from the opening G sharp minor chord to the resolution of the vocal line into E major at b. 14 is a musical journey worthy of the song's title.

There is a distinct resonance here of other later (and better known) songs about death, and presentiment of release from earthly cares. The most famous of these is *Der Tod und das Mädchen* D531, composed in the following month. *Trost* shares that great work's bittersweet majesty, all the more remarkable for being evoked within the space of a few bars in duple time. *Schwanengesang* D744 also comes to mind – not the great cycle from 1828, but the 1822 Senn setting that achieves the same Schubertian mix of elegiac departure and exaltation. In all three songs the dactylic death motif plays a part – a long-short-short rhythm where a crotchet or minim is followed by two notes of half its length. In a song like this, with its ambivalence between major and minor keys, Schubert is on territory of which he was a special master. The opening of the song is in G sharp minor and by b. 6 we have reached B major. There is then a sudden shift to G major for four bars – a sinking into the deepest introspection. The home key, E major, is at last attained in b. 12 as if the singer were straining towards the light. This is a touching little chronicle of a journey: the progress from torment, out on a harmonic limb, to tonic key consolation derived from the hope of rejoining a loved one. The postlude with its gentle decoration on the penultimate crotchet is like the pouring of balm on a wound – the kindly embrace of Death the deliverer, perhaps.

Autograph:	Missing or lost
First edition:	Published as Vol. 7 no. 2 in Friedlaender's edition by Peters, Leipzig in 1885 (P477)
Subsequent editions:	Peters: Vol. 7/9; AGA XX 292: Vol. 5/5; NSA IV: Vol. 11/78
Arrangements:	Arr. Tilman Hoppstock (b. 1961) for guitar accompaniment, in *Franz Schubert: 110 Lieder* (2009)
Discography and timing:	Fischer-Dieskau I 9[9] 2'37
	Hyperion I 21[7]
	Hyperion II 17[14] 2'55 Edith Mathis

← *Die Liebe* D522   *Der Alpenjäger* D524 →

TROST   Consolation
(Mayrhofer) **D671** [H434]
E♭ major   October 1819

(38 bars)

Hörnerklänge rufen klagend	Horn-calls sound plaintively
Aus des Forstes grüner Nacht,	From the green night of the forest;
In das Land der Liebe tragend,	Their magic power is at work,
Waltet ihre Zaubermacht.	Transporting us to the land of love.
Selig, wer ein Herz gefunden,	Happy is he who has found a heart
Das sich liebend ihm ergab!	That yields itself in love.
Mir ist jedes Glück entschwunden,	For me all happiness has vanished,
Denn die Teure deckt das Grab.	For my love lies buried in the grave.
Tönen aus des Waldes Gründen	When horn-calls from the depths of the forest
Hörnerklänge an mein Ohr,	Ring in my ears,

Glaub' ich wieder sie zu finden,	I imagine I have found her once more,
Zieht es mich zu ihr empor.	And am drawn up towards her.
Jenseits wird sie mir erscheinen,	Beyond the grave she who gave herself to me in love
Die sich liebend mir ergab,	Will appear to me.
O welch' seliges Vereinen,	Ah, what a blissful reunion!
Keine Schrecken hat das Grab.	The grave holds no terror for me.

JOHANN MAYRHOFER (1787–1836)

This is the thirty-fifth of Schubert's forty-seven Mayrhofer settings (1814–24). See the poet's biography for a chronological list of all the Mayrhofer settings.

This is a slight song, but a delightful one – the smallest of the Mayrhofer settings from 1819. The accompaniment is based on the sound of a horn call in E flat in its characteristic thirds and sixths, and this brings to mind the alphorn music of another fine Mayrhofer setting, *Abschied* D475 of 1816. John Reed points out the similarity of the song to the gently ruminative Schober setting, *Trost im Liede* D546. In the fifth bar of the introduction the addition of a D flat adds a note of doubt and longing which resonates with modern undertones (by Schubertian standards) of the new Romantic age characterized by fragment and acrostic, fairy tale and folksong, dream and nightmare. This D flat, pulling the music down into the darker realms of A flat major, plays a significant part throughout the song.

Although Schumann could not have known this setting before 1844, it is rather surprising that the song seems one of the closest to that composer's musical world. We detect here the same love of the magic of wood and forest that is part of so many Schumann songs (cf. the mood of *Im Walde* from the Op. 39 *Liederkreis* – also in § – and the fanfare of horn calls that begins *Waldesgespräch* from the same cycle). Schubert did not belong to an age where there was much interest in authentic folksong, although he might have discovered it if he had lived another twenty years. Instead he wrote his own folksongs (as Ravel once remarked of Poulenc), and there is a simplicity and directness here, combined with an air of mysterious melancholy (the title is 'Consolation' after all) which we find again and again in Schumann's river and forest settings of Eichendorff and Kerner. The song leaves one with a sense of unease, probably due to the succession of subtle interrupted cadences in the second half where every statement, however bold, is undermined by harmonic doubt. Once again this is more typical of the age of Schumann than of Schubert. The final cadence 'Denn die Teure deckt das Grab' (from b. 32) with ominous shifts in the falling bass line is again reminiscent of *Im Walde* Op. 39 no. 11 – at 'Und mich schauert's im Herzensgrunde' (compare the dotted minims of 'Grab' – in bb. 34 and 36 of *Trost* – and 'schauert's' in the Schumann song, both floating above stealthy harmonic skulduggery in the bass).

Only two verses of the poem appear in the song's original autograph, enough to make up a complete musical strophe. The repeat marks at the end suggest that Schubert intended two further strophes to be sung, and the listener is only too happy to hear the music of this rare song once again. These verses are printed in italics in the NSA and there is some doubt as to whether they are by Mayrhofer. The poem was printed in neither of the poet's collections (1824 and 1843) and it was not unknown for publishers to commission stray hacks to provide extra words. As Mayrhofer died thirteen years before the printing of the song's first edition (where Verses 3 and 4 appear for the first time) he was in no position to deny authorship. This printing also includes an *ossia* beneath the opening bars that shows different right-hand phrasing in another copy of the song. The marking in the first edition is 'Lebhaft', and this too may go back to the composer himself. It is certainly a warning against interpreting the 'Mässig' tempo marking (the marking in contemporary copies of the song, not in the autograph) in too lugubrious a manner. A significant difference between the NSA and all other earlier editions is the placement of the repeat marks: in the NSA these stand right at the beginning of the song so that the introduction is heard once again as an interlude between the two musical verses. When the words to be heard directly after this interlude are 'Tönen aus des Waldes Gründen' this seems to be a correct reading of Schubert's intentions.

Autograph:	Conservatoire collection, Bibliothèque Nationale, Paris (first draft)
First edition:	Published as Book 44 no. 1 of the *Nachlass* by Diabelli, Vienna in 1849 (P366)
Subsequent editions:	Peters: Vol. 6/38; AGA XX 367: Vol. 6/60; NSA IV: Vol. 12/114
Arrangements:	Arr. Tilman Hoppstock (b. 1961) for guitar accompaniment, in *Franz Schubert: 110 Lieder* (2009)
Discography and timing:	Fischer-Dieskau II 3[10] 2'38
	Hyperion I 29[16]
	Hyperion II 22[9] 2'10 Marjana Lipovšek

← *Die Sternennächte* D670   *Die Liebende schreibt* D673 →

TROST. AN ELISA   Consolation, for Elisa
(MATTHISSON) **D97** [H34]
C major   1814

(26 bars)

Lehnst du deine bleichgehärmte Wange	Are you still resting your cheek, pale with grief,
Immer noch an diesen Aschenkrug?	On this urn of ashes?
Weinend um den Toten, den schon lange	Weeping for the dead man who, long since,
Zu der Seraphim Triumphgesange	On the wings of perfection
Der Vollendung Flügel trug?	Soared up to the Seraphim's triumphant song?
Siehst du Gottes Sternenschrift dort flimmern,	Can you see God's starry script shimmering,
Die der bangen Schwermut Trost verheisst?	Promising comfort for anxious sorrow?
Heller wird der Glaube dir nun schimmern,[1]	Your faith will now shine more brightly
Dass hoch über seiner Hülle Trümmern	So that high above his mortal remains
Walle des Geliebten Geist!	Your beloved's spirit will live!

[1] Matthisson has 'Heller wird der Glaube *nun dir* schimmern'.

Wohl, o wohl dem liebenden Gefährten	Happy the loving companion
Deiner Sehnsucht, er ist ewig dein!	Of your longing, he is for ever yours!
Wiedersehn, im Lande der Verklärten,	Patient sufferer, in the land of the blessed
Wirst du, Dulderin, den Langentbehrten,	You will see again the one you have long yearned for,
Und wie er unsterblich sein!	And be immortal, as he is!

FRIEDRICH VON MATTHISSON (1761–1831); poem written in 1783

This is the fifth of Schubert's twenty-nine Matthisson solo settings (1812–17). See the poet's biography for a chronological list of all the Matthisson settings.

Schubert's course of training with Salieri included all manner of exercises in counterpoint, choral writing and the invention of melodies supported by strong bass lines. Some of these are credible compositions in their own right, but it was not long before Schubert's technical studies bore fruit in the songs themselves: the Matthisson settings of 1814 are a marriage (something borrowed, something new) of schooled practice and new invention. Even Schubert needed someone to help him open the floodgates, and Salieri encouraged the flow of sensuous melody that a German-speaking teacher of the old school might have staunched. The hallmark of the Matthisson songs is graceful melodic invention, but they also show an ability and touching desire to serve the lyric, rather than merely to press it into service. This respect for poet and poetry is a characteristic of the dutiful North German masters who averred that musical invention should not obscure the poetry.

But how best really to serve a lyric? Zumsteeg would have had no doubt that his prime responsibility was to conserve the metre of the text; Schubert, aware of metre most of the time, ocasionally overrules its demands when he feels that it is more important for the music to reflect the mood and situation of a poem. *Trost. An Elisa* is a case in point: Matthisson's classical metre is more or less ignored in this case. Schubert might have reasoned that the words are an impassioned attempt to console Elisa, and in real life (which interested him more and more in the full bloom of late adolescence) one does not actually sing a set-piece song to someone in the depths of bereavement. Instead, Schubert imagines the poet *speaking* to Elisa, using the full weight of his persuasive rhetoric and religious conviction to reason with her. Recitative seems the musical form most appropriate to the task, mirroring spontaneous emotion and reflecting the shape and meaning of the words as the poem unfolds. Modulation occurs in an almost unpremeditated way, and compound time is used only when melody intrudes at odd moments, as at the end of Verse 2 (b. 15) and in the impassioned b. 23. The final cadence appears to turn around a corner, so that the piano's radiant consolation of C major directs the listener's gaze into the infinity of the afterlife. The recitative style of this song is a long way from that of Mozart and Italy; Gluck was no doubt one of the models, but Schubert's hybrid owes much to Zumsteeg too. It is also a study, as Brigitte Massin avers, for the extraordinary *Szene aus 'Faust'* D126 that Schubert would compose at the end of the year where Mephistopheles (or 'Böser Geist') taunts a girl rather than consoles her, but uses a similarly fluid conversational tone. A number of the songs of this period, including some of the Ossian settings, prophesy Wagner in the creative and flexible way that word and tone are made to combine in heightened speech. Wagner could not have known *Trost. An Elisa* but he was a student in Leipzig when some of the most innovative songs in the Schubert Nachlass were first published. Like Schubert himself, that master magpie developed his style from the legacy of what had gone before. For a discussion of Johann Michael Vogl's wayward performing version of this song *see* ORNAMENTATION.

Autograph:	Missing or lost
First edition:	Published as part of the AGA in 1894 (P541)
Subsequent editions:	Not in Peters; AGA XX 19: Vol. 1/154; NSA IV: Vol. 7/6;
	Bärenreiter: Vol. 5/104 (high voice), 99 (medium/low voice)
Bibliography:	Einstein 1951, p. 67
	Massin 1977, pp. 548–9
Discography and timing:	Fischer-Dieskau I 2[1] 2'54
	Hyperion I 12[12]
	Hyperion II 3[6] 2'51 Adrian Thompson

← *Adelaide* D95   *Andenken* D99 →

TROST IM LIEDE   Comfort in song
(Schober) **D546** [H360]

The song exists in two versions, the first of which is discussed below:
(1) March 1817; (2) Before June 1827

(1) 'Etwas bewegt'   F major   §   [41 bars]

(2) 'Mässig'   F major   §   [42 bars]

Braust des Un-glücks Sturm em-por, halt ich mei-ne Har-fe vor,

(42 bars)

Braust des Unglücks Sturm empor:	When the tempest of misfortune roars
Halt' ich meine Harfe vor.	I hold up my harp.
Schützen können Saiten nicht,	Strings cannot protect,
Die er leicht und schnell durchbricht:[1]	The storm breaks them swiftly and easily,
Aber durch des Sanges Tor	But through the portals of song
Schlägt er milder an mein Ohr.	It strikes my ear more gently.
Sanfte Laute hör ich klingen,	I hear sweet sounds
Die mir in die Seele dringen,	That pierce my soul;
Die mir auf des Wohllauts Schwingen	On the wings of harmony
Wunderbare Tröstung bringen;	They bring me mysterious comfort.
Und ob Klagen mir entschweben,	And even if threnodies escape my lips,
Ob ich still und schmerzlich weine,	And I weep in silence and sorrow,
Fühl' ich mich doch so ergeben,	Yet I feel such humility
Dass ich fest und gläubig meine:	That I firmly and devoutly believe
Es gehört zu meinem Leben,	It is part of my life
Dass sich Schmerz und Freude eine.	That pain and joy should be mingled.

[1] Schober writes 'Die er *schnell und leicht* durchbricht'.

Franz von Schober (1796–1882)

This is the third of Schubert's fourteen Schober solo settings (1815–27). See the poet's biography for a chronological list of all the Schober settings.

This remarkable song has a text that comes as near as anything Schubert ever set to being a credo of his belief in the healing powers of music. The piece is contemporary with the famous *An die Musik* D547 but, as Einstein points out, it expresses Schubert's attitude more subtly than 'that other somewhat "homely" thanksgiving song in D major'. Walther Dürr suggests that the two texts actually belong together, were composed together and became forever separated – at least as far as the public was concerned – by a divergent fate at the hands of different publishers. Did Schubert and Schober ever discuss the ambivalence of life as reflected in musical harmony? This poem seems to express views that Schober could only have learned from the composer himself, suggesting that Schubert, at least with those close friends who had a smattering of musical learning, was able to talk about the means by which his own special harmonic world was created.

In any case Schober has given him an ideal text with which to highlight the play between the light and shade of differing tonalities. The music is cast in § and has the air of a rather melancholy serenade or *sicilienne*. No sooner is the introduction over in the major key than the vocal line turns into the relative minor. We might believe that this song is entirely in D minor: only when the portals of song are mentioned ('des Sanges Tor' at bb. 11–12) do we revert to the calm of the major. The whole of the third verse (from b. 26) is miraculous: the insistent repetitious threnodies and unresolved dissonances in the piano part (a dotted quaver followed by three semiquavers in the right hand, a cell that is repeated seven times) underpin a vocal line of the sweetest sorrow, and the lift from the second inversion of F minor (b. 29) to D flat major for 'Fühl' ich mich doch so ergeben' (b. 30) is expressive of a kind of ecstatic humility before music's imponderable Delphic mysteries. Let us not forget that this song comes from Schubert's Mayrhofer-inspired 'Greek' period, that its manuscript also contains *Der Jüngling und der Tod* D545, not to mention *An die Musik* (how precious these four sheets of paper are), and that *Ganymed* D544 was composed in the same month. The last two lines of verse might well serve as an epitaph for Schubert's art, and he finds self-effacing music, pure and Mozartian, to set them to. John Reed is surely correct in pronouncing the song flawless.

The NSA prints two versions of the song. The first was composed in March 1817 (the marking is 'Etwas bewegt'); the second (marked 'Mässig'), with slightly smoother passage-work in the accompaniment, was prepared for the printing of the song in June 1827 when it appeared as a supplement in Johann Schickh's *Wiener Zeitschrift für Kunst, Theater, Literatur und Mode.*

Autograph:	Missing or lost
Publication:	First published as part of the NSA in 1985 (P786; first version)
	First published as a supplement to the *Wiener Zeitschrift für Kunst, Literatur, Theater und Mode* on 23 June 1827; subsequently published as Op. post. 101 no. 3 by H. A. Probst, Vienna in December 1828 (P179; second version)
Subsequent editions:	Peters: Vol. 6/83; AGA XX 313: Vol. 5/184; NSA IV: Vol. 5/156 & 159; Bärenreiter: Vol. 4/54
Bibliography:	Einstein 1951, p. 143
	Fischer-Dieskau 1977, p. 83
	Newbould 1997, pp. 142–3

Discography and timing: Fischer-Dieskau I 9²⁸   2'10
                           Hyperion I 3¹¹
                           Hyperion II 18¹¹   2'48   Ann Murray

⟵ *Der Jüngling und der Tod* D545   *An die Musik* D547 ⟶

TROST IN TRÄNEN   Consolation in tears

(GOETHE) **D120** [H52]
F major – F minor   30 November 1814

(23 bars)

Wie kommt's, dass du so traurig bist,	How come that you are so sad
Da alles froh erscheint?	When everything appears so joyful?
Man sieht dir's an den Augen an,	One can see from your eyes,
Gewiss, du hast geweint?	For sure, you have been crying.
'Und hab ich einsam auch geweint,	'And if, in solitude, I have been weeping,
So ists mein eigen Schmerz,	It is my own sorrow,
Und Tränen fliessen gar so süss,	My tears flowing so very sweetly,
Erleichtern mir das Herz.'	Comfort my heart.'
Die frohen Freunde laden dich,	Your joyful friends bid you,
O, komm' an unsre Brust!	Come to our hearts!
Und was du auch verloren hast,	And whatever you have lost,
Vertraue den Verlust.	Confide to us that loss.
'Ihr lärmt und rauscht und ahndet nicht,	'You revel and make merry, and cannot guess
Was mich, den Armen, quält.	What torments this poor man.
Ach nein! Verloren hab ich's nicht,	No, I have not lost what I grieve for,
So sehr es mir auch fehlt.'	Although I feel its absence sorely.'
So raffe dich denn eilig auf,	So pull yourself together.
Du bist ein junges Blut.	You are a young man.
In deinen Jahren hat man Kraft	At your age men have strength
Und zum Erwerben Mut.	And the courage to achieve.
'Ach nein! erwerben kann ich's nicht,	'Alas, I cannot achieve what I desire,
Es steht mir gar zu fern.	It lies too far away from me.
Es weilt so hoch, es blinkt so schön,	It dwells high and shines as fair
Wie droben jener Stern.'	As yonder star above.'

Die Sterne, die begehrt man nicht,	One does not covet the stars,
Man freut sich ihrer Pracht,	But rejoices in their splendour,
Und mit Entzücken blickt man auf	And gazes up in delight
In jeder heitern Nacht.	On every night that's clear.

'Und mit Entzücken blick ich auf,	'I do gaze up in delight
So manchen lieben Tag,	On many a sweet day.
Verweinen lasst die Nächte mich	Let me weep away my nights
So lang' ich weinen mag.'	As long as I wish to weep.'

JOHANN WOLFGANG VON GOETHE (1749–1832); poem written in 1803?

This is the third of Schubert's seventy-five Goethe solo settings (1814–26). See the poet's biography for a chronological list of all the Goethe settings.

The tradition of setting this poem for voice and piano spans a number of generations, leaving us with a succession of modest and simple songs by Zelter (1803), Reichardt (final version published in 1809), Schubert (1814) and Brahms (1858). The most ambitious setting falls outside the scope of the lied – a four-part a cappella chorus, with elaborate variations of mood and rhythm, by Peter Cornelius (1872). Loewe also set the poem as a simple three-part unaccompanied chorus. But the first four composers named above, who were proud to be part of a continuing tradition, muster an eerie unanimity. There is something ineffably German about a folksong framed in question and answer dialogue: simplicity and repetition are to be relished rather than avoided, as if one's most musically limited brethren are to be included in the sing-song, and the text reflects the German temperament as tears are wept into the beer for the sheer enjoyment of it all. Goethe wrote another poem on similar lines, *Wonne der Wehmut* – 'Delight in Melancholy' (set by both Beethoven Op. 83 no. 1 and Schubert D260). Lorraine Byrne explains this duality by comparing it to the eponymous hero's confession in the *Vor dem Tor* scene from Faust: 'Two souls alas are lodged within my breast. Each seeks separation from the other.' These 'two facets of the poet's psyche reveal the tension between the provinces of his personality'.

The Zelter setting of *Trost in Tränen* is in E minor throughout, apart from a consoling G sharp in the final cadence. This last-minute lift to the major key, as well as Zelter's § rhythm, was to be adopted by Schubert. Reichardt's song seems to have influenced Schubert even more: he uses Reichardt's key of F major (which also falls into F minor for the woebegone replies) and the shape of Schubert's melodic line (in F minor with a change of key signature, from b. 9) also stems from this setting. The Schubert song can be seen as a homage to the past: instead of being taken up by the next table at a beer hall, the song is taken up and subtly modified by succeeding generations. When Brahms came to write his setting, he had relatively recently been welcomed by Schumann into the fold of sacred torch bearers. He elaborates the end of each verse, as earlier generations had declined to do, with a piano postlude. This elongation does remarkably little to improve a dialogue where there are a few too many self-conscious bows to the past. Brahms's setting is in § of course, in the major key for the exhortations and in the minor for the replies. When a wan smile shines through the tears, the song melts back into the major, although not surprisingly it is Schubert who best achieves this effect. Schubert, after all, was ideally placed in history to write successful strophic songs. Those by his antecedents can all too easily sound dull and timid, those by his successors deliberately archaic and hopelessly nostalgic for the simplicity of former times.

When the song was published as part of the *Nachlass* a spurious introduction of a single bar with upbeat was added with a forte marking. This is to be avoided by present-day interpreters.

Autograph:	Wienbibliothek im Rathaus, Vienna (fair copy for Goethe)
First edition:	Published as Book 25 no. 3 of the *Nachlass* by Diabelli, Vienna in October 1835 (P310)
Subsequent editions:	Peters: Vol. 2/230; AGA XX 33: Vol. 1/198; NSA IV: Vol. 7/56; Bärenreiter: Vol. 6/2
Bibliography:	Byrne 2003, pp. 198–200
	Capell 1928, p. 86
	Sternfeld 1979, p. 80
Further settings & arrangements:	Johann Friedrich Reichardt (1752–1814) *Trost in Tränen* (1809)
	Carl Friedrich Zelter (1758–1832) *Trost in Tränen* (1803)
	Ludwig Berger (1777–1839) *Trost in Tränen* Op. 33 no. 3 (1829–33)
	Carl Loewe (1796–1869) *Trost in Tränen* Op. 80, book 2 no. 2 (1836)
	Peter Cornelius (1824–1874) *Trost in Tränen* Op. 14 for five voices and piano ad lib (1872–3)
	Johannes Brahms (1833–1897) *Trost in Tränen* Op. 48 no. 5 (1858)
	Arr. Tilman Hoppstock (b. 1961) for guitar accompaniment, in *Franz Schubert: 110 Lieder* (2009)
Discography and timing:	Fischer-Dieskau I 2[14] 3'40
	Hyperion I 12[19]
	Hyperion II 4[8] 3'42 Adrian Thompson

←— *Schäfers Klagelied* D121   *Ammenlied* D122 —→

Franz Schubert, coloured miniature (1829) by Robert Theer.

U

ÜBER ALLEN ZAUBER LIEBE

(Mayrhofer) **D682** [H439]
(Fragment) G major   *c.* 1820

Love above any magic

Sie hüpf - te mit mir auf grü - nem Plan,

(30 bars)

Sie hüpfte mit mir auf grünem Plan,[1]	She skipped with me on the green plain
Und sah die falbenden Linden an[2]	And gazed at the greying linden trees
Mit trauernden Kindesaugen;	With her sad child's eyes;
'Die stillen Lauben sind entlaubt,	'The silent arbours are leafless,
'Die Blumen hat der Herbst geraubt,	'Autumn has stolen the flowers,
'Der Herbst will gar nichts taugen.	'Autumn is good for nothing.
'Ach, du bist ein schönes Ding,	'Ah, you are a lovely thing,
'Frühling!	'Spring!
'Über allen Zauber Frühling.'	'You are above all magic – spring!'
Das zierliche Kind, wie's vor mir schwebt!	I see the dainty child in my mind's eye,
Aus Lilien und Rosen zart gewebt,	Delicately woven of lilies and roses,
Mit Augen gleich den Sternen; –	With eyes like stars.
'Blüht mir dein holdes Angesicht,	'When your sweet face glows before me,
'Dann mag, fürwahr ich zage nicht,	'Then – and in truth I'm not afraid to say it –
'Der Mayen sich entfernen.	'May can stay away.
'Färbet nur des Lebens Trübe	'Love alone brings colour to life's gloom,
'Liebe:	'Love!
'Über allen Zauber Liebe.'	'Above all magic – love!'

Johann Mayrhofer (1787–1836)

This is the thirty-seventh of Schubert's forty-seven Mayrhofer solo settings (1814–24). See the poet's biography for a chronological list of all the Mayrhofer settings.

Of all the Schubert fragments this is one of the most alluring. The greater part of the music is by Schubert himself – only four bars are needed to complete the setting (assuming Schubert

---

[1] Mayrhofer writes (*Gedichte*, 1824) 'Sie hüpfte *vor* mir auf grünem Plan'. For an explanation of the background to these alternative Mayrhofer readings see Editorial Note at the beginning of Johann Mayrhofer.
[2] Mayrhofer (*Gedichte*, 1824) has 'fahlenden' rather than 'falbenden'.

envisaged a strophic song, which seems possible, if not certain). If the composer had provided these missing bars himself, and had the song been printed in the Peters Edition, it is hard to imagine what would have prevented *Über allen Zauber Liebe* from being far better known. Probably the last of Schubert's Mayrhofer settings to be composed when Schubert still lived under the poet's roof in the Wipplingerstrasse, it is the only one to have remained an incomplete fragment.

The opening prelude is a lovely inspiration; the gently falling sequences of the little four-note cell are perfectly descriptive of summer memories shot through with autumn melancholy. The very shape of the piano writing on the page, bracketed in two-bar phrases, suggests the shelter of a fading tree, branches in an arbour gently swaying in the wind and fast losing their leaves. Everything is of the utmost delicacy and understatement. When the little girl begins to speak there is a long D pedal (from b. 13 beginning on 'Die stillen Lauben sind entlaubt') lasting seven bars. Autumn mist is built into music that floats while remaining suspended in the dominant, resisting a return to the tonic. Even when it wants to do so (at 'Der Herbst will gar nichts taugen' b. 19) the harmony is coloured by the wistfulness of F natural, the flattened seventh in G major. This seems to promise a plagal shift to C major, but there is a surprise in store: the setting of the word 'Ach' on a high G (b. 22) is supported instead by A^7, also in first inversion.

Even with a switch of mood and a change of time signature to $\frac{2}{4}$ (a tempo change is not marked, but is definitely implied) the harmony remains fixed on this inversion for '*Ach, du bist ein* schönes Ding'. The music only now seems to describe the skipping (hüpfen) mentioned in the first line. The lively dotted rhythm in each bar of the left-hand accompaniment suggests a movement both skittish and delicate. The harmony veers between A^7 (still in first inversion), the second inversion of G major, G^7 and C major. Throughout the song the effect of this continued distancing from the tonic is tantalizing, a perfect musical description of the search for something that has been lost, irretrievable except through memory. In this respect, and in the alternation between fast and slow tempi, the song is prophetic of another G major piece about spring's past happiness – *Frühlingstraum* from *Winterreise* D911/11. The only real cadence into an uncomplicated G major is on the very last word 'Frühling', but this is part of the Hoorickx completion (i.e. after b. 30). We have no idea what different and new ideas Schubert might have had up his sleeve had he bothered to finish the song. It is hard to guess why he never completed it.

The second verse actually refutes the assertions of the first: spring is not the most beautiful thing of all – May can stay away. It is *love* that colours everything. Thus it may be rather simplistic to imagine that Schubert would have been satisfied with a strophic solution using the same music and here, indeed, might lie the reason for the song's abandonment. While fitting the underlay of Mayrhofer's second verse to the music of the first is no problem (apart from the need to adopt the 'Ach' from the first verse (b. 22) that does not occur in the second), it is always possible that Schubert had something completely different in mind for the new mood. Nevertheless, Hoorickx's completion works well enough, and the music of the first strophe does good service for some of the imagery of the second – the delicate weave of lilies and roses, for example, are aptly pictured by the tendrils of those falling piano sequences. Not least because of these, *Über allen Zauber Liebe* remains a real *trouvaille*, a tiny piece of poignantly drifting Schubertian enchantment.

Autograph:	Wienbibliothek im Rathaus, Vienna (fragment)
First edition:	Published as part of the AGA in 1895; subsequently completed by Reinhard Van Hoorickx (P721)
Subsequent editions:	Not in Peters; AGA XX 599: Vol. 10/123; NSA IV: Vol. 12/224
Bibliography:	Winter 1978, p. 499

Further settings: Anselm Hüttenbrenner (1794–1868) *Über allen Zauber Liebe*
Discography and timing: Fischer-Dieskau   —
                      Hyperion I 34[16]
                      Hyperion II 22[14]   3'06   Martyn Hill

← *Strophe aus 'Die Götter Griechenlands' D677*   *Die Sterne D684* →

ÜBER WILDEMANN   Above Wildemann
(SCHULZE) OP. 108 NO. 1, **D884** [H601]
D minor   March 1826

(83 bars)

Die Winde sausen	The winds whistle
Am Tannenhang,	Over the pine-slopes,
Die Quellen brausen	The streams rush
Das Tal entlang;	Along the valley;
Ich wand're in Eile[1]	Hurriedly I tramp
Durch Wald und Schnee,	Through forest and snow,
Wohl manche Meile	For many a mile
Von Höh zu Höh.	From peak to peak.
Und will das Leben	And even though life
Im freien Tal	In the open valley
Sich auch schon heben	Is already stirring
Zum Sonnenstrahl;	To meet the sun's rays,
Ich muss vorüber	I must pass on,
Mit wildem Sinn	Troubled in spirit,
Und blicke lieber	Preferring to look
Zum Winter hin.	Towards winter.
Auf grünen Heiden,	In green fields,
Auf bunten Aun,	In many-coloured meadows
Müsst' ich mein Leiden	I would only contemplate
Nur immer schaun,	My suffering ceaselessly,
Dass selbst am Steine	Knowing that from the very stones,

[1] Schulze writes (*Poetische Schriften*, 1819) 'Ich *wandr*' in Eile'.

Das Leben spriesst,	Life burgeons
Und ach! nur Eine	And, alas, that only one creature
Ihr Herz verschliesst.	Closes her heart.
O Liebe, Liebe,	O love, o love,
O Maienhauch!	O breath of May!
Du drängst die Triebe	You force the shoots
Aus Baum und Strauch!	From tree and bush.
Die Vögel singen	The birds sing
Auf grünen Höhn,	On green hilltops;
Die Quellen springen	The springs gush forth
Bei deinem Wehn!	When you stir.
Mich lässt du schweifen	You leave me to roam
Im dunklen Wahn	With my dark imaginings,
Durch Windespfeifen	In whistling winds
Auf rauher Bahn.	Along the rough path.
O Frühlingsschimmer,	O gleam of spring,
O Blütenschein,	O sheen of blossom,
Soll ich denn nimmer	Shall I never again
Mich dein erfreun?	Delight in you?

ERNST SCHULZE (1789–1817); poem written 28 April 1816

This is the last of Schubert's ten Schulze solo settings (1825–6). See the poet's biography for a chronological list of all the Schulze settings. An outline of a suggested performing version for a Schulze cycle is listed under 'Auf den wilden Wegen'.

Schulze's title for this poem is a long-winded one, but it is helpful too: 'Overlooking Wildemann: a small town in the Harz mountains, 28 April 1816'. We can immediately piece together the picture: at this time of year spring has arrived in the valleys, but up in the mountains winter still holds sway. The poet looks down towards where the hope of a new season blossoms, conscious of a two-tiered existence where spring and winter fight for ascendancy, a metaphor for the conflict in his own mind. The path towards vernal fulfilment is blocked to him. The beautiful valley is utopian fantasy; the winter landscape of his soul will prevail whatever the season in the world of nature.

It is possible that Schubert himself thought of the 1826 Schulze settings – *Im Frühling* D882, *Lebensmut* D883 and *Über Wildemann* D884 – as a triptych showing different faces of spring remembered or anticipated. The wild mood swings between these three songs, almost certainly composed within days, if not hours, of each other, suggest the same organizational hand that was to make the *Winterreise* D911 sequence more than the sum of its parts. The contrasts and inconsistencies of the poet's moods are taken on with undisguised relish. *Über Wildemann* was probably the last of the Schulze songs to be composed and we can imagine Schubert's impatience for an encounter with another aspect of the poet's complex emotional situation. His musical responses to the overlay of winter and madness in this song show that he was already unconsciously preparing the way for the winter traveller. Susan Youens has pointed out a number of these similarities, prophetic of the later cycle. *Über Wildemann* shares the tonality of *Gute Nacht* D911/1, the alternation between unison texture and fuller harmonization of *Die Wetterfahne* D911/2, the incessant, restless motion of *Erstarrung* D911/4, as well as the winter tempests that shake the reverie of *Der Lindenbaum* D911/5, and it prefigures the rhythmical monomania of *Rückblick* D911/8. A similar disposition of the accompaniment between the hands is heard in *Die Krähe* D911/15 at the vocal climax of that song ('Treue bis zum Grabe!'); voice and piano in *Über Wildemann* reinforce one another for added stark strength as in *Der stürmische Morgen* D911/18 – and so on. Maurice Brown notes that a passage modelled on *Über Wildemann* appears in the C sharp minor episode of the last movement (bb. 323–57) of another masterpiece of 1826, the G major String Quartet D887.

In Verse 1 there is a lack of harmony in every sense. The high spirits of *Lebensmut* are here made to seem exceedingly hollow. A succession of hard-driven unisons is devoid of softening inner harmonies as the left hand pursues the right, always a quaver rest apart, with the tenacity of an animal chasing its own tail. Schulze is stripped of his bravado and is revealed bare and exposed in every sense. Jagged accents on the fourth beats of the bar create an impression of blind panic: there is no trusty steed here as in *Auf der Bruck* D853; the poet is alone with the elements and there is the suggestion not only of the howling of wind and rushing of streams, but also of a deranged person running hither and thither in search of his own shadow. A vivid impression of climbing up and down is given with the wide intervals in the vocal line throughout the song. The third and fourth lines of the verse are set twice, and 'Von Höh' zu Höh' ('from peak to peak') is sung three times in all. The notes for these four words in bb. 15 and 19 seem to trace the jagged outline of a mountain range on the stave.

Verses 2 and 3 have different music entirely, moving into the warmer regions of D major as life in the valley below is contemplated for a moment before being summarily dismissed. In Verse 2 (from b. 26) the singer rushes through the words, and there are none of the repetitions that have characterized the opening strophe. At the end of Verse 3 mention of the beloved, the 'one creature who closes her heart', prompts an anguished repeat of 'nur Eine / Ihr Herz verschliesst' (bb. 42–6). Verse 4 (where the word 'love' is repeated in pathetic distress in b. 52) is marked off as a separate and isolated moment; this is the heart of the work which its creator allows to beat for only a few moments – the better to highlight the icy body of music and madness that surrounds it. The 'shoots from tree and bush' put forth their flowers, and the harmonies blossom accordingly, coaxed into life by the inner fingers of the pianist's right hand as they warm into action. The key of A major prompts yet another comparison with a song from *Winterreise*, and another hopeless evocation of springtime happiness, *Frühlingstraum* D911/11. The music for Verse 5 is more or less a repeat of the opening verse.

This technique of using matching strophic bookends to contain the inner substance of a song is used elsewhere in the Schulze settings from the *Poetisches Tagebuch*, and for the same purpose: the depiction of energy that can achieve nothing, stunted as it is by the immovable limits of the poet's own psyche. The bewildered Schulze is caught like an insect in the web of his dark imaginings; the confines of Schubert's strophic reformatory (where song form is groomed for a new and more useful life) are where the poet's fate has found its only enduring musical metaphor.

The marking of the song in the printed edition is 'Schnell' but the fair copy prepared by Schubert for the publishers – the so-called 'Stichvorlage' – has 'Nicht zu schnell'. The piece is in common time and not *alla breve,* which should be warning enough against adopting a tempo that hurtles out of control and turns the text into a gabble. For performers for whom this aspect of the weighing of speeds is not familiar, Schubert's original marking (we do not know if he saw a proof of this song published soon after his death) should be taken seriously.

Autograph: Wienbibliothek im Rathaus, Vienna (fair copy)
First edition: Published as Op. post. 108 no. 1 by M. J. Leidesdorf, Vienna in
                        January 1829 (P193)

Subsequent editions:	Peters: Vol. 3/80; AGA XX 500: Vol. 8/216; NSA IV: Vol. 5a/120; Bärenreiter: Vol. 4/33
Bibliography:	Brown 1958, p. 274
	Capell 1928, p. 216
	Hoorickx 1976[2], pp. 260–63
	Youens 1996, pp. 297–302
Discography and timing:	Fischer-Dieskau II 8[9] 2'10
	Hyperion I 18[21]
	Hyperion II 32[7] 2'11 Peter Schreier

← *Lebensmut* D883   *Dithyrambe* D801 →

JOHANN LUDWIG UHLAND (1787–1862)

THE POETIC SOURCE
Gedichte von Ludwig Uhland. Stuttgart und Tübingen, in der J. G. Cotta'schen Buchhandlung, 1815

THE SONG
September 1820   *Frühlingsglaube* D686 [p. 54, no. 2 of sub-section entitled *Frühlingslieder*]

Of the many great German poets who have lived and worked in the beautiful university town of Tübingen (among them Hölderlin and Mörike), Ludwig Uhland was the only one to have been born there (on 26 April 1787). He displayed precocious gifts and studied law from the age of fourteen. His friendship with Justinus Kerner (a poet set by Schumann within Schubert's lifetime) dates from these early years, as does his love of folksong and medieval poetry. Uhland was soon regarded as a leading member of the so-called Swabian School of the Romantic movement. He visited Paris as a young man in order to study the Code Napoléon, and also researched medieval manuscripts in the Bibliothèque Nationale. His *Gedichte* were published in 1815 and the bulk of his creative work dates from his early years. His *Wanderlieder* (1813) were much admired by Wilhelm Müller and thus influenced the Schubert of the great cycles, and not only poetically. It is likely that Schubert knew *Frühlingslieder* and *Wanderlieder*, the two Uhland cycles Opp. 33 and 34 composed by Conradin Kreutzer (1780–1849) sometime before 1818. The *Wanderlieder* seem to have played a significant part as models for the shape and mood of

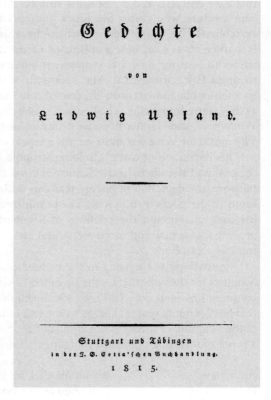

First edition of Uhland's *Gedichte* (1815).

Winterreise D911, and Schubert is known to have admired them, on one occasion claiming that he would have been proud to have composed them. Schubert might well have deliberately refrained from setting more poems by Uhland because he regarded the poet as 'belonging' to the older Kreutzer, much in the same way that Schubert's own name had become linked to Goethe's poetry (there is but a single Kreutzer setting of Goethe – a mirror image of the position with Schubert and Uhland). Schubert's ballad-writing phase as a composer was over by the time he became aware of Uhland's poetry – it is in the story-telling ballads that this poet was a supreme master.

Uhland had a distinguished career as a lawyer, and as a politician representing both Tübingen and Stuttgart as a member of parliament. He combined these roles with that of an even more highly regarded literary scholar. Although he wrote a volume of patriotic verses in 1817, his reputation was as a liberal (he was unpopular with many conservatives), and he was shocked by the repressive measures taken against students and intellectuals. He was briefly a member of the new German parliament in Frankfurt (1848/9) which was the outcome of the revolutions of 1848.

The poetry of Uhland was much admired by Mayrhofer (who would have been aware of his liberal anti-demagogic sympathies) and it could have been Mayrhofer who introduced Schubert to *Frühlingsglaube*. Walther Dürr has suggested that the poem itself may have had political implications: Uhland wrote it in 1812 when a new political spring, and freedom from Napoleonic domination, was around the corner. Perhaps Mayrhofer read the text and imagined a political Utopia in Vienna without censorship and police repression. Nevertheless, Schubert's interpretation of the poem

Ludwig Uhland after a painting by Morst, frontispiece in *Moosrosen Taschenbuch für 1826*.

seems personal rather than political. When he published the song as part of his Op. 20 he chose to group it with *Sei mir gegrüsst* D741 and *Hänflings Liebeswerbung* D552. These songs were dedicated to Justina von Bruchmann, the mother of his friend Franz von Bruchmann, who in 1820 was recovering from the death of her daughter Sybilla. The commentary on *Sei mir gegrüsst!* suggests the elegiac possibilities of that song, and *Frühlingsglaube* might also have been intended in this context as a consolatory gesture to its dedicatee. Schumann, Brahms and Richard Strauss later all set Uhland's verse with enthusiasm. The poet died in Tübingen on 13 November 1862.

UM MITTERNACHT   At midnight
(SCHULZE) OP. 88 NO. 3, **D862** [H580]

The song exists in two versions, the second of which is discussed below:
(1) December 1825; (2) March 1826?

(1) 'Sehr mässig'   B♭ major $\frac{2}{4}$ [82 bars]

(2)   B♭ major

Keine Stimme hör' ich schallen,	I hear no voice,
Keinen Schritt auf dunkler Bahn,	No footstep on the dark path;
Selbst der Himmel hat die schönen	Even heaven has closed
Hellen Äuglein zugetan.	Its beautiful bright eyes.
Ich nur wache, süsses Leben,	I alone am awake, sweet life,
Schaue sehnend in die Nacht,	Gazing longingly into the night
Bis dein Stern in öder Ferne	Until, out of the bleak distance,
Lieblich leuchtend mir erwacht.	Your star comes out to me with its lovely
	radiance.
Ach, nur einmal, nur verstohlen	Ah, if I could see your beloved image
Dein geliebtes Bild zu sehn,	But once, secretly,
Wollt' ich gern in Sturm und Wetter[1]	I would gladly stand long into the morning
Bis zum späten Morgen stehn!	In storm and tempest.
Seh' ich's nicht von ferne leuchten?[2]	Do I not see it shining in the distance?
Naht es nicht schon nach und nach?	Is it not gradually approaching?
Ach, und freundlich hör' ich's flüstern:	Ah, I hear it whispering gently:
Sieh, der Freund ist auch noch wach.	'See your friend is already awake.'
Süsses Wort, geliebte Stimme,	Sweet words, dear voice
Der mein Herz entgegenschlägt!	At which my heart beats in sympathy
Tausend sel'ge Liebesbilder	Your breath has stirred within me
Hat dein Hauch mir aufgeregt.	A thousand blissful images of love.
Alle Sterne seh' ich glänzen	I see all the stars gleaming
Auf der dunklen blauen Bahn,[3]	On their deep-blue course;

[1] Schulze writes (*Poetische Schriften*, 1819) 'Wollt' ich gern *im* Sturm und Wetter'.
[2] Schulze writes (*Poetische Schriften*, 1819) 'Seh' ich's nicht *schon* ferne leuchten?'
[3] Schulze writes (*Poetische Schriften*, 1819) 'Auf der *dunkelblauen* Bahn'.

Und im Herzen hat und droben	The sky has cleared, up above
Sich der Himmel aufgetan.	And within my heart.
Holder Nachhall, wiege freundlich	Sweet echo, lull now
Jetzt mein Haupt in milde Ruh',	My head to gentle rest;
Und noch oft, ihr Träume, lispelt	Dreams, whisper often to me
Ihr geliebtes Wort mir zu!	Her beloved words.

ERNST SCHULZE (1789–1817); poem written 5 March 1815

This is the fifth of Schubert's ten Schulze solo settings (1825–6). See the poet's biography for a chronological list of all the Schulze settings. An outline of a suggested performing version for a Schulze cycle is listed under 'Auf den wilden Wegen'.

Schulze wrote this poem 'on 5th March 1815, at midnight'. The sleepless poet imagines an encounter with a star, the beloved Adelheid's special representative and messenger. Schulze overhears the heavenly body reporting back to Adelheid: 'See, your friend is already awake.' This is enough to conjure up all the fantasies of the love he imagines has passed between them. Schubert excised the date from the title, preferring the piece to have a less specific date. B flat major is a favourite key for the composer in nocturnal mood; one thinks of *Wandrers Nachtlied* II D768, *Der Winterabend* D938 and the gloriously ethereal *Nachthelle* D892 for men's chorus and 'damnably high tenor'. The piano writing suggests a scoring for flutes and bassoons – a wind serenade from an earlier century. The recurring double-dotted figure (a major difference this, between the first version and the second) lends a courtly, old-fashioned gait to the proceedings.

The poem has seven strophes, and Schubert uses two of the poet's verses to make one of his, giving us three and a half musical verses. Thus, apart from the surprise of the ending seeming to come sooner than we expect, the form is an extremely simple strophic one. Indeed, compared to that stirring nocturne from a few years earlier, *Die junge Nonne* D828, the approach seems minimalist. In the course of that intricate, *durchkomponiert* setting, the narrator undergoes a mystical experience that fundamentally changes her life (or death), as can be heard in the ever-developing music. The poem of *Um Mitternacht* might have suggested a similar scope for development – initial loneliness, the disembodied and almost supernatural appearance of a star, Adelheid's plenipotentiary, who acts as an intermediary between the poet and his beloved. This is followed by the clearing of the heavens and transfigured bliss on a starlit night (cf. the Bruchmann setting *Schwestergruss* D762). But Schubert's decision to keep the song uneventfully strophic comes from an attentive and utterly intuitive reading of the real Ernst Schulze behind the text. The composer has decided that the poem has nothing to do with a real beloved, but concerns Schulze's fantasy of someone he can summon with the help of poetry's magic lamp, as if he were Aladdin stranded on a desert island, or locked up in a cell. He *is* locked up, but in a state of mind called 'undying love'. Because nothing really happens in the poem, we hear no real change in his condition from first to last.

On the other hand the poetry is of indisputable beauty and it is a hallmark of Schulze's gift that despite the narcissism and the narrow parameters of his inner world he has the power to summon some of Schubert's most wonderful ideas. The opening of this song is no exception. A falling sequence (in $\frac{3}{4}$) of accented second beats and weak first beats evokes 'heavy sighing . . . depression and descent' (Susan Youens). The repetition of six mezzo staccato quavers on a single chord (in bb. 2–3, and later at bb. 24–5) is a time-honoured motif denoting stars (see Eric Sams's contribution to the 'Lied' article in the *New Grove Dictionary of Music and Musicians*, 1980, Vol. 10, p. 840). For Susan Youens, on the other hand, this is prophetic of *Winterreise* where the motif is seminal to *Gute Nacht* D911/1 and *Der Wegweiser* D911/20. So rich and multi-faceted is Schubert's motivic language that we can all hear different things, or rather more than one thing, in any one idea. For example, the whole first verse of the poem seems prefigured in the music of this introduction: although the poet says 'no voice' and 'no footstep', the composer illustrates these things nonetheless. The falling sequences are pleadingly vocal, the staccato chords footsteps (cf. the left-hand chords of the walking moon in *An den Mond in einer Herbstnacht* D614) and the repeated chords and cadential flourish when repeated in a higher register are perfect for the bright starry eyes of heaven.

This is music of the spheres, a stately dance to the music of timelessness, an impression that deepens as strophe follows strophe. In a slower, more courtly version of that cosmic moto perpetuo *Die Sterne* D939, the poet's troubles are played out against a background of stars which continue their round dance regardless of his woes. In bb. 12–13 the voice's eloquent leap of a ninth on 'Hellen Äuglein' (echoed in the piano in bb. 14–15) is distressingly touching. It is also disarming, for the vocal line has the innocence of childhood, or of madness – and the same self-contained dignity. With this observation another song in B flat written earlier in 1825 comes to mind. In *Der blinde Knabe* D833 there is an air of pathetic and naive sweetness that much resembles the tone and happy self-delusion of *Um Mitternacht*. The blind boy, also trapped in darkness, is locked in his own world; he does not want to see the light because he has his fantasy and imagination with which to see anything he pleases. He is king of his own world where any woman might be as beautiful as he chooses to imagine. In the same way Schulze summons the indifferent, even hostile Adelheid Tychsen to his side with the help of a star, an imaginary celestial go-between, and she somehow becomes Adelheid the compassionate. Schubert, who had eyes in the back of his head when it came to sizing people up, has perfectly understood that at the witching hour of night and dreams, blindness is something that can afflict both madmen and poets.

Autograph:	Missing or lost
Publication:	First published as part of the NSA in 1979 (P772; first version)
	First published as Op. 88 no. 3 by Thaddäus Weigl, Vienna in December 1827 (P139; second version)
Subsequent editions:	Peters: Vol. 2/162; AGA XX 499: Vol. 8/212; NSA IV: Vol. 4a/104 & Vol. 4b/236; Bärenreiter: Vol. 3/72
Bibliography:	Capell 1928, p. 217
	Fischer-Dieskau 1977, p. 227
	Youens 1996, pp. 281–7
Discography and timing:	Fischer-Dieskau II 8[8] 3'27 (strophes 1–4 and 7 only)
	Hyperion I 18[14]
	Hyperion II 31[3] 6'04 Peter Schreier

←— *Der liebliche Stern* D861   *O Quell, was strömst du rasch und wild* D874 —→

Dem UNENDLICHEN   To the infinite one
(KLOPSTOCK) **D291** [H177 & H178A]

The song exists in three versions, the second of which is discussed below:
(1) 15 September 1815; (2) Late 1815; (3) Late 1815

(1) 'Sehr langsam'   F major – E♭ major   **C**   [71 bars]

(2)   F major – E♭ major

Sehr langsam

Wie er-hebt sich das Herz, wenn es dich, Un-end-li-cher, denkt!

(71 bars)

(3)   'Sehr langsam'   G major – E♭ major   𝄴   [72 bars]

Wie erhebt sich das Herz, wenn es dich,	How the heart surges when it thinks of you,
Unendlicher, denkt! wie sinkt es,	Infinite One! How it sinks
Wenn es auf sich herunterschaut!	When it gazes down upon itself!
Elend schauts wehklagend dann, und Nacht und Tod!	Lamenting, it sees but misery, night and death!
Allein du rufst mich aus meiner Nacht, der im Elend, der im Tode hilft!	You alone call me from my night, you alone help me in misery and death!
Dann denk' ich es ganz, dass du ewig mich schufst,	Then I know that you created me for eternity,
Herrlicher! den kein Preis, unten am Grab', oben am Thron,	Lord of Glory, for whom no praise is sufficient, in the grave below or by your throne above,
Herr Gott! den dankend entflammt, kein Jubel genug besingt.	Lord God, no paeans of thanks are worthy of you.
Weht, Bäume des Lebens, ins Harfengetön!	Sway, trees of life, to the music of the harps!
Rausche mit ihnen ins Harfengetön, kristallner Strom!	Murmur with them to the harps' music, crystal streams!
Ihr lispelt, und rauscht, und, Harfen, ihr tönt	You whisper and murmur, and, harps, you play,
Nie es ganz! Gott ist es, den ihr preist!	But never fully enough; it is God whom you praise!
Welten, donnert, in feierlichem Gang,	Thunder, you spheres
Welten, donnert, in der Posaunen Chor![1]	In solemn motion, to the choir of trumpets!
Tönt, all' ihr Sonnen auf der Strasse voll Glanz,	Resound, all you suns on your shining course,
In der Posaunen Chor!	To the choir of trumpets!
Ihr Welten, ihr donnert,[2]	You thunder, spheres,
Du, der Posaunen Chor, hallest	Choir of trumpets, you blaze forth,
Nie es ganz: Gott – nie es ganz: Gott,	But never fully enough;
Gott, Gott ist es, den ihr preist!	It is God, God whom you praise.

FRIEDRICH GOTTLOB KLOPSTOCK (1724–1803); poem begun in 1764

This is the eighth of Schubert's thirteen Klopstock solo settings (1815–16). See the poet's biography for a chronological list of all the Klopstock settings.

[1] Schubert reverses the first two words of Klopstock's line, which is 'Donnert, Welten, in feierlichem Gang, in der Posaunen Chor!' The following line ('Du Orion, Wage, du auch!') is cut by Schubert.
[2] The second 'ihr' in this line is inserted by Schubert who also cuts 'Und' at the beginning of the second line.

We know that Schubert admired the Klopstock odes: he attempted to write one of his own in the poet's high-flown manner sometime in 1813, but the manuscript is now lost. Even today it is hard to resist the grandeur and eloquence of Klopstock's style when he is on a 'roll', a word as suitable for his writing as for the imposing vibrations of a clap of thunder. He was one of the earliest poets (in terms of historical chronology) whom Schubert was to set with relative frequency. Klopstock's old-fashioned language (his idol was Milton) is ideally suited to his subject matter which, with the exception of some exquisite love lyrics, is largely religious or historical (cf. the Teutonic ballad *Hermann und Thusnelda* D322). Pyrker was indebted to him, of course, as were numerous other poets of a later generation who wrote on religious or patriotic themes. It was to Klopstock that Goethe owed his experiments in unrhymed verse – works such as *Ganymed* and *Prometheus*.

The song suggests delivery from the pulpit, so closely does it simulate the fiery oratory of an inspired preacher. This commentary discusses the second version (which begins in F major) rather than the third that begins in G major. There is some likelihood that the third represents Schubert's final thoughts (the key relationship of its two sections preserves his favourite conjunction of tonic and flattened sixth in E flat), but it is the second of the two F major versions that is familiar to most singers through the Peters Edition. In fact the variations between the three songs are scarcely discernible to the average listener. There is a crucial, yet small, modulation in the opening recitative, and this is the major difference; the main body of the work, the long paean of praise to God in E flat major, is essentially the same in all three versions, although there are some alterations to the layout of the accompaniment.

The music begins with dotted rhythms in the style of Handel: a dotted quaver in the bass followed by the reverberation of fanfare-like demisemiquavers. There are two such flourishes, the first grounded in the earth, the second aspiring to heaven, and then, as if the idea were gathering force, they spread like wildfire across the stave, the original fanfare motifs spawning chords in dotted semiquavers that traverse the keyboard in ecstatic proclamation (b. 2). We land on a C major semibreve in b. 3 and the voice, unfettered by accompaniment, enters with 'Wie erhebt sich das Herz'. This is a style of which the eighteen-year-old Schubert is already master – recitative imbued with the outlines of memorable melody. The upward gaze to heaven is mirrored by a glance downwards at the inadequacies of man, sung as if from on high. The piano's fanfares in the middle of the keyboard are more muted in b. 5, and the vocal line is pulled downwards into the chest register by the imagery of night and death. The four-bar piano interlude ('Mit mehr Bewegung' bb. 9–12) consists of ceremonial mezzo staccato quavers heard in sequential flourishes traversing three different registers. These phrases seem to ponder mortality with music that is reminiscent of the deathbed musings of *Verklärung* D59, a setting of a Pope translation and one of the exceptional songs of 1813.

The recitative continues at b. 13 ('Allein du rufst mich aus meiner Nacht') and, true to the meaning of the words, the music begins once more to struggle towards the source of heavenly light, the piano supporting the voice at crucial points. This succession of phrases is remarkable for superb word-setting. The sequence of rising chords after 'der im Tode hilft!' (b. 14) is like an ever-tightening winch pulling the weight of mankind's misery out of the mire. After two bars this lands the music in a distant B major (b. 16) where the piano's chord is held beneath the phrase 'Dann denk' ich es ganz, dass du ewig mich schufst'. On the word 'schufst' ('created') there is a shift to an unsurprising E minor chord but what follows is worthy of the split-second moment when something made of granite acquires the breath of life before our eyes. On the third beat of the bar a bass line of two falling staccato quavers (plus right-hand chords) leads us into the sunshine of C major (last crotchet of b. 17), the elemental key that conveys the brightness of Creation itself. We remain there just long enough to look God in the face for an off-beat setting of 'Herrlicher!' which plunges an octave between the first and second syllables, and then the voice is launched into a remarkable passage of recitative. Goodness knows how on earth (or heaven) Schubert brings this off! The depth of 'Grab' ('grave') and the height of 'Thron' ('throne') are pointedly contrasted within different ends of the same octave in an extraordinary vocal span that shines a spotlight on the heavens so wide-ranging that it seems in danger of spinning out of control. The voice goes on a high, starry walkabout while the piano holds the reins of power. We hardly notice the inexorable rise of the accompaniment's bass (a long progression in bb. 19 and 20 from low F to B flat in semitones) but the tension generated by this slow ascent deep in the heart of the music makes the launch into the next section quite thrilling. A vocal plunge from the high A flat of 'Jubel' into a new E flat aria ('den dankend entflammt, kein Jubel genug besingt') is supported by a resounding B flat^7 chord in b. 21; the arrival of the spinning E flat major sextuplets of the new section feels as inevitable as the turning of the world, or the progression of the seasons.

There could scarcely have been a more effective build-up to a ringing peroration. And the aria itself (marked 'Langsam, mit aller Kraft') does not disappoint. This is mighty music, painted with a generously broad brush, and only a large voice could really do it justice. Schubert must have had in mind a powerful singer like Anna Milder, whom he had earlier heard in the great Gluck operas. *Dem Unendlichen* would certainly have been beyond Therese Grob, the soprano in the Liechtenthal parish church choir and, it is said, the earliest object of Schubert's affections.

Throughout this hymn to the Creator the right hand is engaged in flowing sextuplets. With typical Schubertian ingenuity these represent, all at the same time, the wind-blown undulations of the branches of the trees of life, the arpeggios of sacred harps and the rippling of crystal streams. The music associated with this last image is a powerful pre-echo of the brook music for *Wohin?* D795/2 in *Die schöne Müllerin* – particularly at the words 'Ihr lispelt, und rauscht' (bb. 30–32) with the diminished-chord harmony suggesting something secret and confidential. The right hand, however, is relatively unimportant here; the source of the music's imposing grandeur lies in the glorious interplay between the majestic vocal line and the left-hand octaves. These variously thunder and resound, more in the trombone register than that of the 'choir of trumpets' suggested by the translation. The German word 'Posaune' covers both: 'trumpets' sounds more elegant in English, but surely Schubert had the larger instrument in mind, considering trombones were commonly heard in Vienna at the graveside *equali* of burial services.

At the end of the third strophe the word 'Gott' on a minim (b. 35) stops the music in its tracks, as if inspiring awe and veneration. The sextuplets cease and, as the singer holds on to the word for nearly three beats on an E flat, the piano shifts from chords of E flat major to C minor to A flat major, each a single sforzato crotchet. This, unique in the song, surely represents three ways of looking at God – a trinity of viewpoints. At the end of the phrase 'den ihr preist!' the sextuplets resume in b. 39 and the voice traverses an octave, finishing on a stentorian low B flat at the beginning of that bar.

The final two strophes recycle and develop the music already heard, with subtle changes of tonal emphasis and tessitura to ensure an overwhelming sense of climbing excitement and fervour and a final vocal cadence ending in the tonic of E flat major rather than B flat. Settings of the word 'Gott' on the song's final page (bb. 59 and 61) are a subtle succession of rising notes of ever-increasing intensity: first a simple minim, then a crotchet tied over the bar line with a semitone ascent only on the last quaver; then a high G flat that seems poised to shine for ever in the heavens. This is, in fact, only a minim tied to a dotted quaver, with the two final words 'ist es' brilliantly added when one thinks that the singer must be nearly out of breath. The effect is of a gush of dizzying emotion such as someone speaking in tongues might experience. Everything about this song is extraordinary – it blazes with such inner fire that it could easily be taken as evidence of the composer's passionate belief in God and all his works. But knowing Schubert's enormous gift for empathy with his poets it could also be seen as a portrait of Klopstock's own convictions and a tribute to the Messianic faith of an earlier epoch.

Autographs:	Gesellschaft der Musikfreunde, Vienna (first draft; first version)
	Pierpont Morgan Library, New York (fair copy; second version)
	Staatsbibliothek Preussischer Kulturbesitz, Berlin with a heading
	of 'deutsche Gedichte' as if this song was to be one of an
	assembled, and unknown to us, group of lieder (third version)
Publication:	First published as part of the AGA in 1895 (P588; first version)
	First published as Book 10 no. 1 of the *Nachlass* by Diabelli,
	Vienna in April 1831 (P262; second version)
	First published as part of the AGA in 1895 (P589; third version)
Subsequent editions:	Peters: Vol. 5/31; AGA XX 145a–c: Vol. 3/85; NSA IV: Vol. 9/72, 78 & 84

Discography and timing:	Fischer-Dieskau I 5^{24}	4'43	
	Hyperion I 5^{14}	4'39	Elizabeth Connell (2nd version)
	Hyperion I 31^3	4'20	Christine Brewer (3rd version)
	Hyperion II 10^{12}	4'39	Elizabeth Connell
	Hyperion II 10^{14}	4'20	Christine Brewer

← *Die frühen Gräber* D290　　　　　　　　　　　*Shilrik und Vinvela* D293 →
← *Shilrik und Vinvela* D293　　　　　　　　　　　*Erlkönig* D328 →

UNGEDULD *see Die SCHÖNE MÜLLERIN* D795/7

JOHANN KARL UNGER (1771–1836?)

THE POETIC SOURCES
S1 [manuscript in Unger's own hand] *Joh. Ungers Lieder. Nachgeahmt oder Von ihm selbst gedichtet und in Musik gesetzt*

S2 *Österreichisches Taschenbuch für das Jahr 1804.* Wien

THE SONGS
January 1818	*Die Geselligkeit* (also known as *Lebenslust*) D609 [S1: pp. 31–2] [S2: pp. 49–51]
April or earlier, 1821	*Die Nachtigall* D724 [S1: pp. 21–2]

Johann Unger was born in Rissdorf, Zips in Hungary (now Ruskinova in the Slovak Republic) on 13 April 1771. He was a sometime lawyer, teacher, writer and singer. He studied theology in Neutra (now Nitra in Slovakia) but soon decided to become a lawyer and moved to Vienna. He took up a position as private tutor to a Hungarian nobleman, Baron Ignaz Forgács, spending his winters in Vienna and his summers on the Baron's Moravian estates. He was a published poet by the age of twenty-eight (*Gedichte*, 1797 – one of which is a translation of Dryden's *The Invention of the First Instrument* from *A Song for St Cecilia's Day*, 1687) and contributed to a number of almanacs. He also wrote travel books: his 'Journey through the mountainous regions of Austria and Styria' was published in Vienna in 1803,

Gedichte by Unger (Vienna, 1797). The frontispiece is a portrait of the dedicatee of the volume who took her nickname from a famous Italian contralto of the 1720s.

as was a travellers' guide to Hungary in the same year. Legal textbooks were another sideline.

Unger was well connected with the Hungarian nobility. He was responsible for introducing Schubert to the Esterházy family when the count was seeking a live-in music teacher for his two daughters during the summers. This resulted in Schubert's paid employment in the summer months of 1814 and 1824 at Zseliz in Hungary. Unger married above his station – his wife was the Baroness Anna Cavarese Karminsky. He was the father of the celebrated mezzo soprano Karoline Unger (1803–77) who later composed songs under her married name of Sabatier. Karoline was a singing pupil of Vogl and the first mezzo soprano to sing in Beethoven's Ninth Symphony Op. 125. In February 1821 Schubert was appointed to a temporary post as repetiteur

Johann Karl Unger after a painting by Johann Niedermann.

by the Kärntnertortheater, and he was responsible for coaching Karoline in the role of Dorabella in *Così fan tutte* [see SINGERS]. Johann
Unger died in 1836.

Schubert set two texts by Unger, *Die Geselligkeit* in 1818 for SATB quartet and, in 1821,
Die Nachtigall for male quartet, which was an
immediate hit. Neither of these appears in the
volume of lyrics by Unger that had been
published in 1797. Unger's aspirations as a
poet are well documented, but it is an almost
unknown fact that he was also a rather talented
amateur composer and took pleasure in setting
his own poems. Indeed, he set both *Die Geselligkeit* and *Die Nachtigall* as solo songs. Some
years ago I acquired a slim volume of his lieder
(possibly the only one) – fifty-six pages scrupulously handwritten in sepia ink, and beautifully bound and labelled. This volume was
almost certainly Schubert's source for the two
poems he set as vocal quartets. Pictured right
is a page from Unger's manuscript of his own
setting of *Die Nachtigall*. Note the sudden
eruption of a piano cadenza that depicts the
warbling of the bird. Unlike Schubert, Unger
the amateur composer did not dare ask such
virtuosity of his singers.

Unger's own solo setting of *Die Nachtigall*, from
a volume of his vocal compositions. Among these
is *Die Geselligkeit*, the other Unger poem set by
Schubert.

Der UNGLÜCKLICHE   The folorn one
(PICHLER) OP. 87 NO. 1, **D713** [H464]

The song exists in two versions, the second of which is discussed below:
(1) January 1821; (2) appeared August 1827

(1) 'Langsam'   B minor $\frac{12}{8}$ [85 bars]

(2) B minor

Die Nacht bricht an,_____ mit lei - sen Lüf - ten sin - ket sie

(153 bars)

Die Nacht bricht an, mit leisen Lüften sinket	Night falls, descending with light breezes
Sie auf die müden Sterblichen herab.	Upon weary mortals.
Der sanfte Schlaf, des Todes Bruder, winket,	Gentle sleep, death's brother, beckons,
Und legt sie freundlich in ihr täglich Grab.	And lays them fondly in their daily graves.
Jetzt wachet auf der lichtberaubten Erde	Now only malice and pain
Vielleicht nur noch die Arglist und der Schmerz;	Perchance watch over the earth, robbed of light;
Und jetzt, da ich durch nichts gestöret werde,	And now, since nothing may disturb me,
Lass deine Wunden bluten, armes Herz!	Let your wounds bleed, poor heart.
Versenke dich in deines Kummers Tiefen,	Plunge to the depths of your grief,
Und wenn vielleicht in der zerriss'nen Brust	And if perchance half-forgotten sorrows
Halb verjährte Leiden schliefen,[1]	Have slept in your anguished heart,
So wecke sie mit grausam süsser Lust!	Awaken them with cruelly sweet delight!
Berechne die verlornen Seligkeiten,	Consider your lost happiness,
Zähl' alle Blumen in dem Paradies,	Count all the flowers in paradise,
Woraus in deiner Jugend goldnen Zeiten	From which, in the golden days of your youth,
Die harte Hand des Schicksals dich verstiess!	The harsh hand of fate banished you!
Du hast geliebt, du hast das Glück empfunden,	You have loved, you have experienced a happiness
Dem jede Seligkeit der Erde weicht.	Which eclipses all earthly bliss.
Du hast ein Herz, das dich verstand, gefunden,	You have found a heart that understands you,
Der kühnsten Hoffnung schönes Ziel erreicht.	Your wildest hopes have attained their fair goal.
Da stürzte dich ein grausam Machtwort nieder,	Then the cruel decree of authority dashed you down
Aus deinen Himmeln, und dein stilles Glück,	From your heaven, and your tranquil happiness,
Dein allzuschönes Traumbild, kehrte wieder[2]	Your all-too-lovely dream vision, returned
Zur bessern Welt, aus der es kam, zurück.	To the better world from which it came.
Zerrissen sind nun alle süssen Bande;	Now all the sweet bonds are torn asunder;
Mir schlägt kein Herz mehr auf der weiten Welt!	No heart now beats for me in the whole world!
[(. . . 6 lines . . .)]	[(. . . 6 lines . . .)]

KAROLINE PICHLER (1769–1843)

This is the last of Schubert's four Pichler solo settings (1816, a song of an unknown date, and 1821). See the poet's biography for a chronological list of all the Pichler settings.

Der Unglückliche is one of the few Schubert songs for which there is an extant skeleton sketch (AGA *Revisionsbericht* No. 390 and NSA Volume 4b p. 257). This gives us a glimpse into the composer's workshop and reminds us that he conceived at least some (perhaps all) of his songs in a type of shorthand – the vocal line supported by the bass line, leaving most of the accompaniment to be added at a later stage. Concentrating on the movement of the voice supported by the bass in a short score of two staves, and writing at considerable speed, the composer's

---

[1] Pichler writes (*Olivier*, 1803 and 1821) '*Verjährte, halb vergess'ne* Leiden schliefen'.
[2] Pichler writes (*Olivier*, 1803 and 1821) '*Das allzu schöne* Traumbild, kehrte wieder'.

First edition of *Der Unglückliche* and two other songs, Op. 87 (1827).

highest priorities were evidently spontaneous melodic flow, the correct prosody of the vocal line and a strong basic architecture of shape and harmony. Although the piano part seems to have been left until last, it is probable that Schubert simply kept his ideas for the accompaniment safely in his head until the time came to go one step further: the making of a first draft with the piano writing filled in, or even a fair copy. There are no corrections in this sketch, and it is amazing how near this ground plan is to the final version of this song. The initial time signature of 𝄽 which survived in the song's first version was subsequently changed to §, suggesting a slower, heavier tempo with stronger, more forlorn downbeats.

The song is divided into five main sections. Pichler's poem is printed in four strophes of eight lines each (only two lines of the final strophe are set by the composer). The last six lines of text, not set by Schubert, portray a kind of redemption through duty, and end in a slightly more optimistic mood than is suggested by the rest of the poem:

Was ist's, das mich in diesem Schattenslande,	What is it that keeps me here
In dieser toten Einsamkeit noch hält?	In this deathlike solitude?
Nur einen Lichtstrahl seh ich von ferne blinken;	I can see but one ray of light shining from afar,
Im Götterglanz erscheint die heilge Pflicht:	It is this divine radiance that reveals my sacred duty.
Und wenn des müden Geistes Kräfte sinken,	And should the strength of my weary spirit fail,
So sinkt der Mut, den sie mir einflösst, nicht.	The courage it inspires in me shall not do so.

The opening marking is 'Langsam' for an elegiac introduction in B minor – a tonality of high passion in Schubert's work, but also of depression and derangement (cf. *Die liebe Farbe* D795/16 from *Die schöne Müllerin* written two years later). We are introduced to the pessimistic nature of the wanderer and, in the sections that move into the major, the modifying consolation of nightfall. This opening passage owes a great deal to the 'Andante' movement of the A major Piano Sonata D664. It is possible that this work was written in Steyr, Vogl's home town, while the composer was on holiday with the singer in the summer of 1819; it was perhaps this sonata that Anton Stadler had intended to identify as being a favourite of Vogl's. If this was the case it is likely that Schubert was deliberately quoting from the D major movement of the Sonata to further associate the singer with music which he already admired. The opening of the 'Andante' is heard almost note for note in the bar of accompaniment after the words 'sinket sie' (bb. 11–12). Incidentally, Schubert, understandably, ignores the separation of the verb 'sinken' (at the end of the first line of Pichler's printed poem) from its subject 'sie' at the beginning of the next. The poet's scansion is not the only source of awkwardness: Schubert's emphasis of the word 'auf' – given almost an entire bar of music at b. 13 – is not exactly a miracle of prosody. It is a sign of Schubert's mature style (as opposed to his ballad style of earlier years) that he seeks to unify such a long piece, in a number of sections, by ensuring that the time signature remains the same until the very end – where it changes to dramatic effect. On the repeated words 'in ihr täglich Grab', there is a tender imitation between voice and piano (bb. 24–5), gently appropriate to a text that describes a reciprocated gesture of friendship.

Under cover of night the dark forces of depression emerge to taunt the wretched protagonist, like wolves slinking out of a forest. At b. 31 ('Etwas geschwinder') semiquavers begin to rustle in the right hand, disturbing the calm established in the opening section. For a moment the pianist settles on unison octave Bs including a right-hand tremolando, but then the left hand sinks down to A followed by G, before climbing menacingly in a carefully plotted slow and surreptitious chromatic ascent over the following twelve bars. It is as if an emotional cauldron is on a slow boil, bringing suppressed feelings to the surface. This is transformation music, a highly chromatic bridge passage between night's calm and its more sinister torments.

This paves the way for the powerful music of Pichler's second strophe – 'Versenke dich in deines Kummers Tiefen' (from b. 48). These words are both heralded and accompanied by a strident left-hand motif of angry staccato semiquavers in octaves. In b. 49 the vocal line, unusually for Schubert, plunges down a major seventh from D to E flat and then, as the words 'Versenke dich' are repeated in higher sequence, from F down to G flat (bb. 52–3). Under the words 'Und wenn vielleicht in der zerriss'nen Brust' the accompaniment, now back in § triplets, has reached a plateau in B flat minor (at b. 55), but not for long. The contradiction of the words 'mit grausam süsser Lust!' (bb. 65–7) is the clue to the almost crazed mood that is established with a maelstrom of chromaticism: the deliberate intermingling of conflicting feelings (the happiness of the past, the pain of the present) is suggested by the presence of both minor and major harmonies. By the time we reach 'Berechne die verlornen Seligkeiten' the music blazes in mostly major-key triumph, as if yearningly reinhabiting the golden days of which the poem speaks. This departure from the sadness of the minor only heightens the tension in one of the most unhinged passages in Schubert's songs of grief, intensely demanding in its relentlessly climbing vocal tessitura. It is as if the singer is wildly lashing out in a futile attempt to grasp the lost flowers of paradise. A highly unusual accelerando – 'Geschwinder werdend' – is marked from b. 74 as the accompaniment throbs in syncopations between the hands, half desperate and half exultant, generating ever-greater momentum and threatening to take off. But instead, the 'harsh hand of fate' becomes a clenched fist as dotted minims, acting as gigantic musical brakes, are struck in unison between the hands in bb. 85–9, stopping the hysteria in its tracks. These blows of immutable destiny bring the section to a close.

There is no change of key signature, but the marking is now 'Geschwind'. It is probably this section in B major, and still in §, that persuaded Richard Capell that Schubert was writing to a formula – 'more parade of emotion than emotion itself'. Perhaps Pichler's poem is too far removed from the composer's own experience; he might have responded better if the plaint had been written more directly in the first person (as is the case with the *Winterreise* poems) rather than framed as a rhetorical address to the protagonist's own heart. Schubert's 1821 was a year of personal freedom, successful publishing ventures, parties and, some would say, dissolute living. It would not be long before words like these would resound for the composer with an all too harsh personal significance – but not quite yet. The music for this third strophe is in his

Schiller style – music that can sound staged in rather a lofty manner, as if destined for display beneath an old-fashioned proscenium arch. It is meant to convey a flashback to better days, although there is a danger that the bouncing rhythm can sound more banal than carefree. Seven years later in *Die Post* D911/13 from *Winterreise*, also a flashback to a happier moment when the narrator was in touch with his beloved, Schubert uses the same rhythm to more haunting effect. At b. 114 the jaunty music is interrupted by rumbling basses and dramatic right-hand chords: one and a half lines of poetry make up a quasi-operatic *recitativo stromentato*, suddenly in common time, with a dramatic jump of a tenth for 'stürzte dich'. From 'und dein stilles Glück' ('Langsam', once again **§**, b. 118) Schubertian intimacy firmly re-establishes itself: the rhythm of the opening is reintroduced, now unequivocally in G major (without an actual change of key signature from the original two sharps), with a pathos and stillness that recalls the mood of the song *Strophe aus 'Die Götter Griechenlands'* D677 where there is a plea for a return to the ideals of the past ('Kehre wieder, / Holdes Blütenalter der Natur!'). Here is the 'all-too-lovely dream vision' that has returned ('kehrte wieder') to heavenly realms. From b. 126 this passage is repeated almost note for note – a metaphor for the return of the angelic spirit to its origin. This section ends on an F sharp major chord (b. 140), the dominant of B minor and the means of introducing the final section of the song. We have now reached the last strophe of the poem where Schubert will cut the poet off after only two lines.

In returning to the opening key we rediscover the desperation of a character who has lost even the right to dream of the past. The tempo marking from b. 140 is 'Mässig' in *alla breve* time. The angular dotted rhythms are like the whiplash of a terrible reality. After their appearance in the minor key, the lines are repeated louder and higher in D major (from b. 145), and the higher tessitura causes them to sound even more final. The ghost of the Handelian double-dotted overture (although here a postlude) gives the passage a stagey feel, again recalling several Schiller settings. The tonality of B minor has given the whole song a flavour of Schiller's *Sehnsucht* D636 – a similar type of cantata and probably composed in the same year. But these final lines are even more reminiscent of the closing section ('Ach, kein Steg will dahin führen') of a later song, also to a Schiller text, *Der Pilgrim* D794. In that song the postlude also begins in B minor; dotted rhythms and the interplay of minor and major tonality suggest that the travelling outcast embraces his fate with a grim determination that borders on self-destructive joy.

Sadly Pichler's poem does not enjoy the literary provenance of *Der Pilgrim*. The lyric is embedded in a novel, *Olivier*, that is Biedermeier in tone: love and marriage are stymied by Olivier's love for a woman who has no money or status until – lo and behold! – she is rich and noble after all without realizing it, and everything ends happily ever after. In the novel (on p. 166 of the 1821 edition) the lyric is sung by the beautiful Adelinde to her own harp accompaniment, having been taught by her luckless mother. The glowering Olivier is so moved by this music that he strides out of the room and out of earshot before the final verse is completed. Schubert might have justified his cut to the poem by claiming he had brought the song to an end at the point where the novel's hero could no longer hear it. Olivier has been raised without a musical education but as he develops (this is an *Entwicklungsroman* – a novel showing a character's development) he realizes that he can best express his innermost feelings when singing. Pichler herself, a genuine admirer of Schubert, prided herself on being a musical connoisseur.

See also Die Nacht, the second – and only recently rediscovered – setting of these words by Schubert.

Autograph:	Wienbibliothek im Rathaus, Vienna (first version)
Publication:	First published as part of the AGA in 1895 (P688; first version)
	First published as Op. 84 no. 1 (later changed to Op. 87 no. 1) by
	A. Pennauer, Vienna in August 1827 (P131; second version)

Subsequent editions:	Peters: Vol. 4/70; AGA XX 390a & b: Vol. 6/168; NSA IV: Vol. 4a/80 & Vol. 4b/209 & 257 (sketch); Bärenreiter: Vol. 3/52
Bibliography:	Capell 1928, pp. 169–70
	Einstein 1951, p. 179
	Fischer-Dieskau 1977, p. 140
Discography and timing:	Fischer-Dieskau II 4¹⁰ 6'04
	Hyperion I 15⁵
	Hyperion II 24⁶ 7'24 Margaret Price

← *Die Nacht* (not in Deutsch)   *Versunken* D715 →

URANIENS FLUCHT   Urania's flight
(MAYRHOFER) **D554** [H366]
D major – B♭ major   April 1817

Lebhaft ... // Recit. Lasst uns, ihr Himm-li-schen, ein Fest be-ge-hen!

(394 bars)

(1) 'Lasst uns, ihr Himmlischen, ein Fest begehen!'   'Let us, Immortals, hold a feast!'
    Gebietet Zeus –¹   Commands Zeus.
    Und von der Unterwelt, den Höh'n und Seen,   And from the underworld, the hills and lakes,

    Steigt Alles zum Olympus unverweilt.   All climb up to Olympus without delay.

(2) Der Rebengott verlässt, den er bezwungen,   The god of the vine departs the fabled flowery banks

    Des Indus blumenreichen Fabelstrand: Of the Indus, which he has conquered,
    Des Helikons erhabne Dämmerungen   Apollo the sublime shade of Helicon
    Apoll, und Cypria ihr Inselland.   And Cypria her native island.

(3) Die Strömerinnen moosbesäumter Quellen,   River nymphs from mossy springs,
    Dryadengruppen aus dem stillen Hain,   Dryads from the silent grove,
    Und der beherrscht des Oceanes Wellen,²   And he who rules the ocean waves
    Sie finden willig sich zum Feste ein.   Gladly join the feast.

(4) Und wie sie nun in glänzenden Gewanden   And as they now in radiant attire
    Den ew'gen Kreis, an dem kein Wechsel zehrt,   Dance the eternal, unchanging, round-dance

¹ Schubert truncates this line of poetry. Mayrhofer writes (*Gedichte*, 1824) 'Gebietet Zevs – *sein rascher Bote eilt*'. It is notable that Zeus is spelled *Zevs* throughout in the poet's original. For an explanation of the background to these alternative Mayrhofer readings see Editorial Note at the beginning of Johann MAYRHOFER.
² Mayrhofer writes (*Gedichte*, 1824) '*Wie* der beherrscht des Oceanes Wellen'.

| | Den blühenden, um unsern Donn'rer wanden, | About our Thunderer, |
| | Da strahlt sein Auge jugendlich verklärt. | His eyes sparkle with the light of youth. |

(5) Er winkt: und Hebe füllt die goldnen Schalen,[3] He gives the sign, and Hebe fills the
                                                        golden cups;

     Er winkt: und Ceres reicht Ambrosia,[4]   He gives the sign, and Ceres offers
                                                        ambrosia;

     Er winkt: und süsse Freudenhymnen schallen;   He gives the sign, and sweet hymns of joy
                                                        resound;

     Und was er immer ordnet, das geschah.   Whatever he commands comes to pass.

(6) Schon rötet Lust der Gäste Stirn' und Wange,   Already the guests' brows and cheeks
                                                        blush with pleasure

     Der schlaue Eros lächelt still für sich: And sly Eros smiles silently to himself.
     Die Flügel öffnen sich – im sachten Gange   The doors open – and with soft steps
     Ein edles Weib in die Versammlung schlich.   A noble woman creeps into the company.

(7) Unstreitig ist sie aus der Uraniden   Without doubt she is of the race
     Geschlecht', ihr Haupt umhellt ein   Of the Uranides; around her head is a
        Sternenkranz;   bright crown of stars,
     Es leuchtet herrlich auf dem lebensmüden   And a wonderful heavenly radiance shines
     Und bleichgefärbten Antlitz Himmelsglanz.   Upon her pale, life-weary face.

(8) Doch ihre gelben Haare sind verschnitten,   But her bloud hair is cropped,
     Ein dürftig Kleid deckt ihren reinen Leib.   And a wretched garment covers her pure
                                                        body.

     Die wunden Hände deuten, dass gelitten   Her sore hands reveal that the divine
                                                        woman
     Der Knechtschaft schwere Schmach das   Has suffered the heavy shame of servitude.
        Götterweib.

(9) Es spähet Jupiter in ihren Zügen: Jupiter studies her features.
     'Du bist – du bist es nicht, Urania!'   'You are – you are not Urania?'
     'Ich bin's'. – Die Götter taumeln von den   'I am.' The gods lurch from their cups,
        Krügen
     Erstaunt, und rufen: wie? Urania!   Astonished, and cry: 'What? Urania!'

(10) 'Ich kenne dich nicht mehr. In holder Schöne'   'I no longer know you,' says Zeus. 'In your
                                                        beauty and grace

     Spricht Zeus – 'zogst du von mir der Erde zu.[5] You left me and went to the earth.
     Den Göttlichen befreunden ihre Söhne[6]   You were to acquaint her sons with the
                                                        gods
     In meine Wohnung leiten solltest du.'   And lead them to my abode.

---

[3] Mayrhofer writes (*Gedichte*, 1824) 'Er winkt: und Hebe *füllet Krug'* und Schalen'.

[4] Mayrhofer writes (*Gedichte*, 1824) 'Er winkt: *der Trojer reicht* Ambrosia'. This reference to the Trojan Ganymede, strictly a Phrygian, but son of Tros, was possibly considered too obscure by Schubert. Or the replacement of this famously sensual name by Ceres may have been Mayrhofer's original intention in a poem that criticizes sensuality.

[5] Mayrhofer writes (*Gedichte*, 1824) 'Spricht Zevs – zogst du der Erde zu' ('von mir' is Schubert's addition).

[6] Mayrhofer writes (*Gedichte*, 1824) '*Dem* Göttlichen befreunden ihre Söhne'.

(11)	'Womit Pandora einstens sich gebrüstet,	'The finery which Pandora once flaunted
	Ist unbedeutend wahrlich und gering,	Was truly meagre and insignificant
	Erwäge ich, womit ich dich gerüstet,	When I consider the jewels
	Den Schmuck, den meine Liebe um dich hing.'	With which I, in my love, adorned you.'

(12)	'Was du, o Herr, mir damals aufgetragen,	'The task with which you entrusted me then,
	Wozu des Herzens eigner Drang mich trieb,	To which my own heart, my lord, urged me,
	Vollzog ich willig, ja ich darf es sagen;	I fulfilled willingly, that I will say;
	Doch dass mein Wirken ohne Früchte blieb.'	But my work remained fruitless.

(13)	'Magst du, o Herrscher, mit dem Schicksal rechten,	'You, my lord, may dispute with fate,
	Dem alles, was entstand, ist untertan:	To which every living thing is subject.
	Der Mensch verwirrt das Gute mit dem Schlechten,	But man confuses good with evil;
	Ihn hält gefangen Sinnlichkeit und Wahn.	Lust and delusion hold him captive.

(14)	'Dem einen musst' ich seine Äcker pflügen,	'For one I had to plough his fields;
	Dem Andern Schaffnerin im Hause sein,	For another I had to be housekeeper;
	Dem seine Kindlein in die Ruhe wiegen,	For one I had to rock his children to sleep;
	Dem Andern sollt' ich Lobgedichte streu'n.	For another I had to broadcast eulogies.

(15)	'Der Eine sperrte mich in tiefe Schachten,	'One locked me in deep shafts
	Ihm auszubeuten klingendes Metall;	To dig out jangling metal for him;
	Der Andre jagte mich durch blut'ge Schlachten	Another hunted me down through bloody battles
	Um Ruhm – so wechselte der Armen Qual.	For glory – thus were the varied torments of the poor wretches.

(16)	'Ja dieses Diadem – die goldnen Sterne –	'Even this diadem – these golden stars
	Das du der Scheidenden hast zugewandt,	You gave to me when I departed,
	Sie hätten es zur Feuerung ganz gerne	They would gladly have burnt up as kindling
	Bei winterlichem Froste weggebrannt.'	During winter frosts.'

(17)	'Verwünschte Brut, herrscht Zeus mit wilder Stimme,[7]	'Accursed race,' cries Zeus with angry, imperious voice.
	'Dem schnellsten Untergang sei sie geweiht!'[8]	'It shall be condemned to swift ruin!'
	Die Wolkenburg erbebt von seinem Grimme[9]	The palace amid the clouds quakes at his fury,
	Und Luft und Meer und Land erzittern weit.	And air, sea and land tremble far around.

[7] Mayrhofer writes (*Gedichte*, 1824) 'Verwünschte Brut, *ruft* Zevs mit wilder Stimme'.
[8] Mayrhofer writes (*Gedichte*, 1824) 'Dem schnellsten Untergang sei *du* geweiht'!
[9] Mayrhofer writes (*Gedichte*, 1824) 'Die Wolkenburg erbebt *vor* seinem Grimme'.

(18)   Er reisst den Blitz gewaltsam aus den Fängen   Violently he tears the lightning from the
                                                                  eagle's talons;
       Des Adlers; über'm hohen Haupte schwenkt   High above his head he brandishes
       Die Lohe er, die Erde zu versengen,   The flames to burn the earth,
       Die seinen Liebling unerhört gekränkt.   Which shamefully had hurt his darling.

(19)   Er schreitet vorwärts, um sie zu verderben,   He steps forward to destroy it.
       Es dräut der rote Blitz, noch mehr sein Blick.   The red lightning threatens, his
                                                                  countenance is more menacing still.
       Die bange Welt bereitet sich zu sterben –   The world, in trepidation, prepares to die –
       Es sinkt der Rächerarm, er tritt zurück,[10]   But the avenger's arm sinks down, and he
                                                                  steps back.

(20)   Und heisst Uranien hinunter schauen.   He bids Urania look down.
       Sie sieht in weiter Fern' ein liebend Paar   In the far distance she sees a loving couple
       Auf einer grünen stromumflossnen Aue,[11]   On a green meadow lapped by a stream;
       Ihr Bildnis ziert den ländlichen Altar,   Her own image adorns the rustic altar;

(21)   Vor dem die Beiden opfernd niederknieen,   Before this the pair kneel in sacrifice,
       Die Himmlische ersehnend, die entflohn: Yearning for the goddess who had fled
                                                                  from there.
       Und wie ein mächtig Meer von Harmonien[12]   And, like a mighty ocean of harmonies,
       Umwogt die Göttin ihres Flehens Ton.   The sound of their entreaties envelops the
                                                                  goddess.

(22)   Ihr dunkles Auge füllet eine Träne,   Tears fill her dark eyes;
       Der Schmerz der Liebenden hat sie erreicht;   The lovers' sorrow has touched her.
       Ihr Unmut wird, wie eines Bogens Sehne   Like a bowstring in the moist dew
       Vom feuchten Morgentaue, nun erweicht.[13]   Her displeasure is now softened.

(23)   'Verzeihe,' heischt die göttliche Versöhnte: 'Forgive me,' begs the goddess, appeased.
       'Ich war zu rasch im Zorn, mein Dienst, er gilt   'I was too swift in my anger; my duties
       Noch auf der Erde: wie man mich auch   On earth are still valued; though I was
              höhnte,   scorned
       Manch frommes Herz ist noch von mir erfüllt.'   Many a pious heart still holds me dear.

(24)   'O lass mich zu den armen Menschen steigen,   'Oh let me descend to wretched mankind
       Sie lehren, was dein hoher Wille ist,   To teach them your noble will
       Und ihnen mütterlich in Träumen zeigen   And, like a mother, show them in dreams
       Das Land, wo der Vollendung Blume spriesst.'   The land where the flower of perfection
                                                                  blooms.'

(25)   'Es sei,' ruft Zeus, 'reich will ich dich bestatten;   'It shall be so,' cries Zeus. 'I shall deck you
                                                                  out richly.

---

[10] Mayrhofer writes (*Gedichte*, 1824) 'Es sinkt *des Rächers Arm*, er tritt zurück'.
[11] Mayrhofer writes (*Gedichte*, 1824) 'Auf einer grünen stromumflossnen *Auen*'.
[12] Mayrhofer writes (*Gedichte*, 1824) 'Und wie ein *Ocean* von Harmonien'.
[13] In this line the adjective 'feucht' in 'Vom *feuchten* Morgenthaue' is Schubert's addition.

Zeuch, Tochter, hin, mit frischem starken Sinn!	Go forth, daughter, with new strength of purpose!
Und komme, fühlst du deine Kraft ermatten,[14]	And should you feel your powers wane,
Zu uns herauf, des Himmels Bürgerin.'	Return to us, citizen of heaven.

(26)	'Oft sehen wir dich kommen, wieder scheiden,	'Often we shall see you come and depart again;
	In immer längern Räumen bleibst du aus,	For ever longer periods you shall remain away,
	Und endlich gar – es enden deine Leiden	And finally your sufferings will cease,
	Die weite Erde nennst du einst dein Haus.'	And you will call the wide world your home.

(27)	'Da, Dulderin! wirst du geachtet wohnen,[15]	'You who have suffered will dwell there
	Noch mehr, als wir. Vergänglich ist die Macht,	More highly revered than we are. The power we enjoy
	Die uns erfreut; der Sturm fällt unsre Thronen,[16]	Shall end; the storm may destroy our thrones,
	Doch deine Sterne leuchten durch die Nacht.'	But your stars shall shine through the night.'

JOHANN MAYRHOFER (1787–1836)

This is the twenty-sixth of Schubert's forty-seven Mayrhofer solo settings (1814–24). See the poet's biography for a chronological list of all the Mayrhofer settings.

In terms of length and obscurity this song at first seems to be the Greek-inspired counterpart to the medieval *Adelwold und Emma* D211. It was spurned by Fischer-Dieskau in his 1970s survey of the lieder, and probably for those reasons – it is very long, and at a glance lacks any particular distinction. Denied the kudos earned by *Adelwold und Emma* for being Schubert's longest song, *Uraniens Flucht* is in our own time certainly the least discussed of the Mayrhofer settings – perhaps of all the ballads – and yet it shares its date with an outpouring of the most distinguished mythological songs. In Schubert's lifetime, on the other hand, the work was more highly prized. It appears written out in various contemporary lieder albums (including Franz von Schober's) and in 1835 Moritz von Schwind planned a Mayrhofer wall (next to one dedicated to Goethe) in a room he intended to decorate with themes from the Schubert lieder. In a letter to Bauernfeld from Italy, Schwind mentions the Mayrhofer songs *Einsamkeit* D620 and *Urania* in connection with this project (which was sadly never realized); the sketches for the Urania panel survive and are pictured on p. XXV of the introduction to Volume 11 of NSA. In April 1825, when Franz von Schober organized a concert to take his leave of Breslau, having tried and failed to make a life there as an actor, his farewell recitation was Mayrhofer's *Uraniens Flucht* while his own poem, *Viola* (earlier set by Schubert, D786), was declaimed by a female colleague.

The work owes its present-day obscurity partially to its text; stories that derive from plays by Aeschylus or Sophocles are easier to understand than this tale of Mayrhofer's own invention, seemingly without mythological foundation, about a goddess mistreated by mankind. Is she Urania, one of the nine Muses? Her crown of stars in Verse 7 suggests this is the case, but

---

[14] Mayrhofer writes (*Gedichte*, 1824) 'Und komm, *gewahrst* du deine Kraft ermatten'.

[15] Mayrhofer writes (*Gedichte*, 1824) '*Du* Dulderin! wirst *dort* geachtet wohnen'.

[16] Mayrhofer writes (*Gedichte*, 1824) 'Die uns erfreut; der Sturm *droht unsren* Thronen'.

Venus Urania.

Ueber die Natur der Liebe, über ihre Veredlung
und Verschönerung.

Erster Theil.

Von

Fried. Wilh. Basil. von Ramdohr.

Leipzig,
bey Georg Joachim Göschen. 1798.

Frontispiece and title page of *Venus Urania* (1798) by Friedrich Wilhelm Ramdohr.

Mayrhofer's poem relates not at all to the Urania of astrology who is, in any case, merely a semi-deity. The poet chooses instead to lavish his long poem on the Urania who is the little-known incarnation of the goddess Aphrodite or Venus. For his reason for this we have to read, as Mayrhofer surely had, one of the most famous German books on love published in the eighteenth century – *Venus Urania* by Friedrich Wilhelm Basilius von Ramdohr (1757–1822). This four-volume work from 1798 was an important Enlightenment text – a history of love that encompasses, within its copious philosophical ramblings, reflections on Grecian attitudes to same-sex romantic friendship – the Sacred Band of Thebes and so on. (Biedermeier reactions to the book were less tolerant: my copy had its previous owner's name cut from the title pages, as if he or his heirs wished to preserve his anonymity and respectability.) Venus Urania also appears in Plato's *Symposium*, the most famous classical work on this subject and almost certainly read in German by Mayrhofer, perhaps in Stolberg's 1795 translation.[17] There, a distinction is drawn between the goddess Aphrodite (or Venus) born of a man ('Venus Uranos') and Aphrodite born of a woman ('Venus Dione'). In the 1860s, Karl Ulrichs, the first fighter for gay rights (*see* below) labelled men who were attracted to men as 'Urnings' and those attracted to women as 'Dionings'. Ulrichs's work was the culmination of a long tradition in eighteenth- and nineteenth-century German philology where the Greeks' attitude to same-sex relationships was examined by writers such as Johann Matthias Gesner (1691–1761) in his *Socrates sanctus paederasta*, 1734; Christoph Meiners (1747–1810), professor of philosophy at Göttingen, in an essay on the 'Männerliebe der Griechen' published in 1775 (in which relationships between Achilles and Patroclus or Orestes and Pylades are compared with the chivalric link between medieval knight and squire); and Basilius von Ramdohr.

[17] The explanation, by Pausanias, of the two very different Aphrodites begins on p. 172 of the Viennese edition (1803) of Stolberg's translation (*Das Gastmahl*) of Plato's *Symposium*.

Verse 1: In the preface to his translation of the *Iliad*, E. V. Rieu writes that 'the comic element is introduced almost solely on occasions when gods are shown together'. Like the Schiller setting *Dithyrambe* D801, the beginning of this ballad shows the gods having a party, their joviality untainted by the presence of mortals. This is excellent curtain-raising music and one can almost hear the merry clinking of glasses and a hubbub of chatter. The higher music that tinkles in the treble clef at bb. 7–8 is vividly prophetic of a passage in the Schiller setting *Sehnsucht* D636 (bb. 33–8) that refers to 'Harmonien' and 'Töne süsser Himmelsruh'. Between bb. 12 and 15 Zeus (written 'Zevs' by Mayrhofer) strides centre stage and issues a summons: all creatures great and small are bidden to rise up to the heavenly realms and attend a feast. This is followed by piano writing that suggests a musical hydraulic lift, as if it were one of the mechanical marvels in the Olympian opera house, and pedal-powered by a rumbling tremolo on A for thirteen bars (bb. 18–30). The principle is the same as for the rather more sinister chromatic ascent in the introduction to *Gruppe aus dem Tartarus* D583, but the effect is here entirely genial.

Verses 2–3: 'Mässig' (from b. 31) with a change of key signature to A major. The gathering of the gods is in a moderate ⅜, as if they have all the time in the world – as indeed they do. There is a fancifully ornate vocal line at 'blumenreichen Fabelstrand' (bb. 34–6) and again at 'Dryaden-gruppen aus dem stillen Hain' (bb. 44–7), but the most beautiful effect of this section is where the tune of 'Helikons erhabne Dämmerungen' (heard in bb. 36–8) is repeated by the piano in bb. 47–9, while the voice part stays, quasi parlando, on one note in the middle of the texture with the intoned words 'Und der beherrscht des Oceanes Wellen'. This melody, and the way it is treated twice in these different ways, is identical with the lines 'Rausche, Fluss, das Tal entlang' and 'Was, von Menschen nicht gewusst' in the second setting of Goethe's *An den Mond* D296 (bb. 30–32 of that song, and then bb. 50–52).

Verse 4: 'Majestätisch' with a change to F major key signature from b. 53. The round dance at the court of Zeus is taken at the same unhurried pace; from b. 57 the accompanying quavers ascend in stately staccato (harps – what else?) and one is reminded of how Schubert would later thus evoke the ethereal music of the harps of fairyland in *Ellens Gesang I* D837.

Verses 5–6: The wonderful things that happen at a nod from Zeus prompt music of the utmost charm. The felicities of the Schiller setting *Elysium* D584, composed five months later, are here rehearsed for the first time. There is a change to 'Geschwind' at b. 75. The piano interludes following the serving of Hebe's wine (bb. 75–85) and Ceres' ambrosia (bb. 87–97) are different in colour rather than substance (red and white perhaps?), a pouring of refreshments that vary only in key and register. In both cases the mellifluous sliding of thirds and sixths in the accom-paniment's inner parts suggests the pouring and ingestion of the smoothest of liquids. Anywhere else this would lead to an outbreak of earthy lust, but here even Eros smiles with a radiant innocence. For Schubert such unsullied celestial happiness conjures up Mozart. The music of Verse 6 ('Schon rötet Lust') and its introduction, a miniature piano sonatina movement at bb. 102–5 marked 'Sanft, etwas geschwind', is as pithy a homage to that master as Schubert ever penned. Even the repetitions of 'für sich' (bb. 116–19) might have come directly from a Mozart opera. Eros is here described less than sympathetically and Mayrhofer surely implies that the mischievous god of sexual love is amused by the sufferings that Urania will soon recount. A new musical section in F minor (marked 'Langsam' and *alla breve*, b. 121) begins on the last two lines of Verse 6; the manner in which Urania slips into the gathering ('in die Versammlung schlich', bb. 132–4) is suggested by a beautifully crafted chromatic ascending bass line in the piano that begins at b. 130.

Verses 7–9: The static nature of the music for Verse 7 describes not so much Urania's entrance as the effect it has on the heavenly throng – they are numb with shock at her bedraggled appearance. This is Schubert's 'Kundry moment' albeit with less musical tumult than the first appearance of that character in Wagner's *Parsifal*. The party is brought to a halt and the accompanying minim chords seem to change harmony with difficulty (bb. 138–42). The music moves into crotchets and quavers at Verse 8, a sign of Zeus' quickening curiosity. By Verse 9 there is an accelerando ('Geschwinder werdend' from b. 169) and Urania admits her identity. Zeus' confident, almost arrogant, questioning is countered by Urania's heartbreaking reply ('Ich bin's'), music of helpless vulnerability within a suddenly 'Langsam' tempo marking (b. 173). The 'chorus' is suitably shocked (stage whispers of 'What! Urania?!' within a four-bar recitative marked 'Schnell', bb. 174–7) and in operatic manner we are all set for a big aria from Zeus.

Verses 10–11: From b. 177, 'Mässig' in E major. This is something of a disappointment: head gods can be pompous bores. Dotted rhythms in the grand manner suggest that someone important is speaking, and someone large to boot. A glimmer of feminine interest is provided by the flashing jewels between bb. 190 and 202 ('Den Schmuck, den meine Liebe um dich hing') that shimmer like pearl-drop earrings in a quivering setting of staccato left-hand quavers.

Verses 12–16: From b. 205 Urania's recounting of her fate ('Sehr langsam' in F minor, $\frac{2}{4}$) fails to strike the ear as exceptional, but Schubert has obviously worked hard at cultivating for her a vocal line of meek, but not servile, deference in the presence of Zeus. She describes a mankind that has utterly lost its way. The abuse she has endured is that love has been misused in her name – as if she has to suffer personally all the slights that are motivated by the *Sinnlichkeit* (lust) that has replaced the highest ideals of real love. The love between men and women has been besmirched by unkindness and inequality. There is a reference to women being hunted and presumably raped in battle conditions (bb. 252–4) but most of the atrocities are of a domestic nature. Thus Urania describes the woman who is made to share the hard physical work of her husband (at the plough or down the mine), or who must be his faithful housekeeper, or lavish praise on him even if undeserved, or rock the cradle. This latter duty is depicted in gently oscillating left-hand quavers (bb. 240–41) but it is clear that Urania does not consider it a noble task. On the contrary, Mayrhofer appears to be suggesting, via Urania, that copulation and childbirth, indeed all the functions of marriage, debase love as it should be experienced. We must admit that Urania's catalogue of woes fails to excite the listener's sympathy – or that of Zeus, it seems. It is only after the recitative of Verse 16 (from b. 261), when he hears that mankind has considered burning as winter fuel a diadem that was his gift to Urania, that he is roused to action.

Verses 17–19: After the preceding long, slow exchanges between father and daughter, Mayrhofer's Wotan and Brünnhilde prototypes, the ear longs for some fast music, and Schubert duly provides it ('Schnell' with all flats neutralized into naturals at b. 269). But the composer has thundered to much mightier effect in other songs. Too many earth-threatening events are crammed into too small a musical space: there is only so much excitement to be generated by swashbuckling tremolandi, and here this is not quite enough to engage the listener. Zeus prepares to destroy the world as if intending to rain fire and brimstone down on Sodom – except in this case it is for undeniably heterosexual behaviour. At b. 307 the direction is suddenly 'Zurückhaltend'. The music for suspended motion ('Es sinkt der Rächerarm', bb. 308–10) is effective enough, as is the way Zeus points downwards with the tessitura of his vocal line ('hinunter schauen') as he bids Urania look earthward (bb. 313–14).

Verses 20–22: The marking is now 'Langsam' and the key signature has changed to three flats since the previous 'zurückhaltend'. The words 'in weiter Fern'' inspire for this passage a suggestion of muted horns; the key of E flat and the hint of a far-off hunt have denoted distance in many a piece of romantic music. Zeus has spotted a 'loving couple' whose blameless existence is the exception that will save mankind from destruction. All is idealized love, with never a discordant note in the idyllic thirds and sixths, and although it is no more 'real' than the earlier leaden posturings of Zeus, this passage is probably the most beautiful in the piece. At mention of the 'mighty ocean of harmonies' of the couple's entreaties, the music breaks into effulgent semiquaver triplets (b. 328). To put something of a smile on Urania's face Schubert lifts the music from E flat to E major at b. 333.

Verses 23–4: The triplets cease and from b. 336 a new duplet figure signals another outpouring for Urania – the length of an entire song in its own right. (It is not impossible to envisage performing this long piece with two singers – a high baritone combining the roles of narrator and Zeus, and a high mezzo for Urania.) The music for the goddess is reminiscent of the section beginning 'Die grünen Bäume rauschen dann' in the Mayrhofer *Nachtstück* D672. This aria would sound effective enough if it had made an appearance in a different context; lost within this gigantic ballad it fails to provide the dramatic 'lift' now required. Urania resolves to return to mankind and direct the gaze of mortals to the land where the 'Blume der Vollendung' – the flower of perfection – blooms. This is doubtless the much sought-after 'blue flower' known to readers of Novalis, and the land itself can be nowhere else than Mayrhofer's Utopia, the city-state Heliopolis.

Verses 25–7: A rather perfunctory recitative for Zeus (bb. 349–54) is followed by his closing aria in B flat marked 'Mit Gefühl'; in character and movement this is not unlike the final section of *Adelwold und Emma*. Schubert is aiming for the lofty and judicious tone of an Olympian peroration and, taken on its own, it is a splendidly crafted piece, reflecting emotions of paternal kindness and sacerdotal blessing. Zeus even predicts that, thanks to Urania's fostering of love and humanism, mankind will learn to abandon the gods themselves in favour of goodness and rational behaviour. The qualities of Zeus, the father figure who votes himself out of a job, are less apparent than they could be in this context, principally because the 'libretto' has insufficient variation of mood and pace.

This song has all the hallmarks of a work set by Schubert to please the poet – composed out of respect and friendship rather than because the composer was galvanized by the text. Schubert abandoned a number of pieces in his career where he encountered similar problems to those which cramped his style in *Uraniens Flucht*, but in this case he stuck it out. Mayrhofer almost certainly set great store by having a musical setting of these words – more so perhaps than the composer. It is worth asking why the poet cared so much for Urania's plight, a fate moreover which, unlike his Philoctetes, Orestes, Antigone and Oedipus, does not derive from one of the great Greek plays. If the setting does not tell us a great deal about Schubert it tells us much about Mayrhofer.

As mentioned above, Urania was later to be considered the protector of the cult of the Uranians (as homosexual men were later called). 'Urning' and 'Uraniaster' were pre-Freudian terms for homosexuals used in treatises in the 1860s by Karl Friedrich Ulrichs (1825–1895), a now revered pioneer in the championing of gay rights in Germany. Ulrich's most important essay, published in 1868, was *Memnon: Die Geschlechtsnatur des mannliebenden Urnings*. (The title of another Schubert–Mayrhofer collaboration, *Memnon* D541, may not be coincidence, particularly as it is a fable about a lost and suffering soul.) It is possible that these labels, comprehensible only to initiates, were not entirely invented by Ulrichs; perhaps similar terms derived from Greek mythology were in select and private use much earlier.

Urania's bedraggled, persecuted appearance and tales of demeaning punishments are counterpointed with mention of a 'liebend Paar' – a loving pair, whom the poet avoids identifying by gender. Reference to a cult suggests a temple visited only by special initiates in a land where perfection flowers. Jehovah destroyed Sodom and Gomorrah for so-called sin, but here the pagan god threatens to destroy a world of cruelty, intolerance and persecution, a world where lust (presumably of every sort) has taken the place of elevated Platonic ideals. Zeus refrains from going through with the world's destruction because he accepts that, with Urania's help, romantic (but not sexual) friendship between men is something that can save it. It is a measure of Mayrhofer's terrible isolation, but also of his fervent idealism, that he really seems to have believed in a society that rejected sex entirely. And it is rather ironic that such a view should be propounded on high by Zeus, someone who had been responsible for the abduction of the shepherd boy Ganymede.

Uraniens Flucht is thus far from an apologia for the practice of homosexuality; indeed it condemns sexual indulgence of any kind. Ordinary men, Urania tells us, have robbed her of her dignity by enslaving her in marriage, and the rearing of children is a consequence of their lust. One is reminded of something that Schubert wrote in his diary on 8 September 1816, a thought that seems to have come straight from Mayrhofer: 'to a free man matrimony is a terrifying thought in these days: he exchanges it [freedom] either for melancholy or crude sensuality'. The poet's advice would probably have been to abjure marriage – indeed to turn one's back on a sexual life of any kind. Mayrhofer's tragedy, at least as perceived in twenty-first-century terms, was that he was a self-loathing homosexual who sought to deal with his passionate emotions by suppressing them. We have no idea how successful he was in this reining-in, and whether he strayed from the upright path he set himself; in any case he condemned himself to a life of loneliness. It is significant that Mayrhofer did not seek to deny his sympathies, affiliations and passions for his male friends; instead he demanded that these passions be evaluated separately from the uncontrolled behaviour of those who allowed their affections to be sullied by sexual actions. This combative attitude is to be found in the third volume of *Venus Urania* by Basilius von Ramdohr who accepted that same-sex friendships were indeed erotically charged. Like D. H. Lawrence a century later, Ramdohr wrote that there could be no true friendship without a core of sexual feelings. Close male friends experience love for each other, but any attempt to express these feelings physically causes love to evaporate and turn into something base. Ramdohr thus endorses homoeroticism, but restricts it to the platonic level. This is indeed the credo by which Mayrhofer seems to have led his life. In this poem the mercy of Zeus–Mayrhofer suggests that a couple who renounce lust for a loving friendship can achieve much in society and merit the admiration and gratitude of their peers, as well as the mercy of the gods.

Whether Schubert was aware of all the layers of Mayrhofer's motivation in penning this text is uncertain; indeed his fitful musical engagement with the subject suggests he was not absolutely au fait with Mayrhofer's extended metaphor or, if he was, found it too remote to bring to life. In the composer's reaction we sense no disapproval, merely occasional bewilderment. After he had made such a delightful musical personality for 'the sly Eros', the free-wheeling morality of the gods is suddenly exchanged for a lesson in Platonic morality. A poem of this kind was never destined to make a great musical setting, built as it is on a curious combination of furtiveness and missionary zeal, and of sexual guilt with an almost messianic pride in the elite nature of Urania's dream protégés. Despite the fact that the text has a heroine, the poem has a misogynistic edge; it is as if the poet were still the inmate of a seminary that considered the daughters of Eve (and those who cohabit with them) to be responsible for mankind's woes. In an inversion of biblical storytelling it is married men, not the Sodomites, who bring the world to within an inch of destruction. Zeus is like an all-powerful abbot who would prefer his novices to love each other rather than to fall for the temptation of women. Mayrhofer, who studied theology for some years and had entered a monastery, considered that he had broken off with the church. Yet, not for the first or last time in his work, the song enthusiast is struck by a reading of the Greek classics that reinforces, by rather more subtle means, the guilt and anguish first implanted by religion when the poet was a lonely adolescent. Although Ramdohr's writings had brought some comfort to a stricken minority, it was not until Ulrichs in 1868 that the amazing idea was

postulated that 'Urnings' had a perfect, and constitutional right to a full life without criminaliza-
tion – the opening salvo in a fight that would last for more than a hundred years in German
lands, and continue elsewhere into the twenty-first century.

Autograph:	Conservatoire collection, Bibliothèque Nationale, Paris
First edition:	Published as part of the AGA in 1895 (P673)
Subsequent editions:	Not in Peters; AGA XX 319: Vol. 5/99; NSA IV: Vol. 11/118
Bibliography:	Dürhammer 1999, p. 128
Discography and timing:	Fischer-Dieskau —

Hyperion I 14^{10}
Hyperion II 18^{17} 18'08   Thomas Hampson

← *Auf der Donau* D553   *Liebhaber in allen Gestalten* D558 →

JOHANN PETER UZ (1720–1796)

THE POETIC SOURCES

S1 *Sämmtliche poetische Werke von J. P. Uz*
Erster und Zweyter Theil, Wien. Gedruckt für
Franz Anton Schrämbl bei Ignaz Alberti, 1790

S2 *Poetische Werke von Johann Peter Uz*
Zweyter Band Nach seinen eigenhändigen
Verbesserungen herausgegeben von Christian
Felix Weisse, Wien, bey J. V. Degen Buch-
drucker und Buchhändler 1804 (reprinted
1805)

The fact that all of Schubert's Uz settings are
to be found within a single volume of the
Degen Edition (as opposed to spread between
two volumes of the earlier, and even handier,
Schrämbl Edition), is an argument in favour of
the Degen edition as the composer's source.

Uz's *Werke* (Vienna, 1790).

THE SONGS

1816	*Die Nacht* D358 [S1: Erster Theil p. 128] [S2: p. 116]
	An Chloen D363 [S1: Erster Theil pp. 14–15] [S2: pp. 13–14]
June 1816	*An die Sonne* D439 Quartet (SATB) with piano [S1: Zweyter Theil pp. 123–6] [S2: pp. 233–5]
	Die Liebesgötter D446 [S1: Erster Theil pp. 63–4] [S2: pp. 58–9]
	Gott im Frühlinge D448 [S1: Zweyter Theil pp. 158–9] [S2: pp. 263–4]
	Der gute Hirt D449 [S1: Zweyter Theil pp. 162–3] [S2: pp. 267–8]

Undated works   *Gott im Ungewitter* D985 Quartet (SATB) with piano [S1: Zweyter Theil
                 pp. 160–1] [S2: pp. 265–6]
                 Gott der Weltschöpfer D986 Quartet (SATB) with piano [S1: Zweyter Theil
                 pp. 167–75] [S2 pp. 272–9]

Johann Peter Uz was born in Ansbach on 3
October 1720. He was the son of a goldsmith
and lost his parents early. He went to Halle to
study law but was also drawn to philosophy
and history. His favourite authors were Horace
and Anacreon, and he loved painting as much
as poetry. In Halle he met Johann Wilhelm
Gleim, a poet favoured by Beethoven and
Haydn, whose protégé he became. Uz survived
on very little money, but gradually worked his
way up in various civil service positions in
Ansbach and Nuremberg. His poetry soon
graduated beyond Gleim's entertaining style
and aspired to the seriousness and scope of
Klopstock, including a substantial leaning
towards religious poetry. On the other hand, a
number of Uz's poems were modelled on
anacreontic metre and themes, advocating
the hedonism of wine, women and song; he
adopted a stance that attempted to combine
this epicurean bent with a rational eighteenth-
century Christianity. That he was influenced
by French literature is something that almost
goes without saying for the poets of his generation. In *Gott im Frühlinge*, by far the best
known of Schubert's settings of his verse, there
even seems to be a touch of pantheism. Uz
later received the approbation of Herder who
commented that even if he did not compose
poetry in the metrical form of Horace, the
content and enthusiasm of his odes owed
much to the Roman master.

Uz's modesty was legendary: he lived in
Ansbach where almost no one was aware of his
publications. The ruling Markgraf (military
governor) heard of them from other people,
and Uz was eventually named Geheimer Rat
(privy councillor), a position he declined. He
died in Ansbach, working to the end, on 12

J. P. Uz, engraving by J. F. Baufe (1776).

May 1796. His *Sämmtliche Poetische Werke*
were published in Leipzig in 1768, although it
is likely that Schubert encountered the poet's
output in one of the later Viennese editions.
The Anacreontic lyrics of Uz seem to have
been even more popular in Austria than in
Germany if the number of Viennese printings
is any indication: as well as those listed above,
there were published editions of the *Gedichte*
by Trattner (1769) and Alberti. The 1804
edition published by Joseph Degen (two
magnificent folio volumes with a fine engraving
of the poet) was probably the most sumptuous
presentation of any poet's work to appear in
Vienna during Schubert's lifetime. The young
composer is unlikely to have had access to
these volumes, but Degen reprinted the collection in 1805 in a much smaller and cheaper
format.

KARL AUGUST VARNHAGEN VON ENSE (1785–1858)

THE POETIC SOURCES
S1 *Musenalmanach auf das Jahr 1804*, Herausgegeben von L. A. v. Chamisso und K. A. Varnhagen, Leipzig, bei Carl Gotthold Schmidt 1804

S2 *Vermischte Gedichte* von K. A. Varnhagen von Ense Frankfurt am Main bei Franz Varrentrapp 1816

On the title page there is a couplet from Goethe: 'Ach wie traurig sieht in Lettern / Schwarz auf weiss, das Lied mich an!' ('Ah, how sadly the poem, in letters of black and white, looks up at me!')

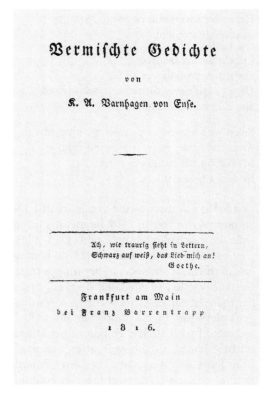

Varnhagen's *Vermischte Gedichte* (1816).

Nächtlicher Schall, the long unidentified source of the middle movement of Schubert's *Der Hirt auf dem Felsen* D965.

THE SONG

October 1828   *Der Hirt auf dem Felsen* D965: The second and first strophes of Varnhagen's poem provide the text for the fifth and sixth strophes of Schubert's song-cantata. In this *minore* middle section (bars 127–218), sandwiched between two different poems by Wilhelm Müller, Schubert reverses the order of the first two strophes as printed by Varnhagen in the *Vermischte Gedichte* and begins with 'In tiefem Gram vezehr ich mich'. In the poet's version the verse beginning 'So sehnend klang im Wald das Lied' is cast as an introduction and inverted commas are opened for 'In tiefem Gram' which pertain until the end of the poem. [S1: p. 60, with the title 'Romanze' where the strophes Schubert uses are the third and first as printed in this *Musenalmanach*] [S2: p. 15, with the title 'Nächtlicher Schall']

The remainder of Varnhagen's six-strophe poem runs thus in *Vermischte Gedichte* (Varnhagen cuts one verse from the earlier version printed in the 1804 *Musenalmanach*):

Der Himmel mir die Liebe gab,
Ich lebte nur in ihr:
Der Menschheit Last mir sank hinab,
Ich fand den Himmel hier!

'Heaven gave me love,
In love alone I lived:
The burden of humanity fell from me,
Here I found heaven!

Der Himmel mir die Liebe gab,
Doch die Geliebte nicht,
Mir strahlt ihr hohes Bild herab
Im hehren Sternenlicht.

Heaven gave me love,
But not my beloved;
Her noble image shines down upon me
In sublime starlight.

Nach der Geliebten sehn' ich mich,
Sie ist auf Erden nie!
Beglückt hier nimmer wähn' ich mich!
Im Himmel nur ist sie!

I yearn for my beloved,
She is never on this earth.
Here I shall never consider myself blessed.
She is in heaven alone!

Voll Sehnsucht sie empor mich zieht
Schon wird das Herz mir leicht!
Der letzte Hauch im Lied entflieht,
Im Lied das Herz entweicht!

Filled with longing she draws me upwards,
And already my heart is growing light!
My last breath escapes in song,
In song my heart flees.'

Karl August Varnhagen von Ense was born in Düsseldorf on 21 February 1785. He studied medicine in Berlin, but after postponing plans to follow in his father's footsteps as a doctor, he became a teacher to the children of a rich Jewish household and developed his interests in literature and philosophy. In 1804 he founded a *Musenalmanach* with Adelbert von Chamisso based around the literary friendships of the so-called 'Nordsternbund'. Varnhagen's early lyrics (including the one that Schubert used, in part, for *Der Hirt auf dem Felsen*) were published in the three years of this almanac's existence, although as a poet he lacked both originality and great talent. He was more gifted as a journalist and an observer of life. In 1807 he met his future wife, the much older Rahel Levin (1771–1833) (her baptized name was Robert) who became one of the great *salonistes* of her time, a cosier German version of Madame de Staël, under her married name, Rahel Varnhagen. Varnhagen's devotion to his more famous wife is indicated by his tireless editing of her letters, initially issued in the year after her death (*Ein Buch des Andenkens für ihre Freunde* in three volumes), a project that was continually amplified until Varnhagen's own death, achieving its definitive publication only in 2012.

Karl August Varnhagen von Ense, unsigned engraving.

During a spell living in Tübingen he encountered Kerner, Uhland and the publisher Cotta. In 1809 he embarked on a career as a soldier, fighting at the battle of Wagram where he was wounded as a member of the forces led by the Archduke Karl of Austria. Varnhagen convalesced in Vienna where he met Karoline Pichler and soon became connected with celebrated names of his time including Brentano, Jean Paul, Beethoven, Metternich (who was to become a powerful enemy) and Goethe (who remained Varnhagen's lifelong idol and lodestar). He married Rahel in Berlin in 1814 and returned to the Austrian capital as a member of the Prussian delegation to the Congress of Vienna. Varnhagen ascended the greasy pole of civil-service power in Prussia but became thoroughly unpopular with conservatives due to his increasingly progressive political views.

Transferred back to Berlin at the devastating request of Metternich, he abandoned the world stage; his life with Rahel encompassed work as a tireless historian and biographer. During these Berlin years the Varnhagens came into frequent contact with the great opera star Anna Milder-Hauptmann for whom *Der Hirt auf dem Felsen* D965 was written. It is not impossible that it was part of Milder's brief to Schubert, if and when she commissioned this work from him, to include these words that salute the power of song, and thus the art of the singer. It is difficult to see how otherwise Schubert might have come across this unexceptional poem (however attuned it might have been to his feelings for music) in either of the two rare sources; the *Musenalmanach*, however, is more likely to have come into his hands than the *Vermischte Gedichte* issued by an obscure Frankfurt publisher.

It was in the field of autobiography, and as a voluminous diarist, that Varnhagen achieved his greatest fame. His self-referential anecdotes – lively, witty and penetrating – seemed unbearable to his enemies, some of whom had an anti-Semitic agenda on account of his wife, and many of whom regarded his exposure of the scandals of Prussian court life as treasonable. He excited the same sort of rage in the establishment as the expatriate Heine, without being in the same class of creative artist. He was close friends with Bettina von Arnim and Alexander von Humboldt, and had a lively correspondence with Carlyle. His fascination with the marital life of the warring Carlyles at Cheyne Walk in London was typical of his passion for personalizing history in the most inquisitive journalistic tradition. Varnhagen has remained a controversial character for those attempting to assess his importance. He died on 10 October 1858. His name was added to the list of Schubert's poets in 2008 thanks to the researches of Till Gerrit Waidelich.

Der VATER MIT DEM KIND

The father with his child

(BAUERNFELD) **D906** [H611]

D major   January 1827

(59 bars)

Dem Vater liegt das Kind im Arm,	The child lies in its father's arms,
Es ruht so wohl, es ruht so warm,	Resting so snug, resting so warm.
Es lächelt süss: 'Lieb' Vater mein!'	'My dear father!'
Und mit dem Lächeln schläft es ein.	And smiling falls asleep.
Der Vater beugt sich, atmet kaum,	The father stoops, scarcely breathing,
Und lauscht auf seines Kindes Traum;	Listening to his child's dream;
Er denkt an die entschwund'ne Zeit	He thinks of times past
Mit wehmutsvoller Seligkeit.[1]	With wistful happiness.
Und eine Trän' aus Herzensgrund	And a tear from deep in his heart
Fällt ihm auf seines Kindes Mund;	Falls on his child's mouth;
Schnell küsst er ihm die Träne ab,	Quickly he kisses the tear away,
Und wiegt es leise auf und ab.	And rocks the child gently to and fro.
Um einer ganzen Welt Gewinn	He would not give up his beloved child
Gäb er das Herzenskind nicht hin;–	For all the world.
Du Seliger schon in der Welt,	Happy are you in this world,
Der so sein Glück in Armen hält!	Who hold thus your happiness in your arms!

EDUARD VON BAUERNFELD (1802–1890)

This is the last of Schubert's three Bauernfeld solo settings (1826–7). See the poet's biography for a chronological list of all the Bauernfeld settings.

In *Sea Drift*, Whitman wrote of 'the cradle endlessly rocking', and in this song we hear (also without respite) music for a child being cradled in its father's arms, perhaps the most original piano figuration ever designed for a berceuse; the composer is unafraid of repeated pianistic motifs (as in *Geheimes* D719 for example) which in lesser hands would be tedious. There is something about the circumscribed world of babyhood that makes the ritual of this repeated movement appropriate and touching. The song was originally cast in $\frac{12}{8}$, which would have given the piece more of an obviously rocking motion, but in $\frac{2}{4}$ the repetition of the tiny two-note accompanying motif, punctuated by a quaver rest, conjures up the smallness and delicacy of a child and its wordless colloquy with its parent. The piano part clings yearningly to the warm security of the more assured voice. At b. 19 the father bends to look at his child, holding his breath as he does so (b. 20); this is illustrated in two adjacent bars by contrasting means – the

[1] Bauernfeld writes (*Gedichte*, 1872) 'Mit wehmutsvoller *Zärtlichkeit*'.

first a downward movement where the piano writing is at one with the vocal line, the second a B⁷ chord rooted to the spot while the singer's vocal line hovers diffidently in the middle of the stave. As always when the accompaniment is halting or fragmentary, the composer invents a flowing vocal line above it. It is tempting to believe that these loving vocal curves are inspired by Schubert's projection of closeness to his own father – someone he loved very much but who seems to have been a source of conflict and misunderstanding in his life.

A short middle section in B flat (from b. 22) suggests some family tragedy (already implied by the words 'entschwund'ne Zeit' in the preceding bars); perhaps the child's mother has died in childbirth – a heartbreaking song for Dietrich Fischer-Dieskau to sing where this scenario represented his own reality. The dynamic changes to a more impassioned mezzo forte at b. 32. It is interesting that *Der Vater mit dem Kind* is in D major, with its key relationship to the B minor of *Vor meiner Wiege* D927 (Leitner), a song about the poet's mother; a feature of both works is the echoing imitation in the piano of phrases proposed by the voice, a musical analogue for the idea of the child as the image of its parents, a follower in their footsteps. This imitation and repetition, the subliminal teaching of the mother tongue, or a baby copying the delighted parent's facial expressions, is heard in bb. 24–6 and again in bb. 49–52. In the latter bars, with the words 'Du Seliger schon in der Welt', the love given by the father seems returned, via the accompaniment, by the child.

Der Vater mit dem Kind.

Dem Vater liegt das Kind im Arm,
Es ruht so wohl, es ruht so warm,
Es lächelt süß: „Lieb Vater mein!"
Und mit dem Lächeln schläft es ein.

Der Vater beugt sich, athmet kaum,
Und lauscht auf seines Kindes Traum;
Er denkt an die entschwund'ne Zeit
Mit wehmuthsvoller Zärtlichkeit.

Illustration for *Der Vater mit dem Kind* from *Album für Deutschlands Töchter* (1863).

Both poet and composer must have been aware of the resemblance of the poem's opening to Goethe's *Erlkönig*, where a father holds his son in his arms with similar imagery ('Er hat den Knaben wohl in dem Arm / Er fasst ihn sicher, er hält ihn warm'). In that song, where the background is illness and fear of death, the *Bewegung* is famously turbulent; in this song, where time is made to stand still, exactly the opposite is the case. The domesticity of *Der Vater mit dem Kind* has some of the qualities of the Leitner setting *Der Winterabend* D938 where the beauties of a 'schöne verschwundne Zeit' within a background of bereavement are also the subject of rapt contemplation. But another Leitner setting, written later in 1827 and also in D major, comes even more strongly to mind, *Der Kreuzzug* D932: being a parent is a crusade of sorts, a long and hazardous journey not to be undertaken lightly. Both songs are about sacred responsibility; the closing bars of each, music for two very different guardians of high ideals, are similar in layout. The father's teardrop falling on the child's mouth, and being kissed away, is symbolic emotional lactation showing his feelings of inadequacy, as a mere man, looking after the child by himself.

As published in the Diabelli Nachlass (and also in Peters) the song has a spurious E minim (instead of the correct C sharp) in b. 4 of the piano introduction; the equally inauthentic minor-key colouring on the word 'Trän'' in b. 33 indicates the kind of egregious 'correction' inflicted on Schubert's posthumous songs by this publisher. The NSA consulted a handwritten copy of Bauernfeld's early 'Jugend-Gedichte' in the Wienbibliothek im Rathaus which contains a version of the words which is nearer to Schubert's setting than the poem as printed in Bauernfeld's *Gedichte* of 1872 – a surprisingly late first publication of the poet's verse.

Autograph:	Gesellschaft der Musikfreunde, Vienna (first draft)
First edition:	Published as Book 17 no. 2 of the *Nachlass* by Diabelli, Vienna in May 1832 (P286)
Subsequent editions:	Peters: Vol. 3/172; AGA XX 514: Vol. 8/261; NSA IV: Vol. 14a/22; Bärenreiter: Vol. 4/66
Discography and timing:	Fischer-Dieskau II 8[20] 3'40
	Hyperion I 6[11]
	Hyperion II 32[18] 4'34 Anthony Rolfe Johnson

← *An die Laute* D905   *Frühlingslied* D919 →

VATERLANDSLIED   Song of the fatherland
(KLOPSTOCK) **D287** [H173]

The song exists in two versions, both of which are discussed below:
(1) 14 September 1815; (2) Date unknown

(1) 'Mässig'   C major $\frac{2}{4}$ [14 bars]

(2) C major

Ich bin ein deutsches Mädchen!	I am a German girl!
Mein Aug' ist blau und sanft mein Blick,	My eyes are blue, my gaze is soft,
Ich hab' ein Herz	I have a heart
Das edel ist, und stolz und gut.	That is noble, proud and good.
Ich bin ein deutsches Mädchen!	I am a German girl!
Zorn blickt mein blaues Aug' auf den,	My blue eyes look with anger on him,
Es hasst mein Herz	My heart hates him
Den, der sein Vaterland verkennt!	Who does not prize the fatherland
Ich bin ein deutsches Mädchen!	I am a German girl!
Erköhre mir kein ander Land	I would choose no other country
Zum Vaterland,	For my fatherland
Wär mir auch frei die grosse Wahl!	Even if I had a free, wide choice.
[...3...]	[...3...]
Ich bin ein deutsches Mädchen!	I am a German girl!
Mein gutes, edles, stolzes Herz	My good, noble, proud heart

Schlägt laut empor.	Surges and beats loud
Beim süssen Namen: Vaterland!	Of the sweet name: Fatherland!
So schlägt mir einst beim Namen	Thus it will beat one day only at the name
Des Jünglings nur, der stolz wie ich	Of the youth who is as proud as I am
Aufs Vaterland,	Of the fatherland,
Gut, edel ist, ein Deutscher ist!	And is good, noble and a German!

FRIEDRICH GOTTLOB KLOPSTOCK (1724–1803); poem written late 1770

This is the fourth of Schubert's thirteen Klopstock solo settings (1815–16). See the poet's biography for a chronological list of all the Klopstock settings.

1815 was the last year when every Viennese, our composer among them, was an unquestioning patriot. In the wake of the Napoleonic wars and the so-called Wars of Liberation, when Germany and Austria threw off the French yoke, there was a feeling among certain intellectuals that the German-speaking states should stick together and perhaps even unite into one country. It would be more than another half-century before this dream became a reality, and then only as a result of the ruthless machinations of Bismarck. There was certainly little sinister about German patriotism of this time. Twentieth-century hindsight renders the proud boasting of blue-eyed and blond-headed Germans somewhat disturbing, but if the many Jewish residents of German states were not yet counted as truly 'belonging' to the land of their birth, the same could be said of their status in Britain. In England's patriotic songs of the period, John Bull is an exclusively Anglo-Saxon stereotype.

Klopstock wrote these verses for his future wife Johanna Elisabeth von Winthem in 1770, a good deal before the Napoleonic Wars. Just as the patriotic poetry of Körner (*Leyer und Schwert* particularly) was pressed into new service by supporters of Bismarck and the German Reich, historical circumstances provided Klopstock's verses with a new lease of life some forty-five years after they were written. They were popular in their own time, however, and were set many times to music. Matthias Claudius made a riposte to these verses (1781) by inventing a male version of the words: 'Ich bin ein deutscher Jüngling! / Mein Haar ist kraus, breit meine Brust' ('I am a German youth; my hair is curly, my chest is broad'). Schubart in his *Deutsche Chronik* published an upmarket version of the words by one 'Charlotte von Y . . .' which were meant to parody Klopstock's verses on the pretext that his sentiments were fit for peasants but far too unrefined for the bourgeoisie. Even Klopstock later wrote a dialect version of his own poem. It is clear from this that nationalism was an issue among certain German (rather than Austrian) artists long before Napoleon placed it in the forefront of the popular political agenda. It was the Wars of Liberation, however, when Prussia and Austria were allies, which temporarily induced Schubert and his contemporaries to enthuse over the prospect of one united 'fatherland'. The composer quickly lost interest in these sentiments when it became obvious that, in the interest of retaining the status quo of power, Metternich was willing to repress free speech and expression in the name of a bogus patriotism that did more to limit the cultural and intellectual influence of neighbouring countries than to encourage a free market of thought between the different regions of the German-speaking world.

The direction 'Mässig' stands at the head of the first version, but the second version is marked 'Etwas geschwind, mit Feuer'; it is rather unusual to find a song written for a woman which is required to be sung 'with fire'. The tune is in the composer's best *Singspiel* style in the 'open' ceremonial key of C major, with the piano doubling the voice part throughout. The accompaniment bristles with activity and conveys an element of pomp, particularly evident in the piano's final bars where the music jumps and leaps with pride. The filled-out chords, played quickly and staccato, make this one of the composer's more tricky postludes, especially for such a simple song. The touch of arrogance evident in this music has to be heard in historical perspective: it is a paean of joy three months after the Battle of Waterloo, a thumbing of the German nose at the thwarted world-ruling ambitions of the French. The first version has a somewhat different postlude and it takes different harmonic and melodic turns from the second which seems to be more kindly written for the voice in terms of tessitura. The high Gs in bb. 2 and 7 of the first version are replaced by a rather more singable and less strident vocal line.

There are eight strophes in Klopstock's poem. Of these 1, 2, 3, 7 and 8 are printed above. For the Hyperion recording only strophes 1 and 7 were performed.

Autograph:	Staatsbibliothek Preussischer Kulturbesitz, Berlin (first draft)
Publication:	First published as part of the AGA 1895 (P583; first version)
	First published as part of the AGA in 1895 (P584; second version)
Subsequent editions:	Not in Peters; AGA XX 141a & b: Vol. 3/76; NSA IV: Vol. 9/62 (first version) & 9/64 (second version)
Bibliography:	Fischer-Dieskau 1977, p. 47
	Friedlaender 1902, Vol. 2, pp. 127–30
Further settings:	Christoph Willibald von Gluck (1714–1787) *Vaterlandslied* (1785)
Discography and timing:	Fischer-Dieskau —
	Hyperion I 22[21]
	Hyperion II 10[8] 0'54 Lorna Anderson

← *Selma und Selmar* D286   *An Sie* D288 →

Der VATERMÖRDER   The parricide
(PFEFFEL) **D10** [H5]
C minor   26 December 1811

(83 bars)

(1) Ein Vater starb von des Sohnes Hand.[1]	A father died by his son's hand.
Kein Wolf, kein Tiger, nein!	No wolf, no tiger,
Der Mensch allein, der Tiere Fürst, erfand[2]	But man alone, the prince of beasts,
Den Vatermord allein.	He alone invented parricide.
(2) Der Täter floh, um dem Gericht	To cheat the law of its victim,
Sein Opfer zu entziehn,	The murderer fled

[1] In this line 'des' is Schubert's addition.
[2] In this line 'allein' is Schubert's addition.

	In einen Wald, doch konnt er nicht	Into a wood, yet he could not
	Den innern Richter fliehn.	Escape the inner judge.

(3)   Verzehrt und hager, stumm und bleich,   Consumed and haggard, silent and pale,
Mit Lumpen angetan,   Dressed in rags,
Dem Dämon der Verzweiflung gleich,   Like the demon of despair
Traf ihn ein Häscher an.   He was found by a henchman.

(4)   Voll Grimm zerstörte der Barbar   Filled with rage, the savage man
Ein Nest mit einem Stein,   Destroyed a nest with a stone
Und mordete die kleine Schar   And murdered the little brood
Der armen Vögelein.   Of poor fledglings.

(5)   Halt ein! rief ihm der Scherge zu,   Stop, cried the henchman,
Verruchter Bösewicht![3]   Accursed murderer!
Mit welchem Rechte marterst du,   By what right do you torture
Die frommen Tierchen so?   These harmless creatures?

(6)   Was fromm, sprach jener, den die Wut   Harmless? he replied, stammering,
Kaum hörbar stammeln liess;   Barely audible in his fury,
Ich tat es, weil die Höllenbrut   I did it because this hellish brood
Mich Vatermörder hiess.   Called me a parricide.

(7)   Der Mann beschaut ihn: seine Tat   The henchman looked at him
Verrät sein irrer Blick,   Whose crazed look betrayed his deed.
Er fasst den Mörder, und das Rad   He seized the murderer, and the rack
Bestraft sein Bubenstück.   Punished him for his villainy.

(8)   Du, heiliges Gewissen, bist   You, sacred conscience, are
Der Tugend letzter Freund;   Virtue's last friend;
Ein schreckliches Triumphlied ist   To her enemy your thunder
Dein Donner ihrem Feind.   Is an awesome song of triumph.

GOTTLIEB CONRAD PFEFFEL (1736–1809); poem written before 1802

This is Schubert's only setting of a Pfeffel text. See the poet's biography.

This is Schubert's fourth vocal composition with piano accompaniment – leaving aside two earlier Baumberg fragments. The first had been *Hagars Klage* D5, with a text inspired by the Bible. The second and third were Schiller settings – *Des Mädchens Klage* D6 and *Leichenfantasie* D7. The choice of *Der Vatermörder* as a text, and of *Leichenfantasie* (which describes the burial of a son, with the grieving father looking on) seems to underline a fact that is obvious throughout Schubert's story – that the composer and his father seldom saw eye to eye. This was confirmed much later by 'Mein Traum' (July 1822, Deutsch Documetary Biography p. 226), a kind of prose-poem allegory in which Schubert recounts a dream that centres on his alienation from, and reconciliation with, his father. It is with the onset of puberty that sons tend to have difficulties

---

[3] Pfeffel writes 'Verruchter *Schadenfroh!*' to rhyme with 'Tierchen so' in the strophe's fourth line.

with their fathers, and vice versa. Schubert senior was strong-willed and somewhat authoritarian, and it is probable that on more than one occasion Franz rebelled on some issue, and was punished.

It is well known that Christmas holidays, when families come together (in Schubert's case, in cramped circumstances), can be occasions of misunderstanding and tension. *Der Vatermörder*, written on 26 December 1811 as if in a flash of anger, raises the grisly idea of parricide and then, as if horrified by even contemplating such a thing, roundly punishes the guilty party. If there was no personal reason for the choice of words, they were certainly not selected for their literary merit, or because the story they lamely describe is an interesting one. The poem is piffle by Pfeffel, more ridiculous than almost any of the early ballads. It is likely that Schubert found it in a Viennese school textbook: the first of two volumes entitled *Sammlung Deutscher Beyspiele zur Bildung und Styls* pp. 40–41. In that publication it is not printed as above, in eight strophes convenient for discussion of the music in sections, but in one continuous block of print with indentations. Setting it probably allowed Schubert to discharge his adolescent anger onto long-suffering paper, airing in the musical arena personal problems that he found impossible to discuss in real life, and achieving some kind of solution or reconciliation. The music both describes the problem and seems to be the therapy that assuages it.

Hagars Klage D5 had been modelled on the Zumsteeg ballad of the same name which served as a ground plan on which Schubert built his own tellingly different version, but *Der Vatermörder* is the first Schubert setting with a Mozartian impetus. The song opens with an extended piano introduction where the syncopations and left-hand arpeggios are inspired by the Queen of Night's first aria in B flat, 'O zittre nicht'. This is here transposed to the C minor of Tamino's struggle with the serpent; the piano writing suggests an orchestra, or at least a short score of one, and the three flats of the key signature proclaim a *Zauberflöte* work. It is possible that Schubert knew this opera through an early vocal score, but the sheer physicality of *Der Vatermörder* suggests that he wrote it with the sound of singing, in a bold high tessitura, ringing in his ears – in which case he had heard the Mozart opera in performance as early as 1811. In asking Tamino to rescue her daughter in Mozart's aria, the Queen of Night is all but inciting him to kill Sarastro, Pamina's father; Schubert's fourteen-bar introduction is a type of overture or prologue, describing the murder of another father offstage before the first sung words proclaim it a fait accompli. It is astonishing how many times the young Schubert extrapolated tonal analogues from works he already knew and admired, employing them for situations found in narrative ballads of this sort. In *Lied des Orpheus* D474, for example, music for Eurydice's spouse at the gates of hell prompts musical parallels of Mozart's Tamino under pressure.

There is much in *Der Vatermörder* that betrays the inexperienced youngster. The tessitura is both unreasonably low and high – a distance of two octaves between the low B flat in b. 132 and the high B flats in bb. 23, 25, 46, 95 and 111 – making for an extremely taxing vocal line. In addition, much of the piano writing is wooden. We are denied the subtleties of Mozart's orchestration, and the piano in this mood suggests sub-Beethoven in *Sturm und Drang* mode. We look in vain for the humour, fantasy and felicity of *Die Zauberflöte* itself but Pfeffel's text militates against this of course. At the beginning of Verse 3 (from the 'Andante' at b. 63) there is an echo of the slow dotted chords that open Mozart's opera and recur at important moments, and the counterpoint in Verse 7 ('Allegro vivace' from b. 125) is doubtless inspired by the duet of the two Men in Armour in the Finale. The stammering of the piano writing after the words 'stammeln liess' in Verse 6 (from b. 119) is a nice touch, and a moment of unintentional respite from the horror that is so over the top that it becomes both tedious and almost laughable. Some of the piano figurations, particularly those ostinati that are meant to stir up the emotions to boiling point, are re-used in *Der Taucher* D77, a work in which Schubert employs with considerable panache all the tricks of stagecraft learned in his earlier ballads.

Autograph: Wienbibliothek im Rathaus, Vienna (first draft)
First edition: Published as part of the AGA in 1894 (P530)
Subsequent editions: Not in Peters; AGA XX 4: Vol. 1/40; NSA IV: Vol. 6/46;
                              Bärenreiter: Vol. 5/38
Bibliography: Fischer-Dieskau 1977, pp. 27–8
                              Schnapper 1937, pp. 98–9
Discography and timing: Fischer-Dieskau I 1² 5'40
                              Hyperion I 12¹
                              Hyperion II 1⁶   6'15   Adrian Thompson

← *Leichenfantasie* D7   *Des Mädchens Klage* D6 →

VEDI QUANTO [T']ADORO   See how much I still love [you]
(Didone abbandonata)   (Dido abandoned)
(Metastasio) **D510** [H327 & H328]

The song exists in four versions, the second and fourth of which are discussed below:
(1) December 1816?; (2) December 1816?; (3) December 1816; (4) December 1816?

(1)   No tempo indication   E♭ major   **C**   [122 bars]

(2)   E♭ major

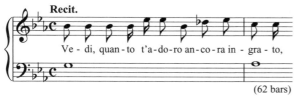

(62 bars)

(3)   'Andante'   E♭ major   **C**   [131 bars]

(4)   E♭ major – F minor

(136 bars)

Vedi quanto [t'] adoro ancora ingrato!   See how much I still love [you] ungrateful man!
Con uno sguardo solo¹   With a [your] single glance
Mi togli ogni difesa, e mi disarmi.   You remove all my defences, and disarm me.
Ed ài cor di tradirmi? E puoi lasciarmi?   Do you have the heart to betray me? And then to
                                            leave me?

¹ Metastasio writes 'Con *un tuo* sguardo'.

Ah! non lasciarmi, no,	Ah, do not leave me,
Bell' idol mio:	My beloved,
Di che mi fiderò	Whom shall I trust
Se tu m'inganni?	If you deceive me?
Di vita mancherei	My life would fail me
Nel dirti addio;	As I said farewell to you.
Chè viver non potrei	I could not live
Fra tanti affanni.	With such grief.

PIETRO METASTASIO (1698–1782); poem written in 1723

This is the tenth of Schubert's fourteen Metastasio solo settings (1812–27). See the poet's biography for a chronological list of all the Metastasio settings.

The text is taken from *Didone abbandonata*, a full-length Metastasio opera libretto from 1724. This aria comes at the end of Act II Scene 4 when the Queen of Carthage engages in a long dialogue with Aeneas (here Enea) who in leaving Carthage asks her to grant a pardon to Jarba, King of the Moors. She eventually accedes to this request and then, still in love with Aeneas, upbraids him while begging him to stay. (One is reminded of Donna Elvira's 'Mi tradì' in the second Act of Mozart's *Don Giovanni*.) The text had been set by Antonio Salieri and published in 1803 as No. 9 of his *Dodici divertimenti vocali*, a work that Schubert almost certainly knew. Schubert's manuscript (containing the first, second and third versions of the aria) was punctiliously vetted and amended by Salieri himself. The work was written right at the end of the young composer's four-year working period with the Italian maestro – Walther Dürr has written of it as Schubert's 'Gesellenstück', the final piece of work submitted by an apprentice before going out into the world. Even if Schubert had officially left Salieri as a teacher before the concert for his fiftieth anniversary in the summer of 1816 (*see Beitrag zur fünfzigjährigsten Jubelfeier des Herrn von Salieri* D407) he might have had a particular need to ask once more for the maestro's advice. At this time of his life Schubert was looking for a job in an opera house (he had tried and failed to land one in Laibach – Ljubljana – in Slovenia) and he may have intended to impress his prospective employers with a piece of flawless *bel canto* word-setting. Salieri remained the best man to consult as master of Italian prosody and style. The autograph is full of his corrections.

And yet Salieri was not Schubert's only model when it came to musical representation of a scorned or abandoned queen or princess. The words 'misera abbandonata' are to be found in Joseph Haydn's *Arianna a Naxos* Hob XXVIB:2, an extended cantata for voice and piano that was given its debut performance during Haydn's first London visit in 1795, and which was received with ecstatic enthusiasm in the British capital. The similarities between the pieces, Haydn's and Schubert's, both devoted to wronged women from classical mythology, seem too great to be coincidental. The Haydn piece is a real cantata – much longer, subdivided into a number of arias and recitatives, but like the fourth version of Schubert's setting of *Didone abbandonata*, it begins with a stately *stromentato* recitative in E flat and ends with passionate invective in the key of F minor. In the latter section particularly, it is difficult to believe that Schubert did not have Haydn's panting, gasping music in his head as a model. Rhythmic excitement is generated by similar means, and though Dido's words, unlike Ariadne's, are meant to cajole and plead, they end up sounding angry in similar vein. This is something to do with the imperious and daunting range of Schubert's vocal line. The whole piece mimics the majesty of *opera seria* – the opening trills in the piano part, the vocal cadenza, the middle section in the relative major leading back to the *da capo*. Haydn's *Arianna a Naxos* has long been a favourite recital opener for mezzo sopranos. Schubert's cantata has never achieved anything like the same popularity with sopranos but it cries out for more frequent performance.

As described above, the song's autograph contains no fewer than three incomplete sketches and a fair copy. All four versions are printed in Volume 11 of the NSA. Only the second version (p. 221) is different enough to be considered as something of a separate setting. We owe the excavation and amplification of this sketch (which mostly consists of melody and bass line) to the indefatigable industry of the late Reinhard Van Hoorickx; it was recorded as a separate piece in the Hyperion Schubert Edition. Schubert's final recitative for the fourth version is an elaboration of the simple and concise one written here; but the main body of the aria ('Ah, non lasciarmi, no, / Bell' idol mio') is rather different. The key of F minor is common to the second and fourth versions, and there is a middle section in the relative major in both, but the melodies, and the shapes of the phrases, are not the same. Hoorickx's simple accompaniment (and Schubert's marking of 'Andante con moto' rather than the final 'Allegro affettuoso') makes this music more accessible to ordinary performers than the final version that requires a high C and towering vocal stamina. There is more anger in the final version, whereas the second has a mood approaching gentle sadness. In working his way towards the definitive setting Schubert started with a core of melody and harmony – vocal line plus bass – and gradually dressed it up in increasingly dramatic clothes. If this earlier music is less showy than the final version of *Vedi quanto [t']adoro*, it also appears less of a pose and more heartfelt, more Schubert perhaps than Haydn or Salieri.

A word here about Schubert's deficient Italian. Having copied down the text ('t'adoro' in line one) accurately for the first two versions, he leaves out the accusative 't' in the next two settings. If we look at the manuscript of the fair copy we can see Salieri adding 't'a' in red pencil above the stave; he also corrects Schubert's 'uncora' to 'ancora'. The NSA's policy is to print what Schubert wrote as text, even if it departs from the poet's original; in this case the word ancora is printed because 'uncora' is nonsense, but we also have 'adoro' instead of 't'adoro'. Schubert's instincts when departing from a poet's texts in his own language are sometimes inspired and usually understandable, but in this case his manuscript offers no feasible improvement on Metastasio. The second line is also problematic: Metastasio wrote 'Con *un tuo* sguardo' and the singer should almost certainly sing this rather than Schubert's uglier 'Con uno sguardo solo' – a phrase he miscopied and even wrote (more than once) as 'con uno squardo'. This is surely a warning against treating the composer's departures from Italian texts (for example the *Vier Canzonen* D688) with too much earnest respect.

Autographs:	Wienbibliothek im Rathaus, Vienna (three incomplete sketches and a fair copy)
Publication:	First published as part of the NSA in 1999 (P819; first version)
	First published as part of the NSA in 1999 (P820; second version)
	First published as part of the NSA in 1999 (P821; third version)
	First published as part of the AGA in 1895 (P705; fourth version)
Subsequent editions:	Not in Peters; AGA XX 573: Vol. 10/40; NSA IV: Vol. 11/58, 221, 223 & 226
Bibliography:	Capell 1928, p. 127
	Litschauer 2001, pp. 74–83
Arrangements:	Arr. Paul Angerer (b. 1927) for voice and string quartet
Discography and timing:	Fischer-Dieskau —
	Hyperion I 9² 4'28 Arleen Auger (4th version)
	Hyperion I 32¹⁰ 3'05 Ann Murray (2nd version)

Hyperion II 17⁵   4'28   Arleen Auger (4th version)
Hyperion II 17⁶   3'05   Ann Murray (2nd version)

← *Licht und Liebe* D352   *An den Tod* D518 →

Die VERFEHLTE STUNDE   The missed opportunity
(A. VON SCHLEGEL) **D409** [H244]

The song exists in two versions, the second of which is discussed below:
(1) April 1816; (2) April 1816?

(1) 'Unruhig'   F minor   **C**   [24 bars]

(2)   F minor

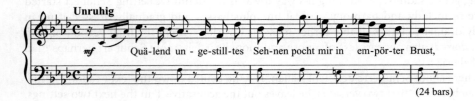

(24 bars)

Quälend ungestilltes Sehnen	The torment of unquiet longing
Pocht mir in empörter Brust.	Beats within my raging breast.
Liebe, die mir Seel' und Sinnen	Love, you knew how to win
Schmeichelnd wusste zu gewinnen,	My soul and my senses with your flattery;
Wiegt dein zauberisches Wähnen	Does your magic illusion lull me
Nur in Träume kurzer Lust,	To dreams of fleeting pleasure,
Und erweckt zu Tränen?	Only to awaken me to tears?
Süss berauscht in Tränen	O to be drunk with sweet tears,
An des Lieben Brust mich lehnen,	Leaning on my beloved's breast,
Arm um Arm gestrickt,	My arms entwined in his arms,
Mund auf Mund gedrückt,	My lips pressed to his lips –
Das nur stillt mein Sehnen!	This alone will still my longing!
Ach, ich gab ihm keine Kunde,	Ah, I gave him no indication,
Wusst' es selber nicht zuvor;	I myself did not know beforehand
Und nun beb' ich so beklommen:	And now I tremble so anxiously:
Wird der Traute, wird er kommen?	Will my beloved come?
Still und günstig ist die Stunde,	The hour is silent and favourable;
Nirgends droht ein horchend Ohr	Nowhere does an eavesdropper threaten
Dem geheimen Bunde.	Our secret bond.
Treu im sel'gen Bunde	O to lean on my beloved's breast
An des Lieben Brust mich lehnen,	In true, blissful union,
Arm um Arm gestrickt,	My arms entwined in his arms,
Mund auf Mund gedrückt,	My lips pressed to his lips –
Das nur stillt mein Sehnen!	This alone will still my longing!

Hör' ich leise Tritte rauschen,	When I hear soft footsteps
Denk' ich: ah, da ist er schon!	I think: ah, here he is!
Ahndung hat ihm wohl verkündet,	A presentiment must have told him
Dass die schöne Zeit sich findet,	That the fair hour is at hand,
Wonn' um Wonne frei zu tauschen. –	The hour to exchange joy freely.
Doch sie ist schon halb entflohn	But already it is half gone,
Bei vergebnem Lauschen.	Passed in vain waiting.
Mit entzücktem Lauschen	O to lean on my beloved's breast
An des Lieben Brust mich lehnen,	In rapturous communion,
Arm um Arm gestrickt,	My arms entwined in his arms,
Mund auf Mund gedrückt,	My lips pressed to his lips –
Das nur stillt mein Sehnen!	This alone will still my longing!
Täuschen wird vielleicht mein Sehnen,	I had hoped that the joy of song
Hofft' ich, des Gesanges Lust.	Might perhaps delude my longing,
Ungestümer Wünsche Glühen	And that gentle melodies might quench
Lindern sanfte Melodien–	The fire of impetuous desire.
Doch das Lied enthob mit Stöhnen	But the song escaped from my heart,
Tief eratmend sich der Brust,	Groaning and panting,
Und erstarb in Tränen.	And died in tears.
Süss berauscht in Tränen	O to be drunk with sweet tears,
An des Lieben Brust mich lehnen,	Leaning on my beloved's breast,
Arm um Arm gestrickt,	My arms entwined in his arms,
Mund auf Mund gedrückt,	My lips pressed to his lips –
Das nur stillt mein Sehnen!	This alone will still my longing!

AUGUST WILHELM VON SCHLEGEL (1767–1845); poem written in 1791

This is the second of Schubert's ten August von Schlegel solo settings (1816–26). See the poet's biography for a chronological list of all the August von Schlegel settings.

In some ways this is a companion piece to the Matthisson setting for tenor, *Entzückung* D413, composed later in the same month. It is a better song, but it takes similar risks. With *Die verfehlte Stunde* Schubert writes one of his most demanding songs for the female voice. The singer here needs to be of a similar temperament to the tenor of *Entzückung*: over the top, especially in terms of tessitura. We are reminded of the composer's ability to find an astonishingly varied tone of voice for his women's songs: *Gretchen am Spinnrade* D118 had marked Schubert out as having an extraordinary insight into female psychology, and by 1816 he had also written songs for Goethe's heroines Mignon and Klärchen, Schiller's Thekla, Amalia and Andromache, and settings of the poetess Gabriele von Baumberg. These are all subtly different musical portraits of passionate and decisive characters, but the Schlegel poem introduces a nameless protagonist who takes the characteristics of strength and determination to a more intense level.

Die verfehlte Stunde is a portrait of a woman who knows exactly what she wants, and who is volubly articulate on the subject. Schlegel's highly charged poem dates from 1791, the heady days of the French Revolution when women were equal citizens of a new order. It comes as no surprise to learn that Schlegel later spent a great deal of time as the literary adviser and travelling companion of Anne-Louise Germaine de Staël, one of the intellectual giants of the time. Madame de Staël in love no doubt presented a formidable challenge to the gentlemen of her choice. If the lover fails to materialize in *Die verfehlte Stunde*, it is possibly for fear of confronting a woman far more intelligent, and demanding, them himself.

A certain overwrought tone in the music is due to a tessitura that cranks up the tension to the maximum. The placing of the phrase 'Nur in Träume kurzer Lust' (b. 7) is particularly impractical, but the stratospheric vocal line is only one of this song's technical challenges. The metre of the poem makes long-spanned phrases inevitable: a glance at the dense first page of music shows that there is not a rest to be had, and the singer is forced to snatch breaths between long phrases that hover relentlessly in the most awkward part of the voice. And, of course, *Die verfehlte Stunde* requires stamina. It is a strophic song where the mounting tension of the scenario requires all four verses to be sung. Because of this it is more than twice the length of *Entzückung*.

The song's tonality and the pattern of the accompaniment bring Mozart's wonderful *Das Lied der Trennung* K519 to mind in a much more frenetic incarnation (Schubert's piece is marked 'Unruhig'). The pulsating semiquavers, nudged forward by left-hand quavers on the beat, represent the restless beating of an impatient heart. The word 'Liebe' (bb. 3–4) is set as a descending chromatic wail that lasts no fewer than five beats. This audacity is highly effective in the first verse but less so in the second where the word 'und' inevitably receives the same treatment. Each of Schlegel's verses is twelve lines long; the poem seems too unwieldy to yield to strophic form and a more cautious composer would have thought twice about choosing it. But Schubert, once engaged, battles gamely on. The poet indents the last five lines of each verse, and the composer engineers a new mood and a new speed (the relatively rarely used marking 'Schnell') for this new section (from b. 10). Although the fit of the words into the musical metre is awkward, the characterization of a woman beside herself with longing is helped by the resulting dislocations of stress and symmetry. Scuttling semiquavers in A flat major (ideally descriptive of 'Süss berauscht in Tränen') suddenly cease at b. 15 for 'Das nur stillt mein Sehnen!'. The stilling of longing stills the movement of the music itself. The vocal line is now in minims perched high in the stave and supported by sliding chromaticisms in pianissimo crotchets which temporarily take the music into the distant regions of C flat major at b. 17. The repeat of these words then leads into a marvellous, and typically Schubertian, use of a chromatically decorated dominant–tonic cadence at 'Das nur <u>stillt</u> mein Sehnen!'. The final word, 'Sehnen', is set to an expressive melisma in which an F is sung against an E flat[7] chord before plunging a seventh and surfacing to return to the tonic. The eloquent four-bar postlude that concludes the song is built of feminine dreams and sighs; a submissive cadence (where we hear the 'stillt' progression again in the penultimate bar) gently returns the music to A flat major.

But this has been anything but a submissive song. As far as Schubert's nameless heroine is concerned, the gentle tenderness is a case of a tactical retreat in order to gather her resources for the next onslaught. Another verse looms, and more restless F minor anguish (the key incidentally of the abandoned Dido in *Vedi quanto t'adoro* D510). As has been pointed out, the subsequent strophes are not as aptly aligned to the musical imagery as the first. It would be some years before Schubert consistently mastered the art of incorporating the verbal subtleties of various verses into music that does multiple service for different images. Nevertheless, he makes good use of the fact that each long strophe ends with five lines of veiled sexual imagery (ideal for those fast pulsating semiquavers) and that 'Das nur stillt mein Sehnen!' is the refrain that ends each verse. In a performance we hear this passage four times, and each time it sounds extraordinarily modern and inventive. If *Die verfehlte Stunde* cannot be counted one of the great songs, it is clearly by a great composer. It is surely forgivable that his youthful enthusiasm, and his identification with a text of unfulfilled longing, should have led him to ask his singer to live dangerously, and at the limits of vocal practicability.

The NSA prints an 'Erste Fassung' of *Die verfehlte Stunde*, a version almost certainly from earlier in April 1816, less finished in terms of phrasing and dynamics, but differing only in tiny details.

Autographs:	Maeda Ikutoku Kai Foundation in Nanki Music Library, Tokyo (first version, first draft)
	Staatsbibliothek Preussischer Kulturbesitz, Berlin (second version, fair copy)
Publication:	First published as No. 26 of *Neueste Folge nachgelassener Lieder und Gesänge* by J. P. Gotthard, Vienna in 1872 (P452; first version)
	First published as part of the NSA in 2002 (P834; second version)
Subsequent editions:	Not in Peters; AGA XX 206: Vol. 4/76; NSA IV: Vol. 10/128 & 132
Bibliography:	Capell 1928, p. 125
	Einstein 1951, p. 135
Discography and timing:	Fischer-Dieskau —
	Hyperion I 32[18]
	Hyperion II 13[20] 5'05 Christine Schäfer

← *Echo et Narcisse: 'O combats, o désordre extrême'*   *Sprache der Liebe* D410 →
   D Anhang IIb

VERGEBLICHE LIEBE   Love in vain
(BERNARD) **D177** [H83]
C minor   6 April 1815

(58 bars)

Ja, ich weiss es, diese treue Liebe	Yes, I know, my wounded heart
Hegt unsonst mein wundes Herz!	Harbours this true love in vain.
Wenn mir nur die kleinste Hoffnung bliebe,	If only the slightest hope remained for me
Reich belohnet wär' mein Schmerz!	My sorrow would be richly rewarded.
Aber auch die Hoffnung ist vergebens,	But even hope is in vain,
Kenn ich doch ihr grausam Spiel!	For I know Her cruel game!
Trotz der Treue meines Strebens	Despite my constant endeavour
Fliehet ewig mich das Ziel!	My goal forever eludes me!
Dennoch lieb' ich, dennoch hoff ich, immer	Yet I love, yet I hope unceasingly,
Ohne Liebe, ohne Hoffnung treu;	Faithful, even without love or hope;
Lassen kann ich diese Liebe nimmer!	I can never forsake this love,
Mit ihr bricht das Herz entzwei!	Yet with it my heart breaks in two!

JOSEF CARL BERNARD (1781–1850)

This is Schubert's only setting of a Bernard text. See the poet's biography.

The emotional resonance of this poem is similar to that of one set to music two days later, *Sehnsucht der Liebe* D180. This Bernard setting is also about 'Sehnsucht' and 'Liebe', a hopeless passion sustained through thick and thin. The opening is a wonderfully rhetorical *stromentato* recitative: it is as if we open a door to enter into the music, and discover a dramatic scene already under way, the first phrase an impassioned reply to an offstage warning that the lover is deluded and has been wasting his time. Note that the word 'treue' (b. 4) has a long-lasting note value to match its meaning; only 'Schmerz' (b. 11) is longer still. Blazing conviction yields to melancholic introspection. The introduction of a devious C flat on the word 'Spiel' in b. 15 (as out of place here as cruel and manipulative games should be in a love affair) continues as a harmonic red herring throughout the passage at the end of Verse 2 in which the poet complains of a goal always eluding him. This leads to a chord in the dominant (b. 19) and, with a sudden change of tempo, the second part of the song (Verse 3).

The new marking from b. 20 is 'Schnell. Mit steigendem Affekt' with a new time signature of ⅜. At b. 31, after seven bars of rising sequences and four of emotional dithering, the music suddenly becomes 'Langsamer'. This is a page of wild and unreasonable determination, halfway between aria and recitative, with the piano's sudden awkward stabbing octaves interrupting the proceedings like gasps of pain (bb. 36 and 40 with fermate on the third beats). The composer adds the repetitions of 'immer' (bb. 25–6) and 'nimmer' (bb. 44–5) and his own exclamation marks. The first time the words 'Mit ihr bricht das Herz entzwei' appear (bb. 36–9) they simulate a howl of inconsolable grief. The setting of the final line (the third time we hear 'Mit ihr bricht das Herz entzwei!') is prophetic of the ending of another dramatic song – also in C minor – from two years later, *Gruppe aus dem Tartarus* D583. In that famous Schiller setting the shape of the phrase 'Bricht die Sense des Saturns entzwei' has Saturn's scythe breaking in two (with the descent of a fifth, as in bb. 55–6) in the same way that the poet's heart is rent in two in *Vergebliche Liebe*. By association, it seems the composer sees the condition of unrequited love as a form of living hell, a kind of death sentence. Raymond Joly's verdict on this song of 'odd bits, fits and starts' (there are no fewer than eight fermate in the vocal line) is 'an excellent bridging scene in an opera'. It is hardly surprising to discover, therefore, that Bernard was a relatively famous opera librettist, providing texts for Spohr and Kreutzer.

Autograph:	In private possession, Nagold, Germany
First edition:	Published as Op. post. 173 no. 3 by C. A. Spina, Vienna in 1867 (P409)
Subsequent editions:	Peters: Vol. 6/114; AGA XX 58: Vol. 2/88; NSA IV: Vol. 8/28; Bärenreiter: Vol. 6/122
Bibliography:	Einstein 1951, p. 108
Discography and timing:	Fischer-Dieskau I 3[10] 2'16
	Hyperion I 10[5]
	Hyperion II 6[2] 1'59 Martyn Hill

← *Die Sterne* D176   *Liebesrausch* D179 →

VERGISSMEINNICHT
(Schober) **D792** [H516]
F minor – E major   May 1823

Forget-me-not

(268 bars)

(1) Als der Frühling sich vom Herzen
Der erblühten Erde riss,
Zog er noch einmal mit Schmerzen
Durch die Welt, die er verliess.[1]

When Spring tore himself from the heart
Of the burgeoning earth
He walked sorrowfully one last time
Through the world that he was leaving.

(2) Wiesenschmelz und Saatengrüne
Grüssen ihn mit hellem Blühn,
Und die Schattenbaldachine
Dunklen Walds umsäuseln ihn.

Radiant meadows and green cornfields,
Blooming brightly, greeted him,
And the shady canopy
Of the dark forest rustled about him.

(3) Da im weichen Samt des Mooses
Sieht er, halb vom Grün verdeckt,
Schlummersüss, ein kummerloses
Holdes Wesen hingestreckt.

There, in the soft, velvet moss,
Half concealed by the greenery, he espied
A lovely, carefree creature
Stretched out in sweet slumber.

(4) Ob's ein Kind noch, ob's ein Mädchen,
Wagt er nicht sich zu gestehn.
Kurze blonde Seidenfädchen
Um das runde Köpfchen wehn.

Whether it was a child still or a maiden
He was loth to say;
Short, blonde threads of silk
Waved about her little round face.

(5) Zart noch sind die schlanken Glieder,
Unentfaltet die Gestalt,[2]
Und doch scheint der Busen wieder
Schon von Regungen durchwallt.

Her slender limbs were still delicate,
Her figure undeveloped,
And yet her breast already seemed
To heave with emotion.

(6) Rosig strahlt der Wangen Feuer,
Lächelnd ist der Mund und schlau,
Durch der Wimpern duft'gen Schleier
Äugelt schalkhaft helles Blau.

A rosy glow shone from her cheeks;
Her mouth smiled slyly.
Through the fragrant veil of her eyelashes
Her bright blue eyes looked out mischievously.

(7) Und der Frühling, wonnetrunken
Steht er, und doch tief gerührt;
In das holde Bild versunken,
Fühlt er ganz, was er verliert!

And Spring, drunk with ecstasy
Yet deeply moved, stood up;
Enraptured by the sweet sight
He fully realized what he was losing.

---

[1] Schober writes (*Gedichte*, 1842) 'Durch die *Flur*, die er verliess'.
[2] Schober writes (*Gedichte*, 1842) '*Unentwickelt* die Gestalt'.

(8) Aber dringend mahnt die Stunde,	But the hour urgently reminded him
Dass er schnell von hinnen muss.	That he had to leave quickly.
Ach! da brennt auf ihrem Munde	Ah, his ardent parting kiss
Glühend heiss der Scheidekuss.[3]	Burned her lips!
(9) Und in Duft ist er entschwunden.–[4]	And he vanished in a haze.
Doch das Kind entfährt dem Schlaf,	But the child awoke from her sleep;
Tief hat sie der Kuss entzunden,	The kiss had inflamed her deeply
Wie ein Blitzstrahl, der sie traf.	As if lightning had struck her.
(10) Alle Keime sind entfaltet,	Every bud concealed
Die ihr kleiner Busen barg,	Within her little bosom unfolded;
Schnell zur Jungfrau umgestaltet,	Swiftly transformed into a young woman
Steigt sie aus der Kindheit Sarg.	She rose from the coffin of childhood.
(11) Ihre blauen Augen schlagen	Her blue eyes opened,
Ernst und liebelicht empor,	Solemn and radiant with love;
Nach dem Glück scheint sie zu fragen,	She seemed to enquire after the happiness
Was sie ungekannt verlor.[5]	That, unknowing, she had lost.
(12) Aber Niemand gibt ihr Kunde,	No one can enlighten her;
Alle sehn sie staunend an,	All gazed at her in astonishment,
Und die Schwestern in der Runde,	And her sisters in a circle
Wissen nicht wie ihr getan.	Did not know what had happened to her.
(13) Ach sie weiss es selbst nicht! – Tränen	Alas, she herself did not know! Her tears
Sprechen ihren Schmerz nur aus,	Expressed nothing but her sorrow,
Und ein unergründlich Sehnen	And an unfathomable longing
Treibt sie aus sich selbst heraus;	Drove her out of herself;
(14) Treibt sie fort, das Bild zu finden,	Drew her away to find the image
Das in ihrem Innern lebt,	That lived on within her
Das ihr Ahnungen verkünden,	That for her conjured up intimations
Das in Träumen sie umschwebt.	That hovered over her in her dreams.
(15) Felsen hat sie überklommen,	She clambered over rocks,
Berge steigt sie ab und auf;	She climbed up and down mountains
Bis sie an den Fluss gekommen,	Until she reached the river
Der ihr hemmt den Strebelauf.	That checked her impetuous course.
(16) Doch im Ufergras dem feuchten,[6]	But in the damp grass on the bank
Wird ihr heisser Fuss gekühlt,	Her burning feet were cooled,
Und in seinem Spiegel leuchten	And she saw her own image shining
Siehet sie ihr eignes Bild.	In the mirror of the water.

[3] Schober writes (*Gedichte*, 1842) 'Glühend heiss *sein* Scheidekuss'.
[4] This and the following two lines were changed for the second edition of Schober's *Gedichte* 1865: *Und wie in Duft verschwindet / Fährt* das Kind *aus tiefem* Schlaf.
[5] Schober writes (*Gedichte*, 1842) '*Das* sie ungekannt verlor'.
[6] Schober writes (*Gedichte*, 1842) '*Hier*, im Ufergras dem feuchten'.

(17)	Sieht des Himmels blaue Ferne,	She saw the distant blue of the sky,
	Sieht der Wolken Purpurschein,	Saw the crimson glow of the clouds,
	Sieht den Mond und alle Sterne; –	Saw the moon and all the stars;
	Milder fühlt sie ihre Pein.	And she felt her pain less keenly.
(18)	Denn es ist ihr aufgegangen:[7]	For she has realized
	Dass sie eine Seele fand,	That she had found a soul
	Die ihr innigstes Verlangen,	Which understood her innermost longing,
	Ihren tiefsten Schmerz verstand.	Her deepest sorrow.
(19)	Gern mag sie an dieser Stelle[8]	She would gladly build herself
	Sich die stille Wohnung bau'n,	A tranquil dwelling on this spot;
	Der verklärten sanften Welle	She could trust implicitly
	Kann sie rückhaltslos vertrau'n.	The gentle, radiant waves.
(20)	Und sie fühlt sich ganz genesen,	And she felt entirely healed
	Wenn sie zu dem Wasser spricht,	As she spoke to the waters
	Wie zu dem geahnten Wesen:	As if to that figure of her dreams:
	O vergiss, vergiss mein nicht!	O forget, forget me not!

FRANZ VON SCHOBER (1796–1882)

This is the twelfth of Schubert's fourteen Schober solo settings (1815–27). See the poet's biography for a chronological list of all the Schober settings.

The forget-me-not flower is to be found in King Henry IV's arms ('souveigne de moi') and was worn by supporters of the house of Lancaster. In a footnote to his poem 'The Keepsake' (1800) Samuel Taylor Coleridge tells us the following about the forget-me-not: 'One of the names (and meriting to be the only one) of the *Myosotis Scorpioides Palustris*, a flower from six to twelve inches high, with blue blossom and bright yellow eye. It has the same name over the whole Empire of Germany (*Vergissmein nicht*) and I believe in Denmark and Sweden.' A quarter of a century later, the forget-me-not was common currency in the language of flowers; it was used as a charm – 'Think of the one you wish to be thinking of you when you pull a sprig of forget-me-not, and you will immediately have a place in his – or her – thoughts.' The flower described by Coleridge, about 50 cm high, is known as *Sumpfvergissmeinnicht* in Germany; there is a variety of 20–40 cm (*Ackervergissmeinnicht* or *Myosotis arvensis*) and a wood and meadow variety (*Wald-Vergissmeinnicht* or *Myosotis sylvatica*) that can be the smallest of all. It is perhaps the last of these that is meant by Schober (who was no botanist) if we are to take seriously the site of the flower in the poem.

This lengthy song was the second flower ballad that Schubert set to the words of his close friend Franz von Schober. He had completed *Viola* D786 two months before, in March 1823, and *Vergissmeinnicht* is something of a sequel. It is possible that both poems were a kind of farewell present to Schubert from Schober before he left Vienna to pursue – unsuccessfully – the life of an actor in Breslau. Both poet and composer seem to have been working towards a larger song form and a means of telling an extended story; this experimentation was to bear fruit later in the year with the composition of *Die schöne Müllerin* D795 in which, by chance, the forget-me-not also figures (in Verse 3 of *Des Müllers Blumen* D795/9) as well as an invented black

---

[7] Schubert here switches the order of the poem's strophes. In Schober's *Gedichte*, 1842, this is Verse 19, not 18.
[8] This strophe is Verse 18, not 19 in Schober's *Gedichte*, 1842.

flower called the 'Vergissmein' – literally the Forget-me – in one of the poems in Wilhelm Müller's cycle that Schubert did not set to music.

There are a number of myths about the naming of the flower (including a French one concerning the drowning of Knight Roland) but Schober seems to be creating his own storyline here, combining it with the myth of Narcissus.

Verse 1: The song opens in a muted mood of searching and longing, emphasized by the questing change of chord that harmonizes the identical rising octave figuration in bb. 6 and 7. The vocal line that begins in b. 9 is arioso – half tune and half recitative, a technique Schubert was to perfect, for example, in the opening section of *Der Neugierige* D795/6 in *Die schöne Müllerin*.

Verse 2 ('Etwas langsamer'): A motif of dotted crotchet plus two semiquavers established in the vocal line of the first verse – on 'Herzen' in b. 11 – is now employed as the basis for the accompaniment to a gently rocking and rustling movement in A flat. The image of a canopy at 'Schattenbaldachine' (bb. 24–5) inspires a canopy of repeated notes on the vocal line, as if they were providing shade for the pianist's stave. (There is something similar in *Im Freien* D880, on that occasion inspired by the image of the poet's faithful friend sleeping beneath the roof of a house.) There is a sinuous *bel canto* melisma on 'umsäuseln ihn' (bb. 27–8) and a sense of gentle well-being throughout. At b. 34 there is a modulation into E major (with change of key signature) – a favourite destination in many a journey from A flat via a bridging bar in A flat minor (b. 31). After two bars the time signature changes to ⅜.

Verses 3–7 ('Langsam', from b. 36): This E major movement is the most charming in the piece, and some commentators have even suggested that it might be performed as a separate song. It is remarkable how Schubert now seems completely to ignore Schober's verse structure (the composer's musical recapitulations are likely to occur halfway through one of the poet's strophes) in order to make a seamless aria of the greatest beauty. This is definitely the hand that was soon to create the immortal 'O Bächlein meiner Liebe' section in *Der Neugierige*. There is the same effortless suggestion of an Italianate vocal line (utterly singable with the most grateful of vocal flourishes) suffused with the deepest German feeling. The sensual overtones are everywhere apparent in this music as Spring the seducer (an urgent motif quickens the pulse in the piano's left hand at b. 77, just before Verse 7) surveys the delicate young flower, a maiden who manages to appear mischievous ('schalkhaft') even as she slumbers. The rapture of his 'wonnetrunken' gaze (bb. 81–2) is aptly caught in a vocal line overflowing with semiquavers. Schober's own reputation in the Schubert circle for lascivious behaviour is scarcely contradicted by the veiled sexual overtones of these verses.

Verses 8–9 ('Geschwinder' from b. 91): This is a bridge passage for the swift disappearance of spring: cold winds tinged with A minor, then F minor and F sharp minor, rush through the music culminating on an anguished chord on 'Scheidekuss' (bb. 103–4). After this, most of Verse 9 ('Geschwind' from b. 110) is another arioso, beginning in F sharp minor, accompanied by a tremolo motif in the piano (derived from the idea of 'Blitzstrahl' – a flash of lightning – mentioned in b. 115). These linking passages suggest the beginnings of tunes, but they fail to flower into melody.

Verse 10 to the first line of Verse 13: This B major aria is the 'transformation' music of the piece. Like a nature film speeded up to show the unfolding of a flower's petals, it fairly bristles with the energy of nature. The cello-like motif in the piano's left hand (from b. 119) pushes upwards from the depths as if driven by the life force. The short two-bar phrases and the snatched crotchet rests in the pianist's right hand give a feeling of panic, even shame. This flower has been awakened in every sense and, no longer virginal ('Was sie ungekannt verlor'), she cannot expect the support and understanding of her sisters. Indeed the kiss of Spring has transformed her into a new and perplexing being. We hear this in bb. 168 to 172 in an astonishingly anguished line of recitative at the beginning of Verse 13 ('Ach sie weiss es selbst nicht!') set to pitches rising by semitones as if the flower is trying to stretch ever upwards to grasp the key to her inner salvation.

Second line of Verse 13 to Verse 17 ('Etwas geschwind', from b. 172): This is a B minor aria richly reminiscent (particularly in its rhythm) of the 'Unfinished' Symphony D759, a work from more or less the same period. It is also a sister of *Suleika I* D720 (also in B minor) and a cousin of both *Der Zwerg* D771 and *Du liebst mich nicht* D756. Only Schubert could get away with using this insistent and unchanging motor rhythm for nearly sixty bars; it powers and preserves the tension and sorrow of the forget-me-not's plight, the better to contrast with the acceptance music of the final section from Verse 18. There are so many fascinating things happening in the inner harmonies in this section that the true Schubertian could scarcely support the charges of monotony sometimes levelled against the work. The aptness of the composer's response to the words at Verses 16–17 is particularly impressive: the cooling of burning feet can be heard in the change of harmony (b. 205); the shining of the flower's image in the stream is apparent in the mirroring interplay between vocal line and bass; the playing of moon and stars in the river shines with colours achieved by the miraculously watery conjunction of voice and piano in these registers. The little piano postlude to this section (bb. 226–33) is a felicitous touch.

Verses 18–20 (Langsam from b. 214, with a return to a key signature of E major): This concluding section is unlike any other in all Schubert. Over an accompaniment of rising and falling arpeggios that would serve as a background to many an anonymous Italian aria (but in this case evokes 'The gentle, radiant waves') the composer weaves musical spells redolent of healing and self-acceptance. The opening line of Verse 20 ('Und sie fühlt sich ganz genesen', bb. 253–4) pours balm on the wound with a succession of sixths between voice and piano. The final cry from the heart that is both urgent plea and naming of a flower, the harmonies prophetic of the chromaticism of a later age, is as haunting a six-bar phrase as Schubert ever wrote. One is left with the distinct impression that for the two creators of this work there was a symbolic importance to the text that we shall never quite understand. 'Und sie fühlt sich ganz genesen' ('And she felt herself entirely healed') are especially moving words for Schubert to have set to music at a time when a cure from his syphilitic illness was his dearest wish, and presumably the poet's too, on his behalf. Schober is said to have exerted a powerful influence on Schubert in encouraging him to sexual openness and experiment. It is hard not to see in this song a parable of someone coming to terms with the forces of sexual awakening. Rejected by siblings, the flower has to move far away from home to find acceptance and self-acceptance; in the end the only solution to the pains and betrayals of life lies within, and in declining to blame oneself or others in a frenzy of guilt. At a time, when the composer was coming to terms with his terrible diagnosis, it seems likely that both *Viola* and *Vergissmeinnicht* contain a hidden personal agenda. In the Liedlexikon 2012 (pp. 629–30) Siegfried Schmalzriedt, while writing that the music has 'a stark homophile component', postulates that the two flower ballads have different characteristics, each linked to a different member of the Castor and Pollux team that composer and poet had become, especially during the composition of *Alfonso und Estrella* D732: *Vergissmeinnicht* with its happy ending referring to the narcissistic and upbeat Schober, and *Viola* to Schubert in the wake of his illness – heartbroken, afraid and ashamed.

Autograph:	Pierpont Morgan Library, New York
First edition:	Published as Book 21 no. 2 of the *Nachlass* by Diabelli, Vienna in February 1833 (P298)
Subsequent editions:	Peters: Vol. 5/112; AGA XX 430: Vol. 7/114; NSA IV: Vol. 13/104

Bibliography: Capell 1928, pp. 178–9
                           Dürhammer 1999, pp. 270–72
                           Einstein 1951, p. 253
Discography and timing: Fischer-Dieskau   —
                           Hyperion I 19[7]
                           Hyperion II 27[4]   12'36   Felicity Lott

← *Pilgerweise D789*   *Das Geheimnis* D793 →

VERKLÄRUNG   Transfiguration
(POPE trans. HERDER) **D59** [H24]
A minor   4 May 1813

The text is a translation of Pope's poem 'The Dying Christian to his Soul Ode'.[1] A literal
rendering of Herder's translation is followed by Pope's original poem, printed in italics.

Lebensfunke, vom Himmel ertglüht,   Spark of life, kindled by heaven,
Der sich loszuwinden müht!   That strives to twist itself free;
Zitternd-kühn, vor Sehnen leidend,   Bold yet trembling, aching with longing
Gern und doch mit Schmerzen scheidend – Parting gladly, yet with pain –
End', o end' den Kampf, Natur!   Cease, o cease this struggle, Nature!
Sanft ins Leben   Let me soar upwards
Aufwärts schweben   Gently into life,
Sanft hinschwinden lass mich nur.   Let me dwindle away gently.

Horch! mir lispeln Geister zu: Spirits whisper to me: 'Hark!
'Schwester-Seele, komm zur Ruh!'   Sister-soul, come to rest!'
Ziehet was mich sanft von hinnen?   Am I drawn gently hence?
Was ist's, was mir meine Sinnen   What is this, that threatens
Mir den Hauch zu rauben droht?   To steal my senses and my breath?
Seele, sprich, ist das der Tod?   Speak, soul, is this death?

Die Welt entweicht! Sie ist nicht mehr! The world recedes, it is no more!
Engel-Einklang um mich her![2]   Angelic harmonies surround me.
Ich schweb' im Morgenrot![3] –   I float in the dawn.

---

[1] Herder's title is *Popens sterbender Christ an seine Seele.*
[2] Herder (*Zerstreute Blätter*, 1796) has *Harmonieen* um mich her.
[3] Herder has 'Ich *schwimm*' im Morgenroth'.

Leiht, o leiht mir eure Schwingen:	Lend, o lend me your wings;
Ihr Bruder: Geister! helft mir singen:	Brother-spirits, help me sing:
'O Grab, wo ist dein Sieg? wo ist dein	'O grave, where is your victory?
Pfeil, o Tod?'	O death, where is your sting?'

I

Vital spark of heav'nly flame!
Quit, oh quit this mortal frame:
Trembling, hoping, ling'ring, flying,
Oh the pain, the bliss of dying!
Cease, fond Nature, cease thy strife,
And let me languish into life.

II

Hark! they whisper; Angels say,
Sister Spirit, come away.
What is this absorbs me quite?
Steals my senses, shuts my sight,
Drowns my spirits, draws my breath
Tell me, my Soul, can this be Death?

III

The world recedes; it disappears!
Heav'n opens on my eyes! my ears
With sounds seraphic ring:
Lend, lend your wings! I mount! I fly!
O Grave! where is thy Victory?
O Death! where is thy Sting?

ALEXANDER POPE (1688–1744), trans. JOHANN GOTTFRIED HERDER (1744–1803)

This is Schubert's only setting of a Pope text, although it is the first of two translations by Herder
(1813 and 1827). See the biographies of both these poets.

Einstein believed that the composer could not have done any better with this text many years later in his career; it is indeed a very considerable achievement for a sixteen-year old. Schubert's preoccupation with the diffuse ballad form is so great in this early period that we can all too easily overlook the handful of much smaller songs that are simultaneously imitations of the past and intimations of Schubertian glories to come. In the ballads he was influenced by Zumsteeg and Reichardt, but in the miniatures there are other models: the Mozartian melody of *Der Jüngling an der Quelle* D300, the poise and gravity of Zelter in the exquisite miniature *Klaglied* D23 (with Rochlitz's words themselves an imitative tribute to Gretchen's plaint at the spinning wheel), and the mellifluous meanderings, again Mozartian, of the Matthisson setting *Die Schatten* D50, where we hear an early attempt to create a vocal line that is halfway between recitative and aria. These pieces however do not attempt to grip or surprise us, only to delight.

Verklärung is a new departure for Schubert in that it seeks to do a ballad's stirring work in a very short time; within the miniature format of song, it unites stretches of aria with the colour and drama of storytelling recitative. The eighteenth-century rhetoric of the opening (bb. 1–4) leads to an all-purpose recitative (bb. 5–12), although the pianistic echo of the word 'zitternd' at b. 7, while scarcely dramatic, shows that the young composer's response to textual details is already flourishing. The 'Adagio' aria in D major–B minor that begins with the words 'Sanft ins Leben' at b. 13 is full of the necessary pathos – the existence of ghosts is announced by the gentle shudder in the piano commentary in b. 18. These voices address the soul in music of enormous tenderness. A recitative of some desperation (bb. 22–8) breaks into this soothing invitation, and the protagonist dies. The drama of 'Die Welt entweicht! Sie ist nicht mehr' is utterly simple and underplayed yet amazingly telling. It is now up to the music to describe what the soul is experiencing on the other side of the great divide. In the passage beginning at b. 29 (marked 'Im vorherigen Tempo') there is a return to the Adagio in D major–B minor. For 'Ihr Brüder: Geister! helft mir singen' (b. 35) the music has settled in E minor, the whole passage having been planned in such a way that the harmonies seem to gradually sink by stages into a comforting unconsciousness and acceptance. The final recitative ('O Death! where is thy sting?') returns the music to A minor.

The drama of death is stylized in pompous and old-fashioned oratorio style; its exalted tone brings to mind Handel and some of C. P. E. Bach's settings of poems by Gellert and Sturm. This eighteenth-century musical treatment is appropriate for the specifically Christian context of the text. Alexander Pope originally wrote a poem, inspired by the Emperor Hadrian, entitled *The Heathen to his Departing Soul*, before being challenged by Richard Steele to write a Christian equivalent that eventually became famous throughout Europe. Many and various were Schubert's successes when he shifted between recitative and aria at text-inspired will, but here we encounter the melange for the first time in a manageable song-sized serving. It might, however, be argued that *Verklärung* is a cantata fragment more than a true lied because it lacks idiomatic piano writing; it could be most felicitously accompanied by strings with touches of oboe. In this way it is related to the aria exercises written (in Italian of course) for Salieri, although none of them is as potent and original as *Verklärung*; the composer setting his mother tongue is what makes the difference. Whatever the mature Schubert's doubts concerning the faith of his fathers, it is probable that in 1813 he was still a papal enthusiast by default (the appropriately named Pope was, after all, a Roman Catholic). Schubert had yet to meet the friends (Mayrhofer, Schober and others) who would foster the schism between him and the establishment attitudes unswervingly held by his parents.

Autograph:	Missing or lost
First edition:	Published as Book 17 no. 4 of the *Nachlass* by Diabelli, Vienna in May 1832 (P288)
Subsequent editions:	Peters: Vol. 5/86; AGA XX 10: Vol. 1/68; NSA IV: Vol. 6/73; Bärenreiter: Vol. 5/64 (high voice), 5/60 (medium/low voice)
Bibliography:	Capell 1928, p. 82
	Einstein 1951, p. 50
	Fischer-Dieskau 1977, p. 24
Discography and timing:	Fischer-Dieskau I 1[7] 3'29
	Hyperion I 11[13]
	Hyperion II 2[20] 3'08 Brigitte Fassbaender

← *Sehnsucht* D52   *Ein jugendlicher Maienschwung* D61 →

Die VERSCHWORENEN D787

Such was the Imperial Censor's fear of plots against the Metternich regime that the original title of Schubert's *Singspiel* from April 1823, *Die Verschworenen* ('The Conspirators') had to be replaced by the more innocuous *Der häusliche Krieg* ('The Domestic War'). This is despite the fact that the conspirators in this plot were all women. The librettist was Ignaz Castelli (qv). The story is derived from the *Lysistrata* of Aristophanes, via a 'comédie en un acte et en prose, mêlée de vaudevilles' by François-Benoît Hoffmann, presented in Paris in 1802. Schubert was bitterly disappointed that the libretto had also been composed by Georg Abraham Schneider (1770–1839) and was a great success in 1824. The character of Helene (wife of Astolf) is one of four named 'conspirators' – two sopranos and two mezzos – all anti-war wives who withdrew their favours from their spouses. Helene's husband is away at the Crusades and at the beginning of the opera she is missing him. She sings the following aria (Act I Scene 2) as she looks listlessly out of the window:

ROMANZE (Ich schleiche bang und still herum)
(CASTELLI) **D787/2** [H509+]
F minor   Completed April 1823

I creep around, anxious and silent

(56 bars)

Ich schleiche bang und still herum,	I creep around, anxious and silent;
Das Herz pocht mir so schwer,	My heart beats so heavily.
Das Leben däucht mich öd' und stumm,	Life to me seems so mute and desolate,
Und Flur und Burg so leer.	Castle and meadow so empty.
Und jede Freude spricht mir Hohn,	Every joy is a mockery to me,
Und jeder Ton ist Klageton,	Every sound a sound of mourning
Ist der Geliebte fern,	When my beloved is far away,
Trübt sich des Auges Stern.	And the star of my eye grows dim.
Ach! Was die Liebe einmal band,	Ah what love once united
Soll nie sich trennen mehr,	Shall never more be sundered.
Was suchst du in dem fremden Land,	What do you seek in that distant land
Und weit dort über'm Meer?	Far across the sea?
Wenn dort auch buntre Blumen blüh'n,	Even if flowers there bloom more brightly
Kein Herz wird heisser für dich glüh'n.	No heart will burn more ardently for you.
O bleib' nicht länger fern,	Stay away no longer,
Du, meines Lebens Stern!	Star of my life!

IGNAZ FRANZ CASTELLI (1781–1862); poem written in 1820

The soprano Helene sings this aria before being drawn into the plot whereby a group of women decide to teach their husbands a lesson. The original scoring of this aria (a gentle undulation of strings with a descending scale for the cello now and then) is dominated by a pair of clarinets in A, one of which, a quasi-operatic soloist, is given a line of sinuous beauty. The bassoon also plays a part in the plaintive mood of the piece as a whole. In the Hyperion Edition this aria (arranged by Fritz Spiegel (1926–2003)) was included on the disc as a companion piece to *Der Hirt auf dem Felsen* D965 for Arleen Auger to sing with clarinet obbligato played by Dame Thea King. This arrangement is sanctioned by neither composer nor tradition, but it rescues a little-known piece from obscurity and reminds us of Schubert's interest in the clarinet as an obbligato instrument at least five years before *Der Hirt auf dem Felsen*. This voice/clarinet combination was to surface again a month later (May 1823) in the beautiful duet for Emma and Eginhard in the Finale to Act I of Schubert's grand opera *Fierabras* D796. In that work the musical *coup de grâce* is the melting change of A minor (the tenor's aria) to A major for the entrance of the soprano voice, as if in womanly benediction. A touch of the same transforming power of love is heard in Helene's aria when the voice part surprises us with a modulation into the major key on its penultimate note. A wife such as this, the music seems to be saying, could never seriously punish her husband.

First edition: Published as part of the AGA in 1889
Subsequent editions: Peters: Vol. 6/127; AGA XV: Vol. 3/144; NSA XV: Vol. 3/144 (aria
                           in full score)
Discography and timing: Fischer-Dieskau   —
                           Hyperion I 9⁶
                           Hyperion II 26¹⁶   3'02   Arleen Auger & Thea King (clarinet)

← *Wehmut* D772   *Drang in die Ferne* D770 →

VERSCHWUNDEN SIND DIE SCHMERZEN

Sorrow has vanished

Unaccompanied, TTB

(ANONYMOUS) **D88** [H28+]
G major   15 November 1813

Ver-schwun-den sind die Schmer-zen, weil aus be-klemm-ten Her - zen
                                                             (34 bars)

Verschwunden sind die Schmerzen,	Sorrows have vanished,
Weil aus beklemmten Herzen	For from oppressed hearts
Kein Seufzer wiederhallt.	Sighs no longer resonate.
Drum jubelt hoch, ihr Deutsche,	Then rejoice, Germans,
Denn die verruchte Peitsche	For the loathsome whip
Hat endlich ausgeknallt.	Has finally cracked its last.

ANONYMOUS/UNKNOWN

This canon (a celebration of the victory of the allies at the Battle of Leipzig on 19 October 1813) is one of the very few pieces of music in Schubert's output that reflects the politics of the time. It is rather ironic that two days after this battle, the bureaucracy of the state functioned well enough for the Emperor Franz to send a memorandum from the field concerning (among other things, admittedly) the poor school grades of Franz Schubert: as a result of the pressure put on him to improve his academic work, Schubert left the Konvikt and began his training as a schoolteacher. The opening notes of the canon are strangely reminiscent of one of the most famous quartets in opera, 'Mir ist so wunderbar' from *Fidelio*, which is also of course canonic. Something wonderful had indeed happened for the Germans. For the canon the composer took only one strophe of a much longer anonymous poem that he used in its entirety in another work – *Auf den Sieg der Deutschen* D81 (qv) – written for solo voice, two violins and a cello in the autumn of 1813.

Autograph:	Wienbibliothek im Rathaus, Vienna	
First edition:	Published as part of the AGA in 1892	
Subsequent editions:	AGA XIX 21: p. 77; NSA III: Vol. 4	
Bibliography:	Dürhammer 1999[2], p. 128	
Discography and timing:	Fischer-Dieskau —	
	Deutsche	Peter Schreier, Horst
	Grammophon 0'59	Laubenthal & Dietrich Fischer-Dieskau
	Schubert Terzette	
	Hyperion I 12[7] 1'20	Adrian Thompson, John Mark
	Hyperion II 2[26]	Ainsley & Richard Jackson

← *Son fra l'onde* D78   *Der Taucher* D77 →

VERSUNKEN   Rapt absorption
(GOETHE) **D715** [H465]

The song exists in two versions, the first of which is discussed below:
(1) February 1821; (2) July 1825

(1)   A♭ major

(125 bars)

(2)   'Geschwind'   F major   2/4   [125 bars]

Voll Locken kraus ein Haupt so rund!–	A head so round, so full of curly locks!
Und darf ich dann in solchen reichen Haaren,	And when I am allowed to fill my hands
Mit vollen Händen hin und wider fahren,	With this abundant hair, and run them to and fro,
Da fühl' ich mich von Herzensgrund gesund.	Then I feel good from the depths of my heart.
Und küss ich Stirne, Bogen, Auge, Mund,	And when I kiss her forehead, eyebrows, eyes and mouth,

Dann bin ich frisch und immer wieder wund.	I am afflicted afresh and ever again.
Der fünfgezackte Kamm, wo sollt' er stocken?	This five-toothed comb, where should it stop?
Er kehrt schon wieder zu den Locken.	Already it returns to her curls.
Das Ohr versagt sich nicht dem Spiel,	The ear, too, cannot refrain from joining in the game;
[(. . .)]¹	[(. . .)]
So zart zum Scherz, so liebeviel!	So delicate it is in playful dalliance, so full of love!
Doch wie man auf dem Köpfchen kraut,	But he who fondles this little head
Man wird in solchen reichen Haaren	Will, in such abundant hair,
Für ewig auf und nieder fahren.	Move his hands up and down for ever.
[(. . . 2 lines . . .)]²	[(. . . 2 lines . . .)]

[The poem's first line is repeated at the end of the song.]

JOHANN WOLFANG VON GOETHE (1749–1832); poem written in 1814

This is the fifty-seventh of Schubert's seventy-five Goethe solo settings (1814–26). See the poet's biography for a chronological list of all the Goethe settings.

As a result of the mysterious word 'Locken' in Goethe's diary, this poem has been suggested as the first of the *West-östlicher Divan* to be written. The inspiration was not Marianne von Willemer but a combination of Goethe's first encounter with the poetry of Hafiz and his enchantment, on 19 May 1814, with the hair of Caroline Ulrich, his part-time secretary and possibly lover. The extraordinary energy of *Versunken* is a characteristic of Schubert's writing in this period. A similar incessant movement of semiquavers in the accompaniment is to be found in *Im Walde* (*Waldesnacht*) D708 from the end of 1820, as well as in two works which the composer never completed – the second version of *Mahomets Gesang* D721 and *Johanna Sebus* D728. There are a few songs from earlier years, *Rastlose Liebe* D138 (1815) for example, where similar pianistic prestidigitation is required, but even that yields in its middle section to triplets, the better to return to passionate semiquavers in the final section. Unyieldingly fast and mercilessly metronomic piano writing is sometimes to be found in the songs of the Berlin masters Reichardt and Zelter, composers who greatly influenced Schubert. (Zelter's pupil, Felix Mendelssohn, wrote many songs where excitement is generated by such unbending tempi.) It is also likely that Schubert was influenced by the technical wizardry of some of the solo pianists active in Vienna; the name of performer–composer Hummel has remained relatively famous, but there were many less well-known pianists of the time who best expressed their musical personalities through virtuosic display.

Few accompanists would deny that *Versunken* is one of the trickiest of all Schubert piano parts, a veritable etude, and hair-raising in every sense. This type of writing, relatively short-lived in the composer's career, seems to have been part and parcel of the confidence that Schubert felt at this point (an optimism sadly soon to be dented by illness), a desire to conquer the world by beating it at its own game. Thus, if the public judged the success of a composer by his achievements in the opera house, then he would write operas! Similarly, if virtuosic display at the keyboard was what people found impressive, Schubert was more than equal to the challenge. If

---

¹ The missing line (where it is easy to sympathize with Schubert's disinclination to set the supremely unpoetic word 'Fleisch' to music) is 'Hier ist nicht Fleisch, hier ist nicht Haut' ('Here is neither flesh nor skin').
² The missing lines are 'So hast du Hafis auch gethan, / Wir fangen es von vornen an' ('You, too, did that, Hafiz; We begin again').

it was not the means of expression that came most naturally to him, it was at least part of his armoury. The composer was beginning to be fascinated by the possibilities of song as symphony, where organic unity is achieved with the help of moto perpetuo accompaniments. It is no accident that *Suleika I* D720 dates from the same period, written just after Schubert's experimentation with more rumbustious accompaniments; a later song like *Der Zwerg* D771 uses the same technique to devastating effect. In these works the semiquavers are equally incessant, but they murmur (rather than clatter) in the manner of strings played with a bow as opposed to struck with a hammer. The repetitive background pulse, the foundation of a work made up of long unfolding melodic phrases, underpins the vocal line rather than swamps it. Schubert finds the means of generating tension and establishing a sense of unity on a scale never before achieved in the realm of lieder.

Versunken is one of Schubert's few energetically erotic songs. The sweet-natured composer whom we were brought up to revere is more familiar to the listener as the master of the gently seductive, but here we have a rare chance to hear him rampant, and it makes some of the commentators uncomfortable. John Reed rightly cites *Suleika I* as an erotic masterpiece, but considers *Versunken* less successful in this regard; indeed it is as if he finds it hard to imagine the corpulent Schubert enmeshed in 'the physical realities of love'. Nevertheless in this song we discover an earthier and more physical Schubert than we might normally expect. To sing and play this music is to set the pulses racing. The hands of this lover, like the pianist's, are not quite 'everywhere', but in the caressing of the lover's head we sense a prelude to the further exploration (if ever permitted) so wonderfully described by John Donne nearly a quarter of a millenium earlier:

License my roaving hands, and let them go
Before, behind, between, above, below.
O my America! my new-found-land,
                        Elegie XIX: To His Mistris going to Bed

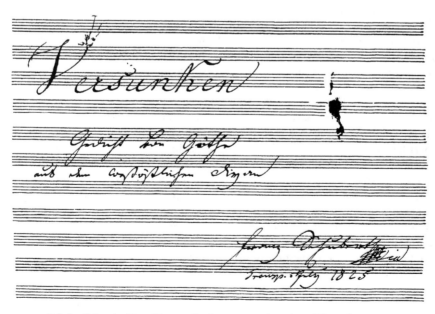

Schubert's handwritten title page for the transposed version of *Versunken*, 1825.

Neither is Donne impervious in this poem to the erotic power of hair, referring to it as a 'Diademe which on you doth grow'.

The idea of the five-toothed comb in Goethe's lyric is an ideal spur to piano writing where all five fingers of the right hand are equally exercised in separating the tangled flow of sound into even strands, each semiquaver equidistant from the next. In the meantime the left hand is free to jump and wander at will, its naughty explorations discreetly masked by the grooming tasks of the right. The writing for the left hand here, quick jumps between low bass notes and chords much higher in the stave, is strongly reminiscent of the second section, the *cabaletta*, of the second *Suleika* song ('Ach um deine feuchten Schwingen' D717). This style of piano writing is one argument in favour of the theory that *Suleika II* was contemporary with *Versunken*, and not written some time later (another theory places that song in 1824).

Schubert's delight in the discovery of the *West-östlicher Divan* is evident; we hear him falling in love with Goethe all over again, and his response to this poem is almost as original as his setting of *Gretchen am Spinnrade* D118 seven years earlier. In the meantime he has learned much about song-writing, not least that certain phrases and words do not sound well in performance. Thus he cuts the tenth line of the poem ('Hier ist nicht Fleisch, hier ist nicht Haut') that refers to 'flesh and skin', as well as Goethe's reflective final couplet where there is a reference to Hafiz (the great Persian poet who inspired the *Divan*) that would only serve to confuse the issue.

The form of the work is one of its most fascinating characteristics. Schubert is now such a master of songs, both strophic and *durchkomponiert*, that he is able to mix the genres and create various hybrid species at will. *Versunken* is essentially through-composed, but it has certain repetitions that give it some of the attributes of a strophic song. (*An Schwager Kronos* D369 is another Goethe setting in which certain passages are recycled, giving a strophic feel to a through-composed work.) *Versunken* is framed by the phrase 'Voll Locken kraus ein Haupt so rund!' (bb. 6–14 at the beginning, and bb. 113–21 at the end). Goethe's first line is set twice (with different music) to make an eight-bar opening phrase, and the song closes with the same words and a matching eight-bar phrase – albeit with different music. After this introduction, one of the song's most arresting inspirations is the explosion of *joie de vivre* for 'Und darf ich dann in solchen reichen Haaren' (bb. 16–20). This memorable music of surging excitement is repeated some pages later with different words (from b. 72), and the ear cannot resist registering the song's close weave as a strophic construction. This musical phrase is worthy of closer examination. A rush of exhilaration in the accompaniment gathers momentum to reach a climactic point where the music explodes, subsides and explodes again, like waves breaking on a rocky promontory. The vocal line is borne aloft (on 'solchen reichen', bb. 18–19) and touches a high A flat for a heady split second before subsiding amidst a foam of swirling semiquavers; the same process is repeated within seconds at 'vollen Händen'.

Schubert has imagined the beloved's flowing locks in terms of his favourite water imagery; the pianist must swim for his life in the swirling hairy rapids, while the singer can only hope to be washed into calmer waters where he might be allowed to practise his breast stroke. This use of unusual arpeggio figures, ornamented with clashes of adjacent minor seconds to give the music a kaleidoscopic glint, is already familiar from another piece of water music, the accompaniment for *Die Forelle* D550. In that song the trout moves hither and thither in his element, breaking the surface of the water as the conventional arpeggio includes adjacent accidentals (G flat and G natural added as piquant decoration to a D flat major chord). In *Versunken* the poet's hands are also in their element as they dart about in his beloved's hair, glimpses of white skin visible from time to time as a background to the dark tresses.

After this ever-shifting recklessness, 'Und küss ich Stirne, Bogen, Auge, Mund, / Dann bin ich frisch und immer wieder wund' (from b. 36) seems rooted in the same harmonic ground with repetitive patterns. This suggests something enjoyed again and again in a never-ending circular repetition: love-making ever freshly experienced with a beloved partner, ever new, ever exciting. There then follows a section ('Der fünfgezackte Kamm, wo sollt' er stocken?') that introduces, from b. 59, an element of uncertainty: how far is too far? The panting rhythms and syncopations of the left hand introduce a tense middle section. Somewhat fussy in matters of grooming, the poet wonders where the pronged comb (a metaphor for his hand of course) should go next and the song focuses once more on the glorious head of hair. The music of the tumbling waves of passion is repeated for 'Das Ohr versagt sich nicht dem Spiel' and, as we have already observed, this is a masterstroke on Schubert's part as he plaits disparate parts of the song together with matching braids. A short interlude with a repetition of the phrase 'Doch wie man auf dem Köpfchen kraut' (bb. 85–92) is beautifully engineered: the return to the A flat tonic is delayed by a bar or two, just long enough to make the most of the ever-giddier intoxication as the lover's roving hands return to their playground and we hear once again the wave-tumbling music of 'Man wird in solchen reichen Haaren'.

From the point of view of harmony, *Versunken* is a feast of joyous explorations and sly detours. At the song's opening we are not permitted to reach the home key until the tenth bar, and even then it hardly seems an inevitable arrival, so disorientated are we by this lover's giddy progress. It is only towards the end that we arrive into a settled tonality. As in some of Schubert's aquatic music (particularly *Der Strom* D565), it is as if flowing hair, like wavy water, cannot stay in one place, nor retain any one shape, long enough to be defined by a long stretch in a single key. During the fourth line ('Da fühl' ich mich von Herzensgrund gesund'), before 'Und küss ich Stirne, Bogen, Auge, Mund', there is a shift from the home tonality of A flat to C flat major via the dominant. This also occurs after the first verse of another A flat major song, *Ganymed* D544, where there is a similar intimation ('Ach, an deinem Busen / Lieg ich und schmachte') of sexual intimacy. This particular tonal shift within A flat major seems to have been one of Schubert's favourites, and it is frequently associated with Goethe in erotic mood (it occurs at crucial points in *An den Mond* D296, *Die Liebende schreibt* D673 and *Geheimes* D719).

The postlude of *Versunken* owes a great deal to the throwaway ending of *Rastlose Liebe* D138. It looks back to the earlier Goethe settings at the same time as being something utterly new in terms of harmonic and pianistic daring. It is perhaps because there is no other song quite like *Versunken*, and because it is unfamiliar Schubert, that it is passed over by performers. There can be no excuse that this song must only be sung by tenors: it is one of the few lieder where we know that Schubert actually approved of a transposition into the baritone key and played it. He made a copy of it in F major (perhaps to be sung by Johann Michael Vogl or Albert Stadler) dating from the summer of 1825 (printed as the second version of the song in Volume 13 of the NSA on p. 15). This varies in a few details from the A flat major version. Professional accompanists, taxed sufficiently by the work in the original key, will be relieved to learn that the composer preferred not to transpose this tricky work at sight.

Autographs:	Österreichische Nationalbibliothek, Vienna (first draft)
	Wienbibliothek im Rathaus, Vienna (fair copy)
Publication:	First published as Book 38 no. 3 of the *Nachlass* by Diabelli, Vienna in 1845 (P353; first version)
	First published as part of the NSA in 1992 (P807; second version)
Subsequent editions:	Peters: Vol. 3/207; AGA XX 391: Vol. 6/178; NSA IV: Vol. 13/8 & 15
Bibliography:	Capell 1928, p. 155
	Einstein 1951, pp. 218–19
	Fischer-Dieskau 1977, pp. 144–5

Discography and timing: Fischer-Dieskau II 4[11] 2'05
                        Hyperion I 28[1]
                        Hyperion II 24[7]   2'00   John Mark Ainsley

← *Der Unglückliche* D713   *Grenzen der Menschheit* D716 →

VIEL TAUSEND STERNE	Many thousand stars	Quartet,
PRANGEN (EBERHARD) **D642** [H10]	shine	SATB
D major 1812?		

(72 bars)

Viel tausend Sterne prangen	Many thousand stars shine forth
Am Himmel, still und schön,	Fair and silent in the heavens,
Und wecken mein Verlangen,	And awaken my longing
Hinaus aufs Feld zu gehn.	To go out into the fields.

O ewig schöne Sterne,	Eternally lovely stars
In ewig gleichem Lauf,	On your eternally unchanging course,
Wie blick' ich stets so gerne	How I always love to gaze
Zu eurem Glanz hinauf. – –	Up at your radiance.

[(. . . 10 . . .)]   [(. . . 10 . . .)]

AUGUST GOTTLOB EBERHARD (1769–1845)

Such is the accomplishment of this choral piece, lost for a long period and resurfacing in 1924, that Otto Erich Deutsch dated it 1819. This accounts for the high catalogue number. As a result of paper studies, and on the grounds of the composer's use of choral clefs and such terms as 'Clav' (for piano), the second edition of the Deutsch catalogue (with the subsequent agreement of the NSA) dates it to 1812 (with a question mark).

The text is the first eight lines of a much longer poem by Eberhard entitled *Das Feuerwerk*. The theme of a dazzling firework display is only developed in the poem after the initial nocturnal description, and it thus makes no sense to use this explosive title for the work. Instead it is published under the poem's first line and, as such, is the first of many songs, great ones among them, where Schubert indulged his fascination with the musical depiction of starlight and the night sky. *Viel tausend Sterne prangen* seems especially to be the musical forbear of *Nachthelle* D892, that extraordinary night piece for tenor and chorus composed in 1826 to a poem of Seidl. The accompaniment's repeated semiquavers on a pedal C sharp in the second verse (from b. 40 at 'O ewig schöne Sterne') are absolutely prophetic of that work where twinkling stars are depicted, in similar fashion, with repeated chords in semiquavers. There is no real change of tempo in the piece, only the filling-out of note values that first appear as spacious crotchets and quavers and are then made to bristle with demisemiquavers (from b. 61) towards the end. There is something of the Gluckian 'engine' behind the build-up of energy in the piece, but Gluck is only one of the masters who was involved in the birth of this music.

In some ways, and perhaps with hindsight, this is obviously an early Schubert work: the piano writing is unambitious, mainly doubling the voices, and the interludes have an eighteenth-century feel to them, Haydn-like in their cheery demeanour. But mention of that master reminds us how much all composers had learned from *Die Schöpfung* which, in 1812, was still relatively modern, having first appeared in 1798. Haydn had been able to capture a sense of the vastness of the cosmos and the breadth of the skies, and the young Schubert here creates a surprisingly imposing heavenly canvas. The piece ends in a blaze of fortissimo glory, impressive in its way (and here Mozart's *Die Zauberflöte* seems to be the presiding influence), but the most moving thing about it is the quiet music at the beginning. In some ways the opening twelve bars, though they contain no ground-breaking harmony, are among the most mature of the composer's youthful achievements. In this choral writing we can hear that Schubert is already capable of rejoicing in the grandeur and beauty of Creation, while remaining aware that the time given to us to enjoy it is all too short. Goodness knows how a boy of fifteen had the technical and emotional means to achieve this. If the work was performed by the composer's fellow students at the Konvikt (as Alfred Orel, the scholar who rediscovered this piece, believed it was) we can understand why the young Schubert quickly became a legend among his contemporaries.

Autograph:	Wienbibliothek im Rathaus, Vienna
First edition:	Published by Universal Edition in 1937 and subsequently as part of the NSA in 1986 (P794)
Subsequent editions:	Not in AGA; NSA III: Vol. 2a/3
Discography and timing:	Hyperion I 33²⁵ 2'54 The London Schubert Chorale Hyperion II 2⁵ (dir. Stephen Layton)

←— *Quell'innocente figlio (Aria dell'Angelo)* D17/2   *Klaglied* D23 —→

VIER CANZONEN
(Vittorelli and Metastasio) **D688**
January 1820

The simplicity of the style of these four songs is doubly astonishing when compared with another work written at the same time, one of Schubert's most complex settings of metaphysical exalt-ation, the Novalis song *Nachthymne* D687. But for Schubert's purposes on this occasion a work like *Nachthymne* would not have been appropriate. These four songs are a clear indication of Schubert's respect for Italian music – despite the capacity of its runaway success in Vienna to ruin his hopes as a composer of German opera. These songs are not exercises for Salieri like some of the earlier Italian material; neither were they aiming to please a great singing virtuoso like Lablache (the *Drei Gesänge* D902 of 1827); and unlike the aria for Josef von Spaun (D749) they were not meant as Italian operatic parody. Walther Dürr suggests that the inspiration for the *canzone* style is probably Beethoven's famous Carpani setting of 1806, *In questa tomba oscura* WoO 133. The songs were composed, admittedly as a superior type of singing exercise, for a girl of whom Schubert was probably very fond – Franziska von Ronner, known as Fanny in the circle, and later the beloved wife of the composer's oldest and best friend, Josef von Spaun. Fanny was obviously no virtuoso, but it is clear that she was no disgrace as a singer either. The vocal range is never excessive, yet the music requires breath control. The composer has affectionately crafted vocal lines that are challenging without being impossible, and always in the spirit of *bel canto* as he understood it. If anything, drama plays too little a part in his conception: we hear traces of Rossini's early style of course, but we cannot expect Schubert to have prophesied Bellini and Verdi. Word illustration and local highlights of atmosphere are generally absent, sacrificed willingly to the shapeliness and general expressiveness of melody. The sources of the Vittorelli poetry, and the place of the third and fourth songs of the set in Metastasio's libretti, are discussed in the two poets' biographical articles.

Autograph:	Schubert-Bund, Vienna, deposited in the Historisches Museum der Stadt Wien
First edition:	Published as *5 Canti per una sola voce con accompagnamento di Pianoforte composti da Fr. Schubert* (Op post.) by J. P. Gotthard, Vienna in 1871 (P420–23)
Arrangement:	Arr. Paul Angerer (b. 1927) for voice and string quartet
Bibliography:	Fischer-Dieskau 1977, p. 132

I NON T'ACCOSTAR ALL'URNA   Do not approach the urn
(VITTORELLI) **D688/1** [H443]
C major

(44 bars)

Non t'accostar all'Urna,[1]	Do not approach the urn
Che l'osse mie rinserra,[2]	Which contains my bones;
Questa pietosa terra	This compassionate earth
È sacra al mio dolor.	Is sacred to my sorrow.
Ricuso i tuoi giacinti[3]	I refuse your hyacinths
Non voglio i tuoi pianti:[4]	I do not want your weeping;
Che giovan agli estinti	What use to the dead
Due lagrime, due fior?[5]	Are a few tears and a few flowers?

[1] Vittorelli's first line as printed in *Anacreontiche* (1798) and *Rime* (1806) is 'Non t'*accostare a l'Urna*'. By the 1815 edition of *Rime* this has changed to 'all'Urna'.
[2] This line is almost correct as it stands in *Anacreontiche* (1798) and *Rime* (1806) where 'ossa' is printed rather than 'osse'. By 1815 Vittorelli had changed this line to '*Che il cener* mie rinserra'.
[3] Vittorelli writes '*Odio gli affanni tuoi*'.
[4] Vittorelli writes '*Ricuso i tuoi giacinti*' (the words Schubert uses for the first line of the second strophe).
[5] Vittorelli writes '*Due lagrime, o due fior*'.

Empia! Dovevi allor[6]	Cruel one! You should have come
Porgermi un fil d'aita,	To help me
Quando traea la vita	When my life was ebbing away
In grembo dei sospir.[7]	In slight and suffering.
A che d'inutil pianto	With what futile weeping
Assordi la foresta?	Do you assail the woods?
Rispetta un'Ombra mesta,	Respect a sad shade,
E lasciala dormir.	And let it sleep.

JACOPO VITTORELLI (1749–1835); poem written before 1815

This is the first of Schubert's two Vittorelli solo settings (1820). See the poet's biography for a chronological list of the Vittorelli settings.

The first of the texts (which, like the second, was by Vittorelli, not Metastasio as was thought for many years, and as Schubert himself clearly believed) was to be set ten years later in 1830 by no less a composer than the young Giuseppe Verdi, who makes much greater drama of the pathos of dying unloved. Schubert's setting, somehow genuinely pious, has dignity and avoids sentimentality. At b. 15 the accompaniment flowers into triplets, and the vocal line takes on a chromatic tinge in bb. 16 and 20. A short three-bar recitative (bb. 24–7) returns the singer to triplet-accompanied arioso that is, in turn, a preparation for a written-out *da capo* whereby the vocal line is ornamented and extended in florid manner for the song's conclusion.

Subsequent editions:	Peters: Vol. 6/171; AGA XX 575: Vol. 10/48; NSA IV: Vol. 12/141
Further settings:	Giuseppe Verdi (1813–1901) *Non t'accostare all'urna* (1830, pub. 1838)
Discography and timing:	Fischer-Dieskau —
	Hyperion I 9[13]
	Hyperion II 23[1] 3'00 Arleen Auger

← *Nachthymne* D687   *Guarda, che bianca luna* D688/2 →

II GUARDA, CHE BIANCA LUNA   Look how bright the moon is
(VITTORELLI) **D688/2** [H444]
G major

Guard - da, che bian - ca lu - na,

(30 bars)

---

[6] Vittorelli writes 'Empia! Dovevi allor*a*'.
[7] Vittorelli writes 'In *braccio* dei sospir' (1798), and later 'Fra *palpiti e* sospir' (1806) and '*Nell'ansia e nei* sospir' (1815).

Guarda, che bianca luna!	Look how bright the moon is,
Guarda che notte azzura!	And how blue the night!
Un'aura non susurra,	Not a breeze whispers,
Nò, non tremola uno stel.[1]	Not a twig quivers.
L'usignuoletto solo	A lone nightingale
Va da la siepe all'orno,[2]	Flies from the hedge to the elm-tree
E sospirando intorno	And sighing all the while
Chiama la sua fedel.	Calls to his faithful love.
Ella, che'el sente oppena,[3]	She, who scarcely hears him,
Vien di fronda in fronda,[4]	Flies from leaf to leaf,
E pare che gli dica[5]	And seems to say to him:
Nò, non piangere, son qui.[6]	'No, do not weep. I am here!'
Che gemiti son questi![7]	What tears,
Che dolci pianti, Irene,[8]	What sweet laments, Irene!
Tu mai non me sapesti[9]	You could never
Rispondere così![10]	Answer me thus.

JACOPO VITTORELLI (1749–1835); poem written before 1815

This is the second of Schubert's two Vittorelli solo settings (1820). See the poet's biography for a list of the Vittorelli settings.

The slightly see-sawing introduction is very nearly banal, but seen in the right light its jumps of open fifths and sixths convey the clarity and simplicity of moonbeams. This music is both an interlude at bb. 27–30 and a postlude at bb. 53–6. Using a split-triplet accompanimental figure that was to serve him well in a number of his lieder, Schubert constructs a seamless vocal line in the Italian manner. One is reminded that the famous *Ungeduld* D795/7 from *Die schöne Müllerin* (to take only one example), with very similar accompaniment, sounds extremely 'Italian' when taken for practice purposes at the slow tempo of this song. The middle section (beginning at b. 15) is in B minor for two bars, and then moves into the major key from b. 27. The Italian influence went to the heart of all Schubert's music; it became so grafted onto the German root that it is sometimes hard to separate the national branches in the composer's mature style.

Subsequent editions: Peters: Vol. 6/171; AGA XX 576: Vol. 10/50; NSA IV: Vol. 12/144
Further settings: Giuseppe Verdi (1813–1901) *Notturno* for soprano, tenor, flute obbligato and piano (1838)

[1] The addition of 'Nò' in this line is Schubert's.
[2] In earlier editions (1798, 1806) this appears as '*a l'orno*'.
[3] Vittorelli writes 'Ella, *che il* sente *appena*'.
[4] Vittorelli writes '*Già* vien di fronda in fronda'.
[5] Vittorelli writes 'E *par* che gli *risponda*'.
[6] The addition of 'Nò' to this line is Schubert's. In the 1806 edition of *Rime* this line is printed in italics.
[7] Schubert here adopts the second line of Vittorelli's strophe as his first.
[8] Schubert here adopts the first line of Vittorelli's strophe as his second, but adapts it from the poet's original 'Che dolce *affetti, o* Irene'.
[9] Vittorelli writes '*Ah mai tu non* sapesti'.
[10] Vittorelli writes 'Rispon*dermi* così!'.

Discography and timing: Fischer-Dieskau   —
                                            Hyperion I 9¹⁴
                                            Hyperion II 23²   3'04   Arleen Auger

← *Non t'accostar all'urna* D688/1   *Da quel sembiante appresi* D688/3 →

III DA QUEL SEMBIANTE APPRESI   From that face I learnt to sigh
(Metastasio) **D688/3** [H445]
B♭ major

(24 bars)

Da quel sembiante appresi	From that face I learnt
A sospirar' d'amore;[1]	To sigh with love;
Sempre per quel sembiante	For that face
Sospirerò d'amore.[2]	I shall always sigh with love.
La face, a cui m'accesi,	The flame which kindled my love
Solo m'alletta, e piace,	Alone delights and pleases me.
È fredda ogn'altra face[3]	Every other flame is too cold
Per riscaldarmi il cuore.[4]	To warm my heart.

PIETRO METASTASIO (1698–1782); poem written in 1752

*This is the eleventh of Schubert's fourteen Metastasio solo settings (1812–27). See the poet's
biography for a chronological list of all the Metastasio settings.*

After another piano introduction that in its chromatic descent runs the risk of sounding musically commonplace, the opening vocal phrase of this little aria is irresistibly reminiscent of the
celebrated rondo 'Non più mesta', the closing display piece of Rossini's *La Cenerentola* (with the
oscillation of a major third in b. 5 turned the other way around; that is to say that Rossini's
vocal line falls a third, Schubert's rises by the same interval). Whether or not Schubert could
have known this famous piece is a moot point. Rossini's work was premiered in Rome in 1817;
the hit numbers must have found their way to Vienna by 1820. The music enters a *minore*
section in b. 13 – an excuse to dally in D flat major for a few bars before returning to the home
key. The descending postlude is identical to the introduction. Despite the major-key tonality
the piece is more highly strung than it may first appear to be; the desperation of Metastasio's
text (*L'Eroe Cinese*, Act I Scene 3) is indicated by Lisinga's reply to Ulania before she embarks

[1] Metastasio writes 'A *sospirare amante*'.
[2] Metastasio writes 'Sospirerò *d'amor*'.
[3] Metastasio writes 'È fredda *ogni* altra face'.
[4] Metastasio writes 'Per riscaldarmi il *cor*'.

on this song, 'Taci, crudel; tu mi trafiggi il core' ('Be silent, cruel man; you have pierced my heart').

Subsequent editions: Peters: Vol. 6/176; AGA XX 577: Vol. 10/50; NSA IV: Vol. 12/148
Discography and timing: Fischer-Dieskau —
                          Hyperion I 9[15]
                          Hyperion II 23[3]   2'00   Arleen Auger

← *Guarda, che bianca luna* D688/2   *Mio ben ricordati* D688/4 →

IV MIO BEN RICORDATI   Remember, beloved
(Metastasio) **D688/4** [H446]
B♭ minor

(21 bars)

Mio ben ricordati,	Remember beloved
Se avvien, ch'io mora:	If it should happen that I die,
Quanto quest' anima	How this faithful soul
Fedel t'amò.	Loved you.
E se pur amano[1]	And if cold ashes
Le fredde ceneri,	Can love
Nell' urna ancora	In the urn,
T'adorerò.[2]	I shall still love you.

Pietro Metastasio (1698–1782); poem written in 1729

This is the twelfth of Schubert's fourteen Metastasio solo settings (1812–27). See the poet's biography for a chronological list of all the Metastasio settings.

This song, in the unusual key of B flat minor and the only one of the four pieces to be in triple metre, is perhaps the most successful and interesting of the group. It has more than just the manner and style of Italian music – it has a measure of southern temperament as well. The passage in B flat major (after the double bar line at b. 13) manages to be typically Schubertian and Italian at the same time (Schubert was also to achieve this wonderful telescoping of styles in the first of the pieces written for Lablache in 1827, *L'incanto degli occhi* D902/1). The melancholy vocal line and the elegant fioritura of its ornamentation would scarcely seem out of place

[1] Metastasio writes '*Io, se pur amano*'.
[2] Metastasio writes '*Ti adorerò*'.

in the *Composizioni da camera* of Bellini. The aria, sung by Gandarte (one of King Poro's generals – although Schubert allows the song to be sung by a female voice) occurs in Metastasio's *Alessandro nell'Indie* (Act III Scene 7). Gandarte takes his leave of his lover Erissena with the following words, before launching into the aria:

Addio, mia vita.	Farewell, my love.
Non mi porre in obblio,	Do not consign me to oblivion,
Se questo fosse mai l'ultimo addio	Even if this were the final farewell.

Subsequent editions: Peters: Vol. 6/178; AGA XX 578: Vol. 10/53; NSA IV: Vol. 12/150
Further settings: Mikhail Glinka (1804–1857) *Mio ben ricordati* (1828)
Discography and timing: Fischer-Dieskau   —
                         Hyperion I 9¹⁶
                         Hyperion II 23⁴   2'26   Arleen Auger

← *Da quel sembiante appresi* D688/3   *Die Vögel* D691 →

VIER ELEMENTE, INNIG GESELLT *see* PUNSCHLIED D277

VIER REFRAIN-LIEDER
(Johann Gabriel Seidl) Op. 95, **D866**
Summer 1828

As these four poems in popular style did not appear in the three-volume edition of Seidl's works published between 1826 and 1828, the texts must have been given to the composer in autograph. This could have happened at any time (and stylistically one may be inclined, like Deutsch, to assign a date before 1828). But the discovery in 1970 of a sketch for *Die Unterscheidung* (the first of these 'Four Refrain Songs') on the same autograph as the last movement of the C minor Sonata D958 suggests the songs (if initially conceived as a group) were written in haste in the summer of Schubert's last year. They were then rushed to publication by Thaddäus Weigl in the hope of commercial success. The publisher's announcement, which appeared in the *Wiener Zeitung* of 13 August 1828, read as follows: 'The public has long cherished the wish to have, for once, a composition of a merry comic nature from the pen of this song composer of genius. This wish has been gratified in a surprising manner by Herr Schubert in the present four songs, which in part are truly comic and in part bear in them the character of ingenuousness and humour.'

In these words ('in part . . . for once . . . truly comic') one can discern the publisher's disappointment that he was unable to announce a set of songs with a comic content which he had clearly hoped Schubert would deliver. The composer's 'surprising manner' was obviously most of all a surprise to Weigl. Only *Die Unterscheidung* and *Die Männer sind mechant!* could possibly be thought to fall into a comic category, and even they display a musical refinement that is hardly typical of the humorous ditties beloved of the populace. The piano writing in particular makes little concession to the amateur. The two remaining songs in the set are hardly funny. *Bei dir allein!* is a straightforward love song (admittedly rather Italianate in manner and thus perhaps associated, in Schubert's mind at least, with a touch of affectionate parody), while *Irdisches Glück* depicts the Viennese homespun philosopher who has been the mouthpiece of some of Schubert's

Title page of four Seidl settings Op. 95, second edition. Once Diabelli had bought the copyright of the songs from Thaddäus Weigl he dropped the original title of *Vier Refrain-Lieder* (1828).

lighter – though not necessarily humorous – songs. It is likely that Weigl had to scratch his head for some time to come up with the – hardly inspiring – title *Refrain-Lieder* which sounds like a compromise description invented specifically to unite all four Seidl songs. It must have seemed much less commercially viable to Weigl than a complete set of truly humorous and popular pieces. The addition, and dubious distinction, of exclamation marks after the titles of the second and third songs (ignored by the Deutsch catalogue but reinstated by the NSA) seems like a vain attempt to persuade the potential buyer that this music is going to be *fun*. In Diabelli's later reprint of these songs, an exclamation mark is also bestowed on *Irdisches Glück* (not adopted by the NSA). Not for the first time Schubert had revealed his innate inability to travel truly downmarket. As far as we know, the pieces, despite being well received in the press, had no particular success with the public in commercial terms.

One further aspect of Weigl's promotion of these *Vier Refrain-Lieder* should be mentioned. It must have been his decision to insert into the publication two engraved pages (after the title page) that listed all the opus numbers by Schubert that had been issued up to that time. Diabelli had done something similar in 1827 in his edition of *Die Rose* D745 Op. 73 where the titles of all the published works up to Op. 87 had appeared. This is surely an indication of Schubert's rising fame and his status as an emerging national treasure; connoisseurs of music would make use of such a list to survey the composer's output in order to complete their collections of his songs, part-songs, piano pieces and so on – something that would be of benefit to all his publishers. In August of 1828, even if Schubert had not been particularly proud of his latest set of Seidl settings, the appearance of this highly impressive list must have given him a certain measure of satisfaction.

First edition: Published as Op. 95 by Thaddäus Weigl, Vienna in August 1828
                         (P169–72)
Dedicatee: Johann Gabriel Seidl
Publication reviews: *Wiener allgemeine Theaterzeitung*, no. 105 (30 August 1828) p. 420
                         [Waidelich/Hilmar Dokumente I No. 632]

I DIE UNTERSCHEIDUNG
D866/1 [H664]
G major

The distinction

(38 bars)

Die Mutter hat mich jüngst gescholten	Mother recently scolded me,
Und vor der Liebe streng gewarnt.	And warned me sternly against love.
'Noch jede,' sprach sie, 'hat's entgolten:	'Every woman,' she said, 'has paid its price;
Verloren ist, wen sie umgarnt.'	She who is ensnared by love is lost.'
D'rum ist es besser, wie ich meine,	And so I think it better
Wenn keins von uns davon mehr spricht:	If neither of us speaks of it again.
Ich bin zwar immer noch die Deine. –	I am in truth still yours for ever,
Doch lieben, Hans! – kann ich dich nicht!	But love you, Hans – this I cannot do!

[. . .]¹

[. . .]

Bei jedem Feste, das wir haben	Whenever we have a holiday,
Soll's meine grösste Wonne sein,	It will be my greatest joy
Flicht deine Hand des Frühlings Gaben	If your hands twine the gifts of springtime
Zum Schmucke mir in's Mieder ein.	To adorn my bodice.
Beginnt der Tanz, dann ist, wie billig,	When the dancing begins, then – as is only fair –
Ein Tanz mit Gretchen deine Pflicht;	It will be your duty to dance with Gretchen;
Selbst eifersüchtig werden will ich,	I shall even be jealous.
Doch lieben, Hans! kann ich dich nicht.	But love you, Hans – this I cannot do!

Und sinkt der Abend kühl hernieder,	And when cool evening descends
Und ruh'n wir dann recht mild bewegt,	And we rest, filled with tender emotion,
Halt' immer mir die Hand an's Mieder,	Keep your hand on my bodice,
Und fühle, wie mein Herzchen schlägt!	And feel how my heart beats!
Und willst du mich durch Küsse lehren,	And if you wish to teach me with kisses
Was stumm dein Auge zu mir spricht,	What your eyes silently tell me,
Selbst das will ich dir nicht verwehren,	Even that I shall not deny you,
Doch lieben, Hans! kann ich dich nicht.	But love you, Hans – this I cannot do!

This is the eighth of Schubert's twelve Seidl solo settings (1826–8). See the poet's biography for a chronological list of all the Seidl settings.

Reed writes that this song resembles Lieschen's aria 'Der Vater mag wohl immer Kind mich nennen' in *Die Zwillingsbrüder* (D647/3, 1819). In terms of its tonality, and in certain other musical aspects this is true; the difference is that Lieschen's is a tender song of sexual awakening,

---

¹ There is an extra verse in this poem as later published in the almanac *Das Veilchen*, 1835.

a plea for independence from her father (and as such it is meant to be taken seriously) whereas this Seidl setting feigns propriety merely to inflame passion. This applies in even richer measure to the third song in the set, *Die Männer sind mechant!* One is reminded of Edwardian music hall songs written for so-called schoolgirls (in reality adult performers) where punters were delighted – and titillated – by the mock interplay of the performers' innocence and precocious experience. Schubert's willingness to publish a song of this type was simply a career move, equivalent to the efforts (usually successful) of some of today's classical singers to beat the pop world at its own game. The poet Seidl, seven years Schubert's junior, to whom the songs are dedicated, was something of a go-getter. Only in his early twenties, but already well known, newly appointed editor of the almanac *Aurora* and ambitious for success in all spheres, he almost certainly played a part in persuading the composer to write and publish the songs.

The music is earthy and illustrative and the vocal line has a teasing bounce and flounce to it. The piano part is a clever depiction of the scolding mother, her jabbing remonstrative finger playing repeated notes in the strident heights of the treble (bb. 2–3). In the gesturing of this piano music, with crushed notes for emphasis, there is a prophetic hint of the crabby lecturing of Hugo Wolf's Mörike setting *Rat einer Alten* (1888). For the fifth line of each verse (at bb. 18 and 50 in the NSA printing) the song moves to the key of B flat, suggesting an abrupt change of subject and a quick readjustment of dress. Indeed, Hans is never far away, his wandering hands written into the very bodice of the song. The girl's first 'Doch lieben Hans! kann ich dich nicht' (bb. 28–9) seems to lure the boy towards her in a fine example of Biedermeier doublespeak (given piquant musical life by Schubert's interrupted cadence), but the repeat of the words (bb. 31–3) pushes him away, although not before having toyed with the verb 'lieben' as a promise of things to come. The chromatic hocketing of the piano writing in bb. 35 and 37 is unfamiliar to the fingers of the Schubert song pianist – perhaps it was a contemporary pianistic commonplace that Schubert normally preferred to avoid. As in Hugo Wolf's *Auf dem grünen Balkon*, the eyes (and the voice) say 'Yes', the fingers (and the accompaniment) say 'No.' This dichotomy was ever thus in courtship, but here we are made to understand that she would be able to love him (in other words marry him) only if the price were right. It tips on its head a Biedermeier semantic hypocrisy: if the young are not permitted to 'love' they will just have to make do with sex.

Subsequent editions: Peters: Vol. 4/83; AGA XX 508: Vol. 8/240; NSA IV: Vol. 5a/37 & Vol. 5b/257; Bärenreiter: Vol. 3/172
Discography and timing: Fischer-Dieskau   —
                          Hyperion I 13[2]
                          Hyperion II 36[4]   3'59   Marie McLaughlin

← *Lebensmut* D937   *Bei dir allein!* D866/2 →

II BEI DIR ALLEIN!   With you alone!
D866/2 [H665]
A♭ major

Nicht zu geschwind, doch feurig

Bei dir al - lein_____ em - pfind ich, dass ich_ le - be,

(137 bars)

Bei dir allein	With you alone
Empfind' ich, dass ich lebe,	I feel that I am alive,
Dass Jugendmut mich schwellt,	That I am fired by youthful vigour,
Dass eine heit're Welt	That a bright world
Der Liebe mich durchbebe;	Of love thrills through me;
Mich freut mein Sein	I rejoice in my being
Bei dir allein!	With you alone!
Bei dir allein	With you alone
Weht mir die Luft so labend,	The breeze blows so refreshingly,
Dünkt mich die Flur so grün,	The fields seem so green,
So mild des Lenzes Blüh'n,	The flowering spring so gentle,
So balsamreich der Abend,	The evening so balmy,
So kühl der Hain,	The grove so cool,
Bei dir allein!	With you alone!
Bei dir allein	With you alone
Verliert der Schmerz sein Herbes,	Pain loses its bitterness,
Gewinnt die Freud' an Lust!	Joy gains in sweetness!
Du sicherst meine Brust	You assure my heart
Des angestammten Erbes;	Of its natural heritage;
Ich fühl' mich mein	I feel I am myself
Bei dir allein!	With you alone!

This is the ninth of Schubert's twelve Seidl solo settings (1826–8). See the poet's biography for a chronological list of all the Seidl settings.

The publishing history of the *Vier Refrain-Lieder* is set out above. The argument for an 1828 date for *Bei dir allein!* is strengthened by the similarity of its accompaniment to the Rellstab setting *Frühlingssehnsucht* (D957/3) from *Schwanengesang*. In this work (also a 'Refrain-Lied' in its way) we find the same time signature and a similar ardour and almost reckless intensity. The two pieces both boast an extended introduction of unceasing triplets (nine bars for the Seidl and twelve for the Rellstab – playing these is like being on a roller coaster) with a similar ingenious manipulation of the chords' inner voices where fast-shifting harmonies build up to the entry of the singer. Both songs demand an impassioned vocal flourish to end with followed by a diminuendo and hushed chords in the piano (compare the last three bars of each piece where both postludes are marked 'piano', with identical spacing of crotchet chords, rests and concluding minims with fermata). A preliminary sketch for *Frühlingssehnsucht* D957/3 proposes a very different song (in terms of key and prosody) than the one that was eventually composed. *Bei dir allein!* with its priapic energy – it is also very much a spring song – may be the missing link between the discarded ideas embodied in that sketch and *Frühlingssehnsucht* as we know it.

Schubert made little concession to the amateur market in terms of technical difficulty. *Bei dir allein!* is a tricky piece, very low in places for a tenor and too high for most high baritones. The piano writing is also difficult, requiring a nimble left hand to snatch at the correct basses and an untiring right hand to negotiate changes of chord at quite a quick pace. The one concession to popular taste here is a gushing operatic style where a singer can impress with his ardour and bravado. An unusual feature of the vocal line is the number of decorative mordents on the word 'dir' (bb. 29, 31, 39, 41 and so on); these add a hint of an Italianate sob to the protestations of love. Apart from the fact that the language is German, one could easily see this as a tenor variant of the style of the three Italian songs written for the famous bass Luigi Lablache in 1827 (D902).

The fire of youthful vigour to which the poet refers occasions a fervent vocal line that leaps as much as a tenth on the word 'Liebe' (b. 23) and unashamedly indulges in all sorts of tonal pirouettes of which Schubert was master. For the final two lines of the first strophe we find ourselves, via an astonishing shift sideways, in the key of G flat. After six bars the singer breaks out of this thicket of flats with an extended 'allein' on D natural (bb. 34–6, the note is held for five beats as if to promise an eternity of devotion) and then, just as suddenly, we are back in A flat for a repeat of the words, where 'Mich freut' is set to a high A flat (b. 37).

The middle section (the poem's second strophe) moves into E major (the enharmonic change from F flat major to four sharps hardly seems designed to appeal to the sight-reading skills of amateurs). This verse is altogether more gentle with deliciously melismatic settings of 'die Luft so labend' (bb. 58–60) and 'So balsamreich der Abend' (bb. 68–71) where the quavers of the vocal line waft as if they are being coaxed up the stave by the caressing winds. The words 'So kühl der Hain' are echoed by delightful little piano interludes in descending quaver octaves (b. 76 and again at b. 79) that swoon as if the singer were about to faint in rapture. Schubert seems to be smiling at this slightly overheated mood; perhaps that is why he regarded *Bei dir allein!* as a lighter song – without going so far as to make fun of it.

The shift back to the home key (via a modulation that puns on the fact that G sharp in E major is enharmonically A flat) reminds us that this has been advertised as a 'Refrain-Lied'. At this point one feels that the composer is reining in a natural tendency to make the music more ornate and complicated – a solution that would better suit the text of the third verse. However, this new strophe is set to music almost identical with that of the opening, even if there are a few minor adjustments in the word-setting. The final mini-cadenza on the word 'dir' is a new, and operatic, touch typical of this song's expressive extravagance. Capell waxes lyrical about *Bei dir allein!* and Reed refers to it as 'irresistible'. To me the song has always seemed to offer more on paper than it delivers in performance: it is awkwardly written for the voice and not quite large and showy enough to be a proper blockbuster. The composer might have felt he could improve on it; it is also for this reason that a link with *Frühlingssehnsucht* – a far greater song – seems a possibility.

Subsequent editions:	Peters: Vol. 3/66; AGA XX 509: Vol. 8/243; NSA IV: Vol. 5/42; Bärenreiter: Vol. 3/176
Bibliography:	Capell 1928, pp. 223–4
Discography and timing:	Fischer-Dieskau II 8[17] 2'20
	Hyperion I 37[3]
	Hyperion II 36[5] 2'14 Michael Schade

← *Die Unterscheidung* D866/1   *Die Männer sind mechant!* D866/3 →

III DIE MÄNNER SIND MECHANT! Men are wicked!
D866/3 [H666]

A minor

(28 bars)

Du sagtest mir es, Mutter:
Er ist ein Springinsfeld!
Ich würd' es dir nicht glauben,
Bis ich mich krank gequält!
Ja, ja, nun ist er's wirklich;
Ich hatt' ihn nur verkannt!
Du sagtest mir's, o Mutter:
  'Die Männer sind mechant!'

Vor'm Dorf im Busch, als gestern
Die stille Dämm'rung sank,
Da rauscht'es: 'Guten Abend!'
Da rauscht' es: 'Schönen Dank!'
Ich schlich hinzu, ich horchte;
Ich stand wie festgebannt:
Er war's mit einer Andern –
  'Die Männer sind mechant!'

O Mutter, welche Qualen!
Es muss heraus, es muss! –
Es blieb nicht bloss bei'm Rauschen,
Es blieb nicht bloss bei'm Gruss!
Vom Grusse kam's zum Kusse,
Vom Kuss zum Druck der Hand,
Vom Druck, ach liebe Mutter! –
  'Die Männer sind mechant!'

You told me, mother:
He's a young rogue!
I would not believe you
Until I had tormented myself sick.
Yes, I now know he really is;
I had simply misjudged him.
You told me, mother:
  'Men are wicked!'

Yesterday, as dusk fell silently,
In the copse outside the village,
I heard a whispered 'Good evening!'
And then a whispered 'Many thanks!'
I crept up and listened;
I stood as if transfixed:
It was he, with someone else –
  'Men are wicked!'

O mother, what torture!
I must be out with it, I must!
It didn't just stop at whispering,
It didn't just stop at greetings!
It went from greetings to kisses,
From kisses to holding hands,
From holding hands . . . ah, dear mother,
  'Men are wicked!'

This is the tenth of Schubert's twelve Seidl solo settings (1826–8). See the poet's biography for a chronological list of all the Seidl settings.

Of Schubert's four *Refrain-Lieder*, only this song (and possibly the first, *Die Unterscheidung*) fulfilled the publisher's hopes that Schubert would write comic songs to capture the market. The *Sinsgpiel* audiences of Vienna, like their later counterparts in the London music hall, had an endless appetite for risqué material; in that realm of double entendre and role play, where the most experienced woman dressed years younger than her age, this kind of schoolgirl-inspired ditty was highly popular. In the end there was nothing very 'amusing' about two of the songs, one of them (*Bei dir allein!*) a love song in the Italian manner, the other (*Irdisches Glück*) a piece of homespun philosophizing. Even *Die Männer sind mechant!*, which takes the palm as Schubert's most suggestive song (one can imagine the sighs of relief at the offices of the publisher Thaddäus Weigl), is not fabulously funny. It is performed endlessly these days by sopranos hopeful of finding an easily accessible entrée to the Schubert lied via Broadway-style cabaret, but the laughs are always fewer than hoped for in performance.

The young Seidl understood what would appeal to the public at the same time as being sufficiently ambiguous to pass the censor. This poor girl has been duped and betrayed by a naughty man; what can men now do to comfort her? The presence of a mother adds a prurient edge to the subtext. Nothing is what it seems – even the title actually means the exact opposite of what it says: men are horrid certainly, but they're really 'absolutely loverly'. There is no greater composer than Schubert for the expression of real innocence, but on this occasion the girl's hurt and wide-eyed shock sound completely phoney, and that is probably exactly how they *should* sound; singers who attempt to bring a sincere sense of desolation to the conclusion of the story are on a hiding to nothing.

The tempo marking suggests a slowly swinging two beats in a bar, something pendulous, but the tempo has to vary with the verses. The music must be slow enough for the words to register: at certain moments the story is spun out to titillate the voyeur (voyeurs in the audience can take pleasure in the girl's own voyeurism at one remove) but at other times the pulses race. The middle of the song (lines five and six of each verse, before the refrain) consists of three sequences of mounting intensity (bb. 14–16, 16–18 and 18–20) that lead to a surprisingly ecstatic affirmation of the tonic major considering that the girl is supposedly upset and that men are being berated. The snatched beats' rest in this section (in the middle of bb. 12, 16 and 18) suggest the panting of the pantyless, and the crossing of hands, unusual in Schubert's solo song accompaniments (here at b. 9) is suggestive of hanky-panky, a reminder that male and female piano duettists were well known for intensifying their acquaintance thanks to such keyboard antics. The final two chords, marked suddenly piano after a forte postlude, suggest a knowing wink at the audience.

The singer of today finds it almost impossible to recapture the freedom and spontaneity of the strophic song (or the 'Refrain-Lied') as it was understood in Schubert's time. The three strophes have to be differentiated. The first can be a more or less straightforward mother to daughter conversation, while the second can take more time to tell the story of a meeting between a working girl and her client, with the singer doing her best to differentiate between the two roles – the man's 'Good evening' in a slightly lower register and the woman's 'Many thanks' for his interest – or payment. (Another option is for both the 'Guten Abend' and the 'Schönen Dank' to be done silkily in the same female voice.) Up to this moment the girl who is spying on her supposedly faithful boyfriend with a more experienced woman has not as yet, in her lack of awareness of the birds and bees, tumbled on the reason for the al fresco meeting. (As Christian Strehk observes in the *Liedlexikon* 2012, p. 714, what is a nice girl doing skulking around the bushes anyway, and spying on people into the bargain?)

Every young man in Schubert's Vienna with a sweetheart from a respectable family (who would have kept her favours firmly under wraps until after marriage) would understand the scenario. It is incredibly unlikely, considering the moral climate of the time, that such a hastily progressed meeting could take place in the open air between a young man and woman, and brand new acquaintances at that, *without* money changing hands.

The whole point of the story is this third verse and it takes a real command of German and of narrative folksong style to put the text across clearly at a tempo that encompasses both excitement and lascivious enjoyment. It is surely a mistake for the singer to end this song in a mood of anger and disappointment (although the first and second strophes must be terminated in this way). Having glimpsed what her boyfriend is doing with the other woman, and having described it in a manner that excites her (as well as her audience), it is a necessary twist that her anger should be overtaken by her curiosity to do the very same thing. A broad smile at the last 'Männer sind mechant' is to be recommended, with a quickening of the postlude as if the singer were impatient to exit and find her friend so that he can be 'mechant' with her too. This is a case of 'Men are naughty, but nice' and bears absolutely no relation to the way a real woman would react under these circumstances. It is very rare for Schubert to use French-derived slang in his lieder (indeed he excised French-derived words from Leitner's poem for *Der Winterabend* D938). The singer unschooled in Viennese French should be aware that 'mechant' is not pronounced in the conventional French way (it is written without the e acute – é – of genuine French), but must rhyme with 'verkannt', 'gebannt' and 'der Hand' including the final 't' consonant that is unpronounced in French. (In French it would in any case be 'méchants'.)

Subsequent editions:	Peters: Vol. 4/88; AGA XX 510: Vol. 8/248; NSA IV: Vol. 5a/47; Bärenreiter: Vol. 3/180
Discography and timing:	Fischer-Dieskau —
	Hyperion I 13[3]
	Hyperion II 36[6] 2'25 Marie McLaughlin

← *Bei dir allein!* D866/2   *Irdisches Glück* D866/4 →

IV IRDISCHES GLÜCK   Earthly happiness

D866/4 [H667]
D minor

(41 bars)

So mancher sieht mit finst'rer Miene	So many people look with grim faces
Die weite Welt sich grollend an,	And resentment on the wide world;
Des Lebens wunderbare Bühne	Life's wondrous stage
Liegt ihm vergebens aufgetan.	Lies open to them, though in vain.
Da weiss ich besser mich zu nehmen,	But I know better what to do,
Und fern, der Freude mich zu schämen,	And, far from being ashamed of joy,
Geniess' ich froh den Augenblick:	I gladly delight in the moment:
Das ist denn doch gewiss ein Glück!	That, for sure, is happiness!
Um manches Herz hab ich geworben,	I have wooed many a heart,
Doch währte mein Triumph nicht lang,	Though my triumph did not last long,
Denn Blödheit hat mir oft verdorben,	For my stupidity often ruined
Was kaum mein Frohsinn mir errang.	What my cheerful spirit had only just won.
D'rum bin ich auch dem Netz entgangen;	And so I escaped the net;
Denn, weil kein Wahn mich hielt umfangen	For since no illusion held me captive,

Kam ich von keinem auch zurück:	I had none to escape from:
Und das ist doch gewiss ein Glück!	And that for sure, is happiness.
Kein Lorbeer grünte meinem Scheitel,	No laurels have adorned my locks;
Mein Haupt umstrahlt' kein Ehrenkranz;	No halo of glory has shone about my head.
Doch ist darum mein Tun nicht eitel	Yet my life is not in vain;
Ein stiller Dank ist auch ein Kranz!	Quiet thanks are also a halo!
Wem, weit entfernt von kecken Flügen,	He who, far from bold flights,
Des Tales stille Freuden g'nügen,	Is content with the peaceful pleasures of the valley,
Dem bangt auch nie für sein Genick:	Need never fear for his neck:
Und das ist doch gewiss ein Glück!	And that, for sure, is happiness.
Und ruft der Bot' aus jenen Reichen	And when one day the messenger from the world beyond
Mir einst, wie allen, ernst und hohl,	Calls me, as he does all, with grave, hollow voice,
Dann sag ich willig, im Entweichen,	Then, in parting, I shall gladly
Der schönen Erde 'Lebe wohl!'	Bid this lovely world farewell.
Sei's denn, so drücken doch am Ende	Maybe, after all, the hands of true friends
Die Hand mir treue Freundeshände,	Will at the end press my hand,
So segnet doch mich Freundesblick:	And friendly eyes will bless me:
Und das ist, Brüder, doch ein Glück!	And that, brothers, is surely happiness!

This is the eleventh of Schubert's twelve Seidl solo settings (1826–8). See the poet's biography for a chronological list of all the Seidl settings.

Of the four Seidl *Refrain-Lieder* this is the most rough-hewn and simple. Even the look of the music on the printed page resembles the Viennese popular songs of the period, with slightly crass accents on some of the offbeats in the piano writing, and lumbering Alberti basses. This is all done deliberately in the interests of heartiness, and Schubert must have worked hard to divest himself of the natural elegance of his piano writing. This is as near as the composer ever came to parodying the type of *Singspiel* ditty for the working people that made mediocre composers a lot of money. *Irdisches Glück* may not have been as funny as the publisher Weigl wished, but the musical tone (and the simplicity of the vocal line) is reminiscent of such contemporary 'masters' of the comic style as the publisher's brother Joseph Weigl, Wenzl Müller (*see* COMPOSERS), Franz Gläser and Josef Drechsler. (The harmonic vocabulary of these composers sounds impoverished and lacking in imagination to modern ears, and it is sometimes hard to imagine why people should have so delighted in their work.) The vocal line is largely doubled by the piano, driving home the philosophical points that the singer is making, as if they are being banged into us. (Images of Schubert the schoolmaster and unwilling disciplinarian are conjured up here!) There is an element of lecturing and finger-wagging – as there usually is when self-appointed sages dispense their wit and wisdom. These figures, stock clowns of Viennese farce (and not unlike the more humble characters in Shakespeare's plays) waste no time in reassuring the public that they – as opposed to the toffs or intellectuals – have a common-sense attitude to life. As Capell puts it, the message here is 'take life as it comes and don't cry for the moon'.

The D minor tonality of the original key puts us in mind of *Wie Ulfru fischt* D525, the Mayrhofer setting with a similar working-class earthiness – if a song with a fishing theme may be described as earthy rather than watery. *Ulfru* is more appealing as a piece of music, however; in *Irdisches Glück* Schubert depicts rather too well the limited imagination of the ever-so-humble protagonist. The tempo is a relatively brisk 'Ziemlich geschwind', but the four-square rhythm ensures that the music is a march not against the philistines but with them – at least in the minor-key section that takes up the first half of each strophe. Seidl's verses are divided in two for musical purposes: the fifth to eighth lines constitute a major-key section which enumerates the narrator's reasons for happiness (the refrain at the end of each verse is a variation of the phrase 'Und das ist doch gewiss ein Glück!' with 'denn' added in the first verse and 'Brüder' in the last) and the music is much more typically Schubertian. This change of key is introduced by a cadence on 'vergebens <u>aufgetan</u>' (line four of the first verse bb. 13–15), after which the piano echoes this rather woeful complaint with a three-bar interlude of some charm (bb. 15–17) but no great originality.

With the change to D major the music becomes more playful. At first, true to form, the piano doggedly shadows the voice. However, when the tune of 'Da weiss ich besser mich zu nehmen' at b. 18 reverts to the piano (played at bb. 25–6 an octave higher as if it were a flute solo) the vocal line (beginning 'Und fern, der Freude mich zu schämen', from b. 26) is treated as an obbligato where the words are spoken interjections to this lilting little melody. The influence here is Mozart in *Singspiel* mood rather than any of the minor Viennese tunesmiths. There is a hearty seven-bar postlude (bb. 35–41, that march again!) which finishes each verse in mock defiance. The leaps in the left hand (beginning in bb. 33–8) feel strangely familiar under the pianist's hand – a type of stride-bass *avant la lettre* which is a feature of the accompaniment of *Die Taubenpost* D965A composed some two months later. Schubert was experimenting at the time with these insouciant antics in the bass clef, and it seems likely that the poems of *Die Taubenpost* and *Irdisches Glück* were part of the same consignment of poems from Seidl. If we did not have firm evidence that these *Refrain-Lieder* date from the summer of 1828 (*see* above), not earlier as Deutsch thought, this would be a stylistic thumb-print to place them there.

A little of this music goes a very long way, as is the case with much music conceived as an up-to-the-minute reflection of popular taste. If this is a song for the Biedermeier age, one is reminded that 'Biedermeier' derives from the German adjective 'bieder', meaning unsophisticated and stolid. Perhaps Schubert took ironic pleasure in writing something that gloried in its own mediocrity (he was apparently given to chortling in a rather snide way on occasion). One would prefer to think of him amusing himself at his fellow composers' expense rather than having to write music of this kind purely for financial reasons.

There are four verses in this strictly strophic song (which John Reed rightly pronounces 'a little dull and monotonous'), three of which were deemed sufficient for the Hyperion recording. Singers of the day might have expected to vary the tempo and mood of each strophe according to the words. It is interesting to speculate what Schubert might have felt in reading the verse describing the lack of laurels celebrating the singer's fame. There is a possibility that Seidl wrote these lines thinking of Schubert, and the composer might equally have lobbed the inference back in the poet's direction by dedicating these songs to him. In the last verse the call of the messenger 'from the world beyond' would come far more quickly for Schubert than he, or anyone else, could ever have dreamed.

Subsequent editions: Peters: Vol. 4/91; AGA XX 511: Vol. 8/250; NSA IV: Vol. 5/49;
                            Bärenreiter: Vol. 3/182
Discography and timing: Fischer-Dieskau II 8[18]   5'16   (4 strophes)
                            Hyperion I 37[4]
                            Hyperion II 36[7]   4'10   Michael Schade

← *Die Männer sind mechant!* D866/3   *Das Echo* D990C →

Die VIER WELTALTER

(SCHILLER) **D391** [H231]
G major   March 1816

The four ages of the world

(16 bars)

Wohl perlet im Glase der purpurne Wein,	The crimson wine sparkles in the glass;
Wohl glänzen die Augen der Gäste,	The guests' eyes shine;
Es zeigt sich der Sänger, er tritt herein,	The minstrel appears and enters,
Zu dem Guten bringt er das Beste.	To the good things he brings the best;
Denn ohne die Leier im himmlischen Saal	For without the lyre joy is vulgar,
Ist die Freude gemein auch beim Nektarmahl.	Even at a nectar banquet in the hall of the gods.
Ihm gaben die Götter das reine Gemüt,	The gods gave him a pure soul,
Wo die Welt sich, die ew'ge, spiegelt,	In which the eternal world is reflected,
Er hat alles gesehen, was auf Erden geschieht,	He has seen all that happens on earth
Und was uns die Zukunft versiegelt,	And what the future has sealed from us,
Er sass in der Götter urältestem Rat	He sat in the most ancient council of gods
Und behorchte der Dinge geheimste Saat.	And listened in on the world's innermost secrets.
[. . . 3 . . .]	[. . . 3 . . .]
Erst regierte Saturnus schlicht und gerecht,	First Saturn ruled, simply and justly,
Da war es heute wie Morgen,	Then one day was like the next;
Da lebten die Hirten, ein harmlos Geschlecht,	Then shepherds lived, a carefree race;
Und brauchten für gar nichts zu sorgen,	They did not need to worry about anything.
Sie liebten, und taten weiter nichts mehr,	They loved, and did nothing else,
Die Erde gab alles freiwillig her.	The earth yielded everything of its own accord.
Drauf kam die Arbeit, der Kampf begann	Then came work, and the struggle began
Mit Ungeheuern und Drachen,	With monsters and dragons;
Und die Helden fingen, die Herrscher, an,	Heroes emerged, and rulers,
Und den Mächtigen suchten die Schwachen,	And the weak sought the man of might;
Und der Streit zog in des Skamanders Feld,	And the battle came to Scamander's fields,
Doch die Schönheit war immer der Gott der	But Beauty was always the god of the world.
Welt.	
Aus dem Kampf ging endlich der Sieg hervor,	Struggle eventually gave rise to victory,
Und der Kraft entblühte die Milde,	And from force gentleness blossomed;
Da sangen die Musen im himmlischen Chor,	Then the muses sang in celestial choir,
Da erhuben sich Göttergebilde!	Then images of gods arose!

Das Alter der göttlichen Phantasie,	The age of divine imagination
Es ist verschwunden, es kehret nie.	Has vanished: it will never return.

[. . . 4 . . .] [. . . 4 . . .]

FRIEDRICH VON SCHILLER (1759–1805); poem written in January 1802

This is the twenty-fifth of Schubert's forty-four Schiller solo settings (1811–24). See the poet's biography for a chronological list of all the Schiller settings.

The music, prophetic of the greatest Schubertian drinking song set on Olympus, *Dithyrambe* D801, is typical of the choruses that Schubert wrote for convivial occasions. In this case he failed to think through the consequences of his all-too-easily written repeat marks: the tune is simple enough to remember after a few repetitions, but the number of repeats that would be welcome in performance would very much depend on the plenitude of wine at hand, and whether there is audience participation. For the recitalist, the song raises a number of awkward performance choices. For the poem to be worthy of Schiller's title it has to be performed complete – but (in concert circumstances certainly) the patience of an audience would be severely challenged by this decision. For the Hyperion Edition the example of Fischer-Dieskau was followed and a selection of four out of Schiller's twelve verses (Verses 1, 6, 7 and 8) was sung; these, while not doing justice to the scope of Schiller's scenario, at least tell part of the story in a more or less logical sequence. A further complication is that, according to the autograph, Schubert intended the second strophe to be sung but he did not take a great deal of care regarding the underlay and correct accentuation of the text. There is a suggestion as to how to rectify this as a footnote to the song in Volume 10 of the NSA – and the strophes as printed above are numbered there according to their position in the original poem to avoid confusion. Verse 2 of the poem printed above does not appear in the Hyperion recording.

To make it clear that the minstrel is hymning the four ages of the world with the possible transition into a fifth, Verse 5 would be necessary, but this cannot be included without Verses 3 and 4. When the first two verses have been used as a kind of introduction, and the character of the minstrel takes over at the beginning of the sixth verse, the singer must get across the fact that he is impersonating the narration of 'Der Sänger' from that point. In our proposed version the singer has to be content to leave the story of mankind before the advent of Christianity and the courtly love tradition. For the afficianado of song history the loss of Verse 11 is a pity because the whole era of the Minnelied is encapsulated by the lines 'Die Flamme des Liedes entbrannte neu / An der schönen Minne und Liebestreu'. Verse 12 predicts an age in which 'Gesang und Liebe' will work together in wonderful conjunction. For the true German-speaking enthusiast all the verses are printed in the AGA, although a complete performance of all twelve verses when set to this simple music seems too high a price to pay to hear these words. Schiller's 'elevated sentiments' are not best served by Schubert's 'jolly little tune' (as John Reed puts it). The rollicking piano interlude at the end of each verse (with slurred semiquavers in the inner voice of the accompaniment that might possibly suggest inebriation) is adapted from the postlude to an earlier Schiller setting for chorus and piano, *Punschlied* D277.

Autograph:	Missing or lost
First edition:	Published as Op. post. 111 no. 3 by Josef Czerny, Vienna in February 1829 (P199)
Publication review:	*Allgemeiner Musikalischer Anzeiger* (Vienna) No. 5 (31 January 1829) p. 19f. [Waidelich/Hilmar Dokumente I No. 688]

Subsequent editions: Peters: Vol. 4/130; AGA XX 196: Vol. 4/56; NSA IV: Vol. 10/62
Arrangements: Arr. Tilman Hoppstock (b. 1961) for guitar accompaniment, in
                            Franz Schubert: 110 Lieder (2009)
Discography and timing: Fischer-Dieskau I 6[19]   2'12
                            Hyperion I 16[13]
                            Hyperion II 13[4]   2'01   Thomas Allen

← *Die Entzückung an Laura* D390   *Ritter Toggenburg* D397 →

Der *VIERJÄHRIGE POSTEN* D190   The four-year sentry duty

Der vierjährige Posten was composed to a published play by the poet Körner (the composer was
proud of having met this hero who died in battle in August 1813). The work was completed in
eleven days in May 1815. This is a spectacular enough feat – the work has eight substantial
numbers and a full score of 108 pages – without taking into account that Schubert was also busy
on songs (Hölty's *An den Mond* D193 among them) in these very same days. The plot of the
opera concerns the tenor hero, Duval, who has been put on sentry duty by a regiment that
marches away without relieving its sentinels. After many days on duty, he tires of his post,
descends to the nearest village, finds his comrades gone and falls in love with Kätchen. Four
years later the regiment returns. To avert the charge of desertion, Duval pretends to have been
on sentry duty all that time. Things look dangerous for him for a little while at which point
Kätchen utters her prayer (Scene 5 of the play). Because it is a prayer of sorts, and also because
the vocal tessitura is so perilously high, we are tempted to surmise that Schubert extracted this
aria from *Der vierjährige Posten* especially for Therese Grob, the soprano who sang at the
composer's parish church of Liechtenthal, and with whom he was said to have been in love.

Illustration for *Der vierjährige Posten* from the *Prachtausgabe* of Körner's *Sämmtliche Werke* (1882).

GOTT, HÖRE MEINE STIMME   Hear my voice, o God
(Körner) **D190/5** [H91+]
E♭ major   8–19 May 1815

(229 bars)

Gott! Gott! Höre meine Stimme,	Hear my voice, o God
Höre gnädig auf mein Fleh'n!	In mercy heed my entreaty.
Sieh, ich liege hier im Staube!	See, I lie here in the dust.
Soll die Hoffnung, soll der Glaube	Should hope and faith
An dein Vaterherz vergeh'n?	In your paternal heart perish?
Er soll es büssen mit seinem Blute,	Should he atone with his blood
Was er gewagt mit frohem Mute,	For what he had ventured with joyous heart,
Was er für mich und die Liebe getan?	For what he did for me, for love?
Sind all die Wünsche nur eitle Träume,	Are all wishes but vain dreams?
Zerknickt die Hoffnung die zarten Keime,	Does hope crush the tender seeds?
Ist Lieb' und Seligkeit nur ein Wahn?	Are love and bliss but a delusion?
Nein, nein, das kannst du nicht gebieten,	No, no, you cannot allow it,
Das wird dein Vaterherz verhüten.	Your paternal heart will forbid it.
Gott, du bist meine Zuversicht!	God, you are my trust.
Du wirst zwei Herzen so nicht trennen,	You will not sunder two hearts
Die nur vereinigt schlagen können!	Which can only beat united.
Nein, Vater! nein, das kannst du nicht!	No, no, that you cannot do.

THEODOR KÖRNER (1791–1813)

Despite the large number of arias in his operas (a treasure trove of riches largely unexplored by all but the most ardent of enthusiasts), Schubert chose to make his own piano-accompanied arrangements of them in only three instances. There are two substantial pieces (one for tenor, one for bass) from the opera *Alfonso und Estrella* D732 (qv) arranged in 1822, four items from *Rosamunde* D797 (qv) in 1823 (a solo song and three choruses) and the piano reduction for this aria, presumably made at the time of the *Singspiel*'s composition in 1815.

This piano reduction is a model of clarity and economy, qualities that arrangers of operatic vocal scores seldom achieve. In the original orchestration the opening 'Adagio con moto' is exquisitely scored for woodwinds only but as the aria progresses the full weight of the orchestra is deployed behind the ardent heroine. The orchestrated aria is composed for some imaginary steel-throated canary able to achieve both height and volume – like a young and inexperienced composer of today who, on the strength of his visits to the opera house, writes music that could only be sung by a Joan Sutherland or Edita Gruberova. When it came to singer-friends, however, the composer was infinitely more careful and as an arranger he seems to have carefully catered for his sweetheart's voice. Then, as now, composers of operas who write for an instrument of their fantasies rather than for actual existing voices, are doomed to the greatest disappointments. Over the years, the more opportunities Schubert had to work with professional singers (above all the renowned Johann Michael Vogl) the more realistic were his vocal demands.

Autograph:	University Library of Lund, Sweden
First edition:	Published as part of the AGA in 1888 as part of the opera; and in this arrangement as part of the NSA in 1988 (P799)
Subsequent editions:	Not in Peters; AGA XV: Vol. 2/58 (as part of opera); NSA IV: Vol. 14b/244
Discography and timing:	Fischer-Dieskau —

Hyperion I 9[3]
Hyperion II 6[11]   4'49   Arleen Auger

← *An die Freude* D189   *Des Mädchens Klage* D191 →

VIOLA   Violet
(SCHOBER) **D786** [H513]
A♭ major   March 1823

(334 bars)

(1) Schneeglöcklein, o Schneeglöcklein!   Snowdrop, snowdrop,
    In den Auen läutest du,   You ring through the meadows,
    Läutest in dem stillen Hain,   You ring in the silent grove.
    Läute immer, läute zu, läute immer zu!   Ring on, ring on for ever!

(2) Denn du kündest frohe Zeit,   For you herald a time of joy;
    Frühling naht, der Bräutigam,   Spring approaches, the bridegroom,
    Kommt mit Sieg vom Winterstreit,   Victorious from his struggle with winter,
    Dem er seine Eiswehr nahm.   From whom he wrested his icy weapon.

(3) Darum schwingt der goldne Stift,   Hence your golden stem swings
    Dass dein Silberhelm erschallt,   So that your silver bell resounds,
    Und dein liebliches Gedüft   And your sweet fragrance wafts gently away,
    Leis' wie Schmeichelruf entwallt: Like an enticing call:

(4) Dass die Blumen in der Erd   So that the flowers in the earth
    Steigen aus dem düstern Nest   Rise from their gloomy nests,

Und des Bräutigams sich wert	And to prove worthy of the bridegroom
Schmücken zu dem Hochzeitsfest. –	Adorn themselves for the wedding feast.

(5) Schneeglöcklein, o Schneeglöcklein!   Snowdrop, snowdrop,
In den Auen läutest du,   You ring through the meadows,
Läutest in dem stillen Hain,   You ring in the silent grove,
Läut' die Blumen aus der Ruh'!   Ring the flowers from their sleep!

(6) Du Viola, zartes Kind,   Violet, tender child,
Hörst zuerst den Wonnelaut,   Is the first to hear the joyful sound;
Und sie stehet auf geschwind,   She rises quickly,
Schmücket sorglich sich als Braut,   And adorns herself carefully as a bride.

(7) Hüllet sich ins grüne Kleid,   She wraps herself in a green gown,
Nimmt den Mantel sammetblau,   Takes a velvety blue mantle,
Nimmt das güldene Geschmeid,   Her golden jewels
Und den Brilliantentau.[1]   And her dewy diamonds.

(8) Eilt dann fort mit mächt'gem Schritt,[2]   Then she hastens forth with powerful gait,
Nur den Freund im treuen Sinn,   With thoughts only of her beloved in her faithful heart,

Ganz von Liebesglück durchglüht,   Inflamed with ardent love,
Sieht nicht her und sieht nicht hin.   Looking neither this way nor that.

(9) Doch ein ängstliches Gefühl   But a feeling of apprehension
Ihre kleine Brust durchwallt,   Troubles her tiny breast,
Denn es ist noch rings so still   For all around it is still so quiet,
Und die Lüfte wehn so kalt.[3]   And the winds blow so cold.

(10) Und sie hemmt den schnellen Lauf,   She checks her rapid course.
Schon bestrahlt von Sonnenschein,   Already the sun shines on her,
Doch mit Schrecken blickt sie auf –   But she looks up in terror,
Denn sie stehet ganz allein.   For she is quite alone.

(11) Schwestern nicht – nicht Bräutigam –   No sisters! No bridegroom!
Z u g e d r u n g e n!   She has been *too pressing*! She has been *rejected*!
und v e r s c h m ä h t! –
Da durchschauert sie die Scham,   Then she shudders with shame
Fliehet wie vom Sturm geweht.   And flees, as if swept away by the storm.

(12) Fliehet an den fernsten Ort,   She flees to the remotest spot,
Wo sie Gras und Schatten deckt,   Where grass and shade conceal her;
Späht und lauschet immerfort: She constantly peers and listens
Ob was rauschet und sich regt.   To see if anything rustles or stirs.

---

[1] Schober writes (*Gedichte*, 1842) 'Und den *Diamantentau*'.
[2] Schober writes (*Gedichte*, 1842) 'Eilt dann fort mit *em'sgem* Schritt'.
[3] Schober writes (*Gedichte*, 1842) 'Und die Lüfte wehn *noch* kalt'.

(13) Und gekränket und getäuscht	Hurt and disappointed
Sitzet sie und schluchzt und weint;	She sits sobbing and weeping,
Von der tiefsten Angst zerfleischt	Tormented by the profound fear
Ob kein Nahender sich zeigt. –[4]	That no one will come near.
(14) Schneeglöcklein, o Schneeglöcklein,	Snowdrop, snowdrop,
In den Auen läutest du,	You ring through the meadows,
Läutest in dem stillen Hain,	You ring in the silent grove;
Läut die Schwestern ihr herzu!	Call her sisters to her.
(15) Rose nahet, Lilie schwankt,	The rose approaches, the lily sways,
Tulp' und Hyazinthe schwellt,	The tulip and hyacinth swell;
Windling kommt daher gerankt,	The bindweed trails along,
Und Narciss' hat sich gesellt.	And the narcissus joins them.
(16) Da der Frühling nun erscheint,[5]	And now, as spring appears
Und das frohe Fest beginnt,	And the happy festival begins,
Sieht er alle die vereint,	He sees them all united,
Und vermisst sein liebstes Kind.	But misses his dearest child.
(17) Alle schickt er suchend fort	He sends them all off to search
Um die eine, die ihm wert,	For the one he cherishes,
Und sie kommen an den Ort,	And they come to the place
Wo sie einsam sich verzehrt.	Where she languishes alone.
(18) Doch es sitzt das liebe Herz	But the sweet creature sits there
Stumm und bleich, das Haupt gebückt –	Dumb and pale, her head bowed;
Ach! der Lieb' und Sehnsucht Schmerz	Alas, the pain of love and longing
Hat die Zärtliche erdrückt.	Has crushed the tender one.
(19) Schneeglöcklein, o Schneeglöcklein	Snowdrop, snowdrop,
In den Auen läutest du,	You ring through the meadows,
Läutest in dem stillen Hain,	You ring in the silent grove;
Läut, Viola sanfte Ruh!	Ring for Violet's sweet repose!

FRANZ VON SCHOBER (1796–1882)

This is the tenth of Schubert's fourteen Schober solo settings (1815–27). See the poet's biography for a chronological list of all the Schober settings.

For Schubert, 1823 was a year of tragedy (his ongoing illness) and of two grand projects – one of which was doomed to obscurity, the other set to conquer the world. The opera *Fierabras* D796 and the song cycle *Die schöne Müllerin* D795 were the two big vocal works: twenty-five ensembles and arias gathered together to make one opera, twenty songs to make a cycle. But Schubert was also experimenting with other means of joining strands together to make a satisfying musical sequence. Many years earlier he had completed his apprenticeship in the

---

[4] Schubert changes Schober's line 'Ob kein Nahender erscheint', to the detriment of the rhyme scheme.
[5] Schober writes (*Gedichte*, 1842) '*Als* der Frühling nun erscheint'.

composition of extended narrative ballads, and the flower ballad *Viola* is one of the pieces where all this earlier work pays handsome dividends. Here is true vocal chamber music, constructed in such a way that it might easily have served as an instrumental finale in rondo form.

The poet Franz von Schober was certainly Schubert's closest friend (in the *Liedlexikon* 2012, in the entry for this song, p. 624, Siegfried Schmalzriedt, basing his account of this period on Ilija Dürhammer's study of the emotive undercurrents of the composer's circle, goes so far as to call him Schubert's 'life-partner for a while'). Whether or not Schober merited the composer's admiration and love has been a moot point among Schubertians ever since. He was handsome and gregarious; he was also feckless and vain. He was said to have encouraged the composer to enjoy himself with a prostitute in 1822, the terrible consequences of which were evident by the end of the year. At a time when Schubert must have felt very ill indeed, the two men collaborated in writing a song about a lovesick and abandoned flower (at this time, more or less, Schober decided to leave Vienna to live in Breslau, so Schubert might have felt equally abandoned). A century later the subject of this work seemed passingly amusing to Richard Capell who felt himself inveigled into a tour of a horticultural show, but for those with a knowledge of the biographical context, the choice of subject is horrifyingly apt. A story of trampled innocence succumbing to a powerful blighting force is disguised in metaphor within a song of musical power. As Donald Francis Tovey (who wrote a famous analysis of the piece) says, 'Its love and longing too great for its strength, Viola wastes away in solitude and shame.' In 1823 Schubert understood the feeling all too well.

Unlike in many of the earlier ballads that liberally employ recitative, the structure of this piece gives a feeling of seamless continuity. We shall never know whether the poem's structure with its repeating refrain was originally Schober's idea or something developed at Schubert's suggestion. Nevertheless the pleasure felt by composer and poet in creating this piece between them is almost palpable; somehow one imagines that Schober was more involved than usual in the work's birth-pangs.

Verse 1: The gentle sound of bells is heard in the very first bars, a 'signature' motif for the snowdrop, a flower that suggests a bell in its appearance – hence its German name, 'Schneeglöcklein'. This opening music, both simple and memorable, is of the kind that one might hear as a 'theme' in an instrumental set of variations. The innocence of this brings to mind another 'theme' in A flat major – the second of the *Moments Musicaux* D780 where the opening bars hover suspended in the treble clef in a similar manner. The piano introduction of *Viola* (bb. 1–8) traces in musical shorthand the contours of the vocal-line melody that begins at b. 9. This is framed in crotchets and dotted crotchets, music that is demure to the point of temerity. Even on the printed page there is the impression of an unsullied and transluscent purity. What this bell actually signifies is only discovered at the end of the song.

Verses 2–4: At b. 21 there is a change of rhythm – a mini-fanfare suggesting a festive gathering, in this case a vernal ceremony, a wedding of sorts. This motif with a delicate spring in its step was to reappear (in slightly more sophisticated form) as harp music for the spotless Ellen, a Viola of sorts, in the Walter Scott setting *Ellens Gesang I* D837. At Verse 3 (from b. 30) Schober's imagery is of music resounding (hence the accompanying semiquavers that rebound off the melody notes, as if reverberations, from b. 32) at the same time as suggesting an inviting and wafting fragrance. Between bb. 34 and 39 Schubert masterfully evokes this perfume in an accompanimental texture that changes only at the beginning of each bar, as if the flower's scent, hanging in the air, were being reassessed by a sensitive nose (or in this case, ear) after every bar; indeed the fragrance gradually dies away, being most apparent in b. 35 and becoming less powerful with the chromatic descent of the right-hand palpitations in semiquavers. These bring the voice with them down to the level at the bottom of the stave where Viola shyly resides; as if searching for the song's heroine the singer plumbs that earthy terrain in bb. 42–3. The word 'Hochzeitsfest' (bb. 47–8) occasions a celebratory melisma which sets off piano writing of unashamed jubilance to suggest the priapic energy of spring and to accompany a repeat of the strophe's last line – 'Schmücken zu dem Hochzeitsfest'.

Verse 5: After a piano interlude of five bars (bb. 53–7) the music for Verse 1 – the song's refrain – returns. The vocal line is identical, but the accompaniment, while retaining the sober right-hand minims and crotchets that have formerly shadowed the voice, is now animated by the 'second-violin' register of the music's four-part texture. This is all achieved without a change of tempo. A pulsation of repeated quavers (E flats and Fs at the bottom of the treble stave) is given added edge by the tripping semiquavers that provide something new – a hidden polonaise rhythm at the heart of the music. This suggestion of a dance fits the general mood of celebrative expectancy.

Verses 6–8: At b. 74 there is a change of key signature to F major, and the marking is 'Etwas geschwind'. The narrator now addresses Viola directly in a gentle cantilena where dancing dotted rhythms are underpinned by flowing semiquavers; in another context these might have suggested water music. When reading through Schober's poem this passage is easy enough to mock (considering that the addressee is a flower), but Schubert's musical conviction is such that he carries his performers (and listeners) with him in tender music that never seems ridiculous. At b. 84 the left hand finds a new rhythmic vitality in gently leaping octaves, and the energy gener-ated by these propels the music forward in describing Viola's party preparations. Schober's 'sammetblau' reminds us of Mayrhofer's 'In dem sammtnen Blau' in *Nachtviolen* D752, written the previous year. It would be easy to believe that it was Mayrhofer's choice of flower imagery that inspired Schober (an amateur poet in comparison to his older mentor) to take up the violet theme as a means of illustrating innocence besmirched (and specifically Schubertian inno-cence). After 'Brilliantentau', an image whereby the dew on the flower seems like an array of diamonds, the piano writing sparkles and exults in an interlude between bb. 97 and 100. Verse 8 continues in this vein with the left hand playing an increasingly important part in describing Viola's unlikely perambulations. Throughout this passage the left hand, its elegant phrasing enhancing the depiction of the flower's feminine grace, steers the music forward in the manner of an impassioned cellist performing a duet with the voice. The music for this strophe concludes with a repeat (between bb. 113 and 116) of the interlude heard earlier, music that takes the pianist into the higher reaches of the treble clef.

Verses 9–10: At b. 117, and utterly without warning, a chill enters the song. There is a sudden switch into the minor key, and a throbbing rhythm between the hands in staccato articulation suggests racing pulses, breathlessness and panic. The harmonic changes here are extraordinary. The bass line slides downwards from F natural (F minor) to F flat, thence to E flat (second inversion of A flat minor), D and C sharp (second inversion of F sharp minor), a descent that reflects the draining away of Viola's confidence and her fear of being alone. By the beginning of Verse 10 (b. 134) the marking has changed to 'Etwas langsamer' and the momentum of the previous musical activity comes gradually to a halt. The last two lines of Schober's Verse 10 are set to something approaching dramatic recitative (while being cleverly integrated into the overall flow of the music without any sense of a division between sections). The announcement that the terrified Viola stands all alone is accompanied by a succession of stentorian chords in dotted minims (from b. 139). These settle on a D pedal at b. 143 that prepares the way for a modulation (with change of key signature) into G minor.

Verses 11–13 ('Sehr langsam' from b. 147): This music of oscillating right-hand tremolos supported by basses in open fifths is an ominous interlude made up of a succession of shivers and frozen trepidation. This is music of the coldest rejection. Schubert was sometimes wary of allowing the shape of a poem to dictate his musical shape, thus here the new section marked 'Geschwind' (at b. 153) occurs halfway through Schober's Verse 11. This music for Viola's flight (where the vocal line is in continual musical conversation with the roving left hand in the cello register) is hugely effective, with a long arch-like sweep that could feature in a violin sonata. From b. 169 until b. 193 (with the exception of bb. 179–80 and bb. 183–4) there is a magnificently extended pedal point on C. As we have seen, the last line of this verse is not exactly what Schubert wrote in his autograph. He changed Schober's 'Ob kein Nahender erscheint' to 'Ob kein Nahender sich zeigt'. The NSA of course adopts this, as is their policy, but why Schubert should have ruined his poet's rhyme to add the prosaic 'sich zeigt' is unexplained. The twelfth verse had ended 'sich regt' and it is well known that such patterns tend to stick subliminally in the mind of someone swiftly copying text, especially in the heat of composition.

Verse 14: The return of the main theme in A flat (at b. 197 with a change of key signature) is nothing less than a masterstroke prepared by a wonderful shift into E flat major (not the F minor the ear may have expected) at b. 193. The burbling semiquavers now calm down into four bars of ever-smoothening quavers. The 'Geschwind' tempo initiated at b. 154 is still very much in operation and we hear the rondo theme ('Schneeglöcklein, o Schneeglöcklein') at the same speed as at the beginning of this long song. It *sounds* the same at this tempo because the refrain is written out in note values that are double the length. Thus the dotted minim and crotchet of b. 197 when played 'Geschwind' are exactly equal to the dotted crotchet and quaver of b. 9 when played 'Mässig'. Once again the accompaniment to this rondo theme is newly inflected in the second-violin register of the piano part. In this case the burbling quavers have lost the perkiness of their previous polonaise rhythm. Instead, a new colour is provided by the intrusion of G flats into the harmony (from b. 206), a hint of the danger and agony that are suggested in the surrounding text – and the text of the refrain itself has been adapted for this new purpose.

Verse 15 ('Ziemlich langsam' with a change to ⅜): This section of the piece is one of Schubert's loveliest and shows the hand of a master orchestrator – someone capable of conceiving his accompaniments in terms other than purely pianistic. The voice here sings in counterpoint with a courtly bassoon-like bass line that begins its sonorous descent, in two-bar phrases, on the offbeat (bb. 225–8). For this solemn convocation of flowers (minus Viola of course) it is clear that all the other varieties of bloom have made their way to the spring festivities without mishap. The composer sets the words of the strophe once in general terms (bb. 229–38), then repeats them in order to allow each flower its own bow in front of the curtain: there is special appearance for the rose (bb. 241–2) and the lily (bb. 243–4), followed by tulip, hyacinth and narcissus.

Verse 16: At b. 254 Spring, the guest of honour, host of this flowery throng of attendants, makes his appearance. This passage is marked 'Etwas geschwinder' and once again we hear the festivity music of Verse 2. This skilfully winds down to the point where Viola, apparently Spring's dearest protégée, is missed (with suddenly dramatic music from b. 265), and a search party is sent out in double-quick time.

Verse 17 (with a change of key signature to B major at b. 269): There is a good deal of walking, strolling and sauntering in Schubert's music (his weight probably governed the speed of his country excursions), but this is a rare example of running. Here the panic is not Viola's, but rather those who have been sent to find her. Both the first edition and the AGA have a marking here of 'Sehr geschwind' with a change to *alla breve* that seems logical and necessary. Although this marking is not reprinted in the NSA, it is unlikely that this did not come from Schubert's hand at some point, considering that the fair-copy autograph that was used for the printing of the first edition has been lost and the publisher Pennauer was quite capable of making mistakes (cf. *Die junge Nonne*). However, excited quavers jostle between the hands as the vocal line gushes with many a textual repetition. There is an interlude of panic-stricken music between bb. 281

and 288 (with scurrying chords that scramble awkwardly across the keyboard in left-hand quavers) followed by a key change to two sharps at b. 286. This coincides with the line 'Und sie kommen an den Ort' halfway through Schober's Verse 17.

Verses 18–19 (from b. 299): With a further change of key signature to a single flat, and a marking of 'Langsam', we have music for the discovery of a crushed flower. Viola has been destroyed by the 'pain of love and longing' and Schubert makes of this sixteen-bar passage Viola's elegy where single-bar phrases in the accompaniment sigh in desperation. The enharmonic modulation from this plaintive D minor to the home key of A flat (bb. 311–14) is, as Tovey points out, especially fine. The return to the refrain for a final requiem, where once again the music is as simple as at the song's opening, is very moving. The marking here (b. 315) is again 'Langsam' although there has been nothing in the score to cancel out the preceding 'Langsam' at b. 300. The gentle pealing of the snowbell is now revealed as that of a passing bell, the 'Zügenglöcklein' (cf. *Das Zügenglöcklein* D871), also in A flat major, that was rung in Catholic communities to signal a death. Indeed, perhaps it has been Schubert's intention from the beginning for the 'Schneeglöcklein' to ring in memory of Viola, the whole of the narrated story being a flashback during the flower's funeral obsequies. The ethereal postlude is a new idea (bb. 329–34); it seems (in a *Ganymed* kind of way) to signal Viola's apotheosis and transport to a flowery heaven.

According to Beethoven's factotum Anton Schindler, this was one of the sixty songs by Schubert that he passed over to Beethoven for the great man to study in 1827. Beethoven was fascinated by the music and immersed himself in Schubert's works for hours on end. (This story has its doubters.) The older composer was said to be amazed that some of the settings were long enough, as he remarked, to contain music sufficient for ten ordinary songs. As *Viola* is specifically mentioned by Schindler as having been one of the songs concerned it is almost certain that Beethoven's observation (if genuine) related to this very music.

The violet referred to as the heroine of this poem is possibly the flower described by Leopold Trattinnick, the famous Viennese botanist, as particularly undervalued and easily overlooked (in his *Österreichischer Blumenkranz* of 1819, p. 80). This is *Viola biflora*, a plucky little plant with golden-yellow flowers that, as described by Trattinnick, shyly inhabits the colder regions of mountains and beautifies areas that are otherwise barren. However, it is just as likely that Schober had no specific idea about which member of the violet family he had in mind.

Autograph:	Pierpont Morgan Library, New York (not an autograph but a copy with annotations in Schubert's hand)
First edition:	Published as Op. post. 123 by Anton Pennauer, Vienna in November 1830 (P258)
Subsequent editions:	Peters: Vol. 3/110; AGA XX 423: Vol. 7/76; NSA IV: Vol. 13/70
Bibliography:	Capell 1928, pp. 178–9
	Fischer-Dieskau 1977, pp. 172–3
	Kohlhäufl 1999, p. 311
	Robertson 1946, p. 187
	Tovey 1944, pp. 137–41
Discography and timing:	Fischer-Dieskau II 5[21] 12'40
	Hyperion I 3[10]
	Hyperion II 27[1] 14'49 Ann Murray

←— *Abendröte* D690   *Lied (Des Lebens Tag ist schwer)* D788 —→

JACOPO ANDREA VITTORELLI (1749–1835)

A SELECTION OF POETIC SOURCES

S1 *Le Anacreontiche del Vittorelli* Editione Quarta notabilmente accresciuta In Venezia MDCCXCVIII [1798]
'A Jacopo Andrea Vitterelli Uomo de singular ingegno e de singular probita Due Candidi Amice offrono e consecrano questa nuova edizione delle incomparabili sue Anacreontiche.'

There is an earlier edition of Vittorelli's *Rime* (Bassano, 1784) that includes the Sonnets and Epigrams but not the anacreontic verse.

S2 *Rime di Iacopo Vittorelli* Nuova Edizione, Dall' Autore medesimo accrescuita, e unicamente approvata, Bassano, Dalla Tipografia Remondiniana, 1806

S3 *Rime di Jacopo Vittorelli, Parte Seconde. Anacreontica*, Bassano dalla stamperia Baseggio, 1815. This version is cited in Schochow 1974.

S4 *Rime Edite ed Inedite Di Jacopo Vittorelli* Colla Traduzione Latina a Fronte Dell'Abate Giuseppe A. Trivellato Già maestro nel Seminario Di Padova Volume II Padova Pei Tip della Minerva MDCCCXXV (1825)

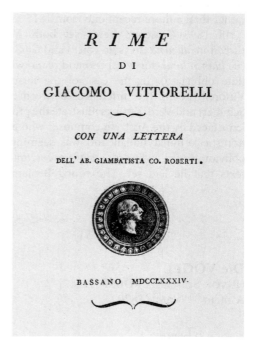

RIME
DI
GIACOMO VITTORELLI

CON UNA LETTERA

DELL' AB. GIAMBATISTA CO. ROBERTI.

BASSANO MDCCLXXXIV.

Vittorelli's *Rime* (1784).

THE SONGS

January 1820   *Non t'accostar all'urna* D688/1 [S1: No. XXI, no page number] [S2: p. 123 under title 'Anacreontica XIII'] [S3: p. 30 under title 'Anacreontica X'] [S4: p. 26]
Guarda, che bianca luna! D688/2 [S1: No. VII, no page number] [S2: p. 115 under title 'Anacreontica V'] [S3: p. 27 under title 'Anacreontica' VII] [S4: p. 16 under title 'Anacreontica VIII']

Jacopo Andrea Vittorelli was born in Bassano, Venetia, on 10 November 1749 and educated by the Jesuits. He lived in Venice between 1787 and 1797; the date of his departure suggests that he chose to leave the city only when it became occupied by Napoleonic forces. He was headmaster of the Ginnasio di S. Giustina in Padua from 1809 until 1814. In 1816 he was employed as a book censor by the occupying Austrian government. His enormously popular anacreontic verses, *Anacreontiche a Irene*, first published before Schubert was born, had reached Vienna in various editions (separately and as part of the *Rime*) long before 1820.

Vittorelli is one of those invisible collaborators, like Marianne von Willemer and Ernestine von Krosigk, whose words Schubert set to music without knowing the names of their authors. The fact that he confused them with ones by the infinitely more famous Metastasio indicates that the composer was working from copies of the texts (and somewhat corrupt ones at that) rather than directly from a volume of verse. As is often the case, it is difficult to say which of the deviations from Vittorelli's text were Schubert's own adaptations and which were simply a result of following inaccurate copies of the verses that had come his way. The source of these probably goes back to an edition of the *Anacreontiche* from the 1790s rather than a more recent one from 1815.

In 1838 Giuseppe Verdi set both *Non t'accostare all'urna* (for solo voice) and *Guarda che bianca luna* (for vocal trio and piano with flute obbligato). In the case of the former Vittorelli poem, the differences between the Schubert and Verdi settings illustrate the problems faced by the Austrian composer who did not speak much Italian and was seemingly oblivious to the awkwardness of the corrupted texts that he had set. The young Benjamin

Britten setting French (Hugo and Rimbaud) and Italian (Michelangelo) comes to mind in terms of a composer's youthful insouciance with a foreign language, although some of Schubert's earlier Italian settings were actually spared this type of confusion thanks to the presence of Antonio Salieri as his guide and teacher until 1817. By 1820 Schubert was no longer showing his work to Salieri, although he might have done so if he had ever seriously considered preparing these songs for publication. The poet died on 12 June 1835 in Bassano, where he had been born.

Die VÖGEL   The birds
(F. VON SCHLEGEL) **D691** [H447]
A major   March 1820

(55 bars)

Wie lieblich und fröhlich,	How delightful and exhilarating it is
Zu schweben, zu singen;	To soar and to sing,
Von glänzender Höhe	To look down on the earth
Zur Erde zu blicken!	From the radiant heights!
Die Menschen sind töricht,	Men are foolish:
Sie können nicht fliegen.	They cannot fly.
Sie jammern in Nöten,	They lament in their distress;
Wir flattern gen Himmel.	We fly up to the heavens.
Der Jäger will töten,	The huntsman whose fruit we pecked
Dem Früchte wir pickten;	Wants to kill us;
Wir müssen ihn höhnen,	But we should mock him
Und Beute gewinnen.	And snatch our spoils.

[1] This tempo marking is found not in the autograph but in contemporary copies. This marking in the first edition (1865) is 'Allegretto'.

This is the the ninth of Schubert's sixteen Friedrich von Schlegel solo settings (1818–25). See the poet's biography for a chronological list of all the Friedrich von Schlegel settings. See also the article about the cycle of which this song is part – Abendröte.

This is a delightful little tune, so full of inevitable Schubertian singability and charm (the marking on contemporary copies of the song is 'Lieblich') that to question how the composer manages to spin out a melody of this kind would be like asking the birds how they are able to fly. Birds are bird-brained, and it is no surprise that their harmonic vocabulary is not large; however, within their own parameters they are kings. Schubert, king of *Ländler* (and almost as highly revered by his friends for his dance music as for his lieder), makes his birds sing in the rhythm of a village dance. These birds regard anyone unlike them as stupid – just as the countryman looks down on the town dweller, who in turn dismisses the yokel as part of a lesser species. In their innocence and happiness in their own environment they have no interest in intellectual pursuits; these birds are both wonderfully balanced and incredibly complacent.

The song is adorable but we would not wish Schubert to compose like this all the time. We know how Schumann used the *Ländler* form in ⅜ in *Das ist ein Flöten und Geigen* Op. 48 no. 9 from *Dichterliebe* to paint the earthbound musical banalities of village life, and it is part of Schubert's wry humour to point out that a flock of birds is as clannish and self-satisfied as the common herd of humanity. This song is also prophetic of another wryly comic lied, *Des Antonius von Padua Fischpredigt* where Mahler parodies *Ländler* commonplaces in order to underline that fishy behaviour is not confined to the deep; he was master of the sinister and even brutal overtones of country life as expressed through the banalities of popular music. The modern listener who thinks of Alfred Hitchcock's film *The Birds* might be persuaded to find a hint of menace behind the very Austrian charm of this song, for unalloyed sweetness is sometimes a sign of danger in Vienna. The exploration of the darker side of Austrian *Gemütlichkeit* intensified as the nineteenth century grew older, but in the setting of *Täuschung* D911/19 from *Winterreise*, another *Ländler*, Schubert demonstrates that he too understood how tragedy can be played out to the accompaniment of a lilting waltz.

Of course here, as always, Schubert responds to the text in his peerless way. Words like 'lieblich', 'fröhlich' and 'singen' flit from branch to branch; but 'schweben' floats on one note (b. 7) as if gliding on an air current. Thus the shape of a tune is decided by verbal images. The notes of the next phrase are almost an exact repeat, apart from 'Erde', which jumps the octave (b. 13), and 'blicken' (b. 14) which answers the upward inflection of 'singen' with a downward lilt. This surge upwards followed by a dropping interval conjures a vantage point high in the sky, from where our ears are musically directed to follow the birds' gaze earthward. We may be sure that this sort of mastery was second nature to our composer, and that he scarcely rated these felicities as anything special. In the middle section the birds look down on mankind in every sense. Schlegel undoubtedly knew *The Birds* of Aristophanes, where the eponymous high-flyers pity men as 'dwellers by nature in darkness … poor plumeless ephemerals'. The human race is thickheaded, and we hear this in the droning left-hand open fifths under 'Die Menschen sind töricht' (bb. 18–20).

Goethe talks of 'der stumpfe Bursche' – 'the dull lad' – in *Der Musensohn* D764 and we meet the species again here. This music is also appropriate for the lamenting tone in the following phrase, the accented passing note of 'jammern' (an E major chord crushed by a passing A sharp, b. 29) illustrative of a human moan, and a complete contrast to 'flattern gen Himmel' (bb. 33–4) which is not weighed down by an extraneous accidental and is thus free to float, light as air. The hunter makes an appearance (one is reminded of *Der Jäger* Op. no. 4 by Brahms which is also a dance of this kind) but there is no minor key to imply the danger of being shot. These birds take the prospect of death as lightly as life itself. As in *Der Schmetterling* D633 we feel that the implacable dance rhythm behind the music is the composer's means of depicting ongoing rituals that are governed by instinct rather than morality. In human terms, the birds might be thieves, the butterfly a promiscuous roué, but Nature has ordained it thus. Accordingly there is no sign of regret, guilt, fear or sadness in either of these charming songs. Walther Dürr adds a warning in the *Liedlexikon* 2012 that it is possible that *Die Vögel* was composed as late as 1823, although the strong probability of 1820 still holds sway.

Autograph:	Wienbibliothek im Rathaus, Vienna (fair copy)
First edition:	Published as Op. post. 172 no. 6 by C. A. Spina in 1865 (P406)
Subsequent editions:	Peters: Vol. 6/104; AGA XX 373: Vol. 6/86; NSA IV: Vol. 12/156
Discography and timing:	Fischer-Dieskau II 3[15] 1'04
	Hyperion I 27[10]
	Hyperion II 23[5] 1'03 Matthias Goerne

← *Mio ben ricordati* D688/4   *Der Fluss* D693 →

VOLLENDUNG   Fulfilment
(MATTHISSON) **D579A** (FORMERLY D989) [H382]
A major   September/October 1817

Langsam, feirlich

Wenn ich einst das Ziel er - run - gen ha - be,

(loco)   ³(15 bars)

Wenn ich einst das Ziel errungen habe,	When one day I reach my journey's end
In den Lichtgefilden jener Welt,	In the radiant fields of the world beyond,
Heil, der Träne dann an meinem Grabe	Then I shall hail the tears which fall on the roses
Die auf hingestreute Rosen fällt!	Scattered upon my grave.
Sehnsuchtsvoll, mit banger Ahnungswonne,	Full of yearning, with anxious joy of anticipation,
Ruhig, wie der mondbeglänzte Hain,	As calm as the moonlit grove,
Lächelnd, wie beim Niedergang die Sonne,	Smiling, as at the setting sun,
Harr' ich, göttliche Vollendung, dein!	I shall await you, divine fulfilment!
Eil', o eile mich empor zu flügen,	Hasten, o hasten to wing me on high,
Wo sich unter mir die Welten drehn,	To where the spheres turn beneath me,
Wo im Lebensquell sich Palmen spiegeln,	Where palm trees are mirrored in the spring of life,
Wo die Liebenden sich wieder sehn.	Where lovers are reunited.

FRIEDRICH VON MATTHISSON (1761–1831); poem written in 1784/5

This is the twenty-eighth of Schubert's twenty-nine Matthisson solo settings (1812–17). See the poet's biography for a chronological list of all the Matthisson settings.

This is one of a pair of Matthisson songs (the other is *Die Erde* D579B) that were rediscovered by Christa Landon as recently as 1970. The poem describes with ecstatic confidence (and no trace of irony) the poet's expectations of heavenly fulfilment and the Christian (as opposed to the mythological) afterlife. How different this is from the charmingly sly irony of *Seligkeit* D433, a text that seems far more authentically Schubertian. In the foreword of the 1794 edition of his poems Matthisson himself describes his *Die Vollendung* as 'youthful and very immature'. There remains a temptation to question the provenance of accompaniments where the disposition of much of the piano writing is untypical of Schubert, if not downright banal. The last line of each verse (from b. 10 where the quaver triplets suddenly throb with a mood reminiscent of another Matthisson setting, *Stimme der Liebe* D187) seems suddenly authentic, flesh and blood after wood. It would hardly be surprising if the work were a collaboration between Schubert and one of his composer friends (Anselm Hüttenbrenner for example) and that he had written only the vocal line and part of the accompaniment. In the absence of an autograph, the heading of the manuscript copy of the songs, found in the papers of the Wiener Männergesang-Verein, is the only factual evidence of their authenticity. Whoever wrote this song, it is a far from negligible response to Matthisson's ardent text. To question its authorship is not to belittle its efficacy. Schubert certainly had a hand, but possibly not much more than that, in its composition. Walther Dürr suggests (NSA IV Vol. 11 p. XXVII) that Schubert's brother Ferdinand may have asked for these songs to be written for performance at the orphanage where he was a teacher. Some of the music is such that it suggests the hand of Ferdinand rather than Schubert himself.

See also DUBIOUS, MISATTRIBUTED AND LOST SONGS.

Autograph:	Missing or lost
First edition:	Published as part of the NSA in 1968 and subsequently as the first of *Zwei Lieder* ed. Christa Landon by Bärenreiter, Kassel in 1970 (P732)
Subsequent editions:	Not in Peters; Not in AGA; NSA IV: Vol. 11/170
Bibliography:	Landon 1970, p. 200
Discography and timing:	Fischer-Dieskau —
	Hyperion I 11[6]
	Hyperion II 19[16] 2'32 Brigitte Fassbaender

←— *Der Knabe in der Wiege* D579   *Die Erde* D579B —→

Der VOLLMOND STRAHLT (ROMANZE/ARIETTE) *see ROSAMUNDE, FÜRSTIN VON ZYPERN* D797/3B

VOM MITLEIDEN MARIÄ   Mary's suffering
(SPEE/F. VON SCHLEGEL) **D632** [H411]
G minor   December 1818

(28 bars)

Als bei dem Kreuz Maria stand,	As Mary stood by the cross
Weh über Weh ihr Herz empfand	She felt woe upon woe in her heart,
Und Schmerzen über Schmerzen;	And sorrow upon sorrow;
Das ganze Leiden Christi stand	All Christ's suffering
Gedruckt in ihrem Herzen.	Was impressed upon her heart.
Sie ihren Sohn muss bleich und tot,	She had to watch her son
Und überall von Wunden rot,	Suffer on the cross, deathly pale,
Am Kreuze leiden sehen.	His whole body red with wounds;
Gedenk, wie dieser bitt're Tod	Ponder how this bitter death
Zu Herzen ihr musst' gehen.	Must have gone to her heart.
In Christi Haupt durch Bein und Hirn,	On Christ's head many sharp thorns pierced
Durch Augen, Ohren, durch die Stirn',	Through bone and brain,
Viel scharfe Dornen stachen,	Through eyes, ears and brow;
Dem Sohn die Dornen Haupt und Hirn,	The thorns broke the son's head and brain,
Das Herz der Mutter brachen.	And the mother's heart.

FRIEDRICH VON SPEE (1591–1635) & FRIEDRICH VON SCHLEGEL (1772–1829)

This is the the second of Schubert's sixteen Friedrich von Schlegel solo settings (1818–25) and the only setting of a Spee text. See the biographies of both these poets.

There were a number of important forces in early nineteenth-century German philosophy and literature that contributed to the popularity of lyrics of this kind: the religious writings of Friedrich Schleiermacher as an antidote to the impersonal rationality of the Enlightenment; the mysticism of Friedrich Schelling; the neo-medievalism of Ludwig Tieck and Novalis. The intensity of the Catholic revival represented by this lyric has engendered in Schubert a sense of historical style that borders on pastiche. The composer was reasonably well acquainted with what we now term 'early music'; a letter written to him by his brother Ferdinand on 3 July 1824 tells us that Schubert had asked for Bach fugues, either to play them or for teaching purposes with his young pupils, the Esterházy countesses in Zseliz. He was easily able to write in a variety of 'old' styles (the Bachian *Agnus Dei* of the first Mass D105 for example) and certain song texts also prompted this response. Here, the austere three-part texture and the restless chromaticism suggest Passion music of another age. Schubert would have perhaps known the Gellert and Cramer settings of C. P. E. Bach and it is the style of those religious odes for voice and piano which this setting brings to mind. Schubert's study of three-part counterpoint with Salieri stood

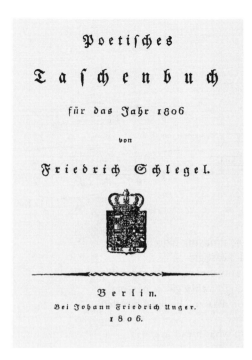

Schlegel's *Poetisches Taschenbuch* (1806).

him in good stead for writing where the voice and each hand of the pianist form a trinity of intertwined equality.

Schubert went through a phase of great enthusiasm in 1819 and 1820 for the *Abendröte* poems, but he began his exploration of Schlegel by setting two poems from *Poetisches Taschenbuch für das Jahr 1806 von Friedrich Schlegel*, 1806 – the songs *Blanka* D631 and this *Vom Mitleiden Mariä* (pp. 200–201 of that source). The latter poem appeared in a section of the almanac that gathers together some of the poems that first appeared in a collection of religious folksongs entitled *Trutznachtigall* by Friedrich Spee von Langenfeld (1591–1635). *Vom Mitleiden Mariä* is not from *Trutznachtigall* but Schlegel's reworking of Verses 2–4 of a hymn by Spee entitled 'Von unser lieben Frawen mit Leiden'. The old German original of these three verses is printed in the biographical article on Friedrich Spee (qv).

We do not know for certain when Schubert met Friedrich Schlegel, who had lived in Vienna since 1808, but it is possible that the composer was drawn into his circle through the intermediary influence of Franz von Bruchmann. By this time in the middle 1820s Schubert had already composed his great Schlegel settings and Schlegel was a very different character from the pantheist who had written the poems of *Abendröte* (qv). In *Vom Mitleiden Mariä* we encounter the poet on the threshold of a life-changing reconversion to Catholicism. It is little wonder that the words, a reworking of the Latin *Stabat Mater*, encourage a moving musical response to the human tragedy of the crucifixion and a mother's grief. The self-imposed hieratic austerity of the 'old' style still allows for the inner glow of Schubertian compassion. The benumbed grief described here was also to be depicted, in rather similar manner, in the third of the *Gesänge des Harfners aus Wilhelm Meister* of 1816, An die Türen will ich schleichen D478/3.

Autograph:	In private possession (Leopold Cornaro, Vienna) (fair copy)
First edition:	Published as Book 10 no. 4 of the *Nachlass* by Diabelli, Vienna in April 1831 (P265)
Subsequent editions:	Peters: Vol. 5/39; AGA XX 349: Vol. 5/238; NSA IV: Vol. 12/64
Bibliography:	Berke 1969, p. 485
	Black 2003, p. 65
	Capell 1928, p. 145
	Dürr, NSA Volume 12, p. 240
	Einstein 1951, p. 42
	Fischer-Dieskau 1977, pp. 120 & 126
Discography and timing:	Fischer-Dieskau II 2[11] 2'21 (first two strophes only)
	Hyperion I 21[24]
	Hyperion II 21[5] 3'16 Edith Mathis

← *Blanka* D631   *Hoffnung* D637 →

VON IDA

Ida

(KOSEGARTEN) **D228** [H119]

F minor   7 July 1815

(11 bars)

Der Morgen blüht,	The morning blooms,
Der Osten glüht;	The east glows;
Es lächelt aus dem dünnen Flor	The sun smiles, weak and sickly,
Die Sonne matt und krank hervor.	Through a thin gauze of cloud.
Denn, ach, mein Liebling flieht!	For, alas, my beloved has fled!
Auf welcher Flur,	On what meadows,
Auf wessen Spur,	On what track
So fern von Iden wallst du itzt,	Do you tarry now, so far from Ida?
O du, der ganz mein Herz besitzt,	You, you possess my whole heart
Du Liebling der Natur!	Darling of nature!
Vernimmst du auch	Do you also hear
Im Morgenhauch	In the morning breeze
Das Ach, das Idens Brust entächzt,	The cry that escapes from Ida's breast,
Das Sehnen, drinn ihr Herz zerlechzt,	The longing that pines within her heart
Im kühlen Morgenhauch?	In the cool morning breeze?
Was ahnest du	What do you know,
Der Idens Ruh	You who took away Ida's peace
Und Idens Freuden mit sich nahm?	And her happiness?
Ach, ahnest du wohl Idens Gram,	So you have an inkling of Ida's grief,
Und fliehst für Idens Ruh.	And do you pray for Ida's peace?
O, kehre um!	O return,
Kehr' um, kehr' um!	Return, return!
Zu deiner Einsamtraurenden!	To her who grieves alone,
Zu deiner Ahnungschaurenden!	To her who shudders with foreboding!
Mein Einziger, kehr' um!	Return, my one and only love!

LUDWIG KOSEGARTEN (1758–1818)

This is the third of Schubert's twenty-one Kosegarten solo settings (1815–17). See the poet's biography for a chronological list of all the Kosegarten settings, as well as a discussion of Morten Solvik's Kosegarten Liederkreis and this song's place within it.

This is music of disarming simplicity, a perfect little three-part invention where the vocal line entwines with the two simple voices in the piano with masterful precision. The way the vocal line dips as the piano rises in bb. 7–8, as if in mirror image, is prophetic of the writing in *Ganymed* D544 (at bb. 80–84 and 95–9 of that song) where the text ('Umfangend umfangen!') encompasses both the act of embracing and the pleasure of being embraced. Schubert adds a note more or less to alert his performers to the fact that this deployment of resources will only sound well if the singer is a soprano: 'NB. Wird dieser Gesang im Tenor gesungen, so fällt die Begleitung durchgehends um eine Oktave herab'. As a tenor voice sounds an octave lower than written, the composer directs that the accompaniment should also be played an octave lower if the singer is a tenor. For this reason one would hope that the song is never sung by a tenor (and the text should be sufficient discouragement in itself) because the ethereal tessitura of the piano writing is what gives the song its considerable charm. The ascending chromatic scale (in bb. 9–10) is deliciously underpinned by the sighing little coda of bb. 10–11.

Both Deutsch and Reed were incorrect to say that it was Schubert who changed Kosegarten's original 'Agnes' because 'Ida' was easier to sing. It is true that the poem's title is 'Von Agnes' in the 1788 printing of the *Gedichte*, but by the time the poet issued his *Poesien* of 1798 and the *Poesien* of 1802 (Schubert's source, or if not, the Viennese *Nachdruck* printed by Bauer) Kosegarten himself had amended the name. It seems that Ida was indeed the name of his beloved in his teenage years, but the name was changed by him to Agnes to protect her identity (*see* the poet's biography) for the publication of 1788. By the time the later editions of his poems came to be published he had reverted to the original name of Ida. Most confusingly, after he died, his heirs changed the name back to Agnes for the complete edtion of Kosegarten's works – an attempt to establish a kind of posthumous respectability concerning the poet's youthful escapades.

The poem is written in the same metre as *Der Abend* D221 ('Der Abend blüht, / Temora glüht') – this is a morning, as opposed to an evening, song. There are five strophes, all of them printed above. For the Hyperion Edition 1, 2 and 5 were recorded.

Autograph:	Humanities Center, University of Texas, Austin
First edition:	Published as part of the AGA in 1895 (P567)
Subsequent editions:	Not in Peters; AGA XX 91: Vol. 2/174; NSA IV: Vol. 8/118
Bibliography:	Holmes 2004
Discography and timing:	Fischer-Dieskau —
	Hyperion I 7[12]
	Hyperion II 8[2] 1'49 Elly Ameling

← *Idens Nachtgesang* D227   *Die Erscheinung (Erinnerung)* D229 →

VOR MEINER WIEGE   At my cradle
(LEITNER) OP. 106 NO. 3, **D927** [H652]
B minor   Autumn 1827–early 1828

(78 bars)

Das also, das ist der enge Schrein,	So this is the narrow chest
Da lag ich einstens als Kind darein,[1]	Where I once lay as a baby;
Da lag ich gebrechlich, hilflos und stumm	Where I lay, frail, helpless and dumb,
Und zog nur zum Weinen die Lippen krumm	Twisting my lips only to cry.
Ich konnte nichts fassen mit Händchen zart,	I could grip nothing with my tiny, tender hands,
Und war doch gebunden nach Schelmenart;[2]	Yet I was bound like a rogue;
Ich hatte Füsschen und lag doch wie lahm,	I possessed little feet, and yet lay as if lame,
Bis Mutter an ihre Brust mich nahm.	Until mother took me to her breast.
Dann lachte ich saugend zu ihr empor,	Then I laughed up at her as I suckled,
Sie sang mir von Rosen und Engeln vor,[3]	And she sang to me of roses and angels;
Sie sang und sie wiegte mich singend in Ruh,	She sang and with her singing lulled me to sleep,
Und küsste mir liebend die Augen zu.	And with a kiss lovingly closed my eyes.
Sie spannte aus Seide gar dämmerig grün	She spread a cool tent of dusky green silk
Ein kühliges Zelt hoch über mich hin;	Above me.
Wo find ich nur wieder solch friedlich	Where shall I find such a peaceful chamber
Gemach?[4]	again?
Vielleicht, wenn das grüne Gras mein Dach.	Perhaps when the green grass is my roof!
O Mutter! lieb' Mutter, bleib' lange noch hier;	O mother, dear mother, stay here a long time yet
Wer sänge dann tröstlich von Engeln mir?	Who else would sing to me comforting songs of
	angels?
Wer küsste mir liebend die Augen zu	Who else would close my eyes lovingly with a kiss
Zur langen, zur letzten und tiefesten Ruh'?	For the long, last and deepest rest?

KARL GOTTFRIED VON LEITNER (1800–1890); poem written in 1823

This is the sixth of Schubert's eleven Leitner solo settings (1822–3 and 1827–8). See the poet's biography for a chronological list of all the Leitner settings.

This poem must have touched Schubert, who lost his own mother at the age of fifteen, enormously; the end of the song has a fleeting image of a man who realizes that he will have to face death without the parental support on which he has relied – such, after all, is the way of the world. Leitner's words clearly made Schubert think of his own long-term future: he had long struggled with a malady that seemed at last to be cured but, just when he felt better, another bout of illness reminded him that his health had been permanently impaired since the diagnosis of syphilis in late 1822 or early 1823. The lack of physical equilibrium also has a psychological dimension. If we are to attach any significance to Schubert's famous prose poem *Mein Traum* (1822) it is clear that even before the diagnosis of his illness he longed to be embraced by his strict and difficult-to-please father and accepted for who he was; at the same time he missed the loving mother who had died early. This gives the music a depth and seriousness that make it a worthy piece to have been composed between the two parts of *Winterreise* D911.

[1] Leitner writes (*Gedichte*, 1825) 'Da lag ich *in Windeln* als Kind darein'. Schubert avoids mentioning a baby's nappy.
[2] Leitner writes (*Gedichte*, 1857) 'Und war doch gebunden nach *Diebesart*'.
[3] Leitner writes (*Gedichte*, 1825) 'Sie sang mir von Rosen und *Engelein* vor'.
[4] Leitner writes (*Gedichte*, 1825 and 1857) '*Wann* find ich *nun* wieder solch friedlich Gemach?'

The tight melodic range of the opening takes its cue from the poetic imagery of 'enge Schrein' – the contained and narrow cradle in which the poet lay as a baby. (We later learn that he has been bound in swaddling clothes – the phrase 'gebunden nach Schelmenart' picturesquely likens his condition to that of a criminal tied up in a straitjacket. The poet made this image clearer with an alteration to the text in the 1857 edition of the poems where the phrase 'gebunden nach Diebesart' is used – 'bound like a robber', rather than like a rogue – Schelm.) The austere four-bar introduction where B minor momentarily melts into D major gives little hint of the flowering to come. In tune with the words the vocal line is in itself constrained and moves within a narrow compass. The biggest jump is for the word 'Weinen' (b. 12), a leap upwards of a fifth; the twisted lips of the crying baby are depicted in the vocal line with a little motif in falling quavers (b. 13) that is taken up and elaborated by the piano in a touching – but somehow helpless – little interlude (bb. 14–15 with upbeat). The second strophe of the poem is set to more or less the same music for the first seven bars (bb. 16–22 with upbeat). That is until the poet remembers the arrival of his mother (in b. 23) who picks him up from his cradled imprisonment and puts him to her breast. The F sharp minor interlude we have already heard in the accompaniment that depicts the sound of the whimpering child, a lachrymose motif in wafting sixths, is suddenly transformed: the music is inflected into F sharp major thanks to the simple addition of an A sharp and a D sharp (bb. 24–6 with upbeat); this change gloriously encompasses that tiny, quixotic distance between a grimace and a sunlit smile, an instantaneous transformation, as we hear it here – although this is only the first stage on the way to Schubert's depiction of the unparalleled rapture that a very young child feels in its mother's arms. These two interludes where the piano more or less echoes the voice reflect the mimetic nature of babyhood, the baby without speech, but able to take his every cue from the mother, to give back the love as it is received.

At b. 27 there is a change of key signature into B major. This is one of the composer's truly miraculous transformations, and it is impossible to imagine him achieving it without having already written such a song as *Frühlingstraum* D911/11 (from *Winterreise*) where the almost interchangeable boundaries between pleasure and pain are shown to melt one into the other. In the upbeat D sharp ('Dann') at the end of b. 26, quite high in the treble stave, we are aware of a sudden change of height in the position of the baby who has now been picked up in loving arms. Such is Schubert's genius that the very feeling of the child adapting to his new position and nestling into the breast with pleasure and relief is entirely captured in the accented and ornamented passing note of 'lachte' falling to its resolution (b. 27). After this everything is unalloyed bliss. The mood is reminiscent of one of the composer's most famous piano pieces – the G flat Impromptu (D899/3), probably composed a few months before this song. In comparison to this, how earthbound and matter-of-fact is that other suckling song in the lieder repertoire, *An meinem Herzen, an meiner Brust* from Schumann's *Frauenliebe und -leben* Op. 42 no. 7. This is no doubt because in that song a male poet recounts the pleasure from the elated mother's point of view, whereas with Schubert the more ineffable emotion is the child's who narrates through the memory of the poet.

Such is the prodigality of this infinitely generous melody, it is as if we have passed through the portals of long-buried primal experience into a magically reconstituted world of limitless maternal love. Schubert's mother almost certainly sang to him as a very young child, and in this song we feel that he is drawing on enormous reserves of empathy and longing. The inseparable bond of mother and child is reflected in an intertwining of voice and piano (the child's little fingers clutching the breast, the little finger of the pianist's right hand pressing out the melody). In performing this passage singer and pianist feel similarly entwined. For the singer the passage is far from easy, not least because of the length of these *bel canto* lines, and the very few places in the score – bb. 36 and 46 – where the melody pauses for breath. Neither the tempo nor the manner of performance should suggest the unprompted gushing of an open tap. Rather is it as if singer and pianist are gently drawing the music from a well of bounty, the flowing of the cantilena, like mother's milk, an unconditional gift of nature prompted by the most intimate love, but only to be drawn on at a comfortable pace for both donor and receiver. Time stands still for both mother and child, and so it is with the music that moves forward in serene and seraphic manner while hovering and staying put. How seraphic will of course depend on the singer's breath control, but slowness is not the paradigm here; many a performance has foundered because singer and pianist have unaccountably opted to take a slower and more sentimental tempo for this middle section than the *alla breve* set in the opening.

The tent of green silk (bb. 47–50) seems to refer back to a particular memory: is this the cupola of a large cradle lined in silk (unlikely in something already described as a 'narrow chest') or simply a shawl that the mother employs to breastfeed her child with a measure of modesty? Another poem of Leitner, *Der Sarg* (The Coffin), quoted by Susan Youens, makes it clear that the poet also imagines a grave to be 'green-canopied' as if the sleeper were buried under a friendly tree. The idea of a green tent under which there is an exchange of love (life is for the living after all) reminds us of the branches of *Der Lindenbaum* D911/5 from *Winterreise* written a few months earlier. And lo and behold, in bb. 50 and 54–5 (and nowhere else in the song) we find undulations in tell-tale sixths in right-hand triplets similar to those that have curvaceously described the green swaying branches of the linden tree. This is typical of how this composer's mind responded to verbal imagery and nothing to do with knowing self-quotation – had Leitner's 'tent' been blue we probably would have had completely different music.

Now Schubert allows the accompanying triplets to cease gradually and gently as if the child were being laid back into his cradle after being fed. Two-armed engagement (as far as the pianist is concerned) ends at b. 55; after this a ghost of the triplet accompaniment continues in bb. 56–9 as if one hand were continuing to cradle the child, the other to rearrange his bedding. From the semibreve-accompanied b. 60 the baby is on its back again and feeling abandoned. Poet and composer now have to face their own mortality. The cry from the heart that is the arioso of bb. 59–62 ('Vielleicht, wenn das grüne Gras mein Dach') is an extraordinary mixture – fear and pain are mingled with an almost joyful longing for release, the implication being that only death will recapture that sense of peace and freedom from care first experienced as a baby. In the case of Leitner this definitely includes dwelling in a Christian heaven; with Schubert we are less sure. The final strophe of the poem (from b. 65 with upbeat) occasions a change of key signature, back to the dark realms of the B minor opening. The D major sections of this music now seem to indicate the softer gently lit beams of a heaven-haven. The repetition of the poem's final line (bb. 72–3 in B minor, bb. 74–5 in B major) echoes the mimetic nature of the opening verse. This music is simple yet there are signs of uncertainty and fear in the eerie elongation of the final 'tiefesten' in b. 75. The depth of the imagery inspires something paradoxically high in the stave and we might imagine the child within the composer crying out in its fear of desertion, aware, however intuitively, of his imminent demise.

This, however, would be to exaggerate the import of this passing intimation of mortality and to overload the music with a biographical significance it does not have. At the age of twenty-seven and still unmarried, the poet Leitner may reasonably suppose that his mother would live on for many more years (as it turned out it was his wife who was to die an early death). In the last major-key repetition of 'Zur langen, zur letzten und tiefesten Ruh?' there is a graceful sense of acceptance built into the music – the awareness that each generation must inevitably hand over to the next. This music may also be heard as an invocation of 'das Ewig-Weibliche' – the eternal feminine that inspires and guides mankind to noble endeavour. Despite occasional echoes of *Winterreise* it is inappropriate to overdramatize this music, performing it as if it were a Wilhelm Müller song; instead it shares the essential sanity and warmth, gratitude and even-keeled qualities of the other Leitner settings. Schubert seldom allows a song to overreach the message and intentions of its poet: we are left with an impression, true to Leitner himself, that he does indeed believe, and gratefully so, in the loving security of that 'letzte und tiefeste Ruh'.

Autograph:	Hungarian National Library, Budapest
First edition:	Published as Op. 106 no. 3 by Schober's Lithographisches Institut, Vienna in February 1828 (P160)
Dedicatee:	Marie Pachler
Subsequent editions:	Peters: Vol. 4/109; AGA XX 546: Vol. 9/108; NSA IV: Vol. 5a/112; Bärenreiter: Vol. 4/27
Bibliography:	Black 2003, p. 192
	Capell 1928, p. 245
	Fischer-Dieskau 1977, pp. 253–4
	Kecskeméti 1969, pp. 564–8
	Porter 1961, pp. 114–15
	Youens 2002, pp. 249–65
Discography and timing:	Fischer-Dieskau II 9^8 5'33
	Hyperion I 6^{10}
	Hyperion II 35^5 5'31 Anthony Rolfe Johnson

←— *Das Weinen* D926   *Des Fischers Liebesglück* D933 —→

JOHANN HEINRICH VOSS (1751–1826)

For the poetic sources and the list of songs associated with Voss's editorial work on Hölty's poems, *see* the biographical article on that poet, Vol. I/900–901. Of Schubert's twenty-three solo Hölty settings there are nine where Voss's changes were substantial: *An die Nachtigall* D196, *Seufzer* D198 (originally entitled *Die Nachtigall* by Hölty), *Auf den Tod einer Nachtigall* D399 (Hölty's title was *Elegie auf einer Nachtigall*), *Die Knabenzeit* D400, *Minnelied* D429, *Die frühe Liebe* D430 (original title *Minnehuldigung*), *Blumenlied* D431 (*Minnelied*), *Seligkeit* D433 (another *Minnelied*) and *Mailied* D503 (*Maylied*). The original Hölty poems for these, before Voss altered them, are printed in Schochow Vol. 1 pp. 172–94.

Voss was born on 20 February 1751 in Sommersdorf bei Waren in Mecklenberg. The poverty of his background and his strongly Protestant beliefs made him a formidable worker and tough opponent. Illegitmate, he carried a chip on his shoulder all his life against wealth and privilege. Although he had been a friend of Friedrich Leopold von Stolberg (qv) he turned against that poet when Stolberg became Catholic, initiating a notorious literary feud. Voss's industry was extraordinary: editor of various almanacs, author of the famous idyll *Luise. Ein ländliches Gedicht* (1795) and a successful translator of the the epics of Homer, he embarked on a complete Shakespeare trans-

Johann Heinrich Voss, lithograph (1826) from a painting by Wilhelm Tischbein.

lation with his sons at the end of his career. When the Viennese edition of *Shakspeares* [*sic*] *dramatische Werke* appeared in 1826 (read at least in part by Schubert) it included translations of *King Lear* and *Macbeth* by Voss. He died in Heidelberg on 29 March 1826.

Voss appears in this book on account of his editing and rewriting the poems of his former colleague, Ludwig Hölty (qv) who had died at the age of twenty-seven in 1776. Voss was a senior and founding member of the famous 'Göttinger Hainbund' (he gave the group its name), a circle of poets, mainly students at Göttingen University, who made a symbolic vow of friendship one night in 1772 as they danced around an oak tree swearing allegiance

to the Romantic ideals exemplified by the poetry of Klopstock (the classicism of Wieland was anathema to them). The Hölty poems as set by Schubert (and by Brahms and other lieder composers) were in fact the compositions of two distinguished poets in a kind of posthumous collaboration.

Schubert would have read Voss's full name, either on the title page of Hölty's *Gedichte* (Hamburg, Bohn, 1804) or the Viennese edition (*Gedichte*, Wien, Kaulfuss & Ambruster, 1815) where it appears under a rubric indicating the edition had been newly prepared and expanded ('neu besorgt und vermehrt') since the 1785 edition made by Voss with Stolberg's collaboration.

Schubert, watercolour by Wilhelm August Rieder, 1825.

Der WACHTELSCHLAG
(SAUTER) OP. 68, **D742** [H479]
A major   1822?

The quail's cry

(28 bars)

Ach! mir schallt's dorten so lieblich hervor:[1]	Ah, how sweet to me that sound from yonder seems:
Fürchte Gott!	'Fear God!'
Fürchte Gott!	'Fear God!'
Ruft mir die Wachtel ins Ohr!	The quail calls into my ear.
Sitzend im Grünen, von Halmen umhüllt,	Sitting amid the greenery, hidden by the corn,
Mahnt sie den Horcher im Schattengefild:[2]	It exhorts the listener in the field:
Liebe Gott!	'Love God!
Liebe Gott!	'Love God!
Er ist so gütig, so mild.	'He is so gracious and so kind.'
Wieder bedeutet ihr hüpfender Schlag:	Again its leaping call signifies:
Lobe Gott!	'Praise God!
Lobe Gott!	'Praise God!
Der dich zu lohnen vermag.	'For He can reward you.'
Siehst du die herrlichen Früchte im Feld?[3]	Do you see the wonderful fruits of the field?
Nimm es zu Herzen, Bewohner der Welt:	Reflect on them in your hearts, dwellers on this earth.
Danke Gott!	'Give thanks to God!
Danke Gott!	'Give thanks to God!
Der dich ernährt und erhält.	For He nourishes and sustains you.'
Schreckt dich im Wetter der Herr der Natur:[4]	If the Lord of Nature terrifies you in the storm,
Bitte Gott!	'Pray to God!'
Bitte Gott!	'Pray to God!

[1] On the whole Beethoven's deviations from the text (almanac edited by C. Lang, 1799) are also Schubert's, but Sauter and Beethoven have the less personal 'Ach! *wie* schallt's dorten'.
[2] In AGA and Peters Edition the last word in this line was changed to 'Saatengefild' (as in Beethoven) but the NSA restores 'Schattengefild' from Schubert's autograph – only possibly intentional on Schubert's part.
[3] Sauter writes 'Siehst du die herrlichen *Früchten* im Feld?'
[4] Sauter writes 'Schreckt *mich* im Wetter der Herr der Natur'.

Ruft sie, er schonet die Flur.	'He spares the fields when they call to Him.'
Machen Gefahren der Krieger dir bang:[5]	If the perils from warriors make you fearful,
[...][6]	[...]
Traue Gott!	'Trust in God!
Traue Gott!	'Trust in God!
Sieh', er verziehet nicht lang.	See, He does not tarry long.'

SAMUEL FRIEDRICH SAUTER (1766–1846); poem written 23 June 1796

This is Schubert's only setting of a Sauter text. See the poet's biography.

Schubert's songs contain many references to bird life. One thinks of feathered creatures as diverse as the ominous crow (*Die Krähe* D911/15) from *Winterreise* and the enchanting nightingale which stars in the quartet *Die Nachtigall* D724, as well as in poems by Hölty and Claudius, both titled *An die Nachtigall* (D196 and D497), and also makes a crucial guest appearance in *Ganymed* D544. Doves are to be heard in *Die Mainacht* D194 and *Lebensmelodien* D395 (the eagle otherwise dominates this song, and the swan also glides serenely through it) and Schubert's last song, *Die Taubenpost* D965A, was memorably devoted to the pigeon, trusty messenger of love. We also enjoy the sprightliness of the lark in Shakespeare's *Ständchen* D889, and in Mayrhofer's *Sehnsucht* D516 where the bird is cast as an operatic diva and where cranes feature in the song's sublime closing section. The cuckoo makes appearances here and there, the best of which is in Mayrhofer's *Einsamkeit* D620, and there is also a tiny suggestion of his call, a descending major third, at the end of the piano's opening ritornello in *Frühlingstraum* from *Winterreise* D911/11, a song where the raucous cock-crow has the starring role. There is, of course, also *Die Vögel* D691, a Schlegel setting where no particular species is mentioned, but the whole feathered race is characterized as flighty, cheeky and birdbrained.

The nightingale's song is variously characterized by trills and tripping little scales, but Schubert is no exacting ornithologist and atmosphere is more important than a Messiaen-like *Catalogue d'oiseaux*. In *Der Wachtelschlag*, however, the actual sound of the quail's call is evoked in the dotted figuration that dominates the piece – three repeated notes interpreted by the poet as denoting various supposedly pious aspects of the bird's nature. These notes (albeit not in dotted rhythm, but marked mezzo staccato) are to be heard high in the treble clef in bb. 9–10 of the Mayrhofer setting *Schlaflied* D527 where the fluting of the quail is mentioned in the poem's second strophe. The call of the bird, *Coturnix coturnix*, has been rhythmically characterized in English as 'quick-wee-wick' or 'wet my lips' but, as Capell points out, English-speakers, for whom quails' eggs are mostly a foreign delicacy, do not have the same relationship with this species as the Germans, or even the French. We do not warm to this song in the same way as those who have heard the call of the quail from childhood. In Germany the bird has long been a part of folklore, regarded as a wise and God-fearing creature. Sauter's poem (published in Carl Lang's almanac of 1799 and, for some time, thought to derive from Metastasio) was a reworking of an old lyric which later appeared in *Des Knaben Wunderhorn* (1819). The other possibility is that those rather casual anthologists Arnim and Brentano collected an adaptation of Sauter and passed it off as age-old.[7]

Beethoven set these words as a piano-accompanied mini-cantata in 1803 (WoO 129, published 1804); later, in the *Pastoral* Symphony Op. 68, he was to assign this bird-call in dotted rhythm

---

[5] Sauter writes 'Machen Gefahren *des Krieges mir* bang'.
[6] There is a line missing here in both Beethoven and Schubert's settings. It is 'Tröstet mich wieder der Wachtelgesang' – 'The quail's song once again comforts me'.
[7] A poem entitled *Wachtelwacht* appears in Vol. 1 (p. 159) of this famous anthology with the opening line 'Hört wie die Wachtel im Grünen schön schlagt'.

to the oboe, with the flute impersonating the nightingale and the clarinet the cuckoo. Schubert usually quails before Beethoven, but here he quails after him – he adopts some of his ideas and textures by way of homage. It is clear that a printed copy of Beethoven's song, rather than Lang's *Almanach und Taschenbuch für hausliche und gesellsehaftliche Freuden* (1799), was in Schubert's possession on the day he composed his own setting. The younger composer opted for a more straightforward treatment, for there is a side to his nature that was as smitten by the older traditions of strophic-song simplicity as by the musical experiments that marked him out as rather avant-garde in the eyes of the public. It is as if he felt a sense of historical responsibility to keep the North German traditions going, at the same time as supplanting them. It took texts of this kind, with thoroughly old-fashioned associations, to summon up the part of his creative process that relished folksong simplicity, earthbound in the least pejorative sense. John Reed points out that Schubert was likely at this period of his life to have been concerned with the 'strength and the simplicity of the vocal line'. This was probably an antidote to his interest in extravagant piano accompaniments at the end of 1820 and the beginning of 1821.

The song shares its tonality with *Die Vögel*. That it is well made and somewhat Beethovenian is hardly surprising, although the three crucial notes that form the basis of the whole piece are somehow prophetic of the tiny elfin trumpets we hear in the accompaniment of *Ständchen* ('Horch!, horch! die Lerch') D589. The quail's cry (almost always on three repeated notes in the introduction, and also within the main body of the song) is sometimes rendered on two adjacent notes in the vocal line, a higher note for the first syllable. There is thus a clash of a major second between voice and piano at 'Liebe Gott' in the first verse (bb. 12–13) which somehow gives the birdcall (or 'Schlag') a more abrasive, outdoor flavour. The music is otherwise strophic, with a change into the tonic minor for the third verse which refers to war (from b. 16 where the sharps of the key signature are cancelled). It is here that Schubert's music seems not quite grand or dramatic enough for the words, whereas Beethoven takes up the challenge more elaborately (losing a sense of avian proportion while doing so), with rumbling basses to depict the thunder of fire on the battlefield. Schubert's song ends with a repeat of the four-bar introduction.

The Italian translation that appeared beneath the German text in the song's second edition (Diabelli, May 1827) is printed in the NSA where the whole song is given the alternative title of *Il canto della quaglia*. (The Italian text is also reprinted in Schochow 1974, Volume 2, p. 503.) Because Beethoven did not acknowledge a poet in the first edition of his song Schubert was also at a loss. It was clearly thought by such collectors as Wittezcek, Weiser and Kreissle that the poem was by Metastasio, and this idea probably came from Schubert himself. In the absence of any matching text by Metastasio, it is likely that an Italian translation in Metastasio style was made by Nicolaus Craigher de Jachelutta. This was surely also part of Schubert's scheme, hatched together with this poet, to extend the commercial viability of his songs in non-German-speaking lands. As none of Diabelli's other publications of Schubert's songs exist in two languages (the original issue of *Der Wachtelschlag* as a supplement in the *Wiener Zeitschrift* on 30 July 1822 was in German only) this bilingual aspect of the 1827 publication must have been at Schubert's behest.

It is worth remarking that the most ebullient quails in the entire song literature (Verlaine's 'Milles cailles / Chantent, chantent dans le thym') are to be found in the *Avant que tu ne t'en ailles*, the sixth song of Fauré's *La Bonne Chanson*. Here the song of the quail is depicted in exactly the same dotted rhythm as we find in Schubert and Beethoven, although in melodic terms the three-note motif begins with a rising perfect fourth followed by a fall of a major second.

Autograph:	Missing or lost
First edition:	Published as a supplement to the *Wiener Zeitschrift für Kunst, Literatur, Theater und Mode* on 30 July 1822; subsequently published as Op. 68 by Diabelli, Vienna in May 1827 (P120)

Subsequent editions: Peters: Vol. 2/134; AGA XX 401: Vol. 7/2; NSA IV: Vol. 3a/132;
                            Bärenreiter: Vol. 2/158
Bibliography: Capell 1928, p. 173
                            Friedlaender 1902, Vol. 2, p. 450
                            Reid 2007, pp. 117–20
                            Shackleton 2012
Discography and timing: Fischer-Dieskau II 5[1]   2'07
                            Hyperion I 28[10]
                            Hyperion II 25[5]   1'47   Maarten Koningsberger

← *Ihr Grab* D736   *Naturgenuss* D422 →

WALDESNACHT *see* IM WALDE D708

Der WALLENSTEINER LANZKNECHT BEIM TRUNK
(LEITNER) **D931** [H654]
G minor   November 1827

Wallensteiner's infantryman drinking

(32 bars)

He! schenket mir im Helme ein,	Here, pour it into my helmet;
Der ist des Knappen Becher,	That's the squire's cup!
Er ist nicht seicht und, traun, nicht klein,	It's not shallow or, indeed, small,
Das freut den wackern Zecher.	Which pleases the lusty drinker.
Er schützte mich zu tausendmal	It has protected me a thousand times
Vor Kolben, Schwert und Spiessen,	From club, sword and spear;
Er dient mir jetzt als Trinkpokal	Now it serves me as a drinking cup,
Und in der Nacht als Kissen.	And at night as a pillow.
Vor Lützen traf ihn jüngst ein Speer,	At Lützen lately it was hit by a spear;
Bin fast ins Gras gesunken,	I almost sank to the ground.
Ja, wär' er durch, – hätt' nimmermehr	Yes, had it gone through
Ein Tröpfelchen getrunken;	I would never have drunk another drop.
Doch kam's nicht so, ich danke dir,[1]	But it was not so, thanks to you
Du brave Pickelhaube!	My good helmet!
Der Schwede büsste bald dafür	The Swede soon paid the price
Und röchelte im Staube.	And bit the dust.

[1] Leitner writes '*Doch's kam* nicht so, ich danke dir'.

Nu! tröst' ihn Gott! Schenkt ein, schenkt ein!	Well, God comfort him! Pour, pour!
Mein Krug hat tiefe Wunden,	My tankard has deep wounds
Doch hält er noch den deutschen Wein,	But it can still hold German wine
Und soll mir oft noch munden.	And I shall often relish it.

KARL GOTTFRIED VON LEITNER (1800–1890); poem written in 1819

This is the seventh of Schubert's eleven Leitner solo settings (1822–3 and 1827–8). See the poet's biography for a chronological list of all the Leitner settings.

The rise and fall of Albrecht Wenzel von Wallenstein (1583–1634) is one of the most dramatic stories of seventeenth-century German history. The tragic aspects of this extraordinary soldier and warlord's life prompted Friedrich von Schiller to write a trilogy of plays between 1797 and 1799, comprising *Wallensteins Lager, Die Piccolomini* and *Wallensteins Tod. Des Mädchens Klage* (set by Schubert as D6, D191 and D389) is a poem taken from the second of these plays, sung by Wallenstein's daughter Thekla. Two songs to the same poem entitled *Thekla (eine Geisterstimme)* purport to be a report on Wallenstein's afterlife when both father and daughter are reunited in the afterlife. These were set as D73 and D595.

Wallenstein's long and complicated career had as its background the Thirty Years War and the rivalry of the German states with the Holy Roman Empire ruled by the Habsburg dynasty in Vienna. For the first time since the Middle Ages, Wallenstein's efforts made the military might of the Empire something to be reckoned with. However, he became too powerful in his own right and was assassinated at the command of his former masters. Wallenstein was a mercenary and an operator, but Schiller's plays did much to ennoble his reputation. His betrayal at the hands of the emperor in Vienna was considered a perfidious disgrace, and a noble Styrian like the poet Leitner would have seen him as a hero. Rather than put words into the mouth of such a great character, Leitner contents himself with allowing us to glimpse something of the Wallenstein legend through the memories of a soldier in his cups. Mention of Lützen in the third verse denotes the famous battle of 16 November 1632. Wallenstein himself was to survive only two more years. The brag about the dying Swedish soldier in the fourth verse refers obliquely to the great Swedish King Gustavus Adolphus who was also killed on that day in Lützen, something any German-speaking schoolchild knew at the time. On that occasion the Swedish troops prevailed over Wallenstein's forces, but this was only one battle lost in a continuing war. For Wallenstein himself Lützen marked the beginning of the end; he had grown so mighty and self-sufficient that the emperor in Vienna regarded him as a dangerous traitor. Only his stout-hearted men loved him to the end (they are the real heroes of the first of the Schiller plays) and we can hear this in Leitner's poem which gives voice to one of that intrepid band, a foot soldier ('Lanzknecht' derives from 'Landsknecht' and has nothing to with a lancer) who rejoices in his memories. The Styrian poet was a staunch admirer of Schiller and no avid supporter of the Metternich regime; in the same year that Schubert composed this song, the poet had fallen foul of the censors in Vienna (*see* poet's biography).

This portrait of an off-duty soldier has much in common with Schubert's many evocations of fishermen, hunters and other working types. The idea of viewing an episode of history through the eyes of the 'little people', small in importance but large of heart, goes back to Shakespeare, and was greatly appreciated by German-speaking poets of Goethe's generation. This miniature, ostensibly a drinking song, is probably meant to pack a stronger punch than it does. Einstein finds the music 'nothing like powerful enough', but Schubert, not a man in love with violence, has fashioned music for a military man who possibly did not play as significant a part on the battlefield as he now boasts – a sort of Germanic Falstaff. In the midst of descriptions

Albrecht Wenzel von Wallenstein, hero of Schiller's
trilogy.

of bloodshed there is a Don Quixote-like geniality. Aware that he was dealing with a seventeenth-century character, Schubert adopts the archaic style that he employs to evoke an earlier century. The sturdy music in a rollicking rhythm, veering between G minor and B flat major 'in a reckless way', as Capell puts it, suggests the modes without actually being modal. (The soldier and his battle-scarred helmet are certainly not *à la mode*.) Much of the music, where both the pianist's hands are on the same notes, is scarcely harmonized. That it does not sound thin at this point is a result of Schubert's ability to imply harmonies without actually writing them. The 𝄴 *Bewegung* and the unisons between the hands in the accompaniment recall another determined Schubertian character from earlier in 1827, the surly hunter of *Jägers Liebeslied* D909, but there is an even greater match in tonality and time signature with another superannuated old-timer from 1823 – *Der zürnende Barde* D785.

The illustration of Wallenstein (*left*) is one that Schubert himself might well have known. It is taken from the *Gesamtausgabe* of Schiller's work that was published in Vienna in 1810 by Anton Doll, the composer's source for all his Schiller settings.

Autograph:	Wienbibliothek im Rathaus, Vienna
First edition:	Published as a supplement to Anton Strauss's *Gemeinnütziger und erheiternder Haus-Kalendar für das oesterreichische Kaiserthum* in Vienna in 1830; subsequently published as Book 27 no. 1 of the Nachlass by Diabelli, Vienna in October 1835 (P312). The song had been advertised by Haslinger in January 1829 as one of his publications 'Unter der Presse'. This song, along with several others including *Der Winterabend* D938 was clearly sold to Diabelli before the appearance of the Haslinger edition.
Subsequent editions:	Peters: Vol. 3/198; AGA XX 548: Vol. 9/112; NSA IV: Vol. 14a/72; Bärenreiter: Vol. 4/100
Arrangements:	Arr. Tilman Hoppstock (b. 1961) for guitar accompaniment, in *Franz Schubert: 110 Lieder* (2009)
Discography and timing:	Fischer-Dieskau II 9[9] 3'20
	Hyperion I 36[14] 3'11 Gerald Finley
	Hyperion II 35[7]

← *Des Fischers Liebesglück* D933   *Der Kreuzzug* D932 →

Die WALLFAHRT

(Rückert) **D₂778A** [H524]
(Sketch) F minor   1823?

The pilgrimage

(16 bars)

Meine Tränen im Bussgewand	My tears in penitential robes
Die Wallfahrt haben	Set off this pilgrimage
Zur Kaaba der Schönheit angetreten;	To the Kaaba of beauty;
In der Wüste brennendem Sand	In the desert's burning sand,
Sind sie begraben,	They are buried
Nicht hingelangten sie anzubeten.	For they did not arrive to worship.

FRIEDRICH RÜCKERT (1788–1866)

This is the last of Schubert's six Rückert solo settings (1822–3). See the poet's biography for a chronological list of all the Rückert settings.

This is a relatively recent discovery – the music emerged only in 1968. The late Reinhard Van Hoorickx discovered a copy of the song (not the autograph) as a result of his excavations in the Cornaro family's library, a source of a number of significant Schubertian treasures. The text was later identified as coming from the *Östliche Rosen* of Rückert, the collection of that poet's work, published in 1822, from which all the other Schubert Rückert settings were taken. In that volume the poem is printed opposite 'Dass der Ostwind Düfte' (p. 368) which Schubert set as *Dass sie hier gewesen* D775. As he was working on that song, the composer's eye was probably drawn to page 369, and these sixteen bars were almost certainly the result of a few minutes' work.

Schubert probably did not consider *Die Wallfahrt* worth preserving. The other Rückert songs (*Sei mir gegrüsst* D741, *Dass sie hier gewesen* D775, *Du bist die Ruh* D776, *Lachen und Weinen* D777, *Greisengesang* D778) all have love as their *raison d'être* but this sombre lyric of a futile, love-related pilgrimage does not seem truly to have inspired the composer. The poem is a short one, and thus also the song, its effect limited by the brevity of the text. If Schubert had bothered to persevere, the music might well have been reworked into a more sophisticated form (we are reminded that the first version of *Greisengesang* had none of its subsequently enlivening coloratura). *Die Wallfahrt* seems more like a sketch for bass voice, simple and noble, though hardly memorable, and it is just possible to read into this simplicity a Middle Eastern atmosphere, as if a chant were being intoned from a minaret.

The phrase 'Kaaba der Schönheit' (bb. 6–7) requires some explication. The Kaaba, a cuboid stone structure, 43 feet high, is the most sacred site in Islam, standing at the centre of the great mosque in Mecca. It is said to have been built by Abraham and his son Ishmael (who appears, wordlessly, as a child in *Hagars Klage* D5). Every follower of Islam aspires to visit the Kaaba in pilgrimage at least once in their lives. In a way that might give offence to a devout Muslim, Rückert (always able to bring his immense knowledge of oriental culture to his verse) imagines a temple of beauty unconnected with the Islamic religion, a metaphor perhaps for someone so beautiful that they embody beauty itself as a sacred quality. Schubert, attracted to medieval imagery involving the Crusades (cf. the subject matter of the operas *Fierabras* D796 and *Der Graf von Gleichen* D918), is a dab hand at pilgrimages, and often manages a tone of holy consecration. We can see the beginning of something of the like here; and the Leitner setting *Der Kreuzzug* D932 from 1827 is a fully realized (and westernized) version of a similar idea.

Autograph:	Missing or lost
First edition:	Published as *Die Wahlfahrt* ed. Reinhard Van Hoorickx, by Bärenreiter, Kassel in 1969 and subsequently as part of the NSA in 1992 (P808)
Subsequent editions:	Not in Peters; Not in AGA; NSA IV: Vol. 13/64
Discography and timing:	Fischer-Dieskau —
	Hyperion I 35[9]
	Hyperion II 27[12] 0'58 Maarten Koningsberger

← *Du bist die Ruh* D776   *Rosamunde: Romanze* D797/3b →

Der WANDERER   The wanderer
(Schmidt 'von Lübeck') Op. 4 no. 1, **D489** [H308]

The song exists in three versions, the third of which is discussed below:
(1) October 1816; (2) Zseliz, summer 1818?; (3) appeared end of May 1821

(1)   'Langsam'   C♯ minor – E major   ¢   [74 bars]

(2)   'Langsam'   B minor – D major   ¢   [72 bars]

(3)   C♯ minor – E major

Ich komme vom Gebirge her;	I come from the mountains;
Es dampft das Tal, es braust das Meer,[1]	The valley steams, the ocean roars.
Ich wandle still, bin wenig froh,	I wander, silent and joyless,
Und immer fragt der Seufzer – wo?	And my sighs for ever ask: Where?
Die Sonne dünkt mich hier so kalt,	The sun seems so cold here,
Die Blüte welk, das Leben alt;	The blossom faded, life old,

[1] In Schubert's most likely source, Deinhard-Deinhardstein's anthology *Dichtung für Kunstredner*: 'Es dampft das Tal, es *rauscht* das Meer'.

Und was sie reden, leerer Schall, –	And men's words mere hollow noise;
Ich bin ein Fremdling überall.	I am a stranger everywhere.

Wo bist du, mein geliebtes Land?	Where are you, my beloved land?
Gesucht, geahnt und nie gekannt,	Sought, dreamt of, yet never known!
Das Land, das Land, so hoffnungsgrün,	The land so green with hope,
Das Land, wo meine Rosen blüh'n;	The land where my roses bloom,

Wo meine Freunde wandeln geh'n,[2]	Where my friends walk,
Wo meine Toten aufersteh'n,	Where my dead ones rise again,
Das Land, das meine Sprache spricht,	The land that speaks my tongue,
O Land, wo bist du?[3]	O land, where are you?

Ich wandle still, bin wenig froh,	I wander, silent and joyless,
Und immer fragt der Seufzer – wo? –	And my sighs for ever ask: Where?
Im Geisterhauch tönt's mir zurück.	In a ghostly whisper the answer comes:
'D o r t, wo du n i c h t bist, dort ist das G l ü c k!'[4]	'*There*, where you are *not*, is *happiness!*'

GEORG PHILLIP SCHMIDT ('VON LÜBECK') (1766–1849); poem written before 1808

This is Schubert's only setting of a Schmidt text. See the poet's biography.

If Schubert's youthful opera-going had fired his imagination, his apprenticeship as a composer of long narrative texts was equally crucial. Without having worked on all those lengthy, episodic early works, it is unlikely that he could have written a mini-cantata like this, made up of different elements, while preserving a strong sense of unity. *Der Wanderer* captured the public's imagination like few other Schubert songs. Only *Erlkönig* D328 could rival its reputation in the composer's own lifetime. It was said to have earned the publisher Diabelli 27,000 florins within forty years – this according to Capell, rightly angered on Schubert's behalf that the composer had been deftly fleeced of his rightful reward.

The song still seems relevant today, although Schubert regularly set much better poems than this. The tragic events of the twentieth century – war and genocide on a scale undreamed of in the nineteenth – gave the words a new resonance, in the same way as the longing to return home of Goethe's 'Kennst du das Land?' seemed more powerful in the wake of the Holocaust and the Second World War. Added to this, the works of Sigmund Freud and his disciples have made us all conversant with neurosis, introspection and the psychological effects of alienation. The wanderer is more likely to be one of us than a shadowy picture painted by Caspar David Friedrich. Indeed, even the itinerant concert artist of the time was no stranger to feelings of disorientation and emptiness, the longing for home and the sound of his own language. And so the situation remains with many a travelling performer.

The song begins with throbbing right-hand triplets in the piano – something else that *Der Wanderer* shares with *Erlkönig*. But the drama is generated by harmony rather than rhythm. (The song is marked 'Sehr langsam', although an *alla breve* time signature and the composer's metronome marking keep the music flowing.) The right hand plays hushed C sharps in triplets, while the left, deep in the bass clef, spells out the first three notes of a C sharp major arpeggio:

[2] In *Dichtung für Kunstredner*: 'Wo meine Freunde *wandelnd* geh'n'.
[3] The line 'O Land, wo bist du?' is Schubert's own interpolation. In *Dichtung für Kunstredner* the strophe ends with the lines 'Und a l l e s hat, was mir gebricht?' ('And has *all* that I lack.')
[4] The second 'dort' in this line is Schubert's own addition.

C sharp – E sharp – G sharp. There is something typically Schubertian about the way a song in the minor key begins with major-key harmony. Each bar from b. 1 to b. 7 begins on this low C sharp pedal and climbs in different directions; bar by bar the right hand makes tiny changes to vary the harmonies of the triplets – a D natural is added to the single C sharps to make a minor second which then opens out into three notes in a diminished chord for the third bar. The widening harmonies are a metaphor for the stain of grief that spreads slowly over both staves and seeps into the fabric of the song. The diminished-seventh harmony, aided by a crescendo, leads to a new outpost – F sharp minor in second inversion (b. 4). The right hand then moves to another diminished chord on the C sharp pedal – four notes in the right hand for the first time (b. 5). This built-in intensification adds to a sense of deepening doom. And then we are back to where we began, in C sharp major, with a piano dynamic. Having surveyed the bleak emotional landscape of the wanderer's mind, the pianist can find no avenue of harmonic escape. It is astonishing how much, and how little, can happen in thirty seconds of music.

The entry of the singer ushers in a mirror image of the accompaniment's fruitless journey. In a sequence of short phrases he tells us that he has come from the mountains and finds himself between valley and sea. 'Ich komme vom Gebirge her' is an unaccompanied trudge up the stave where the dotted rhythms shudder with the infinite weariness of a noble and tortured soul. This initial fragment of seeming recitative (it should conform to the song's overall tempo but seldom does) lifts the musical argument into a higher tessitura; the following interjections (the oppressive weather report of 'Es dampft das Tal' and 'es braust das Meer') are sung, separated by an eloquent gap, against a background replay of the opening six bars, cranked up a perfect fourth to F sharp minor. This rise in tension is abetted by the sudden forte outburst of 'es braust das Meer'; a fortissimo repetition of these words leads us back into C sharp minor. For the second time in the song we have come full circle, a metaphor for the fate of the wanderer himself.

A two-bar interlude of right-hand triplets and solemn left-hand minims (bb. 14–15) makes the connection between C sharp minor and E major with gravity and unhurried nobility. At the change to the new key, the piano's bass line vanishes, leaving etiolated triplets in the right hand over which the voice emerges in legato tones, infinitely sweet and long-suffering – 'Ich wandle still, bin wenig froh'. This beautiful fragment of tune makes us realize that eloquent piano writing from the beginning had led us to mistake accompanied recitative or arioso for real melody, and is the song's first real test for the singer. This is a classic example of Schubert's use of the major key to convey suffering, and it confirms the status of the wanderer as a forerunner of the *Winterreise* protagonist. (The haunting and confessional mood of *Der Lindenbaum* D911/5, also in E major, comes to mind.) At b. 18, deep in the cello register, the pianist's left hand echoes 'Ich wandle still'– this is a real colloquy between voice and piano, as if the singer were communing with an inner voice that prompts, guides and haunts him. Mention of a sigh ('Seufzer') at b. 20 brings the vocal line into a higher register: those Es and D sharps in a pianissimo dynamic are a real challenge for someone with a voice deep enough to negotiate the lower passages. 'Immer wo?' (bb. 21–2) is especially testing: these notes oscillating at a distance of a semitone suggest someone trying in vain to focus, scanning the horizon for an answer to an unanswerable question. The sighing and angst of the text are built into the music's technical demands. This section ends with a fermata, in G sharp major.

The following arietta in C sharp minor (beginning 'Die Sonne dünkt mich') lies at the heart of the work. The dactylic rhythm of the accompaniment is the inspiration for the ebullient opening of Schubert's *Wanderer-Fantasie* for solo piano D760 of 1822, but it is only in that work's slow movement that we hear the magisterial elaboration of the eight-bar harmonic sequence that John Reed calls Schubert's 'Sehnsucht' motif. Otherwise the *Fantasie* is a celebration of energy and virtuosity that transcends the pain and solemnity of the original. Schubert employs dactyls to depict forces of nature; in *Der Wanderer* this rhythm (long-short-short) seems to denote the withdrawal of the life force giving light and heat. As well as gloomy links with *Der Tod und das Mädchen* D531 it is noteworthy that the image of faded or withered flowers ('Die Blüte welk') is embedded in a dactylic dead march; in *Trockne Blumen* D795/18 from *Die schöne Müllerin* it inspires a similar tonal analogue. This traveller is not just a victim of bad luck, he is doomed to a living death like the Flying Dutchman or the Wandering Jew. The vocal line is almost rooted to the spot, pivoting around G sharp in obsessive and repetitive fashion. 'Ich bin ein Fremdling überall' (bb. 28–30) is inexplicably poignant. Twice the vocal line stretches upwards – once at 'ein <u>Fremd</u>ling' and again at '<u>ü</u>berall'. In this rise and fall there is the infinite sadness and vulnerability of someone we take to be a noble man. (Schubert makes much use of the power of these intervals in the *Wanderer-Fantasie*.) The technical difficulty for the singer (who risks cracking the higher notes) adds to the tension of the moment. This eight-bar passage, though hardly the equal of the opening page, is expressive in its mood of bleak emptiness (ideal for the meaning of 'Schall').

The next section (marked 'Etwas geschwinder' from b. 32) requires a fine performance to avoid banality and the impression of a trite, rum-ti-tum march. The pianist has to ensure the imploring nature of the chords in thirds, phrased away in a dying fall. These accompany the singer's impassioned questions – 'Wo bist du, mein geliebtes Land?' The change between A major and A minor following the word 'geahnt' (bb. 37–8) is a classic Schubertian illustration of a dream dissolving into disillusionment. Here there are links with *Strophe aus 'Die Götter Griechenlands'* D677, an A major/minor song of 1819 where dotted rhythms invoke, and fail to summon, another lost land, the 'schöne Welt' of ancient Greece. The repeated words 'Wo bist du' are common to both songs.

The wanderer is now getting into his stride. At the song's beginning he seems scarcely to have had the energy to embark on a description of his surroundings. From b. 41, as the music moves into a different rhythm and a faster tempo ('Geschwind' in $\frac{6}{8}$), he becomes almost vehement in his description of what he has lost. This passage is often performed at a ridiculously fast tempo which nullifies the gravity of the character at a stroke, especially if the words are unintelligible. In unsafe hands the Viennese waltz (beginning at 'Das Land, wo meine Rosen blüh'n') can be a disconcertingly jolly affair. This is surely an early ironic use of the cosiness of dance rhythm, as in the unhinged waltz of *Täuschung* D911/19 from *Winterreise* that depicts the brightly lit, human world from which the winter traveller is excluded. The poem is at its weakest here: if the rhyming of 'so hoffnungsgrün' and 'wo meine Rosen blüh'n' (the wanderer as displaced gardener!) seems corny, the roaming of friends ('Wo meine Freunde wandeln geh'n') paired with the resurrection of his dead relations ('Wo meine Toten aufersteh'n') is even more ungainly. The rising sequence of harmonies between bb. 50 and 53 (C sharp major – F sharp minor – E major – A minor) culminating in 'Das Land, das meine Sprache spricht' implies that the absence of his home language is the last straw. In a fine performance of the song these obsessive repetitions of 'meine' can be thrilling in their intensity.

The anguished cadence into E major ('O Land, wo bist du?') interrupts the jingle at just the right time: Schubert sweeps away the second half of Schmidt's rhyming couplet ('Und alles hat, was mir gebricht') in favour of a rhetorical question ('O Land, wo bist du?') of his own devising. This ushers in the concluding section marked 'Wie anfangs; sehr langsam' ('As at the beginning, very slow'). It is here, above all, that *Der Wanderer* justifies its reputation. Three bars of piano interlude (bb. 55–7) move solemnly from E major and back again via F sharp minor with such magisterial dignity that the wanderer's plight seems overwhelmingly moving. Those exposed E major thirds, once again a weary, almost etiolated pulsation in the pianist's right hand, symbolize his vulnerability. The haunting melody of 'Ich wandle still, bin wenig froh' is again superimposed on this background and the skilfully engineered recapitulation of this music gives a symphonic (and thus larger than life) dimension to what might have appeared merely sentimental.

Once more the wanderer sighs his rhetorical question, 'wo?', on a high-lying line where D sharps and Es nudge each other in the head voice (bb. 63–4). The final section is in eight bars where there is a return to the elements of a recitative. At 'Im Geisterhauch tönt's mir zurück' piano and voice descend the stave together into the nether regions ('zurück' requires a low, resonant G sharp). These hushed unisons usher in the last of the poem's challenges to the singer: a phrase in inverted commas spoken, or rather sung, by the 'Geisterhauch' itself, the grim voice of fate, or perhaps the wanderer's own inner voice, the self-punishing anguish that drives him on. The answer to the wanderer's 'immer wo?' encapsulates the horror of his predicament – the discovery that happiness can only exist where he is not. The falling B major triad on 'Dort, wo du [nicht bist]' (b. 67) is a thumbs-down answer to the questing three-note motif of a rising arpeggio with which the song began. 'Dort ist das Glück!' is only a conventional 6-4 cadence but, spread over three spacious bars, it is among the most impressive that Schubert ever composed. It is the lucky singer who can convincingly encompass the low E of the final 'Glück', the very depth of the tone negating the word's meaning. (The composer provides an *ossia* where the upper E is also allowable.) The three-bar postlude is a moving miniature commentary on the sadness of the situation, reflecting elements both of the protagonist's world-weariness and the composer's compassion. Schubert then has the courage and imagination to end this manifestly masculine song with the dying fall of a feminine cadence (cf. the closing bar of *Erster Verlust* D226).

This poem, the creation of an otherwise obscure writer, achieved a certain fame in its own time and was much anthologized in various almanacs. Its derivative nature is nevertheless

Second edition of *Der Wanderer* with an unsigned engraving.

obvious; Schmidt 'von Lübeck' owes his closing phrase to the final line of Schiller's *Der Pilgrim* (qv Schubert's setting of this poem, D794) which ends 'Und das Dort ist niemals hier'. Kreissle tells us that Schubert was made aware of the poem by one Reverend Horni; in any case there was a version of Schmidt's poem in Deinhard-Deinhardstein's *Dichtungen für Kunstredner*. There it had the title of *Der Unglückliche* and was falsely ascribed to the celebrated and charismatic cleric Zacharias Werner (qv) whose name duly appears on the autograph of the first version of the song. When Schubert wrote out a second version (transposed into B minor) for his summer employer the amateur bass Count Esterházy in the summer of 1818, he was still undecided about the title so he gave it three: 'Der Wanderer, / oder / Der Fremdling / oder / Der Unglückliche'. (This transposed version confirms that the vocal challenge of the song has always been in the higher, rather than the lower, reaches of the stave.) When the song was published as Op. 4 no. 1 in September 1821 (the third version, now at last with the correct identity of poet) Schubert probably avoided *Der Unglückliche* as a title because he had composed a Karoline Pichler setting of this name (D713) at the beginning of the same year.

Autograph:	Gesellschaft der Musikfreunde, Vienna (first version, first draft, from the collection of Johannes Brahms)
	In private possession, the Esterházy family (second version)
Publication:	Published as part of the AGA in 1895 (P659; first version)
	Published as part of the NSA in 1970 (P747; second version)
	Op. 4 no. 1 by Cappi & Diabelli, Vienna in May 1821 (P7; third version)
Dedicatee:	Johann Ladislaus Pyrker von Felsö-Eör
First known performance:	19 January 1821 *Abend-Unterhaltung* of the Gesellschaft der Musikfreunde, Vienna. Soloist: August Ritter von Gymnich (see Waidelich/Hilmar Dokumente I No. 67 for full concert programme)
Publication reviews:	*Allgemeine musikalische Zeitung* (Vienna) No. 6 (19 January 1822), col. 43ff. [Waidelich/Hilmar Dokumente I No. 142]
	F. von Hentl, 'Blick auf Schubert's Lieder', *Wiener Zeitschrift für Kunst, Literatur, Theater und Mode* No. 36 (23 March 1822), p. 289f. [Waidelich/Hilmar Dokumente I No. 146; Deutsch Doc. Biog. No. 278]
Subsequent editions:	Peters: Vol. 1/184; AGA XX 266a & b: Vol. 4/217; NSA IV: Vol. 1a/26 & Vol. 1b/200 & 204; Bärenreiter: Vol. 1/20
Bibliography:	Capell 1928, pp. 114–15
	Fischer-Dieskau 1977, pp. 80–82
Further settings and arrangements:	Anselm Hüttenbrenner (1794–1868) *Der Wanderer* (date unknown)
	Arr. Franz Liszt (1811–1886) for solo piano, no. 11 of *Lieder von Schubert* (1837–1838) [*see* TRANSCRIPTIONS]
	Arr. Robert Fanta (1901–1974) for medium voice and orchestra (1947)
Discography and timing:	Fischer-Dieskau I 8[14] 5'47
	Hyperion I 32[21]
	Hyperion II 16[10] 6'03 Christopher Maltman

← *Gesang der Geister über den Wassern* D484   *Der Hirt* D490 →

Der WANDERER   The wanderer
(F. VON SCHLEGEL) OP. 65 NO. 2, **D649** [H417]

The song exists in two versions, the second of which is discussed below:
(1) February 1819; (2) appeared November 1826

(1) 'Langsam'   D major   **C**   [27 bars]

(2)   D major

(27 bars)

Wie deutlich des Mondes Licht	How clearly the moon's light
Zu mir spricht,	Speaks to me,
Mich beseelend zu der Reise:	Inspiring me for my journey:
'Folge treu dem alten Gleise,	'Follow faithfully the old track,
Wähle keine Heimat nicht.	Choose nowhere as your home,
Ew'ge Plage	Lest bad times
Bringen sonst die schweren Tage;	Bring endless cares.
Fort zu andern	You will move on, and go forth
Sollst du wechseln, sollst du wandern,	To other places,
Leicht entfliehend jeder Klage.'	Lightly casting off all grief.'
Sanfte Ebb' und hohe Flut,	Thus, with gentle ebb and swelling flow
Tief im Mut,	Deep within my soul,
Wandr' ich so im Dunkeln weiter,	I walk on in the darkness.
Steige mutig, singe heiter,	I climb boldly, singing merrily,
Und die Welt erscheint mir gut.	And the world seems good to me.
Alles reine	All things pure I see
Seh' ich mild im Widerscheine,	In gentle reflection.
Nichts verworren	Nothing is blurred
In des Tages Glut verdorren:	Or withered in the heat of the day:
Froh umgeben, doch alleine.	There is joy all around, yet I am alone.

FRIEDRICH VON SCHLEGEL (1772–1829); poem written in 1800/1801

This is the fourth of Schubert's sixteen Friedrich von Schlegel solo settings (1818–25). See the poet's biography for a chronological list of all the Friedrich von Schlegel settings. See also the article about the cycle of which this song is part – Abendröte.

This is a song of strange and haunting beauty. As the first two lines make clear it is that oldest of wanderers, the moon, who shares his unique and privileged viewpoint of planet earth with a terrestrial traveller, the poet Friedrich von Schlegel. It is a fittingly atmospheric introduction to the second half of that poet's *Abendröte* poems where twilight has given way to night. In the first half of the collection, mountains, birds, boy, river, rose and butterfly have had their say, but it was this second section of the poetic cycle that first inspired Schubert to music. In his younger years the composer was susceptible to aphorism and homily, both as reader and writer, and this poem seems to have chimed with his mood; indeed 'Steige mutig, singe heiter' ('I climb boldly, singing merrily'), which seems custom-made to describe his unremitting industry and no-nonsense attitude to work, reads like an entry from his 1816 diary. But other images in the text also seem appropriate to his life. He follows the 'old tracks', firmly grounded in the tradition of Mozart and Beethoven, but at the same time he is determined to carve out a separate path from his great predecessors, 'moving on and going forth to other places'. He also needs to leave home, his succession of lodgings over the years perhaps betokening an unwillingness to settle down. The motto 'I see all things clearly in their gentle reflection' is apt for a composer of Schubert's sensibility – it is something that John Keats might have said as he wrote the poems that are contemporary with this song. Above all the last phrase, 'Froh umgeben, doch alleine' ('There is joy all around, yet I am alone'), has utterly Schubertian resonances. Even the most devoted lover of this composer's music can have little idea of the solitary nature of creativity on this scale. Schubert's towering achievements (and they could already be thus described in 1819) were unrecognized even by his closest friends. But loneliness is not only to do with a lack of profound appreciation from others: to write as much music as Schubert did required an iron discipline and thousands of hours of solitary labour. This meant less time in the company of other human beings than an essentially gregarious man might find congenial. Furthermore, every morning as he sat at his work desk, Schubert inhabited his own solar system where the language was spoken by him alone. When he returned from those uncharted territories of mind and imagination, there was no one with whom he could share the experience. Friends who saw him at work found him 'transfigured' by the heat of inspiration. To live and work in a high and starry space inaccessible to one's friends and contemporaries is both blessing and curse, and Schlegel's poem captures this dichotomy as well as the composer's desire to honour his musical forbears ('the old track') while finding new paths and solutions.

Schubert was always drawn to night pictures, and some of his greatest nocturnes were already behind him. We might be tempted to associate the composer's younger years with somewhat melodramatic evocations of dark mystery and foreboding (as in *Der Geistertanz* D116, for example, and the Ossian setting *Die Nacht* D534) and his later years with more spiritual evening pictures (such as *Im Freien* D880 and *Nachthelle* D892), but both genres of night-piece co-exist throughout his oeuvre. He was capable of writing lucid and transparent tributes to moonlight from early on, and some of the most beautiful (*An den Mond* D193, *Die Mondnacht* D238, *Die Sommernacht* D289, and *Klage (an den Mond)* D₂436) are from his teenage years. *Der Wanderer* is somewhat later, but from its mood and texture it belongs to their number; it stands on the threshold between Schubert's youth and maturity.

The word 'deutlich' ('clearly') in the poem's opening phrase governs the mood of the work which is gently luminous throughout. The key is the same as that for *Der Pilgrim* D794 and the much later *Der Kreuzzug* D932, a clear sign that the composer felt that this traveller was on an important spiritual journey. More important than either of these is the Novalis *Nachthymne* D687, also in D major; as the pianist begins *Der Wanderer* the opening of that future transcendental journey takes shape under the fingers.

Harmonic ambivalence sets in right at the beginning: the second crotchet in the accompaniment is a G sharp that misleads the ear into thinking that the song is really in A major; when the vocal line begins it seems to be in the subdominant rather than the tonic. We never quite recover from this deliberate disorientating effect which lends a gentle plagal ambience to much of the song, as if it were floating unanchored in heavenly space. The use of the flattened sixth on 'schweren Tage' (b. 9), 'jeder Klage' (b. 13) and at the end on 'alleine' (b. 25) adds a twist of world-weariness and other-worldliness to what appears, at first glance, to be simple music. The moon is inspiration and companion, a guiding light in the dark world. This is symbolized by the doubling of the voice and bass line, extensive even by Schubert's standards, a technique he used to underline the import of words. Leo Black, in his article 'Voice Doubling Bass', described this as a symbol of submission to a higher force. The moon's aphoristic advice in inverted commas ('Folge treu dem alten Gleise') is given emphasis in this way, but the doubling serves also as a steadying guide-rail, enabling the singer to 'follow faithfully the old track'. At b. 11 and 'Fort zu andern / Sollst du wechseln' he progresses up a chromatic scale (more or less) and then picks his way down the stave in graduated steps of descending fourths (b. 12). On these journeys through the wilds he is still gently shadowed and supported, perhaps one may say directed, by the piano's left hand.

After the haunting cadence of 'jeder Klage' we are ushered into the second verse, for Schubert has turned the poet's lines of irregular length, seemingly composer-unfriendly, into a flowing strophic song – of the modified variety of course. We are almost unaware of the difficulties of the poem's shape, so smoothly and inevitably does one part progress to the next. The vocal line of the second part of the song is more or less the same as that of the first, but the accompaniment is another matter. In bb. 16–18 it is the right hand that shadows the vocal line (under 'Ebb' und hohe Flut, / Tief im Mut, / Wandr' ich so im Dunkeln weiter'), as if the guiding light were clearer still, streaming over the wanderer's right shoulder rather than his left. This doubling continues for only three bars. At 'Steige mutig, singe heiter' the voice finds itself undoubled for the first time, although not unaccompanied. The dotted-rhythm chords accompanying 'singe heiter' briefly establish a new concerted tone of resolve between voice and piano. 'Alles reine / Seh' ich mild im Widerscheine' ends with one of the most touching of Schubertian cadences in b. 22, a crucial difference from the corresponding passage in the first verse. For a moment we can imagine the composer himself singing these words, transfigured, as his friends described, by a glimpse of beauty beyond the comprehension of lesser mortals.

An inner voice in the accompaniment doubles the last phrase, emblematic of the inner understanding that changes the blurred and confusing into something lucid and clear. A hushed cadence with almost religious overtones ends one of the few songs in Schubert's canon which rank as both a personal and an artistic credo. (Others are *An die Musik* D547, *Trost im Liede* D546 and *Des Sängers Habe* D832.)

The NSA prints a first version of this song in Volume 3b. For reasons explained by Walther Dürr in the preface to Volume 3 (p. XXV) the so-called first version (the only surviving autograph – there is no first draft) may be nearer Schubert's final thoughts than the second version used for the publication of Op. 65 (where the text was wrongly ascribed to A. W. Schlegel). It thus behoves performers, especially pianists, to consult this 'first' version and carefully compare it with the second. There are a number of details of phrasing and articulation (mezzo staccato marked for the song's opening chords for example, a turn in b. 22), that add a colour to the song not present in the more familiar version, the first edition reproduced in Peters.

Autograph:	Wienbibliothek im Rathaus, Vienna (first version, fair copy)
Publication:	Published as part of the NSA in 1982 (P784; first version)
	Published as Op. 65 no. 2 by Cappi & Czerny, Vienna in November 1826 (P110; second version)
Publication reviews:	*Berliner allgemeine musikalische Zeitung*, No. 11 (14 March 1827), p. 81ff. [Waidelich/Hilmar Dokumente I No. 461; Deutsch Doc. Biog. No. 826]

WANDERER AN DEN MOND

Subsequent editions:	Peters: Vol. 4/58; AGA XX 351: Vol. 6/5; NSA IV: Vol. 3a/126 & Vol. 3b/234; Bärenreiter: Vol. 2/154
Bibliography:	Black 2001, p. 89
	Capell 1928, pp. 164–5
	Einstein 1951, pp. 187–8
	Fischer-Dieskau 1977, pp. 121–2
Discography and timing:	Fischer-Dieskau II 2[13] 3'33
	Hyperion I 27[15]
	Hyperion II 21[11] 3'36 Matthias Goerne

← *Die Gebüsche* D646   *Der Schmetterling* D633 →

Der WANDERER AN DEN MOND   The wanderer's address to the moon
(SEIDL) OP. 80 NO. 1, **D870** [H594]
G minor   1826

Ich auf der Erd', am Himmel du,[1]
Wir wandern beide rüstig zu:
Ich ernst und trüb, du mild und rein,
Was mag der Unterschied wohl sein?

Ich wandre fremd von Land zu Land,
So heimatlos, so unbekannt;
Bergauf, bergab, waldein, waldaus,
Doch bin ich nirgend, ach! zu Haus.[2]

Du aber wanderst auf und ab
Aus Ostens Wieg' in Westens Grab, –[3]
Wallst Länder ein und Länder aus,
Und bist doch, wo du bist, zu Haus.

I on earth, you in the sky,
Both of us travel briskly on;
I solemn and gloomy, you gentle and pure,
What can be the difference between us?

I wander, a stranger, from land to land,
So homeless, so unknown;
Up and down mountains, in and out of forests,
Yet, alas, nowhere am I at home.

But you wander up and down,
From the east's cradle to the west's grave,
Travel from country to country
And yet are at home wherever you are.

[1] By the 1851 edition of *Lieder der Nacht* this line had been changed to 'Auf Erden – ich, am Himmel-du'.
[2] Seidl writes (*Lieder der Nacht*, 1826) 'Doch *nirgend bin ich* ach! zu Haus'.
[3] Seidl writes (*Lieder der Nacht*, 1826) 'Aus *Westens* Wieg' in *Ostens* Grab'. The fact that in later editions of his poems the poet inverted this image, and changed it to the more logical and scientific text printed above, suggests that he realized he had made a simple mistake. The line 'Aus Westens Wieg'' is to be found in the Peters Edition following the song's first edition, but it is corrected in the AGA. The NSA prints the incorrect version because that is exactly how it appears in Schubert's autograph.

Der Himmel, endlos ausgespannt,	The sky, infinitely extended,
Ist dein geliebtes Heimatland:	Is your beloved homeland;
O glücklich, wer, wohin er geht,	O happy he who, wherever he goes,
Doch auf der Heimat Boden steht!	Still stands on his native soil!

JOHANN GABRIEL SEIDL (1804–1875)

This is the fourth of Schubert's twelve Seidl solo settings (1826–8). See the poet's biography for a chronological list of all the Seidl settings.

It is no accident that the opening tune in G minor has a down to earth quality – that is exactly where the wanderer is, his feet condemned to trudge the unfriendly earth. After a four-bar prelude the vocal line starts in the lower part of the voice as if the singer at 'Ich auf der Erd' is looking down at his feet. At 'am Himmel du' (bb. 4–5) he gazes up at the moon, the tune suddenly jumping an octave into the heavens (b. 6). Both travellers – the moon and its ambulatory admirer – then occupy the middle of the stave at 'Wir wandern beide rüstig zu' (bb. 7–8). In the third line of the first verse this contrast of tessitura also serves to underline a contrast in moods – the traveller's 'ernst und trüb' (b. 11) and the moon's 'mild und rein' (b. 12). It all feels so natural and apt that one needs to remind oneself that it takes a special composer to reflect word to music details in such a way that we take them for granted. There are other things in this song that we scarcely notice on first hearing: the contrasts 'Ich' and 'du' in the first line have been harmonized by the straightforward apposition of G minor and D major chords, tonic and dominant; in the third line the moon music of 'mild und rein' is underpinned by D minor which gives a plaintive modal twist to the proceedings. The question 'Was mag der Unterschied wohl sein?' ends the verse in this same key (b. 15); Schubert then simply changes F natural to F sharp in two chords (D minor – D major) and, lo and behold, we are in the dominant of the home key of G minor. It could not be simpler, but who but Schubert could have done it?

The tune of the second verse (from b. 17) is exactly the same as for the first but for the last three notes that fall earthward as they bitterly sum up the traveller's fate (bb. 27–8). Such a tiny difference as this – an upward inflection for a question ('Was mag der Unterschied wohl sein?') and a downward one for the answer ('Doch bin ich nirgend, ach! zu Haus') – is typical of Schubert's genius for the modified strophic song.

But the greatest marvel is to come – the healing balm of moonlight streaming out in the major key. Up until now the accompaniment has consisted mainly of strongly accented chords, so simple on the page that they could be strummed on a guitar, the traditional instrument of the traveller. Some of the chords are rolled in a no-nonsense manner that helps establish a mood of hearty self-reliance, and the strong dotted rhythm of the jaunty little interlude (bb. 9–10) that introduces the third line of the first verse suggests a certain type of grim courage, even defiance. At the beginning of the third verse ('Du aber wanderst') everything changes as the music softens into the major key. Instead of the heavy accented footfall of the traveller we hear the moon (thanks to flowing semiquavers of the accompaniment and a touch of pedal) floating in a pool of light and well-being. Even more exceptional is that envy, bitterness or unhappiness are banished as the protagonist is overcome by admiration and love; in music of the greatest tenderness he salutes the moon as a marvel of nature. This song is thus a textbook case of Schubert's use of the polarity of major and minor ('the contrast', in Fischer-Dieskau's words, 'of masculine and feminine, of hardness and softness, of light and shade, of day and night') to depict that special realm of the spirit that is far removed from banal reality.

The final verse is a compromise between the hearty opening and the dreamy atmosphere when G major was first introduced into the picture. Compromise is the order of the day, for now the traveller can go on with life with a new perspective; in wishing happiness to those luckier than himself he has recovered his spirits. The four bars of the postlude allow him to walk offstage accompanied by a beam of light, as content as he will ever be.

The tempo of the song is a moot point because 'Etwas bewegt' is not the clearest of markings – what is the 'somewhat' of 'etwas', and how fast is the 'con moto' of 'bewegt'? There has been many a performance at sprightly tempo, taking as its cue the words 'Wir wandern beide rüstig zu' ('we both travel briskly on'). But we have to avoid depicting this wanderer as too cheerful. Here the watch-words imply someone more misanthropic (at least until the intervention of the moon's healing rays), tired of life on the open road, more 'ernst und trüb', less fit and determined. A tempo that suggests a trudge is surely better than one suitable for a sprightly walk. The word 'rüstig' implies vigour and determination rather than speed. In musical terms it must be the performance of the dotted figuration in b. 10 that determines the tempo – this has to allow the fleeting demisemiquaver to *sound* sprightly rather than as a convulsive hiccup.

It is worth noting that the words 'Aus Westens Wieg' in Ostens Grab' in the first edition of Seidl's poems (and thus faithfully set by Schubert) were altered by Seidl himself in later editions of his poems (*Lieder der Nacht*, Sollinger, Wien 1851 p. 23) and can safely be corrected in performance to 'Aus Ostens Wieg' in Westens Grab'. One or two things in twenty-first-century life are as fixed and reliable for us as they were for the composer, including, thank heavens, the workings of the sun and moon – although there have been justifications advanced for the validity of the poet's first version (see Christian Strehk in *Liedlexikon*, 2012, pp. 718–19 for an alternative viewpoint).[1]

Autograph:	Staatsbibliothek Preussischer Kulturbesitz, Berlin (probably an autograph copy of a lost first draft)
First edition:	Published as Op. 80 no. 1 by Tobias Haslinger, Vienna in May 1827 (P125)
Dedicatee:	Josef Witteczek
First known performance:	26 March 1828 at the Musikverein, Vienna as part of the Schubert 'Privatkonzert'. Soloist: Johann Michael Vogl (see Waidelich/Hilmar Dokumente I No. 603 for full concert programme). (The song had also been performed privately at a Schubertiad on 21 April 1827 – see Deutsch Doc. Biog. No. 855)
Performance reviews:	*Allgemeine Musikalische Zeitung* (Leipzig), No. 19 (7 May 1828), col. 307f. [Waidelich/Hilmar Dokumente I No. 613; Deutsch Doc. Biog. No. 1067]. N.B. This reviewer refers not to *Der Wanderer an den Mond*, but to *Fischerweise*, which featured in an earlier draft of the programme and was subsequently removed in favour of D870, probably at Johann Michael Vogl's request. It is clear, therefore, that the critic was not present at the concert (see Waidelich/Hilmar Dokumente II Nos. 599a, 602, 603 and 603a). *Abend-Zeitung* (Dresden), No. 141 (12 June 1828), p. 564 [Waidelich/Hilmar Dokumente I No. 620] *Allgemeine Musikalische Zeitung* (Berlin), No. 27 (2 July 1828), p. 215 [Waidelich/Hilmar Dokumente I No. 624; Deutsch Doc. Biog. No.1069]
Publication reviews:	*Wiener allgemeine Theaterzeitung*, No. 82 (10 July 1827), p. 336 [Waidelich/Hilmar Dokumente I No. 512]

[1] At dawn and twilight both sun and moon are visible in the sky. The rising sun in the East dims the moon (thus 'Ostens Grab') while the setting sun in the West cradles it into new life ('Westens Wieg'').

Allgemeine Musik-Zeitung (Offenbach) No. 23 (19 September 1827), col. 184 [Waidelich/Hilmar Dokumente I No. 526]

Münchener allgemeine Musik-Zeitung, No. 1 (6 October 1827), col. 8 [Waidelich/Hilmar Dokumente I No. 530; Deutsch Doc. Biog. No. 955]

Allgemeine musikalische Zeitung (Leipzig) No. 4 (23 January 1828), col. 49ff. [Waidelich/Hilmar Dokumente I No. 569; Deutsch Doc. Biog. No. 1014]

Allgemeiner Musikalischer Anzeiger (Vienna) No. 19 (9 May 1829), p. 74 [Waidelich/Hilmar Dokumente I No. 726]

Berliner allgemeine musikalische Zeitung, No. 20 (14 May 1828), p. 157f. [Waidelich/Hilmar Dokumente II No. 613a]

Subsequent editions:	Peters: Vol. 4/59; AGA XX 506: Vol. 8/234; NSA IV: Vol. 4/3; Bärenreiter: Vol. 3/2
Bibliography:	Fischer-Dieskau 1977, pp. 197–8
Discography and timing:	Fischer-Dieskau II 8[15] 2'10
	Hyperion I 15[12] 1'55 Margaret Price
	Hyperion I 26[17] 2'08 Richard Jackson
	Hyperion II 31[17] 2'08 Richard Jackson

←— *Das Zügenglöcklein* D871   *Im Freien* D880 —→

Das WANDERN *see Die SCHÖNE MÜLLERIN* D795/1

WANDRERS NACHTLIED (I)[1]   Wayfarer's night song
(GOETHE) OP. 4 NO. 3, **D224** [H115]
G♭ major   5 July 1815

(16 bars)

Der du von dem Himmel bist,
Alles Leid und Schmerzen stillst,
Den, der doppelt elend ist,
Doppelt mit Entzückung[2] füllst,
Ach! ich bin des Treibens müde!
Was soll all der Schmerz und Lust?
Süsser Friede,
Komm, ach komm in meine Brust!

You who are from heaven,
Who assuage all grief and suffering,
And fill him who is doubly wretched
Doubly with delight, new life?
Ah! I am weary of striving!
To what end is all this pain and joy?
Sweet peace,
Enter my heart!

[1] In both songs entitled *Wandrers Nachtlied* (D224 and D768) Schubert changes Goethe's title of *Wanderers Nachtlied*.
[2] Goethe's original is 'mit *Erquickung füllest*' – fills with refreshment.

JOHANN WOLFGANG VON GOETHE (1749–1832); poem written 12 February 1776

This is the sixteenth of Schubert's seventy-five Goethe solo settings (1814–26). See the poet's biography for a chronological list of all the Goethe settings.

Schubert followed the setting of this poem with two other masterpieces on the same day, *Der Fischer* D225 and *Erster Verlust* D226. After writing this ineffably haunting *Wandrers Nachtlied* most other composers (having spent a lifetime trying in vain to achieve a similar level of concentration in their music) would have taken the rest of the day off. This song is in every way a distillation, the very essence of the lied.

Lorraine Byrne points out that 'the figure of the wanderer is as recurrent in Goethe's poetry as it is in Schubert's songs'. Goethe in his *Dichtung und Wahrheit* relates how he was called 'the wanderer' in his early Frankfurt years – 'a personal association is immediately identifiable'. The poem was written at the beginning of Goethe's stay in Weimar (where he was to remain for most of his life), and in the early stages of his relationship with the aristocratic Charlotte von Stein who was to soften the rough edges of the young firebrand and help to change him into a courtier and a statesman. Like many of the poet's finest lyrics of the period it was sent to Charlotte as an enclosure in a letter. It was her refined example and her schooling of the poet that made the youthful Goethe realize that a lifetime of *Sturm und Drang* was a ridiculous prospect for a grown man; he had been forever on the move and now he needed to settle down both physically and mentally.

By setting Goethe's 'stillest' and 'füllest' into monosyllables ('stillst' and 'füllst'), Schubert ignores the careful balancing of the poet's alternating masculine and feminine rhymes (originally bist / ist; stillest / füllest; müde / Friede; Lust / Brust). This is the kind of cavalier treatment by a musician that Goethe might have taken great exception to; nevertheless this musician perfectly captures the classical gravity of the words and the poet's yearning for quietus. The choice of tonality reminds us that *Nähe des Geliebten* D162, another comparatively short utterance by the same poet, was composed earlier in 1815 and was also in G flat major. The music's profound emotional content seems appropriately reflected in the orthographic complexity of these six flats (on paper at least, and Schubert's songs all have a life of their own as written artefacts). It is as

Schubert's autograph for *Wandrers Nachtlied*, the copy for Goethe, 1816.

if the composer has selected this exotic tonality to put such songs in a realm of their own – like exquisite timepieces by Fabergé where decorative detail encases and enriches something essentially simple and designed for practical use. For the pianist the effect is of music elevated above the ordinary – also *physically* elevated because much of it is played on the black keys.

The music is a kind of hymn with that slow dactylic rhythm (in the song's opening two bars at least) that in Schubert's music almost always implies an elemental force beyond the control of man – such as the twinkling of stars, or the turning of the earth on its axis. At the opening there surely was never a more profound change between the tonic major (the opening two beats) and the relative minor (beats three and four). We are immediately aware that something sublime is in the making. The solemn yet ardent vocal line begins its slow but ineffable ascent, rising a third in the first bar, with a sequential repetition in the second, as if the singer's gaze is lifting slowly heavenwards. There is a sense of suspended motion on 'stillst', which is accompanied by a dominant seventh chord that opens the door into a world of the deepest yearning. For the third and fourth bars the voice takes wing supported by an acceleration of changing harmonies (G flat major to E flat minor to B flat major with a palindromic return to G flat major for 'Entzückung füllst'). In this music we sense the poet's restlessness and his longing for greater stability – and this before he even tells us that he is weary of striving. When he does so ('Ach! ich bin des Treibens müde!') we encounter an early example of Schubert's mastery of arioso – a way of treating the vocal line with some of the freedom of recitative but with enough melodic interest to ensure a seamless continuity in the song's architecture. (In this respect the song is prophetic of the middle section of *Der Neugierige* D795/6 from *Die schöne Müllerin*.) This 'Ach' and the phrase following it constitute a sigh from the heart of infinite spiritual weariness (the passing note on 'müde' serves to emphasize this malaise); the second half of the section (b. 6 with upbeat) contains one of the most poignant questions in all the song repertoire – what is all this pain and joy *for*? – and the setting of the word 'Lust' rises a semitone mid-vowel, suggesting the uplifted face of a questioning supplicant, begging for an answer to one of life's mysteries.

Via the dominant on 'Lust' we return unequivocally to the tonic, and there we more or less stay, as if anchored at last and secure in our bearings. The impassioned phrase beginning 'Süsser Friede' is an answer to the poet's entreaty, while remaining a plea with a hint of urgency (encompassed by Schubert's 'Etwas geschwinder' marking at b. 7). It is the composer's very special decision to repeat not only the last two lines of Goethe's poem, but also his music for them. The first phrase (bb. 7–8) is marked pianissimo, the second, more ardently, with a forte dynamic that quickly fades into a rapt pianissimo for the end of the song. The single bar of postlude with its gently repeated plagal cadences suggests a prayer answered. The whole of this extraordinary page has suggested a religious experience without involving the slightest sense of churchiness.

The poem was published first in 1780 in the *Christliches Magazin* where its title was *Um Friede* and where it was no doubt taken to be a prayer addressed to God in heaven. And yet something about Goethe's poem (and Schubert's setting of it) widens the context of the poet's address and removes it from the realm of a straightforward Christian hymn. A reader and listener accustomed to the mythological pantheism of *Ganymed* and the classicism of many other Goethe poems will find it easier to imagine the poet addressing the heavens and the gods (as in Mayrhofer's *Lied eines Schiffers an die Dioskuren* D360) rather than Heaven and God. One has the impression that Goethe would have been infinitely more at ease conversing with the Delphic oracle than with Christian dignitaries. Nevertheless, when Schubert was gathering a group of songs together in 1821 to dedicate to that powerful prince of the church, Ladislaus Pyrker, this song clearly came to mind as an eminently suitable epilogue to his Op. 4. There was some justification in ending a set of songs that had begun with the tormented *Der Wanderer* D489 with a song that culminated in a glow of solved problems and peaceful rapprochement.

Autographs:	British Library, London (first draft)
	Staatsbibliothek Preussischer Kulturbesitz, Berlin (fair copy)
First edition:	Published as Op. 4 no. 3 by Cappi & Diabelli, Vienna in May 1821 (P9)
Dedicatee:	Johann Ladislaus Pyrker von Felsö-Eör
First known performance:	7 March 1825, Deutsches Theater, Amsterdam in a benefit concert for the singer Carl Schütz. Soloist: Carl Schütz (see Waidelich/Hilmar Dokumente II No. 318b for concert announcement)
Performance reviews:	*Wiener allgemeine Theaterzeitung* No. 45 (14 April 1825), p. 184 [Waidelich/Hilmar Dokumente I No. 326]
Publication reviews:	*Allgemeine musikalische Zeitung* (Vienna), No. 6 (19 January 1822), col. 43ff. [Waidelich/Hilmar Dokumente I No. 142]
	F. von Hentl, 'Blick auf Schubert's Lieder', *Wiener Zeitschrift für Kunst, Literatur, Theater und Mode* No. 36 (23 March 1822), p. 289f. [Waidelich/Hilmar Dokumente I No. 146; Deutsch Doc. Biog. No. 278]
Subsequent editions:	Peters: Vol. 2/8; AGA XX 87: Vol. 2/70; NSA IV: Vol. 1a/34; Bärenreiter: Vol. 1/27
Bibliography:	Byrne 2003, pp. 121–3
	Capell 1928, p. 102
	Einstein 1951, p. 110
	Fischer-Dieskau 1977, pp. 43–4
Further settings and arrangements:	Johann Friedrich Reichardt (1752–1814) *Wanderers Nachtlied* (1794) and in four-part setting (1796)
	Philipp Christoph Kayser (1755–1823) *Um Friede* (1777)
	Carl Friedrich Zelter (1758–1832) *Wanderers Nachtlied* (1807)
	Carl Loewe (1796–1869) *Der du von dem Himmel bist* (1828)
	Fanny Mendelssohn (1805–1847) *Wanderers Nachtlied* (1825)
	Franz Liszt (1811–1886) *Der du von dem Himmel Bist*, four versions (1843, arr. piano solo 1843; 1856, 1860, 1870)
	Hugo Wolf (1860–1903) *Wanderers Nachtlied* (1887)
	Hans Pfitzner (1869–1949) *Wanderers Nachtlied* Op. 40 no. 5 (1932)
	Alexander Zemlinsky (1871–1942) *Wanderers Nachtlied* Op. 27 no. 12 (1937)
	Nikolai Medtner (1879–1951) *Wandrers Nachtlied I*, no. 1 of *12 pesen Gyote* [12 Goethe-Lieder] Op. 15 no. 1 (1905–7)
	Joseph Marx (1882–1964) *Wanderers Nachtlied* (1906)
	Arr. Tilman Hoppstock (b. 1961) for guitar accompaniment, in *Franz Schubert: 110 Lieder* (2009)
Discography and timing:	Fischer-Dieskau I 4[7] 1'51
	Hyperion I 1[8]
	Hyperion II 7[15] 1'35 Janet Baker

← *Lieb Minna* D222   *Der Fischer* D225 →

WANDRERS NACHTLIED (II)[1]   Wayfarer's night song
(Goethe) Op. 96 no. 3, **D768** [H551]
B♭ major   Before 25 May 1824

Über allen Gipfeln	Over all the peaks
Ist Ruh',	There is peace;
In allen Wipfeln	In all the treetops
Spürest du	You feel
Kaum einen Hauch	Scarcely a breath of air;
Die Vöglein schweigen im Walde.	The little birds in the forest are silent.
Warte nur, balde	Wait!
Ruhest du auch.	Soon you too will be at rest.

JOHANN WOLFGANG VON GOETHE (1749–1832); poem written 6/7 September 1780

This is the seventy-first of Schubert's seventy-five Goethe solo settings (1814–26). See the poet's biography for a chronological list of all the Goethe settings.

This is a conjunction of the purest genius: one of the greatest poems in the world, and one of the greatest single pages of music – only fourteen bars long but perfect in every way, the ideal combination of simplicity and deep feeling. It is extremely rare that we encounter at this exalted level a total unanimity of approach and understanding between poet and composer. The lyric has inspired others to do their best: Zelter's *Ruhe* (1814) is a fine song that really creates an atmosphere, and Loewe's setting (*c.* 1817), with its pulsating crotchet accompaniment, is also satisfying; Schumann's *Nachtlied* (1850), one of the underestimated songs from his last period, weaves a mood of profound stillnesss; even Liszt set the poem (in two versions, 1848 and 1860) with what seems admirable restraint in comparison to some of his treatment of song texts; Fanny Mendelssohn, Reger and Ives have all had a go too. But nothing compares with Schubert's song which captures the poignancy of this text like no other.

The poem dates from September 1780. It was first written in pencil on the wall of a small room on the upper floor of a hunting chalet or hermitage belonging to the Duke of Weimar on the Gickelhahn, the highest of the mountains in the vicinity of Ilmenau, near Weimar. Goethe was an energetic thirty-one-year old tasked with civil-service duties on behalf of his noble employer. On this day he had climbed up high to view the sunset. 'Apart from the smoke rising here and there from the charcoal-kilns, the whole scene is motionless', he wrote to Charlotte von Stein. He returned there in August 1813, a few weeks before his sixty-fourth birthday, and renewed the writing on the wall. But it was on his last visit on 27 August 1827, the day before his eighty-second birthday, when these words struck him as a forceful reminder of his own

---

[1] Schubert changes Goethe's title *Ein gleiches* ('Similar One') (*Gedichte*, 1815) to *Wandrers Nachtlied* II. This is no doubt because the poem follows on from *Wanderers Nachtlied* ('Der du von Himmel bist') in that edition. For both songs Schubert changes 'Wanderer' to 'Wandrer'.

The hunting chalet at Ilmenau, burnt down in 1870.

mortality. When Goethe himself described this incident to his friend, the Berlin composer Karl Friedrich Zelter (letter of 4 September 1831), his observations were dryly philosophical; he reflected on how much had happened in the intervening time, how much life had changed – in effect, how much water had passed under the bridge. But on that day at Ilmenau the poet had been in the company of Berg-Inspektor Johann Christian Mahr who left a much more emotional description of the incident: 'Goethe read these lines and tears flowed down his cheeks. Very slowly he drew a snow-white handkerchief from his dark brown coat, dried his eyes and spoke in a soft, mournful tone: "Yes, wait! Soon you too will be at rest!"'

This story is even more moving if we reflect that when the poet dried his tears, Franz Schubert had already been dead for nearly three years. Goethe, in his letter to Zelter, wrote of *Wanderers Nachtlied* as a poem 'that you, on the pinions of music, have so sweetly and movingly drawn through the world'. Zelter's setting is effective, but not nearly as heart-stopping as the song that Schubert had composed in Vienna some nine years before the poet's last visit to the hunting lodge. Goethe was right: these words *have* resounded through the world thanks to music – not Zelter's, however, but Schubert's. And how many countless friends has the poet made who otherwise would never have heard of him (particularly in the English-speaking world) had it not been for music? That Goethe is revered by English-speakers is partly thanks to *Faust*, but no other single work, or body of work from the purely literary standpoint, can rival the amplification of his fame on account of the worldwide reception of the lied. Countless listeners, first enamoured of German song, have come to revere German literature through music.

The poem was published under the title *Ein gleiches* ('A Similar One') so that it is a pendant to the first *Wanderers Nachtlied* D224 – 'Der du von dem Himmel bist', set by Schubert in 1815. It is a model of concision and conceals the logic and clarity of Goethe the scientist. The massive peace of which the poem speaks comes in ordered stages and pervades the whole of Creation. First the mountain peaks ('Gipfeln'), the mineral world on which the poet was a considerable authority. Then, in the treetops (Wipfeln) scarcely any movement can be detected: Flora is still. We ascend the ladder of Creation. Next comes the repose of Fauna as the birds fall silent ('Die Vöglein schweigen'). And finally, at the summit, Man – nature's greatest achievement – who will soon rest also. Everything is so ordered and logical that we can scarcely believe the overwhelming poetic effect; but therein lies the power of Goethe. This is a perfect example of his greatness – the extraordinary balance in his nature between artist and scientist, between fantasy and truth (*Dichtung und Wahrheit*, if you will), between the wise judgement of Apollo (who weighs each syllable and tests the truth of each statement) and Dionysus (who fills what might otherwise have been dry and learned with a rush of sensual feeling). This poem truly contains the completeness of Goethe – the clinical eye of observation tempered by the great-hearted compassion so much more extraordinary than a sentimental story about a snow-white handkerchief. There is unerring ability to live in the present, to celebrate what is actually happening at any given moment. At the same time the poet is able to perceive the larger picture, in terms of both time and space (for this view from Ilmenau is a vast and glorious panorama, no matter how pithy the poem). Goethe understood something that English writers (and composers) after Shakespeare had forgotten, and not yet re-learned in 1780, or even much later: the greatest art of the most learned poet could take the form of a simple lyric – truthful, unpretentious, yet serious, and eminently suitable for musical setting.

The key is B flat major, one of Schubert's more neutral tonalities, although one can think of other spellbinding night-scenes in this key such as *Nachthelle* D892 and *Der Winterabend* D938. On reflection, because the scene is beyond emotion and in a sense impersonal, one understands the choice. The introduction in solemn dactyls announces something softly significant and universal and we immediately sense the inscrutable majesty of a defining moment in nature. The piano sound is cushioned and smooth, the spacing of the chords suggesting the solemnity of ceremonial within the tessitura of tenor and bass singing in close harmony; at this pitch we might hear the mournful tone of an alphorn resounding across the valleys. (Schubert also chose B flat major to depict the wide open spaces of *Der Hirt auf dem Felsen* D965.) There is a hint of a melodic shape in the introduction that pre-shadows the contour of the vocal line, and the 6-4/5-3 cadence in b. 1 makes magic of a harmonic cliché. In b. 2 a dominant-tonic cadence is another commonplace somehow turned to gold. With Spartan economy Schubert later uses this figure as the accompaniment to the song's two closing bars, including the single bar of postlude.

At the entry of the voice both singer and audience are already in the grip of an atmosphere where profound emotion has been conjured from thin air. The singing observer is very still; the vocal line begins on a level plateau of B flats. There is a small upward inflection as his gaze takes in the sight of the peaks (at 'Gipfeln') until a return to B flat on 'Ruh', where Goethe has provided his own vowel-music for a word that sounds ineffably peaceful. At 'in *allen* Wipfeln' (b. 4) there is a jump of a fourth as the singer refocuses his gaze to the middle distance and sees the treetops, all of them. The eye is at work, but the body is stationary. This tranquillity must be reflected by the singer's seamless *mezza voce* legato. At 'Wipfeln / Spürest du' (b. 5) the introduction of a German sixth in the accompaniment adds the first note of chromatic poignancy and mystery, and we are witness to a sight so mighty that a shiver runs down the spine. In the semiquaver syncopations between the hands we hear the last stirrings of nature before complete repose. At 'Kaum einen Hauch' (supported by a diminished-seventh harmony, b. 6) the concentration deepens. There is 'scarcely' a breath of air, but the accompaniment tells us there is still some movement in the distance. The dotted crotchet D flat on 'kaum' has the observer transfixed, waiting to see whether a trace of wind remains in the treetops, straining to hear the dying music of nature. The tree-rustlings have been depicted in the lower octaves of the piano, and from b. 7 the birds twitter over a lighter, clearer piano texture. They are not yet silent (that moment is to come); they are in the process of falling silent, and Schubert allows himself to repeat 'schweigen' (b. 8) with a touch of affectionate vocal cantilena for their fading strain.

There is a moment of silence for the voice (only a quaver) after 'im Walde' and we hear the last rustling in B flat major from the piano. Then the devastating change to G minor for 'Warte nur' – the beginning of Goethe's immortal closing sentence. Richard Stokes describes it as '*Momento mori*, lyric and epigram all in one: the comma after "Warte nur" is hair-raising – the threat is real'. We have arrived at nature's total silence, something almost as eerie as a total eclipse, and the point of the whole song. Only the observer standing on the hill is not at rest. From our privileged vantage point we have viewed all the various aspects of Creation and we are reminded that we are no less susceptible to change and decay than they are. It is difficult to say whether what follows is meant as a warning or a promise of release, and Schubert pitches his music in such a way as to include both possibilities. In b. 9 the two settings of 'Warte nur' (descending phrases in dotted rhythm, first in G minor, then opening out to F^7) are rather stern. But in the

Misty valleys at Ilmenau, sketch by Goethe, 1776.

setting of 'balde', and a return to the tonic chord of B flat major, we encounter something consolatory, as if the voice and soul in their twinned upward flight to the heady realms of *mezza voce* have touched the hem of the divine garment. This tiny word, 'soon' – a gentle horn-call in b. 10 where voice and piano part in contrary motion – promises ineffable peace. But it also mirrors our fear of the unknown, and our reluctance to leave all this beauty behind us. The preceding bars (from 'Warte nur') are now repeated, although rebarred in a subtly different way. This near-symmetry is a masterstroke; only the greatest composers are unafraid to repeat their ideas. This makes of the closing of the song a solemn ritual and a benediction where the gravitas of inevitability ('Soon you too will be at rest') sets the seal on an imperishable masterpiece. The ornamentation of the word 'balde' in bb. 10 and 12 that exists as an *ossia* in the song's first edition is surely unnecessary, although some singers have liked to add the turn to the second appearance of the word. Again this adds nothing to the original – the phrase is difficult enough to sing perfectly as it is.

It is not possible to set an exact date to the song beyond the fact that it must have been written well before May 1824 when Schubert set off for his long summer sojourn in Zseliz and whence he refers to it, not in his possession at the time, in a letter. Deutsch places the song as the last of the five important Goethe settings composed in December 1822, thus the last Goethe setting of all (apart from the Mignon settings of 1826, reworkings of poems that had already occupied Schubert for some years). John Reed supports Deutsch's hypothesis although it is also possible, as Walther Dürr points out, that the song was written as early as 1820.

Autograph:	Missing or lost
First edition:	Published as a supplement to the *Wiener Zeitschrift für Kunst, Literatur, Theater und Mode* on 23 June 1827; subsequently published as Op. 96 no. 3 by Schober's Lithographisches Institut, Vienna in the summer of 1828. The same piece appeared shortly afterwards as Op. 101 no. 4 published by H. A. Probst, Leipzig in late 1828 (P167)
Dedicatee:	Maria Karolina Fürstin von Kinsky (in Op. 96)
Subsequent editions:	Peters: Vol. 1/229; AGA XX 420: Vol. 7/70; NSA IV: Vol. 5/66; Bärenreiter: Vol. 3/197

Bibliography:	Capell 1928, pp. 182–3
	Dürr, Introduction to NSA IV Volume 5a p. XXII
	Einstein 1951, p. 254
	Fischer-Dieskau 1977, pp. 187–8
Further settings and arrangements:	Carl Friedrich Zelter (1758–1832) *Ruhe* (1814)
	Carl Loewe (1796–1869) *Über allen Gipfeln ist Ruh* Op. 9 no. 3 (*c.* 1817)
	Fanny Mendelssohn (1805–1847) *Über allen Gipfeln ist Ruh* (1835)
	Robert Schumann (1810–1856) *Nachtlied* Op. 96 no. 1 (1850)
	Franz Liszt (1811–1886) *Über allen Gipfeln ist Ruh* for male chorus, three versions (1844, 1849, 1856)
	Max Reger (1873–1916) *Abendlied* Op. 14 no. 2, duet for soprano and alto (1894)
	Charles Ives (1874–1954) *Ilmenau*, 'Wandrers Nachtlied' (*c.* 1903)
	Herbert Howells (1892–1983) *Wanderer's Night Song* from *In Green Ways* Op. 43 no. 4 (1928) with piano or orchestral accompaniment
	Arr. Tilman Hoppstock (b. 1961) for guitar accompaniment, in *Franz Schubert: 110 Lieder* (2009)
Discography and timing:	Fischer-Dieskau II 5[18] 2'32
	Hyperion I 34[19]
	Hyperion II 29[6] 1'55 Simon Keenlyside

← *Gondelfahrer* D809   *Gebet* D815 →

JOHANN CHRISTOPH WANNOVIUS (1753–1814)

THE POETIC SOURCES

This text possibly appeared in an issue, from the early 1780s, of the rare almanac, *Poetische*   *Blumenlese der Preussichen Staaten*.

THE SONG

25 August 1815   *Das Leben ist ein Traum* D269 [Trio, SSA]

Very little is known about Wannovius, the poet of Schubert's vocal trio (he is not listed in Goedeke). He was born on 4 November 1753 in Königsberg, formerly the easternmost city in Germany and now Kaliningrad in the Russian Federation. He studied there and worked as a lawyer, becoming 'Hofgericht Advocat' in 1779. He was known as an opera librettist rather than a poet – *Lenore* (based on Bürger's poem) was published in Danzig in 1779. He died in 1814.

WAS IST SILVIA, SAGET AN *see* GESANG (AN SILVIA) D891

WASSERFLUT *see* *WINTERREISE* D911/6

Der WEGWEISER *see* *WINTERREISE* D911/20

Die WEHMUT (Salis-Seewis) *see* Die HERBSTNACHT D404

WEHMUT   Melancholy
(M. VON COLLIN) OP. 22 NO. 2, **D772**[1] [H509]
D minor   1822 or early 1823

(39 bars)

Wenn ich durch Wald und Fluren geh',[2]	When I walk through the woods and fields,
Es wird mir dann so wohl und weh	I feel so happy and yet so sad
In unruhvoller Brust.[3]	In my unquiet heart;
So wohl, so weh, wenn ich die Au	So happy and so sad when I behold
In ihrer Schönheit Fülle schau',	The meadows in the fullness of their beauty,
Und all die Frühlingslust.[4]	And all the joy of spring.
Denn was im Winde tönend weht,	For all that blows and echoes in the wind,
Was aufgetürmt gen Himmel steht,[5]	All that towers up towards heaven,
Und auch der Mensch, so hold vertraut[6]	And man himself, communing so fondly
Mit all der Schönheit, die er schaut,	With all the beauty he beholds
Entschwindet, und vergeht.	All shall vanish and perish.

MATTHÄUS VON COLLIN (1779–1824)

This is the fourth of Schubert's five Matthäus von Collin settings (1816, 1822–3). See the poet's biography for a chronological list of all the Matthäus von Collin settings.

The commentators vie with each other to praise this song, and rightly so. For Capell it is 'luxurious in its expression of grief', and for Einstein it contains 'the whole greatness and unaffected simplicity of Schubert in a nutshell'. The work is only a page long in the Peters Edition (an over-generous three in the NSA, a format that seems to contradict the music's concision) but it has the stature and grandeur of a much longer song, so much is packed into its modest span. The key to it all is the ambiguity between 'wohl' and 'weh', between major and minor, the transient joy that brings tears. Spring was always a poignant season for Schubert, and the whole idea of 'Frühlings-lust' was double-edged; in *Im Frühling* D882 and *Frühlingsglaube* D686 he composed some of his greatest music that combines happiness with melancholy. His setting of *Wehmut* makes us grateful that he encountered Collin's poem in its earlier version, as printed in Ignaz Castelli's almanac *Selam* in 1813. The changes that Collin later made to it are somehow less Schubertian – the springtime imagery of 'Frühlingslust' is replaced by the poet's second thoughts – 'grüne Lust'

---

[1] The poem as printed here is exactly as Schubert found it in Castelli's almanac *Selam*, 1813. The alterations listed in the footnotes represent Collin's later thoughts regarding the poems as printed in the posthumous edition of his works.
[2] Collin (in *Naturgefühl*, published posthumously in *Nachgelassene Gedichte*, 1827) later writes: 'Wenn ich *auf hohem Berge steh*'.
[3] Collin later writes 'In *tiefer, stiller* Brust'.
[4] Collin later writes 'Und all die *grüne* Lust'.
[5] Collin later writes 'Was aufgetürmt *zum* Himmel steht'.
[6] Collin later writes 'Und auch der Mensch, so *eng* vertraut'.

(green happiness). These are admirable words, especially in terms of today's threatened planet, but the heart-stopping setting of the compound noun 'Frühlingslust' in this song, miraculous grace notes and all, would have been lost to us. In the revised text the narrator stands and observes from a high mountain ('auf hohem Berge') while the original, as set by Schubert, places the poet in the woods and fields, preferring not to give mankind the opportunity, in this instance, to look down on nature. For those who might have imagined that Schubert had altered these words himself (and that was the theory before the discovery of the *Selam* source) one would have to point out that Matthäus von Collin was a very powerful man in Vienna, an extremely useful friend and patron, and Schubert would certainly have thought twice before simply rewriting the poem to the extent that commentators once believed. It is likely that *Wehmut* was composed at the end of 1822, at the same time as *Der Zwerg* D771 – the ballad of the queen and her dwarf that is entitled *Treubruch* in its Selam printing of 1813 (also set by Schubert almost without alteration – although Collin himself later considerably amended the text).

In *Wehmut* the drama and poignancy of the world's re-birth (and to what purpose? – it will all soon die again) is amply foreshadowed by the piano's two bars of weighty introduction, and the voice enters over a repeat of these same harmonies. The tug of the unquiet heart (we feel this almost physically in bb. 7–8 on the accented words '<u>un</u>ruh<u>vo</u>ller Brust') pervades the song up to the ravishing shift into F sharp major at b. 11. With this, and the word 'Schönheit' (b. 11), the picture is suffused with the glow of the irresistible beauties of the here and now. The spread chords played by the open hand in bb. 11–13 leave the pianist with the curious feeling of wanting physically to stretch out and embrace these meadows while being unable to do so. The decorative turn on the word 'Frühlingslust' enshrines a similar regret in the vocal line. In modern times those feeling this impulse on looking at such a beautiful landscape would reach for a camera (or mobile phone) in an attempt to preserve the vision, but it is precisely this, in the absence of Caspar David Friedrich at his elbow, that the poet is unable to do. The sight, like beauty itself, slips from his eyes and, by extension, from the pianist's fingers; the interlude at bb. 14–15 is a sad echo of the vocal line of bb. 12–13.

The music begins to shiver in muted tremolando, inspired obviously enough by the wind in the poem, but on another level, deeper than tremor or earthquake: what is really happening is a sea change of perception. The harmonic metamorphoses are slow-moving but ineluctable – from A in the bass climbing to B flat to B natural, with that last note as the foundation for a change (with tiny shifts of finger, now in the right hand) from B major up a semitone to E minor (G at the top), up a further semitone to E major (G sharp at the top); once this chord of E major in second inversion has been reached (where it sustains and supports a wonderfully arched setting of the word 'Schönheit', the second such in the song) the bass rises from B to B sharp to C sharp. From C sharp minor there is another tiny shift of finger to the second inversion of A^7 and the inevitable return to D minor in b. 25. This whole section is a metaphor for the passage of time, with harmonies shifting in a stealthy pincer movement that gradually squeezes human beings out of the picture; listening to this music is like watching a speeded-up film of the seasons, one melding into the other, with mankind reduced to a puny supporting role in the drama.

As ever, Schubert is masterful in his unleashing of a middle section that leaves the reprise subtly yet irrevocably altered by what has been learned in the storm. This technique is used to devastating effect in the slow movements of some of the late piano sonatas and in the String Quintet D956. When this song comes to its 'recapitulation' at b. 25 (the semiquaver oscillations cease and there is a return to chords in minims) the musical idea of the song's opening is treated differently. The first three bars (bb. 25–7) have the same harmony as bb. 3–4 in elongated form. The second time the word 'entschwindet' appears (bb. 26–7) the falling bass line (now plunging in semibreves) somehow conveys humility before the forces of nature and an acceptance of mankind's inevitable fate. This is followed by the wide-open spaces of the song's coda where there is nothing but chords in inexorable semibreves. The hushed void of *Meeres Stille* D216 comes to mind, and the same feeling of being adrift within a boundless sea or destiny beyond mortal control. The change from major to minor under the first appearance of the word 'vergeht' (bb. 32–4) takes all the colour from life, and seems to drain all memory of nature's beauty before our very ears. The second 'vergeht' (bb. 36–7) and the bleak jump of a downward fifth in the vocal line returns mankind to the arms of nescience. The two-bar postlude has something bitter about it, as if the sentence of the cruellest judge were being confirmed on appeal. Cruelty and death are also themes of another Collin setting, *Der Zwerg*, which was published with *Wehmut* in May 1823 as the first song of Op. 22, and during the greatest crisis of the composer's life. These songs clearly belong with each other, and not only because they share the same poet.

Autograph:	Missing or lost
First edition:	Published as Op. 22 no. 2 by Sauer & Leidesdorf, Vienna in May 1823 (P40)
Dedicatee:	Matthäus von Collin
Publication reviews:	*Allgemeine musikalische Zeitung* (Leipzig), No. 26 (24 June 1824), col. 425–8 [Waidelich/Hilmar Dokumente I No. 282; Deutsch Doc. Biog. No. 479]
Subsequent editions:	Peters: Vol. 3/15; AGA XX 426: Vol. 7/102; NSA IV: Vol. 1a/168; Bärenreiter: Vol. 1/134
Bibliography:	Capell 1928, pp. 184–5
	Einstein 1951, p. 255
	Fischer-Dieskau 1977, p. 172
	Newbould 1997, pp. 154 & 156
	Youens 2002, pp. 50–79
Discography and timing:	Fischer-Dieskau II 6² 3'03
	Hyperion I 5⁴
	Hyperion II 26¹⁵ 3'10 Elizabeth Connell

← *Nacht und Träume* D827   *Die Verschworenen (Ich schleiche bang und still herum)* D787/2 →

Der WEIBERFREUND The Ladies' man
(COWLEY/RATSCHKY) **D271** [H157]
A major   25 August 1815

A literal rendering of Ratschky's free version is given here. The first three verses of Cowley's original poem, entitled 'The Inconstant', are printed after it (from the 1684 edition) in italics. (The complete seven-strophe poem and six-strophe translation are in Schochow 1974, Volume 2, pp. 462–3.)

Noch fand von Evens Töchterscharen	Among the daughters of Eve
Ich keine, die mir nicht gefiel.	I have never yet found one that displeased me.
Von fünfzehn bis zu fünfzig Jahren	From fifteen years to fifiy
Ist jede meiner Wünsche Ziel.	Each one is the object of my desires.
Durch Farb' und Form, durch Witz und Güte,	Everything about them delights me –
Durch alles fühl' ich mich entzückt—	Colour and shape, wit and goodness
Ein Ebenbild der Aphrodite	Each one that my eyes behold
Ist jede, die mein Aug' erblickt.	Is an image of Aphrodite.
Selbst die vermag mein Herz zu angeln,	Even she in whom all charms are deemed lacking
Bei der man jeden Reiz vermisst:	Has the power to win my heart:
Mag immerhin ihr alles mangeln,	It matters not that she lacks everything
Wenn's nur ein weiblich Wesen ist!	As long as she is a female creature!
[. . . 3 . . .]	[. . . 3 . . .]

> *I never yet could see that face*
> *Which had no dart for me;*
> *From fifteen years, to fifties space,*
> *They all victorious be.*
> *Love thou'rt a* Devil: *if I may call thee* One,
> *For sure in* Me *thy name is* Legion.
>
>   Colour, *or* Shape, *good* Limbs, *or* Face,
>   Goodness, *or* Wit *in all I find.*
>   *In* Motion *or in* Speech *a grace,*
>   *If all fail, yet, 'tis* Woman-kind;
>   *And I'm so weak the* Pistol *need not be*
>   Double, *or* treble charg'd *to murder* Me.
>
>   *If Tall, the Name of* Proper *slays;*
>   *If Fair, she's pleasant as the* Light;
>   *If Low, her* Prettiness *does please:*
>   *If* Black, *what* Lover *loves not* Night?
>   *If Tallow-haired, I Love, lest it should be*
>   T *h' excuse to others for not loving* Me.

[. . . 4 . . .]

ABRAHAM COWLEY (1618–1667) translated by JOSEPH FRANZ VON RATSCHKY (1757–1810)

This is Schubert's only setting of Cowley, and his only setting of a translation by Ratschky.
See both poets' biographies.

This is the least known of all the songs to texts by British poets. In the company of the great Scott songs, the Colley Cibber song *Der blinde Knabe* D833 and the three well-known Shakespeare settings, it is of no great consequence. It is in John Reed's words 'a pretty trifle . . . but a well crafted one'. It is also by far the most risqué of the English texts, coming as it does from the period of Restoration comedy. Ratschky's version is shorter and more personal than the original – a little gem of courtly elegance. The spectrum of women's ages, between fifteen and fifty, seems less shocking in the light of the age of consent being ten in Cowley's time. The predominant influence, as in *Der Traum* D213, is Papageno. Even the shape of the melody here is reminiscent of his 'Der Vogelfänger bin ich ja' from *Die Zauberflöte*. It is not hard to see why it has never caught on as a recital item as its tessitura makes it very hard to sing. It was written on an exceptional day: 25 August 1815 also saw the composition of two vocal quartets with piano, a trio, one setting each by Baumberg, Tiedge and Matthisson, and two songs to anonymous texts, including *Lilla an die Morgenröte* D273. It seems that the composer's psyche (his guiding influence in his choice of texts) maintained an unconscious balance between poems that placed love on a romantic pedestal and those (such as this, in the hot summer days of 1815) which concentrate on pressing matters in hand – love as something more immediate and physical.

Autograph:	Wienbibliothek im Rathaus (first draft)
First edition:	Published as part of the AGA in 1895 (P575)
Subsequent editions:	Not in Peters; AGA XX 128: Vol. 3/57; NSA IV: Vol. 9/15
Discography and timing:	Fischer-Dieskau I 5[12] 0'34 (first strophe only)
	Hyperion I 10[16]
	Hyperion II 9[18] 1'52 Martyn Hill

← *An die Sonne* D270 *An die Sonne* D272 →

Das WEINEN Weeping
(LEITNER) OP. 106 NO. 2, **D926** [H651]
D major Autumn 1827

(27 bars)

Gar tröstlich kommt geronnen	The sacred source of tears
Der Tränen heil'ger Quell,	Flows comfortingly,
Recht wie ein Heilungs-Bronnen,	Like a healing spring
So bitter, heiss und hell,	So bitter, hot and clear.
Darum du Brust voll Wunden,	Therefore, my heart, full of wounds,
Voll Gram und stiller Pein,	Grief and silent pain,
Und willst du bald gesunden,	If you would recover quickly
So tauche da hinein.	Immerse yourself there.
Es wohnt in diesen Wellen	A secret, magic power
Geheime Wunderkraft,	Dwells in these waters
Die ist für wehe Stellen	That is gentle balm
Ein linder Balsamsaft.	To wounds.
Die wächst mit deinen Schmerzen,	It increases with your suffering,

Und fasset, hebt und rollt	And seizes, lifts and rolls away
Den bösen Stein vom Herzen,	From your heart the evil stone
Der dich zerdrücken wollt'.	That would crush you.
Das hab' ich selbst empfunden	I have felt this myself
Hier in dem Trauerland,	Here in this land of sorrow,
Wenn ich, vom Flor umwunden,	When, swathed in crepe,
An lieben Gräbern stand.	I stood at the graves of dear ones.
Da schalt in irrem Wähnen	There, in demented frenzy,
Ich selbst auf meinen Gott,	I cursed my God;
Es hielten nur die Tränen	Only my tears kept
Der Hoffnung Schiffchen flott.	The ship of hope afloat.
Drum, hält dich auch umfangen	Therefore, when you too are ensnared
Der Schwermut trübste Nacht,	In the darkest night of sorrow,
Vertrau' in allem Bangen	In your anguish trust
Der Tränen Zaubermacht.	The magic power of tears.
Bald, wenn vom heissen Weinen	Soon, when from bitter weeping
Dir rot das Auge glüht,	Your eyes glow red,
Wird neu der Tag erscheinen,	A new day will appear,
Weil schon der Morgen blüht.	For already morning is radiant.

KARL GOTTFRIED VON LEITNER (1800–1890); poem written in 1821

This is the fifth of Schubert's eleven Leitner solo settings (1822–3 and 1827–8). See the poet's biography for a chronological list of all the Leitner settings.

In a letter written from Vienna on 26 April 1828 Johann Baptist Jenger informs posterity which of Schubert's lieder were completed during the composer's stay in Graz in 1827. It is addressed to Marie Pachler, Schubert's hostess in that city, and the dedicatee of a collection of songs about to be published:

> *Vienna, 26 April, 1828. The booklet of songs by friend Schubert which he dedicates to you – and which Fräulein Irene Kiesewetter, your deputy, has accepted in your name – has already been passed for engraving. It contains the following songs: 1. Heimliches Lieben 2. Das Weinen 3. Vor meiner Wiege (the last two by Leitner). 4. Altschottische Ballade. The first and last composed in your house. When Schubert and I come to you – which will doubtless be at the end of August – we shall bring some copies with us for you . . .*

From this it appears that *Das Weinen* was not written in Graz itself, but only sometime later – any time between October 1827 and early 1828. It also reveals that Schubert had plans to recapture the mood of the happy summer of 1827 by returning to Styria in 1828. In the event these plans had to be abandoned for financial reasons. The rather bloodthirsty *Eine altschottische Ballade* D923 – called *Edward* in Loewe's solo and Brahms's duet settings – was abandoned as part of this printed garland of songs for Marie Pachler; it had certainly been written in her house and at her encouragement, but in the end the more approachable and charming *Gesang (An Silvia)* D891 was considered a more suitable final song for the collection. Schober no doubt played some part in this choice as the book of songs was first issued by the Lithographisches Institut of which he was the somewhat hapless manager.

With the exception of *Der Wallensteiner Lanzknecht beim Trunk* D931, *Das Weinen* is the least ambitious of the Leitner songs, although its publication in Volume 2 of Friedlaender's Peters Edtion shows that at some point in the last quarter of the nineteenth century it was popular with singers. This is no longer the case – one now hears this song on the concert platform very rarely, if at all. The 'pilgrimage' key of D major has obvious links with the reverential *Der Kreuzzug* D932 and the *innig* character of the music with such Leitner masterpieces as *Vor meiner Wiege* D927 and *Der Winterabend* D938. Mention of the curative power of tears brings to mind a number of other songs: Goethe's *Wonne der Wehmut* D260 which deals with the tears of unrequited love rather than bereavement, and some of the contemporary songs of *Winterreise*, particularly the strophic *Wasserflut* D911/6 with its powerful image of a river of tears capable of melting ice. But *Das Weinen* is a great deal more soft edged and sentimental than the Müller song; were Leitner to be judged on this text alone it would be difficult to understand what persuaded Marie Pachler to recommend the poet to the composer so wholeheartedly.

Among the commentators only Fischer-Dieskau sees Schubert's choice of text as having some connection with his desperation at the resumption of his syphilitic symptoms in the autumn of 1827. Fischer-Dieskau quotes the song's first verse to make his point, but this nevertheless remains a contentious opinion – although the work's dedication to Marie Pachler (as well as the fact that Schubert wrote to her mentioning the return of his 'usual headaches' – perhaps the ongoing consequences of mercury poisoning) suggests that she might have been his confidante, perhaps even in connection with his health worries. Marie Pachler was, after all, a highly sophisticated artist and, despite living in the provinces, a woman of the world. It is also possible that Jenger, who was well informed on all aspects of Viennese gossip, discreetly informed the Pachlers of the background, a censored version perhaps, regarding Schubert's illness.

The somewhat pious mood of *Das Weinen* is familiar from such pieces as *Vom Mitleiden Mariä* D632 and *Pax Vobiscum* D551. The music adopts the style of a chorale without actually being one – it is less rigid and more flowing as befits the water imagery of the poem. The gentle introduction begins as a descent in a single strand of crotchets in the right hand's treble register; this piano line is almost immediately irrigated into two, three and then finally four parts, an analogue for a well-spring of tears that is heard flowing from both hands. The entry of the vocal line at the end of b. 4 initiates a melody, gently yearning and exploratory, sensual without being erotic, which is doubled throughout by the piano. With most other composers this is a rather dull ploy, but Schubert can use it effectively to suggest containment and, in this case, a mood of chastened sobriety.

The music for the first four lines of each verse (the song is utterly strophic) leads from D major to B minor (b. 13). Then the lines 'Darum du Brust voll Wunden / Voll Gram und stiller Pein' take us to C sharp minor (b. 17) where the softening addition of a major third confirms its position as the dominant of F sharp minor. This twice progresses to B minor and thence back to D major. These little journeys into the valley of death and out again are cleverly planned. The composer must have scanned all four verses and found the key words 'wounds', 'suffering', 'frenzy' and 'weeping' at the end of the fifth line of each; these variations on a single mood are a veritable invitation to a strophic song and in each case these lines lie at the heart of the song's darker middle section. The vocal line at the end of each verse (including the melismas at both appearances of 'So tauche da hinein' in the first strophe, bb. 17–24) is curiously reminiscent of the piano writing in gently wafting quavers that closes each verse of *Der Kreuzzug*. This figuration in another form is also to be found in both the vocal and piano writing of one of the great Leitner settings, *Des Fischers Liebesglück* D933. The four-bar postlude is suitably heartfelt but also more resolute as if the singer has already glimpsed the morning radiance described at the end of the poem. This once again recalls the choral-like aspects of *Der Kreuzzug*.

Autograph:	Hungarian National Library, Budapest
First edition:	Published by Schober's Lithographisches Institut, Vienna initially without opus number in the spring of 1828, and as Op. 106 no. 2 in the spring of 1828 (P159)
Dedicatee:	Marie Pachler
Subsequent editions:	Peters: Vol. 2/199; AGA XX 546: Vol. 9/106; NSA IV: Vol. 5/109; Bärenreiter: Vol. 4/25
Bibliography:	Fischer-Dieskau 1977, pp. 252–3
	Youens 2002, pp. 236–49
Discography and timing:	Fischer-Dieskau II 9[7] 4'00 (Strophes 1, 2 and 4 only)
	Hyperion I 36[11]
	Hyperion II 35[4] 4'36 Juliane Banse

← *Sie in jedem Liede* D896A   *Vor meiner Wiege* D927 →

WENN ALLE UNTREU WERDEN *see* GEISTLICHES LIED D661

WENN ICH DICH, HOLDE, SEHE *see ALFONSO UND ESTRELLA* D732/13

WENN ICH IHN NUR HABE *see* GEISTLICHES LIED D660

WER KAUFT LIEBESGÖTTER?   Who will buy these Cupids?
(GOETHE) **D261** [H147]

The song exists in two versions, the first of which is discussed below:
(1) 21 August 1815; (2) 1816

(1)   C major

(24 bars)

(2)   'Mässig, lieblich'   C major $\frac{2}{4}$ [42 bars]

Von allen schönen Waren,	Of all the beautiful things
Zum Markte hergefahren,	Brought here to market,
Wird keine mehr behagen,	None will please you more
Als die wir euch getragen	Than those we bring you
Aus fremden Ländern bringen.	From foreign lands.
O höret was wir singen!	Hear our song!
Und seht die schönen Vögel,	See the fine birds!
Sie stehen zum Verkauf.	They are for sale.

Zuerst beseht den grossen,	First look at this big one,
Den lustigen, den losen!	This jolly, rakish fellow.
Er hüpfet leicht und munter,	Chirpily, lightly,
Von Baum und Busch herunter;	He hops down from bush and tree,
Gleich ist er wieder droben.	Now he is up there again.
Wir wollen ihn nicht loben.	We are not going to sing his praises.
O seht den muntern Vogel!	Look at the chirpy fellow!
Er steht hier zum Verkauf.	He is for sale.
Betrachtet nun den kleinen,	Now take a look at this little one.
Er will bedächtig scheinen,	He pretends to be thoughtful,
Und doch ist er der lose,	But he's every bit as rakish
So gut als wie der grosse;	As the big fellow.
Er zeiget meist im Stillen	In his quiet way he shows
Den allerbesten Willen.	The best will in the world.
Der lose kleine Vogel,	This rakish little fellow
Er steht hier zum Verkauf.	Is for sale.
O seht das kleine Täubchen?	See this little dove,
Das liebe Turtelweibchen!	This sweet turtle dove.
Die Mädchen sind so zierlich,	Girls are so dainty,
Verständig und manierlich;	So understanding and well-mannered.
Sie mag sich gerne putzen	She likes to spruce herself
Und eure Liebe nutzen.	And to serve your love.
Der kleine, zarte Vogel,	This delicate little bird
Er steht hier zum Verkauf.	Is for sale.
Wir wollen sie nicht loben,	We are not going to sing their praises,
Sie stehn zu allen Proben.	You can try them out as you wish.
Sie lieben sich das Neue;	They love novelty,
Doch über ihre Treue	But as for their constancy,
Verlangt nicht Brief und Siegel;	Do not ask for any promises!
Sie haben alle Flügel.	They all have wings.
Wie artig sind die Vögel!	What charming birds!
Wie reizend ist der Kauf!	What a delightful buy!

JOHANN WOLFGANG VON GOETHE (1749–1832); poem written in 1795

This is the twenty-eighth of Schubert's seventy-five Goethe solo settings (1814–26). See the poet's biography for a chronological list of all the Goethe settings.

This poem was written by Goethe as part of an intended sequel to *Die Zauberflöte* – a duet for that bird-catching duo Papageno and Papagena, with each character singing alternate verses or, as pointed out by Walther Dürr in NSA Vol. 8 p. xxx, the first and fifth verses to be sung by both characters together, Papagena Verses 2 and 4 and Papageno Verse 3. The poet revered Mozart whom he had once seen when the infant prodigy (seven years younger than himself) visited Frankfurt. Of course Goethe had no success in finding a composer adequate to the task of setting such a libretto, but on this showing he might have done worse than Schubert, who needed no encouragement to pay homage to his idol Mozart, or to make a musical bow in the direction of the greatest of all *Singspiele*. The Zelter setting with its marking of 'Schalkhaft' ('Roguishly') is also a delight: the piano writing with its impudent opening acciaccaturas is highly characterized, and in the last two lines of each verse the vocal line goes into three parts.

The tessitura of Schubert's setting – as in *Die Spinnerin* D247 – is cruelly high; when the song appeared in the Nachlass it was transposed down a minor third to A major, just as *Mignon* (Kennst du das Land?) D321 was transposed down a major third. Perhaps these songs were conceived in this tessitura because Schubert's first collaboration with the soprano singing voice was with Therese Grob who was apparently able to sing a D in alt. Most of the birds in this poem are unidentified, but reference to the 'Turtelweibchen' is to *Streptopelia turtur*, the now rare turtle or mourning dove, known simply as the turtle in Shakespeare (in his poem *The Phoenix and the Turtle* and frequently in the plays).

This song would be performed more often if there was more time for the singer to breathe, and if the words, at this pert tempo, were not such a mouthful. Perhaps for this reason it would be a good idea to restore this work to its duet status (although Schubert himself gives no indication that he thought of it as such). The song is printed in the NSA in two almost identical versions, the first dated 21 August 1815, the second from 1816 – part of the second Lieder album prepared for Goethe and never dispatched to Weimar.

Autographs:	Gesellschaft der Musikfreunde, Vienna (first version)
	Wienbibliothek im Rathaus, Vienna (second version)
First edition:	Published as Book 47 no. 2 of the Nachlass by Diabelli, Vienna in spring 1850 (P376)
Subsequent editions:	Peters: Vol. 6/52; AGA XX 118: Vol. 3/43; NSA IV: Vol. 8/199 & 201
Bibliography:	Fischer-Dieskau 1977, p. 45
	Shackleton, 2012
Further settings:	Johann Friedrich Reichardt (1752–1814) *Wer kauft Liebesgötter?* (1796)
	Carl Friedrich Zelter (1758–1832) *Wer kauft Liebesgötter?* (1802)
	Václav Tomášek (1774–1850) *Wer kauft Liebesgötter?* (1815)
Discography and timing:	Fischer-Dieskau I 5[7] 2'29
	Hyperion I 7[15]
	Hyperion II 9[8] 2'25 Elly Ameling

←— *Wonne der Wehmut* D260   *Die Fröhlichkeit* D262 —→

WER NIE SEIN BROT MIT TRÄNEN ASS (I)

He who has never eaten his bread with tears

(GOETHE) **D478**[first version]/**2**(first setting)
[in D₁ D480/1] [H304]
A minor   September 1816

(14 bars)

Wer nie sein Brot mit Tränen ass,[1]	He who has never eaten his bread with tears,
Wer nie die kummervollen Nächte	Who, through nights of grief,
Auf seinem Bette weinend sass,	Has never sat weeping on his bed,
Der kennt euch nicht, ihr himmlischen Mächte!	Knows you not, heavenly powers!
Ihr führt ins Leben uns hinein,	You bring us into life,
Ihr lasst den Armen schuldig werden,	You let the poor wretch fall into guilt,
Dann überlasst ihr ihn der Pein:	Then you abandon him to his agony:
Denn alle Schuld rächt sich auf Erden.	For all guilt is avenged on earth.

JOHANN WOLFGANG VON GOETHE (1749–1832); poem written no later than 1783

This is the forty-third of Schubert's seventy-five Goethe solo settings (1814–26). See the poet's biography for a chronological list of all the Goethe settings.

The celebrated *Gesänge des Harfners* Op. 12, published in 1822, are the composer's final thoughts on the three poems of the Harper from *Wilhelm Meisters Lehrjahre*. The first of these songs, 'Wer sich der Einsamkeit ergibt' D478/1, was the second setting (1816) of a text that had originally been set in 1815 as D325. The last of the set, 'An die Türen will ich schleichen' D478/3, seems to have given Schubert little trouble. When he came to publish the cycle in 1822 the composer made only minor revisions to the 1816 versions of both these songs.

'Wer nie sein Brot mit Tränen ass', the middle panel of the triptych, was a more complicated matter, however. Two settings of the poem date from the same period of 1816, and both were found wanting in 1822 when Schubert composed an entirely new third setting for the publication of Op. 12. It is unfortunate that in putting together a line-up of masterpieces for this opus, two fine, though very different, earlier songs have been eclipsed. The first of these, the strophic setting considered here, in a gently rocking rhythm, was originally titled 'Harfenspieler No. 3' in Schubert's autograph. The A minor tonality seems fixed in Schubert's mind as appropriate for the majority of his *Wilhelm Meister* settings. The simplicity of this song on the page belies a profound intensity when heard in performance although it is the only one of the *Wilhelm Meister* settings that is entirely strophic. Folksong-like at the beginning, the words 'Auf seinem Bette weinend' (bb. 4–6) prompt an excursion into chromaticism that effectively characterizes the Harper's tortured guilt. The extraordinary postlude (bb. 12–14) strays into the higher regions of the keyboard and seems to depict the wandering of a stricken mind. Perhaps Schubert was dissatisfied with this song because it was a little too similar in mood and cast of melody to D325, the 1815 song 'Wer sich der Einsamkeit ergibt', qv.

Autograph:	Wienbibliothek im Rathaus, Vienna
First edition:	Published as part of the AGA in 1895 (P654)
Subsequent editions:	Not in Peters: AGA XX 256: Vol. 3/186; NSA IV: Vol. 1b/291
Discography and timing:	Fischer-Dieskau —
	Hyperion I 24[14]
	Hyperion II 16[5] 2'08 John Mark Ainsley

← *Lied eines Schiffers an die Dioskuren D360   Wer nie sein Brot mit Tränen ass D478/2b* →

---

[1] This poem was originally published with the old-fashioned spelling for 'Brot', thus 'Brod'.

WER NIE SEIN BROT MIT TRÄNEN ASS (II)

He who has never eaten his bread with tears

(Goethe) **D478**[first version]/**2**
(second setting) [in D₁ 480/2] [H304A]
A minor   September 1816

See previous entry for poem and translation

JOHANN WOLFGANG VON GOETHE (1749–1832); poem written no later than 1783

This is the forty-fourth of Schubert's seventy-five Goethe solo settings (1814–26). See the poet's biography for a chronological list of all the Goethe settings.

This setting turns its back on the simplicity of most of the other *Wilhelm Meister* songs – it is more sophisticated (one may almost say more ambitious) in terms of its accompaniment and harmonic changes. Of all the Schubert songs inspired by Goethe's novel, this is undoubtedly the quickest ('Etwas geschwind') and most restless. It paints a figure of hand-wringing neuroticism. Schubert retains the key of A minor from his first setting and moves from there to F sharp minor, a real upward turn of the screw at 'Der kennt euch nicht, ihr himmlischen Mächte!' (bb. 11–12). This sounds frankly crazed. The second verse begins in this key (with a change of key signature) and progresses thence through E flat minor (b. 26), B⁷ (b. 29) and E⁷ (b. 30). Then, by sharpening the bass note E sharp (to emphasize the word 'kennt'), Schubert takes us into the first inversion of C sharp⁷ only to return to F sharp minor – but this for a mere four semiquavers. In the middle of b. 14 the bass F sharp falls to F natural and thence to E and before we know it we are back in A minor after a dizzy harmonic ride. The passage between bb. 28 and 31 with its partially tremolando left-hand accompaniment can be compared to the 'Es schwindelt mir' section of the renowned, and final, *Mignon* setting, 'Nur wer die Sehnsucht kennt' D877/4.

Despite what is perhaps too great an intensity within too short a time frame, this is a fine tenor song (with the caveat of an unkind final low A) and deserves to be better known and performed from time to time as an alternative picture of the Harper. Nevertheless this histrionic portrayal is at odds with Goethe's description of this enigmatic character. The agitation of the setting fails to capture the essentially depressive nature of the man, and Schubert obviously realized this in 1822 when he decided to compose another – definitive – setting of these words.

Autograph: Wienbibliothek im Rathaus, Vienna
First edition: Published as part of the AGA in 1895 (P655)
Subsequent editions: Not in Peters; AGA XX 257: Vol. 4/187; NSA IV: Vol. 1b/226;
                       Bärenreiter: Vol. 1/214

Discography and timing: Fischer-Dieskau   —
                         Hyperion I 24¹⁵
                         Hyperion II 16⁶   1'44   John Mark Ainsley

← *Wer nie sein Brot mit Tränen ass D478/2*   *Der Sänger am Felsen D482* →

WER NIE SEIN BROT MIT TRÄNEN ASS & WER SICH DER EINSAMKEIT ERGIBT *see GESÄNGE DES HARFNERS* D478 [second version]

<table>
<tr><td>

WER SICH DER EINSAMKEIT ERGIBT (Harfenspieler)
(GOETHE) **D325** [H203]
A minor   13 November 1815

</td><td>

He who gives himself up
to solitude

</td></tr>
</table>

(40 bars)

Wer sich der Einsamkeit ergibt,	He who gives himself up to solitude,
Ach, der ist bald allein;	Ah, he is soon alone;
Ein jeder lebt, ein jeder liebt,	One man lives, another loves
Und lasst ihn seiner Pein.	And both leave him to his suffering.
Ja! lasst mich meiner Qual!	Yes, leave me to my suffering!
Und kann ich nur einmal	And if I can just once
Recht einsam sein,	Be truly lonely,
Dann bin ich nicht allein.	Then I shall not be alone.
Es schleicht ein Liebender lauschend sacht,	A lover steals softly, listening:
Ob seine Freundin allein?	Is his sweetheart alone?
So überschleicht bei Tag und Nacht	Thus, day and night,
Mich Einsamen die Pein,	Suffering steals upon me,
Mich Einsamen die Qual.	Torment steals upon me in my solitude.
Ach, werd' ich erst einmal	Ah, once I'm lying
Einsam im Grabe sein,	Lonely in the grave,
Da lässt sie mich allein!	Then my torment will leave me alone.

JOHANN WOLFGANG VON GOETHE (1749–1832); poem written by 1783

This is the thirty-third of Schubert's seventy-five Goethe solo settings (1814–26). See the poet's biography for a chronological list of all the Goethe settings.

This poem comes from Chapter 13 of the second book of *Wilhelm Meisters Lehrjahre* where Wilhelm Meister visits the Harper in the hope that the old man's music will cheer him up. Some

Wilhelm Meister and the Harper by Ferdinand Piloty.

hope! It eventually transpires that this enigmatic figure (who has introduced himself with the ballad *Der Sänger* D149) has been maddened by grief after an unintentionally incestuous relationship with his sister, and her subsequent death after bearing him a daughter who is also lost to him. His music is far from cheerful; indeed the lyrics sung by this character inspired some of Schubert's darkest and most introverted music.

Wilhelm is directed to a lodging house in a remote corner of town, and climbs up to a garret from whence come 'heart-moving, mournful tones, accompanied by a sad and dreary singing'. On overhearing a song, 'Wer nie sein Brot mit Tränen ass', Wilhelm enters the room. He asks the old man to continue, and this second text is sung, once again to the Harper's own accompaniment. Goethe gives a number of clues as to how he imagines the Harper's songs should be performed: 'the few stanzas . . . sometimes chanted, sometimes in recitative, were repeated more than once . . . the old man looked upon his strings, and after touching them softly, by way of prelude, he began and sang'. In Schubert's later setting of the poem from 1816 (Op. 12, D478, second version, no. 1) he provides, true to Goethe, a quietly strummed, and most beautiful, introduction. The lack of it in the first version might suggest that the composer did not yet know the entire novel; if this was the case he would have had to have access to a German edition of Goethe's works (*Gedichte*, Zweiter Band, Tübingen, 1815) which contains the poems from *Wilhelm Meister* separated from their context in the novel.

The key is A minor, with a middle section in F major; these characteristics at least were conserved in the final setting. But this song lacks the wayward, even unhinged passion engendered by obeying the poet's direction that the Harper's lament should waver between aria and recitative. It has a saner, gentler melancholy and a time signature of § (the accompanimental flow is possible harp music) which reminds us of the last setting of Mignon's 'Nur wer die Sehnsucht kennt' D877/4, a song also in A minor but with a searing world-weary intensity of which Schubert was more capable in 1826. However, this piece, written towards the end of 1815, shows the direction in which the composer was surely moving. He had written many huge ballads, and many slight and charming miniatures; he was now learning how to distil the drama of the ballad form into tiny lyrics. It was in this historic fusion that Goethe was to continue to be his most important collaborator.

Richard Stokes has pointed out that in this poem the 'ei' vowel occurs twenty-five times in sixteen lines. In employing this kind of assonance, Goethe depicts the obsessional character of the Harper. The same vowel recurs frequently in *Mein!* D795/11 sung by the love-struck miller boy in *Die schöne Müllerin*. Brian Newbould has shown that the postlude of this version of *Wer sich der Einsamkeit ergibt*, with its swaying parallel sixths over pedal harmony, is reminiscent of the slow movement, also in A minor, of Beethoven's 'Razumovsky' String Quartet Op. 59 no. 3. The pervasive nature of that composer's influence on Schubert is never to be underestimated.

Autograph:	Wienbibliothek im Rathaus, Vienna (first draft on two separate sheets)
First edition:	Published as part of the AGA in 1895 (P610)
Subsequent editions:	Not in Peters; AGA XX 173: Vol. 3/187; NSA IV: Vol. 1b/218; Bärenreiter: Vol. 1/212
Bibliography:	Newbould 1997, p. 55
Discography and timing:	Fischer-Dieskau —

Hyperion I 10^{19}

Hyperion II 11^{16} 3'08   Martyn Hill

⟵ *Klage der Ceres* D323   *Lorma I* D327 ⟶

FRIEDRICH LUDWIG ZACHARIAS WERNER (1768–1823)

THE POETIC SOURCES

S1 *Wanda, Königin der Sarmaten* Eine romantische Tragödie mit Gesang in fünf Akten, published as a supplement to *Das Kreuz an der Ostsee* Ein Trauerspiel von Friedrich Ludwig Zacharias Werner Wien 1813 Im Verlage bey Joh. Bapt. Wallishausser

This play is clearly modelled on Metastasio's *Ruggiero*. Schubert was later to write an operatic fragment *Rüdiger* D791 to a libretto of Ignaz von Mosel with the same characters, Rüdiger and Balderon, found in Werner's play.

S2 *Die Harfe* Herausgegeben von Friedrich Kind Zweites Bändchen Leipzig bei Georg Joachim Göschen 1815. This almanac (in larger format than is usual for the period) included contributions from Theodor Hell, Louisa Brachmann, Herder, Meissner and de la Motte Fouqué among many others.

Wanda, Königin der Sarmaten (1813).

S3 *Die Söhne des Thal's* [*sic*] *Ein Dramatisches Gedicht* von Friedrich Ludwig Zacharias Werner [Frontispiece Illustration of 'Iacob Bernhard von Molay'] *Erster Theil Die Templer auf Cypern*, Berlin bei I.D Sander 1807. The 'Personen' list informs us that Molay was the last grand master of the order of Templars.

THE SONGS

January 1817   *Jagdlied* D521 [S1: Act I pp. 242–3]

1817?   *Nur wer die Liebe kennt* D513A [S2: p. 362, No. 8 of *Blätter aus Tinas Stammbuche* with the title *Impromptu, in Tharand's Ruinen geschrieben*]

1820   *Morgenlied* D685 [S3: Act I, Scene 2 pp. 41–2]

Zacharias Werner was born in Königsberg, Prussia, on 18/19 November 1768. As a young man he spent some years in Warsaw in the German civil service. There he led a life of considerable debauchery and married three times (all three marriages were dissolved). When he resigned from the civil service he devoted himself to writing. He had begun as a poet (*Gedichte*, 1789) but his real forte was as a playwright – his dramas usually have a historical background overlaid with a mystical streak. His writing suited the Romantic mood of the period and his importance in the theatre of the time was considerable. *Die Söhne des Tals* was followed by *Das Kreuz an der Ostsee* (1806), and then a play about Martin Luther (1807) which provided a sympathetic portrait of the great reformer. Werner's influential *Schicksalstragödie*, written at Goethe's behest (and first performed in Weimar in 1810) was entitled *24 Februar* (the day in 1804 when both the author's mother and his best friend died). This continued a technique employed in *Die Söhne des Thales* and *Wanda, Königin der Sarmaten* where the action takes place, as far as is possible, in real time. *24 Februar* is about a curse that besets different generations of the same family on the same day of the year, and it established a vogue for writing of this kind, comparable to the fashion for grisly *Friday the Thirteenth-style* movies in our own time. Werner, whose appearance was striking and unusual, had a charismatic personality bordering on charlatanism. Goethe had a love-hate relationship with him – disliking the plays at first, yielding to the man's personal charm in 1808 and then finally feeling repulsed when Werner demanded that his readings be taken as seriously as some kind of holy ritual.

Werner was readily embraced by Viennese theatregoers. In spring 1812 Beethoven excused himself to the Archduke Rudolph for not having responded to a summons because he had been at the Theater auf der Wieden, at a performance of *Wanda, Königin der Sarmaten*, a play about the queen of the nomadic Sarmatian tribe in the eighth century AD. Perhaps the action on stage was spectacular enough to interest a man who could not hear the dialogue, or perhaps Beethoven was still able to hear

Werner giving a reading of his *Die Söhne des Thales*.

Frontispiece to Werner's *Die Söhne des Thales* (1807).

something of the stirring choral music that was part of it. Thomas Aigner has argued that the lost libretto of Schubert's opera *Rüdiger* D791 was based on this Werner play.

Werner was brought up as a Protestant but he converted to Catholicism in 1810 and was ordained in 1813. He had been acquainted with Madame de Staël and her secretary August von Schlegel, but by the time he reached Vienna he had defected to the side of the other Schlegel brother, Friedrich, who was the nexus of an ultra-Catholic circle. In 1814 Werner fully recanted the pro-Protestant views expressed in his play *Martin Luther, order die Weihe der Kraft* and became one of the most famous Catholic preachers at St Stephen's in Vienna (he was appointed honorary canon). Although he was the poet of only three Schubert songs (all taken from plays) it is clear that this redemptorist cleric of slightly ominous appearance was a name to conjure with in the Vienna of Schubert's time; he certainly had a huge following and a charisma as far as women were concerned

which made him a somewhat sinister figure. Perhaps Schubert was first drawn to the poem for *Der Wanderer* D489 because Werner was such a well-known celebrity; the lyric by Schmidt von Lübeck had been incorrectly attributed to the playwright in *Dichtung für Kunstredner*, the anthology in which the composer found the text. It is quite possible that Schubert later met Werner personally in the salon of Karoline Pichler, but it seems unlikely that he would have been much attracted to the poet-cleric's brand of hocus-pocus.

Werner died on 17 January 1823. If he had lived today he would have made a fortune out of screenplay adaptions of airport novels of the *Da Vinci Code* variety – although he would have scrupulously avoided any questioning of Catholic orthodoxies. The poet would doubtless have been flattered that his play *Attila, König der Hunnen* was much later to be the inspiration for Giuseppe Verdi's opera *Attila* (1846).

Bibliography: Aigner 2002

WEST-ÖSTLICHER DIVAN

Goethe's fascination with the poetry of the East was awoken in childhood by biblical stories told to him by his mother. The religious poetry of Klopstock and his meeting with Herder in Strasbourg stimulated these interests further. Herder's engagement with Eastern literature was broad – he was acquainted with the poetry of Hafiz decades before Goethe made his own study of this great Persian poet. Goethe's study of the Koran led to his beginning (though not completing) the drama *Mahomet* (qv the two incomplete settings of *Mahomets Gesang* D549 and D721).

Despite writing *Der Gott und die Bajadere* in 1797 (*see* Schubert's song D254), Goethe was always more interested in the Muslim Middle East than India, a country which he found, according to Heine, 'bizarre, bewildering and obscure'. However, Friedrich von Schlegel's *Über die Sprache und Weisheit der Inder* (1808) launched the wider literary exploration of that subcontinent in no uncertain terms. The increased awareness of the link between Sanskrit and the main European languages resulted in profound oriental studies (one thinks of the work of the poet Friedrich Rückert and, later, that of Sir Max Müller, son of the poet of *Die Winterreise* and professor of oriental languages at Oxford), and both Goethe and Schubert shared a fascination with Kālidāsa's *Sākuntala* (the subject of the composer's opera fragment D701).

Europe's first orientalist journal appeared in Schubert's home town; between 1809 and 1818 the great Viennese orientalist Joseph Hammer-Purgstall edited and published a richly illustrated periodical entitled *Fundgruben des Orients*, and in 1814 a volume of his own translations of the Persian poet Hafiz – the pseudonym of Mahomed Shams ud-Din (*c.* 1315–1390). This great poet, contemporary with Chaucer, revered in the Middle East as much as Shakespeare is esteemed in the West, was born and died in Shiraz in Persia (Iran). To this day his tomb in the Musalia Gardens, along the banks of the Ruknabad river, is a much-visited shrine and a cultural focal point of the town (there is also a Hafiz–Goethe memorial in Weimar). Although he married and had a child, Hafiz was in love all his life with Shakh-e Nabat, a woman of incredible beauty, a Beatrice to his Dante. The meaning of Hafiz – 'one who remembers' – is a designation for those who have mastered the Koran by heart; he also memorized the works of his fellow poets and exemplars, Attar, Rumi and Nizami. He spent most of his life in Shiraz, but after he fell out of favour with one of its rulers, Mubariz Muzzafar, he was forced to live in exile in Isfahan for some years, at odds also with many of the orthodox clergy. His poetry of wine and women, also boys on occasion (Goethe broached even this latter theme in *Setze mir nicht, du Grobian*, as set in Schumann's *Myrten*, Op. 25 no. 6) belonged to a freedom of thought in certain versions of Sufi philosophy that was controversial in his day, and has remained so. Some of the work of Hafiz brings to mind Omar Khayyám, better known in English-speaking countries thanks to Edward Fitzgerald's popularizing translations. It was Fitzgerald who called Hafiz 'the best musician of Words', and Sir Arthur Conan Doyle has Sherlock Holmes observe, 'There is as much sense in Hafiz as in Horace, and as much knowledge of the world.'

The re-emergence of a gigantic historical personality of this kind, a sage and focal point of Eastern literature, was exactly the impetus that Goethe needed; he must have sensed a kindred spirit across the ages. In terms of his poetic themes Goethe was in the habit of refashioning and reworking material that came from other sources, and which served his all-encompassing inspiration. Joseph Hammer-Purgstall was a scholar of several languages (Degen in Vienna had published his translations of Edmund Spenser's sonnets in a sumptuous bilingual edition) but he was an uninspiring poet in his own right. If there was to be a German version of Hafiz, Goethe would make one – with much less accuracy, certainly, but to far greater artistic purpose.

In July 1814 an enjoyable Rhineland excursion gave the poet an exploratory sense of rejuvenation and discovery. His meeting with the young Marianne von Willemer (qv), whom he found attractive and amazingly clever, sharpened his desire to create something new which would also

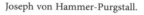
Joseph von Hammer-Purgstall.

(*right*) Design for Goethe's *West-östlicher Divan*, 1827.

give him a chance to initiate a correspondence that included a kind of literary role play. Both Marianne and Goethe were married, and for Goethe in his middle fifties an emotional affair that was confined to letter-writing was probably a sufficiently rewarding outlet – in fact the excitement for both of them lay in the intimacy of games of words and hidden meanings, and in the creative fruits thereof.

On returning to Weimar, Goethe began to arrange his poems into a 'Divan', a Persian word that originally referred to a meeting place, the main room of a customs house lined with couches (thus the connection of this word with sofa-like furniture), where much negotiation and business was done between East and West. 'Divan' is pronounced 'diwan' in Arabic and this is the origin of the French word for customs, *douane*. Goethe applied himself to further reading, including seventeenth-century English tracts on oriental subjects by Thomas Hyde and the famous William Jones, as well as Herbelot's *Bibliothèque orientale*. It was not long before he hit on the idea of finding names for a symbolic couple: the woman's name was Suleika (or more properly Zuleika in English transcription); she was Potiphar's wife (in the biblical legend of Joseph) according to a commentary on the Torah by the medieval Sefer HaYashar. Thus Jussuf and Zuleika were the pair who were purportedly having an affair behind the back of Potiphar. The character of Joseph soon evolved to Hatem, and it was with this name that Goethe metaphorically wooed his own newly incarnated Zuleika.

A visit to the Willemer household in August and September 1815 deepened Goethe's attraction to Marianne and his determination to complete a work (first published in 1819) that has remained a memorial to one of the most fruitful literary exchanges in history. Heine, in his *Die*

Illustration for Goethe's *West-östlicher Divan* by
F. Simm (1882).

(*right*) Zuleika and her retinue, illustration by F. Simm.

romantische Schule (1833), described the *West-östlicher Divan* as 'so light, so charming, so softly inspired, that we wonder that it could be done in German . . . Everything is perfumed and glows like a harem full of amorous odalisques with gazelle-like eyes darkened with *kohl*, and yearning snow-white arms.' Marianne, no passive recipient of Goethe's lyrics, played a full part in recip-rocating his thoughts in poetry of her own. The role she assumed in this poetic dialogue was first revealed as late as 1857 (*see* WILLEMER).

In early 1826 Schubert began work on his opera *Der Graf von Gleichen* D918 (with Eduard von Bauernfeld as librettist). The tale was rather a steamy one concerning the Saracen princess Suleika who is brought home by the hero of the opera to live in a *ménage à trois* with his wife. This storyline was nothing to do with Goethe of course, but is an indication of how quickly his character, Suleika, had taken root in the German literary world.

Schubert's song settings from this collection were the following:

1821

Im Gegenwärtigen Vergangenes (vocal quartet) D710. This is the twelfth poem in the first book of the *West-östlicher Divan*, *Moganni Nameh* – in the *Buch des Sängers* (Book of the Singer), pp. 22–3 (page references refer here to the first edition of the work, published by Cotta in 1819)

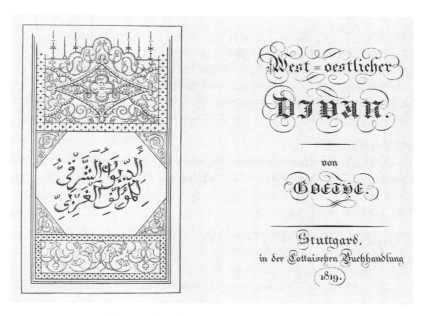

Title page of Goethe's *West-östlicher Divan* (1819).

West-östlicher Divan, Viennese edition (1820) with a design of Sufi inspiration.

1821, March

Versunken D715. This is the fourth poem in the third book of the *West-östlicher Divan, Usch Nameh* – in the *Buch der Liebe* (Book of Love), p. 52

Geheimes D719. This is the eleventh poem in the third book of the *West-östlicher Divan, Usch Nameh* – in the *Buch der Liebe* (Book of Love), p. 60

Suleika I D720. This is the thirtieth poem in the seventh book of the *West-östlicher Divan, Suleika Nameh* – in the *Buch Suleika* (Book of Zuleika), p. 161

1824(?); (or also possibly) 1821

Suleika II D717. This is the thirty-third poem in the seventh book of the *West-östlicher Divan, Suleika Nameh* – in the *Buch Suleika* (Book of Zuleika), p. 166

Bibliography: Byrne 2003, pp. 368–82

Die WETTERFAHNE *see WINTERREISE* D911/2

WIDERSCHEIN   Reflection
(SCHLECHTA) **D639** & **D₁949** [H413]

The song exists in two versions, both of which are discussed below:
(1) appeared September 1820; (2) May 1828?

(1) 'Langsam, zögernd'   D major   **C**   [65 bars]

(2) 'B♭ major

Fischer harrt am Brückenbogen	A fisherman has for so long been waiting
Ach so lange Zeit;	At the arch of the bridge;
Blicket sehnlich in die Wogen,	He gazes longingly into the waters,
Denn sie ist noch weit! –	For she is still so far away.
Und sie schleicht um den Hügel,	And she steals around the hill,
Und das holde Bild	And her sweet image
Leuchtet aus dem Wellenspiegel	Gleams in the mirroring waves,
Lächelnd und so mild.	Smiling and gentle.

Und er sieht's. Und durch Blumenränder	And he sees it! Through fringes of flowers
Schwimmt der süsse Schein –	Her sweet radiance glides.
Und er hält sich am Geländer,	And he holds fast to the railings,
Sonst zieht's ihn hinein!	Lest he should be drawn in.

FRANZ XAVER VON SCHLECHTA (1796–1875); poem written *c.* 1818

This is the second of Schubert's six Schlechta solo settings (1815–26). See the poet's biography for a chronological list of all the Schlechta settings.

Widerschein, first printing (1820).

Of all Schubert's lieder there is scarcely one with a more complicated literary background than this one. Schlechta's poem first appeared in the *Wiener Zeitschrift* on 18 August 1818, beginning with the words 'Fischer harrt am Brückenbogen / Auf die liebe Maid'. The final strophe of the poem shows that it was influenced by the scenario of Goethe's *Der Fischer* (qv D225). Schubert set *Widerschein* in 1819/20 to a revised version of the poem (the 'liebe Maid' is changed, among other things) that was later published in W. G. Becker's *Taschenbuch zum geselligen Vergnügen* for the year 1821 (p. 399). It was not unusual at the time for musical supplements to be commissioned for some of the poems that were printed in almanacs. Schubert's song (in which, to complicate matters, he made some textual changes of his own) appeared as a supplement to that publication in the high key of D major (a version reprinted in the NSA in Volume 5 p. 138). It was only the second of Schubert's songs to appear anywhere in print. Because of some technical problem it seems that this supplement was delivered late, which explains why there are no copies of the almanac to be found today that include Schubert's song. However, a second musical supplement to a different text and composed by Franz Schubert of Dresden – it was the editor's joke to include two Schuberts – is loosely folded into my own copy of the little book.

Seven years later, in preparing the song for publication in 1828, the composer transposed it from his merry fisherman's tonality of D major (cf. the Schlechta setting *Fischerweise* D881) to the more contemplative B flat major for lower voice, possibly to suit the singer Johann Michael Vogl. By this time Schlechta had rewritten his poem (for a third time) and had published it in his *Gedichte* of 1824. There it begins 'Harrt ein Fischer auf der Brücke / Die Geliebte säumt', but for his 1828 version Schubert (understandably) kept to the version of the poem he had set originally. At this point the song was not yet in print apart from its short-lived almanac incarnation. After Schubert's death the poet revised his lyric for the fourth time and seems to have prevailed upon the Nachlass publisher Diabelli to allow him to alter the words, over Schubert's dead body as it were, before the song was properly published at last in 1832. In this version the text reads 'Tom lehnt harrend auf der Brücke, / Die Geliebte säumt'. Between 1832 and about 1894 this was taken to be the song's definitive text.

When Mandyczewski came to publish his *Gesamtausgabe*, lacking the 1821 almanac or Schubert's manuscripts, he took exception to the bad prosody of 'Tom lehnt harrend' where the second word, an important verb of dalliance, is allocated to a snatched semiquaver. Mandyczewski was of course aware of Diabelli's tendency to meddle (although in this instance it was Schlechta's fault rather than Diabelli's) and he realized that this was not a genuine piece of Schubertian word-setting. He decided to go back to what he mistakenly believed was the original source of Schubert's text – Schlechta's *Gedichte* of 1824. Thanks to this misapprehension, yet another version of the poem appears in the AGA, and still not the correct one! Until 1985 the only two available editions of *Widerschein* (Peters and the AGA) were both incorrect; the song's original D major version and its later 1828 revision (with the same text for both) were printed at last in NSA. It might come as no surprise that the poem, shorn of any music (but still claiming a connection with Schubert), appeared in a considerably altered *fifth* version in Schlechta's *Ephemeren* published in 1876.

This is reflective music in every sense and is a mirror not only of the fisherman and his beloved, but also of Schubert's growing skill as a songwriter in the optimistic and experimental period of 1819–20. Watery depths are depicted from the very beginning of the accompaniment, and they are also the depths of the fisherman's longing, and his uncertainty – when on earth will she come? He has been waiting for so long that it is perhaps already early evening, at least in Schubert's mind. We guess this from the similarity of the song's introduction to the opening bars of *Der Abend* D221 and of *Abendlied* D499. In the introduction the lover's reflection, still visible in the failing light, looks back up at him as the pianist seems to peel petals from the stalks of the right-hand chords – 'she loves me . . .' (b. 1), 'she loves me not' (b. 2). With the unusual (for him) marking of 'zögernd' the composer actually asks for this hesitant and lingering approach. When the voice enters on tiptoe, quaver rests break up the line in b. 5, one of Schubert's favourite means to suggest the suspense of romantic assignations (cf. *Die Erwartung* D159 and *Das Geheimnis* D250). Yearning cadences on 'so lange Zeit' (bb. 6–8) and 'sie ist noch weit' (bb. 12–14) show how time and distance stretch the fisherman's patience. (The music of these phrases only makes sense with the original words, and not those of Schlechta's alterations – something that seems not to have occurred to the poet or publisher in the slightest degree.) In the meantime the fisherman (Schubert never knew that he was later to be named Tom) looks at himself in the water and from time to time his reflection is momentarily broken up by a ripple of dotted-rhythm passing notes in the vocal line (bb. 16 and 18), a darting movement of a fish or a tiny eddy. The arrival of the girl is announced in tripping feminine triplets (from b. 26) and he sees *her* reflection. This is the musical turning point of the song; but the fisherman does not turn around to greet her for by now he is more hooked on fantasy than reality.

From b. 32 the vocal writing takes on the quality of Italian cantilena. The recapitulation (from b. 45) has an other-worldly feel, the music of someone transfixed. Throughout this section the piano's right hand, supported by triplets deep in the bass, sings a counter-melody as if a Lorelei were luring the fisherman to the depths. Although he manages to remain bodily on dry land, the postlude follows his dreams into a world of underwater calm, her reflection lying beneath the surface. The song prompts two comparisons with *Die schöne Müllerin*: the first of these is with the song *Tränenregen* D795/10 where the miller boy is so beguiled by the brook that he seems unable to look at his beloved who is sitting by his side awaiting his attention. The haunting final bars of *Der Müller und der Bach* D795/19 from the same cycle are brought to mind by the extraordinarily effective postlude of *Widerschein* where the pianist's right hand, already in the bass clef in b. 60, seems drawn by an inexorable current down into the watery depths via the remaining five bars of piano music. Particularly in this lower key of B flat major we are aware of the dangerous power of water to drown sorrows and care in gentle oblivion.

Autograph:	Missing or lost
Publication:	Published as a supplement to *W. G. Beckers Taschenbuch zum geselligen Vergnügen* in September 1820 and subsequently as part of the NSA in 1985 (P785; first version)
	Published as Book 15 no. 1 of the Nachlass by Diabelli, Vienna in January 1832 (P280; second version)
Publication reviews:	*Allgemeiner Musikalischer Anzeiger* (Vienna), No. 5 (31 January 1829), p. 19f. [Waidelich/Hilmar Dokumente I No. 688]
Subsequent editions:	Peters: Vol. 3/148; AGA XX 553: Vol. 9/130; NSA IV: Vol. 5a/138 & 143; Bärenreiter: Vol. 4/46
Bibliography:	Fischer-Dieskau 1977, p. 139
	Kohlhäufl 1999, p. 183
	Youens 2002, pp. 345–52
Discography and timing:	Fischer-Dieskau II 9[15] 4'01
	Hyperion I 2[4]
	Hyperion II 21[7] 4'23 Stephen Varcoe

← *Hoffnung* D637   *Abend* D645 →

WIDERSPRUCH   Contrariness   Chorus (TTBB) (and solo song)
(SEIDL) OP. 105 NO. 1, **D865** [H590]
D major   1826? or between Spring and August 1828

(133 bars)

Wenn ich durch Busch und Zweig	When I beat my way through bush and branch
Brech auf beschränktem Steig:	On the steep, narrow path,
Wird mir so weit, so frei,	I feel so elated and so free,
Will mir das Herz entzwei.	My heart would break in two.
Rings dann im Waldeshaus	Then, in the wooded house,
Rücken die Wänd' hinaus,	The walls all around spread outwards,
Wölbt sich das Laubgemach	The leafy chamber arches up
Hoch mir zum Schwindeldach,	To form a roof of giddy height.
Webt sich der Blätter schier	Each of the leaves is woven
Jedes zur Schwinge mir,	Into a pinion,
Dass sich mein Herz, so weit,	That my elated heart
Sehnt nach Unendlichkeit.	Longs for infinity.

Doch wann im weiten Raum[1]	But when, in the wide expanse
Hoch am Gebirgessaum	High on the mountain ridge,
Über dem Tal ich steh,	I stand above the valley
Nieder zum Tale seh,	Looking down into it,
Ach, wie beschränkt, wie eng	Ah, how constricted and confined I feel
Wird mir's im Luftgedräng;	In the oppressive air.
Rings auf mein Haupt so schwer	Around me the clouds
Nicken die Wolken her,	Bow heavily on to my head;
Niederzustürzen droht	Around me the sunset threatens
Rings mir das Abendrot,	To tumble down,
Und in ein Kämmerlein	And my heart longs to be
Sehnt sich mein Herz hinein!	Inside a tiny room!
Wenn ich durch Busch und Zweig . . .[2]	When I beat my way . . .

JOHANN GABRIEL SEIDL (1804–1875)

The dating of this quartet that can also be performed as a solo song is difficult and contested.
For these purposes it is placed as the first of Schubert's twelve Seidl solo settings (1826–8). See
the poet's biography for a chronological list of all the Seidl settings.

This TTBB chorus headed the collection of works that happened to be published on the day of Schubert's funeral. The others – all solo songs – were *Wiegenlied* D867, *Am Fenster* D878 and *Sehnsucht* D879, a complete Seidl opus in fact. *Widerspruch* was issued with a rider that explained that it could be performed either by four voices or as a solo song using the first tenor line. This made sense only commercially. Some of the song-buying public may have been disconcerted to find a choral work rubbing shoulders with lieder (although this was not the first time Schubert had mixed the two in an opus) which might have made Opus 105 seem bad value for money for an aspiring soloist. From a musical point of view, however, that *Widerspruch* could also be sung as a solo song was a controversial idea. There was no modification by the composer between the two versions, and the sturdy piano part, suitably hale and hearty for the chorus, seems stolid by Schubert's standards when accompanying a single voice. Most of the vocal line is relentlessly doubled by the piano, and in unimaginative hands this consigns the song to the schoolroom. It is likely that this 'two-for-the-price-of-one' concept was a brainwave of the publisher, Josef Czerny, and that Schubert had been too ill to gainsay the idea in the last weeks of his life. Czerny's advertisement in the *Wiener Zeitung* of 21 November 1828 actually states that *Widerspruch* is also available as a quartet, falsely implying that the solo song represented the composer's original thoughts. The solo version was published separately for the first time in Volume 5 of the *Neue Schubert-Ausgabe*, although it was ignored by Mandyczewski in the AGA. This said, there are performers, the baritone Wolfgang Holzmair and his accompanist Imogen Cooper, for example, who, having discovered the song in the NSA publication of 1985, have performed it regularly since.

The key is D major, a symphonic key for Schubert, and there is something symphonic about this music; the introduction immediately takes us out into the open air. The poem appears in a section of the 1826 edition of Seidl's poetry entitled *Jägerlieder* ('Hunting Poems'), and the piano introduction bids us stride through the countryside where we can hear the sound of the hunting-horn somewhere in the inner parts. In bb. 8–9 a succession of falling thirds (another hunting

[1] Seidl writes 'Doch wenn *in weitem* Raum'.
[2] Schubert repeats the opening verse in order to conclude the song.

motif perhaps) are hammered out in unison double octaves. The insistence on this interval is reminiscent of a similar figure in the first movement of the A minor Piano Sonata D784. The poem has two verses with a rhyme scheme in couplets that result in a relentless succession of two-bar phrases. This is bracing stuff, a tonal analogue for physical exertion and breathlessness, the dactylic rhythms imparting a sense of exhilaration in nature.

The first four lines have the poet beating his way through forest thickets. With the discovery of a clearing in the undergrowth Seidl's text implies a breakthrough into a constricted yet magical space, and Schubert follows suit with a shift from D major into the subdominant, G major (at 'Wölbt sich das Laubgemach', b. 28). Uri Liebrecht compares this altered state of consciousness with *Alice in Wonderland* where, instead of falling down a rabbit hole, the narrator enters another kind of secret world and perceives the forest around him as an edifice with walls and a roof that arches skyward. This produces an ecstatic reaction, the heightened intensity of four bars in B flat major (at 'Jedes zur Schwinge mir', bb. 32–5) followed by a return to the tonic via an extended A pedal (the tonic in second inversion). Being enclosed in this way by a canopy of greenery initiates in the poet's mind thoughts of infinity.

The eleven-bar interlude (bb. 44–54) is a close variant of the introduction, but the second verse beginning with the word 'Doch' proposes another kind of hike in different terrain. For no fewer than twenty-two bars (bb. 55–76) all four voice parts and piano are in hushed unison. This successfully paints the sense of awe, even fear, as the poet stands in the mountains looking down at sunset in the valley. It is here, surely, that he should think of infinity, but this is not the case. He clearly has no head for heights and these words are something of a confessional. The 'Luftgedräng' of the second verse at b. 66 is the shortness of breath that goes together with his discomfort. A short interlude of two bars of double-octave C sharps played softly on the piano, again in dactylic rhythm (bb. 77–8), contributes to the musical suspense. Where are we going?

Safely back home in the twinkling of an eye, that's where! The flowering into F sharp major for the passage beginning 'Und in ein Kämmerlein' (bb. 78–88) transports the narrator into a more comfortable place. Indeed it is musically transporting in every way. In the choral version four-part harmony, after so much unison singing, conveys a luxurious domestic tenderness. The song's title is here illustrated: Seidl paradoxically feels free in the constrictions of the forest and imprisoned by vast open spaces of the mountains. When faced with the latter, he is happier at home in Vienna in his 'Kämmerlein'. This song is thus as much about agoraphobia as the poem for *Nachthelle* D892 (also Seidl) is about the exact opposite – claustrophobia and the irresistible temptation to break out of doors into the starlit night. The poet dislikes open spaces as far as the mountains are concerned, but he rejoices in the wide firmament of the starlit heavens.

In the text of *Widerspruch* Seidl finishes the poem with his longing to be indoors; but Schubert will have none if it. He repeats the first verse of the poem and its music, as if the poet's 'Widerspruch' has been merely a momentary aberration. This is a chorus for hunters after all and there must be music to march them happily home via an obligingly dense forest. Schubert is here very aware of the pleasure taken by choral singers in a stirring peroration – often the case in his part-songs. The piano music of the introduction serves as a postlude.

Autograph:	Missing or lost
First edition:	Both solo and choral versions published as Op. 105 no. 1 by Josef Czerny, Vienna in November 1828 (two days after Schubert's death) (P174)
First known performance:	27 November 1828, *Abend-Unterhaltung* of the Gesellschaft der Musikfreunde at the Musikverein, Vienna, directed by Herr Bogner (see Waidelich/Hilmar Dokumente I No. 650 for full concert programme)

Publication reviews: *Conversationsblatt* (Vienna), No. 116 (28 September 1820),
                        p. 1045f. [Waidelich/Hilmar Dokumente I No. 59]
Subsequent editions: Not in Peters; AGA XVI 12: p. 93 (chorus only); NSA III: Vol. 3
                        (chorus) & IV, Vol. 5/80 (solo song); Bärenreiter: Vol. 4/2
Arrangement: Arr. Josef Stransky (1810–1890) for cello and piano, *Widerspruch*
Discography and timing: Hyperion I 26[16]   The London Schubert Chorale
                        Hyperion II 31[13]   3'39   (dir. Stephen Layton)

←— *Leb' wohl, du schöne Erde (Abschied von der Erde)* D829   *Wiegenlied* D867 —→

WIE ULFRU FISCHT   Ulfru fishing
(MAYRHOFER) OP. 21 NO. 3, **D525** [H338]

The song exists in two versions, the second of which is discussed below:
(1) January 1817; (2) by June 1823

(1) 'Etwas bewegt'   D minor   ¢   [25 bars]

(2) D minor

(25 bars)

Der Angel zuckt, die Rute bebt,	The rod quivers, the line trembles,
Doch leicht fährt sie heraus.	But it comes up easily.
Ihr eigensinn'gen Nixen gebt	You capricious water-sprites
Dem Fischer keinen Schmaus.	Give the fisherman no feast.
Was frommet ihm sein kluger Sinn,	What use is his cunning?
Die Fische baumeln spottend hin;	The fish saunter away mockingly;
Er steht am Ufer fest gebannt,	He stands spellbound on the shore,
Kann nicht ins Wasser, ihn hält das Land.	He cannot enter the water, the land holds him fast.
Die glatte Fläche kräuselt sich,	The smooth surface is ruffled,
Vom Schuppenvolk bewegt,	Disturbed by the scaly shoals
Das seine Glieder wonniglich	Whose members swim blithely
In sichern Fluten regt.	In the safe waters,
Forellen zappeln hin und her,	Trout dart to and fro,
Doch bleibet des Fischers Angel leer.	But the fisherman's rod stays empty,
Sie fühlen, was die Freiheit ist;	They feel what freedom is;
Fruchtlos ist Fischers alte List.	The fisherman's well-tried guile is in vain.

Die Erde ist gewaltig schön,	The earth is surpassingly beautiful,
Doch sicher ist sie nicht!	But safe it is not!
Es senden Stürme Eiseshöh'n;	Storms blow from the icy peaks,
Der Hagel und der Frost zerbricht	Hail and frost destroy,
Mit einem Schlage, einem Druck,	At one stroke, with one blow,
Das gold'ne Korn, der Rosen Schmuck –	The golden corn, the rose's beauty –
Den Fischlein unter'm weichen Dach,	The little fish beneath their soft roof
Kein Sturm folgt ihnen vom Lande nach.	Are pursued by no storm from the land.

JOHANN MAYRHOFER (1787–1836)

This is the seventeenth of Schubert's forty-seven Mayrhofer solo settings (1814–24). See the poet's biography for a chronological list of all the Mayrhofer settings.

Auf der Donau D553, *Der Schiffer* D536 and *Wie Ulfru fischt* were published together in June 1823 as Opus 21. By this time Schubert's days of setting Mayrhofer's verses were over, apart from the four miraculous solo songs and single part-song of 1824. There may have been a rift of sorts between poet and composer during 1821 and it could be that the dedication to Mayrhofer of this music from their shared past was Schubert's peace offering. The composer was in need of friends in that summer of 1823; he had fallen prey to syphilis and later spent a period in hospital. As he looked through his old songs, selecting a group for publication, the intimations of mortality in *Auf der Donau*, written six years earlier, must have struck him as stark prophecy. Indeed Schubert himself penned a poem (almost in Mayrhofian style) in May 1823 which includes the lines:

Take my life, my flesh and blood,
Plunge it all in Lethe's flood . . .

The three songs that Schubert chose for the Opus 21 set were united not only by their poet and vocal range but also by water. The set was advertised as *Drei Fischerlieder von Meyerhofer* [sic] *für den Bass*. The ponderings of Ulfru foreshadow W. H. Auden's poem 'Fish in the Unruffled Lakes' in which mankind turns an envious look 'On each beast and bird that moves'; creatures like fish are able to function serenely within nature's plan because unlike mankind they are not tormented by 'Duty's conscious wrong, / The Devil in the clock, / The goodness carefully worn / For atonement or for luck'. Because no man can feel safe on land the fisherman longs for the underwater security of the fish. Ulfru's music with its little shrugs and sighs and wry smiles is a very Viennese combination of charm and pessimism, an aquatic companion piece to *Der Alpenjäger* D524, that other Mayrhofer song for a working-class rustic. Schubert offers no better example than this of a striding bass line which accounts for the almost jazz-like casual mood of the piece.

Ulfru is more of a character than his unnamed colleagues in *Fischerlied* (Salis-Seewis D351 and D562) and Schlechta's *Fischerweise* D881; he is neither a hero nor very good at his job, but he is a survivor who has the precious gift of self-awareness, a Shakespearean clown who philoso-phizes in a merry minor key. Much more prized by singers is the Byronic *Der Schiffer* D536 which expresses Schubert's musical confidence in 1817 as well as the proselytizing desire of Mayrhofer's 'Bildung' circle to direct the moral compass of the impressionable young. But the musings of *Wie Ulfru fischt* reflect the bitter-sweet paradox of Schubert's own less idealistic view of the world in that devastating summer of 1823 when the song went to press. Raymond Joly has summarized how cleverly the composer managed the strophic structure of a potentially tricky poem: 'In the first two verses, line 4 has three accents and ends with a full stop; in the last strophe it has four accents and the syntax runs on to the end of line 6. Solution: repeat lines 7–8 in the first two strophes, lines 1–2 in strophe 3.'

The NSA prints an earlier version of the song in Volume 1b, p. 269, a copy made by Josef Huttenbrenner of a lost autograph from January 1817. The marking here is an 'Etwas bewegt' that Schubert later moderates. Also different are such things as dotted notes and the articulation of the piano part and Schubert clearly used it as the basis for his 1823 revisions for the publisher.

Autograph:	Missing or lost
Publication:	Published as part of the NSA in 1970 (P757; first version)
	Published as Op. 21 no. 3 by Sauer & Leidesdorf, Vienna in June 1823 (P43; second version)
Dedicatee:	Johann Mayrhofer
Publication reviews:	*Allgemeine musikalische Zeitung* (Leipzig), No. 26 (24 June 1824), col. 425–8 [Waidelich/Hilmar Dokumente I No. 282; Deutsch Doc. Biog. No. 479]
Subsequent editions:	Peters: Vol. 4/16; AGA XX 296: Vol. 5/18; NSA IV: Vol. 1a/158 & Vol. 1b/269; Bärenreiter: Vol. 1/126
Bibliography:	Kohlhäufl 1999, p. 185
	Newbould 1997, p. 148
Discography and timing:	Fischer-Dieskau I 9[13] 2'10
	Hyperion I 2[12]
	Hyperion II 17[16] 2'34 Stephen Varcoe

←— *Der Alpenjäger* D524   *Fahrt zum Hades* D526 —→

WIEDERSEHN   Reunion
(A. VON SCHLEGEL) **D855** [H574]
G major   September 1825

Nicht zu langsam

Der Früh - lings - son - ne hol - des Lä - cheln

(25 bars)

Der Frühlingssonne holdes Lächeln	The sweet smile of the spring sun
Ist meiner Hoffnung Morgenrot;	Is the dawn of my hope;
Mir flüstert in des Westes Fächeln	In the stirring of the west wind
Der Freude leises Aufgebot.	I hear joy's softly whispered call.
Ich komm', und über Tal und Hügel,	I am coming! And over hill and dale,
O süsse Wonnegeberin,	Sweet bestower of delight,
Schweb, auf des Liedes raschem Flügel,	May love sail to greet you
Der Gruss der Liebe zu dir hin.	On swift wings of song.

Der Gruss der Liebe von dem Treuen,
Der ohne Gegenliebe schwur,
Dir ewig Huldigung zu weihen
Wie der allwaltenden Natur;
Der stets, wie nach dem Angelsterne
Der Schiffer, einsam blickt und lauscht,
Ob nicht zu ihm in Nacht und Ferne
Des Sternes Klang hernieder rauscht.

Heil mir! ich atme kühnes Sehnen
Und atm' es bald an deiner Brust
Und saug' es ein mit deinen Tönen
Im Pulsschlag namenloser Lust.
Du lächelst, wenn mein Herz umfangen
Von deiner Näh', dann wilder strebt,
Indes das selige Verlangen
Der Güt' um deine Lippe schwebt.

Du liebst mich, göttlich hohes Wesen!
Du liebst mich, sanftes zartes Weib!
Es gnügt. Ich fühle mich genesen,
Und Lebensfüll an Seel' und Leib.
Nein, noch mit dem Geschick zu hadern,
Das schnell mich wieder von dir reisst,
Verschmäht mein Blut, das durch die Adern
Mit stolzen leichten Wellen kreist.

It is love's greeting from one who is devoted,
Who, without requital, swore
To pay eternal homage to you
As to all-powerful nature;
Who for ever watches and listens alone,
Like the sailor for the pole star,
For the sound of that star to come down to him
Through the remote expanses of the night.

What bliss! I sigh with bold yearning
And shall soon sigh upon your breast,
And drink it in with the sound of your voice
As I pulsate with nameless pleasure.
You smile as my heart, enveloped
By your presence, beats more wildly,
Whilst a happy longing
To be kind hovers about your lips.

You love me, noble, celestial creature!
You love me, gentle, tender woman!
It is enough, I am made well again,
And abundant life fills my soul and body.
No, the blood which ripples lightly, proudly,
Through my veins, disdains
To struggle against the fate
That tears me so quickly from you again.

AUGUST WILHELM VON SCHLEGEL (1767–1845); poem written in 1791

This is the eighth of Schubert's ten August von Schlegel solo settings (1816–26). See the poet's biography for a chronological list of all the August von Schlegel settings.

This is one of the most enchanting of Schubert's unknown songs. It would certainly have won greater fame if it had been published in the Peters Edition and thus made accessible to more singers. The music has the measured tread of joy to be found in some of Handel's music where steady mezzo staccato chords underpin a vocal line that unfolds with spacious elegance (for instance 'Va tacito e nascosto' from *Giulio Cesare*, 1724). A seamless legato melody challenges the singer with leaps and tessitura changes, while the accompaniment maintains its own quietly bouncing momentum; this crotchet movement is irresistible and sets the toe quietly tapping. The introduction even manages to suggest the presence of an obbligato instrument in the Handelian manner, although a duet between voice and accompaniment fails to materialize, except in a few cadential exchanges. In the second half of the song the movement of parts within seemingly simple chords in the accompaniment, and the discoveries of new beauties within an old vocabulary (the suspension under 'Liedes raschem Flügel' for example, b. 19), show the skill of an eighteenth-century master. The word 'Aufgebot' (b. 11) is given an elegant turn which is answered by a similar ornament in the piano in b. 12. (Ornamentation of this kind in Schubert's music sometimes suggests the influence of Vogl who may indeed have been the first to perform this song, albeit in a lower key than the original.)

It might seem puzzling that *Wiedersehn* dates from the holiday in Upper Austria (Steyr, Gmunden, Gastein) in 1825, about the same time that Schubert wrote the Great C major Symphony D944 and *Die Allmacht* D852, for it is as intimate as the Pyrker setting is monumental. But Schubert was always capable of working on many different-sized canvases at the same time. Another underestimated song comes to mind from the same period – the serenade of *Florio* D857/2 from Schütz's *Lacrimas* – which also boasts a rather ornate vocal line over a simple strummed accompaniment. After a long period of depression over his illness, the composer, on holiday at last, was happy again, and this is reflected in *Wiedersehn*, music that manages to be both joyful and relaxed. The simplicity of the song is deceptive, for it is full of Schubertian mastery at every turn, above all in the shaping of the melody that has an irresistible flow. Note the deliciously cheeky jump of a seventh at 'Lächeln' in the poem's first line (b. 6), and the way that even the shape of the music illustrates the text: on the printed page 'Ich komm', und über Tal und Hügel' descends by stages to the valley (b. 14), and then moves up the stave again to hilly territory (b. 15) – a veritable map of the composer's summer perigrinations with Vogl. The word 'Flügel' (wings) prompts the biggest interval in the piece at b. 19, an octave jump in Schubert's best open-hearted manner. We are fooled into believing that the phrase 'Schweb, auf des Liedes raschem Flügel, / Der Gruss der Liebe zu dir hin' is to be repeated in its entirety, but at the last moment an ornamented cadence, with triplets in the vocal line that occur only at this point, introduces a new musical idea and brings the strophe to its end. The toe is still tapping, and we are ready for the *da capo*. The piano has played such a minimal part in this song in terms of Schubert's usual use of motifs and figurations that we feel we have listened to an aria rather than a lied, but *Wiedersehn* is none the worse for that. Indeed, here simplicity is the result of distillation rather than any lack of inspiration.

The first publication of *Wiedersehn* (1843).

Autograph:	Staatsbibliothek Preussischer Kulturbesitz, Berlin (first draft)
First edition:	Published as a supplement to the book *Lebensbilder aus Österreich* in 1843; subsequently published as No. 1 of *Neueste Folge nachgelassener Lieder und Gesänge* by J. P. Gotthard, Vienna in 1872 (P427)
Subsequent editions:	Not in Peters; AGA XX 481: Vol. 8/156; NSA IV: Vol. 13/169
Bibliography:	Capell 1928, p. 218
Discography and timing:	Fischer-Dieskau II 7[11] 2'26
	Hyperion I 27[4]
	Hyperion II 30[11] 2'41 Matthias Goerne

← *Fülle der Liebe* D854   *Abendlied für die Entfernte* D856 →

WIEGENLIED
(KÖRNER) **D304** [H184]
F major   15 October 1815

Cradle song

Schlumm're sanft! Noch an dem Mutterherzen
   Fühlst du nicht des Lebens Qual und Lust;
Deine Träume kennen keine Schmerzen,
   Deine Welt ist deiner Mutter Brust.

Ach! wie süss träumt man die frühen Stunden,
   Wo man von der Mutterliebe lebt;
Die Erinnerung ist mir verschwunden,
   Ahnung bleibt es nur, die mich durchbebt.

Dreimal darf der Mensch so süss erwarmen,

   Dreimal ist's dem Glücklichen erlaubt,
Dass er in der Liebe Götterarmen
   An des Lebens höh're Deutung glaubt.

Liebe gibt ihm ihren ersten Segen,
   Und der Säugling blüht in Freud' und Lust,
Alles lacht dem frischen Blick entgegen;
   Liebe hält ihn an der Mutterbrust.

Wenn sich dann der schöne Himmel trübte,
   Und es wölkt sich nun des Jünglings Lauf:
Da, zum zweiten Mal, nimmt als Geliebte
   Ihn die Lieb' in ihre Arme auf.

Doch im Sturme bricht der Blütenstengel,
   Und im Sturme bricht des Menschen Herz,
Da erscheint die Lieb' als Todesengel,
   Und sie trägt ihn jubelnd himmelwärts.

Slumber softly! Still in your mother's arms
   You do not feel life's joy and torment.
Your dreams know no sorrows;
   Your whole world is your mother's breast.

Ah, how sweetly we dream in those early hours
   When we live by our mother's love;
My memory of them has faded;
   Just an impression remains to thrill through
     me.

Three times a man may experience such sweet
     warmth;
   Three times the happy man is permitted
To believe in the higher meaning of life,
   Embraced by the divine arms of love.

Love gives him her first blessing,
   And the infant blooms in joy and happiness,
All smile at his fresh gaze;
   Love holds him to his mother's breast.

When the fair heavens cloud over
   And the young man's path becomes obscure,
Then for the second time love takes him
   In her arms, as his darling.

But in the storm the flower-stem snaps,
   And in the storm a man's heart breaks;
Then love appears as an angel of death,
   And bears him jubilantly up to heaven.

Theodor Körner (1791–1813)

This is the twelfth of Schubert's sixteen Körner solo settings (1815–18). See the poet's biography for a chronological list of all the Körner settings.

This is one of seven songs written on 15 October 1815, almost every one of which is a 'hit' – which is not to say well known. The composer seems to have been in an exceptionally tender and loving mood, for who but someone with a full heart could have produced in a single day the two ravishing Stoll settings *Labetrank der Liebe* D302 and *An die Geliebte* D303? Not content with intimate lyricism alone, Schubert went on to write a winsome *Mein Gruss an den Mai* D305, a hearty *Skolie* D306, *Das gestörte Glück* D309 and the magisterial *Die Sternenwelten* D307. This *Wiegenlied* belongs to the tender and rhapsodic world of the Stoll songs, for it shares their seamless melodic flow and unhurried sensuality.

The key is a tonality often associated with sleep (cf. the Mayrhofer *Schlaflied* D527, for example). An air of ineffable calm reigns over the song's opening and Schubert uses the favourite device of keeping the accompaniment in the treble regions (for the first three bars at least) to give the picture of mother and child, viewed by the male narrator, an air of innocence and freshness. Emotive words like 'Qual' and 'Schmerzen' on the other hand are decorated by expressive little melismas (bb. 5 and 8). The setting of 'deine Welt' in bb. 9–10 is astonishing. Schubert has poised these two words high in the stave (on an F and held G) as if their tessitura represents the vantage point from which the whole world may be viewed; in this part of a healthy tenor voice we are left in no doubt that the outlook is exhilarating. After this epic high point (proof if any were needed that this is no conventional lullaby), '... ist deiner Mutter Brust' descends to nestle in the warmth of the body of the music in the middle of the stave. The composer must have been pleased with this phrase for he repeats it at the end of the strophe.

Wiegenlied from *Deutsche Lieder in Volkes Herz und Mund* (1864).

Performers are faced with something of a dilemma. After the first two introductory strophes the next four hang together only as a progressive story – a type of Three Ages of Man where the infant is cuddled, the lover caressed and the dying man embraced by the angel of death. The choice therefore is between a song that is rather short (two strophes) and fails to make the poet's point, or too long (all six). The shorter version would also suit female performance. Mention of 'three times' in the third verse initiates imagery that makes little sense unless the song is taken to its conclusion. It is only on reading the last verse (printed above, but not recorded for the Hyperion Edition) that we realize that *Wiegenlied* is related in Schubert's mind to the poet's early death on the battlefield. He had met and been enchanted by Körner two years earlier, and he must have been deeply affected by the poet's tragic fate. *Vor meiner Wiege* D927 (Leitner) also begins with contemplation of the cradle and ends with intimations of mortality. With this in mind, the dactylic 'death motif' of a minim and two crotchets in more than half of the accompaniment is a pre-echo of *Der Tod und das Mädchen* D531. No matter how gifted, famous, or loved we are, death awaits us all from the moment of birth. Schubert uses this dactylic cell not just for death, but as an analogue for the turning of the world, the pulsating of the stars, the inevitable rhythms of nature.

Together with the more robust *Das gestörte Glück*, *Wiegenlied* is 1815's farewell to Theodor Körner who was such an influential, albeit posthumous, presence in that great year of song. There was to be a single return to the poet in 1818 with *Auf der Riesenkoppe* D611.

Autograph: Österreichische Nationalbibliothek, Vienna (fair copy)
First edition: Published as part of the AGA in 1895 (P591)
Subsequent editions: Not in Peters; AGA XX 152: Vol. 3/117; NSA IV: Vol. 9/135
Bibliography: Youens 1996, pp. 140–41
Discography and timing: Fischer-Dieskau —
    Hyperion I 20[29]
    Hyperion II 10[20] 2'28 John Mark Ainsley

← *An die Geliebte* D303   *Mein Gruss an den Mai* D305 →

WIEGENLIED   Lullaby
(ANONYMOUS) OP. 98 NO. 2, **D498** [H315]
A♭ major   November 1816

Schlafe, holder, süsser Knabe,
Leise wiegt dich deiner Mutter Hand;
Sanfte Ruhe, milde Labe
Bringt dir schwebend dieses Wiegenband.

Schlafe in dem süssen Grabe,
Noch beschützt dich deiner Mutter Arm,
Alle Wünsche, alle Habe
Fasst sie liebend, alle liebwarm.

Schlafe in der Flaumen Schosse,
Noch umtönt dich lauter Liebeston,
Eine Lilie, eine Rose,
Nach dem Schlafe werd' sie dir zum Lohn.

Sleep, dear, sweet boy,
Your mother's hand rocks you softly.
The swaying cradle strap
Brings you gentle peace and tender comfort.

Sleep in the sweet grave;
Your mother's arms still protect you.
All her wishes, all her possessions
She holds lovingly, with loving warmth.

Sleep in the down, soft as a lap;
Pure notes of love still echo around you.
A lily, a rose
Shall be your reward after sleep.

ANONYMOUS/UNKNOWN

This is the twelfth of Schubert's nineteen solo settings of an anonymous poet. See Anonymous/
Unknown for a chronological list of all the songs for which the poets are unknown.

This beautiful little melody seems the most fragile, heartfelt Schubert, yet on paper it is hardly more than an oscillation between tonic and dominant. Richard Strauss half quoted it in *Ariadne auf Naxos* Op. 60 (the trio for Najade, Dryade and Echo in the opera's closing scene). Schubert's music has an inevitability and economy that every composer since must have envied. Apart from the composer's misapprehension that Claudius was the poet (it now appears he was not) there is one perplexing factor – the mystery of the middle verse, which is either a Romantic way of describing a cradle as a sweet grave (peaceful and comfortable) or something that actually relates to a child's death. Uri Liebrecht observes that the author of the poem is probably a woman – someone well practised in the mechanics of cradle control.

John Reed believes that Schubert was thinking mainly of the first verse when he wrote his music: 'The shadow of the grave, which obtrudes here as in so many early Romantic pieces on this subject, finds no place in Schubert's music.' Certainly the illustrations for this famous lyric in nineteenth-century anthologies depict a happy mother and a living child. Nevertheless, infant mortality was an everyday occurrence; indeed only a few months after the supposed date of the song's composition (for it is not dated in the composer's hand, only entered as November 1816 in a copy in the Witteczek-Spaun collection), the composer's half-brother Theodor Kajetan Anton died when only a few months old. It is highly unlikely that the song is related to this family bereavement, but it seems hauntingly prophetic. Its mood captures the contentment and wonder of parenthood, but there is also a note of consolation, a feeling of almost holy gratitude for life, however short. In masterpieces of this kind – *Frühlingsglaube* D686 is another example – Schubert's use of the major key encompasses an unobtrusive melancholy, a poignant undertone that ruffles complacency and raises questions such as these.

One final point concerns the last verse where the child is promised a gift for sleeping – a common enough ruse among mothers. But mention of flowers – hardly a gift that a child would appreciate – makes an eerie impression, as if they were to adorn a coffin. Needless to say there are many who love this song for what it appears to be on first hearing, a tender lullaby without any disturbing subtext, and it can be enjoyed as such. But Schubert's music reminds us, one way or another, that such moments of cloudless enchantment are hauntingly evanescent.

Autograph:	Missing or lost
First edition:	Published as Op. 98 no. 2 by Diabelli, Vienna in July 1829 (P229)
Publication reviews:	In his article of 23 March 1822, Friedrich von Hentl makes reference to a 'Wiegenlied'; although D498 was unpublished at the time, a copy, in the hand of Albert Stadler, was in circulation and it is possible that this is therefore the song mentioned by Hentl. See F. von Hentl, 'Blick auf Schubert's Lieder', *Wiener Zeitschrift für Kunst, Literatur, Theater und Mode* No. 36 (23 March 1822), p. 289f. [Waidelich/Hilmar Dokumente I No. 146; Deutsch Doc. Biog. No. 278] and Waidelich/Hilmar Dokumente II No. 146
Subsequent editions:	Peters: Vol. 2/194; AGA XX 277: Vol. 4/239; NSA IV: Vol. 5/76; Bärenreiter: Vol. 3/205
Bibliography:	Capell 1928, p. 120
	Einstein 1951, p. 161

Arrangements:	Arr. Leopold Godowsky (1870–1938) for solo piano, *Cradle Song* (1927, 2nd revised edition 1937) [*see* TRANSCRIPTIONS]
	Arr. Tilman Hoppstock (b. 1961) for guitar accompaniment (2 arrangements), in *Franz Schubert: 110 Lieder* (2009)
Discography and timing:	Fischer-Dieskau —
	Hyperion I 8[15]
	Hyperion II 16[19] 2'50 Sarah Walker

← *An die Nachtigall* D497   *Abendlied* D499 →

WIEGENLIED (Ottenwalt) *see* Der KNABE IN DER WIEGE D579

WIEGENLIED   Lullaby

(SEIDL) OP. 105 NO. 2, **D867** [H591]

A♭ major   1826?

(131 bars)

Wie sich der Äuglein	How carelessly
Kindlicher Himmel,	The eyes' childlike heaven
Schlummerbelastet,	Closes,
Lässig verschliesst! –	Laden with slumber!
Schliesse sie einst so,	Closes them thus, when one day
Lockt dich die Erde:	The earth calls you:
D r i n n e n i s t H i m m e l,	*Heaven is within you;*
A u s s e n i s t L u s t!	*Outside is joy!*
Wie dir so schlafrot	How your cheeks glow
Glühet die Wange!	Red with sleep!
Rosen aus Eden	Roses from Eden
Hauchten sie an:	Have breathed upon them;
Rosen die Wangen,	Your cheeks are roses,
Himmel die Augen,	Your eyes are heaven,
H e i t e r e r M o r g e n,	*Bright morning,*
H i m m l i s c h e r T a g!	*Heavenly day!*
Wie des Gelockes	How the golden waves
Goldige Wallung	Of your locks
Kühlet der Schläfe	Cool the edge

Glühenden Saum.	Of your glowing temples!
Schön ist das Goldhaar,	Your golden hair is lovely,
Schöner der Kranz drauf:	And even lovelier the garland upon it;
T r ä u m ' d u v o m L o r b e e r ,	*Dream of the laurel*
B i s e r d i r b l ü h t .	*Until it blooms for you.*
Liebliches Mündchen,	Sweet little mouth,
Engel umweh'n dich:	The angels hover round you;
Drinnen die Unschuld,	Inside is innocence,
Drinnen die Lieb';	Inside is love!
Wahre sie Kindchen,	Guard them, my child,
Wahre sie treulich:	Guard them faithfully:
L i p p e n s i n d R o s e n ,	*Lips are roses,*
L i p p e n s i n d G l u t .	*Lips are warmth!*
Wie dir ein Engel	As an angel
Faltet die Händchen;	Folds your little hands,
Falte sie einst so,	Fold them thus
Gehst du zur Ruh';	One day when you go to rest!
Schön sind die Träume,	Dreams are beautiful
Wenn man gebetet:	When you have said your prayers,
U n d d a s E r w a c h e n	*And your awakening*
L o h n t m i t d e m T r a u m .	*Is rewarded as is your dream.*

JOHANN GABRIEL SEIDL (1804–1875)

This is the second of Schubert's twelve Seidl solo settings (1826–8). See the poet's biography for a chronological list of all the Seidl settings.

The gifted Johann Gabriel Seidl was seven years younger than Schubert; he was born and he died in the same year as the very much greater poet, Eduard Mörike. He was infinitely ambitious, talented and versatile, and destined for success in Vienna, though not real world fame. The poems set by Schubert are the work of a man in his early twenties, and what he lacks in depth he makes up for in flair and atmosphere. His poetry often induces in Schubert a type of hypnotic musical response which almost constitutes a style of its own. The composer always finds a spellbinding atmosphere, but the poetry somehow meanders and lets him down in terms of follow-through or development. The Seidl songs (apart from the *Vier Refrain-Lieder* D866 written for commercial reasons) are always ravishing pieces of music, but they remain static. In *Im Freien* D880, for example (where the poem is imitative of Goethe), Schubert writes a work of heavenly length but the song does not develop or flower in the manner of a Goethe setting. A great poet is able to usher the composer into new and deeper levels of expression, and the young Seidl, gifted though he may have been, was not Goethe's equal here. This can also be said of *Das Zügenglöcklein* D871, *Am Fenster* D878 and *Wiegenlied*. Only in *Die Taubenpost* D965A is Schubert's genius served as well as can be imagined by Seidl's talent.

Thus is explained the only limitation of this song: a length which would lead to monotony if it were not for the composer's genius. Nevertheless this is the purest Schubert; he has lavished music on this lullaby that glows with innocence and unalloyed delight. The idea of delicacy is apparent in the very first bar: the first figuration, an arpeggio of four quavers ascending through both staves in the key of A flat, both hands together only on the third of these, is as perfectly formed as a baby's fingers; the fact that each works perfectly is the kind of miracle that no parent can quite believe. The pianist must cultivate a mother's touch, gentle and sensuous. The momentum of the accompaniment is self-powering, a small engine having about it the naturalness of a cat's contented purr. The A flat arpeggio is repeated in the second half of the bar before the music shifts into the second inversion of the subdominant with the least amount of effort. The little finger of the pianist's left hand remains curled reassuringly around the bass A flat, and the fingers of the right have to shift only a semitone upwards. This is like 'first steps at the keyboard', but if it is baby language it is the kind spoken by a besotted adult. Seidl's poem is of course precisely this, its short lines attempting to mirror the sort of simplicity that a child could grasp.

The move to the dominant seventh at the beginning of b. 3 continues the interplay of simple chords, weaving a cat's cradle of an accompaniment, mostly lovingly legato, but here and there enlivened by a tripping staccato glint (as in b. 9). The fourth bar introduces a cross-rhythm which is the gentlest of teases, a sudden smile flickering across the baby's face, perhaps, that causes the maternal heart to miss a beat. A parent's love is as basic and unquestioning as this, all sophistication reduced to the fundamentals of a loving response, and only Schubert can mirror this in music without toppling into sentimentality. Each of Seidl's strophes (the second half of which is indented on the page in the manner of a chorus) makes one musical verse. There is a change of mood and a move to the relative minor at 'Schliesse sie einst so' (from b. 15), and the trickle of murmured quavers in the vocal line is replaced by a broader cantilena of minims and crotchets. A felicitous contrast of harmony underlines the difference between 'drinnen' (b. 19) and 'aussen' (b. 21).

The second verse moves to F major at b. 40 rather than F minor, and we realize that although small details of word-setting are carefully changed in each strophe, these must not disturb the hypnotic nature of the music. These tiny modifications are as subtle and private as the exchange of love between mother and child: each moment of interaction brings a new emotional inflection almost inaudible, and certainly invisible, to outsiders.

The third verse (from b. 55) is sometimes omitted, particularly by German singers who find it too sentimental by a hair, with mention of garlands of laurel hopelessly outdated. But the song is usually performed in its entirety, unimpeded by embarrassment or concern at its length. We are drawn into another world and we stay there, under Schubert's spell, until the child falls asleep and the composer allows us to leave the room.

Autograph:	Missing or lost
First edition:	Published as Op. 105 no. 2 by Josef Czerny, Vienna in November 1828 (two days after Schubert's death) (P175)
Publication reviews:	*Allgemeiner Musikalischer Anzeiger* (Vienna), No. 5 (31 January 1829), p. 19f. [Waidelich/Hilmar Dokumente I No. 688]
Subsequent editions:	Peters: Vol. 3/72; AGA XX 572: Vol. 8/252; NSA IV: Vol. 5/84; Bärenreiter: Vol. 4/6
Bibliography:	Capell 1928, p. 224
	Einstein 1951, p. 304
Discography and timing:	Fischer-Dieskau II 8[19] 4'06 (Strophes 1, 2, 4 and 5 only)
	Hyperion I 26[15] 5'45 Christine Schäfer
	Hyperion II 31[14]

←— *Widerspruch* D865   *Totengräber-Weise* D869 —→

WILHELM MEISTERS LEHRJAHRE

This novel by Goethe, a landmark of German literature, inspired Schubert to no fewer than eighteen musical settings. The manuscript of an earlier version of the novel, *Wilhelm Meisters theatralische Sendung* (1777–85) was only discovered in 1909 and is sometimes referred to as the 'Urmeister'. Goethe was persuaded to return to work on it by the generous encouragement of Friedrich Schiller (qv) who was deeply involved in his Kantian aesthetical studies at the time; the conflict between duty and inclination that runs through the published version of *Wilhelm Meister* can be traced back to this bracing influence. If we take into account the sequel, *Wilhelm Meisters Wanderjahre*, the final form of which was published posthumously in 1829, Goethe was preoccupied with the project, as he was with *Faust* (qv), for most of his adult life.

Wilhelm Meisters Lehrjahre is a picture of an ideal society drawn by an artist of liberal persuasion who had begun his novel before the upheaval of the French Revolution and who, in these pages at least, quietly assimilated political changes while neither vaunting nor decrying them. Nationalism, in the absence of a nation state, is represented by Wilhelm's absorption in the theatre which goes back in turn to Schiller's dream of founding a national theatre as a stepping stone to political unity. There is little attention paid to class (the *Spottlied* set to music by Hugo Wolf in 1889 is a hilarious exception) although, in the latter part of the book, America with its new Constitution is promoted as the land of the future. (Perhaps this is why Friedrich von Schlegel (qv) took the publication of the novel to be 'a political act'.) Artists are treated with dignity as significant members of the community; religion and the church play almost no role as far as the novel's hero is concerned. This was society as Goethe wished it to be, and as he was lucky enough to experience it for much of his life.

What had begun as a *Künstlerroman* (artist's novel) became a *Bildungsroman* (educational novel). Wilhelm's desire to educate himself, to make the best of his abilities, was later reflected in the formulation of a 'law of culture' by Thomas Carlyle, Goethe's friend and translator: 'Let each become all that he was capable of being.' Perhaps Carlyle was one of the few to understand that Goethe took education to be the formation of 'the whole human being'. Goethe's literary model had probably been Christoph Wieland's *Geschichte des Agathon* (1766–7) where the eponymous Athenian youth takes a pathway of learning that leads him towards enlightened manhood. In a similar way the Goethe novel concerns the process of a young man's apprenticeship to life itself. The works that followed in the wake of *Wilhelm Meister* are legion, and not only by German-speaking authors such as Gottfried Keller (*Der grüne Heinrich*, 1855) and Adalbert Stifter (*Der Nachsommer*, 1857). Stendahl's *Le Rouge et le noir* (1830), Charles Dickens's *David Copperfield* (1850) and Gustave Flaubert's *L'Éducation sentimentale* (1869) owe more than a little to Goethe's novel. The

Wilhelm Meisters

Lehrjahre.

Ein Roman.

Herausgegeben

von

Goethe.

Zweyter Band.

Berlin.
Bei Johann Friedrich Unger.
1795.

Title page of *Wilhlem Meisters Lehrjahre* (1795).

rippling effects of the influence of *Wilhelm Meisters Lehjahre* extend well into the twentieth century with such works as *A Portrait of the Artist as a Young Man* (James Joyce, 1916), *Der Zauberberg* (Thomas Mann, 1924), *Amerika* (Franz Kafka, 1927) and *À la recherche du temps perdu* (Marcel Proust, published 1913–27). Isaiah Berlin's description of Goethe's *Meister* style (and this includes the more diffuse *Wanderjahre* sequel) might almost refer to Joyce's experiments in *Ulysses* (1922): 'From a piece of sober prose, or a scientific description of, say, the temperature of water or a particular kind of garden, Goethe suddenly goes off into ecstatic, poetical, lyrical accounts of one kind and another and bursts into poetry and then as sharply and as quickly returns to perfectly melodious but severe prose.'

Wilhelm Meister is born into a prosperous middle-class background. As a child he writes plays for puppets, but as an adult his infatuation with the actress Marianne leads him to the warm-blooded world of live theatre. In Book III of the eight-book novel (published in four volumes by Unger, Berlin, 1795) he eventually finds inspiration in Shakespeare (hence, perhaps, the first name of Goethe's protagonist) – an enthusiasm that furthers his resolve, against his parents' wishes, to spend his life on the stage and to found a German national theatre.

After his father dies Wilhelm, now financially independent, meets the flirtatious actress Philine. The earlier books of the novel include characters such as Marianne (Wilhelm's first love, mother of his son Felix, whom he wrongly believes has betrayed him) and the actors Werner, Melina, Laertes, Philine (to whom a lyric is given – *Singet nicht in Trauertönen* – set to music by both Schumann Op. 98a no. 7 and Wolf as *Philine*, 1888) and the stage-manager Serlo and his sister, the highly strung Aurelie. Wilhelm encounters a group of tightrope walkers and sees their act during which an androgynous child, whom he learns is named Mignon, is required to contort hearself into painful acrobatic positions. Later he sees her mistreated and he buys her freedom after threatening the troupe leader with punishment for abducting her. She attaches herself to Wilhelm's retinue which includes other actors and the mysterious Harper whose deeply pessimistic songs both move and disturb Wilhelm. Mignon confesses that she regards Wilhelm as her father. The characters of Mignon and the Harper, who stand somewhat outside the main story (but are the focus of interest for Schubertians and lieder-lovers), are described by Hellmut Ammerlahn as Wilhelm's 'tragic doubles', each representing an unresolved aspect of his own struggle for maturity and the longed-for mastery that is part of his fictional surname. The theatrical troupe prepares a performance of Shakespeare's *Hamlet*. After the tipsy revelry following the first night Mignon observes Philine entering Wilhelm's bedroom and is inconsolable. After a rehearsal for the second performance the Harper starts a fire which consumes the actors' lodgings; he also attempts to kill the child Felix. The Harper, seemingly deranged, returns singing the last of his lyrics, *An die Türen will ich schleichen*. After conversing with him kindly, Wilhelm arranges for him to be looked after; he even replaces the harp which has been burnt in the fire. Matters begin to unravel in terms of Wilhelm's relationship with his actors. It is clear by the end of Book V that this phase of his life is over.

After failing as an actor – having no talent, as Goethe informs us – Wilhelm falls in with a circle of enlightened aristocrats who belong to the *Turmgesellschaft*, the Fellowship of the Tower. The figure of Lothario, who has apparently fought in the American War of Independence on the side of the rebels, seems to be modelled on Karl August, Duke of Weimar, and Wilhelm's place in this entourage equates with Goethe's privileged position at the court of Weimar. (Some commentators believe that the character of the Abbé was inspired by Herder.) In Book VIII when Wilhelm visits Natalie, Lothario's sister, he once again encounters Mignon, to whom Natalie has given shelter. The girl is failing in mind and body and Natalie recounts the circumstances in which she sings the last of her lyrics, 'So lasst mich scheinen'. Shortly afterwards Mignon succumbs to a seizure and dies. The secular funeral service for her was set to music by Schumann in 1849 as *Requiem für Mignon* Op. 98b. The Marchese, Mignon's aristocratic Italian

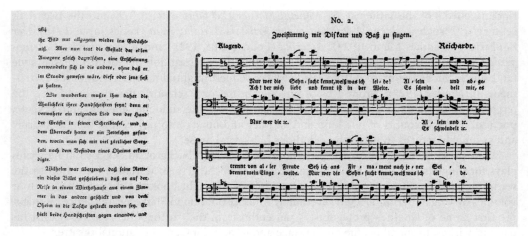

Facing p. 264 in Vol. II of the first edition of *Wilhlem Meister* is a fold-out musical supplement with music by
Reichardt for the duet *Nur wer die Sehnsucht kennt* (1795).

uncle, identifies the body as that of his niece and we learn a great deal more about her background (*see* MIGNON LIEDER: AN OVERVIEW as well as HARFNERLIEDER). Wilhelm eventually
finds happiness with Natalie whom he has earlier known as 'the Amazon'. The Marchese makes
over Mignon's family home in Italy to Wilhelm in gratitude for what he did to look after her
during her short lifetime.

Wilhelm Scherer noted of this work that 'complete unity of composition is wanting; motives
are let drop, inconsistencies may be pointed out, and the style becomes inferior towards the
close'. It was of course this very lack of conventional unity and predictability that appealed to
early Romantics like Friedrich von Schlegel, although the mystical Novalis (qv) found the work
'unfortunate and absurd – unpoetic in the extreme as far as the spirit is concerned'.

There is no denying that many modern readers would agree with Novalis, and most find
Wilhelm Meisters Lehrjahre difficult. 'In order to enrich us with knowledge, Goethe leads us
to the fairest goals by the longest and roughest roads', wrote Henry James, a champion of the
work which, criticism aside, is a turning point in literary history. Scherer reminds us why:
'Goethe treats with sympathetic toleration, one may say with equal love, bad and good, mean
and noble characters. He was not the first to employ this manner, but he brought to its culmination the movement which was started in protest against [Samuel] Richardson's unnaturally
virtuous heroes.' The Victorians dismissed Goethe's novel as immoral, but George Eliot
refuted that charge in 1865. She wrote that Goethe 'brings us into the presence of living,
generous humanity – and erring and self-deluding, but saved from utter corruption by the
salt of some noble impulse, some disinterested effort, some beam of good nature'. Goethe's
sympathy for the benighted characters of Mignon and the Harper is evident, but neither is
allowed to survive after they have served their purpose. They both fall by the wayside as the
novel's hero, his understanding of life deepening, approaches a classical ideal of balanced
humanity and wins for himself the maturity that can only be achieved through 'Bildung' of
this kind.

In the novel's first edition there are no illustrations but eight fold-out songs are included.
These are settings by Johann Friedrich Reichardt (four Harper texts, three of Mignon and one
for Philine) – a measure of the importance that Goethe attached to music as being complementary to his poetry and prose. It is perhaps true that musical literacy was assumed among
the readership of higher-class novels at the time in Germany, but it was also an indication

that the ability to read and appreciate music was part of the poet's ideal concept of what 'Bildung' should be. There is certainly no musical equivalent to be found in the publication of late eighteenth-century English novels.

Schubert's song-settings from this novel were the following:

February 1815
Der Sänger D149 ('Was hör ich draussen vor dem Tor') Op. post 117

18 October 1815
Sehnsucht (Mignon) (I) D310 ('Nur wer die Sehnsucht kennt') In two versions

23 October 1815
Mignon ('Kennst du das Land?') D321 (title otherwise *Mignons Gesang*)

13 November 1815
Wer sich der Einsamkeit ergibt I D325 (title otherwise *Harfenspieler*)

September 1816
Sehnsucht D359 *(Mignon) (II)* ('Nur wer die Sehnsucht kennt') (title otherwise *Lied der Mignon*)
Mignon Fragmente (2) D469 ('So lasst mich scheinen')
Wer nie sein Brot mit Tränen ass D478/2 (first setting) (D480/1)
Wer nie sein Brot mit Tränen ass D478/2 (second setting) (D480/2)
Sehnsucht (Mignon) (III) D481 ('Nur wer die Sehnsucht kennt')

1816–22
Gesänge des Harfners I D478/1 ('Wer sich der Einsamkeit Ergibt')
Gesänge des Harfners III D478/3 (D479) ('An die Türen will ich Schleichen')

April 1819
Sehnsucht D656 *(Mignon) (IV)* ('Nur wer die Sehnsucht kennt') Version for male vocal quintet

April 1821
Mignon I D726 ('Heiss mich nicht reden')
Mignon II D727 ('So lasst mich scheinen')

Autumn 1822
Gesänge des Harfners II D478/2 (third setting) (D480/3) Op. 12 no. 2 ('Wer nie sein Brot mit Tränen Ass')

January 1826
Gesänge aus Wilhelm Meister I D877/1 with the title *Mignon und der Harfner* ('Nur wer die Sehnsucht kennt') Duet version
Gesänge aus Wilhelm Meister II D877/2 with the title *Lied der Mignon* ('Heiss mich nicht reden')
Gesänge aus Wilhelm Meister III D877/3 with the title *Lied der Mignon* ('So lasst mich scheinen')

Bibliography: Adler 2012
                  Ammerlahn 2000, pp. 347–9
                  Berlin 1999
                  Cave 2011
                  Scherer 1883, 1886

MARIANNE VON WILLEMER (1784–1860)

THE POETIC SOURCE
Johann Wolfgang von Goethe: *West-östlicher Divan* Stuttgart [*sic*] in der Cottaischen Buchhandlung, 1819.

THE SONGS

March 1821	*Suleika* I D720 [p. 161 without any acknowledgement from Goethe that Marianne von Willemer was the co-author]
March 1821? or December 1824?	*Suleika* II D717 [p. 166 without any acknowledgement from Goethe that Marianne von Willemer was the co-author]

The story of Goethe's passion for Marianne von Willemer is a late chapter in a long life governed by an extraordinary succession of amorous influences: Annette Schönkopf (Leipzig), Friederike Brion (Sesenheim), Charlotte Buff (Wetzlar), Lili Schönemann (Frankfurt), Charlotte von Stein, Corona Schröter and Christiane Vulpius (all three in Weimar, the latter eventually becoming his wife). In terms of significant new female friends in Goethe's life, only the painful and embarrassing episode of Ulrike von Levetzow in Marienbad post-dates that of the Willemer liaison (if a relationship may be termed thus when its consummation was highly unlikely). The meeting with Marianne coincided with the poet's visit to the Rhineland in 1814 and his interest in the poetry of the Persian poet Hafiz (*c.* 1315–*c.* 1390) whose work had been recently translated by the Austrian Joseph von Hammer-Purgstall (1774–1856).

Maria Anna Katharina Theresia Pirngruber was the illegitimate daughter of an instrument maker from Linz named Jung and a Viennese actress named Pirngruber. Dark of complexion and attractive, she had come to Frankfurt from Austria in a ballet company at the age of fourteen and caught the eye of the twice-widowed banker from Frankfurt, J. J. von Willemer. Goethe's character Mignon comes as powerfully to our minds as it must have to the poet's when he heard the story of Marianne's early life. In 1800 Willemer took her under his wing and educated her with his own children. The meeting with Goethe took place when Willemer, an old friend of the poet, and Marianne (aged thirty by this time)

visited Goethe in Wiesbaden, a few weeks before their marriage – the banker's third. The poet was strongly attracted to her, and she to him. Goethe visited the couple at their summer home once before their marriage and again a fortnight afterwards. Almost a year later (August 1815) he returned to see the Willemers, and they spent three days with him in Heidelberg in the September of that year. A correspondence had been initiated in which Marianne was dubbed 'Suleika' and was wooed by her distinguished new friend in the guise of

Marianne von Willemer, 1809.

Marianne von Willemer, 1819.

informing Goethe that the mule ('Maultier') seeking its way in the mist on the mountain pass in the 1780s has now been superseded by 'a Phaeton with a span of fast horses'. The correspondence between them lasted to the end of Goethe's life and masked a fact of which no one was aware until long after the poet's death when, in the 1850s, she confessed to Hermann Grim her authorship of some of the poems in the *West-östlicher Divan* (qv). Marianne von Willemer had so fully entered into the spirit of Goethe's oriental game that she had written highly skilful replies (as 'Suleika') to his 'Hatem' poems. These were included in the collection published in 1819 by Goethe as if he himself had penned them. There is a precedent for this kind of collaboration with an *inamorata* in the Goethe song texts: *An den Mond* ('Füllest wieder Busch und Tal') D295 and D296 owes some of its finest lines to a reworking by Charlotte von Stein of the first version of the poem after she felt abandoned by Goethe's unannounced flight to Italy.

Of the two Zuleika poems set to music by Schubert (Schumann and Wolf set others) the first, 'Ostwind', was written on the way to see Goethe in Heidelberg in September 1815 (thus the 'hohe Mauern' are the walls of that old and picturesque city), and the second, 'Westwind', on the way back. It is true that the poet changed a few details in Marianne's poems (not always for the better according to her admirers) but he must have regarded this unacknowledged collaboration as the greatest literary compliment (discreet perhaps because of both her marriage and his) he was able to pay a fellow artist. Here is the original of Marianne von Willemer's fourth and fifth stanzas of her Zuleika poem:

the venerable oriental sage 'Hatem'. Thus although Goethe and Marianne were in personal contact from time to time during a fourteen-month period (and we are not certain whether her husband was an effective chaperone) their main communication was literary – and they remained correspondents for the next seventeen years – even if less frequently than Marianne might have wished.

Marianne's knowledge of Goethe's work was extraordinarily detailed. She delighted in allusion and quotation: in a letter to Goethe of December 1825 her reference to her, the writer's, 'eternal feelings' ('die ewigen Gefühle der Schreibenden') is actually a quotation from the second strophe of the poem Schubert set as *Nachtgesang* D119. On a visit to Italy in 1828 she alludes to one of the most famous lines in 'Kennst du das Land?' (Schubert's D321),

Und mich soll sein leises Flüstern
Von dem Freunde lieblich grüssen,
Eh' noch diese Hügel düstern,
Sitz ich still zu seinen Füssen.

Und du magst nun weiterziehen,
Diene Frohen und Betrübten,
Dort wo hohe Mauern glühen,
Finde ich den Vielgeliebten

And its gentle whispering is sent
As a dear message from my lover;
Even before these hills darken,
I shall be sitting quietly at his feet.

And now you may pass on,
And serve the happy and the sad;
There, where the high walls glow,
I shall find my dearly beloved.

Compare what Goethe makes of the poem's fourth verse when he rewrites it:

Und *mir bringt* sein leises Flüstern	And its soft whisperings brings me
Von dem Freunde *tausend Grüsse*;	A thousand greetings from my beloved;
Eh' noch diese Hügel dustern,	Before these hills grow dark
Grüssen mich wohl tausend Küsse.	I shall be greeted by a thousand kisses.

As Lorraine Byrne points out, these revisions achieve 'greater musical fluency, a finer vowel gradation and a richer oriental colour, yet the tone of the verse is changed. Marianne's equanimity is reciprocated by a thousand kisses; her potent image of love replaced . . .' In fact it is Marianne, not a great poet, though a fine one, who writes with greater personal honesty, and Peter Gülke (*Liedlexikon* 2012) avers that these words could easily be substituted in performances of the song and that academic considerations (that Schubert did not know the real Willemer text) should not get in the way. Sitting at Goethe's feet in admiration of the great man's discourse was probably what actually happened, rather than the kisses of the poet's imagining.

In 1824, long after the epistolary passion had calmed to a level of cherished memory and a shared secret, Goethe wrote to Marianne referring to the song of the west wind (the music clearly not by Schubert): 'How often I've heard the song sung, how often have I heard it praised, and in secret smilingly appropriated what should, in the most beautiful sense, be called my own.'

Marianne herself seems also to have been proud of their joint deception. The truth was revealed only after Goethe's death – Schubert and Schumann were never aware of whose words they were really setting. But there is one more irony: it was Marianne von Willemer who first praised Schubert's music (without naming the composer) to Goethe. In a letter of 16 April 1825 she tells the great poet how she sent to a music shop for a copy of Beethoven's Goethe setting 'Herz, mein Herz, was soll das geben' (*Neue Liebe, neues Leben* Op. 75 no. 2); at the same time, someone imaginatively helpful at the music establishment sent her a copy of the 1821 edition of Schubert's Op. 14 – the first *Suleika* song, D720, published together with *Geheimes* D719. In her letter to Goethe she refers to the music as a 'recht artige Melodie' ('a very pretty tune'). She was to live long enough to be a correspondent of one of Schubert's greatest admirers – Johannes Brahms, who rated the first *Suleika* higher than any other Schubert song.

See also WEST-ÖSTLICHER DIVAN.

Bibliography: Byrne 2003, pp. 368–82

WILLKOMMEN UND ABSCHIED   Hail and farewell
(GOETHE) OP. 56 NO. 1, **D767** [H503 & H503A]

The song exists in two versions, the second of which is discussed below:
(1) beginning of December 1822; (2) appeared July 1826

(1)   'Geschwind' D major   **C**   [104 bars]

(2)   C major

Geschwind

Es schlug mein Herz,   ge-schwind   zu Pfer - de,
Mi   bat - te'l   cor!   o - là! il   de - strie - ro!

(105 bars)

Es schlug mein Herz, geschwind zu Pferde!	My heart was beating. Quick, to horse!

Es schlug mein Herz, geschwind zu Pferde!
Es war getan fast eh' gedacht;
Der Abend wiegte schon die Erde,
Und an den Bergen hing die Nacht:
Schon stand im Nebelkleid die Eiche,
Ein aufgetürmter Riese, da,
Wo Finsternis aus dem Gesträuche
Mit hundert schwarzen Augen sah.

Der Mond von einem Wolkenhügel
Sah kläglich aus dem Duft hervor,
Die Winde schwangen leise Flügel,
Umsausten schauerlich mein Ohr;
Die Nacht schuf tausend Ungeheuer;
Doch frisch und fröhlich war mein Mut:
In meinen Adern welches Feuer!
In meinem Herzen welche Glut!

Dich seh ich, und die milde Freude[1]
Floss von dem süssen Blick auf mich,
Ganz war mein Herz an deiner Seite,
Und jeder Atemzug für dich.
Ein rosenfarbnes Frühlingswetter
Umgab das liebliche Gesicht,
Und Zärtlichkeit für mich – Ihr Götter!
Ich hofft' es, ich verdient' es nicht!

Doch ach, schon mit der Morgensonne
Verengt der Abschied mir das Herz;
In deinen Küssen welche Wonne!
In deinem Auge, welcher Schmerz!
Ich ging, du standst und sahst zur Erden,
Und sahst mir nach mit nassem Blick:
Und doch, welch Glück geliebt zu werden!
Und lieben, Götter, welch ein Glück!

My heart was beating. Quick, to horse!
No sooner thought than done.
Evening was already cradling the earth,
And night hung about the mountains.
Already the oak stood in a cloak of mist,
A towering giant, there
Where darkness gazed from the bushes
With a hundred coal-black eyes.

From a bank of cloud
The moon gazed plaintively out through the haze;
The winds softly beat their wings,
Whistling eerily about my ears.
The night begat a thousand monsters,
Yet my mood was bright and cheerful;
What fire in my veins!
What ardour in my heart!

I see you and a gentle joy
Flowed over me from your sweet gaze;
My whole heart was with you,
And my every breath was for you.
A rosy springtime
Enveloped your lovely face,
And tenderness for me – ye Gods!
I had hoped for this, but never deserved it!

But alas, with the morning sun
Farewell already oppresses my heart.
In your kisses what ecstasy!
In your eyes what sorrow!
I went; you stood looking down,
And gazed after me with moist eyes:
And yet, what happiness it is to be loved!
And to love, O gods, what happiness!

[1] Dich *sah* ich (past tense) is the reading in all other editions of Goethe. Schubert follows with what he found in the Viennese edition of *Gedichte* (1810), perhaps a misprint.

JOHANN WOLFGANG VON GOETHE (1749–1832); poem written in spring 1771

This is the seventieth of Schubert's seventy-five Goethe solo settings (1814–26). See the poet's biography for a chronological list of all the Goethe settings.

Illustration of Goethe and Friederike Brion for a Viennese edition of *Dichtung und Wahrheit* (1819).

Goethe wrote this poem at the time he was courting Friederike Brion in Sesenheim, a horse-ride away from where he was studying at the University of Strassburg (today Strasbourg in France). The first ten lines were found among Friederike's papers. In Strassburg the poet sat at the feet of the celebrated Johann Gottfried Herder who opened his younger colleague's eyes to the simplicity and power of folksong, and to the plays of Shakespeare. The freshness of the young Goethe's love affair thus coincided with a new type of lyric that came from the heart, unburdened by the poetic formalities of an earlier age. The delightful *Mit einem gemalten Band* (set to music by Beethoven Op. 83 no. 3) is another example of this. In *Willkommen und Abschied* (arguably influenced by Beethoven's triplet-accompanied *Neue Libe, neues Leben* Op. 75 no. 2) Schubert mirrors the excitement and ardour with one of his equestrian set pieces, not quite as successful and substantial in musical terms as *An Schwager Kronos* D369 and *Auf der Bruck* D853, but something of a companion to that other night journey, *Erlkönig* D328. Like another Goethe setting of the time, *An die Entfernte* D765, this song is a clever marriage of aria and recitative, an ingenious compromise between the German lied style and the powerful world of Italian opera.

This is no ordinary narrative recounted in the past tense; unlike *Erlkönig* D328, *Willkommen und Abschied* is not a ballad. Rather is it self-confessedly autobiographical. The title informs us that at the end of the first leg of this horse-ride there is a welcome awaiting the poet: moments – perhaps hours – of pleasant dalliance before he has to tear himself away from Friederike. The poem encompasses the entire experience of a day – setting off from Strassburg, arriving in Sesenheim, and setting off in the opposite direction. It is typical of Goethe that it is impossible for us to work out the timetable from his own words which are confessional only up to a point.

Whether or not young Goethe's courtship of Friederike Brion incorporated a sexual element is something that has always been discussed at length – and largely dismissed as improbable. It is surely possible to spend rapturous hours in the company of the beloved without actually making love. Goethe, however, was not entirely insensible to everyday male vanities and there was a side to him that would have preferred his readers to imagine him as at least a possible ardent Lothario (however discreet) years before he could claim to be sexually experienced. Accordingly the parameters of this impassioned visit are kept deliberately vague. The first two verses take place in the evening and night; the third is touched with the light of dawn – as we may guess from 'Ein rosenfarbnes Frühlingswetter' – and the final verse faces the return journey in the morning sunlight. Between the excitement of the journey to Sesenheim and the return

Illustration for *Willkommen und Abschied* by Edmund Kanoldt.

to Strassburg there is a period when Goethe dismounts from his horse. Whether he had a secret assignation with Friederike outside, under cover of darkness, or first thing in the morning in the garden; whether he stole secretly into her father's house; or whether he passed the night chastely as a guest of the family (much more likely) – all this information is elided in a narrative that has more poetry than truth about it. It is no surprise that the poet's autobiography was to bear the title *Dichtung und Wahrheit*.

No doubt inspired by the poem's opening words, Schubert elected to set it as a moto perpetuo horse-ride (these words would be an invigorating challenge to any composer) but he found himself with a musical problem when it came to the episodes of introspective recall that lie between, and during, the poet's outward and return journeys. In truth the aria he composed would have been infinitely more suited to a one-way journey, with the poet's arrival at his beloved's side coinciding with the triumphant ending of the song. As it is, Schubert keeps Goethe on horseback more or less throughout; to make up for this, the music slows down here and there in an attempt to incorporate those flashbacks and gaps in the narrative where the listener should be less aware of the horse-ride than the poet's deeper feelings. The trouble is that Goethe's poem (with the exception of the anomalous 'seh' in the edition footnoted in Verse 3 and 'Verlengt der Abschied' in Verse 4) is entirely in the past tense, while Schubert's music seems conceived in the present with on-the-spot reactions to emotions and experiences. It is up to the performers to make this conflict of interests somehow work on the concert platform: naturally there are parts of the song that benefit enormously from the excitement of the here-and-now, the feeling that the singer is in the middle of an impetuous journey, but there are other passages where images of tenderness and doubt, ill reconciled with the sound of a thundering gallop, come to the surface via the narrator's memory. The music as a whole is conceived as an excitable aria of considerable momentum – it has something of a display piece about it and it strives for unity – but the subtleties outlined above make it unacceptable to rush through it in hectoring fashion, and it is equally inappropriate to come to a grinding halt in those passages marked 'Langsam' or 'Langsamer'. There are few other Schubert songs where the composer tinkers so extensively with nuances of tempo, and none where the initial concept of a moto perpetuo has to be moderated in the interests of a somewhat inconvenient narrative scenario. Chugging triplets between the hands in the accompaniment (easy to play in comparison to *Erlkönig* D328) propel the music forward in splendid fashion. The published key of C major is rather too low to be comfortable for a tenor, but it suits a high baritone with high G at his disposal. One suspects the transposition from the original key of D major (a version for which tenors can still opt) was made to suit the voice of Johann Michael Vogl. With such a slew of words throughout the singer has to work hard at his diction, and the pianist needs to be aware that the tempo marking is 'Geschwind' and not 'Schnell', a meaningful distinction in Schubert. In the first strophe there has to be time to register the size of the mist-garlanded giant oak tree, and to make us feel the shudder of fear (remarkably expressed in the spiky chordal interjection of b. 18) as the rider passes what seem to be a hundred coal-black eyes. The second strophe shifts into F minor for a picture of the moon peeping out of the clouds – the same tonality as for that famous moonlit song to a Hölty poem, *An den Mond* D193, and with similar imagery. In this music the journey on horseback continues via the accompaniment, but for these few bars the triplets must seem to waft, rather than thunder, through the staves.

At the beginning of the third verse Schubert follows the probably erroneous 1810 Viennese edition where Goethe's 'Dich sah ich' (b. 48) is changed to 'Dich seh ich', the tense thus shifted from past to present so that the poet's memory of having seen the beloved waiting for him is turned into an experience in the present. The pianist, who has subtle gradations of tempo and musical impulse at his or her command, must keep the journey going here in a mood totally different from that of the demonic energy of the opening – the accompaniment's triplets need to simmer and shimmer rather than boil and toil. As far as the poem is concerned, Goethe has already arrived in Sesenheim and surely dismounted, but for reasons of musical architecture Schubert keeps his narrator in the saddle. When I first heard this song the music suggested to me that the poet was more concerned with completing his aria than with stopping to speak to Friederike – he seems simply to gallop right past her. Hans Pfitzner, in his fine setting of 1922, solves this problem by ending the tumultuous journey at the right dramatic moment, and the music for a thundering horse-ride is not heard again. In Schubert's song it is only in the last lines of the third verse ('Ihr Götter! / Ich hofft' es, ich verdient' es nicht!' from b. 69) that the composer allows the poet to dismount (following a last-minute accelerando in bb. 66–8). The piano's accompanying triplets cease, the marking is 'Langsam' for seven bars and the vocal writing takes on the quality of recitative. The singer has to understand that these bars represent the poet's only time actually spent with his beloved and must perform this passage in a mood of grateful wonderment ('I don't deserve this love, but how very lucky I am to have it!'). Indeed, these few bars free of the piano's galloping are the only place in the song where it is musically possible to imagine the couple in each other's arms.

At the beginning of the fourth verse the musical structure demands that the singer return to his steed and begin his homeward journey (the marking is 'Wie oben' from b. 76). The lines 'In deinen Küssen welche Wonne! / In deinem Auge welche Schmerz!' are given the *canzone* treatment that has already characterized much of the song. Throbbing triplets in the accompaniment suggest that the narrator is on the move again and that whatever has passed between man and maid was crammed into those seven meagre bars of recitative. This was indeed a lightning visit – and, who knows, Goethe may have galloped all the way to Sesenheim for a few minutes with Friederike. Schubert's self-contained *moto perpetuo* is thus more or less preserved, and the sweep of the music brushes literary reservations aside.

Goethe unwittingly plays one more trick on Schubert which reveals the weakness of the composer's telling a story that has taken place in the multi-layered past, while employing the immediacy of the Italian musical style. The return to Strassburg on horseback has already been under way for some ten bars in musical terms when the words 'Ich ging, du standst und sahst zur Erden, / Und sahst mir nach mit nassem Blick' are sung (from b. 76). These lines are clearly unsuitable for rumbustious musical treatment. Even if 'ich ging' were translated as 'I was leaving', with Goethe in motion and Friederike stationary, how much of her downcast gaze would it be possible to perceive from a galloping horse? Schubert has no option here but to keep going in triplets, albeit with a rider that moderates the overdrive. He recapitulates the F minor moon music of b. 22 and marks this passage (at b. 86) 'Etwas langsamer', thus warning performers that Friederike's forlorn demeanour must, temporarily, take precedence for a few bars.

This highlights the conflict of interest throughout the work between Goethe's words and Schubert's exciting Italianate aria. However moist Friederike's eyes, however downcast her gaze, it is essential that this '*Etwas* langsamer' (my italics) is merely a shade slower than the original tempo; the narrator has only just begun his return journey and it is impossible to rein in the galloping horse so soon after it has set off. Added to this, the wonderful peroration of the closing page is very near, and this must be launched with the right amount of energy behind it (in my experience a real and sudden 'Langsam' at b. 86 makes for a very disjointed pair of closing pages for the song as a whole). The word 'doch' (b. 94) is here the linchpin on which the mood of the whole coda is dependent; the composer manages the gradual return to C major superbly in order to engineer a suitable atmosphere of relief and triumph for the closing bars.

Although the broad brushstrokes of *Willkommen und Abschied* fail to do justice to the changing details of the poem, Schubert at least matched the poet's overall passion with an impressive dramatic sweep. The year 1822 was one of Italian domination in the opera house in Vienna and it seems that Schubert was trying to appeal to the prevailing taste; in any case, a part of him was always in love with Italian style. The vocal line achieves an intensity on the final page which, despite itself, owes much to the final page of Gluck's 'Che farò senza Euridice'. It was probably the poet Craigher de Jachelutta who provided Schubert with an Italian singing translation of the poem (*Felice arrivo e congedo*) that was published in the first edition (the first line runs 'Mi batte 'l cor! o là! il destriero!'). This was part of a plan to broaden the appeal of the Schubert lieder to other countries – a not particularly successful ploy at the time. For the first edition the work was also transposed from its original key of D to C major, thus bringing it within the capabilities of a high baritone. There is no great difference between the two versions, the biggest change in the C major edition being a more protracted setting (double the length) of the word 'doch' in the second-last line of the poem at b. 94 – we have already noted what an important word this is here – announced by the marking 'Wie oben' in b. 94.

Willkommen und Abschied employs a subtle variant of modified strophic technique. There is nothing conventionally strophic about the work except that certain key cells are repeated or varied throughout: for example, the four-bar phrase first heard at 'Der Abend wiegte schon die Erde / Und an den Bergen hing die Nacht' (bb. 6–10) is repeated at bb. 33–7 (beginning 'In meinen Adern welches Feuer!') and again at bb. 81–5 ('In deinen Küssen welche Wonne!'). (The lack of verbs in this latter part of the poem is an ellipsis engineered to increase verbal excitement.) In the first strophe this phrase is followed by an episode in E flat; in the second by the Gluckian *Orfeo* phrase mentioned above. A combination of these phrases concludes the song with the interpolation of material from the beginning of the second strophe. Strophe 3 remains on its own for reasons of constrast. The piano writing receives the same recapitulative treatment as the vocal line. Phrases, fragments of phrases and variants of phrases are woven together and plaited into the song structure to serve as building struts, giving the work a powerful impression of inevitability and unity. The way the song is built up of cells that reproduce and proliferate is, coincidentally, a musical mirror of Goethe's botanical observations of the growth of plants (cf. his poem *Die Metamorphose der Pflanzen*).

The story of Goethe and Friederike inspired countless articles and stories, even a Lehár operetta entitled *Friederike* that featured the great Richard Tauber hit *O Mädchen, mein Mädchen*. Over the years curiosity grew about the circumstances of Goethe's early amatory life. It is said that when nineteenth-century Goethe scholars visited Sesenheim to interview the old people there about their memories of the poet and his Friederike, they came across an elderly lady who remembered the incident well. 'Oh, that poor girl,' she recalled, 'she was so in love! And then all of a sudden that Goethe went away . . . and since then no-one has heard anything of him' ('und seitdem hat kein Mensch von ihm gehört').

The cover of Lehár's operetta *Friederike* (1928) with Goethe's profile in the foreground.

The pastor's house in Sesenheim with Friederike Brion's signature.

Autograph:	Staatsbibliothek Preussischer Kulturbesitz, Berlin (first version, first draft)
Publication:	Published as part of the AGA in 1895 (P692; first version)
	Published as Op. 56 no. 1 by Anton Pennauer, Vienna in July 1826 (P102; second version)
Dedicatee:	Karl Pinterics
Publication reviews:	*Allgemeiner musikalischer Anzeiger* (Frankfurt), No. 2 (8 July 1826), p. 10f. [Waidelich/Hilmar Dokumente I No. 395; Deutsch Doc. Biog. No. 672]
Subsequent editions:	Peters: Vol. 3/25 (second version); AGA XX 419a & b: Vol. 8/58 (first version) & 64 (second version); NSA IV: Vol. 3a/61 (second version) & Vol. 3b/176 (first version); Bärenreiter: Vol. 2/98
Bibliography:	Capell 1928, pp. 181–2
	Friedlaender 1902, Vol. 2, p. 171
Further settings:	Johann Friedrich Reichardt (1752–1814) *Willkommen und Abschied* (1794)
	Hans Pfitzner (1869–1949) *Willkommen und Abschied* Op. 29 no. 3 (1922)

Discography and timing:	Fischer-Dieskau II 5[17]	3'18	
	Hyperion I 6[9]	3'31	Anthony Rolfe Johnson (first version)
	Hyperion I 28[21]	3'45	John Mark Ainsley (second version)
	Hyperion II 26[8]	3'31	Anthony Rolfe Johnson
	Hyperion II 26[9]	3'45	John Mark Ainsley

⟵ *Am Flusse* D766   *Am See* D746 ⟶

KARL GOTTFRIED THEODOR WINKLER (Theodor Hell) (1775–1856)

THE POETIC SOURCES
S1 *W. G. Becker's Taschenbuch zum Geselligen Vergnügen*, Herausgegeben von Friedrich Kind. Fünf und Zwanzigster Jahrgang, 1815. Leipzig bei Joh. Friedrich Gleditisch

This source mentions 'Musik von Dotzauer' underneath the heading *Das Heimweh*. This refers to the composer and cellist Justus Johann Friedrich Dotzauer (1783–1860) who lived and worked in Dresden from 1811 until his death. He was not at all known as a composer of lieder. There seem to have been no song supplements printed for this almanac.

S2 *Die Lyra. Eine Auswahl deutscher Gedichte, Monologen, Dialogen, Reden, Erzählungen, und dramatischer Scenen, ernsten und launigen Inhalts, mit Erläuterungen über den Vortrag derselben zum Behuf des Unterrichts auf Schulen und der Uebung in der Deklamation. Herausgegeben von C. F. Solbrig, Deklamator.* Leipzig 1816 bei Carl Friedrich Franz

These sources are both unknown to the NSA, but one of them at least was clearly known at some point to Mandyczewski because all six verses are printed in the AGA exactly as they appear in the Becker *Taschenbuch* and *Die Lyra*. Since that time the AGA has remained the only known source of the complete text of *Das Heimweh*.

Becker's Taschenbuch zum geselligen Vergnügen for 1815 source of *Das Heimweh*.

THE SONG
July 1816   *Das Heimweh* D456 [S1: pp. 6–62]
[S2: p. 31, No. IX of 'Gedichte ernsten Inhalts']

Theodor Hell was the pseudonym for Karl Gottfried Theodor Winkler, who truly seems to have been as bright a spark as the name under which he wrote. He was born on 9 February 1775 in Waldenburg and was well known in Dresden not only as a poet but as an impresario and journalist. Indeed he seems to have been a leading light in the musical life of that city, taking almost every role possible, from assistant director of the court theatre to founder-editor of the *Dresdner Abendzeitung* and long-time editor of the renowned almanac *Penelope*. We know that he travelled as far afield as Egypt because his poem about homesickness (*Heimweh*, set by Schubert in 1816) was written in Alexandria in 1813. He published his poetry (three volumes in all, 1821 and 1830) under the title *Lyratöne*, designating each as a 'Tonreihe', or a sequence of melodies. These volumes were published too late to have been used by Schubert. Winkler was a colleague of two other Schubert poets from Dresden, each responsible for a single solo song: Friedrich Kind (*Hänflings Liebeswerbung* D552), and Karl August Engelhardt, pseud-

onym Richard Roos (*Ihr Grab* D736). Winkler/Hell is perhaps best remembered for his connection with Carl Maria von Weber, whose orphaned children were placed in his care. He made the German translation of the English libretto for *Oberon* and provided Weber with a fine original libretto for *Die drei Pintos*.

Karl Winkler (Theodor Hell), unsigned engraving.

Winkler was also a specialist in the translation of French plays. He had a tiny personal connection with Schubert through his work as a critic on the *Abendzeitung*. As a result of the failure of Helmina von Chézy's *Rosamunde* (qv, for which Schubert had written the incidental music) in December 1823, a vituperative review by the editor of the Vienna *Theaterzeitung* was posted to Dresden for publication. Weber had recently taken offence at Schubert's manifest lack of enthusiasm for *Euryanthe*, but was embarrassed by this critical attack. More on Chézy's behalf, perhaps, than Schubert's, Winkler refused to publish the article. He could not have known that seven years earlier one of his poems had been beautifully set to music by the very composer whose work he now refused to see torn to pieces in his newspaper. He died in Dresden on 24 September 1856.

Der WINTERABEND

(LEITNER)[1] **D938** [H657]
B♭ major   January 1828

The winter evening

(96 bars)

Es ist so still, so heimlich um mich,[2]
Die Sonne ist unter, der Tag entwich.
Wie schnell nun heran der Abend graut! –
Mir ist es recht, sonst ist mir's zu laut.
Jetzt aber ist's ruhig, es hämmert kein Schmied,
Kein Klempner, das Volk verlief und ist müd,

Und selbst, dass nicht rassle der Wagen Lauf,
Zog Decken der Schnee durch die Gassen auf.

Wie tut mir so wohl der selige Frieden!
Da sitz' ich im Dunkeln, ganz abgeschieden,[3]
So ganz für mich – nur der Mondenschein
Kommt leise zu mir in's Gemach.[4]

It is so silent and secret all around me;
The sun has set, the day has vanished.
How swiftly now the evening grows grey!
It suits me well; day is too loud for me.
But now it is peaceful, no blacksmith hammers,

And no plumber. The people have dispersed, tired.

And, lest carts should rattle on their way,
The snow has even draped blankets through the streets.

How welcome to me is this blissful peace!
Here I sit in the darkness, quite secluded,
Quite self-contained; only the moonlight
Comes softly into my room.

[1] Leitner's title for his poem is simply *Winterabend*.
[2] Leitner writes (*Gedichte*, 1825) 'Es ist so still, *und* heimlich um mich'.
[3] Leitner writes 'Da sitz' ich im *Dunkel*'.
[4] Schubert leaves out the word 'herein' (the rhyme for 'Mondenschein') at the end of this line.

[(. . . 3 lines . . .)]⁵   [(. . . 3 lines . . .)]

Er kennt mich schon und lässt mich schweigen.   It knows me and lets me be silent,
Nimmt nur seine Arbeit, die Spindel, das Gold,   And just takes up its work, the spindle, the gold,
Und spinnet stille, webt und lächelt hold,⁶   And spins and weeps silently, smiling sweetly,
Und hängt dann sein schimmerndes   And then hangs its shimmering veil
   Schleiertuch
Ringsum an Gerät und Wänden aus.   Over the furniture and walls all around.
Ist gar ein stiller, ein lieber Besuch,⁷   It is a silent and beloved visitor
Macht mir gar keine Unruh' im Haus'.   That causes no disturbance in my house.
Will er bleiben, so hat er Ort,   If it wishes to stay, there is room,
Freut's ihn nimmer, so geht er fort.   If it is not happy, then it goes away.

Ich sitze dann stumm im Fenster gern'   Then I like to sit silently at the window,
Und schaue hinauf in Gewölk und Stern.   Gazing up at the clouds and stars,
Denke zurück, ach weit, gar weit,   Thinking back to long, long ago,
In eine schöne, verschwundne Zeit.   To a beautiful, vanished past.
Denk' an sie, an das Glück der Minne,   I think of her, of love's happiness,
Seufze still und sinne und sinne. –   And sigh softly, and muse.

KARL GOTTFRIED VON LEITNER (1800–1890); poem written in 1823

This is the tenth of Schubert's eleven Leitner solo settings (1822–3 and 1827–8). See the poet's biography for a chronological list of all the Leitner settings.

This masterpiece is one of the great song achievements of Schubert's final year, but it still receives a bad press from certain critics who are determined to blame the composer for self-indulgent performances of a work they consider too long and lacking in incident. But how could *Der Winterabend* be anything other than long? Winter evenings, by definition, *are* long – and that is part of their magic. The unfolding of these musical mysteries, a sequence of musings and memories, is not to be hurried. This is one of those works which brings home to us the hectic pace of our own benighted century; even by the standards of Schubert's Vienna this portrait of Styrian country life defies the haste and pressure of the metropolis. After his visit to Graz Schubert compared his home city, Vienna, unfavourably: 'There is so much confused chatter . . . and one rarely or never achieves any inward contentment.' In this song we can hear his delight in one of the few safe havens of artistic sympathy he found outside Vienna – the home of the Pachler family. 'In Graz,' Schubert wrote, 'I soon recognized an artless and sincere way of being together.' It was Marie Pachler who reintroduced Schubert to the poetry of her fellow Styrian Karl von Leitner (the composer had set one Leitner poem already in 1823) and this song is aglow with the warmth of domesticity and small-town life. The singer could be one of the citizens addressed bitterly by the traveller in *Im Dorfe* D911/17 from *Winterreise* but Schubert, a few months after completing his great cycle, was all too willing to allow the bourgeois world of comfortable carpet slippers to find a spokesman of its own. With unerring accuracy the composer suggests the singer's maturity of age and experience; a mellow

⁵ The following three lines were left out by Schubert probably because of their use of French-influenced colloqualisms:

Brauche mich aber nicht zu geniren,   But I don't need to be on my best behaviour,
Nicht zu spielen, zu conversiren,   Or play cards, or make small-talk,
Oder mich sonst attent zu zeigen.   Or show myself attentive in any other way.

⁶ Schubert, almost certainly as the result of a slip of the pen (b. 50), writes 'still' here instead of 'hold'. This makes nonsense of the rhyme of course and although 'still' is printed in the NSA, the performer should opt for Leitner's 'hold'.
⁷ The addition of the second 'ein' in this line is Schubert's. Leitner's line reads 'Ist gar ein stiller, lieber Besuch'.

flow of contemplation (for the song has also suffered from performances that swoon to the point of stasis) proceeds in a manner as leisurely as a spiral of smoke from a pipe.

The comfort of being indoors on a winter evening is marvellously conveyed in the introduction. The joy and security of the fireside on a stormy night was to be given rapturous expression twelve years later in Schumann's Kerner setting *Lust der Sturmnacht* Op. 35 no. 1, but there are no raging elements here, only the gently falling snow. Perhaps this is what Schubert means to convey in what Capell calls the 'patter of soft semiquavers' in the accompaniment, as soothing as gentle rain on the roof at bedtime, or the sound of time ticking ineluctably away. This undertow pervades the song and is perhaps the secret of its hypnotic restfulness; it is the discreet work of those inner fingers of the pianist's right hand to simulate a string quartet's second violin and viola. The little finger sings the first violin's beautiful melody which is later taken up by the voice and which is the main theme of this nocturnal impromptu.

What a skilfully constructed theme this is – a great, wide-spanned melody in B flat major, uninterrupted in its flow and unpunctuated by rests. It begins on a plateau of repeated notes in the first bar, then lifts a third, only to fall with a sigh, a pattern (stillness followed by the stretching out of longing resolving into acceptance) which is repeated and developed in sequence before being rounded off by a tiny cadential figure of four semiquavers in b. 5. This last gruppetto is a motif that varies with the greatest ingenuity at the close of each reappearance of the refrain, and which is a tonal analogue for 'sinnen', the process of turning thoughts over in the mind. Only Schubert could suggest the exquisite combination of contentment and pain outlined by this great melody. We are left in no doubt that these notes represent the thoughts (for this is an interior drama) of a sitting figure. We will later discover in the denouement of the song's final pages the reason for the ache in the music – and also its hard-won joy.

We begin by listening, through the narrator's ears, to the world about us. When we hear that the tradesmen of the town have stopped their work, that the people are tired (the stretch and yawn of the turn at 'und ist müd', b. 19) and that the street noises are muffled by a blanket of snow, we are ready to begin (from Verse 2, upbeat to b. 20) a gradual retreat from the here and now. The solitary thinker needs to find his way into the past in order to rediscover his precious memories. He moves through one harmonic portal after another on a journey which only Schubert could arrange. The first of these important doorways is the magical modulation from the home key of B flat into G major that leads us into the next important panel of the song at 'Wie tut mir so wohl' (from b. 31). The narrator sits in the dark (the piano's commentary after 'der selige Frieden' in b. 33 recalls the writing in the left hand in *Der blinde Knabe* D833) until the arrival of the light of the moon at 'nur der Mondenschein / Kommt . . .' (b. 40). This prompts a further journey into E flat major and initiates an extended soliloquy about the narrator's heavenly guest. During the course of this lunar interlude there is another breathtaking modulation at b. 56 (at 'Ist gar ein stiller, ein lieber Besuch'), this time into D major, and we have reached the song's inner sanctum of tranquillity and reflection. The music gradually retraces its steps to B flat major via G major, and to what at first seems to be a straightforward recapitulation of the opening theme at 'Ich sitze dann stumm' (b. 67). But Schubert has not yet played the final hand of the evening: at b. 73 the unexpected A flat bass for the first inversion of F minor under 'denke zurück' is more than a shift of harmony – it signifies a shift of time and a searching of the memory that costs the narrator a certain amount of pain.

The real recapitulation is soon at hand and everything comes into focus as the narrator is at last in touch with profound memories of his beloved wife, lost to him in person perhaps, but alive once more in his mind. Significantly, she makes her reappearance not in some distant tonality but in the home key at b. 78, her presence signified by a glorious counter-melody in the piano at 'Denk' an sie' (surely a deliberate extra variation of the B flat *Rosamunde* music that inspired the piano Impromptu D935/3) which serves as a descant to our song's by now familiar vocal theme. This passionate combination, a metaphor for partnership, transfigures what we now realize has only been half of the whole, half of the music for a story of shared lives. As the husband's theme joins the wife's we briefly hear the complete story. The memory of happiness prompts a moment of exaltation, for there is life in the old boy yet. The vocal line is turned on its head: instead of F rising note by note to B flat, which we have heard on the first appearance of 'Denk' an sie, an das Glück der Minne', those words are repeated slightly more histrionically from b. 85, starting on the F an octave higher (the highest and longest note in the piece) and falling to B flat via an affecting appoggiatura on the word 'sie'. Just for a moment we hear the energy and gallantry of a young lover as the passion of time gone by reasserts itself – Ah yes, he remembers it well. The moment of passion soon passes; the motif of four contemplative semiquavers for the word 'und', plus a plaintive cadence, is repeated again and again for 'und sinne'. Schubert never wrote a more eloquent melisma on a seemingly inessential word. At b. 94 the postlude stretches upwards to embrace the distant key of D major for one last time, but with a smile (or is it perhaps tears?) sinks back into the armchair comfort and solitude of B flat.

In this quintessential portrait of Biedermeier life nothing has happened of very great import. Only the sympathetic listener will detect a masterful musical evocation of those feelings of which Hardy wrote in his poem 'I Look Into My Glass', when the 'fragile frame at eve' is shaken with 'throbbings of noontide'. And there is the key word for the pianist who has to set this tempo: it is not a quick song by any means, but the quiet pulsations, the *throbbing* (not plodding) of those semiquavers, are at the heart of the music's flow. Performance of this song by a man should convey a spirit of quiet gallantry, like an old soldier in retirement living alone, with only his memories for company – a portrait, as it happens, of Karl von Leitner in later life.

The carefully corrected state of the autograph – in particularly beautiful condition – suggests that Schubert envisaged immediate publication of this piece, and that his autograph was meant to go straight to the printer. Tobias Haslinger intended to publish the piece in 1829, but failed to do so, instead selling the song to Diabelli who established something of a monopoly in Schubert's posthumous songs. *Der Winterabend* had to wait seven years after the composer's death to appear in print when Diabelli accorded the song an entire issue of the Nachlass.

Autograph:	Pierpont Morgan Library, New York (fair copy)
First edition:	Published as Book 26 of the Nachlass by Diabelli, Vienna in October 1835 (P311). The song had been advertised by Haslinger in January 1829 as one of his publications 'Unter der Presse'. This song, along with several others including *Der Wallensteiner Lanzknecht beim Trunk* D931 was clearly sold to Diabelli before the appearance of the Haslinger edition.
Subsequent editions:	Peters: Vol. 5/148; AGA XX 551: Vol. 9/118; NSA IV: Vol. 14/83; Bärenreiter: Vol. 4/110
Bibliography:	Capell 1928, p. 246
	Fischer-Dieskau 1977, p. 270
	Youens 2002, pp. 284–98
Further settings:	Heinz Winbeck (b. 1946) *Winterreise. Stationen für 19 Solostreicher* (based on *Der Leiermann* D911/24 and *Der Winterabend*)
Discography and timing:	Fischer-Dieskau II 9[12] 6'59
	Hyperion I 15[11]
	Hyperion II 35[10] 8'35 Margaret Price

← *Al par del ruscelletto (Cantate für Irene Kiesewetter)* D936   *Die Sterne* D939 →

WINTERLIED

Winter song

(HÖLTY) **D401** [H266]

A minor   13 May (deciphered as 'March' by Deutsch) 1816

(14 bars)

Keine Blumen blühn;	No flowers bloom;
Nur das Wintergrün	Only the winter green
Blickt durch Silberhüllen;	Peeps through its silver mantle;
Nur das Fenster füllen	The window is filled
Blumen rot und weiss,	Only with red and white flowers,
Aufgeblüht aus Eis.	Blossoming from the ice.
Ach! kein Vogelsang	Ah, no birdsong
Tönt mit frohem Klang;	Rings out with joyous tones;
Nur die Winterweise	Only the wintry strains
Jener kleinen Meise,	Of the titmouse
Die am Fenster schwirrt,	That flutters at the window
Und um Futter girrt.	Chirping for food.
Minne flieht den Hain,	Love flees the grove
Wo die Vögelein	Where the birds
Sonst im grünen Schatten	Once made their nests
Ihre Nester hatten;	In the green shade;
Minne flieht den Hain,	Love flees the grove
Kehrt ins Zimmer ein.	And comes into this room.
Kalter Januar,	Cold January,
Hier werd' ich fürwahr,	Here, in truth,
Unter Minnespielen,	Among love games,
Deinen Frost nicht fühlen!	I shall not feel your frost.
Walte immerdar,	Reign for ever,
Kalter Januar!	Cold January!

LUDWIG CHRISTOPH HÖLTY (1748–1776); poem written in early 1773. Adapted for
publication in 1804 by JOHANN HEINRICH VOSS (1751–1826)

*This is the sixteenth of Schubert's twenty-three Hölty solo settings (1813–16). See the poet's
biography for a chronological list of all the Hölty settings.*

This is a song written on a remarkable day, 13 May 1816. Within the same twenty-four hours
Schubert wrote *Frühlingslied* D398, *Auf den Tod einer Nachtigall* D399 and *Die Knabenzeit*
D400. All these settings were by Hölty. For *Winterlied* the composer did not need his

imagination to picture a colder part of the year: 1816 was famously the year 'without summer', the notorious 'Eighteen Hundred and Froze to Death' during which European and American weather suffered the catastrophic results of volcanic ash in the atmosphere caused by the eruption of Mount Tambora in Indonesia. There were food shortages throughout Europe and sharp frosts in August. Schubert was always at his best when observing the natural world, and the extraordinary eloquence of this little song surely owes something to the aberrations of the weather.

Winterlied is typical of a type of A minor style in Schubert's song-writing of 1816. It shares this tonality with *Lied* ('Ins stille Land') (March 1816, D403), the Salis-Seewis setting that eventually led in 1826 to the final version of Mignon's 'Nur wer die Sehnsucht kennt' D877/4. The song is also related to another 1816 work, the D minor version of Mignon's lyric, *Sehnsucht* (II) D359. If the prevailing colours of *Frühlingslied* are blue and green (where he *would* have had to use his imagination in this coldest spring on record), in *Winterlied* the composer effectively suggests tones of grey and white. The tune has all the economy and plainness of a denuded branch of a tree, while the accompaniment is easy enough to play with stiff, frozen fingers. A tiny detail that is typical of Schubert's mastery is the means by which he manages to set the enjambement of the second and third lines of the first verse: instead of placing the word 'blickt' on the strong first beat of the bar, it is put on the second beat of the preceding bar (bb. 4–5, thus connecting it to 'grün') with a tie across the bar line that makes the declamation sound utterly natural. The long note on the beginning of 'aufgeblüht' (bb. 10–11), followed by a flow of quavers, suggests blossoming after a period of waiting. As always with strophic songs, these effects are much better suited to some verses than others. The work as a whole has a tone of gentle nostalgia and melancholy that makes the last verse difficult to bring off: the mood of the words changes here to joy in the cosy life indoors with the beloved – let cold January reign for ever! This is similar to the mood of *Der Winterabend* D938, or Kerner's poem *Lust der Sturmnacht*, set by Schumann in 1840, Op. 35 no. 1. Schubert might have chosen to engineer for this verse one of his miraculous changes from A minor to A major, but he preferred to preserve the minimalistic severity of a strophic song.

Autograph:	Library of Congress, Washington
First edition:	Published as part of the AGA in 1895 (P638) and subsequently as part of the NSA in 2009
Subsequent editions:	Not in Peters; AGA XX 220: Vol. 4/102; NSA IV: Vol. 10/98
Bibliography	McKay 2001
Further settings and arrangements:	Johann Friedrich Reichardt (1752–1814) *Winterlied*, two settings (1778 and 1792)
	Minna Brandes (1765–1788) *Winter-Lied* (1788)
	Arr. Tilman Hoppstock (b. 1961) for guitar accompaniment, in *Franz Schubert: 110 Lieder* (2009)
Discography and timing:	Fischer-Dieskau I 7[10] 0'56 (Strophes 1 and 4 only)
	Hyperion I 17[10]
	Hyperion II 14[18] 2'09 Lucia Popp

← *Die Knabenzeit* D400   *Die Erwartung* D159 →

WINTERLIED (Trinklied im Winter)   Winter song
(HÖLTY) **D** DEEST [H133]
(Fragment) F♯ minor   1815

(10 bars)

Das Glas gefüllt!	Fill your glasses!
Der Nordwind brüllt;	The north wind roars,
Die Sonn' ist niedergesunken!	The sun has gone down.
Der kalte Bär	The cold Bear
Blinkt Frost daher!	Glitters frost.
Getrunken, Brüder, getrunken!	Drink, brothers, drink!
Die Tannen glühn	The pine logs glow brightly
Hell im Kamin,	In the hearth,
Und knatternd fliegen die Funken!	And crackling sparks fly.
Der edle Rhein	The noble Rhein
Gab uns den Wein!	Has given us wine!
Getrunken, Brüder, getrunken!	Drink, brothers, drink!
Der edle Most	The noble must
Verscheucht den Frost	Scares off the frost
Und zaubert Frühling hernieder:	And conjures up spring:
Der Trinker sieht	The drinker sees
Den Hain entblüht,	The grove in bloom,
Und Büsche wirbeln ihm Lieder!	And songs swirl from the bushes!
[. . . 3 . . .]	[. . . 3 . . .]

LUDWIG HÖLTY (1748–1776). Adapted for publication in 1804 by
JOHANN HEINRICH VOSS (1751–1826)

This is the simplest and heartiest of communal songs, an ideal invitation to the warmth of a party on a winter night. And what better piece for a convivial Schubertiad than *Winterlied*? It has the archaic feel of modal folksong – Schubert invents a background for the piece as if it were the traditional, age-old music of rousing wassail. The Deutsch catalogue fails to list this version of the song which is in the collection of the Musikverein in Vienna and has come to light only since 1978. It was published privately by Reinhard Van Hoorickx and then in Volume 8 of the NSA. The original (D242) version, *Trinklied im Winter*, is exactly the same music sung by unaccompanied vocal trio (two tenors and bass). It is quite possible that Schubert needed to provide a piano part for rehearsal purposes and that this 'version' was born of such practical considerations. On the other hand it is equally likely that he wrote this out on the spur of the moment as a contribution to an autograph album. For either of these reasons the piano part is merely a straightforward reduction of the vocal parts and shows no sign of elaboration. As it happens, the instrument's percussive strength suits the mood well. For the Hyperion recording we made a compromise between the choral nature of D242 and the solo layout of D deest: on the disc the tenor leads the song, but the bibulous invitation to the brotherhood prompts the entry of the men's chorus.

Autograph: Missing or lost (choral version); Gesellschaft der Musikfreunde, Vienna (piano-accompanied version)

First edition: Accompanied version published privately by Reinhard Van Hoorickx. See below for details of unaccompanied Terzett (P853)

Subsequent editions: Not in Peters; Not in AGA (original Terzett in XIX 18, p. 74); NSA IV: Vol: 8/152 (solo version); NSA III: Vol. 4/48 (terzett only)

Discography and timing: Hyperion I 20[1]   0'52   John Mark Ainsley & the London
                        Hyperion II 8[16]   Schubert Chorale (dir. Stephen Layton)

← *Alles um Liebe* D241   *Die Bürgschaft* D246 →

WINTERREISE
(Müller) OP. 89 **D911**

Winter journey

Autographs: Pierpont Morgan Library, New York: Part One (first draft), Part Two (fair copy)
                      Wienbibliothek im Rathaus, Vienna (copy (Abschrift) of Part One with corrections in Schubert's hand)

First edition: Published in two volumes as Op. 89 by Tobias Haslinger, Vienna: Part One appeared on 14 January 1828, Part Two on 30 December 1828 (just over a month after the composer's death)

First Performances: Three separate songs were sungs were sung in public in 1828/9, but it is not known when the complete cycle was performed for the first time. Bauernfeld mentions *Winterreise* as having been performed by Vogl 'deep in old age' (thus in the late 1830s, probably at the home of Karl von Enderes) without clarifying whether he meant the entire cycle.
                      It is possible than Julius Stockhausen sang his first complete *Winterreise* as early as 1851, in London, deciding to present the work in the order of Müller's *Gedichte*, 1824.

Publication reviews: Part One:
                      Wiener allgemeine Theaterzeitung, No. 39 (29 March 1828), p. 156 [Waidelich/Hilmar Dokumente I No. 606; Deutsch Doc. Biog. No. 1070]
                      Wiener Zeitschrift für Kunst, Literatur, Theater und Mode, No. 69 (7 June 1828), p. 559f. [Waidelich/Hilmar Dokumente I No. 619; Deutsch Doc. Biog. No. 1107]
                      Berliner allgemeine musikalische Zeitung, No. 26 (25 June 1828), p. 206f. [Waidelich/Hilmar Dokumente I No. 622; Deutsch Doc. Biog. No. 1112] This review mentions the forthcoming 'sequel'.

Part Two:

Wiener Zeitschrift für Kunst Literatur, Theater und Mode, No. 30 (10 March 1829), p. 252 [Waidelich/Hilmar Dokumente I No. 707]

Parts One and Two:

Allgemeiner Musikalischer Anzeiger (Vienna) No. 3 (17 January 1829), p. 10ff. [Waidelich/Hilmar Dokumente I No. 684]

Subsequent editions:	Peters: Vol. 1/54–121; AGA XX 517–40: Vol. 9/2–77; NSA IV: Vol. 4a/110–91; Bärenreiter: Vol. 3/78–145
Further settings:	Julius Harrison (1885–1963) *Winter and Spring* (a combination of *Winterreise* and *Schwanengesang* for mixed choir and piano or orchestra) (1936)
	Rainer Bredemeyer (1929–1995) *Die Winterreise* for baritone, horn and piano (1984, rev. 1987 and 2004)
	Friedhelm Döhl (b. 1936) *Winterreise* for string quintet (1985) and string orchestra (1986)
	Hans Zender (b. 1936) *Schuberts Winterreise. Eine komponierte Interpretation* for tenor and chamber orchestra (1993)
	Ingomar Grünauer (b. 1938) *Winterreise*, Opera in eleven scenes. Libretto by Francesco Micieli (1994)
	Werner Weiß (b. 1944) *Winterreise-Skizzen* for female voices (1996)
	Wolfgang Florey (b. 1945) *Winterreise – heimatlos* for horn, guitar and percussion (1997)
	Arr. Yukikazu Suzuki (1954–2010) for voice and orchestra (1997)
	Klaus Karlbauer (b. 1960) *Schubert lebt*, compositions to accompany Karlbauer's film, *Winterreise* (1985)
Bibliography:	Armitage-Smith 1974, pp. 20–36
	Gülke 1991, pp. 216–61
	McKay 1977, pp. 94–100
	McKay 1999, p. 111
	Moore 1975, pp. 75–172
	Newbould 1997, pp. 261–3 & 300–307
	Youens 1991

WILHELM MÜLLER AND HIS POEMS FOR *WINTERREISE*

The first twelve poems of this cycle were written in the winter of 1821/2. These were published in autumn 1822 in the almanac *Urania* for the year 1823. By March 1823 another ten poems were ready which appeared in the periodical *Deutsche Blätter für Poesie, Literatur, Kunst und Theater*. The last two poems to be written (in 1824) were *Die Post* and *Täuschung*; Müller took all twenty-four poems, reordered them (*see* below) and published them in the second volume of *Gedichte aus den hinterlassenen Papieren eines reisenden Waldhornisten* in Dessau in 1824. (The first volume of this collection 'from the posthumous papers of a travelling horn-player', containing *Die schöne Müllerin*, had been entitled *Sieben und siebzig Gedichte* – thus the first seventy-seven poems – *aus den hinterlassennen Papieren* etc., had appeared in 1821.) Whether the poems reflect any of Müller's own amatory experiences is a moot point.

In the *Vermischte Schriften von Wilhelm Müller* (posthumously edited by the poet Gustav Schwab, five volumes, 1830) the first of these handsomely produced little books leads off (after a substantial biography of the poet) with the first three groups of poems exactly as published in the *Sieben und siebzig Gedichte* (1821): *Die schöne Müllerin* (with the subtitle 'To be read in Winter'), followed by the short narrative cycle *Johannes und Esther* ('To be read in Spring') – inspired by a friend's love for a beautiful young Jewish girl – then sixteen *Reisebilder* beginning with a stirring paean, *Grosse Wanderschaft* ('Das Wandern, das Wandern!'). This section includes the nine-poem cycle *Wanderlieder eines rheinischen Handwerksbursche* (Travel Songs of a Rhenish apprentice lad). Schwab editorially adds the figure I to this last group, thus *Reisebilder* I. The twenty-four *Winterreise* lyrics then appear as *Reisebilder* II. *Reisebilder* III comprises nine further travel poems, including *Der ewige Jude* and a touching poem about returning home, *Heimkehr*. These groupings arranged by Schwab, one of the recently deceased author's closest friends, confirm that both cycles set by Schubert, if not actually sequential, belonged in Müller's mind to the same 'Songs of Travel' genre, and that there are many poems in the same vein by this poet that have never been set to music.

It is a minor tragedy for the Schubert scholar that the poet's library in Dessau was destroyed by fire, and with it most of his personal papers. The surviving pages of his *Tagebuch*, unearthed in 1900 by the poet's philologist son, the Oxford don Sir Max Müller, mention a love affair in Brussels in 1814 during the time the young Wilhelm found himself there as a soldier with the Prussian army. The nine *Brüsseler Sonette* give us some indication of the grief and agitation this relationship cost him. The third of these ends with the lines: 'Und weiter führt mich meines Lebens Reise / Als Fremdling fort in ferne, ferne Weiten' ('So, onward my life's journey leads me / A stranger, away to distant, distant fields'). Young Wilhelm's departure from Brussels on 18 November 1814 was marked down as a day of enormous importance and its anniversary was noted in his diary. He tells us, mysteriously, that he wrote a letter in connection with this relationship that had cost him and his father many tears. These factors may have contributed something to the background of the cycle of poems he named *Die Winterreise*, and yet the poet was happily married to Adelheid Basedow (*see* poet's biography) when he wrote it. In the *Tagebuch* we read of the Brussels affair as being already something from the past; by the time the journal begins (October 1815) Müller is in love with Luise Hensel and his sometimes painful experiences in courting her undoubtedly influenced the poetry of that first great Schubert cycle, *Die schöne Müllerin* D795. We also get a sense of how the evasive tactics of the winter traveller – walking away from romantic confrontation – owe something to the poet's own nature: he writes (entry for 15 October 1815) that he has often been in love but only seldom been loved in return, that he is too shy to declare his passion openly, and that he blushes and hides from the girls he finds attractive for fear of betraying his feelings with his 'blood-red' face.

The title *Winterreise* is taken from the Swabian poet Ludwig Uhland (qv) whose *Gedichte* had been published in 1815. A subsection of nine poems in that volume (pp. 63–8) is a group of *Wanderlieder*. The sixth of these, in three quatrains, is entitled *Winterreise* and it tells of the traveller who warms his hands when he reaches a village on the other side of the forest, but who can never warm his heart for love has been extinguished. The whole set of Uhland's *Wanderlieder* was set by Schubert's contemporary Conradin Kreutzer (*see* COMPOSERS), and the precocious Richard Strauss, aged seven, set the single *Winterreise* poem in 1871. Uhland's concise little set of poems, anodyne in comparison with Müller's, was clearly an inspiration to the younger poet (the first twelve poems of *Die Winterreise* were initially published in *Urania* under the rubric *Wanderlieder*), but there were other influences, including the age-old legend of the Wandering Jew. In Müller's poem *Der ewige Jude* he writes lines ('Fremd bin ich in jewedem Land' and 'Ich wandre sonder Rast und Ruh') that are unmistakable echoes of phrases in the *Winterreise* poems *Gute Nacht* (No. 1) and *Der Wegweiser* (No. 20).

Müller fails to single out *Die Winterriese* for mention in his surviving correspondence and it is impossible to know his state of mind at the time he wrote this group of poems. But we are at least aware of the other projects that were occupying his attentions. The writing of original

Portrait of Wilhelm Müller, pencil drawing by Wilhelm Hensel (1822).

poetry was a luxury made financially possible only by his assiduous work as a critic and his contributions to journals and magazines. He was beginning work on the selection and editing of ten volumes of seventeenth-century German poetry (beginning with Paul Flemming, Martin Opitz and Andreas Gryphius). The poems of Gryphius in particular, written in the wake of the Thirty Years War, engage with the subject of death in a stark and touching manner. The directness and simplicity of this aspect of his literary heritage strengthened Müller's efforts to rid his own work of pretension. Influenced by the humility and concision of old German poetry, he was also drawn to English poetry by a modern master. Müller's intimate knowledge of the language had led him to make a study of the man he revered as both a poet and a fellow-supporter of the cause of Greek independence – George Gordon, Lord Byron. His work on Byron, for an encyclopaedia article, began when the English poet was still very much alive; Byron's death at Missolonghi in 1824, supporting the cause of Greek independence, only strengthened Müller's hero-worship. The German poet who published three sets of Greek lyrics (1821–3) was accorded the nickname Griechen-Müller. And yet, unlike Byron, his philhellenism remained theoretical: he was never able to visit the country to which he had devoted so much creative energy.

Müller's distance from the gossip of literary London was sufficient for him to avoid any detailed discussion of the 'mad, bad and dangerous to know' behaviour that had brought Byron such opprobrium in Britain. In the German poet's biographical article (234 pages in the posthumous *Vermischte Schriften*, 1830, though lacking much key information) there is no mention, for example, of the rumours of Byron's incestuous relationship with his sister and the birth of a daughter by this union. This would have made of Byron a latter-day Harfner from *Wilhelm Meister*, although he sported neither the Harper's beard nor shouldered his overwhelming guilt. Instead Müller presents Byron as a martyr to the narrow-mindedness of the English and the hyprocisy of their morals. He quotes from Byron's poem of farewell on leaving London after the failure of his marriage, words that show the bitterness of a man who is forced to begin a long journey as a result of female perfidy and circumstances beyond his control:

> Fare thee well! thus disunited,
>   Torn from every nearer tie,
> Sear'd in heart, and lone, and blighted,
>   More than this I scarce can die.

It comes as no surprise that the genesis of *Winterreise* coincides with Müller's close reading of *Childe Harold's Pilgrimage*, the heartbroken, partly autobiographical chronicle of Byron's

Thomas Phillips' portrait of Byron aged eighteen.

journeys, published between 1812 and 1818 and reflecting his experiences on his Continental travels from as early as 1809 (and thus long before the debacle of his marriage). In the manner of an eighteenth-century grand tour, the whole of Europe is a literary canvas for Byron's reflections and exploits. The work, in four cantos, is very extensive when taken as a whole, but it is manageably subdivided into smaller pieces of verbal mosaic. Each section is a small lyric poem, a separately numbered Spenserian stanza, nine lines long (eight lines of iambic pentameter followed by a single alexandrine). The juxtaposition of these concise cells of poetic thought, linked but at the same time disjointed, gives the impression of a succession of vivid snapshots; sudden changes of locale or subject frequently occur between one stanza and the next. The reader is left to fill in the gaps that have brought the traveller from one place to the next. This unpredictability is both disconcerting and exciting, and the hero emerges as someone impulsive, disturbed, self-destructive and subject to mood swings:

> But soon he knew himself the most unfit
> Of men to herd with Man; with whom he held
> Little in common
> [. . .]
> Proud though in desolation; which could find
> A life within itself to breathe without mankind.
> $\qquad$ [Canto III/XII]

> [. . .]
> Self-exiled Harold wanders forth again,
> With nought of hope left, but with less of gloom;
> The very knowledge that he lived in vain,
> That all was over on this side the tomb,
> Has made Despair a smilingness assume . . .
> $\qquad$ [Canto III/XVI]

Anyone who knows Schubert's cycle and Müller's poems can see what *Die Winterreise*, as a cycle of poems, owes to Byron's example. Müller is much less ambitious, of course, more determinedly German than pan-European: if Byron salutes the Rhine ('The river nobly foams and flows / . . . And all its thousand turns disclose / Some fresher beauty'), Müller is content in *Auf dem Flusse* (No. 7) to salute an anonymous tributary ('Der du so lustig rauchtest / Du heller, wilder Fluss'). And if Byron's epic largely takes place in warm, southern climes (the better to show the contrast with English weather), Müller prefers the bleak winter German landscape he knows so well. Müller's poems are narrated in the first person; Byron's are a mixture of narration and personal observation. What is undeniably Byronic is the restless desire of Müller's protagonist to travel in a doomed attempt to remove himself from emotional pain. This impetus leads to the disorientation and undeserved suffering that contrast strongly with the comfort of the prevailing bourgeois complacency with which Müller felt himself so much at odds in Biedermeier Germany. Müller's *Byron-Biographie* glows with the kind of praise for its subject that Müller could not bring himself to shower on his most famous German contemporary, Goethe, his admiration for whom was tempered by egalitarian disappointment with the old man's *grandeur*. One might almost conclude that the town through which the winter traveller scornfully passes in *Im Dorfe* (No. 17) is self-satisfied Weimar. Byron, on the other hand, was a great modern; he was a traveller and a man of action on a scale that the ever-restless Müller might have wished to achieve for himself. Müller writes that Byron's motto could be 'I have not loved the world, nor the world me'; yet the poet, it seems, stands far above the pettiness of rancour or revenge. (As a parallel to this one thinks of the unexpected tenderness of the final strophe of *Gute Nacht* in *Winterreise*, the song that sets the tone for Schubert's cycle.)

There is no question of Müller's attempting to match Byron's scope, or his astonishing sweep, but we surely owe to the English lord some aspects of the winter traveller's itinerary, as well as his pride, even at his lowest moments. The narrator of Müller's cycle is a commanding, authoritative figure, not a pitiable down-and-out. Some commentaries have likened Müller's cycle to a Passion story, each stage of the journey a Station of the Cross. But Müller is far less likely to have fashioned a Christ-like hero than one inspired by Byron. Some of the most successful performances of this cycle have been by singers (including, perhaps unsurprisingly, quintessential Englishmen like Peter Pears and Ian Bostridge) who, aided by Schubert's music of course, bring a Byronic stature to the work. This might be described as a passionate and frank engagement with the here and now combined with a certain mysterious reserve and phlegm that could be thought of as aristocratic, or English, or both. This combination of passion tempered by noble restraint was clearly admired by the Anglophile Müller and it suited a composer like Schubert whose Romantic expressiveness was firmly counterbalanced by the discipline of his classical background. Something of this marriage of searing intensity and dignified sangfroid was transmitted, via Müller to Heinrich Heine, and thence to the poetic character of Schumann's *Dichterliebe* Op. 48. Goethe's *Die Leiden des jungen Werthers* also played a part in the evolution of Byronism, as did Shakespeare's *Hamlet*, both works well known to the poet of *Winterreise* and to his generation. The most famous literary figures in the Germany of Schubert's time, apart from Goethe of course, were the rediscovered Shakespeare (newly translated by August von Schlegel as if the Elizabethans were still alive), Sir Walter Scott and, indeed, Byron himself.

The heavy-handed Wozzeck-like expressionism favoured by some performers of *Winterreise* today, in any case ill-tuned to Schubert's musical style, is badly suited to the self-referential irony of Müller's Byronic model. Lord Macaulay's definition of the Byronic hero is closer to Emily Brontë's Heathcliffe: 'a man proud, cynical, with defiance on his brow, and misery in his heart, a scorner of his kind, implacable in revenge, yet capable of deep and strong affection'. Whatever the intensity of the Romantic overlay, Byron, via *Childe Harold*, initiated a new relationship between a writer and his public (including Müller) that involved the strong pull of biographical cross-currents beneath the writing's surface. This has been mirrored by the relationship initiated by *Winterreise* between the composer and his listeners in the concert hall. It was never intended as an autobiographical work, yet this cycle stirs in its listeners a stronger curiosity regarding Schubert's life story than any other of his works: it has that kind of Byronic glamour.

Winterreise – the vignette for the front cover of the first edition (Part 2, 1828).

BRINGING *WINTERREISE* TO ORDER

The growing popularity of *Winterreise* in the concert halls of the world, and among singers (increasingly of both sexes, although Elena Gerhardt sang it to universal acclaim as long ago as the Schubert centenary in 1928), would have surprised Schubert's contemporaries. When they first heard the work they were taken aback not only by its pessimism and unrelenting melancholy but also by the sparse textures and (when compared to the other Schubert songs they knew) its lack of charm. The composer had seemed somewhat gloomy during the composition of the cycle, so much so that Josef von Spaun asked him what was the matter. 'You will soon hear it and understand,' the composer replied. Spaun, who was the most reliable of Schubert's friends both in life and in the authenticity of his memoirs, continues the story: 'One day he said to me, "Come to Schober's today, I will sing you a cycle of spine-chilling songs. I am anxious to know what you will say about them. They have affected me more than has been the case with any other of my lieder."' The invitation to hear the songs at Schober's house was for the evening of 4 March 1827. That Schubert, without excuse or explanation, never appeared at this, his own party, is probably less an indication of his forgetfulness than of his illness (the diagnosis of syphilis had hung over him since late 1822) which, apart from the physical symptoms, induced in him from time to time a disturbed and distracted state of mind.

In any case, on this occasion, or rather non-occasion, the composer would have been able to play only the first twelve songs of the cycle as we know it. He was convinced that the work was already complete, having set as many poems as had come to hand. He had found Müller's texts in the almanac entitled *Urania, Taschenbuch auf das Jahr 1823*, where only twelve poems were printed. At that time Schubert was staying with Franz von Schober, and it was almost certainly in that cultured dilettante's library that he had found the small but thick volume (556 pages) published four years previously. In a letter to Kreissle von Hellborn many years after he had left Vienna to live in Weimar, and some forty years after Schubert's death, Schober mentioned the small library that he had put together for the composer among whose volumes Schubert had found the Müller poems. (The composer was not a great book collector, money being a problem, and many of the volumes of poetry he used for his work were loans from friends.) The wording on p. 207 of *Urania* is significant: *Wanderlieder von Wilhelm Müller – Die Winterreise. In 12 Liedern*. This implies that Müller himself regarded the cycle as complete when it went to press. (As with Byron and *Childe Harold's Pilgrimage*, Müller had reserved the right to publish cantos of his work in different instalments.) The trouble was that Schubert was behind the times with Müller's later outpourings. He put the word 'Fine' ('The End') after the twelfth song, showing that he was unaware that the poet had amplified and reamplified his original conception after the printing of *Urania* – in 1823 and 1824 to be exact. It is also significant that the composer, in this first version of *Winterreise*, had composed the song *Einsamkeit* in D minor, as if to bring the cycle, full circle, to a conclusive end in the tonality in which it had begun.

Imagine Schubert's feelings when he discovered, probably in the Schobers' library, the 1824 edition of Müller's poems that included a further twelve *Winterreise* texts. These poems were new to Schubert, some of them interspersed between the lyrics that he had already set. We shall never know whether the composer was overjoyed at finding more poems in the vein that had so appealed to him, or whether he was dismayed. In either case it was immediately obvious that the poet had had a very different running order in mind when considering the work as a whole. This becomes clear if we place Schubert's cycle (as he eventually completed it) side by side with Müller's sequence. We do not know exactly when the composer came across the full edition of the poems but it may have been as late as the autumn of 1827:

MÜLLER

'Die Winterreise' (1824) with numerous small alterations to the poems as published in 1823

SCHUBERT

Winterreise D911 (1827) where the first twelve songs follow Müller's *Urania* sequence (1823)

PART ONE (February 1827)

	MÜLLER	SCHUBERT
1	Gute Nacht	Gute Nacht
2	Die Wetterfahne	Die Wetterfahne
3	Gefrorne Tränen	Gefrorne Tränen
4	Erstarrung	Erstarrung
5	Der Lindenbaum	Der Lindenbaum

So far so good. But now Müller began to interpolate new lyrics (here marked*) into the old, and now outdated, *Urania* sequence. In so doing he had to recycle four of the original and earlier items which he now placed towards the end of his new, expanded cycle of poems.

	MÜLLER	SCHUBERT
6	Die Post*	Wasserflut
7	Wasserflut	Auf dem Flusse
8	Auf dem Flusse	Rückblick
9	Rückblick	Irrlicht
10	Der greise Kopf*	Rast
11	Die Krähe*	Frühlingstraum
12	Letzte Hoffnung*	Einsamkeit

PART TWO (October 1827)

	MÜLLER	SCHUBERT
13	Im Dorfe*	Die Post
14	Der stürmische Morgen*	Der greise Kopf
15	Täuschung*	Die Krähe
16	Der Wegweiser*	Letzte Hoffnung
17	Das Wirtshaus*	Im Dorfe
18	Irrlicht	Der stürmische Morgen
19	Rast	Täuschung
20	Die Nebensonnen*	Der Wegweiser
21	Frühlingstraum	Das Wirtshaus
22	Einsamkeit	Mut!
23	Mut!*	Die Nebensonnen
24	Der Leiermann*	Der Leiermann

If Schubert wished his Part One to correlate with Müller's first twelve lyrics he would have to interpolate settings of four new poems and shunt four songs already completed into the as yet uncomposed second half. While this would have been highly inconvenient from the point of view of publication plans for the work, which were probably already in hand at the firm of Haslinger's, it was surely more than business expediency that stopped the composer from making a last-minute revision. His way out of the *Winterreise* problem is a perfect example of the participation of chance, like a turn of the cards or roll of the dice, in determining a new direction. It was the easiest solution, which has led some people to think that it must have been entirely casual and not thought out. Schubert simply began his Part Two with the lyrics that he had not already set, and progressed to the end, naturally leaving out the poems that he had already composed. Necessity here transpired to be the mother of sublime invention, for the sequence of poems which emerged on taking this route was more perfectly in tune with his musical needs than any ordering of the series that the poet might have devised. Schubert's order concentrates the dark elegiac poems of *Der Wegweiser, Das Wirtshaus* and *Die Nebensonnen* together at the end of the cycle, mitigated by the short, contrasting mood of *Mut!* On the other hand, *Irrlicht, Frühlingstraum* and so on, which break up the screw-turning succession of songs in Müller's order, belong in Schubert's Part One; in this earlier position they cannot lighten the ever-darkening landscape of the traveller's mind. It is at the end of the cycle that Schubert shows that he is, after all, in control of the game, and that he is not content to keep without question every card he has been dealt. He makes one tiny but crucial adjustment to his hand to show us that the ordering of the work is more than fortuitous serendipity, placing *Die Nebensonnen* as the penultimate song of the cycle rather than *Mut!* The last two items are thus linked in the matchless hypnotic succession that is the crowning glory of the work in almost any performance. That he refused to meddle with the integrity of the twelve songs already completed speaks volumes not only of how satisfied he was with his first cycle (and this includes how one song progresses to the next), but how he regarded it as a finished work in its own right and already something from his past. In fact *Winterreise*, like Wolf's *Italienisches Liederbuch* (1891 and 1896), is two separate song cycles, and was published as such in two volumes. The fact that both the Schubert and the Wolf masterpieces are regarded by the public as single works is to do with the power of the composers' imaginations and their ability to weld music together from different periods to make a believable whole.

A glance at Müller's order shows us that poet and composer had different outcomes in mind for the winter traveller. Müller's placement of *Mut!* before *Der Leiermann* and the earlier positioning of *Der Wegweiser* and *Das Wirtshaus* suggest a crisis surmounted, a positive, if gradual, re-entry into the world after a lonely journey. One can even claim a hint of optimism: the story is a type of *Bildungsroman* where disappointment and bitterness are cured by communion with nature, and the man is rendered fit to rejoin his fellow human beings, starting off with the pathetic figure of a hurdy-gurdy player. How often in Schubert's earlier life would he have been sympathetic to this bright-eyed view of the world! He was after all the personification of man's endless capacity for optimism and enjoyment of the here-and-now, of *Frühlingsglaube* – a perpetual faith in spring. But the frightening thing about *Winterreise* (and it frightened the composer too that he should have such negative feelings) was that this faith was no longer there, at least not in 1827. The cycle was composed at a time of coming to terms with his mortality, just as the first Müller cycle, *Die schöne Müllerin*, was a cathartic work written in the year that he discovered and experienced the devastating symptoms of his illness. Josef von Spaun described the atmosphere when the Schubert circle eventually heard the completed work: 'In a voice wrought with emotion, he [Schubert] sang the whole of the *Winterreise* through to us. We were quite dumbfounded by the gloomy mood of these songs and Schober said he had only liked one song, *Der Lindenbaum*. To which Schubert only said, "I like these songs more than all the others, and you will get to like them too." '

If Schubert had come across Müller's order at the beginning of 1827 it is probable that he would have set it as it was and the music might have been rather different. It is also possible that he would have regarded a twenty-four-song cycle (which would have been an early 1827 work as opposed to straddling the whole year) as too great an undertaking at that stage. We owe the shape of the work as it is to a series of accidents, but this is true of many masterpieces and it is not for us to rescue and recast the work. Schubert knew what he was doing: if he was the victim of chance in this matter, or simply unfortunate in not having the correct edition of poems in his possession at the right time, he turned everything to his artistic advantage. Is this not, after all, the least we might expect from a composer-magician of his stature? If we felt, at the end of the cycle, that there was something about it which did not work, perhaps we should have to take the matter into our own hands and reorder the cycle (as did Stockhausen and others) according to Müller. But *Winterreise* needs no rescue team. It is certain that the majesty and power of this cycle, in countless performances over 170 years, is directly ascribable to the controlling hand of one of music's most steel-willed, if apparently unassuming, masters.

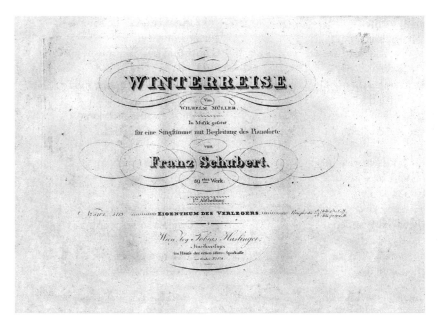

Winterreise – the title page of the first edition (Part 1, 1828).

Sometimes one can be quite daunted when one opens the *Winterreise* – there seems to be nothing on the page . . .

Benjamin Britten: *On Receiving the First Aspen Award* (1964)

PART ONE
Completed February 1827

I GUTE NACHT   Good night
Op. 89 no. 1, **D911/1** [H613]
D minor

(105 bars)

Fremd bin ich eingezogen,[1]	**I** arrived a stranger,
Fremd zieh' ich wieder aus.	A stranger I depart.
Der Mai war mir gewogen,	May blessed me
Mit manchem Blumenstrauss.	With many a bouquet of flowers.
Das Mädchen sprach von Liebe,	The girl spoke of love,
Die Mutter gar von Eh'—	Her mother even of marriage;
Nun ist die Welt so trübe,	Now the world is so desolate,
Der Weg gehüllt in Schnee.	The path concealed beneath snow.
Ich kann zu meiner Reisen	I cannot choose the time
Nicht wahlen mit der Zeit,	For my journey;
Muss selbst den Weg mir weisen	I must find my own way
In dieser Dunkelheit.	In this darkness
Es zieht ein Mondenschatten	A shadow thrown by the moon
Als mein Gefährte mit,	Is my companion;
Und auf den weissen Matten	And on the white meadows
Such' ich des Wildes Tritt.	I seek the tracks of deer.
Was soll ich länger weilen,	Why should I tarry longer
Dass man mich trieb' hinaus?[2]	And be driven out?
Lass irre Hunde heulen	Let stray dogs howl
Vor ihres Herren Haus.	Before their master's house.
Die Liebe liebt das Wandern –	Love delights in wandering
Gott hat sie so gemacht—	God made it so
Von Einem zu dem Andern—	From one to another.
Fein Liebchen, gute Nacht!	Beloved, good night!

[1] The punctuation for the first twelve texts of the cycle is taken from Schubert's source, *Urania*, 1823. The first letter of the poem printed in bold is common to both the original *Urania* source and the *Gedichte* (1824).
[2] For the 1824 edition of *Gedichte eines reisenden Waldhornisten* (the first edition of the complete set of twenty-four poems), Müller changes this line (likewise, notes 3 and 4) to '*Bis* man mich trieb' hinaus'.

Will dich im Traum nicht stören,	I will not disturb you as you dream,
Wär' Schad' um deine Ruh';	It would be a shame to spoil your rest.
Sollst meinen Tritt nicht hören –	You shall not hear my footsteps;
Sacht, sacht die Türe zu!	Softly, softly the door is closed.
Schreib' im Vorübergehen[3]	As I pass I write
An's Tor dir G u t e N a c h t[4]	'Good night' on your gate,
Damit du mögest sehen,	So that you might see
An dich hab' ich gedacht[5]	That I thought of you.

This is the twenty-first of Schubert's forty-six Müller solo settings (1823, 1827 and 1828). See the poet's biography for a chronological list of all the Müller settings.

Müller took the idea of starting his cycle with a 'Good Night' almost certainly from an English source. In the first canto of Byron's *Childe Harold's Pilgrimage* the hero is assigned a song in ten stanzas ('Adieu, adieu! my native shore') which begins and ends with 'My native land – Good Night!' This song is introduced with the line 'Thus to the elements he pour'd his last "Good Night"'. The same may be said of the winter traveller: the poem is addressed to his lover *in*

Autograph of *Gute Nacht*, 1827.

[3] Müller writes (1824) '*Ich schreibe nur im Gehen*'.
[4] Müller writes (1824) 'An's Tor *noch gute Nacht*'.
[5] Only on one occasion in this song does Schubert change one of Müller's lines as printed in *Urania*, 1823: the last line of the poem reads in Müller '*Ich hab' an dich* gedacht'.

absentia (she is safely asleep) and he is already trudging through the snow. Profoundly interested as Müller was in Byron and his circle, it is possible that he also knew Shelley's amorous 'Good Night' from *Posthumous Poems* published in 1824 ('Good night? Ah! no; the hour is ill / Which severs those it should unite'). If, in Müller's cycle, the winter traveller is anything but flirtatious in taking leave of his former beloved, Schubert's music adds a gallant and heartbreaking note of devotion.

From the very beginning we are on the move. The first thing we hear in the accompaniment is the throb of chords in D minor that drive the music forward. These repeated mezzo staccato quavers will be heard elsewhere in the cycle as a kind of 'fate' motif, uneventful on the surface but powerful and ominous in the body of the music. We sense that although the narrator is not exactly in a hurry (it is impossible to walk quickly through heavy snow) he feels there is no time to lose in making his departure. We learn that he cannot choose the time for the journey. It would have been so much easier to leave by day, but he must depart by night, braving the bitter winter weather. The tempo indication is 'Mässig' ('Moderato'), but in the autograph it was originally 'In gehender Bewegung' ('At walking pace'). The singer should beware of too slow a tempo for this song (it is in two, not four, to a bar). The *Winterreise* of many a rising star has been launched into the musical firmament only to fall heavily earthward during this opening song. It is true that the traveller carries with him a substantial amount of emotional luggage, but at this early stage of his flight it must not weigh him down, nor undermine his determination to leave without further ado. John Reed has compared the pacing rhythm of this song to the second movement ('Andante con moto') of the Piano Trio in E flat D929.

In the foreground of the accompaniment, above those quietly pulsating chords, four quavers descend the stave, culminating in a tiny dotted phrase made prominent by an fp marking in b. 2. This figure of a dotted semiquaver + demisemiquaver is intensely physical in its effect and adds a thrust of resolute determination to the implacable trudge. The melody is perhaps too determined and grim to be beautiful (at least until it reaches its metamorphosis in the major key) but it has a grandeur which is a mark of the composer in his last years – a King Lear phase in an artistic development that has become Shakespearean in scope. In this *Vorspiel* we have a masterful musical encapsulation of disappointment and anger, but the anger is contained, and although it is tempting to hammer the tune out on the piano (and then to bellow it in the voice), performers must hold back, aware that they have a long distance to travel.[1] Although the opening marking is piano, the suddenness of this departure is disruptive and dislocating – emphasized subtly with offbeat accents on the last quavers of bb. 3 and 4. The use of a brusque mordent to ornament one of the descending semiquavers in the fifth bar suggests the shaking off of a former life – like snow on a coat, or shuddering at the first blast of cold air encountered outside the door. We can only guess what awful showdown has preceded this decision to part without further ado. Have angry words been exchanged, or will this moonlight flit surprise the occupants of the house when they wake? Will they be grief-stricken or relieved? These are things we are never to know, and Müller meant it so.

The singer's opening words echo a line in Act V Scene 1 of Schiller's play *Die Räuber* spoken by the Moor family retainer, Daniel: 'Leer kam ich hieher – leer zieh ich wieder hin' ('I came here empty-handed, and I leave empty-handed'). The melody is already familiar to us because it has been partially prefigured in the accompaniment. The tune of 'Fremd bin ich eingezogen' (bb. 7–10) is matched and balanced by 'Fremd zieh' ich wieder aus' (bb. 10–12) and the vocal landscape is plotted thus throughout: often a descending two-bar phrase followed by an ascending one, or vice versa, and static quavers mirrored by more eventful semiquavers in the subsequent phrase. The first two lines of this strophe (and those following) are sung only once, giving the

[1] Elmar Budde in *Schuberts Liederzyklen* believes that this is this same descending motif that makes a vehement reappearance, much faster, in *Die Wetterfahne* D911/2 (the last semiquaver of b. 1 and the first three quavers of b. 2).

singer's utterances a terse and compact character, as if in code. This is the perfect musical counterpart to his phlegmatic attitude in explaining (or rather not explaining) the breakdown of his relationship. Musical repetition is reserved for the second half of Müller's eight-line strophe where we discover a little more of the background to the narrator's predicament. At the end of b. 16 with 'Das Mädchen sprach von Liebe / Die Mutter gar von Eh'', D minor cedes briefly to F major as if to retreat into happier memories (this use of the major tonality as a time-shifter will become a notable feature of the cycle). When the girl is mentioned for the first time we hear a bald statement of fact: 'Das Mädchen sprach von Liebe' is centred around four quavers on the same F (b. 16), reminiscent of the accompaniment's motif at the very opening. But Schubert repeats these lines, and the second mention of the marriage-that-might-have-been is a sequence this time, in a higher tessitura, sadder and more world-weary (bb. 19–23).

Müller's words, taken on their own, de-personalize 'Das Mädchen' and 'Die Mutter' – the beloved no longer has a name. Most composers would have found it easy to set this angrily (as, say, Wolf might have done) in order to emphasize the girl's insincerity and the mother's opportunism. Instead we are reminded of how hard it was for Schubert to turn love away and express hate in his music: we sense that if someone were to speak to him lovingly he would reply in like fashion, and here we glimpse his essential graciousness. A tiny conversational counter-melody flowers shyly under the pianist's fingers (at 'Das Mädchen sprach von Liebe') in the treble clef in b. 16 as the maiden plights her troth; this is echoed in the bass clef as the mother adds her support ('Die Mutter gar von Eh''). There is a kind of mild gallantry in these bars: Müller blames the girl unequivocally, but the traveller, because he speaks in Schubert's voice, seems to ruefully acknowledge that some of the fault for the breakdown in relations (perhaps he blames himself for his impecuniousness) may have been his.

All memories of a companionable life are banished by the bleak contrast of what follows. The two-bar piano interlude (bb. 24–5) is a repeat of a three-note motif (incorporating a dotted figure and an fp marking) which is sharp with stabbing pain and foot-dragging depression. The final two lines of the verse ('Nun ist die Welt so trübe, / Der Weg gehüllt in Schnee') are set twice; musically these phrases are almost identical apart from their two concluding bars: the first time there is an ascent at the cadence (bb. 28–9), while the second descends like a thumbs-down verdict and heavy sentence (bb. 32–3). On both occasions 'Nun ist die Welt so trübe' is accompanied by a repeat of the piano interlude described above that is now incorporated into the accompaniment. In this amazingly economical work Schubert wastes nothing and recycles everything to the greatest effect. In conventional strophic-song manner, the bridging *Zwischenspiel* leading to the second verse is the same music as the introduction – once again that determined trudge, both driven and weary, pitiable and noble. Schubert had had a lifetime (albeit a short one) of writing strophic songs, but there was never one greater (nor more technically difficult to sing) than this. Years of apprenticeship, including the fine strophic songs in *Die schöne Müllerin* D795, had been leading to the achievement of *Gute Nacht* where the music for the second verse seems every bit as appropriate for the words as for the first – sometimes even more so. For example, the key of D minor at 'In dieser Dunkelheit' (bb. 13–15 in the repeat) makes a splendidly dark background from which 'Es zieht ein Mondenschatten' emerges in F major, the music bathed in the soft glow of moonlight. The descent of the vocal line at 'Und auf den weissen Matten / Such' ich des Wildes Tritt' is ideally pitched, at the words' repeat, to suggest the traveller bending over to scrutinize deer or other animal tracks in the moonlit landscape.

A repeat sign suffices for the first two strophes because they are musically identical, but Schubert took the trouble to write out the third verse separately because he wanted to make some minuscule changes. These are scarcely evident to the listener but they show the composer's infinitely subtle hand when it came to modifying tiny details. The musical settings of the verbs 'weilen' (b. 41) and 'heulen' (b. 45) rise in minor thirds instead of the adjacent notes of the opening strophes. This gives an impatient thrust to 'weilen', and an appropriate wail to 'heulen', the fall and rise of the whole of that phrase ('Lass irre Hunde heulen') subtly suggestive of a canine howl. Conversely, the two opening words of the phrase 'Die Liebe liebt das Wandern' are set (bb. 47–8) as adjacent semitones instead of a fourth apart, and this makes love something gentle, insinuating and perhaps dishonest. Once again it is difficult to decide whether the words of this strophe are ironic, bitter and sarcastic, or whether the passage shows the philosophical understanding of a man of the world who accepts that faithlessness, or at least flightiness, is part of human nature. Or, taking our cue from a century of flagrant double standards, are we to believe that infidelity is considered especially reprehensible in a woman? Do these words blame mankind merely or perhaps God himself ('Gott hat sie so gemacht')? Despite the use of major tonality, the repeat of this phrase conveys a sense of world-weary resignation – where Müller accuses, Schubert's tendency is to forgive. What has already been called the 'conversational counter-melody' occurs, in this verse, under 'Die Liebe liebt das Wandern'. The ambulatory semiquavers first heard in the accompaniment at b. 48 seem wonderfully appropriate here for the idea of delight in wandering, of moving from one lover to another – and they are also suitable in a slightly different form to depict the traveller passing by at 'Schreib' im Vorübergehen / An's Tor dir Gute Nacht' in the last verse.

We now encounter the most astonishing use of the major key – not the relative major this time, but the tonic major (with a change of key signature to two sharps). For the last verse the by now familiar tramping interlude in D minor moves into calm waters, like a storm-tossed vessel finding safe haven at last. The cadence taking us into this new territory is a simple V-I, but it is anything but simple for the pianist to execute, and deeply moving in its effect. When the voice sings its first F sharp on 'Will dich im Traum nicht stören' (b. 71) we are suddenly led through a magical window into the inner portals of Schubert's tender and forgiving heart. If Heine had written these words they would surely have been intended sarcastically: the girl has utterly ruined the traveller's life, but he wouldn't wish to disturb her precious rest – oh dear me, no. Elaborate and exaggerated courtesy as disguised insult is a Heine trademark, but neither Müller, influenced by the gallantry of Byron, nor Schubert can imagine the winter traveller being so petty. Wounded though he may be, he still cares deeply for the girl he has to leave. In any case how could this composer set words like 'Traum' and 'Ruh'' ironically when they are fundamental to his vocabulary of magical sounds and spellbinding melody?

And magic is what he gives us here in abundant measure. What has seemed querulous and driven in the minor key blossoms into something infinitely gentle if rueful. In this music we hear how much our traveller – and our composer – have to give, and how vulnerable this makes them. The three-note dotted motif (the two-bar interlude that also accompanies the repeat of 'Schreib' im Vorübergehen') has winced with pain in its minor-key form but is here softened in the major key into something as gentle as a caress (bb. 87 and 88). When he sings 'An dich hab' ich gedacht' (Schubert's change of Müller's original word-order miraculously focuses 'dich' on the strong beat of the bar) the jump of a sixth in the vocal line (b. 86) betokens something akin to happiness, but only at a distance, as if through a veil of memory. The repeat of these words in the suddenly re-established minor key is a masterstroke: the sweetness of longing for the past is replaced by the all-too-brutal present and a chilling awareness of how much happiness has been lost. The desperate sigh of a heavy heart is emphasized by the simple marking 'un poco rit.' (used only once elsewhere in the cycle – in *Erstarrung*, No 4) which is devastating in its effect. The six-bar postlude contains, twice buried within its chords, the melody of 'An dich hab' ich gedacht'. Also buried within this song is the happiness of the narrator's life, as well as the reasons for the relationship's demise.

Does he literally write 'Good night' on the gate – a graffiti artist *avant la lettre*? We cannot pursue this line of enquiry: the work has much of the quality of a dream, and does not submit well to the scrutiny of prosaic chronology. It is perhaps for this very reason that this song cycle so fascinated Samuel Beckett (1906–1989) who was mesmerized over many years by Fischer-Dieskau's recording of the work. The Irish playwright's last play, *What Where* or, in German, *Was Wo* (1983) was commissioned for performance in Graz, a town that Schubert visited in the year he composed *Winterreise* (and where he may even have worked on Part Two of the cycle). Beckett was aware of this and his play intentionally mirrors the song cycle's seasonal scenario, beginning with the mention of May (in *Gute Nacht*) and ending in the frozen depths of winter:

It is winter
Without journey
Time passes,
That is all,
Make sense who may.
I switch off.

As Alex Ross has written in the *New Yorker*, 'Those lines are almost a précis of the music itself'; '*Winterreise . . .* unfolds like a Beckett play, in a landscape as vivid as it is vague.'

First edition:	Published as Op. 89 no. 1 by Tobias Haslinger, Vienna on 14 January 1828 (P141)
Subsequent editions:	Peters: Vol. 1/54; AGA XX 517: Vol. 9/2; NSA IV: Vol. 4a/110; Bärenreiter: Vol. 3/78
First known performance:	10 January 1828 *Abend-Unterhaltung* of the Gesellschaft der Musikfreunde, Vienna. Soloist: Ludwig Tietze (see Waidelich/Hilmar Dokumente I No. 558 for full concert programme)
Bibliography:	Youens 1991, pp. 119–30
	Ross *New Yorker* 4 January 2010
Arrangements:	Arr. Franz Liszt (1811–1886) for solo piano, no. 1 of *Winterreise* (1838–9) [*see* TRANSCRIPTIONS]
	Arr. Leopold Godowksy (1870–1938) for solo piano as *Good Night* (1927, 2nd revised edition 1937) [*see* TRANSCRIPTIONS]
	Arr. Tilman Hoppstock (b. 1961) for guitar accompaniment, in *Franz Schubert: 110 Lieder* (2009)
Discography and timing:	Fischer-Dieskau III 2[1] 5'22
	Pears–Britten 5'53
	Hyperion I 30[1]
	Hyperion II 33[1] 5'14 Matthias Goerne

← *Frühlingslied* D919   *Die Wetterfahne* D911/2 →

II Die WETTERFAHNE   The weathervane
Op. 89 no. 2, **D911/2** [H614]
A minor

(51 bars)

Der Wind spielt mit der Wetterfahne	The wind is playing with the weathervane
Auf meines schönen Liebchens Haus:	On my fair sweetheart's house.
Da dacht' ich schon in meinem Wahne,	In my delusion I thought
Sie pfiff' den armen Flüchtling aus.	It was whistling to mock the poor fugitive.
Er hätt' es eher bemerken sollen,[1]	He should have noticed it sooner,
Des Hauses aufgestecktes Schild,	This sign fixed upon the house;
So hätt' er nimmer suchen wollen	Then he would never have sought
Im Haus' ein treues Frauenbild.	A faithful woman within that house.
Der Wind spielt drinnen mit den Herzen,	Inside the wind is playing with hearts,
Wie auf dem Dach, nur nicht so laut.	As on the roof, only less loudly.
Was fragen sie nach meinen Schmerzen? –	Why should they care about my grief?
Ihr Kind ist eine reiche Braut.	Their child is a rich bride.

This is the twenty-second of Schubert's forty-six Müller solo settings (1823, 1827 and 1828). See the poet's biography for a chronological list of all the Müller settings.

This is one of the more violent songs in the cycle – a whirlwind contrast to the poetic introspection of what has gone before. The weathervane, blown hither and thither by the winter storms, is a metaphor for inconstancy and fickleness; and of course this emblem sits atop the house of the beloved, a warning the traveller has not heeded soon enough. Any piano student who has been schooled with classical restraint in terms of Schubertian rubato has to throw discretion to the winds here. Schubert initially added the word 'unruhig' to the tempo marking on his autograph, but thought better of it when he came to have the work printed (the danger being that performers will exaggerate such indications). The very unpredictability of the wintry gusts demands an impetuous freedom of response that can never be entirely rehearsed. Although the musical impression is of something written in a single stroke (and certainly it comes across thus in performance), the autograph shows us that this song gave the composer a great deal of trouble and that he worked hard to achieve its seemingly inevitable flow.

In *Winterreise* the doubling of one hand by the other in octaves is not uncommon; this song opens with ten bars of clattering unisons including the windswept introduction, the most extended example of unharmonized passage-work in the cycle until *Der stürmische Morgen* (No. 18). The dynamic is forte. An A minor arpeggio, the chord in second inversion, surges forcefully up the stave then down; then up again for a brief shudder (a fledgling trill) in oscillating semi-quavers at the top of the stave, followed by the same figuration an octave lower. Thereafter there is another descent in quavers (b. 3) to the B below middle C (the left hand shadowing it an octave lower) for a bone-rattling trill on a dotted crotchet followed by a piano echo of the same motif. These two trills in a counterpoint of contrasting dynamics seem to point to the outer, and louder, drama of the weather as nature's metaphor for the inner shudder of the unquiet heart. The vocal line at 'Der Wind spielt mit der Wetterfahne' surges with an ebb and flow that requires musical shaping of great finesse – or rather a cultivated recklessness where the wildness of the elements undermines the tyranny of the bar line. The next phrase is the first of many in *Winterreise* where the composer's practised genius in recitative, acquired through many years of song-writing apprenticeship, enables the seamless incorporation of quasi-spoken passages into the body of a song. When this happens the accompaniment usually melts to a minimum,

---

[1] Müller (*Urania*, 1823) has 'Er hätt' es *ehr* bemerken sollen'. Schubert's change makes for a far less smooth vocal line.

as if it were the *secco* accompaniment of a Mozart opera recitative, with spare, dry chords. It is the first time that the traveller admits that grief at his personal plight has unhinged him ('Da dacht' ich schon in meinem Wahne', bb. 10–12) and Schubert follows the cue with music equally desperate. The rhythm of this passage is inspired by Müller's terse prosody; the tightness of the dotted figure of 'schon in meinem Wahne' is especially effective. But even more unusual is the inspired perversity of the word-setting at 'Sie pfiff' den armen Flüchtling aus', where tiny melismas in bb. 12 and 13 accentuate vowels off the beat by means of awkward lightning excursions into a higher tessitura. Note the snatched octaves in the piano – acciaccaturas phrased upwards to staccato quavers that accompany the idea of the weathervane whistling derisively at the 'poor fugitive'. (The verb 'auspfeifen' denotes booing or hissing someone off the stage – 'Sie pfiff' den armen Flüchtling aus'.) We will also hear abrasive split octaves in *Frühlingstraum* D911/11 where discordant cocks crow in the middle of the traveller's dream. This indicates that Schubert interpreted 'pfeifen' as synonymous with 'cock-a-doodle-do' and that he had imagined the metallic ornament on the roof as belonging to the same species. (Throughout the cycle the hero is haunted by birds of various sorts – the astonishingly humanized crows in *Rückblick* D911/8, and of course the harbinger of death in *Die Krähe* D911/15.)

The next strophe (beginning 'Er hätt' es eher bemerken sollen', b. 14) is among the most vehement in all Schubert, with words tumbling out in a flood of impassioned intensity. The power of the music is built through an astonishing succession of musical sequences, each of which caps what has gone before. The accompaniment consists of simple quaver chords, first in the left hand and then the right, unusually marked to be spread into arpeggios as well as played staccato. The tritones in the vocal line on 'Er <u>hätt</u>' es eher be<u>mer</u>ken sollen, / Des <u>Hauses</u> aufgestecktes Schild' are ominous in themselves, but the extravagant setting of 'aufgestecktes' in bb. 17–18 broadens these intervals – first to a fifth, and then to an anguished diminished seventh, like a howl of humiliation. The other villagers know that the traveller has been replaced by another man and is effectively a cuckold, or so he imagines. And when one realizes that the old German word for such a risible creature is 'Hahnrei', a word associated with the 'Hahn' or cock, the pain in the second verse and the reason why the weathervane is such a symbol of shame becomes clearer; it is not only because the girl is as flighty and unreliable as a wind-blown instrument, but also because she is unfaithful. This would explain the suggestion of horn-like music (traditionally the theme music for a cuckold) in the opening arpeggios of the song. It also accounts for the increasing musical tension in the last line of the second strophe, where the ironic pianistic support for 'ein treues Frauenbild' (bb. 21–2) consists of the split octaves of the cock-crow that we have already heard under 'Sie pfiff' den armen Flüchtling aus'. Here they achieve their shrillest form, utilizing some of the highest and harshest notes available on Schubert's piano. This passage brings us into D minor, and without further ado there is a piano interlude, fashioned after the shape of the introduction but much shorter (bb. 22–4). This is based on the chord of E^7, something of a harmonic jolt, which ushers in the return to A minor for the second half of the song.

Schubert constructs a whole page of music out of the last of Müller's three verses by repeating the words. 'Der Wind spielt drinnen mit den Herzen' has the same unison-accompanied melody as the song's opening, with the difference that the accompaniment is an octave lower, giving the music a more ominous tone. The fermata on 'Dach' (b. 27) is a clue to the flexible rhythmic approach that the composer had envisaged for this wind-propelled statement. The word 'leise' ('softly') appears in brackets above the singer's stave, making clear that the whole phrase is intended as a theatrically exaggerated (and thus potentially mad or disturbed) contrast to the following outburst ('Was fragen sie nach meinen Schmerzen?'), marked 'laut'. According to the evidence of the autograph, the harmonic and melodic direction of this passage gave Schubert some trouble – a shift into F major progressing, via ever-climbing shifts of harmony, into a snatch of wild *Ländler* music at 'eine reiche Braut' in A major, as if parodying and exaggerating the dancing at the wedding celebration. Schumann's wildly unhappy *Das ist ein Flöten und Geigen* Op. 48 no. 9) from *Dichterliebe* is here momentarily prophesied.

The repeat of Müller's third strophe contrives to be madder still. Instead of unison quavers the vocal line (again marked 'leise') from b. 35 is accompanied by some of Schubert's strangest trills, the notes a minor third apart. In this register, buried deep in the music, they suggest something visceral and 'drinnen' ('within') – wind playing within the heart in ominous palpitations. The 'laut' passage from b. 39, 'Was fragen sie nach meinen Schmerzen?', begins with the same harmonies as before but takes a different direction into G minor when the words are repeated in a mood of anger and contemptuous outrage – 'Why should they care about my grief?' In performance, because of the speed and tessitura of the trill-like semitone intervals, this rhetorical question almost takes on the character of a shout, and the traveller seldom again works himself up into such a pitch of rage. It is this mood which, coming so soon after the tenderness of the final verse of *Gute Nacht*, suggests that his attitude to the girl is alarmingly inconsistent. This is perhaps to the advantage of an interpretation that emphasizes mercurial instability and derangement. Somehow or other a rich suitor has come into the picture. The extended setting of 'eine reiche Braut' (significantly elongated in comparison with the first time we hear the words, as if longer note values were like hoarded gold, suitable for the rich) is mockingly damning. There is a contemptuous vocal roulade of semiquavers on 'eine' and, while the singer holds 'reiche' for nearly two beats, an A major scale (b. 45) ascends the keyboard in one and a half octaves, denoting the range of the parents' ambition and social climbing. Scales exactly of this type occur in the Schlegel setting *Die Berge* D634 (also in §) which talks of the risible aspirations of mortals: 'They desire to fly up / And reach the gods above; / Soaring aloft, man imagines / He has already passed through the clouds.' Immediately after this tidy, upwardly mobile scale we hear a hollow parody of it (b. 46), this time with chromatic complications in A minor, as an upbeat to the postlude: life is a straight path for burghers with their society weddings, but not for the poor traveller. The song ends as it began, the introduction serving as the postlude. In b. 47 one of the semiquaver flourishes is slightly altered to start on a higher note (A instead of F, another afterthought on Schubert's part), giving the music a heightened air of hysteria. The last thing we hear is those amazing juxtaposed trills, the first loud (b. 50), the second a whimper (b. 51).

Schubert's sketch for *Die Wetterfahne* published in Vol. 4b of the NSA is a fascinating glimpse at the bare bones of the composer's initial inspiration. It contains the melodic outline (more or less the pianist's right hand) of the interludes, the vocal line and occasional harmonic pointers at crucial turning points. A long trill under 'Er hätt' es eher bemerken sollen' (bb. 14–16) was later abandoned in favour of snatched staccato chords. The grimly triumphant A major scale under 'reiche Braut' (b. 45) was clearly an idea that was part of the song from the very beginning.

First edition:	Published as Op. 89 no. 2 by Tobias Haslinger, Vienna on 14 January 1828 (P142)
Subsequent editions:	Peters: Vol. 1/58; AGA XX 518: Vol. 9/62; NSA IV: Vol. 4a/115 & Vol. 4b/260 (sketch); Bärenreiter: Vol. 3/82
Bibliography:	Youens 1991, pp. 131–7
Arrangement:	Arr. Tilman Hoppstock (b. 1961) for guitar accompaniment, in *Franz Schubert: 110 Lieder* (2009)
Discography and timing:	Fischer-Dieskau III 2^2 1'47
	Pears–Britten 2'00
	Hyperion I 30^2
	Hyperion II 33^2 1'46 Matthias Goerne

← *Gute Nacht* D911/1   *Gefrorne Tränen* D911/3 →

III GEFRORNE TRÄNEN
Op. 89 no. 3, **D911/3** [H615]
F minor

Frozen tears

(55 bars)

Gefrorne Tropfen fallen
Von meinen Wangen ab:
Ob es mir denn entgangen,[1]
Dass ich geweinet hab?

  Ei Tränen, meine Tränen,
Und seid ihr gar so lau,
Dass ihr erstarrt zu Eise,
Wie kühler Morgentau?

  Und dringt doch aus der Quelle
Der Brust so glühend heiss,
Als wolltet ihr zerschmelzen
Des ganzen Winters Eis.

Frozen drops fall
From my cheeks
Have I, then, not noticed
That I have been weeping?

  Ah tears, my tears,
Are you so tepid
That you turn to ice,
Like the cold morning dew?

  And yet you well up, so scaldingly hot,
From your source within my heart,
As if you would melt
All the ice of winter.

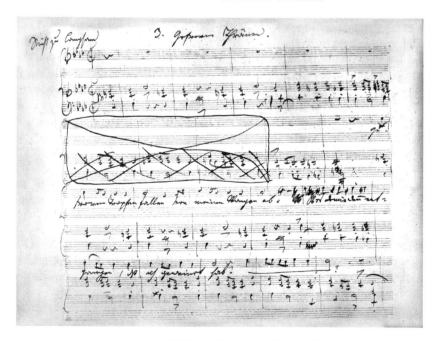

Autograph of *Gefrorne Tränen*, 1827 (first draft).

[1] Müller later (1824) changed this line to '*Und ist's* mir denn entgangen'.

This is the twenty-third of Schubert's forty-six Müller solo settings (1823, 1827 and 1828). See the poet's biography for a chronological list of all the Müller settings.

After the wild outburst of *Die Wetterfahne* (No. 2) we change direction as part of the composer's deliberate (and canny) decision to contrast moods and tempi within the cycle. As John Reed puts it, 'Schubert begins to weave the various strands of the drama into a satisfying pattern.' In musical terms we turn abruptly from the *Sturm und Drang* of *Die Wetterfahne* into a world of frozen classical poise – apt for deep feelings which appear tepid but are in fact red-hot; a front for tears that are hidden and unexpected and for emotions that seem uninvolved but are more intense as a result of their unconscious suppression. The traveller weeps despite himself, at first unaware of how deeply he is mourning his loss. So deep is his grief that he believes his tears should have a more long-lasting effect on the ice. As it is, and contrary to his feelings, they appear to be only lukewarm.

This classicism is expressed in a tightness and strictness of rhythm very different from the rubato and ebb and flow of *Die Wetterfahne*. For the accompaniment the composer chooses as his inspiration the classical format of the string quartet. Most of this piano writing is in four parts, with eloquent solo opportunities for first fiddle in the right hand and cello in the left. There are few other accompaniments in *Winterreise* with the same rigorous economy and the same contrapuntal independence of bass line. Devices that normally provide harmonic filling in the piano (triplets, Alberti basses) are entirely absent; there is scarcely any need for pedal, and left-hand octaves are kept to a minimum.

Schubert has used a string quartet layout for the accompaniment for a very simple reason: the image of a falling tear equates in his mind (and musical ear) with the sound of a string pizzicato. (This analogue became assimilated into Brahms's song-writing vocabulary.) The first two chords in the piano (a crotchet upbeat on the dominant, followed by a crotchet on the tonic) are marked 'staccato' and, fairly obviously, represent teardrops. But the third tear, a solitary C in the treble stave, is longer and louder – a minim with an accent (>). Something has happened to it in midstream, as it were, as the progress of the music is momentarily halted on the syncopated off-beat, first in the right hand (b. 1) and then in the left – another minim on C, an octave lower this time (b. 2). These tears freeze before our very ears and momentarily arrest the flow of music. This is the musical encapsulation of a song's title, something that Schubert manages time and again with a gesture such as this. As we hear the sound properties change we see the tear itself change from water into ice.

The image of a frozen song made up of blocks of ice comes to mind. Schubert was fond of water music of every kind, but here we have its antithesis – music without the fluidity of water, vertical rather than horizontal. In the occasional dactylic rhythms of the poem there is always the potential for the sound of nature on the move, and this is audible on the second page where the poetry speaks of melting ice. But even there it is like large blocks of ice cracking and moving downstream rather than the more familiar Schubertian sound of flowing water. At the beginning the traveller's feelings seem to be constrained by the cold; he sounds emotionally stilted and confused. Some commentators see in this music signs of a limp or stagger, but it is too early in the story for the dragging of weary limbs. Instead there is the numbness of aftershock, the delayed reaction after all the frenzied activity required to extricate himself from the scene of his betrayal and humiliation.

In bb. 5 and 6 of the introduction a descending phrase in dactylic crotchets and quavers is utilized that gives the first clue to the shape and rhythm of the vocal line. The vocal melody (from 'Gefrorne Tropfen fallen', bb. 7–11) is an independent obbligato to its accompaniment which for its first four bars is a slightly varied repeat of the introduction, making it temporarily seem like a descant above a ground bass. This economy of means, and recycling of material, tightens the construction and turns the screw of tension. At 'Dass ich geweinet hab' (bb. 13–15) we find ourselves, rather surprisingly for a mournful image, in the relative major (A flat). The repeat of the words is ornamented by heartfelt little melismas and is an important example of the use of the 'pathetic major': the traveller's vulnerability, and the suggestion that he is giddy and confused, is more touching in the major key than in the minor. Throughout the cycle he achieves moments of martyred nobility, infinitely sad and moving in the context of his disorientated state of mind, and surprisingly often using this harmonic trademark. When he sings in the major key (as at 'Dass ich geweinet hab') he seems to be ruefully speaking to himself, lost in his own world, or living in the past.

After a four-bar interlude in A flat major (bb. 17–20) based on repetitions of the rhythmic cell of 'Gefrorne Tropfen', the poet's second strophe is ushered in by staccatissimo octaves deep in the piano (b. 21). The vocal line at 'Ei Tränen, meine Tränen' is derived from the sixth bar of the introduction. Schubert uses and re-uses his opening material in the interests of watertight cohesion – or perhaps not so watertight as far as the weeping protagonist is concerned. This passage in the voice is shadowed, and often doubled, by the conspiratorial piano, always a sign of emphasis in Schubert's songs and of something deep and serious to say. There is a whispered confidentiality about this passage and we strain our ears in order to hear someone talking not only to himself but actually to his tears, as if they had a life of their own. The staccato accompaniment, crotchets separated by rests in the vocal line, is again vividly evocative of falling tears. Note the startling inflection achieved at 'Dass ihr estarrt' by a sudden change to legato in the piano as the singer ascends a tiny scale covering a minor third (bb. 24–5); also the poignant interval of a diminished fourth on 'kühler Morgentau' (G to C flat, b. 27) which provides a momentary shiver as the music shifts into E flat major.

And then the dams of emotion break. A tiny piano interlude of two bars (bb. 28–9) moves from E flat major to E flat[7] with the right-hand chords rising in degrees in a crescendo: first B flat at the top then C flat – C – D flat. The melodic distance is tiny, the harmonic change not world-shattering, yet the temperature of the poem has risen by many degrees, and the composer more than matches the poet's sharp turn of the emotional screw. The tessitura of the vocal line now sits in the middle of the stave, making frequent excursions to the upper reaches. The heat is on also for the performers, and the second page of the song needs real singing, a heartfelt outburst of scalding emotion. Here we begin to notice that the accented minim in the accompaniment which has represented the frozen tear at the beginning of the song has found a new, more vehement role. This coincides with a remarkably powerful modulation (at 'Als wolltet ihr zerschmelzen / Des ganzen Winters Eis', bb. 33–5) into the distant reaches of G flat major. Instead of sticking out in frozen isolation, these sforzato minims appear in the bass clef, played by the pianist's left hand – or rather the string quartet's eloquent cellist who interacts fiercely with his fellow players in a more heated way. There are six 'cello' D flats in all, loud and low. These *fz* notes are the culmination of a descending scale of left-hand pizzicati, but they are not suddenly arco; what is needed is a different plucked quality, enhanced by vibrato to prolong the sound, and to differentiate it from the smaller tear droplets. They now represent a tear, extremely effective in thermal terms, that hits its mark. (Note too that 'lau' ('tepid') in the previous strophe (b. 24) is set to a similar minim to contrast it with the freezing pizzicato crotchets of the accompaniment.)

Here Schubert has achieved something that one would have thought was all but impossible: translating into music the sound of melting. In the fantasy world of both poet and composer these tears have the power to melt all the winter ice – the sound waves are boiling hot with musical energy and large circles of snow melt in their periphery. (This follows a head-on collision between voice and piano at 'Als wolltet ihr zerschmelzen', bb. 43–5 – the piano's left hand resolutely climbing to counter the voice which falls by a dive-bombing diminished fifth at the beginning of b. 44.) Even in the look of the printed score, the open circle of each minim resembles a newly created crater in the ice. As these pizzicati vibrate on the second and third beats of bb. 45, 46 and 47 they radiate a sonic equivalent of the ripples that emanate from a stone thrown into water. The idea of tears dropping on to snow and melting it in large quantities is certainly fanciful, and Müller has been criticized for this. But Schubert has translated unsound physics into physical sound. He uses the same minim figuration to conjure musical images of both freezing and its mirror image of melting. This, even by his exalted standards, is an extraordinary achievement. As in *Die Wetterfahne*, another song to a three-strophe poem, *Gefrorne Tränen* achieves its formal balance by a repeat of all the words of the final verse as well as repeats of 'Des ganzen Winters Eis' within that strophe. 'Und dringt doch aus der Quelle' has begun in A flat major, and we have already described the powerful shift into G flat major at 'Als wolltet ihr zerschmelzen'. The first 'Des ganzen Winters Eis' is still in this key, but there is a shift to F minor for the second, and thence to a pivotal diminished chord (a tiny moment of hesitation for the performers in b. 39) that clears the way for a moving return to A flat major. This time it is 'Ihr dringt' rather than 'Und dringt', but the music for the entire repeated strophe is the same until the final vocal cadence – the concluding 'Des ganzen Winters Eis' – which is marked 'Stark' and hammers home the tonic F minor in the highest and most awkwardly placed vocal passage in the whole song (bb. 47–9). This has the effect of a desperate *cri de cœur*.

Most brutal of all is the postlude (bb. 49–55) which, in its almost exact return to the music of the opening, instantly deflates the grandeur of the traveller's fantasy about the strength of his tears and import of his grief. We understand by this music that the tears are frozen, solitary and ineffective, just like the narrator himself. Even in the depth of his grief he cannot aspire to the stature of a towering hero. The final staccato bars seem to have retreated into a frightened and timid reticence.

First edition:	Published as Op. 89 no. 3 by Tobias Haslinger, Vienna on 14 January 1828 (P 143)
Subsequent editions:	Peters: Vol. 1/60; AGA XX 519: Vol. 9/8; NSA IV: Vol. 4a/118; Bärenreiter: Vol. 3/84
Bibliography:	Youens 1991, pp. 138–43
Arrangement:	Arr. Tilman Hoppstock (b. 1961) for guitar accompaniment, in *Franz Schubert: 110 Lieder* (2009)
Discography and timing:	Fischer-Dieskau III 2³ 2'18
	Pears–Britten 2'14
	Hyperion I 30³
	Hyperion II 33³ 2'25 Matthias Goerne

← *Die Wetterfahne* D911/2   *Erstarrung* D911/4 →

IV ERSTARRUNG   Numbness
Op. 89 no. 4, **D911/4** [H616]
C minor

(109 bars)

Ich such' im Schnee vergebens	In vain I seek
Nach ihrer Tritte Spur,	Her footprints in the snow,
Wo sie an meinem Arme[1]	Where she walked on my arm
Durchstrich die grüne Flur.	Through the green meadows.
Ich will den Boden küssen,	If only I could kiss the ground
Durchdringen Eis und Schnee	And pierce ice and snow
Mit meinen heissen Tränen,	With my burning tears,
Bis ich die Erde seh'.	Until I see the earth.
Wo find' ich eine Blüte?	Where shall I find a flower?
Wo find' ich grünes Gras?	Where shall I find green grass?
Die Blumen sind erstorben,	The flowers have died,
Der Rasen sieht so blass.	The grass looks so pale.
Soll denn kein Angedenken	Shall I, then, take
Ich nehmen mit von hier?	No memento from here?
Wenn meine Schmerzen schweigen,	When my sorrows are stilled
Wer sagt mir dann von ihr?	Who will speak to me of her?
Mein Herz ist wie erstorben,[2]	My heart is as dead,
Kalt starrt ihr Bild darin:	Her image coldly rigid within it;
Schmilzt je das Herz mir wieder,	If my heart ever melts again
Fliesst auch ihr Bild dahin.[3]	Her image, too, will flow away.

This is the twenty-fourth of Schubert's forty-six Müller solo settings (1823, 1827 and 1828). See the poet's biography for a chronological list of all the Müller settings.

If the preceding piece is inspired by string quartet, we return here to piano writing of unashamed Romantic *Schwung*. The broad sweep and energy of *Erstarrung* is extraordinary, especially in the context of its neighbouring songs that wield their power in a different way. On paper it is the longest in the cycle, occupying five pages in the Peters Edition and eight in the NSA. On the surface Schubert seems to have allowed himself to return to an earlier, more extravagant song-writing style and various commentators have pointed out its similarity to the Schulze setting *Im Walde* D834 which is usually dated from two years earlier (although it is sometimes claimed to have been written in 1827). In reality, *Erstarrung* is more tightly constructed than the Schulze songs, and this is largely due to Müller and Schulze being very different poets, the former much more epigrammatic than the latter.

Gefrorne Tränen (No. 3) seemed to be the music of physical numbness, the frozen tears an outward manifestation of feelings that were so shocked that they could not yet measure the

---

[1] Müller later (1824) changed the third and fourth lines of this strophe to 'Hier, wo wir oft gewandelt / Selbander durch die Flur'. 'Selbander' is old German for 'miteinander' or 'zusammen', thus the poet is still describing walking out with his girl.
[2] Müller's line, in both *Urania* and *Gedichte 1824*, is 'Mein Herz ist wie *erfroren*'. AGA substitutes this word, but Peters (following the first edition) and NSA (following the autograph) retain 'erstorben'.
[3] Müller has '*das* Bild' as does Schubert in his autograph. It is possible that the composer changed this in proof in late 1827 when he was preparing the song for publication. By this time perhaps he was already aware of Heine's great poem for which he himself created the title: *Ihr Bild* (D957/9).

extent of their loss. *Erstarrung* ('numbness') is perhaps misleading as a title, however, for the song begins as a battle against numbness of feeling, rather like the panic of someone with the tingling of pins and needles in arm or leg who desperately hopes it is a temporary phenomenon and not a symptom of something more sinister. When pianists are gripped by fear of this kind, as they frequently are, they move and stretch their hands to get the circulation going – but they may just as well play *Erstarrung* to encourage blood-flow to arms and fingers. The song is dominated by triplets that are (mostly) in the right hand and make their crab-like way around the keyboard while a powerfully shaped melody in the bass clef holds an impassioned dialogue with the vocal line. Despite all the bustling activity from the piano, it is the strength of this two-part writing that gives the song its taut eloquence. (A warning to pianists: there have been countless over-rushed performances of this song and it is useful to remember the moderating 'Ziemlich' of the marking and that Schubert first described the tempo on his autograph as 'Nicht zu geschwind'.)

It is fond memories that bring sensation back to the benumbed heart (as we shall discover in *Der Lindenbaum* No. 5), but here the traveller seeks in vain for some physical manifestation of them – footprints, flowers – and remembrances to take away, or 'Angedenken' as he calls them. This then is the music of fruitless searching and the panic and despondency which accompany it. The first thing we hear is restless melody in the left hand: three crotchets followed by a triplet with an investigative character, betokening scrutiny and disappointment, as if one turns over a leaf only to discover it comes from the wrong tree. These restless crotchets rove up and down the bass stave, while the fourth beat of the first and third bars of the phrase is ornamented with triplets, forever searching and worrying. The singer has his own eloquent melody working superbly in partnership with the pianist's left hand. The vocal line moves hither and thither like someone desperately looking for a lost key-ring in the dark, while the pianist's triplets suggest hands parting the undergrowth, investigating one frond after another. Of course the landscape is a wintry one, but the memories of happier times are populated by summer greenery, and the denseness of the writing suggests someone lost in a forest of emotions. The last word of each line – 'vergebens', 'Spur', 'Arme', 'Flur' – comes to a temporary halt in suspended motion, phrased away as if to say 'no, not there; I must look elsewhere'. These final words are all set to a crotchet, the strong beat of the bar, falling away to a minim; this phrasing subtly conveys uncertainty, disappointment and the wilting of hopes.

The form of this song in five strophes is basically ABCAB. For the second strophe there is a modulation from C minor into G minor (from b. 25), and the triplets are transferred to the left hand where they take up a more conventional accompanying function. The voice now duets with octaves in the pianist's right hand. The musical phrase 'Ich will den Boden küssen' (bb. 24–6) bends earthward, but the accompaniment's determined octaves rising up the stave signify a welling up of feelings, a flood of tears coming to the surface. The setting of 'Mit meinen heissen Tränen' (bb. 28–31) is one of the most impassioned phrases in the whole cycle, and the voice reaches a top A flat on 'meinen' (note how Schubert emphasizes an unimportant part of a word to accentuate derangement and grief; cf. *Die Wetterfahne*, No. 2) which is one of the high points of the cycle in sheerly vocal terms. These burning tears in crotchets roll down the cheeks of the stave, shadowed by the piano octaves sounding a third and a tenth higher. As the traveller imagines the melting of the snow at 'Bis ich die Erde, die Erde, seh'' there is a fleeting, but marvellous, tonal picture of a landscape clear of snow and ice. The second 'die Erde seh'' (bb. 32–4) climbs a fifth to higher, clearer regions, while the bass, still firmly grounded on G for 'die Erde', suddenly moves under the crucial verb 'seh'' ('see'), into more attenuated harmonic territory at b. 34 (a diminished chord with a rising bass line of A flat, B natural, then D). This breaking up of thick minor-key arpeggios into diminished chord fragments, plus a vocal line rising to the surface, suggests snow melting as the mists lift.

The third verse begins with the piano music of the opening (in C minor, from b. 44) but after only two bars the triplets veer suddenly and exquisitely into the submediant (A flat). The pianist has to be careful in turning this corner, a manoeuvre that requires skill and Schubertian experience. This switch into the major is a trademark of the cycle, denoting a retreat to the past, and to happier May weather. For the first time the accompaniment is not a duet between triplets and driven crotchets: there are now triplets in both hands, and the effect is of sudden tranquillity, suspended and floating in memories as if the traveller were treading water in a still lagoon. A lesser composer might have continued the panicky search with distressed music for the words 'Wo find' ich eine Blüte?', but mention of flowers takes Schubert immediately into a warmer season and a stiller land. The appoggiaturas of longing, leaning against the bar line on 'Blüte' (b. 49) and 'Gras' (b. 51) are as pathetic as anything written by Donizetti for the mad scenes of his Lucia or Anna Bolena. There too, madness and the fragile world of the once-proud and beautiful unhinged by their fate are admirably caught in major-key passages where childlike musical simplicity equates to a world of lost innocence. Not uniquely in this cycle we note that Italianate and operatic turns of phrase are fully absorbed into this composer's armoury and transfigured into the purest Schubert. There is a hint of the icy blast which kills the flowers in the semitone rise in the bass (and *fp* marking) in the change under 'Der Rasen sieht so blass' (at b. 55).

The fourth verse is a musical recapitulation of the first, but Schubert inserts a remarkable bridge passage for the return to C minor. The first two lines from the third strophe ('Wo find' ich eine Blüte? / Wo find' ich grünes Gras?') are repeated passionately, as if the traveller has suddenly snapped out of his reverie, no longer lost in the past (bb. 59–63). After a momentary idyll, desperation and ache return to the music in redoubled measure, and with these six bars the composer engineers a superbly turbulent, yet carefully controlled, return to the home key. At 'Soll denn kein Angedenken' the music is the same as for the opening but, as always with the best of Schubert's strophic songs, the new words fit equally well. The rise and fall of 'Wenn meine Schmerzen schweigen' (bb. 68–70) is especially eloquent; the apex of the climbing phrase is on the verb 'schweigen' ('to still') and is superbly paradoxical, underlining that the traveller's sorrows, however he suppresses them, will never be stilled.

The fifth verse mirrors the second. The triplets are once again transferred to the left hand, and once again the voice duets with right-hand octaves. When we come to the passage where, in the second verse, the snow has melted to reveal the earth, there are some interesting parallels and contrasts. This strophe speaks of the beloved's image concealed within the singer's heart. At the first appearance of 'Fliesst auch ihr Bild, ihr Bild dahin' in bb. 87–91, a picture beneath the surface coming into focus through the mist, the ascending diminished arpeggios dissolve the singer's frozen corporeal self to reveal the picture 'darin'. But the difference between the ends of the second and fourth lines ('darin' ('within') and 'dahin' ('there and away')) is crucial. The traveller realizes that if his heart melts he will lose the image of his beloved for ever. The second time we hear 'ihr Bild, ihr Bild dahin' (bb. 98–101) the diminished chord on A flat at 'dahin' refuses to do what it did before – move upwards and dematerialize. Instead it moves down a semitone in b. 102 and, aided by 'un poco ritard', makes a doggedly defiant statement. This is grounded firmly on the dominant which is part of the elongated final cadence, itself something near a howl of distress. He is damned by the pain of carrying the picture within him; he is equally damned by the fear of losing it – the only memento of her he possesses – should his heart melt. What has begun as a search for the tracks of summer ends with an insistence on the frozen status quo. Numbness will at least keep the pain intact within him, and it is only the pain that keeps him alive.

Schubert never set a poem more typical than this of the new Romantic movement that had swept through German literature. The six-bar postlude is derived from the introduction, as is almost always the case in this cycle where new literary ideas are subject to many old-fashioned disciplines of strophic song. The combination, which takes the best from both old and new, is formidably expressive.

The sketch of this song is printed in Volume 4b of the NSA (p. 263). The introduction is hastily laid out and is much the same as we know it, although the left-hand harmonies in bb. 3 and 4 as noted here, no doubt at lightning speed, are crucially changed in the final version by transposing the melody up a fourth – a great enrichment of the song's harmonic palette. Other than this the composer soon loses interest in filling out the accompaniment and concentrates on planning the vocal line. In many respects this sketch, produced in the white heat of inspiration, is amazingly near the final version, but Schubert returned to polish the song and enlarge its scope by repeating whole phrases and diverting the harmonies into slightly different directions. This makes the song longer than he first thought: for example, the crucial change into A flat major ('Wo find' ich eine Blüte?') at b. 47 occurs at b. 41 of the sketch. Despite these adjustments and refinements it is truly amazing that the song seems conceived in a single flash of inspiration, with many of its greatest ideas put down directly from the composer's mind onto paper.

First edition:	Published as Op. 89 no. 4 by Tobias Haslinger, Vienna on 14 January 1828 (P144)
Subsequent editions:	Peters: Vol. 1 /62; AGA XX 520: Vol. 9/10; NSA IV: Vol. 4a/120 & Vol. 4b/263 (sketch); Bärenreiter: Vol. 3/86
Bibliography:	Youens 1991, pp. 144–50
Arrangement:	Arr. Franz Liszt (1811–1886) for solo piano, no. 5 of *Winterreise* (1838–9) [*see* TRANSCRIPTIONS]
Discography and timing:	Fischer-Dieskau III 2[4] 3'00
	Pears–Britten 3'12
	Hyperion I 30[4]
	Hyperion II 33[4] 3'11 Matthias Goerne

← *Gefrorne Tränen* D911/3   *Der Lindenbaum* D911/5 →

V Der LINDENBAUM   The lime tree
OP. 89 NO. 5, **D911/5** [H617]
E major

Am Bru - nen vor dem To - re,

(82 bars)

Am Brunnen vor dem Tore	By the well, before the gate,
Da steht ein Lindenbaum:	Stands a linden tree;
Ich träumt' in seinem Schatten	In its shade I dreamt
So manchen süssen Traum	Many a sweet dream.

Ich schnitt in seine Rinde
So manches liebe Wort;
Es zog in Freud' und Leide
Zu ihm mich immer fort.

Ich musst' auch heute wandern
Vorbei in tiefer Nacht,
Da hab' ich noch im Dunkel
Die Augen zugemacht.

Und seine Zweige rauschten,
Als riefen sie mir zu:
Komm her zu mir, Geselle,
Hier findst du deine Ruh'!

Die kalten Winde bliesen
Mir grad' in's Angesicht;
Der Hut flog mir vom Kopfe,
Ich wendete mich nicht.

Nun bin ich manche Stunde
Entfernt von jenem Ort,
Und immer hör' ich's rauschen:
Du fändest Ruhe dort!

In its bark I carved
Many a word of love;
In joy and sorrow
I was ever drawn to it.

Today, too, I had to walk
Past it at dead of night;
Even in the darkness
I closed my eyes.

And its branches rustled
As if they were calling to me:
'Come to me, friend,
Here you will find rest.'

The cold wind blew
Straight into my face,
My hat flew from my head;
I did not turn back.

Now I am many hours' journey
From that place;
Yet I still hear the rustling:
'There you would find rest.'

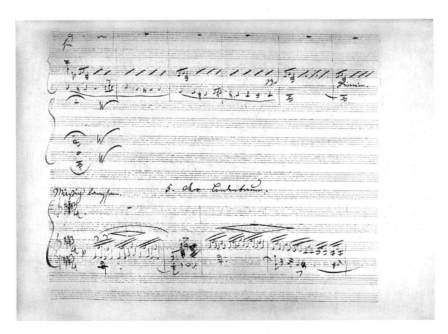

Autograph of opening of *Der Lindenbaum*, 1827.

This is the twenty-fifth of Schubert's forty-six Müller solo settings (1823, 1827 and 1828). See the poet's biography for a chronological list of all the Müller settings.

This is one of the most famous songs of all time. Indeed, many thousands of people who know its melody by heart have no idea that it comes from *Winterreise*. With this deeply serious song Schubert had the sort of 'hit' that he achieved neither in his operatic work nor in his deliberately populist comic songs. It is printed in Erk's *Deutscher Liederschatz* with a simplified accompaniment that ignores altogether the minor change of the third verse and the storm interlude of the fifth. The melody has long been elevated to the status of folksong and, to the wider public, its provenance and context have been unimportant. However, even to those who encounter it in its bowdlerized form, it is clear that the words refer to the idyllic past of small-town life, a time when lovers could sit a-courting on the village green in the shade of that most German of trees. It is perhaps difficult for the English-speaker to understand what a potent image the linden tree is in the Teutonic imagination. Heine writes of it in his history of Geman literature (1833) as a meeting place for lovers: 'it is their favourite tree, probably because the linden-tree leaf is in the form of a heart'. Among Schubert's other poets, Rückert, Uhland and Mayrhofer have all written movingly about the broad cultural shadow cast by the linden tree, and the last of Mahler's *Lieder eines fahrenden Gesellen* (1885) owes much to the example of *Der Lindenbaum*. In Thomas Mann's *The Magic Mountain* Schubert's song is praised for its marriage of lied and folksong styles. It is a tribute to the inevitability of the music that it seems always to have been part of mankind's melodic inheritance.

Müller's autograph for *Der Lindenbaum*.

In the context of the cycle it is a haven of peace – one of only two songs in Part One that begin in the major key – and a perfect foil for *Erstarrung* (No. 4). The accompaniment is a miracle of beauty and invention. In *Erstarrung* we have had triplets that describe a circular search for footprints, flowers, mementos. But in *Der Lindenbaum* the triplets (semiquavers this time) finger lovingly through the invisible pages of memory rather than through the undergrowth. Schubert has deliberately contrived that the speed of the triplets in the adjacent songs should be related, different sides of the same coin. The rustling figuration has an obvious link with the sound of wind gently passing through the branches of the linden tree. But it is more than this: it is a homage to Wolfgang Amadeus Mozart and his song *Abendempfindung* K523, one of the first great German lieder. The undulating sixths in the piano, like so much else in Schubert, derive from Mozart, and the kinship of the songs originates in similar philosophical reflections, thoughts at eventide, intimations of mortality and, in this case, the death of love. (The accompaniment of another fine Schubert song, *Abendbilder* D650, is also inspired by *Abendempfindung*.)

The first bar of rustling semiquaver triplets culminates in a temporary resting point on the dominant (b. 2).[1] This second bar is decorated by a tiny figure, a C sharp semiquaver that falls to an adjacent minim B. This tiny gesture is one of the most memorable features of the accompaniment: it might suggest an ear cocked, straining to listen, with the concentration necessary to recall every detail of the past. (Later in the song we will meet these two notes again, in different guise.) Another bar of triplets, an octave higher this time, is accompanied by C sharp – B, now incorporated in the bass line and an echo of what has gone before in the treble. The triplets slide down the stave and shift into C sharp minor, where they hover for a bar, before opening out into slightly portentous quavers that suggest the slow rising of a stage curtain (second half of b. 6). As the triplets sidle upwards in the right hand the bass line descends an octave, the contrary motion of the hands suggestive of the opening up, before our very eyes, of a rolling vista of landscape. The right hand reaches an *fp* chord on the notes F sharp and A, the left ends up on a low B. The resulting chord of B^7 in b. 7 forms part of a tiny fanfare figure (descending horn music in demisemiquaver thirds and fifths) that resounds on its own through an entire bar. Once again there is a sense of echo when the same 'fanfare' is repeated ppp (b. 8). That Schubert associated the sound of E major horn music with country life is evident as early as 1816 in the Pichler setting *Lied* ('Ferne von der grossen Stadt') D483, but here it has a scene-setting stature unlike any other. These horn-calls are some of Schubert's most Romantic musical gestures (like those haunting bass trills at the beginning of the B flat major Piano Sonata D960), almost Mahlerian in their impact. They rejoice in the pastoral beauty of the wooded countryside and sigh at the sadness of the human condition at sunset. These emotions were evoked at almost the same time by Alfred de Vigny in *Le cor* (1825) ('Dieu! que le son du cor est triste au fond des bois!') and mournful horn music was later described by Verlaine in *Le son du cor s'afflige vers les bois* – an instance of German Romanticism and French Impressionism listening to the same sounds:

Le son du cor s'afflige vers les bois	The sound of the horn wails towards the woods
D'une douleur on veut croire orpheline	With a grief so close to bereavement
Qui vient mourir au bas de la colline	Which fades away at the foot of the hill
Parmi la bise errant en courts abois.	Amid the gust of the fierce North Wind.

At the end of b. 8 the voice enters with a melody that is simple almost beyond analysis. It descends in steps of thirds ('Am Brunnen vor dem Tore') and finishes with a straightforward little progression up and down the scale ('Da steht ein Lindenbaum'). The accompaniment is content to hug the vocal line in earnest studiousness, as if played by a village musician, not highly talented but working lovingly at the church harmonium. This is part of the music's all-embracing humanity and accessibility. When his heart is in it, Schubert can write for the ordinary man, and ordinary musician, with an instinct for the popular (in the best sense) equal to Shakespeare's. After the first vocal phrase an interlude of horn music reappears in quavers (b. 12). The next two lines repeat the music we have already heard and it becomes clear here that Schubert has decided to use two of Müller's verses to make one of his own. 'Ich schnitt in seine Rinde' (b. 17) shifts to a bass of A sharp in the first inversion of the supertonic; the effect is to take us suddenly out of a floating reverie with a sense of narrative progress as the young man remembers cutting into the tree's bark with his penknife. This line brings us back to the

---

[1] Elmar Budde in *Schuberts Liederzyklen* discerns in the melodic shape traced by the higher notes of the right-hand figurations (thus E – D sharp – E – G sharp – F sharp – E) a transposed echo of the left-hand melody in crotchets at the opening of *Erstarrung* D911/4 (C – B natural – C – E flat – D – C).

dominant (the demisemiquavers of the introduction's horn-call are fleetingly reintroduced in b. 20). The last line of the strophe is a repeat of this music, adapted at the final cadence to return to the tonic. It sounds so simple, and so it is, but it breathes deeply in the air of the calm, healing countryside. However much or little we know about Schubert and the circumstances of the winter traveller, we feel the great aura of this music, a leafy-branched cupola of tenderness and regret, sweetness and longing, hanging over us and protecting us from the cares of the outside world.

This is the bit that the folksong enthusiasts liked, and they were quite content to sing the tune three times through without variation. But *Der Lindenbaum* is a lied, no more a real folk-song than *Ellens Gesang III (Ave Maria)* D839 is a piece of church music. The E major of the opening strophe has been a photograph of the past, sunlit in a way that cannot be associated with winter. We return to the chilling present with a verse (Müller's third) beginning in the minor. As an introduction the rustling leaves motif is shifted to minor-key tonality, and the falling semiquaver motif of the introduction appears in both the treble and bass clefs. Instead of C sharp – B, we now hear C natural – B (b. 28), an ominous adjustment that emphasizes that the present has deeper and sadder resonances than the past. This interval, as we shall see, will be the musical foundation for the stormy weather soon to come. For 'Ich musst' auch heute wandern' and the rest of the verse, the shape of a familiar melody stays the same, although it has been darkened into E minor. The accompaniment, however, is more eventful – dragging triplets followed by a dotted quaver + semiquaver figure that limps along and pulls against the flow of the vocal line. As soon as we return to the past tense (at 'Und seine Zweige rauschten'), and the healing properties of the linden tree make themselves apparent, as well as its magical ability to speak to the traveller, the music shifts again into E major (a change of key signature before b. 37). Those dragging footsteps in the accompaniment are now softened into a gentle curve rather than a leaden droop. With these shifts between major and minor we move between present and past like a picture moving in and out of focus – a cinematic trick from a composer whose visualizing imagination encompassed such legerdemain a century before it became common currency in the film world.

That change back to the major key makes what happens next – the song's central section – more of a surprise. There is no modulation, only the sudden contrast between E major and its flattened submediant, in effect the harmony of C major. This is the starting point for a sequence of stormy semiquaver triplets in sixths – a magnificent evocation of a stormy wintry blast, almost volcanic in its brilliant depiction of shuddering change. (This music is all the more effective because it has been so cleverly transformed from the rustlings of the introduction.) This C pedal (from bb. 45 to 52) is only a semitone away from B, the dominant of the home key, and of course this is an augmentation of the tiny motif given to the piano (in bb. 26 and 28) that has introduced the minore verse, a falling C natural to B. Roaming right-hand triplets are underpinned by the pedal C which twice (at bb. 46 and 48) sinks a semitone amidst a flurry of B minor arpeggios, right hand following left. These oscillations are prophetic of the music for the crow (*Die Krähe*, No. 15) later in the cycle. This is Schubert at his most illustrative and one could not wish for a better storm-tossed moment of drama as the pianist insistently drums those low Cs under 'Der Hut flog mir vom Kopfe' (bb. 50–51). The stoic insistence of 'Ich wendete mich nicht', a decisive point for the story and the continuation of the journey, is tell-ingly conveyed by repeated Cs in the vocal line (awkwardly low for tenors, bb. 51–3) to match those of the accompaniment. Then something magical happens on 'nicht' (b. 53). The bass line on C again falls to a low B, but this time it is not harmonized as the tonic of B minor but rather as the second inversion of E major. This is our gateway to a final flurry of triplets rising and falling in chromatic undulation while low Bs toll in the bass (bb. 53–8). This spine-chilling music brilliantly, and uncannily, evokes the sound of the howling wind. These four bars make a perfect transition to the final strophe, but not before a repeat of the B^7 horn-calls from the opening.

The composer has gathered all the ingredients he needs for the final strophe, and the extended interlude has set it up to achieve a magical and eloquent effect. The E major melody we already know and love, but the accompaniment is transfigured. Like the closing pages of the slow movements of the late piano sonatas and the String Quintet D956, a flicker of the preceding storm lingers as a haunting reminder that (as the Greeks said) one cannot step into the same river twice: one can never return to the same linden tree and find it unchanged. The accompaniment (triplets + dotted quavers + semiquavers) is similar in shape to that of the walking music of the minore verse, but there is an added figure of staccato quavers in the accompaniment at the end of each bar that gives the music new determination and impetus. It is this which reminds us of the recent disruption to the music during the storm and the loss of the traveller's hat. This verse is a middle ground between past and present. Having taken the irrevocable decision not to turn around, even to retrieve his hat – precious protection against the cold – the traveller must continue on his way. But the memories of warmth and security are sufficiently strong for their major-key glow to be cast onto the remainder of the song. This final appearance of an immortal melody warms to its theme, and from b. 67 the accompaniment broadens into right-hand octaves that inevitably bring a richer texture and heightened intensity. This passage contains a quietly magical moment – 'Du fändest Ruhe dort!' – when the tree seems to whisper to the traveller. The postlude, a shortened version of the introduction, fades away into the distance with a feminine cadence, the final E major chord off the beat in a moment of renunciation. The song began with the traveller standing still, stopped in his tracks as he cherished his memories. It ends with the resumption of the journey and his inevitable exit from the scene of past happiness.

First edition:	Published as Op. 89 no. 5 by Tobias Haslinger, Vienna on 14 January 1828 (P145)
First known performance:	22 January 1829 *Abend-Unterhaltung* of the Gesellschaft der Musikfreunde, Vienna. Soloist: Johann Karl Schoberlechner (see Waidelich/Hilmar Dokumente I No. 685 for full concert programme). *Im Dorfe* D911/17 was also performed.
Subsequent editions:	Peters: Vol. 1/67; AGA XX 521: Vol. 9/16; NSA IV: Vol. 4a/128; Bärenreiter: Vol. 3/92
Bibliography:	Youens 1991, pp. 151–69
Further settings and arrangements:	Arr. Franz Liszt (1811–1886) for solo piano, no. 7 of *Winterreise* (1838–9) [*see* TRANSCRIPTIONS]
	Arr. Arnold Schoenberg (1874–1951) for orchestra (fragment, 1916–17)
	Franz Koringer (1921–2000) *Hommage an Franz Schubert* (this song included in mixture of Lieder) (1996)
	Arr. Tilman Hoppstock (b. 1961) for guitar accompaniment, in *Franz Schubert: 110 Lieder* (2009)
Discography and timing:	Fischer-Dieskau III 2^5 4'37
	Pears–Britten 5'08
	Hyperion I 30^5
	Hyperion II 33^5 4'43 Matthias Goerne

← *Erstarrung* D911/4   *Wasserflut* D911/6 →

VI WASSERFLUT   Flood
Op. 89 no. 6 **D911/6** [H618]
F♯ minor, changed to E minor for publication[1]

(32 bars)

Manche Trän' aus meinen Augen	**M**any a tear has fallen
Ist gefallen in den Schnee:	From my eyes into the snow;
Seine kalten Flocken saugen	Its cold flakes eagerly suck in
Durstig ein das heisse Weh.	My burning grief.
Wenn die Gräser sprossen wollen,[2]	When the grass is about to shoot forth,
Weht daher ein lauer Wind,	A mild breeze blows;
Und das Eis zerspringt in Schollen,	The ice breaks up into pieces
Und der weiche Schnee zerrinnt.	And the soft snow melts away.
Schnee, du weisst von meinem Sehnen:	Snow, you know of my longing;
Sag', wohin doch geht dein Lauf?[3]	Tell me, where does your course lead?
Folge nach nur meinen Tränen,	If you but follow my tears
Nimmt dich bald das Bächlein auf.	The brook will soon absorb you.
Wirst mit ihm die Stadt durchziehen,	With it you will flow through the town,
Muntre Strassen ein und aus –	In and out of bustling streets;
Fühlst du meine Tränen glühen,	When you feel my tears glow,
Da ist meiner Liebsten Haus![4]	There will be my sweetheart's house.

This is the twenty-sixth of Schubert's forty-six Müller solo settings (1823, 1827 and 1828). See the poet's biography for a chronological list of all the Müller settings.

Like *Gefrorne Tränen* (No. 3) before it and *Auf dem Flusse* (No. 7) after it, this poem shows Müller's obsession with water imagery (we remember that he was also the poet of *Die schöne Müllerin* D795 where the stream is a dominant character). In *Wasserflut* he returns to ruminations on the stark contrast between the traveller's heated emotions and the coldness of ice. Once his tears mingle with the snow it is his strange (not to mention unhinged) belief that they will recover their heat in the melted stream (like sensitized material encountering a radiation hot spot) simply as a result of flowing past the house of the beloved. This is an aquatic reworking of the theme of the poem *Trockne Blumen* D957/18 in *Die schöne Müllerin*, where dead flowers come to life as a result of the girl's graveside visit. The traveller addresses the snow as a living

[1] Because Schubert decided on a straightforward transposition here, the copy in F sharp minor does not qualify as a version (*Fassung*) in its own right in NSA. The AGA, however, prints only the F sharp minor version.
[2] Müller writes (*Urania*, 1823) 'Wann die Gräser sprossen wollen'.
[3] Müller writes (in both 1823 and 1824 editions) 'Sag' *mir*, wohin geht dein Lauf?'.
[4] In the *Gedichte*, 1824, Müller emphasizes the first word of the line with double spacing: '*D a* ist meiner Liebsten Haus!'

thing. He sees it as rapaciously capable of feeding, vampire-like, on his grief-stricken tears, and assumes that it will be able to feel the rekindled heat of his tears, within its own body as it were, amidst the melted slush. The poet's imagination has carried him downstream and landed him in a logjam of wooden, and less than productive, imagery. Apart from such fancies, this is one of the less eventful songs in *Winterreise*. It tells us nothing new about our hero and advances the story not a jot. He will reflect on ice and water once again in *Auf dem Flusse*, but the poetic pictures there lend themselves more obviously to illustration and tonal analogue.

Nevertheless, Schubert makes of this philosophical reflection, based on highly dubious physics, a strangely moving plaint with undeniable power. The piano plays less of a role here than in any other song in the cycle, for there is little in the rather abstract poem that encourages the creation of a particularly illustrative or lively accompaniment (apart from the title, that is – the music flows on with scarcely a rest in the piano part, and this is admirably right for a *Wasserflut*). Like an aria with a discreet background accompaniment, it is almost exclusively the vocal line which regulates speed, shape and colour and, as the portrait of the protagonist is filled out in musical and emotional (rather than narrative) terms, the piano takes a back seat. This places more responsibility on the singer who must not allow the music to sag. A sentimental performance has turned many a *Wasserflut* into a backwater of self-indulgence.

The four-bar introduction has a quality of frozen eloquence. With the exception of the bleak octave arpeggios (omitting the third of the scale) which stand at the beginning of the first two bars, everything lies within the compass of a minor sixth. The music pivots around a repetitive exploration of this tiny area, as if obsessively ruminating and getting nowhere, the mind doing its best to stretch and encompass a point, trying again (b. 2 is an exact repetition of b. 1) and then giving up, defeated. The left hand seems unable to move outside the most rudimentary harmonies, mainly in E minor, although these unremarkable chords are the subject of an old controversy: should the left-hand semiquavers come together with the right-hand triplet (as was often the practice of the time) or after it (as is strictly the case in musical terms)? Britten believed in the former and Gerald Moore in the latter. Moore liked the feeling of dislocation as his final left-hand semiquavers limped just after the right-hand triplet, but modern opinion finds this fussy in a song which is, after all, about flowing water rather than trudging feet.[1]

After this rather static introduction the vocal line has a grand and noble sweep. At 'Manche Trän'' it soars up the stave, and down again for 'aus meinen Augen', spanning an octave and a half (bb. 5–6). Although Schubert has chosen to accent 'Manche' (hardly a key word), placing it on the first beat of the bar rather than as an upbeat, he compensates by highlighting the emotive 'Trän'' ('tear'), setting it at the apex of the arpeggio phrase and elongating the vowel's duration to a dotted crotchet. Something similar happens on 'meinen Augen'. (The recurring accent on the second beat of the bar gives the music the characteristic of a sarabande; this suggestion of a stately dance only reinforces the eerie impression of the wanderings of a distraught mind.) On the other hand, when the melody calls for it, Schubert does not shy away from emphasizing and lengthening the first (and unimportant) word of the next phrase ('Ist'). The dotted rhythms of 'Ist gefallen in den Schnee' are accompanied by unchanging B major chords (bb. 7–8) that effectively suggest something pointed and repetitive, such as the monotonous dripping of tears on the ice. 'Seine kalten Flocken saugen', back on the tonic, is an exact repeat of 'Manche Trän' aus meinen Augen'; but 'Durstig ein das heisse Weh' (bb. 11–12) contains new and exciting material. The phrase rises dramatically from the bottom of the stave and reaches its apogee on an extraordinary 'Weh' (b. 12), an unusual melisma where the highest note, an F,

---

[1] Elmar Budde avers that this song is in the nature of a sarabande; this not only affects its tempo (performers should avoid taking it too slow) but the dance rhythm, with its accent on the second beat of the bar, can be clear only if the triplet and semiquaver in right and left hands coincide.

comes both high in the stave and off the beat. This eccentric setting, supported by strong and (temporarily) dissonant chords in the piano, contains the very wail of the winter wind and the traveller's distress. It also seems that Schubert has been fascinated by the verb 'einsaugen' – 'to suck in' – an unusual image in a lieder text: 'kalten Flocken saugen' descends and, as we have seen, 'Durstig ein das heisse Weh' goes in the opposite direction – action and reaction, something falling, something being taken up, with a different part of the separable verb 'einsaugen' in each half. The ascent of this phrase and its culmination in an *fp* chord as abrupt as the closing of a Venus flytrap is a vivid tonal equivalent of the act of greedy slurping and swallowing – the tears pulled up through the stave into the mouth of the snow. It is a feature of this song that the last line of each strophe is repeated, always in an antithetical mood to what has gone before. Here, the second 'Durstig ein das heisse Weh' (bb. 13–14) falls disconsolately to the tonic in complete contrast to the wildness of its first appearance.

There is now a four-bar interlude (bb. 15–18) that begins like the introduction, but which turns the music into G major by means of a tiny but crucial adjustment in the left-hand harmony in b. 17. As always in this cycle, such a change into a related major key presages an opening of a door into another time and place, usually the past. Here we have a fantasy about the imagined future. As in *Erstarrung* (No. 4), the strophe beginning 'Wenn die Gräser sprossen wollen' takes us to a kinder season, in this case the first signs of spring which will come to melt the snow and ice. The playful vocal arpeggio (in the purest G major) at 'Weht daher ein lauer Wind' is wonderfully evocative of a gentle spring breeze (bb. 21–2), and the phrase 'Und der weiche Schnee zerrinnt' is similarly taken up by pleasant springtime auguries. The repeat of this last line (marked 'Stark') in a mood of vehement fear, anger and desperation is a masterstroke. G major is peremptorily pushed aside by a grandiose E minor arpeggio with the range of a tenth. This harks back to the last verse of *Erstarrung* in which the springtime thaw is seen as an enemy that will melt the beloved's image which will then be irrevocably lost to the traveller. The violence of the verb 'zerrinnt' (bb. 27–8) here comes into its own.

The second half of the song is an exact musical repeat of the first. Schubert is far too great a hand at strophic songs not to ensure that all the lines fit second time around with appropriate illustrative and illuminating meaning. Accordingly, in the second line of the third strophe, he changes Müller's 'Sag' mir, wohin geht dein Lauf?' to his own 'Sag', wohin doch geht dein Lauf?' (bb. 7–8 repeated), the better to accommodate the prosody and to avoid stressing 'wohin' on its first syllable. 'Muntre Strassen ein und aus' in the final verse is set to the same uncomplicated G major arpeggio that was used for the breezes of spring, an appropriate enough evocation of bustling town life. The first mention of the beloved's house, 'Da ist meiner Liebsten Haus', in G major seems chillingly genial, but of course this is counterbalanced by the sudden madness of the repeat in E minor, a tirade as heartfelt and unhinged as anything shouted by King Lear on the heath. This vision of the house seems all the more frighteningly self-deluding in the context of the crestfallen postlude (the four-bar introduction adapted for a final cadence), so quickly does the traveller switch in mood from anger to depression.

This commentary refers throughout to *Wasserflut* in its published key of E minor. Schubert initially composed it in F sharp minor and we do not know what persuaded him to change a tonality that sounds more unhinged, as well as being eminently related to the B minor of *Irrlicht* D911/9 and *Einsamkeit* D911/12. It was perhaps changed for purely practical reasons on the advice of the singer Vogl (who would certainly have found it impossible to sing in that key). On the other hand it is also possible that Schubert wished to link the song more closely to *Der Lindenbaum* (No. 5) by moving from E major to E minor in the adjacent songs.

Publication: Published as Op. 89 no. 6 by Tobias Haslinger, Vienna on 14 January 1828 (P146); version in F sharp minor published as part of the AGA in 1895 (P697)

Subsequent editions:	Peters: Vol. 1/71; AGA XX 522: Vol. 9/20 (F sharp minor); NSA IV: Vol. 4a/134; Bärenreiter: Vol. 3/96 & 222 (F sharp minor)
Bibliography:	Youens 1991, pp. 170–75
Arrangements:	Arr. Franz Liszt (1811–1886) for solo piano, no. 6 of *Winterreise* (1838–9) [*see* TRANSCRIPTIONS]
	Arr. Tilman Hoppstock (b. 1961) for guitar accompaniment, in *Franz Schubert: 110 Lieder* (2009)

Discography and timing:	Fischer-Dieskau III 2[6]	4'14	
	Pears–Britten	3'49	
	Hyperion I 30[6]		
	Hyperion II 33[6]	4'09	Matthias Goerne

← *Der Lindenbaum* D911/5   *Auf dem Flusse* D911/7 →

VII AUF DEM FLUSSE   On the river
OP. 89 NO. 7, **D911/7** [H619]

The song exists in two versions, the second of which is discussed below:

(1)   'Mässig'   E minor $\frac{2}{4}$ [74 bars]

(2)   E minor

(74 bars)

Der du so lustig rauschtest,	**Y**ou who rippled so merrily
Du heller, wilder Fluss,	Clear, boisterous river,
Wie still bist du geworden,	How still you have become;
Gibst keinen Scheidegruss!	You give no parting farewell.
Mit harter, starrer Rinde	With a hard, rigid crust
Hast du dich überdeckt,	You have covered yourself
Liegst kalt und unbeweglich	You lie cold and motionless,
Im Sande ausgestreckt.[1]	Stretched out in the sand.
In deine Decke grab' ich	On your surface I carve
Mit einem spitzen Stein	With a sharp stone
Den Namen meiner Liebsten	The name of my beloved,
Und Stund' und Tag hinein:	The hour and the day.
Den Tag des ersten Grusses,	The day of our first greeting,
Den Tag an dem ich ging,	The date I departed.

---

[1]In the *Gedichte*, 1824, Müller changes this line to 'Im Sande *hin*gestreckt'.

Um Nam' und Zahlen windet   Around name and figures
Sich ein zerbrochner Ring.   A broken ring is entwined.

  Mein Herz, in diesem Bache   My heart, do you now recognize
Erkennst du nun dein Bild? –   Your image in this brook?
Ob's unter seiner Rinde   Is there, I wonder, beneath its crust
Wohl auch so reissend schwillt?   Likewise a seething torrent?

This is the twenty-seventh of Schubert's forty-six Müller solo settings (1823, 1827 and 1828). See the poet's biography for a chronological list of all the Müller settings.

After the static misery of *Wasserflut* (No. 6) we are once more on the move. The traveller remains heartbroken but we are no longer submerged in the abject mood of that song, and for the moment we hear no more of tears. The first stage of mourning is over and we embark, in John Reed's words, on 'the beginning of a new act in the drama'. The introduction, minimalist music in Schubert's most pithy manner, is among the most fascinating in the cycle. The bass line is in single staccato quavers on the beat, first falling to the submediant then curving upwards back to the home key of E minor. The right hand, also staccato, fills in simple harmonies with complementary chords off the beat. These four bars have the majesty of a great Purcellian ground bass: they are empty of significance in themselves, but pregnant with possibilities. This is no passacaglia – Schubert's century had other musical fashions. Nevertheless, before a note has been sung, the traveller's lament, like Dido's, has been set up with an underlying sense of tension and pathos.

The vocal line is almost mysteriously legato over these staccato quavers in the piano. Not since the second version of Goethe's *An den Mond* D296 and *Die schöne Müllerin* D795 has a singer addressed a river or stream in such urgent and confidential tones. The season is not the same of course. The 'heller, wilder Fluss' behaves very differently in *Eifersucht und Stolz* D795/15 where watery semiquavers tumble volubly and angrily through the summer landscape. *Auf dem Flusse* has much more in common with *Trockne Blumen* D795/18 from the same cycle. Even on the printed page the similarity is striking: dry quavers in E minor at the beginning flower into semiquavers in E major later in the song. In *Trockne Blumen* the miller boy imagines the flowers to be deep beneath the ground, with him in his grave. But their dried state is only temporary, and they will spring into life when the maid of the mill thinks loving thoughts. The inactivity of the river in *Auf dem Flusse* is also temporary and it too will return to its former seething state for all to see. For the moment, however, everything is suppressed beneath a layer of ice, a 'harte, starre Rinde'. Right from the outset we can hear in the tightness of the rhythm and the directional thrust of the vocal line the concealed energy of the river beneath the surface. One of the greatest moments of harmonic surprise in the whole cycle is the slip into the second inversion of D sharp minor at 'Wie still bist du geworden' (bb. 8–10), a miraculous musical device for an altered state. We hear, as well as see, the turning point, the moment when water glazes over into ice. The singer is asked to sing very quietly (the passage is marked 'Sehr leise') and we might imagine it is his icy breath blowing through the stave that has effected the change of temperature. Perhaps the little mordent on 'keinen Scheidegruss!' (b. 11) betokens a shiver of apprehension, but its gestural formality, like the flourish of an old-fashioned obeisance, has something ironic, even sinister about it. A chord of D sharp minor needs only a tiny adjustment in hand position (A sharp rising to B) to turn it into B major, and thus we are in the dominant key of the song as an upbeat to a return to E minor. Eight mezzo staccato semiquavers, a tiny hint of the river's power and energy held in reserve, form the miniature interlude (b. 13) that leads us into the next strophe, an exact musical repetition of the first.

The staccato quavers of the opening make a reappearance and are an ideal dry and precise accompaniment to 'Mit harter, starrer Rinde'. Once again that change into D sharp minor proves a perfect mirror for 'Liegst kalt und unbeweglich'. At this point the outside temperature seems to fall by many degrees, amazingly achieved with a downward slip of only half a degree of the scale. The river is stretched out in the sand ('Im Sande ausgestreckt') and the dryness of the staccato chords is appropriately descriptive. The little interlude of eight semiquavers (b. 22) makes a reappearance, this time leading us into E major with a change of key signature. This gives a sense of great intimacy on 'In deine Decke grab' ich'. Not for the first time in Schubert's Müller songs the protagonist directs to the stream the thwarted tenderness that he cannot give to his paramour, and we catch a glimpse of his own loving heart. We do not know the extent of the traveller's intimacy with the girl, but he here penetrates the surface of the ice in her frigid memory. Taking a sharp stone, he engraves into the frozen surface of the river the name of his beloved (how curious we would be to read this), together with details of the dates that mark the birth and death of their relationship – a tombstone in ice. The mezzo staccato semi-quaver motif (which has served until now as an interlude) is the perfect accompaniment to depict such a bizarre ceremony. These notes scratch against the smooth surface of the vocal line in little bursts of activity as they attempt to chisel the poignant runes of failed love – a childish task as doomed as building sandcastles. At 'Den Namen meiner Liebsten', mention of the beloved is set a third higher in the stave than the adjacent notes. In this context the stretch of longing in the vocal line seems enormous and poignantly hopeless, as if the 'Liebste' is well beyond reach.

At 'Den Tag des ersten Grusses' (bb. 31–3) the traveller becomes more immersed in his memories than in his engraver's task. The accompanying semiquavers change into gently throb-bing triplets, lifting the music into the fragrant reaches of springtime memory. As pulses quicken, emotions can be heard to burgeon as he warms to his theme and to his task. At 'Stund' und Tag hinein' in the previous verse the accompaniment had been shared between the hands, but the triplets now occupy both of them, as if something has come together in his mind and the power of recall has been successfully marshalled. We sense that the singer is really experi-encing those happy moments again – the setting of 'Der Tag des ersten Grusses' is lovingly elongated, and even 'Den Tag, an dem ich ging' here seems coloured by nostalgia and gentle regret rather than bitterness. (This mood is familiar to lovers of Schubert in the song *Im Frühling* D882.) He speaks of the broken ring which he has etched into the ice to surround the rest of his design, symbolic, of course, of a relationship torn apart. (The poet Josef von Eichendorff had already expanded on this theme in his famous poem *Das zerbrochene Ringlein*, 1813.) Here the semiquaver triplets are no longer working in tandem, as if hands together were a symbol for holding hands; instead they are separated between the treble and bass staves in an interlude of tiny shudders, marked 'diminuendo' (from b. 38). Thus the dream of those happy courting days evaporates before our ears and eyes. We can also almost sense the protagonist absent-mindedly allowing the sharp stone, the implement with which he can delicately carve his story on the ice, to drop from his hands in the numbed silence of b. 40.

The remainder of the song, almost half the music, is a setting (with repetitions) of the impas-sioned final strophe of the poem. The traveller moves inward; he no longer addresses the stream but questions his own heart. The music mirrors this and the shape of the vocal line at the begin-ning of the song is now heard in the pianist's left hand. This accompanies a new vocal line which is a rhetorically powerful parlando set against a background of familiar melody, an operatic practice that prefigures a composer like Verdi. Thus the traveller's dialogue with his heart is underpinned (bb. 41–4) by a pianistic version of the melody of 'Der du so lustig rauschtest' (which refers to the stream) and Schubert answers the questions in Müller's final strophe: the heart recognizes its similarity to the stream, and there is indeed a torrent raging beneath its surface that matches these seething rapids. A first indication of its power is provided by the left-hand eruption following 'Erkennst du nun dein Bild?' We are already familiar with the sidestepping modulation into D sharp minor, but we are hardly prepared for the violent demisemiquaver motif that suddenly animates a bar which had been icebound in the first two strophes. Dry and phlegmatic quavers, symbols of a frozen surface, are replaced by a left-hand arpeggio that lunges up the stave and lands menacingly on an accented passing note in the middle of b. 47. This is like the cracking of ice and it opens the floodgates for the extraordinary passage of water music in G sharp minor that follows. At 'Ob's unter seiner Rinde' the same left-hand piano melody (now transposed) shadows a vocal line of almost wild eloquence, while off-the-beat demisemiquavers churn in storm-whipped rapids (bb. 48–51). A modified repetition of the words ('Ob's wohl auch so reissend schwillt?') and an intensification of the vocal line, now high in the stave and decorated with melismas, lead us back to E minor, and we recognize the ominous bass trill in b. 52 from *Auf der Donau* D553 that also concerns the hidden history of a powerful river.

No sooner is this passage over than we slip back (from b. 54) into the remarkable parlando mood which has opened the verse, now almost unbearably poignant because the traveller's state of mind has switched so suddenly. The abrupt shift into G major after 'Mein Herz' (b. 56) is one of the most touching moments in the cycle, and the setting of the tiny phrase 'in diesem Bache' rends the heart with its tenderness. It is as if the traveller is blessing the river as he sings, and this gentleness strikes a note of madness which elicits our compassion. Details like this allow us to build up a portrait of the traveller's disturbed mental state, but this atmosphere of other-worldly disorientation does not last long. The bass line slips down a semitone, turning the mood quickly vehement. 'Erkennst du nun dein Bild?' is heard this time to the key of F sharp minor (bb. 58–60) and, when the ice-cracking motif returns, two bars of these thrusting arpeggio figures in the left hand are needed to return the music (via B[7]) into the home key of E minor for 'Ob's unter seiner Rinde' (bb. 61–3). As before, the left hand sings the river's melody while the right oscillates in stormy mood and the voice rises in desperate colloquy. The next phrase ('Wohl auch so reissend schwillt?') climbs into G minor and the left-hand trill introduces another repetition of the words with a spectacular interrupted cadence on 'schwillt'. This dramatic moment of hiatus launches the vocal peroration, a final repetition of 'Ob's wohl auch so reissend schwillt?' (b. 68) which pushes the voice even higher in the stave – a howl of despair where images of raging river and tormented heart are heard as one. A ghost of the introductory tune is heard deep in the left hand as the right shudders in aftershock. The final three bars (from b. 72) re-establish the dry and empty quavers of the opening. The river is still frozen, the heart is still numb with grief, and the traveller must continue on his way.

Publication:	Published as Op. 89 no. 7 by Tobias Haslinger, Vienna on 14 January 1828 (P147); first version published as part of the NSA in 1979 (P777)
Subsequent editions:	Peters: 1/74; AGA XX 523: Vol. 9/22; NSA IV: Vol. 4a/136 & Vol. 4b/266 (first version); Bärenreiter: Vol. 3/98
Bibliography:	Youens 1991, pp. 176–86
Discography and timing:	Fischer-Dieskau III 2[7] 3'27
	Pears–Britten 3'34
	Hyperion I 30[7]
	Hyperion II 33[7] 3'17 Matthias Goerne

←— *Wasserflut* D911/6   *Rückblick* D911/8 —→

VIII RÜCKBLICK
Op. 89 no. 8, **D911/8** [H620]
G minor

Backward glance

Nicht zu geschwind

Es brennt mir un-ter bei-den Soh-len,

(69 bars)

Es brennt mir unter beiden Sohlen,
Tret' ich auch schon auf Eis und Schnee;
Ich möcht' nicht wieder Atem holen,
Bis ich nicht mehr die Türme seh'.

Hab' mich an jeden Stein gestossen,[1]
So eilt' ich zu der Stadt hinaus;
Die Krähen warfen Bäll' und Schlossen
Auf meinen Hut von jedem Haus.

Wie anders hast du mich empfangen,
Du Stadt der Unbeständigkeit!
An deinen blanken Fenstern sangen
Die Lerch' und Nachtigall im Streit.

Die runden Lindenbäume blühten,
Die klaren Rinnen rauschten hell,
Und ach, zwei Mädchenaugen glühten!—
Da war's geschehn um dich, Gesell!

Kommt mir der Tag in die Gedanken,
Möcht' ich noch einmal rückwärts sehn,
Möcht' ich zurücke wieder wanken,
Vor i h r e m Hause stille stehn.

The soles of my feet are burning,
Though I walk on ice and snow;
I do not wish to stop to catch my breath
Until I can no longer see the towers.

I tripped on every stone,
Such was my hurry to leave the town;
The crows threw snowballs and hailstones
On to my hat from every house.

How differently you received me.
Town of inconstancy!
At your shining windows
Lark and nightingale sang in rivalry.

The round linden trees blossomed,
The clear fountains plashed brightly,
And, ah, a maiden's eyes glowed;
Then, friend, your fate was sealed.

When that day comes to my mind
I should like to look back once more,
And stumble back
To stand before *her* house.

This is the twenty-eighth of Schubert's forty-six Müller solo settings (1823, 1827 and 1828).
See the poet's biography for a chronological list of all the Müller settings.

In *Auf dem Flusse* (No. 7) the pianist's hands alternate in dry quavers or, when the traveller recognizes the hidden turbulence beneath the ice as that of his own heart, in shuddering bursts of demisemiquavers. Here the accompaniment also consists of alternation between the hands, this time in rapid semiquavers. It is as if the metaphor of stormy torrents has spilled from one song and flooded the next; in *Rückblick* the helter-skelter retreat from the place of the traveller's

---

[1]Müller writes 'Hab' ich an *jedem* Stein gestossen'. This represents an interesting change from 'each stone gets in his way' (the dative 'jedem') and, literally, 'he knocked into every stone' (the accusative 'jeden').

unhappiness carries him along like so much flotsam and jetsam. This is the speediest song in the cycle since *Erstarrung* (No. 4); it is part of Schubert's mastery to place the faster lieder at strategic intervals, and skilled programme-planners know how important these judicious changes of tempo and key are to keep the audience's attention. *Rückblick* is certainly one of the most hectic of the *Winterreise* songs, its impression of speed reinforced by the choppy nature of the piano writing. Nevertheless, the composer's moderating hand can be felt on the tiller with the direction 'Nicht zu geschwind' ('Not too fast'). Gerald Moore, after a lifetime's experience with all practical aspects of performance, points out the dangers: 'There are several reasons why a quicker tempo is impracticable: the singer has many words to articulate and they will be extremely difficult to enunciate clearly and therefore unintelligible to the listener also, voice and pianoforte tumbling over one another in such confusion that everything develops into a grand muddle. Rhythmic control must be exercised.'

Control in the midst of a whirr of confusion is a paradox typical of this particular song, but this is seldom apparent in performance. The key is G minor, a minor third higher than *Auf dem Flusse*, and this upward harmonic shift raises the sense of tension. Another telling contrast with *Auf dem Flusse* is the way the bass line rises, rather than falls, in the introduction. Here the chords are the same in each hand (although an octave apart) and they chase each other up the stave at the distance of a semiquaver. They begin as open fifths – G and D; the Ds in each hand remain a constant, forming a ceiling of repeated notes underneath which rising G minor scales squeeze the intervals together with the determination of a torturer's thumbscrews. When these can be tightened no further both hands converge on these Ds, at which point they freeze and shake: the second bar of the introduction (b. 2) contains nothing but this note pitched across the whole range of the keyboard – left-hand octaves on the strong beats, and oscillating semi-quavers in the right hand. These two contrasting bars are a powerful musical analogue for full-ness followed by emptiness, frenzied activity followed by stasis. Their juxtaposition signifies going forward and then looking back; simultaneous attraction and repulsion; not knowing whether one is coming or going. This idea is repeated and amplified. At b. 5 the same musical pattern is transposed a fourth higher, and a C minor scale culminates in a bar of Gs, even more dramatic because higher pitched. This is one of the longest introductions in the cycle – ten tumultuous bars pressing determinedly forward while at the same time giving a strong impression of confusion and enforced retreat.

Once the vocal line begins it sweeps up the stave in a long, arched phrase lasting two and a half bars. There is a strong push towards the cadence in D minor at b. 13, the end of the poet's line, that shifts the emphasis away from the home key. This obscuring of G minor so recently insisted on in the introduction adds to the sense of disorientation; a satisfying cadence on the tonic always seems just outside the grasp of hand or ear. One of Schubert's most daring metrical experiments adds to the song's manifold ingenuities: the music is in ⅜, but the scansion of the text seems to call for ²⁄₄ – which is precisely how a lesser composer would have set it. One can almost rebar the vocal line into ²⁄₄, but the fact that it is staggered into triple time adds powerfully to a sense of alienation and awkwardness. The feeling of being pursued from within, as well as by outside forces, is mirrored by the bass line in canon with the voice at the distance of a crotchet. This imitation persists throughout the outer sections of the song, even if it is often only frag-mentary. After 'Eis und Schnee' and again after 'die Türme seh'' there are tiny convulsive outbursts in the piano that are expanded to even greater illustrative effect after 'Hab' mich an jeden Stein gestossen' and 'So eilt' ich zu der Stadt hinaus'. Schubert has here invented one of his great all-purpose accompaniments which manages to convey both the throbbing pain of incipient frostbite ('Es brennt mir unter beiden Sohlen') and the pounding pulses and breathless-ness of physical exertion and emotional panic. The verb 'sich stossen' (to knock into) seems to have been an important inspiration: in right-hand jabbing semiquaver chords, played off the beat and sometimes perversely accented, we can hear the physical shock of impact as the shaken wanderer trips over stones and is hit by falling snow.

Müller now introduces the bizarre imagery of maniacal crows which throw snowballs at the poor demented man (bb. 20–26). This tricky aspect of the poem is clarified by Susan Youens: 'The birds roosting on the pointed eaves of houses shift position and move about, dislodging pieces of ice ('Schlossen', 'hailstones') and snowballs. The wanderer, acutely conscious of his alienation from society, sees hostile intentions where none exist.' Youens also persuasively argues that the whole song is a '*Rückblick*', or glance back into the past, rather than just the middle section (which is the usual interpretation). Even though the poem is written in the present tense, the scene of fleeing the city does not actually take place in its appointed place in the cycle but rather as a nightmare of tormented remembrance. This explains the puzzling detail, commented on by Capell, of a hat mentioned in the second strophe, despite its having already been lost in *Der Lindenbaum* (No. 5). And how can the protagonist, a third of the way through the cycle, still be in such a hurry to leave the town and the sight of its towers when we know from *Der Lindenbaum* that he has already travelled 'many hours' journey from that place'? It makes no sense here for us to find him back at the scene of his initial humiliation. Another explanation is that the whole thing is a frightening dream (with the nightmare horrors of malevolent crows and so on) or a heightened recollection of his original exit which he remembers as being more humiliating than it actually was. After all, when we first encounter the traveller in *Gute Nacht* D911/1, he quits the village (hardly a town if we are to believe the traveller's description in the first song, of white meadows and deer tracks) walking, not running, determined to take his leave as quietly as possible.

In any event the poem's first two strophes serve as a single breathless musical verse. The next two strophes (from b. 27) are also joined together to make an achingly beautiful glance back to a happier past, and this excursion into memory, as always in this cycle, occurs in the major key (in this case with a change of key signature into G major). If the first section has been a confrontation with the unhappy events of, say, a week before, here we glance further back to the Maytime happiness of the lover. That ceiling of Ds which we have heard in the introduction in unfriendly, driven mood is here recast in bb. 27 to 34 as a sheltering roof, a haven of urban bliss framed in terms of an Arcadian bower – and so this roof-like run of notes appears on the printed page. Schubert had already used this visual pun in *Im Freien* D880 for the lines 'Unter seinem trauten Dach / Schläft mein liebster Freund' ('Beneath the house's cosy roof / Sleeps my dearest friend'). The vocal line here takes on a lyrical folksong quality that is reminiscent of *Der Lindenbaum* (linden trees are mentioned here as well) and the piano bass line, cello-like, duets with the voice in tender euphony like the duo of lark and nightingale mentioned in the text. (This in itself is a surreal idea: the song of the lark is harbinger of dawn, the nightingale's of dusk. But as we have seen, chronology means little in this context.) Suggestion of horn music at intervals between the voice and the pianist's left hand evokes magical far-off times, lost in the idealized forest of memory. But horn intervals, as we saw in *Die Wetterfahne* (No. 2), are also symbolic of the cuckold, and can imply danger and betrayal. Perhaps this is Schubert's subtle response to the image of 'Stadt der Unbeständigkeit' ('town of inconstancy', bb. 30–31) which is pointedly not a signal for minor-key commiseration. The smooth progress of this suave G major music is interrupted by sudden palpitations at the mention of the girl's glowing eyes, and we return to the rapid alternation between the hands to depict the prickly heat of newborn infatuation. The first setting of 'Da war's geschehn um dich, Gesell!' (bb. 41–3) outlines a rueful shrug, an acceptance of fate that we might imagine from Schubert himself. It is still in the major key, another indication of this composer's apparent reluctance to blame others for the complexities of the human condition. The repeat of this phrase is set within a higher tessitura, with a resulting touch of desperation but still no trace of bitterness. A two-bar interlude (a run of semiquavers in G major on the way up at b. 47, and G minor on the way down in b. 48) leads to a recapitulation of the music of the opening.

As often in *Winterreise* Schubert uses a single strophe of Müller's poem as a peroration, expanding four lines of text through repetition and emphasis to make something substantial of the song's close. Here the traveller imagines that he stands in front of his lover's house, a theme Schubert would explore with more ominous overtones in *Der Doppelgänger* D957/13 from *Schwanengesang*. Once again this shows the affinity between the work of Müller and his admirer Heinrich Heine. As in the second strophe of *Der Lindenbaum*, Schubert places half the strophe in the minor key of hard reality and half in the major key of dream and fantasy. Instead of a glance backwards we have a glance forwards into an improbable future. Never has the traveller shown more clearly his affinity with the miller boy: *Die böse Farbe* D795/18 also envisages a pathetic return to the girl's threshold – a visit designed, should it ever really occur, to make her feel thoroughly wretched and guilty. Schubert's depiction of the stumbling traveller, simultaneously radiant with love and humiliated by it, is masterful. Note the setting of 'Vor i h r e m Hause' on a painfully long high G (bb. 63–4), as if her house – and no other – has taken on the attributes of a shrine. The addition of an F natural in the bass line as the harmony is softened to G^7 powerfully suggests the traveller's deranged tenderness. On the repeat of these words it is 'stille' which is held on a minim (b. 67), a solitary moment of repose that roots the music to the spot as if transfixed. The vocal triplets before this contain a ghostly prophecy of the *Ständchen* D957/4 from *Schwanengesang* ('Leise flehen meine Lieder'), as if a stillborn serenade in front of the beloved's dwelling is a part of the traveller's vigil. Once again the song ends in a short postlude that suggests crestfallen retreat – a shudder or a whimper.

First edition:	Published as Op. 89 no. 8 by Tobias Haslinger, Vienna on 14 January 1828 (P148)
Subsequent editions:	Peters: Vol. 1/78; AGA XX 524: Vol. 9/26; NSA IV: Vol. 4a/140; Bärenreiter: Vol. 3/102
Bibliography:	Moore 1975, pp. 105–10
	Youens 1991, pp. 187–95
Discography and timing:	Fischer-Dieskau III 2^8 2'19
	Pears–Britten 2'23
	Hyperion I 30^8
	Hyperion II 33^8 2'26 Matthias Goerne

← *Auf dem Flusse* D911/7   *Irrlicht* D911/9 →

IX IRRLICHT[1]   Will-o'-the-wisp
Op. 89 no. 9, **D911/9** [H621]
B minor

(43 bars)

[1]The title of the poem in Müller's *Gedichte* is '*Das* Irrlicht'.

In die tiefsten Felsengründe
Lockte mich ein Irrlicht hin:
Wie ich einen Ausgang finde,
Liegt nicht schwer mir in dem Sinn.

   Bin gewohnt das Irregehen,[2]
's führt ja jeder weg zum Ziel:
Unsre Freuden, unsre Leiden,[3]
Alles eines Irrlichts Spiel!

   Durch des Bergstroms trockne Rinnen
Wind' ich ruhig mich hinab—
Jeder Strom wird's Meer gewinnen,
Jedes Leiden auch sein Grab.[4]

A will-o'-the-wisp enticed me
Into the deepest rocky chasms.
How I shall find a way out
Does not trouble my mind.

   I am used to straying;
Every path leads to one goal.
Our joys, our sorrows
All are a will-o'-the-wisp's game.

   Down the dry gullies of the mountain stream
I calmly wend my way;
Every river will reach the sea;
Every sorrow, too, will reach its grave.

Autograph of *Irrlicht* (second page), 1827 (first draft).

This is the twenty-ninth of Schubert's forty-six Müller solo settings (1823, 1827 and 1828).
See the poet's biography for a chronological list of all the Müller settings.

The phenomenon of *ignis fatuus* (literally 'a foolish fire', known as the will-o'-the-wisp, or jack-o'-lantern) is rich in symbolism for the weary traveller. When approached, it retreats and remains ever distant. Magical in appearance (it has frequently been mistaken for a UFO by the

[2]Müller writes 'Bin gewohnt das *irre Gehen*'.
[3]Müller writes 'Unsre Freuden, unsre *Wehen*'. Schubert's change dispenses with the poet's rhyme.
[4]Müller writes 'Jedes Leiden auch *ein* Grab'.

gullible of our own century), it is the result of an emission of naturally occurring gassy vapour kindled in the air and producing a thin phosphorescent glow. It is chiefly to be seen on summer nights in meadows, marshes and other moist places. *Ignis fatuus* is out of place in bitter winter weather, and this, like the question of the traveller's hat, leads to another problem of chronology in terms of the story. It is usually assumed that the will-o'-the-wisp appears to the traveller in the midst of his winter journey, but the verb 'lockte' ('enticed') is in the past tense and it is not clear how much time has elapsed since he followed the dancing flame. Perhaps the traveller here recalls chasing the will-o'-the-wisp in warmer days, or it is possible that he identifies the imagery with the girl who had lured him into her clutches during the summer months of courtship.

Müller would no doubt have known the Walpurgisnacht scene in the first part of Goethe's *Faust* where there is a small speaking role for 'Irrlicht', an *ignis fatuus* that lights the way to the Witches' Sabbath while trying to overcome, out of fear of Mephistopheles, its tendency to move in a wayward fashion ('zickzack' as Goethe puts it). This is the beginning of a journey into the frightening realms of the supernatural, and the role of the 'Irrlicht' assumed a similarly sinister function in the works of those who had read their Goethe, Müller included. A poem entitled *Das Irrlicht* by Schubert's friend Josef Kreil, published in Mayrhofer's 1817 journal-anthology *Beiträge zur Bildung für Jünglinge* (pp. 320–21), describes two brothers walking hand in hand until one of them breaks away, lured to follow a will-o'-the-wisp that he wrongly believes to be a star, and never returns. In this case the 'Irrlicht' is a metaphor for deadly temptation. The Viennese artist Kolomán Moser took this 'Irrlicht' to be an embodiment of a femme fatale, as is obvious from the illustration he made (reproduced on the right) for the Schubert centenary in 1897.

Perhaps Müller's traveller is still in the backward-glancing mood of *Rückblick*, and the will-o'-the-wisp is a metaphor for his plight: once he was beguiled by the capricious girl, he yielded to his fate like a lamb to slaughter, with no wish to escape ('How I shall find a way out / Does not trouble my mind'). The 'Felsengründe' are, then, a metaphor for the emotional chasms in which he finds himself. Of the number of poems in *Winterreise* which might have made the composer shudder in empathy, this is one of the most poignant, particularly in light of the widely held belief that Schubert's syphilitic infection was the result of a dalliance with a prostitute in late 1822. A glance through the poem in this context gives it an interesting slant: led astray by the will-o'-the-wisp of sexual attraction ('I am used to straying' is something the headstrong composer himself might have said according to friends' descriptions of his sensual nature), he accepts his fate and stoically, at least on the surface, faces his inevitable end. This reading gives the 'deepest rocky chasms' into which he has been tempted a powerful significance worthy of Freud, and the moment of pleasure is such that he is little concerned about finding his way out.

There is also a musical link with the past that gives further pause for thought. Brian Newbould has drawn attention to the relation of *Irrlicht* to another B minor song, the infinitely less complex *Abschied (Lebe wohl! Du lieber Freund!)* D578 which was written ten years earlier, in 1817, when Franz von Schober left Vienna. The poem, most unusually, was by the composer himself. The pianist's fingers are powerfully reminded of that song by the similarities in terms of keyboard geography – in the falling phrases of both introductions, their triple time, their mournful resignation and the way they modulate into the relative major like a sudden burst of sunlight. What was it about Schubert's response to imagery that made him draw on similar tonal analogues for both songs? The verb 'irrgehen' means 'to go astray' and other forms include 'to be led astray'. Was the unreliable but devastatingly charismatic Schober something of a will-o'-the-wisp figure in Schubert's mind, someone representing temptation and the good life, whom he would have followed anywhere but who was then (in August 1817) vanishing into the distance? Or had the composer, as he sang his farewell, imagined Schober himself trapped between a rock and a hard place, distressed about his brother's health (Axel Schober subsequently died) and his upcoming journey full of uncertainty? If this is the case then the change to the major key envisages a 'way out' out of the impasse, Schubert's optimistic prediction that things would work out, that Schober would survive somehow. In either case the solution hangs by a thread: the endangered traveller must hope for the best and live by his wits.

The German word 'Irrlicht' combines 'light' ('Licht') with the adjective for 'insane' ('irre'), and the composer seems to play on this conjunction. This is particularly interesting in view of the theory put forward by Elizabeth McKay in her Schubert biography – that the composer was a chronic sufferer from cyclothymia, or mood swings of a mildly manic-depressive nature. If this is so, *Irrlicht* is a song drawn from experience as well as empathy. Just as *Rückblick* has counterpointed and contrasted the physical movements of the traveller, pushed forward while at the same time being pulled back, *Irrlicht* outlines a similar portrait of his temperament, the backward-and-forward movement, as it were, of the mind and spirit. Almost every two-bar phrase (in a song almost entirely made up of two-bar phrases) stands as a contrast, both musical and emblematic, to what has gone before or what is to come.

The song opens with two bars that droop downwards, quavers phrased away to crotchets, B to F sharp, followed by a similar plunge to complete the octave, from E to B. The skeleton of a plagal cadence in the second bar aids an atmosphere of withdrawn mournfulness created with seemingly little effort. And then suddenly there is a pick-me-up. The direction

LOCK-TE MICH EIN IRR-LICHT HIN:

Koloman Moser's depiction of *Irrlicht*, 1897.

(and mood) is reversed by a bar of semiquaver triplets, six of them marked 'mezzo staccato'. The harmonic plan of this bracing little ascent is basically V-I and, once we are back in B minor, the tonic is decorated with a tiny dotted flourish that sounds light-headed and capricious, mad yet merry, despite the minor key. The pattern of drag followed by push thus established is the exact opposite of the introduction to *Rückblick*. The vocal line is initially built on a repeat of the introduction. Appropriately enough, it descends deep into the 'Felsengründe' (tenors dislike the low Bs) before being lured up the stave by the gleaming light of the will-o'-the-wisp. The semiquaver triplets first heard in b. 3 are ideally illustrative of an insubstantial, wandering pinpoint of light. The next two lines are similarly contrasted. 'Wie ich einen Ausgang finde' implies anxiety to find a way out of the rocky terrain; at bb. 9 and 10 dotted demisemiquavers fall onto accented crotchets an augmented fourth lower, betraying a note of panic. And then, as if blithely to allay any concern, the bravado of 'Liegt nicht schwer mir in dem Sinn' has the martial precision of a seasoned military campaigner: there will be no trouble at all in getting out of this valley, and there is nothing to be frightened about. Here the lack of accompaniment for the first quavers of the bar may well be saying, 'I'm all right on my own.' When the piano does join the voice it is in the banal music of empty bluster. The insistence on dotted rhythms is disturbing, bringing to mind the image of a madman playing at toy soldiers. And then Schubert does something which is the prerogative of composers who see more than one meaning in a text: he repeats it with a change of musical nuance. This is neither the first nor the last time he does this in *Winterreise*, but it is perhaps the most telling. The second 'Liegt nicht schwer mir in dem Sinn' (bb. 13–14) could not be more different. It completely changes our impression of the traveller's state of mind – or rather it shows us that he is continually in two minds. Instead of the earlier knee-jerk macho reaction to his troubles we hear the doubts and confusions of a dreamer. The delicate tracery of the demisemiquaver melismas in b. 13 and the eloquent curve and stretch of the cadence remind us that he is a poet and artist – unbalanced perhaps, wounded certainly, but nevertheless a person of exquisite imagination and refinement. The interlude in the piano (bb. 15–17) echoes the shape of these last two bars.

The poem's second verse receives a similar musical treatment to the first. The accompaniment is exactly the same, but the vocal line is ornamented in remarkable fashion for the first line, 'Bin gewohnt das Irregehen' (bb. 17–18). Just as the deepest rocky chasms of the opening strophe had inspired an austere melodic plunge, here the music of the wanderer moves quixotically upwards, nonchalant as well as gently unhinged. As in the first verse, ambiguity of response to the text is shown in the contrasted settings of the phrase 'Alles eines Irrlichts Spiel!' The first emphasizes the hollow, jolly qualities of 'Irrlichts Spiel', the second the mystery and madness of the same phrase, the melisma on the word 'Irrlichts' touching a wayward F sharp at the top of the stave in b. 25. The vocal writing here recalls another 1827 song, *Des Fischers Liebesglück* D933, also about a pale light gleaming through the willows – this time the bedroom candle of the fisherman's sweetheart. It flickers, the poet Leitner says, like a will-o'-the-wisp ('Es gaukelt / Wie Irrlicht').

The third strophe produces music entirely new. For the first time we have a four-bar phrase that contrasts strongly with the obsessive two-bar structure where depression is always followed by elation. There is a broad and inevitable sweep for 'Durch des Bergstroms trockne Rinnen / Wind' ich ruhig mich hinab'. This grand vocal line, supported by dramatic dotted figures in the piano, climbs down in various stages (between bb. 28 and 32) to cover the interval of a ninth. In it we can trace, as if on an ordnance map, the winding path of the river as it is pulled to the sea. That these gullies are dry is also audible in the jagged dotted rhythms, the least liquid stream in all Schubertian literature. The word 'hinab' descends to a low B, where the next phrase starts on the word 'jeder'. In b. 32 the harmonies change from B major to G^7 and this pivotal bar launches the singer's next soaring flourish up the phrase in C major, 'Jeder Strom wird's Meer gewinnen' (b. 33). The confidence of this almost triumphant statement of nature's inevitability (C major) is followed by a heartbreaking repetition of the words – a poignant reflection on human vulnerability and the certainty of the grave. These two phrases are so powerfully eloquent that the composer is able to repeat them almost note for note as a vocal peroration from b. 36. The only change is tiny yet telling: on the final 'auch sein Grab' the voice stretches a semitone higher with a G at the summit of the phrase (in b. 39) instead of an F sharp. In the Peters Edition a pause sign is printed on the note itself, but an examination of the autograph makes it clear that the composer intended the whole phrase to lie under the fermata (as printed in the AGA and the NSA). The postlude is a slightly ornamented version of the introduction.

| First edition: | Published as Op. 89 no. 9 by Tobias Haslinger, Vienna on 14 January 1828 (P149) |
| Subsequent editions: | Peters: Vol. 1/82; AGA XX 525: Vol. 9/30; NSA IV: Vol. 4a/145; Bärenreiter: Vol. 3/106 |

Bibliography: Youens 1991, pp. 196–202
Discography and timing: Fischer-Dieskau III 2⁹   2'31
                                 Pears–Britten   2'19
                                 Hyperion I 30⁹
                                                           2'22   Matthias Goerne
                                 Hyperion II 33⁹

←— *Rückblick* D911/8   *Rast* D911/10 —→

X RAST   Rest
OP. 89 NO. 10, **D911/10** [H622]

The song exists in two versions, the second of which is discussed below:

(1)   No tempo indication   D minor   ²/₄   [67 bars]

(2)   C minor

(67 bars)

Nun merk' ich erst, wie müd' ich bin,	**O**nly now, as I lie down to rest,
Da ich zur Ruh' mich lege;	Do I notice how tired I am.
Das Wandern hielt mich munter hin	Walking kept me cheerful
Auf unwirtbarem Wege.	On the inhospitable road.
Die Füsse frugen nicht nach Rast,	My feet did not seek rest
Es war zu kalt zum Stehen,	It was too cold to stand still
Der Rücken fühlte keine Last,	My back felt no burden;
Der Sturm half fort mich wehen.	The storm helped to blow me onwards.
In eines Köhlers engem Haus	In a charcoal-burner's cramped cottage
Hab' Obdach ich gefunden;	I found shelter.
Doch meine Glieder ruhn nicht aus:	But my limbs cannot rest
So brennen ihre Wunden.	Their wounds burn so.
Auch du, mein Herz, in Kampf und Sturm[1]	You too, my heart, so wild and daring
So wild und so verwegen,	In battle and tempest;
Fühlst in der Still' erst deinen Wurm	In this calm you now feel the stirring of your
	serpent,
Mit heissem Stich sich regen!	With its fierce sting!

[1]In his *Gedichte*, 1824, Müller changed this line in a tiny detail: 'Auch du mein Herz, *im* Kampf und Sturm'. In *Urania*, 1823, the line reads as it stands above, and as Schubert set it.

*This is the thirtieth of Schubert's forty-six Müller solo settings (1823, 1827 and 1828). See the
poet's biography for a chronological list of all the Müller settings.*

Winterreise is a cycle preoccupied with Shakespearean antitheses – melting and freezing, remem-
bering and forgetting, repulsion and attraction, sinking and soaring, all translated into musical
imagery with unparalleled acuity. *Rast* continues this catalogue of conflicts; the physical nature
of pain and exhaustion is shown to be subject to the power of the mind. On the other hand the
traveller's heartbreak, originating in and nurtured by his mental state, cannot be vanquished or
assuaged by physical means. In this juxtaposition of corporeal and non-corporeal pain, rest has
nothing to do with peace; the physical rigours of the winter journey, considerable though they
are, cannot compare in intensity to the traveller's mental anguish. The second verse of music
(Schubert uses two of Müller's to make one of his own) expands the metaphor. Whereas his
retreat into fantasy can make the traveller oblivious to the cold, this release from reality is bought
at a cost. Also nurtured by his unbalanced mind are the stirrings of the stinging serpent buried
in his heart. If madness gives the traveller a noble stoicism, it also feeds the monsters waiting
to consume him from within.

Verschneite Hütte (1827) by Caspar David Friedrich.

For the first time in the cycle the wanderer
pauses in his journey. But instead of a moment
of respite, the travel music continues in his
head, reflected in the unceasing trudge of the
accompaniment. The journey itself is gradually beginning to rival the girl as the traveller's
idée fixe. In the second verse we learn that he
has taken refuge in a charcoal-burner's hut,
although it is never clear whether that humble
worker is with him, or whether his dwelling,
like his occupation, is abandoned for the
winter months. (This is yet another detail to
occupy the song detectives who insist on plot-
ting this journey in Baedeker terms, charting
the wanderer's movements as if he were
subject to a tourist's normal logic.) Although
we might have guessed by the first strophe
that the traveller has found shelter with the
words 'zur Ruh' mich lege', the indoor snapshot of the cramped cottage in the second
would have tempted almost any other composer to music newly composed for the
change of circumstance. Schubert's strophic
scheme, however, is merciless. It emphasizes
in its plainness that the traveller, whether he finds himself indoors or out, takes the harsh winter
of the soul with him as his only constant companion. Even if the charcoal-burner had been
present, and compassionate and hospitable, the protagonist would scarcely have noticed him;
this voyager is oblivious to everything except himself.

The tempo marking 'Mässig' and Schubert's earlier original key of D minor suggests a
strong connection between this song and *Gute Nacht* (No. 1). There is a similar sense of determination in both songs and it is an intentional paradox that a song entitled *Rast* is conceived
in a tempo that drives relentlessly forward, however much the traveller is impeded by physical
strictures. Instead of the four well-ordered quavers with which the cycle began we are reduced

to a straggling two in each hand. This down-at-heel music seems less together than *Gute Nacht* in every way: stripped of his former respectability the wanderer and his garments even *sound* shabbier, but the determination to travel ever onwards remains unwavering. The accented second beat is approached from beneath by an upbeat quaver; each step spans only six inches on the keyboard but it has a groan behind it which costs the effort of a mile hike. These 'toilsome strides', as Gerald Moore calls them, are the responsibility of the right hand. The left drags behind: stolidly earthbound on the first beat, it bumps or stumbles on the final quavers (marked 'staccatissimo') of each bar. Because the harmonic changes occur within a tiny radius of the keyboard (there is a pedal C in the bass and both hands seem all but rooted to the spot) there is a feeling of constricted shuffling, and in those accented second beats we hear the eye-watering twinges of painfully throbbing feet. From the pianist there is an obvious need for a subtle rubato – nothing too exaggerated, but some suggestion that the footfalls are not effortlessly uniform, that they are costing the traveller too much to be a well-regulated march.

Performers should beware of too slow a tempo, however. The traveller's spirits are still determined, and this is in itself a sign of derangement more disturbing perhaps than ranting and raving; he seems able to use the word 'munter' ('cheerful') without a jot of irony. Tiredness is painted in the vocal line by the heavy passing note at 'wie müd' ich bin' and by the expressive droop on 'lege' (b. 10), but the music flows on, nevertheless, despite the suggestions of shudder and jolt. There is no such thing as rest, even when the traveller is lying down. On the lines 'Das Wandern hielt mich munter hin / Auf unwirtbarem Wege' (bb. 13–15) we hear a tiny pre-echo of the song *Das Wirtshaus* (No. 21) in the progression of four legato quavers, fully harmonized with left-hand chords, and longing for the hospitality of that most certain of resting places, the graveyard. We have already noted that *Rast* and *Gute Nacht* share a similar tempo, and *Der Wegweiser* (No. 20) is also prophesied in the music's momentum. We are reminded how cleverly Schubert has distributed walking songs throughout the piece (Nos 1, 10, 20, all 'Mässig' and in ⅔) to propel the story forward when there is a danger of contemplative stasis.

There is a marked difference between the almost English sangfroid of some of the traveller's words ('Walking kept me cheerful') and the accompaniment that deals in the cold realities of physical exhaustion. At 'Die Füsse frugen nicht nach Rast' the accents in the piano are shifted to the second quavers of the bar in wincing off-beat emphasis. The accompaniment at the heart of the music reflects the twinges racking the traveller's body, perhaps his feet especially, but he is so taken up with his epic journey that he cannot feel them. This is evident from the remarkable music, marked 'Leise' ('softly'), for 'Der Rücken fühlte keine Last' (bb. 20–22). An oppressive load is miraculously taken off the traveller's shoulders. Melismas in the vocal line, marked pp, fancifully embroider a diminished-seventh chord with wafting semiquavers, music that suddenly sidesteps the harmonic rigours of the C minor journey and floats free. The follow-up to this phrase is a return to the home key for a loud 'Der Sturm half fort mich wehen' (bb. 23–5). Now the elements are quixotically cast as the traveller's friends, and the arpeggio figurations, in a no-nonsense C minor, are strident and wide-ranging, with a mighty stretch of a tenth between 'half' and 'fort' in b. 24. Not content with this startling juxtaposition of contrasting phrases, Schubert sets these two lines again. This time 'Der Rücken fühlte keine Last' settles on the submediant on A flat, with a potent added F sharp, which is equally mysterious and etiolated in effect. For the second 'Der Sturm half fort mich wehen' (bb. 29–31) there is a return to a C minor arpeggio, exactly the same music as before. These extraordinary sideways retreats from the normality and logic of the home key, using two differently harmonically shaded chords, make time stand still. The music crosses the threshold of insanity and enters a region free of logic, free of pain.

The introduction of the second strophe is an unadorned repeat of the song's opening bars. Perhaps one appreciates more the second time around the exhausted eloquence of the fermata (b. 36) before the entry of the voice. This device, a cliché in the hands of other composers, appears in only one other song in *Winterreise*, hence its potency when used in connection with this 'poor fellow' who is 'dog-tired' – in Gerald Moore's words. Because we have heard the melody before, mention of the charcoal-burner, without a new melody of his own, seems remarkably perfunctory – and so it is, for he is only a bit-part player in the drama, or more likely an offstage member of the otherwise non-existent dramatis personae (until the very last song that is). The rising phrase of 'So brennen ihre Wunden' (bb. 43–5) is marvellously apt for the meaning, the vocal climax reaching its apex on the very word ('wounds') which needs to throb and glow. It is not unusual for Schubert in the greatness of his maturity to reveal his most powerful surprise in the second verse of a strophic song, but here he excels himself. The melismatic phrases which have spoken in the poem's second strophe of two images – the lifting of burdens and the blowing of storms – now serve the single image of a stinging serpent. It would be difficult to believe that the composer did not have the poem's fourth strophe at the forefront of his mind right from the start, so perfectly do the successive vocal phrases uncoil and writhe in sinister fashion, before the full might of 'Mit heissem Stich sich regen!' is unleashed with the power of a large snake striking at his prey (bb. 53–5). As before, these linked phrases are heard twice with shifts of harmonic emphasis – 'Leise' bars contrasted with those marked 'Stark'. The introduction also serves as a postlude and this drives home that the journey must continue, come what may. Indeed the journey has become an end in itself, the star-turn that gives the cycle its title. We sense that in a lifetime of failure and broken relationships the traveller now realizes that at last he is involved in a great and noble venture. After all, it is this journey that will make him immortal.

Schubert composed this song in D minor but directed on the autograph that it should be transposed down to C. This change was probably a result of the tonal scheme of the first part of the cycle that originally began and ended in D minor. A song in that key so near to *Einsamkeit* (No. 12) would have stolen the tonal thunder of what Schubert, in early 1827, took to be the concluding song of the set.

Volume 4b of the NSA prints both the sketch of the song and its first draft version – a fascinating documentation of the metamorphosis of many tiny details that come together, third time lucky, nay blessed, in the perfection of the second, definitive, version. Both the sketch and the first version are in D minor, as opposed to C minor. There is many a tenor who might be tempted to revert to this tonality, if only to avoid digging down to make enough tone for the middle Cs in the vocal line.

Publication:	Published as Op. 89 no. 10 by Tobias Haslinger, Vienna on 14 January 1828 (P150); first version published as part of the AGA in 1895 (P698)
Subsequent editions:	Peters: Vol. 1/84; AGA XX 526: Vol. 9/32 (C minor) & 34 (D minor); NSA IV: Vol. 4a/147 & Vol. 4b/270 (sketch) & 272 (first version, D minor); Bärenreiter: Vol. 3/108 & 224 (D minor)
Bibliography:	Youens 1991, pp. 203–7
Discography and timing:	Fischer-Dieskau III 2[10] 2'54
	Pears–Britten 3'20
	Hyperion I 30[10]
	Hyperion II 33[10] 3'05 Matthias Goerne

← *Irrlicht* D911/9   *Frühlingstraum* D911/11 →

XI FRÜHLINGSTRAUM
Op. 89 no. 11, **D911/11** [H623]

Dream of spring

The song exists in two versions, the second of which is discussed below:

(1) 'Etwas geschwind'   A major   §   [88 bars]

(2) A major

(88 bars)

Ich träumte von bunten Blumen,	**I** dreamt of bright flowers
So wie sie wohl blühen im Mai,	That blossom in May;
Ich träumte von grünen Wiesen,	I dreamt of green meadows
Von lustigem Vogelgeschrei.	And merry birdcalls
Und als die Hähne krähten,	And when the cocks crowed
Da ward mein Auge wach;	My eyes awoke
Da war es kalt und finster,	It was cold and dark,
Es schrieen die Raben vom Dach.	Ravens cawed from the roof.
Doch an den Fensterscheiben	But there, on the window panes,
Wer malte die Blätter da?	Who had painted the leaves?
Ihr lacht wohl über den Träumer,	Are you laughing at the dreamer
Der Blumen im Winter sah?	Who saw flowers in winter?
Ich träumte von Lieb' um Liebe,	I dreamt of mutual love,
Von einer schönen Maid	Of a lovely maiden
Von Herzen und von Küssen,	Of embracing and kissing,
Von Wonne und Seligkeit.[1]	Of joy and rapture.
Und als die Hähne krähten,	And when the cocks crowed
Da ward mein Herze wach;	My heart awoke;
Nun sitz' ich hier alleine	Now I sit here alone
Und denke dem Traume nach.	And reflect upon my dream.
Die Augen schliess' ich wieder,	I close my eyes again,
Noch schlägt das Herz so warm.	My heart still beats so warmly
Wann grünt ihr Blätter am Fenster?	Leaves on my window, when will you turn green?
Wann halt' ich mein Liebchen im Arm?[2]	When shall I hold my love in my arms?

[1]Müller writes 'Von *Wonn*' und Seligkeit'.
[2]In both *Urania*, 1823 and *Gedichte*, 1824, Müller writes 'Wann halt' ich *dich*, Liebchen im Arm?' By avoiding the personal pronoun, Schubert increases the emotional distance between the traveller and his former beloved.

This is the thirty-first of Schubert's forty-six Müller solo settings (1823, 1827 and 1828). See the poet's biography for a chronological list of all the Müller settings.

Once again we have a song about contrasts: dreaming is juxtaposed with waking and, in musical terms, the classical style with the Romantic. In the stormy and dark world of *Winterreise* this song is an oasis of calm and pastoral delight – or at least it begins as such. There is nothing harder to play in the entire cycle than this song's introduction. The pianist feels balanced 'on point' as if a ballerina, so exactly judged must be all the nuances, so beautifully turned the mordents, so controlled the tone in the balance between right hand and left. In hearing this music so simple, so fragile, so ineffably beautiful, we think of another dream of spring, Mozart's song *Sehnsucht nach dem Frühlinge* K596, also in a wafting §, which inspired the last movement of the Piano Concerto in B flat major, K595. The traveller dreams of an idealized world of springtime, before the Fall as it were, and for Schubert, Mozartian transparency represented just this purity and innocence. The world as Mozart knew it was changed for ever by the French Revolution and the rise of Napoleon. The traveller's world was torn apart by the treachery of his girl; anything before this was his golden age. Thus we have fourteen Mozartian bars, almost entirely free of chromatic complications. Music as purely diatonic as this is rare in *Winterreise* and, in Susan Youens's phrase, it is 'a privileged moment in the cycle'. There are other influences at work too. Nothing could be more old-fashioned and stylized than the bergerette convention of music in §. Haydn, for one, wrote a number of songs in this genre, and Schubert was also an old hand at this pastoral style. (*Schäfers Klagelied* D121 begins with a similarly lilting dotted rhythm, and the Hölty setting *Mailied* D503, another enchantingly melodic song in §, also comes to mind as Müller mentions the month of May at the beginning of his poem.) The opening of *Frühlingstraum* is pastoral music as if raised to a higher power; it is almost too beautiful to be true, as if conceived for a music-box with a perfect mechanism that includes human feeling. Schubert writes here in a style worthy of the shepherds and shepherdesses depicted on the wallpaper of a nursery – not real people, but enchantingly Arcadian. And this brings us back to the traveller and his childlike dreams of the past which are heightened by longing and simplified by memory into something more perfect than they could ever have been. The song begins with an evocation of a picture-book springtime, right down to the two notes of the cuckoo which bring this prelude to a close. The poignancy of this music, in a tonality that is always special for Schubert, is to do with its hapless idealization of the past. We recall at least two great songs in the same A minor/major about impossible dreams – the thwarted love-at-a-distance of *Abendstern* D806, and the heartfelt plea for the return of the classical world in *Strophe aus 'Die Götter Griechenlands'* D677 ('Kehre wieder / Holdes Blütenalter der Natur!' – 'Return again, / Sweet springtime of nature!').

The melody, outlined relatively high on the keyboard, is instantly and touchingly memorable and the vocal line derives from it unashamedly. Two delicate mordents (trills in the song's first version) emphasize the music's eighteenth-century quality, as if it might be played on a harpsichord but for the smoother addition of an overlay of romanticism that requires the piano. This impression is continued with the voice with its gallant appoggiatura on 'bunten <u>Blumen</u>' (bb. 5–6), its delicate rise and fall within an arpeggio to paint the pastoral undulation of the fields at 'Wiesen' (b. 10) and its ornate little decorative passage on 'Vogelgeschrei' (bb. 11–12) where the unimportant word 'von' is graced with a tripping little downward scale passage. In a brilliant reading of Müller's use of the hearty word 'lustig' and the raucous 'schrei', Schubert has realized that these merry birdcalls are linked to the cock-crow of the next verse. The traveller has heard these strident sounds in his sleep and, in the moments before he wakes, his unconscious has attributed the unwelcome intrusion to the chocolate-box birds of his dreams. Sleeping and waking are thus elided and merged. It is a universal experience that dreams are at their most vivid the moment before surfacing, but most people wake from a nightmare to a world of calm reality, whereas the traveller wakes from an idyll to face a nightmare. 'Vogelgeschrei' in b. 12 is set as a melisma to the notes A – C sharp – E, a major-key version of the horn-call arpeggio that opens *Die Wetterfahne* (No. 2): E – A – C natural – E. As we have seen in the commentary on that song, the weathervane in the shape of a cockerel is not only a symbol of the girl's fickleness but also a taunting reminder that the traveller, though unmarried, was all but a cuckold. It is perhaps significant that *Die Wetterfahne* is the only other song in the cycle so far to have been in the key of A.

The awakening is sudden and brutal as Mozart's world is replaced by Beethoven's. A gentle piano dynamic is replaced by music much louder, and the ambling 'Etwas bewegt' by an unequivocal 'Schnell' ('fast') from the upbeat to b. 15. (The first version of the song requires merely an 'Etwas geschwind' at this point, but this must have been a mistake because the tempo of the song from the beginning in this version is also 'Etwas geschwind'.) 'Schnell' is the signal for nothing less than a musical whiplash. The piano's chords are short and brutal, like slaps in the face of a tortured prisoner forced to return to consciousness. The split octaves that the composer employs to mimic the sound of the cock-crow are a variation of the octave jumps in *Die Wetterfahne* under the words 'Sie pfiff' den armen Flüchtling aus'; these punctuate the short vocal phrases, each utterance only a line long, as if the newly aroused dreamer has difficulty in getting his thoughts together. Underneath these shudders of sound marked forte the left hand crunches adjacent notes together in ominous discords (bb. 16, 18 and 20). The introduction of ravens produces a shift into A minor via a strong cadence on the words 'die Raben vom Dach' (bb. 21–2). The metal weathervane of tinny and easily swayed affections has been replaced on the roof by real birds that signify death. The last two lines of the strophe are repeated. Rumbling left-hand octaves establish a pedal on A for five tempestuous bars (bb. 22–5); discords, including the clash of the flattened supertonic, are in the right hand this time and evoke the abrasive sound of cawing. There is a suggestion of complete disorientation as the traveller wakes in the dark and cold from the sleep of the exhausted and finds himself swimming in a half-conscious world of unfriendly sounds and sensations. The passage ends with a dramatic A minor arpeggio in octaves in both hands (b. 26).

If we have started this song with Mozart and continued with *Sturm und Drang* music worthy of Beethoven's 'Pathétique' Sonata Op. 13, we continue with music that only Schubert, of all the great classical masters, could have written. The composer had originally placed a new key signature at the double bar but decided against it (it was scratched out and is illegible on the autograph). From b. 27 the marking is 'Langsam' and 𝄴 is replaced by ¾. Right-hand octave oscillations have been a feature of the stormy middle section but, as the traveller slips gently back into a half-dreaming state, these split octaves slow down and are transformed into stretches of yearning. Bare As, off the beat in the treble, are supported by an A major chord moving up in steps in the bass, from tonic to first inversion and then to second inversion, each step a retreat from the horrors of reality. The creation of a seventh chord by the addition of a left-hand G natural (b. 30) enables a heart-stopping sidestep into D major for a few bars at the entrance of the voice ('Doch an den Fensterscheiben'). Thus the major-key soliloquy, one of the glories of the cycle, begins on the subdominant – always a magical realm for Schubert who here uses this harmonic region to spirit us away into a kinder world. The major key heightens the sense of pathos and vulnerability and, in performance, this page is a demanding test of the singer's innate sense of poetry and fantasy, not to mention vocal technique.

Childlike, the wanderer asks who has painted leaves on the windowpanes. Of course it is the crystalline patterns formed by ice on the glass that resemble leaves, and winter itself, the old enemy, is the cunning artist. This image recalls another wintry tale: in *The Last Leaf* the American O. Henry (pseudonym of W. S. Porter, 1862–1910) wrote a short story about a dying girl who believes she will live only as long as the last leaf is visible from her window. An old man goes out in the snow and paints one on the wall, catching his death in the process, but saving her life. The sight of a leaf, even one made of ice, seems to save the traveller from the death of all his hopes. It is the nearest he can come to reconciling his wretchedly grey life with the multicoloured springtime beauties glimpsed in his dream. In the song *Letzte Hoffnung* (No. 16) we shall see an even stronger connection with this kind of fatalism.

The phrase 'Wer malte die Blätter da?' (bb. 30–32) takes us back from D major into A major, and the first two lines of the strophe are heartbreakingly repeated. The first time the question has been posed we hear a note of upbeat curiosity but the second time (bb. 34–6) there is only a sigh of relinquishment in the way the phrase falls at 'die Blätter da'. In this we can hear the gesture of a man, too exhausted or ill to move, who can only point at something distant and unattainable. From b. 37 'Ihr lacht wohl über den Träumer' shifts into D minor as a preparation for the re-establishment of the tonic key. Note that the word 'dreamer' ('Träumer', b. 38) is set on the first inversion of A minor to avoid anchoring it in the tonic (and thus reality), and that the actual return of the home tonality is reserved for the piano interlude – two bars of empty repeated As, marking time in a harmonic void, exploring the memory and lost in the miasma of dreams (bb. 42–3).

Schubert has used three verses of Müller's poem to make a three-part musical structure (ABC), and the next three verses repeat this shape exactly to make one of his most inspired strophic songs. At b. 44, as if emerging from the murky depths of the unconscious, a simple A major arpeggio marked 'mezzo staccato' signals the return of the 'Etwas bewegt' music of the song's opening. Where people are generally said to sink into dreams, here, in the topsy-turvy world of inverted values, the traveller rises to his. (Pianists are much occupied with the problem of whether to play this transitional bar in the marked 'Etwas bewegt' or in a tempo still some-what influenced by the 'Langsamer'.) Beethoven lovers will recognize in this passage the transi-tion (a similar ascending arpeggio, also in § although in G major; surprisingly simple and unexpectedly sublime) into the inverted fugue (bb. 135–6) in the finale of that composer's Piano Sonata in A flat, Op. 110.

The lilting melody of the introduction that reappears has to be played, if possible, even more beautifully than at the opening. The longing for spring is now particularized into a sad story of love. Even though the key is A major, mention of the 'schönen Maid' and his courtship with her seems surrounded by a halo of unreality. Were things ever as beautiful as he describes them? The fast middle section has gentler words from Müller: the crowing cocks are just as raucous but the ravens who have inspired the Beethovenian discords are replaced by gentler, sadder thoughts of solitude (bb. 66–70). When combined with this music, however, being alone with one's memories is frightening, something to bring on madness. The 'Langsam' section is just as moving second time around, if not more so. 'Die Augen schliess' ich wieder' is beautifully served by the pianist's gentle right-hand figures where the completion of the octave seems a musical metaphor for the closing of eyes – the eyelid falls softly as the pianist's little finger gently tips the upper note (bb. 77–8). The offbeat syncopation of the same right-hand figure, together with the all-important left-hand pulse in mezzo staccato quavers, suggest a heartbeat ('Noch schlägt das Herz so warm', bb. 79–80). The minor-key question of 'Wann grünt ihr Blätter am Fenster?' answers itself – the leaves will never be green for this traveller, and he will never hold his love in his arms. This is amply confirmed by the chilling finality of the spread A minor chord with which the song ends – the shutting of a door, the sealing of the traveller's fate.

The first version of this song, printed in the NSA Volume 4b p. 275, differs in tiny details: 'Etwas geschwind' in this version is later replaced by the more moderate 'Etwas bewegt'. The change of tempo for the cock-crows here is also 'Etwas geschwind' – as such it must be a mistake; this is later replaced by the more shocking 'Schnell'. The middle section of the first version is marked 'Langsamer' rather than the unequivocal 'Langsam' of the second version, and so on. In cases like these the composer seems to anticipate misunderstandings of his intentions from performers as a result of his previous markings. *Frühlingstraum* is written out at first as a strophic song with repeats; later Schubert prefers to give it a *durchkomponiert* appearance.

Publication: Published as Op. 89 no. 11 by Tobias Haslinger, Vienna on 14
                                             January 1828 (P151); first version published as part of the NSA in
                                             1979 (P778)
Subsequent editions: Peters: Vol. 1/86; AGA XX 527: Vol. 9/36; NSA IV: Vol. 4a/150 &
                                             Vol. 4b/275 (first version); Bärenreiter: Vol. 3/110
Bibliography: Youens 1991, pp. 208–15
Arrangement: Arr. Tilman Hoppstock (b. 1961) for guitar accompaniment, in
                                             Franz Schubert: 110 Lieder (2009)
Discography and timing: Fischer-Dieskau III 2[11]   3'52
                                             Pears–Britten   4'38
                                             Hyperion I 30[11]
                                             Hyperion II 33[11]   5'01   Matthias Goerne

←— *Rast* D911/10   *Einsamkeit* D911/12 —→

XII EINSAMKEIT   Loneliness
OP. 89 NO. 12, **D911/12** [H624]
D minor, changed to B minor for publication[1]

Wie ei - ne trü - be_ Wol - ke durch heit - re Lüf - te_ geht,

(48 bars)

Wie eine trübe Wolke	**A**s a dark cloud
Durch heitre Lüfte geht,	Drifts through clear skies,
Wenn in der Tanne Wipfel[2]	When a faint breeze blows
Ein mattes Lüftchen weht:	In the fir-tops;
So zieh' ich meine Strasse	Thus I go on my way,
Dahin mit trägem Fuss,	With weary steps, through
Durch helles, frohes Leben,	Bright, joyful life,
Einsam und ohne Gruss.	Greeting, and greeted by, no one.
Ach, dass die Luft so ruhig!	Alas, that the air is so calm!
Ach, dass die Welt so licht!	Alas, that the world is so bright!
Als noch die Stürme tobten,	When storms were still raging
War ich so elend nicht.	I was not so wretched.

[1] The NSA prints both a sketch and first version of the song in D minor. The AGA also prints the song in both keys.
[2] In his *Gedichte*, 1824, Müller changes 'Wenn' to 'Wann'.

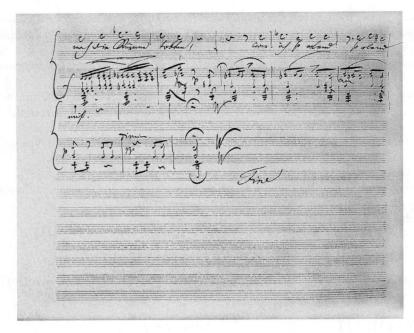

Autograph of *Einsamkeit* (fourth page, with 'Fine'), 1827 (fair copy).

This is the thirty-second of Schubert's forty-six Müller solo settings (1823, 1827 and 1828). See the poet's biography for a chronological list of all the Müller settings.

There is a change of weather here, but no change of mood for the protagonist. In the Ur-*Winterreise* of February 1827 this was the final song, and Schubert wrote 'Fine' with a flourish at the end of it, believing that he had composed the complete cycle. In the first published sequence of poems it showed the emergence of the traveller from the depths of his journey; at the end the reader bids him farewell, trying to imagine what will become of him. Müller left him worse off than he would eventually be – at least the cycle in its final form gave the traveller the companionship of the hurdy-gurdy man. After pitting his energies against winter, a tough but like-minded opponent, the traveller finds that the unaccustomed brightness only underlines his alienation. Intimations of a change of season (clear skies, the beginnings of what might be a spring breeze) emphasize how out of tune he is with his environment. He has dreamed of spring in the previous song, but that was an idealized spring of many months past. The spring of the present will make no difference to him; the leaves may turn green, but he will never hold his loved one in his arms. Indeed he now realizes he felt less wretched in the companionable bluster of stormy weather. Thus the shorter twelve-song version of the cycle leaves the traveller at the end of his journey surrounded by 'bright, joyful life' (how this is manifested is not made clear), but sealed as it were into his own loneliness. In Müller's reordering of his poetic cycle the poem stands third to last, although there it is followed by another change in the weather, the snowstorm of *Mut!*

Of course everything changes when *Einsamkeit* marks the mid-point of the cycle rather than its culmination. Müller's poem does not actually mention the arrival of spring, and this comparatively clement weather can simply be read as a temporary brightening, a lull before the winter storms that the traveller will face once again in *Der stürmische Morgen* (No. 18) and *Mut!* (No. 22). The song was originally written in D minor and presumably it was the composer's plan to bring the cycle full circle in terms of tonalities. A glance at the sequence of original keys in this first completed *Winterreise* is revealing. The cycle is framed by two songs in D minor and A minor at the beginning, and two in a reversed order (A and D) at the end. Within these poles the songs are linked by key relationships, often a third apart. The F sharp minor of *Wasserflut* (No. 6), an odd man out in terms of the sequence, was changed to E minor so that there are three consecutive songs based on E major/minor. And the D minor of *Rast* (No. 10) was changed to C minor to give the key of *Einsamkeit* more impact. When Schubert realized that *Einsamkeit* was not to finish the full cycle he transposed it into B minor, but the range of Vogl's voice doubtless also played some part in the decision. And interestingly enough, he did not change the key of *Rast* back to D minor which would have been a more comfortable juxtaposition with the B minor of *Irrlicht* (No. 9).

The final impression is of a composer sensitive to key relationships but not obsessed with them. Any programme planner knows the advantage of taking into account the tonalities of songs to build a successful group, but changes of mood and tempo are even more important. As he moved from one song to the next, Schubert certainly bore tonality in mind as a means of heightening a sense of sequence or contrast. But to ascribe to the whole of *Winterreise* a premeditated tonal ground plan, such as one may claim to discover in some of Schumann's cycles, seems pointless. Of course some of the key sequences in the work are crucial (for instance, keeping the last two songs in the same tonality), and it is unarguable that performances in the composer's original keys are preferable wherever possible. But the power of Schubert's music, and the cumulative sense of the cycle's unity, has always been more dependent on the quality of singing and playing than on key relationships preserved at all costs, especially at the expense of vocal comfort. The ability to communicate at one's vocal best is paramount in this cycle. When it came to singers Schubert was, above all, a practical man.

After a succession of strophic songs of various kinds and complexities *Einsamkeit* is in essence *durchkomponiert*, although within strophes there are near-repetitions of musical phrases which give the impression of organic unity; also of simplicity in a complicated creative process. The song begins with mournful open fifths in the left hand. We are not to hear these again until *Der Leiermann* (No. 24), hinting that Schubert was determined to use this forlorn musical idea at the end of the cycle, whether of the original twelve-song set or of the final version. Not for the first time the hands alternate, but here without the sense of driving purpose found in *Auf dem Flusse* (No. 7), *Rückblick* (No. 8) or *Rast* (No. 9). In its original D minor, the chords of the opening bar (reading upwards) are D – A (bass clef) – F – D (treble clef), the same notes that propelled forward most of the opening song, *Gute Nacht*. But here we have only the ghost of that song's energy; the traveller's determination is fractured and split apart between the hands. It is clear that he is only a shadow of his former self. The phrase 'mit trägem Fuss' ('with weary steps', bb. 17–18) is the key to the feeling that this music is always pulling slightly behind the beat. On the second beat of b. 3 in the introduction we hear a motif of a quaver and two semiquavers leading to a quaver on the beat. These flourishes in various registers ornament the plodding sixths in almost baroque fashion, as if for flute and oboe with string accompaniment. One might even imagine this as Passion music by a contemporary of Bach. It certainly describes tortured martyrdom and another station of the wanderer's cross.

The vocal line is set in the middle register which makes it seem lacking in brilliance and energy. The voice drifts somewhat aimlessly, moving with the aid of weary little melismas to depict the scudding of the black cloud across the skies and the stirrings of a faint breeze. Underneath 'Durch heitre Lüfte geht', and again at 'Ein mattes Lüftchen weht' there is an echo of the trudging piano motif of *Rast*. This aptly conveys the pain and drudgery of the traveller's laborious progress, and it is significant that this figure makes its reappearance here as a commentary on two verbs of movement. (In bb. 10 and 12 the crotchet on the second beat of the bar is preceded by an upbeat where the lower parts of the chord are tied to the second beat, as if the player is too weary to re-strike them.) 'Durch helles, frohes Leben' (bb. 18–20) is accompanied by dark, accented chords. The word 'helles' (bright) is purposefully negated by its underlay, a thick-textured chord in the bass clef singularly inappropriate to illustrate the word itself but expressive of the wanderer's contemptuous reaction to the bright life led by others. The phrase 'Einsam und ohne Gruss' (bb. 20–22) is accompanied by a classic Schubertian signature employed when he wishes to denote loneliness or solitariness: the vocal line is doubled by the piano which also doubles itself – the notes are the same in each hand, an octave apart.

The last of the poem's three strophes is expanded by word repetitions and the musical language of magnificent rhetoric and pathos. This is the basis of at least half the song. As if to reflect feeling rising from the depths of the singer's being, the piano, still in unison octaves, struggles up the stave in bb. 22 to 23, a progress mainly made up of minor thirds. This leads with a crescendo to a tremolando eruption on a diminished chord (b. 24). The only pianistic effect of its kind in the whole cycle, this prompts a similar burst of visceral emotion from the voice at 'Ach, dass die Luft so ruhig! / Ach, dass die Welt so licht!' The absence of a verb in these phrases underlines their epigrammatic desperation. Once again the piano writing contradicts the words: the agitated movement of the tremolo is anything but 'ruhig', and its harmony denotes anything but 'licht'. Another masterstroke is the tiny but searing motif of a falling semitone in bb. 25 and 27, the hands once again an octave apart, which punctuates and frames these outbursts, adding to their power.

And then something quite unexpectedly volcanic happens: semiquaver triplets begin in the bass clef and, as if borne by molten lava, spread through the keyboard, culminating in two dramatic quavers, snatched and hammered on 'tobten' (b. 30). Of course this is a reflection of the storm mentioned in the words ('Als noch die Stürme tobten'), but it is equally descriptive of the raging of storms within the traveller's soul. Throbbing sextuplets like these have played a similarly impassioned role in *Die böse Farbe* D795/17 from *Die schöne Müllerin*, and to pianists who have played both cycles the two passages feel familiar and related. Just as suddenly as this music has changed character, there is a reversion (at 'War ich so elend') to the weary quavers and semiquavers of the opening which has already been referred to as baroque Passion music for a martyr. It calls for (and receives) the listener's compassion in similar fashion. The way we are made to wait for the crucial 'nicht' by the splitting of the poet's phrase into two ('War ich so elend' and then 'so elend nicht') is highly unusual, even by the standards of Schubert's inventive word-setting. It takes two attempts for the traveller to speak the entire phrase, which implies huge emotion and stuttering bewilderment.

In a feat of canny musical planning Schubert now repeats the music we have already heard for this strophe, but at different pitches and with different harmonic implications. The impression at first is of a decrease in tension, but this is only a means of stepping back for a moment, all the better to wring our withers. The Sisyphean push up the stave (bb. 34–5) and the vocal phrase 'Ach dass die Luft so ruhig!' (bb. 35–7) are at a lower pitch than earlier, but 'Ach, dass die Welt so licht!' (bb. 37–9) and the 'volcano' music of bb. 40–42 are repeats of what we have already heard. They seem even more highly strung, however, and more in the style of a peroration, because they have been approached differently. The effect of the final line of the song is also heightened by its context. In fact it is almost exactly the same music we heard earlier for 'War ich so elend nicht' but for the tiny detail that the voice is taken to a high-pitched wail on the final 'so elend nicht' (bb. 45–6). The postlude is a shrunken version of the introduction; it insists once again on alternating chords – bleak open fifths in the left hand, sixths in the right. The dynamic is pianissimo, and the composer marks a diminuendo. At the end of the first half of the cycle the wanderer shuffles off the stage with dragging footsteps (which might have been the last we saw of him had Schubert not discovered more Müller poems). He is subject to terrible moments of pain but he is incapable of sustaining emotional outbursts for any length of time. The broken chords of the final bars denote an equally broken man.

As Ian Bostridge has proved on various occasions it is not impossible to programme the twelve songs of the Ur-*Winterreise* as the first or even second part of a recital (depending on what else is sung). In fact it is fascinating to hear from time to time the cycle as Schubert first conceived it in its twelve-song form. Bostridge sings the closing *Einsamkeit* in D minor – the tonality of the opening *Gute Nacht*. Although the sketch for the song (NSA Volume 4b, p. 278) breaks off after one page, there is no doubt that the composer thought of *Einsamkeit* in D minor in the first place.

Publication:	Published as Op. 89 no. 12 by Tobias Haslinger, Vienna on 14 January 1828 (P152); first version published as part of the AGA in 1895 (P699)
Subsequent editions:	Peters: Vol. 1/90; AGA XX 528: Vol. 9/40 (D minor) & 42 (B minor); NSA IV: Vol. 4a/155 & Vol. 4b/278 (sketch, D minor); Bärenreiter: Vol. 3/114
Bibliography:	Reed 1985, p. 497 (a thematic and stylistic link between this song and 'Andante un poco mosso' of the G major String Quartet D887) Youens 1991, pp. 216–22
Arrangement:	Arr. Tilman Hoppstock (b. 1961) for guitar accompaniment, in *Franz Schubert: 110 Lieder* (2009)
Discography and timing:	Fischer-Dieskau III 2[12] 2'38
	Pears–Britten 2'54
	Hyperion I 30[12]
	Hyperion II 33[12] 2'41 Matthias Goerne

← *Frühlingstraum* D911/11   *Jägers Liebeslied* D909 →

PART TWO[1]
Completed October 1827 or perhaps by the end of September[2]

XIII Die POST   The post
Op. 89 no. 13, **D911/13** [H635]
E♭ major

Von der Stra - sse her ein Post-horn klingt.

(94 bars)

---

[1] For the twelve songs in the second part of *Winterreise* the punctuation given here is taken from Schubert's source, Müller's *Gedichte*, 1824.

[2] The beginning of the autograph of Part Two is dated 'Oct. 1827' with 'S' crossed out (September?) and overwritten with 'O'. If this date refers to the writing out of the whole of the fair copy of Part Two, rather than the single song's composition, Part Two may already have been complete by the end of September. See also footnotes on pp. 716 and 720.

Von der Strasse her ein Posthorn klingt.	**A** post horn sounds from the road
Was hat es, dass es so hoch aufspringt,	Why is it that you leap so high,
Mein Herz?	My heart?
Die Post bringt keinen Brief für dich.	The post brings no letter for you.
Was drängst du denn so wunderlich,	Why, then, do you surge so strangely,
Mein Herz?	My heart?
Nun ja, die Post kommt aus der Stadt,[3]	But yes, the post comes from the town
Wo ich ein liebes Liebchen hatt',	Where I once had a beloved sweetheart,
Mein Herz!	My heart!
Willst wohl einmal hinübersehn,	I expect you just want to go over to look
Und fragen, wie es dort mag gehn,	And ask how things are there,
Mein Herz?	My heart?

This is the thirty-third of Schubert's forty-six Müller solo settings (1823, 1827 and 1828).
See the poet's biography for a chronological list of all the Müller settings.

The music of horn-calls is to be found elsewhere in Schubert's music. He wrote songs with horn accompaniment for outdoor performance, and *Auf dem Strom* D943 for tenor, horn and piano is one of his two great vocal works with obbligato instruments. It is, however, the sound of the hunting-horn (as in *Die schöne Müllerin* D795) emanating from the dark forest, crucial symbol of romanticism, that plays a substantial part in the song repertoire – from Schubert, via Schumann, to Mahler. The post horn is another matter: although the metaphorical coachman's fanfare that concludes *An Schwager Kronos* D369 is unforgettably rousing, postilion music is not common in serious song. Despite being an inspiration for polka and quadrille, the sound of the post horn is romantic in its own urban way: it not only signals the excitement of departure and foreign travel (as in Beethoven's 'Les Adieux' Piano Sonata Op. 81a) but also the arrival of someone returning from a long voyage – the reuniting of parted lovers, perhaps. And there is also the dual role of the post-chaise that carries mail as well as people; it speeds love letters on their way to distant destinations, and brings them from afar. In our own day we have traded this happy musical signal of departures and homecomings for the drone of aeroplanes overhead; the ringing of the doorbell is all that has remained of the thrilling sound of the brass fanfare signifying the arrival of the mail, and even that is replaced increasingly by email, heralded by a computer's ping. Nevertheless, as W. H. Auden says in *Night Mail*: 'And none will hear the postman's knock / Without a quickening of the heart, / For who can bear to feel himself forgotten?'

It is this almost involuntary quickening of the heart that gave rise to this song. *Einsamkeit* left the traveller in the trough of lassitude and despair, but depression often has a cyclical nature and hope can be rekindled. When Schubert returned to write Part Two of *Winterreise* after a gap of some months (we are not sure how many) the work needed to be re-launched in every way, and this music triumphantly achieves that. Many a dramatic work needs an overture, and an entr'acte can revitalize the interest, quicken the pulse and whet the appetite. Performers will feel in their audiences, as this song begins, a palpable sense of relief at the change of mood, however temporary.

The advantage of a merry post-horn motif from Schubert's point of view is that the excuse for fast music and dancing arpeggios is an important counterpoint for the plight of the wanderer.

---

[3] In Müller (1824) 'Nun ja, die Past *kömmt* aus der Stadt'. The erasure of the conditional 'would come' makes the protagonist's expectations seem a little less sane.

There is as much opportunity for the pathos of contrast between the workings of the outer world and the protagonist's inner life as between the bouncing accompaniment and a vocal line that is only temporarily seduced into the rhythms and melody of its surroundings. The poem's second and fourth strophes open a window into his suffering, albeit with the horn music still in the distance. It is in some ways a perfectly logical continuation from *Einsamkeit* where the protagonist has referred to his aversion to 'helles, frohes Leben' ('bright, joyful life'), one of the sounds of which might include the merry arrival of the mail coach.

All but three of Müller's poems in the cycle are written in quatrains. In *Gute Nacht* (No. 1) the verse scheme is eight lines long; *Die Nebensonnen* (No. 23) consists of ten lines of rhyming couplets; *Die Post* is exceptional for its rhyming couplets followed by a refrain, each three-line strophe making up a separate verse. This gives a spring to the music's step, and the singer's statements are all remarkably pithy, as if written in telegraphese (appropriately of course). Only Schubert could have made something so individual out of the unadulterated E flat major arpeggios and flourishes of bb. 1–6, and this is proved by the relative banality of Conradin Kreutzer's setting of the same poem (1826). The canter of the horse trotting over the cobblestones is vividly suggested by the staccato left-hand triplets; in the right, the cheeky announcement of the post horn. The dotted rhythm here sounds authentically illustrative of that instrument, but the composer has already calculated that

The Letter Post from O. E. Deutsch's edition of Adalbert Stifter's *Aus dem alten Wien.*

this must serve also as symbol of racing pulses and a palpitating heart. In the midst of all this spiky music for tongued brass, legato phrasing binds together six quavers in b. 4 and again in b. 6. This implies that the fanfare, energetically depicted in dotted rhythm, is to be heard as only a part of the right-hand melody, and the legato quavers suggest an echo effect, perhaps the cocked-ear response of those listening, or layers of resonance and echo building up in the frosty winter air. (In any case, if the phrasing is ignored and Schubert's tune is treated as a seamless melody, it would be an impossible challenge for any postilion at this speed, and in one breath.) The introduction in b. 7 of a D natural in the left hand after so much pure E flat major harmony is a masterstroke; it sets up a recurring cadence of dominant to tonic that becomes stuck in a groove as if suspended in time – a metaphor for unfinished business.

In b. 9 the voice enters, the beginning of its hopes dovetailing with the end of the coachman's prelude. 'Von der Strasse her ein Posthorn klingt' is set above three repetitions of this simple V–I cadence. In b. 12 the fourth of these B flat major pulsations moves to E flat[7], as if to imply that we are sidestepping the tonic to move into the subdominant (A flat major), but this too is deception. In b. 13, under 'Was hat es, dass es so hoch aufspringt', the pianist swiftly pounces on prancing dotted rhythms on A flat[7] that last for two bars. This in turn leads to the inevitable shift into D flat major for the rhetorical leap of 'Mein <u>Herz</u>?' at b. 15. This dizzy progress into a distant key, always one step ahead of expectation, is remarkably effective in painting the excitement and uncertainty of a beating heart and suggesting that a satisfactory conclusion, either harmonic or personal, will remain outside the traveller's grasp. After the 'high' of the forte passage on 'Mein Herz' the bottom begins to drop out – literally – of the traveller's hopes: the bass line falls in semitones – D flat to C flat – and finishes on a diminished chord with a G flat in the right hand (b. 18). For the repeat of 'Was hat es, dass es so hoch aufspringt' this rises gently into G natural and an E flat major chord. But even this return to the tonic key is undermined by the fact that the E flat chord is in second inversion – still uncertain ground where hope is mixed with uncertainty. It is only with the repetitions of 'Mein Herz?' that we return at last to E flat major in root position (b. 24). Here the accompaniment fades away in two bars of convulsive shudders, leaving a bar of silence and nothingness (b. 26) which betokens suspense and frozen thought-processes. The traveller has asked a question and he now ponders the answer, his sense of logic, it seems, pitifully impaired by his journey.

The contrast between the outer world of bustle and activity and the inner one of desolation could not be more clearly marked by the musical change. The rattling post-chaise triplets are replaced by a throb where gentle crotchets alternate with quavers. The simple expedient of the tonic minor is wonderfully effective for 'Die Post . . . [note the lump in the narrator's throat suggested by the intervening rests in the vocal line] . . . bringt keinen Brief für dich'. The modulation into D flat major for 'dich' (b. 30) adds a note of heartbreaking tenderness; the poor traveller addresses his heart in the same tone of voice as the stream in *Auf dem Flusse* (No. 7), as if it were another being. The shift to G flat major (b. 33) reinforces the impression of meditative introspection far from the galloping banality of the tonic. Of course all expectation of a letter waiting for him is nonsense, and he knows it. Nevertheless, the sound of the horn has aroused in him a longing for some sort of communication with the outside world that he barely understands. This is beautifully conveyed by a further question: 'Was drängst du denn so wunderlich, / Mein Herz?' The preceding two phrases are an example of a parlando style, bordering on recitative, which is a feature of the second batch of *Winterreise* songs as well as the later Heine settings. The vocal intervals are kept small to suggest the naturalness and spontaneity of speech. After a two-bar interlude (bb. 36–7) the whole of the second strophe is repeated, this time set to new music, higher in pitch and more openly sung. Schubert, with composer's licence, inserts two extra settings of 'Mein Herz' (bb. 43–6) after 'Die Post bringt keinen Brief für dich' that heighten the intensity of the self-questioning. 'Why, oh why', he asks his heart, 'are you getting so excited?' These nine bars (bb. 37–46) are built on a B flat pedal that raises the sense of tension. The final 'Mein Herz' rewards these expectations with a return to the E flat major of the opening (in b. 46), and the music of the post horn.

The renewed sound of the postilion's bugle call shakes the traveller's frozen memory. The post-chaise has come in from the very place where he used to live with his girl, the town which he refers to simply as 'die Stadt' as if it were too painful to name it. 'Nun ja' – now he understands why it has moved and disturbed him so. The contrasting two-part AB structure that has served the first and second verses is now used for the third and fourth with scarcely a change – merely minor alterations of rhythmic quantities to facilitate word-setting. The strophic structures of Schubert's maturity are created to have a double or triple life; in each case the words of successive verses appropriately fit the music in miraculous fashion. Thus the gap of a bar between 'Stadt' (b. 56) and its subordinate clause 'Wo ich ein liebes Liebchen hatt'' (beginning at the end of b. 57) is no miscalculation but rather a catching of breath at the mention of the town of his humiliation. The passage of descending semitone basses before the repeat of 'Wo ich ein liebes Liebchen hatt'' seems to be a descent into the half-forgotten reaches of the traveller's memory; the second-inversion chords supporting the words give the music a glow of rueful nostalgia – the past tense of 'hatt'' makes it feel as long ago as a fairy tale.

The E flat minor music for the fourth verse (beginning b. 72) is also well suited to the words. The traveller's conversation with his heart, a mysterious parlando, suggests painful diffidence and covert intrigue. The repeat of 'Willst wohl einmal hinübersehn, / Mein Herz?' takes a bolder path and we glimpse another of his wild fantasies, as in *Rückblick* (No. 8) when he imagined stumbling back to stand before his lover's house in abject reproach. His heart wishes to fly out of his breast, not only to ask 'how things are there' but to speed there, in the opposite direction of the mail coach, on wings of musical sound. But there is an undertow of irony here, and the gallant use of the major key as the song comes to a close has the grandeur of sarcastic jest. As we have noted, horn music, for all its romantic connotations, also contains the sound of inconstancy and betrayal: the horn-call, symbol of love and communion with nature, has its reverse image as music for the cuckold. Two simple little chords from the piano close this chapter. The girl is not referred to in the cycle again, although in *Die Nebensonnen*, at the end of the work, her sun-like eyes are raised to a higher power in the traveller's memory – at least in one of various interpretations of those mysterious words.

First edition:	Published as Op. 89 no. 13 by Tobias Haslinger, Vienna on 30 December 1828 (P181)
First known performance:	18 December 1828 *Abend-Unterhaltung* of the Gesellschaft der Musikfreunde, Vienna. Soloist: Johann Karl Schoberlechner (see Waidelich/Hilmar Dokumente I No. 663 for full programme)
Subsequent editions:	Peters: Vol. 1/92; AGA XX 529: Vol. 9/44; NSA IV: Vol. 4a/158; Bärenreiter: Vol. 3/116
Bibliography:	Youens 1991, pp. 223–33
Further settings and arrangements:	Arr. Franz Liszt (1811–1886) for solo piano, no. 4 of *Winterreise* (1838–9) [*see* TRANSCRIPTIONS] Rainer Bredemeyer (1929–1995) *Post Modern* for chorus and four horns (1988)
Discography and timing:	Fischer-Dieskau III 2[13] 2'17
	Pears–Britten 2'00
	Hyperion I 30[13]
	Hyperion II 34[6] 2'21 Matthias Goerne

← *Eine altschottische Ballade* D923   *Der greise Kopf* D911/14 →

XIV Der GREISE KOPF
OP. 89 NO. 14, **D911/14** [H636]
C minor

The hoary head

(88 bars)

Der Reif hat einen weissen Schein[1]
Mir über's Haar gestreuet.
Da glaubt' ich schon ein Greis zu sein,[2]
Und hab' mich sehr gefreuet.

The frost has sprinkled a white sheen
Upon my hair:
I thought I was already an old man,
And I rejoiced.

---

[1] Müller writes 'Der Reif *hatt*' einen weissen Schein'. This 'hatt', a contraction of 'hatte' (had) places the narration of this story more in the past tense. Schubert's change into the present ('hat' – has) though sounding no different to the ear, renders the suffering of the traveller more immediate in written terms.
[2] Müller writes 'Da *meint*' ich schon ein Greis zu sein'.

Doch bald ist er hinweggetaut,	But soon it melted away;
Hab' wieder schwarze Haare,	Once again I have black hair,
Dass mir's vor meiner Jugend graut—	So that I shudder at my youth.
Wie weit noch bis zur Bahre!	How far it is still to the grave!
Vom Abendrot zum Morgenlicht	Between sunset and the light of morning
Ward mancher Kopf zum Greise.	Many a head has turned grey.
Wer glaubt's? Und meiner ward es nicht	Who will believe it? Yet mine has not done so
Auf dieser ganzen Reise!	Throughout this whole journey.

This is the thirty-fourth of Schubert's forty-six Müller solo settings (1823, 1827 and 1828). See the poet's biography for a chronological list of all the Müller settings.

In Wilhelm Müller's *Tagebuch* for 7 October 1815, the poet's twenty-first birthday, he recalls having written a letter to his father a year earlier that had cost both of them many tears. Without going into detail concerning the crisis, the poet writes: 'the past year lies so far behind me, or in front of me, it is as if, since then, I have turned from a child into an old man, [von einem Kinde zum Greise] or from an old man into a child'. This family altercation may have been part of the background to *Winterreise*. In any case, his description of an imaginary accelerated ageing process was surely the beginning of this poem in Müller's mind.

Der greise Kopf marks an important change in the traveller's preoccupations. In contrast to *Die Post* (No. 13) where his beloved, someone living, is the main theme, the not-so-hidden agenda of *Der greise Kopf*, and of many songs which follow, is death. Indeed, the girl makes no further direct appearance. The poetic imagery of death pervades the cycle, joining hands with the idea of journeying purposefully towards that goal. The music takes on an increasingly sombre and exalted aspect, and in this song the traveller bays at the moon in a manner worthy of King Lear.[3] With its sparse accompaniment and the baleful majesty of its long arched phrases, imposing and crazy at the same time, this is music that wanders in the head and creaks with the painful joints of an old man. But the traveller remains, despite himself, young; he is denied the venerable status of old age and its consequent guarantee of impending release. Too young for a bypass (including the shortcut of death) and not yet eligible for a bus pass, he must continue his journey on foot.[4] In its extraordinary mixture of portentous melody and unhinged recitative, Schubert creates a unique monologue of dramatic power and pathos.

The shape of the melodic phrase that opens this song seems to have been inspired by the words of the final strophe, 'Vom Abendrot zum Morgenlicht / Ward mancher Kopf zum Greise' ('Between sunset and the light of morning / Many a head has turned grey'). The idea of a fixed span of time where the birth and death of a day equates with the life-cycle is effectively traced in the four bars of the piano's introduction. A long, almost symmetrical curved arch of notes (made up of two bars of ascent and two of descent) starts on a middle C and returns to it. After two bars of climbing by stages, the sun reaches its apogee on a high A flat (b. 3) where it is poised in the firmament for only a moment before tumbling beneath the stave that the composer here marks as the point of his horizon. We know how enthusiastically Schubert had toyed with visual translations of sunset imagery in such songs as *An die untergehende Sonne* D457 and *Freiwilliges Versinken* D700. In this introduction he invents a musical symbol that stands as much for the inevitable process of ageing (the progression from conception to death – a climb to a high point, then downhill all the way) as for the progress of a single day from dusk to dawn

---

[3] By chance, Lear is pictured on the first plate of *Urania*, 1823, the almanac in which Schubert found the first twelve poems of the cycle.
[4] Residents of London are eligible for a 'bus pass' from the age of sixty, thus free travel on public transport.

and back again. The two ideas are conflated by the poet's imagery: it takes a lifetime to make one's hair grey, yet the traveller is astonished that, with everything that has happened to him, his hair has not gone grey overnight in the manner of a ghost story and this celebrated outward sign of deep suffering has not yet manifested itself.

The entry of the voice mirrors this opening prelude almost exactly. In bb. 7 and 8 the singer adds two mordents of his own on 'Haar' and 'gestreuet', shakes and shudders contributing to the chilliness of the frozen day, and perhaps even suggesting the quavering voice of an old man. Once again we note the versatility of Schubert's figurations. Whatever else it represents, the descending arpeggio on a diminished chord of 'über's Haar gestreuet' (immediately echoed by the piano) is a perfect illustration of a floating shower of snow (if not actually frost) descending on someone's head. The major difference between vocal line and piano introduction is the highest note of the phrase which is an F instead of an A flat; by this stage in his career Schubert has a fine feeling for what is possible, and impossible, for the human voice. There are higher notes in the cycle, but here a brilliant vocal A flat at the peak of the phrase would denote youth and vigour, and this is not what the song is about. There is even something slightly doddering about 'Da glaubt' ich schon ein Greis zu sein, / Und hab' mich sehr gefreuet'. We hear the painful movement of prematurely aged bones at the pivotal change of harmony at 'Und hab'' (bb. 12–13), and the sweetly complacent downward spiral of 'hab' mich sehr gefreuet' – set to wandering triplets as the phrase moves into the cosy key of G major – seems ineptly fond.

Bitter disappointment restores the traveller's vitality and puts him back unwillingly in touch with his youth. We have heard little as bitingly angry as the snatched quaver chords under 'Doch bald ist er hinweggetaut' (bb. 15–17) since the middle section of Die Wetterfahne (No. 2). (The chordal shudders accompanying the crowing of the cocks in Frühlingstraum (No. 11) were equally biting and a shock to the sleeping traveller, but they did not signify anger.) In Die Wetterfahne the traveller has also allowed himself to be deceived by appearances; there he realizes that he should have noticed sooner that the weathervane signified inconstancy. In Der greise Kopf he has also been duped, by winter this time, as a result of trusting his eyes too easily. (Where did he get a mirror, we must prosaically ask; perhaps he saw his white hair reflected in a stream, or in a shop window in the town?) The words, spoken between gritted teeth in their terse disappointment and self-directed anger (as if to say 'What a fool I was!'), are set in the manner of recitative, and the arpeggiated shudder of the accompaniment suggests a mane of hair shaken angrily to remove the last traces of perfidious snow. There is a tradition here that the tempo of the music should move forward freely to reflect the anguish of the discovery and Schubert makes this passage as dramatic as the sudden operatic unmasking of a black-hearted villain. The dawning realization that his hair is still black (the words 'schwarze Haare' are set as a howl of protest, bb. 19–20) is achieved by a series of strong and exciting harmonic progressions that follow hard on each other's heels: G major – C minor – first inversion of E flat^7 and then A flat. The next line takes us back via another series of chromatic steps into the relative major, E flat. This phrase ('Dass mir's vor meiner Jugend graut') is almost overwhelming in its power – a shuddering confrontation between man and his own image which is related to Der Doppelgänger D957/13. The rise of the vocal line in semitones (bb. 20–22) and the changing harmonization of 'graut' (E flat major slinking into A flat minor and back again) seems a compressed version of the recognition music, the chromatic turn of the thumbscrews, in the Heine song beginning at the words 'Du Doppelgänger! du bleicher Geselle!'

The last line of the strophe, 'Wie weit noch bis zur Bahre!', summons some of the most disturbing music of the song: the piano makes a mournful ascent up the bass stave in an E flat major scale (b. 24) and gathers up the voice in wearied unisons that now descend the stave with the greatest lassitude. The introduction of an F sharp on the shocking word 'Bahre' is especially ominous. This music, dreadfully sparse, looks back on two lieder already written, rather than on *Der Doppelgänger* which, after all, was still to be composed. The first is *Greisengesang* D778, a portrait of an old man in very different mood, but one that uses a similar vocabulary of musical unisons to depict creaking joints and the draining of colour from hair and complexion. Even more closely related is *Totengräbers Heimwehe* D842 where voice and piano come together in sombre unison in the same register at the passage beginning 'Von allen verlassen / Dem Tod nur verwandt'. These words speak of abandonment and of a longing for death that eerily predict this powerful passage in *Der greise Kopf*. There is a similar group of shuddering upbeat acciaccaturas under the word 'Tod' in the gravedigger's song as we find in *Der greise Kopf* under the word 'weit' (b. 25). At bb. 26 to 28 this line is repeated a minor third lower, bringing the music to a unison D on 'Bahre'. This, together with the uncomfortable F sharp on the first appearance of the word, has prepared the ear for an implied D major harmony that leads to a sumptuous minim chord in the bass register. For a moment we hear the calm repose, deep in the ground, of which the traveller dreams. However, this is no tonic come-to-rest, not even a straightforward dominant. This is a G^7 chord, and in that seventh is buried the inevitability of a return to ground level, and the C minor of the beginning.

The last verse is a variant of the first. We have already noticed the significance of the shape of the phrase at 'Vom Abendrot zum Morgenlicht / Ward mancher Kopf zum Greise'. After the vocal line rises to a high point and then falls to earth, the piano poignantly echoes the descent a minor third higher (bb. 33–5). The phrase beginning 'Wer glaubt's?' is set with the freedom of a recitative. The response seems almost humorous, and 'Und meiner ward es nicht' sounds somewhat offhand, as if the traveller is shrugging at a strange little phenomenon. There is a touch of madness here, and the major key can be more ominous in depicting this than the minor. Even 'Auf dieser ganzen Reise!' is framed within the mild manners of a cadence from G^7 to C major, although we hear the size and extent of the journey in the wide sweep of the vocal line. It is in the twisted emotion of the repeat of these words that we understand how bitterly disappointed the traveller has been to discover that there is no short cut to age and death. The agony and heartbreak of the entire journey seems encapsulated by the second 'Auf dieser ganzen Reise!' (bb. 39–42). We plunge into the subdominant (F minor) for the weary triplets of 'dieser ganzen' where the addition of an added sixth to the bass provides an edge of uncertainty: when will the journey end? The elongation of 'Reise' (b. 41) is underlined by an imposing cadence in the dominant, ornamented by a passing note, which gives it a baroque grandeur. It is like seeing 'Reise', the title of the cycle (or half of it) up in lights for the first time. We are given to understand that this journey is no small thing, that it is important in its own right. And it is for the journey that the traveller will be remembered, rather than for his failed love affair. The means of escape from unhappiness has now become an end in itself: the winter journey has become the anti-hero of *Winterreise*, the work named in its honour. The postlude is the same phrase of descending triplets (infinitely challenging for the pianist in the subtlety and variety of its tonal colour and rubato) that has followed on from the second line of the first and last strophes.

First edition:	Published as Op. 89 no. 14 by Tobias Haslinger, Vienna on 30 December 1828 (P182)
Subsequent editions:	Peters: Vol. 1/96; AGA XX 530: Vol. 9/48; NSA IV: Vol. 4a/162; Bärenreiter: Vol. 3/120
Bibliography:	Youens 1991, pp. 234–9
Discography and timing:	Fischer-Dieskau III 2[14] 2'56
	Pears–Britten 2'51
	Hyperion I 30[14]
	Hyperion II 34[7] 2'45 Matthias Goerne

← *Die Post* D911/13   *Die Krähe* D911/15 →

XV Die KRÄHE

The crow

Op. 89 no. 15, **D911/15** [H637]
C minor

Etwas Langsam

Ei - ne Krä - he war mit mir

(43 bars)

Eine Krähe war mit mir
Aus der Stadt gezogen,
Ist bis heute für und für
Um mein Haupt geflogen.

Krähe, wunderliches Tier,
Willst mich nicht verlassen?
Meinst wohl bald als Beute hier
Meinen Leib zu fassen?

Nun, es wird nicht weit mehr gehn
An dem Wanderstabe.
Krähe, lass mich endlich sehn
Treue bis zum Grabe!

A crow has come with me
From the town,
And to this day
Has been flying ceaselessly about my head.

Crow, you strange creature,
Aren't you going to leave me?
Do you intend soon
To seize my body as prey?

Well, I can't walk much further,
Even with my staff.
Crow, let me at last see
Faithfulness unto the grave!

Autograph of *Die Krähe*, 1827.

This is the thirty-fifth of Schubert's forty-six Müller solo settings (1823, 1827 and 1828). See the poet's biography for a chronological list of all the Müller settings.

Schubert pointedly stays in the C minor tonality of *Der greise Kopf* (No. 14) and the link seems especially eerie as one song melts into the other. If old age (with its badge of white hair) is one pathway to death, there are always others – and it this continuity of thought which the juxtaposition suggests. Suicide is something that does not really occur to the traveller – or, if it does, it is an option which he is unable to act upon (differentiating him from that other Müller protagonist, the miller boy). However, there is a death-wish fantasy at work here, and the image of the black bird of death is a strong one. In Müller's revised (1824) order for his twenty-four-poem cycle, *Die Krähe* stands only two songs down the road from *Rückblick* (No. 8) where crows have thrown balls of snow at the hapless traveller. The implication may be that one of these birds has detached itself from its fellows and is now shadowing the cycle's narrator.

Thanks to this song, the crow has the most significant billing of all avian predators in lieder, but its relative, the raven, is bigger-billed and has an even more sinister reputation. The most grisly appearance of lieder ravens is in Schumann's *Muttertraum* Op. 40 no. 2 (Hans Andersen translated by Chamisso) where a mother's baby son is one day destined to be executed and hanged from the ramparts, his body thrown to the scavengers. These caw over the cradle in gruesome anticipation of a pecking order in the battlements' brasserie. In *Die Krähe* the traveller's fate is much less clear. Is he soon to fall by the wayside where he will be helped with beak and claw into another world? Those who collapsed in the deserts of the Wild West were said to be torn apart by vultures before they were dead, but such an outcome is unlikely here. This 'Krähe' is no 'Geier' ('vulture'), and even if it is a carrion crow, the traveller ascribes to his overhead companion sinister ambitions beyond its powers – after all, he is still fit enough to walk. This crow cannot provide death, only benefit from it. But in this cycle we have long since left logic behind. Schubert takes the traveller's perceptions seriously, and the music is conceived through his eyes and with his unbalanced vision. As Fischer-Dieskau remarks: 'One would have to go back to an Altdorfer, a Rembrandt or a Goya to find images of comparable intensity.' As to the type of crow described in this song, Andrew Shackleton explains that the carrion crow (*Corvus corone*) and the hooded crow or hoodie (*Corvus cornix*) 'live in separate regions of Europe and interbreed along the boundary between . . . It so happens that the species boundary passes near both Müller's home town of Dessau (on the Elbe) and Vienna, which is well populated with hybrid crows ('Rakelkrähen') coloured black and sooty grey.'

Both *Der greise Kopf* and this song are marked 'Etwas langsam', but a change of tempo (tactically necessary to keep the cycle journeying on its way) is implicit in the flowing semiquaver triplets of *Die Krähe*. There is no song with a more insidiously sinister gait than this, seemingly innocuous on first hearing but revealing hidden dangers on closer acquaintance. The traveller feels himself marked out, and instead of recoiling in horror he embraces the crow as a companion and faithful friend. But the piano music that shadows the vocal line like the tenacious crow who never lets the traveller out of its sights has a grotesque character of its own and never lets the listener forget the underlying menace. In contrast to other Schubertian birds, this crow is too angular and bedraggled to dart or pirouette with grace. Instead it lollops through the viscous atmosphere. Mugginess and claustrophobia are in the sickly air that is both its breath of life and the traveller's whiff of death. There are great artists who like to take this song quickly; one famous tenor moves through it like lightning in order to dally as little as possible with the challenging low Cs towards the end of the song. He argues that this swiftness reflects with greater accuracy the flight of a bird on the wing. But this is no ordinary bird with delicate bone structure – the crow is all gristle and sinew, more chew than swallow. The sticky quality of the music should suggest effort – on the part of both the traveller who struggles and stumbles, and of the crow who circles and hovers, forever concentrating on his prey-to-be.

The opening melody is haunting, announced high in the treble register of the piano. The supporting left-hand triplets are also in the treble clef. Indeed, for this accompaniment, as Gerald Moore notes, Schubert employs a tessitura that is to be found scarcely anywhere else in his lieder. This is especially noticeable at the song's impassioned climax. The right-hand melody, in the upper reaches of the keyboard and in even quavers, traces the slowly circling flight. This lies within the range of a fourth and gives an impression of hovering, as if treading water in the sky. The left-hand accompanying triplets denote the flapping of wings. Thus from the very beginning we both see the crow and hear it. When played at a tempo which is 'etwas langsam' and with a minimum of pedal, the sound of feathers cleaving the air takes on a sinister aspect – if wings could be said to creak, they do so here. The introduction of the flattened supertonic in b. 3 (D flat in the key of C minor) adds to an impression of 'dirty work afoot' or, in this case, on the wing. If the first two bars of the introduction have hovered, the subsequent pair descends the stave with something like a slow swoop. The Phrygian flavour of a C minor scale with an added D flat also gives the music a malign colouring. The final bar of the introduction is a series of C minor broken chords ascending the stave in triplets. It is this which directs the traveller's gaze skywards for the entrance of the voice in b. 5.

On paper the vocal line is exactly doubled with left-hand quavers in the same octave. In actual fact the male voice sounds an octave lower than written so the piano, instead of its habitual role as voice supporter, creates a musical canopy over the singer and shadows the voice in the role of the crow. This reversal of the usual procedure contributes to the song's unearthly atmosphere. It is a paradox that this device of unisons (something which Schubert often uses to denote solitariness or loneliness) is here used to describe a relationship of sorts. Of course the crow, hardly a human companion, is a symbol of the traveller's desire for death, and it might be said that a man who relies on a predator for friendship is truly alone. The right hand, off the beat, is now responsible for the second and third notes of the triplets; these bounce off the left-hand quavers that trace the melody. It is here that a major feature of the accompaniment establishes itself: semiquaver rests in the treble stave, before the two remaining notes of the triplets. Each pair of these is punctiliously phrased with a slur. Schubert took enormous care to write these rests, 128 of them, and it is a pity that their effect is often lost in over-pedalled performances. Each of them looks like 'the sign of the crow' on manuscript paper – the imprint of a crow's foot in ink. Because the left hand in effect provides the first note of the triplet, the rest is not heard as a silence. But observing it scrupulously changes how the adjacent notes are played. Instead of the smooth, mellifluous underlay so often encountered in performances of this song, observant phrasing reveals the sound of galumphing wings, flapping in the leathery-skinned manner of a pterodactyl. There is nothing here of the fast-moving fluff and feathers of a bird song such as *Die Vögel* D691. This added touch of character highlights and counterpoints the mournful legato of the vocal line that unfolds in an apathetic succession of uninflected quavers. At the words 'Um mein Haupt geflogen' (bb. 12–13) the music moves into E flat, the relative major. This change of key sets up a meeting. The crow seems to come more directly into the traveller's line of vision, and the two-bar piano interlude that moves chromatically sideways before settling back into E flat major suggests that the bird has perhaps come to rest on a branch nearby. The whole of the following section depicts an interview that is apparently conducted face to face.

This introduces one of the strangest and most wonderful passages in *Winterreise*. Time seems suspended, as are the long legato phrases which have denoted flying. The triplets are now less expressive of flapping wings, more suggestive of something hovering, a mental presentiment as much as physical stasis. The oscillations of the left hand and the gradually climbing chromatics add to the mood of unanchored diffidence; the harmonic haze is a metaphor for confusion and uncertainty.

From b. 16 the traveller speaks to the bird, man to man as it were, with a courtesy born of derangement. The vocal line is modelled on the naturalness of speech together with just the right number of hesitations between phrases to suggest a heightening sense of horror. This is recitative with melody built into its fabric. The phrase 'Krähe, wunderliches Tier' is one of the most memorable moments in the cycle, a perfect encapsulation of the pathos of the traveller's condition, as well as his gentleness and a long-unsatisfied craving for intimacy. That he must find it here with this bedraggled creature, alongside the danger of death, is as unbearably sad as imagining Schubert searching for a sign of warmth and love in the stews of Vienna where he too flirted with death. The phrase is also a chilling pre-echo of the closing strophe of the cycle when the traveller addresses the hurdy-gurdy man as 'Wunderlicher Alter'.

At bb. 18–19, on the words 'Willst mich nicht verlassen?' ('Aren't you going to leave me?') we note how close the music of the left hand is to that of the right – closer than ever in fact. This is a perfect metaphor for the tenacious possessiveness of the crow who will not let his prey out of his sight. At the moment the traveller's mind is at his beck and call, and he only has to wait for the body to be within range of beak and claw. The words also imply a pathetic gratitude – at last the traveller has found a companion who, unlike the faithless girl, actually wants to stay by his side. Once again there is a biographical parallel of buying intimacy at a dreadful cost. The mounting tension of the remaining words of the strophe, underlined by a succession of chromatic harmonies, speaks for itself as a slow and deliberate stalking of vulnerable prey. In the setting of 'Meinen Leib zu fassen' (bb. 22–3) we hear the ambivalence of the traveller's fears and hopes as he imagines the grip of talon and incision of beak. The image is awful; the music is in the major key. Here the left hand is freed from its minuscule chromatic oscillations and returns to its melodic role. Perhaps this signals that the crow, after a few moments' rest on a branch, is returning to the air. If so, this resumption of its flight is depicted by a short interlude that returns the music from this climactic point on a D major chord (b. 23) to the C minor of the opening (from b. 25).

When the melody begins again we may be fooled into thinking that this is one of those songs where the composer is content to repeat the first strophe after an intervening middle section. The first four bars of the vocal melody (bb. 25–8) are indeed an exact music repeat of what has gone before. But nothing can prepare us for the outbreak of violent, searing emotion that transforms a gently grotesque song into one which tests the traveller's (and the singer's) capacity for the expression of the extremes of passion and pain. As if to signify that these extremes lie on the borders of sanity, at b. 29 the voice plunges down to the bottom of its register (for 'Krähe, lass mich'), then up the octave for 'endlich sehn', and then further upwards for a chilling C minor scale ascending on 'Treue bis zum Grabe!' (bb. 31–3). This last phrase culminates on a profoundly anguished forte minim G on 'Grabe'. During these vocal alarms and excursions the right hand plies its triplets in unaccustomed heights. Gerald Moore speculates that Schubert did not often use this area of his piano for his figurations because he was not fond of the stringy, tinny sound of the upper strings. But here, of course, it serves his purpose perfectly to suggest the raw cawing of the menacing bird. The second syllable of the word 'Grabe' sets off a precipitous descent on a diminished chord which leads to a repeat of the last two lines of the strophe. On the second airing the words 'Treue bis zum Grabe' reflect the depth and the inevitability of the grave ('Grabe' set to a mercilessly final drop of a fifth in a perfect cadence at bb. 37–8) rather than the anguished height of the traveller's panic. The postlude is exceptionally moving. The changes here that Schubert has made to the music of the introduction are tiny but eloquent. Most importantly we hear the flight music for the first time an octave lower than before, and this makes a very dark effect. The descent of quavers in the right hand, faithfully followed by the retinue of semiquaver triplets, signifies an ineluctable, one-way journey to the grave. The mezzo staccato repeated middle Cs in the penultimate bar (b. 42), each harmonized differently by left-hand triplets sinking ever deeper, make for a portentous extended upbeat to a final minim C. The last writhings of death lead to stillness: the unusual spacing of the ultimate chord, with its third (E flat) thickly placed in the bass register, makes for an especially woeful closing sonority.

First edition:	Published as Op. 89 no. 15 by Tobias Haslinger, Vienna on 30 December 1828 (P183)
Subsequent editions:	Peters: Vol. 1/98; AGA XX 531: Vol. 9/50; NSA IV: Vol. 4a/164; Bärenreiter: Vol. 3/122
Bibliography:	Fischer-Dieskau 1977, p. 264
	Shackleton 2012
	Youens 1991, pp. 240–44
Arrangement:	Arr. Tilman Hoppstock (b. 1961) for guitar accompaniment, in *Franz Schubert: 110 Lieder* (2009)
Discography and timing:	Fischer-Dieskau III 2^{15} 2'01
	Pears–Britten 2'20
	Hyperion I 30^{15}
	Hyperion II 34^{8} 2'31 Matthias Goerne

← *Der greise Kopf* D911/14   *Letzte Hoffnung* D911/16 →

XVI LETZTE HOFFNUNG   Last hope
Op. 89 no. 16, **D911/16** [H638]
E♭ major

Hie und da ist an den Bäumen[1]
Manches bunte Blatt zu sehn,[2]
Und ich bleibe vor den Bäumen
Oftmals in Gedanken stehn.

    Schaue nach dem einen Blatte,
Hänge meine Hoffnung dran;
Spielt der Wind mit meinem Blatte,
Zittr' ich, was ich zittern kann.

Here and there on the trees
Many a colourful leaf can be seen
I often stand, lost in thought,
Before those trees.

    I search for the single leaf
And hang my hopes upon it;
If the wind plays with my leaf
I tremble to the depths of my being.

---

[1] Müller writes '*Hier* und da'.
[2] Müller's line is '*Noch ein buntes* Blatt zu sehen'.

Ach, und fällt das Blatt zu Boden,	Ah, and if the leaf falls to the ground
Fällt mit ihm die Hoffnung ab,	My hopes fall with it;
Fall' ich selber mit zu Boden,	I, too, fall to the ground
Wein' auf meiner Hoffnung Grab.[3]	And weep on the grave of my hopes.

This is the thirty-sixth of Schubert's forty-six Müller solo settings (1823, 1827 and 1828). See the poet's biography for a chronological list of all the Müller settings.

Perhaps it was the three crisp syllables 'Hie und da' that suggested the staccatissimo hither-and-thither of the vocal line, and thence the accompaniment. Müller's poem begins with the more liquid 'Hier und da', and Schubert's change is tiny but significant. Or perhaps it is just that the leaves are detached. The image of their falling at random from a tree (why should one cling to the branch seconds, or weeks, longer than its fellows?) inspired the composer to a rhythmic ground plan unique in his lieder where pairs of joined quavers straddle the bar line to disorientate the ear – an analogue both for the fickleness of nature and the traveller's unhinged state of mind. (There is a tiny reappearance of this motif in the introduction to *Mut!* (No. 22)) Even on the printed page the notes look out of kilter, as if the engraver has suddenly taken leave of his senses and placed the bar line a quarter of an inch out of place. Spiky quavers come at us from all directions – first from the piano's middle register, then higher, then much lower. The four introductory bars end with both hands deep in the bass clef, tracing an uneven progress from tree to ground level; but events along the way suggest hectic disintegration, of something out of control and collapsing all around. (Any pianist knows the formidable concentration needed to avoid being swept away into disaster in these bars as the hand and mind struggle to dart and jab in the prescribed directions.) The whole of this wonderful introduction, based on various permutations of diminished chords followed by resolutions, accents the very nature of life and death. In the winter of our existence each of us will die, ripped from the branch of the tree of life by a cold gust of wind. This can happen at a moment's notice, and in no particular sequence related to logic or merit. Schubert's achievement here is that he finds a musical means of illustrating the fitful nature of leaf-fall as a metaphor for the random selection process of death itself. Here the traveller focuses his attention on the fortunes of a particular leaf as a symbol of the survival or extinction of his hopes; as we are buffeted through life, our happiness depends on a play of the dice, a turn of the cards, a fall of the leaf.

The fermata on the dominant at the end of four bars of introduction provides a momentary hope of a return to a normal harmonic world, but Schubert is set on a course where, in John Reed's words, 'music renounces pulse, tune and tonality, all the usual marks of stability and order'. As often happens in this cycle, the first appearance of the vocal line is accompanied by a repeat of part of the introduction. It is significant that, in the poem's second line, the composer has changed Müller's 'Noch ein buntes Blatt' ('still one many-coloured leaf') to 'Manches bunte Blatt' ('many a coloured leaf'). The more trees there are within the traveller's gaze, the more leaves there are to fall, and Schubert has already created a musical image to begin the song that paints a freefall of random profusion. 'Manches bunte Blatt zu sehn' is harmonized in a courtly phrase, suddenly legato, which closes in E flat major, the tonic key. It has taken eight bars to have any such intimation of the home tonality and even in the depth of the traveller's confusion and anguish he (like Schubert, we suspect, in similar circumstances) is able to take momentary pleasure in nature's beauty. Disruption immediately follows in b. 8 with the resumption of the staccatissimo quavers, dry as withered leaves. This time they rise in the left hand, rather than falling, a tiny bridge to an exact repeat (for 'Und ich bleibe vor den Bäumen') of the by now

[3] The impassioned repetitions of 'Wein' in Schubert's setting are not reflected in the printed poem.

familiar diminished-chord quavers of the opening. The harmonization of 'Oftmals in Gedanken stehn' (bb. 11–13) begins with the same music as its equivalent phrase in the strophe's second line but it suddenly veers in another direction. Instead of a cadence into E flat there is a dramatic interruption as the word 'Gedanken' settles on an F sharp at b. 12, a sudden and complete stillness which suggests the feverish marshalling of concentration. All the traveller's mental resources bear down on the single leaf that will occupy his attention in the next strophe. The hands of the pianist, drawn into the obsession as accomplices, come together on a dotted minim F sharp an octave apart.

As soon as this held note edges up a semitone to G (b. 13) the music takes off in a shuddering series of bobbing staccatissimo chords descriptive of nervous jitters. The traveller has placed the outcome of his entire life on the fate of an arbitrarily chosen leaf. If this is a game it is one in deadly earnest, like Russian roulette. As already remarked in the commentary on *Frühlingstraum* (No. 11), this is reminiscent of the O. Henry story *The Last Leaf* (1907) where a young girl, dangerously ill with pneumonia, believes she will die if the last of five leaves blows off the vine visible from her Greenwich Village window. Without her knowing, an old man paints a leaf on the wall, and the power of auto-suggestion allows the girl to survive the winter because her 'last leaf' remains in view.

The prevalence of diminished-chord harmonies and the lack of a tonal centre make for increased suspense. There are no fewer than five repetitions, like a nervous tic, of the same motif – A flat to G in the treble, then two jumping thirds across the bar line followed by A flat to G in the bass. This mad, machine-like music accompanies the lines 'Schaue nach dem einen Blatte, / Hänge meine Hoffnung dran' (bb. 14–18). The traveller obviously has only one thing on his mind: he has reduced his whole tragedy to a tiny focal point the size of a leaf. There is a momentary move into G major at b. 18, but the dominant of C minor is no resting place; it merely facilitates a further tightening of the loose screws as the same process is repeated a third higher under 'Spielt der Wind mit meinem Blatte'. This is an example of the tension-increasing device known as 'Terzensteigerung'. 'Zittr' ich, was ich zittern kann' moves on to the chord of B flat, the dominant of the home key. This conventional progression is ornamented in a grotesque manner: the interlude that follows has a bass line that veers madly between B flat and its neighbouring C flat for two bars (bb. 22–4). The first of these is in the spiky quavers which have been musically descriptive of freezing weather since Purcell's time (and the Cold Scene in *King Arthur*). But deluded fear is even worse than cold. These biting and aggressive chords give way to a bar of semiquaver oscillations in the pianist's right hand, as the whole of the traveller's body begins to shake involuntarily ('Zittr' ich, was ich zittern kann'). Whatever awaits him in terms of mental disintegration, we have reached the most physically unbalanced moment of the cycle.

There is a moment of respite after the shuddering bar – four quavers of silence in b. 24 – before jabbing quavers across the bar line begin again, this time C flat to A flat in three different registers of the piano. These notes form a musical gateway into the tonic minor, and the traveller's worst-case scenario – the possibility of *his* leaf falling to the ground. Left-hand quavers in staccato octaves are chased by ricocheting semiquavers in the right hand, tracing the imagined leaf-fall in a variation of an E flat minor scale (bb. 26–9). The vocal line at 'Ach, und fällt das Blatt zu Boden' ironically rises to its highest point for 'fällt', an E flat held for a dotted crotchet as if postulating something which stands out as a horrible eventuality, and then traces a wayward progress, leaflike, which touches the ground as the word 'Boden' falls an octave – C flat in the middle of the stave to C flat low in the voice. But we have not yet hit rock-bottom. The piano continues its fluttering alternation of staccato semiquavers an octave apart, as if wafting the leaf to deeper and more mysterious regions, the depths of despair in the traveller's mind. For the first time in the song frenetic quavers yield to a slower tempo (marked 'Etwas langsamer') and at the beginning of the phrase 'Fällt mit ihm die Hoffnung ab' the voice touches the lowest note

'Träumen sich manches, was sie nicht haben' the music moves into dreamlike regions built on a pedal A, first inversions of the tonic chord and A^7. The second inversion of D minor is a prelude to the revelation that these dreams will not last into the morning. The flattened C natural on 'was sie nicht haben' is touchingly needy, as if the traveller momentarily sympathizes with the have-nots in the light of his own desolation (another instance of Schubert being more forgiving than Müller). In this section the rumbling semiquavers float into the right hand in the inverted world of the subconscious, a mirror image of life. There is nothing exceptional in either the melody or harmony, but the composer has built a slow-moving structure in blocks of harmony, the cumulative effect of which has the grandeur of Bruckner-in-the-bud. The traveller is invested with the majesty of a prophet expounding his credo in the wilderness.

The cadence of 'Und morgen früh ist Alles zerflossen' (bb. 17–18) is one of the cycle's magical moments. The evanescent half-light of a new day is announced in the tonic minor (b. 16) and, as the vocal line descends into the regions of banal reality, the pianist's right hand surfaces from the subconscious to meet it, the coming together facilitated by a 'ritard'. Under the word 'zerflossen' the left hand plunges deep into the void and rumbles in tuneless antithesis to the sweet harmonies of dreams. The villagers must now rise to meet the realities of day. At the other end of the keyboard spectrum a new section of the song is announced by right-hand mezzo staccato Ds in quaver triplets (b. 19), an inverted pedal that shelters the harmonic movement beneath it, a roof of notes suggesting domestic cosiness. The whole of this section can be sung with the greatest sincerity, as if the traveller would dearly love to be part of the villagers' dreams. In some great performances (including Pears and Britten) this is the case; as we have seen, maliciousness and sarcasm do not come easily to Schubert. The music next moves into G major, the magic realm of the subdominant so dear to this composer.

But there is something more disturbing here too, something about the insistence of those repeated notes which recalls *Die liebe Farbe* D795/16 in *Die schöne Müllerin*, a song that is poetic while being heavy with ironic sarcasm. In that case the word 'liebe' is really meant to be 'böse', and in *Im Dorfe* the sweetness of the traveller's response seems similarly loaded. Can it be that the gentle repetitions between bb. 19 and 22 of 'Je nun' and 'Und hoffen' (such beautiful music) are hidden taunts? Heard in this light, all those Ds suggest the sarcasm of someone harping on a theme and determined to drive it home; home, of course, is far too refined to contain any dirty linen. At the culmination of the phrase beginning 'Doch wieder zu finden' we return to D major with the domestic resonance of the word 'Kissen' (pillow, b. 26); this sets the seal on the irony – a discussion of this refinement of bedding seems almost obscene in the context of the traveller's homelessness. A two-bar piano interlude makes a spiralling descent (bb. 27–8) back to the Land of Nod, and the predictability of this music is an inspired depiction of the uninspired cycle of bourgeois routine, where villagers expect that their lovely, unfinished dreams will continue when they next take to their beds. Then again, some travellers would long for the comfort of fresh bedlinen and would bid goodbye to this secure life with the greatest regret. The colour of this whole section depends on how performers choose to 'produce' it; as it happens, the music can encompass either viewpoint.

The final section of the song is announced by rumbling basses of A and B flat and an A^7 chord with a bitter edge (bb. 29–30), and this sets up the return of the music of the opening at 'Bellt mich nur fort'. The motif here serves to depict the growling dogs. The recapitulation has been beautifully engineered and the traveller's message gains enormously in stature. His renunciation of the dreamworld of these sleepers is something toweringly majestic. At 'Ich bin zu Ende' (bb. 35–6) the rise of a semitone (and thus the suggestion of a new phase in life) is especially eloquent, as is the change of harmony and the shift into the distant regions of the flattened submediant (B flat major) for 'mit allen Träumen'. Most impressive of all is the baroque breadth of cadence at 'Was will ich unter den Schläfern säumen?' (bb. 37–40), suddenly supported by broad chords of dotted minims and crotchets. There is a plagal flavour to this music that suggests the organ, the church and the Schubert Masses, and it would be tempting to read into this setting (and the even more grandiose cadence with which the song closes) a sign of the composer's renunciation of the conventional religious faith of his fathers and their dreams of everlasting life. It certainly speaks to all artists, black sheep of the family or those at odds with society who have come from safe, small-minded backgrounds that they have found necessary to leave for survival's sake. Keeping company with the sleepers becomes impossible for those who have to go on a significant journey. With the line 'Ich bin zu Ende mit allen Träumen' (bb. 39–42) Schubert cannot resist an ascent into the very dream-world that he renounces (another breathtaking shift into B flat major) and the repeat of 'Was will ich unter den Schläfern säumen?' provides the most magisterial of cadences. Despite the fact that the traveller says he will not linger, the word 'säumen' is illustrated by a vowel elongation of five beats. Never has the traveller appeared more like an abdicating monarch, infinitely noble and grandly mournful. Here we briefly sense that he is sorry to go and that in all acts of walking away from the past there are regrets. Nevertheless, in the postlude the left-hand accompaniment plunges by stages ever lower into the bass clef while an immutable D major chord pulsates in triplets in the right. The inexorable descent emphasizes that this traveller now longs for nothing less than the total release of the grave; being buried alive in the provinces is a feather-bedded option no longer open to him.

First edition:	Published as Op. 89 no. 17 by Tobias Haslinger, Vienna on 30 December 1828 (P185)
First known performance:	22 January 1829 *Abend-Unterhaltung* of the Gesellschaft der Musikfreunde, Vienna. Soloist: Johann Karl Schoberlechner (see Waidelich/Hilmar Dokumente I No. 685 for full concert programme). *Der Lindenbaum* D911/5 was also performed
Subsequent editions:	Peters: Vol. 1/102; AGA XX 533: Vol. 9/56; NSA IV: Vol. 4a/169; Bärenreiter: Vol. 3/126
Bibliography:	Youens 1991, pp. 251–60
Arrangement:	Arr. Franz Liszt (1811–1886) for solo piano, no. 12 of *Winterreise* (1838–9) [*see* TRANSCRIPTIONS]
Discography and timing:	Fischer-Dieskau III 2[17] 3'38
	Pears–Britten 4'12
	Hyperion I 30[17]
	Hyperion II 34[10] 3'55 Matthias Goerne

←— *Letzte Hoffnung* D911/16   *Der stürmische Morgen* D911/18 —→

XVIII Der STÜRMISCHE MORGEN   The stormy morning
OP. 89 NO. 18, **D911/18** [H640]
D minor

(19 bars)

Wie hat der Sturm zerissen
Des Himmels graues Kleid!
Die Wolkenfetzen flattern
Umher in mattem Streit.

    Und rote Feuerflammen
Ziehn zwischen ihnen hin.
Das nenn' ich einen Morgen
So recht nach meinem Sinn!

    Mein Herz sieht an dem Himmel
Gemalt sein eignes Bild—
Es ist nichts als der Winter,
Der Winter kalt und wild!

How the storm has torn apart
The grey mantle of the sky!
Tattered clouds fly about
In weary conflict.

    And red flames
Dart between them.
This is what I call
A morning after my own heart.

    My heart sees its own image
Painted in the sky.
It is nothing but winter—
Winter, cold and savage.

Autograph of *Der stürmische Morgen*, 1827.

This is the thirty-eighth of Schubert's forty-six Müller solo settings (1823, 1827 and 1828). See the poet's biography for a chronological list of all the Müller settings.

This is the shortest song in the cycle and among the most energetic. It follows hard on the heels of *Im Dorfe* (No. 17) and Schubert obviously intended the tonalities of D major and D minor to be linked in ironic conjunction. The change from major to minor is here an inversion of normal musical imagery: in *Im Dorfe*, the nocturnal sounds of barking dogs and the traveller's disdain for the village sleepers had been cast in the gentleness of the major key; in *Der stürmische Morgen* the realities of a newly breaking day are depicted with grim relish in the minor. We have already encountered the same harmonic axis in the switch between dreaming (major) and waking (minor) in *Frühlingstraum* (No. 11). In *Einsamkeit* (No. 12) the traveller had complained of the relative mildness of the weather; he felt less wretched when surrounded by storms. In *Der stürmische Morgen* his wish for stormier surroundings is granted. He encounters a morning that he tells us is 'after my own heart', and for a brief moment of manic delight this energizes him and the music. The insertion of a quick song is highly necessary at this point in the cycle. Every composer knows the importance of varying pace and tonality to keep the listener's attention. Not since *Die Wetterfahne* (No. 2) have we heard such wind-whipped energy. In that song much of the piano writing had been doubled in the hands an octave apart, and here there is even more persistent doubling of voice and accompaniment. Apart from the explosive cadence at the end of the introduction, the hands are linked together for seven and a half bars, and the vocal line also hugs the same note. This device depicts the solitary state of the traveller, but it also implies resolution and a marshalling of resources. The traveller finds a new (if temporary) upbeat determination, and the weather is also determined on its course; howling winds blowing over open wastes suggest doubled octaves in the Schubertian musical vocabulary. The lack of any harmonic filler emphasizes the bareness of the landscape, and the impossibility of taking cover from these cruel gusts of wind.

The introduction is made up of two contrasting ideas – essentially an ascent followed by a descent, as inevitable as manic delight followed by an aftermath of depression. In the first bar a flourish of four semiquavers and two staccato quavers is followed by a sequence a third higher, an example of the so-called 'Terzensteigerung'. This opening strain is ambiguous in its singular lack of harmonic detail. We hear an implication of the major key (the third beat of the bar starting pointedly on an F sharp) but, at the same time, the subdominant key of G minor is suggested, where the F sharp is heard as its leading note. There follows a rush of eight slurred semiquavers in an ascending chromatic scale beneath a ceiling of Ds. This is a close variant of the chord pattern which introduced *Rückblick* (No. 8). The apex of the phrase is reached with a sforzato crotchet on a diminished chord: B – D – F – G sharp in both hands, the first of the diminished chords we hear in the song. There are only three such chords possible in terms of chromatic harmony, and in *Der stürmische Morgen*, uniquely in *Winterreise*, the composer uses them all. After a quaver's rest as short as a snatched breath we glimpse the other side of the coin as the proposal is rebutted, and antithesis pursues thesis. There is another pair of flourishes, this time falling semiquaver triplets which land first on a B at the beginning of b. 3, then a staccatissimo A. This last note serves as the launching-pad for the right hand's leap of nearly two octaves into the treble for a snatched cadence – an unequivocal V–I which suggests whiplash violence and demonic energy.

The vocal line is not modelled on the introduction but continues its mood. Before something as large as the sky is torn apart, holes first have to made in it. The violence of the verb 'zerrissen' is depicted in two stages – first by the dagger-edged staccatissimo at 'Des Himmels graues Kleid!' (b. 5) and then by the diminished seventh chord (here symbolic of harmony rent asunder, and the heavens falling apart) at 'Die Wolkenfetzen flattern' (b. 6). Displaced accents off the beat on 'Umher in mattem Streit' indicate a tug-of-war between the elements. The fall of more than an octave, E flat down to D, for the repeat of 'Umher in mattem Streit' (illustrative of exhaustion as a concomitant of warlike struggle) sets off one of the cycle's rare virtuoso outbursts of pianism, a swirling succession of downwardly spiralling triplets based on the diminished chord encountered in the song's introduction. To underline the idea of conflict, of currents of air meeting head-on with stormy consequences, the left-hand accompaniment, in contrary motion to the right, hammers out incisive quavers in a reckless collision course. They meet on the A below middle C and this sets off a clap of thunder, another of those snatched V–I cadences. This loud outburst marks the halfway point of the song.

The middle section is a vigorous march, firmly rooted in the submediant (B flat). In its tonality as well as the robust character of its hammered dotted rhythms, this marche militaire-like passage recalls the Schulze setting *Lebensmut* D883 from 1826. The mention of red flames ('rote Feuerflammen') is unusual in this cycle which is otherwise bereft of the imagery of colour. *Lebensmut*, however, had a purple patch where the poet's heart was tinged with blood ('blutig färben'). 'So recht nach meinem Sinn!' is followed by defiantly repeated B flats (end of b. 13) as if to emphasize: 'Yes, this is what I like!' This B flat is the pivotal note that unlocks the key of the closing section, another visit to a diminished-seventh broken chord in the vocal line. 'Mein Herz sieht an dem Himmel / Gemalt sein eignes Bild' has exactly the same music as the third and fourth lines of the first strophe, a rather original means of binding the threads of a semi-strophic song together in the interests of airtight unity. This means that new music has to be found for the final two lines, and here Schubert excels himself in an exciting pair of collaborative bars where both voice and piano are at full tilt. In *Letzte Hoffnung* (No. 16) we have already noted music reminiscent of Purcellian shiver (the Cold Scene from *King Arthur*), and the setting of 'Es ist nichts als der Winter' depicts the hoary old man in a similarly age-old way. (Schubert could not have known Purcell's music but, as Deryck Cooke points out in *The Language of Music* (1959), this kind of imagery has been somehow shared by composers throughout the ages.) At b. 16 no fewer than nine repetitions of the same insistent chord unmask winter in his true, grizzled colours. This is the last of the three diminished chords available to the composer (here it is based on E flat, with the voice holding to that note in bleak triumph for 'Es ist nichts als der Winter' and dropping an octave from its perch only for the last syllable). This exploration of the different possibilities of diminished harmony has been exhaustive and has finally resulted in recognition, revelation and something that passes for exultation. This fulmination briefly resolves on a second-inversion G minor chord, and another set of shivering chords (A^7 in first inversion) hammers home the same words in less equivocal, even gleeful, harmony.

But a musical echo from a musical past much nearer than Purcell reveals to us that there is terror here also, especially in the context of the song's D minor tonality. Whenever Schubert uses this key in a dramatic context we suspect the ghost of the Commendatore, the shadow of the statue from Mozart's *Don Giovanni*, and the most famous diminished seventh in musical history. Schubert reverses Mozart's progression (A^7 to diminished seventh) but we hear this famous crushing chord (albeit in a different inversion) in *Der stürmische Morgen*. This statue-music depicts winter itself – something huge and white and implacable – as it comes to claim the traveller, hence the involuntary tremors. All this is masterfully planned as an extended upbeat to the final line of the poem, which is spat out in the same falling melodic outline that has ended the first verse (at 'in mattem Streit'). The postlude is a superb commentary on the words 'kalt und wild', but we have heard this music before – another collision course of downwardly rolling arpeggios and upwardly grasping left-hand quavers. And once again the verse snaps shut with a perfect cadence, an A major chord crashing onto a D minor thunderclap.

First edition:	Published as Op. 89 no. 18 by Tobias Haslinger, Vienna on 30 December 1828 (P186)
Subsequent editions:	Peters: Vol. 1/106; AGA XX 534: Vol. 9/60; NSA IV: Vol. 4a/174; Bärenreiter: Vol. 3/130
Bibliography:	Youens 1991, pp. 261–5
Arrangement:	Arr. Franz Liszt (1811–1886) for solo piano, no. 11 of *Winterreise* (1838–9) [*see* TRANSCRIPTIONS]

Discography and timing: Fischer-Dieskau III 2¹⁸ 0'53
Pears–Britten 0'55
Hyperion I 30¹⁸
Hyperion II 34¹¹ 0'51 Matthias Goerne

⟵ *Im Dorfe* D911/17 *Täuschung* D911/19 ⟶

XIX TÄUSCHUNG Illusion

OP. 89 NO. 19, **D911/19** [H641]
A major

(43 bars)

Ein Licht tanzt freundlich vor mir her;	**A** light dances cheerfully before me.
Ich folg' ihm nach die Kreuz und Quer;	I follow it this way and that;
Ich folg' ihm gern und seh's ihm an,	I follow it gladly, knowing
Dass es verlockt den Wandersmann.	That it lures the wanderer.
Ach, wer wie ich so elend ist,	Ah, a man as wretched as I
Gibt gern sich hin der bunten List,	Gladly yields to the beguiling gleam
Die hinter Eis und Nacht und Graus	That reveals to him, beyond ice, night and terror,
Ihm weist ein helles, warmes Haus,	A bright, warm house,
Und eine liebe Seele drin—	And a beloved soul within
Nur Täuschung ist für mich Gewinn!	Pure delusion is a boon to me!

This is the thirty-ninth of Schubert's forty-six Müller solo settings (1823, 1827 and 1828).
See the poet's biography for a chronological list of all the Müller settings.

Why should this particular melody have come into Schubert's mind when he read Müller's text? On one level the answer is simple. This is the only instance in all his lieder when the composer openly quotes and recycles a substantial melody from his operatic output, in this case *Alfonso und Estrella* D732, written in 1821/2. (This is quite apart from the arias from *Claudine von Villa Bella* D239 that have entered the Schubert lied repertory thanks to their inclusion in the Peters Edition.) The second act of *Alfonso und Estrella* begins with an extended scene between the eponymous hero, Alfonso, and his father, the exiled king of Leon. (The AGA incorrectly gives his name as Troila, but the eighth-century Spanish king on whom the character was modelled was Freula, and Froila is now the accepted spelling.) The section which includes the *Täuschung* music is a set piece and not part of the dramatic action. Alfonso begs Froila to sing him the old lay of the Cloud Maiden, a Lorelei-like figure who inhabits the wild mountain terrain. In this ballad the seductive witch is encountered by a hunter who is struck by her devastating beauty; he gladly accepts her wheedling invitation to her fairy-tale castle that can be seen at the mountain summit. Once he has climbed the hazardous peaks, maiden and castle evaporate in the mist and the hunter falls to his death. The inclusion of such a ballad in an opera was rather a novel practice in 1822, but later composers were to make much of it, including Wagner in *Der fliegende Holländer* (premiered in 1843). It is noteworthy that another Viennese creation, Lehár's *Die lustige Witwe* (1905), contains 'Vilja', a ballad of a supernatural 'witch of the wood' ('Es lebt' eine Vilja, ein Waldmägdelein').

This story of someone being lured to his death by false promises and the beauties of a dangerously deceitful woman has obvious parallels with the fate of the traveller. The idea of Müller's dancing light ('Ein Licht tanzt freundlich vor mir her') and the ethereal dancing presence of the Cloud Maiden in Schober's libretto ('Sie tanzte über Felsenstufen / Durch dunkle Schlünde leicht ihm vor' – 'She danced lightly in front of him, / Over rocky steps, through dark gorges') are similar enough to have jogged the composer's memory about the work composed five years earlier. However, it is Schubert's usual practice when confronted by words recalling an earlier composition not to quote from that work *in extenso*. He prefers to draw on his own private library of tonal analogues (a musical phrase or idea that is the equivalent of a verbal phrase or idea) to write newly minted music. Thus similar verbal imagery in different song texts is subtly and intricately related in musical terms but, apart from celebrated appearances of song melodies in chamber music, hardly ever by deliberate quotation. An example of the normal relationship between songs with poetic ideas in common is the shared water imagery of floating semiquaver melismas in *Irrlicht* (No. 9), *Auf dem Wasser zu singen* D774 and *Des Fischers Liebesglück* D933. It is extremely unlikely that the composer deliberately crafted a cross reference between these three songs; any similarities are interesting chiefly because they show us how his creative mind functioned when confronted with similar verbal ideas, and the amazing consistency of his response to words throughout his output.

Many-layered must have been the thoughts running through the composer's mind when he decided to lift a chunk from an opera. Chief among these is the fact that his whole musical life had been governed by the illusion that if only he worked hard enough he could become a successful opera composer. Indeed, it might be said that this is what he wished for most ardently in his career, and that his failure as a composer of grand opera cost him more pain in his life than almost anything else. *Alfonso und Estrella* was a work embarked on by the friends Schubert and Schober in a bout of defiant (and ill-founded) optimism (there is even a theory that they were lovers at the time – see *Liedlexikon* 2012, p. 624). This was despite the warnings of others in the composer's circle, notably Vogl, who is said to have remarked that Schubert had 'lost his way' – an interesting comment in the light of *Täuschung*. Whether or not the composer came to agree with Vogl's verdict is doubtful. However, it was an irony probably not lost on Schubert that by quoting from *Alfonso* in *Winterreise*, Vogl, the cycle's first notable interpreter, would be forced to sing a fragment of the very opera he had condemned. Other words in Müller's poem evoke the world of opera, though only by chance. 'Haus' is commonly used in German, as in English, for a theatre; and the phrase 'ein helles, warmes Haus' can be read to denote the bright lights of success and the warm enthusiasm of the public. This is surely what any aspiring opera composer would long for; and yet for most of his career Schubert had pressed his nose to the window from out in the cold, to look in at other – and mostly lesser – men's operatic successes.

Another resonance concerns the librettist Schober, who is said to have been the 'seducer' (an epithet used by others in the Schubert circle) who encouraged the composer to visit a prostitute in 1822. This was at a time when Schober's influence on the composer was at its height. *Alfonso und Estrella* was a newly composed work and its fortunes still hung in the balance. The ballad's storyline of a young man sweet-talked into his death had only an abstract meaning for the composer in 1822, but by 1827 the significance was all too obvious. The word 'Täuschung' thus seems to stand for 'Enttäuschung' ('disappointment') in Schubert's bad luck across the board in his business and personal dealings. His enormous faith in *Alfonso und Estrella* and its librettist was based on illusion, and here it comes back to haunt the winter traveller as if that poor man was somehow the composer himself.

In the opera, Froila's aria begins in G major; gentle harp arpeggios suggest the king's skill on that instrument. There is nothing yet which sounds like *Täuschung*, although the dancing rhythms of flute and oboe resemble the repeated octaves heard in the song's introduction. As the narration turns to the enchantress's seductive patter the music modulates into E flat major, but it is only when we enter the magical realms of B major (pivoting around an enharmonic E flat/D sharp to do so) that there is a blossoming of the melody familiar to lovers of *Winterreise* (on 'Er folgte ihrer Stimme Rufen').

Schubert chooses A major as his key in the context of the cycle. This harks back to *Frühlingstraum* (No. 11), another song of dreamlike illusion with a lilting melody that has more complicated overtones than first meet the ear. A succession of mezzo staccato Es in a tripping alternation of crotchets and quavers provides a ceiling beneath which the left hand plays a jaunty succession of upwardly sweeping triplet figurations (marked 'staccatissimo') leading towards an accented crotchet on the second beat of each bar. (In *Alfonso und Estrella* this music is given to the bassoon.) There is a charming right-hand lift from E to E sharp in b. 9 that occasions a brief modulation to the relative minor of F sharp. The suddenness of the return to A major at b. 11 is the first of a series of slightly disjointed jolts to show that underneath the superficial Viennese charm of *Ländler* or waltz lies something wild and disturbing. Susan Youens has interestingly described the song as a *danse macabre* for a ball in Bedlam. Schubert has changed the gravely lyrical music of a noble king into the babbling of someone deranged. Time has indeed moved on for him.

In some ways the song is a companion piece of *Irrlicht*: both talk of more or less the same thing – a will-o'-the-wisp light dancing before the eyes. But the music here is very different from the mercurial waywardness of that earlier song. It seems driven and obsessive, yet strangely fixed in one place – in the traveller's deluded brain perhaps – rather than subject to the movement ('nach die Kreuz and Quer') suggested by the words. The right hand occasionally makes jabbing little excursions into the higher reaches of the piano, only to return to home base as soon as possible. The rhyming couplets of the ten-line verse, a form found only in this song within the cycle, also help to suggest the doggerel of the deranged and damned. The third and fourth lines of the poem are set to more or less the same eerily jaunty music as the first and second. At 'Ach, wer wie ich so elend ist' (from b. 22) we move into A minor as if to suggest that the traveller is momentarily in touch with some aspect of reality in his plight, a glimmer of self-awareness. (The melodic line from here on, incidentally, is all new invention, and not to be found in the opera.) There is a predictable move to the dominant (E major) at 'Gibt gern sich hin der bunten List' (bb. 24–7) as the music resumes its former major-key garb of naive simplicity. This ironic use of Viennese musical charm, horribly misplaced, reaches its climax in a bridge passage for both voice and piano that flirts chromatically around E major, and ornaments and prevaricates around the return to A major in a teasing fashion suggestive of Johann Strauss the younger at his most *gemütlich*. The pianist is required to make a slight rubato in an oh-so-Viennese manner to edge the music into the tonic key after the word 'Graus', so that the return to the home key occurs most elegantly on the words 'Ihm weist' (bb. 30–31). It is as if the musician were taking part in the malicious act of pointing the poor deluded traveller in the wrong direction – smiling, as it were, while sending him to his execution. The enthusiastic mention of a bright warm house seems in this context a tauntingly cruel jest. The closing three lines of the poem are set as if we had returned to the beginning, but of course three lines of poetry, instead of four, don't permit the symmetry of the first page. This results in the song sounding prematurely curtailed in an unbalanced manner that is a mirror of the traveller's unhinged state of mind. In b. 40 the piano's echo of 'ist für mich Gewinn', with its suddenly hectic leap upwards (a fifth in octaves), is emblematic of snatching at straws. Pathetically grateful, the traveller is content to take the first option and close the deal (and the song), even if it means being short-changed and betrayed. Never before has a seemingly innocuous dance piece had such a hidden agenda, where images of happiness and warmth mean their exact opposite, and where every aspect of music normally taken to be the epitome of congenial fellowship emphasizes a sorry state of loneliness and despair.

A passage in Müller's *Tagebuch* for 12 November 1815 recounts the experience that possibly inspired this poem. The young poet's beloved, Luise Hensel, attended a ball to which he had not been invited, and he resolved to spy on what was happening from the outside. He fantasized about the scenario before he got there: 'I had imagined it all to be truly romantic; the dance music, the bright lights and the smart gentlemen and coiffed ladies who, here and there, appeared at the window – below in the darkness, the unfortunate lover.'[1] It is remarkable, or a remarkable coincidence, that Schubert provides dance music for *Täuschung* while nothing in the poem itself refers to a social occasion. But then the composer might often have felt like a voyeur at the many balls where, seated at the piano and rooted to the spot, he was expected to provide the music for young lovers determined to enjoy themselves.

First edition:	Published as Op. 89 no. 19 by Tobias Haslinger, Vienna on 30 December 1828 (P187)
Subsequent editions:	Peters: Vol. 1/108; AGA XX 535: Vol. 9/62; NSA IV: Vol. 4a/176; Bärenreiter: Vol. 3/132
Bibliography:	Müller 1903, p. 43 Newbould 1997, pp. 304–5 Youens 1991, pp. 266–71
Arrangement:	Arr. Franz Liszt (1811–1886) for solo piano, no. 9 of *Winterreise* (1838–9) [*see* TRANSCRIPTIONS]
Discography and timing:	Fischer-Dieskau III 2[19] 1'31 Pears–Britten 1'10 Hyperion I 30[19] Hyperion II 34[12] 1'18 Matthias Goerne

← *Der stürmische Morgen* D911/18   *Der Wegweiser* D911/20 →

XX Der WEGWEISER   The signpost
OP. 89 NO. 20, **D911/20** [H642]
G minor

(83 bars)

[1] The original German for this passage reads 'Ich dachte es mir recht romantisch aus; die Tanzmusik, die hellen Lichter, und die geputzten Herren und Damenköpfe, die sich hie und da an den Scheiben sehen lassen – unten in der Finsterniss der unglückliche Liebhaber . . .'

Was vermeid' ich denn die Wege,	**W**hy do I avoid the roads
Wo die andern Wandrer gehn,[1]	That other travellers take,
Suche mir versteckte Stege	And seek hidden paths
Durch verschneite Felsenhöhn?	Over the rocky, snow-clad heights?
Habe ja doch nichts begangen,	Yet I have done no wrong,
Dass ich Menschen sollte scheun—	That I should shun mankind.
Welch ein törichtes Verlangen	What foolish yearning
Treibt mich in die Wüstenein?	Drives me into the wilderness?
Weiser stehen auf den Wegen,[2]	Signposts stand on the roads,
Weisen auf die Städte zu,	Pointing towards the towns;
Und ich wandre sonder Massen,[3]	And I wander on, relentlessly,
Ohne Ruh', und suche Ruh'.	Restless, and yet seeking rest.
Einen Weiser seh' ich stehen	I see a signpost standing
Unverrückt vor meinem Blick;	Immovable before my eyes;
Eine Strasse muss ich gehen,	I must travel a road
Die noch Keiner ging zurück.	From which no man has ever returned.

This is the fortieth of Schubert's forty-six Müller solo settings (1823, 1827 and 1828).
See the poet's biography for a chronological list of all the Müller settings.

The change of mood between *Täuschung* (No. 19) and this song could not be more extreme. The moment of mad and inappropriate merriment is over and we must resume the journey. For all its dancing movement, the previous song, strangely surrealist, has felt somewhat stationary, as if the traveller were running on the spot, Alice-like, to keep still. To keep the journey on course, Schubert now engineers a return to the time signature and tempo marking of the opening song, *Gute Nacht* (No. 1), with its innate 'gehende[r] Bewegung'. In rehearsal, performers do well to measure the tempo of one song against the other and resist any temptation to take the later song at a more dragging pace in the hope of deepening its significance. On the other hand, similar tempi in *Gute Nacht* and this song cannot disguise a huge change of character in the traveller after the trials of his journey. The chords of the opening ritornello in *Gute Nacht* seem effulgently euphonious when compared to the spare textures of *Der Wegweiser*, a song as bare as the wooden post of its title, and also emblematic of someone thin and ill, stripped to the bone mentally (if not quite physically) and humbled by hardship. The broad sweep of the opening song's vocal line now seems almost imperious in retrospect; most of *Der Wegweiser* lies within a much less ambitious musical compass – indeed a compass that points in only one direction. The traveller, having been rejected by the world, is now locked into his own ascetic world, the self-obsessed monasticism of the inveterate loner. We hear this in the frugality of the part-writing, where every mezzo staccato quaver is made to count like a drop of water in the wilderness. He shuns the company of others and makes a rod for his own back, as the text tells

---

[1] Müller writes 'Wo die *andren* Wandrer gehn'.
[2] Müller writes 'Weiser stehen auf den *Strassen*'. Schubert's alteration suppresses the poet's rhyme, but the composer's supremely sensitive ear for language seems to have found something unsuitably banal about the word 'Strassen' in this context.
[3] 'Sonder' is archaic German for 'ohne' [without].

us, by avoiding the easy paths and deliberately choosing the difficult ones. As if to illustrate this, the music stops and starts, shifts its footing and redefines its direction, culminating in the realization that the only signpost of any importance is the one that leads to the grave. All this is a hollow mockery of the determined march that the song purports to be. There is nothing random about this stage of the voyage of self-discovery – it all seems 'written', and the traveller is a passive object of fate. This starkly contrasts with his unstoppable personal energy in *Gute Nacht*, music that flowed from first to last in a torrent of sound and emotion, sure footed in comparison with the cycle's subsequent music of stagger and stumble.

Another earlier song comes to mind, *Gefrorne Tränen* (No. 3). *Der Wegweiser* is the only other song in the cycle that contains contrapuntal part-writing, particularly in terms of the independence of the bass line which suggests a string quartet rather than a piano. Apart from its searing emotion, Schubert never wrote a song more technically pure and perfect than this, an achievement as astonishing as the construction of a miniature timepiece, hermetically sealed and flawless, and thus, paradoxically, impervious to time. The cogs and wheels of musical science are here deployed to interact with such precision that there is no possibility of any margin of error, even of a single semiquaver. This Bach-like perfection and lucidity (which even Schubert must have worked hard to achieve), when married with Romantic imagery and shorn of its religious context, is eerie in its effect. The traveller's end is preordained, but not his salvation. Even if his trudge falters, the directional pull of fate never wavers. As he sings he is transported, in both senses: sometimes the music is so rapt, grave and almost serene, that it is clear that he already belongs to another world; at the same time he is inexorably driven along tracks that have been programmed to end in the charnel house, and we hear bouts of agitated anguish. At this point in the journey the poor traveller, reduced to the status of a helpless refugee, is the victim, rather than the cause, of the pauses and delays that shunt him into wasteland sidings. He may think it is his decision to choose certain routes over others, but fate has decided for him. As he is moved on to the next stage of the pitiless journey, the ingenious gliding harmonic changes of the song's last verse are like the ominous switching of railway points, ensuring no deviation from the timetable of death.

The melodic line of the introduction begins with a two-semiquaver upbeat (G and A harmonized in sixths) leading to the repetition of B flats as part of four repeated G minor chords. In these insistent mezzo staccato quavers we hear the ghost of the opening of *Gute Nacht*. The melodic shape also recalls the opening of the C minor Impromptu for piano D899/1 where a similarly ambulatory melody is transcribed in crotchets, rather than quavers. The second full bar ends with an exhausted drooping minor third. (So far this is music ordinary enough to have been composed by any of Schubert's contemporaries.) Suddenly a canonic imitation at the fifth below begins in the left hand and we might imagine that the music had been composed in an earlier century; this time, the motif in mezzo staccato quavers is harmonized by a diminished seventh chord that moves to a French sixth and thence to a V–I cadence, ornamented with a tiny baroque flourish. This is old music and weary, but the underlying Romantic angst is unmistakable. We expect the voice to make its appearance at the end of the fourth bar in order to take part in the return to the tonic. But no – the pianist reaches the tonic alone in b. 5 and the voice begins, wrong-footed from the start, only at the end of this bar. There could be no better illustration of the verb 'vermeiden' ('to avoid') in the poem's opening. The vocal line opens with what at first seemed the slightly unpromising melody of the opening, but thanks to Schubert's sorcery this potential banality is transformed into something searingly memorable. Those four repeated notes that originally seemed merely an accompanimental figure immediately become central to the melody's powerfully tragic stature. The little finger of the right hand doubles the voice part almost entirely. This normally deadens the vocal colour, but here it adds to the sense of urgency as if the pianist were charged with policing the traveller and keeping him on the prescribed paths. At 'Suche mir versteckte Stege / Durch verschneite Felsenhöhn?' (bb. 10–14) the mournful descent of the vocal sequences (harmonized in falling chromatic semitones) is followed by an outbreak of activity in the bass line by way of commentary. As the singer makes his way down the hidden rocky paths, he seems to miss his footing. This off-the-beat scuffing occurs on two occasions as the traveller struggles to secure his foothold: crushed and jabbed grace notes become clumsy as stones and pebbles are dislodged by the slips of shoe or boot. He finds himself on more even ground (though in the remote key of F minor) for the repeat of these words, and the music trudges on in grim determination. Again it is the left hand that provides the commentary: the mirthlessly jaunty dotted semiquaver figure under 'versteckte Stege' and 'Felsenhöhn' (which triggers a dotted rhythm in the voice) is reminiscent of a similar frisson in *Der Wanderer an den Mond* D870, another G minor/major song about a lonely traveller far from home.

The change into G major for the second verse (at b. 22 with change of key signature) is one of the cycle's glories and another echo of D870. The little interlude linking the verses has insisted on repeated Gs, the last two bars of which have been mezzo staccato and unharmonized. Nevertheless, however many times we have heard the tonic, the emergence of the *major* third (B natural) at this point is perfectly timed to be both a surprise and heartbreaking in its sudden switch to a mood of intimate confession. For the first time the traveller points out that he is not guilty of anything and that his compulsion to avoid mankind is not logical. He questions how it is that he has come to be in the grip of feelings he is unable to justify or control. This music, a major-key variant of the first verse, opens its heart to us, and the traveller's gentle bewilderment wrings our withers. The touch of canonic imitation that has been a feature of the song from the beginning comes into its own at 'Welch ein törichtes Verlangen / Treibt mich in die Wüstenein?' (bb. 26–31). Here the accompaniment drives the vocal line forward in case it should be tempted to dally on a word like 'Verlangen'. The piano writing is in octaves, giving the music the force of a proclamation. As the voice rises to repeated Es (the highest note in the song so far) on 'törichtes Verlangen', the piano replies with repeated Bs as if to answer the singer's question with, 'It is *this* foolish yearning – listen to it – and move on!' Counterpoint always suggests a weaving of life's forces, and here the traveller is caught as if enmeshed in a web. The repeat of the words 'Treibt mich in die Wustenein' (bb. 31–3) renounces harmony and imitation in favour of complete unison between voice and piano, a perfect use of Schubert's motif of solitude to describe the loneliness of the wilderness. The sparse texture of the piano interlude (bb. 33–9) also suggests a withered wasteland. The repeated mezzo staccato quavers, now in the treble register, now in the bass, continue to haunt the ear. A bar of isolated Bs (b. 33) is followed by one harmonized in B major (b. 34), then two in B minor (bb. 35–6); then a slide down to a B flat and the chord of G minor in root position (b. 37). Or was this only a mirage of the home key? A bar of harmonic prevarication on a chord of the German sixth confuses the traveller's weary senses before we reach the dominant, a D major chord, and silence – only three quavers' rest, but signifying a world of crushed hopes.

The third strophe is a modified repeat of the first. We return to a key signature of G minor and, as always in the greatest strophic songs, certain details in the accompaniment seem more potent second time around. Thus the canonic entry of the bass line after 'Weiser stehen auf [den Wegen]' (bb. 41–2) seems to illustrate, uncannily, the act of pointing, as if the jutting wooden post has come to life as a finger of the pianist's left hand. The vocal line at 'Ohne Ruh', und suche Ruh'' (bb. 47–9) is recast to give a new note of desperation to 'suche Ruh'' (a high G flat). Schubert's repeat of that phrase sets the unessential word 'und' as the highest musical note in a deliberate disruption of the practices of judicious word-setting. The absence of 'Ruh'' ('peace' or 'rest') is perfectly caught by the dotted semiquaver 'Wanderer an den Mond' figure, descriptive of a shudder of disquiet, and this time found only in the piano line. As at the end of the first strophe, there is another succession of solitary Gs in the accompaniment (bb. 55–6), but nothing can prepare us for the last verse which is utterly unlike the preceding three.

It is also unlike anything else in *Winterreise*. Indeed, this passage is the apotheosis of the use of pedal in Schubert's songs – not the piano's sustaining pedal (which should be largely absent from this passage anyway) but the musical device whereby an extended passage is built around an unchanging bass, or elsewhere in the harmonic texture (an inverted pedal). The repeated F sharps of *Die liebe Farbe* D795/16 from *Die schöne Müllerin* are a famous instance of an adventurous use of a pedal note, as is the E flat upper pedal in *Das Zügenglöcklein* D871, and it is no coincidence that both those songs have death as their theme. For four bars the voice intones on G while the piano screws the tension to a higher pitch by basses that rise a semitone with each bar. The extraordinary progression harmonizes 'Einen Weiser seh' ich' (bb. 55–6) on a diminished seventh on C sharp; 'stehen / Unver . . .' on G minor in second inversion (bass on D); '. . . rückt vor meinem' on an E flat⁷ chord (b. 59); 'Blick; / eine' on another diminished seventh, this time on E natural. All this while the voice holds to its repeated Gs. At 'Eine Strasse muss ich gehen' it climbs to a B flat for two bars, then rises another minor third to D flat (b. 63) for a repeat of the words that now glow with the grandeur of a brilliantly engineered harmonic onslaught. We almost expect the voice to go on rising in minor thirds – F flat to A double flat and so on, but in that direction it can never find release, never return to its point of departure harmonically spelled in the same way. (We wonder at Schubert's tortured, and amazingly modern, orthography, where a vocal D flat co-exists with a C sharp in the piano in bb. 63–4.) At 'noch Keiner ging zurück' (bb. 64–7) the voice rises a semitone and from the vantage point of D⁷ spies a way out of the harmonic maze. But it is not yet his time to continue his journey down the one-way street of death. The return to the home key is marked by two bars of ominous mezzo staccato quavers on the G below middle C.

In the many passages in this cycle where one struggles to describe the uniquely imaginative quality of Schubert's genius, there can be few more moving than the following. The vocal line on those Gs and B flats is partially repeated, but it is now harmonized by chords of a completely different spectrum. The traveller, who has seen any number of signposts on the road, can now see only one, in the same way that he had focused all his concentration on one leaf in *Letzte Hoffnung* D911/16. This marker points to death, and everything else is pushed to the outer fields of his vision. As a tonal analogue for this, the pedal note of G stands centre stage (doubled in the vocal line, and in the alto register of the keyboard, played by the right thumb) and pushes other harmonies to the extremities of the picture – within reach of the little finger of the left hand deep in the bass, and the little finger of the right in the treble stave. At b. 69 the significance of the terrible signpost is emphasized (at 'Einen Weiser seh' ich stehen'), with the extraordinarily chilling interval of a tritone – the *Diabolus in musica* – B natural and F natural at opposite poles of the keyboard. The outer notes of the treble and bass, bell-like minims, converge in contrary motion in a death march of menacing power. Bar by bar and semitone by semitone the basses rise and the treble line falls while the fate of the traveller is squeezed in a slowly tightening vice. The singer's chant – as already noted, a differently harmonized repeat of what has gone before – suggests someone transfixed with horror by the contemplation of their own fate. Once again there is an exit from the maze at 'Die noch Keiner ging zurück', using the same chord progression (bb. 75–7) as previously. Once again we are reminded that there is no easy release for this traveller. Those words are set, yet again, for a last time in a chilling postlude where the quaver movement is finally stilled and replaced by funereal crotchets. In an astonishing (and probably unconscious) link with one of Schubert's earliest compositions, this passage recalls the phrase 'Nimmer gibt das Grab zurück' (also in crotchets, also in G minor with a plunging bass line) which concludes the Schiller epic ballad *Leichenfantasie* D7 (1811). John Reed has also pointed out the similarities between *Der Wegweiser* and the contemporary

C minor Impromptu. The repeated notes and contrapuntal imitation of the opening pages of that work (which tricks the ear into believing it begins in G minor) bring *Der Wegweiser* strongly to mind.

First edition:	Published as Op. 89 no. 20 by Tobias Haslinger, Vienna on 30 December 1828 (P188)
Subsequent editions:	Peters: Vol. 1/110; AGA XX 536: Vol. 9/64; NSA IV: Vol. 4a/178; Bärenreiter: Vol. 3/134
Bibliography:	Youens 1991, pp. 272–7
Arrangement:	Arr. Anton Webern (1883–1945) for voice and orchestra (1903) [*see* ORCHESTRATIONS]
Discography and timing:	Fischer-Dieskau III 2[20] 3'55
	Pears–Britten 3'52
	Hyperion I 30[20] 3'47 Matthias Goerne
	Hyperion II 34[13]

← *Täuschung* D911/19   *Das Wirtshaus* D911/21 →

XXI Das WIRTSHAUS   The inn
OP. 89/21, **D911/21** [H643]
F major

Auf ei-nen To-ten-a-cker hat mich mein Weg ge-bracht,

(31 bars)

Auf einen Totenacker	**M**y journey has brought me
Hat mich mein Weg gebracht.	To a graveyard.
Allhier will ich einkehren:	Here, I thought to myself,
Hab' ich bei mir gedacht.	I will rest for the night.
Ihr grünen Totenkränze	You green funeral wreaths
Könnt wohl die Zeichen sein,	Might as well be the signs
Die müde Wandrer laden	Inviting tired travellers
In's kühle Wirtshaus ein.	Into the cool inn.
Sind denn in diesem Hause	Are all the rooms
Die Kammern all' besetzt?	In this house taken, then?
Bin matt zum Niedersinken	I am weary to the point of collapse,
Bin tödlich schwer verletzt.[1]	I am mortally wounded.
O unbarmherz'ge Schenke,	Pitiless tavern,
Doch weisest du mich ab?	Do you nonetheless turn me away?
Nun weiter denn, nur weiter,	On, then, press onwards,
Mein treuer Wanderstab!	My trusty staff!

[1] Müller writes '*Und* tödlich schwer verletz'. The repetition of 'bin' is Schubert's own.

Autograph of *Das Wirtshaus*, 1827.

This is the forty-first of Schubert's forty-six Müller solo settings (1823, 1827 and 1828).
See the poet's biography for a chronological list of all the Müller settings.

The traveller's encounter with a graveyard on his journey occasions the grandest vocal hymn that Schubert ever wrote. Certainly there are louder and longer songs that praise Jehovah in the highest (for example *Die Allmacht* D852, *Dem Unendlichen* D291) and these too are wonderful. But *Das Wirtshaus* is perhaps the greatest of a number of Schubert lieder where the trappings of conventional religion play only a subliminal part in music of spiritual significance (for example, the Novalis settings). Its noble amplitude is unlike anything else in the cycle, except perhaps *Die Nebensonnen* (No. 23) which is still to come. The song's key of F major, the tonality of pastoral repose (we know nothing of the graveyard's locale – whether in barren field or sheltered valley), is also unique in *Winterreise*, completely at variance with the G minor of the songs either side of it. With the slowest tempo marking in the cycle, the composer has insisted on four-in-a-bar rather than the customary two-in-a-bar. In earlier songs an *alla breve* often moderates the indication 'very slow' when the speed is governed by the minim, in eighteenth-century fashion, rather than the crotchet – but there is no need for that corrective here. An almost cosmic weariness is built into the character of the singer who longs to be delivered from the servitude of life. It is only breath control and an ability to sustain a long legato line that will limit the breadth of tempo at which the song is performed.

There is an inherent simplicity in this utterance which lends it the stature accorded only to music that is both popular and uncomplicated – like a folksong or a hymn, which speak immediately to all. The other song in the cycle of which this can be said is the much better-known *Der Lindenbaum* (No. 5). *Das Wirtshaus* is music of the highest sophistication, but somehow built into it is the down-to-earth accessibility of harmonium-accompanied communal worship and mourning. It is a plaint from the heart couched in the four-square rigours of the hymnal, yet it goes beyond the conventional functions of small-town church music to convey the nobility and dignity of Everyman. The composer's depiction of the dispossessed in *Das Wirtshaus* is both personal and universal, and its mixture of pain and sensuality is entirely typical of his music. This suggests (to me, at least) an unusual and fortuitous link with the great African-American spirituals. Although this is a huge leap across the barriers of geography and culture, *Das Wirtshaus* happens to share the fervour and humility of many a spiritual, music that is simultaneously enslaved by establishment hymnbook convention, and subversively free of it. Even Müller's poem reminds us of the metaphors to be found in this faraway repertory: the traveller longs for room in the graveyard inn as he might beg to cross 'over Jordan . . . into camp ground'. For earlier generations of the enslared singers of spirituals, only the grave brought deliverance, and they wooed it with an ardour that our traveller would have understood only too well.

Much has been written about the origin of the hymn music itself. The musicologist Thrasybulos Georgiades avers that the whole song is based on the F-centred Kyrie of the plainchant Requiem Mass, known to the composer from his schooldays as choirboy in the Hofkapelle. Force is lent to this argument by Schubert's other large-scale composition from 1827, the *Deutsche Messe* D872, which features a paraphrase of this same Kyrie in the opening movement (*Zum Eingang*), a setting of Neumann's *Wohin soll ich mich wenden?* In playing through that unpretentious little F major hymn (with words that say 'Where shall I turn when sorrow and pain press me?') the suggested link between the plainchant *Kyrie* and *Das Wirtshaus* seems convincing. In *Schubert durch die Brille* No. 23 (1999), Elizabeth McKay expands on this theme, uncovering another similarity between bb. 13–15 of the *Gloria* of the *Deutsche Messe* and the final three bars of *Das Wirtshaus*. One can just about detect the foundations of the traveller's inn or graveyard (and, by implication, church) but it is doubtful whether it is wise to construct, on this evidence, theories concerning Schubert's own religious faith, or that of the cycle's protagonist. If the cemetery is a symbol for an inn, and graveyard wreaths are also reminiscent of the evergreen garlands on inn doors that signify the time of the 'Heurige', or new wine, then the use of a church music as the harmonic ground plan of a secular lied merely extends that metaphor. The composer uses the juxtaposition of sacred and profane to mirror Müller's similarly ambiguous verbal imagery of graveyard and inn.

Under the hands this feels unlike any other Schubert song. There is a spaciousness about the chords as well as an airiness denoted by their mezzo staccato articulation that calls for the help of pedal resonance. Entering the key of F major in this context, where the preceding songs have been searingly intense, is like ducking under the lintel and walking into an old stone-walled Austrian inn, dark and cool on a scorching summer day. Or a church, of course. As the cycle has progressed the coldness of winter has become less of a reason for complaint; the relative merits of heat and cold have changed places and are now those expressed by Schubert's gravedigger in *Totengräbers Heimwehe* D842 (1825): 'Im Leben, da ist's ach! so schwül! . . . Im Grabe so friedlich, so kühl!' ('Life, alas, is so sultry . . . The grave is so peaceful, so cool!'). The Heine poem set by Brahms also comes to mind: 'Der Tod, das ist die kühle Nacht; / Das Leben ist der schwüle Tag' ('Death is cool night; living is sultry day'). The traveller longs for the coolness of death in much the same way as he has rejoiced in the winter cold of *Der stürmische Morgen* (No. 18). The second verse refers to 'the cool inn' and by an imaginative miracle Schubert conveys the idea of coolness-in-music throughout *Das Wirtshaus*. Within sight of most graveyards there is a church. Perhaps the implied churchly setting, cryptic and crypt-like, with organ-like chords, aids the cool impression; the slow tempo and use of the pedal also suggest a resonance and echo that we associate with thick-walled, and thus cool, buildings (in this connection another F major song comes to mind, *Am Fenster* D878). And perhaps it is something to do with the tempo and harmony where chords move one to the other in a stately yet understated way, descriptive of something grander than the temporal heat of everyday emotion. In great Schubert songs, dactylic rhythm such as this seldom denotes the sweat of human endeavour, rather the inscrutable workings of Nature where death is her most important henchman.

The first two bars of introduction are a mixture of the simple and imposing; the phrase ends on a 4-3 cadence as the second inversion of the tonic falls to the dominant. We are briefly tricked into believing that the next bars will repeat the same music, but after a crotchet and two quavers we hear one of the most famous harmonic changes in *Winterreise*. Instead of another F major chord on the third beat of the third bar there is an F^7, a telling E flat added to the harmony. This is as 'cool' or as 'blue' as anything Schubert ever wrote. The music changes colour as it leans into this 'blue' harmony which then sinks sensuously on its way to the subdominant. It is in this uncanny presentiment of jazz that shades of Schubert and the plantation slaves seem to slip into the same deep, cool river of musical repose. (We discover later in the song that this F^7 chord signifies tiredness in the composer's mind, the desire to sink down into rest, just as any dominant seventh chord eagerly awaits the repose of its resolution.)

Once the introduction has reached the subdominant (B flat major) in b. 4 it moves through other keys like an organ improvisation; we reach the relative minor, and then the dominant of that key (an A major chord approached by a mordent almost impossible to play quietly enough in its pianissimo filigree). The C^7 chord that suddenly follows is another surprise. The semitone drop in the melodic line is unexpectedly audacious and once again the addition of a seventh seems rather jazzy, for want of a less anachronistic epithet. At the same time it indicates shared music-making – the gathering note given by the organist to enable the faithful to sing their hymn in unison. As in *Der Wegweiser* (No. 20) the voice part enters later than we expect, here due to the asymmetrical length of the introduction (five bars). The vocal melody, which is mostly doubled by opulent piano chords, has all the qualities of a stirring hymn (S. S. Wesley's tune for 'The Church's One Foundation' comes to mind). That it is performed pianissimo, and in the most rapt musical manner possible, adds to its power. In the manner of good singable hymns there are stirring shifts in the bass line on the first and third beats of the bar that give the music some of the impetus of a processional. The interlude after this first verse is more or less a repeat of the third and fourth bars of the introduction, including that heart-stopping F^7 chord, once again a gateway to a short dalliance with the subdominant.

In terms of melody and essential harmony the second verse (from b. 11) is a repeat of the first, but the descant brought out by the little finger of the right hand adds an air of almost unbearable pathos. Many an Austrian burial used to be accompanied by the 'Blaskapelle', the solemnity of open-air music for brass; Beethoven, for example, wrote a set of trombone *Equali* for just this purpose. The custom remains in the countryside. Robert Holl, the great Dutch bass-baritone who lives in Austria, believes that no one can truly understand this song without experiencing an Austrian country funeral with open-air music played by brass instruments. There are in fact horns and three trombones in the orchestration of Schubert's *Wohin soll ich mich wenden?* from the *Deutsche Messe*, although the tessitura of the descant in *Das Wirtshaus* suggests the higher register. These extra notes stand out from the main melody, emerging from the vocal texture mostly when the piano is not doubling the vocal line. This descant limns the music with a touch of brightness that again gives forward impetus to the solemn processional. At the same time it forms a doleful and poignant commentary on the words where Müller's graveside imagery is at its strongest. The two-bar interlude that follows is an octave higher than it was between the first and second verses (bb. 16–17). This intensifies the atmosphere for the devastating moment of rejection when the traveller loses his cool, just as the music does, and discovers there is no room at the inn. (Here the piano's melody prophesies the great spiritual 'Were you there when they crucified my Lord?')

For 'Sind denn in diesem Hause' (bb. 17–18) we depart from the strophic structure of the song's first page and hear a new melody. The falling shape of the phrase is ideal for the deflation of the traveller's hopes expressed in a question sung with innocence and wide-eyed wonder. The radiance of this music would have befitted the disappointed enquiries of Joseph and Mary in

Bethlehem. In being rebuffed by the hard-hearted landlord, the traveller can scarcely believe his misfortune. The progression of F^7 to B flat, which has already provided some of the most moving moments of the song, is the underlying harmony of the passage. This is one of the most devastating instances of the pathetic major in the whole cycle, where childlike vulnerability and madness conjoin in a moment of the greatest pathos. This crucial dominant seventh chord (F^7) is also the underlay for 'Bin matt zum Niedersinken', and it is surely here that we discover the significance of this harmony in the composer's mind, linking the key word 'matt' (weary) with the harmony that supports it. This 'matt', the first note in b. 20, is perhaps the most difficult single note to sing in the cycle, particularly for baritones, with its sudden exposed leap into the *passaggio* of the voice for a note that must remain hushed and covered, true to the word's meaning. Felicitous details (if so they may be called in the context of this tragic music) abound: the tiny semiquaver movement in the piano that ornaments the plagal cadences in quasi-baroque fashion at 'diesem Hause' and 'Niedersinken' bend the knee or make the sign of the Cross in deference to the implied religious imagery; the unexpected flattening of the submediant – a D flat on 'Bin tödlich schwer verletzt' (b. 21) – calls on an illustrative twist of chromatic harmony worthy of the great madrigalists. The first musical indication that the traveller must be on his way is a fleeting glance back to *Der Wegweiser*: the interlude between the third and fourth strophes in b. 22 is a reappearance of the 'travelling' mezzo staccato quaver chords that have been a governing feature of that song, and of *Gute Nacht* (No. 1).

In a peroration of grandeur and immense moral authority the traveller gathers all his strength and rounds on the 'unbarmherz'ge Schenke' in a moment of Lear-like bitterness more typical of earlier songs in the cycle. Although no change of dynamic is marked here, there are two separate crescendo markings unique to this strophe that surely imply a growth of intensity, a slow eruption of emotion. The sudden change into F minor at 'O unbarmherz'ge Schenke' (b. 23) hardens the heart of the music, and steels the traveller's resolve. The unusual, augmented chord on 'Doch weisest du mich ab?' emphasizes 'Why me? Why am I singled out for rejection from the grave?' The pointed use of the verb 'weisen' triggers another tiny reminiscence of *Der Wegweiser*: in the bass line, at the end of b. 24, two rising semiquavers echo the opening upbeat of the preceding song. Thus, before he sets off again, the traveller wearily gathers around him references to his journey like so much paraphernalia, including the 'Wanderstab'' ('walking-stick' or 'staff') which we have heard mentioned at the end of *Die Krähe* (No. 15) and nowhere else. This is music of the most heartbreaking fortitude. For the first time in the song, lines of poetry are repeated: 'Nun weiter denn, nur weiter, / Mein treuer Wanderstab!' (The fact that there has been no repetition of words earlier in the song has deepened its mood of exhaustion and defencelessness.) But now, *so be it!* If the first setting of 'nur weiter' seems declaimed within a crescendo, the second stretches even higher as the traveller's mind endeavours to encompass a journey without end. Twice (in bb. 25 and 27) we hear the change of C minor to A flat between the two words 'weiter denn', a powerful harmonic metaphor for the bleak vistas of the interminable future open before the traveller. Like Wagner's Dutchman he seems cursed to voyage for ever through the seas of life, but in this case there is no hope of redemption through a woman's love. The first setting of 'Wanderstab' (b. 26) contains a quickening of intention in its dotted rhythms, but the drooping appoggiaturas of the second imply someone on the move at last, however exhausted. The postlude is problematic for the pianist. Many performers prefer to return to the muted tones of the opening for the final reappearance of the ritornello. The two crescendo markings in the penultimate line of music are never cancelled, however, and it seems likely that, as a transition to the mood of *Mut!* (No. 22), the diffidence of the introduction has undergone a metamorphosis into music of greater grim purpose and determination. Brigitte Fassbaender encouraged her pianists to play this postlude with a burning sense of determination, as well as disappointed anger; in the last two lines of music the traveller recommenced his journey in a new mood of bitter re-engagement with his unrelenting fate. Other artists, like Pears and Britten, preferred to retain throughout the mood of elevated pathos with which the song had begun.

First edition:	Published as Op. 89 no. 21 by Tobias Haslinger, Vienna on 30 December 1828 (P189)
Subsequent editions:	Peters: Vol. 1/114; AGA XX 537: Vol. 9/68; NSA IV: Vol. 4a/182; Bärenreiter: Vol. 3/138
Bibliography:	Georgiades 1967
	Mckay 1999
	Youens 1991, pp. 278–84
Arrangements:	Arr. Franz Liszt (1811–1886) for solo piano, no. 10 of *Winterreise* (1838–9) [*see* TRANSCRIPTIONS]
	Arr. Tilman Hoppstock (b. 1961) for guitar accompaniment, in *Franz Schubert: 110 Lieder* (2009)
Discography and timing:	Fischer-Dieskau III 2[21] 4'08
	Pears–Britten 4'30
	Hyperion I 30[21]
	Hyperion II 34[14] 4'55 Matthias Goerne

← *Der Wegweiser* D911/20   *Mut!* D911/22 →

XXII MUT!   Courage!
OP. 89 NO. 22, **D911/22** [H644]

The song exists in two versions, the second of which is discussed below:

(1) 'Mässig, kräftig'   A minor $\frac{2}{4}$ [30 bars][1]

(2) G minor

(64 bars)

Fliegt der Schnee mir in's Gesicht,	**W**hen the snow flies in my face
Schüttl' ich ihn herunter.	I shake it off.
Wenn mein Herz im Busen spricht,	When my heart speaks in my breast
Sing' ich hell und munter.	I sing loudly and merrily.
Höre nicht, was es mir sagt,	I do not hear what it tells me,
Habe keine Ohren,	I have no ears;
Fühle nicht, was es mir klagt,	I do not feel what it laments.
Klagen ist für Toren.	Lamenting is for fools.

[1] It is possible that the first version of this song, un-numbered, was composed in Graz in September 1827 before Schubert had decided to compose a complete Part Two. *See* also footnote p. 720. Elmar Budde believes that the change of key to G minor was undertaken on the publisher Haslinger's initiative. The AGA publishes the song only in A minor.

Lustig in die Welt hinein	Cheerfully out into the world,
Gegen Wind und Wetter!	Against wind and storm!
Will kein Gott auf Erden sein,	If there is no God on earth,
Sind wir selber Götter.	Then we ourselves are gods.

This is the forty-second of Schubert's forty-six Müller solo settings (1823, 1827 and 1828).
See the poet's biography for a chronological list of all the Müller settings.

The mood of this brief and rather manic outburst of energy is in the same mould as *Der stürmische Morgen* (No. 18). In the wake of *Das Wirtshaus* (No. 21), the air is cleared for *Die Nebensonnen* (No. 23) and *Der Leiermann* (No. 24) that plumb even greater depths of emotion. In embarking on the second part of *Winterreise* in the autumn of 1827, Schubert followed the sequence of Müller's 1824 version of the cycle in his own apparently casual way: he went through the list of twenty-four poems and set those which were new to him. This determined the order of this half of the cycle (*see* introduction to this section). But the placement of *Mut!* in the sequence is the exception that proves the rule – in this case Schubert's ability to rule his own works (as well as occasionally his own manuscript paper) and order them as he saw fit. Müller had *Mut!* as the penultimate poem; it launches the traveller back into the real world and his encounter with the hurdy-gurdy player. Schubert, on the other hand, envisaged a darker *Der Leiermann* and a very different precursor to it, the heartbreaking *Die Nebensonnen* that Müller had placed before *Mut!* This single, yet absolutely crucial, change belies any theory of carelessness on the composer's part – it is the most powerful argument against performing Schubert's cycle in Müller's 1824 order.

After the epic calm and contained anguish of *Das Wirtshaus* this song comes as a shock. Having dispatched *Der stürmische Morgen* the pianist might imagine himself safe from further tempests. But he has to summon all his energy for one last explosion, one last gleam of rage before the dying of the light. In its short span the song offers more virtuoso challenges for the accompanist than any other song in the cycle: leaps and jumps, scales and arpeggio figures, rattling double octaves (although these are hardly Lisztian either in terms of difficulty or quantity). In fact the song is not that hard to play in itself, but any pianist who has journeyed through a public *Winterreise* will testify to its unexpectedly formidable challenges when performed in context. This wrong-footing of the pianist is a fitting match for the traveller's confusion: the poem's context in the musical cycle, particularly in Schubert's inspired positioning, renders it disturbing rather than wholesome and invigorating. Following hard on the heels of *Der Wegweiser* (No. 21) and *Das Wirtshaus*, and immediately followed by *Die Nebensonnen*, such bravado is unconvincing. Even the exclamation mark after the title seems rather forced. All this fist-brandishing optimism is as pathetically illusory as the *Gemütlichkeit* of *Täuschung* (No. 19). It is not that the traveller lacks courage, or that he even realizes he is lying to himself. He is beyond any dissembling. We have listened to him in the grip of depression often enough, and here he lives out the moment of manic exuberance which is the other side of the coin. This quasi-Nietzschean outburst makes sense on its own as a manifesto of self-reliant fortitude. In a sense the macho mood is real: he does shake the snow off, he does sing, he is deaf to the heart's fear, he does think lamenting is for fools. And he is right. And yet, in the context of Schubert's cycle, if not Müller's, all of this is heartbreakingly inept. If it is tempting to cite the last verse in particular as evidence of the composer's own sympathy for atheism, we are reminded that the traveller's bold assertions are made only to be knocked down; as we shall soon see, he is in no position to avail himself of the strength and independence he advocates. This is the protest music of Prometheus raging against the gods, but just as Prometheus defies the gods for an explosive moment before succumbing to the horrors of his fate, the traveller proclaims his god-like independence before revealing himself more mortal, and mortally wounded, than ever.

As the pianist pounds out the opening ritornello, the hollow ring of this music is announced immediately after the first lacerating G minor chord: bare octaves are shared between the hands in an energetic rising sequence. Elsewhere in Schubert, doubled octaves denote loneliness or determination; in *Letzte Hoffnung* (No. 16), for example, they imply the gathering of concentration. In *Mut!* they reinforce a strand (and stand) of bravery with an extra layer of bold (but eventually unconvincing) affirmation – Dutch courage in music. The upward climb of these octaves is punctuated by an underlay of punched staccatissimo chords (G minor to C minor) that straddle the bar line in the manner of *Letzte Hoffnung* – nowhere else do we see this unusual way of grouping quavers. The invigorating rise of these octaves is followed by a bar of falling quavers and semiquavers (b. 3), with clashes and harmonic holes in the texture that occur nowhere else in the song. The music pretends to be bravely military, but there is something discordant and empty about it and the equally empty flourish of a perfect cadence. All this perfectly conveys a macho huffing and puffing, effortful but without substance. In contrast to *Der Wegweiser* and *Das Wirtshaus*, the voice enters bang on cue at the beginning of the bar after a symmetrical four-bar introduction, a parody of textbook normality.

The vocal melody at 'Fliegt der Schnee mir in's Gesicht' (G – A – B flat, b. 5) hammers home the song's indebtedness to *Der Wegweiser*, with the principal motivic idea that opens that song – the same notes in similar semiquaver upbeats in $\frac{2}{4}$. Moreover, the entry of the piano at the end of the bar in canonic imitation, as if both echoing the singer's line and pressing it forward, also brings to mind the layered counterpoint of the same song. The phrase ends with bb. 6 and 7 and a tentative doubling of voice and piano ('mir in's Gesicht') and the strangely bare II–V harmonization of 'Gesicht' in which we can hear the chill of something wind-borne and ominous. This introspective passage is perhaps madder than any of the louder bluster, and it seems possible that this echo of the music signposting death was deliberate self-quotation on Schubert's part. These three intense bars (the elongation of the phrase engenders suspense at its outcome) are emblematic of death and are set up to be contradicted, countermanded, vanquished. Any idea of contrapuntal subtlety is peremptorily banished with the four-square certainties of 'Schüttl' ich ihn herunter' (bb. 8–9), one of the heartiest phrases in the cycle. It is earthed in the certainties of the dominant and finishes with a cadence ending on a heavy-footed and defiant conclusion to the phrase. (This is a feature of the song that will come into its own in the louder, and cruder, third strophe where this two-crotchet figure might just as well signify a defiant, two-finger gesture.) The two-bar interlude, by way of pianistic commentary (bb. 10–11), embroiders the dance-like pattern with a run of eight semiquavers and two accented crotchets, perfect also of course to mirror the idea of shaking off a flurry of snow. It is interesting to note that Schubert marks this interlude forte and that the singer's line has until now remained piano, as if the winter traveller is still locked within his own internal drama. The effect of a sudden outbreak of loud music frees him from freeze-frame inertia and brings a vivid picture to mind: the poor man, carried away by a rush of elation, makes a clumsy whirl in the snow. He attempts to dance, but manages only the shuffle of injured feet that move ponderously within a tight circle of tonic and dominant. (The composer's 'Ziemlich geschwind' marking should moderate any temptation to make the music mercurial.)

This passage, ending in the dominant, is balanced by a similar seven bars for 'Wenn mein Herz im Busen spricht, / Sing' ich hell und munter'. Three tentative bars (where the idea of dialogue with the heart is beautifully caught by canonic imitation) are brushed aside by four bars in the manner of mindless communal singing where any attempt at introspection is silenced ('Sing' ich hell und munter'). The chief difference in the second half of this strophe is that the composer engineers a shift back into the tonic key where the exuberant interlude of bb. 17–18 (again a sudden forte) moves into G major to chime with the idea of a merry sing-song.

For the second strophe the whole of this construction is repeated exactly. After the explosive introduction the canonic interplay between voice and piano in an asymmetrical three-bar phrase ('Höre nicht, was es mir sagt', bb. 23–5) is ideally illustrative of straining to catch a message that is difficult to decipher. In brushing aside the subtleties of harmony and counterpoint, the peremptory outburst of 'Habe keine Ohren' (bb. 26–7) makes any attempt at listening impossible. 'What do I care?' is the subtext. In a similar manner, the idea of feeling sensitivity is debunked in the next phrase where the traveller refuses to hear the lament of his heart and says that complaining is for fools. The stiff upper lip advocated here has a very British feel, and many a Victorian must have been heartily stirred by these sentiments in early *Winterreise* performances. Robert Louis Stevenson subtitled his poem 'The Vagabond' (later set by Vaughan Williams as the opening number of *Songs of Travel*), 'To an air of Schubert', without naming the song he had in mind. In fact, Stevenson's poem beginning 'Give to me the life I love, / Let the lave[1] go by me' fits *Mut!* exactly, if sung twice through. It is almost certain that Stevenson heard the famous English baritone Harry Plunket Greene (*see* SINGERS) performing this cycle (in English translation) in the mid-1890s.

We have reached G major at the end of the second verse (b. 34, followed by a two-bar interlude also in G major). For the third verse we stay there, celebrating the defeat of the blues by an official change of key signature into a single sharp (from b. 37). The minor-key music of dialogue and doubt haunts the traveller's ears no more, and everything is bracing and incisive. Schubert wrote music like this from time to time in his piano works, both solo and duet – an ultra-masculine Beethovenian manner implying the ceremonial of the fatherland and the military fascination of the patriotic. The stirring music for 'Lustig in die Welt hinein / Gegen Wind und Wetter!' (bb. 37–40) is derived from the rebuttal music of the earlier strophes. For the first time the piano writing of the interludes aspires to the virtuosity of right-hand octaves (bb. 41–2). This phrase ends in the dominant. The music for 'Will kein Gott auf Erden sein, / Sind wir selber Götter' is very similar, and in a similarly assertive manner leads us back to G major. The music marches up and down the hill as if commanded by the grand old Duke of York, and with similarly minimal effect – everything is for show. The whole of the verse is now repeated in a process common enough in the cycle, where the elaboration of the setting of the concluding verse provides the material for half the song. 'Lustig' has been the key word of the G major section, but the reminder of the traveller's unendingly grim struggle with the elements brings out his fighting spirit. The grit of G minor is reintroduced at 'Welt hinein' (b. 50), and the crucial B flat of this key enables a surprising Schubertian shift at bb. 51–2 into B flat major for 'Gegen Wind und Wetter!' – to be sung and played with relish. There is a bracing frisson to this music, ideal for someone whistling down the wind. The final 'Wetter' (b. 52) plunges down the octave, by far the most dramatic of the song's phrase-endings, and this sets off a piano interlude that jumps higher into the upper reaches of the piano than anything else in the cycle. Not even the wiry circling crow (*Die Krähe* No. 15) has wingtipped the twanging B flat in alt – a part of his piano that Schubert seems to reserve for grotesque or magical effects.

In b. 57 the final vocal phrase touches a high G at 'Sind wir selber Götter' in a reckless moment of Promethean defiance. Perhaps too reckless. Schubert originally wrote this song in A minor (printed in the NSA Volume 4b p. 242) but changed it into G minor at some stage before publication. In attempting to guess his reasoning one may imagine that he preferred to reserve this tonality for his final two songs. In any case a high A at this stage of the proceedings, in a song that is mostly placed in the middle and lower registers of the voice, is comfortable for few performers. (Perhaps the glance back into the G minor music of *Der Wegweiser* at the beginning also encouraged this revision.) Lusty tenors with a lusty top register may make something of an argument, however, for a reversion to the A minor of the composer's first

[1] Stevenson means 'let the flow go by me' – 'lave' is used in the context of 'flow on by'.

thoughts. The marking of the first version is 'Mässig kräftig' which is a warning to the performer that this song was meant to be on the slower side of the later, definitive marking, 'Ziemlich geschwind, kräftig'.

Autograph:	In private possession (first version, in A minor)
Publication:	Published as Op. 89 no. 22 by Tobias Haslinger, Vienna on 30 December 1828 (P190); first version published as part of the NSA in 1979 (P773)
Subsequent editions:	Peters: Vol. 1/116; AGA XX 538: Vol. 9/70; NSA IV: Vol. 4a/184 & Vol. 4b/242 (first version, A minor); Bärenreiter: Vol. 3/140 & 228 (first version)
Bibliography:	Youens 1991, pp. 285–8
Further settings and arrangements:	Arr. Franz Liszt (1811–1886) for solo piano, no. 3 of *Winterreise* (1838–9) [*see* TRANSCRIPTIONS]
	Rainer Bredemeyer (1929–1995) *Einmischung in unsere Angelegenheit* for bass and orchestra (with quotations from *Mut!*) (1985)
	Arr. Tilman Hoppstock (b. 1961) for guitar accompaniment, in *Franz Schubert: 110 Lieder* (2009)
Discography and timing:	Fischer-Dieskau III 2²² 1'24
	Pears–Britten 1'31
	Hyperion I 30²²
	Hyperion II 34¹⁵ 1'22 Matthias Goerne

← *Das Wirtshaus* D911/21   *Die Nebensonnen* D911/23 →

XXIII Die NEBENSONNEN   The phantom suns
OP. 89 NO. 23, **D911/23** [H645]

The song exists in two versions, the second of which is discussed below:

(1) 'Mässig'   A major   ¾   [33 bars]¹

(2) A major

¹ The first version, un-numbered, was in the possession of the Pachler family in Graz until at least 1842. This suggests that Schubert either composed the song in Graz in September 1827 and left it with Marie Pachler as a gift, or that he sent it to her from Vienna as a token of this gratitude – perhaps together with the libretto of *Alfonso und Estrella* that he promised to send her some days after his 'bread-and-butter' letter of 27 September. This would indicate that it was a song of which he was especially proud.

Drei Sonnen sah ich am Himmel stehn,	**I** saw three suns in the sky;
Hab' lang' und fest sie angesehn;	I gazed at them long and intently.
Und sie auch standen da so stier,	And they, too, stood there so fixedly,
Als wollten sie nicht weg von mir.[2]	As if unwilling to leave me.
Ach, m e i n e Sonnen seid ihr nicht!	Alas, you are not *my* suns!
Schaut Andren doch in's Angesicht!	Gaze into other people's faces!
Ach, neulich hatt' ich auch wohl drei:[3]	Yes, not long ago I, too, had three suns
Nun sind hinab die besten zwei.	Now the two best have set.
Ging' nur die dritt' erst hinterdrein!	If only the third would follow,
Im Dunkeln wird mir wohler sein.[4]	I should feel happier in the dark.

This is the forty-third of Schubert's forty-six Müller solo settings (1823, 1827 and 1828). See the poet's biography for a chronological list of all the Müller settings.

Nothing can prepare the first-time listener to *Winterreise* for the profundity of *Die Nebensonnen*; and the first thing one notices is that it is also profound in the physical sense. No other accompaniment in the cycle is written solely in the bass clef. Like the eclipse of the sun which it suggests, albeit metaphorically, the tessitura of this piano writing is something quite out of the ordinary. The hands move within a surprisingly small compass, as if feeling their way in the dark from chord to chord. The steady pace and sudden change of emotional temperature come as a shock after the hectic outburst of *Mut!* (No. 22). Some commentators see this song as the culmination of the cycle with *Der Leiermann* (No. 24) as a ghostly coda; the transfigured anguish of the music certainly suggests that the traveller has crossed a threshold and reached the nadir of his destiny. Or perhaps the apex. To explain his mood as madness is far too easy. *Die Nebensonnen* inhabits an emotional landscape beyond insanity; the suffering is so intense that pain is transfigured into a radiance that may be described as 'saintly', for want of a better word, the key signature's three sharps being a sign of stigmata. In the stature of this music (and the mysterious beauty of this most enigmatic of Müller's poems) the traveller seems at one with such great mystics as St John of the Cross who wrote of the 'Dark Night of the Soul'. Never has the composer used his beloved key of A major, and its inevitable contrast with A minor in the following song, to more ennobling effect.

In *Gute Nacht* (No. 1), the cycle's opening song, winter and darkness were crucial narrative ingredients, but so much has changed in the meantime. We have arrived at a point in the pilgrimage where season and time of day are truly immaterial; even the setting of suns has nothing to do with nightfall in a literal sense. The music is grounded in the sonorous lower reaches of the piano, yet it floats in lofty spiritual regions. In the last songs of the cycle this winter journey takes on a new dimension of freedom; the traveller, no longer conscious of his body, bares his soul in music that seems to come from another world. But does it? In fact much of the musical material in the final songs derives from Viennese life and custom: the hurdy-gurdy depicted in *Der Leiermann* was to be heard on many a street corner; *Das Wirtshaus* (No. 21) took the simplicity of hymn-singing as its inspiration; the hearty certainties of *Mut!* parody the vigorous energy of the military march and popular quadrille to show the traveller in the grip of optimistic folly; and, as we shall see, the 'mock suns' are made up of earthly matter

---

[2] Müller writes 'Als *könnten* sie nicht weg von mir'.
[3] Müller (*Gedichte*, 1824) writes 'Ja' instead of 'Ach', but 'Ach' is found in the fair copy of the autograph, the first edition and NSA. Friedländer in Peters Edition, believing the second 'Ach' in the poem to be an unintended repetition, reverts to the poet's 'Ja'. His reckoning is supported by the fact that 'Ja' is also to be found in the song's first version (*see* Footnote 1).
[4] Müller writes 'Im *Dunkel* wird mir wohler sein'. Schubert's change to 'Dunkeln' darkens the colour of the word, when sung, to marvellous effect.

rather than extra-terrestrial elements. All of this duly undergoes an astonishing Schubertian metamorphosis, but it is surely the echoes of everyday life in the high art of these songs that deepen their universality.

On first hearing, this sonorous music in ⅜ could be taken to be another hymn. Closer listening reveals the ghost of a popular dance, albeit in a tempo more fitting for a funeral than a marriage. The hysterical gaiety of *Täuschung* (No. 19) is long past, but that music of self deception was also in A major, and there is a generic link between the songs. The muted melody of *Die Nebensonnen* reveals itself as a dance tune – but in half tempo. It illustrates a different type of confusion – a distortion of aural perception which is a perfect analogue for the visual delusions of the poem. Instead of the *Täuschung* waltz, where the invitation is open to everyone (except the traveller, of course), we hear a stately sarabande for a solitary dancer. The spacing and tessitura of the chords suggest brass music – a mournful chorale rather than the tinkling strains of a merry gathering. Schubert significantly marks the music 'Nicht zu langsam' to preserve something of a lilt. To discover the *Ländler* hidden in this song one has only to play the first page of the accompaniment at double the tempo, with the dotted quavers and semiquavers smoothed out; an upward transposition of, say, a sixth would add a touch of sparkle. Schubert has simply lowered the pitch and muted the mood in order to raise the dance to a higher power. But the slow swing that animates the melody remains, and its courtly gait adds to its spiritual weight.

All this height and depth far exceed what one might expect from glancing at the song's modest musical means on paper. Not that this Schubertian alchemy was new. Throughout his career the composer was renowned for his dance music, always able to create tiny jewels, sparkling with joy or, as here, reflecting the deepest *Sehnsucht*, from unpromisingly banal raw material. Some of Schubert's most intense inspirations must have evaporated in the moment of their creation as he sat at the piano improvising for his dancing friends. As he played hour after hour for their merrymaking he was naturally unable to dance himself, and was excluded from the romantic embraces which his music encouraged. With his keyboard as the only thing that he could lovingly touch all evening, it is hardly surprising that he should associate dancing with being on the outside looking in (cf. *Täuschung*), and that many of his dances are suffused with an almost physical sense of longing.

Another viewpoint on the origins of this passage is that of Elizabeth McKay (*Schubert durch die Brille* 23, 1999), who draws attention to the similarity of the opening melody of the song and the *Zum Sanctus* of the *Deutsche Messe* D872 (at the words 'Heilig, heilig, heilig, [heilig ist der Herr]'). The *Deutsche Messe* was written in the German language in demotic style. The inspiration for *Die Nebensonnen*, whether secular or religious, seems to have had its roots in popular, rather than highbrow, culture.

Much has been written on the significance of the three suns. As we have seen in the commentary on *Die schöne Müllerin*, Müller was a scholar of English literature: certain images in *Ungeduld* D795/7 from the earlier cycle derive from Edmund Spenser, he translated Marlowe, and he must have known his Shakespeare. In *Henry VI Part 3* Act II Scene 1 the following lines occur, signifying the ascendancy of the House of York:

EDWARD [later King Edward IV]: Dazzle mine eyes, or do I see three suns?
RICHARD [later King Richard III]: Three glorious suns, each one a perfect sun:
Not separated with the racking clouds,
But sever'd in a pale clear-shining sky.
See, see! they join, embrace, and seem to kiss,
As if they vow'd some league inviolable:
Now are they but one lamp, one light, one sun.
In this the heaven figures some event.

To explain Müller's imagery, English commentators have fielded more complicated explanations, for once, than their German counterparts. A. H. Fox Strangways put forward the idea that they represent Faith, Hope and Life, and experienced Schubertians of the old school, Gerald Moore and Richard Capell among them, have accepted this explanation. The suns of Faith and Hope have set for the traveller and only that of Life remains, something that he would dearly wish to be without. This idea, however, derived from St Paul, seems too complicatedly theological for Müller. Because the poet has already described the occurrence of *ignis fatuus* in *Irrlicht* (No. 9), it is possible that he had in mind here another purely natural phenomenon – *parhelia*, or Mock Suns (sometimes known as Sundogs), which can be seen as neighbouring images of the sun, appearing on either side of it at the same height. The apparently magical vision of Shakespeare's kings-to-be would be explained by this trick of nature, which is caused by the refraction of light by ice crystals in the clouds, best seen when the sun is low in the sky. These Mock Suns, visible at any time of year and regardless of the ground temperature, can be bright and distinct, or mere smudges in the sky. They are red-coloured towards the sun and are sometimes partially green and blue. This mixture of physics and poetry reminds us of Goethe's *Phänomen* (set by Wolf and Brahms) where a lunar rainbow is explained in the light of his colour theory and used as a metaphor for the white hair of old age. Although Müller's simple poetry normally eschewed the occasional Goethean tendency to use verse as a mirror of philosophy and science, his knowledge of Shakespeare may have led him to introduce these curious Mock Suns into his *Winterreise* text. Neverthless, the traveller's mention of his 'besten zwei' surely also refers to the eyes of the beloved, which he has lost in being cut off from her gaze. Among German musicologists 'the eyes have it', and this explanation has long been taken as clarification enough of the whole poem. But this is perhaps rather too simple. The traveller refers to the suns he sees in the heavens and the eyes he calls 'my suns' as separate things. The question remains as open as ever.

The poem is a single ten-line strophe that Schubert has fashioned into a musical construction in three sections. The first section uses four lines of Müller's text, likewise the second, and the last musical verse is made up of a two-line coda. There is a four-bar introduction which, in the manner typical of *Winterreise*, serves as the accompaniment to the first musical phrase. The simplicity of the harmony belies its sophisticated use, and the emotional scope of the melody is an astonishing achievement considering that it is constructed within the range of a fourth. The pianist has the impression, under the fingers, of being centred on the chord of A major around which other rudimentary chords pivot. First there is a conventional visit to the dominant (E major) followed by an A^7 chord that leads to the subdominant and then immediately back to A major. An E^7 chord ornamented with an accented passing note on C sharp leads to A major yet again, and this progression is repeated within a pianissimo echo after an eloquent turn that recalls the *bel canto* grace of an Italian aria. It goes without saying that the banality of this description does no justice to the haunting beauty of the music. But the sensation of always returning to A major, as a fixed point of reference as it were, seems to signify something moving in and out of focus. It is as if the home key is the centre of the solar system, and the chords of IV and V, in close proximity, are two further suns glimpsed from time to time but which soon disappear from view. In feeling their way around the keyboard as if in the dark, the pianist's wandering fingers represent the traveller's confused state of mind. The pathos of that lean into the subdominant in b. 2, and the way we are not allowed to dally there long (the music quickly melts back into A major), are perfect to illustrate the loss of something that was once reality but which has slipped out of one's grasp into the realms of fantasy. The sad emphases in the vocal line on 'sah' – very much in the past tense – and 'fest' heighten the eloquence of the plaint.

An astonishing feature of this song is its range of dynamics, and how they are juxtaposed suddenly, almost violently. 'Hab' lang' und fest sie angesehn' ends in a pianissimo and, after a mezzo forte interlude, the next line, 'Und sie auch standen da so stier', occasions a forte outburst. Here the music moves into the relative minor and its subdominant; the idea of constancy occasions a tragic, rather than a happy, response, and the words 'Als wollten sie nicht weg von mir' (bb. 11–13) remind us of the 'Willst mich nicht verlassen?' phrase from *Die Krähe* (No. 15). The idea of being close to anything, or anybody, now seems impossible, even repugnant, to the traveller. The short interlude following this phrase is divided into two contrasting gestures, the first forte (as if struggling against something, bb. 13–14), answered by the second, a falling piano phrase (inexorably defeated, bb. 14–15).

The song's middle section uses the next four lines of Müller's ten-line strophe, and completely departs from any idea of a slow-motion *Ländler*. Here the traveller moves into a type of half-spoken, half-sung arioso. As he awakes from the intensity of his reverie of self-communing, the music shifts into A minor. From b. 16, at 'Ach, m e i n e Sonnen seid ihr nicht!' a line of repeated C naturals harmonized in this key are echoed (b. 17) by mezzo staccato E major chords in the piano. Thus the traveller, for the first time in the cycle, vocalizes an important motif that has run like a thread of silver frost through the accompaniment from the very first notes of the cycle, disappearing altogether in some songs only to reappear in others. These repeated quavers, half insistently lyrical, half detached, have signified the process of travel 'in gehender Bewegung'. Here they trigger a slight quickening of the tempo, a brushing aside of the strange vision of the suns in order to press on to journey's end. A minor to C major is a fairly traditional transition, but here, between bb. 18 and 20, the power of the modulation defies analysis. Schubert (whether intentionally or not) modifies Müller's text and substitutes a world-weary 'Ach' for 'Ja', as an upbeat to 'neulich hatt' ich auch wohl drei', the accented 'auch' on an F natural, the highest note of the song, encapsulating a world of irreparable loss. The ceremonial broadness of C major and the rise of vocal tessitura give the passage enormous rhetorical power. The downward progress in tiered stages of 'auch wohl drei' (b. 21), followed by the sequences 'Nun sind hinab' and 'die besten zwei' (bb. 21–2), trace the setting of the suns in a physical manner typical of the composer (cf. *Freiwilliges Versinken* D700, *An die untergehende Sonne* D457). The piano interlude continues this descent and returns the accompaniment to the lower reaches of the keyboard and a bare E major chord denuded of its fifth – the musical equivalent of a blackout (b. 25).

It might be thought that there is nothing particularly special about A major following E major, but this carefully prepared recapitulation of the opening music (at 'Ging' nur die dritt' erst hinterdrein!') is a masterstroke. The music is bathed in a ray of unearthly light, a sun that is not of our own world. We are reminded all over again of how extraordinary that transfigured *Ländler* melody is, and how Schubert so often excels himself in the contrast between A minor and major – a magical and almost holy harmonic region as far as he is concerned. The simplicity of the traveller's renunciation of the warmth and comfort of earthly love and hope is overwhelming. The harmony under 'Im Dunkeln wird' (b. 28) is subtly different from its equivalent earlier passage at 'Als wollten sie nicht weg von mir', a bass E sharp drawing the harmony into the darker regions of F sharp minor. The composer cannot resist word-painting, and often makes such tiny alterations as he goes.

The music remains in the minor for only a moment. This song is in A major, and it is this most beloved of keys that is the pivot around which the postlude moves in a state of uncanny meditative grace. How could any composer hope to find music to follow this for the last song in the cycle?

Autograph:	Gesellschaft der Musikfreunde, Vienna (first version, fragment lacking bb. 13–19)
Publication:	Published as Op. 89 no. 23 by Tobias Haslinger, Vienna on 30 December 1828 (P191); first version published as part of the NSA in 1979 (P774)

Subsequent editions:	Peters: Vol. 1/118; AGA XX 539: Vol. 9/72; NSA IV: Vol. 4a/187 & Vol. 4b/244 (first version); Bärenreiter: Vol. 3/142
Bibliography:	Heiberg 1993, p. 98
	Mckay 1999, pp. 111–21
	Youens 1991, pp. 289–94
Arrangements:	Arr. Franz Liszt (1811–1886) for solo piano, no. 2 of *Winterreise* (1838–9) [*see* TRANSCRIPTIONS]
	Arr. Tilman Hoppstock (b. 1961) for guitar accompaniment, in *Franz Schubert: 110 Lieder* (2009)

Discography and timing:	Fischer-Dieskau III 2[23]	2'43
	Pears–Britten	3'02
	Hyperion I 30[23]	
	Hyperion II 34[16]	2'48 Matthias Goerne

←— *Mut!* D911/22   *Der Leiermann* D911/24 —→

XXIV Der LEIERMANN   The hurdy-gurdy man
Op. 89 no. 24, **D911/24** [H646]
B minor, changed to A minor for publication[1]

(61 bars)

Drüben hinter'm Dorfe	There, beyond the village,
Steht ein Leiermann,	Stands a hurdy-gurdy player;
Und mit starren Fingern	With numb fingers
Dreht er was er kann.	He plays as best he can.
Barfuss auf dem Eise	Barefoot on the ice
Wankt er hin und her;[2]	He totters to and fro,
Und sein kleiner Teller	And his little plate
Bleibt ihm immer leer.	Remains for ever empty.
Keiner mag ihn hören,	No one wants to listen,
Keiner sieht ihn an;	No one looks at him,
Und die Hunde knurren[3]	And the dogs growl
Um den alten Mann.	Around the old man.
Und er lässt es gehen	And he lets everything go on
Alles, wie es will,	As it will;
Dreht, und seine Leier	He plays, and his hurdy-gurdy
Steht ihm nimmer still.	Never stops.

[1] Because Schubert (if it really was the composer himself) decided on a straightforward transposition here, the song in B minor does not qualify as a version (*Fassung*) in its own right in NSA (where there is no printed version in B minor). The AGA, however, prints the song in both keys.
[2] Müller writes '*Schwankt* er hin und her'.
[3] Müller writes 'Und die Hunde *brummen* ['growl']'.

Wunderlicher Alter,   Strange old man,
Soll ich mit dir gehn?   Shall I go with you?
Willst zu meinen Liedern   Will you turn your hurdy-gurdy
Deine Leier drehn?   To my songs?

Autograph of *Der Leiermann* (fair copy).[1]

This is the forty-fourth of Schubert's forty-six Müller solo settings (1823, 1827 and 1828).
See the poet's biography for a chronological list of all the Müller settings.

On his walks around Vienna and on visits to various towns in the Austrian provinces, Schubert would almost certainly have encountered players of the hurdy-gurdy. This was an ancient instrument, originally from the East, which was ubiquitous in the Middle Ages. Although it enjoyed a second lease of life in the eighteenth century it was fast going out of fashion again by the 1820s; hurdy-gurdy music was for those who were behind the times, not to say down-and-out. The instrument has two sets of strings, one melody and one drone, and a wooden wheel that acts as a bow on the strings when rotated by a crank. There is a keyboard played by the left hand, with tangents that press on the melody strings to make them speak. The hurdy-gurdy responds best to the skilful performer, but anyone can sound the drone strings by turning the wheel with the right hand, and a rudimentary melody can be picked out in the left without calling for the normal acuity of the trained string player. From medieval times this enormously popular instrument was to be found in churches, palaces and on village greens. It enjoyed a renewed vogue

---

[1] Elmar Budde believes that it was the publisher Tobias Haslinger's decision, not Schubert's, to change the autograph keys of *Mut* (originally A minor) and *Der Leiermann* (originally B minor), transposing them each a tone lower. (It is generally attested, however, that Schubert saw the proofs of the second part of the cycle.) The key of *Der Leiermann* should, said Budde, mirror the B minor of *Einsamkeit* that brought the first part of the cycle to a close.

with the French court's whimsical delight in rusticity at the time of Marie-Antoinette. Haydn wrote for it, as did Mozart in one of his Minuets (K601) and one of his German Dances (K602). Donizetti used it to accompany arias in *Linda di Chamonix*, where its plangent sound represents the innocence of country life and nostalgia for the past. During the nineteenth century, as pilgrims and itinerant minstrels faded into the background of history, the instrument was inherited by peasants and beggars. The modern revival of the hurdy-gurdy (Drehleier) as a concert instrument has been spearheaded by the virtuoso Matthias Loibner who has recorded an entire *Winterreise* with hurdy-gurdy accompaniment from first note to last. This is a real technical feat, even if the banishing of the piano's expressive possibilities diminishes the work's *raison d'être*. Loibner gives a new and uncomfortable slant to the cycle, as if the meeting with the hurdy-gurdy player in *Der Leiermann* has eerily taken place in the very first song, and the whole of the cycle is experienced as a kind of flash-back.

Hurdy-gurdy player (known as 'Old Sarah'). Engraving from a daguerreotype, reproduced in Henry Mayhew's *London Labour and the London Poor* (1851).

The distinctive sound of the instrument is suggested in the very first bar of Schubert's introduction, an open fifth, A to E, written as a dotted minim in the left hand and ornamented with a D sharp grace note. We find this drone effect more regularly in old French music than in German, suggesting how important the hurdy-gurdy was in eighteenth-century *musettes*. Indeed, this *bourdon* effect became a cliché in collections of old French airs such as Weckerlin's *Echos du temps passé*. Later, composers of *mélodie* were pleased to employ it as one of their time-shifting tricks in writing period pastiches. But there are some powerful hurdy-gurdy effects in lieder too. Apart from *Der Leiermann*, we hear it concealed in the whirling textures of Schumann's *Das ist ein Flöten und Geigen* from *Dichterliebe*, and at the opening of the first song of Mahler's *Lieder eines fahrenden Gesellen* (both these latter examples describe wedding music tinged with the false note of jarring unhappiness); in Wolf's *Die Bekehrte* where it evokes a bergerette in the French manner; and in the same composer's *So lasst mich scheinen* as Mignon accompanies herself on the zither, another instrument with a drone

bass. Earlier than any of these was Weber's *Reigen* (an 1815 setting of words by Voss) which also begins with two open-fifth chords, plus twanging acciaccaturas. This is a yokel and yodel picture of village life, far from town, in a country setting where the archaic nature of the hurdy-gurdy seems to find employment. (Note that Müller has placed his player 'Drüben hinter'm Dorfe' – not even in a village, but beyond it.) The last of Brahms's Thirteen Canons, Op. 113, for unaccompanied women's voices is a reworking of *Der Leiermann*: sopranos sing Schubert's melody, while the bare fifths are shared between the altos. The text is a Rückert fragment, 'Einförmig ist der Liebe Gram' ('The suffering of love is monotonous'). The poem includes the word 'mitsummen' ('to hum along') and here one great composer hums along with the work of another as a mark of fellow-feeling and shared desolation.

The left hand continues with its open fifths throughout *Der Leiermann* (the acciaccaturas feature only in the two introductory bars, although some pianists have seen fit to continue the grace notes throughout). Above this the right hand traces the ghost of a tune, more like a formula of notes, which is the foundation of the entire accompaniment. Four semiquavers are followed by four quavers, all contained within the interval of an augmented fourth. This suggests the random musical doodling of beggars (then, as now), who take up an instrument without training – blowing tuneless wails on the mouth-organ, or plucking aimlessly at the ill-tuned strings of a guitar. Two bars follow (bb. 4 and 5) with the stilted little flourish of tonic-to-dominant cadences, A minor to E major; the clash of this right-hand music with the unchanging open fifths of the left hand adds to a harmonic sense of alienation and emptiness. Another bar of four semiquavers and four quavers balances the first in a type of echo sequence, and two bars of cadences, dominant back to tonic, suggest a kind of symmetry. Perhaps this player has some musical skill after all. Even sadder than the untrained would-be musician are those beggars who have once had the ability to play an instrument well but can no longer do so, often victims of a catalogue of personal disasters, alcoholism and other sicknesses.

What has brought the hurdy-gurdy player in Müller's poem to this frostbitten point in his story is not clear, but in the course of the song we find out something about him: he is poorly clothed, barefoot and frozen; his music is not good enough to interest, much less enrapture, the public or earn him any money – on the contrary, he is an embarrassment that nobody wants to see or hear. Even the dogs do not like the look of him. And yet he is a musician of sorts, even if terribly down on his luck. Any successful professional musician who passes such a fellow-'artist' (for want of a less charitable word) cannot fail to feel a twinge of conscience: 'There, but for the grace of God, go I.' The words of a Schumann song, the Andersen/Chamisso *Der Spielmann* Op. 40 no. 4, come to mind: 'Bin selber ein armer Musikant' ('I myself am a poor musician').

When the vocal line appears for the first time in b. 9 the piano's right hand vanishes, leaving the singer accompanied only by those bare fifths. From the beginning the voice matches the primitive level of the hurdy-gurdy player's artistry and technique. Schubert has succeeded in the almost impossible: he has written a memorable tune using melodic ingredients of such simplicity that the music is simultaneously negligible and self-evidently the work of a great master. Perhaps this is the earliest example of the power of minimalism and a tune so rudimentary in terms of its invention that it remains in the heads of the most unmusical of people. Whilst brilliantly controlling this descent into banality, Schubert remains a peerless word-setter. The melody rises and falls and retraces itself in its own tracks, conveying the progress of numb fingers over the same patches of the keyboard, as well as the player's tottering movement described in 'Wankt er hin und her'. The fruitless and repetitive nature of his work is emphasized by the repeat of the strophe's last line – no matter how much he plays, his little begging bowl remains empty. The first 'Und sein kleiner Teller / Bleibt ihm immer leer' ends on the dominant (still underscored by the A minor drone, of course) and after a two-bar interlude (bb. 23–4) the repeat of these words returns, with an implied shrug, to the tonic. There is an awful symmetry about the way these phrases answer each other, as if to imply acceptance of fate.

In an interlude that is longer than anything since the introduction (bb. 27–30), the right hand climbs a full octave in steps of a minor sixth and a major third, a craggy path of keyboard accomplishment that we suspect is beyond the frozen stretch of the old man. It is as if the composer has interceded in a twinge of compassion and allowed the numbed fingers a momentary echo of a possible former virtuosity. The lonely high A at the apex of this phrase, unharmonized and supported only by what sound remains of the left-hand chord, is as powerfully mournful as anything in the cycle. We hear it three times, at the end of each of the song's musical sections, and always with increasing intensity.

Schubert has thus used two of Müller's verses to make a single musical verse. 'Barfuss auf dem Eise' (b. 17) did not mark the beginning of a new musical section, but sounded as the seamless continuation of the first. The song continues in like fashion where the next two strophes are again linked in an exact musical repeat of what has gone before. The repetitions and the deadness of the musical atmosphere have already worked their uniquely hypnotic spell. In the suspension of the rich harmonic activity we have experienced over twenty-three songs, time seems to stand still, music itself seems to freeze. The hurdy-gurdy player who carries on regardless, impervious even to snarling dogs, seems either the passive puppet of fate or something much more powerful and ominous. Müller tells us that no one wants to listen, but is this mere indifference or is it fear? The unceasing music could be taken as a metaphor for the monotonous but implacable work of the Reaper. Everyone tries to avoid Death – even the dogs feel his icy presence and growl – but he carries on regardless with the work that he has to do. In this light the figure of the hurdy-gurdy player becomes something much more disturbing, much more final, than we might have supposed from the tentative and stumbling mood of the opening. The four-bar interlude at the end of the repetition of the words 'Dreht, und seine Leier / Steht ihm nimmer still' (bb. 49–52) is more frightening than pathetic in its hollow impassivity. (There has been no dynamic change, however, and the song remains pianissimo.)

And then comes one of the most inspired codas in musical history. Müller's poem contains five strophes, so after a pattern which marries off the first four in pairs, the composer is free to do what he will with the dangling remnant. These are the last words that the listener hears in the cycle, and they remain to haunt him. 'Wunderlicher Alter', asks the traveller, who has somehow approached the hurdy-gurdy player without the slightest musical suggestion of trudge or tramp. Only once before in the cycle has he initiated a conversation, and that was when he questioned the crow (*Die Krähe* (No. 15)) in similar manner, addressing it as 'wunderliches Tier' – 'strange creature'. Strange and peculiar of course, but also awesome and wonderful in every sense. We are by now familiar with the little accompanying figure that has closed the introduction, as well as the second strophe – a hiccup or musical tic where a fragment of melody rises a third and returns to the tonic, all within one bar. Against a continuing repetition of this musical cell, the traveller whispers to the old man. The vocal line is suddenly parlando, a succession of Es with a remarkable upward inflection of a fourth on '<u>Al</u>ter', implying a pull at the sleeve, or an interlocking of glances. The question 'Soll ich mit dir gehn?' (bb. 54–5) combines curiosity with exquisite and courtly tenderness, wide- rather than wild-eyed. At 'Willst zu meinen Liedern / Deine Leier drehn?' (bb. 56–7) both the pianist's hands support the vocal line: until now it has only been the left-hand drone. Thus the full musical resources of the accompaniment are engaged with those of the singer, and we have a tiny demonstration of the proposed collaboration. In fact, duos for voice with hurdy-gurdy were common among itinerant musicians and beggars: there is one such with a soprano described in Book 2, Chapter 6 of a Dostoyevsky's *Crime and Punishment*: 'I love', Raskolnikov says 'when they sing to the accompaniment of a hurdy-gurdy on a cold, dark, damp evening of autumn . . . or better yet when a wet snow is falling.' This takes place in a poverty-stricken corner of St Petersburg where two beggars stand a better chance of being heard than one. Perhaps such a business partnership is what Schubert's traveller has in mind. As if attempting to give an example of his wares, he leaves the reaches of speech and sings his heart out with leaps of an octave, as if energized at last by a solution to his woes. This all occurs within a piano marking, but perhaps Schubert did not need to make a crescendo given the contour of the vocal line – a point for performers to ponder. For a single bar, the beginning of the closing interlude is marked forte (b. 58) and the end of the singer's phrase – a mournfully elongated E natural on 'drehn' for three beats – is also drawn into this louder dynamic. Thus a powerful streak of colour suddenly appears, comet-like, in the bleak winter sky, and just as quickly disappears. Is this a twinge of recognition that life will go on like this for ever – the making of music to which no one will listen, the isolation of internment without release? Or is it the parting gasp of a soul at the portals of death? The postlude leaves the matter as open as the bare fifths which continue their dull knell in the left hand (and here one realizes it is a mistake to have considered importing the acciaccaturas throughout). The aimless explorations of the right hand are inexplicably (and frighteningly) forte in b. 58, but their outcome is as uncertain as ever. Even the final A minor chord (the dynamic has returned to pianissimo) provides no answers, only the lingering resonances of unanswered questions, and our awe at the masterpiece that has come to an unlikely end. In failing to reach a thundering peroration, *Winterreise* has evaporated into icy mist before our very ears.

The unstoppable crescendo of popularity for this cycle – once one of the least heard of Schubert's works, and now perhaps the victim of a surfeit of well-meant but anodyne perform-ances by singers who assay this work too early in their careers – has ensured an iconic place for the figure of both the traveller and the organ-grinder in world literature. A recent example of a work inspired by these characters from *Winterreise* is *El Viajero del siglo*, an award-winning novel by the Argentinian author Andrés Neuman (b. 1977), published in Spain in 2009.

Publication:	Published as Op. 89 no. 24 by Tobias Haslinger, Vienna on 30 December 1828 (P192); first version published as part of the AGA in 1895 (P700)
Subsequent editions:	Peters: Vol. 1/120; AGA XX 540: Vol. 9/76 (A minor) & 74 (B minor); NSA IV: Vol. 4a/189; Bärenreiter: Vol. 3/144 & 228 (B minor)
Bibliography:	Aries 1976
	Berke 2002, p. 83
	Youens 1991, pp. 295–306
Further settings and arrangements:	Arr. Franz Liszt (1811–1886) for solo piano, no. 8 of *Winterreise* (1838–9) [*see* TRANSCRIPTIONS]
	Arr. Johannes Brahms (1833–1897) *Einförmig ist der Liebe Gram* Op. 113. no. 13, in which the melody and ostinato bass are presented in six-part unaccompanied canon for female voices
	Rainer Bredemeyer (1929–1995) *Lieder auf der Flucht* for mezzo soprano and piano (1985)
	Heinz Winbeck (b. 1946) *Winterreise. Stationen für 19 Solostreicher* (based on *Der Leiermann* and *Der Winterabend* D938)
	Arr. Tilman Hoppstock (b. 1961) for guitar accompaniment (2 arrangements), in *Franz Schubert: 110 Lieder* (2009)
Discography and timing:	Fischer-Dieskau III 2²⁴ 3'33
	Pears–Britten 3'19
	Hyperion I 30²⁴
	Hyperion II 34¹⁷ 3'54 Matthias Goerne

←— *Die Nebensonnen* D911/23   *Der Hochzeitsbraten* D930 —→

AFTERWORD: MUSIC IN THE STREET, AND IN THE MIND

Weil er zu vertraut war,	Because he'd been too intimate
wird er nun fremd.	He now becomes a stranger.

Seine Wanderer trafen	His wanderings met
auf wenig Freundlichkeit,	with little kindliness;
immer verschlossen sich	again and again the houses
die Häuser, die Nachbarn	shut in his face, the neighbours
waren aus Stein,	were of stone,
die Mädchen deren Bild	the girls whose pictures
er bewahrte, gehörten	he held on to belonged
andern, und	to others and
sein Winter endete	his winter was
nicht.	without end.
Er wusste, die Erde	He knew the earth
kühlt aus.	was growing cold.

Peter Hartling (b. 1933)

Schubert heard countless musicians of every kind on the streets of Vienna. His youth was spent in a time of military mobilization and he must have walked in step with many a military band playing their unsophisticated *marches militaires*. In this city almost everyone aspired to be a musician. Performers ranged from the relatively sophisticated *Bankelsänger*, who sang popular and topical songs accompanying themselves on harps and guitars, to the infinitely less skilled itinerant street-musicians, many of whom were blind, crippled or maimed. These vagabonds, many of them still children, had to make their living somehow. They lined the city walls and hid in dark passages with their harps and guitars, hoping for a few coins thrown by passers-by in exchange for their striking up a familiar melody. As he walked home to his lodgings, one of which was located in the city walls near the Karolinentor (in late 1826 and early 1827), the composer must often have had these strains ringing in his ears.

The topic of street music had long been an emotive one and so it has remained. The dignity of art and indignity of destitution can be a highly uncomfortable combination when confronted at close quarters. It is only the occasional street-musician who gives the kind of musical pleasure that results in money falling in large quantities into his hat. It is far more usual for badly played music to accompany acts of grudging, or embarrassed, compassion.

The skeletal figure of Death is sometimes represented playing the hurdy-gurdy in medieval iconography, and it is not surprising that *Der Leiermann* is often taken to be 'Freund Hain' – or Death – as depicted in the frontispiece of the works of Matthias Claudius. Perhaps this is what Müller intended but as he was no musician his choice of ending seems either arbitrary, or eerily predestined for Schubert who was no doubt both attracted to and troubled by the poem on a number of levels. This sudden and strangely appropriate mention of a musician at the last moment in the cycle may well have been the clinching factor that motivated the composer to expand the Ur-*Winterreise* into a twenty-four-song work. Schubert must have been familiar with the problem of penury among musicians whose talents had been eroded by misfortune and illness. Even a tiny accident can render a player unable to work, and Schubert's hand-to-mouth existence was not protected by such things as insurance and pension plans, much less a Musicians' Benevolent Fund.

In ordinary circumstances he need never have feared the loss of his musical capital. After Beethoven's death in March 1827 he must have known that he had inherited the great man's mantle, and had more musical talent in either of his little fingers than anyone else in Vienna – nay, probably the world – but this depended on his fingers being able to function more efficiently than those of Müller's hurdy-gurdy player. Since late 1822 there had been a long and dark shadow across his life: syphilis. The disease had a number of alarming prognoses, chief among them was that after a number of years it was likely to attack the brain and, with it, the powers of thought and creativity. By 1827 four years had already elapsed but 'What does the future hold for me?' is a question that must have obsessed him.

Of course, we know what Schubert could not foresee – that he was to die within thirteen months of completing *Winterreise*, spared the effects of tertiary syphilis and still at the height of his musical powers. But it was a real possibility that, in the normal course of his venereal infection, the river of Schubertian melody would dry up. Perhaps he would be left, like the similarly afflicted Baudelaire, endlessly repeating the same words, parrot-fashion, like a record-playing needle stuck in the same groove of the brain. Even if he hoped that he had been cured of syphilis by the stringent, painful mercury treatments he had to endure, there was always the threat that the old ill would return. In the hospital where he wrote part of *Die schöne Müllerin* D795 in 1823 he would have seen the effects of syphilis on patients at later stages of the illness. There must have been plenty of anecdotal evidence about those who had felt well again for years, only for the illness to claim them in the most tragic manner. While at times Schubert might have truly believed himself to be cured (doctors attempted to convince their patients that they had earned their fees), at other moments he must have felt that he lived under the Sword of Damocles. One of these times was mid-October 1827 when Schubert complained in a letter to Frau Pachler that his 'usual headaches' were once more assailing him. Thus it seems likely that the composer was coping with the after-effects of the old illness, or its treatment by mercury, at the very time that he was putting the finishing touches to *Winterreise*.

It is far too simplistic to imagine the character of the winter traveller as a self-portait. The character is in a sense bigger than Schubert, as King Lear is bigger than Shakespeare. The hero of this cycle achieves an eloquence and stature that are reserved for the mightiest characters in opera. *Winterreise* is a dramatic event and cannot be explained solely by the sad fate of its creator who was largely able to forget himself and his problems when he was in the throes of composing. As we have seen, many songs in the cycle refer back to earlier works and can be interpreted simply as a development of Schubert's pioneering achievements in the genre, something quite separate from the special pleading of biographical parallels. But there is documentary evidence that Schubert was shaken to the core in writing the first half of this work and that he was strangely moody and withdrawn during its gestation. If he felt this way after composing the first twelve songs of the cycle, we can only imagine what his reaction might have been after his encounter with Müller's *Der Leiermann*. With its barren and bleak landscape, it is the only song in Schubert's output that is denuded of music itself. There is no real harmonic movement, and the repetitive musical phrases go round in circles. The stumbling fingers of the old man are numb with cold, but perhaps they are also impeded by illness (any musician's nightmare – arthritis, multiple sclerosis, some other neurological complaint, or syphilis perhaps). In this way the hurdy-gurdy player on the ice does not seem to be a symbol of death as we understand it, but of something which, in Schubert's eyes and ears, would surely have been far worse – *living* death, or, in this case, life without *real* music. One need look no further than the later years of both Schumann and Wolf for an illustration of the protracted period of humiliating disability in the antechamber of death. In some of the failing music of the last periods of both these masters we can detect the chilly grip and numb fingers of the hurdy-gurdy man.

Der Leiermann was not drawn from the composer's own experience; the eerie tune was not formed from the large bank of musical allusion and tonal analogue at his disposal throughout the rest of the cycle; nor could the song benefit from the unending fount of melody from which Schubert could draw at any time he chose. For example, the dactylic rhythm of Death, a fingerprint found in *Der Tod und das Mädchen* D531 and elsewhere, is nowhere to be heard. Where then does this music come from? The future, perhaps. The composer's future that is. This song is a moonscape, a projection of an unknown tomorrow. 'What will become of me?' the traveller asks. 'Am I to go with you, hurdy-gurdy man? Will your music be a fitting accompaniment for my poems?' And Schubert allows himself to ask the same thing: 'Will this music be like the music *I* will compose one day – sans tune, sans harmony, sans everything? Is this how life – my life at least – will come to an end? A descent into non-music, just like those poor street people who call themselves musicians?' At the beginning of the cycle the traveller could not have imagined himself having anything in common with an itinerant musical beggar. But Schubert could now anticipate his own musical abilities having something in common with the incompetent drone and stumble of a hurdy-gurdy player.

On 8 May 1823 Schubert had written a poem entitled *Mein Gebet* ('My Prayer') that included the lines 'Take my life, my flesh and blood, / Plunge it all in Lethe's flood'. In the penultimate song (*Der Müller und der Bach* D795/19) of the other great Müller cycle, *Die schöne Müllerin*, the young miller boy drowns himself in the millstream. It was perhaps in sacrificing his protagonist, and experiencing death alongside the young miller in musical terms, that Schubert found the strength to continue with what remained of his own life – five matchless years of unimpeded creativity. This was a cathartic act of self therapy by someone *in extremis*, a composer whose artistic survival was in danger of extinction, and who used the most powerful thing he had – his own art – to overcome the crisis.

Someone who imagines the worst and puts it down on paper, or turns it into art, might be considered a pessimist or hypochondriac. But the belief in knowing your enemy, looking him in the eye and disarming him *before* the moment of meeting is an ancient one. In Stone Age culture, rock paintings depicted the successful hunt in anticipation of the event; in medieval times those wishing to be spared the plague simulated its symptoms in a *Totentanz*, a dance of death. In *Western Attitudes Toward Death: From the Middle Ages to the Present* the French historian Philippe Ariès describes how people in ages past attempted to 'tame' death by preparing for it, thus ensuring they lived well and died with grace. Just as Schubert had drowned the miller boy in his stead, he encourages the winter traveller to sing non-music with a hurdy-gurdy player, even composing non-music for the two of them. As the cycle ends, they go off together into the distance, and the composer remains behind. It is as if in staging their meeting, the composer has avoided being overcome himself. The composition of *Der Leiermann* perhaps enabled him to look into the bleakest regions of the future while keeping his ability to write melody intact; in short, he had remained in control. Thus do artists flirt with their own creations, identifying closely with what they are, but retaining a distance, a barrier against being destroyed by the forces they have called into life. (Mary Shelley's contemporary *Frankenstein* can be seen as a warning against creators who fail to do this.)

Once he had given musical form to his worst nightmare Schubert may have felt less frightened by a lifetime destitute of melody, hidebound by the winter fog of a degenerative illness. He may even have felt he was less likely to succumb to it. His subsequent music, the masterpieces composed between the end of 1827 and his death a year or so later (a death not directly related to tertiary syphilis) are a massively reassuring affirmation that what may have been the composer's worst nightmare never became reality. This *Leiermann* remains a powerful and haunting creation, but even if the hurdy-gurdy player was the figure of Death, he was not given the last *musical* word. The traveller's rhetorical questions, 'Wunderlicher Alter, / Soll ich mit dir gehn? / Willst zu meinen Liedern / Deine Leier drehn?', seem to be answered with a 'Yes' as far as the hurdy-gurdy player is concerned, but with a firm and silent 'No' from the composer. A year after completing *Winterreise* Schubert penned his final work which later became the last of his so-called *Schwanengesang*, a sequence of very different songs, on his own terms. This was *Die Taubenpost* D965A, a miracle of melody, animated by an unimpeded awareness of everything to do with love and longing. The song's beauty is heartbreaking, but it remains graceful, articulate, unimpaired by any trace of illness or self-pity.

Das WIRTSHAUS *see WINTERREISE* D911/21

WOHIN? *see Die SCHÖNE MÜLLERIN* D795/2

WOLKE UND QUELLE   The cloud and the stream
(LEITNER) **D896B** [H648]
(Fragment) C major   Between autumn 1827 and beginning of 1828

(96 bars)

German	English
Auf meinen heimischen Bergen,	On the mountains of my native land
Da sind die Wolken zu Haus'	The clouds are at home;
Bin mitten ihnen gestanden,	I have stood among them
Und sah in's Tal hinaus.	Looking out into the valley.
Sie aber flogen von dannen,	But they flew away,
Wie Schwäne, so licht und leicht;	As light and as weightless as swans;
Wär' gerne mit ihnen gezogen,[1]	I would gladly have flown with them
So weit der Himmel reicht.	To the ends of the sky.
Es drängt mich fort in die Fremde[2]	A wild urge drives me
Zur Ferne ein wilder Trieb;	To distant foreign lands.
Doch jetzt erscheinen mir Heimat	But now my home and surroundings
Und Nähe gar heilig und lieb.	Are dear and sacred to me.
Nun sehn' ich mich nimmer in's Weite,	Now I never yearn to be far away
Hinaus in's nebelnde Blau;	In the misty azure;
Nun späh' ich mit stillem Verlangen	Now I gaze with silent longing
Hinab in die schmale Au.	Down into the narrow valley.
Was nickt dort unten am Fenster	What is that nodding down there by the window,
Und blühet wie Morgenlicht?	Blossoming like the dawn?
Ist's ihre Ros' am Gesimse?	Is it her rose on the sill,
Oder ihr holdes Gesicht?	Or her sweet face?
Viel Glück ihr Wolken zur Reise!	I wish you a good journey, clouds.
Ich ziehe nimmer mit euch;	I shall never come with you.
Was aber locket und lispelt	But what is that enticing and whispering to me
Da drüben im Lenzgesträuch?	Over there amid the spring foliage?

[1] Leitner writes (*Gedichte*, 1857) '*Gern wär' ich* mit ihnen gezogen'.
[2] Leitner writes 'Es *drängte* mich fort in die Fremde'.

Bist du es, o Quelle, die flüstert?
Ja, ja! ich eile mit dir;
Du kennst ja die kürzesten Wege,
Hinunter, hinunter zu ihr.

Is it you whispering, o stream?
Yes, yes! I shall hasten with you;
For you know the shortest way
Down to her below!

KARL GOTTFRIED VON LEITNER (1800–1890)

This is the fourth of Schubert's eleven Leitner solo settings (1822–3 and 1827–8). See the poet's biography for a chronological list of all the Leitner settings.

The three unknown Leitner settings (the others are *Fröhliches Scheiden* D896 and *Sie in jedem Liede* D896A) are the more interesting for being more or less contemporary with the songs for the second half of *Winterreise*, and being the last of the composer's lieder to remain as incomplete fragments. Schubert sketched all three on the same sheet of manuscript paper, and it seems clear that they were conceived at the same time, probably the work of a single day. As was the composer's usual practice, the vocal lines were outlined but, although he allowed space for an accompaniment, the songs were abandoned before they were taken to the next stage of development. We are thus in possession of a great deal of genuine Schubertian melody in the treble clef with scarcely an indication of harmony and little idea of what pianistic motifs might have been used to fashion the accompaniments. Just occasionally the composer has jotted down a few notes in the empty piano staves to remind himself of what had occurred to him in this regard.

Schubert's intentions regarding two of the poems is also something of a problem. While *Fröhliches Scheiden* has Leitner's lyrics (with title but no acknowledgement of author) written out by the composer, the others have no words under the notes. Reinhard Van Hoorickx came up with the idea that the remaining two songs were also Leitner settings (surely highly likely), and having examined the Leitner poems in Schubert's possession at the time (the *Gedichte* published in 1825) he proposed that the missing texts were *Wolke und Quelle* and *Sie in jedem Liede*. Hoorickx published a private edition of these songs with his suggested textual underlay, as well as an accompaniment which is typical of his work in this field: he never pretended to be a skilled composer, but his completions are simple enough to allow us to hear Schubert's melodies with a harmonic and pianistic background that does its best not to take attention away from the genuine core of the setting. Of course Hoorickx always incorporates the few genuine accompanimental notes that Schubert had written in a sort of musical shorthand on the piano staves.

The editors of the *Neue Schubert-Ausgabe* rather grudgingly concede that *Wolke und Quelle* is, in all probability, the correct poem for the music, but at first were less convinced by *Sie in jedem Liede*. These reservations were based on the fact that at certain points the poem has been made to fit the music with some difficulty. In the absence of any alternative suggestions, however, the Leitner titles suggested by Hoorickx have been adopted by the second edition of the Deutsch catalogue and the NSA. The problems of fitting the words exactly into the musical sketch might well have been ironed out by the composer had he done any further work on the songs.

The gentle rocking gait of *Wolke und Quelle* brings to mind another quasi-waltz song in ⅜, also with a Leitner text – *Drang in die Ferne* D770. Of course the mood suggested by the text has been governed in this instance by Hoorickx's piano part (he has opted for something much less impassioned, and dreamier, than *Drang in die Ferne*) but the link with a possible Leitner style is obvious. What is also clear is that Schubert is writing with a certain singer in mind – almost certainly a tenor. Nowhere else in the songs of the late period is the vocal line placed so high, except of course in the famous choral piece for tenor and men's chorus, *Nachthelle* D892. That was one of the great works of 1826 performed at the beginning of 1827 at a Musikverein concert with Ludwig Tietze as the lead tenor. The solo part was written 'für . . . verdammt hohen Tenor' – 'for a damnably high tenor' (Schubert's friend Ferdinand Walcher described it thus in a letter to the composer on 25 January 1827). It may have been that Tietze had asked Schubert to write him some new songs, and that these sketches are an attempt to do so: they are scattered with high notes, and the tessitura hovers around high Gs and As more than is usual in Schubert's lieder. In both *Fröhliches Scheiden* and *Sie in jedem Liede* there are a number of high B flats (authentic), and the latter song boasts a high C towards the end which is a Hoorickx suggestion for a passing note.

It is interesting that the only work dedicated to Ludwig Tietze was the *Offertorium* in C, D136. Perhaps the composer and singer had a disagreement some time in the autumn of 1827, or perhaps Schubert abandoned these three songs because he had little enthusiasm for writing music styled to show off the strong points of a particular voice. (This failure to deliver a promised group could easily have engendered Tietze's disappointment and anger.) In any case one has the impression that this singer was more of a technician with a fine instrument than a deeply interesting artist; in contemporary accounts we read of the special feeling and understanding of Vogl or Schönstein, but Tietze's singing was always praised more for his timbre and his command of the upper tessitura than for the depth of his artistry (*see also* SINGERS).

Looking at the mellifluous shape of the vocal line (as printed in the *Neue Schubert-Ausgabe* with a great deal of empty space for the accompaniment) one regrets more than ever that Schubert did not complete the task. Here surely the character of the accompaniment could have made all the difference in the world. Hoorickx's realization is gentle and unpretentious; he chooses to mark the piece 'Ruhig' where some parts of the poem – 'Es drängt mich fort in die Fremde', for example – might have suggested a more urgent interpretation. As a result there is a sentimental note to the music that conveys the salon. It is true that this tone is also struck in *Heimliches Lieben* D922, written at the same time, but music that is cosily Biedermeier in character is a Schubertian rarity. One could also argue that this style was another of Schubert's occasional commercial ploys – an attempt to reach a wider market. What is interesting, however, is that the airy idea of floating clouds and the flowing imagery of the stream are both beautifully captured in the vocal line, and that if the composer was looking for a text for a high voice then this poem was eminently suited for the purpose by the 'head in the clouds' mood of its subject matter.

Autograph:	Wienbibliothek im Rathaus, Vienna (fragment)
First edition:	Published in Richard Heuberger's *Franz Schubert* in 1902; performing version by Reinhard Van Hoorickx. Subsequently published as part of the NSA in 1988 (P805)
Subsequent editions:	Not in Peters; Not in AGA; NSA IV: Vol. 14b/278
Discography and timing:	Fischer-Dieskau —
	Hyperion I 36[8]
	Hyperion II 35[1] 5'17 Juliane Banse

←— *Der Hochzeitsbraten* D930   *Fröhliches Scheiden* D896 —→

Die WOLKENBRAUT *see* DUBIOUS, MISATTRIBUTED AND LOST SONGS

WONNE DER WEHMUT
(GOETHE) **D260** [H146]
C minor   20 August 1815

Delight in melancholy

(20 bars)

Trocknet nicht, trocknet nicht,	Do not grow dry, do not grow dry,
Tränen der ewigen Liebe!	Tears of eternal love!
Ach, nur dem halbgetrockneten Auge	Ah, even when the eye is but half-dry
Wie öde, wie tot die Welt ihm erscheint!	How desolate, how dead the world appears!
Trocknet nicht, trocknet nicht,	Do not grow dry, do not grow dry,
Tränen unglücklicher Liebe!	Tears of unhappy love!

JOHANN WOLFGANG VON GOETHE (1749–1832); poem written in summer 1775

This is the twenty-seventh of Schubert's seventy-five Goethe solo settings (1814–26). See the poet's biography for a chronological list of all the Goethe settings.

Most singers prefer Beethoven's setting of this poem (Op. 83 no. 1, 1810) which is undoubtedly eloquent but also somewhat 'stagey' as Einstein puts it. In Schubert there is no trace of self-indulgence, and we note an urgency that gives a completely different slant to the poem. The Schubert song lasts well under a minute but a wounded vulnerability is created by a single curved line of the song-writer's brush. A certain note of personal experience is sounded – even by 1815 Schubert knew something of love, although it is also possible that he did not grasp the full measure of the poem. His music (especially when sung 'Etwas geschwind' as marked) strikes an urgent if not desperate note – its short-breathed phrases give the impression of someone pleading (and almost panting) in distress. On the other hand, Beethoven, lover of many women and canny preserver of his own creative privacy, understood the text's paradox to a more sophisticated extent: the 'delight' of the title is every bit as important as the 'melancholy'. The poet uses love's ups and downs as a kind of stimulant to activity, just as Schiller was said to have kept musty apples in a drawer for the same purpose. Goethe luxuriates in his unhappiness (self-indulgence, albeit in a rarefied Goethean way, is very much part of the picture) and Beethoven writes music in the major key that perfectly reflects the rather leisurely pleasure taken by the poet in that pain – as if he were examining tears and their effect on the artist as a quasi-scientific phenomenon. For Goethe the 'poet-in-love' is a valuable and fruitful pose, and love that causes tears is worthwhile because it keeps the imagination working at full tilt. As Lorraine Byrne puts it, 'It is only when tears are permitted to flow unimpeded, or sorrow set free, that the poet can experience an emotional release.' The word 'trocknen' is both transitive and intransitive. Uri Liebrecht makes the point that this poem could also be read as an imprecation to us, the readers, not to wipe away these tears but to indulge in our feelings of melancholy – they do us good. The presence of the comma at the end of the poem's first line works against this theory.

It is difficult to believe that the woman loved by Goethe at this time (Elisabeth 'Lili' Schönemann, 1758–1817) was more than a cardboard cut-out whose role was simply to be cast as one of his changing lovers in the ongoing drama of his life. Schubert of course had neither the

Autograph of *Wonne der Wehmut* from the album for Goethe, 1816.

self-absorption nor the arrogance to indulge in these mind-games, and he took the words a mite too seriously; in 1815 he lacked any sense of the delectation of experience that is at the heart of this poetic pondering. There is a marked similarity between this song and the musical ideas in the second movement of his unfinished piano sonata known as the 'Reliquie' D840. In this C minor movement the *Bewegung* of the semiquavers, sometimes staccato, has something of the nervy and impassioned character of the song. One might imagine that this was not a favourite of Schubert's from the fact that it is one of the few Goethe settings not published in his lifetime, but he liked it well enough to place it opposite *Heidenröslein* D257 in the album of songs written out for the great poet in 1816. And he also quoted it, including the original Goethe text, twelve years later (with doubled note values – quavers rather than semiquavers) as part of his last, and never finished, opera *Der Graf von Gleichen* D918. There it is the Gräfin's aria, no. 13 of the work (Act II, Scene 2), and transposed into G minor, a rather more comfortable tonality. Perhaps integrating orchestrations of his already composed lieder into his operas was something that Schubert intended to pursue in his subsequent stage works.

Autographs:	Gesellschaft der Musikfreunde, Vienna (first draft)
	Staatsbibliothek zu Berlin (fair copy made for Goethe)
First edition:	Published as Op. post. 115 no. 2 by M. J. Leidesdorf, Vienna in June 1829 (P219)
Subsequent editions:	Peters: Vol. 4/141; AGA XX 117: Vol. 3/42; NSA IV: Vol. 8/198
Bibliography:	Byrne 2003, pp. 74–6
	Einstein 1951, p. 111
Further settings and arrangements:	Johann Friedrich Reichardt (1752–1814) *Wonne der Wehmut* (1788)
	Carl Friedrich Zelter (1758–1832) *Wonne der Wehmut* (1807)
	Ludwig van Beethoven (1770–1827) *Wonne der Wehmut* Op. 83 no. 1 (1810)

Robert Franz (1815–1892) *Wonne der Wehmut* Op. 33 no. 1 (1864)
Franz Salmhofer (1900–1975) *Wonne der Wehmut* Op. 5 no. 3 (1923)
Arr. Tilman Hoppstock (b. 1961) for guitar accompaniment, in *Franz Schubert: 110 Lieder* (2009)

Discography and timing: Fischer-Dieskau I 5[6]   1'06
Hyperion I 1[11]
Hyperion II 9[7]   0'48   Janet Baker

← *An den Mond* D259   *Wer kauft Liebesgötter?* D261 →

One of the plaster casts of Schubert's death mask.

Z

ALOIS ZETTLER (1778–1828)

THE POETIC SOURCES
S1 *Selam. Ein Almanach für Freunde des Mannigfaltigen auf das Jahr 1814.* Von I. F. Castelli. Wien Gedruckt und in Verlage bey Anton Strauss

S2 *Nachgelassene Gedichte* von Alois Zettler Mit einer Vorrede herausgegeben von Chr. Kuffner, Wien. Bei Schmidl's Witwe und Ig. Klang 1836 Gedruckt bei Franz Ludwig

THE SONG
12 April 1815   *Trinklied* D183 [S1: p. 222 with the title 'Freundschaft und Wein, Rundgesang']
                [S2: p. 113 with the title *Trinklied*]

Alois Zettler was an older contemporary of Schubert's whose life was spent in the employ of the Austrian civil service. He was born to poor parents in Brüx (today Most in northern Bohemia) but by dint of hard work and the study of oriental languages he achieved distinction in Vienna, eventually reaching high office in the Imperial Censor's office where the poet Mayrhofer also worked. His works were published in various Viennese periodicals between 1811 and 1816 and Schubert discovered this poem in the same 1814 edition of the almanac *Selam* in which he found *Die Sternenwelten* D307 and *Die Macht der Liebe* D308, among other poems (*see* SELAM CYCLE). In the absence of other settings by the composer, Zettler's greatest claim to fame is that he died only twelve days before Schubert in November 1828, and of the same generalized complaint ('Nervenfieber') as that which appears on the composer's death certificate. The poet Christoph Kuffner (whom Schubert also set only once – the song *Glaube, Hoffnung und Liebe* D955) introduced and edited a volume of Zettler's verse in 1836.

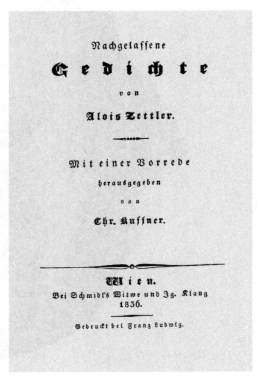

Title page of Kuffner's 1836 edition of Zettler's *Gedichte*.

Das ZÜGENGLÖCKLEIN   The passing bell

(SEIDL) OP. 80 NO. 2, **D871** [H593]

The song exists in two versions, the second of which is discussed below:
(1) 1826; (2) appeared May 1827

(1) 'Langsam'   A♭ major   ¢   [60 bars]

(2)   A♭ major

Kling' die Nacht durch, klinge,   Ring, ring the night through,
Süssen Frieden bringe   Bring sweet peace
  Dem, für den du tönst!   To him you toll for!
Kling in weite Ferne,   Ring out in the far distance;
So du Pilger gerne   Thus you reconcile pilgrims
  Mit der Welt versöhnst!   With the world.

Aber wer will wandern   But who would wish to journey
Zu den lieben Andern,   To the loved ones
  Die vorausgewallt?   Who have gone before?
Zog er gern die Schelle?   Did he gladly ring the bell,
Bebt er an der Schwelle,   Does he tremble on the threshold?
  Wann 'Herein' erschallt?   When a voice cries 'Enter'.

Gilt's dem bösen Sohne,   Is it meant for the wicked son
Der noch flucht dem Tone,   Who still curses its sound
  Weil er heilig ist?!   Because it is sacred?
Nein, es klingt so lauter   No, it rings so pure
Wie ein Gottvertrauter   When a man who trusts in God
  Seine Laufbahn schliesst.   Concludes his life's journey.

Aber ist's ein Müder,   But if it is a weary man
Den verwaist die Brüder, –   Deserted by his kin,
  Dem ein treues Tier   Whose faith in the world
Einzig liess den Glauben   Has been saved
An die Welt nicht rauben, –   Only by a faithful beast,
  Ruf ihn Gott zu Dir!   Call him unto You, O God!

Ist's der Frohen Einer,   If it is one of the blessed,
Der die Freuden reiner   Who partakes of the joys
  Lieb' und Freundschaft teilt,   Of love and friendship,

Gönn' ihm noch die Wonnen   Then grant him yet more or continued bliss
Unter dieser Sonnen   Beneath this sun,
  Wo er gerne weilt!   Where he gladly tarries!

JOHANN GABRIEL SEIDL (1804–1875)

This is the third of Schubert's twelve Seidl solo settings (1826–8). See the poet's biography for a
chronological list of all the Seidl settings.

This beautiful song, with its deathbed poem of slightly doubtful taste, is from 1826, the height
of Schubert's maturity and a climactic point in the history of the Schubertiads, those splendid
gatherings where Schubert was able to present his music to a group of discerning music lovers.
These exalted occasions, when the composer accompanied Johann Michael Vogl and other
singers, were remembered by each of those friends, with awe-struck gratitude, to the ends of
their collective lives.

   Johann Gabriel Seidl, a recent addition to the circle and never truly an intimate, was a young
man inclined to wear his heart on his sleeve. His uncomfortably sentimental text is translated
into great art by the sheer force of the composer's craftsmanship. Schubert binds word and
tone into a single circular graveside wreath, the beginning and ending woven into one. Like *Auf
dem Wasser zu singen* D774 in the same key, the piece is partially an impromptu for a pianist
who is entrusted with the central idea behind the work – the sound of the small bell rung when
one of the faithful is dying (the Zügenglöcklein is the Austrian equivalent of the German 'Sterbe-
glocke'), summoning the deceased's friends to pray for him. The equivalent in English is the
passing bell, or death knell. Shakespeare rings 'fancy's knell' in *The Merchant of Venice*, and
Wilfred Owen, in his 'Anthem for Doomed Youth' (set in Britten's *War Requiem*), asks 'What
passing-bells for these who die as cattle?' Roger Quilter (1877–1953) wrote a duet entitled *The
Passing Bell* (words by Winnifred Trasker) and it can scarcely be coincidental that this cultivated
composer's little lament for the death of spring was also conceived in the key of A flat major
with a recurring E flat in the piano's tenor register.

   As in Schubert's long rondo-ballad *Viola* D786 (where a snowdrop or 'Schneeglöcklein' rings
its own passing bell, also in A flat major, in requiem for the eponymous violet) the pianist's right
hand is entrusted with the task of pricking out a death knell in pinging E flat octaves – nearly
200 of them. The ingenious accompaniment would be perfectly adequate without this gentle
but persistent resonance, an aural overlay, but its inclusion *en dehors* in almost every bar, an
inverted pedal sounding above the main texture of the work, is the illustrative spur that set the
composer's brain ringing. There is no doubt that it was the challenge associated with this depiction that led Schubert to set such a mawkish text. Thoughts of mortality are clothed in subtly
different music over four of the five verses. This is no straightforward strophic structure,
although a casual listener, hypnotized by the song's campanology, may perceive it as such. The
uniting theme is of death and the compassion of the onlooker, and everything is a variation on
that. The beauty of the music underlines the poignancy of someone, somewhere, passing away
to the sound of this bell and its surrounding Schubertian harmonies – a heavenly death indeed.
The end of the poem suggests that with music as beautiful as this in our ears we should be saved
by the bell and simply refuse to die.

   The song opens with a four-bar introduction that acts as something of a recurring rondo
theme: after its appearance in bb. 1–4, we hear it again in shortened form (without b. 2) in bb.
13–15, 24–6, 35–7, 46–8 and as part of the postlude – elongated with two further bars. When
Schubert writes an extended song in A flat major he can rarely resist the temptation to move
into A flat minor (with its flattened third of C flat) and from there to C flat major, and this song

is no exception. A brief shift into A flat minor (bb. 19–20), followed by a significant move into C flat major (at b. 21) is the composer's response to the welcoming words at the end of the second verse ('Wann "Herein" erschallt'); it is as if he were standing on harmonic tiptoe, hesitating on the threshold of the better life, tentatively glimpsing what is on offer on the other side. In comparison with the poet's own radiant beliefs (or at least his projection of them in the sanctimonious terms required for the popular religious market) the considerably less religious Schubert may well have seen himself as a 'böser Sohn', but he set the third verse (from b. 27) without irony, and the fourth verse (from b. 38, concerning 'the faithful beast' and its redemptive powers)

Illustration by Sorrieu for the French edition of *Das Zügenglöcklein* (1838).

without embarrassment. There is, after all, a painting by Kupelwieser, *Gesellschaftsspiel der Schubertianer in Atzenbrugg* (1821), that indicates that the composer was fond of animals, or they of him; a dog apparently named Drago sits happily under his piano (*see* Vol. II/542). Such confidence carries the day, especially for the listener who is less interested in analysing the text than in appreciating the delights that unfold in the music.

The fifth and last verse (from b. 49) is nearest the music of the opening and almost certainly the one the composer liked best; it hymns the pleasures of the present and the incalculable blessings of friendship. It is here that the poem reveals itself, almost mischievously, as a variation on Hölty's *Seligkeit* D433, where the beauties of Laura here on earth are such as to make the poet simply decide, in the final strophe, not to die. In Seidl's lyric, friendship and good company stand high on the list of reasons to prefer life to death. Indeed, after the pathos of the earlier verses, death is brushed aside in a last-minute reprieve. However restful and soothing the offerings of heavenly eternity may seem, the poet (not to mention the composer) would much rather tarry down below for the time being. The bell, now given an unexpected new lease of life, chimes along as if in affirmation of these cheerier sentiments, vindicating the song's major-key tonality. Unexpectedly, the effect of this sudden change of register is uplifting, almost triumphant, rather than risible, but this is due entirely to the power of Schubert's music and the sense of inevitability and organic unity that carries all before it.

The lilting cadential bars decorated with semiquavers at bb. 12–13, 23–4, 34–5, 45–6 and 56–7 seem to have made an indelible impression on Johannes Brahms. A slightly modified version of this figure is quoted in his Op. 69 no. 3, *Ich sah als Knabe Blumen blühn* (*Heimweh III*). This too is a song of mourning – in this case for the irretrievably lost years of that composer's youth.

The first version of *Das Zügenglöcklein* was unknown to the early editors; it is similar to the second but with fewer left-hand staccato markings (the addition of these was carefully noted in the second version) and other occasional differences of notation.

Autograph:	Staatsbibliothek Preussicher Kulturbesitz, Berlin (first version autograph copy, probably made from a vanished first draft)
	Kolbenheyer Gesellschaft, Nürnberg (second version, fair copy)
Publication:	First published as part of the NSA in 1979 (P770; first version)
	First published as Op. 80 no. 2 by Tobias Haslinger, Vienna in May 1827 (P126; second version)
Dedicatee:	Josef Witteczek
Publication reviews:	*Wiener allgemeine Theaterzeitung* No. 82 (10 July 1827), p. 336 [Waidelich/Hilmar Dokumente I No. 512]
	Allgemeine Musik-Zeitung (Frankfurt), No. 23 (19 September 1827), col. 184 [Waidelich/Hilmar Dokumente I No. 526; Deutsch Doc. Biog. No. 944a]
	Münchener allgemeine Musik-Zeitung No. 1 (6 October 1827), col. 8 [Waidelich/Hilmar Dokumente I No. 530; Deutsch Doc. Biog. No. 955]
	Allgemeine musikalische Zeitung (Leipzig), No. 4 (23 January 1828), col. 49ff. [Waidelich/Hilmar Dokumente I No. 569; Deutsch Doc. Biog. No. 1014]
	Berliner allgemeine musikalische Zeitung, No. 20 (14 May 1828), p. 157f. [Waidelich/Hilmar Dokumente II No. 613a]
	Allgemeiner Musikalischer Anzeiger (Vienna), No. 19 (9 May 1829), p. 74 [Waidelich/Hilmar Dokumente I No. 726]
Subsequent editions:	Peters: Vol. 3/36; AGA XX 507: Vol. 8/237; NSA IV: Vol. 4a/6 & Vol. 4b/195; Bärenreiter: Vol. 3/4
Bibliography:	Capell 1928, p. 222
	Youens 2002, pp. 390–95
Arrangement:	Arr. Franz Liszt (1811–1886) for solo piano under the title *Das Sterbeglöcklein*, no. 3 of *Sechs Melodien von Schubert* (1838) [*see* TRANSCRIPTIONS]
Discography and timing:	Fischer-Dieskau II 8[16] 4'02
	Hyperion I 11[10]
	Hyperion II 31[16] 4'37 Brigitte Fassbaender

←— *Totengräber-Weise* D869   *Der Wanderer an den Mond* D870 —→

Der ZÜRNENDE BARDE   The indignant bard
(BRUCHMANN) **D785** [H511]
G minor   February 1823

Geschwind, kraftvoll

Wer wagt's, wer wagt's, wer wagt's, wer will mir die Lei-er zer-bre - chen,

(90 bars)

Wer wagt's, wer wagt's, wer wagt's,	Who dares, who dares, who dares,
Wer will mir die Leier zerbrechen,	Who wishes to shatter my lyre?
Noch tagt's, noch tagt's, noch tagt's,	It is still day, still day, still day;
Noch glühet die Kraft, mich zu rächen.	The strength to avenge myself still burns within me.
Heran, heran, ihr Alle,	Draw near, draw near, all of you,
Wer immer sich erkühnt,	Whoever will make so bold;
Aus dunkler Felsenhalle	My lyre burgeoned
Ist mir die Leier ergrünt.	From dark rocky vaults.
Ich habe das Holz gespalten	I split the wood
Aus riesigem Eichenbaum,	From the giant oak tree
Worunter einst die Alten	Beneath which our ancestors
Umtanzten Wodans Saum.	Once danced around Wotan's grove.
Die Saiten raubt' ich der Sonne,	As strings, I stole from the sun
Den purpurnen, glühenden Strahl,	Its glowing, crimson rays
Als einst sie in seliger Wonne	As once it sank in blissful ecstasy
Versank in das blühende Tal.	Into the flowering valley.
Aus alter Ahnen Eichen,	You lyre, made of the oaks of our ancient forebears
Aus rotem Abendgold,	Will never waver as long
Wirst, Leier, du nimmer weichen,	As the gods smile upon me.
So lang' die Götter mir hold.	

Franz von Bruchmann (1798–1867)

This is the last of Schubert's five Bruchmann solo settings (1822–3). See the poet's biography for a chronological list of all the Bruchmann settings.

Between 1821 and 1823 Schubert was close friends with the Bruchmann family. In their company he enjoyed their hospitality and much convivial music-making, and his friendship with Franz, the son and heir of the family, brought to his notice the young man's poetry which he would certainly not have encountered otherwise. Not all the verse written by Schubert's friends was good, but not all of it was awful either – there was a considerable range of talent, with Johann Mayrhofer in leading position. Bruchmann, though not as crude a poetaster as the young and enthusiastic Josef Kenner at his 'Gothick' worst, does not belong at the top of the league. The imagery of the very short *Am See* D746 and of *Im Haine* D738 are pretty enough without being masterful, and the text of *An die Leier* D737 is an adaptation of an already extant translation from the Greek by Degen, but the poem for *Schwestergruss* D762, inspired by Novalis, is self-dramatizing and sanctimonious. Kenner's juvenile balladry is far less sophisticated, but it is good-hearted and far less pretentious. That *Schwestergruss* is miraculously transfigured by great music has very little to do with Bruchmann.

Bruchmann's poetry, reflecting the self-absorbed manner of its creator, is very 'I' orientated. *Schwestergruss* recounts a personal fantasy at the end of which the poet imagines himself invested with the spiritual imprimatur to 'spread the word'. One might imagine that the poem of *Der zürnende Barde* had been written in sympathy for Schubert's plight as he was forced to take stock of his future on learning of his illness. But it is just as likely that Bruchmann cast himself as the indignant bard of the poem. He was to prove something of a specialist in feeling indignant, and promises of vengeance sound far more like him in one of his tempers than Schubert. Reference to 'ancestors' and 'ancient forbears' seems much more applicable to a knight of the realm (Bruchmann's inherited title was 'Ritter') than to a schoolteacher's son.

Bruchmann was among the students arrested and interrogated by the police, together with Schubert and the Tyrolean poet Johann Senn, in March 1820. On that occasion, Bruchmann weighed in with what the authorities called 'insulting and opprobrious language'. There is nothing in his poetry that is remotely seditious or dangerous (he became, in later life, an arch-member of the establishment) but *Der zürnende Barde* seems to protest that he and his close friend Senn are far too well-born and talented to be muzzled by impertinent policemen. Bruch-mann would emerge from the incident unscathed while Senn was exiled.

Schubert was in the middle of a grave personal crisis when he composed this work, and it was a month when no other songs were written (he was fully occupied with the Piano Sonata in A minor D784). Bruchmann, for all his posturing, was the good-looking and healthy son of a well-to-do family, and it is perhaps for this reason that one can detect a certain lack of conviction in this music, and it is not one of the most towering of Schubert's utterances. It is possible that Schubert somehow identified with the lyric's anger for either political or personal reasons, but if he were really angry we would expect a more imposing demonstration than this. It is hard not to imagine that the poem was set at the poet's special request, for it bears the marks of something written in haste for a party on the same night. Apart from a touch or two of magic, the music avoids the *innig*; it seems conceived as an opera aria for a character, the whole thing distanced from deeper involvement by the inverted commas of an invisible stage or soap-box. The rum-ti-tum accompaniment is the first clue that this is the case, a Gilbert and Sullivan-like introduction in a rollicking $\frac{6}{8}$, two bars in the tonic minor, two in the submediant (E flat), followed by a cadential tag bringing the music back to G minor. By Schubert's standards this is drinking-song note-spinning – one of those introductions, func-tional rather than inspired, which sounds as if it might have been added by the publisher Diabelli at a later date, although in this song this was not the case.

There is a fine sense of bustle in the first two strophes, the sort of thing that sounds impres-sive in a voice with a glamorous timbre. Some of the Schiller settings (*Der Kampf* D594, for example) also begin with this kind of masculine huffing and puffing. A succession of 'Wer wagt's' in G minor, repeated perhaps just a little too automatically, neatly counterbalance the line begin-ning 'Noch tagt's' (B flat major) from b. 10 with upbeat, but this outrage does not come from within (compare the genuinely angry opening of *Prometheus* D674). Rage is a tricky thing to convey in music and, with rare exceptions, Schubert is the composer of love, compromise and forgiveness rather than confrontation and vengeance. Use of diminished sevenths in the second strophe (bb. 16 and 18–19) does little to make the minstrel genuinely menacing; indeed the interlude between Strophes 3 and 4, a dance-like juxtaposition of E flat major and B flat[7] (bb. 23–6), suggests the wandering minstrel of *The Mikado* rather than a druid at the end of his tether. This amiable music ('close to triviality' – Fischer-Dieskau) is the basis of the accompani-ment to the third strophe, and it does little justice to the image of dancing in Wotan's grove; there is nothing here of the Ossianic atmosphere that Schubert had conjured in the past, music really worthy of the tribal rites of age-old cultures.

The next strophe of the song is more harmonically adventurous, with a pleasing modulation to D flat major (b. 38) appropriate to the 'selige Wonne' of the setting sun, an event mirrored by the fall of the vocal line at 'Versank in das blühende Tal' (bb. 44–7). This is followed by a bridge passage back to G minor (bb. 55–8) and Schubert adapts the music of the opening to fit the beginning of the poem's closing strophe. Here four lines of text are expanded through music to last for an entire page (the words are heard twice with various further repetitions); there is a suddenly touching reference, in G major, to the smile of the gods – 'So lang' die Götter mir hold' (bb. 66–9 with upbeat) – and a generous coda with flourishes of bravery and determination where the elongated setting of 'nimmer', a word extrapolated from the poem's second-last line, shows glowering defiance (again one is reminded of the closing of an aria) before the curtain falls on more hearty G major chords. The final dominant–tonic cadence (bb. 86–8) is unusually unsophisticated for a work with a serious text.

The § rhythm was perhaps not an ideal choice for these words; in this metre we are more used to Schubert as a writer of charming barcarolles, plaintive pastorales or merry drinking songs – lilting music with a spring in its step. Capell calls the song 'spirited' and that is about right; it has too much of the communal song about it, and it challenges the ear (and the accompanist) rather too little. *Der zürnende Barde* is closely related to the Leitner setting *Der Wallensteiner Lanzknecht beim Trunk* D931 (in the same key and metre) where a soldier recalls heroic deeds with greater charm than is managed by Bruchmann's incensed minstrel. We cannot fail to notice how distant Bruchmann's bard is from the inspired minstrel of Mayrhofer's *Nachtstück* D672. In a group of Schubert songs in performance, the work's brisk *Bewegung* could make it a useful link between two slower works of greater significance if sung with conviction and beautiful tone.

Autograph:	In private possession (Hunziker family, Switzerland; first draft)
First edition:	Published as Book 9 no. 1 of the Nachlass by Diabelli, Vienna in April 1831 (P259)
Subsequent editions:	Peters: Vol. 5/26; AGA XX 421: Vol. 7/71; NSA IV: Vol. 13/65
Bibliography:	Capell 1928, p. 176
	Fischer-Dieskau 1977, p. 158
Discography and timing:	Fischer-Dieskau II 5^{19} 1'51
	Hyperion I 35^3
	Hyperion II 26^{18} 2'06 Maarten Koningsberger

← *Drang in die Ferne* D770   *Abendröte* D690 →

Der ZÜRNENDEN DIANA   To the angry Diana
(MAYRHOFER) OP. 36 NO. 1, **D707** [H458]

The song exists in two versions, the second of which is discussed below:
(1) December 1820; (2) December 1820

(1)   'Entschlossen'   A major   ₵   [169 bars]

(2)   A♭ major

Ja, spanne nur den Bogen, mich zu töten,	Yes, draw your bow to slay me,
Du himmlisch Weib! im zürnenden Erröten[1]	Divine lady! In the flush of wrath
Noch reizender. Ich werd' es nie bereuen:	You are still more enchanting. I shall never regret
Dass ich dich sah am buschigen Gestade	That I saw you on the flowering bank,
Die Nymphen überragen in dem Bade;	Outshining the nymphs as they bathed,
Der Schönheit Funken in die Wildnis streuen.	Scattering the sparks of beauty through the wilderness.
Den Sterbenden wird noch dein Bild erfreuen.	Your image will gladden me even as I die.
Er atmet reiner, er atmet freier,[2]	He who has beheld your unveiled radiance
Wem du gestrahlet ohne Schleier.	Will breathe more purely and more freely.
Dein Pfeil, er traf, – doch linde rinnen	Your arrow hit its mark, yet warm waves
Die warmen Wellen aus der Wunde:	Flow gently from the wound.
Noch zittert vor den matten Sinnen	My failing senses still tremble
Des Schauens süsse letzte Stunde.	At that last sweet hour when I observed you.

JOHANN MAYRHOFER (1787–1836)

This is the fortieth of Schubert's forty-seven Mayrhofer solo settings (1814–24). See the poet's biography for a chronological list of all the Mayrhofer settings.

In *Der entsühnte Orest* D699, composed in September 1820, Diana (Artemis) is the guardian and saviour of Orestes. She is also the protecting deity in *Iphigenia* D573. Here in her towering anger she is a force of destruction, albeit a dazzlingly beautiful one. Actaeon was the son of Aristeus, son of Apollo. He was a famed hunter who was savaged by his own dogs on Mount Cithaeron. This was explained in a number of ways: jealous Zeus wanted to punish the young man for being in love with Semele (actually Actaeon's aunt) and it was probably Zeus who led him into a situation where he looked on Artemis (Diana) in her nakedness as she bathed with her attendant nymphs in a spring. In revenge the goddess changed Actaeon into a deer and incited the pack of hounds to tear their master to pieces. Mayrhofer declines to allow either dogs or deer into his narrative, but in other respects it is a reworking of the Actaeon myth.

It seems that the dedicatee of this song is directly, and audaciously, related to its poetic content. Katharina von Lászny (spelled Lacsny in its German form) was the 'Dame aux Camélias' of Vienna, a singer and courtesan who, according to one of her besotted admirers Moritz von Schwind ('What a woman!'), was 'in ill repute all over the city'. Like Dumas' Marguerite Gautier, she suffered from consumption and, again according to Schwind, seems to have known Schubert for a long time. Katharina von Lászny (she had performed under her maiden name of Catarina – or Catinka – Buchwieser) was also perhaps the inspiration behind the stage direction 'A hall at the naked lady's' in Scene 7 of the Schubertiad charade of 1 January 1826 (Deutsch *Documentary Biography* p. 497). There is a link between Frau von Lászny and Schwind's lunette painted for the Vienna Opera House (1869), illustrating a selection of Schubert's works (*see* above right). In the centre of the three-panel mural is an illustration of the opera *Die Verschwornenen* D787, to the left *Erlkönig* D328 and to the far right *Der Fischer* D225. Also in this right-hand

---

[1] Mayrhofer writes (*Gedichte*, 1824) 'Du himmlisch Weib! im *zornigen* Erröten'. For an explanation of the background to these alternative Mayrhofer readings see Editorial Note at the beginning of Johann MAYRHOFER.
[2] Mayrhofer writes (*Gedichte*, 1824) 'Er atmet reiner, atmet freier'. The second 'er' in this line is thus Schubert's addition.

Design by Moritz von Schwind for a half-moon fresco illustrating Schubert's works. On the right *Der zürnenden Diana* and *Der Fischer*.

Actaeon and Diana from *Der Mythos alter Dichter* (1815).

panel a naked female figure wielding a bow represents the song *Der zürnenden Diana*. Recent research by Clemens Höslinger has revealed that this was a depiction of Lászny herself. She seems to have been an object almost of veneration among the young men who knew her; quite apart from her talents as a singer, her intelligence and conversation were legendary as was her ability to reconcile her style of life with a sense of dignity and worth. To have dedicated this song to her says much for Schubert's lack of regard for petty Viennese gossip.

This song has a symphonic breadth and intensity, built on as wide and arched a span as the huntress-goddess's bow; it is entirely typical of the bold musical experiments of the 1820s. On the printed page the poem is rather short but, unusually for his treatment of this poet's texts, the composer reserves the right to repeat passages at will. This is entirely appropriate for Actaeon's states of mind and body: obsessed by physical beauty (repetition is a sign of obsession after all) and then wounded and in a delirium as his life trickles away. The tempo marking in the first version is 'Entschlossen', the second 'Risoluto' (both versions are printed in the NSA). The tempo marking of the first in the AGA, 'Feurig', is more helpful in that it suggests Diana's towering rage in the ten-bar introduction. As a student, and influenced by the steady pace of the Fischer-Dieskau/Moore recording, I had learned the song at a rather deliberate tempo. Practising it one day at the Britten–Pears School in Aldeburgh, Sir Peter Pears burst through the door of the rehearsal room, eyes flashing with Olympian displeasure. He demanded a faster tempo forthwith – a real *alla breve* – that would better reflect the terrifying rage of Diana. Of course this 'Schwung' also helps launch the vocal line with enormous bravura, whereas in many a performance it remains grounded. The accompanying figure, an onrush of triplets that find their mark as they bear down on the accented third beat, sweeps forward for thirty-two bars. A defiant 'Ich werd' es nie bereuen' (b. 35 with upbeat) changes the texture of the triplets by way of interlude (bare octaves rather than sensual chords), and then we are off for another fourteen bars of cushioned triplets. We remain uncertain as to whether the marvellous reckless momentum of the vocal line is propelled by Diana's anger in the piano, or shudders of ecstasy from the protagonist, now displaying his open hubris with nothing to lose because he is dying anyway.

Diana slays Actaeon with her arrows. Detail from a Greek vase of the seventh to fifth centuries BC.

At b. 53 the key signature changes to A major and there is a repeat of the music for 'Ich werd' es nie bereuen' in a slightly different word order; this time there is only a two-bar interruption by minims that temporarily stem the ongoing slew of visceral triplets. At b. 74, after a six-bar piano interlude largely consisting of oscillating octaves treading water to maintain the suspense, the four sharps melt into the naturals of C major and the triplets are replaced by a succession of tiny semiquaver tremors in the left hand (transferring to the right at b. 84). This is one of Schubert's most brilliant and original tonal analogues: blood flows as it is pumped from a wounded body thanks to a pulse and flickering heartbeat (those semiquavers), and during the song these gradually weaken in intensity as Actaeon dies. 'Den Sterbenden wird noch dein Bild erfreuen' is worthy of a swansong, heady in the extreme (when it is repeated from b. 91 the vocal line becomes even more ardent). A yearning passing note in the piano on the third beat of the bar as it falls to the fourth is repeated ten times (bb. 74–83) as we are suspended in a sweet daze of masochistic, death-defying ecstasy. The long passing note on 'Schleier' in bb. 86–7 is a metaphor for the veil that momentarily conceals the heavenly harmony of Diana's limbs, before falling away to expose the chord in its unadorned nakedness. (In Schwind's illustration, on p. 749 above, an artfully coiled veil winds around Diana's left arm and descends conveniently to mask her pudenda.)

At b. 109, after 'Dein Pfeil, er traf' (four bars of octaves between the hands marked 'Stark' that derive from the earlier music for 'nie bereuen', the music that refuses to atone) the triplets return (from b. 112) but drained of their strength and anger. When 'Dein Pfeil, er traf' is recapitulated (from b. 145) the last four lines of the poem are repeated in their wake. For 'doch linde rinnen / Die warmen Wellen aus der Wunde' (bb. 147–53) Schubert achieves a vocal line that burbles in a viscous trickle of sound suggestive of the flow of blood. All the singer's reserves of strength and emotion are called on one last time for an impassioned *Liebestod*; he is required to find a succession of high Gs in bb. 155–7, and there is a wonderful suspension on the word 'matten' (marked 'leise') in b. 157. Pauses and gaps in the vocal line signify failing strength and loss of consciousness (between 'süsse' b. 160 and 'letzte' b. 162 stands a vocally silent b. 161) as the life force ebbs away before our ears. The death of Actaeon, chastened and yet happily unrepentant, is marvellously pictured on the song's last page as the music winds down in a mood of bliss while its pulse, like that of its protagonist, grows weaker and weaker.

Richard Capell wrote that the youth's feelings seem 'unnatural and picturesque'. We may not believe in this Actaeon as a real-life figure, but his words would have seemed instantly sympathetic in their passion and sensuality to most of the young men of the Schubert circle. This is despite the fact that the poet is probably making the point that the price for acquiring knowledge of this libidinous kind is death – that the gods (and goddesses) will punish those who cross a certain threshold in their sexual behaviour. Schubert's reading of the poem seems to be that man should happily take responsibility for living life to the hilt; careful, judicious behaviour denying the life force is impossible for the passionate, poetic being, and it is better to grasp one's chances with both hands, whatever the consequences – as Goethe commands in *An Schwager Kronos* D369: 'Rasch ins Leben hinein!' Mayrhofer himself, in *Die Locke*, published posthumously in 1843, writes a poem about ageing which is in fact a gloss on the Actaeon–Diana legend. This ten-line strophe ends, 'It is sure that you, in a state of bliss, have seen what few mortals have seen. / You have lived intoxicated by ecstasy and you will die from your secret happiness.' This sounds as if Mayrhofer ruefully wished he had had the courage to act on his desires – for those who had done so, old age and death were more bearable. Schubert himself seems to have played the role of the brave and reckless Actaeon just long enough to catch the venereal infection that blighted the last five years of his life. In various sad letters he bemoans his state of health in that period, but it is notable that he never once voiced regret for having given himself up to the passions that led to the illness ('Ich werd' es nie bereuen') and neither, as far as we know from any of his letters, did he ever subscribe to the notion that such an illness was punishment from on high.

Both autographs of the song have *Die zürnende Diana* in Schubert's hand (this may have been the result of a simple misreading on Schubert's part), later corrected to the dative form, *Der zürnenden Diana*, for the song's publication. Walther Dürr suggests in the NSA Revisionbericht for Volume 2 (p. 104) that this alteration was at the express wish of Mayrhofer who certainly later published his poem (1824) with the revised title. The first version of the song as printed in both the AGA and NSA is a semitone higher, thus in the key of A major. It varies in a few details (including some added ornamentations) from the second version, but not sufficiently to be regarded as anything like a separate setting.

Autograph:	Gesellschaft der Musikfreunde (first version, first draft)
	Wienbibliothek im Rathaus, Vienna (second version, fair copy for Carl von Schönstein)
Publication:	First published as part of the AGA in 1895 (P687; first version)
	First published as Op. 36 no. 1 by Cappi & Co., Vienna in February 1825 (P75; second version)
Dedicatee:	Katharina Lászny von Folkusfálva
First known performance:	24 February 1825, as part of an *Abend-Unterhaltung* given by the Gesellschaft der Musikfreunde, Vienna. Soloist: Johann Hoffmann (See Waidelich/Hilmar Dokumente I No. 317 for full concert programme)

Subsequent editions:	Peters: Vol. 2/75; AGA XX 387a & b: Vol. 6/133; NSA IV: Vol. 2a/113 & Vol. 2b/210; Bärenreiter: Vol. 2/15
Bibliography:	Capell 1928, pp. 161–2
	Einstein 1951, p. 192
	Fischer-Dieskau 1977, p. 204
	Höslinger 2013, pp. 45–69
Discography and timing:	Fischer-Dieskau II 4[7] 5'21
	Hyperion I 14[15]
	Hyperion II 23[16] 5'48 Thomas Hampson

← *Im Walde D708*   *Gesang der Geister über den Wassern D705* →

Der ZUFRIEDENE   The contented man
(Reissig) **D320** [H199]
A major   23 October 1815

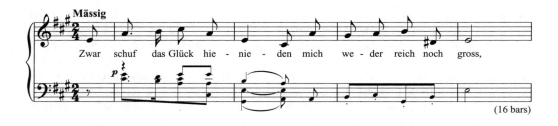

(16 bars)

Zwar schuf das Glück hienieden	Fortune here on earth
Mich weder reich noch gross,	Has made me neither rich nor great,
Allein ich bin zufrieden	But I am contented
Wie mit dem schönsten Loos.	As if with the finest of lots.
So ganz nach meinem Herzen	A friend quite after my own heart
Ward mir ein Freund vergönnt,	Has been granted me.
Denn Küssen, Trinken, Scherzen	For with kissing, drinking and jesting
Ist auch sein Element.	He too is in his element.
Mit ihm wird froh und weise	With him, cheerfully and wisely,
Manch Fläschchen ausgeleert;	Many a bottle is emptied!
Denn auf der Lebensreise	For on life's journey
Ist Wein das beste Pferd.	Wine is the best of steeds.
Wenn mir bei diesem Loose	If, amid this lot of mine,
Nun auch ein trüb'res fällt,	A gloomier fate should overtake me,
So denk' ich: keine Rose	I shall reflect that no rose
Blüht dornlos in der Welt.	Blooms without thorns in this world.

CHRISTIAN LUDWIG REISSIG (1784–1847)

This is Schubert's only setting of a Reissig text. See the poet's biography.

By October 1815 Schubert had already composed a large number of wonderful songs, but he was still fascinated by the compositions of those who had come before him, and humble enough to pay musical homage to his forbears and distinguished contemporaries. On 23 October 1815 a volume of Beethoven songs almost certainly lay before him on his desk – not the complete *Lieder* in the single Peters Edition volume available today, but the collection of six songs of Op. 75, published in 1810. Schubert composed two songs of his own on 23 October 1815, both of them using poems that appear in this Beethoven opus: Goethe's *Mignon* ('Kennst du das Land?') D321 and Reissig's *Der Zufriedene*. Moreover, Beethoven's songs are both in A major and Schubert follows suit in his choice of key; he also takes his cue from the Beethoven songs in terms of time signature ($\frac{2}{4}$) and the use of semiquaver triplets in the accompaniments. After studying these Schubert songs it is curious to encounter those by Beethoven that were composed first. There is a similar sense of déjà vu when one encounters a ballad by Zumsteeg which seems already half familiar from the Schubert setting of the same lyric. It is as if the young composer has reverently applied tracing paper to the works of an established master and come up with a copy magically superior to the original. Zumsteeg's classical models are rendered almost unrecognizable by the exuberance of an apprentice touchingly aware of his debt to those who have gone before him while at the same time revelling in his superior powers. Thus in some cases we have an extraordinary mixture of homage to, and unintentional annihilation of, one composer's achievement by another.

There is not much to choose between the two settings of *Der Zufriedene*; neither is among their composers' masterpieces. Beethoven referred to Reissig as a scoundrel, and the poem seems not unsuited to an old soldier with the gift of the gab, not altogether honest in his dealings. Both songs are exuberant and cheeky, but Schubert wins on grounds of melodic memorability. Beethoven stays in his chosen key throughout the strophe, whereas Schubert is rather more subtle. After the first two lines of poetry the piano's interlude modulates briefly into E major (b. 4), as if the achievement of coming up in the world requires a lift to the dominant – an apt illustration of 'reich' and 'gross'. At 'Allein bin ich zufrieden' the vocal line slides down into G major (at b. 9), as if contented to sink back into a more humble tonal position in life. The ambitions of the E major digression and the diffidence of the G major retreat are then both eschewed in favour of a quick return to the middle path of A major for the rest of the verse. Like Wolf's Mörike setting *Gebet* (1888), the song is about 'holdes Bescheiden', blessed moderation. Tiny details these, but they are telling enough to show how Schubert could see dramatic possibilities in lyrics that had seemed uneventful to older musicians. More than any composer before him (and possibly since), Schubert found subtle musical analogues for the poetry he set, often so deeply woven into the music's fabric that it takes a practised ear to discern the ingenuity at work and identify exactly what made the composer respond to the text. Thanks to Schubert, the art of song-writing had come on in leaps and bounds between 1810, when Beethoven's Op. 75 was written, and 1815.

Walburga Litschauer has suggested that the inspiration for Schubert's song may have been Antonio Salieri's setting of the same text (also in A major), advertised for sale in the *Wiener Zeitung* at the end of November 1815 (thus after the composition of Schubert's version). Litschauer makes the point that Schubert may have known this work before it appeared in print. It also raises the intriguing possibility that Salieri may have composed this work in the wake of his ex-pupil's selection of the text – or that both composers had been inspired by Beethoven's example at more or less the same time.

Autograph:	Österreichische Nationalbibliothek, Vienna (first draft), loan from the Österreichische Münze
First edition:	Published as part of the AGA in 1895 (P606)
Subsequent editions:	Not in Peters; AGA XX 167: Vol. 3/154; NSA IV: Vol. 9/175
Bibliography:	Litschauer 2001, pp. 74–83
	Reid 2007, pp. 120–22
Discography and timing:	Fischer-Dieskau I 6[1] 1'21 (strophes 1, 2 and 4 only)
	Hyperion I 20[8]
	Hyperion II 11[11] 2'15 John Mark Ainsley

← *Luisens Antwort* D319   *Mignon* 'Kennst du das Land?' D321 →

ZUFRIEDENHEIT (I)   Contentment
(CLAUDIUS) **D362** [H207]
A major   1815 or 1816

(32 bars)

Ich bin vergnügt, im Siegeston
   Verkünd' es mein Gedicht,
Und mancher Mann mit seiner Kron
   Und Szepter ist es nicht.
Und wär'er's auch; nun, immerhin!
   Mag er's doch! so ist er, was ich bin.

Des Sultans Pracht, des Mogols Geld
   Des Glück, wie hiess er doch,
Der, als er Herr war von der Welt,
   Zum Mond hinauf sah noch?
Ich wünsche nichts von alle dem,
   Zu lächeln drob fällt mir bequem.

Z u f r i e d e n s e i n, das ist mein Spruch!
   Was hülf' mir Geld und Ehr?
Das, was ich hab', ist mir genug,
   Wer klug ist, wünscht nichts sehr;
Denn, was man wünschet, wenn man's hat,
   So ist man darum doch nicht satt.

Und Geld und Ehr ist oben drauf
   Ein sehr zerbrechlich Glas,

I am happy, my verses
   Proclaim it triumphantly,
And many a man with his crown
   And sceptre is not.
And even if he is, well, all the better!
   Let him be: he is as I am.

The sultan's splendour, the mogul's wealth,
   The good fortune of – what was his name?
He who, when ruler of the world,
   Still gazed up at the moon.
I desire none of that;
   I prefer to smile at it.

To be content, that is my motto!
   What use would I have for wealth and honour?
What I have is enough for me.
   He who is wise does not desire much;
For when people have what they desire
   They are still not satisfied with it.

Moreover, gold and honour
   Form a very brittle glass;

Der Dinge wunderbarer Lauf,	The strange course of events
(Erfahrung lehret das)	(So experience teaches)
Verändert wenig oft in viel	Often transforms little into much
Und setzt dem reichen Mann sein Ziel.	And sets the rich man his limits.
Recht tun und edel sein und gut	To do right, to be generous and good,
Ist mehr als Geld und Ehr;	Is more than wealth and honour
Da hat man immer guten Mut	Such a man is always in good spirits,
Und Freude um sich her,	With joy around him;
Und man ist stolz und mit sich eins,	He is proud and at one with himself
Scheut kein Geschöpf und fürchtet keins.	Shuns no creature and fears no one
Ich bin vergnügt, im Siegeston	I am happy, my verses
Verkünd' es mein Gedicht, *etc.* . . .	Proclaim it triumphantly, *etc.* . . .

Matthias Claudius (1740–1815); poem published in 1771

This is the second of Schubert's thirteen Claudius solo settings (1816–17). See the poet's biography for a chronological list of all the Claudius settings.

Claudius, in his persona as the Wandsbek Messenger, introduced the poem printed above thus: 'The following song seems to have something in common with *My mind to me a kingdom is* in the *Reliques of Ancient English Poetry*. Whether it is a free translation of this song or a slavish imitation, or neither, I will let the reader decide.' It is in fact a very free rendition of the eleven-stanza poem published in the *Reliques*. The first verse of the original runs thus:

My minde to me a kingdome is;
    Such perfect joy therein I finde
As farre exceeds all earthly blisse,
    That God or nature hath assignde;
Though much I want, that most would have,
Yet still my mind forbids to crave.

Percy (qv) tells us that it is a sixteenth-century poem (before 1588), quoted by Ben Jonson in his play *Every Man out of his Humour*, and that he found it in 'a thin quarto music book entitled "Psalmes, Sonets and Songs of Sadnes and Pietie, made into Musicke of five parts &c. By William Byrd, one of the Gent. Of the Queenes Majesties honorable Chappell"'. A link between Schubert and William Byrd, however distant, is to be savoured. Later scholars have attributed the poem to Sir Edward Dyer (1543–1607) but it is probably not by him.

   The breezy character of the lyric must have appealed to Claudius's independent North German spirit. Mention of 'Des Sultans Pracht' in the second verse puts us in mind of the orientalism of another Claudius setting by Schubert for either solo voice or chorus, *Klage um Ali Bey* D140 and D496A. The composer was to set *Zufriedenheit* twice, the other version (D501) written for bass (*see* below). The most delightful thing about this first setting, and certainly the most individual, is the insouciant postlude (bb. 30–32) that winks and smiles, ducks and weaves. Together with the cheeky bar of prelude that struts at the opening, this aptly frames the ditty of a self-sufficient and satisfied man – not a very deep one perhaps, but a merry soul. The style verges on that of the drinking song, and one has the impression that a modicum of booze plays its part in keeping this singer satisfied with his lot in life.

Because *Zufriedenheit* appears on the same manuscript as *Cronnan* D282, Ernst Hilmar dates the song to 1815. Walther Dürr believes it more likely that it dates to 1816–17 (with the other Claudius settings) and that in using the space after *Cronnan*, Schubert was merely appropriating the first piece of manuscript paper that came to hand.

Schubert only placed a single strophe of text verse under the music, adding repeat marks. The AGA prints two verses, Strophes 1 and 2 (as recorded in the Hyperion Edition) but the NSA prints all six as translated above.

Autograph:	Wienbibliothek im Rathaus, Vienna (first draft)
First edition:	Published as part of the AGA in 1895 (P662)
Subsequent editions:	Not in Peters; AGA XX 280: Vol. 4/244 (as 'Lied'); NSA IV: Vol. 11/38
Discography and timing:	Fischer-Dieskau I 8[24] 1'00
	Hyperion I 23[28]
	Hyperion II 12[2] 1'00 Christoph Prégardien

← *Das Grab* D330   *Klage um Ali Bey* D140 →

ZUFRIEDENHEIT (II)   Contentment
(CLAUDIUS) D501 [H319]

The song exists in two versions, the first of which is discussed below:
(1) November 1816; (2) November 1816?

(1)   E major

Mässig geschwind

Ich bin ver - gnügt, im Sie-ges- ton

(36 bars)

(2)   'Vergnügt'   G major   ¢   [36 bars]

See previous entry for poem and translation

MATTHIAS CLAUDIUS (1740–1815); poem published in 1771

This is the third of Schubert's thirteen Claudius solo settings (1816–17). See the poet's biography for a chronological list of all the Claudius settings.

Schubert's second setting of this Claudius text is dated November 1816. Neither song is to be found in the Peters volumes, which accounts for the fact that they are seldom, if ever, heard in recital programmes. At first glance one wonders why Schubert bothered to return to a poem for which he had already provided an attractive and genial setting. However, as cheery as the first setting is, the second is more memorable and has a stronger character, and Schubert's decision to try again seems justified.

The first setting (*see* above) was for tenor, in the key of A major. The second, in E major, suits the bass-baritone tessitura. There is a substantial ten-bar *Vorspiel*, and a complete recasting of the melody. Where the first version has a cheeky charm that suggests a young man, Schubert has made of the second a vehicle for someone who *sounds* older and richer in experience – a Falstaffian philosopher whose girth is suggested by the vocal range and the slightly portly gait to the music. This is a mini-portrait of a homespun philosopher, conceived as if it were a cameo role in an opera (like Mozart's Bartolo or Curzio). We can sense Schubert's enjoyment of a person of his own creation – slightly ponderous, self congratulatory, but still somehow loveable and endearing. He is a relation of the solitary man by the fire in *Der Einsame* D800, a real character in an uneventful domestic soap. The latter song, written a decade later, is more poignant, but this second setting of *Zufriedenheit* also hymns the virtues of Biedermeier life while incorporating the composer's amused smile in observing it. At moments like this, where music allows the 'little person' to live unfettered in his own world, Schubert's genius appears even more than usually Shakespearean.

There is a hint of orchestration in the introduction: bouncing strings and winds in the right-hand quavers, slower horn-calls in the descending thirds and sixths stretching out in the left (from b. 4). These are almost gestural, a self-satisfied yawn at the incomprehensible ambition of others. We are about to hear wise words, but we are made to wait for them as the protagonist gathers his thoughts. Musical flourishes (stately old-world mordents, like dance steps executed by limbs creaky yet gallant, bb. 5–6) suggest introductory bows and niceties. We arrive at a cadence in the tonic that is comically extended for two further bars, a last-minute clearing of the throat by someone who is about to hold forth. As the voice enters with a G sharp on 'Ich', the accompanying seventh chord on A sharp – an upbeat to a 6-4 chord in E major – accentuates self-importance; the harmony pauses mid-suspension and calls the whole assembly to attention. The jump of a sixth down to a low B for 'bin' (b. 11) denotes gravitas. At 'im Siegeston' (bb. 12–13) voice and piano are doubled in a rising arpeggio as a metaphor for battle or manly endeavour. The phrase 'mit seiner Kron . . . / Und Szepter ist es nicht' is punctuated by the strutting right-hand motif that has opened the song. The vocal descent down to a low B at 'ist es <u>nicht</u>' (b. 23) implies a shrug of dismissal. The strophe's last two lines are interrupted by a delicious interlude of suspensions in minims (bb. 27–9); the singer needs time to think of the next line, or perhaps he is taking a draw on his pipe. Either way he is making us wait for his conclusion with all the flair of a pub rhetorician. When this comes (at 'Mag er's doch! so ist er, was ich bin') the musical phrase starts unaccompanied, and unexpectedly high in the voice – a throwaway line in a different register, registering indifference.

The subsequent strophes are not quite so neatly tailored to the music. It is not clear whether the introduction is included in the *da capo*, or whether the singer is meant to go straight to his next verse. In the performance for the Hyperion Edition, where 1, 2, 4 and 5 of the six strophes printed in the NSA are performed (for the sixth strophe of his poem Claudius simply repeats his first verse), we offer a compromise: the delightful introduction is heard twice, and on two occasions the strophes are connected without an interlude.

This song was transposed up into G major (D501, second version) for its appearance in the Therese Grob songbook, a collection of songs which Schubert reputedly put together for the young singer's birthday in November 1816, but which seems to have belonged instead to her brother Heinrich. Therese might have been better able to sing it in this higher key, but such an upward transposition robs the music of its essential character. Although hardly suitable for female voice, Schubert might have wanted Therese to take the text to heart, particularly if it was true that the composer's lack of financial prospects was the reason for their parting. According to research by Rita Steblin, the relationship was not one of mutually acknowledged sweethearts: 'Therese was not aware of the intensity of Schubert's love for her.' Perhaps the inclusion of a song like this was designed to give the Grob family a clue to the composer's philosophy of life, particularly if Therese's brother or parents were the types to measure success by material standards alone.

Autograph:	Missing or lost (first version)
	In private possession in Switzerland (second version as part of the Therese Grob album)
Publication:	First published as part of the AGA in 1895 (P663; first version)
	First published as part of the NSA in 1999 (P814; second version)
Subsequent editions:	Not in Peters; AGA XX 281: Vol. 4/246 (as 'Lied'); NSA IV: Vol. 11/40 & 44
Bibliography:	Steblin 2002
Further settings:	Johann Friedrich Reichardt (1752–1814) without a title and with the marking 'Vergnügt aus freier offner Brust' (1779)
Discography and timing:	Fischer-Dieskau —
	Hyperion I 32[19]
	Hyperion II 16[23] 3'04 Stephen Varcoe

← *Phidile* D500   *Am Bach im Frühlinge* D361 →

ZUM PUNSCHE   In praise of punch
(MAYRHOFER) **D492** [H311]
D minor   October 1816

(20 bars)

Woget brausend, Harmonien,	Swell, ring out, harmony!
Kehre wieder, alte Zeit;	Old times, return!
Punschgefüllte Becher, wandert	Let cups brimming with punch pass
In des Kreises Heiterkeit!	Around the cheerful circle!
Mich ergreifen schon die Wellen,	The waves already engulf me,
Bin der Erde weit entrückt;	I am far removed from this world;
Sterne winken, Lüfte säuseln—	Stars beckon, breezes whisper,
Und die Seele ist beglückt.	And my soul is enraptured.

Was das Leben aufgebürdet,	The burden of life
Liegt am Ufer nebelschwer;	Lies heavy as mist on the shore;
Steu're fort, ein rascher Schwimmer,	Head off, fast swimmer,
In das hohe Friedensmeer.	Towards the high sea of peace.
Was des Schwimmers Lust vermehrt,	What enhances the swimmer's pleasure
Ist das Plätschern hinterdrein;	Is the splashing behind him;
Denn es folgen die Genossen,	For his companions follow him;
Keiner will der Letzte sein.	No one wants to be the last.

Johann Mayrhofer (1787–1836)

This is the eleventh of Schubert's forty-seven Mayrhofer solo settings (1814–24). See the poet's biography for a chronological list of all the Mayrhofer settings.

This song is one of the least musically complicated of all the Mayrhofer settings. The poet himself did not think enough of the text to include it in the slim volume of his poems privately printed in 1824; it does feature, however, in the posthumous volume edited by Feuchtersleben in 1843.

At the end of 1816 the greatest Mayrhofer songs were still to come as far as Schubert was concerned. He had already set nine of the poems to music, but had not yet embarked upon the sequence of works inspired by the Greek classics that stand at the centre of their collaboration. Although the composer had known the poet since 1814 it took some time for Schubert (younger by ten years) to understand what was new and extraordinary about his friend's work. This song implies a social side of Mayrhofer which, in terms of his day to day behaviour, became less typical as the years went on. Someone more unlikely to join in a light-hearted sing-song could not be imagined and, were he to do so, there would be something lugubrious about his vocal contribution. When we look deeper into the text this mood is exactly what is revealed: instead of real merrymaking we find the type of escapist philosophy that is the result of too much introspection when one is in one's cups.

The music, marked 'Feurig' ('fiery'), is full of weighty unisons between voice and piano, as well as piano interludes of hearty staccato octaves (as in bb. 6–7) supported by muscular left-hand chords thick with fistfuls of notes. D minor is rather a serious key for a drinking song (it has something of the grimness of Don Giovanni's final feast about it), although the composer seems to have allowed himself a touch of humour with a phrased jump of a fifth in the right-hand piano part (bb. 7 and 13) that might well be taken as an inebriated hiccup. Otherwise one can see how Schubert already equates the poet's philosophy with one of tough masculine endeavour in the manner of the ancient Greeks. Indeed, the 'old times' mentioned by the poet suggest the athletic and manly world of antiquity when competitive young men preferred swimming to drinking. There is a similarly homoerotic tinge to Matthisson's poem *Badelied* which describes young men swimming and disporting themselves in the Elbe.

Although the song appears in Peters, AGA and NSA as a solo, the first draft of the manuscript seems to have been headed 'Chor', as if Schubert had originally envisaged the work as a chorus. As this does not appear in a later copy the performance recorded for the Hyperion Edition was a compromise between the two ideas: part of the strophe was presented as a solo for baritone, part as a chorus. There are tiny differences between the piano interludes and postludes in Peters (Diabelli-modified) and the AGA/NSA (Schubert's manuscript), particularly in the tessitura of the piano writing at the end of the strophe. In the heady spirit of punch-drunk party improvisation the recorded performance for Hyperion includes features from both versions, although this is scarcely noticeable without scouring the two scores.

Autograph:	Österreichische Nationalbibliothek, Vienna (first draft)
First edition:	Published as Book 44 no. 3 of the Nachlass by Diabelli, Vienna in 1849 (P368)
Subsequent editions:	Peters: Vol. 6/42; AGA XX 270: Vol. 4/226; NSA IV: Vol. 11/22
Arrangement:	Arr. Tilman Hoppstock (b. 1961) for guitar accompaniment in *Franz Schubert: 110 Lieder* (2009)
Discography and timing:	Fischer-Dieskau I 8[18] 1'23

Hyperion I 32[8]   1'57   Christopher Maltman with Toby
Hyperion II 16[13]   Spence, Daniel Norman & Neal
                                Davies

← *Geheimnis (An Franz Schubert) D491*   *Der Geistertanz D494* →

~~~~~~~~~~~~~~~~~

ZUR GUTEN NACHT   Goodnight
(Rochlitz) Op. 81 no. 3, **D903** [H608]
D major   January 1827

Der Vorsitzende:	The Spokesman:
Horcht auf! Es schlägt die Stunde,	Hark! The hour strikes,
Die unsrer Tafelrunde	Bidding each one at our table
Verkündigt: Geh' ein jeder heim,	To go home
Hat er sein Glas geleeret,	When he has emptied his glass,
Den Wirt mit Dank geehret,	Thanked mine host
Und ausgesungen diesen Reim!	And finished singing this rhyme.

Alle:	*All:*
Erst sei dies Glas geleeret,	First let us empty this glass,
Der Wirt mit Dank geehret,	Thank mine host
Und ausgesungen dieser Reim!	And finish singing this rhyme.

Der Vorsitzende:	The Spokesman:
Wir dürfen fröhlich gehen;	We should go merrily;
Was wir gehört, gesehen,	What we have heard, seen
Getan – das darf kein Mann bereun;	And done, no man should regret.
Und das, was wir empfunden,	Our shared experience,
Was enger uns gebunden	Binding us more closely
An Freund und Kunst, darf ihn erfreun.	To friends and to art, should gladden us.

A l l e:	All:
Ja, ja, was wir empfunden,	Yes, our shared experience,
Was enger uns gebunden	Binding us more closely
An Freund und Kunst, darf uns erfreun!	To friends and to art, should gladden us.

D e r V o r s i t z e n d e:	The Spokesman:
Schlaft wohl; und träumt, wie Bräute!	Sleep well, and dream like brides!
Kommt nächstens gern, wie heute!	Come gladly next time, as you did today.
Seid auf manch neues Lied bedacht!	Think upon many a new song.
Und geht einst Einer abe	And if, one day, one of us
Zu seiner Ruh im Grabe,	Should go to his rest in the grave,
Singt ihm mit Liebe: gute Nacht!	Sing to him, with love, 'Good night!'

A l l e:	All:
Ja, geht einst Einer abe,	Yes, if one day one of us
Zu seiner Ruh im Grabe,	Should go to his rest in the grave,
Singt ihm mit Liebe: gute Nacht![1]	Sing to him, with love, 'Good night.'

JOHANN FRIEDRICH ROCHLITZ (1769–1842); poem written in 1816

Zur guten Nacht is strictly speaking a choral piece, but it contains a major solo and was published as part of a group of Rochlitz solo settings. Accordingly, the work is listed here as the second of Schubert's four Rochlitz solo settings (1812–27). See the poet's biography for a chronological list of all the Rochlitz settings.

Although this song does not strictly belong to the canon of Schubert's lieder, the composer (or more likely the publisher Haslinger) thought it a good way to conclude Opus 81; it is also to be found in Series IV of the NSA, though not in the *Liedlexikon* (2012). The music is fairly evenly divided between a solo voice ('Der Vorsitzende') and a four-part male chorus ('Alle'). Like a good many of Schubert's songs for male voices, the music is simple, heartfelt and very Germanic. (It is difficult to imagine a group of British men sitting around a table singing this song ('Ja, ja, was wir empfunden, / Was enger uns gebunden') about death and parting, tears pouring into their beer. Because this is music from 1827 there is something memorable and touching about it, moving on a D major–B minor axis with noble and solemn tread. One is reminded of another strophic work from 1827 that appears banal on paper but is strangely gripping in performance: *Eine altschottische Ballade* D923. The final three bars of *Zur guten Nacht* ('Dieser Reim, dieser Reim!' in the first verse) have a hauntingly mournful quality in four-part harmony, although they are nothing more than an elaboration of an ordinary perfect cadence. What sets this music apart from countless other choral pieces in the same vein is the streak of Schubertian tenderness of which only he seems capable, particularly at this late stage of his career.

Autograph:	Wienbibliothek im Rathaus, Vienna (first draft)
First edition:	Published as Op. 81 no. 3 by Tobias Haslinger, Vienna in May 1827 (P130)
Dedicatee:	Friedrich Rochlitz (dedicated by Haslinger)
Publication reviews:	*Allgemeine Musik-Zeitung* (Frankfurt), No. 23 (19 September 1827), col. 184 [Waidelich/Hilmar Dokumente I No. 526; Deutsch Doc. Biog. No. 944a]

---

[1] Rochlitz writes for this last line 'Singt *unsre Lieb'* ihm: gute Nacht'.

Münchener allgemeine Musik-Zeitung No. 1 (6 October 1827), col. 8 [Waidelich/Hilmar Dokumente I No. 530; Deutsch Doc. Biog. No. 955]

Allgemeine musikalische Zeitung (Leipzig), No. 4 (23 January 1828), col. 49ff. [Waidelich/Hilmar Dokumente I No. 569; Deutsch Doc. Biog. No. 1014]

Berliner allgemeine musikalische Zeitung, No. 20 (14 May 1828), p. 157f. [Waidelich/Hilmar Dokumente II No. 613a]

Allgemeiner Musikalischer Anzeiger (Vienna), No. 20 (16 May 1829), p. 77 [Waidelich/Hilmar Dokumente I No. 727]

Subsequent editions: Not in Peters; AGA XVI 11: p. 91; NSA IV: Vol. 4/26

Discography and timing: Hyperion I 6[16]

Hyperion II 32[15]   3'52   Anthony Rolfe Johnson & male chorus

← *Grab und Mond* D893   *Alinde* D904 →

ZUR NAMENSFEIER DES HERRN ANDREAS SILLER

(ANONYMOUS) **D83** [NOT IN HYPERION]
G major   28 October–4 November 1813

To celebrate
the name-day
of Herr
Andreas Siller

Voice with
harp & violin

(39 bars)

Des Phöbus Strahlen	Phoebus's beams
Sind dem Aug entschwunden	Have gone from sight
Hinweg vom Horizont,	Beyond the horizon,
Und o!	And oh,
Des Feierabends frohe Stunden	The happy hours of this evening celebration
Beleuchtet nun der Mond	Are now illumined by the moon.

ANONYMOUS/UNKNOWN

This is the second of Schubert's nineteen solo settings of an anonymous poet. See Anonymous/Unknown for a chronological list of all the songs for which the poets are unknown.

This is a piece of occasional music for voice with harp and violin accompaniment from Schubert's sixteenth year. Although we no longer have any idea who Andreas Siller was, we can work out that Schubert had prepared the piece to be ready in plenty of time for the name-day itself, 10 November, even going to the trouble of making a preparatory sketch (NSA Volume 14b p. 298) at the end of October. Perhaps Siller was someone who was important to the profession of

Schubert senior – a family friend like Josef Spendou for whom Schubert composed a celebratory cantata for solo voices, chorus and orchestra (D472, 1816). The music is Haydnesque (to be sung by a baritone voice from the point of view of tessitura) and there is a somewhat ebullient introduction for the violin. The harp part is extremely undemanding. A feature of the music is that between bb. 9 and 24 the voice is accompanied by the violin alone, sometimes with pizzicato chords. The poem is something of an amateur effort and one might well imagine that the young Schubert wrote it himself. There was almost certainly more to the poem – probably praising Siller – than was preserved on the autograph.

Autograph:	Wienbibliothek im Rathaus, Vienna
First edition:	Published as part of the AGA in 1895 (P707)
Subsequent editions:	AGA XX 582: Vol. 10/72; NSA IV: Vol. 14b/194 (preliminary sketch)
Discography and timing:	Fischer-Dieskau —
	Hyperion I —
	Hyperion II

ZUR NAMENSFEIER MEINES VATERS

(SCHUBERT) D80 [NOT IN HYPERION]
A major   27 September 1813

To celebrate
the name-day
of my father

Trio, TTB
& Guitar

(88 bars)

Ertöne, Leier	Ring out, o lyre,
Zur Festesfeier!	For the celebration!
Apollo steig' hernieder	Descend, Apollo,
Begeistre uns're Lieder!	Inspire our songs!
Lange lebe unser Vater Franz!	Long live our father Franz,
Lange währe seiner Tage Chor!	Long may the chorus of his days last!
Und im ewig schönen Flor	And may his life's garland
Blühe seines Lebens Kranz.	Bloom eternally fair.
Wonnelachend umschwebe die Freude	May joy envelop with smiling bliss
Seines grünenden Glückes Lauf.	The verdant course of his happiness.
Immer getrennt vom trauernden Leide	Forever sundered from mournful sorrow
Nehm' ihn Elysiums Schatten auf.	May the shades of Elysium receive him;
Endlos wieder töne, holde Leier,	Sweet lyre, when the year brings back this time,
Bringt des Jahres Raum die Zeit zurück,	Sound once more, without end,
Sanft und schön an dieser Festes-Feier.	Soft and lovely on this festive day.
Ewig währe Vater Franzens Glück!	May our father Franz's happiness last forever!

FRANZ SCHUBERT (1797–1828)

This is Schubert's only song written specifically for guitar accompaniment (qv GUITAR). It is likely that he played the instrument himself while his brothers Ignaz, Ferdinand and Karl took the vocal parts for two tenors and bass in a piece to honour their father on his name-day (4 October). The first seventeen bars are declaimed in an Andante – as grandiose as is possible for a domestic trio with rather a weak-toned accompanying instrument. But the intention is imposing: the poem itself is a feast of exclamation marks, with no less than three after the little cantata's title on the autograph! From b. 18 the tempo marking is Allegretto and there is a change to §. The singers are instructed to sing fortissimo and the guitar is allowed two bars by way of arpeggiated interlude, pianissimo. At b. 33 there is another guitar solo, more complicated this time, which is what leads us to think of the composer as the likely executant. The voices are then allowed an unaccompanied passage of six bars, followed by a tiny touch of imitation between them. A jolly time is had by all and the music brims with affection. This was a patriotic time in Austrian history and it so happens that the emperor's name was the same as that of Schubert's father. It was common enough to refer to the emperor as father of the nation and so in honouring the name of 'Father Franz' the composer was simultaneously wishing long life to Austria's ruler, who at the time was busy fighting the French and was especially popular.

Autograph:	Wienbibliothek im Rathaus, Vienna
First edition:	Published as part of the AGA in 1892 (P523)
Subsequent editions:	AGA XIX 4: p. 48; NSA III: Vol. 3
Discography and timing:	Fischer-Dieskau —
	Hyperion I —
	Hyperion II

ZWEI SZENEN AUS LACRIMAS D857

Christian Wilhelm von Schütz (1776–1847); verse drama written before 1803, and wrongly credited to August Wilhelm von Schlegel in the first edition
September 1825

The play *Lacrimas* appeared in Berlin in 1803. It might have come to Schubert's notice because of Schütz's link with the Schlegel brothers: Friedrich von Schlegel lived in Vienna, and in the 1820s Schubert almost certainly had some contact with him through Karoline Pichler, Franz von Bruchmann or Matthäus von Collin. Einstein notes that Wilhelm von Schütz was the author of a drama entitled *Der Graf und Gräfin von Gleichen*, but this connection with Schubert's operatic plans at the end of his life (with Bauernfeld as librettist) was almost certainly coincidental. As the two *Lacrimas* songs date from the end of Schubert's stay in Upper Austria in 1825 he may have discovered the play in the library of a friend's house during that time. In the first edition the author's name is left out, but Friedrich's brother August von Schlegel (described as the play's editor) wrote an introductory poem. This laudatory dedication ('An den Dichter des *Lacrimas*') makes it unlikely that Schubert, as late as 1825, would have thought that Schlegel himself was the author of the play. Nevertheless, the posthumous first edition of the songs (1829) attributes the two poems to the elder Schlegel – music publishers are not always well versed in literary matters. My own copy of the first edition of the play has Schütz's name entered on the title page in a nineteenth-century hand – quite possibly many years after its publication.

Lacrimas was rather famous in its day. Its complex plot unfolds with a beauty of language enriched by the contemporary fashion for oriental fantasy, something to which Schubert himself was rather partial as we know from his settings of poems from Goethe's *West-östlicher Divan*, the opera *Fierabras* D796 and his projected opera *Der Graf von Gleichen* D918. East versus West, and Christian versus Muslim, were long-standing obsessions in a Vienna that had once been besieged by the Turks. There was something about these conflicts and contrasts that had appealed to Schubert, an avid enthusiast of Mozart's *Die Entführung aus dem Serail* K384, even at the beginning of his career: the three songs of *Don Gayseros* D93 tell the story of Donna Clara and her love for Don Gayseros, a Moorish king in disguise. Gayseros is slain by his beloved's brothers, and the lady, who has at first been shocked to discover her lover's religion, pines away.

Lacrimas explores similar themes. The first two acts take place near Malaga where the local high-born Spaniards are susceptible to strange visits from ship-borne foreigners. The eponymous hero, newly arrived on Spanish shores, is educated and charming, but like Don Gayseros (qv) he is not what he seems; although he is taken for an Italian, Lacrimas comes from North Africa. He falls in love with the beautiful Ismene and confesses to her that he is not a Christian. She is at first shocked, but resolves to elope with him nevertheless. The second pair of lovers, in a sub-plot, interested Schubert more. Ismene's cousin Florio, son of Antonio of Aredo, conceives a passion for a slave-girl, also part of the ship's company that has docked in Malaga. He is enchanted by her voice when he hears her singing songs of her homeland (like that other slave-girl, Berlioz's *Zaïde*). Believed to be Italian in origin, her name is Delphine – a name that had resonated throughout Europe the year before the appearance of Schütz's play; Madame de Staël's novel, the marginally racy *Delphine* of 1802, had occasioned that great intellectual's exile from Napoleon's Paris. Returning to Schütz's similarly sensual character, it seems that Delphine had been purchased in Italy and was destined to be part of a sultan's harem in a faraway land. Florio resolves to rescue and woo her, no matter what the dangers. The third act unfolds in the oriental realm of Elmadina where Zumrud is Pasha. Lacrimas and Ismene have sailed here of course, and Florio also – the two young Spaniards in oriental disguise. It transpires that Delphine is in reality the long-lost daughter of Zumrud's overlord, Amru, Sultan of Merameris. She had been kidnapped by Bedouins as a child, sold into slavery and brought up as a Christian; her return to her homeland as a princess is not the dastardly act of slave-trafficking that Florio, ignorant of her true identity, continues to believe. She is imprisoned by her overprotective father in a palace surrounded by a garden and Florio can only be near her by working as a woodcutter.

The song that Schubert set, 'Nun, da Schatten niedergleiten' (*see Florio*), comes from the ninth scene of this long act. Florio watches Delphine arranging flowers on her terrace as he tells of the pains of love; she sees him as he sings, recognizes her distant suitor from Spain, and secretly gives him her heart. This he has no way of knowing at the time. She later tests him by sending Onaiza, her lady-in-waiting, disguised as the king's daughter, to seduce him. Florio proves his fidelity by telling the 'Sultanin' that he can only think of Delphine. The second scene of the fourth act begins with a monologue for Delphine, now helplessly in love with her mysterious serenader, which Schubert set to music. Ismene's parents, as well as Florio's, arrive from Malaga for a series of denouements, chief among which is the solving of the question of Florio's parenthood. Inevitably he turns out to be Amigad, long-lost son of the sultan Tansor, and thus the perfect bridegroom for Delphine. The two lovers meet and speak to each other only in the final two pages of the play. At the end there is a mood of general reconciliation and understanding between Christian and Muslim. In the same way, at the end of *Fierabras* D796, Boland, Prince of the Moors, is reconciled to the marriage of Roland and Florinda. In *Lacrimas* the unlikely outcome is a Muslim kingdom ruled by two people brought up as Christians.

Autograph: Missing or lost
First edition: Published as *Zwey Szenen aus dem Schauspiel Lacrimas* Op. post. 124 by
                  A. Pennauer, Vienna in October 1829 (P236 and 237)

I DELPHINE   Delphine

D857/1 [H576]
A major

(133 bars)

Ach, was soll ich beginnen	Ah, how shall I begin,
Vor Liebe?	For love?
Ach, wie sie innig durchdringet	Ah, how profoundly it penetrates
Mein Innres!	My inmost being!
Siehe, Jüngling, das Kleinste	See, young man, the smallest part of me,
Vom Scheitel	From my head
Bis zur Sohl' ist dir einzig	To the soles of my feet,
Geweihet.	Is dedicated to you alone.
O Blumen! Blumen! verwelket,	O flowers, fade!
Euch pfleget	The soul
Nur, bis sie Lieb' erkennet,	Tends you
Die Seele.	Only until it knows love.
Nichts will ich tun, wissen and haben,	I wish to do nothing, know nothing, have nothing;
Gedanken	All I wish is to cherish
Der Liebe, die mächtig mich fassen,[1]	Thoughts of love,
Nur tragen.	Which has held me in its power.
Immer sinn' ich, was ich aus Inbrunst	I for ever reflect on what else I might do
Wohl könne tun,	In my ardour,
Doch zu sehr hält mich Liebe im Druck,	But love holds me too tightly in its grasp,
Nichts lässt sie zu.[2]	It permits me nothing.
Jetzt, da ich liebe, möcht' ich erst brennen,	Being in love has taught me what lust for life is,
Und sterbe.	And I die.
Jetzt, da ich liebe, möcht' ich hell brennen,	Being in love makes me want to burn brightly,
Und welke.	And I wither.
Wozu auch Blumen reihen und wässern?	What is the good of planting rows of flowers and watering them?
Entblättert!	Flowers, shed your leaves!
So sieht, wie Liebe mich entkräftet,[3]	Thus he sees

---

[1] Schütz writes (1803) 'Der Liebe, die mächtig mich *fasste*'.
[2] Schubert precedes the musical setting of these words (bb. 60–61) with the word 'nichts' set twice (bb. 58 and 59).
[3] Schubert has reversed the word order of Schütz's original: 'So sieht, wie mich *Liebe* entkräftet'.

Sein Spähen.	How love weakens me.
Der Rose Wange will bleichen,	The rose's cheek will fade,
Auch meine.	And so, too, will mine.
Ihr Schmuck zerfällt, wie verscheinen	Her lustre is ruined, as clothes
Die Kleider.	Grow threadbare.
Ach Jüngling, da du mich erfreuest	Ah, young man, if you bring me joy
Mit Treue,[4]	With your devotion,
Wie kann mich mit Schmerz so bestreuen	How can that joy fill me
Die Freude?	With such pain?

This is the first of Schubert's two Schütz solo settings (1825). See the poet's biography for a chronological list of all the Schütz settings.

Delphine's song is that of a virgin; there is an element of containment about it counterbalancing its erotic qualities. She is on the threshold of sexual discovery; tremulous curiosity is to be heard in the shimmering staccati of the right-hand accompaniment (as if scored for strings), the left reminiscent of a bassoon line. Yet the piece, bedevilled by performances that are too fast, is marked in moderate tempo ('Mässige Bewegung'), and as such it is slower than the 'Etwas lebhaft' of *Suleika I* D720. Its exact mood is hard to capture for, as well as its girlish qualities, Schubert intended it to display womanly passion in the oriental manner where quasi-Islamic pudeur and sensuality conjoin in evocations of veiled eroticism. Fischer-Dieskau writes that this song is 'universally condemned as unperformable' but that for a big voice it offers 'extremely interesting possibilities'. The 'condemnation' is, and was, far from universal: in a letter of 25 March 1863 the singer Ottilie Hauer reported that she and Brahms had gone through 'the whole of Schubert – and a favourite song of his was *Delphine*'. Because of its unusual high C, its length and a rather dense accompaniment, the piece has often been consigned to big voices, not always the most telling of song performers.

The majority of *Delphine* requires a pianissimo dynamic, and the vocal line moves with a sinuous grace that many opulent voices cannot negotiate. It falls between two stools: too high and dramatic at the end for many a lyric voice, too delicate and curvaceous of line for a barn-storming Brünnhilde. Above all, the sentiment of the poem is too delicate for a dramatic soprano, its halting metre a mixture of inexperienced modesty, flushed curiosity and real emotional pain. In many performances Delphine can all too easily sound like an Amazon on the warpath. Pianists are often to blame for inflating the scale of the piece by thundering away at the accompaniment in such a way that the singer has no choice but to go into battle mode. Despite the high C, this piece was not intended for Anna Milder-Hauptmann, the former Iphigenie who sang the *Suleika* songs and *Der Hirt auf dem Felsen* D965. It is, nevertheless, an orientalism. The rather ludicrous eastern scenario allows Delphine to be more forthright in the expression of her sexual desires than might have been seemly in a character of German origin.

There are any number of delightful touches: the way Delphine's vocal line moulds itself lovingly to the masculine bass in lithe duet; the almost bosom-baring excursion into C sharp major at line 6 (bb. 23–4); the way the flowers (line 9 of the text) first blossom then fade in drooping sequences (bb. 34–9) together with the heroine herself; the bass line's agitation suggesting nascent love after 'Gedanken / Der Liebe' (b. 45 and again at b. 47); the meaningful excursion into the relative minor at 'welke' (bb. 73–5). The long passage (lines 25 to 32, bb. 75–91), warning that the body will wither without love, brings forth a succession of musical phrases that fold in on themselves like the leaves

---

[4] Schütz writes (1803) '*Durch* Treue'.

of a parched lotus flower, the voice, in its dejection, drooping in a succession of long notes in a sinking tessitura. For pianists using the high-voice Peters Edition (Volume 3), attention must be drawn to b. 52 where the second quaver in the left hand is wrongly printed as a B flat instead of A – a reading that is as awkward to play as it is harmonically unlikely. Volume 13 of the NSA confirms that the passage as printed in the AGA (with an A) is correct.

The final pages are passionate indeed, even more so than the closing pages of *Suleikas II* D717. The peroration of that song touches a high B flat almost in passing, but *Delphine* boasts a much longer high B flat: the F below – the word is 'Freude' – acts as a springboard, and the singer must remain in the heights for four whole beats (bb. 99–101). This moment of vocal drama is soon capped, however: at bb. 121–3 the F is once more a springboard, but this time the voice must climb to a high C and stay there on an ungrateful word ('was' – it is really hard to avoid an ugly slide in the middle of this vowel) in mid-sentence. This final page of the song has certainly precluded it from the repertoire of many an aspiring performer. The perfect voice for *Delphine* is that of that rare operatic creature, the ideal Anne Truelove in Stravinsky's *The Rake's Progress* who must also face a high C at the end of her aria. This is a role of some delicacy that should not be cast on the basis of that high C alone. *Delphine* appears in the programmes of some singers less experienced but sumptuous of voice because they believe it may give them a quasi-operatic chance to shine at the final stretch. This has resulted in many unsatisfactory performances whereby an already elusive song appears hectic and boring; if this music has to depend for its validity on a merely ornamental top note in passing, a remarkable piece of music has been assigned to the wrong pair of vocal chords.

Subsequent editions:	Peters: Vol. 3/126; AGA XX 484: Vol. 8/146; NSA IV: Vol. 13/172	
Bibliography:	Black 2003, p. 145	
	Capell 1928, p. 218	
	Fischer-Dieskau 1977, p. 220	
Discography and timing:	Fischer-Dieskau	—
	Hyperion I 9^{12} & 26^3	4'51 Arleen Auger
		4'51 Christine Schäfer
	Hyperion II 30^{13}	4'51 Christine Schäfer

←— *Abendlied für die Entfernte* D856   *Florio* D857/2 —→

II FLORIO   Florio
D857/2 [H577]
E major

(56 bars)

Nun, da Schatten niedergleiten,	Now that the shadows glide down,
Und die Lüfte zärtlich wehen,	And the breezes blow gently,
Dringet Seufzen aus der Seele,	Call forth sighs from the soul
Und umgirrt die treuen Saiten.	And caress the faithful strings.

Klaget, dass ihr mit mir sterbet	Lament that you die with me
Bittern Tod, wenn die nicht heilet,	A bitter death, unless she cures me –
Die den Becher mir gereicht,	She who handed me the poisoned cup,
Voller Gift, dass ich und ihr verderbet.[1]	To destroy you and me.
Erst mit Tönen, sanft wie Flöten,	First with sounds as soft as flutes
Goss sie Schmerz in meine Adern;	She poured pain into my veins;
Sehen wollte sie der Kranke,	The invalid desired to see her,
Und nun wird ihr Reiz ihn töten.	But now her charms will kill him.
Nacht, komm her, mich zu umwinden	Come, O night, and envelop me
Mit dem farbenlosen Dunkel!	In your colourless darkness!
Ruhe will ich bei dir suchen,	With you I will seek the rest
Die mir not tut bald zu finden.	Which I need to find quickly.

This is the second of Schubert's two Schütz solo settings (1825). See the poet's biography for a chronological list of all the Schütz settings.

Just before Florio sings his song, Delphine, from her balcony, has been admiring his prowess as a woodcutter as he fells cypress trees, hatchet in hand. How delightful it would be, she says, if he were to pick up a lute instead and pluck its strings in serenade. Schubert has taken his cue from Delphine's words and given Florio a strummed lute accompaniment with mezzo staccato quavers in the right hand. The temptation to sing this song *alla breve*, as a jolly serenade, should be avoided. One of the reasons it is seldom sung is because its tempo is so hard to judge. The words are full of pain and longing, for the young suitor is at his most desperate, yet he remains tender-hearted; he has no way of being in close proximity to the object of his adoration, and can only admire her at a distance. In Schütz's original, Florio compares the charms of Delphine metaphorically to the oriental delights of sherbet, yet this delicacy is poisoned (in the manner of many an old tale of intrigue in the harem) and will kill him unless she provides the antidote. Schubert baulks at setting the words 'in süssem Scherbet' to music in a song of this poignancy, and replaces them with 'dass ich und ihr verderbet' (bb. 27–8), a substitute rhyme of which he was probably proud. Nevertheless he responds to the idea of slow poisoning with a meltingly beautiful series of progressions in the middle section of the song. At 'Erst mit Tönen, sanft wie Flöten, / Goss sie Schmerz in meine Adern' (from b. 29) the vocal line descends in stately steps underpinned by harmonic suspensions; these not only suggest the strange fascination of Delphine's singing of Moorish songs that first enchanted Florio, but are also an unmistakable tonal analogue for the idea of a powerful substance seeping through the veins of the lover.

A little figure of four quavers, which made its first sinister appearance in the bass after mention of the poison (b. 28), reappears in the alto voice of the accompaniment (bb. 30–31 and 34) and then slides into the tenor register (b. 35). Thus the body of the music droops stage by stage through the veins of the stave as the spirits of the lover are drugged by a surfeit of unconsummated love. After 'Und nun wird ihr Reiz ihn töten' (bb. 35–8) the whole accompaniment has slipped to the bottom of the piano, as if it has lost consciousness, only recovering to lead us, via a delicious modulation, back to the home key for the last verse. The wafting breezes mentioned in the second line of the poem (bb. 8–10) inspire melismas, even on such insignificant words as 'Und die Lüfte' as well as the more important 'zärtlich'; these add to the oriental flavour of the piece as a whole. Something about gently dancing decorations of this kind suggested nocturnal serenade to the composer. Compare the music following 'Wenn euer Lied

---

[1] Schütz writes (1803) 'Voller Gift *in süssem Scherbet*' (see commentary).

das Schweigen bricht' in *Der Einsame* D800, and the melismas of 'Ihre Saiten rühren kann' from *Des Sängers Habe* D832, both composed in the same period.

Till Gerrit Waidelich (*Liedlexikon* 2012) observes that Schubert had composed something new with these two scenes and that they are not bona fide lieder. The heightened vocal demands of *Delphine* in particular suggest a novel kind of piano-accompanied vocal work. After failing to get his operas performed, perhaps it was the composer's intention to embark on a whole series of scenes from stage plays, a new quasi-operatic genre. He had, after all, published some of the arias from his own opera *Alfonso und Estrella* D732 (qv) with piano accompaniments.

The first edition of Deutsch follows Mandyczewski, placing *Florio* first and *Delphine* second within D857. This is also the order of the songs as they occur in the play. The second (1978) Deutsch catalogue reverses this and lists the songs in the order they were published in the first edition. The *Neue Schubert-Ausgabe* follows suit.

Subsequent editions:	Peters: Vol. 3/132; AGA XX 483: Vol. 8/143; NSA IV: Vol. 13/183
Bibliography:	Black 2003, p. 145
	Capell 1928, p. 219
	Fischer-Dieskau 1977, p. 220–21
	Liedlexikon 2012, p. 703

Discography and timing: Fischer-Dieskau II 7[13]   2'21   (Here entitled 'Szene I aus dem Schauspiel Lacrimas')

Hyperion I 26[4]
Hyperion II 30[14]   3'23   Richard Jackson

← *Delphine* D857/1   *An mein Herz* D860 →

Der ZWERG[1]   The dwarf
(M. von Collin) Op. 22 no. 1, **D771** [H507]
A minor   November 1822?

(150 bars)

(1)   Im trüben Licht verschwinden schon die Berge,   In the dim light the mountains already fade;

Es schwebt das Schiff auf glatten Meereswogen,   The ship drifts on the sea's smooth swell,
Worauf die Königin mit ihrem Zwerge.[2]   With the Queen and her Dwarf on board.

---

[1] The poem's title in Castelli's almanac *Selam* (1813) is *Treubruch*. This was probably Schubert's source.
[2] 'Worauf die Königin' is correct as it appeared in *Selam*, 1813. Collin writes (*Nachgelassene Werke*, 1827) 'Worin die Königin mit ihrem Zwerge'.

(2) Sie schaut empor zum hochgewölbten Bogen,
Hinauf zur lichtdurchwirkten blauen Ferne;

Die mit der Milch des Himmels blass durchzogen.

She gazes up at the high arching vault,
At the blue distance, interwoven with light,

Streaked with the pale milky way.

(3) 'Nie habt ihr mir gelogen noch, ihr Sterne,'[3]
So ruft sie aus, bald werd' ich nun entschwinden,

'Ihr sagt es mir, doch sterb' ich wahrlich gerne.'

'Stars, never yet have you lied to me,'
She cries out. 'Soon now I shall be no more.

You tell me so; yet in truth I shall die gladly.'

(4) Da tritt der Zwerg zur Königin, mag binden[4]

Um ihren Hals die Schnur von roter Seide,
Und weint, als wollt' er schnell vor Gram erblinden.[5]

Then the Dwarf comes up to the Queen, begins

To tie the cord of red silk about her neck,
And weeps, as if he would soon go blind with grief.

(5) Er spricht: Du selbst bist schuld an diesem Leide,

Weil um den König du mich hast verlassen,

Jetzt weckt dein Sterben einzig mir noch Freude.[6]

He speaks: 'You are yourself to blame for this suffering,

Because you have forsaken me for the king;

Now your death alone can revive joy within me.

(6) Zwar werd' ich ewiglich mich selber hassen,[7]
Der dir mit dieser Hand den Tod gegeben,

Doch müsst zum frühen Grab du nun erblassen.

'Though I shall forever hate myself
For having brought you death by this hand,

Yet now you must grow pale for an early grave.'

(7) Sie legt die Hand auf's Herz voll jungem Leben,

Und aus dem Aug' die schweren Tränen rinnen,
Das sie zum Himmel betend will erheben.

She lays her hand on her heart, so full of youthful life,

And heavy tears flow from her eyes
Which she would raise to heaven in prayer.

(8) Mögst du nicht Schmerz durch meinen Tod gewinnen!
Sie sagt's, da küsst der Zwerg die bleichen Wangen,
Drauf alsobald vergehen ihr die Sinnen.

'May you reap no sorrow from my death!'

She says; then the Dwarf kisses her pale cheeks,
Whereupon her senses fade.

---

[3] Schubert follows the word order of *Selam* in this line, and adds a repetition of 'nie'; Collin's later version reads '*Ihr habt mir nie* gelogen noch, ihr Sterne'.
[4] Collin writes (in all editions) 'Da *geht* der Zwerg zur Königin'.
[5] Schubert sets the text as in *Selam*. Collin's later version reads 'Und weint als wollt' *vor Gram er schnell* erblinden'.
[6] Schubert sets the *Selam* text as printed above. Collin's later version of this line is '*Nun macht* dein Sterben einzig mir *nur* Freude'.
[7] Schubert sets the *Selam* (1813) text as printed above. Collin's later version of this line is '*Mich selber* werd' ich ewiglich *wohl* hassen'.

(9)   Der Zwerg schaut an die Frau, vom Tod   The Dwarf looks upon the lady in the
        befangen,   grip of death;
      Er senkt sie tief ins Meer mit eignen Handen.   He lowers her with his own hands deep
                                                                    into the sea.

      Ihm brennt nach ihr das Herz so voll Verlangen, His heart burns with such longing for her,
      An keiner Küste wird er je mehr landen.   He will never again land on any shore.

MATTHÄUS VON COLLIN (1779–1824)

*This is the third of Schubert's five Matthäus von Collin settings (1816, 1822–3). See the poet's
biography for a chronological list of all the Matthäus von Collin settings.*

All Schubert's work on gruesome Gothic ballads in his youth finds its final and most refined
expression in this subtle apotheosis of the horror genre from his maturity. The rhythmic impetus
(an extended upbeat of three quavers falling to the first beat of the bar) is the animating force
of two of Schubert's most celebrated works, the 'Unfinished' Symphony D759 and the first
Suleika song D720. The construction of *Der Zwerg* is equally symphonic in that it suggests a
self-contained sonata movement (without actually being one) rather than an ordinary lied. The
spirit of Beethoven, brandishing the rhythm of Fate from the C minor Symphony Op. 67, is
blatantly evident at the forte outburst of bb. 80–81, but this motif has quietly pervaded the
accompaniment from the beginning. Here it is both erotic (as in the *Suleika* song) and associated with destiny, as in Beethoven. If *Der Zwerg* dates from the end of 1822 or later – about the
time Schubert discovered his illness – it is no surprise that sexual desire and death are woven
more closely together, and more destructively, than in any of his other songs.
      The extraordinary poem, and the subject of dwarves in general, has been discussed at length
– and fascinatingly – by Susan Youens, where even the minuscule Napoleon makes an appearance as a potential inspiration for the bête noire. Leo Black mentions the Norse goddess Freya,
famous for her wanton and covetous nature, and the four dwarves with whom she sleeps in
return for the beautiful necklace known as 'Brisingamen'. This necklace of the Brisings
(mentioned in *Beowulf*) may have a distant relationship – in Collin's mind at least – with the
blood-red cord that is the instrument of death for the Queen. In some versions of the legend,
Freya strangles her consort with the necklace.
      The poem in nine strophes is conceived as three groups of three in the manner of the cele-
brated *Terzine* of Dante's *The Divine Comedy*: thus aba-bcb-cdc – although the purity of this
conception is slightly spoiled by the four-line strophe at the end. The composer plans the
unfolding of the story carefully; in film-making terms this is a move from the long shot of the
opening lines to the close-up of the murder, and in this the poet (provider of the screenplay) is
Schubert's closest collaborator. Collin opens the ballad with a sea picture, a description of
twilight ('Im trüben Licht') where evening mist obscures distant detail. The mountains in the
background are already disappearing on the horizon, and we can barely make out the small boat
that bobs in the distance. The range of the piano writing is hemmed in – as constricted as our
vision. Twilight seems almost palpable and there is a claustrophobic sense of drama: something
evil is afoot, although we do not yet understand what has generated the suspense. The ominous
left-hand rhythm contributes greatly to this. The movement of the right-hand semiquavers,
whereby the little finger is scarcely permitted to cross the barrier of A above middle C, as if it
were a kind of upper pedal, suggests the movement of a vessel on water. True to Collin's phrase
'glatten Meereswogen', Schubert provides the pull of an undercurrent (in the left-hand quavers)
depicting 'the sea's smooth swell'. The effect is wonderfully contradictory: a tense calm, an
excitement that is all the more dramatic because it is, for the moment, eerily contained.

With the word 'Worauf' (bb. 15–16) the narrator permits us to zoom in on the boat directly (as if allowed a place in the cameraman's helicopter), and identify the two starring actors in his drama: 'the Queen' (as if Collin assumes that we are familiar with the kingdom into which we have been spirited) and 'her Dwarf'(as if it were the most natural thing in the world for these two characters to find themselves alone in a boat at sunset). The throwaway nature of these words allows a most unusual situation to be passed off as normal. We are in a kind of song-theatre of the absurd, a realm where a different kind of logic prevails. We are never told why the Queen seems to be the masochistically willing victim of a heinous crime. Collin's achievement, perhaps influenced by the 'Schicksal' dramas of Zacharias Werner (qv), is to tell us as little as possible and leave us to piece together the story as best we can.

The five-bar interlude immediately after the words 'mit ihrem Zwerge' (bb. 19–23) requires the pianist's right hand to sidle awkwardly across the keyboard, while the left has mid-bar accents in bb. 19 and 20. This music, misshapen by these emphases, waddles across the stave, imitating and echoing the vocal line. The Dwarf moves awkwardly around the boat as he prepares his dastardly deed. By contrast the Queen in Verse 2 (from b. 23) is a model of static purity and musical symmetry. The perfect fifth interval for the word 'empor' (bb. 24–5) is a measure of her artless submission; her eyes move skywards but she seeks neither advice nor help from a Christian heaven. The pagan context of a court where astrology seems more important than religion is part of the text's deliberate strangeness. In bb. 32–3 the distant blue that frames this picture is streaked with light – a description that is marvellously reflected by the change into F major at the end of Verse 2 (bb. 27–35). From b. 37 the Queen addresses the stars directly and the musical tension is increased by the change into C minor.

Both male and female singers can perform this song. Men have to find a *mezza voce* for the Queen's voice without descending (or ascending) into the kind of falsetto parody that can result in unintentional comedy. (We must disregard the interpretative exaggerations that the singer Vogl almost certainly got away with during his career.) In today's recital world it is perhaps easier for female singers to find a menacing colour for the murderer's pronouncements than for male performers to vary the colour between narrator, Queen and Dwarf. The Queen seems to regard the stars as her counsellors; her astrological chart has told her that she is doomed to die, and she is transfixed by this and passively fatalistic. Now that she is alone in a boat with the Dwarf she welcomes the fulfilment of the prophecy – indeed she seems to regard it as deserved, almost a relief ('doch sterb' ich wahrlich gerne'). As yet there is no sign of resistance or struggle from her. It may be that she longs to be released from an unhappy marriage.

The Dwarf's three strophes (Verses 4–6) slump down into B minor (from b. 51). The pianist is here in a tonality where the impulses of this motor rhythm are eerily familiar from an earlier song (*Suleika I* in B minor). The binding of the Queen's neck with a cord of red silk in preparation for the murder feels all the more ominous because the vocal line is doubled, note for note, by the pianist's left hand. This melody, going back on itself in falling sequences, seems to incorporate the grotesque hobbling of the aggrieved jester (for this was almost certainly his role in the royal retinue), simultaneously aggressive and obsequious. Schubert's Dwarf is surely the grandfather of Wagner's Alberich. At bb. 58–9 this doubling ceases and intervals open up between vocal line and accompaniment that perfectly suggest the twisted facial grimaces of the weeping murderer (on the repeated word 'weint'), blinded by grief. From b. 64, with a return to C minor, he addresses the Queen directly, and here the doubling of voice and piano is heard again. This remonstrance explains something of the skewed background to the story: 'It is your own fault', he tells the Queen, 'you have brought it on yourself.' Once again we encounter the absurd logic that governs this text: the Queen (who must have been married to a king in order to procure her title) is accused of abandoning the Dwarf in favour of her husband! One might expect the king to be treated as the injured party in this story, but this is a deliberate reversal of what is sane and accepted. Even the title of the poem as it appears in the 1813 journal *Selam* (and on a contemporary copy of the song) is odd: *Treubruch*, or *Perfidy*. The Queen is guilty of betrayal, but surely she has betrayed the king by having an affair with the Dwarf? It is only in the twisted eyes of her accuser that he is the injured party. Possibly the Dwarf and the Queen, as a princess, grew up together in the same court. If so, like the savage lion in Schumann's Chamisso setting *Die Löwenbraut* Op. 31 no. 1, the Dwarf is incapable of understanding her 'infidelity' and would sooner kill the thing he loves than see it possessed by someone else.

The awakening of joy that he expects to find in her death is mirrored in exultant phrases, high in the stave for a baritone, and in a wild C major (bb. 70–74). Almost immediately he admits, with a change of key and in a lower tessitura, that he will forever hate himself for killing her. A terrible fortissimo reiteration of the fate motif in the accompaniment's left hand (bb. 80–81) on a falling diminished fifth (in musical terms a synonym for the tritone, symbol of *Diabolus in musica*) precedes the eerily muted pronouncement of the death sentence (bb. 81–6). As the Dwarf tells the Queen she is to go to an early grave the hovering minims in the vocal line appear deathly pale on the stave. With the dip of a fifth in the vocal line at 'erblas*sen*' the Dwarf stoops in his imagination as he sees himself in the act of carefully laying the Queen's body to its final rest in the sea. This tenderness, twisted though it may be, is conveyed by the wonderful change to major on the last syllable of 'erblassen'.

This switch from A minor to A major (from b. 86, beginning of Verse 7) signals inevitable pathos. All the romantic longing of its familiar usage is turned on its head as surely as the roles of master and servant have been reversed in this scenario. The composer looks deeper into the Queen's mind and a kind of masochistic joy seeps into the music's fabric. Her plight is self-inflicted: she is a lost soul caught up with the Dwarf we know not how; perhaps she still loves him and believes she deserves her fate. In a more modern scenario we might imagine a perverted game with fatal consequences. When tears run (b. 94) the tonality is once again flattened into A minor. At b. 102 (Verse 8) the Queen begins to plead (Schubert places her words high in the stave, realizing that the *mezza voce* of the baritone voice will sound very different from the rest of the song), hoping that the Dwarf will not regret what he is about to do. He suddenly loses patience and the murder is accomplished in the middle of her speech. There is a high leap of strangled terror in the voice part on the words 'sie sagt's' (b. 105) as the silk cord, placed around her neck earlier, is pulled brutally tight. This is a masterstroke by Schubert: the unusual sound of a singer jumping a sudden sixth in mid-sentence, and on an unimportant word, depicts, surely, the deft *coup de grâce* that has taken place from behind. The Dwarf accords his mistress this mercy at the very least.

Nevertheless, death is not instantaneous and a slow process of strangulation now begins, with the Queen described as being 'in the grip of death' rather than already slain. She lies dying on the floor of the boat, growing paler as she does so. Everything stops save tremolandi on a broken octave, supported by ominous basses falling in semitones – a suspenseful musical void that continues for ten bars (bb. 105–14). In the meantime the Dwarf kisses the pale cheeks of the Queen as life-giving harmony, the oxygen of music, drains out of the song.

From b. 118 (Verse 9) the Dwarf looks balefully at his victim. The fate motif of diminished fourths and fifths in the bass (bb. 118–19, 120–21 and 122–5) indicates that the stars' prophecies have been fulfilled, but the harmony tells us that nothing has been resolved. He pushes her overboard with his own hands, a burial at sea hardly easy for someone of his stature. Schubert only allows him to accomplish his grisly task on his second attempt – depicted by the musical repeat contained within the setting of 'Er senkt sie tief' (bb. 123–5) – while his heart burns in sorrow and longing. The Queen is unconscious, certainly, but we cannot be certain that she has died before she is consigned to the deep. The reaction to this is the vocal climax of the song: poet and composer conjoin the roles of villain and narrator – the singer's rant and word repetitions could easily be in the first, rather than third, person with music of this howling intensity. Underpinning this, in the piano's left hand, is a terrifying restatement of the Dwarf's weeping motive from bb. 58–61, this time in strident octaves, the loudest music in the piece, suggesting a storm of tears.

The accompaniment for *Der Atlas* D957/8 from *Schwanengesang* is prophesied in this music – a common theme between the two songs relates to stunted growth due to a weight of worldly woes, and both accompaniments have a low ceiling under which only the left hand is able to articulate a melody. The Dwarf remains in the grip of a violent, festering passion, the only way out of which is suicide, as we learn elliptically in the final verse. (In a dissenting view, Uri Liebrecht claims that suicide is not part of the dwarf's character; it is more likely that he condemns himself to a 'Flying Dutchman' life of relentless, unremitting agony on the waves. If the dwarf were to drown himself, says Liebrecht, he and the queen might well bump into each other.) The final drop of a fifth (awkwardly low for most singers) at b. 148 (on 'lan<u>den</u>') leaves most of us in no doubt that he drowns himself by slipping deep into the water. In sinking his own boat at sea he shares a fate with Britten's Peter Grimes: both characters leave behind them the same empty seascape with which their respective dramas began, horizons of enormous loneliness. Only a few months separate the composition of *Der Zwerg* and *Die schöne Müllerin* where there is a similarly other-wordly waterscape in *Des Baches Wiegenlied* D795/20, following the death of the miller boy. Each of these victims – both drowned for loving unwisely and too intensely – receives a requiem. (Cf. also the wonderful extended postlude for the intrepid diver, besotted by the princess, drowned at the end of *Der Taucher* D77, 1814.)

There is a story from the contemporary composer Benedict Randhartinger, usually unreliable as a witness, that Schubert, under pressure from the printer, finished *Der Zwerg* in a hurry while at the same time keeping up a conversation with a friend. The only thing that gives this tale any credence is that Schubert had recently broken with Cappi & Diabelli and had decided to switch to Sauer & Leidesdorf for the publication of his songs. The new firm clearly needed a distinguished work with which to establish their link with Schubert, and it is conceivable that they nagged him to write something specially for them with a dedicatee of some importance – in this case the poet Collin himself, who was tutor of Napoleon's son, the Duc de Reichstadt. Nevertheless, it seems impossible to imagine even Schubert writing a song of this quality without 100 per cent concentration. Indeed concentration is what *Der Zwerg* is all about – it compresses a whole opera plot into a few pages. In modern times it is one of the most frequently performed Schubert songs, a mixed blessing for a work that contains so many challenges for its often inexperienced student artists.

Autograph:	Missing or lost
First edition:	Published as Op. 22 no. 1 by Sauer & Leidesdorf, Vienna in May 1823 (P39)
Dedicatee:	Matthäus von Collin
First known performance:	13 November 1823, Musikverein, Vienna as part of an *Abend-Unterhaltung* given by the Gesellschaft der Musikfreunde. Soloist: Josef Preisinger (See Waidelich/Hilmar Dokumente I No. 216 for full concert programme)
Publication reviews:	*Allgemeine musikalische Zeitung* (Leipzig), No. 26 (24 June 1824), cols 425–8 [Waidelich/Hilmar Dokumente I No. 282; Deutsch Doc. Biog. No. 479]
Subsequent editions:	Peters: Vol. 2/55; AGA XX 425: Vol. 7/95; NSA IV: Vol. 1a/160; Bärenreiter: Vol. 1/128
Bibliography:	Black 2001, p. 89
	Dürhammer 1999, p. 43
	Youens 2002, pp. 13–50

Discography and timing: Fischer-Dieskau II 6[1]   5'26
                            Hyperion I 3[12]
                            Hyperion II 26[13]   5'23   Ann Murray

← *An die Leier* D737   *Nacht und Träume* D827 →

Der Zwerg by Martha Griebler (2005). In the original pencil drawing the single thread connecting the hands of the
dwarf with the tip of Schubert's pen is coloured blood red – as is the dwarf's heart.

CATALOGUES AND ADDENDA

ACCORDING TO DEUTSCH

The dates of songs given here are as they appear in the second Deutsch catalogue of 1978 [D$_2$]. Since that time, some of these dates have been revised by the editors of the *Neue Schubert-Ausgabe*, sometimes quite dramatically.

Many of the songs' dates given here were in place only for the second edition of the Deutsch catalogue, reflecting the progress in Schubert studies between the early 1950s and late 1970s. The original numbering established Otto Erich Deutsch's chronology of Schubert's works contemporary with the catalogue's first appearance in 1951 (D$_1$). The biggest deviations between D$_2$ and D$_1$ are shown here. There is now a definite need for a new D$_3$ to include information about many revised songs. An example of how scholarship has advanced over the years may be seen from D965. D$_1$ attributed the middle section of this work to the poet Helmina von Chézy; D$_2$ added a question mark to her name; D$_3$ will name the real poet whose identity was discovered only in 2011. It is clearly too late to change the Deutsch numbers allocated to Schubert's works which have remained more or less unchanged.

The H numbers to the right of the Deutsch numbers (*see also* How to Use this Book, Vol. I/xxix–xxx above) reflect the song sequence used for the chronological version of the Hyperion Schubert Song Edition (Hyperion II). This is also the sequence adopted for the Song Calendar.

All entries refer to solo songs with piano, unless otherwise indicated.

Before 1810(?)
D1A	H1	*Lebenstraum* (*Gesang in c* in D$_2$) (Baumberg) (first setting, fragment). This song does not appear in D$_1$	**II/135**

30 March 1811
D5	H3	*Hagars Klage* (Schücking)	**I/820**

1811 or 1812
D6	H6	*Des Mädchens Klage* (Schiller) (first setting)	**II/289**

1811(?)
D7	H4	*Leichenfantasie* (*Eine Leichenphantasie* in D$_1$) (Schiller)	**II/146**

26 December 1811
D10	H5	*Der Vatermörder* (Pfeffel)	**III/242**

c. 1812
D15	H7	*Der Geistertanz* (Matthisson) (first setting, fragment)	**I/672**
D15A	H8	*Der Geistertanz* (Matthisson) (second setting, fragment)	**I/672**

1812(?)
D17	H9	*Quell' innocento figlio* (Metastasio) (composition exercises)	**II/622**

1812
D23   H11   *Klaglied* (Rochlitz)   **II/63**

24 September 1812
D30   H12   *Der Jüngling am Bache* (Schiller) (first setting) **II/16**

September–October 1812
D33   H13   *Entra l'uomo allor che nasce* (Metastasio)   **I/499**
                             (composition exercises)
D35   H14   *Serbate, o Dei custodi* (Metastasio) (composition **III/135**
                             exercises)

25–7 December 1812
D37   H15   *Die Advokaten* (Engelhardt) (comic trio)   **I/70**

Beginning of 1810(?)   The date in D₁ is 1813(?)
D39   H2   *Lebenstraum* (*Ich sass an einer Tempelhalle am* **II/142**
                             Musenhain in D₁) (Baumberg) (second setting,
                             fragment)

No date given in D₂. The date in D₁ is 1813
D42   H17 & 19   *Misero pargoletto* (Metastasio) (composition   **II/370 & 371**
                             exercises)

19 January 1813
D44   H20   *Totengräberlied* (Hölty)   **III/364**

29 March 1813
D47   H21   *Dithyrambe* (Schiller) (first setting, soloists and **I/416**
                             chorus)

12 April 1813
D50   H22   *Die Schatten* (Matthisson)   **II/726**

15–17 April 1813
D52   H23   *Sehnsucht* ('Ach, aus dieses Tales Gründen')   **III/94**
                             (Schiller) (first setting)

4 May 1813
D59   H24   *Verklärung* (Pope/Herder)   **III/478**

8 May 1813
D61   H24+   *Eine jügendlicher Maienschwung* (Schiller)   **I/470**
                             (composition exercise)

22–3 August 1813
D73   H25   *Thekla* (*eine Geisterstimme*) (Schiller) (first **III/327**
                             setting)

29 August 1813
D75   H26   *Trinklied* ('Freunde sammelt euch im Kreise')   **III/401**
                             (Schäffer) (quartet)

7 and 13 September 1813
D76   H27   *Pensa, che questo istante* (Metastasio)   **II/513**

17 September 1813–5 April 1814 (first version); second version completed
  beginning of 1815

D77	H29	*Der Taucher* (Schiller). In D₁ the number D111 is assigned to the second version	**III/304**

18 September 1813

D78	H28	*Son fra l'onde* (Metastasio)	**III/218**

Completed 27 September 1813

D80		*Zur Namensfeier meines Vaters* (Schubert) (trio with guitar)	**III/763**

Autumn 1813

D81		*Auf den Sieg der Deutschen* (Anonymous) (song with violin and cello accompaniment)	**I/241**

28 October–4 November 1813

D83		*Zur Namensfeier des Herrn Andreas Siller* (Anonymous) (song with violin and harp accompaniment)	**III/762**

15 November 1813

D88	H28+	*Verschwunden sind die Schmerzen* (Schiller) (unaccompanied trio)	**III/482**

1815(?)   In D₁ the assigned date is 1814(?)

D93	H30–H32	*Don Gayseros* (de la Motte Fouqué)	
		(i) 'Don Gayseros, Don Gayseros, wunderlicher schöner Ritter'	**I/425**
		(ii) 'Nächtens klang die süsse Laute'	**I/428**
		(iii) 'An dem jungen Morgenhimmel'	**I/429**

1814

D95	H33	*Adelaide* (Matthisson)	**I/54**

1814   In D₁ the assigned date is April(?) 1814

D97	H34	*Trost. An Elisa* (Matthisson)	**III/416**

Autumn 1814   In D₁ the assigned date is April(?) 1814

D98	H44	*Erinnerungen* (Matthisson)	**I/512**

April 1814

D99	H35	*Andenken* (Matthisson)	**I/217**
D100	H37	*Geisternähe* (Matthisson)	**I/669**
D101	H36	*Erinnerung* (Matthisson)	**I/510**

Autumn 1814   In D₁ the assigned date is April(?) 1814

D102	H45	*Die Betende* (Matthisson)	**I/301**

16 May 1814

D104	H38	*Die Befreier Europas in Paris* (Mikan)	**I/283**

July 1814 (first version)

D107	H39	*Lied aus der Ferne* (Matthisson)	**II/213**

July 1814

D108	H41	*Der Abend (Purpur malt die Tannenhügel)* (Matthisson)	**I/1**
D109	H40	*Lied der Liebe* (Matthisson)	**II/219**

17 September 1814 (first version)

D113	H42	*An Emma* (Schiller)	**I/193**

September 1814

D114	H43	*Romanze* (*Das Fräulein im Turme* in D₁) (Matthisson)	**II/659**

2–7 October 1814

D115	H46	*An Laura, als sie Klopstocks Auferstehungslied sang* (Matthisson)	**I/196**

14 October 1814

D116	H47	*Der Geistertanz* (Matthisson) (third setting)	**I/674**

16 October 1814

D117	H48	*Das Mädchen aus der Fremde* (Schiller) (first setting)	**II/284**

19 October 1814

D118	H49	*Gretchen am Spinnrade* (Goethe)	**I/792**

30 November 1814

D119	H50	*Nachtgesang* (Goethe)	**II/423**
D120	H52	*Trost in Tränen* (*Thränen* in D₁) (Goethe)	**III/420**
D121	H51, H418A	*Schäfers Klagelied* (Goethe)	**II/720**

December 1814

D122	H53	*Ammenlied* (Lubi)	**I/126**

3 December 1814   In D₁ the assigned date is 7 December 1814

D123	H54	*Sehnsucht* ('Was zieht mir das Herz so?') (Goethe)	**III/99**

7 December 1814 (second version)

D124	H55	*Am See* ('Sitz ich im Gras') (Mayrhofer)	**I/113**

12 December 1814 (second version)

D126	H56	*Szene aus 'Faust'* (Goethe)	**III/292**

1815(?)

D134	H57	*Ballade* (Kenner)	**I/275**

19 May 1815   In D₁ the assigned date is simply 1815(?)

D138	H96	*Rastlose Liebe* (Goethe)	**II/625**

1815

D140	H208	*Klage um Ali Bey* (Claudius) (trio)	**II/60**
D141	H58	*Der Mondabend* (Ermin)	**II/372**

1815 or 1816   In D₁ the assigned date is 1815

D142	H59, H59A	*Geistes-Gruss* (Goethe)	**I/675**

1815
D143   H60   *Genügsamkeit* (Schober)   **I/686**

April 1816   In D₁ the assigned date is 1815 or 1816
D144   H249   *Romanze* (Stolberg) (fragment)   **II/663**

February 1815
D148   H63   *Trinklied* ('Bruder, unser Erdenwallen') (Castelli)   **III/403**
                              (solo and chorus)

February 1815 (first version)
D149   H61   *Der Sänger* (Goethe)   **II/698**

17 January 1816   In D₁ the assigned date is February 1815–17 January 1816
D150   H219   *Lodas Gespenst* (Macpherson)   **II/259**

2 February 1815
D151   H64   *Auf einen Kirchhof* (Schlechta)   **I/257**

8 February 1815
D152   H65   *Minona* (Bertrand)   **II/357**

10 February 1815
D153   H66   *Als ich sie erröten sah* (Ehrlich)   **I/96**

11 February 1815
D155   H67   *Das Bild* (Anonymous)   **I/304**

May 1816 (first version)   In D₁ the assigned date is 27 February 1815
D159   H267   *Die Erwartung* (Schiller)   **I/535**

27 February 1815
D160   H68   *Am Flusse* (Goethe) (first setting)   **I/107**

27 February 1815 (first version)
D161   H69, H71A   *An Mignon* (Goethe). D161 also encompasses the   **I/203**
                              undated second version)

27 February 1815
D162   H70   *Nähe des Geliebten* (Goethe)   **II/442**
D163   H71   *Sängers Morgenlied* (Körner) (first setting)   **II/709**

March 1815
D164   H72   *Liebesrausch* (Körner) (first setting, fragment)   **II/193**

1 March 1815
D165   H73   *Sängers Morgenlied* (Körner) (second setting)   **II/711**

1 March 1815 ('in five hours')
D166   H74   *Amphiaraos* (Körner)   **I/128**

9 March 1815
D168   H75   *Nun lasst uns den Leib begraben* (*Begräbnis* in D₁)   **II/461**
                              (Klopstock) (chorus with piano)

D168A   H76   *Jesus Christus unser Heiland, der den Tod*   **II/12**
                              überwand (Klopstock) (chorus with piano).
                              This part song does not appear in D₁

12 March 1815

D169	H77	*Trinklied vor der Schlacht* (Körner) (double chorus with piano)	**III/411**
D170	H78	*Schwertlied* (Körner) (song for solo and chorus)	**III/77**
D171	H79	*Gebet während der Schlacht* (Körner)	**I/645**
D172	H80	*Der Morgenstern* (Körner) (fragment)	**II/386**

26 March 1815

D174	H81, H281	*Das war ich* (Körner) (first setting and second setting – D450A)	**I/399 & I/400**

6 April 1815

D176	H82	*Die Sterne* ('Was funklet ihr so mild mich an?') (Fellinger)	**III/250**
D177	H83	*Vergebliche Liebe* (Bernard)	**III/471**

8 April 1815

D179	H84	*Liebesrausch* (Körner) (second setting)	**II/194**
D180	H85	*Sehnsucht der Liebe* (Körner)	**III/113**

12 April 1815

D182	H86	*Die erste Liebe* (Fellinger)	**I/530**
D183	H87	*Trinklied* ('Ihr Freunde und du gold'ner Wein') (Zettler) (song for solo and chorus)	**III/404**

May 1815

D186	H88	*Die Sterbende* (Matthisson)	**III/248**
D187	H89	*Stimme der Liebe* ('Abendwölke schweben hell') (Matthisson) (first setting)	**III/265**
D188	H90	*Naturgenuss* (Matthisson) (first setting)	**II/449**
D189	H91	*An die Freude* (Schiller)	**1/162**

8–19 May 1815

D190	H91+	*Die vierjährigen Posten* (Körner)	**III/505**
		(No. 5) *Gott, höre meine Stimme* – arranged for voice and piano	**III/509**

15 May 1815

D191	H92	*Des Mädchens Klage* (Schiller) (second setting)	**II/293**
D192	H93	*Der Jüngling am Bache* (Schiller) (second setting)	**II/18**

17 May 1815

D193	H94	*An den Mond* ('Geuss, lieber Mond') (Hölty)	**I/147**
D194	H95	*Die Mainacht* (Hölty)	**II/304**

19 May 1815

D195	H97	*Amalia* (Schiller)	**I/123**

22 May 1815

D196	H98	*An die Nachtigall* ('Geuss nich so laut') (Hölty)	**I/178**
D197	H99	*An die Apfelbäume, wo ich Julien erblickte* (Hölty)	**I/158**
D198	H100	*Seufzer* (Hölty)	**III/137**

25 May 1815

D201	H101	*Auf den Tod einer Nachtigall* (Hölty) (first setting, fragment)	**I/243**

26 May 1815
D206   H102   *Liebeständelei* (Körner)   **II/195**

29 May 1815
D207   H103   *Der Liebende* (Hölty)   **II/186**

29 May (first version)
D208   H106   *Die Nonne* (Hölty). In D₁ the second version of   **II/452**
                         this song is D212; in D₂ D208 is valid for both
                         versions

January 1815   In D₁ the assigned date is June–12 December 1815
D209   H62   *Der Liedler* (Kenner)   **II/240**

3 June 1815
D210   H104   *Die Liebe* (*Klärchens Lied* in D₁) (Goethe)   **II/178**

5–14 June 1815
D211   H105   *Adelwold und Emma* (Bertrand)   **I/57**

17 June 1815
D213   H107   *Der Traum* (Hölty)   **III/399**
D214   H108   *Die Laube* (Hölty)   **II/116**

20 June 1815
D215   H109   *Jägers Abendlied* (Goethe) (first setting)   **II/3**
D215A   H110   *Meeres Stille* (Goethe) (first setting). This setting   **II/226**
                         does not appear in D₁

21 June 1815
D216   H110a   *Meeres Stille* (Goethe) (second setting)   **II/328**

22 June 1815
D217   H111   *Kolmas Klage* (*Colmas Klage* in D₁) (Macpherson   **II/87**
                         after 'Ossian'/unknown)

24 June 1815
D218   H112   *Grablied* (Kenner)   **I/770**

25 June 1815
D219   H113   *Das Finden* (Kosegarten)   **I/553**

15 July 1815   In D₁ the assigned date is July 1815
D221   H125   *Der Abend* ('Der Abend blüht') (Kosegarten)   **I/3**

2 July 1815
D222   H114   *Lieb Minna* (Stadler)   **II/176**

5 July 1815
D224   H115   *Wandrers Nachtlied* ('Der du von dem Himmel   **III/550**
                         bist') (Goethe)
D225   H116   *Der Fischer* (Goethe)   **I/555**
D226   H117   *Erster Verlust* (Goethe)   **I/532**

7 July 1815
D227   H118   *Idens Nachtgesang* (Kosegarten)   **I/917**
D228   H119   *Von Ida* (Kosegarten)   **III/524**

D229	H120	*Die Erscheinung (Erinnerung)* (Kosegarten)	**I/527**
D230	H121	*Die Täuschung* (Kosegarten)	**III/299**

8 July 1815

D231	H122	*Das Sehnen* (Kosegarten)	**III/92**

11 July 1815

D232	H123	*Hymne an den Unendlichen* (Schiller) (quartet with piano)	**I/914**

15 July 1815

D233	H124	*Geist der Liebe* (Kosegarten)	**I/664**
D234	H126	*Tischlied* (Goethe)	**III/335**

24 July 1815

D235	H128	*Abends unter der Linde* (Kosegarten) (first setting)	**I/32**

20 July 1815   In D₁ the assigned date is 25 July 1815

D236	H127	*Das Abendrot* ('Der Abend blüht, der Westen glüht') (Kosegarten) (trio with piano)	**I/28**

25 July 1815

D237	H129	*Abends unter der Linde* (Kosegarten) (second setting)	**I/34**
D238	H130	*Die Mondnacht* (Kosegarten)	**II/376**

Begun on 26 July 1815

D239	H138++	*Claudine von Villa Bella* (Goethe)	
		No. 3 *Ariette der Lucinde* ('Hin und wieder fliegen die Pfeile')	**I/352**
		No. 6 *Ariette der Claudine* ('Liebe schwärmt auf allen Wegen')	**I/353**

27 July 1815

D240	H131	*Huldigung* (Kosegarten)	**I/909**
D241	H132	*Alles um Liebe* (Kosegarten)	**I/82**

August 1815(?)

D242		*Trinklied im Winter* (Hölty)	**III/619**

August 1815

D246	H134	*[Winterlied]*[1]	**I/326**
D247	H139	*Die Bürgschaft* (Schiller)	**III/235**
D248	H149	*Die Spinnerin* (Goethe)	**II/256**
		Lob des Tokayers (Baumberg)	

1 August 1815

D249		*Die Schlacht* (Schiller) (first setting, fragment). There is no incipit for this fragment in D₁	**II/756**

7 August 1815

D250	H135	*Das Geheimnis* (Schiller) (first setting)	**I/657**
D251	H136	*Hoffnung* (Schiller) (first setting)	**I/905**

12 August 1815

D252	H137	*Das Mädchen aus der Fremde* (Schiller) (second setting)	**II/286**

[1] *Winterlied*, first printed in NSA in 2009, is a solo song arrangement of the trio *Trinklied in Winter*.

18 August 1815

| D253 | H138 | *Punschlied. Im Norden zu singen* (Schiller) | **II/612** |
| D254 | H140 | *Der Gott und die Bajadere* (Goethe) | **I/762** |

19 August 1815

D255	H141	*Der Rattenfänger* (Goethe)	**II/629**
D256	H142	*Der Schatzgräber* (Goethe)	**II/728**
D257	H143	*Heidenröslein* (Goethe)	**I/833**
D258	H144	*Bundeslied* (Goethe)	**I/336**
D259	H145	*An den Mond* ('Füllest wieder Busch und Tal') (Goethe) (first setting)	**1/140**

20 August 1815

| D260 | H146 | *Wonne der Wehmut* (Goethe) | **III/737** |

21 August 1815

| D261 | H147 | *Wer kauft Liebesgötter?* (Goethe) | **III/566** |

22 August 1815

D262	H148	*Die Fröhlichkeit* (Prandstetter)	**I/613**
D263	H150	*Cora an die Sonne* (Baumberg)	**I/387**
D264	H151	*Der Morgenkuss* (*Der Morgenkuss nach einem Ball* in D₁) (Baumberg)	**II/378**

23 August 1815

| D265 | H152 | *Abendständchen. An Lina* (Baumberg) | **I/35** |

24 August 1815

| D266 | H153 | *Morgenlied* ('Willkommen, rotes Morgenlicht') (Stolberg) | **II/380** |

25 August 1815

D267	H154	*Trinklied* ('Auf! Jeder sei nun froh') (Anonymous)	**III/406**
D268	H155	*Bergknappenlied* (Anonymous) (male quartet with piano)	**I/295**
D269	H159	*Das Leben* (Wannovius) (trio with piano)	**II/123**
D270	H156	*An die Sonne* ('Sinke, liebe Sonne') (Baumberg)	**I/183**
D271	H157	*Der Weiberfreund* (Cowley/Ratschky)	**III/561**
D272	H158	*An die Sonne* ('Königliche Morgensonne') (Tiedge)	**I/185**
D273	H160	*Lilla an die Morgenröte* (Anonymous)	**II/250**
D274	H161	*Tischlerlied* (Anonymous)	**III/333**
D275	H162	*Totenkranz für ein Kind* (Matthisson)	**III/377**

28 August 1815

| D276 | H163 | *Abendlied* ('Gross und rotenflammet') (Stolberg) | **I/12** |

29 August 1815

| D277 | H164 | *Punschlied* ('Vier Elemente, innig gesellt') Schiller | **II/614** |

1815   In D₁ the assigned date is September(?) 1815

| D278 | H165 | *Ossians Lied nach dem Falle Nathos* (Macpherson after 'Ossian'/Harold) | **II/496** |

September 1815

D280	H166	*Das Rosenband* (Klopstock)	**II/680**
D281	H167	*Das Mädchen von Inistore* (Macpherson after	**II/287**
		'Ossian'/Harold)	

5 September 1815

| **D282** | H168 | *Cronnan* (Macpherson after 'Ossian'/Harold) | **I/391** |

6 September 1815

| **D283** | H169 | *An den Frühling* (Schiller) (first setting) | **I/137** |
| **D284** | H170 | *Lied* ('Es ist so angenehm') (Schiller) | **II/205** |

12 September 1815

| **D285** | H171 | *Furcht der Geliebten/An Cidli* (Klopstock) | **I/634** |

14 September 1815

D286	H172	*Selma und Selmar* (Klopstock)	**III/130**
D287	H173	*Vaterlandslied* (Klopstock)	**III/460**
D288	H174	*An Sie* (Klopstock)	**I/214**
D289	H175	*Die Sommernacht* (Klopstock)	**III/216**
D290	H176	*Die frühen Gräber* (Klopstock)	**I/619**

15 September 1815

| **D291** | H177, H178A | *Dem Unendlichen* (Klopstock) | **III/432** |

20 September 1815

| **D293** | H178 | *Shilric und Vinvela* (Macpherson after 'Ossian'/ | **III/142** |
| | | Harold) | |

1815 or 1816(?)[1] In D₁ the assigned date is Autumn 1815(?) and 1817(?)

| **D295** | H212 | *Hoffnung* ('Schaff', das Tagwerk meiner Hände') | **I/903** |
| | | (Goethe) | |

1815 or 1816(?)   In D₁ the assigned date is Autumn 1815(?)

| **D296** | H213 | *An den Mond* ('Füllest wieder Busch und Tal') | **I/143** |
| | | (Goethe) (second setting) | |

Spring 1817(?)   In D₁ the assigned date is October(?) 1815

| **D297** | H340 | *Augenlied* (Mayrhofer) | **I/263** |

October 1815

| **D298** | H180 | *Liane* (Mayrhofer) | **II/170** |

1816 or 1817(?)   In D₁ the assigned date is 12 October 1815

| **D300** | H376 | *Der Jüngling an der Quelle* (Salis-Seewis) | **II/22** |

12 October 1815

| **D301** | H181 | *Lambertine* (Anonymous). In both D₁ and D₂ the | **II/112** |
| | | poem is attributed to J. L. Stoll | |

15 October 1815

| **D302** | H182 | *Labetrank der Liebe* (Stoll) | **II/107** |
| **D303** | H183 | *An die Geliebte* (Stoll) | **I/168** |

---

[1]In 2012 [NSA Vol. 9] D295 and D296 were re-dated in the *Neue Schubert-Ausgabe*. Both songs were composed after February 1820.

D304	H184	*Wiegenlied* ('Schlummre sanft') (Körner)	**III/591**
D305	H185	*Mein Gruss an den Mai* (Ermin)	**II/330**
D306	H186	*Skolie* ('Lasst im Morgenstrahl des Mai'n') (Deinhardstein)	**III/214**
D307	H187	*Die Sternenwelten* (Jarnik/Fellinger)	**III/263**
D308	H188	*Die Macht der Liebe* (Kalchberg)	**II/273**
D309	H189	*Das gestörte Glück* (Körner)	**I/723**

18 October 1815

| **D310** | H190, H190A | *Sehnsucht* ('Nur wer die Sehnsucht kennt') (Goethe) (first and second settings) | **III/102** |

19 October 1815

D312	H191	*Hektors Abschied* (Schiller)	**I/852**
D313	H192	*Die Sterne* ('Wie wohl ist mir im Dunkeln') (Kosegarten)	**III/251**
D314	H193	*Nachtgesang* ('Tiefe Feier schauert um die Welt') (Kosegarten)	**II/425**
D315	H194	*An Rosa I* ('Warum bist du nicht hier') (Kosegaten)	**I/206**
D316	H195	*An Rosa II* ('Rosa, denkst du an mich?') (Kosegarten)	**I/208**
D317	H196	*Idens Schwanenlied* (Kosegarten)	**I/919**
D318	H197	*Schwangesang* (Kosegarten)	**III/73**
D319	H198	*Luisens Antwort* (*Louisens Antwort* in D₁) (Kosegarten)	**II/268**

23 October 1815

| **D320** | H199 | *Der Zufriedene* (Reissig) | **III/752** |
| **D321** | H200 | *Mignon* ('Kennst du das Land?') (Goethe) | **II/344** |

27 October 1815

| **D322** | H201 | *Hermann und Thusnelda* (Klopstock) | **I/871** |

9 November 1815 to June 1816

| **D323** | H202 | *Klage der Ceres* (Schiller) | **II/53** |

13 November 1815

| **D325** | H203 | *Harfenspieler (Wer sich der Einsamkeit ergibt)* (Goethe) | **III/571** |

28 November 1815

| **D327** | H204 | *Lorma* (Macpherson after 'Ossian'/Harold) (first setting) | **II/265** |

October 1815(?)   In D₁ the assigned date is late autumn 1815

| **D328** | H179, H201A | *Erlkönig* (Goethe) | **I/517** |

23 December 1815

| **D329** | H205 | *Die drei Sänger* (Bobrik) (fragment) | **I/444** |

28 December 1815

| **D330** | H206 | *Das Grab* (Salis-Seewis) (song with chorus) (first setting) | **I/767** |

c. 1816
D331   H235+   *Der Entfernten* (Salis-Seewis) (first setting,
                         unaccompanied male quartet)
D342   H214   *An mein Klavier* (*Seraphine an ihr Klavier* in D₁)   **I/201**
                         (Schubart)

August 1816   In D₁ the assigned date is *c.* 1816
D343   H293   *Am Tage aller Seelen (Litanei)* (Jacobi)   **I/121**

1816(?)
D344   H215   *Am ersten Maimorgen* (Claudius)   **I/103**
D350   H235   *Der Entfernten* (Salis Seewis) (second setting)   **I/497**
D351   H236   *Fischerlied* (Salis-Seewis) (first setting)   **I/558**
D352   H326   *Licht und Liebe* (M. von Collin) (duet)   **II/173**

1816
D356   *Trinklied* ('Funkelnd im Becher') (Anonymous)   **III/407**

1816(?)   In D₁ the date is assigned definitively to 1816
D358   H210   *Die Nacht* ('Du verstörst uns nicht') (Uz)   **II/43**

1816
D359   H211   *Sehnsucht* ('Nur wer die Sehnsucht kennt') (*Lied*   **III/104**
                         der Mignon in D₁) (Goethe) (second setting)
D360   H303   *Lied eines Schiffers an die Dioskuren* (Mayrhofer)   **II/228**
D361   H320   *Am Bach im Frühlinge* (*Am Bach im Frühling* in   **I/100**
                         D₁) (Schober)

1815 or 1816(?)   In D₁ the date is assigned defintively to 1816
D362   H207   *Zufriedenheit* (*Lied – Ich bin vergnügt* in D₁)   **III/754**
                         (Claudius)

1816
D363   H209   *An Chloen* (Uz) (fragment)   **I/134**

Beginning of 1816
D367   H220   *Der König in Thule* (Goethe)   **II/78**

Beginning of 1816(?)
D368   H221   *Jägers Abendlied* (Goethe) (second setting)   **II/5**

1816   In D₁ the assigned date is the beginning of 1816
D369   H222   *An Schwager Kronos* (Goethe)   **I/210**

January 1816
D371   H216   *Klage* ('Trauer umfliesst mein Leben')   **II/51**
                         (Anonymous). This first version of this song
                         was D292 in D₁

15 January 1816
D372   H217   *An die Natur* (Stolberg)   **I/181**
D373   H218   *Lied* ('Mutter geht durch ihre Kammern') (de la   **II/211**
                         Motte Fouqué)

February 1816
D375   H223   *Der Tod Oskars* (Macpherson after 'Ossian'/Harold)   **III/337**

10 February 1816
D376   H224   *Lorma* (Macpherson after 'Ossian'/Harold)   **II/267**
                            (second setting, fragment)

11 February 1816
D377   H225   *Das Grab* (Salis Seewis) (third setting, male   **I/767**
                            chorus with piano)
24 February 1816
D381   H226   *Morgenlied* ('Die frohe neubelebte Flur')   **II/382**
                            (Anonymous)
D382   H227   *Abendlied* ('Sanft glänzt di Abendsonne')   **I/14**
                            (Anonymous)

March 1816
D387   *Die Schlacht* (Schiller) (second setting,   **II/756**
                            fragment)
D388   H228   *Laura am Klavier* (Schiller)   **II/117**
D389   H229   *Des Mädchens Klage* (Schiller) (third setting)   **II/295**
D390   H230   *Die Entzückung an Laura* (Schiller)   **I/504**
                            (first setting)
D391   H231   *Die vier Weltalter* (Schiller)   **III/506**
D392   H237   *Plügerlied* (Salis-Seewis)   **II/523**
D393   H238   *Die Einsiedelei* (Salis-Seewis) (second setting)   **I/488**
D394   H239   *An die Harmonie* (*Gesang an die Harmonie* in D_1)   **I/169**
                            (Salis-Seewis)
D395   H243   *Lebensmelodien* (A. von Schlegel)   **II/127**
D396   H233   *Gruppe aus dem Tartarus* (Schiller) (first setting,   **I/809**
                            fragment)

13 March 1816
D397   H232   *Ritter Toggenburg* (Schiller)   **II/649**

13 May 1816   In D_1 the date assigned to D398–D401 is 13 March 1815
D398   H263   *Frühlingslied* ('Die Luft ist blau') (Hölty)   **I/626**
D399   H264   *Auf den Tod einer Nachtigall* (Hölty) (second   **I/244**
                            setting)
D400   H265   *Die Knabenzeit* (Hölty)   **II/76**
D401   H266   *Winterlied* (Hölty)   **III/617**

18 March 1816
D402   H234   *Der Flüchtling* (Schiller)   **I/570**

27 March 1816
D403   H240   *Lied (Ins stille Land)* (Salis-Seewis)   **II/208**

March 1816   In D_1 the assigned date is end of March–April 1816
D404   H242   *Die Herbstnacht* (*Wehmut* in D_1) (Salis-Seewis)   **I/867**

April 1816 (first version)   In D_1 the assigned date is end of March–April 1816
D405   H246   *Der Herbstabend* (Salis-Seewis)   **I/863**

March 1816   In D_1 the assigned date is end of March–April 1816
D406   H241   *Abschied von der Harfe* (Salis-Seewis)   **I/46**

16 June 1816   In D₁ the assigned date is spring 1816 and (i) is assigned the number D441

D407	H268,	*Beitrag zur fünfzigjährigen Jubelfeier des Herrn*	**I/290**
	H268A–C	*von Salieri* (Schubert?)	
		(i) *Gütigster, Bester* (quartet of male voices with piano)	
		(ii) *So gut als Weisheit strömen mild* (solo tenor with piano)	
		(iii) *Unser aller Grosspapa* (unaccompanied canon for three voices)	

April 1816

D409	H244	*Die verfehlte Stunde* (A. von Schlegel)	**III/460**
D410	H245	*Sprache der Liebe* (A. von Schlegel)	**III/238**
D411	H247	*Daphne am Bach* (Stolberg)	**1/397**
D412	H248	*Stimme der Liebe* ('Meine Selinde') (Stolberg)	**III/268**
D413	H251	*Entzückung* (Matthisson)	**I/502**
D414	H252	*Geist der Liebe* (Matthisson) (first setting)	**I/666**
D415	H253	*Klage* ('Die Sonne steigt, die Sonne sinkt') (Matthisson)	**II/50**
D416	H250	*Lied in der Abwesenheit* (Stolberg)	**II/233**

29 April 1816

D418	H254	*Stimme der Liebe* ('Abendgewölke schweben hell') (Matthisson) (second setting)	**III/267**

30 April 1816

D419	H255	*Julius an Theone* (Matthisson)	**II/30**

1822(?)   In D₁ the assigned date is end of May 1816 and February 1822

D422	H480	*Naturgenuss* (Matthisson) (Male quartet with piano, second setting)	**II/450**

May 1816

D429	H256	*Minnelied* (Hölty)	**II/355**
D430	H257	*Die frühe Liebe* (Hölty)	**I/617**
D431	H258	*Blumenlied* (Hölty)	**I/319**
D432	H259, H259A	*Der Leidende* (Anonymous) (two versions)	**II/155**
D433	H260	*Seligkeit* (Hölty)	**III/128**
D434	H261	*Erntelied* (Hölty)	**I/525**

12 May 1816 (first version)

D436	H262	*Klage* ('Dein Silber schien durch Eichengrün') (*Klage an den Mond* in D₁) (Hölty)	**II/47**

June 1816

D439	H269	*An die Sonne* (Uz) (SATB quartet with piano)	**I/186**
D442	H270	*Das grosse Halleluja* (Klopstock) (solo or chorus with piano)	**I/807**
D443	H271	*Schlachtlied* (*Schlachtgesang* in D₁) (Klopstock) (solo or chorus with piano)	**II/761**
D444	H272	*Die Gestirne* (Klopstock)	**I/721**
D445	H273	*Edone* (Klopstock)	**I/467**

D446	H274	*Die Liebesgötter* (Uz)	**II/191**
D447	H276	*An den Schlaf* (Anonymous)	**I/154**
D448	H275	*Gott im Frühlinge* (Uz)	**I/754**
D449	H277	*Der gute Hirt* (Uz)	**I/816**
D450	H280	*Fragment aus dem Aeschylus* (Mayrhofer)	**I/588**

July 1816

D454	H282	*Grablied auf einen Soldaten* (Schubart)	**I/772**
D455	H283	*Freude der Kinderjahre* (Köpken)	**I/595**
D456	H284	*Das Heimweh* ('Oft in einsam stillen Stunden') (Hell)	**I/841**

May 1817 In D₁ the assigned date is July 1816 (May 1817)

| **D457** | H285 | *An die untergehende Sonne* (Kosegarten) | **I/189** |

30 July 1816

| **D458** | H286 | *Aus Diego Manazares [recte Manzanares]: Ilmerine [recte Almerine]* (Krosigk). In both D₁ and D₂ the poem of this song is attributed to Schlechta | **I/265** |

August 1816

D462	H288	*An Chloen* ('Bei der Liebe reinsten Flammen') (Jacobi)	**I/135**
D463	H289	*Hochzeit-Lied* (*Hochzeitslied* in D₁) (Jacobi)	**I/890**
D464	H290	*In der Mitternacht* (Jacobi)	**I/950**
D465	H291	*Trauer der Liebe* (Jacobi)	**III/397**
D466	H292	*Die Perle* (Jacobi)	**II/516**
D467	H287	*Pflicht und Liebe* (Gotter)	**II/521**

7 August 1816

| **D468** | H294 | *An den Mond* ('Was schauest du so hell') (Hölty) | **I/149** |

September 1816

D469	H296, H297	*Mignon* ('So lasst mich scheinen') (Goethe) (first setting, two fragments)	**II/349**
D473	H299	*Liedesend* (Mayrhofer)	**II/349**
D474	H295	*Lied des Orpheus, als er in die Hölle ging* (Jacobi)	**II/221**
D475	H300	*Abschied, nach einer Wallfahrtsarie* (Mayrhofer)	**I/44**
D476	H301	*Rückweg* (Mayrhofer)	**II/696**
D477	H302	*Alte Liebe rostet nie* (Mayrhofer)	**I/98**

September 1816 (first version) and 1822 (second version)

| **D478** | H304, H304A, H492, H493, H494 | *Gesänge des Harfners aus Wilhelm Meister* (Goethe)
(i) 'Wer sich der Einsamkeit ergibt' – 2 versions
(ii) 'Wer nie sein Brot mit Tränen ass' – 3 settings
(iii) 'An die Türen will ich schleichen'
In D₁ the 'Harfenspieler' I, II and III are assigned D478, 479 and 480 | **I/698–706 &
III/568–70** |

September 1816

| **D481** | H298 | *Sehnsucht* ('Nur wer die Sehnsucht kennt') (*Lied der Mignon* in D₁) (Goethe) (third setting) | **III/105** |

D482	H305	*Der Sänger am Felsen* (Pichler)	**II/704**
D483	H306	*Lied* ('Ferne von der grossen Stadt') (Pichler)	**II/207**
D484	H307	*Gesang der Geister über den Wassern* (Goethe) (first setting, fragment)	**I/710**

October 1816   In D₁ this song shares the catalogue numbers D489 and D493

| D489 | H308 | *Der Wanderer* ('Ich komme vom Gebrige hier') (*Der Unglückliche* in D₁ under D489) (Schmidt) | **III/538** |

October 1816

D490	H309	*Der Hirt* (Mayrhofer)	**I/885**
D491	H310	*Gehemnis* ('Sag an, wer lehrt dich Lieder') (*Geheimnis an Franz Schubert* in D₁) (Mayrhofer)	**I/661**
D492	H311	*Zum Punsche* (Mayrhofer)	**III/758**

November 1816

| D495 | H312 | *Abendlied der Fürstin* (Mayrhofer) | **1/18** |
| D496 | H313 | *Bei dem Grab meines Vaters* (Claudius) | **I/285** |

This song does not appear in D₁

D496A	H313A	*Klage um Ali Bey* (Claudius) (solo song version of trio D140)	**II/61**
D497	H314	*An die Nachtigall* ('Er liegt und schläft') (Claudius)	**I/180**
D498	H315	*Wiegenlied* ('Schlafe, schlafen holder süsser Knabe') (Anonymous)	**III/593**
D499	H316	*Abendlied* ('Der Mond ist aufgegangen') (Claudius)	**I/15**
D500	H318	*Phidile* (Claudius)	**II/525**
D501	H319	*Zufriedenheit* (*Lied* in D₁) (Claudius) (second setting)	**III/756**
D502	H321	*Herbstlied* ('Bunt sind schon die Wälder') (Salis-Seewis)	**I/865**
D503	H322	*Mailied* ('Grüner wird die Au') (Hölty) (third setting)	**II/303**

4 November 1816

| D504 | H317 | *Am Grabe Anselmos* (Claudius) | **I/110** |

December 1816

D507	H323	*Skolie* ('Mädchen entsiegelten, Brüder, die Flaschen') (Matthisson)	**III/215**
D508	H324	*Lebenslied* (Matthisson)	**II/125**
D509	H325	*Leiden der Trennung* (H. von Collin)	**II/152**
D510	H327, H328	*Vedi quanto adoro* (Metastasio) (2 versions, fragment)	**III/465**

A spurious version of *Der Leidende* is included in D₁ as D512

1817(?)

| D513 | H344 | *La pastorella al prato* (*La Pastorella* in D₁) (Goldoni) (first setting, male quartet with piano) | **II/105** |

D513A	H330	*Nur wer die Liebe kennt* (Werner). This song does not appear in D₁	**II/463**
D514	H331	*Die abgeblühte Linde* (Széchényi)	**I/39**
D515	H332	*Der Flug der Zeit* (Széchényi)	**I/573**

1816(?)   In D₁ the assigned date is 1817(?)

D516	H341	*Sehnsucht* ('Die Lerche wolkennahe Lieder') (Mayrhofer)	**III/108**

April 1817   In D₁ the assigned date is simply 1817

D517	H364	*Der Schäfer und der Reiter* (de la Motte Fouqué)	**II/717**

1816 or 1817   In D₁ the date is assigned definitively to 1817

D518	H329	*An den Tod* (Schubart)	**I/155**

1817(?)   In D₁ the assigned date is January(?) 1817

D519	H371	*Die Blumensprache* (Platner[?])	**I/320**

January 1817 (first version)

D520	H333	*Frohsinn* (Castelli)	**I/615**

January 1817

D521	H334	*Jagdlied* (Werner) (chorus with piano)	**II/10**
D522	H335	*Die Liebe* ('Wo weht der Liebe hoher Geist?') (Leon)	**II/181**
D523	H336	*Trost* ('Nimmer lange weil ich hier') (Anonymous)	**III/413**
D524	H337	*Der Alpenjäger* ('Auf hohem Bergesrücken') (Mayrhofer)	**I/89**
D525	H338	*Wie Ulfru fischt* (Mayrhofer)	**III/586**
D526	H339	*Fahrt zum Hades* (Mayrhofer)	**I/544**
D527	H342	*Schlaflied* (Mayrhofer)	**II/764**
D528	H343	*La pastorella al prato* (Goldoni) (second setting)	**II/106**

February 1817

D530	H345	*An eine Quelle* (Claudius)	**I/192**
D531	H347	*Der Tod und das Mädchen* (Claudius)	**III/343**
D532	H346	*Das Lied vom Reifen* (Claudius)	**II/235**
D533	H348	*Täglich zu singen* (Claudius)	**III/298**
D534	H349	*Die Nacht* ('Die Nacht is dumpfig und finster') (Macpherson after 'Ossian'/Harold)	**II/202**
D535		*Lied* ('Brüder, schrecklich brennt die Träne') song for soprano and orchestra	**II/736**

1817(?)   In D₁ the assigned date is March(?) 1817

D536	H352	*Der Schiffer* ('Im Winde, im Sturme befahr ich den Fluss') (Mayrhofer)	**II/736**

March 1817

D539	H353	*Am Strome* (Mayrhofer)	**I/119**
D540	H350	*Philoktet* (Mayrhofer)	**II/527**
D541	H351	*Memnon* (Mayrhofer)	**II/331**
D542	H354	*Antigone und Oedip* (Mayrhofer)	**I/220**
D543	H356	*Auf dem See* (Goethe)	**I/230**
D544	H357	*Ganymed* (Goethe)	**I/637**

D545	H359	*Der Jüngling und der Tod* (Spaun)	**II/28**
D546	H360	*Trost im Liede* (Schober)	**III/418**
D547	H361	*An die Musik* (Schober)	**I/175**
D548	H355	*Orest* [in D₁ and D₂ *Orest auf Tauris*] (Mayrhofer)	**II/485**
D549	H358	*Mahomets Gesang* (Goethe) (first setting, fragment)	**II/297**

Between end of 1816 and 1817 (first and second versions); 21 February 1818 (third version); autumn 1820 (fourth version); October 1821 (fifth version)

D550	H391	*Die Forelle* (Schubart)	**I/577**

April 1817

D551	H362	*Pax vobiscum* (Schober)	**II/508**
D552	H363	*Hänflings Liebeswerbung* (Kind)	**I/818**
D553	H365	*Auf der Donau* (Mayrhofer)	**I/250**
D554	H366	*Uraniens Flucht* (Mayrhofer)	**III/443**

May 1817

D558	H367	*Liebhaber in allen Gestalten* (Goethe)	**II/197**
D559	H368	*Schweizerlied* (Goethe)	**III/75**
D560	H369	*Der Goldschmiedsgesell* (Goethe)	**I/746**
D561	H370	*Nach einem Gewitter* (Mayrhofer)	**II/403**
D562	H372	*Fischerlied* (Salis-Seewis) (third setting)	**I/561**
D563	H373	*Die Einsiedelei* (Salis-Seewis) (third setting)	**I/490**
D564	H374	*Gretchen im Zwinger* (*Gretchens Bitte* in D₁) (Goethe) (fragment)	**I/799**

June 1817(?)

D565	H375	*Der Strom* (Anonymous)	**III/274**

June 1817

D569	H377	*Das Grab* (Salis-Seewis) (male chorus with piano, fourth setting)	**I/767**

July 1817

D573	H378	*Iphigenia* (Mayrhofer)	**I/952**

August 1817

D577	H379	*Entzückung an Laura* (Schiller) (second setting, two fragments)	**I/506**

24 August 1817

D578	H380	*Abschied* ('Lebe wohl! Du lieber Freund!') (Schubert)	**I/42**

Autumn 1817   In D₁ the assigned date is September(?) and November 1817

D579	H381	*Der Knabe in der Wiege* (Ottenwalt)	**II/73**

September or October 1817(?)   In D₁ the following two songs do not appear

D579A	H382	*Vollendung* (Matthisson)	**III/520**
D579B	H383	*Die Erde* (Matthisson)	**I/508**

September 1817

D583	H384	*Gruppe aus dem Tartarus* (Schiller) (second setting)	**I/810**

D584	H386	*Elysium* (Schiller)	**I/492**
D585	H385	*Atys* (Mayrhofer)	**I/225**
D586	H387	*Erlafsee* (Mayrhofer)	**I/514**

October 1817 (first version)

D587	H388	*An den Frühling* (Schiller) (third setting)	**I/139**
D588	H389	*Der Alpenjäger* ('Willst du nicht das Lämmlein hüten?') (Schiller)	**I/92**

November 1817

D594	H392	*Der Kampf* (Schiller)	**II/39**
D595	H393	*Thekla (eine Geisterstimme)* (Schiller) (second setting)	**III/329**
D596	H390	*Lied eines Kindes* (Anonymous)	**II/225**

December 1817

D598	H394	*Das Dörfchen* (Bürger) (male quartet with piano)	**I/420**

1818

D607	H398	*Evangelium Johannes* (Bible)	**I/541**

January 1818

D609	H395	*Die Geselligkeit* (*Lebenslust* in D₁) (Unger) (SATB with piano)	**I/718**

March 1818

D611	H396	*Auf der Riesenkoppe* (Körner)	**I/254**

April 1818

D614	H397	*An den Mond in einer Herbstnacht* (Schreiber)	**I/151**

June 1818

D616	H399	*Grablied für die Mutter* (Anonymous)	**I/774**

July 1818

D619	H400	*Sing-Übungen* (wordless) (vocal exercises for two voices in D₁)	**III/180**
D620	H401	*Einsamkeit* ('Gib mir die Fülle der Einsamkeit') (Mayrhofer)	**I/479**

August 1818

D622	H402	*Der Blumenbrief* (Schreiber)	**I/317**
D623	H403	*Das Marienbild* (Schreiber)	**II/307**

September 1818

D626	H404	*Blondel zu Marien* (Anonymous)	**I/312**

November 1818

D627	H405	*Das Abendrot* ('Du heilige, glühend Abendrot!') (Schreiber)	**I/29**
D628	H407	*Sonett* ('Apollo, lebet doch dein hold Verlangen') (*Sonett I* in D₁) (Petrarca/A. von Schlegel)	**III/220**
D629	H408	*Sonett* ('Allein, nachdenklich') (*Sonett II* in D₁) (Petrarca/A. von Schlegel)	**III/223**

December 1818
D630   H409   *Sonett* ('Nunmehr, da Himmel Erde schweigt')   **III/226**
                       (*Sonett III* in D₁) (Petrarca/Gries)
D631   H410   *Blanka* (F. von Schlegel)   **I/306**
D632   H411   *Vom Mitleiden Mariä* (Spee adapted by F. von   **III/522**
                       Schlegel)

Between 1819 and 1823(?)   In D₁ the assigned date is *c.* 1819
D633   H418   *Der Schmetterling* (F. von Schlegel)   **II/784**
D634   H415   *Die Berge* (F. von Schlegel)   **I/293**

Beginning of 1821   In D₁ the assigned date is *c.* 1819
D636   H461   *Sehnsucht* ('Ach, aus dieses Tales Gründen')   **III/96**
                       (Schiller) (second setting)

c. 1819
D637   H412   *Hoffnung* ('Es reden und träumen die Menschen')   **I/907**
                       (Schiller) (second setting)

April 1819 (first version) In D₁ the assigned date is *c.* 1819
D638   H424   *Der Jüngling am Bache* (Schiller) (third setting) **II/20**

September 1820   In D₁ the version that appeared in the Nachlass in 1832
  was assigned the number D949
D639   H413   *Widerschein* (Schlechta)   **III/580**

1812(?)   In D₁ the assigned date is *c.* 1819
D642   H10   *Viel tausend Sterne prangen* (*Das Feuerwerk* in **III/488**
                       D₁) (Eberhard) (SATB with piano)

Beginning of 1819
D645   H414   *Abend* (Tieck) (fragment)   **I/5**

January 1819
D646   H416   *Die Gebüsche* (F. von Schlegel)   **I/647**

February 1819
D649   H417   *Der Wanderer* ('Wie deutlich des Mondes Licht   **III/544**
                       zu mir spricht') (F. von Schlegel)
D650   H419   *Abendbilder* (Silbert)   **I/8**
D651   H420   *Himmelsfunken* (Silbert)   **I/879**
D652   H421   *Das Mädchen* ('Wie so innig, möcht ich sagen')   **II/281**
                       F. von Schlegel
D653   H422   *Bertas Lied in der Nacht* (*Berthas Lied* in D₁) **I/297**
                       (Grillparzer)

March 1819
D654   H423   *An die Freunde* (Mayrhofer)   **I/164**

April 1819
D656   H424+   *Sehnsucht* ('Nur wer die Sehnsucht kennt')   **III/107**
                       (fourth setting, male quintet)

May 1819
D658   H425   *Geistliches Lied* (*Marie* in D₁) (Novalis)   **I/678**

D659	H426	*Hymne I* ('Wenige wissen das Geheimnis der Liebe') (Novalis)	**I/910**
D660	H427	*Hymne II* ('Wenn ich ihn nur habe') (*Geistliches Lied* in NSA) (Novalis)	**I/680**
D661	H428	*Hymne III* ('Wenn alle untreu werden') (*Geistliches Lied* in NSA) (Novalis)	**I/682**
D662	H429	*Hymne IV* ('Ich sag es jedem, dass er lebt') (*Geistliches Lied* in NSA) (Novalis)	**I/684**

June 1819

D663	H430	*Der 13. Psalm* (Bible/Mendelssohn)	**II/591**

10 August 1819

D666	H431	*Kantate zum Geburstag des Sängers Johann Michael Vogl* (*Cantate* in NSA) (Stadler) (trio with piano)	**I/339**

October 1819

D669	H432	*Beim Winde* (Mayrhofer)	**I/287**
D670	H433	*Die Sternennächte* (Mayrhofer)	**III/261**
D671	H434	*Trost* ('Hörnerklänge rufen klagend') (Mayrhofer)	**III/414**
D672	H437	*Nachtstück* (Mayrhofer)	**II/435**
D673	H435	*Die Liebende schreibt* (Goethe)	**II/188**
D674	H436	*Prometheus* (Goethe)	**II/581**

November 1819

D677	H438	*Strophe aus 'Die Götter Griechenlands'* (*Strophe von Schiller* in D₁) (Schiller)	**III/276**

Between 1820 and 1824 In D₁ the assigned date is *c.* 1820

D682	H439	*Über allen Zauber Liebe* (Mayrhofer) (fragment)	**III/423**

1820

D684	H440	*Die Sterne* ('Du staunest, o Mensch') (F. von Schlegel)	**III/253**
D685	H441	*Morgenlied* ('Eh' die Sonne früh aufersteht') (Werner)	**II/383**

September 1820 (first version)

D686	H455	*Frühlingsglaube* (Uhland)	**I/623**

January 1820

D687	H442	*Nachthymne* (Novalis)	**II/429**
D688	H443–H446	*Vier Canzonen* (Vittorelli, i & ii, Metastasio, iii & iv)	**III/489**
		(i) *Non t'accostar all'Urna*	**III/490**
		(ii) *Guarda, che bianca luna*	**III/491**
		(iii) *Da quel sembiante appresi*	**III/493**
		(iv) *Mio ben ricordati*	**III/494**

March 1820

D690	H512	*Abendröte* (F. von Schlegel)	**I/25**
D691	H447	*Die Vögel* (F. von Schlegel)	**III/518**

D692	H449	*Der Knabe* (F. von Schlegel)	**II/71**
D693	H448	*Der Fluss* (F. von Schlegel)	**I/575**
D694	H450	*Der Schiffer* ('Friedlich lieg' ich hingegossen') (F. von Schlegel)	**II/739**

By 19 March 1820(?)

D695	H451	*Namentagslied* (Stadler)	**II/447**

September 1820

D698	H452	*Des Fräuleins Liebeslauschen* (Schlechta)	**I/584**
D699	H453	*Der entsühnte Orest* (Mayrhofer)	**I/500**
D700	H454	*Freiwilliges Versinken* (Mayrhofer)	**I/592**

November 1820

D702	H456	*Der Jüngling auf dem Hügel* (Hüttenbrenner)	**II/24**

December 1820

D705	H459	*Gesang der Geister über den Wassern* (third setting, TTBB chorus, fragment)	**I/713**
D706	H460	*Der 23. Psalm* (Bible/Mendelssohn)	**II/593**
D707	H458	*Der zürnenden Diana* (Mayrhofer)	**III/747**
D708	H457, H460+	*Im Walde (Waldesnacht)* ('Windes Rasuchen, Gottes Flügel') (F. von Schlegel)	**I/941**

March 1821(?)   In D₁ the assigned date is 1821(?)

D710	H470	*Im Gegenwärtigen Vergangenes* (Goethe) (tenor solo and male quartet)	**I/933**

1818(?, first version)   In D₁ the assigned date is 1821(?)

D711	H406	*Lob der Tränen* (*Thränen* in D₁) (A. von Schlegel)	**II/253**

January 1821

D712	H462	*Die gefangenen Sänger* (A. von Schlegel). An unknown earlier setting of this poem is positioned as D369(a) in D₁	**I/650**
D713	H464	*Die Unglückliche* (Pichler) (*Die Nacht*, earlier version without Deutsch number, recorded H463)	**III/438**

February 1821

D715	H465	*Versunken* (Goethe)	**III/483**

March 1821

D716	H466	*Grenzen der Menschheit* (Goethe)	**I/788**

March(?) 1821

D717	H469	*Suleika II* ('Ach, um deine feuchten Schwingen') (Willemer/Goethe)	**III/287**

March 1821

D719	H467	*Geheimes* (Goethe)	**I/654**
D720	H468	*Suleika I* ('Was bedeutet die Bewegung?') (Willemer/Goethe)	**III/283**
D721	H471	*Mahomets Gesang* (Goethe) (second setting, fragment)	**II/300**

April 1821

D724	H474	*Die Nachtigall* (Unger) (male quartet with piano)	**II/433**
D725		*Linde Weste wehen* (Anonymous) (duet, fragment)	**II/252**
D726	H472	*Mignon I* ('Heiss mich nicht reden') (Goethe) (first setting)	**II/350**
D727	H473	*Mignon II* ('So lasst mich scheinen') (Goethe) (second setting)	**II/352**
D728	H475	*Johanna Sebus* (Goethe) (fragment)	**II/13**

September 1821

| **D731** | H476 | *Der Blumen Schmerz* (Mailáth) | **I/314** |

20 September 1821 to 27 February 1822

D732		*Alfonso und Estrella* (Schober) (opera – two arias arranged with piano accompaniment)	
		No. 8 *Doch im Getümmel der Schlacht*	**I/76**
		No. 13 *Wenn ich dich Holde sehe*	**I/78**

1822(?)

| **D736** | H478 | *Ihr Grab* (Engelhardt) | **I/921** |

1822 or 1823(?)   In D₁ the assigned date is 1822(?)

| **D737** | H506 | *An die Leier* (Bruchmann after Anacreon) | **I/172** |
| **D738** | H505 | *Im Haine* (Bruchmann) | **I/937** |

April 1822   In D₁ the assigned date is simply 1822

| **D740** | H483 | *Frühlingsgesang* (Schober) (male quartet with piano) | **I/620** |

Between the end of 1821 and autumn 1822   In D₁ the assigned date is 1822

| **D741** | H495 | *Sei mir gegrüsst* (Rückert) | **III/115** |

Appeared as a supplement on 30 July 1822

| **D742** | H479 | *Der Wachtelschlag* (Sauter) | **III/531** |

Autumn 1822(?)   In D₁ the assigned date is simply 1822

| **D743** | H491 | *Selige Welt* (Senn) | **III/126** |
| **D744** | H490 | *Schwanengesang* (Senn) | **III/1** |

1822

| **D745** | H477 | *Die Rose* (F. von Schlegel) | **II/677** |

1822 or 1823(?)

| **D746** | D504 | *Am See* ('In des Sees Wogenspiele') (Bruchmann) | **I/117** |

January 1822

| **D747** | H481 | *Geist der Liebe* (Matthisson) (second setting, male quartet) | **I/667** |
| **D749** | H482 | *Herrn Josef Spaun, Assessor in Linz* (M. von Collin) | **I/876** |

April 1822

| **D751** | H487 | *Die Liebe hat gelogen* (Platen) | **II/182** |
| **D752** | H484 | *Nachtviolen* (Mayrhofer) | **II/439** |

D753	H485	*Heliopolis I* ('Im kalten rauhen Norden')	**I/855**
		(*Heliopolis* in D₁) (Mayrhofer)	
D754	H486	*Heliopolis II* ('Fels auf Felsen hingewälzet')	**I/857**
		(*Im Hochgebirge* in D₁) (Mayrhofer)	

July 1822

| D756 | H488 | *Du liebst mich nicht* (Platen) | **I/451** |

August 1822

| D757 | H489 | *Gott in der Natur* (Kleist) (SATB quartet) | **I/759** |

September 1822

| D758 | H496 | *Todesmusik* (Schober) | **III/348** |

November 1822

| D761 | H497 | *Schatzgräbers Begehr* (Schober) | **II/731** |
| D762 | H498 | *Schwestergruss* (Bruchmann) | **III/81** |

22 November 1822

| D763 | H499 | *Des Tages Weihe* (*Geburtstagshymne* in D₁) | **II/734** |
| | | (Anonymous) (SATB quartet with piano) | |

Beginning of December 1822

D764	H501	*Der Musensohn* (Goethe)	**II/398**
D765	H500	*An die Entfernte* (Goethe)	**I/160**
D766	H502	*Am Flusse* (Goethe) (second setting)	**I/109**
D767	H503, 503a	*Willkommen und Abschied* (Goethe)	**III/604**

Before July 1824   In D₁ the assigned date is *c*. 1823

| D768 | H551 | *Wandrers Nachtlied* ('Über allen Gipfeln ist Ruh') | **III/554** |
| | | (Goethe) | |

Beginning of 1823

| D770 | H510 | *Drang in die Ferne* (Leitner) | **I/431** |

1822(?)   In D₁ the assigned date is 1823(?)

| D771 | H507 | *Der Zwerg* (Collin) | **III/770** |

1822 or 1823(?)   In D₁ the assigned date is 1823(?)

| D772 | H509 | *Wehmut* ('Wenn ich durch Wald und Fluren geh') | **III/559** |
| | | (M. von Collin) | |

1823

| D774 | H519 | *Auf dem Wasser zu singen* (Stolberg) | **I/239** |

1823(?)

| D775 | H520 | *Dass sie hier gewesen* (Rückert) | **I/401** |

1823

| D776 | H523 | *Du bist die Ruh* (Rückert) | **I/447** |

1823(?)

| D777 | H521 | *Lachen und Weinen* (Rückert) | **II/109** |

Before June 1823   In D₁ the assigned date is simply 1823

| D778 | H522 | *Greisengesang* (Ruckert) | **I/873** |

1823(?)	This song does not appear in D₁		
D778A	H524	*Die Wallfahrt* (Rückert)	**III/537**
February 1823			
D785	H511	*Der zürnende Barde* (Bruchmann)	**III/744**
March 1823			
D786	H513	*Viola* (Schober)	**III/510**
Completed April 1823			
D787	H509+	*Die Verschworenen* (Singspiel)	**III/481**
		No. 2 *Romanze* ('Ich schleiche bang und still herum')	
April 1823			
D788	H514	*Lied (Die Mutter Erde)* ('Des Lebens Tag ist schwer und schwül') (Stolberg)	**II/203**
D789	H515	*Pilgerweise* (Schober)	**II/547**
May 1823			
D792	H516	*Vergissmeinnicht* (Schober)	**III/473**
D793	H517	*Das Geheimnis* (Schiller) (second setting)	**I/659**
D794	H518	*Der Pilgrim* (Schiller)	**II/552**

October–November 1823   In D₁ the assigned date is May to November 1823

D795	H526–H545	*Die schöne Müllerin* (Müller) (song cycle)	**II/799**
		(i) *Das Wandern*	**II/807**
		(ii) *Wohin?*	**II/811**
		(iii) *Halt!*	**II/815**
		(iv) *Danksagung an den Bach*	**II/818**
		(v) *Am Feierabend*	**II/821**
		(vi) *Der Neugierige*	**II/824**
		(vii) *Ungeduld*	**II/829**
		(viii) *Morgengruss*	**II/833**
		(ix) *Des Müllers Blumen*	**II/836**
		(x) *Tränenregen*	**II/839**
		(xi) *Mein!*	**II/844**
		(xii) *Pause*	**II/847**
		(xiii) *Mit dem grünen Lautenbande*	**II/851**
		(xiv) *Der Jäger*	**II/854**
		(xv) *Eifersucht und Stolz*	**II/856**
		(xvi) *Die liebe Farbe*	**II/861**
		(xvii) *Die böse Farbe*	**II/864**
		(xviii) *Trockne Blumen*	**II/869**
		(xix) *Der Müller und der Bach*	**II/872**
		(xx) *Des Baches Wiegenlied*	**II/877**

Autumn 1823			
D797	H525	*Rosamunde, Fürstin von Zypern* (Chézy) (play with music, four items arranged with piano accompaniment)	
		No. 3b *Romanze* ('Der Vollmond strahlt') (*Romanze* in D₁)	**II/672**

No. 4 *Geisterchor* (*Chorus of Spirits* in D₁)		**II/673**
No. 7 *Hirtenchor* (chorus) (*Chorus of Shepherds* in D₁)		**II/674**
No. 8 *Jägerchor* (chorus) (*Chorus of Huntsmen* in D₁)		**II/676**

1824 or February 1825   In D₁ the assigned date is 1824(?)
D799   H554   *Im Abendrot* (Lappe)   **I/923**

Beginning of 1825   In D₁ the assigned date is 1824(?)
D800   H555   *Der Einsame* (Lappe)   **I/475**

Appeared in print on 10 June 1826   In D₁ the assigned date is 1824
D801   H602   *Dithyrambe* (Schiller) (second setting)   **I/418**

Beginning of March 1824
D805   H547   *Der Sieg* (Mayrhofer)   **III/175**
D806   H546   *Abendstern* (Mayrhofer)   **I/37**

March 1824
D807   H548   *Auflösung* (Mayrhofer)   **I/260**

Beginning of March 1824
D808   H549   *Gondelfahrer* (Mayrhofer) (first setting, male quartet)   **I/748**

March 1824
D809   H550   *Gondelfahrer* (*Der Gondelfahrer* in D₁) (Mayrhofer) (second setting, male quartet with piano)   **I/750**

September 1824
D815   H552   *Gebet* (de la Motte Fouqué) (SATB quartet with piano)   **I/641**

31 December 1824
D822   H553   *Lied eines Kriegers* (Anonymous) (solo bass with men's chorus and piano)   **II/226**

Beginning of 1828   In D₁ the assigned date is 1825(?)
D826   H659   *Der Tanz* (Meerau?) (SATB quartet)   **III/302**

Before June 1823   In D₁ the assigned date is 1825(?)
D827   H508   *Nacht und Träume* (Collin)   **II/419**

Beginning of 1825
D828   H556   *Die junge Nonne* (Craigher)   **II/32**

For a performance on 17 February 1826   In D₁ the assigned date is 1825–6
D829   H589   *Leb wohl, du schöne Erde* (*Abschied von der Erde* in D₁) (Pratobevera)   **II/121**

Beginning of 1825(?)
D830   H557   *Lied der Anne Lyle* (Scott, Macdonald/Craigher?; trans. attrib. to Sophie May in D₁)   **II/215**
D831   H558   *Gesang der Norna* (Scott)   **I/715**

February 1825
D832   H559   *Des Sängers Habe* (Schlechta)   **II/705**

April 1825
D833   H562   *Der blinde Knabe* (Cibber/Craigher)   **I/308**

March 1825 (first version)
D834   H561   *Im Walde* ('Ich wandre über Berg und Tal')   **I/946**
                          (Schulze)

1825   In D_1 the assigned date is spring or summer 1825
D835   H566   *Bootgesang* (Scott/Storck) (male quartet with   **III/158**
                          piano)

D836   H567   *Coronach* (Scott/Storck) (female trio with piano)   **III/160**

Between April and July 1825   In D_1 the assigned date is spring or summer 1825
D837   H564   *Ellens Gesang I* ('Raste Krieger') (Scott/Storck)   **III/151**
D838   H565   *Ellens Gesang II* ('Jäger, ruhe von der Jagd')   **III/156**
                          (Scott/Storck)

April 1825
D839   H569   *Ellens Gesang III* ('Ave Maria! Jungfrau mild')   **III/166**
                          (Scott/Storck)

D842   H563   *Totengräbers Heimwehe* (Craigher)   **III/368**
D843   H570   *Lied des gefangenen Jägers* (Scott/Storck)   **III/170**

April 1825   In D_1 the assigned date is summer 1825
D846   H568   *Normans Gesang* (Scott/Storck)   **III/162**

August 1825
D851   H571   *Das Heimweh* ('Ach, der Gebirgssohn') (Pyrker)   **I/843**
D852   H572   *Die Allmacht* (Pyrker)   **I/84**

March or August 1825 (first version)   In D_1 the assigned date is August 1825
D853   H560   *Auf der Bruck* (Schulze)   **I/247**

August 1825
D854   H573   *Fülle der Liebe* (F. von Schlegel)   **I/630**

September 1825
D855   H574   *Wiedersehn* (A. von Schlegel)   **III/588**
D856   H575   *Abendlied für die Entfernte* (A. von Schlegel)   **I/20**
                          In D_1 the order of the following two *Lacrimas*
                          songs is reversed.
D857   H576, H577   *Zwei Szenen aus dem Schauspiel Lacrimas*
                          (Schütz)
                          (i)   *Lied der Delphine*   **III/766**
                          (ii) *Lied des Florio*   **III/768**

December 1825
D860   H578   *An mein Herz* (Schulze)   **I/198**
D861   H579   *Der liebliche Stern* (Schulze)   **II/199**
D862   H580   *Um Mitternacht* (Schulze)   **III/430**

1826(?)

| **D865** | H590 | *Widerspruch* (Seidl) (chorus with piano and solo song) | **III/583** |

Summer 1828(?)   In D₁ the assigned date is 1826(?)

D866	H664–H667	*Vier Refrain-Lieder* (Seidl)	**III/495**
		(i) *Die Unterscheidung*	**III/497**
		(ii) *Bei dir allein!*	**III/498**
		(iii) *Die Männer sind mechant!*	**III/501**
		(iv) *Irdisches Glück*	**III/503**

1826(?)

| **D867** | H591 | *Wiegenlied* (Seidl) | **III/595** |

1826

D869	H592	*Totengräber-Weise* (Schlechta)	**III/373**
D870	H594	*Der Wanderer an den Mond* (Seidl)	**III/547**
D871	H593	*Das Zügenglöcklein* (Seidl)	**III/741**

January 1826(?)

| **D874** | H581 | *O Quell, was strömst du rasch und wild* (Seidl) (fragment) | **II/465** |

January 1826

D875	H583	*Mondenschein* (Schober) (male quintet with piano)	**II/374**
D875A	H584	*Die Allmacht* (Pyrker) (second setting, fragment, chorus with piano)	**I/87**
D876	H582	*Im Jänner 1817 (Tiefes Leid)* (*Ich bin von aller Ruh geschieden* in D₁) (Seidl)	**I/938**
D877	H585–H588	*Gesänge aus 'Wilhelm Meister'* (Goethe)	**I/688**
		(i) *Mignon und der Harfner* ('Nur wer die Sehnsucht kennt') (duet, fifth setting)	**I/688**
		(ii) *Lied der Mignon* ('Heiss mich nicht reden') (second setting)	**I/690**
		(iii) *Lied der Mignon* ('So lasst mich scheinen') (fourth setting)	**I/693**
		(iv) *Lied der Mignon* ('Nur wer die Sehnsucht kennt') (solo song, sixth setting)	**I/696**

March 1826

D878	H596	*Am Fenster* (Seidl)	**I/104**
D879	H597	*Sehnsucht* ('Die Scheibe friert, der Wind ist rauh') (Seidl)	**III/110**
D880	H595	*Im Freien* (Seidl)	**I/926**
D881	H598	*Fischerweise* (Schlechta)	**I/565**
D882	H599	*Im Frühling* (Schulze)	**I/930**
D883	H600	*Lebensmut* ('O wie dringt das junge Leben') (Seidl)	**II/130**
D884	H601	*Über Wildemann* (Schulze)	**III/425**

July 1826   In D₁ the assigned date is beginning of July 1826

D888	H603	*Trinklied* ('Bacchus, feister Fürst des Weins') (Shakespeare/Mayerhofer von Grünbühel)	**III/408**
D889	H604	*Ständchen* ('Horch, horch! die Lerch im Ätherblau') (Shakespeare/A. von Schlegel)	**III/241**
D890	H606	*Hippolits Lied* (Gerstenbergk)	**I/881**
D891	H605	*Gesang* ('Was ist Sylvia, saget an') (Shakespeare/ Bauernfeld)	**I/707**

September 1826

D892	H607	*Nachthelle* (Seidl) (solo with male chorus and piano)	**II/427**
D893	H607+	*Grab und Mond* (Seidl) (male quartet, unaccompanied)	**I/776**

Between autumn 1827 and the beginning of 1828

D896	H649	*Fröhliches Scheiden* (Leitner) (fragment)	**I/611**
		(In D₁ the following two songs do not appear)	
D896A	H650	*Sie in jedem Liede* (Leitner) (fragment)	**III/146**
D896B	H648	*Wolke und Quelle* (Leitner) (fragment)	**III/734**

1827 (before September)

D902	H630–H632	*Drei Gesänge für Bass-Stimme mit Klavier* (Metastasio [i & ii] and Anonymous [iii])	**I/435**
		(i) *L'incanto degli occhi* (second setting)	**I/437**
		(ii) *Il traditor deluso*	**I/439**
		(iii) *Il modo di prender moglie*	**I/441**

January 1827

D903	H608	*Zur guten Nacht* (Rochlitz) (solo with chorus and piano)	**III/760**
D904	H609	*Alinde* (Rochlitz)	**I/79**
D905	H610	*An die Laute* (Rochlitz)	**I/171**
D906	H611	*Der Vater mit dem Kind* (Bauernfeld)	**III/458**

March 1826(?)   In D₁ the assigned date is beginning of January 1827

D907	H627	*Romanze des Richard Löwenherz* (Scott/M. Müller)	**II/665**

February 1827

D909	H625	*Jägers Liebeslied* (Schober)	**II/7**
D910	H626	*Schiffers Scheidelied* (Schober)	**II/742**

Begun February 1827 (Part One); begun October 1827 (Part Two)

D911	H613–H624 (Part One) H635–H646 (Part Two)		
		Winterreise (Müller) (song cycle)	**III/620**
		(i) *Gute Nacht*	**III/630**
		(ii) *Die Wetterfahne*	**III/635**
		(iii) *Gefrorne Tränen*	**III/639**
		(iv) *Erstarrung*	**III/642**
		(v) *Der Lindenbaum*	**III/646**
		(vi) *Wasserflut*	**III/652**

	(vii)	*Auf dem Flusse*	**III/655**
	(viii)	*Rückblick*	**III/659**
	(ix)	*Irrlicht*	**III/662**
	(x)	*Rast*	**III/667**
	(xi)	*Frühlingstraum*	**III/671**
	(xii)	*Einsamkeit*	**III/675**
	(xiii)	*Die Post*	**III/679**
	(xiv)	*Der greise Kopf*	**III/683**
	(xv)	*Die Krähe*	**III/687**
	(xvi)	*Letzte Hoffnung*	**III/691**
	(xvii)	*Im Dorfe*	**III/695**
	(xviii)	*Der stürmische Morgen*	**III/699**
	(xix)	*Täuschung*	**III/703**
	(xx)	*Der Wegweiser*	**III/706**
	(xxi)	*Das Wirtshaus*	**III/711**
	(xxii)	*Mut*	**III/716**
	(xxiii)	*Die Nebensonnen*	**III/720**
	(xxiv)	*Der Leiermann*	**III/725**

June 1827
D917	H628	*Das Lied im Grünen* (Reil)	**II/230**

Spring 1827   In D₁ the assigned date is summer 1817
D919	H612	*Frühlingslied* (Pollak)	**I/627**

July 1827   In D₁ the second version is allocated the number D921
D920	H629	*Ständchen* ('Zögernd, leise') (Grillparzer) (alto with male chorus with piano, and female chorus with piano)	**III/244**

September 1827
D922	H633	*Heimliches Lieben* (Klenke)	**I/837**
D923	H634	*Eine altschottische Ballade* (ballad from Percy's *Reliques*, trans. Herder)	**I/470**

Between autumn 1827 and the beginning of 1828   In D₁ the assigned date is October 1827(?)
D926	H651	*Das Weinen* (Leitner)	**III/563**
D927	H652	*Vor meiner Wiege* (Leitner)	**III/525**

November 1827
D930	H647	*Der Hochzeitsbraten* (Schober) (comic trio with piano)	**I/892**
D931	H654	*Der Wallensteiner Lanzknecht beim Trunk* (Leitner)	**III/534**
D932	H655	*Der Kreuzzug* (Leitner)	**II/98**
D933	H653	*Des Fischers Liebesglück* (Leitner)	**I/562**

26 December 1827
D936	H656	*Al par del ruscelletto* (In D₁ *Kantate zur Feier des Fräulein Irene von Kiesewetter*) (Anonymous) (male and female chorus with piano)	**I/74**

Summer 1828(?)   In D₁ the assigned date is simply 1828
D937   H663   *Lebensmut* ('Fröhlicher Lebensmut') (Rellstab)   **II/133**
                          (fragment)

January 1828
D938   H657   *Der Winterabend* (Leitner)   **III/613**
D939   H658   *Die Sterne* (Leitner)   **III/256**

March 1828
D942   H661   *Mirjams Siegesgesang* (Grillparzer) (solo soprano   **II/262**
                          with SATB chorus and piano)
D943   H660   *Auf dem Strom* (Rellstab) solo voice with horn   **I/233**
                          and piano

April 1828
D945   H662   *Herbst* (Rellstab)   **I/860**

July 1828
D953   H668+   *Der 92. Psalm* (Bible) (unaccompanied baritone   **II/596**
                          solo with SATB chorus)

For 2 September 1828
D954   *Glaube, Hoffnung und Liebe* ('Gott, lass die   **I/725**
                          Glocke glücklich steigen') (Reil) (male quartet,
                          SATB chorus with piano, later orchestral,
                          accompaniment)

August 1828
D955   H669   *Glaube, Hoffnung und Liebe* (Glaube, hoffe,   **I/727**
                          liebe!) (Kuffner)

Begun in August 1828   In D₁ the date is finished in August (October) 1828
D957   H670–H676 (Rellstab Lieder); H677–H682 (Heine Lieder)
                          Schwanengesang (Rellstab – i to vii; Heine – viii   **III/3**
                          to xiii) (posthumously published song cycle)
                          (i)   *Liebesbotschaft*   **III/6**
                          (ii)   *Kriegers Ahnung*   **III/12**
                          (iii) *Frühlingssehnsucht*   **III/16**
                          (iv)   *Ständchen* ('Leise flehen meine Lieder')   **III/20**
                          (v)   *Aufenthalt*   **III/24**
                          (vi)   *In der Ferne*   **III/28**
                          (vii) *Abschied* ('Ade! du muntre, du fröhliche   **III/33**
                          Stadt')
                          (viii) *Der Atlas*   **III/39**
                          (ix)   *Ihr Bild*   **III/43**
                          (x)   *Das Fischermädchen*   **III/47**
                          (xi)   *Die Stadt*   **III/50**
                          (xii) *Am Meer*   **III/54**
                          (xiii) *Der Doppelgänger*   **III/59**

October 1828

D965	H683	*Der Hirt auf dem Felsen* (Müller and Varnhagen von Ense) (soprano with clarinet and piano) (Müller und Helmina von Chézy in D$_1$; Müller und Helmina von Chézy(?) in D$_2$)	**I/886**
D965A	H684	*Die Taubenpost* (Seidl). In D$_1$ *Die Taubenpost* was D957/14	**III/65**

Unknown dates at the end of the catalogue

D985	H278	*Gott im Ungewitter* (Uz) (SATB with piano)	**I/755**
D986	H279	*Gott der Weltschöpfer* (Uz) (SATB with piano)	**I/752**
D990		*Der Graf von Habsburg* (Schiller) D990A, D990C and D990E do not appear in D$_1$	**I/778**
D990A		*Kaiser Maximillian auf der Martinswand* (Collin)	**II/36**
D990C	H668	*Das Echo* (Castelli). In D$_1$ *Das Echo* was assigned the number D868	**I/462**
D990E	H18	*L'incanto degli occhi* (Metastasio) (fragment)	**II/251**

Anhang: Schubert's arrangements of other composers' works:

DII, 3	H243+, ++	*Echo und Narcisse* (opera by Christophe Willibald Gluck)	
		(i) *Rien de la nature*	**I/466**
		(ii) *O combats, o désordres extrème*	**I/466**
DII, 4		*Der 8. Psalm* (setting by Maximillian Stadler arranged and revised by Schubert) (Bible/ Mendelssohn)	**II/589**

Liechtenthal parish church where Schubert's parents were married and where the composer received musical tuition as a boy from Michael Holzer. His Mass in F D105 was first performed here in October 1814.

Panorama of Vienna by Jakob Alt (1830).

A SCHUBERT SONG CALENDAR

The house of Schubert's birth, the schoolhouse at Nussdorferstrasse, 54 in the ninth *Bezirk*.

1797

31 January: Franz Peter Schubert was born in Vienna. His parents, Franz Theodor Schubert, a schoolmaster, and Elisabeth, née Vietz, had both been born in Silesia and moved to Vienna at different times to better their circumstances. They had married on 17 January 1785 in the Liechtenthal parish church and a year later Franz Theodor had become director of the boys' school in the same district. Among Schubert's surviving siblings, Ignaz, the composer's eldest brother and first piano teacher, was twelve in 1797; Ferdinand Schubert, who was to be Franz's favourite brother, was three. In 1912 the cramped house in Vienna's ninth district in which the composer was born (Nussdorferstrasse 54) became a museum, although none of Schubert's music was actually written there.

The house in which Schubert grew up and composed his early songs, Säulengasse, 3 – around the corner from the Nussdorferstrasse.

The Imperial Stadtkonvikt where Schubert went to school in 1808 on a choral scholarship.

1801–3 (aged four to seven)
In 1801 the family moved from the schoolhouse in the Nussdorferstrasse to roomier quarters in the nearby Säulengasse (No. 3); the forecourt is given over to an car-servicing firm ('Schubertgarage') in present-day Vienna. This is the home in which the teenage Schubert composed his first songs, including *Gretchen am Spinnrade* D118 and *Erlkönig* D328. In 1802 he began to play the piano, but the little boy, while deeply musical, was clearly no Mozartian prodigy in performing terms. He was to remain a fluently expressive, rather than a virtuoso, pianist.

1805–7 (aged eight to ten)
Violin studies (from his father) were added to the curriculum. Schubert began to sing in the Liechtental parish church within short walking distance of his home. The choirmaster there, Michael Holzer, instructed the boy in organ, singing and counterpoint and professed himself astonished by his student's gifts. It is possible that Schubert at this time was already composing music that is now lost to us. His father and two brothers joined him in performing string quartets in the home – Franz played the viola.

1808–9 (aged eleven to twelve)
Against stiff competition Schubert won a choral scholarship to the Imperial Konvikt where the audition panel was chaired by the famous composer Antonio Salieri, the senior musician in the emperor's hierarchy. The boy received his education in exchange for singing at the Hofburg – he was in effect a member of the Vienna Boys' Choir. His first term began on 30 September 1808. There was a great deal of music-making at the Konvikt, including an orchestra in which Schubert played the violin. This redeemed the otherwise rather hard and cheerless life of the boarding school; it also provided the boy with a strong background in both theoretical and practical music-making.

1810 (aged thirteen) – *2 solo songs* (October)
Schubert made many friends at the Konvikt, including the generous and protective Josef von Spaun, nine years older, who was principal violinist in the orchestra, but who soon noticed that the young Schubert, standing behind him, played far more rhythmically. When Wenzel Ruzicka, who was in charge of the orchestra, was absent, the young composer progressed to beating time for his fellow students. He also took composition lessons from Ruzicka. Spaun was one of several young men at the Konvikt who had received their earlier education at the boarding school in Kremsmünster, Upper Austria, near Linz. Spaun and his Linz contemporaries played a major part in the circle of supportive friendship that would later surround Schubert. The earliest surviving songs (two incomplete settings of the same extended text by Gabriele von Baumberg) probably date from this year. Schubert's lifelong habit of depending on the artistic and spiritual nourishment of a group of sympathetic friends was established at this time, as well as the practice of borrowing books from those who had access to the kind of private libraries that were not to be found in poorer homes. These, school anthologies of poetry and copies of earlier musical settings by older composers, were the young Schubert's earliest sources for his vocal settings.

See: FRIENDS AND FAMILY: Franz Schubert senior, Elisabeth Vietz, Ignaz
            Schubert, Ferdinand Schubert, Josef von Spaun
            Gabriele von BAUMBERG

HYPERION DISC 1

H1	*Lebenstraum (Gesang in c)* (Baumberg) first setting D1A fragment, 1810[1]	**II/135**
H2	*Lebenstraum* (Baumberg) second setting D39, 1810	**II/142**

1811 (aged fourteen) – *4 solo songs* (March, September, December)
Schubert's literary explorations broadened somewhat to include the larger than life, but
outmoded, writings of Schücking and Pfeffel. In setting the ballads and poems of Friedrich von
Schiller he discovered his first great poet. Several of the texts set in this period mirrored a teenager's typical conflict with a loving but irascible father. The hard-working and religious milieu
into which the composer was born was a strong contrast to the more liberal and well-to-do
background enjoyed by many of the affluent students educated at the same school, boys who
became the composer's close friends. Here was a source of family conflict (Schubert, the scholarship boy, outgrowing his more modestly educated parents and siblings) that was never to be
satisfactorily resolved.

See: Gottlieb Conrad PFEFFEL, Friedrich von SCHILLER
            Clemens SCHÜCKING

DISC 1 continued

H3	*Hagars Klage* (Schücking) D5, 30 March 1811	**I/820**
H4	*Leichenfantasie* (Schiller) D7, c. 1811	**II/146**
H5	*Der Vatermörder* (Pfeffel) D10, 26 December 1811	**III/462**
H6	*Des Mädchens Klage* (Schiller) first setting D6, 1811 or 1812 [*see* second setting H92 and third setting H229]	**II/289**

Some other works of 1810–11: Fantasie in G for piano duet (D1, May 1810); Ouverture in D and
Symphony in D (both unfinished, D2A and 2B, 1811); Six Minuets for Winds (D2D); Ouverture
in C minor for string quintet; *Der Spiegelritter* (Kotzebue) (D11), a *Singspiel* in 3 acts begun at
the end of 1811.

1812 (aged fifteen) – *7 solo songs* (March, September, October)
The first real tragedy in the composer's life was the death of his mother at the age of fifty-six on
28 May 1812. A short time afterwards (18 June) he began composition lessons with Antonio
Salieri, a privilege that was granted only to the most promising of the Konvikt's pupils. On 26
July he marked a choral score with the words 'Schubert, Franz crowed for the last time' – his
voice had broken. Salieri was a benevolent taskmaster; according to Spaun he first taught Schubert twice a week, and later 'almost daily'. The Italian was scrupulous in giving Schubert many
counterpoint exercises, but his teaching had an unashamed vocal bias, and he favoured Metastasio texts for exercises in *bel canto* style. Schubert set these texts for every possible vocal
combination at the same time as pursuing a healthy interest in the literature of his own language

---

[1]*Lebenstraum*: It is possible that one or both settings of this poem (D1A and D39) were composed before 1810.

– Matthisson, Hölty and Rochlitz. This mixture was a compromise that perhaps only a musical education in Vienna at the hands of an Italian teacher could have provided. Far away from the rigours of the North German lieder school, southern sensuality was allowed to coalesce unselfconsciously with Germanic depth and seriousness. In November, in his first surviving letter, Schubert complained to his brother Ignaz about the lack of sufficient food at the Konvikt, and begged for an allowance of a few Kreuzer a month.

See: Ludwig HÖLTY
           Friedrich von MATTHISSON
           Pietro METASTASIO
           Johann Friedrich ROCHLITZ

DISC 2

H7	*Der Geistertanz* (Matthisson) first setting D15 fragment, *c.* 1812	**I/672**
H8	*Der Geistertanz* (Matthisson) second setting D15A fragment, *c.* 1812	**I/672**
	[*see* third setting H47, fourth (unaccompanied) setting H311+]	
H9	*Quell' innocente figlio (Aria dell' angelo)* (Metastasio) D17/1	**II/622**
	composition exercise, solo, *c.* 1812	
H9a	*Quell' innocente figlio (Aria dell' angelo)* (Metastasio) D17/2	**II/622**
	composition exercise, duet, *c.* 1812	
H10	*Viel tausend Sterne prangen* (Eberhard) D642 quartet, *c.* 1812	**III/488**
H11	*Klaglied* (Rochlitz) D23, 1812	**II/63**
H12	*Der Jüngling am Bache* (Schiller) first setting D30, 24 September 1812	**II/16**
	[*see* Second setting H93, third setting H424]	
H13	*Entra l'uomo allor che nasce (Aria di Abramo)* (Metastasio) D33/1	**I/499**
	composition exercise, solo, September–October 1812	
H13a	*Entra l'uomo allor che nasce (Aria di Abramo)* (Metastasio) D33/2	**I/499**
	composition exercise, duet, September–October 1812	
H14	*Serbate, o Dei custodi* (Metastasio) D35/3 composition exercise, 10	**III/135**
	December 1812	
H15	*Die Advokaten* (Engelhardt) D37 comic trio after Anton Fischer, 25–7	**I/70**
	December 1812	

1813 (aged sixteen) – *12 solo songs* (January, April, May, August, September, October)
It was probably at the beginning of this year that Schubert visited the opera for the first time, at the invitation of Josef von Spaun, to see Gluck's *Iphigenie auf Tauris*. The principal singers were Johann Michael Vogl and Anna Milder-Hauptmann, both of whom were to play an important part in Schubert's life. The music of Gluck (Schubert's grand-teacher via Salieri) was a huge influence on the young composer. At the same time he met the already famous young poet Theodor Körner who was living in Vienna at the time and who was soon to die a hero in one of the last battles against the French. Schubert confessed to Körner his hopes for becoming a composer and received encouragement from the poet to follow his dream. The composer's father married Anna Kleyenböck who proved a sympathetic step-mother. It was clear that a youthful period of study at the Konvikt had now come to an end and in the autumn Schubert renounced a scholarship that would have paid for extended musical studies. Instead he took a teacher-training course and became an assistant schoolmaster working for the family 'firm' – an outcome that was at odds with his dreams of being an independent artist. The string quartets of this

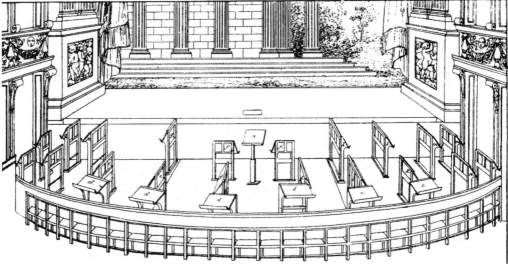

The Kärntnerthor Theatre in Vienna (near the site of the present Hotel Sacher) and its orchestral pit (anonymous drawing from 1821).

period were written for home performance. There is also some evidence of music-making with schoolfriends: *Die Advokaten* from the end of 1812 had been a reworking of a humorous trio by Anton Fischer, a local composer. At this stage of his career Schubert followed models by his elders as assiduously as a trainee painter made copies of the old masters.

See: COMPOSERS: Christoph Willibald von Gluck, Anton Fischer
         FRIENDS AND FAMILY: Anna Kleyenböck
         SINGERS: Johann Michael Vogl, Anna Milder-Hauptmann
         Theodor KÖRNER

DISC 2 continued

H16	*Ombre amene, amiche piante (La Serenata)* (Metastasio) D990F, composition exercise 1813(?)[2]	**II/467**
H17	*Misero pargoletto* (Metastasio) first setting D42 (first setting, second version) composition exercise, 1813(?) [*see* second setting H19]	**II/370**
H18	*L'incanto degli occhi* (Metastasio) first setting D990E composition exercise, 1813(?) [*see* second setting H630][3]	**II/251**
H19	*Misero pargoletto* (Metastasio) second setting D42 composition exercise, 1813(?) [*see* first setting H17]	**II/371**
H20	*Totengräberlied* (Hölty) D44, 19 January 1813	**III/364**
H21	*Dithyrambe* (Schiller) first setting D47 fragment, tenor, bass, chorus and piano, 29 March 1813 [*see* second setting H602]	**I/416**
H22	*Die Schatten* (Matthisson) D50, 12 April 1813	**II/726**
H23	*Sehnsucht* (Schiller) first setting D52, 15–17 April 1813 [*see* second setting H461]	**III/94**
H24	*Verklärung* (Pope/Herder) D59, 4 May 1813	**III/478**
H24+	*Ein jugendlicher Maienschwung* (Schiller) D61 unaccompanied trio, 8 May 1813	**I/470**
H25	*Thekla (eine Geisterstimme)* (Schiller) first setting D73, 22–3 August 1813 [*see* second setting H393]	**III/327**
H26	*Trinklied (Freunde, sammelt euch im Kreise)* (Schäffer) D75 quartet, 29 August 1813	**III/40**
H27	*Pensa, che questo istante* (Mestastio) D76, 13 September 1813	**II/513**
H28	*Son fra l'onde* (Metastasio) D78, 18 September 1813	**III/218**
	[*Zur Namensfeier meines Vaters* (Schubert) D80 trio (TTB) accompanied by guitar, 27 September, 1813]	**III/763**
	[*Auf den Sieg der Deutschen* (Anonymous) D81 song accompanied by two violins and cello, October 1813]	**I/241**
	[*Zur Namensfeier des Herrn Andreas Siller* (Anonymous) D83 song with violin and harp accompaniment, before 4 November 1813]	**III/762**
H28+	*Verschwunden sind die Schmerzen* (Anonymous) D88 unaccompanied trio, 15 November 1813	**III/482**

Some other works of 1812–13: Ouverture in D (D26); *Salve Regina* in F (D27); Piano Trio in B flat (D28); String Quartet in C (D32); String Quartet in B flat (D36); String Quartet in C (D46); String Quartet in B flat (D68); Octet in F for winds (D72); String Quartet in D (D74); Symphony no. 1 in D (D82).

---

[2]*Ombre amene*: Walther Dürr places this aria three years later in 1816(?), thus Dürr198.
[3]*L'incanto degli occhi*: Walther Dürr places this aria three years later in 1816(?), thus Dürr197. This possible chronology was communicated to me some years ago and may not represent Dr Dürr's most recent thinking.

1814 (aged seventeen) – *24 solo songs* (April, May, July, September, October, November, December)

In the autumn of 1813 Schubert had entered the Normal-Hauptschule, a college for trainee teachers; in August 1814 he passed the preliminary examination that qualified him to work in his father's school. Meanwhile events in the outside world were moving fast. The surrender of Napoleon in Paris to the allies at the end of March was marked by a Schubert song – D104 [H38]. The subsequent Congress of Vienna was also a focus of world attention. In May Schubert attended the first performance of the final version of Beethoven's *Fidelio* Op. 72; in September the performance of another work that was enormously influential on Schubert – the Seventh Symphony Op. 92 – reinforced a pecking order in Viennese musical life where Beethoven was cast as a god. The very existence of this overwhelming genius throughout Schubert's life, with the exception of his final year, would remind the younger composer of his shortcomings – a perception that sometimes limited his ability to rejoice in his own achievements. At this time Schubert had no option but to live at home, but his imagination ranged far and wide. His musical activities reached a peak in the autumn: on 16 October his Mass in F (D105) was performed in the Liechtental church, the soprano solo sung by Therese Grob (1798–1875), the girl who was later said to be the focus of his futile romantic longings. A few days later, on 19 October, in the middle of a public holiday celebrating the first anniversary of Austria and Germany's victory over Napoleon, Schubert effected his own Austrian-German synthesis: the poetry of Goethe inspired *Gretchen am Spinnrade* D118, a song that marks the beginning of a fresh chapter in the lied where voice and piano combine in a way that was completely unprecedented. The vocal line, thanks to studies with Salieri, is sinuously operatic, a grateful song for any singer wishing to make an effect. However, the psychological intention, intensified by the remarkable accompaniment, eschews the banalities of virtuosity and is worthy of Goethe's Germanic seriousness. An examination of the many songs from earlier in 1814 shows the painstaking preparation for this great moment with a long line of remarkable Matthisson settings, and a continuing fascination with Schiller, fixed in history as Goethe's alter ego despite the two poets' fundamental differences. It was Goethe who became the lodestar in the composer's life, perhaps because, unlike Schiller, he was still very much alive. Towards the end of the year Schubert met the introspective Viennese poet Johann Mayrhofer and set to music, for the first time, the verses of an Austrian contemporary (D124). For all the young composer's achievements in instrumental music, 1814, like 1815, was also an important year of song.

See:	COMPOSERS: Ludwig van Beethoven
	FRIENDS AND FAMILY: Therese Grob
	Johann Wolfgang von GOETHE
	Friedrich von MATTHISSON
	Johann MAYRHOFER

DISC 3

H29	*Der Taucher* (Schiller) second version D77 (D$_1$111), 13 September 1813–August 1814[4]	**III/304**
	Don Gayseros:[5]	
H30	'Don Gayseros, Don Gayseros' (de la Motte Fouqué) D93/1, *c.* 1814	**I/425**
H31	'Nächtens klang die süsse Laute' (de la Motte Fouqué) D93/2, *c.* 1814	**I/428**

---

[4]*Der Taucher*: The first version of this song was completed on 5 April 1814. At the end of 1814 or beginning of 1815, Schubert revised the second version of the song; so the entire span of the work's composition possibly encompasses September 1813 to early 1815.

[5]*Don Gayseros*: Walther Dürr places this set of three songs later in his ordering (Dürr47) together with the date 1815(?).

H32	'An dem jungen Morgenhimmel' (de la Motte Fouqué) D93/3, *c*. 1814	**I/429**
H33	*Adelaide* (Matthisson) D95, 1814	**I/54**
H34	*Trost. An Elisa* (Matthisson) D97, 1814	**III/416**
H35	*Andenken* (Matthisson) D99, April 1814	**I/217**
H36	*Erinnerung* (*Todtenopfer*) (Matthisson) D101, April 1814	**I/510**
H37	*Geisternähe* (Matthisson) D100, April 1814	**I/669**
H38	*Die Befreier Europas in Paris* (Mikan) D104, 16 May 1814	**I/283**
H39	*Lied aus der Ferne* (Matthisson) D107, July 1814	**II/213**
H40	*Lied der Liebe* (Matthisson) D109, July 1814	**II/219**
H41	*Der Abend* (Matthisson) D108, July 1814	**I/1**
H42	*An Emma* (Schiller) D113, September 1814	**I/193**
H43	*Romanze* (Matthisson) D114 September 1814[6]	**II/650**
H44	*Erinnerungen* (Matthisson) D98, autumn 1814	**I/512**

Disc 4

H45	*Die Betende* (Matthisson) D102, September(?) 1814	**I/301**
H46	*An Laura, als sie Klopstocks Auferstehungslied sang* (Matthisson) D115, 2–7 October 1814	**I/196**
H47	*Der Geistertanz* (Matthisson) third setting D116, 14 October 1814 [*see* first setting H7, second setting H8, fourth setting H311+]	**I/674**
H48	*Das Mädchen aus der Fremde* (Schiller) first setting D117, 16 October 1814 [*see* second setting H137]	**II/284**
H49	*Gretchen am Spinnrade* (Goethe) D118, 19 October 1814	**I/792**
H50	*Nachtgesang* (Goethe) D119, 30 November 1814	**II/423**
H51	*Schäfers Klagelied* (Goethe) first version D121, 30 November 1814 [*see* second version H418a]	**II/720**
H52	*Trost in Tränen* (Goethe) D120, 30 November 1814	**III/420**
H53	*Ammenlied* (Lubi) D122, December 1814	**I/126**
H54	*Sehnsucht* (Goethe) D123, 3 December 1814	**III/99**
H55	*Am See* (Mayrhofer) D124, 7 December 1814	**I/113**
H56	*Szene aus 'Faust'* (Goethe) second version D126, 12 December 1814	**III/292**

Some other works of 1814: *Des Teufels Lustschloss*, a *Singspiel* in 3 acts (D84); String Quartet in E (D87); String Quartet in D (D94); *Salve Regina* in B flat (D106); String Quartet in B flat (D112); Symphony no. 2 in B flat (D125).

1815 (aged eighteen) – *142 solo songs* (every month of the year)

This celebrated *annus mirabilis* of song represents an amazing musical journey in the context of, and in contrast to, the composer's domestic stasis. The year was poor in tabulated biographical events (very few documents have come down to us) and rich in musical creativity. The alarming re-emergence of Napoleon and his defeat at Waterloo were played out while young Franz attempted to reconcile himself to a life of teaching in the ninth *Bezirk*. It was no doubt Napoleon's escape from Elba (the news reached Vienna on 5 March) that made Schubert reach for his copy of Körner's war poems, *Leyer und Schwert*, and initiate a new wave of Körner settings on 12 March. The banality of his own domestic circumstances no doubt seemed a terrible contrast with

---

[6]*Romanze*: The second version of this song was composed on 29 September 1814; the two versions share a Deutsch number.

memories of the fallen hero's bravery. Apart from visits to his friends at the Konvikt, Schubert was stuck at home in the Säulengasse, but he refused to renounce his dreams. Domestic surroundings seemed especially to have favoured the composition of lieder, the epitome of domestic music. In the white heat of inspiration he wrote some 150 songs – sometimes as many as nine in one day (D267–75 on 25 August and eight on 15 October), particularly when he was spared his teaching duties on account of school holidays or weekends. The composer's willpower enabled him to spirit himself away from the dullness of his material circumstances. This extraordinary creativity occasioned neither arrogance nor complacency: he continued his composition lessons with Salieri and maintained links with his schoolfriends. An increasing number of people were becoming his staunch admirers; *Erlkönig* D328 was soon famous among all members of the circle. Schubert's appetite for settable material was voracious – from the older eighteenth-century poets (Klopstock, Hölty, Kosegarten, Stolberg, the supposedly ancient 'Ossian' who inspired a modern cult that would later appeal to Mendelssohn) to moderns like Körner (whom Schubert had actually met) and the perennials Goethe and Schiller who provided the template by which all other poetry was judged. He already nurtured an ongoing relationship with Johann Mayrhofer, ten years his senior and librettist of the *Singspiel, Die Freunde von Salamanka* D326, a work from the end of 1815. The single Mayrhofer song setting of the year, *Liane* (D298) dates from October.

Schubert's literary judgement was more acute than posterity has given him credit for, and he read far more widely than is reflected in the authorship of his own musical settings, broad as that selection of poets was. In 1815 his taste was not yet infallible (the hoary ballads of Bertrand and Bernard) but it would be a mistake to dismiss the indulgence of his friends' poetry (Kenner, Schlechta, Stadler) as a lapse of perception on his part. He was all too aware that they were not great writers, but he was always willing to take seriously the efforts of those who had accorded him their admiration and support – a definition of friendship, perhaps. The musical gatherings of friends, not yet officially known as Schubertiads, achieved their vitality and longevity thanks to an exchange of artistic energy between the composer and his less gifted contemporaries – a youthful symposium that was at the heart of an ever-developing camaraderie crucial to his development. He was acutely aware of the difference between German poets and his less celebrated countrymen (like the Viennese Stoll and the Styrians Fellinger and Kalchberg); he seems to have been willing to admit Austrian provincials into the lieder fold precisely because he identified with their home-grown qualities. Schubert was already able to control the means by which the ordinary text could become the extraordinary song. His willingness to work this alchemy in the case of poetry written by people of whom he was fond was also an indication of a different mindset from that which judges a work only in terms of its quality, or its success with the public. Whether or not Schubert considered his friends' work as 'first rate' is probably beside the point. Isaiah Berlin in *The Roots of Romanticism*, 1999, p. 14, delineates the underlying zeitgeist that had 'shifted consciousness away' from the notion that there were 'universal canons of art, that all human activities were meant to terminate in getting things right'. In the new order, 'the purpose of art is to produce beauty, and if the artist alone perceives that his object is beautiful, that is a sufficient end in life'. It was according to these lights, surely, that much of the poetry within the Schubert circle was received by those for whom it was produced, although it is fortunate that Schubert never allowed himself to judge his own work in this self-satisfied way. In any case these songs were the only gifts the composer was able to make to his friends in his straitened financial circumstances.

See:　　Josef Karl BERNARD
　　　　　Friedrich Anton BERTRAND
　　　　　Johann Georg FELLINGER
　　　　　Johann Nepomuk KALCHBERG

Friedrich Gottlob KLOPSTOCK
Ludwig Theobul KOSEGARTEN
James MACPHERSON ('Ossian')
Franz von SCHLECHTA
Albert STADLER
Friedrich von STOLBERG
Josef Ludwig STOLL

DISC 4 continued

H57	*Ballade* (Kenner) D134, *c.* 1815	**I/275**
H58	*Der Mondabend* (Ermin) D141, 1815	**II/372**
H59	*Geistes-Gruss* (Goethe) third version D142[7]	**I/675**
H59a	*Geistes-Gruss* (Goethe) sixth version D142	**I/675**
H60	*Genügsamkeit* (Schober) D143, 1815	**I/686**
H61	*Der Sänger* (Goethe) D149, February 1815[8]	**II/698**

DISC 5

H62	*Der Liedler* (Kenner) D209, January 1815	**II/240**
H63	*Trinklied* (Castelli) D148, February 1815	**III/403**
H64	*Auf einen Kirchhof* (Schlechta) D151, 2 February 1815	**I/257**
H65	*Minona, oder die Kunde der Dogge* (Bertrand) D152, 8 February 1815	**II/357**
H66	*Als ich sie erröten sah* (Ehrlich) D153, 10 February 1815	**I/96**
H67	*Das Bild* (Anonymous) D155, 11 February 1815	**I/304**
H68	*Am Flusse* (Goethe) first setting D160, 27 February 1815 [*see* second setting H502]	**I/107**
H69	*An Mignon* (Goethe) first version D161, 27 February 1815 [*see* second version H71a]	**I/203**
H70	*Nähe des Geliebten* (Goethe) D162, 27 February 1815	**II/442**
H71	*Sängers Morgenlied* (Körner) first setting D163, 27 February 1815 [*see* second setting H73]	**II/709**
H71a	*An Mignon* (Goethe) second version D161, 1815	**I/203**
H72	*Liebesrausch* (Körner) first setting D164 fragment, March 1815 [*see* second setting H84]	**II/193**
H73	*Sängers Morgenlied* (Körner) second setting D165, 1 March 1815 [*see* first setting H71]	**II/711**
H74	*Amphiaraos* (Körner) D166, 1 March 1815	**I/128**
H75	*Nun lasst uns den Leib begraben (Begräbnislied)* (Klopstock) D168 quartet, 9 March 1815	**II/461**
H76	*Jesus Christus unser Heiland (Osterlied)* (Klopstock) D168A, 9 March 1815	**II/12**
H77	*Trinklied vor der Schlacht* (Körner) D169, 12 March 1815	**III/411**
H78	*Schwertlied* (Körner) D170, 12 March 1815	**III/77**
H79	*Gebet während der Schlacht* (Körner) D171, 12 March 1815	**I/645**
H80	*Der Morgenstern* (Körner) D172 fragment, 12 March 1815	**II/386**
H81	*Das war ich* (Körner) first setting D174, 26 March 1815 [*see* second setting H281]	**I/399**

[7]The Deutsch catalogue ascribes *Geistes-Grüss* to '1815 or 1816'. The NSA, however, places the first version in March 1816, the third version in 1820–21 and the sixth version in 1828, the year of the song's publication. These newer datings are adopted in the commentaries.

[8]*Der Sänger*: This song is part of the outburst of activity in February 1815 and properly belongs somewhere between H63 and H71.

DISC 6

H82	*Die Sterne* (Fellinger) D176, 6 April 1815	**III/250**
H83	*Vergebliche Liebe* (Bernard) D177, 6 April 1815	**III/471**
H84	*Liebesrausch* (Körner) D179, 8 April 1815 [*see* first setting H72]	**II/194**
H85	*Sehnsucht der Liebe* (Körner) D180, 8 April 1815	**III/113**
H86	*Die erste Liebe* (Fellinger) D182, 12 April 1815	**I/530**
H87	*Trinklied* (Zettler) D183, 12 April 1815	**III/404**
H88	*Die Sterbende* (Matthisson) D186, May 1815	**III/248**
H89	*Stimme der Liebe* (Matthisson) first setting D187, May 1815 [*see* second setting H254]	**III/265**
H90	*Naturgenuss* (Matthisson) D188, May 1815	**II/449**
H91	*An die Freude* (Schiller) D189, May 1815	**I/162**
H91+	*Gott, höre meine Stimme* (Körner) D190/5 (aria from *Der vierjährige Posten*), 8–19 May 1815	**III/509**
H92	*Des Mädchens Klage* (Schiller) second setting D191, 15 May 1815 [*see* first setting H6, third setting H229]	**II/293**
H93	*Der Jüngling am Bache* (Schiller) second setting D192, 15 May 1815 [*see* first setting H12, third setting H424]	**II/18**
H94	*An den Mond* (Hölty) D193, 17 May 1815	**I/147**
H95	*Die Mainacht* (Hölty) D194, 17 May 1815	**II/304**
H96	*Rastlose Liebe* (Goethe) D138, 19 May 1815	**II/625**
H97	*Amalia* (Schiller) D195, 19 May 1815	**I/123**
H98	*An die Nachtigall* (Hölty) D196, 22 May 1815	**I/178**
H99	*An die Apfelbäume, wo ich Julien erblickte* (Hölty) D197, 22 May 1815	**I/158**
H100	*Seufzer* (Hölty) D198, 22 May 1815	**III/137**
H101	*Auf den Tod einer Nachtigall* (Hölty) first setting D201 fragment, 25 May 1815 [*see* second setting H264]	**I/243**
H102	*Liebeständelei* (Körner) D206, 26 May 1815	**II/195**
H103	*Der Liebende* (Hölty) D207, 29 May 1815	**II/186**
	[*Die Nonne* (Hölty) first version D212 fragment, 29 May 1815 [*see* second setting H106]]	
H104	*Die Liebe* ('Freudvoll und Leidvoll') (Goethe) D210, 3 June 1815	**II/178**

DISC 7

H105	*Adelwold und Emma* (Bertrand) D211, 5–14 June 1815	**I/57**
H106	*Die Nonne* (Hölty) second version D208, 16 June 1815 [*see* first setting after H103]	**II/452**
H107	*Der Traum* (Hölty) D213, 17 June 1815	**III/399**
H108	*Die Laube* (Hölty) D214, 17 June 1815	**II/116**
H109	*Jägers Abendlied* (Goethe) first setting D215, 20 June 1815 [*see* second setting H221]	**II/3**
H110	*Meeres Stille* (Goethe) first setting D215A, 20 June 1815	**II/326**
H110a	*Meeres Stille* (Goethe) second setting D₂216, 21 June 1815	**II/328**
H111	*Kolmas Klage* (Ossian/Macpherson/translator unknown) D217, 22 June 1815	**II/87**
H112	*Grablied* (Kenner) D218, 24 June 1815	**I/770**
H113	*Das Finden* (Kosegarten) D219, 25 June 1815	**I/553**
H114	*Lieb Minna* (Stadler) D222, 2 July 1815	**II/176**
H115	*Wandrers Nachtlied I* (Goethe) D224, 5 July 1815	**III/550**

| H116 | *Der Fischer* (Goethe) D225, 5 July 1815 | **I/555** |
| H117 | *Erster Verlust* (Goethe) D226, 5 July 1815 | **I/532** |

DISC 8

H118	*Idens Nachtgesang* (Kosegarten) D227, 7 July 1815	**I/917**
H119	*Von Ida* (Kosegarten) D228, 7 July 1815	**III/524**
H120	*Die Erscheinung (Erinnerung)* (Kosegarten) D229, 7 July 1815	**I/527**
H121	*Die Täuschung* (Kosegarten) D230, 7 July 1815	**III/299**
H122	*Das Sehnen* (Kosegarten) D231, 8 July 1815	**III/92**
H123	*Hymne an den Unendlichen* (Schiller) D232 quartet, 11 July 1815	**I/914**
H124	*Geist der Liebe* (Kosegarten) D233, 15 July 1815	**I/664**
H125	*Der Abend* (Kosegarten) D221, 15 July 1815	**I/3**
H126	*Tischlied* (Goethe) D234, 15 July 1815	**III/335**
H127	*Das Abendrot* (Kosegarten) D236 trio, 20 July 1815	**I/28**
H128	*Abends unter der Linde* (Kosegarten) first setting D235, 24 July 1815	**I/32**
H129	*Abends unter der Linde* (Kosegarten) second setting D237, 25 July 1815	**I/34**
H130	*Die Mondnacht* (Kosegarten) D238, 25 July 1815	**II/376**
H131	*Huldigung* (Kosegarten) D240, 27 July 1815	**I/909**
H132	*Alles um Liebe* (Kosegarten) D241, 27 July 1815	**I/82**
H133	*Winterlied* (Hölty) D242 fragment, 27 July 1815[9]	**III/619**
	[*Die Schlacht* (Schiller) first version D249 fragment, 1 August 1815]	**II/756**
H134	*Die Bürgschaft* (Schiller) D246, August 1815	**I/326**
H135	*Das Geheimnis* (Schiller) first setting D250, 7 August 1815 [*see* second setting H517]	**I/657**
H136	*Hoffnung* (Schiller) first setting D251, 7 August 1815 [*see* second setting H412]	**I/905**
H137	*Das Mädchen aus der Fremde* (Schiller) second setting D252, 12 August 1815 [*see* first setting H48]	**II/286**
H138	*Punschlied (Im Norden zu singen)* (Schiller) D253, 18 August 1815	**II/612**
H138+	*'Hin und wieder fliegen Pfeile'* (Goethe) D239/3 (Ariette of Lucinde from *Claudine von Villa Bella*), after 26 July 1815	**I/352**
H138++	*'Liebe schwärmt auf allen Wegen'* (Goethe) D239/6 (Ariette of Claudine from *Claudine von Villa Bella*), after 26 July 1815	**I/353**
H139	*Die Spinnerin* (Goethe) D247, August 1815	**III/235**

DISC 9

H140	*Der Gott und die Bajadere* (Goethe) D254, 18 August 1815	**I/762**
H141	*Der Rattenfänger* (Goethe) D255, 19 August 1815	**II/629**
H142	*Der Schatzgräber* (Goethe) D256, 19 August 1815	**II/728**
H143	*Heidenröslein* (Goethe) D257, 19 August 1815	**I/833**
H144	*Bundeslied* (Goethe) D258, 4/19 August 1815	**I/336**
H145	*An den Mond* (Goethe) first setting D259, 19 August 1815 [*see* second setting H213]	**I/140**
H146	*Wonne der Wehmut* (Goethe) D260, 20 August 1815	**III/737**
H147	*Wer kauft Liebesgötter?* (Goethe) D261, 21 August 1815	**III/566**
H148	*Die Fröhlichkeit* (Prandstetter) D262, 22 August 1815	**I/613**
H149	*Lob des Tokayers* (Baumberg) D248, August 1815	**II/256**

[9] *Winterlied*: This song is dated by Dürr as 1816(?) and is thus placed much later in Dürr's sequence (192).

H150	*Cora an die Sonne* (Baumberg) D263, 22 August 1815	**I/387**
H151	*Der Morgenkuss* (Baumberg) D264, 22 August 1815	**II/378**
H152	*Abendständchen an Lina* (Baumberg) D265, 23 August 1815	**I/35**
H153	*Morgenlied* (Stolberg) D266, 24 August 1815	**II/380**
H154	*Trinklied* (Anonymous) D267, 25 August 1815	**III/406**
H155	*Bergknappenlied* (Anonymous) D268, 25 August 1815	**I/295**
H156	*An die Sonne* (Baumberg) D270, 25 August 1815	**I/183**
H157	*Der Weiberfreund* (Cowley/Ratschky) D271, 25 August 1815	**III/561**
H158	*An die Sonne* (Tiedge) D272, 25 August 1815	**I/185**
H159	*Das Leben ist ein Traum* (Wannovius) D269 trio, 25 August 1815	**II/123**
H160	*Lilla an die Morgenröte* (Anonymous) D273, 25 August 1815	**II/250**
H161	*Tischlerlied* (Anonymous) D274, 25 August 1815	**III/333**
H162	*Totenkranz für ein Kind* (Matthisson) D275, 25 August 1815	**III/377**
H163	*Abendlied* (Stolberg) D276, 28 August 1815	**I/12**
H164	*Punschlied* ('Vier Elemente, innig gesellt') (Schiller) D277, 29 August 1815	**II/614**
H165	*Ossians Lied nach dem Fall Nathos'* (Ossian/Macpherson/Harold) D278, September(?) 1815[10]	**II/496**

DISC 10

H166	*Das Rosenband* (Klopstock) D280, September 1815	**II/680**
H167	*Das Mädchen von Inistore* (Ossian/Macpherson/Harold) D281, September 1815	**II/287**
H168	*Cronnan* (Macpherson) D282, 5 September 1815	**I/391**
H169	*An den Frühling* (Schiller) first setting D283, 6 September 1815 [*see* second setting H388]	**I/137**
H170	*Lied* ('Es ist so angenehm') (Schiller?), D284, 6 September 1815	**II/205**
H171	*Furcht der Geliebten* ('An Cidli') (Klopstock) D285, 12 September 1815	**I/634**
H172	*Selma und Selmar* (Klopstock) D286, 14 September 1815	**III/130**
H173	*Vaterlandslied* (Klopstock) D287, 14 September 1815	**III/460**
H174	*An Sie* (Klopstock) D288, 14 September 1815	**I/214**
H175	*Die Sommernacht* (Klopstock) D289, 14 September 1815	**III/216**
H176	*Die frühen Gräber* (Klopstock) D290, 14 September 1815	**I/619**
H177	*Dem Unendlichen* (Klopstock) first version D291, 15 September 1815	**III/432**
H178	*Shilrik und Vinvela* (Macpherson) D293, 20 September 1815	**III/142**
H178a	*Dem Unendlichen* (Klopstock) second version D291, *c.* 1815	**III/432**
H179	*Erlkönig* (Goethe) D328, October(?) 1815	**I/517**
H180	*Liane* (Mayrhofer) D298, October 1815	**II/170**
H181	*Lambertine* (Anonymous) D301, 12 October 1815	**II/112**
H182	*Labetrank der Liebe* (Stoll) D302, 15 October 1815	**II/107**
H183	*An die Geliebte* (Stoll) D303, 15 October 1815	**I/168**
H184	*Wiegenlied* (Körner) D304, 15 October 1815	**III/591**
H185	*Mein Gruss an den Mai* (Ermin) D305, 15 October 1815	**II/330**
H186	*Skolie* (Deinhard-Deinhardstein) D306, 15 October 1815	**III/214**
H187	*Die Sternenwelten* (Jarnik/Fellinger) D307, 15 October 1815	**III/263**
H188	*Die Macht der Liebe* (Kalchberg) D308, 15 October 1815	**II/273**
H189	*Das gestörte Glück* (Körner) D309, 15 October 1815	**I/723**

[10]*Ossians Lied nach dem Falle Nathos*: Walther Dürr places this song at the beginning of 1815 (Dürr53).

Disc 11

H190	*Sehnsucht (Mignon)* (Goethe) first setting, first version D310, 18 October 1815	**III/102**
H190a	*Sehnsucht (Mignon)* (Goethe) first setting, second version D310A, 18 October 1815 [*see* second setting H211, third setting H298, fourth setting H424+, fifth setting H585, sixth setting H588]	**III/102**
H191	*Hektors Abschied* (Schiller) D312, 19 October 1815	**I/852**
H192	*Die Sterne* (Kosegarten) D313, 19 October 1815	**III/251**
H193	*Nachtgesang* (Kosegarten) D314, 19 October 1815	**II/425**
H194	*An Rosa I* (Kosegarten) D315, 19 October 1815	**I/206**
H195	*An Rosa II* (Kosegarten) D316, 19 October 1815	**I/208**
H196	*Idens Schwanenlied* (Kosegarten) D317, 19 October 1815	**I/919**
H197	*Schwangesang* (Kosegarten) D318, 19 October 1815	**III/73**
H198	*Luisens Antwort* (Kosegarten) D319, 19 October 1815	**II/268**
H199	*Der Zufriedene* (Reissig) D320, 23 October 1815	**III/752**
H200	*Mignon* (Kennst du das Land?) (Goethe) D321, 23 October 1815	**II/344**
H201	*Hermann und Thusnelda* (Klopstock) D322, 27 October 1815	**I/871**
H201a	*Erlkönig* (Goethe) D328 trio version, October(?) 1815	**I/517**
H202	*Klage der Ceres* (Schiller) D323, 9 November 1815[11]	**II/53**
H203	*Wer sich der Einsamkeit ergibt (Harfenspieler)* (Goethe) first setting D325, 13 November 1815 [*see* second setting H492]	**III/571**
H204	*Lorma* (Ossian/Macpherson/Harold) first setting D327 fragment, 28 November 1815 [*see* second setting H224]	**II/265**
H205	*Die drei Sänger* (Bobrik) D329 fragment, 23 December 1815	**I/444**

Disc 12

H206	*Das Grab* (Salis-Seewis) second setting D330, 28 December 1815 [*see* third setting H225, fourth setting H377]	**I/767**
H207	*Zufriedenheit* (Claudius) D362 first setting, 1815 or 1816 [*see* second setting H319][12]	**III/754**
H208	*Klage um Ali Bey* (Claudius) D140 trio version, 1815 [*see* solo version H313a]	**II/60**

Some other works of 1815: Zwölf Walzer, siebzehn Ländler und neun Ecossaisen für Klavier (D145); Sonata in E major for piano (D157); Mass in G (D167); String Quartet in G (D173); Stabat Mater in G minor (D175); *Der vierjährige Posten*, a *Singspiel* with a text by Körner (D190); Symphony no. 3 in D (D200); *Fernando*, a *Singspiel* with a text by Stadler (D220); *Claudine von Villa Bella*, a *Singspiel* with a text by Goethe (D239); Sonata in C for piano (D279); Mass in B flat major (D324).

---

[11]*Klage der Ceres*: This ballad, begun in November 1815, was completed only in June 1816, an unusually long time span for the composition of a solo vocal piece.

[12]*Zufriedenheit*: This song appears on a spare space on the autograph of *Cronnan* D282 from September 1815. Accordingly Ernst Hilmar believes it was composed at this time; Walther Dürr believes that Schubert composed the song in 1816, and to do so used the first piece of spare paper that came to hand. Reed believes the song was probably composed in April 1816.

1816 (aged nineteen) – *112 solo songs* (every month of the year)
In February Schubert attempted to escape the drudgery of his father's school by applying (unsuccessfully) for a job as a music teacher in Laibach, the present-day Ljubljana. An audacious project was developed by Josef von Spaun who envisaged the publication of Schubert's songs gathered together under their poets: two Goethe volumes, one of Schiller, two of Klopstock, one shared between Matthisson, Hölty and Salis-Seewis, and two volumes of Ossian. Spaun's idea was to put this plan to Goethe by letter and, having obtained his approval, to use the great poet's name to convince the sceptical Viennese publishers. This idea came to nothing and Spaun's request in April that Goethe should be dedicatee of the projected first volume was also ignored. The enclosure of a lovingly prepared autograph collection of sixteen Goethe settings was sent back to Vienna from Weimar without comment. As Schubert wrote in a rare diary entry of June 1816 (apropos something else), 'It is quite common to be disappointed by one's expectations.' In the same month the composer took part in the celebrations of the fiftieth anniversary of Salieri's arrival in Vienna. The young composers musical contribution, D407, was one of several heard on a long day where Salieri was surrounded by all his pupils. Schubert's first paid commission (to write the cantata *Prometheus* D451, now lost) dates from the same time. The first outdoor performance of this work at the home of Professor Watteroth was delayed because of bad weather. Elizabeth McKay has pointed out that the European summer of 1816 was exceptionally cold and unsettled because of a volcanic eruption in Indonesia. There is a topical reference to a volcano in the contemporary opera *Die Bürgschaft* D435. By the end of this stormy year much had changed in Schubert's life: the love affair with Therese Grob (such as it was) came to an end, as did his regular association with Salieri. Despite parental opposition he had finally taken the decision to leave the schoolhouse, give up teaching and live in the rooms of his charismatic friend Franz von Schober in the inner city (Tuchlauben 26). This somewhat valiant assertion of independence was to last for about a year.

Perhaps this is why the flood of songs, over one hundred in 1816, continued unabated. There was nothing as overtly dramatic as *Gretchen am Spinnrade* or *Erlkönig* in the offing (although *An Schwager Kronos* D369 was nearly as exciting, and *Der Wanderer* D489 became nearly as famous), but Schubert turned his attention to the achievements of the German composers who were masters of the ballad (Zumsteeg in Stuttgart) and of the strophic song (Reichardt and Zelter in Berlin). In some cases he modelled his own compositions on their example, often bar by bar; as he went along he outstripped the achievements of the older composers almost without trying (as in *Die Erwartung* D159). In 1816 Schubert tackled head-on the problem of the strophic song, the art that conceals art. Here, painstakingly, were laid the foundations of the effortless simplicity of later masterpieces, such as the two Müller cycles, where great emotion is expressed in a pithy, economical way. In 1816 there were fewer Klopstock songs, but there was ongoing work on Ossian, Hölty, Matthisson and Stolberg. Schubert intensified his interest in Schiller and broadened his Goethean outlook to include the lyrics of Mignon and the Harper from *Wilhelm Meisters Lehrjahre*. Some writers are almost entirely linked with the songs of 1816: the Swiss Salis-Seewis in March; Uz in June; Jacobi in August and September. The composer's enthusiasm for these older poets was often occasioned by recently published Viennese reprints of their work which made them appear to be new arrivals on the literary scene, at least as far as he was concerned. There were two Schubart settings in 1816 and a glut of Claudius settings in November, both enthusiasms that would spill into the following year. Significant on the home front were nine Mayrhofer songs, a kind of prelude to the outburst of great settings of that poet in 1817. There was a single setting of his friend Schober, and a sign of the composer's awakening awareness of the salon life of Vienna in two settings of the influential blue-stocking Karoline Pichler.

See: COMPOSERS: Johann Friedrich Reichardt, Carl Friedrich Zelter, Johann Rudolf
            Zumsteeg
            Matthias CLAUDIUS
            Johann Georg JACOBI
            Caroline PICHLER
            Johann Gaudenz von SALIS-SEEWIS
            Christian Friedrich Daniel SCHUBART
            Johann Peter Uz

DISC 12 continued

	[*Trinklied* (Anon) D356 fragment, tenor, chorus TTBB and piano, 1816]	**III/407**
H209	*An Chloen* (Uz) D363 fragment, 1816[13]	**I/134**
H210	*Die Nacht* (Uz) D358, 1816[14]	**II/43**
H211	*Sehnsucht (Mignon)* (Goethe) second setting D359, 1816 [*see* first setting H190 and H190A, third setting H298, fourth setting H424+, fifth setting H585, sixth setting H588]	**III/104**
H212	*Hoffnung* (Goethe) D295, *c.* 1816[15]	**I/903**
H213	*An den Mond* (Goethe) second setting D296, *c.* 1816 [*see* first setting H145][16]	**I/143**
H214	*An mein Klavier* (Schubart) D342, *c.* 1816	**I/201**
H215	*Am ersten Maimorgen* (Claudius) D344, *c.* 1816[17]	**I/103**
H216	*Klage (Trauer umfliesst mein Leben)* (Anonymous) D371, January 1816	**II/51**
H217	*An die Natur* (Stolberg) D372, 15 January 1816	**I/181**
H218	*Lied (Mutter geht durch ihre Kammer)* (de la Motte Fouqué) D373, 15 January(?) 1816	**II/211**
H219	*Lodas Gespenst* (Macpherson) D150, 17 January 1816	**II/259**
H220	*Der König in Thule* (Goethe) D367, early 1816	**II/78**
H221	*Jägers Abendlied* (Goethe) second setting D368, early 1816(?) [*see* first setting H109]	**II/5**
H222	*An Schwager Kronos* (Goethe) D369, 1816	**I/210**
H223	*Der Tod Oscars* (Macpherson) D375, February 1816	**III/337**
H224	*Lorma* (Macpherson) second setting D376, 10 February 1816 [*see* first setting H204]	**II/267**
H225	*Das Grab* (Salis-Seewis) third setting D377, 11 February 1816 [*see* second setting H206, fourth setting H377]	**I/767**
H226	*Morgenlied* (Anonymous) D381, 24 February 1816	**II/382**
H227	*Abendlied* (Anonymous) D382, 24 February 1816	**I/14**
	[*Die Schlacht* (Schiller) second version, D387 fragment, soli, chorus and piano, March 1816]	**II/756**

[13]*An Chloen:* It is possible that this Uz setting, like others by the same poet, was composed in June of this year.
[14]*Die Nacht:* It is possible that this Uz setting, like others by the same poet, was composed in June of this year.
[15]*Hoffnung* (Goethe): This song appears much earlier in Walther Dürr's chronology (Dürr49), at the beginning of the 1815 songs. However, NSA (2011) places it definitively after February 1820, a clear case of a great scholar changing his mind.
[16]*An den Mond* (Goethe): This song appears much earlier in Walther Dürr's chronology (Dürr50) at the beginning of the 1815 songs. Some commentators believe this song was written much later than D295, i.e. in 1819. NSA (2011) places it after February 1820.
[17]*Am ersten Maimorgen:* This song is placed in November(?) 1816 in Walther Dürr's chronology, thus Dürr291.

DISC 13

H228	*Laura am Klavier* (Schiller) D388, March 1816	**II/117**
H229	*Des Mädchens Klage* (Schiller) third setting D389, March 1816 [*see* first setting H6, second setting H92]	**II/295**
H230	*Die Entzückung an Laura* (Schiller) first setting D390, March 1816 [*see* second setting H379]	**I/504**
H231	*Die vier Weltalter* (Schiller) D391, March 1816	**III/506**
H232	*Ritter Toggenburg* (Schiller) D397, 13 March 1816	**II/649**
H233	*Gruppe aus dem Tartarus* (Schiller), first setting D396 fragment, March 1816 [*see* second setting H384]	**I/809**
H234	*Der Flüchtling* (Schiller) D402, 18 March 1816	**I/570**
H235	*Der Entfernten* (Salis-Seewis) second setting D350, 1816?	**I/497**
H235+	*Der Entfernten* (Salis-Seewis) first setting D331 unaccompanied choral, *c.* 1816	
H236	*Fischerlied* (Salis-Seewis) first setting D351, 1816(?) [*see* second setting H372]	**I/558**
H237	*Pflügerlied* (Salis-Seewis) D392, March 1816	**II/523**
H238	*Die Einsiedelei* (Salis-Seewis) second setting D393, March 1816 [*see* third setting H373]	**I/488**
H239	*An die Harmonie* (Salis-Seewis) D394, March 1816	**I/169**
H240	*Lied (Ins stille Land)* (Salis-Seewis) D403, 27 March 1816	**II/208**
H241	*Abschied von der Harfe* (Salis-Seewis) D406, end of March/April 1816	**I/46**
H242	*Die Herbstnacht ('Die Wehmut')* (Salis-Seewis) D404, end of March/ April 1816	**I/867**
H243	*Lebensmelodien* (A. von Schlegel) D395, March 1816	**II/127**
H243+	C. W. Gluck: *'Rien de la nature'* (Tschudi) from *Echo et Narcisse* D Anhang IIA, arr. Schubert, March 1816	**I/466**
H243++	C. W. Gluck: *'Ô combats, ô désordre extrême!'* (Tschudi) from *Echo et Narcisse* D Anhang IIB, arr. Schubert, March 1816	**I/466**
H244	*Die verfehlte Stunde* (A. von Schlegel) D409, April 1816	**III/468**
H245	*Sprache der Liebe* (A. von Schlegel) D410, April 1816	**III/238**
H246	*Der Herbstabend* (Salis-Seewis) D405, April 1816[18]	**I/863**
H247	*Daphne am Bach* (Stolberg) D411, April 1816	**I/397**
H248	*Stimme der Liebe* (Stolberg) D412, April 1816	**III/268**
H249	*Romanze* (Stolberg) D144 fragment, April 1816	**II/663**

DISC 14

H250	*Lied in der Abwesenheit* (Stolberg) D416 fragment, April 1816	**II/223**
H251	*Entzückung* (Matthisson) D413, April 1816	**I/502**
H252	*Geist der Liebe* (Matthisson) first setting D414, April 1816 [*see* second setting as a vocal quartet H481]	**I/666**
H253	*Klage (Die Sonne steigt)* (Matthisson) D415, April 1816	**II/50**
H254	*Stimme der Liebe* (Matthisson) second setting D418, 29 April 1816 [*see* first setting H89]	**III/267**
H255	*Julius an Theone* (Matthisson) D419, 30 April 1816	**II/30**
H256	*Minnelied* (Hölty) D429, May 1816	**II/355**
H257	*Die frühe Liebe* (Hölty) D430, May 1816	**I/617**
H258	*Blumenlied* (Hölty) D431, May 1816	**I/319**

[18] *Der Herbstabend*: The NSA dates the two versions of this song 27 March 1816 and November 1816(?).

H259	*Der Leidende (Klage)* (Anonymous) first version D432, May 1816	**II/155**
H259A	*Der Leidende (Klage)* (Anonymous) second version D432B, May 1816	**II/155**
H260	*Seligkeit* (Hölty) D433, May 1816	**III/128**
H261	*Erntelied* (Hölty) D434, May 1816	**I/525**
H262	*Klage (An den Mond)* (Hölty) D₂436, 12 May 1816	**II/47**
H263	*Frühlingslied* (Hölty) D398, 13 May 1816	**I/626**
H264	*Auf den Tod einer Nachtigall* (Hölty) second setting D399, 13 May 1816 [*see* first setting H101]	**I/244**
H265	*Die Knabenzeit* (Hölty) D400, 13 May 1816	**II/76**
H266	*Winterlied* (Hölty) D401, 13 May 1816	**III/617**
H267	*Die Erwartung* (Schiller) D159, May 1816[19]	**I/535**
H268	*Beitrag zur fünfzigjährigsten Jubelfeier des Herrn von Salieri, Erstem k.k. Hofkapellmeister in Wien* (Schubert?) D407, 'Gütigster, Bester!' trio, by 16 June 1816	**I/290**
H268A	*Beitrag zur fünfzigjährigsten Jubelfeier des Herrn von Salieri, Erstem k.k. Hofkapellmeister in Wien* (Schubert?) D407, 'Gütigster, Bester!' unaccompanied quartet, by 16 June 1816	**I/290**
H268B	*Beitrag zur fünfzigjährigsten Jubelfeier des Herrn von Salieri, Erstem k.k. Hofkapellmeister in Wien* (Schubert?) D407, 'So Güt als Weisheit strömen mild' tenor solo, by 16 June 1816	**I/290**
H268C	*Beitrag zur fünfzigjährigsten Jubelfeier des Herrn von Salieri, Erstem k.k. Hofkapellmeister in Wien* (Schubert?) D407, 'Unser aller Grosspapa' unaccompanied trio, by 16 June 1816	**I/290**
H269	*An die Sonne* (Uz) D439 quartet, June 1816	**I/186**
H270	*Das grosse Halleluja* (Klopstock) D442 choral, June 1816	**I/807**
H271	*Schlachtgesang* (Klopstock) D443 tenor solo and chorus, June 1816	**II/761**
H272	*Die Gestirne* (Klopstock) D444, June 1816	**I/721**
H273	*Edone* (Klopstock) D445, June 1816	**I/467**

DISC 15

H274	*Die Liebesgötter* (Uz) D446, June 1816	**II/191**
H275	*Gott im Frühlinge* (Uz) D448, June 1816	**I/754**
H276	*An den Schlaf* (Anonymous) D447, June 1816	**I/154**
H277	*Der gute Hirt* (Uz) D449, June 1816	**I/816**
H278	*Gott im Ungewitter* (Uz) D985 quartet, 1816(?)	**I/755**
H279	*Gott der Weltschöpfer* (Uz) D986 quartet, 1816(?)	**I/752**
H280	*Fragment aus dem Aeschylus* (Aeschylus/Mayrhofer) second version D450, June 1816	**I/588**
H281	*Das war ich* (Körner) second setting D174A/450A fragment, 1816? [*see* first setting H81]	**I/400**
H282	*Grablied auf einen Soldaten* (Schubart) D454, July 1816	**I/772**
H283	*Freude der Kinderjahre* (Köpken) D455, July 1816	**I/595**
H284	*Das Heimweh* (Hell) D456, July 1816	**I/841**
H285	*An die untergehende Sonne* (Kosegarten) D457, July 1816–May 1817	**I/189**
H286	*Aus 'Diego Manazares [Manzanares]': Ilmerine [Almerine]* (Krosigk) D458, 30 July 1816	**I/265**
H287	*Pflicht und Liebe* (Gotter) D467 fragment, August 1816	**II/521**

---

[19] *Die Erwartung*: This is the date of the first version. The date of the second, probably revised for publication, is unknown.

H288	*An Chloen* (Jacobi) D462, August 1816	**I/135**
H289	*Hochzeit-Lied* (Jacobi) D463, August 1816	**I/890**
H290	*In der Mitternacht* (Jacobi) D464, August 1816	**I/950**
H291	*Trauer der Liebe* (Jacobi) D465, August 1816	**III/397**
H292	*Die Perle* (Jacobi) D466, August 1816	**II/516**
H293	*Am Tage aller Seelen* ('Litanei') (Jacobi) D343, August 1816	**I/121**
H294	*An den Mond (Was schauest du so hell und klar?)* (Hölty) D468, 7 August 1816	**I/149**
H295	*Lied des Orpheus (als er in die Hölle ging)* (Jacobi) D474, September 1816	**II/221**
H296	*Mignon* ('So lasst mich scheinen') (Goethe) first setting D469 I fragment, September 1816	**II/349**
H297	*Mignon* ('So lasst mich scheinen') (Goethe) second setting D469 II fragment, September 1816 [*see* third setting H473, fourth setting H587]	**II/349**
H298	*Sehnsucht (Mignon)* (Goethe) third setting D481, September 1816 [*see* first setting H190 and 190A, second setting H211, fourth setting 424+, fifth setting 585, sixth setting H588]	**III/105**
H299	*Liedesend* (Mayrhofer) D473, September 1816	**II/237**

Disc 16

H300	*Abschied, nach einer Wallfahrtsarie* (Mayrhofer) D475, September 1816	**I/44**
H301	*Rückweg* (Mayrhofer) D476, September 1816	**II/696**
H302	*Alte Liebe rostet nie* (Mayrhofer) D477, September 1816	**I/98**
H303	*Lied eines Schiffers an die Dioskuren* (Mayrhofer) D360, 1816?[20]	**II/228**
H304	*Wer nie sein Brot mit Tränen ass (Harfenspieler III)* (Goethe) first version of first setting D478/2, September 1816	**III/568**
H304A	*Wer nie sein Brot mit Tränen ass (Harfenspieler III)* (Goethe) second version of first setting D478/2B, September 1816 [*see* second setting H493]	**III/570**
H305	*Der Sänger am Felsen* (Pichler) D482, September 1816	**II/704**
H306	*Lied* ('Ferne von der grossen Stadt') (Pichler) D483, September 1816	**II/207**
H307	*Gesang der Geister über den Wassern* (Goethe) first setting D484 fragment, September 1816 [*see* second setting H459]	**I/170**
H308	*Der Wanderer* (Schmidt von Lübeck) D489 (second and third versions previously D493), October 1816	**III/538**
H309	*Der Hirt* (Mayrhofer) D490, 8 October 1816	**I/885**
H310	*Geheimnis (An Franz Schubert)* (Mayrhofer) D491, October 1816	**I/661**
H311	*Zum Punsche* (Mayrhofer) D492, October 1816	**III/758**
H311+	*Der Geistertanz* (Matthisson) fourth setting D494 unaccompanied quintet, November 1816 [*see* first setting H7, second setting H8, third setting H47]	
H312	*Abendlied der Fürstin* (Mayrhofer) D495, November 1816?	**I/18**
H313	*Bei dem Grabe meines Vaters* (Claudius) D496, November 1816	**I/285**
H313A	*Klage um Ali Bey* (Claudius) D₂496A solo version, November 1816 [*see* trio version H208]	**II/61**

---

[20]*Lied eines Schiffers an die Dioskuren*: Walther Dürr places this song earlier in 1816 (Dürr201). John Reed, on the other hand, believes it was possibly composed in 1822.

H314	*An die Nachtigall* (Claudius) D497, November 1816	**I/180**
H315	*Wiegenlied* (Anonymous) D498, November 1816	**III/593**
H316	*Abendlied* (Claudius) D499, November 1816	**I/15**
H317	*Am Grabe Anselmos* (Claudius) D504, 4 November 1816	**I/110**
H318	*Phidile* (Claudius) D500, November 1816	**II/525**
H319	*Zufriedenheit* (Claudius) second setting D501, November 1816	**III/756**
H320	*Am Bach im Frühlinge* (Schober) D361, 1816[21]	**I/100**
H321	*Herbstlied* (Salis-Seewis) D502, November 1816	**I/865**
H322	*Mailied* (Hölty) third setting D503 first solo setting, November 1816	**II/303**

DISC 17

H323	*Skolie* (Matthisson) D507, December 1816	**III/215**
H324	*Lebenslied* (Matthisson) D508, December 1816	**II/125**
H325	*Leiden der Trennung* (H. von Collin) D509, December 1816	**II/152**
H326	*Licht und Liebe* (M. von Collin) D352 duet, 1816(?)	**II/173**
H327	*Vedi quanto adoro (Didone abbandonata)* (Metastasio) first setting D510, December 1816	**III/465**
H328	*Vedi quanto adoro (Didone abbandonata)* (Metastasio) second setting D510A fragment, December 1816	**III/465**
H329	*An den Tod* (Schubart) D518, 1816 or 1817[22]	**I/155**

Some other works of 1816: String Quartet in E (D353); Deutsches *Salve Regina* in F (D379); *Stabat mater* (Klopstock, D383); Sonatas ('Sonatinas') in D major, A minor and G minor for violin and piano (D384, 385, 408); *Salve Regina* in B flat (D386); Symphony no. 4 in C minor ('Tragic' – the composer's own title – D417); *Die Bürgschaft* (Schiller-inspired fragment of *opera seria*, unknown librettist, D435); Rondo in A major for violin and orcherstra (D438); Mass in C major (D452); Symphony no. 5 in B flat major (D485); Magnificat in C major (D486).

1817 (aged twenty) – *65 solo songs* (every month of the year except December)
The early months of the year were particularly rich in songs. The last and perhaps greatest Ossian setting, *Die Nacht* D534, dates from February, as does *Der Tod und das Mädchen* D531. Schubert wrote to the firm of Breitkopf & Härtel in Leipzig enclosing *Erlkönig*. The manuscript was returned after having first been posted back to the wrong composer, the pompous Franz Schubert of Dresden, who achieved immortal notoriety by castigating the publisher for imagining that he were capable of composing such rubbish. A turning point in the spring was Schubert's meeting, arranged by Schober and Spaun, with Johann Michael Vogl, the operatic baritone whom the composer had first heard in 1813 as Orestes in Gluck's *Iphigenia in Tauris*. Vogl's initial chilly self-importance gradually yielded to an almost bewildered, yet devoted, admiration for Schubert's work. The performances that were later given by the baritone and composer-accompanist would be the foundation stones of the professional *Liederabend* and song recital tour. Vogl's classical sympathies (he read Latin and Greek, as well as English) coincided with Schubert's deepening friendship with Johann Mayrhofer, and an increasing absorption in setting those poet's lyrics with a mythological background. There were no fewer than twenty Mayrhofer settings in this year and many of these were ideal material for Vogl.

[21]*Am Bach im Frühlinge*: Walther Dürr places this at the beginning of the 1816 songs (Dürr202).
[22]*An den Tod*: Walther Dürr places this at the beginning of the 1816 songs (Dürr190).

The Goethe setting *Ganymed* D544 and Schiller's *Gruppe aus dem Tartarus* D583 and *Elysium* D584 seem to owe their existence to the same Mayrhofer-inspired enthusiasm for antiquity. It is at this time that Schubert discovered the piano sonata as a rewarding expressive medium and composed a number of important works in this form. Contemporary Viennese personalities like Ludwig Széchényi, Matthäus von Collin and Ignaz Castelli were set to music, a sign that the composer was moving increasingly in important Viennese artistic circles. Franz von Schober (three of whose poems were set in 1817, including *An die Musik* D547) left Vienna in August due to a family crisis; this occasioned the valedictory *Abschied* (D578 'Lebe wohl! Du Lieber Freund!'), the only solo song with piano where the composer set his own words to music. Following Schober's departure there was no option for Schubert but to return to his father's schoolhouse. In December 1817 Franz Theodor Schubert took over a bigger school in the Rossau (Grüntorgasse 11). The composer was needed there as an assistant and he had to work there for seven depressing months. The Schubert circle was enlarged by the arrival in Vienna of Josef Hüttenbrenner, brother of the composer Anselm, who became a self-appointed agent for Schubert's interests, and later a kind of personal assistant. In the period 1817 to 1818 Schubert belonged, together with his painter friend Leopold Kupelwieser, to the *Unsinnsgesellschaft* – a playful fraternity where allusive and highly structured tomfoolery (including the performance of parodies of famous literary works) was the order of the day, and where ridiculous costumes, including drag, were worn with enormous relish. It seems likely that the male-voice quartet *Das Dörfchen* D598 was written for the *Unsinnsgesellschaft*, and quite possibly a number of other songs too.

See: FRIENDS AND FAMILY: Anselm Hüttenbrenner, Josef Hüttenbrenner
       SINGERS: Johann Michael Vogl
       Ignaz CASTELLI
       Matthäus von COLLIN
       Franz von SCHOBER
       Ludwig SZÉCHÉNYI

DISC 17 continued

H330	*Nur wer die Liebe kennt (Impromptu)* (Werner) D₂513A, fragment 1817(?)	**II/463**
H331	*Die abgeblühte Linde* (Széchényi) D514, 1817(?)	**I/39**
H332	*Der Flug der Zeit* (Széchényi) D515, 1817(?)[23]	**I/573**
H333	*Frohsinn* (Castelli) D520, January 1817	**I/615**
H334	*Jagdlied* (Werner) D521 choral, January 1817	**II/10**
H335	*Die Liebe* (Leon) D522, January 1817	**II/181**
H336	*Trost* (Anonymous) D523, January 1817	**III/413**
H337	*Der Alpenjäger* (Mayrhofer) D524, January 1817	**I/89**
H338	*Wie Ulfru fischt* (Mayrhofer) D525, January 1817	**III/586**
H339	*Fahrt zum Hades* (Mayrhofer) D526, January 1817	**I/544**
H340	*Augenlied* (Mayrhofer) D297, early 1817(?)[24]	**I/263**
H341	*Sehnsucht* (Mayrhofer) D516, 1817(?)[25]	**III/108**
H342	*Schlaflied* ('Schlummerlied') (Mayrhofer) D527, January 1817	**II/764**
H343	*La pastorella al prato* (Goldoni) D528 solo version, January 1817	**II/106**

[23]*Die abgeblühte Linde* and *Der Flug der Zeit*: There is a possibility that both Széchényi settings date from 1821 when Schubert was attempting to be elected to the Gesellschaft der Musikfreunde, and a dedication of songs to the poet, powerful in that organization, was considered politically expedient.
[24]*Augenlied*: Walther Dürr places this song some months later in 1817, thus Dürr337.
[25]*Sehnsucht* (Mayrhofer): Walther Dürr and other commentators place this song a year or so earlier in 1816, Reed firmly in 1817, thus Dürr196.

H344	*La pastorella al prato* (Goldoni) D513 quartet, 1817(?)	**II/105**
	[*Lied* ('Brüder, schrecklich brennt die Träne') (Anonymous) D535, soprano with chamber orchestra, February 1817]	**II/202**
H345	*An eine Quelle* (Claudius) D530, February 1817	**I/192**
H346	*Das Lied vom Reifen* (Claudius) D532, February 1817	**II/235**
H347	*Der Tod und das Mädchen* (Claudius) D531, February 1817	**III/343**
H348	*Täglich zu singen* (Claudius) D533, February 1817	**III/298**
H349	*Die Nacht* (Ossian/Macpherson/Harold) D534, February 1817	**II/415**

DISC 18

H350	*Philoktet* (Mayrhofer) D540, March 1817	**II/527**
H351	*Memnon* (Mayrhofer) D541, March 1817	**II/331**
H352	*Der Schiffer* (Mayrhofer) D536, 1817[26]	**II/736**
H353	*Am Strome* (Mayrhofer) D539, March 1817	**I/119**
H354	*Antigone und Oedip* (Mayrhofer) D542, March 1817	**I/220**
H355	*Orest* (Mayrhofer) D548, March 1817	**II/485**
H356	*Auf dem See* (Goethe) D543, March 1817	**I/230**
H357	*Ganymed* (Goethe) D544, March 1817	**I/637**
H358	*Mahomets Gesang* (Goethe) first setting D549 fragment, March 1817 [*see* second setting, also a fragment, H471]	**II/297**
H359	*Der Jüngling und der Tod* (Spaun) D545, March 1817	**II/28**
H360	*Trost im Liede* (Schober) D546, March 1817	**III/418**
H361	*An die Musik* (Schober) D547, March 1817	**I/175**
H362	*Pax vobiscum* (Schober) D551, April 1817	**II/508**
H363	*Hänflings Liebeswerbung* (Kind) D552, April 1817	**I/818**
H364	*Der Schäfer und der Reiter* (de la Motte Fouqué) D517, April 1817	**II/717**
H365	*Auf der Donau* (Mayrhofer) D553, April 1817	**I/250**
H366	*Uraniens Flucht* (Mayrhofer) D554, April 1817	**III/443**

DISC 19

H367	*Liebhaber in allen Gestalten* (Goethe) D558, May 1817	**II/197**
H368	*Schweizerlied* (Goethe) D559, May 1817	**III/75**
H369	*Der Goldschmiedsgesell* (Goethe) D560, May 1817	**I/746**
H370	*Nach einem Gewitter* (Mayrhofer) D561, May 1817	**II/403**
H371	*Die Blumensprache* (Platner or Plattner?) D519, 1817(?)[27]	**I/320**
H372	*Fischerlied* (Salis-Seewis) third setting D562, May 1817 [*see* first setting H236]	**I/561**
H373	*Die Einsiedelei* (Salis-Seewis) third setting D563, May 1817 [*see* second setting H238]	**I/490**
H374	*Gretchen im Zwinger* (*Gretchens Bitte*) (Goethe) D564 fragment, May 1817	**I/799**
H375	*Der Strom* (Anonymous) D565, June(?) 1817[28]	**III/274**
H376	*Der Jüngling an der Quelle* (Salis-Seewis) D300, c. 1817[29]	**II/22**
H377	*Das Grab* (Salis-Seewis) fourth setting D569, June 1817 [*see* second setting H206, third setting H225]	**I/767**

[26]*Der Schiffer*: It seems likely that this song was composed in March, although Reed makes a 'plausible guess' that it dates from the autumn of this year.
[27]*Die Blumensprache*: Dürr places this song about six months later at the end of 1817(?) thus Dürr367.
[28]*Der Strom*: Reed places this song slightly later, in the Autumn of 1817.
[29]*Der Jüngling an der Quelle*: Dürr places this song very much earlier at the beginning of the 1816 songs (Dürr191). On the other hand, Reed believes in 1821 as a possible date for this song.

H378	*Iphigenia* (Mayrhofer) D573, July 1817	**I/952**
H379	*Die Entzückung an Laura* (Schiller) second setting D577 fragments, August 1817 [*see* first setting H230]	**I/506**
H380	*Abschied* ('Lebe wohl! Du Lieber Freund!') (F. Schubert) D578, 24 August 1817[30]	**I/42**
H381	*Der Knabe in der Wiege (Wiegenlied)* (Ottenwalt) D579, Autumn 1817	**II/73**
H382	*Vollendung* (Matthisson) D579A (formerly D989), September/October 1817	**III/520**
H383	*Die Erde* (Matthisson) D579B (formerly D989), September or October 1817	**I/508**
H384	*Gruppe aus dem Tartarus* (Schiller) second setting D583, September 1817 [*see* first setting, fragment, H233]	**I/810**
H385	*Atys* (Mayrhofer) D585, September 1817	**I/225**
H386	*Elysium* (Schiller) D584, September 1817	**I/492**
H387	*Erlafsee* (Mayrhofer) D586, September 1817	**I/514**
H388	*An den Frühling* (Schiller) third setting D587, October 1817 [*see* first setting H169][31]	**I/139**
H389	*Der Alpenjäger* (Schiller) D588, October 1817	**I/92**
H390	*Lied eines Kindes* (Anonymous) D596 fragment, November 1817	**II/225**
H391	*Die Forelle* (Schubart) D550 *c.* 1817[32]	**I/577**

DISC 20

H392	*Der Kampf* (Schiller) D594, November 1817	**II/39**
H393	*Thekla (eine Geisterstimme)* (Schiller) second setting D595, November 1817 [*see* first setting H25]	**III/329**
H394	*Das Dörfchen* (Bürger) D598 (D641 in D₁) quartet, December 1817	**I/420**

Some other works of 1817: Piano Sonata in A minor (D537); Piano Sonata in A flat (D557); Piano Sonata in E minor (D566); Piano Sonata in E flat (D568); Sonata in A major ('Duo') for violin and piano (D557); Piano Sonata in B major (D575); 12 *Variations on a Theme of Anselm Hüttenbrenner* for piano (D576); String Trio in B flat (D581); Symphony no. 6 in C major (D589, begun in 1817); Overtures 'in the Italian Style' in D (D590) and in C (D591). Two Scherzi for piano (D593).

1818 (aged twenty-one) – *17 solo songs* (March, April, June, August, September, November, December)

Schubert worked as a schoolteacher until the summer. Depression regarding his own circumstances seems to have affected his productivity. Meanwhile his works were becoming known to the general public. In February the Mayrhofer setting *Erlafsee* was published as a supplement to an almanac – this was the first Schubert song to appear in print. One of the Overtures in Italian style was performed at the Theater an der Wien (the first of his orchestral works to be played in public). Schubert's application to be a member of the Musikverein was rejected. Always short of money, he jumped at the chance to leave Vienna for a summer job at the country house of Count Esterházy (1777–1834) in Zseliz, Hungary (present day Slovakia), as a music teacher

---

[30]*Abschied*: This song was first published in the *Nachlass* as *Abschied von einem Freunde*.
[31]*An den Frühling*: Hilmar has suggested the second version of the song, in B flat major, may date from as late as 1823.
[32]*Die Forelle* is placed earlier in Dürr's chronology, at the end of 1816 or beginning of 1817, thus Dürr307.

The schoolhouse in the Rossau district (now Grünertorgasse, 11) occupied by the Schubert family from 1818 and where the composer spent many unhappy hours as a schoolmaster.

to his two young daughters, the countesses Marie (1802–1837) and Karoline (1805–1851). Schubert taught them daily and composed singing exercises for them to study together. He was there, not altogether happily, from 7 July to 19 November and missed Vienna dreadfully. Nevertheless he met some interesting people of his own age including the singer Karl von Schönstein who would later sing *Die schöne Müllerin* D795. Settings of the poet Aloys Schreiber probably reflect the noble family's religious enthusiasms. On his return to Vienna it is clear that Schubert could not face living in the parental home. Mayrhofer (whose long poem *Einsamkeit* had been set in Zseliz as Schubert's riposte to Beethoven's cycle *An die ferne Geliebte*) offered to let him share his lodgings in the house of Frau Anna Sanssouci in the Wipplingerstrasse. Here Schubert began work on a commission obtained through Vogl for the Kärntnertor Theatre – this was *Die Zwillingsbrüder* D647, a *Singspiel* that cast Vogl in the role of twin brothers. The three large Petrarch settings date from November and December of this year.

See: FRIENDS AND FAMILY: Marie and Karoline Esterházy
           SINGERS: Karl von Schönstein
           Aloys SCHREIBER

DISC 20 continued

H395	*Die Geselligkeit (Lebenslust)* (Unger) D609 quartet, January 1818		**I/718**
H396	*Auf der Riesenkoppe* (Körner) D611, March 1818		**I/254**
H397	*An den Mond in einer Herbstnacht* (Schreiber) D614, April 1818		**I/151**

H398	*Evangelium Johannis* (Bible) D607, spring 1818	**I/541**
H399	*Grablied für die Mutter* (Anonymous) D616, June 1818	**I/774**
H400	*Sing-Übungen* (wordless) D619 duet, July 1818	**III/180**
H401	*Einsamkeit* (Mayrhofer) D620, July 1818	**I/479**
H402	*Der Blumenbrief* (Schreiber) D622, August 1818	**I/317**
H403	*Das Marienbild* (Schreiber) D623, August 1818	**II/307**
H404	*Blondel zu Marien* (Anonymous) D626, September 1818	**I/312**
H405	*Das Abendrot* (Schreiber) D627, November 1818	**I/29**
H406	*Lob der Tränen* (A. von Schlegel) D711, 1818?[33]	**II/253**

DISC 21

H407	*Sonett* (Petrarca) D628, November 1818	**III/220**
H408	*Sonett* (Petrarca) D629, November 1818	**III/223**
H409	*Sonett* (Petrarca) D630, December 1818	**III/226**
H410	*Blanka* (F. von Schlegel) D631, December 1818	**I/306**
H411	*Vom Mitleiden Mariä* (Spee/F. von Schlegel) D632, December 1818	**III/522**
	[*Der Graf von Habsburg* (Schiller) D990, 1818?]	**I/778**
	[*Kaiser Maximillian auf der Martinswand* (H. von Collin) D₂990A, 1818?]	**II/36**

Some other works of 1818: *Adrast*, Singspiel with a text of Mayrhofer (between 1817 and 1819, D137); a large quantity of piano duets – among them Rondo in D (D608); Sonata in B flat (D617), *Deutscher* in G major (D618), Eight Variations on a French song (D624); *Deutsches Requiem* in G minor (D621)

1819 (aged twenty-two) – *19 solo songs* (January to June, October, November)
On 8 January there was a repeat performance of the cantata *Prometheus* under the auspices of a powerful new supporter, Schubert's exact contemporary Leopold von Sonnleithner (1797–1873). The composer completed a *Singspiel, Die Zwillingsbrüder* a short while later (19 February), and on 28 February a higher transposition of *Schäfers Klagelied* (Goethe) was sung by the tenor Franz Jäger, the first Schubert lied to be performed at a public concert. This received a favourable press notice as far away as Berlin and was repeated by Jäger at further concerts on 25 March and 12 April. Schubert was paid a reasonable sum for the new *Singspiel* in June and he went on holiday (early July to mid-September) with Vogl to the singer's home town of Steyr (from where they also visited Linz and Kremsmünster) as a kind of reward. It was during this holiday that the famous 'Trout' quintet for piano and strings was composed (D677) for the amateur cellist Sylvester Paumgartner, as well as the cantata for three voices and piano written in honour of Vogl's birthday (D666). On his return to Vienna the composer lodged once again at the home of Mayrhofer. The writings of the brothers Schlegel (and the poems printed in Tieck's famous *Musenalmanach* of 1802) now played a significant part in Schubert's songs. Friedrich von Schlegel had lived in Vienna for over a decade and may have been in personal contact with the composer at a later date. This was perhaps the most 'philosophical' phase in Schubert's song-composing career – a period that shows him attracted by pantheism among other alternatives to conventional religion. The year's work included some of his settings from Friedrich von Schlegel's *Abendröte* cycle, the four hymns of Novalis and some of the more profound Mayrhofer texts. Such important settings as Goethe's *Prometheus* D674 and Schiller's *Strophe aus 'Die*

---

[33]*Lob der Tränen*: Dürr places this at the beginning of 1818, thus Dürr368. Reed places the song in the first half of 1818.

Lithograph of Steyr (first visited by Schubert in 1819) by Johann Maximillian Kolb.

Lithograph by Vinzenz Katzler of the monastery of Kremsmünster.

Götter Griechenlands' D677, show a continuing interest in classical mythology. More than at any other time the depth and seriousness of Mayrhofer's literary tastes were strongly reflected in the settings of his musical protégé.

See: FRIENDS AND FAMILY: Leopold von Sonnleithner
NOVALIS
August von SCHLEGEL
Friedrich von SCHLEGEL
Ludwig TIECK

DISC 21 continued

H412	*Hoffnung* (Schiller) second setting D637, *c.* 1819 [*see* first setting H136][34]	**I/907**
H413	*Widerschein* (Schlechta) D639, *c.* 1819[35]	**III/580**
H414	*Abend* (Tieck) D645 fragment, early 1819	**I/5**
H415	*Die Berge* (F. von Schlegel) D634, *c.* 1819[36]	**I/293**
H416	*Die Gebüsche* (F. von Schlegel) D646, January 1819	**I/647**
H417	*Der Wanderer* (F. von Schlegel) D649, February 1819	**III/544**
H418	*Der Schmetterling* (F. von Schlegel) D633, *c.* 1819[37]	**II/780**
H418a	*Schäfers Klagelied* (Goethe), second version in E minor D121, February 1819(?) [*see* first version H51]	**II/720**
H419	*Abendbilder* (Silbert) D650, February 1819	**I/8**
H420	*Himmelsfunken* (Silbert) D651, February 1819	**I/879**
H421	*Das Mädchen* (F. von Schlegel) D652, February 1819	**II/281**
H422	*Bertas Lied in der Nacht* (Grillparzer) D653, February 1819	**I/297**
H423	*An die Freunde* (Mayrhofer) D654, March 1819	**I/164**
H424	*Der Jüngling am Bache* (Schiller) third setting D638, April 1819 [*see* first setting H12, second setting H93]	**II/20**
H424+	*Sehnsucht (Mignon)* (Goethe) fourth setting, choral D656, April 1819 [*see* first setting H190 and 190a, second setting H211, third setting H298, fifth setting H585 and sixth setting H588]	**III/107**
H425	*Geistliches Lied ('Marie')* (Novalis) D658, May(?) 1819[38]	**I/678**

DISC 22

H426	*Hymne* (Novalis) D659, May 1819	**I/910**
H427	*Geistliches Lied* (Wenn ich ihn nur habe) (Novalis) D660, May 1819[39]	**I/680**
H428	*Geistliches Lied* (Wenn alle untreu werden) (Novalis) D661, May 1819	**I/682**
H429	*Geistliches Lied* (Ich sag es jedem, dass er lebt) (Novalis) D662, May 1819	**I/684**
H430	*Der 13. Psalm* (Bible/Mendelssohn) D663 fragment, June 1819	**II/591**
H431	*Cantate zum Geburtstag des Sängers Johann Michael Vogl* (Stadler), D666 trio, before 10 August 1819	**I/339**

[34]*Hoffnung* (Schiller): Reed suggests this song might have been composed in 1817.
[35]*Widerschein*: Dürr places this song later, 'before 13 September 1820', suggesting March 1820 (Dürr419). Schubert revised the song again for publication in 1828 and it is sometimes erroneously dated in that year as a result.
[36]*Die Berge*: John Reed conjectures that this song was written in March 1820.
[37]*Der Schmetterling*: Dürr places this song about a year later in March 1820, thus Dürr633.
[38]*Geistliches Lied*: The AGA published this song as *Mariä*.
[39]The AGA published the three *Geistliche Lieder* D660–62 as *Hymne II, III* and *IV* (in AGA *Hymne* D659 is entitled *Hymne I*).

H432	*Beim Winde* (Mayrhofer) D669, October 1819	**I/287**
H433	*Die Sternennächte* (Mayrhofer) D670, October 1819	**III/261**
H434	*Trost* (Mayrhofer) D671, October 1819	**III/414**
H435	*Die Liebende schreibt* (Goethe) D673, October 1819	**II/188**
H436	*Prometheus* (Goethe) D674, October 1819	**II/581**
H437	*Nachtstück* (Mayrhofer) D672, October 1819	**II/435**
H438	*Strophe aus 'Die Götter Griechenlands'* (Schiller) D677, November 1819	**III/276**

Some other works of 1819: Overture in E minor (D648); Sonata in A major (D664); *Salve Regina* in A major (D676); Mass in A flat (D678)

1820 (aged twenty-three) – *20 solo songs* (January to April, October, November, December) The 'philosophical' period continued in terms of the selection of song texts, but Schubert was not as prolific in 1820 as in some other years. What he did compose, however, showed him at his most experimental and daring. From January came *Nachthymne* of Novalis (D687), as well as the completely different set of four Italian *Canzone* (D688). There could be no better illustration of the composer's ability to write in either his German or Italian styles at will. The oratorio *Lazarus* (D689) was written in February, as groundbreaking and 'modern' a work as Schubert was ever to compose – although he failed to complete it. In March he was involved in a disturbing episode with the police who raided the rooms of the poet Johann Senn and arrested him for questioning, together with Franz von Bruchmann and the composer himself. (Schubert was let off without charge, but Senn was jailed for two months and subsequently exiled to the Tyrol.) In the same month Schubert continued to work on poems from Schlegel's *Abendröte*. His Overture in E minor was performed in Graz in April. This marked the first public performance of his work outside Vienna. On 14 June *Die Zwillingsbrüder*, the *Singspiel* written with a double-starring role for Vogl, had its first night at the Kärntnertortheater and ran for six performances. In July the composer and his friends visited Atzenbrugg outside Vienna for musical parties. On 19 August the *Singspiel*, *Die Zauberharfe* (text by Georg von Hofmann) was produced at the Theater an der Wien (eight performances in 1820 and 1821). In September Schubert returned once more to the poetry of his old schoolfriend Franz von Schlechta, and he also set a solitary song by Ludwig Uhland (his only bow in the direction of a poet he thought the preserve of his admired song-composing contemporary Conradin Kreutzer). Three of the grandest of the Mayrhofer songs were written between September and December 1820, and in November he completed a single setting of Heinrich Hüttenbrenner, but the autumn of this year was one of the composer's least active from the point of view of numbers of works composed. At the end of the year (1 December) August von Gymnich sang *Erlkönig* at a soirée at Sonnleithner's. Some five years after the song's composition it brought down the house, and a group of friends resolved to have it published, together with a selection of Schubert's other lieder. In the end a private arrangement was made with the publishing firm Cappi & Diabelli to issue Opp. 1 to 7 and 12 'on commission'. These printed copies appeared in 1821. This spared the publisher any cost or risk, although the wily Anton Diabelli eventually cottoned on to his best interests, persuading the composer, woefully inexperienced in business matters, to sell back the copyright in 1822. Diabelli thus made a fortune from publishing Schubert's music right up to 1850. At the end of the year Schubert moved out of Mayrhofer's room; the intensity of the poet's inflexible and idealistic nature seems to have precipitated something of an estrangement. For a few months Schubert, relishing his new freedom, took up residence at Wipplingerstrassse 21, very near his former lodgings with the poet.

See: COMPOSERS: Conradin Kreutzer
          OPUS NUMBERS
          PUBLISHERS: Cappi & Diabelli
          SINGERS: August von Gymnich
          Franz von BRUCHMANN
          Heinrich HÜTTENBRENNER
          Franz von SCHLECHTA
          Friedrich von SCHLEGEL
          Johann SENN
          Ludwig UHLAND

DISC 22 continued

H439	*Über allen Zauber Liebe* (Mayrhofer) D682 fragment, *c.* 1820[40]	**III/423**
H440	*Die Sterne* (F. von Schlegel) D684, 1820[41]	**III/253**
H441	*Morgenlied* (Werner) D685, 1820	**II/383**
H442	*Nachthymne* (Novalis) D687, January 1820	**II/429**

DISC 23

	Vier Canzonen	**III/489**
H443	*Non t'accostar all'urna* (Vittorelli) D688/1, January 1820	**III/490**
H444	*Guarda, che bianca luna!* (Vittorelli) D688/2, January 1820	**III/491**
H445	*Da quel sembiante appresi* (Metastasio) D688/3, January 1820	**III/493**
H446	*Mio ben ricordati* (Metastasio) D688/4, January 1820	**III/494**
H447	*Die Vögel* (F. von Schlegel) D691, March 1820	**III/518**
H448	*Der Fluss* (F. von Schlegel) D693, March 1820	**I/575**
H449	*Der Knabe* (F. von Schlegel) D692, March 1820	**II/71**
H450	*Der Schiffer* (F. von Schlegel) D694, March 1820	**II/739**
H451	*Namenstagslied* (Stadler) D695, March 1820	**II/447**
H452	*Des Fräuleins Liebeslauschen* (Schlechta) D698, September 1820[42]	**I/584**
H453	*Der entsühnte Orest* (Mayrhofer) D699, September 1820	**I/500**
H454	*Freiwilliges Versinken* (Mayrhofer) D700, September 1820[43]	**I/592**
H455	*Frühlingsglaube* (Uhland) D686, September 1820	**I/623**
H456	*Der Jüngling auf dem Hügel* (Hüttenbrenner) D702, November 1820	**II/24**
H457	*Im Walde* (F. von Schlegel) D708, December 1820[44]	**I/941**
H458	*Der zürnenden Diana* (Mayrhofer) D707, December 1820	**III/747**
H459	*Gesang der Geister über den Wassern* (Goethe) third setting, D705 choral, fragment, December 1820 [*see* first Setting H307]	**I/713**

DISC 24

H460	*Der 23. Psalm* (Bible/Mendelssohn) D706 quartet, December 1820	**II/593**
H460+	*Im Walde* (F. von Schlegel) D708, December 1820 [alternative performance, *see* H457]	**I/941**

Some other works of 1820: *Sakuntala*, opera in 3 acts (Neumann) for which only sketches remain; Six Ecossaises in A flat for piano (D697)

[40]*Über allen Zauber Liebe*: Both Reed and Winter favour the autumn of 1819 as a date, whereas Walther Dürr places this song at the end of 1820, thus Dürr439.
[41]*Die Sterne*: Reed points out that this song could also possibly have been composed in 1819.
[42]*Des Fräuleins Liebeslauschen*: This song was published in the *Nachlass* simply as *Liebeslauschen*.
[43]*Freiwilliges Versinken*: Both Maurice Brown and John Reed place this song in 1817 together with other lieder with subjects from Greek antiquity. Dürr is tempted by the 1817 conjecture, but comes down in favour of 1820 (see NSA Series IV Volume 12 pp. XXV–XXVI).
[44]*Im Walde*: This song was published in the *Nachlass* as *Waldesnacht*.

1821 (aged twenty-four) – *15 solo songs* (January to April, September)
In January 1821 a musical review by Ignaz Castelli in a Dresden newspaper had spoken of the Schubert songs as 'not yet printed, and only available in copies that go from hand to hand'. The appearance of Schubert songs in print would soon change all that; 1821 was a year of changes, some for the better, some for the worse. In January Schubert put himself forward as a coach at the Kärntnertortheater but proved unsuited to the post in terms of aptitude and reliability. This in itself was a sign of a suddenly different and more carefree lifestyle – if Schubert had still been living with Mayrhofer he might have fulfilled his contractual obligations. At the end of the same month Schober gave a party at which Schubert's songs were sung. This is usually reckoned to have been the first real Schubertiad. In this year Schubert became a member of the Gesellschaft der Musikfremde. From now on their programmes advertised performances of Schubert's works – solo songs, part-songs, orchestral works – with reasonable regularity. In February *Erlkönig* Op. 1 appeared in print at last and a concert was arranged where some hundred copies of the song were sold to members of the public, thus covering the costs of the next issue, *Gretchen am Spinnrade* Op. 2. Another public performance in March of *Erlkönig* (sung by Vogl accompanied by Anselm Hüttenbrenner) at the Kärntnertortheatre was a sensation and marked the beginning of the composer's fame with the general public. Other items on the programme were the male vocal quartet *Das Dörfchen* (well received) and the second setting of Goethe's *Gesang der Geister* for voice and low strings (unfavourably reviewed). In terms of solo songs, 1820 had been a Goethe-free year. Schubert's return to his most revered poet comprised eight solo settings (nine if *Suleika II* was also written in 1821) that included lyrics from the recently published *West-östlicher Divan* (the composer did not realize – and neither did anyone else – that the *Suleika* poems are really by Marianne von Willemer). There were also fresh attempts at *Wilhelm Meister* poems, and the definitive solo version of *Grenzen der Menschheit* D716. In June, Hérold's opera *Das Zauberglöckchen* was produced at the Kärntnertortheater with two extra numbers by Schubert. In July the Schubertians repaired to Atzenbrugg for musical fun and games that were immortalized in drawings by Leopold Kupelwieser. The autumn occasioned a month-long withdrawal from Vienna to St Pölten so that Schubert and his librettist Franz von Schober could work on the new opera they planned to write together, *Alfonso und Estrella* D732. This large task, condemned as a waste of time by Vogl, occupied Schubert almost exclusively until he finished the third act in February 1822.

See: ALFONSO UND ESTRELLA
          WEST-ÖSTLICHER DIVAN
          Marianne von WILLEMER

DISC 24 continued

H461	*Sehnsucht* (Schiller) second setting D636, beginning? of 1821 [*see* first setting H23]	**III/96**
H462	*Die gefangenen Sänger* (A. von Schlegel) D712, January 1821	**I/650**
H463	*Die Nacht* (Pichler) not in Deutsch, first setting of 'Der Unglückliche', before 1821	**II/410**
H464	*Der Unglückliche* (Pichler) D713, January 1821	**III/438**
H465	*Versunken* (Goethe) D715, February 1821	**III/483**
H466	*Grenzen der Menschheit* (Goethe) D716, March 1821	**I/788**
H467	*Geheimes* (Goethe) D719, March 1821	**I/654**
H468	*Suleika I* (Willemer/Goethe) D720, March 1821	**III/283**
H469	*Suleika II* (Willemer/Goethe) D717, March 1821(?)[45]	**III/287**

[45]*Suleika II*: It is very possible that the second Suleika song was only composed in 1824 as a result of the composer's contact with the famous soprano Anna Milder-Hauptmann. Dürr, on the other hand, places both Suleikas in 1821 with *Suleika II* (Dürr432) composed before *Suleika I* (Dürr435).

Ball games at Atzenbrugg, 1821, lithograph after a drawing by Franz von Schober. Schubert is to the right of the group in the foreground while Vogl, in the hat, sits next to him. Moritz von Schwind is standing and playing the violin.

Engraving of St Pölten where Schubert and Schober worked together on the opera *Alfonso und Estrella* D732.

H470	*Im Gegenwärtigen Vergangenes* (Goethe) D710 tenor and male chorus, March 1821	**I/933**
H471	*Mahomets Gesang* (Goethe) second setting D721 fragment, March 1821 [*see* first setting H358]	**II/300**
	[*Linde Weste wehen* (Anonymous) D725 duet, fragment, April 1821]	**II/252**
H472	*Mignon I* ('Heiss mich nicht reden') (Goethe) first setting D726, April 1821 [*see* second setting H586]	**II/350**
H473	*Mignon II* ('So lasst mich scheinen, bis ich werde') (Goethe) third setting D727, April 1821 [*see* first and second settings H296 and H297, fourth setting H587]	**II/352**
H474	*Die Nachtigall* (Unger) D724 quartet, by April 1821	**II/433**

DISC 25

H475	*Johanna Sebus* (Goethe) D728 fragment, April 1821	**II/13**
H476	*Der Blumen Schmerz* (Mailáth) D731, September 1821	**I/314**
	[*Doch im Getümmel der Schlacht* (Schober) D732/8 Aria from *Alfonso und Estrella*, arr. with piano by Schubert (late 1821–2)]	**I/76**
	[*Wenn ich dich, Holde, sehe* (Schober) D732/13 Aria from *Alfonso und Estrella*, arr. with piano by Schubert (late 1821–2)]	**I/78**

Some other works of 1821–2: sketches for a large Symphony in E major (D729); Three Marches Militaires for piano duet (D733); *Tantum ergo* in C D739.

1822 (aged twenty-five) – *33 solo songs* (January, March, April, May, October, November, December)

On 21 January Schubert made a new friend in the person of Eduard von Bauernfeld, one of a new generation of younger Schubertians that also numbered the talented painter Moritz von Schwind. Later in the year the Bavarian Franz Lachner, who was to become a prolific song composer, moved to Vienna; in time he also became one of Schubert's closest younger friends and colleagues, associated particularly with discussions about, and performances of, Schubert's chamber music. Living again in new lodgings with Schober (Göttweiger Hof, Spiegelgasse, 9), the composer was now a regular member at some of the important Viennese salons (where he was in contact with such important luminaries as Matthäus von Collin). On 23 March there was a long and favourable article about his song output in the *Wiener Zeitschrift für Kunst, Literatur, Theater und Mode*. With his new-found confidence Schubert broke with the publisher Diabelli (at least for a while) and moved to Sauer & Leidesdorf, a firm that was bedevilled by financial problems and inefficiency. His friend Franz von Bruchmann returned from a Bavarian visit where he had attended the lectures of Schelling in Erlangen (such journeys were forbidden to students by the Austrian authorities) and where he had spent time in the company of the poet August, Graf von Platen. Schubert received Platen's poems from Bruchmann's hands apparently with the aristocratic poet's express wish that he should set them to music. The composer set two of these poems and a number by Schober at this time, as well as poems by Bruchmann himself, and by Bruchmann's close friend, the exiled Johann Senn. It was a major blow that the Court Opera, biased towards the vogue for Italian repertory, turned down the new opera, *Alfonso und Estrella* (D732). In October Schubert returned dejected to the schoolhouse in the Rossau. On 1 December the eleven-year-old Liszt gave his first public concert in Vienna. Schubert was almost certainly unaware of the beginning of the career of one of his greatest future proselytizers. In the same month he composed four of his most inspired Goethe settings as well as seeing the three *Gesänge des Harfners* through the press as his Op. 12. It is all too probable that in experiencing the first symptoms of syphilis (from December 1822 or, at the latest, in January 1823) Schubert shared the desperate and bitter mood of Goethe's Harper. In the previous two years Schubert had enjoyed his independence, but it seems likely that he had also been over-susceptible to the influence of free-living friends, above all that of Franz von Schober.

See: COMPOSERS: Franz Lachner
FRIENDS AND FAMILY: Eduard von Bauernfeld, Moritz von Schwind
PUBLISHERS: Sauer & Leidesdorf
Franz von BRUCHMANN
August von PLATEN

DISC 25 continued

H477	*Die Rose* (F. von Schlegel) D745, early 1822 [before May]	**II/677**
H478	*Ihr Grab* (Engelhardt) D736, 1822(?)	**I/921**
H479	*Der Wachtelschlag* (Sauter) D742, 1822?	**III/531**
H480	*Naturgenuss* (Matthisson) second setting D422 quartet, 1822(?) [*see* first setting H90]	**II/450**
H481	*Geist der Liebe* (Matthisson) second setting D747 quartet, January 1822 [*see* first setting H252]	**I/667**
H482	*Herrn Josef Spaun, Assessor in Linz* (M. von Collin) D749, January 1822	**I/876**
H483	*Frühlingsgesang* (Schober) D740 quartet, January–April 1822	**I/620**
H484	*Nachtviolen* (Mayrhofer) D752 April 1822	**II/439**
H485	*Heliopolis I* (Mayrhofer) D753, April 1822	**I/855**
H486	*Heliopolis II* (Mayrhofer) D754, April 1822	**I/857**
H487	*Die Liebe hat gelogen* (Platen) D751, before 17 April 1822	**II/182**
H488	*Du liebst mich nicht* (Platen) D756, July 1822	**I/451**
H489	*Gott in der Natur* (Kleist) D757 quartet, August 1822	**I/759**
H490	*Schwanengesang* (Senn) D744, Autumn 1822?	**III/1**
H491	*Selige Welt* (Senn) D743, Autumn? 1822	**III/126**
	Gesänge des Harfners Op. 12	**I/698**
H492	*Wer sich der Einsamkeit ergibt* (Goethe) second setting D₂478/1, 1816 revised for publication in 1822 [*see* first setting H203]	**I/699**
H493	*Wer nie sein Brot mit Tränen ass* (Goethe) second setting D₂478/2, September 1822 [*see* two versions of first setting H304 and H304a]	**I/702**
H494	*An die Türen will ich schleichen* (Goethe) D₂478/3, 1816 revised for publication in 1822	**I/704**
H495	*Sei mir gegrüsst!* (Rückert) D741, between end of 1821 and autumn 1822	**III/115**

DISC 26

H496	*Todesmusik* (Schober) D758, September 1822	**III/348**
H497	*Schatzgräbers Begehr* (Schober) D761, November 1822	**II/731**
H498	*Schwestergruss* (Bruchmann) D762, November 1822	**III/81**
H499	*Schicksalslenker, blicke nieder (Des Tages Weihe)* (Anonymous) D763 quartet, 22 November 1822	**II/734**
H500	*An die Entfernte* (Goethe) D765, December 1822	**I/160**

H501	*Der Musensohn* (Goethe) D764, December 1822	**II/398**
H502	*Am Flusse* (Goethe) second setting D766, December 1822 [*see* first setting H68]	**I/109**
H503	*Willkommen und Abschied* (Goethe) first version in D major D767, December 1822	**III/604**
H503a	*Willkommen und Abschied* (Goethe) second version in C major D767, December 1822[46]	**III/604**
H504	*Am See* (Bruchmann) D746, 1822–3[47]	**I/117**
H505	*Im Haine* (Bruchmann) D738, 1822 or 1823	**I/937**
H506	*An die Leier* (Bruchmann after Anacreon) D737, winter 1822/3(?)	**I/172**
H507	*Der Zwerg* (M. von Collin) D771, 1822 or 1823[48]	**III/770**
H508	*Nacht und Träume* (M. von Collin) D827, 1822 or 1823[49]	**II/419**
H509	*Wehmut* (M. von Collin) D772, 1822 or early 1823[50]	**III/559**
H509+	*'Ich schleiche bang und still herum', 'Romanze'* of Helene from the Singspiel *Die Verschworenen* (Castelli) D787/2, late 1822–3	**III/481**

Some other works of 1822: Sixteen Ländler and Two Ecossaises for piano (D734); Symphony no. 7 ('The Unfinished' – D759); Fantasy in C major for piano ('The Wanderer Fantasy' – D760).

1823 (aged twenty-six) – *29 solo songs* (January, March, April, May, October, November)
The next two years, spent in the shadow of a terrifying illness, were a roller coaster of fear and unhappiness. At the beginning of 1823 Schubert felt extremely unwell and kept to his room; he was unable to accept a commission for a male-voice quartet for the Musikverein. He was proposed as an honorary member of the Musikverein in Graz, an indication of his burgeoning fame. The composer's poem *Mein Gebet* ('My Prayer', 8 May 1823) reveals a deeply depressed, perhaps even suicidal, state of mind; it could be no help that he was forced to endure his confinement at home in the Rossau where his father was probably horrified by the nature of his illness – if he indeed ever knew all the details. *Die Verschworenen* (The Conspirators), a *Singspiel* with a text by Ignaz Castelli, D787 is a light-hearted work about the impracticability of sexual abstinence, and was completed by April. Because of censorship the title had to be changed to *Der häusliche Krieg* – The Domestic War. Schubert began work on the grand opera *Fierabras* (text by Josef Kupelwieser) in May, and Act Two was complete by 5 June. The appearance in 1822 of Friedrich Rückert's collection of poetry entitled *Östliche Rosen* (inspired by Goethe's *West-östlicher Divan*) gave rise to five of Schubert's finest songs. He found temporary refuge at the home of his friend Josef Huber (at Stubenbastei, 14).

At about this time he spent a number of weeks in hospital in an era when treatment for syphilis was very limited in its efficacy, and painful to endure.[51] It was in hospital that he is said to have begun composing his song cycle *Die schöne Müllerin* D795. The composer left Vienna in mid-July and went to recuperate in his beloved Linz and Steyr until mid-September.

---

[46] The second (C major) version of *Willkommen und Abschied* was prepared for publication in July 1826.
[47] *Am See* (Bruchmann) and two other Bruchmann settings (H504–6): Certain scholars place these songs much earlier in the chronology (between October 1819 and March 1821).
[48] *Der Zwerg*: Dürr places this song at the beginning of 1822 rather than at the end of the same year (Dürr447).
[49] *Nacht und Träume*: Dürr places this song in 1823 just before *Die schöne Müllerin* (Dürr480).
[50] *Wehmut*: Dürr places this song at the beginning of 1822 rather than at the end of the same year (Dürr446). Reed thinks it more likely that the song dates from November 1822 at the same time as *Der Zwerg*.
[51] The exact timing of Schubert's hospitalization is contested: Walther Dürr places it in the autumn of 1823, thus after the holiday in Steyr.

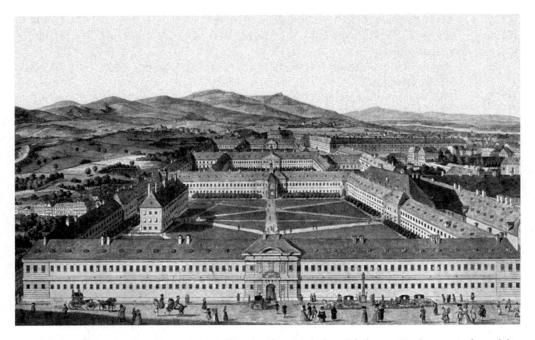

The Allgemeines Krankenhaus (General Hospital) in the Alsergrund where Schubert received treatment for syphilis in 1823.

In the meantime, precisely when Schubert might have wished to rely on his moral support, Schober had left Vienna to pursue unrealistic dreams of an acting career in Breslau, remaining there for the following two years. The composer continued work on *Fierabras* (D796) and Act Three was finished by the end of the month. He returned to Vienna and continued work on his Müller song cycle. At the end of October he met Weber and was blunt regarding the relative merits of the masterpiece *Der Freischütz* and the weaker (in his opinion) opera *Euryanthe*. This frankness no doubt had a negative effect on Weber's willingness to support a staging of *Alfonso und Estrella* in Dresden. At the end of the year Schubert wrote successful incidental music for Helmina von Chézy's play *Rosamunde, Fürstin von Zypern* D797, although the work as a whole was badly received by the critics (Chézy was also librettist of Weber's *Euryanthe*). An added burden for the composer was that his circle of friends was in decline, some of them getting married or moving away. The only positive outcome for posterity was the number of informative letters that were written as a result of this dispersal. A complete edition of these is in preparation by Till Gerrit Waidelich. At the tender age of twenty-six Schubert looked back with nostalgia on the golden era of his youth before all his hopes had withered. The poem of Schober's ballad *Viola* (D786) seems descriptive of his own plight, but fortunately he was spared the self-destruction of the miller boy in *Die schöne Müllerin* who drowns himself – almost in Schubert's stead, as it were.

See: FRIENDS AND FAMILY: Josef Huber
       COMPOSERS: Carl Maria von Weber
       Helmina von CHÉZY
       ROSAMUNDE, FÜRSTIN VON ZYPERN
       Friedrich RÜCKERT
       Franz von SCHOBER
       Franz SCHUBERT, the composer as poet

DISC 26 continued

H510	*Drang in die Ferne* (Leitner) D770, early 1823	**I/431**
H511	*Der zürnende Barde* (Bruchmann) D785, February 1823	**III/744**
H512	*Abendröte* (F. von Schlegel) D690, March 1823[52]	**I/25**

DISC 27

H513	*Viola* (Schober) D786, March 1823	**III/510**
H514	*Lied* (Des Lebens Tag ist schwer) *('Die Mutter Erde')* (Stolberg) D788, April 1823	**II/203**
H515	*Pilgerweise* (Schober) D789, April 1823	**II/547**
H516	*Vergissmeinnicht* (Schober) D792, May 1823	**III/473**
H517	*Das Geheimnis* (Schiller) second setting D793, May 1823 [*see* first setting H135]	**I/659**
H518	*Der Pilgrim* (Schiller) D794, May 1823	**II/552**
H519	*Auf dem Wasser zu singen* (Stolberg) D774, 1823	**I/239**
H520	*Dass sie hier gewesen* (Rückert) D775, 1823(?)[53]	**I/401**
H521	*Lachen und Weinen* (Rückert) D777, 1823(?)	**II/109**
H522	*Greisengesang* (Rückert) D778, by June 1823[54]	**I/873**
H523	*Du bist die Ruh* (Rückert) D776, 1823	**I/447**
H524	*Die Wallfahrt* (Rückert) D778A, 1823(?) (Sketch)	**III/537**
	[*Der 8. Psalm* (Bible/Mendelssohn) D Anhang II, 4; music by Abbé Stadler arranged Schubert [Steyr?], 29 August 1823]	**II/589**
H525	*Romanze (Ariette)* from *Rosamunde* (Chézy) D797/3B, autumn 1823	**II/672**
	[*Geisterchor* 'In der Tiefe wohnt das Licht' from *Rosamunde* (Chézy) D797/4 choral, TTBB with piano, autumn 1823]	**II/673**
	[*Hirtenchor* 'Hier auf den Fluren' from *Rosamunde* (Chézy) D797/7 choral, SATB with piano, autumn 1823]	**II/674**
	[*Jägerchor* 'Wie lebt sichs so fröhlich' from *Rosamunde* (Chézy) D797/8 choral, SATB with piano, autumn 1823]	**II/676**

DISC 28

	Die schöne Müllerin Op. 25	**II/799**
H525+	Der Dichter, als Prolog (Müller) reading	**II/805**
H526	*Das Wandern* (Müller) D795/1, completed by October–November 1823	**II/807**
H527	*Wohin?* (Müller) D795/2, completed by October–November 1823	**II/811**
H528	*Halt!* (Müller) D795/3, completed by October–November 1823	**II/815**
H529	*Danksagung an den Bach* (Müller) D795/4, completed by October–November 1823	**II/818**
H530	*Am Feierabend* (Müller) D795/5, completed by October–November 1823	**II/821**
H531	*Der Neugierige* (Müller) D795/6, completed by October–November 1823	**II/824**
H531+	Das Mühlenleben (Müller) reading	**II/828**
H532	*Ungeduld* (Müller) D795/7, completed by October–November 1823	**II/829**
H533	*Morgengruss* (Müller) D795/8, completed by October–November 1823	**II/833**

[52]*Abendröte*: March 1823 is the date of the fair copy of the autograph of this song, but it is possible that it was composed earlier – as early in fact as 1820.

[53]*Dass sie hier gewesen* and four other Rückert settings (H520–24): Dürr places all these song earlier in 1823.

[54]*Greisengesang*: John Reed suggests the autumn of 1822 as a possible date for this song.

H534	*Des Müllers Blumen* (Müller) D795/9, completed by October–November 1823	**II/836**
H535	*Tränenregen* (Müller) D795/10, completed by October–November 1823	**II/839**
H535+	Ein ungereimtes Lied (Müller) reading	**II/843**
H536	*Mein!* (Müller) D795/11, completed by October–November 1823	**II/844**
H537	*Pause* (Müller) D795/12, completed by October–November 1823	**II/847**
H538	*Mit dem grünen Lautenbande* (Müller) D795/13, completed by October–November 1823	**II/851**
H539	*Der Jäger* (Müller) D795/14, completed by October–November 1823	**II/854**
H540	*Eifersucht und Stolz* (Müller) D795/15, completed by October–November 1823	**II/856**
H540+	Erster Schmerz, letzter Scherz (Müller) reading	**II/860**
H541	*Die liebe Farbe* (Müller) D795/16, completed by October–November 1823	**II/861**
H542	*Die böse Farbe* (Müller) D795/17, completed by October–November 1823	**II/864**
H542+	Blümlein Vergissmein (Müller) reading	**II/867**
H543	*Trockne Blumen* (Müller) D795/18, completed by October–November 1823	**II/869**
H544	*Der Müller und der Bach* (Müller) D795/19, completed by October–November 1823	**II/872**
H545	*Des Baches Wiegenlied* (Müller) D795/20, completed by October–November 1823	**II/877**
H545+	Der Dichter, als Epilog (Müller) reading	**II/882**

Some other works of 1823: Thirty-four 'Valses sentimentales' for piano (D779); *Moments musicaux* for piano (D780 no. 3); Zwölf Ecossaises for piano (D781); 16 Deutsche and two Ecossaises for piano (D783); Piano Sonata in A minor (D784)

1824 (aged twenty-seven) – *6 solo songs* (March, June, December)

This was the least prolific of the composer's years in terms of song, although it contains such uncontested masterpieces as *Abendstern*, *Auflösung* and *Wandrers Nachtlied II*. Schubert continued to have trouble with his health and no doubt suffered from the cure as well as the illness – he had to consume quantities of mercury that had a toxic effect on him. There were five remarkable settings composed in March, all inspired by the publication of Mayrhofer's privately printed *Gedichte*. At this point any breach between composer and poet seems to have been already repaired, though there was no return to their former intimacy. At the end of March Schubert wrote a desperate letter to his friend the painter, Leopold Kupelwieser (who was studying in Rome) and lamented that, like Goethe's Gretchen, he had lost his peace of mind for ever more. He remained ambitious, however, to write a grand symphony and he intended to approach this goal through chamber music. In the same month (27 March) he wrote in a diary entry (one of the few surviving such): 'There is no one who understands the pain or the joy of others! We always imagine we are coming together, and we always merely go side by side. Oh, what torture for those who recognize this.' He was clearly lonely in the absence from Vienna of such close friends as Schober and Kupelwieser. Schubert heard the first performance on 7 May of movements from Beethoven's Choral Symphony, and parts of the *Missa Solemnis*. The summer

Schloss Zseliz, country seat of the Esterházy family. Schubert worked there for the summers of 1818 and 1824, although he was only accommodated as a guest in the house itself for his second visit. Photograph *c.* 1905.

The Music Room in Schloss Zseliz, photograph *c.* 1905.

Schubert's room in Schloss Zseliz, water colour by Franz Seligmann, 1897.

marked his second sojourn at Zseliz, the large country house which was the summer seat of Count Esterházy and his family. He stayed there from May until the middle of October. By this time the Countess Karoline was nineteen years old (she had only been thirteen at Schubert's previous visit) and she had matured into a willowy, if not exactly beautiful, young lady with a gift for playing the piano. The composer was clearly drawn to Karoline and wrote some magnificent four-handed works to play with her. She was the kind of ideal, an unattainable version of Beethoven's 'immortal beloved', whom the lonely Schubert might have fantasized about marrying. Even in the age of Beethoven, a composer who regarded artists as aristocracy in their own right, the disparities between a musician and a countess made any such thoughts wildly unrealistic. As before the amateur singer Baron von Schönstein was a genial house guest at Zseliz, and Schubert returned to Vienna in his coach. The composer's illness manifested itself again and he dragged himself back to the schoolhouse in the Rossau where his family looked after him. He stayed there until February 1825. The year 1824 had been a busy one in terms of chamber music and piano duets, but Schubert's vocal output, apart from a single immortal Goethe setting, is confined to the Mayrhofer songs and to a Fouqué setting, the quartet *Gebet*, which he wrote for the Esterházys to sing *en famille*. *Lied eines Kriegers* to an anonymous text was written for New Year's Eve; this swells the number of songs in 1824 to a grand total of eight.

Disc 29

H546	*Abendstern* (Mayrhofer) D806, March 1824	**I/37**
H547	*Der Sieg* (Mayrhofer) D805, March 1824	**III/175**
H548	*Auflösung* (Mayrhofer) D807, March 1824	**I/260**
H549	*Gondelfahrer* (Mayrhofer) first setting D808, March 1824	**I/748**
H550	*Gondelfahrer* (Mayrhofer) second setting D809 quartet, March 1824	**I/750**

H551	*Wandrers Nachtlied II* (Goethe) D768, before July 1824	**III/554**
H552	*Gebet* ('Du Urquell aller Güte') (de la Motte Fouqué) D815 quartet, September 1824	**I/641**
H553	*Lied eines Kriegers* (Anonymous) D822 solo with men's chorus, 31 December 1824	**II/226**

Some other works of 1824: Variations in E minor for flute and piano (on the song '*Trockne Blumen*') (D802); Octet in F for winds, horn and strings (D803); String Quartet in A minor (D804); String Quartet in D minor ('Death and the Maiden') (D810); *Salve regina* in C (D811); Sonata in C for piano duet ('Grand Duo') (D812); Eight Variations on an original theme in A flat for piano duet (D814); *Divertissement à l'hongroise* for piano duet (D818); Six Grandes Marches for piano duet (D819); Sonata in A minor for arpeggione and piano (D821)

1825 (aged twenty-eight) – *25 solo songs* (January to April, August, September, December)
This year began with the composer once again in poor spirits – and little wonder. At this time the prognosis for syphilis was appalling: unless another fatal illness intervened before the tertiary stage, as turned out to be the case with Schubert, a terrible death was likely (although the doctors of the time seem to have had enormous confidence in their 'cures', giving their patients unreasonable grounds for hope). The exact manner, and timing, of a total disintegration of health remained an arbitrarily suspended Damoclesian sword as far as the sufferer was concerned. In January of this year he may have spent a period in hospital occasioned by some kind of relapse in his illness. The solitary Schubert failed to muster for himself the philosophical jollity of the protagonist of *Der Einsame* D800, the first of two Lappe settings, but he always responded to any poem with an openness worthy of Keats's negative capability. In this way he also found the calm mood necessary for *Im Abendrot* D799, somehow producing a musical landscape that describes perfectly the glorious sunsets seen from Lappe's home on the island of Rügen – which of course the composer had never seen for himself. This is but one example of his almost supernatural musical empathy with the various backgrounds of his many poets. New song enthusiasms of 1825 included Walter Scott (whom Schubert had first read in 1823) as well as the vivid, if overblown, tableaux of Craigher de Jachelutta. In the two settings of this poet, great songs both, Schubert demonstrates beyond dispute his ability to turn base metal into gold. The composer clearly regarded Craigher as worthy of notice because of his business flair and an ability to translate into several languages – there was talk of multi-language editions of songs that would increase their appeal in countries like England and Italy. The intensification of the friendship between Schubert, Bauernfeld and the gifted young painter Moritz von Schwind (both members of the new wave of Schubertians) encouraged the composer to lodge in the suburb of Wieden, next door to the Schwind family residence (today Technikerstrasse 9). As for the older 'first generation' Schubertians, another of Schlechta's poems was set to music in February, and in March it was revealed that Schober had been secretly engaged to Bruchmann's sister. This caused an open breach between factions in the circle. Schubert, as ever, stayed loyal to Schober but the alienation from Bruchmann was permanent.

In mid-May Schubert left Vienna to join Vogl in Steyr. This turned out to be the beginning of the holiday of a lifetime, as well as the first recital tour. In a royal progress from town to town and monastery to castle in Upper Austria, Vogl and Schubert sang and played to small but enraptured, and discerning, audiences. The timetable was as follows: 24 to 27 May – excursion to Linz, St Florian and Steyregg Castle; 4 June – excursion to Gmunden on Lake Traun for a stay of six weeks while Schubert worked on his 'Great' C major Symphony (D944); 25

July – return to Steyr via Linz; 10 August – travel via Salzburg to Gastein, arriving 4 September. In Bad Gastein the pair were received by the poet and cleric Ladislaus Pyrker, Patriarch of Venice, two of whose poems the composer immediately set to music. Vogl and Schubert reached Gmunden by 10 September, arriving back in Steyr on 17 September. The composer had returned to Vienna by 3 October. The seven settings, some solo, some choral, from Walter Scott's *The Lady of the Lake* that Schubert brought back with him from this holiday were immediately snapped up by the Viennese firm of Artaria – after all, this was the man whose engraving (from a portrait of Rieder) was published on 9 December with the words 'composer of genius' printed under his name. There were a number of other significant Schubert poets who emerged in 1825 – Ernst Schulze (in March) whose *Poetisches Tagebuch* inspired a number of song masterpieces, a return of the Schlegel brothers (with three songs between them in August and September) and Wilhelm Schütz, a Schlegel protégé from much earlier, with two songs from the play *Lacrimas*.

See: Nicolaus von CRAIGHER DE JACHELUTTA
Karl LAPPE
Ladislaus PYRKER
Walter SCOTT
Wilhelm von SCHÜTZ
Ernst SCHULZE

DISC 29 continued

H554	*Im Abendrot* (Lappe) D799, early 1825	I/923
H555	*Der Einsame* (Lappe) D800, early 1825	I/475
H556	*Die junge Nonne* (Craigher) D828, early 1825[55]	II/32
H557	*Lied der Anne Lyle* (Scott/Craigher(?)) D830, early 1825?	II/215
H558	*Gesang der Norna* (Scott/Spiker) D831, early 1825	I/175
H559	*Des Sängers Habe* (Schlechta) D832, February 1825	II/705
H560	*Auf der Bruck (Auf der Brücke)* (Schulze) D853, March(?) 1825	I/247
H561	*Im Walde* (Schulze) D834, March 1825	I/946
H562	*Der blinde Knabe* (Cibber/Craigher) D833, April 1825	I/308
H563	*Totengräbers Heimwehe* (Craigher) D842, April 1825	III/368

DISC 30

	Sieben Gesänge aus Walter Scott's Fräulein vom See Op. 52	III/149
H564	*Ellens Gesang I* (Scott/Storck) D837, April–July 1825	III/151
H565	*Ellens Gesang II* (Scott/Storck) D838, April–July 1825	III/156
H566	*Bootgesang* (Scott/Storck) D835 quartet, 1825	III/158
H567	*Coronach (Totengesang der Frauen und Mädchen)* (Scott/Storck) D836 trio of women's voices, 1825	III/160
H568	*Normans Gesang* (Scott/Storck) D846, April 1825	III/162
H569	*Ellens Gesang III* (Scott/Storck) D839, April 1825	III/166
H570	*Lied des gefangenen Jägers* (Scott/Storck) D843, April–July 1825	III/170
H571	*Das Heimweh* (Pyrker) D851, August 1825	I/843
H572	*Die Allmacht* (Pyrker) first setting D852, August 1825 (see second setting H584)	I/84
H573	*Fülle der Liebe* (F. von Schlegel) D854, August 1825	I/630

[55]*Die junge Nonne*: Reed believes this song was possibly composed in late 1824.

H574	*Wiedersehn* (A. von Schlegel) D855, September 1825	**III/588**
H575	*Abendlied für die Entfernte* (A. von Schlegel) D856, September 1825	**I/20**
	Zwei Szenen aus Lacrimas	**III/764**
H576	*Delphine* (Schütz) D857/1, September 1825	**III/766**
H577	*Florio* (Schütz) D857/2, September 1825	**III/768**

DISC 31

H578	*An mein Herz* (Schulze) D860, December 1825	**I/198**
H579	*Der liebliche Stern* (Schulze) D861, December 1825	**II/199**
H580	*Um Mitternacht* (Schulze) D862, December 1825[56]	**III/430**

Some other works of 1825: Piano Sonata in C major D840; Piano Sonata in A minor (D845); Piano Sonata in D major (D850).

1826 (aged twenty-nine) – *24 solo songs* (January, February, March, July)
The earlier months of this year were adorned by the beautiful and talented actress Sophie Müller whose diary mentions music-making with her friends Vogl and Schubert. She heard the first *Suleika* setting and songs from *Die schöne Müllerin* and she was delighted with the Teltscher lithograph of the composer (11 January) whom she clearly regarded as a celebrity. On 25 January Schubert visited her in person and he sang some of his recent Schulze settings. On 28 February Müller expected Schubert to call on her, but he did not come – probably an indication of the uncertain state of his health. In the meantime he composed his farewell to the poetry of Goethe – the four *Gesänge aus Wilhelm Meister* (D877) with the final versions of the three lyrics of Mignon. Maurice Brown averred that these were composed with Sophie Müller's voice in mind. Schubert chose to open and close the group with different settings of 'Nur wer die Sehnsucht kennt', a spell-binding duet as well as a haunting solo song. In March a new Austrian poet entered the Schubert canon – Johann Gabriel Seidl, an ambitious twenty-two-year old who climbed the greasy pole of Viennese literary life in determined fashion. Seidl, a youthful imitator of Goethe, happened to encounter Schubert at just the right stage of the composer's career to ensure that his accomplished poems were encouraged and turned into masterly lieder. It is hard not to be grateful to a poet who, though hardly a new Goethe, could somehow inspire Schubert to the heights of *Im Freien* (D880) and *Nachthelle* (D892).

In April Schubert petitioned the emperor for the official position of Vice-Kapellmeister. He was on the shortlist but the post eventually went to Joseph Weigl, a decision apparently graciously accepted by the younger composer who had known Weigl's music since his childhood. There followed a fallow patch in Schubert's output as if he were in the grip of depression. In April he and Bauernfeld resolved to write an opera together. The subject decided upon was *Der Graf von Gleichen* and Bauernfeld duly wrote the libretto when he was on holiday in Carinthia and delivered it to Schubert at the end of July. (This libretto was banned by the censor on account of its subject – bigamy – but the composer was determined to go ahead with the project.) Short of money, Schubert was unable to afford a summer holiday; instead he spent some time with Schober and the poet's mother in Währing where he composed his three settings of Shakespeare and finished his String Quartet in G major (D887) in a spate of feverish activity. In the autumn he once again lodged with Schober, this time at Bäckerstrasse, 6. At the end of the year Schubert lived alone in the Bastei (in the old city walls) near the Karolinentor. In a new move to improve

---

[56]*Um Mitternacht*: The Witteczek-Spaun collection dates this song to March 1826.

his business dealings with publishers he approached two famous Leipzig publishers, Probst and Breitkopf & Härtel, without success. (The latter publisher would later undertake the composer's complete edition – the *Alte Gesamtausgabe* or AGA – in the 1890s.) The year concluded with a 'big, big Schubertiad' at the home of Josef von Spaun, the occasion that was depicted many years later (in 1868) in a large painting by Moritz von Schwind.

See: Composers: Joseph Weigl
         Posthumous Songs: Probst, Breitkopf & Härtel
         Singers: Sophie Müller
         Johann Gabriel Seidl
         William Shakespeare

Disc 31 continued

H581	*O Quell, was strömst du rasch und wild (Die Blume und der Quell)* (Schulze) D874 fragment, January(?) 1826[57]	**II/465**
H582	*Im Jänner 1817 (Tiefes Leid)* (Schulze) D876, January 1826	**I/938**
H583	*Mondenschein* (Schober) D875 quintet, January 1826	**II/374**
H584	*Die Allmacht* (Pyrker) second setting D875A fragment, soprano and chorus, January 1826 (*see* first setting H572)	**I/87**
	Gesänge aus 'Wilhelm Meister' Op. 62	**I/688**
H585	*Mignon und der Harfner* ('Nur wer die Sehnsucht kennt') (Goethe) fifth setting D877/1 duet, January 1826 [*see* first setting (two versions) H190 and H190a, second setting H211, third setting H298, fourth setting H424+, sixth setting H588]	**I/688**
H586	*Lied der Mignon* ('Heiss mich nicht reden') (Goethe) second setting D877/2, January 1826 [*see* first setting H472]	**I/690**
H587	*Lied der Mignon* ('So lasst mich scheinen') (Goethe) fourth setting D877/3, January 1826 [*see* first setting H296, second setting H297, third setting H473]	**I/693**
H588	*Lied der Mignon* ('Nur wer die Sehnsucht kennt') (Goethe) sixth setting D877/4, January 1826 [*see* first setting (two versions) H190 and 190a, second setting H211, third setting H298, fourth setting H424+, fifth setting H585]	**I/696**
H589	*Leb'wohl, du schöne Erde (Abschied von der Erde)* (Pratobevera) D829, 17 February 1826	**II/121**
H590	*Widerspruch* (Seidl) D865 choral, 1826(?)	**III/583**
H591	*Wiegenlied* (Seidl) D867, 1826(?)	**III/595**
H592	*Totengräber-Weise* (Schlechta) D869, 1826	**III/373**
H593	*Das Zügenglöcklein* (Seidl) D871, 1826[58]	**III/741**
H594	*Der Wanderer an den Mond* (Seidl) D870, 1826	**III/547**

Disc 32

H595	*Im Freien* (Seidl) D880, March 1826	**I/926**
H596	*Am Fenster* (Seidl) D878, March 1826	**I/104**
H597	*Sehnsucht* (Seidl) D879, March 1826	**III/110**

---

[57]*O Quell, was strömst du rasch und wild*: Reed and Hoorickx date the song in March 1826.
[58]*Das Zügenglöcklein*: Reed points out that it is likely that this song was composed at the same time as the other Seidl settings, in March.

H598	*Fischerweise* (Schlechta) D881, March 1826[59]	**I/565**
H599	*Im Frühling* (Schulze) D882, March 1826	**I/930**
H600	*Lebensmut* (Schulze) D883, March 1826	**II/130**
H601	*Über Wildemann* (Schulze) D884, March 1826	**III/425**
	[*Romanze des Richard Löwenherz* D907 belongs here, chronologically, in March 1826. *See* H627]	
H602	*Dithyrambe* (Schiller) second setting D801, by June 1826 [*see* first setting H21][60]	**I/418**
H603	*Trinklied* (Shakespeare/Mayrhofer von Grünbühel) D888, July 1826	**III/408**
H604	*Ständchen* (Shakespeare/A. von Schlegel) D889, July 1826	**III/241**
H605	*Gesang (An Silvia)* (Shakespeare/Bauernfeld) D891, July 1826	**I/707**
H606	*Hippolits Lied* (Gerstenbergk) D890, July 1826	**I/881**
H607	*Nachthelle* (Seidl) D892 tenor solo and choral, September 1826	**II/427**
H607+	*Grab und Mond* (Seidl) D893 unaccompanied choral, September 1826	**I/776**

Some other works of 1826: Deutsche Messe (text by Johann Philipp Neumann – D872); *Grande Marche Héroique* in A minor for piano duet (D885); *Piano Sonata in G major* (D894); *Rondo in B minor for violin and piano* (D895)

1827 (aged thirty) – *46 solo songs* (January, February, April, May, June, September, October, November)

In terms of song composing the year began with three genial Rochlitz settings; the poet was a powerful music critic in Leipzig and it is hard not to suspect that Schubert had been advised to choose these lyrics partly for musico-political reasons. (He was gradually learning the hard lessons of being savvy in the music business.) A single song with a poem by his librettist Bauernfeld was surely intended as more of a personal gift. In February the composer found a group of poems in the almanac *Urania* (1823) printed with the title page 'W a n d e r l i e d e r / *von* / Wilhelm Müller; / Die Winterreise. In 12 Liedern'. Schubert believed that these twelve songs constituted a complete poetic cycle, writing the word 'Fine' (The End) at the end of no. 12, *Einsamkeit*. He was convinced they were the finest of his songs and was later disappointed by the initial reaction of friends who found them too gloomy. In the same month he composed two substantial Schober settings. In March Schubert availed himself yet again of the poet's hospitality – a recurring rondo theme in his domestic arrangements. He stayed in the Schober apartment until a few weeks before his death and benefited from the regular reading parties where he became acquainted with important new literature – authors like Kleist (*Die Marquise von O*) and Heine (*Reisebilder, 1826*, where the poems set in *Schwanengesang* were printed before their appearance in the *Buch der Lieder*). The hearty expansiveness of Schober's *Schiffers Scheidelied* could not be more different from the concentrated tone of *Winterreise* (the composer himself dropped the definite article from the title rendering it even more stark). Still in March, at the salon of the 'grande horizontale' Katharina von Lászny (the dedicatee of several Schubert songs), the composer met the great pianist Hummel and his young student Ferdinand Hiller. Hummel was moved to tears by the impromptu song recital given by Vogl and Schubert, and he improvised on *Der blinde Knabe* D833. It is unlikely, although sometimes mooted, that later in the same month Schubert, in the company of Schindler, Teltscher and the brothers

---

[59]*Fischerweise*: Dürr has suggested that this song could date from as early as 1817 and that the extant autograph material may derive from a lost autograph from nine years earlier.
[60]*Dithyrambe*: The song is ascribed by some commentators to 1824.

Hüttenbrenner, visited Beethoven on his deathbed. With Beethoven's death Schubert must have felt a sense of inner liberation; now he knew himself to be the greatest composer in Vienna, if not the world, and in the eighteen months before his own death this was indeed the case.

In April the Octet D803 was given a public performance. In May Schubert and Schober took a two-month retreat at 'The Empress of Austria', a comfortable hostelry in the picturesque town of Dornbach, west of Vienna. Here *Das Lied im Grünen* D917 was composed. Schubert returned to Vienna in time to provide Anna Fröhlich with music for the birthday of Louise Gosmar, a choral serenade (*Ständchen*, D920); he wrote a version for mezzo soprano and male voices in error but supplied on request a second arrangement with female chorus. In the early autumn there was a pleasurable stay in Graz (3–20 September). This time Schubert travelled with Johann Baptist Jenger, an enthusiastic accompanist of his songs. Their Styrian hosts were Karl and Marie Pachler and their small son Faust, for whose young fingers Schubert wrote a deliberately simplified *Kindermarsch* D928. Marie Pachler, a brilliant pianist and a pupil of Beethoven, was an admirer of the poetry of Karl Gottfried von Leitner, a native of Graz and perhaps the most delightful and endearing of the contemporary Austrians that Schubert set to music. In fact Schubert had already set Leitner's *Drang in die Ferne* (D770) in 1823; he now had the chance to see much more of the poet's work and only narrowly missed meeting him personally. Four or five of the Leitner settings of 1827–8 are among the composer's most beautiful songs, reflecting this happy period in his life and his new-found friendship with the Pachlers. The composer left two settings of Schulze with the Graz publisher Kienreich who published them in 1828.

Schubert returned to Vienna and had a relapse; his compromised health was subject to setbacks of this kind. He was not fit enough to attend Anna Hönig's party in October. The three delightful Italian *canzone* (D902) were written for the great bass Luigi Lablache some time before September. These are the best songs that Rossini, Schubert's arch rival in the operatic sphere, never wrote. It was no doubt a surprise for the composer to discover an edition of 'Die Winterreise' (in the second volume of Müller's *Gedichte eines reisenden Waldhornisten*, 1826) with twenty-four poems. Twelve of these texts, interpolated between the twelve he had already set, were new to him. Müller's book is dedicated to 'Carl Maria von Weber, the master of German song'. This was surely enough both to annoy Schubert and put him on his mettle. The second book of *Winterreise* songs was composed in November as if in open defiance of the poet's assertion. The first book of twelve songs composed in February was left intact, a masterpiece in its own right. Schubert composed Part Two by picking out the poems new to him and setting these in their published

View of the Tuchlauben, Vienna. In the foreground is the original building of the Gesellschaft der Musikfreunde (Musikverein) where Schubert's music was often performed. A few houses away, along the same side of the street, the composer lived with Schober in 1827/8. This was the composer's last dwelling in the inner city.

order – thus Müller's no. 6 (*Die Post*), became Schubert's 13, Müller's 10 (*Der greise Kopf*) became Schubert's 14 and so on, although there was a small but crucial rearrangement of the sequence towards the end. This sounds like a haphazard poetic scenario (Müller would have thought so) but with Schubert's hand on the musical tiller the work's unfolding seems inevitable and sublime. The contrast between this cycle and the vocal trio from the same month, *Der Hochzeitsbraten* D930, makes the two works seem most unlikely contemporaries; the trio was a rare instance of Schubert writing for humorous effect. Schober's text with its double entendres was arguably a portrait of the poet's own behaviour, and the work throws light on the sexual laissez-faire of some members of the circle. The extremely productive year came to an end with a short cantata in thanksgiving for the recuperation of Irene Kiesewetter, music clearly written for a chorus of Italian singers borrowed from the opera. This piece contains the only piano duet vocal accompaniment that Schubert ever wrote.

See: COMPOSERS: Johann Nepomuk Hummel
        FRIENDS AND FAMILY: Anna Hönig, Anna Fröhlich, Karl Pachler,
           Marie Pachler, Faust Pachler
        PIANISTS: Johann Baptist Jenger, Irene Kiesewetter
        SINGERS: Luigi Lablache
        Karl von LEITNER
        Johann Friedrich ROCHLITZ

DISC 32 continued

H608	*Zur guten Nacht* (Rochlitz) D903 tenor solo and chorus, January 1827	**III/760**
H609	*Alinde* (Rochlitz) D904, January 1827	**I/79**
H610	*An die Laute* (Rochlitz) D905, January 1827	**I/171**
H611	*Der Vater mit dem Kind* (Bauernfeld) D906, January 1827	**III/458**
H612	*Frühlingslied* (Pollak) D919, early 1827[61]	**I/627**

DISC 33

	Winterreise Op. 89 Part One	**III/620**
H613	*Gute Nacht* (Müller) D911/1, February 1827	**III/630**
H614	*Die Wetterfahne* (Müller) D911/2, February 1827	**III/635**
H615	*Gefrorne Tränen* (Müller) D911/3, February 1827	**III/639**
H616	*Erstarrung* (Müller) D911/4, February 1827	**III/642**
H617	*Der Lindenbaum* (Müller) D911/5, February 1827	**III/646**
H618	*Wasserflut* (Müller) D911/6, February 1827	**III/652**
H619	*Auf dem Flusse* (Müller) D911/7, February 1827	**III/655**
H620	*Rückblick* (Müller) D911/8, February 1827	**III/659**
H621	*Irrlicht* (Müller) D911/9, February 1827	**III/662**
H622	*Rast* (Müller) D911/10, February 1827	**III/667**
H623	*Frühlingstraum* (Müller) D911/11, February 1827	**III/671**
H624	*Einsamkeit* (Müller) D911/12, February 1827	**III/675**
H625	*Jägers Liebeslied* (Schober) D909, February 1827	**II/7**
H626	*Schiffers Scheidelied* (Schober) D910, February 1827	**II/742**
H627	*Romanze des Richard Löwenherz* (Scott) D907, March 1826[62]	**II/665**

---

[61]*Frühlingslied*: This song probably dates after April of this year considering that the quartet version, D914, was composed in April.

[62]*Romanze des Richard Löwenherz*: Walther Dürr places this song in March 1826(?) Dürr518. The incorrect placing of the song in context here was due to the distribution of songs on the Hyperion discs. Chronologically it belongs after H601 (see above).

H628	*Das Lied im Grünen* (Reil) D917, June 1827	**II/230**
H629	*Ständchen* (Grillparzer) D920 mezzo soprano and male or female chorus, July 1827	**III/244**

Disc 34

	Drei Gesänge für Bass-Stimme mit Klavier Op. 83	**I/435**
H630	*L'incanto degli occhi* (Metastasio) second setting D902/1, 1827 [*see* first setting H18]	**I/437**
H631	*Il traditor deluso* (Metastasio) D902/2, 1827	**I/439**
H632	*Il modo di prender moglie* (Anonymous) D902/3, 1827	**I/441**
H633	*Heimliches Lieben* (Klenke) D922, September 1827	**I/837**
H634	*Eine altschottische Ballade* (Percy's Reliques/Herder) D923, September 1827	**I/470**

	Winterreise Op. 89 Part Two	
H635	*Die Post* (Müller) D911/13, September–October 1827	**III/679**
H636	*Der greise Kopf* (Müller) D911/14, September–October 1827	**III/683**
H637	*Die Krähe* (Müller) D911/15, September–October 1827	**III/687**
H638	*Letzte Hoffnung* (Müller) D911/16, September–October 1827	**III/691**
H639	*Im Dorfe* (Müller) D911/17, September–October 1827	**III/695**
H640	*Der stürmische Morgen* (Müller) D911/18, September–October 1827	**III/699**
H641	*Täuschung* (Müller) D911/19, September–October 1827	**III/703**
H642	*Der Wegweiser* (Müller) D911/20, September–October 1827	**III/706**
H643	*Das Wirtshaus* (Müller) D911/21, September–October 1827	**III/711**
H644	*Mut!* (Müller) D911/22, September–October 1827	**III/716**
H645	*Die Nebensonnen* (Müller) D911/23, September–October 1827	**III/720**
H646	*Der Leiermann* (Müller) D911/24, September–October 1827	**III/725**
H647	*Der Hochzeitsbraten* (Schober) D930 trio, September–October 1827	**I/892**

Disc 35

H648	*Wolke und Quelle* (Leitner) D896B fragment, between autumn 1827 and beginning of 1828	**III/734**
H649	*Fröhliches Scheiden* (Leitner) D896 fragment, autumn 1827	**I/611**
H650	*Sie in jedem Liede* (Leitner) D896A fragment, autumn 1827 or later	**III/146**
H651	*Das Weinen* (Leitner) D926, autumn 1827	**III/563**
H652	*Vor meiner Wiege* (Leitner) D927, autumn 1827–early 1828	**III/525**
H653	*Des Fischers Liebesglück* (Leitner) D933, November 1827	**I/562**
H654	*Der Wallensteiner Lanzknecht beim Trunk* (Leitner) D931, November 1827	**III/534**
H655	*Der Kreuzzug* (Leitner) D932, November 1827	**II/98**
H656	*Al par del ruscelletto (Cantate für Irene Kiesewetter)* (Anonymous) D936 choral with piano-duet accompaniment, 26 December 1827	**I/74**

Some other works of 1827: Eight Variations on a theme from the opera *Marie* by Hérold for piano duet (D908); *Nachtgesang im Walde* for voices and four horns (texts by Seidl) (D913); *Der Graf von Gleichen* – opera in 2 acts (text by Bauernfeld, begun in June 1827) (D918); *Zwölf Grazer Walzer* for piano (D924); Piano Trio in B flat major (D898); Piano Trio in E flat major (D929); Fantasy in C for violin and piano (D934); Four Impromptus for piano Op. 90 (D899); Four Impromptus for piano Op. post. 142 (D935)

1828 (aged thirty-one) – *23 solo songs* (February, March, April, August, October)
In January two of the greatest Leitner settings (*Der Winterabend* D938 and *Die Sterne* D939)
were composed, late fruit from the composer's visit to Graz in the autumn of 1827. Josef von
Spaun married at the end of the month and there was a Schubertiad in his honour. In February
the publishers Probst of Leipzig and Schott of Mainz approached Schubert with business propo-
sitions – this was a clear sign that the composer's fortunes were at last turning for the better,
and that the death of Beethoven was prompting a re-evaluation of the hierarchy of composers
in the music world, as well as a search for new, commercially viable talent. Another indication
of Schubert's growing standing was the great success of the one and only public concert of his
works given in his lifetime (26 March), the first anniversary of Beethoven's death, in fact, and
a kind of modestly disguised announcement that Schubert had taken the great man's mantle on
his own shoulders. For this concert he composed a setting of Rellstab's *Auf dem Strom* for tenor,
horn and piano; close examination of this work with its Beethovenian quotations has revealed
that Schubert was consciously paying homage to the departed master. This mixed programme
of songs and chamber music made a substantial profit. The Handelian flavour of the cantata
Mirjams Siegesgesang D942 (Grillparzer) showed another connection with Beethoven who
possessed a complete edition of Handel's works, a gift from England.

In April Schubert composed another Rellstab setting, a solo song this time, entitled *Herbst*
D945. In May Schubert attended a Paganini recital with Bauernfeld, and at Bauernfeld's home
he played his Fantasie in F minor for piano duet (D940) with his protégé Franz von Lachner.
He went on an expedition in early June to Heiligenkreuz and Baden. He was in the company of
Lachner and Johann Schickh, the editor of the *Wiener Zeitschrift für Kunst, Literatur, Theater
und Mode* (to give this bi-weekly feuilleton its full title) where, between 1821 and 1828, ten of
Schubert's songs had first appeared as folded-in supplements (and three more were to be
published posthumously). The dandy Schickh also provided his *Zeitschrift* subscribers with
some of the most beautiful coloured fashion engravings of the time. Schubert spent much of
the summer out of town, probably in the company of Schober in Währing. In August he began
work on the Rellstab and Heine settings that were to be his *Schwanengesang*, although there was
no indication that he envisaged their publication in a single work. He also set *Psalm 92* D953
in Hebrew for the celebrated cantor Salomon Sulzer. Negotiations with Schott had stalled, but
Probst accepted the E flat major Piano Trio and Schubert wrote to him in August telling him
that it had to be published as Op. 100.

On 1 September the composer moved, on doctor's orders, from Schober's apartment in the
inner city to the Wieden suburb with its newly built and still damp walls (a change for the
worse). He lodged with his brother Ferdinand at Lumpertgasse, 694 (the present Kettenbrück-
enstrasse, 6). At about this time, probably encouraged by the publisher Thaddäus Weigl and the
poet Seidl, he composed a set of *Vier Refrain-Lieder* D866, four lighter songs that were meant
to capture the popular market; in the event they proved not quite light enough. These were no
more than a passing distraction from his more serious ambitions. Schubert was impatient to see
his trio in print and offered Probst further treasures – the three final piano sonatas, the string
quintet and the Heine songs. In the event these were all published posthumously by Viennese
publishers. In the company of friends Schubert went on an extended walking expedition all the
way to Eisenstadt, about 60 kilometres from Vienna (6–8 October) to see Haydn's grave, surely
a foolhardy undertaking for someone who was far from healthy. On his return Schubert ignored
a potentially important letter from Schindler urging the composer to arrange a concert of his
own works in Pest. This month of October was his last period of creativity. On 24 October the
committee of the Musikverein decided that a performance should be given of his Sixth Symphony.
At the request of the great soprano Anna Milder-Hauptmann he composed a new work, a
cantata for voice and piano with clarinet obbligato, *Der Hirt auf dem Felsen* D965, designed to

Interior of the synagogue in Vienna's Seitenstettengasse where Salomon Sulzer was cantor.

The house at Kettenbrückengasse, 6 (formerly Neue Wieden) where Ferdinand Schubert had an apartment and where Franz Schubert died.

The small, narrow room in which Schubert died, now part of a museum.

show off her technical prowess to good advantage. He had admired her singing since he was a teenager, and he indulged her vanity while ennobling her art. He also set to music a stray Seidl poem, *Die Taubenpost* D965A, which is usually counted as his last song.

On 31 October Schubert was taken ill while dining at the 'Red Cross' inn; he complained of having eaten bad fish. He clearly believed, or perhaps he had been told, that fresh air and exercise were necessary. He went for a three-hour walk on 3 November, and the next day attended his first, and only, lesson with the counterpoint specialist Simon Sechter. He dined with friends on 9 or 10 November and visited the baritone Karl von Schönstein. The last nine days or so of his life were spent in his brother's house, but he was still fit enough to be bored. In his last letter (to Schober on 12 November, to which he received no reply) he begged for more reading matter – he listed the novels by Fennimore Cooper he had already devoured, including *The Last of the Mohicans*.

On about 14 November, and at his own request, a performance of Beethoven's String Quartet in C sharp minor Op. 131 was arranged for him at Ferdinand's home; at this time he was also scouring and correcting the proofs (from the publisher Haslinger) of the second part of *Winterreise*. The last friends to visit were Bauernfeld and Lachner (not Schober who seems to have been afraid of infection) who discussed operatic plans. On 17 November the composer became delirious and ceaselessly sang aloud. On 18 November he had hallucinations and fell into a coma. Despite the best efforts of his doctors, Wehring and Wisgrill, he died on 19 November at 3 p.m. The cause of death was given as *Nerven-fieber*, but it is probable that the composer, with an immune system weakened by his ongoing illness and poisoned by mercury treatment, had succumbed to a typhus infection as a result of eating polluted food. His body was taken to the church of St Josef von Margareten on 21 November where there was a performance of *Pax vobiscum* (Schober) with new words provided by the poet. Friends accompanied the body to the Währing cemetery where Schubert was laid to rest next to Beethoven. A graveside monument including a portrait bust by Josef Alois Dialer (erected in 1830) was paid for by a benefit concert in the composer's memory.

See: COMPOSERS: G. F. Handel, Franz Lachner, Simon Sechter
PUBLISHERS: Thaddäus Weigl, Tobias Haslinger
SINGERS: Salomon Sulzer
Heinrich HEINE
Ludwig RELLSTAB

DISC 35 continued

H657	*Der Winterabend* (Leitner) D938, January 1828	**III/613**
H658	*Die Sterne* (Leitner) D939, January 1828	**III/256**
H659	*Der Tanz* (Meerau) D826 quartet, early 1828	**III/302**
H660	*Auf dem Strom* (Rellstab) D943 tenor, horn and piano, March 1828	**I/233**

DISC 36

H661	*Mirjams Siegesgesang* (Grillparzer) D942 soprano solo and chorus, March 1828	**II/362**
H662	*Herbst* (Rellstab) D945, April 1828	**I/860**
H663	*Lebensmut* (Rellstab) D937 fragment, summer(?) 1828[63]	**II/133**
	Vier Refrain-Lieder Op. 95	**III/495**
H664	*Die Unterscheidung* (Seidl) D866/1, summer(?) 1828	**III/497**
H665	*Bei dir allein!* (Seidl) D866/2, summer(?) 1828	**III/498**
H666	*Die Männer sind mechant!* (Seidl) D866/3, summer(?) 1828	**III/501**
H667	*Irdisches Glück* (Seidl) D866/4, summer(?) 1828	**III/503**
H668	*Das Echo* (Castelli) D990c (formerly D868), 1828(?)[64]	**I/462**
H668+	*Der 92. Psalm* (Bible, in Hebrew) D953 baritone and chorus, July 1828	**II/596**
	[*Glaube, Hoffnung und Liebe* (Reil) D954, choral SATB, before 2 September 1828]	**I/725**
H669	*Glaube, Hoffnung und Liebe* (Kuffner) D955, August 1828	**I/727**

DISC 37

	Schwanengesang Part One	**III/3**
H670	*Liebesbotschaft* (Rellstab) D957/1, August 1828	**III/6**
H671	*Kriegers Ahnung* (Rellstab) D957/2, August 1828	**III/12**
H672	*Frühlingssehnsucht* (Rellstab) D957/3, August 1828	**III/16**
H673	*Ständchen* (Rellstab) D957/4, August 1828	**III/20**
H674	*Aufenthalt* (Rellstab) D957/5, August 1828	**III/24**
H675	*In der Ferne* (Rellstab) D957/6, August 1828	**III/28**
H676	*Abschied* (Rellstab) D957/7, August 1828	**III/33**
	Schwanengesang Part Two	
H677	*Der Atlas* (Heine) D957/8, August 1828	**III/39**
H678	*Ihr Bild* (Heine) D957/9, August 1828	**III/43**
H679	*Das Fischermädchen* (Heine) D957/10, August 1828	**III/47**
H680	*Die Stadt* (Heine) D957/11, August 1828	**III/50**
H681	*Am Meer* (Heine) D957/12, August 1828	**III/54**
H682	*Der Doppelgänger* (Heine) D957/13, August 1828	**III/59**
H683	*Der Hirt auf dem Felsen* (Müller/Varnhargen von Ense) D965 soprano, clarinet and piano, October 1828	**I/886**
H684	*Die Taubenpost* (Seidl) D965A, October 1828	**III/65**

Some other works of 1828: Drei Klavierstücke D946: Allegro in a minor for piano duet 'Lebensstürme' (D947); Mass in E flat (D950); Rondo in A major for piano duet (D951); String Quintet in C major (D956); Piano Sonata in C minor (D958); Piano Sonata in A major (D959); Piano Sonata in B flat major (D960).

---

[63]*Lebensmut*: Reed believes that this song fragment was possibly composed in 1827.
[64]*Das Echo*: Walther Dürr places this song in the summer of 1828 (Dürr551). Reed suggests this song may have been written as early as 1826.

INDEX OF SCHUBERT'S POETS AND TRANSLATORS

INDEX OF ARTICLES ON SUBJECTS RELATED TO SCHUBERT'S SONGS

THE HYPERION SCHUBERT EDITION

The Hyperion Schubert Edition came into being because of the initiative and daring of Edward ('Ted') Perry (1931–2003), founder of the record label that modestly conceals his surname in its second and third syllables. Before his death he completed an autobiography that I hope will be published one day; it tells an astonishing story of an amazingly resilient autodidact, a boy from the Midlands, sometime driver of ice-cream vans and minicabs, whose life was transfigured by his love of great music. It was a joy to be caught up in the orbit of Ted's optimism and generosity of spirit. Although he was a canny businessman, he was also something of a mystic. He trusted his own ears, schooled by a lifetime of avidly listening to music, both live and recorded; he had fallen in love with records at a young age – listening to them, handling them as almost magical artifacts, and selling them at the famous EMG Record Shop off London's Oxford Street. Like the legendary entrepreneur Walter Legge (although, thank heavens, Ted had a completely different personality), he was not afraid to follow his instincts when it came to choosing artists for his own label.

Ted Perry had learned the recording business while working for Marcel Rodd of Saga; this had been the first label in the UK to challenge the monopoly of the large recording companies by producing so-called 'budget' recordings. I first met Ted in 1978 when, still in the LP era, he had branched out on his own as co-owner of Meridian Records and I accompanied the tenor Martyn Hill in a French-song recording for that label. Ted took a liking to my work and, when he went on to create Hyperion, I was among the earlier artists to appear on a label that immediately received favourable reviews from the critics – to the growing dismay of the larger companies. EMI and Decca (as well as DGG and Philips from Germany and the Netherlands respectively) had formed between them something of a cartel, despite their obvious rivalries, that had enjoyed decades of unchallenged hegemony in classical music recordings. It was soon clear, however, that Hyperion was a real rival and not simply a budget label like Saga. It aimed for the highest musical and technical values, as well as delightful design and presentation (one of Ted Perry's specialities – he had a marvellous eye and had trained as a printer's apprentice). London was the home base of hundreds of world-class musicians of every kind, the vast majority ignored by EMI and Decca and ripe for collaboration with someone like Ted (this included a number of wonderful choral groups and a burgeoning Early Music Movement). Hyperion and other new British labels gradually displaced the BBC as patrons of less than world-famous artists who now often achieved the international recognition that had hitherto eluded them. 'Auntie's' powerful and often very knowledgeable producers (that great Schubertian Leo Black and the legendary Hans Keller among them) had employed countless British artists (as well as musicians from abroad) at a time when radio broadcasts had been the only conduit for a wider dissemination of the work of those ignored by the large gramophone companies. For nearly thirty years or so after the war, the Third Programme/Radio 3 had filled the wide gap between commercial recordings and live concerts. There were several famous BBC broadcasters (the soprano Ilse Wolf and the pianist Nina Milkina come to mind), and it really meant something to be 'on the BBC books'. But discs, reviewed in papers and magazines and on sale throughout the world, wielded greater power still, and a number of British 'local' artists soon became world names thanks to Hyperion. This innovation came too late for Ilse and many other post-war British artists, but it changed the lives and careers of the younger generation.

The founder singers of The Songmakers' Almanac and myself were members of that happy breed. We featured in a series of LPs (later mostly reissued as CDs): *Voices of the Night*, *Venezia*, *Voyage à Paris*, *España* and *Le Bestiaire*. I then proposed an album of two LPs, a *Schubertiade* featuring these same four singers – Felicity Lott, Ann Murray, Anthony Rolfe Johnson and Richard Jackson – in four, differently themed programmes, one per side, that combined well-known and rarely heard Schubert lieder. Our *Schubertiade* was very well received in early 1985 (there was even a *Gramophone* cover), but what I did not realize was that these discs were an important audition for me, not only as far as Ted was concerned, but also his close friend Lucy Hayward, an ardent Schubertian who had turned pages for me at many a session. One night, when the three of us were having dinner, Ted asked me what I would really like to do in terms of recording. I replied (as would many an accompanist), 'All the Schubert songs, of course.' In a few seconds, over a glass of wine, the deal was done – and a phone call the next morning proved Ted to be a man who kept his word. This project was considered ill-advised by many recording connoisseurs at the time: the great critic Desmond Shawe-Taylor, for instance, assured a colleague that it would never be completed, despite its promising beginnings.

But that is to rush forward in the story; how to begin had been the big question. Ted and I knew that such a bold project needed the support of an auspicious singer to get it started. I had accompanied Dame Janet Baker in several recitals since 1978, and I knew that her Schubert repertoire was extensive. No longer restricted by exclusivity to EMI, she agreed to initiate our series. Although she was nearing the end of her singing career – she had retired from opera five years earlier – Janet was still in glorious voice. She came up with a marvellous mix of songs both famous and unknown, almost exclusively featuring the two most famous poets of German literature, Goethe and Schiller. My only intervention was to suggest that we should drop *Der Unglückliche* D713 (Pichler) because it did not fit into the Goethe–Schiller theme. I regret now that I did not beg the great lady to include all the strophes of the second setting of Goethe's *An den Mond* D296. The recording sessions in February 1987 took place in Elstree over two days of intense and concentrated work. (Sessions would eventually be allotted a more realistic three days, and some of the grander artists demanded – though very few received – four.) Dame Janet's artistry ensured a prizewinning disc: her unique vocal colour, febrile yet vulnerable, and the magisterial conviction with which she governed subtleties of shape and rubato, launched the series with an appropriate mixture of gusto and dignity. It was agreed that I should provide the notes and commentaries, having done so for the Songmakers' LPs. I remember how saddened I was that Gerald Moore (who had died the year before) was not there to send me his customary comments – not only about the music-making itself, but also about the words accompanying the music in the booklet.

At this time the horizons and aspirations of the series were still local. After beginning with a bang, Ted saw it as part of Hyperion's brief to record fine British artists who had not yet come into the sights of the major record companies. After the Baker recording it was understood that we should continue the series with my own, more immediate, contemporaries. Stephen Varcoe, an old friend of mine and a great favourite of Ted's, with a number of acclaimed English song recordings already under his belt, recorded Volume 2 in October 1987. This had a water theme – I had already made so many programmes for live performances of the The Songmakers' Almanac in the past decade that the discipline of thematic programme seemed a viable alternative to giving artists free rein to choose their favourite songs. Although Volume 2 included the first of Schubert's really long ballads (*Der Taucher* D77), at under sixty minutes it was the shortest of the discs. I soon realized that if I was to include all of Schubert's songs in fewer than fifty recordings I would have to use the length of the CDs to better advantage. Time seemed to stretch before us and a year passed before we continued with two further discs by artists whom I had long known and admired. Ann Murray's Volume 3 was recorded in November 1988. A founder member of The Songmakers' Almanac and, by now, a famous singer on the European opera stage, Ann was always the incomparable mistress of her material. A disc by her husband, the tenor Philip Langridge, also a mesmerizing artist, had already been recorded in September, but because it seemed a good idea to alternate issues between male and female singers, Philip's disc emerged after Ann's, as Volume 4. These records (the theme of both is settings of poetry by Schubert's Austrian friends) have been among the most admired in the series. Volume 5, also made in September 1988, was the nature-themed recital by Elizabeth Connell, 'Schubert and the Countryside'. This opulent and exciting voice was ideal for the operatic breadth of the great Schiller ballad *Klage der Ceres* D323.

At the time it was impossible for me to plan out the allocation of songs for the series very far in advance. Hyperion – lacking the clout of a great opera house – could not engage singers years ahead, and artists who were available would usually slip three days of recording into their time-table fairly late in the day, and only in the absence of operatic or orchestral engagements. Who were to be my next singers? I did not really know, yet all the programmes had to be tailor-made with individual voices and personalities in mind. To avoid a pile-up at the end, it was a general rule never to allow any one singer too many well-known songs. Fortunately many of my closer colleagues whom I had worked with on The Songmakers' Almanac trusted me to provide them with suitable material. For example, the night music for Volume 6 (recorded in September 1989), all lullabies and barcarolles, was an exact fit for the seductive vocal talents of Anthony Rolfe Johnson who had already made a disc of Shakespeare settings for Hyperion, not to mention a distinguished Britten recital. Tony died in 2010 after a long and debilitating illness, leaving behind a recorded legacy in opera, oratorio and song that continues to inspire awe and affection in the young artists of today. Philip Langridge also died unexpectedly in 2010, a few months before Tony, and in 2012 Elizabeth Connell. These three wonderful singers, each unique in his or her own way, were sadly not the first to disappear from the roster of Hyperion's Schubertians.

The success of the series up to this point led to an important watershed. Why not, after all, ask artists from abroad to record for us? The redoubtable Elly Ameling came from the Netherlands to Rosslyn Hill Chapel, Hampstead, in August 1989 to sing Schubert. Everything about these sessions was memorable, not least the consummate music-making of Ameling herself (who was reigning queen of European lieder singers) and the amazing working relationship between her own sharp ears and those of our producer Martin Compton. The songs were all from 1815 (the first disc in the series with a time frame) and she agreed to sing such unknown ballads as *Minona* D152 in return for some of the really great songs (or 'plums', as she called them) of the year. I was delighted that in the end she liked *Minona* D152 well enough to programme it in recitals with her regular accompanist Rudolf Jansen. After Ameling's Volume 7 there was no longer any reason to be diffident about asking European singers to join us. More importantly, there was even less reason for them to refuse. Of course the best British singers remained indispensable. Sarah Walker's recital (another record of nocturnal music) was issued as Volume 8, with *Ständchen* D920 as the first piece of extended choral music in the series so far. Sarah and I had worked together many times, in Britain, on tour in America, and also on a disc for Hyperion entitled *Shakespeare's Kingdom*. *Erlkönig* D328 was recorded at the very last moment and in one take, with all the blazing imagination for which this singer is admired.

In October 1989 the extraordinary Arleen Auger, an American resident in Europe, came to Rosslyn Hill to record Volume 9 (songs that had connections with plays and the theatre). She had trained as a violinist (I recall her deciding in rehearsal whether certain vocal phrases were up-bow or down) and her art was based on a musical schooling of the greatest purity and refinement. Having first accompanied Arleen in the late 1970s for a BBC broadcast when she was on the staff at the Frankfurt Conservatoire, I was now astonished by the transformation in her career and self-confidence. She was one of two star sopranos in our series (Lucia Popp was the other) who died – both in 1993 – not very long after their Hyperion recordings. Arleen's rendition of Schiller's *Thekla* D595, a ghostly voice singing from the 'other side', was extremely moving at the time; it now seems to have contained a heartbreaking prophecy.

We continued, making two to three recordings a year. This fitted Ted's idea of how many new Schubert discs from Hyperion the record-buying public could cope with. There was still the ambition to finish by 1997, Schubert's bicentenary, which at the time seemed a long way ahead (although some simple arithmetic might have made us more realistic). In May 1990 Martyn Hill (that fine tenor to whom I owed my initial introduction to Ted) made another splendid record of 1815 songs, issued as Volume 10. A month later, Brigitte Fassbaender recorded Volume 11, 'Songs of Death'. This great singer had suffered a personal bereavement just before the sessions and, not surprisingly, she approached this music with considerable angst. The intensity of her *Ausstrahlung* terrified all of us – the atmosphere at Rosslyn Hill was highly charged as never before or since – but subsequent recital encounters proved her a warm-hearted friend. Right at the end of 1990 the Scottish soprano Marie McLaughlin came into the studio for a mixture of songs, both sacred and suggestive (Volume 13). The settings from Walter Scott's *Lady of the Lake* gave the programme an appropriately Hibernian accent. These performances remain among my personal favourites of the series. When at the end of the sessions the beautiful (and happily married) Marie whispered that she needed a lift home within earshot of the still-'live' microphone, a phalanx of male admirers materialized in seconds, competitively brandishing their car keys. This seemed to me like a contemporary re-enactment of the rivalry between Scott's Malcolm Graeme, Roderick Dhu and the King of Scotland for the affections of Ellen Douglas, whose songs Marie had just recorded.

Some of Schubert's songs, particularly the earlier ones, require somewhat ample voices (the composer was not kind to his singers in the rather impractical first phase of his song-writing career). The generously voiced Adrian Thompson, that most equable, kind-hearted and amusing of colleagues, undertook the demanding songs of 1812–14 for Volume 12, 'The Younger Schubert'. This was in February 1991, and I was already aware that I could not simply leave until last the considerable quantities of earlier music that showed the composer's inexperience as well as his budding genius. There were two further recordings that year, back to back between 5 and 10 October. The first was Thomas Hampson, at the height of his considerable powers, singing texts inspired by Greek mythology. (Of Malcolm Crowthers's many beautiful cover pictures for the series, the one for Volume 14 – disc 18 in Hyperion 2 – of Hampson in front of the Elgin marbles is particularly striking.) Hampson got so exasperated with himself during the recording of *Amphiaraos* D166 that he threw a music stand from one end of the chapel to the other. As it flew by I remember trying to lighten the atmosphere by referring to Custer's last stand. The other recording was a third, and final, programme of Schubert's nocturnal music by Dame Margaret Price, also temperamental in her Celtic way while remaining a very old-fashioned professional. I had accompanied her in recitals all over the world for many years (at the time she lived just outside Munich). Her Volume 15 featured lieder that we had performed together for quite some time on the concert platform. The recording flew by in two days, considerably fuelled by the glasses of gin and tonic provided by Ted Perry (he thought Margaret had come to the end of her first session, but the proffered refreshment simply rekindled her energy for further work). The death of Margaret Price early in 2011 robbed the musical world of one of the greatest of all British sopranos.

1992 was a glorious year for the project – five discs with five star singers. Ted had clearly decided we had to get a move on. It was also the last year that I could allow myself to draw on the ever-diminishing repertoire without giving serious thought to how I was going to shape the final product, the squaring of a seemingly impossible circle. April 1992 saw my first, and sadly only, encounter with Lucia Popp. This mesmerizing woman, dazzlingly intelligent, came briefly into my life, recorded happily, invited me to accompany her in some recitals the following year, and then died of a brain tumour eighteen months later. She shouldered some of the songs of 1816 (issued as Volume 17) with infinite grace and an amused nonchalance that was part of her Slovakian charm. If Arleen's *Thekla* is haunting, brave Lucia's *Litanei* D343 is no less so (she knew she was dangerously ill at the time of the recording; we did not). One cannot go far in a Schubert song volume without confronting intimations of mortality.

There were two recordings in May 1992: with Sir Thomas Allen in a programme of Schiller settings for Volume 16, which he undertook with his customary cheery energy and magical timbre (how well he coped with the heights of the inconsiderate young Schubert's tessitura), and with Peter Schreier (Volume 18, 'Schubert and the Strophic Song'). I had first worked with Peter over a decade earlier in America. His arrival at Bristol for the recording was another turning point for the series; he seemed to bring with him the spirit of the age-old German lieder tradition and bestow its somewhat belated blessing on Hyperion's enterprise. No longer a young singer, and with a lifelong problem with diabetes, he showed unflagging vivacity and an artistic will-power that time and again communicated the ageless enthusiasm of the young lover in the Schulze songs. At the end of June Felicity Lott (not yet a dame), my colleague from Royal Academy of Music days and founder soprano of The Songmakers' Almanac, recorded a programme of songs about flowers and nature (Volume 19). While it is always wonderful to meet new singers and tune in to new temperaments, my very special relationship with 'Flott' allowed me to draw on musical associations that went back decades. I had reserved for this disc a handful of songs that we had often performed together, but as always she was eager to add to her vast repertoire. Music-making with this great artist (she has the most remarkable natural feeling for rhythm and tempo) has been at the core of my own development as a song accompanist. In October 1992 the Swiss soprano Edith Mathis (as it happens one of Schreier's favourite lieder-singing colleagues) contributed an anthology of songs from 1817 (Volume 21). This justly

famous singer gave performances of unfailing style and judicious musicality; she is a real Schubertian and I was heartbroken that her ill-health meant a last-minute cancellation of a Wigmore
Hall recital some time later.

The recordings of 1992 took care of the discs to be issued in 1993 and into 1994, but we were
still only just over halfway. There was by now a new generation of interesting and gifted singers
who merited an appearance with the series. It is here that the concept of the Schubertiad, in
effect the shared recital disc, was once again called into service. Because of the large backlog of
recordings waiting to be issued we only recorded two discs in 1993. These were both Schubertiads (songs from 1815, supplementing Volumes 7 and 10), arranged into two different casts of
four singers each. Volume 20 featured Patricia Rozario, the gifted Indian soprano with whom I
had already worked for a long time; John Mark Ainsley, originally a pupil of Anthony Rolfe
Johnson, with a glorious tenor voice; the sonorous and soulful bass Michael George; and a
bespectacled and highly intelligent young tenor who had impressed me mightily when I had
been a judge at the Walter Grüner lieder competition – Ian Bostridge (I remember thinking
how well his voice suited the microphone during the first play-back sessions). Volume 22
featured the considerable lieder-singing talents of the Scottish singers Lorna Anderson (soprano)
and Jamie MacDougall (tenor), and the distinguished Catherine Wyn-Rogers (mezzo) graces a
cast rounded off by the young Simon Keenlyside (baritone). Although destined to become one
of the country's most exciting operatic singers, he was devoted, by nature and temperament, to
singing lieder (he was to record Volume 2 in the Hyperion Schumann series in 1997) and so he
has remained. We must also not forget the sensitive contributions of the mezzo Catherine
Denley to a number of these ensembles.

These concerted programmes became more and more the order of the day. A Goethe Schubertiad was recorded in May 1994 – the first time since Volume 1 that the series had concentrated on this crucial poet in Schubert's life. Three of the singers, including Simon Keenlyside,
had already appeared on the Hyperion Edition, but this disc (Volume 24) also introduced the
extraordinary German soprano, Christine Schäfer. I had first worked with her in Songmakers'
recitals at the Wigmore Hall, and had been struck by her brilliant ability to colour and inflect
words. She was to record the prizewinning first volume of The Hyperion Schumann Edition in
1995 but was snapped up by DGG for an exclusive contract soon afterwards. This type of exclusivity began to have less and less of a hold as the financial turmoil facing the major recording
labels, and their continuing changes of ownership and administration, undermined the long-
term associations of yore between artists and their recording companies. Classical music was
increasingly becoming a niche market, unable to sustain the extravagances of the past where
artists, like Hollywood stars, were greeted at airports by their recording companies with cars
and bouquets of flowers. Times were changing fast, and the informal style of Ted and Hyperion,
working on a much less extravagant budget, increasingly became the norm rather than the
exception. Hyperion was initially patronized and dangerously underestimated by the big players.
I remember talking to a senior EMI executive who referred, in drawled upper-class nonchalance,
to my work for that 'funny Mr Merry, or Terry, or whatever he is called', who was 'trying so hard
to do his best'. I later learned that this very panjandrum had attempted – and failed – to buy the
Hyperion label from Ted, and for a great deal of money, earlier in the same week over lunch at
the Dorchester.

There was still room in September 1994 for a solo disc with that eloquent German tenor
Christoph Prégardien, a master of contained style (Volume 23). His *Harfner* songs are superb,
and he additionally undertook some of the more obscure songs of 1816 which required, and
received, his great lieder-singing expertise. We also had sessions on *Die schöne Müllerin* with
Anthony Rolfe Johnson at about this time. We had worked together for many years in The
Songmakers' Almanac and I had nearly made a disc of this cycle with him for the Bis label in

Sweden; now seemed the time to make a permanent record of an interpretation that we had often given in the concert hall. In December 1994 the producer Mark Brown and I flew to Berlin to spend the day with Dietrich Fischer-Dieskau who recorded for us (at considerable speed and expense) the poems by Wilhelm Müller that had not been set to music by Schubert. Once the spoken part of the disc was in the can there was a crisis. With the integrity and openness of the great artist that he was, Tony Rolfe Johnson pronounced himself dissatisfied by first edits of this *Müllerin* (he had been fighting a cold at the sessions). We would have to re-do it, but his tightly packed diary did not permit us to do this for some time. We already had the cover picture (seen for the first time on the cover of disc 37 for Hyperion 2) but Ted was understandably impatient to keep up the series' impetus by issuing one of the long-awaited cycles with Fischer-Dieskau's participation. What were we to do? What about Ian Bostridge who could record it immediately? 'Well, Graham', said Ted, 'if you think he can do it, let's go with it!' The rest – after the rapturous reception of Volume 25, *Die schöne Müllerin*, and Bostridge's subsequent EMI contract – is gramophone history.

By this point we had come to realize that completion by 1997 was going to be impossible – there were simply too many loose ends to tidy up. Volume 26, for example ('An 1826 Schubertiad'), contains recordings made in six different sessions in 1994, March 1995 and February 1996 – shortly before its release. Christine Schäfer makes another appearance (a transfigured *Mignon* 'So lasst mich scheinen' D877/3), as does John Mark Ainsley in top form for *Nachthelle* D892 with men's chorus, pronounced 'damnably high' at the time of its composition. One of my closest colleagues from Songmakers' days, the invaluable baritone Richard Jackson, also sings a number of songs on this disc. Hyperion had undertaken to record not just the solo songs but all the piano-accompanied vocal music; this meant the ever-increasing appearance of choral singers at the sessions, more often than not conducted by the brilliant and versatile Stephen Layton. 1993 marked my first meeting with the German baritone Matthias Goerne. His particular genius, apart from his uncanny command of *mezza voce* in the *pasaggio* of the voice (as in the Schlegel *Die Sterne* D684), lies in his awareness of the differing interpretative choices that are possible with the tiniest variations of tempo and emphasis. He came into Hyperion's sights at exactly the right time for two important discs: 'Schubert and the Schlegels' (together with Schäfer, Volume 27) recorded in early 1995, and *Winterreise* (Volume 30) recorded in the summer of 1996. He too 'graduated' to an exclusive recording contract – in his case with Decca – but also, in the longer term, a temporary arrangement.

There was only to be one further solo record, or at least I had hoped it would be a solo disc! This featured the songs of 1819–20, sung by the Slovenian mezzo-soprano Marjana Lipovšek. On the day before the recording sessions in London she announced without apology that the long Mayrhofer setting *Einsamkeit* D620 did not, after all, suit her (she had been initially enthusiastic and had been provided with the music in a suitable key a year earlier). At this late stage of the edition, when every allocation was being carefully measured, there was no scope simply to lose twenty minutes from a CD. So with just under an hour of the disc recorded by Lipovšek, its issue was delayed (it was eventually Volume 29) to allow the gifted Canadian baritone Nathan Berg time to record the 'missing' Mayrhofer cantata. On reflection, it is amazing that there were not many more problems of this kind over the years.

The remainder of the discs were Schubertiads with different time frames. Many of the artists who had contributed to earlier issues were recalled to appear in these closing discs – Ann Murray and Philip Langridge, both as fresh as ever, Stephen Varcoe for the very first Schubert songs of all (Volume 33), and an array of tenors – our old friends Martyn Hill and Adrian Thompson as well as new blood in the form of Paul Agnew, Daniel Norman, Toby Spence and James Gilchrist. Anthony Rolfe Johnson returned for the Heine settings from *Schwanengesang* on the final disc (Volume 37), also one of that great artist's last appearances on record. Neal Davies sang some of the bass songs with skill and relish. On occasion important artists, such as Nancy Argenta and Lynne Dawson, played a smaller role than befitted their experience. Some artists were unable to contribute to the project because of exclusivity contracts with other labels. There were two great British Schubertians, Ian Partridge and the late John Shirley Quirk, highly esteemed colleagues both, whose exclusion was not a matter of choice but simply because life (and diaries) can sometimes work out that way. Their absence from the series remains a matter of regret for me. We were near to securing the services of the great German bass Kurt Moll until the project was scuppered by someone telling him, incorrectly and maliciously, that I had already assigned all the bass songs to Fassbaender. From the beginning there were a number of people who willed the series to fail, some nearer to home than others. Fortunately Ted remained as impervious to these rumblings as he had to takeover bids designed to silence his work (I now realize that giving up on the Schubert series halfway through and selling Hyperion would have made him a rich man). In the 1990s even Dietrich Fischer-Dieskau sketched out a programme with the intention of taking part in the project, but health (and diary) considerations got in the way. Nevertheless, this series, without trying, had turned into an aural snapshot of many of the gifted lieder singers of an entire generation. This provided a growing incentive to include appearances, even if brief, by younger artists who had come to prominence since we had begun in 1987, provided they were happy to sing only a few songs. Thus in the final volumes of the series we find a line-up of international sopranos: the voluminously voiced Christine Brewer, an American star able to negotiate the roller coasters of early Schubert with astonishing ease; the German soprano Juliane Banse (also Schumann Lieder, Volume 3, 1998); the British Geraldine McGreevy (whose *Schwestergruss* D762 is a personal favourite, and we made a Wolf recital for Hyperion in 2000). Among the male singers are the German-Canadian tenor Michael Schade, the British baritone Christopher Maltman (also Schumann Lieder, Volume 5, 2001), the Dutch Maarten Koningsberger (the latter featured prominently in Volume 28), the German Stephan Loges and the Canadian Gerald Finley who plays a large and distinguished role in Volume 36, as well as shouldering the supplementary baritone songs for Volumes 38 to 40 of Hyperion 2 – separately issued as 'Songs by Schubert's Friends and Contemporaries'. These three CDs also feature the compelling artistry of the soprano Susan Gritton, the mezzo Stella Doufexis (also Schumann Lieder, Volume 4, 1998), the perennial Ann Murray, as well as one of the most compelling tenors of the new British wave, Mark Padmore. Once it was decided that the series should include a certain amount of choral music requiring the help of a conductor, we were very fortunate to have had the brilliant collaboration of Stephen Layton directing his own hand-picked singers some of whom have since emerged as well-known soloists. Layton was to play a larger role in the Hyperion Schumann Edition.

Perhaps we have talked enough about the singers. Godfather to the series was the late Eric Sams, whose crucial importance in my life as a writer is described on p. x of the *Foreword and Acknowledgements*. We must not forget four wonderful instrumentalists – the late Dame Thea King (clarinet, Volume 9), David Pyatt (horn, Volume 37), Marianne Thorsen (violin) and Sebastian Comberti (cello) – these last two in the 'Schubert's Friends and Contemporaries' recordings. My wonderful colleague and former pupil Eugene Asti played a piano duet accompaniment with me on Volume 36, as well as being responsible for a remarkable completion of the choral version of *Gesang der Geister* D705 with piano. The work of the late Reinhard Van Hoorickx, fervent Schubertian and indefatigable editor of fragments, features on very many of these discs. The production teams were crucial: the gifted Martin Compton and Antony Howell in the earlier days, the ever-patient and genial Mark Brown and Julian Millard in the later, and on a few occasions Tony Faulkner – all great men in their field without whose work this series could never have been imagined. I have already mentioned the work of the series' photographer, the enchanting Malcolm Crowthers. He spent many hours of thought and effort in his quest to find suitable sites and backdrops for the innumerable sessions for both the Schubert and the Schumann series. I refused to be a part of these covers, calculating that over thirty pictures of me in the company of the singers would both tire the eye and provide rather too graphic a depiction of the passing of time. I was placed, and only at Ted's request, on the cover of Volume 37, the final issue of the series. We must not forget all the stoic piano tuners (will we ever forget the legendary Steinway No. 340 – the star of that firm's hire stock and for a while everybody's favourite piano?), page turners and the singers (here we go again!) who have sung with us in a choral capacity, some of them now very well known in their own right – and that is how it goes.

Despite all manner of setbacks and difficulties Hyperion remains, under Simon Perry's direction, the human face of the beleaguered record industry. His back-up team remains superb and the in-house publishing achievements of Hyperion booklets under the eagle eye of the gifted Nick Flower are matchless. This is all to do with the hovering spirit of Ted. I can still see him during long sessions, hunched over poets' texts and taking notes of performers' departures (for various editorial reasons) from the texts that were to be published in the booklets. He proofread everything personally, and edited all my notes himself. I took it as a great tribute to our beloved Franz Schubert when I saw tears in his eyes during sessions after he had listened to music he had never heard before. We both got better at our work as we went along. But right from the beginning he was behind me every inch of the way: no pianist could have managed such a project without the support of powerful back-up – the singers appeared as if by magic, their fees negotiated, their travel arranged. The discs appeared on time, bright, shiny and perfectly packaged. All I had to do was rehearse, play and write. And Ted allowed me to do just this without any fuss. The series really belongs to him – after all, he paid for it, and not only in terms of money.

It is for this reason that Ted, whom many of us regarded as a mentor, is one of the dedicatees of this book. He was in a sense its 'onlie begetter' – he and Schubert himself, of course. Here's to you Ted, and here's to the great composer who brought us together. To say Hyperion has done him proud would be rash; let us simply say it has done its best (as even the snooty manager from EMI agreed), as did each and every artist involved in the project. And doing one's best is surely what defines the true Schubertian, whatever their level of achievement. That Schubert himself understood this accounts for that unique musical phenomenon, the Schubertiad, where no one who brought their best offering to the table was turned away, and where the composer's genius always encouraged emerging talent.

A complete list of singers taking part in the Hyperion Series is given below. An asterisk denotes the singers who were allocated an entire disc in the series.

John Mark Ainsley (b. 1963)   English tenor
*****Sir Thomas Allen** (b. 1944)   English baritone
*****Elly Ameling** (b. 1934)   Dutch soprano
Lorna Anderson (b. 1962)   Scottish soprano
Nancy Argenta (b. 1957)   Canadian soprano
*****Arleen Auger** (1939–1993)   American soprano
*****Dame Janet Baker** (b. 1933)   English mezzo soprano
Juliane Banse (b. 1969)   German soprano
Nathan Berg (b. 1968)   Canadian baritone
*****Ian Bostridge** (b. 1965)   English tenor
*****Christine Brewer** (b. 1960)   American soprano
*****Elizabeth Connell** (1946–2012)   South African soprano
Neil Davies (b. 1966)   English bass

Lynne Dawson (b. 1956)	English soprano
Stella Doufexis (b. 1968)	German mezzo soprano
*Brigitte Fassbaender (b. 1939)	German mezzo soprano
Gerald Finley (b. 1960)	Canadian baritone
Michael George (b. 1950)	English bass
*Matthias Görne (b. 1967)	German baritone
Susan Gritton (b. 1965)	English soprano
*Thomas Hampson (b. 1955)	American baritone
*Martyn Hill (b. 1944)	English tenor
Richard Jackson (b. 1949)	English baritone
Simon Keenlyside (b. 1959)	English baritone
Maarten Koningsberger (b. 1955)	Dutch baritone
*Philip Langridge (1939–2010)	English tenor
*Marjana Lipovsek (b. 1946)	Slovenian mezzo soprano
Stephan Loges (b. 1972)	German baritone
*Dame Felicity Lott (b. 1947)	English soprano
Jamie McDougall (b. 1966)	Scottish tenor
Geraldine McGreevy (b. 1968)	English soprano
*Marie McLaughlin (b. 1954)	Scottish soprano
Christopher Maltman (b. 1970)	English baritone
*Edith Mathis (b. 1938)	Swiss soprano
*Ann Murray (b. 1949)	Irish mezzo soprano
Daniel Norman (b. 1970)	English tenor
Mark Padmore (b. 1961)	English tenor
*Lucia Popp (1939–1993)	Slovakian soprano
*Christoph Prégardien (b. 1956)	German tenor
*Dame Margaret Price (1941–2011)	Welsh soprano
*Anthony Rolfe Johnson (1940–2010)	English tenor
Patricia Rozario (b. 1960)	Indian soprano
Michael Schade (b. 1967)	German-Canadian tenor
Christine Schaefer (b. 1965)	German soprano
*Peter Schreier (b. 1935)	German tenor
Toby Spence (b. 1969)	English tenor
*Adrian Thompson (b. 1954)	English tenor
*Stephen Varcoe (b. 1949)	English tenor
Brandon Velarde (b. 1975)	American baritone
*Sarah Walker (b. 1943)	English mezzo soprano
Catherine Wyn-Rogers (b. 1958)	English mezzo soprano

The covers of the Hyperion Edition
as illustrated on the following pages were photographed by Malcolm Crowthers (vols 2–31,
and 37). The portrait of Dame Janet Baker (Vol. 1) is a photograph by Zoë Dominic.

Vol. 1   Janet Baker.

Vol. 2   Stephen Varcoe.

Vol. 3   Ann Murray.

Vol. 4   Philip Langridge.

Vol. 5   Elizabeth Connell.

Vol. 6   Anthony Rolfe Johnson.

Vol. 7   Elly Ameling.

Vol. 8   Sarah Walker.

Vol. 9   Arleen Auger.

Vol. 10   Martyn Hill.

Vol. 11   Brigitte Fassbaender.

Vol. 12   Adrian Thompson (pictured), Nancy Argenta, John Mark Ainsley, Richard Jackson.

Vol. 13   Marie McLaughlin, Thomas Hampson.

Vol. 14   Thomas Hampson, Marie McLaughlin.

Vol. 15   Margaret Price.

Vol. 16   Thomas Allen.

Vol. 17   Lucia Popp.

Vol. 18   Peter Schreier.

Vol. 19   Felicity Lott.

Vol. 20   Patricia Rozario, John Mark Ainsley, Ian
Bostridge, Michael George.

Vol. 21   Edith Mathis.

Vol. 22   Loran Anderson, Catherine Wynn Rogers,
Jamie McDougall, Simon Keenlyside.

Vol. 23   Christoph Prégardien.

Vol. 24   Christine Schäfer, John Mark Ainsley, Simon
Keenlyside.

Vol. 25   Ian Bostridge (*Die schone Müllerin*).

Vol. 26   Richard Jackson, Christine Schäfer, John Mark Ainsley.

Vol. 27   Matthias Goerne.

Vol. 28   Maarten Koningsberger, John Mark Ainsley.

Vol. 29   Marjana Lipovšek, Nathan Berg.

Vol. 30   Matthias Goerne (*Winterreise*).

Vol. 31 Christine Brewer (pictured), Patricia Rozario, Lorna Anderson, Catherine Denley, Catherine Wynn Rogers, Brandon Velarde.

Vol. 32 Lynne Dawson, Christine Schäfer, Ann Murray, John Mark Ainsley, Daniel Norman, Christoph Prégardien, Michael Schade, Toby Spence, Christopher Maltman, Stephen Varcoe.

Vol. 33 Marie McLaughlin, Ann Murray, Catherine Wynn Rogers, Philip Langridge, Daniel Norman, Adrian Thompson, Maarten Koningsberger, Stephen Varcoe.

Vol. 34 Lorna Anderson, Lynne Dawson, Patricia Rozario, Marjana Lipovšek, Martyn Hill, Philip Langridge, Daniel Norman, Michael Schade, Gerald Finley, Matthias Goerne, Thomas Hampson, Simon Keenlyside, Stephan Loges, Christopher Maltman, Neal Davies.

Vol. 35 Lynne Dawson, Geraldine McGreevy, Philip Langridge, Thomas Hampson, Maarten Koningsberger, Christopher Maltman, Neal Davies.

Vol. 36 Juliane Banse, Lynne Dawson, Michael Schade, Gerald Finley.

Vol. 37   John Mark Ainsley, Anthony Rolfe Johnson, Michael Schade, Graham Johnson (pictured) (*Schwanengesang*).

Susan Gritton, Ann Murray, Stella Doufexis, Mark Padmore, Gerald Finley (*Songs by Schubert and his Contemporaries*).

BIBLIOGRAPHY

The following bibliography gives full reference information for all those items listed within individual song and poet articles, and also contains a number of additional texts which, by dint of their centrality to Schubert studies, have been included here. Perhaps the five most important general reference texts in this book are *The New Grove Dictionary of Music and Musicians* (in several editions), the German equivalent, *Die Musik in Geschichte und Gegenwart* (MGG), the recent *Schubert Liedlexikon*, Walther Dürr's commentaries for the NSA, Deutsch's Documentary Biography and the even more monumental pair of volumes of documents edited by Waidelich and Hilmar. Full details of each are given here.

Abraham 1946	Gerald Abraham, ed.: *Schubert. A Symposium* (London: Lindsay Drummond Ltd, 1946)
Aderhold 2002	Werner Aderhold: 'Nah und fern. Von zweifacher Übertragung: Hafiz – Rückert – Schubert' in W. Aderhold, M. Kube and W. Litschauer, eds, *Schubert und das Biedermeier. Beiträge zur Musik des frühen 19. Jahrhunderts. Festschrift für Walther Durr zum 70. Geburtstag* (Kassel: Bärenreiter, 2002), pp. 59–81
Adler 2012	Jeremy Adler: 'Towards Infinitude', *Times Literary Supplement*, Vol. 5,676 (13 January 2012), p. 8
AGA	*Franz Schuberts Werke. Kritisch durchgesehene Gesammtausgabe* (Leipzig: Breitkopf & Härtel, 1884–97): Eusebius Mandyczewski, ed.: *XX Lieder und Gesänge*, 10 vols (1894–5)
Aigner 2002	Thomas Aigner: 'Zwei Sagen als stoffliche Vorlagen für Opernprojekte Schuberts', *Schubert durch die Brille*, Vol. 29 (June 2002), pp. 5–14
Ammerlahn 2000	Helmut Ammerlahn: 'Wilhelm Meisters Lehrjahre' in M. Konzett, ed., *Encyclopaedia of German Literature*, 2 vols (Chicago and London: Routledge, 2000), Vol. 1, pp. 347–9
Aries 1976	Philippe Aries: *Western Attitudes Towards Death, from the Middle Ages to the Present*, trans. P. Ranum (London and New York: Marion Boyars, 1976)
Armitage-Smith 1974	Julian Armitage-Smith: 'Schubert's *Winterreise*, Part I: The Sources of the Musical Text', *The Musical Quarterly*, Vol. 60, No. 1 (January 1974), pp. 20–36
Audley 1871	Agathe Audley: *Franz Schubert: sa vie et ses œuvres* (Paris: Didier & Co., 1871)
Badura-Skoda/Branscombe 1982	Eva Badura-Skoda and Peter Branscombe, eds: *Schubert Studies. Problems of Style and Chronology* (Cambridge: Cambridge University Press, 1982)

Badura-Skoda/Gruber 1999   Eva Badura-Skoda, Gerold Gruber et al., eds: *Schubert und Seine Freunde* (Vienna: Böhlau Verlag, 1999)

Batta 1993   András Batta: 'Worte ohne Lieder? Franz Liszts Klavierdichtungen anhand der Schubert-Lieder', *Schubert durch die Brille*, Vol. 11 (June 1993), pp. 65–90

Bauer 1915   Moritz Bauer: *Die Lieder Franz Schuberts. Erster Band* (Leipzig: Breitkopf & Härtel, 1915; repr. Vaduz: Sändig, 1985). Only the first volume of this work was ever published, containing commentaries on settings of Goethe, Schiller, Ossian, Salis-Seewis and eleven further German poets

Baumann 1992   Thomas Baumann: 'Gotter, (Johann) Friedrich Wilhelm' in S. Sadie, ed., *The New Grove Dictionary of Opera*, 4 vols (London: Macmillan, 1992), Vol. 2, p. 493

Bell 1964   Arnold Craig Bell: *The Songs of Schubert* (Lowestoft: Alston Books, 1964)

Berke 1969   Dietrich Berke: 'Zu einigen anonymen Texten Schubertscher Lieder', *Die Musikforschung*, Vol. 22, No. 4 (October–December 1969), pp. 485–9

Berke 1979   Dietrich Berke: 'Schuberts Liedentwurf "Abend" D654 und dessen textliche Voraussetzungen' in O. Brusatti, ed., *Schubert-Kongreß Wien 1978* (Graz: Akademische Druck- und Verlaganstalt, 1979), pp. 305–20

Berke 1999   Dietrich Berke: '"In einem Style, der an die Erhabenheit der Händel'schen Compositionen erinnert" – Schubert und Grillparzer: eine Künstlerfreundschaft?' in E. Badura-Skoda, G. Gruber et al., eds, *Schubert und Seine Freunde* (Vienna: Böhlau Verlag, 1999), pp. 203–14

Berke 2002   Dietrich Berke: 'Mutmaßungen über den *Leiermann*' in W. Aderhold, M. Kube and W. Litschauer, eds, *Schubert und das Biedermeier. Beiträge zur Musik des frühen 19. Jahrhunderts. Festschrift für Walther Durr zum 70. Geburtstag* (Kassel: Bärenreiter, 2002), pp. 83–90

Berlin 1999   Isaiah Berlin: *The Roots of Romanticism*, ed. H. Hardy (London: Chatto & Windus, 1999)

Bird/Stokes 1976   George Bird and Richard Stokes (trans.): *The Fischer-Dieskau Book of Lieder* (London: Victor Gollancz and Pan Books, 1976). This is the English version of Fischer-Dieskau's *Texte Deutscher Lieder* (Munich: Deutscher Taschenbuch-Verlag, 1968), containing over 750 songs, chosen and introduced by the singer

Black 1997   Leo Black: 'Oaks and Osmosis', *Musical Times*, Vol. 138, No. 1852 (June 1997), pp. 4–15

Black 1998   Leo Black: 'Schubert and Fierrabras. A Mind in Ferment', *Opera Quarterly*, Vol. 14, No. 4 (summer 1998), pp. 17–39

Black 2001   Leo Black: 'Voice doubling bass', *Schubert durch die Brille*, Vol. 26 (January 2001), pp. 89–100

Black 2003   Leo Black: *Franz Schubert: Music and Belief* (Woodbridge: Boydell Press, 2003)

Bodendorff 2006	Werner Bodendorff, ed.: *Franz Schubert. Die Texte seiner einstimmig und mehrstimmig komponierten Lieder und ihre Dichter. Band 3: Die Texte der mehrstimmigen Lieder* (Hildesheim and New York: Georg Olms Verlag, 2006; originally published in 1997). *See also* Schochow 1974
Böckh 1822	Franz Heinrich Böckh: *Wiens lebende Schriftsteller, Künstler und Dilettanten im Kunstfache* (Vienna: B. Ph. Bauer, 1822)
Boyle 2000	Nicholas Boyle: *Goethe: The Poet and the Age*, 2 vols (Oxford: Clarendon Press, 1991, 2000)
Branscombe 1982	Peter Branscombe: 'Schubert and the melodrama' in E. Badura-Skoda and P. Branscombe, eds, *Schubert Studies. Problems of Style and Chronology* (Cambridge: Cambridge University Press, 1982), pp. 105–41
Britten 1964	Benjamin Britten: *On Receiving the Aspen Award* (London: Faber and Faber, 1964)
Brody 1982	Elaine Brody: 'Schubert and Sulzer revisited: a recapitulation of the events leading to Schubert's setting in Hebrew of Psalm XCII, D953' in E. Badura-Skoda and P. Branscombe, eds, *Schubert Studies. Problems of Style and Chronology* (Cambridge: Cambridge University Press, 1982), pp. 47–60
Brown 1998	Clive Brown: 'Schubert's tempo conventions' in B. Newbould, ed., *Schubert Studies* (Aldershot: Ashgate, 1998), pp. 1–15
Brown 1954	Maurice J. E. Brown: 'Some unpublished Schubert songs and song fragments', *Music Review*, Vol. 15, No. 2 (May 1954), pp. 93–102
Brown 1955	Maurice J. E. Brown: 'New Light on some Schubert songs', *The Monthly Musical Record*, Vol. 85, No. 972 (December 1955), pp. 260–4
Brown 1958	Maurice J. E. Brown: *Schubert. A Critical Biography* (London: Macmillan, 1958)
Brown 1961	Maurice J. E. Brown: 'Schubert: Discoveries of the Last Decade', *The Musical Quarterly*, Vol. 47, No. 3 (July 1961), pp. 293–314
Brown 1966	Maurice J. E. Brown: 'Some Problematical Publications Considered' in M. J. E. Brown, ed., *Essays on Schubert* (London: Macmillan, 1966), pp. 244–66
Brown 1966[2]	Maurice J. E. Brown, ed.: *Essays on Schubert* (London: Macmillan, 1966)
Brown 1967	Maurice J. E. Brown: *Schubert Songs* (London: British Broadcasting Corporation, 1967)
Brown 1968	Maurice J. E. Brown: 'The Therese Grob Collection of Songs by Schubert', *Music & Letters*, Vol. 49, No. 2 (April 1968), pp. 122–34
Brüggemann 1998	Otto Brüggemann: 'Ein verschollenes Schubert-Lied? *An Gott* D863', *Schubert durch die Brille*, Vol. 20 (January 1998), pp. 75–93

Budde 1997	Elmar Budde: '*Der Flug der Zeit*. Zur Erstveröffentlichung der Schubert-Lieder und zu ihrer Rezeption' in E. Hackenbracht, ed., '*Der Flug der Zeit*'. *Franz Schubert. Ein Lesebuch* (Tutzing: Hans Schneider, 1997), pp. 9–31
Budde 2003	*Schuberts Liederzyklen* (Munich: C. H. Beck; 2nd edn, 2012)
Byrne 2003	Lorraine Byrne: *Schubert's Goethe Settings* (Aldershot: Ashgate, 2003)
Byrne 2004	Lorraine Byrne, ed.: *Goethe: Musical Poet, Musical Catalyst. Proceedings of the Conference hosted by the Department of Music, National University of Ireland, Maynooth, 26 & 27 March 2004* (Dublin: Carysfort Press, 2004)
Byrne/Farrelly 2002	Lorraine Byrne and Dan Farrelly, eds: *Claudine von Villa Bella: Goethe's Singspiel set to Music by Franz Schubert* (Dublin: Carysfort Press, 2002). Performing version with piano reductions of all eight of Schubert's arias in bilingual version
Byrne/Reul 2008	Lorraine Byrne and Barbara M. Reul, eds: *The Unknown Schubert* (Aldershot: Ashgate, 2008)
Capell 1928	Richard Capell: *Schubert's Songs* (London: Ernest Benn, 1928)
Carlyle 1893	Thomas Carlyle: *The Life of Friedrich Schiller. Comprehending an Examination of his Works* (London: Taylor & Hessey, 1825; repr. London: Chapman & Hall, 1893)
Cave 2011	Terrence Cave: *Mignon's Afterlives: Crossing Cultures from Goethe to the Twenty-first Century* (Oxford: Oxford University Press, 2011)
Challier 1885	Ernst Challier: *Grosser Lieder-Katalog. Ein alphabetisch geordnetes Verzeichniss sämmtlicher einstimmiger Lieder mit Begleitung des Pianoforte sowie mit Begleitung des Pianoforte und eines oder mehrerer anderer Instrumente* (Berlin: C. A. Challier & Co., 1885)
Chézy 1858	Helmina von Chézy: *Unvergessenes. Denkwürdigkeiten aus dem Leben* (Leipzig: F. A. Brockhaus, 1858)
Chochlow 1995	Jurij Chochlow: '*Mein Frieden* – Ein Lied vom Wiener oder vom Dresdener Schubert?', *Schubert durch die Brille*, Vol. 15 (June 1995), pp. 107–12
Chusid 2000	Martin Chusid, ed.: *Schwanengesang. Facsimilies of the Autograph Score and Sketches, and Reprint of the First Edition* (New Haven and London: Yale University Press, 2000)
Chusid 2000[2]	Martin Chusid, ed.: *A Companion to Schubert's Schwanengesang: History, Poets, Analysis, Performance* (New Haven and London: Yale University Press, 2000)
Clerk 1870	Archibald Clerk: *The Poems of Ossian in the Original Gaelic, with a literal translation into English*, 2 vols (Edinburgh and London: William Blackwood & Sons, 1870)

Clive 1997	Peter Clive: *Schubert and his World: A Biographical Dictionary* (Oxford: Clarendon Press, 1997)
Clough/Cuming 1952	Francis F. Clough and G. J. Cuming: *The World's Encyclopaedia of Recorded Music*, 3 vols (London: Sidgwick & Jackson, in association with The Decca Record Company, 1952, 1953 & 1957)
Coetzee 2012	John Maxwell Coetzee: 'Storm Over Young Goethe', *New York Review of Books*, Vol. 59, No. 7 (26 April 2012), pp. 19–21
Cone 1998	Edward T. Cone: ' "Am Meer" Reconsidered: Strophic, Binary, or Ternary?' in B. Newbould, ed., *Schubert Studies* (Aldershot: Ashgate, 1998), pp. 112–26
Cottrell 1970	Alan P. Cottrell: *Wilhelm Müller's Lyrical Song-Cycles. Interpretations and Texts* (Chapel Hill: University of North Carolina Press, 1970)
Dahms 1912	Walter Dahms: *Schubert* (Berlin and Leipzig: Schuster & Loeffler, 1912)
Damian 1928	Franz Valentin Damian: *Franz Schuberts Liederkreis* Die schöne Müllerin (Leipzig: Breitkopf & Härtel, 1928)
Davidson 2007	James Davidson: *The Greeks and Greek Love: A Radical Reappraisal of Homosexuality in Ancient Greece* (London: Weidenfeld & Nicolson, 2007)
Davidson/Hillenaar 2008	Michael Davidson and Henk Hillenaar: *Schubert and Mayrhofer* (London: Kahn & Averill, 2008)
De Clercq 1991	Robert de Clercq: 'Zu Umfang der Klavier zu Schuberts Zeit – und weiteres', *Schubert durch die Brille*, Vol. 7 (June 1991), pp. 121–5
Deutsch 1905	Otto Erich Deutsch: *Schubert-Brevier* (Berlin and Leipzig: Schuster & Loeffler, 1905)
Deutsch 1913	Otto Erich Deutsch, ed.: *Franz Schubert. Sein Leben in Bildern* (Munich: Georg Müller, 1913)
Deutsch 1928	Otto Erich Deutsch, ed.: *Franz Schubert's Letters and other Writings*, trans. V. Savile (London: Faber & Gwyer, 1928). First published as *Franz Schuberts Briefe und Schriften* (Munich: Georg Müller, 1919; 2nd edn, 1922)
Deutsch 1946	Otto Erich Deutsch, ed.: *Schubert: A Documentary Biography*, trans. E. Blom (London: J. M. Dent & Sons, 1946). This English-language volume is an expanded version of *Franz Schubert. Die Dokumente seines Lebens* (Munich: Georg Müller, 1914)
Deutsch 1958	Otto Erich Deutsch, ed.: *Schubert: Memoirs by his Friends*, trans. R. Ley and J. Nowell (London: A & C Black, 1958). First published as *Schubert. Die Erinnerungen seiner Freunde* (Leipzig: Breitkopf & Härtel, 1957)
Deutsch 1964	Otto Erich Deutsch, ed.: *Schubert. Zeugnisse seiner Zeitgenossen* (Frankfurt am Main: Fischer Bücherei, 1964)
Deutsch Werkverzeichnis 1 [D_1]	Otto Erich Deutsch: *Schubert. Thematic catalogue of all his works in chronological order.* In collaboration with D. R. Wakeling (London: J. M. Dent & Sons, 1951)

Deutsch Werkverzeichnis 2 [D₂]   Otto Erich Deutsch: *Franz Schubert. Thematisches*
                                   Verzeichnis seiner Werke in chronologischer Folge.
                                   Neuausgabe in deutscher Sprache, ed. W. Aderhold et al.
                                   (Kassel: Bärenreiter, 1978)

Dieckmann 1996   Friedrich Dieckmann: *Franz Schubert. Eine Annäherung*
                                   (Frankfurt am Main: Insel Verlag, 1996)

Dittrich 2007   Marie-Agnes Dittrich: ' "Für die Menschenohren sind es
                                   Harmonien". Die Lieder' in W. Dürr and A. Krause, eds,
                                   Schubert Handbuch (2nd edn, Kassel: Bärenreiter, 2007),
                                   pp. 141–267

Dobersberger 1997   Roland Dobersberger: *Johann Ladislaus Pyrker: Dichter*
                                   und Kirchenfürst (St Pölten: Niederösterreichisches
                                   Presshaus, 1997)

Dürhammer 1996   Ilija Dürhammer: 'Schlegel, Schelling und Schubert.
                                   Romantische Beziehungen und Bezüge in Schuberts
                                   Freundeskreis', *Schubert durch die Brille*, Vol. 16/17
                                   (January 1996), pp. 59–93

Dürhammer 1999   Ilija Dürhammer: *Schuberts literarische Heimat. Dichtung*
                                   und Literaturrezeption der Schubert-Freunde (Vienna:
                                   Böhlau Verlag, 1999)

Dürhammer 1999²   Ilija Dürhammer: ' "Von den lachenden Fluren des
                                   Ideenreichs" oder: "Die schlafenden Jünglinge" –
                                   Schuberts oberösterreichische Dichter-Freunde' in
                                   E. Badura-Skoda, G. Gruber et al., eds, *Schubert und Seine*
                                   Freunde (Vienna: Böhlau Verlag, 1999), pp. 119–36

Dürhammer 2006   Ilija Dürhammer: *Geheime Botschaften: homoerotische*
                                   Subkulturen im Schubert-Kreis, bei Hugo von Hofmannsthal
                                   und Thomas Bernhard (Vienna: Böhlau Verlag, 2006)

Dürr 1971   Walther Dürr: 'Beobachtungen am Linzer Autograph
                                   von Schuberts *Rastlose Liebe*' in *Historisches Jahrbuch*
                                   der Stadt Linz 1970 (Linz: Archiv der Stadt Linz, 1971),
                                   pp. 215–30

Dürr 1982   Walther Dürr: 'Schubert's songs and their poetry:
                                   reflections on poetic aspects of song composition' in E.
                                   Badura-Skoda and P. Branscombe, eds, *Schubert Studies.*
                                   Problems of Style and Chronology (Cambridge: Cambridge
                                   University Press, 1982), pp. 1–24

Dürr 1983   Walther Dürr: 'Schuberts Lied *An den Tod* (D518)
                                   – zensiert?', *Österreiche Musikzeitschrift*, Vol. 38, No. 1
                                   (January 1983), pp. 9–17

Dürr 1989   Walther Dürr: 'Lieder aus dem "Selam": Ein Schubertsches
                                   Liederheft' in G. Brosche, ed., *Beiträge zur musikalischen*
                                   Quellenkunde. Katalog der Sammlung Hans P. Wertitsch in
                                   der Musiksammlung der Österreichischen Nationalbibliothek
                                   (Tutzing: Hans Schneider, 1989), pp. 353–61

Dürr/Feil 1991   Walther Dürr and Arnold Feil: *Franz Schubert* (Stuttgart:
                                   Reclam, 1991)

Dürr/Krause 2007   Wathler Dürr and Andreas Krause, eds: *Schubert*
                                   Handbuch (2nd edn, Kassel: Bärenreiter, 2007)

Eckhardt 1997	Mária Eckhardt: 'Franz von Schober. Schuberts und Liszts Dichter-freund', *Schubert durch die Brille*, Vol. 18 (January 1997), pp. 69–79
Einstein 1951	Alfred Einstein: *Schubert*, trans. D. Ascoli (London: Cassell & Co., 1951)
Erickson 1997	Raymond Erickson, ed.: *Schubert's Vienna* (New Haven and London: Yale University Press, 1997)
Everett 1988	Walter T. Everett: *A Schenkerian view of text-painting in Schubert's Song cycle Winterreise*, PhD thesis, University of Michigan, 1988
Feil 1988	Arnold Feil: *Franz Schubert. Die schöne Müllerin. Winterreise*, trans. A. C. Sherwin (Portland: Amadeus Press, 1988). First published in German under the same title (Stuttgart: Reclam, 1975)
Fernandez 1989	Dominique Fernandez: *Le Rapt de Ganymède* (Paris: Bernard Grasset, 1989)
Fétis	François-Joseph Fétis: *Biographie universelle des Musiciens et bibliographie générale de la musique*, 8 vols (Paris: Didot, 1860–5); 2 further supplementary vols, ed. Arthur Pougin (Paris: Didot, 1881)
Feurzeig 1997	Lisa Feurzeig: *Idea in song: Schubert's settings of Friedrich Schlegel*, PhD thesis, University of Chicago, 1997
Fischer/Schumann 1996	Klaus-Gotthard Fischer and Christiane Schumann, eds: *Schubert-Jahrbuch 1996. Bericht von der Tagung 'Schubert-Aspekte' Xanten, 2. und 3. März 1995.* (Duisburg: Deutsche Schubert-Gesellschaft, 1996)
Fischer-Dieskau 1971	Dietrich Fischer-Dieskau: *Auf den Spuren der Schubert-Lieder: Werden, Wesen, Wirkung* (Wiesbaden: F. A. Brockhaus, 1971). This is the German original of *Schubert's Songs. A Biographical Study*
Fischer-Dieskau 1976	Dietrich Fischer-Dieskau: *Schubert's Songs. A Biographical Study*, trans. K. Whitton (New York: Alfred Knopf, 1976, repr. 1977)
Friedlaender 1902	Max Friedlaender: *Das deutsche Lied im 18. Jahrhundert. Quellen und Studien*, 2 vols (Stuttgart & Berlin: J. G. Cotta, 1902)
Friedlaender 1922	Max Friedlaender, ed.: *Die schöne Müllerin. Ein Zyklus von Liedern gedichtet von Wilhelm Müller, in Musik gesetzt von Franz Schubert* (Leipzig: C. F. Peters, 1922). This critical edition includes an introduction and editorial remarks by Friedlaender
Frisch 1986	Walter Frisch, ed.: *Schubert. Critical and Analytical Studies* (Lincoln and London: University of Nebraska Press, 1986)
Fuchs 1904	Karl Fuchs: *Johann Gabriel Seidl* (Vienna: Carl Fromme, 1904)
Gál 1950	Hans Gál: '[Review:] *Der Charakter der Tonarten*. By Paul Mies', *Music & Letters*, Vol. 31, No. 2 (April 1950), pp. 156–8

Gál 1974   Hans Gál: *Franz Schubert and the Essence of Melody* (London: Victor Gollancz, 1974). Originally publised as *Franz Schubert, oder die Melodie* (Frankfurt: S. Fischer, 1970), Gál subsequently produced the English translation himself

Georgiades 1967   Thrasybulos G. Georgiades: *Schubert. Musik und Lyrik* (Göttingen: Vandenhoeck & Ruprecht, 1967)

Gerstenberg 1963   Walter Gerstenberg, Jan La Rue and Wolfgang Rehm, eds: *Festschrift Otto Erich Deutsch zum 80. Geburtstag am 5. September 1963* (Kassel: Bärenreiter, 1963)

Gibbs 1994   Chistopher H. Gibbs: 'Einige Bemerkungen zur Veröffentlichung und zu den frühen Ausgaben von Schuberts *Erlkönig*', *Schubert durch die Brille*, Vol. 12 (January 1994), pp. 33–48

Gibbs 1997   Christopher H. Gibbs, ed.: *The Cambridge Companion to Schubert* (Cambridge: Cambridge University Press, 1997)

Gibbs 2000   Christopher H. Gibbs: *The Life of Schubert* (Cambridge: Cambridge University Press, 2000)

Gide 1942   André Gide: 'Preface' to *Goethe: Œuvres dramatiques*. Bibliothèque de la Pléaide (Paris: Éditions Gallimard, 1942)

Godowsky 2001   Millan Sachania, ed.: *The Godowsky Collection. Vol. 2: Transcriptions, Arrangements and Cadenzas* (New York: Carl Fischer, 2001).

Goebels 1978   Franzpeter Goebels: ' "Die Forelle del Sig. Baumbach". Eine Anregungsquelle für Schubert?', *Musica*, Vol. 32, No. 2 (March–April 1978), pp. 152–3

Goedeke   Karl Goedeke et al.: *Grundriss zur Geschichte der deutschen Dichtung aus den Quellen*. This publication consists of eighteen volumes, some in a number of sections, which appeared in print between 1859 and 1998. The volumes consulted for this book are listed below, with publication information and reprint dates where later editions have been consulted:
Volume 4: *Vom siebenjährigen bis zum Weltkriege. Erste Abteilung*, ed. E. Goetze (Dresden: L. Ehlermann, 1891; subsequently reissued in five substantially enlarged *Abteilungen*, 1910–60)
Volume 5: *Vom siebenjährigen bis zum Weltkriege. Zweite Abteilung*, ed. E. Goetze (Dresden: L. Ehlermann, 1893)
Volume 6: *Zeit des Weltkrieges. Siebentes Buch, erste Abteilung*, ed. E. Goetze (Dresden: L. Ehlermann, 1898)
Volume 7: *Zeit des Weltkrieges. Siebentes Buch, zweite Abteilung*, ed. E. Goetze (Dresden: L. Ehlermann, 1900, 2nd edn, 1906)
Volume 8: *Vom Weltfrieden bis zur französischen Revolution 1830. Achtes Buch, erste Abteilung*, ed. E. Goetze (Dresden: L. Ehlermann, 1905)

Volume 9: *Vom Weltfrieden bis zur französischen Revolution 1830. Achtes Buch, zweite Abteilung*, ed. E. Goetze (Dresden: L. Ehlermann, 1910)

Volume 10: *Vom Weltfrieden bis zur französischen Revolution 1830. Achtes Buch, dritte Abteilung*, ed. E. Goetze (Dresden: L. Ehlermann, 1913)

Volume 11: *Vom Weltfrieden bis zur französischen Revolution 1830. Achtes Buch, vierte Abteilung (Drama und Theater), Erster Halbband*, ed. C. Diesch (2nd edn, Dusseldorf: L. Ehlermann, 1951)

Volume 12: *Vom Weltfrieden bis zur französischen Revolution 1830. Achtes Buch, fünfte Abteilung*, ed. F. Muncker and A. Rosenbaum (2nd edn, Dresden: L. Ehlermann, 1929)

Volume 13: *Vom Weltfrieden bis zur französischen Revolution 1830. Achtes Buch, sechste Abteilung* [no editor listed] (2nd edn, Dresden: L. Ehlermann, 1938)

Volume 14, part 2: *Vom Frieden 1815 bis zur französischen Revolution 1830. Achtes Buch, siebente Abteilung*, ed. H. Jacob (Berlin: Akademie Verlag & Dusseldorf: L. Ehlermann, 1955)

Volume 14, part 3: *Vom Frieden 1815 bis zur französischen Revolution 1830. Achtes Buch, siebente Abteilung*, ed. H. Jacob (2nd edn, Berlin: Akademie Verlag & Dusseldorf: L. Ehlermann, 1956)

Volume 15: *Vom Frieden 1815 bis zur französischen Revolution 1830. Achtes Buch, achte Abteilung*, ed. H. Jacob (2nd edn, Berlin: Akademie Verlag, 1964)

Volume 17, parts 1–2: [No volume title], ed. H. Jacob (2nd edn, Berlin: Akademie Verlag, 1991). This large volume, divided into two parts, is entirely given over to a listing of translations and translators

Volume 18: *Register I–III*, ed. H. Jacob (2nd edn, Berlin: Akademie Verlag, 1998)

Goertz 2002   Harald Goertz: 'Der Mühle Lied. Myrthen um Mühle und Müllerin' in W. Aderhold, M. Kube and W. Litschauer, eds, *Schubert und das Biedermeier. Beiträge zur Musik des frühen 19. Jahrhunderts. Festschrift für Walther Dürr zum 70. Geburtstag* (Kassel: Bärenreiter, 2002), pp. 73–81

Goldschmidt 1976   Harry Goldschmidt: *Franz Schubert. Ein Lebensbild* (Berlin: Henschelverlag, 1954, repr. Leipzig: VEB Deutscher für Musik, 1976)

Gooch/Thatcher 1991   Bryan Gooch and David Thatcher: *A Shakespeare Music Catalogue*, 5 vols (Oxford: Clarendon Press, 1991)

Gramit 1987   David Gramit: *The intellectual and aesthetic tenets of Franz Schubert's Circle: their development and their influence on his music*, PhD thesis, Duke University, 1987

Griebler 2005   Martha Griebler: *Franz Schubert. Zeichnungen* (Horn: Druckerei Berger, 2005)

Grindea 1998   Miron Grindea: 'Beckett's Involvement with Music' in
                    M. Bryden, ed., *Samuel Beckett and Music* (Oxford:
                    Clarendon Press, 1998), pp. 183–5
Grove 1954   Eric Blom, ed.: *Grove's Dictionary of Music and Musicians*,
                    9 vols (London: Macmillan, 1954)
Grove 1980   Stanley Sadie, ed.: *The New Grove Dictionary of Music and
                    Musicians*, 20 vols (London: Macmillan, 1980)
Grove 2001   Stanley Sadie and John Tyrrell, eds: *The New Grove
                    Dictionary of Music and Musicians*, 29 vols (London:
                    Macmillan, 2001)
Gruber 1999   Gerold Gruber: 'Moritz Graf von Dietrichsteins Lieder' in
                    E. Badura-Skoda, G. Gruber et al., eds, *Schubert und Seine
                    Freunde* (Vienna: Böhlau Verlag, 1999), pp. 311–30
Gülke 1991   Peter Gülke: *Franz Schubert und seine Zeit* (Laaber: Laaber
                    Verlag, 1991)
Gunkel 1999   Rainer Gunkel: 'Franz von Schober in Schnepfenthal',
                    Schubert durch die Brille, Vol. 22 (January 1999), pp. 53–7
Haas/Orel 1929   Robert Haas and Alfred Orel, eds: *Bericht über den
                    Internationalen Kongress für Schubertforschung. Wien 25. bis
                    29. November 1928* (Augsburg: Dr Benno Filser Verlag, 1929)
Hake 1908   Bruno Hake: *Sein Leben und Dichten Kapitel IV: Die
                    schöne Müllerin* (Berlin: Mayer & Müller, 1908)
Hall 2003   Michael Hall: *Schubert's Song Sets* (Aldershot: Ashgate, 2003)
Hallmark 1982   Rufus Hallmark: 'Schubert's "Auf dem Strom"' in
                    E. Badura-Skoda and P. Branscombe, eds, *Schubert Studies.
                    Problems of Style and Chronology* (Cambridge: Cambridge
                    University Press, 1982), pp. 25–46
Hallmark 1996   Rufus Hallmark: *German Lieder in the Nineteenth Century*
                    (New York: Schirmer Books, 1996; 2nd edn, London:
                    Routledge, 2009)
Hanson 1985   Alice M. Hanson: *Musical Life in Biedermeier Vienna*
                    (Cambridge: Cambridge University Press, 1985)
Heiberg 1993   Harold Heiberg: 'Eine Erklärung für die *Nebensonnen*',
                    Schubert durch die Brille, Vol. 10 (January 1993), p. 98
Herbeck 1885   Ludwig Herbeck: *Johann Herbeck: ein Lebensbild von
                    seinem Sohne Ludwig* (Vienna: Gutmann, 1885)
Heuberger 1920   Richard Heuberger: *Franz Schubert* (Berlin: 'Harmonie'
                    Verlagsgesellschaft für Literatur und Kunst, 1902, repr.
                    Berlin: Schlesische Verlagsanstalt, 1920)
Hilmar 1978   Ernst Hilmar: *Verzeichnis der Schubert-Handschriften in
                    der Musiksammlung der Wiener Stadt- und
                    Landesbibliothek* (Kassel: Bärenreiter, 1978)
Hilmar 1988   Ernst Hilmar: *Franz Schubert in his Time*, trans. R. Pauly
                    (Portland: Amadeus Press, 1988). First published as *Franz
                    Schubert in seiner Zeit* (Vienna: Böhlau Verlag, 1985)
Hilmar 1988[2]   Ernst Hilmar: 'Anmerkungen zu Franz Schuberts
                    Erstdrucken' in C.-H. Mahling, ed., *Florilegium
                    Musicologicum. Hellmut Federhofer zum 75. Geburtstag*
                    (Tutzing: Hans Schneider, 1988), pp. 145–54

Hilmar 1989	Ernst Hilmar: *Schubert* (Graz: Akademische Druck- u. Verlagsanstalt, 1989)
Hilmar 1991	Ernst Hilmar: 'Eine spätere Version von *An den Frühling* D587', *Schubert durch die Brille*, Vol. 6 (January 1991), p. 47
Hilmar 1993	Ernst Hilmar: 'Schuberts *Gesang der Geister über den Wassern*. Das "wiederaufgefundene" Autograph von D714', *Schubert durch die Brille*, Vol. 10 (January 1993), pp. 7–24
Hilmar 1993[2]	Ernst Hilmar: 'Ein "geheimes Programm" in den drei wiederentdeckten Manuskripten zum Zyklus *Die schöne Müllerin*', *Schubert durch die Brille*, Vol. 11 (January 1993), pp. 34–47
Hilmar 1997	Ernst Hilmar: *Franz Schubert* (Hamburg: Rowohlt Taschenbuch Verlag, 1997)
Hilmar/Brusatti 1978	Ernst Hilmar and Otto Brusatti, eds: *Franz Schubert. Ausstellung der Wiener Stadt- und Landesbibliothek zum 150. Todestag des Komponisten* (Vienna: Universal Edition, 1978)
Hilmar/Jestremski 1997	Ernst Hilmar and Margret Jestremski, eds: *Schubert-Lexikon* (Graz: Akademische Druck- und Verlagsanstalt, 1997)
Hilmar/Jestremski 2004	Ernst Hilmar and Margret Jestremski, eds: *Schubert-Enzyklopädie*, 2 vols (Tutzing: Hans Schneider, 2004)
Hilmar-Voit 1991	Renate Hilmar-Voit: 'Zu Schuberts "letzten Liedern". Einige Zweifel an überlieferten Daten und Fakten', *Schubert durch die Brille*, Vol. 6 (January 1991), pp. 48–55
Hilmar-Voit 1991[2]	Renate Hilmar-Voit: '*Die schöne Müllerin* und ihre Folgen: Neue Dokumente, neue Quellen und neue Probleme', *Schubert durch die Brille*, Vol. 7 (June 1991), pp. 19–26
Hirsch 1993	Marjorie Wing Hirsch: *Schubert's Dramatic Lieder* (Cambridge: Cambridge University Press, 1993)
Hirsch 2007	Marjorie Wing Hirsch: *Romantic Lieder and the Search for Lost Paradise* (Cambridge: Cambridge University Press, 2007)
Höcker 1987	Karla Höcker: *Franz Schubert in seiner Welt* (2nd edn, Munich: Deutscher Taschenbuch Verlag, 1987)
Höslinger 2013	Clemens Höslinger: 'Schubert, Schwind und die Göttin Diana. Eine Erinnerung an die Sängerin Catinka Buchwieser', *Schubert Perspektiven*, Vol. 10, Book 1 (Stuttgart: Franz Steiner Verlag, 2013), pp. 45–69
Holl 2002	Robert Holl: '*Franz Schubert. Evangelium Johannis 6, Vers 55–58 (D607). Eine Aussetzung*' in W. Aderhold, M. Kube and W. Litschauer, eds, *Schubert und das Biedermeier. Beiträge zur Musik des frühen 19. Jahrhunderts. Festschrift für Walther Durr zum 70. Geburtstag* (Kassel: Bärenreiter, 2002), pp. 45–51
Holmes 2004	Lewis M. Holmes: *Kosegarten: The Turbulent Life & Times of a North German Poet* (New York: Peter Lang, 2004)

Holmes 2005	Lewis M Holmes: *Kosegarten's Cultural Legacy: Aesthetics, Religion, Literature, Art and Music* (New York: Peter Lang, 2005)
Hoorickx 1969	Reinhard Van Hoorickx: 'About some early Schubert Manuscripts', *The Music Review*, Vol. 30, No. 2 (May 1969), pp. 118–23
Hoorickx 1974	Reinhard Van Hoorickx: 'Old and New Schubert Problems', *The Music Review*, Vol. 35, No. 1 (Feb–May 1974), pp. 76–92
Hoorickx 1974[2]	Reinhard Van Hoorickx: 'Schubert's Reminiscences of His Own Works', *The Musical Quarterly*, Vol. 60, No. 3 (July 1974), pp. 373–88
Hoorickx 1976	Reinhard Van Hoorickx: 'Thematic Catalogue of Schubert's Works: New Additions, Corrections and Notes', *Revue Belge de Musicologie*, Vols 28–30 (1974–76), pp. 136–71
Hoorickx 1976[2]	Reinhard Van Hoorickx: 'Un manuscrit inconnu de Schubert', *Revue Belge de Musicologie*, Vols 28–30 (1974–6), pp. 260–3
Hoorickx 1977	Reinhard Van Hoorickx: 'Schubert: Songs and Song Fragments not included in the Collected Edition', *The Music Review*, Vol. 38, No. 4 (November 1977), pp. 267–92
Hoorickx 1978	Reinhard Van Hoorickx: 'Further Schubert Discoveries', *The Music Review*, Vol. 39, No. 2 (May 1978), pp. 95–9
Hoorickx 1980	Reinhard Van Hoorickx: 'A Schubert Song Rediscovered', *Musical Times*, Vol. 121, No. 1644 (February 1980), pp. 97–8
Howard 1995	Leslie Howard: [sleeve notes], *Liszt. The Complete Music for Solo Piano. Vols 31–3: The Schubert Transcriptions, I–III* (Hyperion Records) 1995, CDA66951/3, CDA66954/6, CDA66957/9
Hutchings 1945	Arthur Hutchings: *Schubert* (London: J. M. Dent & Sons, 1945)
Jestremski 2003	Margret Jestremski: '175 Jahre Schuberts "Privatkonzert" – Eine längst fällige Korrektur', *Schubert durch die Brille*, Vol. 30 (January 2003), pp. 115–24
Jolizza 1910	W. K. von Jolizza [Lizzy von Waldheim and Baronin Johanna Krauss]: *Das Lied und seine Geschichte* (Vienna and Leipzig: A. Hartleben, 1910)
Kahl 1938	Willi Kahl: *Verzeichnis des Schrifttums über Franz Schubert, 1828–1928* (Regensburg: Gustav Bosse, 1938)
Kecskeméti 1968	István Kecskeméti: 'Eine wieder aufgetauchte Eigenschrift Schuberts', *Österreichische Musikzeitschrift*, Vol. 23, No. 2 (February 1968), pp. 70–4
Kecskeméti 1969	István Kecskeméti: 'Neu entdeckte Schubert-Autographe', *Österreichische Musikzeitschrift*, Vol. 24, No. 10 (October 1969), pp. 564–8

Kohlhäufl 1999	Michael Kohlhäufl: *Poetisches Vaterland. Dichtung und politisches Denken im Freundeskreis Franz Schuberts* (Kassel: Bärenreiter, 1999)
Kohlhäufl 2002	Michael Kohlhäufl: 'Tod und Verklärung des "*königlichen Poeten*" – der Sänger als Dichterfürst der Goethezeit' in W. Aderhold, M. Kube and W. Litschauer, eds, *Schubert und das Biedermeier. Beiträge zur Musik des frühen 19. Jahrhunderts. Festschrift für Walther Durr zum 70. Geburtstag* (Kassel: Bärenreiter, 2002), pp. 173–84
Kramer 1998	Lawrence Kramer: *Franz Schubert: Sexuality, Subjectivity, Song* (Cambridge: Cambridge University Press, 1998)
Kramer 1994	Richard Kramer: *Distant Cycles. Schubert and the Conceiving of Song* (Chicago: University of Chicago Press, 1994)
Krautwurst 2002	Franz Krautwurst: *George Grove als Schubert-Forscher. Seine Briefe an Max Friedlaender* (Tutzing: Hans Schneider, 2002)
Kravitt 1996	Edward F. Kravitt: *The Lied: Mirror of Late Romanticism* (New Haven and London: Yale University Press, 1996)
Kreissle 1861	Heinrich Kreissle von Hellborn: *Franz Schubert. Eine biografische Skizze* (Vienna: L. C. Zamarski & C. Dittmarsch, 1861). N.B. Despite the printed publication date, this volume appeared in 1860
Kreissle 1865	Heinrich Kreissle von Hellborn: *Franz Schubert* (Vienna: Carl Gerold's Sohn, 1865)
Kreissle 1869	Heinrich Kreissle von Hellborn: *The Life of Franz Schubert*, trans. A. D. Coleridge, 2 vols (London: Longmans, Green & Co., 1869)
Kube 2007	Michael Kube, Walburga Litschauer and Gernot Gruber, eds: *Schubert und die Nachwelt. I. Internationale Arbeitstagung zur Schubert-Rezeption Wien 2003. Kongressbericht* (Munich and Salzburg: Musikverlag Katzbichler, 2007)
Lafite 1928	Carl Lafite: *Das Schubertlied und seine Sänger* (Vienna: Strache Verlag, 1928)
Lambert 2009	Sterling Lambert: *Re-reading Poetry. Schubert's multiple settings of Goethe* (Woodbridge: Boydell Press, 2009)
Landon 1970	Christa Landon: 'New Schubert Finds', trans. G. Deutsch and C. Landon, *Music Review*, Vol. 31, No. 3 (August 1970), pp. 215–31
Lehl 2002	Karsten Lehl: 'Zur Schubert-Diskographie: Nachweisbare Aufnahmen auf Schellack-Platten', *Schubert durch die Brille*, Vol. 29 (June 2002), pp. 229–404
Liedlexikon 2012	Walther Dürr, Michael Kube, Uwe Schweikert and Stefanie Steiner, eds: *Schubert Liedlexikon* (Kassel: Bärenreiter, 2012)
Liess 1954	Andreas Liess: *Johann Michael Vogl. Hofoperist und Schubertsänger* (Graz and Cologne: Hermann Böhlau, 1954)

Litschauer 1986   Walburga Litschauer: *Neue Dokumente zum Schubert-Kreis*
                         [Band 1] (Vienna: Musikwissenschaftlicher Verlag Wien,
                         1986)
Litschauer 1993   Walburga Litschauer: 'Unbekannte Dokumente über
                         Schubert und die Klaviere seiner Zeit', *Schubert durch die*
                         Brille, Vol. 11 (June 1993), pp. 133-6
Litschauer 1993²   Walburga Litschauer: *Neue Dokumente zum Schubert-*
                         Kreis, Band 2 (Vienna: Musikwissenschaftlicher Verlag
                         Wien, 1993)
Litschauer 2001   Walburga Litschauer: 'Schubert und sein Lehrer Salieri',
                         Schubert Perspektiven, Vol. 1, Book 1 (Stuttgart:
                         Franz Steiner Verlag, 2001), pp. 74-83
Littlejohns 2000   Richard Littlejohns: 'Lucinde' in M. Konzett, ed.,
                         Encyclopaedia of German Literature, 2 vols (Chicago and
                         London: Routledge, 2000), Vol. 2, pp. 873-4
Lorenz 2000   Michael Lorenz: 'Dokumente zur Biographie Johann
                         Mayrhofers', *Schubert durch die Brille*, Vol. 25 (June 2000),
                         pp. 21-50
McKay 1977   Elizabeth Norman McKay: 'Schubert's *Winterreise*
                         reconsidered', *The Music Review*, Vol. 38, No. 2 (May
                         1977), pp. 94-100
McKay 1988   Elizabeth Norman McKay: *Franz Schubert. Bühnenwerke.*
                         Kritische Gesamtausgabe der Texte, ed. C. Pollack (Tutzing:
                         Hans Schneider, 1988)
McKay 1991   Elizabeth Norman McKay: *Franz Schubert's Music for the*
                         Theatre (Tutzing: Hans Schneider, 1991)
McKay 1996   Elizabeth Norman McKay: *Franz Schubert: A Biography*
                         (Oxford: Clarendon Press, 1996)
McKay 1999   Elizabeth Norman McKay: 'Einige Querverbindungen
                         zwischen der *Winterreise* und der *Deutschen Messe*',
                         Schubert durch die Brille, Vol. 23 (June 1999), pp. 111-21
McKay 2000   Elizabeth Norman McKay: 'Zu Schuberts Vertonungen
                         von Kosegarten-Texten aus dem Jahr 1815: Aus Anlass
                         einer Aufführung in Oxford im September 1999', *Schubert*
                         durch die Brille, Vol. 24 (January 2000), pp. 141-6
McKay 2001   Elizabeth Norman McKay: 'Schubert and "The Year
                         without Summer" ', *Schubert durch die Brille*, Vol. 27 (June
                         2001), pp. 65-78
McKay 2009   Elizabeth Norman McKay: *Schubert: The Piano and Dark*
                         Keys (Tutzing: Hans Schneider, 2009)
Mackworth-Young 1952   Gerard Mackworth-Young: 'Goethe's "Prometheus" and Its
                         Settings by Schubert and Wolf', *Proceedings of the Royal*
                         Musical Association, 78th Session (1951-2), pp. 53-65
Marston 1998   Nicholas Marston ' "Wie aus der Ferne". "Pastness" and
                         "presentness" in the Lieder of Beethoven, Schubert and
                         Schumann', *Schubert durch die Brille*, Vol. 21 (June 1998),
                         pp. 126-42
Massin 1977   Brigitte Massin: *Franz Schubert* (Paris: Fayard, 1977, repr.
                         1993)

Matthisson 2007	Friedrich Matthisson: *Das Stammbuch Friedrich von Matthissons. Trankription und Kommentar zum Faksimile*, ed. E. Wege, D. Walser-Wilhelm, P. Walser-Wilhelm and C. Holliger (Göttingen: Wallstein Verlag, 2007)
Mayer 1991	Andreas Mayer: 'Zur ersten Veröffentlichung von Liedern aus *Die schöne Müllerin* in Deutschland', *Schubert durch die Brille*, Vol. 7 (June 1991), pp. 29–36
Mayer 1887	Anton Mayer: *Wiens Buchdrucker-Geschichte. 1432–1882*, 2 vols (Vienna: Verlag des Comités zur Feier der vierhundertj. Einführung der Buchdruckerkunst in Wien, W. Frick, 1887)
Mendel/Reissmann 1891	Hermann Mendel, August Reissmann et al.: *Musikalisches Conversations-lexikon. Eine Encylopädie der gesammten musikalischen Wissenschaften für Gebildete aller Stände*, 11 vols plus *Ergänzungsband* (2nd edn, Leipzig: List & Francke, 1890–1)
Menzel 1828	Wolfgang Menzel: *Die deutsche Literatur*, 2 vols (Stuttgart: Gebrüder Franckh, 1828)
Messing 2006	Scott Messing: *Schubert in the European Imagination. Volume 1: The Romantic and Victorian Eras* (Woodbridge: Boydell & Brewer, 2006)
Metzner 1992	Günter Metzner: *Heine in der Musik: Bibliographie der Heine-Vertonungen*. Vols 9–10: *Werke A–D* & *Werke E–Z* (Tutzing: Hans Schneider, 1992). Within this extraordinary twelve-volume set, these two volumes list the Heine settings alphabetically with appended lists of the musical settings associated with each poem
MGG 1949	Friedrich Blume, ed.: *Die Musik in Geschichte und Gegenwart. Allgemeine Enzyklopädie der Musik*, 17 vols (Kassel & Basel: Bärenreiter, 1949–86)
MGG 1994	Ludwig Finscher, ed.: *Die Musik in Geschichte und Gegenwart. Allgemeine Enzyklopädie der Musik*, 29 vols (Kassel: Bärenreiter & Stuttgart: J. B. Metzler, 1994–2008)
Mies 1928	Paul Mies: *Schubert, der Meister des Liedes. Die Entwicklung von Form und Inhalt im Schubertschen Lied* (Berlin: Max Hesse, 1928)
Monson 1992	Dale E. Monson: 'Filosofo di Campagna, Il' in S. Sadie, ed., *The New Grove Dictionary of Opera*, 4 vols (London: Macmillan, 1992), Vol. 2, pp. 204–5
Montgomery 2001	David Montgomery: 'Notation and performance in Schubert: A discussion and review of the relevant sections from Clive Brown's *Classical and Romantic performing practice 1750–1900*', *Schubert durch die Brille*, Vol. 27 (June 2001), pp. 97–116
Montgomery 2003	David Montgomery: *Franz Schubert's Music in Performance: Compositional ideals, notational intent, historical realities, pedagogical foundations* (Hillsdale, NY: Pendragon Press, 2003)

Moore 1975   Gerald Moore: *The Schubert Song Cycles: With thoughts on
                              performance* (London: Hamish Hamilton, 1975)
Moser 1949   Hans Joachim Moser: *Goethe und die Musik* (Leipzig:
                              C. F. Peters, 1949)
Müller 1903   *The Diary and Letters of Wilhelm Müller. With explanatory
                              notes and a biographical index*, ed. and trans. P. S. Allen
                              and J. T. Hatfield (Chicago: University of Chicago Press,
                              1903). N.B. Despite its English title, this is a German-
                              language volume
Müller 1898   Friedrich Max Müller: *Auld Lang Syne* (London:
                              Longmans, Green & Co., 1898)
Muxfeldt 1991   Kristina Muxfeldt: *Schubert Song Studies*, PhD thesis, State
                              University of New York at Stony Brook, 1991
Newbould 1997   Brian Newbould: *Schubert. The Music and the Man*
                              (London: Victor Gollancz, 1997)
Newbould 1998   Brian Newbould, ed.: *Schubert Studies* (Aldershot: Ashgate,
                              1998)
Norton-Welsh 1996   Christopher Norton-Welsh: 'Zur Aufführungpraxis der
                              Schönen Müllerin', *Schubert durch die Brille*, Vol. 16/17
                              (January 1996), pp. 117–22
Nottebohm 1874   Gustav Nottebohm: *Thematisches Verzeichniss der im
                              Druck erschienenen Werke von Franz Schubert* (Vienna:
                              Freidrich Schreiber, 1874)
NSA   *Neue Schubert-Ausgabe* (Kassel: Bärenreiter, 1963–):
                              Dietrich Berke, ed.: *III Mehrstimmige Gesänge*, 5 vols
                              (1974–); Walther Dürr, ed.: *IV Lieder*, 20 vols (1968–
                              2011). Series IV is in 14 numbered volumes, with Vols 1–5
                              and 14 published in two parts each (a and b), thus 20
                              printed volumes in all; Walther Dürr: *Lieder: Kritische
                              Berichte*, 14 vols (Tübingen: Internationalen Schubert-
                              Gesellschaft, 1972–). The volumes are numbered to
                              correspond with the NSA publications. These too-little-
                              known bright-blue paperbacks contain Walther Dürr's
                              meticulously detailed descriptions of the autograph and
                              copy sources of the Schubert songs, as well as explications
                              of editorial decisions taken on behalf of NSA. They
                              represent a life's work – an examination of the nuts
                              and bolts of Schubert manuscripts unequalled in
                              our time
ÖMZ 1958   *Österreichische Musikzeitschrift. Sonderheft: Otto
                              Erich Deutsch zum 75. Geburtstag*, Vol. 13 (autumn
                              1958)
Orel 1930   Alfred Orel: 'Der urpsprüngliche Text zu Schuberts
                              Liebeslauschen' in E. H. Müller, ed., *Festschrift Johannes
                              Biehle zum 60. Geburtstag überreicht* (Leipzig: Kistner &
                              Siegel, 1930), pp. 71–81
Orel 1937   Alfred Orel: 'Kleine Schubertstudien: I. Die authentische
                              Fassung von Schuberts *Lied eines Krieger*', *Archiv für
                              Musikforschung*, Vol. 2, No. 1 (1937), pp. 285–98

Orel 1940	Alfred Orel: *Der Junge Schubert. Mit ungedruckten Kompositionen Schuberts nach Texten von Pietro Metastasio* (Vienna: Musikverlag Adolf Robitschek, 1940)
Ottner 1999	Carmen Ottner: ' "So schön die Welt, und doch so vieles Leiden. So viele Freundschaft, so viel Übermuth!" – Franz von Schlechta, Dichter und Beamter (1796–1875)' in E. Badura-Skoda, G. Gruber et al., eds, *Schubert und Seine Freunde* (Vienna: Böhlau Verlag, 1999), pp. 183–202
Pagnier 2006	Dominique Pagnier: *Mon Album Schubert* (Paris: Éditions Gallimard, 2006)
Panofka 1991	Andreas Mayer: 'Biographie – Franz Schubert [von H. Panofka, 1838]', *Schubert durch die Brille*, Vol. 7 (June 1991), pp. 7–18
Partsch/Scheit 1989	Erich Wolfgang Partsch and Karl Scheit: 'Ein unbekanntes Schubertlied in einer Sammlung aus dem Wiener Vormärz', *Schubert durch die Brille*, Vol. 2 (1989), pp. 15–18
Pascall 1998	Robert Pascall: ' "My love of Schubert – no fleeting fancy." Brahms's Response to Schubert', *Schubert durch die Brille*, Vol. 21 (June 1998), pp. 39–60
Paumgartner 1943	Bernhard Paumgartner: *Franz Schubert* (Zurich: Atlantis-Verlag, 1943)
Pfordten 1916	Hermann von der Pfordten: *Franz Schubert und das deutsche Lied* (Leipzig: Quelle & Meyer, 1916)
Porhansl 1989	Lucia Porhansl: 'Bemerkungen zu Franz Schuberts Textvorlagen nach Johann Mayrhofer und Aloys Schreiber', *Schubert durch die Brille*, Vol. 2 (January 1989), pp. 12–14
Porhansl 1990	Lucia Porhansl: 'Schuberts Textvorlagen nach Salis-Seewis und Kleist – Einige Bemerkungen', *Schubert durch die Brille*, Vol. 4 (January 1990), pp. 11–13
Porhansl 1993	Lucia Porhansl: 'Schuberts Textvorlagen nach Friedrich Wilhelm Gotter und Christian Friedrich Daniel Schubart', *Schubert durch die Brille*, Vol. 10 (January 1993), pp. 69–74
Porhansl 1995	Lucia Porhansl: 'Schuberts Textvorlagen von Ignaz Fraz Castelli', *Schubert durch die Brille*, Vol. 14 (January 1995), pp. 101–4
Porhansl 1996	Lucia Porhansl: '*Der Liedler*: Zu Kenners Textvorlage und zu Schwinds Illustrationen', *Schubert durch die Brille*, Vol. 16/17 (January 1996), pp. 111–16
Porter 1961	Ernest G. Porter: *Schubert's Song Technique* (London: Dennis Dobson, 1961)
Pyrker 1966	Johann Ladislaus Pyrker: *Mein Leben, 1772–1847*, ed. A. P. Czigler (Vienna: Böhlau Verlag, 1966)
Raab 2002	Michael Raab: 'Zu Antonio Diabellis Nachlaßlieferungen' in W. Aderhold, M. Kube and W. Litschauer, eds, *Schubert und das Biedermeier. Beiträge zur Musik des frühen 19. Jahrhunderts. Festschrift für Walther Dürr zum 70. Geburtstag* (Kassel: Bärenreiter, 2002), pp. 217–26
Racek 1956	Fritz Racek: 'Von den Schubert-Handschriften der Stadtbibliothek', in Amt für Kultur und Volksbildung der

Stadt Wien, *Festschrift zum hundertjährigen Bestehen der Wiener Stadtbibliothek, 1856–1956* (Vienna: Verlag für Jugend und Volk, 1956), pp. 98–124

Reed/Gascoyne 1989 Jeremy Reed (trans.) and David Gascoyne: *Novalis. Hymns to the Night* (Petersfield: Enitharmon Press, 1989)

Reed 1972 John Reed: *Schubert. The Final Years* (London: Faber and Faber, 1972)

Reed 1978 John Reed: *Schubert* (London: Faber and Faber, 1978)

Reed 1985 John Reed: *The Schubert Song Companion* (Manchester: Manchester University Press, 1985)

Reed 1987 John Reed: *Schubert* (London: J. M. Dent & Sons, 1987, repr. Oxford: Oxford University Press, 1997)

Reid 2007 Paul Reid: *The Beethoven Song Companion* (Manchester: Manchester University Press, 2007)

Reissmann 1861 August Reissmann: *Das deutsche Lied in seiner historischen Entwicklung* (Kassel: Oswald Bertram, 1861)

Reissmann 1873 August Reissmann: *Franz Schubert. Sein Leben und seine Werke* (Berlin: J. Guttentag, 1873)

Rigney 2012 Anne Rigney: *The Afterlives of Walter Scott: Memory on the Move* (Oxford: Oxford University Press, 2012)

Robertson 1902 John George Robertson: *A History of German Literature* (Edinburgh: Blackwood, 1902)

Robertson 1946 Alec Robertson: 'The Songs' in G. Abraham, ed., *Schubert. A Symposium* (London: Lindsay Drummond Ltd, 1946), pp. 149–97

Rode-Breymann 1999 Susanne Rode-Breymann: 'Schubert's *Sieben Gesänge aus Walter Scotts* Fraulein vom See Op. 52: Kulturhistorische und Zusammenhänge und gattungsübergreifende Tendenzen der zyklischen Anlagen' in D. Berke, W. Dürr, et al., eds, *Franz Schubert – Werk und Rezeption. Bericht über den Internationalen Schubert-Kongress Duisberg 1997. Teil 1: Lieder und Gesänge – Geistliche Werke* (Duisburg: Deutsche Schubert-Gesellschaft, 1999), pp. 31–45

Rosen 1996 Charles Rosen: *The Romantic Generation* (London: HarperCollins, 1996)

Rowland 2000 Herbert Rowland: 'Matthias Claudius' in M. Konzett, ed., *Encyclopaedia of German Literature*, 2 vols (Chicago and London: Routledge, 2000), Vol. 1, pp. 193–5

Sams 1978 Eric Sams: 'Notes on a Magic Flute: The Origins of the Schubertian Lied', *The Musical Times*, Vol. 119, No. 1629 (November 1978), pp. 947–9

Saunders 1894 Bailey Saunders: *The Life and Letters of James Macpherson. Containing a particular account of his famous quarrel with Dr. Johnson, and a sketch of the origin and influence of the Ossianic poems* (London: S. Sonnenschein & Co., 1894)

Scherer 1883 Wilhelm Scherer: *Geschichte der deutschen Literatur* (Berlin: Weidmannsche Buchhandlung, 1883)

Scherer 1886 Wilhelm Scherer: *Aufsätze über Goethe* (Berlin: Weidmannsche Buchhandlung, 1886)

Schilling 1840	Gustav Schilling, ed.: *Encylopädie der gesammten musikalischen Wissenschaften, oder Universal-Lexicon der Tonkunst*, 6 vols and supplement (2nd edn, Stuttgart: Franz Heinrich Köhler, 1840–2)
Schlossar 1906	Anton Schlossar, ed.: *Gedichte von Karl Gottfried Ritter von Leitner* (Leipzig: Reclam, 1906)
Schmid 2002	Manfred Hermann Schmid: 'Die Instrumente der Liedbegleitung', in G. Günther and R. Nägele, eds, *Musik in Baden-Württemberg Jahrbuch*, Vol. 9 (Stuttgart & Weimar: Verlag J. B. Metzler, 2002), pp. 137–49
Schnapper 1937	Edith Schnapper: *Die Gesänge des Junger Schubert vor dem Durchbruch des romantischen Liedprinzips* (Berne and Leipzig: P. Haupt, 1937)
Schneider 1994	Marcel Schneider: *Schubert* (Paris: Éditions du Seuil, 1957, 2nd edn, 1994)
Schober 1891	Thekla von Schober: *Unter fünf Königen und drei Kaisern. Unpolitische Erinnerungen einer alten Frau* (Glogau: Carl Flemming, 1891)
Schochow 1974	Maximilian and Lilly Schochow, eds: *Franz Schubert. Die Texte seiner einstimmig komponierten Lieder und ihre Dichter*, 2 vols (Hildesheim and New York: Georg Olms Verlag, 1974). *See also* Bodendorff 2006
Schroeder 2009	David Schroeder: *Our Schubert. His Enduring Legacy* (Lanham: Scarecrow Press, 2009)
Schubart 1806	Christian Friedrich Daniel Schubart: *Ideen zu einer Ästhetik der Tonkunst* (Vienna: J. V. Degen, 1806). Reissued, ed. Paul Alfred Merbach (Leipzig: Wolkenwanderer-Verlag, 1924)
Schubert 1997	[Exhibition catalogue] *Schubert 200 Jahre: 'Ich lebe und componire wie ein Gott' – Schuberts Leben und Schaffen. Stadtmuseum Lindau 'Schubert im Spiegel der Nachwelt' 3. Mai bis 7. September 1997*, Landratsamt Ravensburg and Kulturamt der Stadt Lindau (Cologne: Druckerei Locher, 1997)
Schulze-Ardey 2003	Ira Schulze-Ardey: *Der Komponist als produzierender Leser. Zum Verhältnis von Text- und Musikstruktur im klavierbegleiteten Sololied am Beispiel der Dichtung Friedrich von Matthissons in den Vertonungen von Franz Schubert* (Frankfurt am Main: Peter Lang, 2003)
Schwandt 1997	Christoph Schwandt: ' "Unausprechlich, unbegriffen". Indizien und Argumente aus Leben und Werk für die wahrscheinliche Homosexualität des Franz Peter Schubert' in H.-K. Metzger and R. Riehn, eds, *Musik-Konzepte 97/98: Franz Schubert 'Todesmusik'* (October 1997), pp. 112–94
Seidlitz [Jeitteles] 1837	Julius Seidlitz [Isaac Jeitteles]: *Die Poesie und die Poeten in Österreich im Jahre 1836*, 2 vols (Grimma: J. M. Gebhart, 1837)
Shackleton 2012	Andrew Schackleton: 'Animals in Schubert's Songs', *The Schubertian*, Vol. 73 (January 2012), pp. 9–18

Smeed 1985   John William Smeed: ' "Süssertönendes Klavier": Tributes to the Early Piano in Poetry and Song', *Music & Letters*, Vol. 66, No. 3 (July 1985), pp. 228–40

Solomon 1989   Maynard Solomon: 'Franz Schubert and the Peacocks of Benvenuto Cellini', *19th-Century Music*, Vol. 12, No. 3 (spring 1989), pp. 193–206

Solvik 1999   Morten Solvik: 'Finding a Context for Schubert's Kosegarten Cycle' in E. Badura-Skoda, G. Gruber et al., eds, *Schubert und Seine Freunde* (Vienna: Böhlau Verlag, 1999), pp. 169–82

Sonnleithner 1860   Leopold von Sonnleithner, 'Bemerkungen zur Gesangkunst IV' in *Recensionen und Mitteilungen über Theater und Musik*, Vol. 45 (1860). Reprinted in G. Braungart and W. Dürr, eds: *Über Schubert. Von Musikern, Dichtern und Liebhabern* (Stuttgart: Philipp Reclam, 1996), pp. 140–7

Steblin 1993   Rita Steblin: 'The Peacock's Tale: Schubert's Sexuality Reconsidered', *19th-Century Music*, Vol. 17, No. 1 (summer 1993), pp. 5–33

Steblin 1994   Rita Steblin: 'Unbekannte Dokumente über Schubert und die Klavierwerkstatt von Conrad Graf in Währing', *Schubert durch die Brille*, Vol. 12 (January 1994), pp. 49–53

Steblin 1998   Rita Steblin: *Die Unsinnsgesellschaft: Franz Schubert, Leopold Kupelwieser und ihr Freundeskreis* (Vienna: Böhlau Verlag, 1998)

Steblin 1999   Rita Steblin: '*Das Dörfchen* and the "Unsinnsgesellschaft": Schubert's Elise', *Musical Times*, Vol. 140, No. 1866 (spring 1999), pp. 33–43

Steblin 2002   Rita Steblin: 'Schubert's beloved singer Therese Grob: New Documentary Research', *Schubert durch die Brille*, Vol. 28 (January 2002), pp. 55–100

Steblin 2002[2]   Rita Steblin: 'The Schober Family's "Tiefe sittliche Verdorbenheit" as revealed in spy report from 1810 about Ludovica and her mother', *Schubert durch die Brille*, Vol. 29 (June 2002), pp. 39–65

Stegemann 1996   Michael Stegemann: '*Ich bin zu Ende mit allen Träumen*': *Franz Schubert* (Munich: Piper Verlag, 1996)

Stein 1971   Jack M. Stein: *Poem and Music in the German Lied from Gluck to Hugo Wolf* (Cambridge, MA: Harvard University Press, 1971)

Sternfeld 1979   Frederick W. Sternfeld: *Goethe and Music. A List of Parodies and Goethe's Relationship to Music: A List of References* (New York: Da Capo Press, 1979)

Stillmark 2000   Alexander Stillmark: 'Buch der Lieder' in M. Konzett, ed., *Encyclopaedia of German Literature*, 2 vols (Chicago and London: Routledge, 2000), Vol. 1, pp. 434–6

Stokes 2005   Richard Stokes (trans.): *The Book of Lieder. The Original Texts of over 1000 Songs* (London: Faber and Faber, 2005)

Stricker 1997	Rémy Stricker: *Franz Schubert. Le naïf et la mort* (Paris: Éditions Gallimard, 1997)
Tovey 1944	Donald Francis Tovey: *Essays in Musical Analysis. Supplementary [seventh] volume: Chamber Music*, ed. Hubert J. Foss (London: Oxford University Press & Humphrey Milford, 1944)
Tschense 2004	Astrid Tschense: *Goethe-Gedichte in Schuberts Vertonungen. Komposition als Textinterpretation* (Hamburg: Bockel Verlag, 2004)
Utz 1989	Helga Utz: *Untersuchungen zur Syntax der Lieder Franz Schuberts* (Munich: Musikverlag Katzbichler, 1989)
Vetter 1934	Walther Vetter: *Franz Schubert* (Potsdam: Akademische Verlagsgesellschaft Athenaion, 1934)
Vetter 1953	Walther Vetter: *Der Klassiker Schubert*, 2 vols (Leipzig: C. F. Peters, 1953)
Voss 1999	Egon Voss: 'Verkannt und doch bewundert – Franz Schubert in der Sicht Richard Wagners', *Schubert durch die Brille*, Vol. 23 (June 1999), pp. 122–30
Waidelich 1996	Till Gerrit Waidelich, ed.: *Rosamunde. Drama in fünf Akten von Helmina von Chézy. Musik von Franz Schubert. Erstveröffentlichung der überarbeiteten Fassung* (Tutzing: Hans Schneider, 1996)
Waidelich 1997	Till Gerrit Waidelich: 'Ein fragmetarischer autographer Entwurf zur Erstfassung von Chézy's Schauspiel *Rosamunde*', *Schubert durch die Brille*, Vol. 18 (January 1997), pp. 46–57
Waidelich 2008	Till Gerrit Waidelich: ' "Torupson" und Franz Schober – Leben und Wirken des von Frauen, Freunden und Biographen umworbenen Schubert- und Schwind-Freundes', *Schubert Perspektiven*, Vol. 6, Books 1–2 (Stuttgart: Franz Steiner Verlag, 2008), pp. 3–237
Waidelich/Hilmar Dokumente I	Till Gerrit Waidelich, ed.: *Franz Schubert. Dokumente 1817–1830. Erster Band: Texte. Programme, Rezensionen, Anzeigen, Nekrologe, Musikbeilagen und andere gedruckte Quellen*. Veröffentlichungen des Internationalen Franz Schubert Instituts, ed. E. Hilmar, Vol. 10/I (Tutzing: Hans Schneider, 1993)
Waidelich/Hilmar Dokumente II	Ernst Hilmar, ed.: *Franz Schubert. Dokumente 1801–1830. Erster Band: Texte. Programme, Rezensionen, Anzeigen, Nekrologe, Musikbeliagen und andere gedruckte Quellen. Addenda und Kommentar*. Veröffentlichung des Internationalen Franz Schubert Instituts, ed. E. Hilmar, Vol. 10/II (Tutzing: Hans Schneider, 2003)
Wells 2002	Stanley W. Wells: *Shakespeare: For All Time* (London: Macmillan, 2002)
Werba 1997	Robert Werba: *Franz Schubert. Ein volkstümlicher Unbekannter in den Augen der Nachwelt* (Vienna: Pichler, 1997)

Wigmore 1988	Richard Wigmore (trans.): *Schubert: The Complete Song Texts* (London: Victor Gollancz, 1988)
Wigmore 2005	Richard Wigmore (trans.): *Schubert: The Complete Song Texts*, Introduction and Calendar by G. Johnson (London: Hyperion Records Ltd, 2005)
Winter 1978	Robert Winter: 'Schubert's Undated Works: A New Chronology', *The Musical Times*, Vol. 119, No. 1624 (June 1978), pp. 498–500
Wolff 1846	Oskar Wolff: *Encyclopädie der deutschen national Literatur*, 4 vols (Leipzig: Otto Wigand, 1846)
Wolff 1982	Christoph Wolff: 'Schubert's "Der Tod und das Mädchen": Analytical and Explanatory Notes on the Song D531 and the Quartet D810', in E. Badura-Skoda and P. Branscombe, eds, *Schubert Studies. Problems of Style and Chronology* (Cambridge: Cambridge University Press, 1982), pp. 143–71
Youens 1991	Susan Youens: *Retracing a Winter's Journey: Schubert's Winterreise* (Ithaca and London: Cornell University Press, 1991)
Youens 1992	Susan Youens: *Franz Schubert: Die schöne Müllerin* (Cambridge: Cambridge University Press, 1992)
Youens 1996	Susan Youens: *Schubert's Poets and the Making of Lieder* (Cambridge: Cambridge University Press, 1996)
Youens 1997	Susan Youens: *Schubert, Müller, and Die schöne Müllerin* (Cambridge: Cambridge University Press, 1997)
Youens 1985	Susan Youens: 'Schubert and the Poetry of Graf August von Platen-Hallermünde', *The Music Review*, Vol. 46, No. 1 (February 1985), pp. 19–34
Youens 2002	Susan Youens: *Schubert's Late Lieder: Beyond the Song Cycles* (Cambridge: Cambridge University Press, 2002)
Youens 2007	Susan Youens: *Heinrich Heine and the Lied* (Cambridge: Cambridge University Press, 2007)
Youens 2007[2]	Susan Youens: ' "So tönt in Welle Welle": Schubert's Pantheist Songs' in A. Dorschel, ed., *Verwandlungsmusik: Über komponierte Transfigurationen* (Vienna, London and New York: Universal Edition, 2007)
Youens 2008	Susan Youens: 'Swan Songs: Schubert's *Auf dem Wasser zu singen*', *Nineteenth-Century Music Review*, Vol. 5, No. 2 (November 2008), pp. 19–42

DISCOGRAPHY OF RECORDINGS REFERRED TO IN THE SONG ARTICLES

Deutsche Grammophon *Schubert Duette* Deutsche Grammophon *Schubert Terzette* Deutsche Grammophon *Schubert Quartette*	Elly Ameling, Janet Baker, Dietrich Fischer-Dieskau, Horst Laubenthal, Peter Schreier and Gerald Moore: *Franz Schubert. Duette, Terzette, Quartette*, 2 discs (Deutsche Grammophon) 2002, 435 596-2. These three recordings, originally released as single LPs, are now available as a 2CD box-set.

Fischer-Dieskau I   Dietrich Fischer-Dieskau and Gerald Moore: *Franz Schubert. Lieder*
                     (1811–1817), Vol. I, 9 discs (Deutsche Grammophon) 1970, 437 215-2
Fischer-Dieskau II   Dietrich Fischer-Dieskau and Gerald Moore: *Franz Schubert. Lieder*
                     (1817–1828), Vol. II, 9 discs (Deutsche Grammophon) 1969, 437 225-2
Fischer-Dieskau III Dietrich Fischer-Dieskau and Gerald Moore: *Franz Schubert. Lieder,*
                     Vol. III: Die schöne Müllerin, Winterreise, Schwanengesang, 3 discs
                     (Deutsche Grammophon) 1972, 437 235-2
Hyperion I   Graham Johnson et al.: *The Hyperion Schubert Edition*, 37 vols
                     (Hyperion Records) 1987–2001, CDJ3301–CDJ33037
Hyperion II   Graham Johnson et al.: *Franz Schubert. The Complete Songs*, 40 discs
                     (Hyperion Records) 2005, CDS44201/40. This is a re-release of
                     Hyperion I with the songs ordered chronologically by date of
                     composition – see H numbers throughout this book
Pears–Britten   There are three recordings of Schubert Lieder by Pears and Britten
                     referred to in this book, all of which have been reissued many times:
                     Peter Pears and Benjamin Britten: *Schubert Songs* (Decca) 1975, SXL
                     6722
                     Peter Pears and Benjamin Britten: *Schubert: Die schöne Müllerin*
                     (Heritage Records) 2012, HTGCD234
                     Peter Pears and Benjamin Britten: *Schubert: Winterreise* (Decca) 2000,
                     466382

ILLUSTRATIONS INDEX

behind him. The absence of a depiction of a post-chaise in this image might have disappointed admirers of Schubert's song. [*Franz Schubert. Sein Leben in Bildern*, Otto Erich Deutsch, 1913, p. 206b.]

I/217 Anacreon by Phidias. This is a Roman marble copy of a bronze original (*c.* 450 BC) by Phidias (*c.* 480–430 BC). [*Propyläen Geschichte der Literatur*, Volume 1, Berlin, 1981 p. 179.]

I/240 First edition of Schubert's Op. 72, 1827. [Auf dem Wasser zu singen| Gedicht von Leopold Grafen zu Stolberg| In Musik gesetzt| für eine Singstimme mit Begleitung des Pianoforte| von| Franz Schubert| 72tes Werk, Eigenthum der Verleger| Wien| bei Ant. Diabelli & Comp. Graben No. 1133.] GJ coll.

I/253 Engraving of Schloss Greifenstein by J. Armann from an oil painting by J. Schwemminger. This appears in: Vesta| Taschenbuch für das Jahr 1835| Auf Kosten des Herausgebers| V. Jahrgang| Gedruckt von Franz Ludwig| Wien. GJ coll. In this almanac the article beginning with Mayrhofer's quote from *Auf der Donau* (p. 11) continues with a history of Greifenstein castle until p. 22. Whether Mayrhofer had ever indicated that this particular castle had inspired his poem is unknown but this issue of the almanac *Vesta* was published within the poet's lifetime. Decades earlier Theodor Körner had written the poem, *Auf dem Greifenstein*, describing his ecstatic emotions climbing high above the Danube and surveying the view from the castle.

I/256 Illustration to Körner's poem *Auf der Riesenkoppe*. [Theodor Körner's| Sämmtliche Werke| Herausgegeben| von Heinrich Laube| Illustrierte Pracht-Ausgabe| Erster Band| Wien, Leipzig, Prag| Verlag von Sigmund Bonsiger| 1882, p. 102.] GJ coll.

I/268 Lithograph of Nikolaus Dumba (1830–1900) by Ignaz Eigner. [*Franz Schubert. Sein Leben in Bildern*, Otto Erich Deutsch, 1913, p. 597.]

I/272 Oil painting of Josef Wilhelm Witteczek (1787–1859) by Johann Peter Krafft. [*Franz Schubert. Sein Leben in Bildern*, Otto Erich Deutsch, 1913, p. 407.]

I/274 A student (perhaps Schubert) in the uniform of the Imperial Konvikt, from a watercolour by Leo Diet. [Lieder von Goethe|komponiert von|Franz Schubert|Nachbildung der Eigenschrift aus dem Besitz der Preussichen Staatsbibliothek|Herausgegeben| von| Georg Schünemann| Verlag Albert Frisch, Berlin| 1943.] GJ coll.

B

I/279 Lithograph of Eduard von Bauernfeld by Stöbler, after Moritz Michael Daffinger, *c.* 1837. [*Franz Schubert. Sein Leben in Bildern*, Otto Erich Deutsch, 1913, p. 302.]

I/280 *Die beiden Edelleute von Verona* by Shakespeare (Vienna, 1825). [Die beiden Edelleute| von Verona| von Bauernfeld| Titel und Vignetten| Lithographiert bei Joseph Trentsensky| in Wien.] In the centre of each title page, vignette engravings by Thompson from designs by Thurston (London, 1825) were adopted for all the volumes in this edition. The vignette illustrated here is of a hat and cloak, Julia's masculine disguise when confronting Proteus in Act V Scene 4 of the play. ['If shame live / In a disguise of love / It is the lesser blot, modesty finds / Women to change their shapes, than men their minds.'] The preceding page of this

small booklet has 'William Shakspeare's [*sic*]| Sämmtliche|Dramatische Werke| übersetzt im Metrum des Originals| II Bändchen| Wien| Druck und Verlag von J. P. Sollinger|1825. GJ coll.

I/281 Antonius| und| Cleopatra| von| Ferd. V. Mayerhofer| 11tes neue Übersetzung| Titel und Vignetten| Lithographiert bei Jos. Trentsensky| in Wien. For this eleventh new translation made for the Viennese Shakespeare Edition, Eduard von Bauernfeld had collaborated with the older Ferdinand Mayerhofer von Grünbühel (1798–1869) and generously allowed him, on the title page, to take full credit for translating the work. The vignette of the Roman riding the crocodile is linked to Antony's lament in Act III Scene 9 of the play: 'Egypt, thou knewst too well/ My heart was to thy rudder tied.' The preceding page of this small booklet has 'William Shakspeare's [*sic*] | Sämmtliche| Dramatische Werke| übersetzt im Metrum des Originals| XXXVI Bändchen| Wien| Druck und Verlag von J. P. Sollinger|1825. GJ coll.

I/282 Gabriele von Baumberg, unsigned oil painting, 1791. [*Franz Schubert. Sein Leben in Bildern*, Otto Erich Deutsch, 1913, p. 542.]

I/286 Illustration of a young man at his father's graveside for the poem *Bei dem Grabe meines Vaters* printed at the end of the first volume of Claudius's complete works (Hamburg and Wandsbeck, 1775). GJ coll. For further details *see* note for I/357.

I/296 Illustration of a German coalminer of the early nineteenth century. [*Deutsche Lieder in Volkes Herz und Mund*, 1864, p. 159.] GJ coll.

I/309 Der blinde Knabe| (The blind boy)| Gedicht von Craigher| In Musik gesetzt| für eine Singstimme mit Beglei. Des Pianoforte| von| Franz Schubert | Op. 101| Neue Ausgabe| Eigenthum der Verleger| Eingetragen in das Vereins-Archiv| Wien,| bei Ant. Diabelli & Comp. Graben Bo. 1133. GJ coll.

I/323 Franz von Bruchmann, pencil drawing by Leopold Kupelwieser (1821). [*Franz Schubert. Sein Leben in Bildern*, Otto Erich Deutsch, 1913, p. 284.]

I/325 Gottfried August Bürger, engraving after a watercolour by J. D. Fiorelli. [*Könnecke Bilderatlas zur Geschichte der deutschen Literatur*, p. 260.]

I/332 Illustration for Strophe 8 of Schiller's *Die Bürgschaft*, one of a cycle of lithographs by Josef Hyrtl after drawings by Moritz von Schwind (*c.* 1822). [*Franz Schubert. Sein Leben in Bildern*, Otto Erich Deutsch, 1913, p. 202.]

I/335 Illustration for the closing section of Schiller's *Die Bürgschaft*. After mighty struggles, Möros returns at the last possible moment to give himself up in return for the life of the hostage about to be crucified. The friends embrace. On the right-hand side of the drawing is the tyrant Dionysos. [*Deutsches Balladenbuch*, 1861, by Heinrich Plüddemann, p. 137.] GJ coll.

I/336 Illustration for Goethe's *Bundeslied*. [*Deutsche Lieder in Volkes Herz und Mund*, p. 154.] GJ coll.

I/338 Schubert at the age of seventeen, drawing possibly by Franz von Schober. [*Franz Schubert. Sein Leben in Bildern*, Otto Erich Deutsch, 1913, p. 20.]

C

I/344 (*left*) Ignaz Castelli, drawing and lithograph by Josef Kriehuber (1800–1876). [*Bilderatlas zur*

II/57 Pluto kidnaps Proserpina. Engraving in Der| Mythos alter Dichter| in| Bildischen Darstellungen| Wien| in Commission bey Cath. Gräffer und Härter| Gedruckt bei Anton Strauss| 1815. GJ coll. The drawing by Redl, engraved by Stöber, faces p. 64 of this pictorial anthology of mythical figures with accompanying commentary.

II/59 Illustration for *Klage der Ceres*. [Schillers Gedichte mit Holzschnitten|nach Zeichnungen von |Böcklin, Keil, Kirchner, Mackart. Carl Piloty, Ferd. Piloty, Ramberg, Rothbart, R. Schnorr, Schwind and Schwoiser| Stuttgart| Verlag der F. G Cottaschen Buchhandlung, p. 271.] Edition issued as a Jubiläums-Ausgabe in 1859 as celebration of the centenary of the poet's birth.

II/66 Contemporary engraving of Ewald Christian von Kleist. [Robert Koenig| Deutsche Literaturgeschichte, fortgeführt von Dr. Paul Weiglin, 1930, p. 174.]

II/67 (*above*) Anna Luise Karsch, née Dürbach (1722–1791), mother of Karoline Klenke, grandmother of Helmina von Chézy. [*Bilderatlas zur Geschichte der deutschen Nationalliteratur*, Gustav Könnecke, 1895, p. 217.]

II/67 (*below*) Gilt cover of *Deutschlands Dichterinnen* | Von | H. Klenke| Berlin| Verlag con Hermann Hollstein. GJ coll. This undated anthology (*c.* 1855) includes selections from the work of forty-three German and Austrian female poets. The poem of *Heimliches Lieben* D922 is not printed in this book, but it is mentioned in a biographical note about Klenke on p. 377. It was this that gave Faust Pachler the clue to the identity of the poet of the song Schubert dedicated to his mother as part of Op. 106. Other chosen contributors to the women's anthology include Karoline Pichler, Helmina von Chézy, Luise Hensel (of *Schöne Müllerin* fame) and Elisabeth Kuhlmann (set by Schumann). The most enduringly famous poet in the book, Annette von Droste-Hüslhoff, was almost entirely ignored by lieder composers.

II/70 (*left*) Oden| von| Klopstock| Wien| gedruckt bey Joh. Thomas Edlen von Trattnern| k.k. Hofdruckern und Buchhändlern| 1784. GJ coll.

II/70 (*right*) Portrait of Klopstock, engraving by F. G. Huck from a painting by Anton Hickel (1798). [*Bilderatlas zur Geschichte der deutschen Nationalliteratur*, Gustav Könnecke, 1895, p. 224.]

II/79 Illustration of Goethe's *Der König in Thule*. [*Die Dichter des deutschen Volkes*| Album| des| Gediegensten und Ausgezeichnetsten| aus| den Werken deutscher Dichter | Mit Original-Zeichnungen deutscher Künstler| Berlin| Verlag von A. Hofmann & Comp.| 1846.] GJ coll.

II/82 Musen-Almanach| fürs Jahr 1795| herausgegeben| von| Johann Heinrich Voss| Hamburg| bey Carl Ernst Bohn. GJ coll. This is the tiniest (10 cm × 6 cm) of all the almanacs associated with the texts of Schubert's songs, the same size as the famous Göttingen almanac series on which it was modelled.

II/84 Pastel drawing, *c.* 1808, of Theodor Körner at the age of seventeen. [*Bilderatlas zur Geschichte der deutschen Nationalliteratur*, Gustav Könnecke, 1895, p. 360.]

II/85 Oil painting of Theodor Körner by Gerhard von Kügelgen, painted in 1810, the year of the poet's

Knospen. [Josef Nadler, *Literaturgeschichte des Deutschen Volkes: Dichtung und Schriftum der deutschen Stämme und Landschaften*, 1938, Vol. 2, p. 662.] GJ coll.

II/86 Theodor Körners| vermischte| Gedichte und Erzählungen| nebst| einer Charakteristik des Dichters| von| C. A. Tiedge| und| biographischen Notizen über ihn von dem Vater| des Verewigten| Leipzig, 1815| bey Johannes Friedrich Hartknoch. GJ coll. The frontispiece of the poet in military uniform is based on a drawing of Körner by his sister Emma.

II/93 Ludwig Theoboul Kosegarten's| Poesieen| Erster Band| Neue verbessere Auflage| Leipzig| bey Heinrich Gräff, 1802. GJ coll. This edition was the source of Schubert's settings. The frontispiece of 'Endymion' is engraved by Anton Karcher, after a painting by H. Tischbein. The 1816 paperback edition by Bauer of Vienna has the same frontispiece.

II/95 (*above*) Portrait of Ludwig Theobul Kosegarten, painted by Jany Weström, engraved by Lips, frontispiece to first volume of *Poesieen*, Leipzig, 1798.

II/95 (*below*) Drawing of Kosegarten by Hyölström, engraving by Friedrich Bolt, 1800. [Josef Nadler, *Literaturgeschichte des Deutschen Volkes: Dichtung und Schrifttum der deutschen Stämme und Landschaften*, 1938, Vol. 2, p. 557.] GJ coll.

II/99 Otto Erich Deutsch proposed this picture as a possible illustration for *Der Kreuzzug* D932. It is in fact a depiction of Charles V, King of Spain and Emperor of Germany, who had abdicated from his thrones and lived in seclusion at the monastery of St-Just (San Jerónimo de Yuste) in Estramdura. The drawing is thus set in the mid sixteenth century rather than the medieval period of the crusades. The drawing is by Peter Fendi, the engraving by Johann Passini. [*Franz Schubert. Sein Leben in Bildern*, Otto Erich Deutsch, 1913, p. 193.]

II/103 Unsigned portrait of Johann Gottfried Kumpf ('Ermin'). [*Deutsch-Österreichische Literaturgeschichte*: Ein Handbuch zur Geschichte der deutschen Dichtung in Österreich-Ungarn, Nagl, Zeidler, Castle, Wien, 1914, Vol. 2, p. 939.]

II/104 Franz Schubert, pencil drawing, *c.* 1825, by Moritz von Schwind. [Ernst Hilmar, *Schubert*, Graz, 1989, p. 29.] In the possession of the Wiener Schubertbund.

L

II/110 Vignette for *Lachen und Weinen* on p. 132 of Östliche Rosen| von| Friedrich Rückert| Drei Lesen| Leipzig| F. A. Brockhaus| 1822. GJ coll.

II/115 Unsigned portrait of Karl Lappe as frontispiece to Karl Lappe's| sämmtliche poetische Werke| Erster Theil| Rostock| Verlag von J. M. Oeberg| 1840. GJ coll.

II/120 Illustration for *Laura am Klavier* of Schiller. [Schillers Gedichte mit Holzschnitten|nach Zeichnungen von |Böcklin, Keil, Kirchner, Mackart. Carl Piloty, Ferd. Piloty, Ramberg, Rothbart, R. Schnorr, Schwind and Schwoiser| Stuttgart| Verlag der F. G. Cottaschen Buchhandlung, p. 3.] Edition issued in 1859 as a Jubiläums-Ausgabe in celebration of the centenary of the poet's birth.

II/138 Baumberg's *Ein Jugendtraum*. [Sämmtliche | Gedichte | Gabrielens | von | Baumberg | Wien |

II/541 (*below*) Schuberts Zimmer. Pen drawing by Moritz von Schwind, 1821. [*Franz Schubert. Sein Leben in Bildern*, Otto Erich Deutsch, 1913, p. 48.]

II/542 Schubert at the piano. Detail from Leopold Kupelwieser's much larger watercolour 'Gesellschaftsspiel der Schubertianer' painted in 1821. The picture depicts a game of charades at Atzenbrugg castle outside Vienna. 'The Fall of Man' is being enacted as a charade while Schubert looks on from the piano (the left-hand side of the picture). The composer's left hand is still on the keyboard as if he has been providing music for the charade; under his seat is the dog Drago. This was one of seven pictures, four in colour and three in black and white, selected by Otto Erich Deutsch in 1922 for sumptuous lithographic reproduction and issued in a large linen folder. [*Die historischen Bildnisse Franz Schuberts in getreuen Nachbildungen*, Verlag Karl König, Wien.] GJ coll.

II/543 Idyllen| von| Carolina [*sic*] Pichler| gebornen von Greiner| Wien| Im Verlage bey Anton Pichler| 1803. GJ coll. This was Pichler's first publication.

II/544 Watercolour of Karoline Pichler by Julius Schoppe, 1818. [Josef Nadler, *Literaturgeschichte des Deutschen Volkes: Dichtung und Schrifttum der deutschen Stämme und Landschaften*, 1938, Vol. 2, p. 649.]

II/545 Two editions of Pichler's *Olivier*: (*above*) Olivier| oder| Die Rache der Elfe| von| Carolina Pichler| gebornen von Greiner| Erster Theil| Wien| Im Verlage bey Anton Pichler| 1803; (*below*) Olivier| Von| Caroline Pichler| gebornen| von| Greiner| Neue verbesserte Auflage| Wien, 1821| Gedruckt und im Verlage bey Anton Strauss| Leipzig| in Commission bey August Liebeskind. Both in GJ coll. The 1821 edition is the eighth volume in the poet's *Sämmtliche Werke* (second edition) in twenty-four volumes. By 1844 Pichler's complete works ran to an edition of sixty volumes.

II/546 Watercolour of Karoline Pichler by L. Krones (1829). [Caroline Pichler geborne von Greiner| Denkwürdigkeiten aus meinem Leben, reprinted 1914, München, Volume 2 p. 264.] GJ coll.

II/556 Ghaselen| von| August Graf v. Platen Hallermünde| Erlangen| Carl Heyder| 1821. GJ coll. A quotation in Arabic is printed on the obverse side of the title page.

II/557 [Cover] Vermischte Schriften| von| August Graf von Platen Hallermünde. The illustration here is of the cover of the work in stiff brown paper. The title page adds Erlangen| bei Carl Heyder| 1822. GJ coll.

II/558 Graf August von Platen. Engraving by C. Barth. [Robert Koenig| Deutsche Literaturgeschichte fortgeführt von Dr. Paul Weiglin, 1930, p. 336.]

II/559 Taschenbuch| zum| geselligen Vergnügen| Fünfzehnter Jahrgang| 1805| Herausgegeben| von| W. G. Becker| Leipzig | bei Christian Adolph Hempel. GJ coll. The poem *Die Blumensprache* is printed on pp. 165–6, and signed simply with 'Pl'.

II/561 The| Works [in red] of| Alexander Pope Esq;| Vol. I [in red]| with| Explanatory notes and additions never before printed| [four line Latin quotation from Tully]| London [in red]| Printed for B. Lintot, 1736. GJ coll. The Ode, *The Dying Christian to his soul* is printed on pp. 100–101 of this volume.

II/566 (*above*) [Cover] Franz Schubert| Sämmtliche Gesänge| Band 1. [Title page] Sämmtliche Gesänge| für eine Singstimme| mit Begleitung des Pianoforte| von| Franz Schubert| Neue Ausgabe. Revidirt von Julius Rietz.| Band 1 || [List of twenty-four songs, Opp. 1–8]|| Leipzig, Verlag von Bartholf Senff. GJ coll. The edition is handsomely produced in twenty slim volumes with silk covers.

II/566 (*below*) Franz Schubert's| sämmtliche Compositionen | VI. Band| Lieder und Gesänge| für eine Contra-Alt-oder-Bass-Stimme| mit Pianofortebegleitung.| Erste vollständige and rechtmässige Gesammtasugabe|revidirt und corrigirt| von H. Sattler| 13 Hefte| Preis 2 Thlr 10 Sgr,| Œuvres complètes de| François Schubert| Volume 6| Airs et chansons| pour une voix de contralto ou basse| avec accompagnement de Piano| Wolfenbüttel| Druck und Verlag von L. Holle| Paris (A Bohne) London (Augener & Co.) New York (Th. Hagen). GJ coll.

II/568 Forty Songs published by J. P. Gotthard, 1872. [Neueste Folge| nachgelassener Lieder| und| Gesänge| von| Franz Schubert| Original-Ausgabe|| List of 40 song-titles in two columns|| Wien bei J. P. Gotthard.] GJ coll.

II/570 Title page of the Mandyczewski *Complete Edition* (AGA), 1894. [Franz Schubert's| Werke.| Kritisch durchgesehene Gesammtausgabe| Serie 20| Lieder und Gesänge.|| List of the ten volumes and their time-frames|| Erster Band 1811–1814| Nr. 1–38| Leipzig. Verlag von Breitkopf & Härtel.] GJ coll., inherited from Gerald Moore, and containing the great accompanist's notes on transposing various songs at sight for the DGG recordings with Fischer-Dieskau, c. 1970.

II/575 Franz Schubert| 1797–1828| Therese Grob| Collection, GJ coll. Privately printed facsimile publication of the seventeen songs in the Therese Grob collection, 31 January 1967. List of contents in typescript. Although some songs are illegible for practical use due to the poor quality of the reproductions, Reinhard Van Hoorickx made separate editions of each of these songs, also privately printed. He appends a note of thanks to the Wilhelm family in Bottmingen, Switzerland, owners of the album, for their permission to publish it.

II/580 Adolf Pratobevera, Freiherr von Wiesborn, unsigned oil painting of 1829.

II/583 Autograph of Goethe's *Prometheus*, Verses 5–7. Beginning 'Ich dich ehren? Wofür?/Hast du die Schmerzen gelindert/Je des Beladenen?' [Illustrierte Geschichte| der| Weltliteratur| von| Dr Johannes Scherr, Zweiter Band, Stuttgart, no date, p. 226.] GJ coll.

II/584 Prometheus, engraving by Stöber after a painting by Schedy. The Titan brandishes fire, his own discovery, and by his side sits a man whom he has created. [*Der Mythos alter Dichter| in| Bildlichen Darstellungen*| Wien| Anton Strauss, 1815, facing p. 18.] GJ coll.

II/585 Prometheus, engraving by C. Teichendorff. [*Goethes Werke*| illustrirt von ersten| deutschen Künstlern| Herausgeber H. Düntzer| Erster Band| Stuttgart und Leipzig| Deutsche Verlagsanstalt vorm. Ed. Hallberger (1882), p. 191.] GJ coll.

II/597 Salomon Sulzer, lithograph of August Prinzhofer, 1846. [*Franz Schubert. Sein Leben in Bildern*, Otto Erich Deutsch, 1913, p. 372.]

Leipzig| F.A Brockhaus| 1819. GJ coll. This is the first edition of the *Poetisches Tagebuch*. The four-volume edition of Schulze's complete works is bound in attractive dappled light-blue covers with yellow spines. The second edition of 1822 ('Sämmtliche poetische Werke', also Brockhaus) is in two volumes bound in black half-leather, and may also have been Schubert's source.

II/926 *Im Walde* and *Auf der Brücke*, two Schulze songs Op. 93. [Im Walde| und| Auf der Brücke| zwei

Gedichte von| Ernst Schulze| In Musik gesetzt| für eine Singstimme| mit| Begleitung des| Piano-Forte| von| Franz Schubert| 93tes Werk| Neue Ausgabe| Wien,| bei Ant. Diabelli Comp. Graben 1133.] Susan Youens collection.

II/927 Endpiece *Schubert* by Martha Griebler (2001). Drawing reproduced by arrangement with Matthias Griebler. Also published in Martha Griebler, *Franz Schubert – Zeichnungen*, Bibliothek der Provinz, Weitra, 2005, p. 23.

VOLUME III Schwanengesang–Z

Frontispiece *Doppelgänger* by Martha Griebler (1997). Drawing reproduced by arrangement with Matthias Griebler. Also published in Martha Griebler, *Franz Schubert – Zeichnungen*, Bibliothek der Provinz, Weitra, 2005, p. 20.

from Schwanengesang

III/3 The printed opening bars of *Liebesbotschaft*, the first song in *Schwanengesang*, from the first edition of 1829 (published by Tobias Haslinger). From the Kralik reprint described in II/804 above.

III/8 Schubert's sketch for *Liebesbotschaft* D957/1 – the bare bones of the song are mapped out on the first of two sparsely filled sides of manuscript paper. [Franz Schubert | *Schwanengesang* | Facsimile of the Autograph Score and Sketches | and Reprint of the First Edition | Edited by Martin Chusid | Yale Univeristy Press, New Haven and London, 2000, p. 44.]

III/9 Autograph, dated August 1828, of *Liebesbotschaft*, the opening song of *Schwanengesang*. [Franz Schubert | *Schwanengesang* | Facsimile of the Autograph Score and Sketches | and Reprint of the First Edition | Edited by Martin Chusid | Yale University Press, New Haven and London, 2000, p. 4.]

III/23 Illustration (1935) for *Ständchen* D957/4 by the Dutch artist Anton Pieck (1895–1987). [Franz Schubert | Bloemlezing, uit zijn Liederen | met zestien Aquarellen van | Anton Pieck| N. V. Uitgeversmaatschij 'Joost van den Vondel' | Amsterdam, facing p. 110.] GJ coll.

III/32 Autograph of *In der Ferne* (conclusion) and *Abschied* (beginning). [Franz Schubert | *Schwanengesang* | Facsimile of the Autograph Score and Sketches | and Reprint of the First Edition | Edited by Martin Chusid | Yale Univeristy Press, New Haven and London, 2000, p. 12.]

III/40 Autograph of *Der Atlas*, the first of the six Heine settings in *Schwanengesang*. [Franz Schubert | *Schwanengesang* | Facsimile of the Autograph Score and Sketches | and Reprint of the First Edition | Edited by Martin Chusid | Yale Univeristy Press, New Haven and London, 2000, p. 27.]

III/51 Illustration (1935) for *Die Stadt* D957/11 by Anton Pieck (1935). [Franz Schubert | Bloemlezing, uit zijn Liederen | met zestien Aquarellen van | Anton Pieck| N. V. Uitgeversmaatschij 'Joost van den Vondel' | Amsterdam, facing p. 107.] GJ coll.

III/55 Autograph of the last seven bars of *Die Stadt* D957/11 and the first two staves of *Am Meer* D957/12. [Franz Schubert | *Schwanengesang* | Facsimile of the Autograph Score and Sketches | and Reprint of the

First Edition | Edited by Martin Chusid | Yale University Press, New Haven and London, 2000, p. 33.]

III/63 Illustration (1935) of *Der Doppelgänger* D957/13 by Anton Pieck. [Franz Schubert | Bloemlezing, uit zijn Liederen | met zestien Aquarellen van | Anton Pieck| N. V. Uitgeversmaatschij 'Joost van den Vondel' | Amsterdam, facing p. 105.] GJ coll.

III/68 Sketch of *Die Taubenpost* D957/14 showing Schubert's method of planning a song on two staves, the vocal line and the bass line without any of the piano detail that was added later. [Franz Schubert | *Schwanengesang* | Facsimile of the Autograph Score and Sketches | and Reprint of the First Edition | Edited by Martin Chusid | Yale Univeristy Press, New Haven and London, 2000, p. 47.]

III/69 Illustration in the almanac Aurora (1844) of *Die Taubenpost*. GJ coll. The picture is by Adolph Teer, engraved by Josef Urmann. The image here (the fifth engraving at the beginning of the small volume and described as inspired by the 'Epoch of romantic chivalry') does not refer to the Seidl poem set by Schubert. It is, nevertheless, furnished with an accompanying poem, almost certainly by Seidl, who was this almanac's editor:

Bist eine Königsmaid,	You're daughter of a king
Und trägst ein Purpurkleid,	And wear a purple gown,
Und schmückst die Scheitel dir	Your brow embellishing
Mit goldner Kronenzier.	There sits a golden crown.
Und blickst zum hohen Haus	Up to yon house on high
Doch sehnsuchtsvoll hinaus,	You gaze with such desire,
Und schickst dein Täubchen fort	Send your pigeon out to fly
Mit süssem Liebeswort.	With sweet words full of fire.
Ach, mehr als Purpurkleid	Ah, more than a purple gown –
Ist Liebesseligkeit!	The bliss that comes with love.
Ach, mehr als Goldgeschmeid'	Ah, more than any crown –
Ist Liebesheimlichkeit.	The secrecy of love.
	(translated by Uri Liebrecht)

[Aurora | Taschenbuch für das Jahr| 1844 | herausgegeben| von | Johann Gabriel Seidl |

Zwanzigster Jahrgang | Wien | Bei Franz Riedl's sel. Witwe und Sohn.] GJ coll.

III/72 (*above*) Schwanen-Gesang[*sic*]| von| Franz Schubert| 1ᵗᵉˢ [filled-in in ink] Abtheilung| Wien, bei Tobias Haslinger. Cover on light blue paper with glued-on printed vignette in white card and hand-numbering. First edition of the cycle published in 1829. [Franz Schubert | *Schwanengesang* | Facsimile of the Autograph Score and Sketches | and Reprint of the First Edition | Edited by Martin Chusid | Yale University Press, New Haven and London, 2000, p. 50.]

III/72 (*below*) Subscribers' sheet ('Prænumerations Exemplar') bound in copies of the first edition of *Schwanengesang* that had been paid for in advance. The name of the subscriber was filled in on this page. [Schubertˢ| Liederzyklen| Die schöne Müllerin, Winterreise| und Schwanengesang.| In verkleinerter Nachbildung| der Originalausgaben| herausgegeben und| einbegleitet| von Heinrich Kralik. || Verlag Steyrermühl, Wien.]

III/79 Illustration for *Schwertlied* in Theodor Körner's| Sämmtliche Werke| Herausgegeben| von Heinrich Laube| Illustrierte Pracht-Ausgabe| Erster Band| Wien, Leipzig, Prag| Verlag von Sigmund Bonsiger| 1882, p. 88. GJ coll.

III/80 Illustration for Körner's *Schwertlied* by Rudolf Eichstaedt (1857–1924), from Koerners [*sic*]| Leyer und Schwert | und Knospen| Berlin | Deutsches Verlaghaus Bong & Co. This late nineteenth-century volume (no given date) is profusely illustrated by Eichstädt's coloured drawings. GJ coll.

III/88 Tales of my landlord| Third Series| Collected and arranged| by| Jedediah Cleishbotham| schoolmaster and parish-clerk of Gandercleugh| [six-line Burns quotation]| In Four Volumes| Vol III| Edinburgh| 1819. GJ coll. Cleishbotham was a pen-name for Scott before he revealed the authorship of his prose. The first tale in this third volume is *The Bride of Lammermoor*; the second, *A Legend of Montrose* (pp. 135–332) continues into the fourth volume where the Annot Lyle lyric (*Lied der Anne Lyle* D830) is to be found on p. 277.

III/89 The Pirate| By the author of 'Waverley,| Kenilworth' &c.| Nothing in him – | But doth suffer a sea-change. Tempest| In three volumes| Vol I| Edinburgh| 1822. GJ coll. Norna's song is on p. 126 of Vol. II of this set. This edition was issued before Scott's authorship of his prose works had been acknowledged.

III/90 (*left*) Walter Scott, frontispiece to Urania| Taschenbuch| auf| das Jahr 1827| Mit acht Kupfern| Leipzig| F. A. Brockhaus| 1827. GJ coll.

III/90 (*right*) Ivanhoe| A Romance| By 'The Author of Waverley' &c.| Now fitted the halter, now traversed the cart| And often took leave, – but seemed loth to depart| [Matthew] Prior| In three volumes| Vol. II| Third edition| Edinburgh| 1821. GJ coll. 'The Crusader's Return' is on p. 43 of this volume. This edition was issued before Scott's authorship had been acknowledged.

III/91 The| Lady of the Lake| A Poem| By| Walter Scott, Esq.| Edinburgh| Printed for John Ballantyne and Co. Edinburgh| And| Longman, Hurst, Rees, and Orme; and William Miller,|London| 1810. Frontispiece of the

author, engraving of Heath after painting by Saxon. GJ coll.

III/117 Vignette for the poem 'O du Entriss'ne mir und meinem Kusse' (Schubert's *Sei mir gegrüsst* D741) in Friedrich Rückert's *Östliche Rosen*, 1822 (p. 321). GJ coll.

III/122 Lieder der Nacht| Elegien| von Alfons von Lamartine| Die Deutung| von| Johann Gabriel Seidl| Wien| Druck und Verlag von J. P. Sollinger, 1826. GJ coll. This 'Songs of the Night' is the second volume of Seidl's *Dichtungen* (the first is Balladen| Romanzen| Sagen und Lieder|) published by Sollinger in 1826 when the poet was twenty-two years old.

III/124 Portrait of Johann Gabriel Seidl in Album| österreichischer Dichter| Wien| Verlag von Pfautsch & Voss| Wien 1850. Seidl's portrait, with his signature, is a separate plate facing p. 322. GJ coll.

III/132 Gedichte| von| Johann Senn| Innsbruck| in der Wagner'schen Buchhandlung| 1838. GJ coll.

III/133 Johann Senn, pencil drawing by Leopold Kupelwieser, 1820. [*Franz Schubert. Sein Leben in Bildern*, Otto Erich Deutsch, 1913, p. 306.]

III/139 (*above*) Front and back cover designs by Moritz von Schwind for the Viennese Shakespeare Edition (1825–6) to which his friend Eduard von Bauernfeld contributed, published by the firm J. P. Sollinger in Vienna. In this form of the edition there were thirty-seven small booklets bound in brown card, each with a different vignette (of English design) on the internal title page. GJ coll.

III/139 (*below*) William| Shakspeare's [*sic*] | sämmtliche Werke| und| Gedichte| Übersetzt im Metrum des Originals| in einem Bande nebst Supplement,| enthaltend| Shakspeare's [*sic*] Leben| nebst| Ammerkungen und kritschen Erläuterungen zu seinen Werken| Wien| Druck und Verlag von J. P. Sollinger| Zu haben bei Rudolph Sammer, Buchhändler| 1826. GJ coll. This substantial single-volume version of the Viennese edition of Shakespeare's works prints the plays in double columns up to. p. 906; the supplement containing an outline of Shakespeare's life by Augustin Skottowe (translated from the English by Adolph Wagner), as well as the poems and sonnets and critical commentary (including essays by A. W. Schlegel, Voss etc.) is a further 186 pages.

III/141 Shakespeare welcomes Schiller into heaven: 'Schillers Empfang in den Räumen des Lichts'. Frontispiece of Minerva| Taschenbuch| für| das Jahr 1820| Zwölfter Jahrgang| Leipzig bei Gerhard Fleischer d. Jüng. GJ coll.

III/149 Engraving by Fleischer after a painting by J. Hübner of the soprano Henriette Sontag (1806–1854) in the role of Elena in Rossini's opera *La donna del lago*. Frontispiece to Die| Jungfrau vom See| Ein Gedicht in sechs Gesängen| von| Walter Scott| Metrisch übersetzt| von| Willibald Alexis| Zwickau, 1827. | Im Verlag der Gebrüder Schumann. GJ coll.

III/152 Vignette by Moritz von Schwind, 1824, for the Viennese printed vocal score of Rossini's *La donna del lago* (The Lady of the Lake).

III/153 Painting of Ellen Douglas (in the opening of Scott's poem) from The Lady of| The Lake| By Sir Walter Scott, Bart.| With illustrations by Howard

W

III/530 Franz Schubert, watercolour (1825) by Wilhelm August Rieder (1796–1880). This is perhaps the best known of all Schubert portraits. [Die historischen Bildnisse Franz Schuberts in getreuen Nachbildungen, Verlag Karl König, Wien.]

III/536 Albrecht Wenzel von Wallenstein, Herzog von Friedland und Sagan, hero of Schiller's *Wallenstein* trilogy. [Frontispiece to Theater| von| Schiller| Vierter Theil| Wien, 1810| In Commission bey Anton Doll. Engraving by Blaschke after a drawing by Ferdinand Jagemann.] GJ coll.

III/542 The second edition of *Der Wanderer* D489 with an unsigned engraving. [Der Wanderer| von Schmidt v. Lübeck| Morgenlied| von Werner| Wandrers Nachtlied| von Göthe| |[unsigned engraving]|für eine Singstimme mit Begleitung des Pianoforte| In Musik gesetzt und| Sʳ Excellenz dem Hochgebornen und Hochwürdigsten Herrn Herrn| Johann Ladislav Pyrker von Felsö-Eör,| Patriarchen v. Venedig, Primas v. Dalmatien, Grossdignitar u. Kroncaplan des Lomb. Venetianischen Königreiches, Sʳ k. k. M. wirkl. Geheimen Rathe &c.| in tiefer Ehrfurcht gewidmet von | Franz Schubert| 4ᵗᵉˢ Werk| Wien| bey Ant. Diabelli u Comp. Graben N° 1133.] GJ coll.

III/551 The autograph of *Wandrers Nachtlied I* D224 from an album prepared for Goethe and sent to him in April 1816, and duly returned to sender. In 1978 this album (in the Deutsche Staatsbibliothek in Berlin, then East Germany) was published in facsimile by the firm of Peters in Leipzig. *Wandrers Nachtlied* is the eighth of the sixteen songs in the album.

III/555 Photograph (before 1870) of the exterior of the hunting chalet on the Gickelhahn, a high mountain in the vicinity of Ilmenau in the Thüringer Wald. Goethe wrote *Wandrers Nachtlied* ('Über allen Gipfeln ist Ruh', a poem he entitled 'Ein Gleiches') on an inner wooden wall of this rather makeshift building on 6/7 September 1780. He returned there in August 1813 and renewed the inscription. He saw it for the last time on 27 August 1831, the day before his last birthday, fifty-one years after having written it. The chalet was burned down in 1870, but a photograph survives of the poem Goethe himself inscribed on the wall. [*Könnecke Bilderatlas zur Geschichte der deutschen Literatur*, p. 282.]

III/557 *Dampfende Täler bei Ilmenau* ('Misty valleys at Ilmenau'), pencil, grey brushwork on blue-grey paper. Drawing by J. W. von Goethe, 1776, in the papers of Charlotte von Stein. [Goethe und die Kunst, herausgegeben von Sabine Schulze, exhibition catalogue, 1999, p. 119.]

III/572 Illustration of Wilhelm Meister and the Harper at their first meeting, by Ferdinand Piloty. [Album| deutscher| Kunst und Dichtung.| Herausgegeben| von| Friedrich Bodenstedt. Berlin| G. Grote'sche Verlagsbuchhandlung p. 145.] GJ coll.

III/573 Wanda| Königin der Sarmaten.| Eine romantische Tragödie| mit Gesang| in| fünf Akten|. This printing of the play is the second part of a volume also containing Werner's Das| Kreuz an der Ostsee. GJ coll. The volume bears the imprint Wien| 1813| Im Verlag bey Joh. Bapt. Wallishausser.

III/574 'Zacharias Werner, sein Drama: Die Söhne des Thales vorlesend' (Werner reading his *Sons of the Valley*). Drawing made by E. T. A. Hoffmann during one of Werner's celebrated readings. [*Könnecke Bilderatlas zur Geschichte der deutschen Literatur*, p. 356.]

III/575 Frontispiece and title page from Die| Söhne des Thal's| Ein| dramatisches Gedicht| von| Friedrich Ludwig Zacharias Werner| [vignette by Iacob Bernhard von Molai]| erster Theil:| Der Templer aus Cypern| [biblical quote: Gott hat das Gedeyen gegeben.| Erste Ep. a. d. Corinther. 3 v. 6]| Zweite durchgängig verbesserte und vermehrte Auflage| Berlin, bei A. D. Sander. 1807. Frontispiece of Act V Scene 4, Eudo and Molay, when Eudo sings the words 'Polykarpos, so wie du'. GJ coll.

III/577 (*left*) Joseph Freiherr von Hammer-Purgstall, k. k. Fidei-Comiss. Bibliothek, Wien. Lithograph by Josef Kriehuber (1843). [Caroline Pichler geborne von Greiner| Denkwürdigkeiten aus meinem Leben, reprinted 1914, München, Vol. 2, p. 80.] GJ coll.

III/577 (*right*) The representative illustration of the *West-östlicher Divan* was made by M. Eichholzer. It is one of a set of fifty-six engravings that was prepared between 1827 and 1840 for the octavo edition (as opposed to the far more popular pocket-size version without illustrations) of Goethe's *Ausgabe letzter Hand*. This drawing was the frontispiece for Volume 5 of this edition of 'Goethe's Werke' published by Cotta in Tübingen. The original artwork involved eleven painters and draughtsmen (including Schubert's friend Moritz von Schwind) and eighteen engravers.

III/578 (*left*) Illustration title page for *West-östlicher Divan*. [Goethes Werke| illustriert von ersten| deutschen Künstlern| Herausgegeber H. Düntzer| Erster Band| Stuttgart und Leipzig| Deutsche Verlagsanstalt vorm. Ed. Hallberger (1882) p. 293.] GJ coll. The drawing is by Franz Simm.

III/578 (*right*) A fanciful illustration by Franz Simm (*c.* 1880) of Zuleika and her retinue. [Goethes Werke| illustriert von ersten| deutschen Künstlern| Hersausgeber H. Düntzer| Erster Band| Stuttgart und Leipzig| Deutsche Verlagsanstalt vorm. Ed. Hallberger (1882) p. 329.] GJ coll.

III/579 (*above*) Frontispiece and title page of the first issue of West-oestlicher| Divan| von| Goethe| Stuttgard [sic] in der Cottaschen Buchhandlung| 1819. GJ coll.

III/579 (*below*) *West-östlicher Divan*, Viennese edition of 1820. [Goethe's| Werke| XXI Band| Original Ausgabe| Vignette.|Wien und Stuttgart 1820.] GJ coll. This is the twenty-first volume of a complete Goethe edition in twenty-six volumes issued as a joint venture between the publisher Cotta in Stuttgart and the Viennese firm of Kaulfuss & Armbruster between 1816 and 1822. It is very likely Schubert knew this edition of the collection rather than the German edition. The engraving is by Ludwig Schnorr von Carolsfeld, a symbolic representation of Sufi teaching with an adherent shielding his gaze from the strength of heavenly light.

III/581 *Widerschein*, a loose supplement in 'W. G. Becker's| Taschenbuch| zum| geselligen Vergnügen| Herausgegeben| von| Friedrich Kind| Auf das Jahr 1821'. Like all almanacs this appeared in the autumn of the preceding year, thus 1820. Copies of the Franz Schubert of Vienna (as opposed to the Franz Schubert

of Dresden) supplement are very rare. [Franz
Schubert, Fünf erste Lieder, in Faksimile-
reproduktionen von Otto Erich Deutsch, 1922.]
GJ coll.

III/590 *Wiedersehen*, supplement to Lebensbild aus
Österreich| Ein Denkbuch vaterländischer
Erinnerungen| unter Mitwirkung sinnverwandter
Schriftsteller und Künstler| zum Besten der bei dem
verheerenden Brande| vom 3 Mai 1842| verunglückten
Familien von Steyr| herausgegeben| von| Andreas
Schumacher| Wien, 1843| Bei Tauer und Sohn|
Schulhof N° 413| und in allen Buchhandlungen der
Monarchie. GJ coll. This is one of a number of Austrian
nineteenth-century anthologies issued to raise money
for fire or flood victims – in this case for victims of a fire
in Steyr, a town Schubert knew and loved.

III/592 Illustration for *Wiegenlied*. [*Deutsche Lieder in
Volkes Herz und Mund*, 1864, p. 179.]

III/598 Title page of first edition of *Wilhelm Meister*,
1795. [Wilhelm Meisters | Lehrjahre| Ein Roman. |
Herausgegeben| von| Goethe| Zweiter Band| Berlin|
Bei Johann Friedrich Unger| 1795.] GJ. coll. This is
the second of four volumes in this first edition of
Goethe's novel.

III/600 Fold-out musical supplement to *Wilhlem
Meister*, Volume II, p. 264. 'No. 2| Zweistimmig mit
Diskant und Bass zu singen| Reichardt| Klagend| Nur
wer die Sehnsucht kennt, weiss was ich leide' etc. This
is the second of eight musical fold-out supplements
composed by Johann Friedrich Reichardt for the first
edition of Goethe's *Wilhelm Meister*: there are two
songs in this volume (Mignon's 'Kennst du das Land'
is the other), three fold-outs in the first volume (*Der
Sänger* and the first two Harper settings), two songs in
the third volume (Philine's song and Mignon's 'Heiss
mich nicht reden') and Mignon's 'So lasst mich
scheinen' at the very end of the fourth volume.

III/602 Marianne von Willemer, pastel portrait by J. J.
Lose, 1809. [Josef Nadler, *Literaturgeschichte des
Deutschen Volkes: Dichtung und Schrifttum der
deutschen Stämme und Landschaften*, 1938, Vol. 3,
p. 14.]

III/603 Marianne von Willemer, engraving (with the
poet's signature) by Doris Raab (1819) from a
miniature painting. [Robert Koenig| Deutsche
Literaturgeschichte fortgeführt von Dr. Paul Weiglin,
1930, p. 300.]

III/606 Illustration of Goethe and Friederike Brion from
a Viennese edition by Kaulfuss & Armbruster of the
poet's works. [Goethe's Werke| XVIII Band: Original-
Ausgabe| Wien und Stuttgart, 1819.] GJ coll. This
volume is Part Two of Goethe's autobiography,
Dichtung und Wahrheit in which he recounts the story
of his relationship with Friederike.

III/607 Illustration for *Willkommen und Abschied* by
Edmund Kanoldt. [Goethes Werke| illustriert von
ersten| deutschen Künstlern| Hersausgeber H.
Düntzer| Erster Band| Stuttgart und Leipzig| Deutsche
Verlagsanstalt vorm. Ed. Hallberger (1882) p. 33.]
GJ coll.

III/610 (*above*) The title page of the vocal score of Franz
Lehár's operetta *Friederike* (1928). GJ coll. The profile
in the foreground is that of Goethe in his twenties; the
profile in the background is that of an imaginary
Friederike.

III/610 (*below*) *Das Pfarrhaus in Sesenheim zu
Friederikens Zeit* ('The pastor's house in Sesenheim in
Friederike's time'), the picture taken from an old oil
painting. Her signature survives, but there is no
surviving image of Friederike herself. [*Könnecke
Bilderatlas zur Geschichte der deutschen Literatur*,
p. 270.]

III/612 (**above**) W. G. Becker's |Taschenbuch| zum|
Geselligen Vergnügen| Herausgegeben| von| Friedrich
Kind| Fünf und Zwanzigster Jahrgang| 1815| Leipzig|
bei Joh. Friedrich Gleditsch. GJ coll. Winkler's
six-strophe poem *Heimweh*, signed 'Alessandria 1813,
Th. Hell' is printed on pp. 61–2 of this almanac.

III/612 (**below**) Karl Winkler (Theodor Hell), unsigned
engraving. [*Franz Schubert. Sein Leben in Bildern*,
Otto Erich Deutsch, 1913, p. 543.]

III/623 Pencil drawing of Wilhelm Müller, 1822, by
Wilhelm Hensel. [Ernst Hilmar, *Schubert*, Graz, 1989,
p. 83.]

III/624 Portrait of George Gordon, Lord Byron, by
Thomas Phillips (1770–1845).

III/626 The vignette pasted on to the dark green paper
wrappers of the first edition of Winterreise (1828).
[Winterreise| von | Franz Schubert| '2'[handwritten in
ink] ᵗᵉˢ Abtheilung | Wien, bei Tobias Haslinger.] GJ
coll. The first part of the cycle had the same vignette
with the number '1' filled in with ink.

III/628 Illustration of a Winter traveller from *English
Echoes* [*sic*] *of German Song*, translated by Wallis,
Morell and D'Anvers, with twelve [unascribed]
engravings on steel. London, Marcus Ward & Co.,
1877, p. 60, opposite an English translation of Salis-
Seewis's *Winterlied*, a poem not set by Schubert.
GJ coll.

III/629 Winterreise | von | Wilhelm Müller | in Musik
gestetzt | für eine Sigstimme mit Begleitung des
Pianoforte | von | Franz Schubert | 89ᵗᵉˢ Werk | Iᵗᵉ
Abtheilung | Eigenthum des Verlegers | Wien bei
Tobias Haslinger | Musikverleger | im Hause der
ersten österr. Sparkasse | am Graben N° 1572. GJ coll.

III/631 Autograph of *Gute Nacht* (No. I of *Winterreise*),
fair copy. [Franz Schubert. Die [*sic*] Winterreise|
Faksimile-Wiedergabe nach der Originalhandschrift |
Bärenreiter-Verlag Kassel.Basel.Paris. London. New
York | 1966.] Although this is a fair copy, the tempo
marking here ('Mässig, in gehender Bewegung') was
almost certainly changed to 'Mässig' at proof stage.
The autograph shown is the first of fifteen fair copies
of songs (including the whole of Part Two) in the
assembled manuscript of the work in the Pierpont
Morgan Library, New York. It is probable that the
songs in fair copy in Part One had been previously
revised and reworked to such an extent that the
composer decided he needed to recopy a clean version
of them for the printer's benefit. The same pertained
to the whole of Part Two which clearly went through
a rigorous revision process, sadly no longer visible
to us.

III/639 Autograph of *Gefrorne Tränen* (No. III of
Winterreise), first draft. [Franz Schubert. Die [*sic*]
Winterreise| Faksimile -Wiedergabe nach der
Originalhandschrift | Bärenreiter-Verlag Kassel.Basel.
Paris. London. New York | 1966.] The autograph
shown is the second of nine songs in first draft in the
assembled manuscript of the work in the Pierpont

Morgan Library, New York. The use of two inks of different shades is visible in these fair copies. Despite his obvious corrections, Schubert clearly believed that his intentions were clear enough to be read by the printers.

III/647 Autograph of the end of *Erstarrung* and beginning of *Der Lindenbaum* (Nos IV and V of *Winterreise*), first draft. [Franz Schubert. Die [*sic*] Winterreise| Faksimile -Wiedergabe nach der Originalhandschrift | Bärenreiter-Verlag Kassel.Basel. Paris. London. New York | 1966.] The autograph shown is the third (and the beginning of the fourth) of nine songs in first draft in the assembled manuscript of the work in the Pierpont Morgan Library, New York. The use of two inks of different shades is visible in these fair copies. Despite his obvious corrections, Schubert clearly believed that his intentions were clear enough to be read by the printers.

III/648 Wilhelm Müller's autograph for *Der Lindenbaum*. [Deutsche Gedichte| in| Handschriften| Im Insel-Verlag zu Leipzig.] GJ coll.

III/663 Autograph of *Irrlicht* (No. IX of *Winterreise*), first draft. [Franz Schubert. Die [*sic*] Winterreise| Faksimile -Wiedergabe nach der Originalhandschrift | Bärenreiter-Verlag Kassel.Basel.Paris. London. New York | 1966.] The autograph shown is the seventh of nine songs in first draft in the assembled manuscript of the work in the Pierpont Morgan Library, New York. The use of two inks of different shades is visible in these fair copies. Despite his obvious corrections, Schubert clearly believed that his intentions were clear enough to be read by the printers.

III/665 Depiction of *Irrlicht* (including a musical quotation from the song) by Koloman Moser (1868–1918), part of a booklet prepared for a ball in Vienna honouring Schubert's centenary in 1897. Reproduced in Susan Youens, *Retracing a Winter's Journey – Schubert's Winterreise*, Cornell University Press, 1991, p. 201.

III/668 *Verschneite Hütte*, 1827, by Caspar David Friedrich (1774–1840). Oil on canvas, 31 × 25 cm. Perhaps it was in a similar snow-covered forest hut that the winter traveller took his refuge. Picture reproduced in *Galerie der Romantik – Katalog der ausgestellten Werke*, Nationalgalerie, Berlin, 1986, p. 55.

III/676 Autograph of end of *Einsamkeit* (No. XII of *Winterreise*), fair copy. [Franz Schubert. Die [*sic*] Winterreise| Faksimile -Wiedergabe nach der Originalhandschrift | Bärenreiter-Verlag Kassel.Basel. Paris. London. New York | 1966.] The autograph shown is different from the rest of this work in that the first three pages of the song are in draft form (including a series of lines, seemingly angry or impatient, cancelling the second page) but the fourth page depicted here, the ending of the song, is in fair copy. The assembled manuscript of the work is in the Pierpont Morgan Library, New York. Despite the cancellation of this single page, Schubert clearly believed that his intentions in the earlier part of the song were clear enough to be read by the printers.

III/681 *Der Briefpost* ('The Letter Post'), engraving by Mahlknecht for Adalbert Stifter's anthology *Wien und die Wiener* where it accompanied an article on the Viennese postal service by the Viennese writer (1805–

1858). This was reprinted in *Aus dem alten Wien, zwölf Studien von Adalbert Stifter*, Herausgegeben von Otto Erich Deutsch, Insel Verlag, 1909, pp. 141–7. GJ coll. Stifter describes a highly convenient postal service – with local pick-ups as well as deliveries – initiated in Vienna following the first outbreak of cholera in the city in 1831. This means of quick communication between the various parts of Vienna itself represented real modernity, although it was nowhere near as speedy as the French *pneumatique*. This is thus the kind of postal delivery that Schubert might have known in Vienna had he lived a few years longer. Stifter's article details the considerable inconveniences of writing letters (particularly those destined for local delivery) before this service began – and thus during Schubert's lifetime. This may account for the scarcity of correspondence between the composer and his circle from within Vienna; his correspondence (apart from notes that were probably hand-delivered by friends) seems mostly to have been written to or from addresses outside the city.

III/687 Autograph of the first page of *Die Krähe* (No. XV of *Winterreise*), fair copy. [Franz Schubert. Die [*sic*] Winterreise| Faksimile -Wiedergabe nach der Originalhandschrift | Bärenreiter-Verlag Kassel. Paris. London. New York | 1966.] The autograph shown is the sixth of fifteen fair copies of songs (including the whole of Part Two) in the assembled manuscript of the work in the Pierpont Morgan Library, New York.

III/700 Autograph of the beginning of *Der stürmische Morgen* (No. XVIII of *Winterreise*), fair copy. [Franz Schubert. Die [*sic*] Winterreise| Faksimile-Wiedergabe nach der Originalhandschrift | Bärenreiter-Verlag Kassel.Basel.Paris. London. New York | 1966.] The autograph shown is the ninth of fifteen fair copies of songs (including the whole of Part Two) in the assembled manuscript of the work in the Pierpont Morgan Library, New York.

III/712 Autograph of the first page of *Das Wirtshaus* (No. XXI of *Winterreise*), fair copy. [Franz Schubert. Die [*sic*] Winterreise| Faksimile -Wiedergabe nach der Originalhandschrift | Bärenreiter-Verlag Kassel.Basel. Paris. London. New York | 1966.] The autograph shown is the twelfth of fifteen fair copies of songs (including the whole of Part Two) in the assembled manuscript of the work in the Pierpont Morgan Library, New York.

III/726 Autograph of beginning of *Der Leiermann* (No. XXIV of *Winterreise*), fair copy. [Franz Schubert. Die [*sic*] Winterreise| Faksimile-Wiedergabe nach der Originalhandschrift | Bärenreiter-Verlag Kassel.Basel. Paris. London. New York | 1966.] The autograph shown is the last of fifteen fair copies of songs (including the whole of Part Two) in the assembled manuscript of the work in the Pierpont Morgan Library, New York. It is probable that these songs had been revised to such an extent that the composer decided he needed to recopy a final version to make his intentions clear to the printers.

III/727 A hurdy-gurdy player (known as 'Old Sarah'). Engraving from a daguerreotype, reproduced in Henry Mayhew's *London Labour and the London Poor*, 1851. This engraving was also reproduced in George Speaight, *The Entertainments of the Streets* in *The*

A SCHUBERT CALENDAR

together on the opera *Alfonso und Estrella* D732. [Ernst Hilmar, *Schubert*, Graz, 1989, p. 125.]

III/846 The Allgemeines Krankenhaus (General Hospital) in the Alsergrund where Schubert received treatment for syphilis in 1823. Coloured engraving by Josef and Peter Schaffer. [*Franz Schubert. Sein Leben in Bildern*, Otto Erich Deutsch, 1913, p. 124.]

III/849 (*above*) Schloss Zseliz, country seat of the Esterházy family. Schubert worked there for the summers of 1818 and 1824, although he was only accommodated as a guest in the house itself for his second visit. Photograph *c.* 1905 taken by the owner of the time, Marie, Gräfin von Goudenhove. [*Franz Schubert. Sein Leben in Bildern*, Otto Erich Deutsch, 1913, p. 256.]

III/849 (*below*) The Music Room in Schloss Zseliz, photograph *c.* 1905 taken by the owner of the time, Marie, Gräfin von Goudenhove. [*Franz Schubert. Sein Leben in Bildern*, Otto Erich Deutsch, 1913, p. 257.]

III/850 Schubert's room in Schloss Zseliz, watercolour by Franz Seligmann, 1897. [*Franz Schubert. Sein Leben in Bildern*, Otto Erich Deutsch, 1913, p. 258.]

III/856 View of the Tuchlauben, Vienna. In the foreground is the original building of the Gesellschaft der Musikfreunde (Musikverein) where Schubert's music was often performed. A few houses away, along the same side of the street, the composer lived with Schober in 1827–8. This was the composer's last dwelling in the inner city. [Ernst Hilmar, *Schubert*, Graz, 1989, p. 151.]

III/860 (*above*) Interior of the synagogue in Vienna's Seitenstettengasse where Salomon Sulzer was Cantor. Engraving by J. Enderle. [*Franz Schubert. Sein Leben in Bildern*, Otto Erich Deutsch, 1913, p. 373.]

III/860 (*below*) The house at Kettenbrückengasse, 6 (formerly Neue Wieden) where Ferdinand Schubert had an apartment and where Franz Schubert died. [*Franz Schubert. Sein Leben in Bildern*, Otto Erich Deutsch, 1913, p. 129.]

III/861 The small, narrow room in which Schubert died, now part of a museum. [Ernst Hilmar, *Schubert*, Graz, 1989, p. 157.]

III/936 Endpiece *Schubert* by Martha Griebler, 1997. Detail from *Grillparzer* (the poet is depicted on the left-hand side of the drawing). Drawing reproduced by arrangement with Matthias Griebler. Also published in Martha Griebler, *Franz Schubert – Zeichnungen*, Bibliothek der Provinz, Weitra, 2005, p. 52.

ERRATA in VOLUME ONE

p. 219, under Anonymous/unknown   For the date of *Zur Namensfeier des Herrn Andreas Siller* D83 read 28 October–4 November, not 20 October–4 November.

p. 238, under Bibliography   For Black 2000 read Black 2003.

p. 301, under Bibliography   For Bodendorff 1996 read Bodendorff 2006.

p. 312   For the date of the second version of *Blondel zur Marien* D626 read 1818, not 1812.

p. 332, caption   For Hyrtll read Hyrtl.

p. 338   Further settings of *Bundeslied* D258 should include Ludwig van Beethoven (1770–1827) Op. 122 (c. 1795 rev. 1820s).

p. 345, under Bibliography   For Pohansl read Porhansl.

pp. 404, 450 and 788 For the name of the writer in the Bibliographies read Aderhold, not Adelhold.

p. 456, under Bibliography   For Brügemann read Brüggeman.

p. 459, under Bibliography   For Schochow read Chochlow

pp. 495 and 508, under Bibliography   For Stebin 1999² read Stebin 1999.

pp. 558 and 704, under Bibliography   The date for Capell should read 1928.

p. 699   Read Wer sich der Einsamkeit ergibt, not Wer Sich der Einsamkeit Ergibt.

p. 702   Read Wer nie sein Brot mit Tränen ass, not Wer nie sein Brot mit Tränen Ass.

p. 704   Read An die Türen will ich schleichen, not An die Türen Will Ich Schleichen.

p. 711, caption   For Engraving read Oil painting.

pp. 750, 758, 792 and 946, under Bibliography   For Black 2000 read Black 2001.

p. 953   For Goethe's *Iphigenia in Tauris* read *Iphigenie in Tauris*.

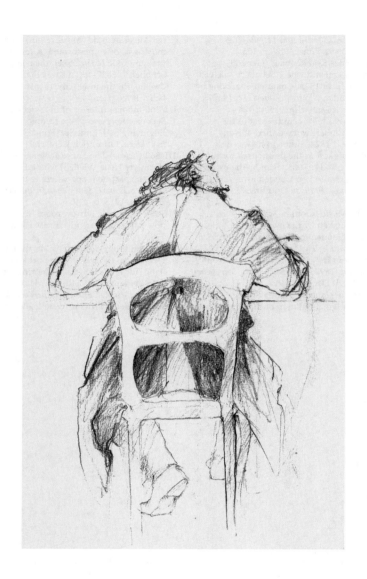